Thailand

China Williams

Mark Beales, Tim Bewer, Catherine Bodry,

Austin Bush, Brandon Presser

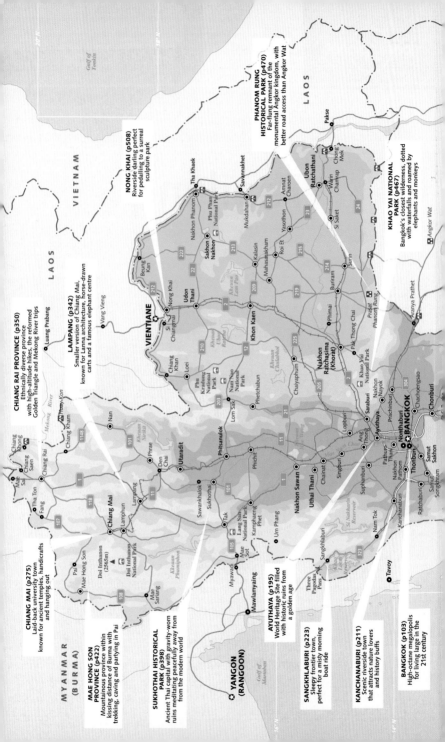

CHIANG RAI PROVINCE (p350)
Ethnically diverse province with high-altitude hikes, the reformed Golden Triangle and Mekong River trips

NONG KHAI (p508)
Riverside darling perfect for pedalling to a surreal sculpture park

PHANOM RUNG HISTORICAL PARK (p470)
Far-flung remnant of the monumental Angkor kingdom, with better road access than Angkor Wat

LAMPANG (p342)
Smaller version of Chiang Mai, known for Lanna architecture, horse-drawn carts and a famous elephant centre

KHAO YAI NATIONAL PARK (p467)
Bangkok's closest wilderness, dotted with waterfalls and roamed by elephants and monkeys

CHIANG MAI (p275)
Laid-back university town known for ancient temples, handicrafts and hanging out

MAE HONG SON PROVINCE (p422)
Mountainous province within kissing distance of Burma with trekking, caving and partying in Pai

SUKHOTHAI HISTORICAL PARK (p398)
Ancient Thai capital with gravity-worn ruins meditating peacefully away from the modern world

AYUTHAYA (p195)
World Heritage Site filled with historic ruins from a golden age

SANGKHLABURI (p223)
Sleepy frontier town, perfect for a misty morning boat ride

KANCHANABURI (p211)
Scenic riverside town that attracts nature lovers and history buffs

BANGKOK (p103)
High-octane megalopolis for living large in the 21st century

CAMBODIA

VIETNAM

HO CHI MINH CITY (SAIGON)

PHNOM PENH

Mekong River

Tonle Sap

Sihanoukville

SOUTH CHINA SEA

GULF OF THAILAND

ANDAMAN SEA

INDIAN OCEAN

MALAYSIA

PHETCHABURI (p549)
Break up the beach sojourn with a touch of old Siam and its attractions above and below ground

CHA-AM (p553)
A weekend beach getaway for Thais who prefer dining on seafood to sunbathing

KO CHANG (p258)
A beach resort merging mod-con comfort with a jungle-clad interior; escape to the nearby islands for sand and solitude

KO TAO (p610)
Dive until you grow gills on this pint-sized island surrounded by coral gardens

KO PHA-NGAN (p595)
Master the art of hanging out on its bohemian beaches

KO SAMUI (p575)
Eager-to-please beach resorts for holiday pop-ins

SONGKHLA (p729)
Take a slice of southern provincial life from the seafood piers and curry shacks

KHAO SOK NATIONAL PARK (p639)
Land-before-time jungle with muddy treks and wildlife spotting

KHAO LAK (p640)
Embark on live-aboard dive trips to the world-class Similan and Surin Islands

KRABI PROVINCE (p681)
The prettiest playground around, with stunning karst mountains rising out of the sea

PHUKET (p649)
Thailand's most famous beach resort, with plenty of rest and recreation

KO PHI-PHI (p692)
The prettiest beach of them all – you'll see

TRANG (p704)
Historic southern city famous for its Hokkien coffee and pine-rimmed beaches catering to Thais

KO TARUTAO MARINE NATIONAL PARK (p720)
Collection of parkland ranging from the barely inhabited to the next best thing, Ko Lipe

ELEVATION
1000m
500m
200m
100m
0

LEGEND
Freeway
Primary Road
Secondary Road
Railway

0   150 km
0   90 miles

Chanthaburi
Trat
Ko Chang
Ko Kut
Rayong
Pattaya
Sattahip
Ko Samet

Kaeng Krachan National Park
Cha-am
Hua Hin
Prachuap Khiri Khan
Thap Sakae
Bang Saphan
Chumphon
Isthmus of Kra
Ranong
Mergui

Ko Tao
Ko Pha-Ngan
Ko Samui
Ang Thong Marine National Park

Surat Thani
Chaiya
Khao Sok National Park
Khao Lak
Similan Islands
Surin Islands
Phang-Nga
Phuket
Ko Yao Yai
Ko Phi-Phi
Krabi
Ko Lanta

Nakhon Si Thammarat
Thung Song
Trang
Kantang
Ko Tarutao Marine National Park
Thaleh Ban National Park
Satun
Langkawi

Ranot
Phatthalung
Thaleh Luang
Songkhla
Hat Yai
Sadao
Alor Setar
Keroh
Sungai Petani

Pattani
Yala
Narathiwat
Betong
Kota Bharu

On the Road

CHINA WILLIAMS
Coordinating Author

In the evenings, after I'd finished snooping around guesthouses and checking off map items, I'd strap my son onto my back and we'd hit the streets together, like a strange variation of an elephant and mahout. Here we are waiting for a *sŏrng·tăa·ou* in Chiang Mai (p275).

BRANDON PRESSER A hike, a bus, a taxi and a long-tail boat – my trek to the Trang Islands (p709) was a tiring one. When I arrived, all I wanted to do was drop my bags and take a nap. But the water was impossibly clear and the sky incredibly blue, so I slipped on my trunks, grabbed my snorkel-mask and rushed into the sea, smiling. I had finally found it – the perfect beach.

MARK BEALES Hiring a quad-bike to reach the remote southern beaches of Ko Samet (p245) was by far the best (and most fun) way to get around. Rainy season conditions soon turned the dirt track into a quagmire, which made for a challenging but rewarding ride along the stunning coastline.

AUSTIN BUSH This pic was taken at the top of Wat Phra That Doi Kong Mu (p423), a hilltop temple in my favourite province, Mae Hong Son. In fact, I liked the place so much that I based myself there temporarily to complete much of the writing for this book!

CATHERINE BODRY This photo was taken at the Saturday market in Dan Singkhon (p567). I'd heard about this early morning event, where Burmese cross the border to sell orchids. I decided to see for myself, so I rented a car and convinced a new Thai friend to drive me there early one Saturday morning.

TIM BEWER No, it's not the Rainforest Cafe. It's Wat Pho Ban Nontan (p496) in Khon Kaen, my adopted hometown. TAT doesn't promote it and some of my Thai friends had never heard of it, but one day while out for a walk I wandered in and found one of the country's most wonderfully odd temples. Just another of those regular reminders you get in Thailand that there's always something new and exciting to see.

For full author biographies see p794.

Traveller Highlights

On these pages, travellers and Lonely Planet staff and authors share their top experiences in Thailand. Do you agree with their choices, or have we missed your favourites? Go to lonelyplanet.com/thailand and tell us your highlights.

MICHAEL COYNE

1 CHIANG MAI

Having never ridden a motorbike before, renting a scooter and riding up the mountain overlooking Chiang Mai to the Buddhist temple Wat Phra That Doi Suthep (p296) was probably not the smartest thing to do. But joining the chaos of túk-túks, scooters and cars on the multi-lane moat road was certainly exhilarating, and experiencing the ancient temple and its views over the city was infinitely rewarding.

Robyn Loughnane, Australia

VIVIANE PO

❷ ELEPHANT NATURE PARK, CHIANG MAI

Feed elephants, bathe elephants and walk beside elephants at this sanctuary (p298) for elephants outside of Chiang Mai. Incomparable experiences and photo opportunities aside, whether visitor or volunteer, your support will help save the lives of elephants abused or decommissioned from logging and tourism industries. It's an experience, like the elephants, you won't forget.

Debra Herrmann, Australia

AUSTIN BL

❸ ANG THONG MARINE NATIONAL PARK

As an Australian travelling overseas, I had been a bit underwhelmed by much-hyped beaches. But Ang Thong Marine National Park (p623) is as close to tropical paradise as I've ever seen – soft white sand, turquoise water, lush palm trees and all totally unspoilt. Not even getting seasick and being dramatically ill on a pristine stretch of beach could ruin it for me.

Emma Chapple, Australia

MAE HONG SON

Most visitors return south after a stay in Chiang Mai or Chiang Rai, but if you're going between November and January, Mae Hong Son (p422) is a must. Perched on the hills north of Chiang Mai, this province, lost in the clouds, is the stuff dreams are made of.

oranutt (online name)

JOE CUMMINGS

4

ANDREW LUBRAN

ĐÔM YAM

My personal mission in Bangkok was to seek out the best *đôm yam* (p86)! This involved tireless research, which at one point meant three serves of the delightful concoction in one day! The winner? A túk-túk driver recommended a family run eatery across from Hualamphong station. Kaffir lime, lemon grass, tamarind, mushrooms, spring onion, galangal, ginger and bok choy... yum!

Martine Power, Australia

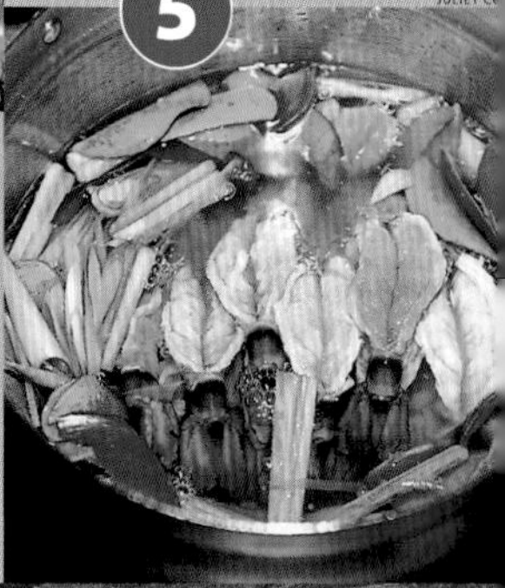

5

JULIET C

6

THE OTHER SIDE OF THE (FULL) MOON

Ko Tao may be considered the hidden gem of Thailand's islands (particularly if you're into diving), but the quieter side of Ko Pha-Ngan (p595) is well worth exploring. If you left your glow sticks at home and would rather have your mushrooms in an omelette, seek out a beachside view from a hammock on the island's calmer east coast. Sometimes a Full Moon is best appreciated on an empty stretch of beach.

Chris Girdler, Australia

CHRIS M

7

CHIANG RAI

Without a doubt, renting a bike in Chiang Rai (p350) and cycling along the Mekong River through small villages, verdant farmlands and hills dotted with crumbling overgrown temples was a highlight of my trip to Thailand.

Christina Tunnah, USA

DALLAS STRIBLEY

8 KO PHI-PHI

Ko Phi-Phi (p692) is exactly what you dreamed a Thai paradise would be. A photographer's delight, with sunsets over the island and fishing boats in the water as you look out at Phi-Phi Leh (setting for *The Beach*). You'll find plenty of entertainment and friendly people in the small streets full of restaurants, shops and the occasional bar.

Karen Burrows, New Zealand

GREG

9 BANGKOK

There are markets and then there is Chatuchak Weekend Market (p179). This is the market that all markets around the world are measured by. You'll find things here that you didn't know you wanted or needed. And they will come in every size and colour.

Mark Broadhead, Australia

CRAIG PERS

10 KO LANTA

Many travel to Ko Lanta to dive off the famous Hin Daeng and Hin Muang pinnacles (p700), renowned for their exceptional abundance of marine life. If you could ever tire of this, hop on a motorbike and ride virtually the whole coastline of Ko Lanta, popping in to say 'hello' to the sea gypsies along the way. Spend the evening in Saladan eating grilled spicy fish before a well-earned sleep.

Kristian Daely, Australia

RAILAY BEACH

Railay (p688), halfway between the city of Krabi and Ao Nang, is a rock-climber's paradise. Now, I'm not a rock-climber, but the limestone cliffs, thick jungles and beautiful beaches did it for me. I loved kicking back on oversized cushions, eating delicious spicy fish and sipping Chang beer while watching those hasty rock-climbers scaling immense heights. No guilt warranted!

Jessica Racklyeft, Australia

11

ANDREW BAIN

NOBORU K

12 SUKHOTHAI

It's the ruins of a once-great ancient city, reclaimed by deep Southeast Asian jungle, rediscovered in the modern era and transformed into a historical park. Angkor Wat? Good call – but incorrect. This is Thailand's Sukhothai (p397), the ancient walled one-time capital of the kingdom of the same name. Though not as grandiose as Angkor Wat, Sukhothai offers nearly 200 ruins filled with devotional art, sculpture and carvings sprawled out over 70 sq km of jungle. But being subdued isn't necessarily a bad thing. While Angkor Wat is thronged with tourists nearly 365 days a year, Sukhothai is still a mere blip on the Southeast Asia travel map; on some days, it'll be just you and the ghosts of the ancients.

Joshua Samuel Brown, USA

ANTONY

13 SEVEN STEPS WATERFALL

The Seven Steps Waterfall in Erawan National Park (p218), near Kanchanaburi, involved walking for about an hour up a neverending cascade of beautiful limestone pools and waterfalls, watching monkeys leap from trees into the water, jumping out of the water as they approached us intent on our peanuts, and getting nibbled by the large carp that swam in the milky blue pools beneath the waterfalls.

Bruce Evans, Australia

Contents

Destination Thailand

Technically, elephants are not allowed on the streets of Bangkok, but during the right time of year (typically after rice farmers have finished harvesting their crops), you can't help but come across the giant beasts, wandering the congested sois with their owners, largely ignored by just about everybody except foreign tourists. To most visitors it's inconceivable that a creature so large can be so casually disregarded. But this is Thailand, a country where the people have become experts at ignoring the metaphorical elephants in their rooms.

Since the abolition of the absolute monarchy in 1932, political instability has essentially been the norm in Thailand. The most recent period of unrest began in 2006 with the coup d'état (the 18th in 70 years) that saw then Prime Minister, Thaksin Shinawatra, forcibly removed from office, sent into exile and replaced by military rule. Unlike elsewhere where such an event might have had people protesting on the streets, the 'smooth as silk' coup hardly disrupted Bangkok traffic, and Thais, depending on their political allegiances, appeared to accept the changes with restrained joy or quiet resignation.

The following 15 months of caretaker rule were largely seen as ineffectual, and spanned lowlights ranging from limits on press freedom to significant economic slowdown, but public displays of discontent were rare if not non-existent. Long-awaited elections in late 2007 led to the People's Power Party (PPP) of Samak Sundaravej, an alleged Thaksin proxy, gaining a majority in parliament. This sparked a series of street protests led by the People's Alliance for Democracy (PAD), the same anti-Thaksin group whose protests preceded the 2006 coup.

In less than six months, the largely middle-class Bangkok-based PAD had boldly taken over Government House and was demanding Samak's resignation. In response, pro-Thaksin supporters, many of whom are relatively poor farmers, labourers and taxi drivers from Thailand's north and northeast, formed their own pro-government alliance called the United Front of Democracy Against Dictatorship (UDD). Even moderate Thais began taking sides, with PAD supporters wearing yellow (a colour associated with the monarchy), and government supporters sporting red. For the first time in recent Thai history, it appeared that at least one elephant – the vast divide between the urban, educated elite and the rural poor – could no longer be ignored.

In June 2008, after several weeks of PAD occupation of Government House, the country's Constitutional Court found Samak guilty of accepting money to host a cooking program, and he was forced to stand down. Although his dismissal due to this technicality was tantamount to the coup the PAD demanded, they were anything but placated when Sundaravej was subsequently replaced by Somchai Wongsawat, Thaksin's brother-in-law.

Meanwhile, Thaksin and his wife Potjaman remained largely in exile in the UK, with only sporadic visits to Thailand. However in late 2008, the Supreme Court found Thaksin guilty of a corruption charge, sentencing him to two years' imprisonment. Potjaman was subsequently sentenced to three years in jail for tax fraud. The couple's UK visas were later revoked, and any plans to return to the UK or Thailand were inevitably shelved.

In October and November of 2008 confrontations between the PAD and police and pro-government supporters became increasingly violent, leading to the death of two PAD members. Rumours of a military coup were rampant, and more bloody clashes were feared. Events culminated in late November when several thousand PAD protesters took over both

'this is Thailand, a country where the people have become experts at ignoring the meta-phorical elephants in their rooms'

of Bangkok's airports, bringing tourism to a complete standstill for more than a week. It wasn't until the Constitutional Court dissolved the ruling party that the protesters finally agreed to leave the airports.

After a great deal of political wrangling, a tenuous new coalition was formed in December, led by Oxford-educated Abhisit Vejjajiva, leader of the Democrat Party and Thailand's fifth prime minister of 2008. Although Abhisit's appointment ushered a brief period of relative stability, violent protests in early 2009 by red-shirted Thaksin supporters in Bangkok and Pattaya showed that, although still in exile, the former Prime Minister remains the single most influential and polarising figure in Thai politics.

But perhaps the largest elephant of all is the impending but unspoken reality of a Thailand without its current monarch. Thailand's king, Bhumibol Adulyadej, is the world's longest-serving head of state and a figure literally worshipped by the vast majority of Thais for more than 60 years. The king is in his eighth decade now and his health has been failing. It remains to be seen how the Thais will adapt to life without a ruler whose reign most have lived their entire lives under. For certain, the grief felt by Thais will be profound, and the lack of the king's relatively stabilising influence on domestic politics, and the contentious issue of royal succession will have profound implications on Thailand's near future.

Yet, despite the seemingly endless cycle of crises, Thailand continues to progress towards a modern, wealthy society. Bangkok's infrastructure continues to improve, with ambitious plans to expand both the Metro and Skytrain, and the long-awaited airport link scheduled to begin operations in 2009. Elsewhere in the country, virtually all of the communities devastated by the 2004 Boxing Day tsunami have fully recovered. Road links to distant parts of the country are improving, and an abundance of cheap domestic flights makes it easier than ever for those who wish to get off the beaten track.

Political crises have also done little to alter what makes the country arguably the most diverse and rewarding destination in Southeast Asia. A friendly and tolerant population and a solid infrastructure make Thailand an approachable destination for first-time travellers, while destinations and activities ranging from tropical beaches to cooking courses will appeal to even the most jaded traveller.

Throughout Thailand's lengthy and often rocky experiment with democracy, the Thai people's ability to ignore elephants has been a constant factor. But until issues such as class division, Thaksin Shinawatra's polarising influence on politics, and royal succession are acknowledged and dealt with, political instability is bound to define Thailand's future, as well as its past.

FAST FACTS

Area: 514,000 sq km

Border countries: Cambodia, Laos, Malaysia, Myanmar (Burma)

Population: 65,493,296

Inflation: 2.2%

GDP per capita: US$8000

Religion: 95% Buddhist

Literacy: 92.6%

Original name: Siam

Number of coups d'état since 1932: 18

Number of 7-Elevens: currently 3912

Highest Point: Doi Inthanon 2565m

Rice exports: 10.02 million tonnes in 2008 (number-one rice exporter in the world)

Getting Started

Most people find travel in Thailand to be relatively easy and economical. Of course, a little preparation will go a long way towards making your trip hassle-free and fun.

WHEN TO GO

See Climate Charts (p742) for more information.

The best time to visit most of Thailand is between November and February, because it rains the least and it is not too hot. This period is also Thailand's main season for festivals, like Loi Krathong and Songkran.

If you plan to focus on the northern provinces, the hot season (March to May) and early rainy season (June to July) are not bad either, as temperatures are moderate at higher elevations. Northeastern and central Thailand, on the other hand, are best avoided from March to May, when temperatures may climb over 40°C. Because temperatures are more even year-round in the south (because it's closer to the equator), the beaches and islands of southern Thailand are a good choice for respite when the rest of Thailand is miserably hot.

Thailand's peak tourist season runs from November to late March, with secondary peaks in July and August. If you want to avoid crowds and take advantage of discounted room rates, consider travelling during the least crowded months (typically April to June, September and October).

Although the rainy season (roughly July to October) gets a bad reputation, there are some bonuses: temperatures tend to be cooler, tourists are fewer and the landscape is lush and green. Depending on the region and the month, the rains might be hour-long downpours in the afternoon. October, however, tends to be the wettest month.

COSTS & MONEY

Thailand is an inexpensive country to visit thanks to advantageous foreign currency exchanges and an affordable standard of living. Those on a budget should be able to get by on about 600B to 700B per day outside Bangkok and the major beach islands. This amount covers basic food, guesthouse accommodation and local transport but excludes all-night beer binges, tours, long-distance transport or vehicle hire. Travellers with more money to spend will find that for around 1500B or more per day life can be quite comfortable.

Bangkok is a good place to splurge on a hotel for recovery from a long flight or to celebrate returning to 'civilisation'. In the provinces, guesthouses tend to be the best value even for bigger budgets. Market meals

HOW MUCH?

2nd-class air-con sleeper train, Bangkok to Surat Thani 758-848B

Beach bungalow on Ko Pha-Ngan 350-500B

One-day Thai cooking course in Chiang Mai 900B

National park admission 200B

Dinner for two at a midrange restaurant 300-500B

See also the Lonely Planet Index, inside front cover.

DON'T LEAVE HOME WITHOUT...

Pack light wash-and-wear clothes, plus a pullover (sweater) or light jacket for chilly bus rides and the northern mountains. Slip-on shoes or sandals are handy. Laundry is cheap in Thailand, so you only need to travel with a week's supply of clothes.

You can buy toothpaste, soap and most other toiletries almost anywhere in Thailand. International stores like Boots tend to carry tampons and antiperspirants strong enough to fight the tropical malady. See p772 for a list of recommended medical items.

Other handy items include: a small torch (flashlight), sarong (dries better than a towel), waterproof money/passport container (for swimming outings), earplugs and sunscreen (high SPFs are not widely available outside of big cities).

Be sure to check government travel advisories for Thailand before you leave. See Dangers & Annoyances (p743) for general security issues.

TOP PICKS

One of the best ways to get ready for a Thailand tour is to start dreaming about this faraway land. Here are a few highlights:

BEST ECOTOURISM SPOTS

- Chiang Rai – the centre for hill-tribe trekking with a social justice hook; some trekking compa-nies employ hill-tribe guides or foster community development programs (p350)
- Northeastern Thailand – loads of village homestays are sprouting up all over this rural land-scape to put you in touch with the people and rice paddies (p455)
- Chiang Mai – a pretty northern town that is evolving into a cycling mecca for in-town touring and off-roading (p275)

BEST SCENIC JOURNEYS

- Overnight ferry from Chumphon to Ko Tao – it's just a simple fishing boat with mats on the upper deck and winking stars overhead (p622)
- Mahachai Shortline train – this day's diversion from Bangkok trundles through forests, marsh-land and wet markets (p190)
- Mae Sa–Samoeng loop – the mountain equivalent of a rollercoaster ride that climbs, dips and twists along the peaks outside Chiang Mai (p326)
- Bus ride from Kanchanaburi to Sangkhlaburi – the local tin-can bus slides in between the toothy green mountains (p226)

BEST THAILAND MEMORIES

- Smells and bells – rice cooking in the morning, perfume of joss sticks, maniacal honking of long-distance buses, deep bellows of temple bells, 7-Eleven doorbell chimes, barking *jìng·jòk* (house lizards)
- Religious accoutrements – jasmine garlands, amulets dangling from rear-view mirrors and ceremonial cloths tied around sacred trees
- Smoke and cough – belching diesel buses, chilli-laden smoke from a street-stall wok, burning carcasses of *gài yâhng* (grilled chicken)
- Water, water everywhere – fish ponds and roadside water gardens in front of shops and homes, murky *klorng* (canals), sweat pouring out of every pore, 5B plastic water bottles, jewel-toned seas

are cheaper and tastier than guesthouse fare but you'll need a little local language and an adventurous stomach.

ATMs are widespread and are the easiest ways to get Thai baht. Have a ready supply of US dollars in cash, if you need to do a border run (crisp new notes are preferred). Credit cards are accepted in big cities and resort hotels but not in family-run guesthouses or restaurants.

TRAVEL LITERATURE

Cosy up to the kingdom with tales penned by hapless travellers turned insightful scribes or by culture-straddling Thais. The bulk of the genre is B-grade thrillers revolving around bar-girls and gangsters, but the follow-ing titles are culturally acute page-turners.

■ *Fieldwork* (2008), by Mischa Berlinski, is set in a fictional hill-tribe village in northern Thailand, with a complicated cast of anthropologists, missionaries and an aimless journalist all pursuing their own version of the title.

■ *Sightseeing* (2005) is a debut collection of short stories by Rattawut Lapcharoensap that gives readers a 'sightseeing' tour into Thai households and coming-of-age moments.

■ *Thailand Confidential* (2005), by ex–*Rolling Stone* correspondent Jerry Hopkins, weaves an exposé of everything expats and visitors love about Thailand and much they don't.

■ *Bangkok 8* (2004), by John Burdett, is a hard-boiled whodunit on the surface, but the lead character, a Thai-Westerner cop, proves an excellent conduit for understanding Thai Buddhism.

■ *Touch the Dragon* (1992) is the diary of Karen Connelly, a Canadian who worked as a volunteer in a northern Thai village at the age of 17. Her book about culture and culture shock is well circulated amongst paperback-swapping expats posted in rural areas.

■ *The Beach* (1998), by Alex Garland, is the ultimate beach read about a backpacker who finds a secluded island utopia off the coast of Ko Samui.

■ *Jasmine Nights* (1995), by SP Somtow, is a coming-of-age novel set in 1960s Bangkok.

■ *Mai Pen Rai Means Never Mind* (1965), by Carol Hollinger, is the classic tale of befriending Thailand, written by a Bangkok-based housewife in the 1960s.

INTERNET RESOURCES

Lonely Planet (www.lonelyplanet.com) Country-specific information as well as a user exchange on the Thorn Tree forum.

One Stop Thailand (www.onestopthailand.com) Comprehensive tourism guide to popular Thai destinations.

Thai Students Online (www.thaistudents.com) Sriwittayapaknam School in Samut Prakan maintains the largest and most informative website portal on Thai culture and society.

Thailand Daily (www.thailanddaily.com) Part of World News Network, offering a thorough digest of Thailand-related news from English news sources.

ThaiVisa.com (www.thaivisa.com) Extensive info on visas as well as user forums and news alerts.

Tourism Authority of Thailand (www.tourismthailand.org) Contains provincial tourism profiles, travel promotions and festival information from Thailand's national tourism department.

Events Calendar

Religious holidays make up the bulk of Thailand's festival line-up but that doesn't mean that these are solely prayer and incense affairs. Many religious holidays are based on the lunar calendar, causing the exact dates to vary. For specific dates, visit the website of the Tourism Authority of Thailand (TAT) at www.tourismthailand.org. Dozens of smaller festivals offer snapshots of provincial culture; see the respective destination chapters for more information.

JANUARY–FEBRUARY

CHINESE NEW YEAR   Jan-Feb
Called đrùt jeen, Thais with Chinese ancestry celebrate their ancestral lunar new year with a week of house-cleaning and fireworks. Phuket (p649), Bangkok (p103) and Nakhon Sawan all host citywide festivities, but in general Chinese New Year is more of a family event.

MAKHA BUCHA   Feb-Mar
One of three holy days marking important moments of Buddha's life, Makha Bucha (Mah•ká Boo•chah), on the full moon of the third lunar month, commemorates Buddha preaching to 1250 enlightened monks who came to hear him 'without prior summons'. A public holiday, it's mainly a day for temple visits. Organisations and schools will often make merit as a group at a local temple.

APRIL

SONGKRAN   12-14 Apr
Thailand's famous water fight marks the Thai New Year (12 to 14 April; dates vary). The traditional religious activities are held in the morning and involve showing respect to elders and sacred temple images by sprinkling water on them. Afterwards Thais in Chiang Mai (p302) and Bangkok (p148) load up their water guns and head out to the streets for battle: water is thrown, catapulted and sprayed from roving commandos and outfitted pick-up trucks at willing and unwilling targets.

MAY–JUNE

ROYAL PLOUGHING CEREMONY   May
This royal ceremony employs astrology and ancient Brahman rituals to kick-off the rice-planting season. Sacred oxen are hitched to a wooden plough and part the ground of Sanam Luang (p129) in Bangkok. The ritual was revived in the 1960s by the king, and Crown Prince Maha Vajiralongkorn has assumed the ceremony's helm.

ROCKET FESTIVAL   May-Jun
In the northeast, where rain can be scarce, villagers craft bamboo rockets (bâng fai) that are fired into the sky to encourage the rains to be plentiful for the upcoming rice-planting season. This festival is celebrated in Yasothon (p542), Ubon Ratchathani (p481) and Nong Khai (p508).

VISAKHA BUCHA   May-Jun
The holy day of Visakha Bucha (Wí•săh•kà Boo•chah) falls on the 15th day of the waxing moon in the sixth lunar month and commemorates the date of the Buddha's birth, enlightenment and parinibbana (passing away). Activities are centred around the temple.

BUN PHRA WET   Jun
This Buddhist holy day is given a Carnival makeover at the Phi Ta Khon Festival (p525) in Dan Sai village'. Revellers disguise themselves in garish 'spirit' costumes and parade through the village streets wielding wooden phalluses and downing rice whisky. The festival commemorates a Buddhist legend in which a host of spirits (pĕe, also spelt 'phi') appeared to greet the Buddha-to-be (Prince Vessantara or Phra Wet), the penultimate birth.

JULY

ASALHA BUCHA   Jul
The full moon of the eighth lunar month commemorates Buddha's first sermon during Asalha Bucha (Ah•săhn•hà Boo•chah). During Khao Phansaa, worshippers make offerings of candles other necessities to the temples and attend ordinations.

KHAO PHANSAA   Jul
The day after Asalha Bucha marks the beginning of Buddhist Lent (the first day of the waning moon in the eighth lunar month), the traditional time for men to enter the monkhood and the start of

the rainy season when monks typically retreat inside the monastery for a period of study and meditation. In Ubon Ratchathani, candle wax offerings have grown into elaborately carved sculptures that are shown off during the Candle Parade (p484).

AUGUST

HM THE QUEEN'S BIRTHDAY   12 Aug

The Queen's Birthday (12 August) is a public holiday and national mother's day. In Bangkok, the day is marked with cultural displays at Sanam Luang (p129) as well as festive lights lining the royal avenue of Th Ratchadamnoen Klang.

SEPTEMBER–OCTOBER

VEGETARIAN FESTIVAL   Sep-Oct

A holiday from meat is taken for nine days (during the ninth lunar month) in adherence with Chinese Buddhist beliefs of mind and body purification. Cities with large Thai-Chinese populations, such as Bangkok (p163), Trang (p704) and Krabi (p681), are festooned with yellow banners heralding vegetarian vendors, and merit-makers dressed in white shuffle off for meditation retreats. In Phuket the festival gets extreme, with entranced marchers turning themselves into human shish kebabs (p663).

ORK PHANSAA   Oct-Nov

The end of the Buddhist lent (three lunar months after Khao Phansaa) is marked by the *gà·tǐn* ceremony, in which new robes are given to the monks by merit-makers. The peculiar natural phenomenon known as the 'naga fireballs' (p514) coincides with Ork Phansaa.

NOVEMBER

SURIN ELEPHANT ROUND-UP   Nov

Held on the third weekend of November, Thailand's biggest elephant show celebrates this northeastern province's most famous residents. The event in Surin (p473) begins with a colourful elephant parade culminating in a fruit buffet for the pachyderms. Re-enactments of Thai battles showcase mahouts and elephants wearing royal military garb.

LOI KRATHONG   Nov-Dec

One of Thailand's most beloved festivals, Loi Krathong is celebrated on the first full moon of the 12th lunar month. The festival thanks the river goddess for providing life to the fields and forests and asks for forgiveness for the polluting ways of humans. Small handmade boats (called *kràthong* or *grà·tong*) are sent adrift in the country's waterways. The *grà·tong* are origami-like vessels made from banana leaves, they're decorated with flowers, and incense, candles and coins are placed in them. Loi Krathong is a peculiarly Thai festival that probably originated in Sukhothai (p401). In Chiang Mai the festival is also called Yi Peng (p302).

DECEMBER

HM THE KING'S BIRTHDAY   5 Dec

Honouring the king's birthday on 5 December, this public holiday hosts parades and merit-making events; it is also recognised as national father's day. Th Ratchadamnoen Klang in Bangkok (p103) is decorated with lights and regalia. Everyone wears yellow shirts, the colour associated with the king's birthday. Phuket (p649) also holds the Kings Cup Regatta during the first week of the month in honour of the monarch.

Itineraries
CLASSIC ROUTES

JUST A QUICKIE
Two Weeks/Bangkok to Bangkok

Even if you're only doing a Thailand 'pop-in', you can still pack in a full itinerary thanks to the affordability of domestic flights. Start off in **Bangkok** (p103) and then fly to the tropical beach resorts of **Ko Samui** (p575) or **Phuket** (p649). Although both are international superstars, there are plenty of quiet corners, and beaches with personalities to suit every sand hunter. If you find yourself on a spot that fits like a wet bathing suit, shop around the island before plotting your escape route to the next destination.

Once you've tired of sand and sun, fly up to **Chiang Mai** (p275) for a Thai cooking class and temple-spotting. Then explore the surrounding countryside filled with high-altitude road trips and hill-tribe trekking. Pay homage to Thailand's highest peak at **Doi Inthanon National Park** (p334).

Return to Bangkok with a tan, a Thai recipe book and lots of travel tales for the water cooler.

Fly from Bangkok to Ko Samui or Phuket. Return to Bangkok and fly, train or bus to Chiang Mai. Rent a car for trips around Chiang Mai.

A LITTLE BIT OF EVERYTHING

One Month/Bangkok to Nakhon Ratchasima

If you've got a month to wander through all of Thailand, spend a few days in **Bangkok** (p103), then take a slow ride north stopping in the ancient capital of **Ayuthaya** (p195) and the monkey town of **Lopburi** (p205). Visit more historic ruins in **Sukhothai** (p397) and then continue to **Chiang Mai** (p275), the cultural capital of the north. Be a high-altitude hippie in **Pai** (p439) and join a do-good trekking tour in **Chiang Rai** (p350). For more intensive northern immersion, see the Altitude Adjustment trip (p26).

By now the beach is calling so transit back through Bangkok to the classic island stops: **Ko Samui** (p575) for the party scene, **Ko Pha-Ngan** (p595) for beach bumming and **Ko Tao** (p610) for deep-sea diving.

Hop over to the Andaman Coast to see those famous postcard views of limestone mountains jutting out of the sea. **Phuket** (p649) is convenient but **Ko Phi-Phi** (p692) is the prettiest of them all; both require stacks of baht to stay somewhere with an ocean view. Backpackers and rock climbers opt for **Krabi** (p681). On the way back north detour to the rainforests of **Khao Sok National Park** (p639).

Transit again through Bangkok to dip your toes into the agricultural northeast. Crawl through the jungle of **Khao Yai National Park** (p467). Then head to **Nakhon Ratchasima** (Khorat; p458), a transit point for trips to the Angkor ruins at **Phimai** (p465) and the pottery village of **Dan Kwian** (p463).

Train from Bangkok to Ayuthaya, Lopburi and to Phitsanulok. Bus to Sukhothai. Bus to Chiang Mai. Bus to Pai or Chiang Rai from Chiang Mai. Fly, train or bus to Bangkok, then train or bus to Surat Thani and ferry to the Ko Samui archipelago, or fly direct to Ko Samui or Phuket from Bangkok. Bus to Krabi. Ferry to Ko Phi-Phi. Bus or fly (from Phuket) back to Bangkok. Bus to Nakhon Ratchasima, Phimai and Dan Kwian.

BEACH BINGING

Three Weeks/Surat Thani to Khao Lak

If your bragging buddies back home have sent you to Thailand with a long list of must-see beaches, then pack light and prepare for a marathon-run through the islands and coves of the Malay Peninsula. Head to the string of Gulf islands just off the coast of **Surat Thani** (p624) and take your pick from **Ko Samui** (p575), **Ko Pha-Ngan** (p595) or **Ko Tao** (p610).

Then cross the peninsula to conquer the Andaman celebrities of **Phuket** (p649), **Krabi** (p681) and **Ko Phi-Phi** (p692). Don't forget about the back-packer darling **Ko Lanta** (p698).

Pay your respects to **Khao Lak/Lamru National Park** (p641), which was badly bruised by the 2004 tsunami but today boasts long uninterrupted stretches of dunes facing a turquoise bay. From Khao Lak, you are nearby a global diving superstar: **Similan Islands Marine National Park** (p645).

Boat to the Gulf islands from Surat Thani. Bus from Surat Thani to Phuket. From Phuket boat to Ko Phi-Phi or bus to Krabi. Boat to Ko Phi-Phi or Ko Lanta from Krabi. Bus from Krabi to Khao Lak. Boat to Similan Islands.

ROADS LESS TRAVELLED

ALTITUDE ADJUSTMENT   Three Weeks/Mae Sot to Chiang Rai

Climb into the bosom of lush mountains and the ethnic minority villages that cling to the border between Thailand, Myanmar and Laos.

Mae Sot (p411) is a cross-pollinated town of Thai residents and displaced Karen and Burmese nationals. There isn't so much to see but the town is a border crossing for visa runs and is filled with aid workers and opportunities to volunteer in refugee camps and schools. Slightly off the main tourist trail, Mae Sot also has nature tours tailored to flora and fauna fanatics.

Follow the backroads to the trekking towns of **Mae Sariang** (p451) and **Mae Hong Son** (p422) to learn about the ethnic minorities more closely aligned to Myanmar than Thailand that thrive on these forested mountain peaks. Next is **Soppong** (p447) and its underground cave sculptures. Do some hippie-style R&R at **Pai** (p439), a mountain retreat with lots of daytime strolls and night-time carousing. Descend out of the winding mountain route into urban **Chiang Mai** (p275), a base for meditation and massage courses.

More mountains await northwards in **Chiang Dao** (p327), Pai's more sober sister. Then take the backdoor to Chiang Rai by busing to **Fang** (p330) and zig-zagging up the mountain ridge to **Mae Salong** (p358), a Yunnanese tea settlement. Slide into **Chiang Rai** (p350), which has a socially conscious trekking industry run by hill-tribe cooperatives and hill-tribe homestays.

Bus from Mae Sot to Mae Sariang, Mae Hong Son, Soppong and Pai to the transport hub of Chiang Mai. Bus to Chiang Dao, Fang and Mae Salong. Bus to Chiang Rai.

TAILORED TRIPS

SOUTHERN COMFORT & CULTURE

You might come to southern Thailand to recharge your vitamin D reserves on the powdery beaches but take some time to savour southern Thai culture, which has been spiced by ancient traders from China, India, Malaysia and Indonesia. From Bangkok, break up the long journey south in **Phetchaburi** (p549), where you can explore cave sanctuaries, hilltop palaces or the local cuisine. Traipse through the Gulf islands described in Beach Binging (p25). Be a little more adventurous by catching a southern tailwind to **Nakhon Si Thammarat** (p628), the cultural keeper of the southern tradition of shadow puppets. Then drink up the majesty of the province's unspoilt coastline at **Ao Khanom** (p627), a nearly deserted bay as pretty as Samui but without the package tourists. Then follow the windswept coast to **Songkhla** (p729) for seafood and Thai-style beachcombing. Saunter over to **Satun** (p717), a low-key Muslim town nearby the port for boats to **Ko Tarutao Marine National Park** (p720), a collection of beach celebrities like Ko Lipe (p722) and nearly unknowns like Ko Adang (p726).

Stop in at **Trang** (p704) for a caffeine buzz at one of its historic Hokkien-style cafes and then wade out to Ko Muk (p709) and its famously photographed cave lake. Then ricochet between the Andaman queens described in Beach Binging (p25).

CULTURE GEEKS

Do you love wandering around old stuff? If so, Thailand has enough crumbling fortresses, half-destroyed temples and limbless Buddha statues to fill a hard drive with pictures. This trip takes in several former royal capitals and one-time outposts of the Angkor empire, which once stretched into Thailand from western Cambodia.

Start at the ancient capital of **Ayuthaya** (p195), an easy day trip from Bangkok, then continue to **Lopburi** (p205), one of Thailand's oldest towns and a former Angkor centre. Continue north to **Sukhothai** (p397), which is considered the first Thai kingdom and is the best preserved of Thailand's ancient ruins. Nearby is **Si Satchanalai-Chaliang Historical Park** (p404), another collection of ruins set in the countryside.

Take an overnight bus to **Nakhon Ratchasima** (Khorat; p458), a good launching point for the Angkor-era ruins at **Phimai** (p465). Follow the Angkor trail east to Buriram Province where an extinct volcano is topped by the temple complex of **Phanom Rung** (p470), the most important and visually impressive of the Angkorean temples in Thailand. It's a short jaunt from here to **Prasat Meuang Tam** (p472) – known for its remoteness and reflective lily ponds.

MIGHTY MEKONG RIVER RUN

There aren't a lot of big-ticket attractions in Thailand's rural northeast (known as Isan) but cultural chameleons will find an old-fashioned way of life, easygoing people and interesting homestays that mix lodging with lounging around the rice fields. The most scenic route through the region is along the Mekong River, which divides Thailand and Laos. The border towns barely recognise the boundary and often share more cultural attributes with their foreign neighbours than their fellow citizens.

Start in the charming town of **Nong Khai** (p508), a rock-skipping throw from Laos and an easy border-crossing point. If the pace here is too fast, follow the river road east to **Beung Kan** (p516), a dusty speck of a town with a nearby temple built on a rocky outcrop and several neighbouring homestays with forays into wild-elephant territory. Pass through **Nakhon Phanom** (p527) for its picturesque river promenade but base yourself in tiny **That Phanom** (p531), with its famous Lao-style temple, honoured with a vibrant 10-day festival in January/February.

For a little urban Isan, check out **Ubon Ratchathani** (p481), surrounded by the Pha Taem National Park, river rapids and handicraft villages. Afterwards pick up the Culture Geek trip (p27) in reverse.

THAILAND FOR KIDS

Entertain and enlighten the kids without a lot of marathon travel. **Bangkok** (p103) is hyperactive enough for all ages (and it's all the better if your hotel has a swimming pool). Nearby you'll find culture and history bundled into a compact mini-state at **Muang Boran** (p132).

Let their imaginations run with the wild things in **Lopburi** (p205), home to a troop of monkeys who receive (deserved or not) a banquet feast during the town's signature festival. Lopburi is on the train line from Bangkok – a transport highlight for the locomotive fan in the family. Also accessible by train, **Surin** (p473) celebrates an annual elephant round-up with a buffet breakfast for the pachyderms and mock battles.

If your visit doesn't coincide with these festivals, **Kanchanaburi** (p210) is hugged by thick jungle explored by elephant treks and bamboo rafting. Or opt for **Khao Yai National Park** (p467), which is close to Bangkok and filled with as many monkeys as visitors.

End the trip with a beach romp. Steer clear of the Thai beaches (like Hua Hin and parts of Phuket and Samui) dominated by older European tourists who disapprove of children's deficient volume control. **Ko Samet** (p245) is a semi-wild island and an easy trip from Bangkok.

History

PRE-HISTORIC SETTLEMENT

An important question for any history of Thailand is where the Thais originally came from, and how they became Thai. Older studies claim that the ancestors of the Thais migrated from southern China into the fertile mainland of Southeast Asia around the 13th century AD. However, this position has been challenged by the assertion that Thai history should also include the life and legacy of people who preceded the new arrivals. Recently discovered *Homo erectus* fossils in Thailand's northern province of Lampang date back at least 500,000 years. Thailand's most important prehistoric settlement is Ban Chiang in the northeastern province of Udon Thani, which reveals evidence of the development of pottery, bronze tools and rice cultivation as far back as 4000 to 2500 BC.

THE ARRIVAL OF THE TAI

The people who laid the foundations of the contemporary Thai identity arrived in the areas of present-day Thailand about a thousand years ago. They were called 'Tai'.

Lampang Man provides the first evidence of the existence of Homo erectus in Asia outside Indonesia and China.

During the first millennium AD, these immigrants from southern China arrived in consecutive waves in the hinterlands of Southeast Asia. They spoke Tai-Kadai, a family of monosyllabic and tonal languages said to be the most significant ethno-linguistic group in Southeast Asia. They settled in villages as farmers, hunters and close-distance traders. The core of their village networks were *meu·ang*, centres of associations of interrelated villages and of villages under the rule of a lord. *Meu·ang* were the technological starting points for Tai state building.

By the end of the first millennium AD, many Tai were already living in areas of modern Thailand. They had encountered, displaced, assimilated or were co-existing with Mon and Khmer people. Other groups of Tai-Kadai speakers split off and moved through mainland Southeast Asia; into Laos (the Lao people) and Myanmar (the Shan), for example. In the 9th and 10th centuries AD, the empires of southern China (Nanzhao), Vietnam (Champa) and Cambodia (Angkor) were thriving. The Tai, however, with no centralised administration of their own, were still living in the margins of history.

THE RISE OF THE TAI KINGDOMS
Dvaravati, Angkor & Srivijaya

Before the arrival of the Tai, present-day Thailand had been contested by Mon and Khmer in the central plain, by Khmer in the northeast and by Malays in the south.

TIMELINE

4000–2500 BC	6th–11th centuries	10th century
Prehistoric inhabitants of northeastern Thailand develop pottery, rice cultivation and bronze metallurgy.	City-states of Dvaravati thrive in central Thailand, basing their civilisation upon Mon culture and Theravada Buddhism.	Arrival of Tai peoples in Thailand.

Thailand: A Short History
(2003) by David K Wyatt
and *A History of Thailand*
(2005) by Chris Baker
and Pasuk Phongpaichit
are highly recommended
reading.

Thailand's central and northeastern regions from the 6th to 9th centuries AD witnessed the formation of a distinctive Buddhist culture associated with the Mon and the name Dvaravati. The discovery of several coins in Nakhon Pathom bearing the inscription 'Lord of Dvaravati' suggests that Dvaravati was a kingdom whose centre was Nakhon Pathom. It could have been a loose association of city-states sharing Mon and Buddhist culture, including Ku Bua (Ratburi), Srimahosot (Prachinburi), Nakhon Ratchasima and U Thong, with the centre in Nakhon Pathom. Evidence of recovered artefacts from Dvaravati sites and present-day mapping of these sites suggests overland trade routes – west to Burma, east to Cambodia, north to Chiang Mai and Laos, and toward the northeast and the Khorat Plateau.

The urban civilisation of Dvaravati left behind its distinctive art, architecture and Mon-language stone inscriptions. Indian influences colour several aspects of Dvaravati civilisation, such as city names, religious beliefs and material culture. The process of state- and civilisation-building in ancient Southeast Asia, once understood as 'Indianising' or 'Indianisation,' is now often described as 'localisation,' rather than as a reception of Indian culture in a pure form.

In the 11th century, the influence of Mon-Dvaravati city-states declined quickly after the Khmer empire expanded westward across present-day central and northeastern Thailand. Lavo (Lopburi), Sukhothai and Phimai (Nakhon Ratchasima) were regional Khmer administrative centres. Between these centres and the capital at Angkor, roads and temples in Khmer style made travel easier and were a visible symbol of imperial power. Khmer elements – Brahmanism, Theravada Buddhism and Mahayana Buddhism – mark the cultural products of this period in Thailand. Relief carvings at Angkor Wat from the early 12th century depict Tai mercenaries serving in Khmer armies. The Khmer called them 'Syam', a term for the Thai Kingdom which may have eventually become 'Sayam' or 'Siam'.

French historian Georges
Cœdès suggested that
'Indianisation' was a
common experience
among the early states of
Southeast Asia.

Between the 8th and 13th centuries, southern Thailand was under the sway of the maritime empire of Srivijaya which controlled trade between the South China Sea and the Indian Ocean. Chaiya (nearby Surat Thani) was its regional centre. A vital cultural differentiation in Southeast Asia occurred in Srivijaya: the city-state of Tambralinga (Nakhon Si Thammarat) adopted Buddhism, while the Malay city-states further south converted to Islam. By the 15th century, a permanent religious frontier existed on the peninsula between the Buddhist mainland of Southeast Asia and Muslim Malaya.

Srivijaya was the most
important trading empire
of ancient Southeast Asia.
Its centre is believed to
have been in Palembang
on Sumatra.

While these great empires gradually declined in the 12th to 16th centuries, Tai peoples in the hinterlands of Southeast Asia were successfully establishing new states. The Buddhist polities of Lanna and Sukhothai were becoming the centre of the Tai world and were soon joined by Ayuthaya.

1283	1292	1351
Early Thai script invented by King Ramkhamhaeng of Sukhothai.	Chiang Mai becomes the capital of Lanna.	Legendary founding of the Kingdom of Ayuthaya.

The Kingdom of Lanna

The Lanna kingdom was founded by King Mangrai who established Chiang Mai (meaning 'new city') as his capital in 1292. The king's success was based on the creation of a common Tai identity and a network of relationships with important neighbouring Tai rulers, especially King Ngam Muang of Phayao and King Ramkhamhaeng of Sukhothai. His legal work, *The Judgments of King Mangrai*, was humane and reasonable.

In the second half of the 14th century, the learned King Kü Na established the Sinhalese sect of Theravada Buddhism. Lanna assumed cultural leadership of the northern Tai (Tai Yuan). The long reign of King Tilok in the 15th century reinforced the hegemony of Lanna. Another period of generous royal sponsorship for Buddhism in the 1520s led to the creation of the great Pali-language chronicle *Jinakalamali* (which presented the narrative of Buddha's life and the spread of Buddhism). However, Lanna was plagued by dynastic intrigues and many wars, especially against Sukhothai and Ayuthaya. By the mid-16th century, the kingdom had become a victim of the power struggle between Laos and Ayuthaya.

The Kingdom of Sukhothai

In the mid-13th century, Tai rulers Pha Muang and Bang Klang Hao combined forces to expel the main Khmer outpost in the Sukhothai region. With the consent of Pha Muang, Bang Klang Hao was crowned King Sri Indraditya. Under the leadership of his son Ramkhamhaeng, the kingdom of Sukhothai became a regional power with dependencies in the east (Phitsanulok and Vientiane), the south (Nakhon Sawan, Chainat, Suphanburi, Ratburi, Phetburi and Nakhon Si Thammarat), the west (Pegu and Martaban) and in the north (Phrae, Nan, and Luang Prabang). These territories were not necessarily won by force. The southern annexes may have been a product of marriage or kinship between Ramkhamhaeng and families of the local rulers. Siamese Tai was becoming the language of the elite. The king is said to have invented a script variant and earlier version of present-day Thai in 1283. Sukhothai was a major centre of Theravada Buddhism on mainland Southeast Asia, as documented in works of art and the seminal Buddhist text, *Traiphum Phra Ruang*, composed by King Li Thai in 1339. After his death, however, Ramkhamhaeng's empire disintegrated.

The Long Ayuthaya Period

In the mid-14th century a new power, the kingdom of Ayuthaya, arose in the Chao Phraya River basin. Contemporary sources outside Thailand often call it Siam. Its legendary founder, King U Thong, has obscure origins. While he may have been from Phetchaburi or of Chinese origin, sources indicate that he was allied by marriage with the powerful houses of Suphanburi and Lopburi.

Traiphum Phra Ruang (The Three Worlds of King Ruang) describes the Buddhist cosmology. It also reinforces social hierarchy in terms of unequal religious merit, thereby justifying the Sukhothai monarchy.

1518	1569	1688
Ayuthaya concludes its first treaty with a Western nation, a cordial trade agreement with Portugal.	Ayuthaya is defeated by Burma.	King Narai's death is followed by the Palace Revolution, the dramatic fall of the Greek Constantine Phaulkon and the expulsion of the French.

RAMKAMHAENG'S STONE INSCRIPTION

In an inscription of 1292, King Ramkhamhaeng gives a picture of his kingdom as idyllic and free of constraints, and of himself as a benevolent patriarch:

In the time of King Ramkhamhaeng this land of Sukhothai is thriving. There are fish in the water and rice in the fields…whoever wants to trade in elephants, does so; whoever wants to trade in horses, does so;…if any commoner in the land has a grievance…it is easy; he goes and strikes the bell which the King has hung there; King Ramkhamhaeng…hears the call; he goes and questions the man, examines the case, and decides it justly for him.

Translation by AB Griswold and Prasert Na Nagara, Journal of the Siam Society (July 1971)

The rise of Ayuthaya was based on the ruler's ability to recruit an essential labour force and to profit from international trade. Wealth and commercial links gave Ayuthaya particularly advantageous access to Portuguese firearms and mercenaries. The fortified capital city was situated on a small island encircled by rivers.

With 36 kings and five dynasties in a period of 416 years, Ayuthaya's internal politics was a history of violence. The more absolute the king's power over people, land and resources, the fiercer the challenge. Grotesquely, royal victims of court manoeuvrings were wrapped up and beaten to death with a sandalwood club (as sandalwood was rare and luxurious), their sacred blood prevented from seeping into the earth.

Significantly strengthening the kingdom's administrative system, King Trailok (who reigned from 1448 to 1488) promulgated the Law of Civil Hierarchy and the Law of Military and Provincial Hierarchies. Together, they clarified the administrative structure with elaborate lists of official posts with specific titles and ranks. They also defined the place and position of individuals within Ayuthaya's complex hierarchical society. Individual social status was measured in numerical units of *sàk·dì·nah* – the amount of land in his (virtual) possession. Fines and punishments were proportional to the *sàk·dì·nah* of the person involved. Ayuthayan society consisted, roughly, of royalty, nobility and commoners. Commoners were *prai* (freemen) or *tâht* (slaves). Freemen were assigned to a royal or noble overseer. For six months of each year, they owed labour to the ruling elite, doing personal errands, public works or military service. Despite the clear social hierarchy, social mobility was possible, depending on personal skills, connections (including marriage) and royal favour.

Ayuthaya's sphere of influence was reinforced through the frontier towns of Khorat to the east, Kanchanaburi to the west, Phitsanulok to the north, and Nakhon Si Thammarat in the south. Having defeated Angkor in 1431–32, Ayuthaya's elite adopted Khmer court customs, honorific language and ideas of kingship. While the monarch styled himself as a Khmer *devaraja* (divine

Some scholars believe the Ramkhamhaeng inscription is a 19th-century forgery, fabricated to support claims that the Sukhothai region was a historic part of Siam.

Between the 13th and 15th centuries, firearms may have been introduced to Southeast Asians first by the Chinese and Arabs and then the Portuguese.

1767	**1768–82**	**1782**
The disastrous fall of Ayuthaya at the hands of the Burmese.	King Taksin rules from the new capital of Thonburi.	Death of King Taksin; founding of the Chakri dynasty; Bangkok becomes the new capital.

king) rather than Sukhothai's *dhammaraja* (righteous king), Ayuthaya continued to pay tribute to the Chinese emperor, who rewarded this ritualistic submission with generous gifts and enviable commercial privileges. The Siamese kingdom also had vassal states which were obliged, under threat, to provide troops and tributary gifts. Among these states were the kingdoms of Songkhla, Cambodia and Pattani. Submission was expressed symbolically in exquisitely crafted silver and golden trees.

It was an 'Age of Commerce' in Southeast Asia. A political and economic centre, Ayuthaya thrived on maritime trade. It was both the royal city and the major port. The river system connected the hinterlands as well. Coming overland or by sea, foreign trade was of great interest. Besides rice, Ayuthaya's main export was forest products. Its bureaucracy created the Phra Khlang ministry to handle foreign affairs and trade. The ministry held monopolies over selected exports and imports, setting tariffs and prices accordingly. From the 17th century, Ayuthaya's commercial economy expanded.

The historic presence in Ayuthaya of many foreigners is still discernible in the remnants of foreign settlements (Japanese, Dutch and French on the river banks around the island), and in old maps (Chinese, Moorish and English). Accounts by foreign visitors mention Ayuthaya's cosmopolitan markets and court. Foreign residents governed themselves, but leaders of these alien communities were absorbed into the Siamese bureaucracy, making them ever more dependent on the king's favour. Contemporary Westerners were terrified of Siamese law and its harsh physical punishments. In 1664 the Dutch were the first to seek and receive extraterritorial rights, escaping Siamese jurisdiction.

Siam's first *Treatise on Victorious Warfare* was composed to guide the armies of King Ramathibodi II in 1498. In 2008 an authentic version of a treatise of the early Bangkok period was recovered in Phetchabun.

In the 17th century, animal skins were exported to Japan in huge numbers of around 100,000 pieces a year.

KING NARAI'S WORLD

King Narai's interest in the international scene expressed itself in the exchange of embassies in the 1680s with the great rulers of Persia, France, Portugal and the Vatican. Siamese embassies to France created great interest. The king was keen to acquire and consume foreign material, culture and ideas. His court placed orders for items including spyglasses, hourglasses, paper, walnut trees, cheese, wine and marble fountains. Before he joined the French Jesuits to observe the eclipse at his palace in Lopburi, the Siamese monarch had received gifts including a globe from King Louis XIV.

In the 1680s, Narai recruited the services of the Greek adventurer Constantine Phaulkon. While serving the king as an intermediary between the Siamese and the West, Phaulkon abused his power as a high minister and royal favourite.

When the heirless King Narai died, Phaulkon was on the losing side and fell victim to Siamese court scheming during the '1688 Palace Revolution', in which he played an important part. Several contemporary authors have found inspiration to write about the rise and fall of Constantine Phaulkon.

1805	1851–68	1855
Codification of the Three Seals Law.	Reign of King Mongkut (Rama IV); waning Chinese influence; increasing Western influence.	Bowring Treaty concluded between Siam and Britain, stimulating the Siamese market economy and granting extraterritorial rights to British subjects in Siam.

Ayuthaya's impressive wealth and prosperity deriving from revenues and trade profits was a major theme in contemporary European travel literature. The display of wealth was part of the royal propaganda which is still evident today in the historical areas of Ayuthaya.

The glories of Ayuthaya were interrupted and cut short by the expansionist Burmese. In 1569 the city had fallen to the great Burmese king, Bayinnaung, but regained independence under the leadership of King Naresuan.

Then again, in the 1760s, Burma's ambitious and newly established Kongbaung dynasty pushed eastward to eliminate Ayuthaya as a political and commercial rival. Burmese troops laid siege to the capital for a year before destroying it in 1767. The city was devastated, its buildings and people wiped out. The surrounding areas were deserted and left uninhabited. So chilling was this historic sacking and razing of Ayuthaya that the perception of the Burmese as ruthless foes and aggressors still persists in the minds of many Thais to this day.

THE BANGKOK ERA
The Revival

The line of succession of the kings was thus broken. A former general, Taksin, claimed his right to rule. After defeating other contenders, including a brother of the last king of Ayuthaya, the new monarch chose Thonburi as his capital, a settlement downriver with a fort constructed by the French, more defensible and with better access to trade than Ayuthaya. Consolidating his power, King Taksin, the son of a Chinese immigrant father and Thai mother, strongly promoted trade with China. Towards the end of his 15 years on the throne, the king allegedly became mentally unstable and acted inappropriately toward Buddhist monks. In 1782, two of his leading generals mounted a coup and had him executed. One of the generals, Chao Phraya Chakri, was crowned as King Yot Fa (Rama I), founding the Chakri dynasty. Once again, the new monarch decided to move the capital, this time to the other side of the Chao Phraya River. This new location, Bangkok, was hailed as 'Rattanakosin' (Indra's Jewel), or as it is more commonly known, 'Krungthep' (the City of Angels).

In the 70 years between the reigns of King Taksin and King Nangklao (Rama III), the new rulers focused on restoring unity among the Siamese people and reviving Ayuthayan models. Surviving knowledge and practises were preserved or incorporated into new laws, manuals of government practise, religious and historical texts and literature. At the same time, the new rulers transformed their defence activities into expansion by means of war, extending their influence in every direction. Destroying the capital cities of both Laos and Cambodia, Siam contained Burmese aggression and made a vassal of Chiang Mai, which had suffered Burmese attacks as

Recommended European accounts of 17th-century Ayuthaya were written by Jeremias van Vliet, Simon de la Loubère, Nicolas Gervaise and Engelbert Kaempfer.

King Naresuan is portrayed as a national hero and became a cult figure, especially worshipped by the Thai army. His story inspired a high-budget film trilogy, *King Naresuan* by filmmaker Chatrichalerm Yukol.

1868–1910	1874	1890
Reign of King Chulalongkorn (Rama V); modernisation; European imperialism.	Edict abolishing slavery.	Siam's first railway, connecting Bangkok with Nakhon Ratchasima.

THAI WOMEN IN HISTORY

Foreign visitors during the Ayuthaya period noted that women did most of the work in Siam, including trade. But only in 1868 did King Mongkut (Rama IV) abolish a husband's right to sell his wife or her children without her permission. The older provision, it was said, treated the woman 'as if she were a water buffalo'. A mid-19th century work, *Suphasit Son Ying* (Sayings for Ladies), acknowledged that upper-class women wanted to have an influence on the selection of a husband and that they contributed to family businesses. The Sayings gave advice to women on both these matters.

---

well. Defeated populations were resettled and played an important role in increasing the rice production of Siam, much of which was exported to China. King Nangklao was very keen on trading with the Chinese and was interested in their culture. Unlike the Ayuthayan rulers who identified with the Hindu god Vishnu, the Chakri kings positioned themselves as defenders of Buddhism. They undertook compilations and Thai translations of essential Buddhist texts and constructed many royal temples. In the meantime, a new social order and market economy was taking shape.

> The Three Seals Laws were based partly upon the surviving legal texts of Ayuthaya in the first reign of Bangkok. They set the legal standard in the early Bangkok period.

Modernisation & Westernisation

The Siamese elite had admired China, but that fascination died away in the 1850s when Siam opened itself to Western countries. In the process, the ruling elite adopted a limited version of Western modernisation, including scientific knowledge, bureaucratic and military systems, education, infrastructure and legal systems.

Before his accession, King Mongkut (Rama IV) spent 27 years in the monkhood. He founded the Thammayut monastic sect, based on the strict disciplines of the Mon monks he himself had followed. During his long monastic career, he became proficient not only in Pali and Sanskrit, but also Latin and English. He also studied Western sciences. During the reign of Rama III, the first printing press had been brought to Siam by the American missionary James Low. The possibility of printing documents in Thai script advanced further when another American missionary, Dan Bradley, published the first Thai newspaper, the *Bangkok Recorder* in the 1840s and 1860s. King Mongkut and some Thai elite were among the subscribers of this newspaper.

> The *Bangkok Recorder* dealt with local and foreign news, and various topics like science, politics and religion.

An enduring debate inherited from the reign of Rama III centred on the connected issues of the economy, the social order and the handling of Western influence. Reformers reasoned, though their position was not shared by all, that more Western trade, freer labour and access to new technologies would generate economic growth. While expressing disdain for Christianity, King Mongkut was genuinely fascinated by the Western idea of material progress. One of his advisors, Chaophraya Thiphakorawong, wrote a

> Sugar was Siam's most important export commodity until it was replaced by rice from the 1870s.

1892	**1893**	**1909**
New administration: a cabinet government with 12 ministries, part of which became or were predecessors of the Ministries of Defence, Interior Affairs, Justice and Education.	French blockade of the Chao Phraya River (the 'Paknam incident') intensifies the threat of colonialism.	Anglo-Siamese Treaty settles Siam's boundaries.

During the 'Paknam incident' of 1893 Siam responded with military action after the French annexed its territory on the east bank of the Mekong. France sent two gunboats into the Chao Phraya River, demanding concession. The incident resulted in a French-Siamese treaty, which created a clear boundary between Siam and French Indochina along the Mekong River.

collection of essays, *Sadaeng Kitjanukit,* encouraging children to learn Western science but to reject Christianity.

During this reign, Siam concluded treaties with Western powers. In particular, the Bowring Treaty of 1855 forced the kingdom to integrate into the world market system. The Siamese court had to give up royal monopolies and grant extraterritorial rights to British subjects. Other Western powers followed the British example.

Mongkut's son, King Chulalongkorn (Rama V) was to take much greater steps in replacing the old political order with the model of the nation-state. He abolished slavery and the corvée system, which had lingered on ineffectively since the Ayuthaya period. The control of labour suddenly became difficult with the unmanageable influx of Chinese immigrants and frontier peasants, and the extraterritorial rights of the subjects of Western nations. Chulalongkorn's reign oversaw the creation of a salaried bureaucracy, a police force and a standing army. His reforms brought uniformity to the legal code, law courts and revenue offices. As peasant colonisation on the frontiers was increasing, agriculture in Siam's core areas was improved by new irrigation techniques. Schools were established along European lines. Universal conscription and poll taxes made all men the king's men.

In 'civilising' his country, Chulalongkorn relied greatly on foreign advisors, mostly British. Within the royal court, much of the centuries-old protocol was abandoned and replaced by Western forms. The architecture and visual art of state, like the new throne halls, were designed by Italian artists. Defying old traditions, the king allowed himself to be seen in public, photographed, painted and sculpted, and allowed his image to be reproduced on coins, stamps and postcards. (Although King Mongkut was the first Siamese monarch to allow himself to be photographed and seen by commoners in public.)

Klai Ban is available in English, French and German translations.

King Chulalongkorn annexed Lanna, Khorat and Phuket. In 1893 the Ministry of Interior was created to supervise the provinces, and railways were built to connect distant population centres. However, Siam was forced to concede territories to French Indochina (Laos in 1893 and Cambodia in 1907) and British Malaya (three Malayan states in 1909). Siam was becoming

CHULALONGKORN, THE TRAVELLER KING

While still a boy, young King Chulalongkorn travelled to observe the colonial countries of Singapore, Java, Malaya, Burma and India in order to select 'what may be safe models for the future prosperity of Siam'. In 1897, four years after the 'Paknam incident' with the French, he visited Europe, hoping to show that Siam was a civilised country which should be treated like a European power. His second visit in 1907 resulted in *Klai Ban* (Far from Home), a compilation of letters written to his daughter in Siam during his journey. They present an insightful account of early 20th century Europe.

1913	1916	1917
The Nationality Act and Surname Act enacted by King Vajiravudh's government.	The first Thai university, Chulalongkorn University, established.	Siam sends troops to join the Allies in WWI.

a geographically defined country in a modern sense. By 1902, the country no longer called itself Siam but Prathet Thai (the country of the Thai) or Ratcha-anachak Thai (the kingdom of the Thai). By 1913, all those living within its borders were defined as 'Thai'.

In the face of imperialist threats and internal disarray, Western modernisation seemed to the Siamese elite to be the logical response. However, establishing a parliament was too great a step for King Chulalongkorn and his immediate successor to take.

English-educated King Vajiravudh (Rama VI) introduced further reforms, including compulsory education. He converted the Thai calendar to Western models and promoted nationalism with a royalist tinge. In 1917, the new tricolour national flag (red, white and blue representing nation, religion and king respectively) was designed for the Thai contingent sent to fight on the side of the Allies in the European war. Thai people were required to use surnames. The Thai government feared that the Chinese in Siam would become involved with the politics of China, and was concerned about the spread of republican and revolutionary ideas, so it passed the 1913 Nationality Act allowing descendants of Chinese immigrants to become Thai citizens.

> The People's Party originated from a group of Thai students (including Phibul and Pridi) in Paris in the 1920s who shared a vision of a future democratic Thailand based on Western models.

DEMOCRATIC THAILAND
The 1932 Revolution

In 1932 a group of young officers and bureaucrats calling themselves Khana Ratsadon (People's Party) mounted a successful, bloodless coup which transformed the government into a constitutional monarchy and Siam into a democratic state with parliamentary representation. The leaders of the group were inspired by the democratic ideology they had encountered during their studies in Europe. After the abdication and voluntary exile to the UK of King Prajathipok (Rama VII) in 1935, the new democratic government promoted his 10-year-old nephew, Ananda Mahidol, to the throne as Rama VIII. Successfully suppressing royalist reactionaries, in the years after the coup the two factions within the People's Party engaged in their own internal struggle. The military faction was led by General Phibul Songkhram, the civilians by Pridi Phanomyong.

Pridi Phanomyong (1900–83) was a French-educated lawyer, a civilian leader of the 1932 Revolution, figurehead of Seri Thai and Thai prime minister. His work on democratic reforms in Thailand was based on constitutional measures and attempts to restrict by law military involvement in Thai politics. He supported nationalisation of land and labour, state-led industrialisation and labour protection. In 1934, he founded Thammasat University. Attacked for being 'communist', his direct role in Thai politics ended in the mid-1950s. He was named one of Unesco's great personalities of the 20th-century world in 2000.

By command of force, Phibul dominated the contest. His regime, which coincided with WWII, was characterised by strong nationalistic tendencies

1932	1939	1941
Bloodless revolution by young military and civilian officers ends the absolute monarchy.	The country's English name is officially changed from Siam to Thailand.	Japanese forces enter Thailand.

centring on 'nation' and 'Thai-ness'. In 1939 he changed the English name of the country to Thailand, the land of the Thai – the free people.

During the WWII Japanese invasion of Southeast Asia, the Phibul government sided with Japan, hoping to increase its negotiating power in international politics, especially in reclaiming territory from France. Thailand intended to declare war on the US and Britain. Eventually, the anti-Japanese Thai Liberation Movement, Seri Thai, led by Pridi, forced Phibul's resignation. Since Seni Pramoj, the Thai ambassador in Washington and a member of Seri Thai, had refused to deliver the formal declaration of war, Thailand was saved from bearing the serious consequences of defeated-nation status.

The post-war democratic governments were short-lived. Pridi's government passed the 1946 Constitution, which created a fully elective legislature. In that year, young King Ananda Mahidol was shot dead – the circumstances of his death are still unclear. His younger brother became King Bhumibol (Rama IX). In 1947, elements in the military who felt threatened by the liberal and socialist approach of the government overturned it, sending Pridi into exile. Phibul became the head of a new, more radical anti-communist government.

Military Rule & the Cold War

In 1957, General Sarit Thanarat took over, subjecting Thailand to a true military dictatorship: abolishing the constitution, dissolving the parliament and banning all political parties. In the 1950s, the US directly involved itself in Southeast Asia, attempting to contain communist expansion in the region. In the context of the Cold War, the US government gave economic and military support to the Sarit government.

Sarit supported expansion of the royal role, seeing in the king a 'unifying authority' for the nation. King Bhumibol and Queen Sirikit made state visits abroad, presenting an image of Thailand as a traditional but modernised nation. At home they engaged in rural development. The Royal Project Foundation was founded in 1969, to help eradicate opium cultivation among the northern hill tribes and to encourage a balanced utilisation of land and forest for sustainable development.

From 1963 to 1973, military rule was continued under Generals Thanom Kittikachorn and Praphat Charusathien, who allowed the US to station its troops in Thailand during the Vietnam War. A volatile mixture of capitalism, US imperialism, military dictatorship and Marxist ideology set in motion the opposition of intellectuals, students, peasants and workers. In 1973, more than half a million people in Bangkok and in major provincial towns demonstrated, demanding a constitution from the military government. The bloody dispersal of the Bangkok demonstration on 14 October led to the collapse of the regime.

In the following years, the polarisation of right and left, represented by the military and extreme right, and the left-oriented student movement, intensified

---

In 1950, Thailand was the first Asian country to offer troops to support the US in the Korean War. In 1954, it joined the Southeast Asia Treaty Organization (SEATO), a US-led international organisation for collective defence.

In 1988 the Royal Project Foundation received the prestigious Ramon Magsaysay Award for development work.

Prem Tinsulanonda serves as lifelong head of the Privy Council of King Bhumibol.

1942	**1945**	**1946**
Communist Party of Thailand (CPT) re-established.	WWII ends; Thailand is compelled to return territory seized from Laos, Cambodia and Malaya.	Accession of King Bhumibol Adulyadej (Rama IX); Thailand joins the UN.

in Thai society. Finally, anti-communist forces erupted, leading to the massacre of students inside Thammasat University on 6 October 1976. Many students and intellectuals joined with armed communist insurgents in the jungles.

Economic Development & Consequences

The last quarter of the 20th century witnessed skyrocketing economic growth and Thailand's subsequent social transformation. Development indicators such as the rise of consumerism and individualism were accompanied by new problems – the collapse of rural communities, exploitation of workers and increased prostitution. Economic growth also impacted Thai politics.

In the 1980s, the government of the 'political soldier,' General Prem Tinsulanonda, enjoyed a period of political and economic stability. Prem managed to dismantle the communist insurgency through military action and amnesty programs. With economic growth as their priority, the new generation of business people–politicians began to criticise the military, their budgets and their role in politics. In 1988, Prem was succeeded by Chatichai Choonhavan. His Chat Thai Party had close ties with rising provincial business people able to manipulate the local electorate. Under Chatichai, the Ministries of Defence, Interior and Finance were handed over to elected politicians, rather than technocrats and generals. Chatichai's government attempted to shift power away from the bureaucracy and the military in favour of the Cabinet and business interests. Abandoning the Cold War mentality, the government's regional policy aspired instead to transform 'battlefields into marketplaces', to end hostilities in communist Indochina and to take advantage of economic liberalisation.

Increasing 'money politics' during the 1980s provoked a reaction, especially within the urban middle class. In 1985, a former soldier, Chamlong Srimuang, was elected as Bangkok mayor. He promised to clean up corruption. Chamlong's Phalang Tham (Moral Power) party also stood for office in national elections. Meanwhile, Chatichai's government was forced out by a coup in February 1991, undone by excesses such as its notorious 'buffet cabinet', an exploitative rotation of lucrative ministerial posts.

While the military was moving to protect its privileged position in the state, the coup received the assent of the Bangkok business community and the educated class, who were repelled by the money politics of provincial business people–politicians. Anand Panyarachun, a former diplomat turned business-man, was appointed prime minister and worked for liberal economic reforms. Soon the generals' abuse of power for personal benefit raised criticism. In the elections of March 1992, the pro-military party, which included former Chat Thai members, won the largest number of seats and prepared to form a govern-ment, only to have their candidate for prime minister discredited by charges of drug trading. General Suchinda Kraprayoon, the leader of the coup, then stepped in as the new prime minister, a development quite unacceptable to

Chamlong Srimuang is a devout Buddhist affiliated with the anti-materialist, anti-consumerist Santi Asoke sect.

The Democrat Party ('Phak Prachathipat') was founded in 1946 and is the longest surviv-ing political party in Thailand.

1957	1959	1965
The successful coup by Sarit Thanarat starts a period of long military rule that lasts until 1973.	The first tourist authority formed.	Thailand hosts US military bases during the Vietnam War.

Bangkok's middle class. Led by Chamlong Srimuang, on 17 May 1992 around 200,000 protestors launched a mass demonstration in Bangkok. They were dubbed the 'mobile phone mob' – their phones identifying them as members of the rising urban, educated class. In three nights of violence, armed soldiers of the military tried to suppress the demonstrators, as the Thai and international press published full reports of the events. On the night of 20 May, King Bhumibol summoned Chamlong and Suchinda to the palace and ordered them to stop the violence. Anand returned to lead an interim government.

After the 'Black May' events, democracy activists fervently demanded constitutional reform, balance of power between the state and civil society, freeing of the electronic media from military control and democratic decentralisation.

For most of the 1990s, the parliament was dominated by the Democrat Party, which represented the hopes of business and the urban middle class that Thailand would successfully adapt to the globalising economy. Its major support came from the southern Thai urban population of old port towns and a tourism- and export-oriented economy (rubber, tin and fishing). On the other side of the spectrum were the former pro-military politicians based in the central plain and the people of the agrarian northeast in new provincial towns who focused on state-budget distribution to their provinces.

Within months of the 1997 crisis, Thai currency devalued swiftly from 25B to 56B per US$1.

The Democrat-led government under the leadership of Chuan Leekpai returned to the traditional system of compromise between bureaucrats and politicians. Reforms were hardly implemented. The depletion of natural resources, especially in the use of land by government agencies for bureaucratic and private benefit, provoked protests among local people. The Democrats lost their popularity. However, the two subsequent governments led by the Chat Thai and New Aspiration parties were unable to protect Thailand from the devastating effects of the 1997 Asian economic crisis.

From 1985 to 1996, Thailand's economic growth averaged over 9% per year. However, in 1997, the country's economy, already plagued by the burdens of foreign debt, was aggravated further by financial overextension in the real-estate sector. The Thai government failed to defend the baht against massive international speculation and was forced to float the currency. The weakened currency resulted in a devalued stock market and falling prices of other assets. Mushrooming debt in the private sector was coupled with massive layoffs and personal tragedies. The crisis immediately spread through Asia. The International Monetary Fund (IMF), while imposing conditions of financial and legal reforms and economic liberalisation, initiated a rescue program, using more than US$17 billion to stabilise the Thai currency.

In the aftermath of the crisis, the Democrats returned to power uncontested, but their support evaporated as they failed to prevent the economy from worsening over the next three years. Business and the urban middle class strongly voiced their resentment against inefficient politicians, government

1968	1973	1976
Thailand is a founding member state of the Association of Southeast Asian Nations (ASEAN).	Thai students, workers and farmers join together to overthrow the military dictatorship; a democratic government is installed.	Violent suppression of student movement by the military and the rightists.

mismanagement and what they perceived as unfair IMF policies (such as the forced liberalisation/opening up to foreign ownership of Thai business). A new opportunity seemed to appear in the promise of a constitution which would create a better political system. This 'people's constitution' was passed on 27 September 1997. It enshrined human rights and freedom of expression and granted more power to a civil society to counter corruption.

Disappointed by the results of globalisation, spokespersons for rural constituencies and people at the grassroots now began to dominate debate on the country's pattern of development, for example, how to enable rural society to re-absorb large numbers of jobless persons returning home. King Bhumibol emphasised the idea of self-sufficiency in his birthday speech in December 1997: 'What is important is to have enough to eat and to live; and to have an economy which provides enough to eat and live…We need to move backwards in order to move forwards'.

> The Charoen Pokphand (CP) Group, founded in the 1920s by the Chearavanont family, is Thailand's largest business conglomerate and multinational corporation, consisting of agribusiness, retailers, 7-Eleven franchising and telecommunications.

Thaksinocracy

In 2000, the economic crisis began to ease, leaving Thailand in urgent need of a new approach to development policy. Business had long since succeeded the military as the dominant force in politics. In 1998, the telecommunications billionaire and former police officer, Thaksin Shinawatra, founded the Thai Rak Thai (TRT or 'Thai Loving Thai') party, which corresponded with rising nationalism in the country after the Asian economic crisis. Thaksin chose to address two major sectors of society which had been deeply affected by the crisis – business and the countryside. Promising to help business recover, TRT gained support, especially from CP Group and Bangkok Bank. The party's program included community empowerment and bottom-up grassroots development (through agrarian debt relief, village capital funds and cheap health care), which was to earn Thaksin a reputation as a populist.

> Thaksin was the first prime minister in Thai history to complete a four-year term of office.

After winning an almost absolute majority in the national elections of 2001, Thaksin became prime minister. The decisive majority, along with constitutional provisions designed to strengthen the prime minister, made his a stable government. Much more than previous prime ministers, he made use of telecommunications to communicate with his electorate and dominated press and TV news. He quickly delivered what he had promised during the election campaign (on community empowerment and grassroots development). In 2005, Thaksin won an outright majority in national elections. His popularity among the grassroots was immense.

Thaksin was criticised nationally and internationally for his 'war on drugs', which began in 2003. It was seen as his means to shake up influential groups, suspected of having links to drug trafficking, that were dominating local politics and elections. The 'war' took over 2700 lives, many of which appeared to be extrajudicial killings by Thai police, according to human rights groups such as Amnesty International.

1979	1980–88	1988
After three years of military rule, elections and parliament restored.	Prem Tinsulanonda's government works to undermine the communist insurgent movement and eventually ends it with a political solution.	Chatichai Choonhavan becomes first elected PM since 1976; trade opens with Indochina.

Troubles in the Deep South

In 2001, Muslim separatist insurgents began attacking government property and personnel in Thailand's southernmost provinces of Pattani, Narathiwat and Yala. These three provinces once comprised the area of the historic kingdom of Pattani until it was conquered by the Chakri kings. Under King Chulalongkorn's administrative reforms, the provinces came more directly under the sway of the centralised bureaucracy, which replaced the local ruling elite with governors and bureaucrats from Bangkok. During WWII, Phibul's ultranationalist regime set out to enforce a policy of nation-building from above, including the transformation of a multi-ethnic society into a unified and homogenous Thai Buddhist nation. In the 1940s, this policy inflamed resistance in these southern provinces, and gave birth to a strong separatist movement fighting for the independence of Pattani. In the 1980s and 1990s, the Prem administration abolished this forced assimilation policy. Prem promised support for Muslim cultural rights and religious freedoms, offered the insurgents a general amnesty, and implemented an economic development plan. However, the three provinces continue to rank among the least developed (economically and educationally) in the country. In the 1990s, the Chuan government committed to implementing a supposed 'development as security' approach from 1999 to 2003.

However, the Thaksin regime decided to impose greater central control over the southernmost provinces. This change of government policy was a veiled attempt to break up the traditional domination of the Democrat Party in the south. The policy succeeded in weakening relations between the local elite, southern voters and the Democrats who had served as their representatives in parliament. However, it did not take into consideration the sensitive and tenacious Muslim culture of the Deep South. In 2002, the government dissolved the longstanding Southern Border Province Administration Center, which had been a joint civilian-police-military office. Instead, they handed the security of the region over to the police. These tactics displaced the old structure of dialogue between the Thai government and the southern Muslims, replacing it with a more powerful Thai provincial police structure that was abhorred by local Muslim communities. In 2004, in denial of the rebels' separatist spirit, Thaksin described the insurgency as part of an insidious attempt to undermine the country's tourism industry. The government responded harshly and evaded responsibility over two incidents that year: a government force launched a deadly attack on insurgents hiding in the historic Krue Se Mosque, highly revered by local Muslims; and in Tak Bai, hundreds of local people were arrested after demonstrating to demand a release of suspected insurgents – while being transported to an army camp for interrogation, 78 of them suffocated to death in the overcrowded trucks. Those responsible for the two incidents (which together cost the lives of more than 100 Muslims) received minor punishments. In 2005, martial law was declared in the area.

In 2002 Thaksin Shinawatra said 'There's no separatism, no ideological terrorists; just common bandits'.

1991–92	1995	1997
General Suchinda attempts to seize power; King Bhumibol intervenes to halt civil turmoil surrounding 'Black May' protests.	First internet service for the Thai public offered by state enterprises.	Thailand reels under impact of Asian economic crisis; passage of 'people's constitution'.

Human rights abuses have been committed by both sides in this dispute, as reported by various groups including Human Rights Watch. The insurgents have been attacking not only soldiers and policemen and their bases, but also teachers, students and state schools. To date, the conflict has cost more than 3000 lives; most of the casualties have been villagers – Buddhist and Muslim alike. The insurgents' identities remain anonymous and no concrete demands have been put forward by them.

The official website of the royal family is: http://kanchanapisek.or.th

2006–08 POLITICAL CRISIS

In 2006 Prime Minister Thaksin Shinawatra was accused of conflicts of interest, the most glaring example of which was the Shinawatra family's sale of their Shin Corporation stock to the Singaporean government for a tax-free sum of 73 billion baht (US$1.88 billion), thanks to new telecommunications legislation that exempted individuals from capital gains tax. These and a series of lawsuits filed against the prime minister's critics set off a popular anti-Thaksin campaign. His call for a snap election to assure his electoral support was met with a boycott by the opposition Democrats, and the election results were subsequently annulled.

In June, the Thai took a short break from overheated politics to celebrate the 60th year of their king's accession to the throne, the Golden Jubilee. Highly respected King Bhumibol is the world's longest reigning monarch.

On 19 September 2006, the military, led by General Sonthi Boonyaratglin, staged a bloodless coup which forced Thaksin into exile. Retired General Surayud Chulanont was appointed as interim prime minister. In the following year, the Constitutional Court ruled that as a result of electoral fraud, the TRT Party had to be dissolved, barring 111 of the party's executive members from politics for five years. A new constitution was approved in a referendum by a rather thin margin. As promised, the interim government held general elections in December, returning the country to civilian rule. In January 2008, the Thaksin-influenced People's Power Party (PPP) won a majority and formed a government led by Samak Sundaravej.

A 1907 French map put the Phra Wihan temple, but not the area around it, in Cambodia. In 2008 Cambodia wanted to include the disputed area around the temple as part of the would-be World Heritage Site.

In that year Thailand faced great pressure on various levels: the ongoing insurgency in the Deep South, a territorial conflict with neighbouring Cambodia, the global economic crisis, rising oil prices and the extreme political polarisation at home.

After Unesco listed the ancient Khmer temple of Phra Wihan ('Preah Vihear' in Cambodian) as an official World Heritage Site, nationalist emotions ran high on both sides. Cambodia and Thailand moved troops into the disputed area, but returned to talks.

Ousted PM Thaksin returned to Thailand briefly, but then went back into exile (at that time to the UK, but he has since been constantly on the move) to avoid trial, and later, the sentence handed down against him by the Thai court. His wife also faced charges in court.

2001	2003	2004
Telecommunications tycoon, Thaksin Shinawatra, is elected prime minister.	False media reports that a Thai actress accused Cambodia of stealing the Angkor Wat complex from Thailand spurs angry crowds in Phnom Penh; the Thai embassy is burned.	Renewed insurgent violence in the Deep South. A devastating tsunami hits Thailand's Andaman Coast, killing 5000 and damaging tourism and fishing industries.

Samak's PPP-led government was troubled by the extra-parliamentary tactics of the opposition People's Alliance for Democracy (PAD). Demonstrations were led by the ex-mayor of Bangkok, Chamlong Srimuang, and newspaper owner, Sondhi Limthongkul. The movement represented a mixture of anti-Thaksin, anti-PPP (considered Thaksin's proxy) and royalist sentiments. The protesters, wearing yellow (the king's birthday colour) and equipped with plastic hand-clappers, were dubbed 'yellow-shirters'. They included a wide range of middle-class groups and some of the upper class. The PAD were well organised and developed strategies on a daily basis to interrupt the work of the government and cabinet. They seized public spaces and government complexes, setting up camps for months in places such as the Government House. The quasi-permanent gathering, supplied with food and drink and entertained with music and speeches, added to the capital's traffic woes, although it eventually became something of a tourist attraction.

The supporters of Thaksin and the PPP government also organised their own movement, symbolised by red shirts and a formidable trademark of plastic foot-shaped clappers. (A later, milder version was heart-shaped.) The red-shirt protestors represented TRT and PPP supporters. They came mostly from the north and northeast, and included anti-coup activists. Both yellow and red movements found support from politicians and academics in different camps. Some skirmishes in Bangkok and other provinces resulted in more than a dozen deaths. This was seen by some as evidence of the surfacing of a longstanding, suppressed polarisation between classes and between rural and urban sectors in Thailand.

In September 2008, Samak Sundaravej was unseated as PM by the Constitutional Court for violating a conflict of interest law by hosting TV cooking shows while in office. The PAD occupation of Thailand's main airports, Suvarnabhumi and Don Muang, in November 2008, was the boldest and riskiest move to force the resignation of Samak's replacement, Somchai Wongsawat, Thaksin's brother-in-law. The occupation led to a week-long closure of both major airports, causing enormous damage to the Thai economy, especially its tourism and export industries. Throughout the crisis, the military claimed to remain 'neutral', but when an Army Commander in Chief, General Anuphong Phaochinda, called publicly for new elections and a PAD withdrawal, many in the government called it a silent coup.

In the midst of this crisis, Prime Minister Somchai was forced to quit his office by a Constitutional Court ruling which dissolved the PPP because of vote buying, and barred its leaders from politics for five years. After weeks of manoeuvring by the Democrat Party to persuade several minor parties to switch sides, Democrat Abhisit Vejjajiva was elected in a parliamentary vote, becoming Thailand's 27th prime minister. Even as the pro-Thaksin camp remained hostile and active, Abhisit faced the daunting task of re-establishing 'national harmony' and restoring confidence in the Thai economy in the face of the global economic recession.

2006	2007	2008
The nation celebrates King Bhumibol's 60th year on the throne. Demonstrations against Thaksin Shinawatra are followed by the September coup ending his government.	Democratic elections return civilian rule to Thailand in December, Samak is announced as Prime Minister the following month.	A nation in crisis: anti-government demonstrations; dispute with Cambodia over the Phra Wihan temple; the closing of Bangkok's two main airports due to demonstrators; the global economic recession.

Thailand & You
Making the most of your trip

RESPONSIBLE TRAVEL

It is easy to love Thailand: the pace of life is unhurried, the people are generally friendly and the pressures on the short-term visitor are relatively few. A smile goes a long way, chitchat is more important than a to-do list and doling out compliments is a national sport.

That doesn't mean that every Thai is a cheery Pollyanna. So many foreigners pass through the country completely oblivious of the culture and customs that many Thais in the tourism industry suffer from 'foreigner fatigue'. Further complicating matters is that tourism is a relatively lucrative industry attracting sound business people as well as fast operators and con artists. Handicapped by language and culture, many visitors have a hard time spotting the genuine sweethearts from the shysters.

Knowing a little bit more about this place will make you a smarter traveller and a better guest. Emanate a sense of warmth and happiness and the Thais will instinctively respond in kind. Know how to behave politely in public and you'll coax a smile from the disapproving schoolmarms. Learn some of the language and you'll become a fast friend with everyone from the noodle vendor to the taxi driver.

THE CULTURE

Thais are generally tolerant of most kinds of behaviour and assume that the majority of foreigners know nothing about their country. When you do exhibit the slightest bit of etiquette mastery, Thais will beam with gratitude. For information on how to understand Thai culture as a whole, see p54.

www.responsible-travel .org offers common-sense advice on how to travel with a conscience.

Monarchy Etiquette

If you do nothing else, remember to treat the monarchy and the religion (which are often viewed as interconnected) with extreme deference. Thais regard any image of the king and the royal family with religious devotion. Money, which bears images of the king, is never stepped on (in the case of a dropped bill) or kept in one's shoe.

In addition, avoid criticising or disparaging the royal family. Thais are very guarded about discussing negative aspects of the monarchy for fear of offending someone or worse, being charged for lese-majesty, which carries a jail sentence.

It's also considered a grave insult to Thai nationhood, and to the monarchy, not to stand when you hear the national or royal anthems. Radio and TV stations in Thailand broadcast the national anthem daily at 8am and 6pm; in towns and villages this can be heard over public loudspeakers in the streets or in bus and train stations. In Bangkok, the national anthem is played in Skytrain and subway stations. The Thais stop whatever they're doing to stand during the anthem and visitors are expected to do likewise. (It is not necessary to stand if you're inside a home or business.) The royal anthem is played just before films are shown in public cinemas; again, the audience always stands until it's over.

Temple Etiquette

When visiting a temple, it is very important to dress modestly (covered to the elbows and the ankles) and to take your shoes off when you enter any building that contains a Buddha image. Buddha images are sacred objects, so don't pose in front of them for pictures and definitely do not clamber upon them. When sitting in a religious edifice, keep your feet pointed away from any Buddha images. The usual way to do this is to sit in the 'mermaid' pose in which your legs are folded to the side, with your feet pointing backwards.

The dress code at royally associated temples is strictly enforced and trousers or long sarongs are available to rent if tourists are dressed in shorts.

Monks are not supposed to touch or be touched by women. If a woman wants to hand something to a monk, the object should be placed within reach of the monk or on the monk's 'receiving cloth' and not handed directly to him.

Since most temples are maintained from the donations received, when you visit a temple remember to make a contribution.

Social Conventions & Gestures

The traditional Thai greeting is with a prayerlike palms-together gesture known as a *wâi*. If someone shows you a *wâi*, you should return the gesture, unless the greeting comes from a child or a service person. Overusing the *wâi* or placing your hands too low in respect to your face trivialises a very intricate custom.

A smile and a cheery *sà·wàt·dee kráp* if you're male or *sà·wàt·dee kâ* if you're female (the all-purpose Thai greeting) goes a long way towards calming the initial trepidation that locals may feel upon seeing a foreigner.

In the more traditional parts of the country, it is not proper for members of the opposite sex to touch one another, either as lovers or as friends. Hand-holding is not acceptable behaviour outside of the major cities such as Bangkok. But same-sex touching is quite common and is typically a sign of friendship, not sexual attraction. Older Thai men might grab a younger man's thigh in the same way that buddies slap each other on the back. Thai women are especially affectionate with female friends, often sitting close to one another or linking arms.

When hailing a bus or a taxi, Thais extend their arms slightly, with their hand below their waists and wave downward. In the West, we summons someone with a hand gesture that involves waving the hand with the palm towards our faces. In Thailand the same hand gesture is used only to call animals. People are assigned a slightly different gesture: the palm is turned away from the caller's face.

When handing an object to another person or receiving something, the ultimate in polite behaviour is to extend the right hand out while the left hand gently grips the right elbow.

Dress & Hygiene

The Thais hold modesty in personal dress in high regard. Shorts above the knee, sleeveless shirts, tank tops (singlets) and other beach-style attire are not appropriate when you're not at the beach or sporting events, or when you're outside Bangkok. If you insist on wearing less, do it in Bangkok where international standards of skin exhibition are more accepted. And don't exempt yourself because of the humid climate. Covering up with light, loose fabric offers protection from the sun, and frequent showers act as better natural air-conditioning than spaghetti-strap tops.

The importance of modesty extends to the beach as well. Except for urban Bangkokians, most Thais swim fully clothed. For this reason, sunbathing nude or topless is not acceptable and in some cases is even illegal.

Thais are also fastidious in their personal appearance and even in the hottest weather rarely sweat, whereas new arrivals are in a constant state

To be super polite, lower your head slightly when passing between two people having a conversation or when passing near a monk.

Bring a gift if you're invited to a Thai home. Something simple like fruit or beverages (eg beer, wine or Fanta, depending on the economic level) can be bought from the market.

VISITING HILL-TRIBE VILLAGES

The minority tribes of Thailand living in the northern mountains have managed to maintain their own distinct cultural identity despite increased interaction with the majority culture over the last 30 years. Even with the adoption of outside influences, like Christianity or Buddhism or donated Western-style clothes, many hill-tribe villages continue their animistic traditions, which define social taboos and conventions. If you're planning on visiting hill-tribe villages on an organized trek, talk to your guide about do's and don'ts. Here is a general prescription to get you started.

- Always ask for permission before taking any photos of tribespeople, especially at private moments inside their dwellings. Many traditional belief systems view photography with suspicion.
- Show respect for religious symbols and rituals. Don't touch totems at village entrances or sacred items hanging from trees. Don't participate in ceremonies unless invited to join.
- Avoid cultivating a tradition of begging, especially among children. Don't hand out candy unless you can also arrange for modern dentistry. Talk to your guide about donating to a local school instead.
- Avoid public nudity and be careful not to undress near an open window where village children might be able to peep in.
- Don't flirt with members of the opposite sex unless you plan on marrying them. Don't drink or do drugs with the villagers; altered states sometimes lead to culture clashes.
- Smile at villagers even if they stare at you. And ask your guide how to say 'hello' in the tribal language.
- Avoid public displays of affection, which in some traditional systems are viewed as offensive to the spirit world.
- Don't interact with the villagers' livestock, even the free-roaming pigs; these creatures are valuable possessions, not entertainment oddities. Also avoid interacting with jungle animals, which in some belief systems are viewed as visiting spirits.
- Don't litter.
- Adhere to the same feet taboos that apply to Thai culture (see below). Plus don't step on the threshold of a house, prop your feet up against the fire or wear your shoes inside.

of perspiration. One way to avoid the continual drip is to bathe often. Talcum powder is another antidote to moisture and stink and helps prevent prickly heat.

Sandals or slip-on shoes are perfectly acceptable for almost any but the most formal occasions.

Head & Feet Taboos

From practical and spiritual viewpoints, Thais regard the head as the highest and most sacred part of the body and the feet as the dirtiest and lowest part of the body. Many of the taboos associated with the feet have a practical derivation as well. Traditionally Thais ate, slept and entertained on the floor of their homes with little in the way of furniture. To keep their homes and eating surfaces clean, the feet (and shoes) contracted a variety of rules. All feet and head taboos in Thailand come with certain qualifiers and exceptions that will make more sense as you become more familiar with the culture. In the meantime, err on the side of caution with the following tips.

One of the most considerate things you can do in Thailand is to take off your shoes inside private homes or some guesthouses and businesses. (When entering temple buildings, removing your shoes is an absolute must.) Not every establishment asks for shoe removal, but a good sign that this is required is a pile of shoes left at or near the entrance. To Thais, wearing shoes

Master Thai etiquette like a diplomat with this handy online guide (www.ediplomat.com).

indoors is disgusting. Also avoid stepping on the threshold, which is where the spirit of the house is believed to reside.

Don't prop your feet on chairs or tables while sitting, especially at a restaurant or in a guesthouse. This is an obvious one as you wouldn't treat a public place back home like your living room, so why start now in a culture that is foot-phobic? On some buses and 3rd-class trains, you'll see Thais prop up their feet; while this isn't the height of propriety, do notice that they always remove their shoes before doing so. Thais also take off their shoes if they need to climb up onto a chair or seat.

Never step over someone or their personal belongings, even on a crowded 3rd-class train; instead squeeze around them or ask them to move. The same holds for food that might be served on a mat or on the floor, as is commonly seen in rural areas or at temple fairs. When sitting with a group of Thais, remember to use the mermaid pose, with your feet tucked behind you to one side so that the bottoms of your feet aren't pointed at sacred images or people of high status.

Also avoid tying your shoes to the outside of your backpack where they might accidentally brush against someone (like, totally gross) or worse touch someone's head (shame on you).

Westerners often use their feet informally as secondary hands: we might close the refrigerator door with our feet, stop something from blowing away with our feet or point at something with our feet. These are all no-nos in Thailand and will cause gasps from onlookers. If you need to move, motion or touch something, do it with your hands. With enough consideration, all of this will become second nature and you'll soon feel embarrassed when you see these conventions broken.

Now for the head taboos: don't touch Thais on the head or ruffle their hair. This is perceived as an insult, not a sign of affection. Occasionally you'll see young people touching each other's head, which is a teasing gesture between friends. Don't sit on pillows meant as headrests, as this represents a variant of the taboo against head touching.

LOCAL COMMUNITIES

Hair-raising adventures and postcard snapshots make great souvenirs from a trip, but the travel experiences that become lifelong companions are the moments when you stop being an invading alien and connect with someone who may not speak your language or share your culture. A conversation at a bus stop or an invitation to join a family picnic – these are all open doors for 'snapshot' friendships, a temporary connection between strangers that teaches appreciation and commonality. These unscripted interactions aren't available in the midst of a tourist ghetto. You must first place yourself in local communities where people have the time and the curiosity to befriend a stranger.

Community immersion can range from a solo foray into a town or an area of town off the tourist circuit, or better yet you can temporarily adopt a Thai address while giving something back through a volunteer program.

Volunteering

When you travel to another country it is easier to see the divide between the rich and poor and to feel compassion for those trapped at the bottom. A myriad of organisations exist in Thailand to address both the needs of the locals and visitors' desire to help.

Education is the primary source for volunteer opportunities. In Thailand, the public schools offer tuition-free education for 12 years to anyone living legally in the country. The definition of a legal resident

Chiang Mai (p275) is Thailand's 'classroom', where you can study language, culture and cooking.

excludes some hill-tribe villagers in the northern mountains and un-documented Burmese refugees and immigrants, mainly concentrated in the north or in urban centres like Bangkok. Even for members of these groups who do have the proper documentation, the associated fees for attending school (uniforms, supplies, books etc) are often too expensive for families to afford. The incidental fees of an education also exclude many fully recognised but poor citizens living in the northeast. It is estimated that 1.3 million children don't attend school due to economic, geographic or citizenship reasons.

Taking on a teaching position in Thailand elevates your status from forgettable tourist to honourable guest, and it gives you insight and access into a community pleased to have you. Teachers in Thailand are revered professionals and a foreigner who speaks Thai is often assumed to hold this position, which in turn encourages Thais to be on their 'Sunday-best' behaviour.

You can help villagers create jobs in their back-yards by buying locally produced coffee, textiles and handicrafts.

Finding a teaching job is fairly easy, as native English speakers are always in demand. But finding an experience that suits your interests takes some research. If you want more of a cultural challenge than just a job overseas, look into programs in rural areas where English is limited and foreigners are few. In these situations, you'll learn Thai more quickly and observe a way of life with deeper connections to the past.

The following volunteer opportunities are subdivided into their regional placement locations and should be contacted for details on position placements and program costs.

NORTHEASTERN THAILAND

Most volunteer opportunities in the northeast work in rural schools in the country's agricultural heartland.

LemonGrass Volunteering (☎ 08 1977 5300; www.lemongrass-volunteering.com) is a Thai-run organisation that links volunteers teaching English in classrooms and student camps around the Surin area.

Open Mind Projects (☎ 0 4241 3578; www.openmindprojects.org; 856/9 Mu 15, Th Prachak, Nong Khai) offers a lengthy list of volunteering positions, including IT positions, community-based ecotourism projects and English-teaching assignments in schools, temples and orphanages. All volunteers get an ambitious three-day training program before beginning their work.

Travel to Teach (☎ 08 4246 0351; www.travel-to-teach.org; 1161/2 Soi Chitta Panya, Th Nong Khai-Phon Phisai, Nong Khai) offers flexible volunteering positions from two weeks to six months in schools, English camps or in temples teaching monks. Volunteers receive teacher training and there are homestay options and placements in Nong Khai, Mae Hong Son and Chiang Mai.

Volunthai (www.volunthai.com; 86/124 Soi Kanprapa, Bang Sue, Bangkok) is a homey operation that places volunteers in teaching positions at rural schools with homestay accommodation. No previous teaching experience is necessary and the program is best suited for cultural chameleons who want to experience a radically different way of life.

NORTHERN THAILAND

Northern Thailand, especially Chiang Mai and Chiang Rai, has a number of volunteer opportunities working with disadvantaged hill-tribe groups. Chiang Mai and Mae Sot also have distressed communities of Burmese refugees and migrants needing access to schooling and health care.

Akha Association for Education and Culture in Thailand (Afect; ☎ 0 5371 4250, 08 1952 2179; www.akhaasia.multiply.com; 468 Th Rimkok, Chiang Rai) runs a Life Stay program in which volunteers live and work in an Akha village with a local family. Depending on the agricultural season, the days can be quite physical: working in the fields, helping build a house or gathering food in the forest. Stays are from seven days, and places are limited so it is best to arrange in advance of travel. Proceeds from Life Stay are put back into the community for health and education programs.

Cultural Canvas Thailand (☎ 08 6920 2451; www.culturalcanvas.com; Chiang Mai) unites volunteers with positions in a variety of Chiang Mai–based social-justice organisations, such as migrant learning centres and hill-tribe schools. Time commitments vary from one-day art workshops to month-long stints teaching English.

Hill Area and Community Development Foundation (☎ 0 5371 5696; www.hadf.or.th; 129/1 Mu 4, Th Pa-Ngiw, Soi 4, Rop Wiang, Chiang Rai) helps hill tribes deal with problems ranging from environmental management to social development. Currently, volunteering opportunities include teaching English in the Mae Chan/Mae Salong area for six months, but shorter stays may be possible.

Mae Tao Clinic (Dr Cynthia's Clinic; ☎ 0 5556 3644; www.maetaoclinic.org, Mae Sot) was established in 1989 by Dr Cynthia Maung, a Karen refugee, and provides free medical treatment to around 80,000 Burmese migrants a year. The clinic also helps pay for medical care at one of Mae Sot's hospitals if the treatment is beyond its capabilities. If you have medical training, the clinic offers volunteer positions for a minimum of six months. There are also administrative and English-teaching opportunities with three-month commitments.

Mirror Art Group (☎ 0 5373 7412-3; www.mirrorartgroup.org; 106 Moo 1, Ban Huay Khom, Tambon Mae Yao, Chiang Rai) is an NGO working with hill tribes in the Mae Yao area, 15km west of Chiang Rai. Its volunteer teaching program focuses on developing English-language and IT skills. The program goes for a minimum of five days. Donations of books, toys and clothes are also appreciated.

Ban Thai Guest House (p415) in Mae Sot can help visitors find informal volunteer spots in schools, child care and at HIV centres. The minimum commitment is usually one month.

CENTRAL & SOUTHEASTERN THAILAND

Hilltribe Learning Centre is set on a remote hillside 10km south of Sangkhlaburi and is where Buddhist nun Pimjai Maneerat built her outreach school for ethnic minorities. It was a spot where she used to meditate and where she was approached by villagers hoping to obtain a basic education. The rudimentary school has 70 children, mostly ethnic Karen, and they learn Thai language and basic life skills. Mae Chee Pimjai runs the place virtually single-handedly, welcomes volunteers who can teach, especially English language, or help with daily chores. Basic accommodation is available for anyone wanting to stay a few days (contact P Guest House, p225).

Baan Unrak (p225), in Sangkhlaburi, and Pattaya Orphanage (p238), in the resort town of Pattaya, are orphanages with long-term volunteer positions.

Homestays

You can travel independently without isolating yourself from the culture by staying at one of Thailand's local homestays. More popular with domestic tourists, homestays differ from guesthouses in that visitors are welcomed into a family's home, typically in a small village that isn't on the tourist trail. Accommodation is basic: usually a mat or foldable mattress on the floor, or occasionally a family will have a private room. Rates include lodging, meals with the family and cultural activities that highlight a region's traditional way of life, from rice farming to silk weaving. English fluency varies, so homestays are also an excellent way to exercise your spoken Thai.

Every regional Tourist Authority of Thailand (TAT) office has a list of registered homestays; however, do note that the term 'homestay' is sometimes loosely applied to generic guesthouses rather than cultural immersions.

The king has sponsored agriculture projects in northern Thailand since 1969 to stop slash-and-burn practices and to eradicate opium production. About 274 villages in six provinces grow mainly chemical-free produce for the royal project.

EXPLOITED CHILDREN

A struggling or fractured family relies on all members of the family to work, a situation that often leads to children working in the sex industry. Although technically illegal, prostitution in Thailand is a well-established cultural phenomenon that employs many consenting adults. But a disturbing subset of this industry is the brothels and karaoke bars that employ children as well as the street prostitution of children.

Urban job centres such as Bangkok and Chiang Mai and border towns such as Mae Sai and Mae Sot have large populations of displaced and marginalised people (Burmese immigrants, ethnic hill-tribe members and impoverished rural Thais) and an attendant occurrence of underage prostitution (younger than 18) that caters both to a domestic and international clientele. Thailand is also a conduit and destination for people trafficking (including children) from poorer countries like Myanmar and Cambodia.

The Thai authorities have shown some commitment to stopping underage prostitution, which attracts an unwanted type of overseas tourist. Many countries also have extraterritorial legislation that allows nationals to be prosecuted in their own country for such crimes. Responsible travellers can help to stop child-sex tourism by reporting suspicious behaviour on a dedicated **hotline** (☎ 1300) or reporting the individual directly to the embassy of the offender's nationality.

Organisations working across borders to stop child prostitution include **ECPAT** (End Child Prostitution & Trafficking; www.ecpat.net) and its Australian affiliate **Child Wise** (www.childwise.net), which has been involved in providing training to the tourism industry in Thailand to counter child-sex tourism.

The majority of genuine homestays are in the northeast, including the award-winning program in Ban Prasat (p463). Another well-organised option is at Ban Kham Pia (p517), which is walking distance to an elephant wildlife reserve. The village around the Angkor ruins of Prasat Meuang Tam (p472) offers homestays as well. The elephant-raising village of Ban Tha Klang (p476) can find a bed and some elephant encounters for visitors. Dan Sai (p524), the village known for its wild spirit festival, has an English-speaking homestay program that gets rave reviews.

The homestay program on Ko Yao Noi (see p680), a Muslim fishing island, has also been recognised as a sustainable alternative to beach-style tourism. Just a short distance from Chiang Mai, Ban Mae Kampong (p332) is a high-altitude village (free of mosquitoes) with homestay options and glimpses into a community that makes its living from the forest.

THE ENVIRONMENT

Most visitors to Thailand have fairly sophisticated views about the environmental impact of human habitation on sensitive natural environments. If the soporific atmosphere of the Thai beaches has caused environmental amnesia, just take an early morning stroll along the beach before the vendors have had time to do their morning sweep of the litter left behind by high tide and you'll be jolted out of your stupor.

Thailand has made great headway in protecting its natural beauty by enforcing bans on coral dynamiting and creating national parks, but the country has not been as successful at implementing restrictions on commercial development and building the infrastructure needed to properly treat the waste produced by an increased population, especially in tourist centres where visitors often outnumber the full-time residents.

The conscientious visitor might hope for a few incremental do-it-yourself measures to reduce the impact of tourism but these rarely counterbalance the shortcomings of policy and enforcement. One fairly radical approach is to avoid visiting areas that have not yet developed the sanitation systems to

A wonderful online tool for learning more about Thailand through its language can be found at www.thai-language.com.

Planes, trains and automobiles generate CO_2 emissions that contribute to global climate change. To determine the 'carbon footprint' generated by your flight to Thailand, click on the CO_2 calculator at www.co2balance .com.

TIPS FOR BEING NICE TO THE PLANET

- Use public transport or rent a bicycle to cut down on petrol consumption.
- Team up with other travellers to share chartered transport.
- Turn down the air-conditioning by a few degrees.
- Opt for a cold shower.
- Use biodegradable soap to reduce water pollution.
- Leave plastic packaging in your home country to lighten your garbage load.
- Reuse plastic bags or carry your own canvas bags for trips to the market.
- Throw away cigarette butts in the rubbish bin not on the beach, street or ocean.
- Skip the jet skis and motorised vehicles through the jungle, which create noise pollution and disturb animal habitats.
- Pack out all rubbish you brought into a natural environment.
- Don't feed wildlife or marine animals.
- Avoid collecting or buying corals or shells.

TIPS FOR ECO-DIVING

The popularity of Thailand's diving industry places immense pressure on fragile coral sites. To help preserve the ecology, adhere to these simple rules.

- Avoid touching living marine organisms, standing on coral or dragging equipment (such as fins) across the reef. Coral polyps can be damaged by even the gentlest contact.
- When treading water in shallow reef areas, be careful not to kick up clouds of sand, which can easily smother the delicate reef organisms.
- Take great care in underwater caves where your air bubbles can be caught within the roof and leave previously submerged organisms high and dry.
- Join a coral clean-up campaign, sponsored by dive shops on Ko Tao and Ko Samui.

accommodate tourists. In the case of the islands, well-touristed places like Phuket, and to a lesser-extent Phi-Phi, Samui and Samet are better equipped to deal with tourism than the smaller, less-visited islands.

Also consider keeping your outdoor adventures as close as possible to your hotel or guesthouse. For example, dive shops on Ko Samui shuttle divers to sites off the coast of Ko Pha-Ngan and Ko Tao, a journey of two hours in one direction. Meanwhile, visitors who base themselves on Ko Tao need only travel 30 minutes at the most to reach these sites. The same scenario occurs in Chiang Mai, where tour operators will take trekkers on far-flung hiking and caving trips in Mae Hong Son Province. Instead of spending your vacation 'commuting', why not stay where you play: stick to the general guideline of no more than one hour's travelling time from your hotel or guesthouse for any trip or activity.

Volunteering

Many grassroots organisations in Thailand need volunteers to help in animal rescue and environmental conservation efforts.

Elephant Nature Park (☎ 0 5320 8246; www.elephantnaturepark.org; Mae Taeng) Sangduen Chailert's award-winning sanctuary. The park accepts volunteers to help care for the resident elephants. Those with veterinary experience are most welcome but others with strong backs can help out too. Positions are for one, two and four weeks. For more information, see p298.

BANGKOK'S STREET WALKERS

The heat, the hawkers, the hookers – Bangkok is already a zoo at night, and then you'll spot an elephant plodding down the road with a flashing light tied to its tail. The skinny mahout will thrust a bunch of bananas in your hands to feed to the animal in exchange for a fistful of baht. Surreal, indeed. Heartbreaking, most certainly.

Thailand has a pachyderm crisis. Throughout Thai history, these animals were revered for their strength, endurance and intelligence, working alongside their mahouts harvesting teak or transporting goods through mountainous terrain. And then the modern world invaded and promptly made the elephant redundant.

In 1989 logging was banned in Thailand, resulting in decreased demand for trained elephants. Working elephants have a career of about 50 years and are trained at a young age by two mahouts, usually a father-and-son team, who can see the animal through its lifetime. Thai law requires that elephants be retired and released into the wild at age 61. They often live for 80 years or more.

But without a job, the elephants and their dependent mahouts come to the big city, like the rest of the country's economic refugees, in search of work. And what can an elephant do in this era of planes, trains and automobiles? One option is to roam the streets like a beggar.

A promising alternative is the elephant rescue preserves that support themselves through tourism. Lampang's Thai Elephant Conservation Center (p348), Chiang Mai's Elephant Nature Park (p298) and Patara Elephant Farm (p298) are just a few of the creative solutions for ensuring these animals' dignity and quality of life.

Highland Farm Gibbon Sanctuary (☎ 0 9958 0821; www.highland-farm.or; Mae Sot) Gives a permanent home to orphaned, abandoned and mistreated gibbons, a monkey species that has long been hunted in Thailand. Volunteers are asked for a one-month commitment and help with daily farm chores.

Starfish Ventures (☎ 44 800 1974817; www.starfishvolunteers.com) Arranges for volunteers to assist in the Turtle Conservation Centre (p244), a Thai-run, sea-turtle program on a protected island off the coast of Rayong. Other volunteer opportunities include working at a gibbon rehabilitation centre in Phuket, helping to build and repair poor rural schools, and teaching opportunities.

Wild Animal Rescue Foundation (WAR; www.warthai.org) Thai NGO, operates the Phuket Gibbon Rehabilitation Centre (p658) and a sea-turtle conservation project as well as a conservation education centre in Ranong Province on the Andaman Coast. The foundation runs entirely on volunteer labour and donations. Job placements include assisting in the daily care of gibbons that are being rehabilitated for life in the wild or counting and monitoring sea-turtle nests.

Wildlife Friends of Thailand Rescue Centre (p557) Puts volunteers to work caring for sun bears, macaques and gibbons who have been rescued from animal shows or abusive owners.

On the resort islands of Ko Chang and Ko Samui, devoted animal lovers run dog rescue centres (see p262 for Ko Chang and p580 for Ko Samui).

The Culture

THE NATIONAL PSYCHE

Much of Thailand's cultural operating system is hinged upon a value system that emphasises respect for the family, religion and monarchy. Within that system each person knows his or her place and Thai children are strictly instructed in the importance of group conformity, respecting elders and suppressing confrontational views. Thais are also notorious for indifference, especially in public situations where chaos could be avoided with a queue and a dash of chivalry (both foreign concepts in Thailand). But you'll find that most Thais are kind-hearted and place a high value on enjoying life.

Very Thai (2005), by Philip Cornwell-Smith, explains all the quirks in Thailand that you ever wondered about, accompanied by evocative photos shot by John Goss.

Sà·nùk

The Thai word *sà·nùk* means 'fun' and is often regarded as a necessary underpinning of anything worth doing. Even work and studying should have an element of *sà·nùk*, otherwise they automatically become drudgery. This doesn't mean Thais don't want to work, but they labour best as a group, so as to avoid loneliness and ensure an element of playfulness. Nothing condemns an activity more than *mâi sà·nùk* (not fun). The back-breaking work of rice farming, the tedium of long-distance bus driving, the dangers of a construction site: Thais often mix their job tasks with a healthy dose of socialising. Watch these workers in action and you'll see them flirting with each other, trading insults or cracking jokes. The famous Thai smile comes partially out of their desire to enjoy themselves.

Saving Face

Thais believe strongly in the concept of saving face, ie avoiding confrontation and endeavouring not to embarrass themselves or other people (except when it's *sà·nùk* to do so). The ideal face-saver doesn't bring up negative topics in conversation, doesn't express firm convictions or opinions, and doesn't claim to have an expertise. Agreement and harmony are considered to be the most important social graces.

While Westerners might find a heated discussion to be good sport, Thais avoid such confrontations and regard any instance where voices are raised as rude and potentially volatile. Losing your temper causes a loss of face for everyone present and Thais who have been crossed often react in extreme ways.

Minor embarrassments, like tripping or falling, might elicit giggles from a crowd of Thais. In this case they aren't taking delight in your mishap, but helping you save face by laughing it off.

Status & Obligation

Culture Shock: Thailand (2008), by Robert and Nanthapa Cooper, explains Thailand's quirky, curious and practical customs.

All relationships in traditional Thai society – and those in the modern Thai milieu as well – are governed by social rank defined by age, wealth, status and personal or political position. The elder position is called *pôo yài* (literally the 'big person') and is used to describe parents, bosses, village heads, public officials etc. The junior position is called *pôo nóy* (little person) and describes anyone who is subservient to the *pôo yài*. Although this tendency towards social ranking is to some degree shared by many societies around the world, the Thai twist lies in the set of mutual obligations linking the elder to the junior.

Pôo nóy are supposed to show obedience and respect (together these concepts are covered by the single Thai term *greng jai*) towards *pôo yài*. Those

THAI TÊE·O

When it comes to *wan yùt* (holidays), Thais don't stay at home and curl up with a book. Instead they gather up their friends and go on a *têe·o* (trip or journey). University students might pack up their guitars and bottles of whisky for a camping trip at a nearby national park. Middle-class matrons dress up in their most beautiful silk dresses to make merit at a famous temple. And villagers climb into the back of pick-up trucks to go shopping at a secondhand border market. Regardless of the destination, all *têe·o* have a few commonalities. There's usually a lot of chaotic driving (if invited on a *têe·o*, don't sit in the front seat) and more time spent eating than actually visiting the intended destination. Of course every road trip has the obligatory lunch stop and then there are the pit stops for speciality snacks. Before departing, so much time is spent driving around town picking up friends and running unrelated errands that it begins to feel like an episode of the *Keystone Cops*. But the waiting and detours are part of the excursion and go unnoticed by chatting friends.

with junior status are not supposed to question or criticise those with elder status be it in the office, the home or the government. In the workplace, this means younger staff members are not encouraged to speak during meetings and are expected to do their bosses' bidding.

In return *pôo yài* are obligated to care for or 'sponsor' the *pôo nóy*. It is a paternalistic relationship in which *pôo nóy* can, for example, ask *pôo yài* for favours involving money or job access. *Pôo yài* reaffirm their rank by granting requests when possible; to refuse would be to risk a loss of face and status. When dining, touring or entertaining, the *pôo yài* always picks up the tab; if a group is involved, the person with the most social rank pays the bill for everyone, even if it empties his or her wallet. For a *pôo nóy* to try and pay would 'ruin our culture' as a Thai friend once explained. Sharing one's wealth within one's social circle or family affirms a person's position as an elder. This component of familial obligation is often a source of confusion in mixed marriages between Thais and Westerners.

The protocol defined by the social hierarchy governs almost every aspect of Thai behaviour within family units, business organisations, schools and the government. Elected or appointed officials occupy one of the highest rungs on the social ladder and often regard themselves as caretakers of the people, a stark contrast to the democratic ideal of being the voice of the people. The complicated personal hierarchy in Thailand often prevents collaboration, especially between those with competing status.

Most foreign visitors will interact with a simplified version of this elder-junior relationship in the form of *pêe* (elder sibling) and *nórng* (younger sibling). All Thais refer to each other using familial names. Even people unrelated by blood quickly establish who's *pêe* and who's *nórng*. This is why one of the first questions Thais ask new acquaintances is 'How old are you?'.

Thai World View (www .thaiworldview.com) is a culture lesson with lots of handy vocabulary covering everything from body gestures to soap operas.

LIFESTYLE

Individual lifestyles vary tremendously according to family background, income and geography. In many ways Bangkok is its own phenomenon where middle-class Thais wake up to all the mod cons: SMS, instant messaging, fast-food, J-pop music and fashion addictions. The amount of disposable income in Bangkok is unparalleled elsewhere in the country. Meanwhile Bangkok's working classes are usually economic migrants from the northeast provinces or increasingly from across the border in Myanmar. While the rice fields lay fallow, Isan farmers saddle up a Bangkok taxis or join a construction crew catered at lunchtime by an enterprising Isan housewives who whips up northeastern specialities that were merely culinary fables in the capital some 20 years ago. The young 20-somethings from such provinces as Roi Et and Si Saket who aren't college-bound head to service-industry jobs in the guesthouses and form their own urban tribes. The southern resort islands have seen a similar migration pattern: Isan Thais working as housekeeping staff and construction crews, locals working as security guards and educated Bangkokians filling the managerial positions. Regardless of the job, most Thais send a portion of their pay home to struggling parents or to support dependent children.

More traditional family units and professions can be found in the provincial capitals across the country. The civil servants – teachers and government employees who make up the backbone of the Thai middle class – mainly live in nuclear families in terrace housing estates outside the city centre. Some might live in the older neighbourhoods filled with front-yard gardens growing papayas, mangoes and other fruit trees. The business class lives in the city centre, usually in apartments above shopfronts, making for an easy commute but a fairly urban life. In the cool hours of the day, the wage earners and students head to the nearest park to jog, play badminton or join in the civic-run aerobics classes.

Though fewer people toil in the rice paddies than in the past, the villages still survive on the outskirts of the urban grid. Here life is set to the seasons, the fashions are purchased from the market and if the water buffaloes could talk they'd know all the village gossip. In rural areas, female members of a family typically inherit the land and throughout Thailand women tend to control the family finances.

Across the country, motorcycles are emblematic of modern Thai life. Babies are balanced on the handlebars along with the groceries. Students still in short pants scoot around the back alleys. A Thai expression says that if you're old enough to laugh, you're old enough to drive, a social ambivalence that the government has tried to combat with various public-safety campaigns. Cars are still a sign of wealth, and due to favourable taxes pick-up trucks make up the bulk of automobile sales. Mobile phones have infiltrated the daily lives of just about everyone, even humble villagers and lowly market vendors.

In general, Thais are enjoying a higher standard of living than in decades past. The long-distance fan buses that once stopped at every shade tree and collected toothless grannies and young men carrying fighting cocks have been phased out. These days people have their own transport or can afford the air-con bus. From a demographic perspective Thailand is at a crossroads, being transformed from a developing nation to a developed one. Life expectancy has risen to a median age of 70 years for men and 75 years for women; fertility rates have held steady at 1.82. The country's median age is 33, meaning that for the time being there is a workforce that can counterbalance declining birth rates and an ageing population.

Social norms between the sexes are also changing. A decade ago it was considered shameful for women to drink and smoke, and at a proper middle-class party socialising would be segregated by sex. Today much of those taboos have been tossed out. One sign of the times is the popularity of the word *gík*, a slang term that originally meant 'part-time lover' (now it is more broadly used to mean 'girl/boyfriend'), applied to someone with whom you have sex without any emotional or financial responsibility, a relatively new concept distinct from that of traditional sexual partners: a mistress, girlfriend or prostitute. *Gík* can be applied to either gender and is increasingly a source of frustration for married couples who in previous generations might have fought over too many visits to the brothels or the discovery of a mistress. This sexual revolution has begun to take its toll on the domestic prostitution industry as well. According to a 2001 government public health study, sex

Thais have a special language they use to speak to the monarchy. School children study *râht-chá-sàp* (the royal language) but Princess Srindhorn has been known to circumvent the convention by speaking English.

Thai-Blogs (www.thai -blogs.com) peeks into the lives of Thais and expats and their outings to uncommon corners.

DEMOGRAPHIC STATS

▓ Average age for a Thai man/woman to get married: 27/24 years

▓ Bangkok's minimum daily wage: 203B

▓ Nakhon Ratchasima's minimum daily wage: 170B

▓ Entry-level government workers earn around 9000B per month

▓ Service workers earn between 4500B to 6500B per month

▓ Teachers with two decades of seniority make 24,000B per month

---

workers averaged one customer a night instead of 1.5 customers in 1997 and fewer men in their 20s surveyed by the study admitted to visiting brothels, from 55% in 1995 to 10% in 2001.

Despite the unloosening of Thailand's Victorian corset, religion still plays an active and important role in modern society and Thais have yet to adopt a secular world view like their European counterparts. See p65 for more information.

ECONOMY

Thailand is classified as a developing economy with exports constituting about 70% of the gross domestic product (GDP). It is the second-largest economy in Southeast Asia (Indonesia is the largest) and manufactured exports, especially electronics and automobiles, are beginning to eclipse traditional agricultural products, like rice and rubber. Its largest trade partners are the USA, Japan and China.

The country is often touted as the rice basket of the world, though Vietnam and Thailand often vie for the top slot. Agriculture accounts for 11% of the GDP and employs about 37% of the workforce. Other agricultural export products include farm-raised shrimp and cassava. Food processing is also becoming an important industry.

Many Thais will consult with a monk or fortune-teller to determine an auspicious astrological date for a wedding or the opening of a new business.

A more recent accolade has described Thailand as the 'Detroit of Asia'. The automobile industry constitutes 15% of the GDP and Thailand is the largest automobile market and producer among the Asean nations. It is particularly strong in the production and domestic sales of 1-tonne pick-up trucks. Toyota and Isuzu are the largest car manufacturers in Thailand with factories in the industrial suburbs of Bangkok. About half of the 1.2 million vehicles produced in 2006 were exported to foreign markets. However, the recent downturn in the global economy has seen lowered production and sales numbers for automobiles in Thailand.

Despite a fairly robust economy, Thailand's ongoing political stand-off resulting from the military coup in 2006 has compromised the country's projected economic growth rate. It was hoped that 2008 would see a growth rate of 4% to 5%, but this figure was decreased to 2% after the week-long closure of Bangkok's two airports by anti-government protestors in late 2008.

The industry most affected by the political and economic crises is tourism, which made up 6% of the economy and attracted 14 million people in 2007. At the start of 2008, the government hoped to increase the number to 15 million, but by early 2009 a more realistic figure was a contracted 10 million visitors. The closure of Bangkok's airports is estimated to have cost US$3.8 billion in lost revenue and affected cargo shipping, import/export, and passenger services and tourism. The tourism industry is expected to experience a greater and more prolonged slump than it did following the 2004 Indian Ocean tsunami.

Economists are predicting troubled times for Thailand with an estimate of 2% of the workforce (or about one million people) filing as unemployed in 2009, still considerably less than the record high of 4.4% during the 1997 Asian financial crisis.

POPULATION

Estimated to have 63 million people, Thailand is the most populous of the mainland Southeast Asian countries. Over one-third of all Thais live in urban areas, mainly in the capital of Bangkok (6.3 million people) and its industrial suburbs of Samut Prakan (379,000) and Nonthaburi (292,000). Although known for its rural character, the northeast claims two of Thailand's largest cities: Udon Thani (222,000) and Nakhon Ratchasima (205,000). The southern crossroads town of Hat Yai (188,000) and the coastal town of Chonburi (183,000) are other population centres. Meanwhile Chiang Mai (174,000), often considered a cultural capital, barely cracks the top 10 list.

Thailand is categorised as being a homogeneous country but the reality is more complex, especially in provinces that border neighbouring countries or areas that have an historical allegiance to other nations. Thailand's immigrant population consists of mainly Chinese and more recently economic refugees from Myanmar.

The Thai Majority

Some 75% of citizens are ethnic Thais, who can be divided into four groups: Central Thais (Siamese) of the Chao Phraya delta; Thai Lao of the northeast; Thai Pak Tai of the south; and northern Thais. Each group speaks its own dialect and to a certain extent practises customs unique to its region. Politically and economically the Central Thais are the dominant group.

Small minority groups who speak Thai dialects include the Lao Song (Phetchaburi and Ratchaburi); the Phuan (Chaiyaphum, Phetchaburi, Prachinburi); the Phu Thai (Sakon Nakhon, Nakhon Phanom, Mukdahan); the Shan (Mae Hong Son); the Thai Khorat or Suay (Khorat); the Thai Lü (Nan, Chiang Rai); the Thai-Malay (Satun, Trang, Krabi); and the Yaw (Nakhon Phanom, Sakon Nakhon).

The Chinese

People of Chinese ancestry – second- or third-generation Hakka, Teochew, Hainanese or Cantonese – make up 14% of the population. Bangkok and the nearby coastal areas have a large population of immigrants from China who came for economic opportunities in the early to mid-20th century. In northern Thailand there is also a substantial number of Hui-Chinese Muslims who emigrated from Yunnan in the late 19th century to avoid religious and ethnic persecution during the Qing dynasty.

Ethnic Chinese in Thailand probably enjoy better relations with the majority of the population than they do in any other country in Southeast Asia. Many families have intermarried with Thais and have interwoven traditional Chinese customs into the predominant Thai culture. Historically wealthy Chinese introduced their daughters to the royal court as consorts, developing royal connections and adding a Chinese bloodline that extends to the current king.

Other Minorities

The second-largest ethnic minority are the Malays (4.6%), most of whom reside in the provinces of the deep south. The remaining minority groups include smaller percentages of non-Thai-speaking people like the

Thailand is the world's second-largest pick-up truck market after the US.

Thailand has a penchant for Guinness World Records, including longest condom chain, most couples married underwater and most Mini Coopers in a convoy (444 cars parked to spell out 'Long Live the King').

Letters from Thailand (1969), by Botan, is about a Chinese immigrant who came to Thailand after WWII. The hero tells his story of finding success in business and marriage through letters to his mother.

Vietnamese, Khmer, Mon, Semang (Sakai), Moken (*chow lair;* people of the sea, or 'sea gypsies'), Htin, Mabri, Khamu and a variety of hill tribes. A small number of Europeans and other non-Asians reside in Bangkok and the provinces.

Hill Tribes

Ethnic minorities in the mountainous regions of northern Thailand are often called 'hill tribes', or in Thai vernacular, *chow kŏw* (mountain people). Each hill tribe has its own language, customs, mode of dress and spiritual beliefs.

Most are of semi-nomadic origin, having come from Tibet, Myanmar, China and Laos during the past 200 years or so. They are 'fourth world' people in that they belong neither to the main aligned powers nor to the developing nations. Rather, they have crossed and continue to cross national borders, often fleeing oppression by other cultures, without regard for recent nationhood.

Queen of Langkasuka (2008), by Nonzee Nimibutr, is a lavish period piece loosely based on the Malay kingdom of Pattani, a segment of history few non-Malay Thais know much about. The opening weeks of the movie positioned it as the year's highest-grossing movie.

A MODERN PERSPECTIVE ON THE HILL TRIBES

Hill tribes tend to have among the lowest standards of living in Thailand. Although it could be tempting to correlate this quality of life with traditional lifestyles, their situation is compounded, in most cases, by not having Thai citizenship. Without the latter, hill tribes don't have the right to own land, educate their children, earn minimum wages or access health care. In the last couple of decades some members of hill-tribe groups have been issued Thai identification cards, which enable them to access national programs (in theory, though often extra 'fees' might prevent families from being able to afford public schooling and health care). Other hill-tribe families have received residency certificates that restrict travel outside of an assigned district, in turn limiting access to job opportunities and other necessities associated with a highly mobile modern society.

Furthermore, the Thai government has pursued a 30-year policy of hill-tribe relocation, often moving villages from fertile agricultural land to infertile land, in turn removing the tribes from a viable subsistence system in which tribal customs were intact to a market system in which they can't adequately compete and in which tribal ways have been fractured.

Some suggest that the revenue generated by Thai trekking companies helps the hill-tribe groups maintain their separate ethnic identity. Most agree that a small percentage of the profits from trekking filters down to individual families within hill-tribe villages, giving them a small source of income that might prevent urban migration. One guide we spoke to estimated an optimistic 50% of the tour budget was spent on purchasing food, lodging and supplies from hill-tribe merchants at the host village.

In general the trekking business has become more socially conscious than in previous decades. Most companies now tend to limit the number of visits to a particular area to lessen the impact of outsiders on the daily lives of ordinary villagers. But the industry still has a long way to go. It should be noted that trekking companies are Thai-owned and employ Thai guides, another bureaucratic impediment regarding citizenship for ethnic minorities. Without an identification card, guides from the hill tribes do not qualify for a Tourist Authority of Thailand (TAT) tour guide license and so are less than desirable job candidates.

In the past decade, the expansion of tourism into the mountainous regions of the north presents a complicating factor to the independence of hill-tribe villages. City speculators will buy land from hill-tribe farmers for fairly nominal sums only to be resold, usually to resorts, for much higher costs if the documentation of ownership can be procured. (In many cases the hill-tribe farmer doesn't own the land rights and has very little bargaining power when approached by outsiders.) The displaced farmer and his family might then migrate to the city, losing their connection to their rural and tribal lifestyle with few resources to succeed in the lowland society.

Language and culture constitute the borders of their world. Some groups are caught between the 6th and 21st centuries, while others are gradually being assimilated into modern life. Many tribespeople are also moving into lowland areas as montane lands become deforested.

The tribes most likely to be encountered by visitors fall into three main linguistic groups: the Tibeto-Burman (Lisu, Lahu, Akha), the Karenic (Karen, Kayah) and the Austro-Thai (Hmong, Mien). Within each group there may also be several subgroups, eg Blue Hmong, White Hmong; these names usually refer to predominant elements of clothing that vary between the subgroups.

Hilltribe.org (www.hill tribe.org) is an informative resource on hill-tribe culture and history.

The Tribal Research Institute in Chiang Mai recognises 10 different hill tribes but there may be up to 20. The population figures are taken from the most recent estimates. The following comments on dress refer mostly to the females, as hill-tribe men tend to dress like rural Thais, although increasingly hill-tribe villagers wear donated clothes rather than traditional garb. The traditional method of home construction is sometimes replaced with modern materials, like corrugated metal.

AKHA (I-KAW)
Population: 68,600
Origin: Tibet
Present locations: Thailand, Laos, Myanmar, Yunnan
Economy: dry rice, corn, beans, peppers
Belief system: animism with an emphasis on ancestor worship; some groups are Christian
Cultural characteristics: The Akha are among the poorest of Thailand's ethnic minorities and reside mainly in Chiang Mai and Chiang Rai provinces, along mountain ridges or steep slopes 1000m to 1400m in altitude. They are regarded by most Thais as skilled farmers but are often displaced from arable land by government intervention. Their traditional clothing consists of a headdress of beads, feathers and dangling silver ornaments. The well-known Akha Swing Ceremony takes place from mid-August to mid-September, between planting and harvest time. Akha houses are constructed of wood and bamboo, usually atop short wooden stilts and roofed with thick grass. At the entrance of every traditional Akha village stands a simple wooden gateway consisting of two vertical struts joined by a lintel. Akha shamans affix various charms made from bamboo strips to the gateway to prevent malevolent spirits from entering. Standing next to each village gateway are the crude wooden figures of a man and a woman, each bearing exaggerated sexual organs, in the belief that human sexuality is abhorrent to the spirit world.

LAHU (MUSOE)
Population: 102,876
Origin: Tibet
Present locations: south China, Thailand, Myanmar
Economy: dry rice, corn
Belief system: theistic animism (supreme deity is Geusha); some groups are Christian
Cultural characteristics: The Thai term for this tribe, *moo·seu,* is derived from a Burmese word meaning 'hunter', a reference to their skill in the forest. The Lahu tend to live at about 1000m altitude and can be found in remote areas of Chiang Mai, Chiang Rai and Tak provinces. There are five main groups – Red Lahu, Black Lahu, White Lahu, Yellow Lahu and Lahu Sheleh. Traditional dress consists of black-and-red jackets with narrow skirts worn by women; bright green or blue-green baggy trousers worn by men. Houses are built of

wood, bamboo and grass, and usually stand on short wooden posts. Lahu food is probably the spiciest of all the cuisines.

LISU (LISAW)

Population: 55,000
Origin: Tibet
Present locations: Thailand, Yunnan
Economy: rice, corn, livestock
Belief system: animism with ancestor worship and spirit possession
Cultural characteristics: Lisu villages are usually in the mountains at an elevation of about 1000m and occur in eight Thai provinces: Chiang Mai, Chiang Rai, Mae Hong Son, Phayao, Tak, Kamphaeng Phet, Sukhothai and Lampang. The women wear long multicoloured tunics over trousers and sometimes black turbans with tassels. Men wear baggy green or blue pants pegged in at the ankles. Patrilineal clans have pan-tribal jurisdiction, which makes the Lisu unique among hill-tribe groups (most of which have power centred with either a shaman or a village headman). Homes are built on the ground and consist mostly of bamboo and thatched grass. Older homes – today quite rare – may be made from mud brick or mud-and-bamboo thatch.

MIEN (YAO)

Population: 45,500
Origin: central China
Present locations: Thailand, south China, Laos, Myanmar, Vietnam
Economy: dry rice, corn
Belief system: animism with ancestor worship and Taoism
Cultural characteristics: The Mien are highly skilled at crafts such as embroidery and silversmithing. They settle near mountain springs at between 1000m and 1200m with a concentration in Nan, Phayao and Chiang Rai provinces and a few communities in Chiang Mai, Lampang and Sukhothai. Migration into Thailand increased during the American War era when the Mien collaborated with the CIA against Pathet Lao forces; 50,000 Mien refugees have been resettled in the US. Women wear trousers and black jackets with intricately embroidered patches and red furlike collars, along with large dark-blue or black turbans. The Mien are heavily influenced by Chinese traditions and they use Chinese characters to write their language. Kinship is patrilineal and marriage is polygamous. Houses are built at ground level, out of wood or bamboo thatch.

HMONG (MONG OR MAEW)

Population: 151,000
Origin: south China
Present locations: south China, Thailand, Laos, Vietnam
Economy: rice, corn, cabbages, strawberries
Belief system: animism
Cultural characteristics: The Hmong are Thailand's second-largest hill-tribe group and are especially numerous in Chiang Mai Province with smaller enclaves in the other northern Thai provinces. They usually live on mountain peaks or plateaus above 1000m. Tribespeople wear simple black jackets and indigo or black baggy trousers (White Hmong) with striped borders or indigo skirts (Blue Hmong) and silver jewellery. Sashes may be worn around the waist, and embroidered aprons draped front and back. Most women wear their hair in a large bun. Houses are built on ground level. Kinship is patrilineal and polygamy is permitted.

KAREN (YANG OR KARIANG)
Population: 428,000
Origin: Myanmar
Present locations: Thailand, Myanmar
Economy: rice, vegetables, livestock
Belief system: animism, Buddhism, Christianity, depending on the group
Cultural characteristics: The Karen are the largest hill-tribe group in Thailand and number about 47% of the total tribal population. They tend to live in lowland valleys and practise crop rotation rather than swidden agriculture. Their numbers and proximity to mainstream society have made them the most integrated and financially successful of the hill-tribe groups. Thickly woven V-neck tunics of various colours (unmarried women wear white) are typically worn. Kinship is matrilineal and marriage is monogamous. Karen homes are built on low stilts or posts, with the roofs swooping quite low. There are four distinct Karen groups – the Skaw (White) Karen, Pwo Karen, Pa-O (Black) Karen and Kayah (Red) Karen.

EDUCATION

Free public schooling is compulsory for nine years and is available for 12 years. Prior to the creation of a ministry of education in the late 19th century, the Buddhist temples provided the bulk of public education to boys who had entered the monastery. Although education is highly regarded, Thailand's public schools are often criticised for emphasising rote learning over critical thinking. Several attempts to reform the system in the early 2000s introduced child-focused learning methods but the efforts were regarded as having little tangible results. Thai public schools are particularly successful in creating citizens with a cohesive Siamese (or Central Thai) national identity, though this is a point of contention with minority groups like the Malay Muslims in the southern provinces. The classroom is one of the primary microcosms of the deeply ingrained societal hierarchy: students believe that teachers occupy the honoured 'elder' position, which requires compliance and respect. This educational culture is an asset when it comes to interacting within Thai society but is sometimes a handicap when competing academically against other nations.

Thailand's public school system is organised around six years at the bà·tŏm (primary) level, beginning at the age of six, followed by either three or six years of má·tá·yom (secondary) education. The three-year course is for those planning to follow school with three to five years of wí·chah·chêep (trade school), while the má·tá·yom (six-year course) is for students planning to continue at the ù·dom (tertiary) level, ie university. About 69% of the population continues past the mandatory nine years and 15% receives little to no education at all.

Private and international schools for the foreign and local elite are found in Bangkok and Chiang Mai, and in the other large provincial cities. The country boasts over 30 public universities plus roughly 41 teacher training schools (Rajabhat) and nine technical schools (Rajamangala), both of which have been promoted from college to university status. There are also numerous trade schools and technical colleges. Thammasat and Chulalongkorn are two of the country's most prestigious universities.

Panrit 'Gor' Daoruang started documenting his student days on www .thailandlife.com at the age of 12. Now 22 years old, he is serving a three-year prison sentence for drug possession and periodically posts firsthand accounts on www.thaiprisonlife.com.

SPORT
Moo·ay tai

Almost anything goes in this martial sport, both in the ring and in the stands. Moo·ay tai (Thai boxing; also spelt muay thai) is an intense contact sport accompanied by a folksy musical orchestra, a flamboyant ceremonial ritual dance before each match and frenzied betting throughout the stadium.

All surfaces of the body are considered fair targets and any part of the body, except the head, may be used to strike an opponent. Common blows include high kicks to the neck, elbow thrusts to the face and head, knee hooks to the ribs and low crescent kicks to the calf. Punching is considered the weakest of all blows and kicking merely a way to 'soften up' one's opponent; knee and elbow strikes are decisive in most matches.

A *ram moo·ay* (boxing dance) precedes every match. This ceremony usually lasts about five minutes and expresses obeisance to the fighter's guru *(kroo)*, as well as to the guardian spirit of Thai boxing. The complex series of gestures and movements is performed to the ringside musical accompaniment of Thai *ƀèe* (oboe) and percussion.

Fighters wear sacred headbands and armbands into the ring for good luck and divine protection. The headband is removed after the *ram moo·ay*, but the armband, which contains a small Buddha image, is worn throughout the match.

From championship fights to novice spars, matches are staged at provincial rings and temple fairs all over the country. The most competitive are fought at two Bangkok stadiums, Ratchadamnoen and Lumphini.

Thailand won two gold medals at the 2008 Beijing Olympics, one for female weightlifting and the other for male boxing.

Grà·bèe Grà·borng

Another traditional martial art, *grà·bèe grà·borng* focuses on hand-held weapons using the *grà·bèe* (sword), *plorng* (quarter-staff), *ngów* (halberd), *dàhp sörng meu* (a pair of swords held in each hand) and *mái sŭn·sòrk* (a pair of clubs). Nowadays the sport is merely a ritual to be displayed during festivals or at tourist venues but it is still solemnly taught according to a 400-year-old tradition handed down from Ayuthaya's Wat Phutthaisawan. The king's elite bodyguards are trained in *grà·bèe grà·borng;* many Thai cultural observers perceive it as a purer and more aristocratic tradition than *moo·ay tai*.

Modern matches are held within a marked circle, beginning with a *wâi kroo* ceremony and accompanied throughout by a musical ensemble. Thai-boxing techniques and judo-like throws are employed in conjunction with weapons techniques. Although sharpened weapons are used, the contestants refrain from striking their opponents – the winner is decided on the basis of stamina and the technical skill displayed.

Đà·grôr

Sometimes called Siamese football in old English texts, *đà·grôr* involves kicking a woven rattan ball (about 12cm in diameter) between opponents.

The traditional way to play is for players to stand in a circle (the size depends on the number of players) and simply try to keep the ball airborne by kicking it soccer-style. Points are scored for style, difficulty and variety of kicking manoeuvres. This form of the game is often played by friends and office colleagues wherever there's a little room: a vacant lot, school playground and sandy beaches.

A popular variation on *đà·grôr* – and the one used in intramural or international competitions – is played like volleyball, with a net, but with only the feet and head permitted to touch the ball. It's amazing to see the players perform aerial pirouettes, spiking the ball over the net with their feet. Another variation has players kicking the ball into a hoop 4.5m above the ground – basketball with feet, and no backboard!

Popular in several neighbouring countries, *đà·grôr* was introduced to the Southeast Asian Games by Thailand, and international championships tend to alternate between the Thais and Malaysians.

MEDIA

Southeast Asian governments are not typically fond of uncensored media outlets but Thailand often bucked this trend throughout the 1990s, even ensuring press freedoms in its 1997 constitution, albeit with fairly broad loopholes. That era came to end with the ascension of Thaksin Shinawatra, a telecommunications tycoon, and his Thai Rak Thai (TRT) party at the beginning of the new millennium. Just before the decisive 2001 general election, Thaksin's company, Shin Corp, bought a controlling interest in iTV, Thailand's only independent TV station. Shortly thereafter the new board sacked 23 iTV journalists who complained that the station was presenting biased coverage of the election to favour Thaksin and TRT. Almost overnight, the station was transformed from an independent, in-depth news channel to a pro-Thaksin mouthpiece.

With Thaksin winning the prime minister position and his party holding a controlling majority, the press encountered the kind of censorship and legal intimidation not seen since the 1970s era of military dictatorships. In 2002, two Western journalists, Shawn W Crispin and Rodney Tasker working for the Far Eastern Economic Review, were threatened with expulsion after the Thai authorities deemed a 10 January 2002 article to be offensive to the country. In 2004, Veera Prateepchaikul, editor-in-chief of the *Bangkok Post*, was removed from his job due to direct pressure from board members with allegiances to TRT, after Prateepchaikul's critical remarks of Thaksin's handling of the 2003–04 bird flu crisis. The TRT government also filed a litany of defamation lawsuits against critical individuals, publications and media groups who printed embarrassing revelations about his regime.

'the media exercises self-censorship with regard to the monarchy, mainly out of respect for the crown, but also out of fear that political enemies will file lèse majesté charge'

After the 2006 ousting of Thaksin, the media managed to retain its guarantees of press freedoms in the newly drafted constitution but this was a 'paper promise' that did little to rescue the press from intimidation, lawsuits and physical attacks. The military junta and its interim government took great liberties in silencing any pro-Thaksin reports. For example, the military blocked Thai cable and the internet from transmitting a 2007 CNN interview Thaksin gave months after the coup. The pro-Thaksin iTV channel was seized by the military and re-established as Thai PBS, a commercial-free public station. The post-coup election restored power to Thaksin's former party, which inflicted censorship on media outlets that covered the other side of the political divide – the antigovernment protests. The new government also introduced the state-controlled National Broadcasting Thailand (NBT) channel, as a competing 'public' station to Thai PBS, though it was viewed by the public as a government mouthpiece during the brief return of the former TRT in 2008. On two occasions in 2008 the antigovernment Peoples Alliance for Democracy (PAD) protestors stormed the NBT station, disrupting broadcasts and assaulting newscasters.

The country's political strife is essentially a showdown between two media moguls and both have used their own outlets as political tools. The government opposition is co-organised by Sondhi Limthongkul, a former journalist who built a print and broadcast empire that he has used to rally opposition to the Thaksin regime and the post-coup elected government. His privately owned Asia Satellite Television (ASTV) station aired nearly 24-hour live broadcasts of PAD rallies and used the channel to mobilise supporters against police intervention.

Press intimidation in Thailand is made easier because of the country's lèse majesté laws – causing offence against the dignity of the monarchy – which carries a jail term of between three and 15 years. Often the media exercises self-censorship with regard to the monarchy, mainly out of respect for the crown, but also out of fear that political enemies will file lèse majesté charges.

Since 2006, there have been eight charges of lèse majesté filed, most notably by Thaksin and Sondhi against each other, as well as against Thai and foreign journalists. Most charges are never pursued but a recent recipient of a jail sentence was Harry Nicolaides, an Australian national who was sentenced to three years in a Thai jail for putting into print otherwise unprintable stories about the crown prince's indiscretions into a work of fiction. He served a little more than a month of his sentence before receiving a royal pardon and returning home to Australia. More indicative of information suppression is the banning of historical books (and lèse majesté charges filed against the authors) that the government views as presenting a manipulative role by the monarchy in modern politics.

One of the most complete selections of material on Theravada Buddhism is available at Access to Insight (www.accesstoinsight.org).

RELIGION

Religion is alive and well in Thailand and colourful examples of daily worship can be found on nearly every corner. Walk the streets early in the morning and you'll see the solemn progression of the Buddhist monks, with shaved heads and orange-coloured robes, engaged in *bin·dá·bàht*, the daily house-to-house alms food gathering.

Although the country is predominantly Buddhist, the minority religions often practice alongside one another. The green-hued onion domes of the mosques mark a neighbourhood as Muslim in pockets of Bangkok and in southern towns. In urban centres, large rounded doorways inscribed with Chinese characters and flanked by red paper lanterns mark the location of *săhn jôw,* Chinese temples dedicated to the worship of Buddhist, Taoist and Confucian deities.

Buddhism

Approximately 95% of Thai people are Theravada Buddhists, a branch of Buddhism that came from Sri Lanka during the Sukhothai period. The Theravada school is often called the southern school because it travelled from the Indian subcontinent to Southeast Asia, while Mahayana Buddhism was adopted throughout the northern regions of Nepal, Tibet, China and the rest of East Asia.

Prior to the arrival of Sinhalese monks in the 13th century to Thailand, an Indian form of Theravada existed during the Dvaravati kingdom (6th to 10th centuries), while Mahayana Buddhism was known in pockets of the northeast under Khmer control in the 10th and 11th centuries.

Theravada doctrine stresses the three principal aspects of existence: *dukkha* (stress, unsatisfactoriness, disease), *anicca* (impermanence, transience of all things) and *anatta* (insubstantiality or nonessentiality of reality – no permanent 'soul'). These three concepts, outlined by Siddhartha Gautama in the 6th century BC, were in direct contrast to the Hindu belief in *param-atman,* an eternal, blissful self, and are considered a 'heresy' against India's Brahmanic religion. Gautama, an Indian prince-turned-ascetic, subjected himself to many years of severe austerity before he realised that this was not the way to reach the end of suffering. He became known as Buddha, 'the enlightened' or 'the awakened' and spoke of four noble truths that had the power to liberate any human being who could realise them.

The ultimate end of Theravada Buddhism is *nibbana* ('nirvana' in Sanskrit), which literally means the 'blowing out' or extinction of all grasping and thus of all suffering *(dukkha)*. Effectively, *nibbana* is also an end to the cycle of rebirths (both moment-to-moment and life-to-life) that is existence.

In reality, most Thai Buddhists aim for rebirth in a 'better' existence rather than the supramundane goal of *nibbana*. By feeding monks, giving

TEMPLE VISITS

Because Thai Buddhists don't adhere to strict weekly congregational days (though there are lunar holy days), a Thai temple is always open to individuals wishing to make merit. On such visits a worshipper will buy the traditional offering of lotus buds, incense and candles from nearby vendors. They'll place the flowers on the altar, kneel (or stand, in the case of outdoor altars) before the Buddha image and light the three incense sticks, placing these between two palms in a prayerlike gesture. The head is bowed and the hands are then raised between the heart and the forehead three times before the incense is planted at the altar. It is a simple and individualistic ritual. Other merit-making activities include offering food to the temple *sangha* (community); meditating (individually or in groups); listening to monks chanting *suttas* (Buddhist discourse); and attending a *têht* or *dhamma* (teachings) talk by the abbot or some other respected teacher.

donations to temples and performing regular worship at the local wát (local monastery) they hope to improve their lot, acquiring enough merit (*puñña* in Pali; *bun* in Thai) to prevent or at least reduce their number of rebirths. The concept of rebirth is almost universally accepted in Thailand, even by non-Buddhists, and the Buddhist theory of karma is well expressed in the Thai proverb *tam dee, dâi dee; tam chôoa, dâi chôoa* (good actions bring good results; bad actions bring bad results).

All the Tiratana (Triple Gems) revered by Thai Buddhists – the Buddha, the *dhamma* (the teachings) and the *sangha* (the Buddhist community) – are quite visible in Thailand. The Buddha, in his myriad sculptural forms, is found on a high shelf in the lowliest roadside restaurants as well as in the lounges of expensive Bangkok hotels. The *dhamma* is chanted morning and evening in every temple and taught to every Thai citizen in primary school. The *sangha* is seen everywhere in the presence of orange-robed monks, especially in the early morning hours when they perform their alms rounds.

Thai Buddhism has no particular Sabbath day when Thais are supposed to make temple visits. Instead, Thai Buddhists visit whenever they feel like it, most often on *wan prá* (holy days), which occur every seventh or eighth day depending on phases of the moon.

MONKS & NUNS

Socially, every Thai male is expected to become a monk (*bhikkhu* in Pali; *prá* or *prá pík·sù* in Thai) for a short period in his life, optimally between the time he finishes school and the time he starts a career or marries. Men or boys under 20 years of age may enter the *sangha* as a 10-vow novice (*samanera* in Pali; *nairn* in Thai). A family earns great merit when one of its sons 'takes robe and bowl'. Traditionally, the length of time spent in the wát is three months, during the *pan·săh* (Buddhist lent), which begins in July and coincides with the rainy season. However, nowadays men may spend as little as a week to accrue merit as monks.

Monks who live in the city usually emphasise study of the Buddhist scriptures, while those who opt for the forest temples tend to emphasise meditation.

In Thai Buddhism, women who seek a monastic life are given a minor role in the temple that is not equal to full monkhood. A Buddhist nun is known as *mâa chee* (mother priest) and lives as an *atthasila* (eight-precept) nun, a position traditionally occupied by women who had no other place in society. Thai nuns shave their heads, wear white robes and take care of temple chores. Generally speaking, *mâa chee* aren't considered as prestigious as monks and don't have a function in the laypeople's merit-making rituals.

Being Dharma: The Essence of the Buddha's Teachings (2001) is an inspiring collection of talks on Buddhist practice given by the late Thai forest monk, Ajahn Chah.

Over the years there have been some rebels who have sought equal ordination status as monks. One of the most prominent was Voramai Kabilsingh, who went to Taiwan to receive full ordination as a *bhikkhuni* (the female version of a *bhikku*, or male monk) through the Mahayana tradition. She returned to Thailand to found Wat Songtham Kalayanee in Nakhon Pathom. Her daughter, Chatsumarn Kabilsingh, has continued the tradition by seeking a Theravada ordination in Sri Lanka in 2003; she is now the director of the temple her mother founded. Reviving the long-extinct tradition of female monks in Thai Buddhism has caused controversy among the established order, but the quiet resistance continues at the temple with the first ordination of a woman on Thai soil in 2002.

MONARCHY

Historically the Thai king has occupied a revered position in the fundamentals of the country and the religion, often viewed as semi-divine. The present Thai king, His Majesty Bhumibol Adulyadej, has held the position for 62 years, making him the world's longest-reigning monarch. Thai royal ceremonies remain almost exclusively the domain of one of the most ancient religious traditions still functioning in the kingdom, Brahmanism. White-robed, top-knotted priests of Indian descent keep alive an arcane collection of rituals that, it is believed, must be performed regularly to sustain the three pillars of Thai nationhood, namely sovereignty, religion and the monarchy. Such rituals are performed regularly at a complex of shrines near Wat Suthat in Bangkok.

Other Religions

About 4.6% of the population are followers of Islam. The remainder are Christian, including missionised hill tribes and Vietnamese immigrants, as well as Confucianists, Taoists, Mahayana Buddhists and Hindus.

Arts

Thailand has an intensely visual culture and an appreciation of beauty that infuses the audacious temple buildings, the humble old-fashioned houses and the high arts developed for the royal court.

ARCHITECTURE
Traditional Residential Architecture

A harmonious blend of function and style, traditional Thai homes were adapted to the weather, the family and artistic sensibilities. These antique specimens were humble dwellings consisting of a single-room wooden house raised on stilts. More elaborate homes, of the village chief or minor royalty for instance, might link a series of single rooms by elevated walkways. Since many Thai villages were built near rivers, the elevation provided protection from flooding during the annual monsoon. During the dry season the space beneath the house was used as a hideaway from the heat of the day, an outdoor kitchen or as a barn for farm animals. Later this all-purpose space would shelter bicycles and motorcycles. Once plentiful in Thai forests, teak was always the material of choice for wooden structures and its use typically indicates that a house is at least 50 years old.

Thai House: History and Evolution (2002), by Ruethai Chaichongrak, explains the decorative and functional aspects of residential architecture.

Rooflines in central, northern and southern Thailand are steeply pitched and often decorated at the corners or along the gables with motifs related to the *naga*, a mythical sea serpent long believed to be a spiritual protector of Tai cultures throughout Asia.

Geographic differences abound and often reflect influences from neighbouring countries. In Thailand's southern provinces it's not unusual to come upon houses of Malay design, using high masonry pediments or foundations rather than wooden stilts. Residents of the south also sometimes use bamboo and palm thatch, which are more plentiful than wood. In the north, the homes of community leaders were often decorated with an ornate horn-shaped motif called *galare*, a decorative element that has become shorthand for old Lanna architecture. Roofs of tile or thatch tend to be less steeply pitched, and rounded gables (a feature inherited from Myanmar) can also be found further north.

Temple Architecture

Most striking of Thailand's architectural heritage are the Buddhist temples, which dazzle in the tropical sun with wild colours and soaring rooflines. Thai temples (wát) are compounds of different buildings serving specific religious functions. The most important structures include the *uposatha* (*bòht* in central Thai, *sǐm* in northern and northeastern Thai), which is a consecrated chapel where monastic ordinations are held, and the *wí·hǎhn*, where important Buddha images are housed.

Another classic component of temple architecture is the presence of one or more stupas (*chedi* in Thai), a solid mountain-shaped monument that pays tribute to the enduring stability of Buddhism. *Chedi* come in a myriad of styles, from simple inverted bowl-shaped designs imported from Sri Lanka to the more elaborate octagonal shapes found in northern Thailand. Many are believed to contain relics (often pieces of bone) belonging to the historical Buddha. In northern and northeastern Thailand such stupas are known as *tâht*. A variation of the stupa inherited from the Angkor kingdom is the corn cob–shaped *prang*, a feature in the ancient Thai temples of Sukhothai and Ayuthaya. Dotting the grounds of most temples are smaller squarish

---

HOUSES OF THE HOLY

Many homes or inhabited dwellings in Thailand have an associated 'spirit house', built to provide a residence for the plot of land's *prá poom* (guardian spirits). Based on animistic beliefs that predate Buddhism, guardian spirits are believed to reside in rivers, trees and other natural features and need to be honoured (and placated). The guardian spirit of a particular plot of land is the supernatural equivalent of a mother-in-law, an honoured but sometimes troublesome family member. To keep the spirits happily distracted, Thais erect elaborate dollhouse-like structures on the property where the spirits can 'live' comfortably separated from human affairs. To further cultivate good relations and good fortune, daily offerings of rice, fruit, flowers and water are made to the spirit house. If the human house is enlarged the spirit house must also be enlarged, so that the spirits do not feel slighted. Spirit houses must be consecrated by a Brahman priest.

More elaborate spirit shrines stand alongside hotels and office buildings and are sometimes dedicated to a Hindu deity, such as Brahma or Shiva. In Bangkok especially, many of these mega-site spirit houses have earned a reputation for expediting certain types of prayers and have become city-wide shrines filled with beseeching visitors.

---

chedi, known as *tâht grà·dòok* (bone reliquaries) that contain the ashes of deceased worshippers.

Other structures typically found in temple compounds include one or more *săh·lah* (open-sided shelters) that are used for community meetings and *dhamma* lectures; a number of *gù·dì* (monastic quarters); a *hŏr đrai* (Tripitaka library), where Buddhist scriptures are stored; a *hŏr glorng* (drum tower), sometimes with a *hŏr rá·kang* (bell tower); plus various ancillary buildings, such as schools or clinics.

The architectural symbolism of these temple buildings relies heavily on Hindu-Buddhist iconography. *Naga*, the mythical serpent that guarded Buddha during meditation, is depicted in the temple roofline where the green and gold tiles are said to represent the serpent's scales (others say that the tiles represent the land and the king) and the soaring eaves represent its diamond-shaped head. On the tip of the roof is the silhouette of the *chôr fáh*: often bird-shaped decorations the colour of gold. Rooflines are usually tiered into three levels, representing the triple gems of Buddhism: the Buddha, the *dhamma* (Buddhist philosophy) and the *sangha* (the Buddhist community).

The lotus bud is another sacred motif that is used to decorate the tops of the temple gates, veranda columns and spires of Sukhothai-era *chedi*. Images of the Buddha often depict him meditating in a lotus blossom–shaped pedestal. The lotus bud was extensively used before the introduction of monk-like figures depicting the Buddha. It carries with it a shorthand reminder of the tenets of Buddhism. In a practical sense, the lotus plant can create a dramatic flower even in the most rancid pond – a natural phenomenon reminding the faithful of religious perfection. Many Thai markets sell lotus buds, which are used solely for merit-making in Thailand not as secular decorations.

'The architectural symbolism of these temple buildings relies heavily on Hindu-Buddhist iconography'

Contemporary Architecture

Thais began mixing traditional architecture with European forms in the late 19th and early 20th centuries, as exemplified by Bangkok's Vimanmek Teak Mansion (p138), and certain buildings of the Grand Palace (p126).

The port cities of Thailand, including Bangkok and Phuket, acquired fine examples of Sino-Portuguese architecture – buildings of stuccoed brick decorated with an ornate facade – a style that followed the sea traders during the colonial era. In Bangkok this style is often referred to as 'old Bangkok' or 'Ratanakosin'.

HEAVEN ON EARTH

Wander into a temple and you might think that the layout is as haphazard as everything else in Thailand. But if you had a bird's-eye view, you'd look down on an ancient and sacred mandala based on the Hindu-Buddhist belief of a universe composed of different vertical and horizontal planes roughly corresponding to heaven, earth and hell. In the centre of the universe is Mt Sumeru (or Mt Meru in Hindu texts), where Brahma and other important deities reside and around which the sun and moon orbit. Mt Sumeru is often symbolised by a central *chedi* with minor *chedi* placed at the cardinal points to represent minor peaks and oceans encircling Sumeru. The central *chedi* in a Thai temple is often one of the most revered structures and displays distinct characteristics that have defined the various artistic periods (see opposite for more information).

Buildings of mixed heritage in the north and northeast exhibit French and English influences, while those in the south typically show Portuguese influence. Shophouses *(hôrng tǎa·ou)* throughout the country, whether 100 years or 100 days old, share the basic Chinese shophouse design, where the ground floor is reserved for trading purposes while the upper floors contain offices or residences.

In the 1960s and '70s the trend in modern Thai architecture, inspired by the European Bauhaus movement, shifted towards a stark functionalism – the average building looked like a giant egg carton turned on its side. When Thai architects began experimenting with form over function during the building boom of the mid-1980s, the result was high-tech designs such as ML Sumet Jumsai's famous Robot Building on Th Sathon Tai in Bangkok. Rangsan Torsuwan, a graduate of Massachusetts Institute of Technology (MIT), introduced the neoclassic (or neo-Thai) style. A traditional-building specialist, Pinyo Suwankiri designs temples, government buildings and shrines for hospitals and universities. His work is ubiquitous and the blueprint for an institutional aesthetic of traditional architecture.

Bangkok: Thai Interior Design (2006), by Brian Mertens, documents the country's design boom and profiles artists as well as artisans.

In the new millennium, Duangrit Bunnag has excited the design world with his nearly undressed glass boxes offering a contemporary twist on mid-century modernism. The H1 complex on Soi Thonglor in Bangkok is a series of interconnected geometric cubes with flat cantilevered roofs, glass curtain windows and exposed steel ribs, arranged around a courtyard much like a traditional Thai house. Encore performances include the Pier restaurant on Ko Samui and Costa Lanta on Ko Lanta. He has now even built his way into interior design with his minimalist Anyroom design label.

PAINTING & SCULPTURE
Traditional Art

Bangkok's National Museum (p128) offers a comprehensive comparative look at Buddhist art through the ages.

Thailand's artistic repository remains mainly in the temples where you'll find ornate murals depicting Hindu-Buddhist mythology and Buddha sculptures, which define Thailand's most famous contribution to the world of religious art.

Always instructional in intent, temple murals often show depictions of the *jataka* (stories of the Buddha's past life) and the Thai version of the Hindu epic *Ramayana*. Reading the murals requires both knowledge of these religious tales and an understanding of the mural's spatial relationship and chronology. Most murals are divided into scenes, in which the main theme is depicted in the centre with resulting events taking place above and below the central action. Usually in the corner of a dramatic episode between the story's characters are independent scenes of Thai village life: women carrying food in bamboo baskets, men fishing, or a happy communal get-together; all of these simple village folk wear the ubiquitous Thai smile.

THE BUDDHA LINE-UP

Like other Buddhist cultures, Thailand borrowed and adapted the religious iconography and symbolism that first developed in India. Based on rules defined by Indian artists, the Buddha is depicted in poses (mudra) that are symbolic of a particular episode in his life or of certain religious precepts. For example, a standing Buddha with one or both hands raised and the palms facing the viewer represents dispelling fear from his followers. Buddha sitting in the lotus position with hands folded and palms facing upwards represents meditation. When the Buddha is in the basic meditation position, but with the right hand pointing towards the earth, then the figure is subduing Mara, a demon who tried to tempt Buddha. A reclining Buddha represents his dying moment.

Lacking the durability of other art forms, pre-20th century religious painting is limited to very few surviving examples. The earliest examples are found at Ayuthaya's Wat Ratburana (1424; p198), Wat Chong Nonsi in Bangkok (1657–1707; p129) and Phetchaburi's Wat Yai Suwannaram (late 17th century).

Nineteenth-century religious painting has fared better. Ratanakosin temple art is, in fact, more highly esteemed for painting than for sculpture or architecture. Typical temple murals feature rich colours and lively detail. Some of the finest are found at the Buddhaisawan Chapel at Bangkok's National Museum and at Thonburi's Wat Suwannaram. For more information about Bangkok's temple murals see p129.

The study and application of mural painting techniques have been kept alive, and today's practitioners often use improved techniques and paints that promise to hold fast much longer than the temple murals of old.

Alongside the vivid murals in the sacred temple spaces are revered Buddha images that trace Thailand's sculptural evolution. The country is most famous for its graceful and serene Buddhas that emerged during the Sukhothai era, and today the country is a pilgrimage site for art collectors and connoisseurs of religious sculpture.

ARTISTIC PERIODS

The development of Thai religious art and architecture is broken into different periods or schools defined by the patronage of the ruling capital. The best examples of a period's characteristics are seen in the variations of the *chedi* shape and in the features of the Buddha sculptures. *Chedi* styles often vary in the shape of the pedestal and of the central bell before it begins to taper. For Buddha sculpture, artistic periods often show differences in the facial features, the top flourish on the head, the dress and the position of the feet in meditation.

Dvaravati Period (7th–11th Centuries)

This period refers to the Mon kingdom that occupied areas of northwestern and central Thailand. The Buddha sculptures borrowed heavily from the Indian periods of Amaravati and Gupta, with the Buddha's body shape being thick, along with large hair curls, arched eyebrows to represent a flying bird, protruding eyes, thick lips and a flat nose. Examples can be seen at Phra Pathom Chedi (p189) in Nakhon Pathom. Lamphun (p339) in northern Thailand was also an outpost of the Mon kingdom and today contains several temples displaying the needle-like *chedi* spires associated with this period.

Steven Van Beek's *The Arts of Thailand* (1999) is a thorough account of artistic movements in Thailand from the Bronze Age to the Ratanakosin era.

Srivijaya Period (7th–13th Centuries)

A southern kingdom that extended throughout the Malay peninsula and into parts of Indonesia, Srivijaya's artistic creations were closely linked to Indian forms and were more sensual and stylised than what is found in central and northern Thailand. Examples can be found in Chaiya's Wat Phra Boromathat and Nakhon Si Thammarat's Wat Phra Mahathat Woramahawihaan (p629).

Khmer Period (9th–11th Centuries)
The great Angkor empire based in present-day Cambodia, which once carved its artistic signature into Thai soil, is reflected in images of Buddha meditating under a canopy of the seven-headed *naga* and atop a lotus pedestal. The most famous Khmer contribution to temple architecture is the central corn cob–shaped stupa, called a *prang*. Examples can be seen at Sukhothai Historical Park (p398) and Phimai (p465).

Chiang Saen-Lanna Period (11th–13th Centuries)
This northern Thai kingdom drew inspiration from its Lao, Shan and Burmese neighbours in depicting Buddha, who appears with a plump figure and round, smiling face, with both pads of the feet facing upward in the meditation position. Standing Buddhas were often shown in the pose of dispelling fear or giving instruction. Lanna-style temples were typically made of teak and the *chedi* are often indented. Examples can be found in the temples and museums of Chiang Mai (p275) and at Chiang Saen National Museum (p367).

Sukhothai Period (13th–15th Centuries)
Often regarded as the first 'Thai' kingdom, Sukhothai set forth the underlying aesthetic of successive Thai art. Buddha images were graceful and serene and were often depicted 'walking', but without anatomical human detail. The intention was to highlight the Buddha's spiritual qualities rather than his human status. The telltale Sukhothai *chedi* are fairly slim spires topped with a lotus-bud motif. Examples can be seen at Sukhothai Historical Park (p398).

Ayuthaya Period (14th–18th Centuries)
Incorporating elements inherited from the Khmer and Sukhothai kingdoms, Ayuthaya morphed the Buddha image into a king wearing a gem-studded crown and royal regalia instead of an austere monk's robe. The period's bell-shaped *chedi*, with an elongated, tapering spire, can be seen at Ayuthaya Historical Park (p198).

Bangkok-Ratanakosin Period (19th Century–)
The religious artwork of the modern capital is noted for merging traditional Thai styles with Western influences. Wat Phra Kaew and the Grand Palace (p126) are a good starting point.

Contemporary Art
Adapting traditional themes and aesthetics to the secular canvas began around the turn of the 20th century as Western influence surged in the region. In general, Thai painting favours abstraction over realism and continues to preserve the one-dimensional perspective of traditional mural paintings. There are two major trends in Thai art: the updating of religious themes and tongue-in-cheek social commentary. Some of the younger artists often overlap the two.

Italian artist Corrado Feroci is often credited as the father of modern Thai art. He was first invited to Thailand by Rama VI in 1924 and built Bangkok's Democracy Monument and the militaristic Rama I monument that stands at

Rama IX Art Museum (www.rama9art.org) is an online reference focusing on Thai contemporary artists and galleries.

the entry to Memorial Bridge. Feroci founded the country's first fine arts institute in 1933, a school that eventually developed into Silpakorn University, Thailand's premier training ground for artists. In gratitude, the Thai government made Feroci a Thai citizen, with the Thai name Silpa Bhirasri.

In the 1970s, Thai artists began to tackle the modernisation of Buddhist themes through abstract expressionism. Leading works in this genre include the colourful surrealism of Pichai Nirand, the mystical pen-and-ink drawings of Thawan Duchanee, and the fluid naturalist oil and watercolours of Pratuang Emjaroen. Receiving more exposure overseas than at home, Montien Boonma used the ingredients of Buddhist merit-making, such as gold leaf, bells and candle wax, to create abstract temple spaces within museum galleries. Other recognised names include Songdej Thipthong with his spare mandalas, Surasit Saokong with his realist paintings of rural temples, and Monchai Kaosamang with his ephemeral watercolours. Jitr (Prakit) Buabusaya painted in the French impressionist style but is best remembered as an art teacher.

Politically motivated artwork defines a parallel movement in Thai contemporary art. In Thailand's quickly industrialising society, many artists have watched as the rice fields became factories, the forests became asphalt and the spoils went to the politically connected. During the student activist days of the 1970s, the Art for Life Movement was the banner under which creative discontents – including musicians, intellectuals and painters – rallied against the military dictatorship and embraced certain aspects of communism and workers' rights. Sompote Upa-In and Chang Saetang are two important artists from that period.

During and after the boom times of the 1980s, an anti-authority attitude emerged in the work of the artists known as the Fireball school. Manit Sriwanichpoom is best known for his Pink Man on Tour series, in which he depicted artist Sompong Thawee in a pink suit and with a pink shopping cart amid Thailand's most iconic attractions. Less famous are Manit's evocative black-and-white photographic pieces denouncing capitalism and consumerism, typically identified as unwelcome Western imports. Vasan Sitthiket is more blatantly controversial and uses mixed-media installations to condemn the players he views as corrupt. His works have been banned in Thailand and widely criticised as anti-Thai.

Steven Pettifor focuses on the work of some of Thailand's most prominent contemporary artists in *Flavours – Thai Contemporary Art* (2003).

In the 1990s there was a push to move art out of the dead zones of the museums and into the public spaces. An artist and art organiser, Navin Rawanchaikul started his 'in-the-streets' collaborations in his hometown of Chiang Mai and then moved his big ideas to Bangkok where he filled the city's taxi cabs with art installations, a show that literally went on the road. His other works have had a way with words, such as the mixed media piece *We Are the Children of Rice (Wine)* in 2002 and his rage against the commercialisation of museums in his epic painting entitled *Super (M)art Bangkok Survivors* (2004), which depicts famous artists, curators and decision makers in a crowded Paolo Veronese setting. The piece was inspired by the struggles the Thai art community had getting the new contemporary Bangkok art museum to open without becoming a shopping mall in disguise.

The works of Thaweesak Srithongdee are pure pop. He paints flamboyantly cartoonish human figures woven with elements of traditional Thai handicrafts or imagery. In a similar vein, Jirapat Tasanasomboon pits traditional Thai figures in comic book–style fights or in sensual embraces with Western icons. In *Hanuman is Upset!*, the monkey king chews up the geometric lines of Mondrian's famous grid-like painting.

THAI-ED UP IN DESIGN

Thailand has a long history of handicrafts, from woven bamboo baskets used to carry tools and freshly caught fish to ornate lacquerware and celadon pottery that was used to serve the royal court. Although a great deal of the 'traditional' crafts are now mass-produced for tourist markets, the artistic sensibilities remain and have been channelled into a wave of modern industrial design, mainly centred in Bangkok. Many of this movement's designers studied overseas during the boom times of the 1990s and returned to Thailand during the Asian financial crisis to infuse the country with a shot of creative energy. The result is an engaging fusion of such styles as Scandinavian minimalism with tropical materials such as rattan and water hyacinth.

There are now a number of well-known companies and creative individuals working in this new wave today. The design firm Yothaka was one of the first to pioneer the use of water hyacinth, an invasive plant that has long clogged the country's waterways. Planet 2001 has developed some of Thailand's most iconic haute-design rattan chairs, while Jitrin Jintaprecha's award-winning i-Kon Revolving Lounge Chair turns water hyacinth into an artistic version of a beanbag seat. Crafactor is a leading design firm that claims such talent as Eggarat Wongcharit, Thailand's Frank Gehry of furniture design, who creates non-linear moulded plastic pieces; and Paiwate Wangbon, who prefers contorting natural materials into curvaceous shapes.

Kritsana Chaikitwattana works in moody paint-and-collage abstracts, including a series of self-portraits inspired by his years as a Buddhist monk. In contrast, Jaruwat Boonwaedlom explores modern realism, a genre not well populated by Thai artists, with her prism-like paintings of Bangkok street scenes.

Although lacking in commercial attention, Thai sculpture is often considered to be the strongest of the contemporary arts, not surprising considering the country's relationship with Buddha figures. Moving into nonreligious arenas, Khien Yimsiri is the modern master creating elegant human and mythical forms out of bronze. Sakarin Krue-On is often applauded for adapting sculpture and installation. His work *Phawang Si Leuang* (Yellow Simple) fashioned a huge, hollow Buddha head from a mixture of clay, mud, papier-mâché and turmeric. Manop Suwanpinta similarly moulds the human anatomy into fantastic shapes that often intersect with technological features, such as hinged faces that open to reveal inanimate content. Kamin Lertchaiprasert explores the subject of spirituality and daily life in his sculptural installations, which often include a small army of papier-mâché figures. One of his most recent exhibitions, *'Ngern Nang'* (Sitting Money), included a series of figures made of discarded paper bills from the national bank embellished with poetic instructions on life and love.

> 'Classical
> pleng
> tai deum
> (central-
> Thai music)
> features a
> dazzling
> array of tex-
> tures and
> subtleties,
> hair-raising
> tempos and
> pastoral
> melodies'

MUSIC

Throughout Thailand you'll find a diversity of musical genres and styles, from the serene court music that accompanies classical dance-drama to the chest-thumping house music played at dance clubs.

Traditional Music

Classical *pleng tai deum* (central-Thai music) features a dazzling array of textures and subtleties, hair-raising tempos and pastoral melodies. The classical orchestra is called the *ȟèe pâht* and can include as few as five players or more than 20. Among the most common instruments is the *ȟèe*, a woodwind instrument that has a reed mouthpiece; it is heard prominently at Thai-boxing matches. The four-stringed *pĭn*, plucked like a guitar, lends subtle counterpoint, while the *rá·nâht èhk*, a bamboo-keyed percussion instrument resembling the xylophone, carries the main melodies. The slender *sor,* a bowed instrument with a coconut-shell soundbox, provides soaring embellishments, as does the *klòo·i* (wooden Thai flute).

One of the more attention-drawing instruments is the *kórng wong yài,* which consists of tuned gongs arranged in a semicircle and played in simple rhythmic lines to provide a song's underlying fabric. Several types of drums carry the beat, often through multiple tempo changes in a single song. The most important is the *dà·pohn (tohn),* a double-headed hand-drum that leads the entire ensemble. Prior to a performance the players offer incense and flowers to the *dà·pohn,* considered to be the conductor of the music's spiritual content.

Want to know more about Thai music? Check out www.ethaimusic .com where you can read transliterated and translated lyrics and buy popular songs.

The standard Thai scale divides the eight-note octave into seven full-tone intervals, with no semitones. Thai scales were first transcribed by the Thai-German composer Peter Feit (also known by his Thai name, Phra Chen Duriyanga), who composed Thailand's national anthem in 1932.

The *'bèe pâht* ensemble was originally developed to accompany classical dance-drama and shadow theatre, but can be heard these days in straightforward performances at temple fairs and concerts.

Classical Thai music has not been forgotten in the dusty annals of history, but has been fused with international jazz elements. Fong Nam, a Thai orchestra led by American composer Bruce Gaston, performs an inspiring blend of Western and Thai classical motifs that have become a favourite choice for movie soundtracks, TV commercials and tourism promotion. Another leading exponent of this genre is the composer and instrumentalist Tewan Sapsanyakorn (also known as Tong Tewan), who plays soprano and alto sax, violin and *klòo·i* with equal virtuosity.

Lôok Tûng & Mŏr Lam

The bestselling of all modern musical genres in Thailand remains *lôok tûng* (literally 'children of the fields'), which dates back to the 1940s. Analogous to country and western music in the USA, it's a genre that tends to appeal most to working-class Thais. Subject matter almost always cleaves to tales of lost love, tragic early death, and the dire circumstances of farmers who work day in and day out and at the end of the year are still in debt. There are two basic styles: the original Suphanburi style, with lyrics in standard Thai; and an Ubon style sung in Isan dialect.

If *lôok tûng* is Thailand's country and western, then *mŏr lam* is the blues. *Mŏr lam* is a folk tradition firmly rooted in the northeast of Thailand and is based on the songs played on the Lao-Isan *kaan* (a wind instrument devised of a double row of bamboo-like reeds fitted into a hardwood soundbox). The oldest style is most likely to be heard at a village gathering or parade, has a simple but very insistent bass beat topped by vocal melodies, and is often sung in Isan dialect. It has traditionally had a 'country bumpkin' image, often the source of comedic music videos and self-effacing lyrics. *Mŏr lam* has jumped the generational fence and now has an electrified pop version.

Within the past decade, as economic migrants from Isan moved to Bangkok, the two genres have begun to merge, creating a brew called *lôok tûng 'brá·yúk.* Contemporary singers often cross from one style to another with a few songs in between and the terms are often inconsistently applied.

Thailand's most famous *lôok tûng* singer was Pumpuang Duangjan, who rated a royally sponsored cremation when she died in 1992 and a major shrine at Suphanburi's Wat Thapkradan, which receives a steady stream of worshippers. When she died many feared that the genre would pass with her, but gravelly voiced Siriporn Amphaipong helped carry the tradition and is still one of the most beloved *lôok tûng* superstars, although she is beginning to approach retirement age. A promising young replacement is Tai Orathai who can vibrate those dramatic notes like a plaintive cry.

Jintara Poonlarp is a current fixture in the *mŏr lam/lôok tûng Ъráˑyúk* constellation; she's quite nouveau with a trendy haircut and Bangkok-style fashions instead of the farm-girl look. Mike Pirompon excels with the oh-so-sad *lôok tûng* tunes, while Rock Salaeng brings denim cool to the *mŏr lam* stage with songs that are more rock than *lôok tûng*.

Thai Rock & Pop

Check out 365 Jukebox (www.365jukebox.com), which charts the hits for all the popular radio stations including Fat FM 104.5 (alt-rock), Seed FM 97.5 (T-pop), and Luk Thung FM95.0 (*lôok tûng* and *mŏr lam*).

The 1970s ushered in a new style inspired by the politically conscious folk rock of the USA and Europe, which the Thais dubbed *pleng pêuˑa cheeˑwít* ('songs for life'). Chiefly identified with the Thai band Caravan, this style remains the most major musical shift in Thailand since *lôok tûng* arose in the 1940s. Songs of this nature have political and environmental topics rather than the usual love themes. During the authoritarian dictatorships of the '70s many of Caravan's songs were officially banned. Another longstanding example of this style, Carabao, took *pleng pêuˑa cheeˑwít*, fused it with *lôok tûng*, rock and heavy metal, and spawned a whole generation of imitators as well as a chain of barnlike performance venues.

Thailand also has a thriving teen-pop industry – sometimes referred to as T-pop – centred on artists chosen for their good looks, which often means they are *lôok krêung* (half-Thai, half-*faˑràng*) and sport English names. Thailand's king of pop is Thongchai 'Bird' Mcintyre (also known as Pi Bird). His first album came out in 1986 and he has followed up with an album almost every year since. He has Madonna's staying power coupled with a nice-guy persona. Among Thais in their 30s and 40s, Pi Bird often makes up the bulk of their CD collections.

GMM Grammy Entertainment is Thailand's leading music producer having manufactured pop stars for decades. But a few new crooners are bubbling through TV singing competitions like 'Star' and 'Academy Fantasia'.

Pop queens used to be cute 'girls next door', but Tata Young matured from a pop princess into a tart queen with her album *Sexy, Naughty, Bitchy*. In 2006 she started courting overseas approval with the release of two English-language albums and these days Thai teens sniff that she is more of a celebrity than a singer. A counterpoint to Tata is soulful Palmy (half-Thai, half-Belgian), who has cultivated a successful hippy persona. In the heart-throb boys section is Golf + Mike, two teen brothers with a crossover career in Japan. Also popular is Aof Pongsak who melts the girls' hearts with his sweet voice and sensitive songs.

The 1990s gave birth to an alternative pop scene – known as *glorng săiˑree* (free drum), *pleng đâi din* (underground music) or more simply just as 'indie' – pioneered by the independent record label Bakery Music, which captured a youth revolution more musically sophisticated than Grammy's mainstream machine. Bakery Music upstaged Grammy at the 2002 MTV Asia Awards but it has since gone corporate when it was bought by a larger conglomerate. During indie's heyday, Modern Dog, composed of four Chulalongkorn University graduates, orchestrated the generation's musical coming of age. After 10 years on the alt-rock scene, Modern Dog is still a beloved veteran with a much-anticipated album released in 2008. Another indie fixture is Loso (from 'low society' as opposed to 'hi-so' or socialites), which updated Carabao's affinity for Thai folk melodies and rhythms. Both bands are known for their anthem status – most twenty-something Thais can sing their greatest hits by heart.

Thais love to sing and every major band or singer releases video CDs (VCD) specially formatted for karaoke-style singalongs.

There is still a thriving underground scene in Bangkok thanks to smaller record labels like Mind the Gap and compilations of unsigned artists from Sanamluang Zine. Abuse the Youth, the Papers and Slur are all chart toppers at the indie station Fat 104.5 and have MySpace fame. The Kai-Jo Brothers

---

THAI SOUNDTRACK

Looking for tunes from the kingdom? Check out these hits and oddities:

- *Ting Nong Noy* (Modern Dog) – Latest album from Thailand's alt-rock gurus.
- *Thai Pop Spectacular 1960s–1980s* – Sublime Frequencies' LP compilation with such doo-wop hits as 'Look Who's Underwear is Showing'.
- *Made in Thailand* (Carabao) – Thailand's classic classic-rock album.
- *Best* (Pumpuang Duangjan) – Compilation of the late *lôok tûng* diva's most famous tunes.
- *Captain Loma* (Captain Loma) – Easy listening sans the cheesiness; the Captain rocks the toe-tappers too mature to head bang.
- *Newbie Party* – A compilation series of new indie rockers, like Abuse the Youth, Tabasco and other Mind the Gappers.

---

have outfitted the Thai language with a reggae beat and Blue on Blue channels an Asian version of BB King.

THEATRE & DANCE

Traditional Thai theatre consists of six dramatic forms: *kŏhn* (formal masked dance-drama depicting scenes from the *Ramakian* – the Thai version of India's *Ramayana*); *lá·kon* (a general term covering several types of dance-drama); *lí·gair* (a partly improvised, often bawdy folk play featuring dancing, comedy, melodrama and music); *má·noh·rah* (the southern Thai equivalent of *lí·gair*, but based on a 2000-year-old Indian story); *năng* (shadow plays limited to southern Thailand); *lá·kon lék* or *hùn lŏo·ang* (puppet theatre) and *lá·kon pôot* (contemporary spoken theatre).

Kŏhn

In all *kŏhn* performances, four types of characters are represented – male humans, female humans, monkeys and demons. Monkey and demon figures are always masked with the elaborate head coverings often seen in tourist promotional material. Behind the masks and make-up, all actors are male. Traditional *kŏhn* is a very expensive production – Ravana's retinue alone (Ravana is the *Ramakian*'s principal villain) consists of over 100 demons, each with a distinctive mask.

Scenes performed in traditional *kŏhn* (and *lá·khon* performances) come from the epic-journey tale of the *Ramayana*, known as the *Ramakian* in Thai. The central story revolves around Prince Rama's search for his beloved Princess Sita, who has been abducted by the evil 10-headed demon Ravana and taken to the island of Lanka.

Perhaps because it was once limited to royal venues and hence never gained a popular following, the *kŏhn* or *Ramakian* dance-drama tradition nearly died out in Thailand. See the Bangkok chapter (p173) for information on *kŏhn* performances.

Lá·kon

The more formal *lá·kon nai* ('inner' *lá·kon,* performed inside the palace) was originally performed for lower nobility by all-female ensembles. Today it's a dying art, even more so than royal *kŏhn*. In addition to scenes from the *Ramakian, lá·kon nai* performances may include traditional Thai folk tales; whatever the story, text is always sung. *Lá·kon nôrk* ('outer' *lá·kon,* performed outside the palace) deals exclusively with folk tales and features a mix of sung and spoken text, sometimes with improvisation. Both male and female performers are permitted. Like *kŏhn* and *lá·kon nai,* performances are becoming increasingly rare.

Much more common these days is the less-refined *lá·kon chah·đree,* a fast-paced, costumed dance-drama usually performed at upcountry temple festivals or at shrines (commissioned by a shrine devotee whose wish was granted by the shrine deity). *Chah·đree* stories have been influenced by the older *má·noh·rah* theatre of southern Thailand.

A variation on *chah·đree* that has evolved specifically for shrine worship, *lá·kon gâa bon* involves an ensemble of around 20 members, including musicians. At an important shrine like Bangkok's Lak Meuang, four different *gâa bon* troupes may alternate performances and there is usually a list of worshippers waiting to hire them.

Lí·gair

In outlying working-class neighbourhoods in Bangkok you may be lucky enough to come across the gaudy, raucous *lí·gair.* This theatrical art form is thought to have descended from drama rituals brought to southern Thailand by Arab and Malay traders. The first native public performance in central Thailand came about when a group of Thai Muslims staged a *lí·gair* for Rama V in Bangkok during the funeral commemoration of Queen Sunandha. *Lí·gair* grew very popular under Rama VI, peaked in the early 20th century and has been fading slowly since the 1960s.

Most often performed at Buddhist festivals by troupes of travelling performers, *lí·gair* presents a colourful mixture of folk and classical music, outrageous costumes, melodrama, slapstick comedy, sexual innuendo and up-to-date commentary on Thai politics and society. Foreigners – even those who speak fluent Thai – are often left behind by the highly idiomatic, culture-specific language and gestures.

Marionettes

Lá·kon lék (little theatre), also known as *hùn lŏo·ang* (royal puppets), like *kŏhn,* was once reserved for court performances. Metre-high marionettes made of *kòi* paper and wire, wearing elaborate costumes modelled on those of the *kŏhn,* are used to convey similar themes, music and dance movements.

Two to three puppet masters are required to manipulate each *hùn lŏo·ang* by means of wires attached to long poles. Stories are drawn from Thai folk tales, particularly *Phra Aphaimani,* and occasionally from the *Ramakian.* The *hùn lŏo·ang* puppets themselves are highly collectable; the Bangkok National Museum has only one example in its collection. A smaller, 30cm court version called *hùn lék* (little puppets) are occasionally used in live performances.

Another Thai puppet theatre, *hùn grà·bòrk* (cylinder puppets) is based on popular Hainanese puppet shows. It uses 30cm hand puppets carved from wood.

One of the sole surviving Thai puppet masters, Sakorn Yangkhiawsod (nicknamed Joe Louis) helped revive the dying *hùn lék* tradition in the latter half of the 20th century with his popular puppet troupe based in Bangkok. The patriarch died in 2007 but his children continue the tradition at the Aksra Theatre (p174).

Năng

Shadow-puppet theatre – in which two-dimensional figures are manipulated between a cloth screen and a light source at night-time performances – has been a Southeast Asian tradition for perhaps five centuries. Originally brought to the Malay Peninsula by Middle Eastern traders, the technique eventually spread to all parts of mainland and peninsular Southeast Asia; in Thailand it is mostly found in the south. As in Malaysia and Indonesia, shadow puppets in Thailand are carved from dried buffalo or cow hides *(năng).*

Two distinct shadow-play traditions survive in Thailand. The most common, *năng đà·lung,* is named after Phattalung Province, where it developed around Malay models. Like their Malay-Indonesian counterparts, Thai shadow puppets represent an array of characters from classical and folk drama, principally the *Ramakian* and *Phra Aphaimani* in Thailand. A single puppet master manipulates the cut-outs, which are bound to the ends of buffalo-horn handles. *Năng đà·lung* is still occasionally seen at temple festivals in the south, mostly in Songkhla and Nakhon Si Thammarat provinces. Performances are also held periodically for tour groups or visiting dignitaries from Bangkok.

The second tradition, *năng yài* (big hide), uses much larger cut-outs, each bound to two wooden poles held by a puppet master; several masters may participate in a single performance. *Năng yài* is rarely performed nowadays because of the lack of trained *năng* masters and the expense of the shadow puppets. Most *năng yài* that are made today are sold to interior designers or tourists.

CINEMA

When it comes to Thai cinema, there are usually two concurrent streams: the movies that are financially successful and the movies that are considered cinematically meritorious; only occasionally do these overlap.

Popular Thai cinema ballooned in the 1960s and '70s, especially during the period when the government levied a tax on Hollywood imports thus spawning a home-grown industry. The majority of films were cheap action flicks that were often dubbed *'nám nôw'* (stinking water); but the fantastic, even nonsensical, plots and rich colours left a lasting impression on modern-day Thai filmmakers, who have inserted these elements into modern contexts.

The leading couple of the action genre was Mitr Chaibancha and Petchara Chaowarat, a duo who starred in some 75 films together. Their last film was *Insee Thong* (Golden Eagle), in which Mit, playing the film's hero, was tragically killed during the filming of a helicopter stunt.

Another beloved film of the era was *Mon Rak Luk Thung*, a musical rhapsodising Thai rural life. Isan musicals were a theatre darling during this era and re-emerged in 2001 with *Monpleng Luk Thung FM* (Hoedown Showdown) and Pen-Ek Ratanaruang's *Monrak Transistor,* which paid tribute to the music of Suraphol Sombatcharoen. In 2005 comedian-actor-director Petchtai Wongkamlao wrote, directed and starred in *Yam Yasothon,* a colourful homage to the 1970s musicals.

For a country renowned for its sense of fun, comedy will always be a guaranteed local moneymaker. The classic comedy flick of the 1960s was *Ngern Ngern Ngern* (Money, Money, Money), starring comedian Lor Tork. The modern comedies invariably feature *gà·teu·i* (transvestites and transsexuals), another guaranteed laugh in Thai humour. The 2000 film *Satree Lek* (Iron Ladies), directed by Yongyoot Thongkongtoon, dramatised the real-life exploits of a Lampang volleyball team made up almost entirely of *gà·teu·i*.

More important as an artistic inspiration, the director Rattana Pestonji is often credited as the father of Thai new wave. His 1957 movie *Rong Raem Narok* (Country Hotel) is a dark comedy set in a Bangkok bar and filmed using only one camera.

The current era boasts several generations of seriously good directors, a number of whom studied film abroad and are beloved in international film festivals. Nonzee Nimibutr is regarded as the most mainstream (and profitable) of the so-called new wave filmmakers. His 1998 release of *Nang Nak* was a retelling of a famous Thai spirit tale that had seen no fewer than 20 previous cinematic renderings. The film became one of the largest-grossing films in Thai history, out performing even *Titanic*. His follow-up films, like *Ok Baytong* (2003) and *Queens of Langkasuka* (2008), invited the Buddhist majority to learn more about the Muslim minority regions of Thailand.

Criticine (www.criticine.com) is an online magazine about Southeast Asian cinema featuring Bangkok-based movie critics writing in English about new releases and industry news.

A Century of Thai Cinema, by Dome Sukwong, is a glossy coffee-table book giving a visual history of film in the kingdom.

Queens of Langkasuka (2008) was an expensive blockbuster that caught the imagination of domestic and international film-goers; not a surprise, since grand historical epics tend to rake in the baht.

Director Pen-Ek Ratanaruang's films are gritty and satirical, and garner fans of cinema not just fans of Thailand. His debut film was *Fun Bar Karaoke,* a 1997 farce of Bangkok life in which the main characters are an ageing Thai playboy and his daughter. But it is *Ruang Rak Noi Nid Mahasan* (Last Life in the Universe; 2003), written by Prabda Yoon, that will secure him a position in the vault of international cinema classics. His most recent film *Kham Phiphaksa Khong Mahasamut* (Invisible Waves; 2006) has been described as the darkest yet and is set in Macau and Phuket.

One of Thai cinema's proudest moments arrived when Cannes 2002 chose *Sut Sanaeha* (Blissfully Yours) for the coveted Un Certain Regard screening. Helmed by Apichatpong Weerasethakul, Thailand's leading *cinéma-vérité* director, the film dramatises a romance between a Thai woman and an illegal Burmese immigrant. Just two years later Apichatpong's dreamlike *Sut Pralat* (Tropical Malady) won the Cannes Jury Prize. His highly anticipated movie *Sang Satawat* (Syndromes and a Century; 2006) was flagged by Thai censors for inappropriate scenes involving doctors drinking whiskey and kissing in a hospital. Rather than remove the scenes, as requested, the director withdrew the movie from screening in Thailand, which in turn sparked a protest movement against film censorship by the country's independent filmmakers.

Apichatpong has become a role model for the next generation of new wavers, many of whom are working in short films due to budget restrictions. Pimpaka Tohveera has garnered praise for *One-Night Husband* (2003). Thunska Pansittivorakul was recently honoured in 2003 with a government-sponsored Silpathorn Award given to contemporary artists. His documentary *Happy Berry* (2003) follows four hip friends trying to live the Bangkok dream of fashion and music.

Colourful tales that merge myth and reality are vital parts of the Thai imagination. *Fah Talai Jone* (Tears of the Black Tiger; 2000), directed by Wisit Sasanatieng, bridged the gap between new wave and the 1960s action genre with a campy homage, while Jira Malikul's *Mekhong Sipha Kham Deuan Sip-et* (Mekong Full Moon Party; 2002) juxtaposes folk beliefs about mysterious 'dragon lights' emanating from Mekong River with the sceptical Bangkok scientists.

With a tradition of martial arts and a thriving mafia, Thailand is fertile ground for home-grown action flicks. The Pang Brothers (Danny and Oxide) imported movie know how from Hong Kong to Thailand with their 1999 hit *Bangkok Dangerous,* about a deaf-mute hit man. The movie was remade in 2008 and starred Nicholas Cage in the lead (albeit speaking) role. Prachya Pinkaew's *Ong Bak* (2004) and his follow-ups *Tom-Yum-Goong* (2005) and *Ong Bak 2* (2008) created an international *moo·ay tai* hero in Tony Jaa, often likened to a younger Jackie Chan.

The up-and-coming generation of filmmakers have a penchant for horror thanks to Thailand's wealth of ghost stories and occult arts to mine for material. *Art of the Devil I* and *II* (2004/2005) is a set of movies, unrelated except by name, made by a collective of Thai filmmakers called the Ronin Team, specialising in grotesque gore and black magic. Picking from a crowded field, *See Phrang* (4bia) is considered one of 2008's best fright fests with four directors, including Yongyoot Thongkongtoon, telling suspense-filled tales about phobias.

A startling cinema hit, *Rak Haeng Siam* (Love of Siam; 2007), directed by Chookiat Sakveerakul, engaged both the art-house snobs and the love-struck teens. The story is a sombre drama about a family limping along after the loss of a daughter. Character-driven movies are on a roll thanks

All film and print depictions of Anna Leowens in the court of Siam, best known through the 1950s musical *The King & I,* are banned in Thailand.

to screenwriter-turned-director Kondej Jaturanrasamee's *Kod* (Handle Me with Care; 2008), about a three-armed boy and his journey to Bangkok to get surgery to remove his extra appendage.

LITERATURE

The written word has a long history in Thailand, dating back to the 11th or 12th century when the first Thai script was fashioned from an older Mon alphabet. The first known work of literature to be written in Thai is thought to have been composed by Sukhothai's Phaya Lithai in 1345. This was *Traiphum Phra Ruang*, a treatise that described the three realms of existence according to a Hindu-Buddhist cosmology. According to contemporary scholars, this work and its symbolism was, and continues to be, of considerable influence on Thailand's artistic and cultural universe.

Thailand's literacy rate is a whopping 92.6%, though reading anything other than the newspaper or comic books is regarded as an eccentric hobby.

Classical

The 30,000-line *Phra Aphaimani,* composed by poet Sunthorn Phu in the late 18th century, is Thailand's most famous classical literary work. Like many of its epic predecessors around the world, it tells the story of an exiled prince who must complete an odyssey of love and war before returning to his kingdom in victory.

Of all classical Thai literature, however, *Ramakian* is the most pervasive and influential in Thai culture. The Indian source, *Ramayana*, came to Thailand with the Khmers 900 years ago, first appearing as stone reliefs on Prasat Hin Phimai and other Angkor temples in the northeast. Eventually the Thais developed their own version of the epic, which was first written down during the reign of Rama I. This version contained 60,000 stanzas and was a quarter longer than the Sanskrit original.

Although the main themes remained the same, the Thais embroidered the *Ramayana* with more biographical detail on arch-villain Ravana (called Thotsakan, or '10-necked' in the *Ramakian*) and his wife Montho. Hanuman, the monkey god, differs substantially in the Thai version in his flirtatious nature (in the Hindu version he follows a strict vow of chastity). One of the classic *Ramakian* reliefs at Bangkok's Wat Pho depicts Hanuman clasping a maiden's bared breast as if it were an apple.

Also passed on from Indian tradition are the many *jataka* (*chah·dòk* in Thai): life stories of the Buddha. Of the 547 *jataka* in the Pali Tripitaka (Buddhist canon), each one chronicling a different past life, most appear in Thailand almost word for word as they were first written down in Sri Lanka.

A group of 50 extra stories, based on Thai folk tales of the time, were added by Pali scholars in Chiang Mai about 300 to 400 years ago. The most popular *jataka* in Thailand is one of the Pali originals known as the *Mahajati* or *Mahavessantara*, the story of the Buddha's penultimate life.

During the Ayuthaya period, Thailand developed a classical poetic tradition based on five types of verse – *chăn*, *gàhp*, *klong*, *glorn* and *râi*. Each of these forms uses a complex set of strict rules to regulate metre, rhyming patterns and number of syllables. Although all of these poetic systems use the Thai language, *chăn* and *gàhp* are derived from Sanskrit verse forms from India, while *klong*, *glorn* and *râi* are native forms. The Indian forms have all but disappeared from 21st-century use.

Contemporary

The first Thai-language novel appeared in direct imitation of Western models. Unfortunately much of Thai fiction, both past and present, has not been translated into English. For recommendations on travel literature in English see p19.

Considered the first Thai novel of substance, *The Circus of Life* (Thai 1929; English 1994), by Arkartdamkeung Rapheephat, follows a young, upper-class Thai as he travels the world. The fact that the author, himself a Thai prince, took his own life at the age of 26 has added to the mystique surrounding this work.

The late and revered Kukrit Pramoj, former ambassador and Thai prime minister, novelised Bangkok court life from the late 19th century through to the 1940s in *Four Reigns* (Thai 1935; English 1981), the longest novel ever published in Thai. *The Story of Jan Darra* (Thai 1966; English 1994), by journalist and short-story writer Utsana Phleungtham, traces the sexual obsessions of a Thai aristocrat. Praphatsorn Seiwikun's well-tuned, rapid-paced *Time in a Bottle* (Thai 1984; English 1996) turned the life dilemmas of a fictional middle-class Bangkok family into a bestseller. Writing under the pen name – a common conceit with Thai writers – Siburapha, Kulap Saipradit spun many romantic tales, including the novel *Behind the Painting* (1937), about a student who falls in love with a married aristocrat during the postwar era.

In the later half of the 20th century, Thai fiction took a turn towards the grassroots due in part to writers with humble origins having earned Bangkok University degrees. Instead of privileged aristocrats, their stories looked to their parents and neighbours for inspiration and followed the dramatic turns of ordinary, often working-class, Thais in remote corners of the country. Known as a social critic in narrative form, Chart Korbjitti is a two-time winner of the Southeast Asian Writers Award (SEA Write) for *The Judgement* (1981), about a young village man wrongly accused by his nosy neighbours, and for his novel *Time* (1993). The plight of Noi, a widowed fish-gutter, is bittersweetly told in *Of Time and Tide* (1985), by Atsiri Thammachoat, a journalist and newspaper editor often hailed as Thailand's 'bard of the sea'. Writing entirely in English in order to reach a worldwide audience, Pira Sudham captures the struggles of the impoverished northeast in his books *The Force of Karma, Monsoon Country, People of Esarn* and *Shadowed Country*. He was born into a poor farming family and was sent to Bangkok to get an education as a temple boy.

Even middle-class Thais put pen to paper during the later half of the 20th century. In *Married to the Demon King,* Sri Daoruang adapted the *Ramakian* into modern-day Bangkok casting a middle-class family into the epic's lead roles. A fine collection of modern short stories by women writers can be found in *A Lioness in Bloom,* translated by Susan Kepner, which includes helpful cultural and historical notes for context.

Few of the postmodern writers have been translated into English but their subject matter ranges from themes of isolation and modern dislocation to individual perspectives on current events. Prabda Yoon's short story 'Probability' won the 2002 SEA Write award. English-speaking audiences know him best through his screenplay for the *Last Life in the Universe* and other Pen-ek Ratanaruang–directed films.

The ongoing political crisis has provided Thai writers with an opportunity to tap into the collective psyche. Chartvut Bunyarak explores the political tensions preceding the 2006 ouster of then–prime minister Thaksin Shinawatra in the short story 'Thor Sor 2549' ('Taxi 2006'), about a customer ejected from a cab for disagreeing with the pro-Thaksin driver. Writer and poet, Siriworn Kaewkan won the government-sponsored Silpathorn Award for contemporary literature thanks to his wordily titled book, roughly translated as *Tales from a Scribe that a Storyteller Once Told Him.*

Want to read the Thai prize-winners? Silkworm Books publishes *The SEA Write Anthology of Thai Short Stories & Poems.*

English translations of Thai literature are hard to come by but DCO Thai (www.dcothai.com) offers a respectable reading list as well as instructional books on Thai language.

Food & Drink

There's an entire universe of amazing dishes once you get beyond 'pad thai' and green curry, and for many visitors, food is one of the main reasons for choosing Thailand as a destination. Even more remarkable, however, is the love for Thai food among the locals; Thais become just as excited as tourists when faced with a bowl of well-prepared noodles or when seated at a renowned hawker stall. This unabashed enthusiasm for eating, not to mention an abundance of fascinating ingredients and influences, has generated one of the most fun and diverse food scenes anywhere in the world.

STAPLES & SPECIALITIES
Rice

Rice is so central to Thai food culture that the most common term for 'eat' is *gin kôw* (literally, 'consume rice') and one of the most common greetings is *Gin kôw rĕu yang?* (Have you consumed rice yet?). To eat is to eat rice, and for most of the country, a meal is not acceptable without this staple.

There are many varieties of rice in Thailand and the country has been among the world leaders in rice exports since the 1960s. The highest grade is *kôw hŏrm má·lí* (jasmine rice), a fragrant long grain that is so coveted by neighbouring countries that there is allegedly a steady underground business in smuggling out fresh supplies. Residents of Thailand's north and northeast eat *kôw nĕe·o*, 'sticky rice', a glutinous short-grained rice that is cooked by steaming, not boiling. In Chinese-style eateries, *kôw đôm*, 'boiled rice', a watery porridge sometimes employing brown or purple rice, is a common carb.

Appon's Thai Food (www .khiewchanta.com) features a wealth of authentic and well-organised Thai recipes, written by a native Thai.

TASTY TRAVEL

Thailand's cuisine is intensely regional and virtually every town is associated with a specific dish not available (or at least not as tasty) outside the city limits. To help you look (and eat) like local, we've listed a few of the more delicious regional specialties:

- **Ayuthaya**: *gŏo·ay đĕe·o reu·a* ('boat noodles') Rice noodles served with a dark, intense spice-laden broth.
- **Chiang Mai**: *nám prík núm* and *kâab mŏo* (roast chilli 'dip' and deep-fried pork crackling) Available at virtually every market in the city, the two dishes go wonderfully together, ideally accompanied by par-boiled veggies and sticky rice.
- **Hat Yai**: *gài tôrt hàht yài* This city's namesake fried chicken is marinated in a dried-spice mixture, giving it a distinctive red hue.
- **Khon Kaen**: *gài yâhng* Marinated free-range chicken (*gài bâhn*) grilled over hot coals – a northeastern speciality said to be best in this town.
- **Lampang**: *kôw taan* Sticky rice cakes made with watermelon juice and drizzled with palm sugar are a popular treat in this northern town.
- **Nong Khai**: *năam neu·ang* This Vietnamese dish of balls of pork served with rice paper wrappers and a basket of herbs has found a home in northeastern Thailand.
- **Phetchaburi**: *kôw châa* This odd but delicious Mon dish of chilled fragrant rice served with sweet/savoury sides is said to be best in this central Thai town.
- **Trang**: *mŏo yâhng* Roast pig, skin and all, typically eaten as part of a dim sum brunch, is a speciality of this southern town.

(CON)FUSION CUISINE

A popular dish at restaurants across Thailand is *kôw pàt à·me·rí·gan,* 'American fried rice'. Taking the form of rice fried with ketchup, raisins and peas, sides of ham and deep-fried hot dogs, and topped with a fried egg, the dish is, well, every bit as revolting as it sounds. But at least there's an interesting history behind it: American fried rice apparently dates back to the Vietnam War era, when thousands of US troops were based in northeastern Thailand. A local cook apparently decided to take the ubiquitous 'American Breakfast' (also known as ABF, fried eggs with ham and/or hot dogs, and white bread, typically eaten with ketchup) and make it 'Thai' by frying the various elements with rice.

This culinary cross-pollination is only a recent example of the tendency of Thai cooks to pick and choose from the variety of cuisines at their disposal. Other (significantly more palatable) examples include *gaang màt·sà·màn,* 'Muslim curry', a now classic blend of Thai and Middle Eastern cooking styles, and the famous *pàt tai,* essentially a blend of Chinese cooking methods and ingredients (frying, rice noodles) with Thai flavours (fish sauce, chilli, tamarind).

Rice is customarily served alongside main dishes like curries, stir-fries or soups, which are lumped together as *gàp kôw* (with rice). When you order plain rice in a restaurant you use the term *kôw ʼblòw,* 'plain rice' or *kôw sŏoay,* 'beautiful rice', and the grains are usually served by the plate *(jahn)* or in a *tŏh,* a large bowl, lidded to keep the rice warm and moist.

Noodles

It shouldn't take too long in Thailand before you get your tongue around *gŏo·ay dĕe·o,* the intimidating and all-encompassing word for noodle soup. Despite being an import from China, noodles have been entirely integrated into the Thai repertoire of foods, and for most Thais, a day hardly passes without a bowl or two.

You'll find four basic kinds of noodle in Thailand. Hardly surprising, given the Thai fixation on rice, is the overwhelming popularity of *sên gŏo·ay dĕe·o,* noodles made from rice flour mixed with water to form a paste, which is then steamed to form wide, flat sheets. The sheets are folded and sliced into *sên yài* (flat 'wide line' noodles 2cm to 3cm wide), *sên lék* ('small line' noodles about 5mm wide) and *sên mèe* ('noodle line' noodles only 1mm to 2mm wide). At most restaurants or vendor stands specialising in *gŏo·ay dĕe·o,* when ordering you are expected to specify which noodles you want.

The simplest and most ubiquitous dish is *gŏo·ay dĕe·o nám,* a bowl of noodles served most commonly with pork stock along with meatballs and various vegetables, including a garnish of *pàk chee* (coriander leaf). This dish is eaten around the clock as a quick snack before work, after shopping, post-clubbing or in between the real meals.

The most famous *gŏo·ay dĕe·o* dish among foreigners is undoubtedly *gŏo·ay dĕe·o pàt tai,* usually called *pàt tai* for short. Taking the form of thin rice noodles stir-fried with dried or fresh shrimp, bean sprouts, tofu, egg and seasonings, the dish is traditionally served with lime halves and a few stalks of Chinese chives and a sliced banana flower.

Another kind of noodle, *kà·nŏm jeen,* is produced by pushing rice-flour paste through a sieve into boiling water, much the way Italian-style pasta is made. *Kà·nŏm jeen* is a popular morning market meal that is eaten doused with various spicy curries and topped with a self-selection of fresh and pickled vegetables and herbs.

The third kind of noodle, *bà·mèe,* is made from wheat flour and egg. It's yellowish in colour and is sold only in fresh bundles. After being briefly par-boiled, the noodles are mixed with broth and meat, typically barbecued pork or crab, and you have *bà·mèe nám*. Served in a bowl with a small amount of garlic oil and no broth, it's *bà·mèe hâang*. Restaurants or vendors selling *bà·mèe* typically also sell *gée·o*, a square of *bà·mèe* dough wrapped around ground meat.

Finally there's *wún·sên*, an almost clear noodle made from mung-bean starch and water. Sold only in dried bunches, *wún·sên* (literally 'jelly thread') is prepared by soaking in hot water for a few minutes. The most common use of the noodle is in *yam wún sên*, a hot and tangy salad made with lime juice, fresh sliced *prík kêe nŏo* (tiny chillies), shrimp, ground pork and various seasonings. Other uses include *ʼboo òp wún·sên*, bean-thread noodles baked in a lidded clay pot with crab (or sometimes shrimp) and seasonings, or *gaang jèut*, a bland, Chinese-influenced soup containing ground pork, soft tofu and a handful of the noodles.

> *Thai Food* by David Thompson is widely considered the most authoritative book on Thai cooking.

Curries & Soups

In Thai, *gaang* (it sounds somewhat similar to the English 'gang') is often translated as 'curry', but it actually describes any dish with a lot of liquid and can thus refer to soups (such as *gaang jèut*) as well as the classic chilli paste–based curries for which Thai cuisine is famous. The preparation of the latter begins with a *krê·uang gaang*, created by mashing, pounding and grinding an array of fresh ingredients with a stone mortar and pestle to form an aromatic, extremely pungent-tasting and rather thick paste. Typical ingredients in a *krê·uang gaang* include dried chilli, galangal, lemon grass, kaffir lime zest, shallots, garlic, shrimp paste and salt.

Thai curry cuisine revolves around three primary *gaang*. *Gaang pèt* (hot curry) is the most traditional and is often used as a base to create other curries. This curry paste should be quite spicy, with its deep red colour coming from a copious number of dried chillies. *Gaang pá·naang*, by contrast, is a relatively mild curry where the heat is brought down by the presence of ground peanuts. *Gaang kĕe·o wăhn*, literally 'sweet green curry', substitutes fresh green chillies for red, and somewhat unusually, dried spices such as cumin and coriander. A few extra seasonings such as *bai má·gròot* (kaffir lime leaves), *bai hŏh·rá·pah* (sweet basil leaves) and *nám ʼblah* (fish sauce) may be added to taste just before serving.

Most *gaang* are blended in a heated pan with coconut cream, to which the chef adds the rest of the ingredients (meat, poultry, seafood and/or vegetables), along with diluted coconut milk to further thin and flavour the *gaang*. Some recipes omit coconut milk entirely such as *gaang ʼbàh* (jungle curry), a fiery soup that combines a mixture of vegetables and meat.

Most Thais eat curries only for breakfast or lunch, and the average curry shop is open 7am to 2pm only. Among the Thais it is considered a bit odd

---

NOODLE MIXOLOGY

If you see a steel rack containing four lidded glass bowls or jars on your table, it's proof that the restaurant you're in serves *gŏo·ay đĕe·o* (rice noodle soup). Typically these containers offer four choices: *nám sôm prík* (sliced green chillies in vinegar), *nám ʼblah* (fish sauce), *prík ʼbòn* (dried red chilli, flaked or ground to a near powder) and *nám·đahn* (plain white sugar).

In typically Thai fashion, these condiments offer three ways to make the soup hotter – hot and sour, hot and salty, and just plain hot – and one to make it sweet.

The typical noodle-eater will add a teaspoonful of each one of these condiments to the noodle soup, except for the sugar, which in sweet-tooth Bangkok usually rates a full tablespoon. Until you're used to these strong seasonings, we recommend adding them a small bit at a time, tasting the soup along the way to make sure you don't go overboard.

Thai Food Tonight (www
.thaifoodtonight.com)
includes several cooking
videos accompanied by
detailed recipes.

to eat curries in the evening, and hence most restaurants (tourist restaurants excepted) don't offer them on the evening menu.

Another food celebrity that falls into the soupy category is *đôm yam,* the famous Thai spicy and sour soup. Fuelling the fire beneath *đôm yam*'s often velvety surface are fresh *prík kêe nŏo* (tiny chillies) or, alternatively, half a teaspoonful of *nám prík pŏw* (a roasted chilli paste). Lemon grass, kaffir lime leaf and lime juice give *đôm yam* its characteristic tang. Galangal is also added to *đôm yam,* and like its friends, is not meant to be eaten, but rather simply to add flavour – much like bay leaf in Western cooking. Keep also in mind that *đôm yam,* as with all Thai soups and curries, is meant to be taken with rice, not sipped alone.

Of the several variations on *đôm yam* that exist, probably the most popular with Westerners is the milder *đôm kàh gài* (literally 'boiled galangal chicken', but often translated as 'chicken coconut soup'). The chilli is considerably muted in this soup by the addition of coconut milk.

Stir-Fries & Deep-Fries

The simplest dishes in the Thai culinary repertoire are the various stir-fries *(pàt),* introduced to Thailand by the Chinese, who are world famous for being able to stir-fry a whole banquet in a single wok.

The list of *pàt* dishes seems endless. Many cling to their Chinese roots, such as the ubiquitous *pàt pàk bûng fai daang* (morning glory flash-fried with garlic and chilli), the preparation of which is often accompanied by an impressive burst of flame. Some are Thai-Chinese hybrids, such as *gài pàt prík kĭng,* in which chicken is stir-fried with ginger and garlic – ingredients shared by both traditions – but seasoned with chilli paste and fish sauce.

Perhaps the most Thai-like *pàt* dish is the famed lunch meal *pàt gá·prow,* a chicken or pork stir-fry with garlic, fresh sliced chilli, soy and fish sauce, and lots of holy basil. Another classic Thai stir-fry is *pàt pèt* (literally 'hot stir-fry'), in which the main ingredients, typically meat or fish, are quickly stir-fried with red curry paste and tossed with sweet basil leaves.

Thais are among the most
prolific consumers of
garlic in the world.

Tôrt (deep-frying in oil) is mainly reserved for snacks such as *glôo·ay tôrt* (deep-fried bananas) or *ʔo·ʔée·a* (egg rolls). An exception is *ʔlah tôrt* (deep-fried fish), which is a common way to prepare fish. And a very few dishes require ingredients to be dipped in batter and then deep-fried, such as *gài tôrt* (fried chicken) and *gûng chúp ʔâang tôrt* (batter-fried shrimp).

Hot & Tangy Salads

Standing right alongside curries in terms of Thai-ness is the ubiquitous *yam,* a hot and tangy 'salad' typically based around seafood, roast vegetables or meats.

Lime juice provides the tang, while the abundant use of fresh chilli generates the heat. Other ingredients vary considerably, but plenty of leafy vegetables and herbs are usually present, including lettuce (often lining the dish)

SCHOOLS IN SESSION

Do you spend more time hanging around the markets than the temples? Are you packing in four or more meals a day? Then you are a good candidate for a cooking course, which can range from formal, equipment-oriented instructions to simple chop-and-talk introductions. Bangkok, Chiang Mai and the popular tourist islands offer different types of cooking classes, most of which include a market tour. See the respective destination chapters for more information.

THE CULT OF SÔM·ĐAM

Green papaya salad, known in Thai as *sôm·đam*, probably has its origins in Laos, but is today one of the most popular dishes in Thailand. It is made by taking strips of green unripe papaya and bruising them in a clay or wood mortar along with garlic, palm sugar, green beans, tomatoes, lime juice, fish sauce and a typically shock-inducing amount of fresh chillies. *Sôm·đam low*, the 'original' version of the dish, employs heartier chunks of papaya, sliced eggplants, salted field crabs, and a thick unpasteurised fish sauce known as *Ƅlah ráh*. Far more common in Bangkok is *đam tai*, which includes dried shrimp and peanuts, and is seasoned with bottled fish sauce. Almost always made by women, *sôm·đam* is also primarily also enjoyed by women, often as a snack rather than an entire meal – the intense spiciness providing a satisfying mental 'full'.

---

and *kêun chài* (Chinese celery). Most *yam* are served at room temperature or just slightly warmed by any cooked ingredients. The dish functions equally well as part of a meal, or on its own as *gàp glâam*, snack food to accompany a night of boozing.

Perhaps the zenith of this style of cooking is northeastern Thailand's *sôm·đam* (see boxed text, above).

Fruits

Being a tropical country, Thailand excels in the fruit department with exceptionally delicious *sàp·Ƅà·rót* (pineapple), *má·lá·gor* (papaya) and *đaang moh* (watermelon) sold from ubiquitous vendor carts, often accompanied by a dipping mix of salt, sugar and ground chilli. You'll find more exotic fruits sold in produce markets. The king of fruits is the spiky-shelled *tú·ree·an* (durian), an acridly pungent delicacy in Southeast Asia. The fruit smells so strong that it is banned from airlines, air-conditioned buses and some hotels. Other seasonal fruits that you deserve to meet include creamy *nóy nàh* (custard apple), the Velcro tennis-ball shaped *ngó* (rambutan), the purplish skinned *mang·kút* (mangosteen), and the grape-shaped *lá·mút* (sapodilla) and *lam yai* (longan).

Má·môo·ang (mangoes) come in a dozen varieties that are eaten at different stages of ripeness. Some are served green and crisp and taste like apples, while others are ripe and luscious and served in the intoxicating dessert *kôw nĕe·o má·môo·ang* (mangoes and sticky rice).

Sweets

English-language Thai menus often have a section called 'Desserts', but the concept takes two slightly different forms in Thailand. *Kŏrng wăhn*, which translates as 'sweet things', are small, rich sweets that often boast a slightly salty flavour. Prime ingredients for *kŏrng wăhn* include grated coconut, coconut milk, rice flour (from white rice or sticky rice), cooked sticky rice (whole grains), tapioca, mung-bean starch, boiled taro and various fruits. Coconut milk also features prominently in several soupier *kŏrng wăhn*, to which crushed ice is often added to cool the mixture. Egg yolks are a popular ingredient for many *kŏrng wăhn* – including the ubiquitous *fŏy torng* (literally 'golden threads') – probably influenced by Portuguese desserts and pastries introduced during the early Ayuthaya era (see boxed text, p88).

Thai sweets similar to the European concept of pastries are called *kà·nŏm*. Here again the kitchen-astute Portuguese were influential. Probably the most popular type of *kà·nŏm* in Thailand are the bite-sized items wrapped in banana leaves, especially *kôw đôm gà·tí* and *kôw đôm mát*. Both consist of sticky rice grains steamed with *gà·tí* (coconut milk) inside a banana-leaf wrapper to form a solid, almost taffylike, mass.

MUITO OBRIGADO

Try to imagine a Thai curry without the chillies, *pàt tai* without the peanuts, or papaya salad without the papaya. Many of the ingredients used on a daily basis by Thais are in fact relatively recent introductions courtesy of European traders and missionaries. During the early 16th century, while Spanish and Portuguese explorers were first reaching the shores of Southeast Asia, there was also subsequent expansion and discovery in the Americas. The Portuguese in particular were quick to seize the exciting new products coming from the New World and market them in the East, thus introducing modern-day Asian staples such as tomatoes, potatoes, corn, lettuce, cabbage, chillies, papayas, guavas, pineapples, pumpkins, sweet potatoes, peanuts and tobacco.

Chillies in particular seem to have struck a chord with Thais, and are thought to have first arrived in Ayuthaya via the Portuguese around 1550. Before their arrival, the natives got their heat from bitter-hot herbs and roots such as ginger and pepper.

And not only did the Portuguese introduce some crucial ingredients to the Thai kitchen, but also some enduring cooking techniques, particularly in the area of sweets. The bright-yellow duck egg and syrup-based treats you see at many Thai markets are direct descendants of Portuguese desserts known as *fios de ovos* ('egg threads') and *ovos moles*. And in the area surrounding Bangkok's Church of Santa Cruz (p133), a former Portuguese enclave, you can still find *kà·nŏm fa·ràng*, a bunlike snack baked over coals.

Although foreigners don't seem to immediately take to most Thai sweets, one dish few visitors have trouble with is *ai·đim gà·tí*, Thai-style coconut ice cream. At more traditional shops, the ice cream is garnished with toppings such as kidney beans or sticky rice, and is a brilliant snack on a sweltering Thai afternoon.

DRINKS

Coffee, Tea & Fruit Drinks

Written and photographed by the author of this chapter, www .austinbushphotography .com/category/foodblog details food and dining in Thailand.

Thais are big coffee drinkers, and good-quality arabica and robusta are cultivated in the hilly areas of northern and southern Thailand. The traditional filtering system is nothing more than a narrow cloth bag attached to a steel handle. The bag is filled with ground coffee, and hot water poured through producing *gah·faa tŭng* (bag coffee) or *gah·faa boh·rahn* (traditional coffee). The usual *gah·faa tŭng* is served in a glass, mixed with sugar and sweetened with condensed milk – if you don't want either, be sure to specify *gah·faa dam* (black coffee) followed with *mâi sài nám·đahn* (without sugar).

Black tea, both local and imported, is available at the same places that serve real coffee. *Chah tai* derives its characteristic orange-red colour from ground tamarind seed added after curing. *Chah rórn* (hot tea) and *chah yen* (iced tea) will almost always be sweetened with condensed milk and sugar.

Fruit drinks appear all over Thailand and are an excellent way to rehydrate after water becomes unpalatable. Most *nám pŏn·lá·mái* (fruit juices) are served with a touch of sugar and salt and a whole lot of ice. Many foreigners object to the salt, but it serves a metabolic role in helping the body to cope with tropical temperatures.

Beer & Spirits

There are several brands of beer in Thailand but they are largely indistinguishable in terms of taste and quality. The Singha label is considered the quintessential 'Thai' beer and like all others, is an alcohol-strong pilsner. Pronounced sing (not 'sing-ha'), it claims about half the domestic market, and has an alcohol content of 6%. Beer Chang matches the hoppy taste of Singha but pumps the alcohol content up to 7%. There are other varieties of beer, like Leo, that offer more alcohol for the baht. Dutch-licensed but Thailand-brewed Heineken and Singapore's Tiger brand are also popular selections.

When in the company of Thais, beer is rarely consumed directly from the bottle but instead enjoys yet another communal ritual. Each drinker gets a glass, filled with ice, into which the brew is poured. A toast goes round and the younger member of the group is usually in charge of keeping everyone's glass filled with ice and beer. The ice helps keep the beverage cool in a hot climate and combats the dehydrating effects of a hangover.

Rice whisky is a favourite of the working class, struggling students and family gatherings as it's more affordable than beer. Most rice whiskies are mixed with distilled sugarcane spirits and thus have a sharp, sweet taste not unlike rum. The most famous brands are Mekong and Sang Som, which are typically sold in a large bottle *(glom)* or a flask-sized bottle *(bàan)*, and are mixed with ice, soda water and a splash of Coke.

Once spending money becomes a priority, Thais prefer to upgrade to the whiskies produced from barley. Johnnie Walker is of course an immediate status symbol, but for more modest means there are a few cheaper Thai versions (see boxed text, p90).

WHERE TO EAT & DRINK

Prepared food is available just about everywhere in Thailand, and it shouldn't come as a surprise that the locals do much of their eating outside the home. In this regard, as a visitor, you'll fit right in.

Open-air markets and food stalls are among the most popular places where Thais eat. The changing landscape of the vendor carts provides a sun-dial service for judging the time of day. In the mornings stalls selling coffee and Chinese-style doughnuts spring up along busy commuter corridors. At lunchtime, midday eaters might grab a plastic chair at yet another stall for a simple stir-fry, or pick up a foam box of noodles to scarf down at the office. In most small towns, night markets are the provincial equivalent of a restaurant row. These hawker centres set up in the middle of town with a cluster of vendors, metal tables and chairs, and some shopping as an after-dinner mint.

There are, of course, restaurants *(ráhn ah·hǎhn)* in Thailand that range from simple food stops to formal affairs. Lunchtime is the right time to point and eat at the *ráhn kôw gaang* (rice-and-curry shop), which sells a selection of pre-made dishes. The more generic *ráhn ah·hǎhn đahm sàng* (food-to-order shop) can often be recognised by one or more tall refrigerated cabinets with clear glass windows at the front of the shop. These will be filled with many of the raw ingredients – Chinese kale, tomatoes, chopped

---

CAN I DRINK THE ICE?

Among the most common concerns we hear from first-time visitors to Thailand is the safety of the country's ice. At the risk of sounding fatalistic, if it's your first time in Thailand, the ice probably is the least of your concerns – you're almost certainly going to get sick at some point. Considering that you're exposing yourself to an entirely different cuisine and a new and unfamiliar family of bacteria, it's virtually inevitable that your body will have a hard time adjusting.

On the good side, in most cases this will mean little more than an upset tummy that might set you back a day or two. You can avoid more serious setbacks, at least initially, by trying to frequent popular restaurants/vendors where dishes are prepared to order, and only drinking bottled water.

And the ice? We've been lacing our drinks with it for years and have yet to trace it back to any specific discomfort.

THE WHISKY SET

Thai beer is generally more miss than hit, so the next time you're out on the town, why not drink like the Thais do and order a bottle of whisky.

Your first step is to choose a brand. For a particularly decadent night out, the industry standard is a bottle of *bláak* (Johnny Walker Black Label). Those on a budget can go for the cheaper imported labels such as Red Label or Benmore, and a rock-bottom cheap but fun night can be had on domestic spirits such as 100 Pipers or Sang Som. And it's not unusual to bring your own bottle to many Thai bars, although some might charge a modest corkage fee.

As any Thai can tell you, your next immediate concern is mixers. If you're drinking whisky, these will take the form of several bottles of soda water and a bottle or two of Coke, along with a pail of ice. Most waitresses will bring these to you as a matter of course.

Mixing is the easiest step and requires little or no action on your part; your skilled waitress will fill your glasses with ice followed by a shot of whisky, a splash of soda, a top-off of Coke, and finally, a swirl with the ice tongs to bring it all together.

If you can't finish your bottle, shame on you, but don't fret, as it's perfectly normal to keep it at the bar. Simply tell your trusted waitress, and she will write your name and the date on the bottle and keep it for your next visit.

Thai Hawker Food by Kenny Yee and Catherine Gordon is an illustrated guide to recognising and ordering street food in Thailand.

pork, fresh or dried fish, noodles, eggplant, spring onions – for a standard repertoire of Thai and Chinese dishes. As the name implies, the cooks attempt to prepare any dish you can name, a slightly more difficult operation if you can't speak Thai.

For many years, Thais celebrated special occasions with a meal at a Chinese banquet restaurant, a cuisine viewed as more refined than their own, or Chinese-style seafood restaurant. In recent years, Bangkok, Chiang Mai and other internationally influenced cities tend to have more of a Western-style restaurant scene with hip decor and nouveau or imported cuisine.

VEGETARIANS & VEGANS

Vegetarianism isn't a widespread trend in Thailand, but many of the tourist-oriented restaurants cater to vegetarians. That doesn't mean that all Thais are monogamous carnivores; there are, however, home-grown practices of vegetarianism and veganism rooted in a strict interpretation of Buddhism made popular by Bangkok's ex-Governor Chamlong Srimuang. Now there are several nonprofit *rähn ah·hähn mang·sà·wí·rát* (vegetarian restaurants) in Bangkok and several provincial capitals where the food is served buffet-style and is very inexpensive. Dishes are almost always 100% vegan (ie no meat, poultry, fish or fish sauce, dairy or egg products).

During the Vegetarian Festival, celebrated by Chinese Buddhists in October, many restaurants and street stalls in Bangkok, Phuket and in the Chinese business districts of most Thai towns go meatless for one month. Other easy, though less common, venues for vegetarian meals include Indian restaurants, which usually feature a vegetarian section on the menu.

The phrase 'I'm vegetarian' in Thai is *pŏm gin jair* (for men) or *dì·chăn gin jair* (for women). Loosely translated this means 'I eat only vegetarian food', which includes no eggs and no dairy products – in other words, total vegan.

EATING WITH KIDS

Dining with children, particularly with infants, in Thailand is a liberating experience as the Thais are so fond of kids. Take it for granted that your babies will be fawned over, played with, and more than not, carried around, by restaurant wait staff. Regard this as a much-deserved break, not to mention a bit of free cultural exposure.

Because much of Thai food is so spicy, there is also an entire art devoted to ordering 'safe' dishes for children, and the vast majority of Thai kitchens are more than willing to oblige. Many a child in Thailand has grown up on a diet of little more than *gaang jèut,* a bland, Chinese-influenced soup containing ground pork, soft tofu and a handful of the noodles, or variations on *kôw pàt,* fried rice. Other mild options include *kôw man gài,* Hainanese chicken rice, and *jóhk,* rice porridge.

HABITS & CUSTOMS

Like most of Thai culture, eating conventions appear relaxed and informal but are orchestrated by many implied rules. Dining is considered an important social occasion not only to chat with friends but to enjoy many different dishes, which is made easier if there are more mouths interested in sampling. You'll rarely see a Thai dining alone, and solo diners are more common at Thailand's original version of 'fast-food' restaurants, places that serve one-plate dishes.

Whether at home or in a restaurant, Thai meals are always served 'family-style', that is from common serving platters, and the plates appear in whatever order the kitchen can prepare them. Another important factor in a Thai meal is achieving a balance of flavours and textures. Traditionally, the party orders a curry, a steamed or fried fish, a stir-fried vegetable dish and a soup, taking great care to balance cool and hot, sour and sweet, salty and plain.

When eating Thai family-style, all the dishes are arranged on the table and everyone digs in rather than passing the plates to each diner. Reaching over someone to a plate is customary. If you can't reach the platter at all, it's best to hand your plate to someone near the serving platter, who can then place some food on your plate. Most Thais will do this automatically if they notice you're out of platter range. When serving yourself from a common platter, put no more than one spoonful onto your plate at a time. Heaping your plate with all 'your' portions at once will look greedy to Thais unfamiliar with Western conventions.

Originally Thai food was eaten with the fingers, and it still is in certain regions of the kingdom. In the early 1900s, Thais began setting their tables with fork and spoon to affect a 'royal' setting, and it wasn't long before fork-and-spoon dining became the norm in Bangkok and later spread throughout

For the best of Lonely Planet's culinary wisdom, seek out *World Food Thailand* by Joe Cummings.

BEYOND THE STREET STALL

Read any food magazine article about eating in Thailand, and you will inevitably find gushing references to the glories of the country's street food. While much of the food sold from mobile carts and streetside stalls is indeed very tasty, it certainly isn't the case that *only* street food is good. In fact, in our research, we've found that the best places to eat are anything but mobile, but rather are the long-standing, family-owned restaurants typically found in aged Sino-Portuguese shophouses. The cooks at such places have likely been serving the same dish, or limited repertoire of dishes, for several decades, and really know what they're doing. The food may cost slightly more than on the street, but the setting is usually more comfortable and hygienic, not to mention the fact that you're eating a piece of history. While such restaurants rarely have English-language menus, you can usually point to a picture or dish. If that fails, turn to p92 and practise your Thai.

So do indulge in a street cart or two, they're a fun part of the Thailand experience, but be sure to try a few old-school restaurants as well.

THE RIGHT TOOL FOR THE JOB

If you're not offered chopsticks, don't ask for them. Thai food is eaten with fork and spoon, not chopsticks. When *fa·ràng* (Westerners) ask for chopsticks to eat Thai food, it only puzzles the restaurant proprietors.

Chopsticks are reserved for eating Chinese-style food from bowls, or for eating in all-Chinese restaurants. In either case you will be supplied with chopsticks without having to ask. Unlike their counterparts in many Western countries, restaurateurs in Thailand won't assume you don't know how to use them.

---

the kingdom. To use these tools the Thai way, use a serving spoon, or alternatively your own, to take a single mouthful of food from a central dish, and ladle it over a portion of your rice. The fork is then used to push the now food-soaked portion of rice back onto the spoon before entering the mouth.

EAT YOUR WORDS

While some restaurants in Thailand may have English-language menus, most will not. So you'll need to have some stock phrases on hand to tell *pàt tai* from *kôw pàt*. For pronunciation guidelines, see p781.

Useful Phrases

EATING OUT

Not too spicy please.	*kŏr mâi pèt mâhk*
I'd like…	*kŏr…*
glass	*gâaou*
cup	*tôo·ay*
fork	*sôrm*
spoon	*chórn*
plate	*jahn ฿lòw*
napkin	*grà·dàht chét ฿àhk*

Thank you, that was delicious.	*kòrp kun mâhk, aròy mâhk*
Bring the bill, please.	*kŏr bin*

VEGETARIAN & SPECIAL MEALS

I'm allergic to…	*pŏm/dì·chăn páa …*
I don't eat …	*pŏm/dì·chăn gin … mâi dâi*
meat	*néu·a sàt*
chicken	*gài*
fish	*฿lah*
seafood	*ah·hăhn tá·lair*
pork	*mŏo*

Does this dish have meat?	*ah·hăhn jahn née sài néu·a sàt măi*
Please don't use fish sauce.	*gà·rú·nah mâi sài nám ฿lah*
Please don't use MSG.	*gà·rú·nah mâi sài pŏng choo rót*
Don't add salt.	*mâi sài gleu·a*

Food Glossary

STAPLES

ah·hăhn tá·lair	อาหารทะเล	seafood
jóhk	โจ๊ก	thick rice soup or congee
gài	ไก่	chicken
kài	ไข่	egg
kà·nŏm	ขนม	sweet pastries or desserts
kôw jôw	ข้าวเจ้า	white rice
kôw glôrng	ข้าวกล้อง	brown rice

kôw pàt	ข้าวผัด	fried rice
kôw blòw	ข้าวเปล่า	plain rice
kôw	ข้าว	rice
gŏo·ay đĕe·o	ก๋วยเตี๋ยว	rice noodles
gûng	กุ้ง	variety of shrimp, prawn and lobster
mŏo	หมู	pork
néu·a	เนื้อ	beef, meat
bèt	เป็ด	duck
blah	ปลา	fish
blah mèuk	ปลาหมึก	squid; cuttlefish (generic)
boo	ปู	crab

VEGETABLES

pàk	ผัก	vegetables
hèt	เห็ด	mushrooms
má·kĕua	มะเขือ	eggplant/aubergine
má·kĕua·têt	มะเขือเทศ	tomatoes
man fa·ràng	มันฝรั่ง	potatoes
đôw hôo	เต้าหู้	tofu
tòo·a fàk yow	ถั่วฝักยาว	long bean, yard bean, green bean
tòo·a lĕu·ang	ถั่วเหลือ	soybean
tòo·a ngôrk	ถั่วงอก	mung bean sprouts
ká·náh	คะน้า	Chinese kale
pàk bûng	ผักบุ้ง	morning glory (a crispy green vegetable)

CONDIMENTS & SEASONINGS

kĭng	ขิง	ginger
gleu·a	เกลือ	salt
nám jìm	น้ำจิ้ม	dipping sauces
nám blah	น้ำปลา	fish sauce
nám see·éw	น้ำซีอิ๊ว	soy sauce
nám sôm săi chuu	น้ำส้มสายชู	vinegar
nám đahn	น้ำตาล	sugar
pàk chee	ผักชี	coriander leaf
pŏng choo rót	ผงชูรส	monosodium glutamate (MSG)
prík	พริก	chilli
sà·rá·nàa	สะระแหน่	mint

FRUIT

pŏn·lá·mái	ผลไม้	fruit
fa·ràng	ฝรั่ง	guava
glôo·ay	กล้วย	banana
má·kăhm	มะขาม	tamarind
má·lá·gor	มะละกอ	papaya
má·môo·ang	มะม่วง	mango
má·now	มะนาว	lime
mang·kút	มังคุด	mangosteen
má·prów	มะพร้าว	coconut
ngó	เงาะ	rambutan
đaang moh	แตงโม	watermelon

DRINKS

bee·a	เบียร์	beer
chah	ชา	tea
gah·faa	กาแฟ	coffee
krêu·ang dèum	เครื่องดื่ม	beverages

nám	น้ำ	water or juice
nám ôy	น้ำอ้อย	sugar-cane juice
nám dèum	น้ำดื่ม	drinking water
nám kăang	น้ำแข็	ice
nám sôm	น้ำส้ม	orange juice
nám đôw hôo	น้ำเต้าหู้	soy milk
nom jèut	นมเจ็ด	milk

METHODS OF PREPARATION

dìp	ดิบ	raw
nêung	นี่	steamed
pŏw	เผา	grilled (chillies, vegetables, fish and shrimp only)
pàt	ผัด	stir-fried
đôm	ต้ม	boiled
tôrt	ทอด	deep fried
yâhng	ย่ำ	grilled or roasted

Environment

THE LAND

Thailand's odd shape is often likened to the head of an elephant with the shaft of the trunk being represented by the Malay peninsula. More practically, the Thai boundary encompasses 514,000 sq km, making it about the size of France. The capital of Thailand, Bangkok, sits at about N14° latitude – level with Madras, Manila, Guatemala and Khartoum. Because its north–south length of 1650km spans 16 latitudinal degrees, Thailand ends up having the most diverse climate of any country in Southeast Asia.

Northern Thailand is dominated by the Dawna-Tenasserim mountain range, a southeast-trending extension of the Himalayan mountains. Dropping from there into the central region, the topography mellows into a flat rice basket fed by rivers that are as revered as the national monarchy. Thailand's most exalted river is the Chao Phraya, which is formed by the northern tributaries of the Ping, Wang, Yom and Nan – a lineage as notable as any aristocrat's. The country's early kingdoms emerged around the Chao Phraya basin, still the seat of the monarchy today. The river delta spends most of the year in cultivation – changing with the seasons from fields of emerald green rice shoots to the golden harvests. Elegant white egrets dotting the fields add a nice visual accent, but are practically the last wild animals in this highly modified part of the country.

Tracing the contours of Thailand's northern and northeastern border is another celebrated river: the Mekong River. As the artery of Southeast Asia, the Mekong both physically separates and culturally fuses Thailand with its neighbours. It is a workhorse river that has been dammed for hydroelectric power and swells and contracts based on the seasonal rains. In the dry season, riverside farmers plant vegetables in the muddy floodplain, harvesting the fruits of their labour before the river reclaims its territory.

Thailand's tallest mountain is Doi Inthanon (2565m).

The landscape of Thailand's northeastern border is occupied by the arid Khorat Plateau rising some 300m above the central plain. This is a hardscrabble land where the rains are meagre, the soil is anaemic and the red dust stains as stubbornly as the betel nut chewed by the ageing grandmothers.

The kingdom's eastern rivers dump their waters and sediment into the Gulf of Thailand, a shallow basin off the neighbouring South China Sea. The warm, gentle waters of the gulf are an ideal cultivation ground for brilliantly coloured coral reefs that help temper the rollicking tendencies of the open ocean.

From the north, Thailand stretches its long slender 'trunk' of land south along the Malay peninsula, where it is bordered on the east by the Gulf of Thailand and on the west by the Andaman Sea. The Andaman Coast is an especially splendid tropical setting of stunning blue waters and dramatic limestone islands. Onshore, the Malay peninsula is dominated by some final remaining stands of rainforest and ever-expanding rubber and palm-oil plantations.

WILDLIFE

Thailand is 1650km long from north to south with such varied climate and topography that it should come as no surprise this is home to a remarkable diversity of flora and fauna. What is more surprising is that Thailand's environment is still in good shape given the country's long history of resource extraction and an ever-growing push to develop its resources. In part this is the result of courageous environmental heroes such as Seub

THAILAND'S BEST NATIONAL PARKS: SWEATY HIKES & GREAT VIEWS

■ **Doi Inthanon** (p334) Tall granite mountains, views of misty valleys and lots of birdlife; it is best visited November to May.

■ **Doi Phu Kha** (p388) A steep mountain summit overlooking misty valleys, karst caves and silvery waterfalls; it is best visited November to May.

■ **Um Phang Wildlife Sanctuary** (p418) Thailand's biggest, most beautiful waterfall.

■ **Thung Salaeng Luang National Park, Phetchabun/Phitsanulok** (p396) Massive grasslands are home to carpets of flowers (after the rainy season) and varied wild animals and birdlife.

■ **Khao Yai** (p467) A dense monsoon forest famed for its waterfalls, and bird and monkey populations; it is best visited November to April.

■ **Phu Kradung** (p526) A popular mountain hike rewarded with sunset views and lots of camping camaraderie; it is best visited January to May.

■ **Kaeng Krachan** (p552) An energy-sapping 6km hike delivers you to the summit of Phanoen Tung for breathtaking views of misty morning valleys.

■ **Khao Sok** (p639) A pristine southern rainforest, well-suited for jungle safaris and kayak trips; monkeys and hornbills are commonly spotted and if timed just right so is the rafflesia; it is best visited February to May.

Nakasathien (p101) as well as conscientious efforts by governmental and environmental organisations.

Animals

In the northern half of Thailand most indigenous species are classified zoologically as Indo-Chinese, referring to fauna originating from mainland Southeast Asia, while that of the south is generally Sundaic, typical of peninsular Malaysia, Sumatra, Borneo and Java. An extensive overlap between the two zoogeographical and vegetative zones, starting around Prachuap Khiri Khan on the southern peninsula and extending north to Uthai Thani, provides habitat for plants and animals from both zones.

Thailand is particularly rich in birdlife, with over a thousand recorded resident and migrating species – approximately 10% of the world's bird species. The cool mountains of northern Thailand are populated by montane species and migrants with clear Himalayan affinities such as flycatchers and thrushes. The arid forests of Khao Yai National Park in northeastern Thailand are a favourite for hornbills. Marshland birds prefer the wetlands of the central region, while Sundaic species like Gurney's Pitta flock to the wetter climate of southern Thailand.

Besides abundant birdlife, visitors to the country's national parks are most likely to spot monkeys. Thailand is home to five species of macaque, four species of the smaller leaf-monkey and three species of gibbons. Although they face the same habitat loss as other native species, monkeys sometimes survive by living in varying states of domestication with humans. The long-armed gibbons were once raised alongside children in rural villages and macaques can be found living in small wooded patches or unused temples in the midst of human population centres. Monkeys are also used to harvest coconuts in family plots. But Thais' relationship with the monkey see-saws between generosity and cruelty: food is often given to resident monkey troops as an act of Buddhist merit-making, while it isn't unusual to see a monkey kept in a small cage as an ignored pet.

Other species found in the kingdom's parks and sanctuaries include gaur (Indian bison), banteng (wild cattle), serow (an Asiatic goat-antelope), sambar deer, muntjac (barking deer), mouse deer and tapir – to name a few.

Thailand's rainforests are so luxuriant that 200 species of trees have been found growing on a single 100 sq metre plot.

Thai Birding (www .thaibirding.com) is a great online resource for bird-spottings and trip reports.

Thailand has six venomous snakes: common cobra, king cobra, banded krait, green viper, Malayan viper and Russell's pit viper. Although the relatively rare king cobra can reach up to 6m in length, the nation's largest snake is the reticulated python, which can reach a whopping 10m. The country's many lizard species include two commonly seen in homes – *đúk·gaa*, a reclusive and somewhat homely gecko that is usual heard in the early evening coughing its name; and *jîng·jòk*, a spirited house lizard that is usually spotted on ceilings and walls chasing after bugs. The black jungle monitor, which looks like a miniature dinosaur, lives in some of the southern forests.

The oceans on either side of the Malay peninsula are home to hundreds of species of coral, and the reefs created by these tiny creatures provide the perfect living conditions for hundreds of species of fish, crustaceans and tiny invertebrates. You can find the world's smallest fish (the 10mm-long goby) and the largest (the 18m-long whale shark), plus reef denizens such as clownfish, parrotfish, wrasse, angelfish, triggerfish and lionfish. Deeper waters are home to larger species such as grouper, barracuda, sharks, manta rays, marlin and tuna. You might also encounter turtles, whales and dolphins.

Thailand's most famous animals are also its most endangered. The Asian elephant, a smaller cousin to the African elephant, once roamed the forests of Indochina in great herds. The elephant's massive size and intelligence made it a reliable beast of burden, often corralled during important cultural festivals for the purposes of domestication. The elephant is still a national symbol and has served many roles in Thailand's history: war machine, timber logger, royal transport and godlike character in the Hindu-inherited myths. But both the wild and domesticated elephants face extinction and displacement as Thailand's human population increases and modernises. The population of wild elephants in Thailand is estimated at about 2000, but agricultural villages often border the few remaining stands of elephant habitat resulting in battles between farmers and wild elephants who are prone to raiding crops instead of foraging in the forest. Despite the animals' protected status, retaliation or poaching is often seen by struggling farmers as the only solution to this threat to their livelihood.

A Field Guide to the Birds of Thailand (2002), by Craig Robson, is the must-have guide for birders.

The domesticated elephant has become increasingly obsolete in modern society. No longer employable in the timber industry or honoured in ceremonial processions, these elephants and their mahout handlers often wander the streets of the kingdom's major cities reduced to beggars and sideshows. See (p52) for information about elephant sanctuary programs.

Reclusive wild tigers stalk the hinterlands between Thailand and Myanmar but in ever-decreasing numbers. It is difficult to obtain an accurate count

---

THAILAND'S BEST NATIONAL PARKS: BEACHES & CORAL GARDENS

- **Similan Islands** (p645) A well-protected preserve famed for snorkelling and diving; it is best visited November to May.
- **Ko Tarutao** (p720) A series of islands that range from deserted to developed for back-to-naturalists, coral exploration and hiking; best visited November to May.
- **Khao Lak/Lamru** (p641) A coastal park with blonde beaches, crystal-clear water for snorkelling and rainforest hikes; it is best visited January to May.
- **Ko Lanta** (p698) A low-key island combing rainforest hiking with beach-bum activities.
- **Khao Sam Roi Yot** (p562) A coastal mangrove forest filled with birdlife.

of surviving tigers, but experts estimate that around 200 to 300 wild tigers remain in Thailand. Although tiger hunting and trapping is illegal, poachers continue to kill the cats for the lucrative overseas wildlife trade.

Of Thailand's 280 species of mammals, the smallest is called the Kitti's hog-nosed bat, and the largest is the Asian elephant.

The rare dugong (also called manatee or sea cow), once thought extinct in Thailand, is now known to survive in a few small pockets, mostly around Trang in southern Thailand, but is increasingly threatened by habitat loss and the lethal propellers of tourist boats.

Roughly 250 animal and plant species in Thailand are on the International Union for Conservation of Nature (IUCN) list of endangered or vulnerable species with fish, bird and plant species being the most affected. However, the Thai government is slowly recognising the importance of conservation, perhaps due to the efforts and leadership of Queen Sirikit. Many of the kingdom's zoos now have an active breeding and conservation program, and wildlife organisations such as the Phuket Gibbon Rehabilitation Centre are working to educate the public about native wildlife or have initiated wildlife rescue and rehabilitation projects.

Plants

The days of Thailand as a vast jungled landscape are long gone, with the cultivating hand of the farmer and more recently the industrialist, moulding the canopy into field and city. In the remaining protected areas, there are two types of primary forests: monsoon (with a distinct dry season of three months or more) and rainforest (where rain falls more than nine months per year). The most heavily forested provinces are Chiang Mai and Kanchanaburi.

Monsoon forests in the northern parts of the country are comprised of deciduous trees, which are green and lush during the rainy season but dusty and leafless during the dry season. Teak is one of the most highly valued monsoon forest trees but it now exists only in limited quantities.

The Elephant Keeper (1987; directed by Prince Chatrichalerm Yukol) tells the story of an honest forestry chief who tries to protect the wilderness from illegal logging interests; he is assisted by a courageous mahout and his faithful elephant.

In southern Thailand, where rainfall is plentiful and distributed evenly through the year, forests are classified as rainforests with a few areas of monsoon forest. One remarkable plant found in some southern forests is *Rafflesia kerrii*, a squat plant with a huge flower that reaches 80cm across; you can see it at Khao Sok National Park (p639) near Surat Thani.

Most coastal areas are fringed with wetland mangroves that proved to be a helpful buffer during the unexpected 2004 Asian tsunami. Thailand is home to nearly 75 species of these small salt-tolerant trees that are highly adapted to living at the edge of salt water. Unfortunately, mangrove forests are easily dismissed as wastelands and have been heavily depleted by urban development and commercial farming, despite the forests' role as a protective incubator for many coastal fish and animal species.

Flourishing in every backyard large enough to claim sunshine is an incredible array of fruit trees (mango, banana, papaya, jackfruit and occasionally durian). Common in the forests are 60 species of bamboo (more than any other country outside China), tropical hardwoods and over 27,000 flowering species, including Thailand's national floral symbol, the orchid, of which there are 1300 varieties. Commercial plantings in the south include coconut, palm oil, cashew and rubber. In the denuded northeast eucalyptus is planted to prevent erosion and as a cheap and quick timber source, though sadly these plantations have no ecological value.

NATIONAL PARKS & PROTECTED AREAS

With 15% of the kingdom's land and sea designated as park or sanctuary, Thailand has one of the highest percentages of protected areas of any nation in Asia. There are over 100 national parks, plus over a thousand 'nonhunting areas', wildlife sanctuaries, forest reserves, botanical gardens and arboretums. Twenty-six of the national parks are marine parks that protect coastal, insular and open-sea areas. Thailand began its conservation efforts in 1960 with the creation of a national system of wildlife sanctuaries under the Wild Animals Reservation and Protection Act, followed by the National Parks Act of 1961. Khao Yai National Park was the first wild area to receive this new status. In 2005, Khao Yai, along with four other neighbouring parks and sanctuaries were designated a Unesco World Heritage Site, spanning 230km of habitat from Ta Phraya National Park in Cambodia to Khao Yai National Park in Thailand.

Despite promises, official designation as a national park or sanctuary does not always guarantee protection for habitats and wildlife. Local farmers, well-moneyed developers and other business interests easily win out, either legally or illegally, over environmental protection in Thailand's national parks. Few people adhere to the law and there is little government muscle to enforce regulations. Ko Chang, Ko Samet and Ko Phi-Phi are examples of coastal areas that are facing serious development issues despite being national parks.

Thailand's parks are administered by the **National Park, Wildlife & Plant Conservation Department** (DNP; www.dnp.go.th), which assumed control in 2002 from the Royal Forest Department. Its website helps you to book campsites and accommodation in advance, as well as providing lots of other park-related information.

Marine national parks (as well as unprotected areas) along the Andaman coast experienced varying amounts of damage from the 2004 tsunami. Roughly 5% to 13% of the coral in reef systems associated with these parks was estimated to have been heavily damaged by the waves or by debris brought by the waves. None of the damage was extensive enough to interfere with park activities in the long run, and in many areas the reefs seem to be bouncing back.

A Land on Fire: The Environmental Consequences of the Southeast Asian Boom (2003), by James David Fahn, reports on the environmental outcome of Thailand and its neighbours' conversion into modern, tourist-oriented countries.

ENVIRONMENTAL ISSUES
Deforestation, Flooding & Species Loss

Typical of countries with high population densities, Thailand has put enormous pressure on its ecosystems. Natural forest cover now makes up about 32% of the kingdom's land area as compared to 70% some 50 years ago. The rapid depletion of the country's forests coincided with the modern era's shift toward industrialisation, urbanisation and commercial logging. Although these statistics are alarming, forest loss has slowed since the turn of the millennium to about 0.2% per year according to statistics published by the World Bank in 2008.

In response to environmental degradation, the Thai government has created a large number of protected areas since the 1970s and set a goal of 40% forest cover by the middle of this century. In 1989 all logging was banned in Thailand following a disaster the year before in which hundreds of tonnes of cut timber washed down deforested slopes in Surat Thani Province, burying villages and killing more than a hundred people. It is now illegal to sell timber felled in the country, but unfortunately this law merely sent Thai logging companies into neighbouring countries where there is lax enforcement of environmental laws.

Seasonal flooding is a common natural disaster in Thailand, but 2006 was an exceptionally destructive year, especially in Nan Province, which experienced its worst occurrence in 40 years after days of incessant rains. Monsoon rains during this period caused flooding in 46 provinces in northern and central Thailand. Another flood on the Mekong in August

---

YOU CALL THIS A PARK?

Why do some Thai national parks look more like tourist resorts? To be perfectly honest, the government's commitment to enforcement of environmental protection is more firm on paper than practice. Back when forests were natural resources not natural treasures, the Royal Forest Department (RFD) managed the profitable teak concessions. How does a government replace a money-making venture like logging with a money-losing venture like conservation? A sizeable enforcement budget would be a good start, but rarely did the necessary funds materialise to bar moneyed interests from operating surreptitiously in public lands. The conflict between paper legislation and economic realities became most acute in the late 1990s after the Asian currency crisis crippled the RFD's enforcement budget.

Another loophole arises around land ownership and land use: many of Thailand's parks contain local communities, in some cases marginalised ethnic minorities, subsistence farmers or fisherfolk, whose presence pre-dates the area's park status. Villagers can be disrespectful of forest-protection rules that conflict with traditional practices like slash-and-burn agriculture or firewood collection; some even augment incomes through illegal poaching. More obvious though are the southern marine parks where coastal villagers have turned their fishing shacks into bungalows for the emerging tourism industry. In the case of Ko Chang, for example, commercial development of the park was orchestrated by business interests connected to the Thaksin government. The island was once a rural community with a few basic guesthouses and intermittent electricity, but during the Thaksin era the island was given special economic status and touted as an ecotourism model. The end result was a sizeable profit for politically connected land buyers and a mini-Samui.

It is easy to judge Thailand for mismanaging its natural endowments when the West has, in many cases, squandered and auctioned off their own, but the Thai government is still figuring out its commitment to environmental protection and how to deal with temptations of a new revenue source: tourism.

2008 inundated more than 2200 villages and was considered the worst in a century for some areas.

Many environmental experts suspect human alteration of natural flood barriers and watercourses could be responsible for increased occurrences of severe flooding. Increased incidents of flooding along the Mekong River is often linked to upstream infrastructure projects, like dams and removal of rapids for easier navigation, and increasing human populations along the river. Deforestation and destruction of wetlands and river margins are some of the many compounding factors. Another emerging component is the role of climate change in the increase of seasonal rains that overload the ability of the ecosystem to absorb and transport excess water.

Thailand is a signatory to the UN Convention on International Trade in Endangered Species (Cites), and although Thailand has a better record than most of its neighbours, corruption hinders government attempts to protect 'exotic' species from the lucrative global wildlife trade, which is the third largest black-market activity after drugs and arms dealing. As the border between Thailand and Myanmar becomes more stable, it becomes easier for poachers and illegal loggers to move contraband from the unregulated forests of Myanmar into the markets of Thailand and beyond. Southeast Asia is a poaching hot-spot due to the region's biodiversity and because of inconsistent enforcement of wildlife protection laws.

In any case wildlife experts agree that the greatest danger faced by Thai fauna is neither hunting nor the illegal wildlife trade but rather habitat loss – as is true worldwide. Species that are notably extinct in Thailand include the kouprey (a type of wild cattle), Schomburgk's deer and the Javan rhino, but innumerable smaller species have also disappeared with little fanfare.

Ecology Asia (www
.ecologyasia.com) has
an econews section that
archives green headlines
in Thailand.

Coastal Development & Overfishing

Coastal development is putting serious pressure on Thailand's diverse coral reef system and marine environment. It is estimated that about 40% of Thailand's coral reefs have died and that the annual loss of healthy reefs will continue at a rate of 20% a year. Coral's biggest threat is sedimentation from coastal development, like new condos, hotels, roads and houses. Other common problems include pollution from anchored tour boats, rubbish and sewage dumped directly into the sea, and agricultural and industrial run-off. Coastal development and the attendant light pollution also threaten the breeding cycles of the marine turtles who rely on a dark night sky lit by the moon.

The overall health of the ocean is further impacted by large-scale fishing undertaken by Thailand and its neighbours. Fish catches have declined by up to 33% in the Asia-Pacific region and the upper portion of the Gulf of Thailand is no longer as fertile as it once was. Most of the commercial catches are sent to overseas markets and rarely see a Thai dinner table. The seafood sold in Thailand is typically from fish farms, another large coastal industry for the country.

Air & Water Pollution

Bangkok is once one of the most polluted cities in the world with at least a million Bangkok residents suffering from respiratory problems or allergies triggered by air pollution. However, over the past couple years Bangkok has dramatically cut back on air pollution and become a role model in Asia for its remarkable efforts. Even as the number of cars on Bangkok's roads rose by 40%, the average level of air pollution was cut by 47%, placing Bangkok's air quality within permissible standards for cities in the USA.

There are over five million registered cars in Bangkok.

CHAMPION OF THE FOREST: SEUB NAKASATHIEN

Civil servants, no matter their dedication, rarely leave a legacy beyond their professional circle. But Seub Nakasathien turned his salaried position with the Royal Forest Department into an inspiration for stewardship.

In the mid-1970s, Seub Nakasathien began working for the Wildlife Conservation Division of the Royal Forest Department (RFD) at a small wildlife sanctuary in Chonburi Province, where he first encountered the impediments to conservation in Thailand's parks: underpaid staff charged with protecting the forests from exploitative interests, often acting with consent from forestry officials. Many low-rung employees chose to avoid conflict (that could often result in death) by overlooking blatantly illegal activity. Seub managed to find a middle path in which he earned the respect of both his peers and his adversaries.

After completing a master's degree in environmental conservation overseas, Seub returned to Thailand and was promoted to the chief management position at Huay Kha Khaeng Wildlife Sanctuary in 1989. This remote sanctuary is on the border with Myanmar and is one of the hot spots for illegal logging and wildlife poaching. In an attempt to block an RFD-supported logging concession, Seub appealed to Unesco to designate the Thung Yai/Huay Kha Khaeng Wildlife Sanctuary a World Heritage Site.

The sanctuary was approved for World Heritage status a year later but by then Seub had resigned from his struggles by taking his own life in September 1990, or at least it is popularly believed that his death was suicide. Prior to his death, he donated his research gear to a wildlife centre and built a shrine dedicated to the park rangers who had given their lives to protect Huay Kha Khaeng. He was adopted as a martyr and hero of Thailand's environmental movement in the 1990s, and the **Seub Foundation** (www.seub.or.th, in Thai) established in his memory continues the work of conservation and protection for park rangers who stand up to illegal activities.

Chiang Mai, Thailand's second largest city, is also heading towards air pollution issues due to traffic pressures and further augmented by agricultural burning and household rubbish fires, but this city could turn the situation around if it made a commitment similar to Bangkok's.

Water pollution varies according to region but is, as would be expected, most acute in the Bangkok metropolitan area because of the relatively high concentration of factories, particularly east of the city. Chemical run-off from agribusiness, coastal shrimp farming and untreated sewage also pollutes groundwater and coastal areas.

ENVIRONMENTAL ORGANISATIONS

There are a number of nongovernmental organisations (NGO) working on rural- and forest-related issues in Thailand, especially environmental justice regarding minority hill tribes. International funding, research and policy organisations are typically headquartered in Bangkok. Along the Gulf and Andaman coasts are informal village associations that regard the ocean as their backyard and periodically orchestrate beach clean-ups or animal rescues. The following activist or research organisations work on environmental and conservation issues in Thailand. For information on environmental volunteer opportunities, see p52.

Bird Conservation Society of Thailand (☎ 0 2691 4816; www.bcst.or.th/eng) Works to preserve birding sites through public and government outreach.

Friends of Asian Elephant (☎ 0 2509 1200; en.elephant-soraida.com) A Thai NGO that operates an animal hospital in Mae Yao National Park in Lampung Province, treating abused and injured elephants.

Sanithirakoses-Nagapateepa Foundation (www.sulak-sivaraksa.org) An umbrella group working on numerous environmental and social justice issues in the spirit of the 1995 Alternative Nobel Prize winner, Sulak Sivaraksa.

Southeast Asia Rivers Network (Searin; ☎ 0 5340 8873; www.livingriversiam.org/indexE .htm) An activist group working to maintain local communities' access to rivers and waterways and to oppose the development of large-scale damming projects. Its projects focus on the Mekong, Mun and Salween Rivers.

Thailand Environment Institute (TEI; ☎ 0 2503 3333; www.tei.or.th) A nonprofit research institute devoted to sustainable human development and promoting green business models.

Wild Animal Rescue Foundation of Thailand (WAR; ☎ 0 2712 9715; www.warthai.org) One of Thailand's leading conservation NGOs working to protect native species through rehabilitation programs and conservation projects.

World Wide Fund for Nature (WWF; ☎ 0 2524 6128; www.wwfthai.org) Has a Thailand-based office working on reducing human–wild elephant conflicts and protecting the ecosystem of the Mekong River and marine environment.

Bangkok

Formerly the epitome of the steamy Asian metropolis, in recent years Bangkok has gone under the knife and emerged as a rejuvenated starlet, defiantly daring people to guess her age. Her wrinkles haven't totally been erased, but you might not notice them in the ever-expanding and efficient public transportation system, air-conditioned mega-malls and international-standard restaurants. A diverse international community, a burgeoning art scene and a brand-new airport complete the new look, making even frequent visitors wonder what happened to the girl they once knew.

But don't take this to mean that there's no 'real' Bangkok left. The Royal Palace and Wat Phra Kaew still sparkle just as they did more than 200 years ago. You can still taste classic Bangkok cuisine in the shophouses of Banglamphu, and Skytrains and the Metro have had little impact on the canalside houses of Thonburi. The traditional framework that made this city unique is still very much alive and kicking, and can be found a short walk from any Skytrain station or probably just around the corner from your hotel.

To really experience the Bangkok of today, it's necessary to drop all preconceived notions of what the city 'should' be like and explore both of these worlds. Take the air-conditioned Metro to sweltering, hectic Chinatown, or the soggy *klorng* boat ride to the chic Central World mall. Along the way we're sure you'll find that the old personality and the new face culminate in one sexy broad indeed.

HIGHLIGHTS

- Skipping between sightseeing spots aboard the **Chao Phraya Express** (p185)
- Exploring the streets of old Bangkok, including **Ko Ratanakosin** (p141), on foot
- Learning to make authentic Thai dishes at one of Bangkok's numerous **cooking schools** (p144)
- Toasting the stars and the twinkling skyscraper lights atop a rooftop bar, such as **Moon Bar at Vertigo** (p169) or **Sirocco Sky Bar** (p169)
- Getting blissfully pounded into submission at one of the city's terrific value **massage parlours** (p140)
- Eating yourself into a stupor on the streets of **Chinatown** (p164)
- Getting out of the city and visiting the nearby canalside town of **Amphawa** (p190)

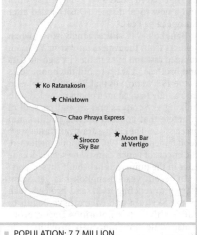

- BEST TIME TO VISIT: NOVEMBER–FEBRUARY
- POPULATION: 7.7 MILLION

HISTORY

The centre of government and culture in Thailand today, Bangkok was a historical miracle during a time of turmoil. Following the fall of Ayuthaya in 1767, the kingdom fractured into competing forces, from which General Taksin emerged as a decisive unifier. He established his base in Thonburi, on the western bank of Mae Nam Chao Phraya (Chao Phraya River), a convenient location for sea trade from the Gulf of Thailand. Taksin proved more of a military strategist than a popular ruler. He was later deposed by another important military general, Chao Phraya Chakri, who moved the capital across the river in 1782 to a more defensible location in anticipation of a Burmese attack. The succession of his son in 1809 established the present-day dynasty, and Chao Phraya Chakri is referred to as Rama I.

Court officials envisioned the new capital as a resurrected Ayuthaya, complete with an island district (Ko Ratanakosin) carved out of the swampland and cradling the royal court (the Grand Palace) and a temple to the auspicious Emerald Buddha (Wat Phra Kaew). The emerging city, which was encircled by a thick wall, was filled with stilt and floating houses ideally adapted to seasonal flooding.

Modernity came to the capital in the late 19th century as European aesthetics and technologies filtered east. During the reigns of Rama IV (King Mongkut) and Rama V (King Chulalongkorn), Bangkok received its first paved road (Th Charoen Krung) and a new royal district (Dusit) styled after European palaces.

Bangkok was still a gangly town when soldiers from the American war in Vietnam came to rest and relax in the city's go-go bars and brothels. It wasn't until the boom years of the 1980s and '90s that Bangkok exploded into a fully fledged metropolis crowded with hulking skyscrapers and an endless spill of concrete that gobbled up rice paddies and green space. The city's extravagant tastes were soon tamed by the 1997 economic meltdown, the effects of which can still be seen a decade later in the numerous half-built skyscrapers.

In recent years Bangkok has yet again started to redefine itself, and projects such as the Skytrain and Metro have begun to address the city's notorious traffic problems, while simultaneously providing the city with a modern face. A spate of giant air-conditioned mega-malls has some parts of the city looking a lot like Singapore, and it's only a matter of time before Bangkok's modernisation reaches the level of other leading Asian capitals.

ORIENTATION

Occupying the east side of Mae Nam Chao Phraya, Bangkok proper can be divided in two by the main north–south railway terminating at Hualamphong train station.

The portion between the serpentine river and the railway is old Bangkok, a district of holy temples, crowded markets and family-owned shophouses. Swarming either side of the train station is the dense neighbourhood of Chinatown, a frenzy of red, gold and neon. Chinatown's chaos is subdued by Ko Ratanakosin, the former royal enclave and Bangkok's most popular tourist district. Charming Banglamphu and the backpacker strip of Th Khao San (Khao San Rd) are north up the river. Crowning the old city is Dusit, a planned homage to the great European capitals, and the easy-going neighbourhood of Thewet.

East of the railway is new Bangkok, a modern Asian city with little charm. Around Siam Square is a universe of boxy shopping centres that attracts fashion-savvy Thai teenagers and shopping-holiday tourists. Th Sukhumvit runs a deliberate course from the geographic city centre to the Gulf of Thailand, and has limblike tributaries reaching into corporate-expat cocoons and the girly-bar scene at Soi Cowboy and Nana Entertainment Plaza.

Bangkok's financial district centres along Th Silom, which cuts an incision from the river to Lumphini Park. Intersecting Th Silom near the river is Th Charoen Krung, Bangkok's first paved road that was once the artery for the city's mercantile shipping interests. Its narrow sois (lanes) branch off through the old *fa·ràng* (foreigners of European descent) quarters that are littered with decaying Victorian monuments, churches and the famous Oriental Hotel. True to the city's resistance to efficiency, there are two main embassy districts: Th Withayu/Wireless Rd and Th Sathon.

On the opposite (west) side of the river is Thonburi, which was Thailand's capital for 15 years, before Bangkok was founded. *Fàng ton* (Thonburi Bank), as it's often called by Thais, seems more akin to the provincial capitals than Bangkok's glittering high-rises.

Bangkok's main international airport, Suvarnabhumi (pronounced *sù·wan·ná·poom*), is located 30km east of the city centre. Some domestic flights still use the old Don Muang Airport, north of the city. For details on how to get to and from these equidistant ports, see p183.

Bangkok Addresses

Any city as large and unplanned as Bangkok can be tough to get around. Street names are intimidating, and the problem is compounded by the inconsistency of romanised spellings as well as a mystifying array of winding streets that never lead where a map dares to propose.

The Thai word thanŏn (Th) means road, street or avenue. Hence Ratchadamnoen Rd (sometimes called Ratchadamnoen Ave) is always Th Ratchadamnoen in Thai.

A soi is a small street or lane that runs off a larger street. So, the address referred to as 48/3-5 Soi 1, Th Sukhumvit, will be located off Th Sukhumvit on Soi 1. Alternative ways of writing the same address include 48/3-5 Th Sukhumvit Soi 1 or even just 48/3-5 Sukhumvit 1. Some Bangkok sois have become so large that they can be referred to both as thanŏn and soi, eg Soi Sarasin/Th Sarasin and Soi Asoke/Th Asoke. Smaller than a soi is a *trok* (*dròrk*; alleyway).

Building numbers are equally confounding; the string of numbers divided by slashes and dashes (eg 48/3-5 Soi 1, Th Sukhumvit) indicate lot disbursements rather than sequential geography. The number before the slash refers to the original lot number; the numbers following the slash indicate buildings (or entrances to buildings) constructed within that lot. The preslash numbers appear in the order in which they were added to city plans, while the postslash numbers are arbitrarily assigned by developers.

Maps

A map is essential for finding your way around Bangkok. The long-running and oft-imitated *Nancy Chandler's Map of Bangkok* is a schematic guide to the city, with listings of out-of-the-way places, beloved restaurants, and colourful anecdotes about neighbourhoods and markets. It is an entertaining visual guide but should be complimented by a more hard-nosed navigator, such as Think Net's *Bangkok* bilingual map with accompanying mapping software. To master the city's bus system, purchase Roadway's *Bangkok Bus Map*. The Thai Marine Department prints

the free map *Boat to All Means*, which shows the routes of all water-bound transport in Bangkok. Ask for a copy at any large river or canal boat pier. For visitors who consider eating a part of sightseeing, check out Ideal Map's *Good Eats* series, which has mapped legendary mom-and-pop restaurants in three of Bangkok's noshing neighbourhoods. For nightcrawlers, Groovy Map's *Bangkok Map 'n' Guide* series makes a good drinking companion.

If travelling to districts outside central Bangkok, invest in *Bangkok & Vicinity A to Z Atlas*, which covers the expressways and surrounding suburbs.

INFORMATION
Bookshops

For a decent selection of English-language books and magazines, branches of **Bookazine** (www.bookazine.co.th) and **B2S** (www.b2s.co.th) can be found at nearly every mall in central Bangkok. The Banglamphu area is home to nearly all of Bangkok's independent bookstores, in addition to at least three branches of Bookazine. Th Khao San is virtually the only place in town to go for used English-language books. You're not going to find any deals there, but the selection is decent.

Asia Books (www.asiabook.com) Soi 15 (Map pp122-3; Soi 15, 221 Th Sukhumvit; Skytrain Asoke); Siam Discovery Center (Map pp120-1; 4th fl, Th Phra Ram I; Skytrain Siam) Also a branch in the Emporium Shopping Centre on Th Sukhumvit (Map pp122–3).

Dasa Book Café (Map pp122-3; ☎ 0 2661 2993; 710/4 Th Sukhumvit, btwn Soi 26 & 28; Skytrain Phrom Phong) Multilingual used bookstore.

Kinokuniya Siam Paragon (Map pp120-1; ☎ 0 2610 9500; www.kinokuniya.com; 3rd fl, Th Phra Ram I; Skytrain Siam) Emporium (Map pp122-3; ☎ 0 2664 8554; 3rd fl, Th Sukhumvit; Skytrain Phrom Phong) The country's largest book store has two branches, both featuring multilanguage selections, magazines and children's books.

RimKhobFah Bookstore (Map pp114-15; ☎ 0 2622 3510; 78/1 Th Ratchadamnoen) This shop specialises in scholarly publications from the Fine Arts Department on Thai art and architecture.

Saraban (Map pp114-15; ☎ 0 2629 1386; 106/1 Th Rambutri) Stocking the largest selection of international newspapers and new Lonely Planet guides on Th Khao San.

Shaman Bookstore (Map pp114-15; ☎ 0 2629 0418; D&D Plaza, 71 Th Khao San) With two locations on Th Khao San and one at 127 Th Tanao, Shaman has the area's largest selection of used books; titles here can conveniently be searched using a computer program.

BANGKOK IN...

For the best of what this city has to offer, try mixing and matching these suggestions.

One Day

Get up as early as you can and take the **Chao Phraya Express** (p185) to **Nonthaburi Market** (p180). On your way back, explore the ancient sites of **Ko Ratanakosin** (p109), followed by an authentic **lunch in Banglamphu** (p161).

After freshening up, get a new perspective on the city with sunset cocktails at one of the **rooftop bars** (p169), followed by dinner downtown such as upscale Thai at **Bo.lan** (p166) or flawless international cuisine at **Cy'an** (p167).

Three Days

Allow the **Skytrain** (p184) to whisk you to various **shopping** (p175) destinations, punctuated by a **buffet lunch** (p168) at one of the city's hotels. Wrap up the daylight hours with a **traditional Thai massage** (p140). Then work off those calories at the dance clubs of **RCA** (p172).

One Week

Now that you're accustomed to the noise, pollution and traffic, you're ready for **Chinatown** (p143). Spend a day at **Chatuchak Weekend Market** (p179) or enrol in a **cooking school** (p144). Fresh air fiends can escape the city at **Ko Kret** (p192), a car-less island north of Bangkok, or charter a long-tail boat to ride through **Thonburi's canals** (p141).

Cultural Centres

Various international cultural centres in Bangkok organise film festivals, lectures, language classes and other educational liaisons.

Alliance Française (Map p124; ☎ 0 2670 4200; www .alliance-francaise.or.th; 29 Th Sathon Tai; Metro Lumphini)

British Council (Map pp120-1; ☎ 0 2652 5480; www .britishcouncil.or.th; Siam Sq, 254 Soi Chulalongkorn 64, Th Phra Ram I; Skytrain Siam)

Foreign Correspondents Club of Thailand (FCCT; Map pp120-1; ☎ 0 2652 0580; www.fccthai.com; Penthouse, Maneeya Center, 518/5 Th Ploenchit; Skytrain Chitlom)

Goethe Institut (Map p124; ☎ 0 2287 0942; www .goethe.de; 18/1 Soi Goethe, btwn Th Sathon Tai & Soi Ngam Duphli; Metro Lumphini)

Japan Foundation (Map pp122-3; ☎ 0 2260 8560; Serm-mit Tower, 159 Soi Asoke/21, Th Sukhumvit; bus 136, 206)

Emergency

If you have a medical emergency and need an ambulance, contact the English-speaking hospitals listed on opposite. In case of a police or safety issue, contact the city hotlines for the following emergency services:

Fire (☎ 199)

Police/Emergency (☎ 191)

Tourist police (☎ 1155; ⏲ 24hr) An English-speaking unit that investigates criminal activity involving tourists, including gem scams. It can also act as a bilingual liaison with the regular police.

Internet Access

There's no shortage of internet cafes in Bangkok competing to offer the cheapest and fastest connection. Rates vary depending on the concentration and affluence of net-heads – Banglamphu is infinitely cheaper than Sukhumvit or Silom, with rates as low as 20B per hour. Many internet shops are adding Skype and headsets to their machines so that international calls can be made for the price of surfing the web. A convenient place to take care of your communication needs in the centre of Bangkok is the **TrueMove Shop** (Map pp120-1; ☎ 0 2658 4449; www .truemove.com; Soi 2, Siam Sq; ⏲ 7am-8pm; Skytrain Siam). It has high-speed internet computers equipped with Skype, sells phones and mobile subscriptions, and can also provide information on city-wide wi-fi access for computers and phones.

Wi-fi, mostly free of charge, is becoming more and more ubiquitous around Bangkok and is available at more businesses and public hotspots than we have space to list here. For relatively authoritative lists of wi-fi hotspots in Bangkok, go to www .bkkpages.com (under 'Bangkok Directory') or www.stickmanbangkok.com.

Libraries

Although Bangkok's libraries may not impress you with their stock, they make a peaceful escape from the heat and noise.

National Library (Map pp112-13; ☎ 0 2281 5212; Th Samsen; admission free; ☽ 9am-6.30pm Mon-Fri, to 5pm Sat & Sun; river ferry Tha Thewet) A few foreign-language resources, but the library's strength is in its astrological books and star charts, as well as recordings by the king and sacred palm-leaf writings and ancient maps.

Neilson Hays Library (Map pp118-19; ☎ 0 2233 1731; www.neilsonhayslibrary.com; 195 Th Surawong; family membership 3300B; ☽ 9.30am-5pm Tue-Sun; Skytrain Surasak) The oldest English-language library in Thailand, with many children's books and a decent selection of titles on Thailand.

Media

Daily newspapers are available at streetside newsagents. Monthly magazines are available in most bookstores.

Bangkok 101 (www.bangkok101.com) A monthly city primer with photo essays and reviews of sights, restaurants and entertainment.

Bangkok Post (www.bangkokpost.net) The leading English-language daily with Friday and weekend supplements covering city events.

BK Magazine (www.bkmagazine.com) Free weekly listings mag for the young and hip.

The Nation (www.nationmultimedia.com) English-language daily with a heavy focus on business.

Medical Services

Thanks to its high standard of hospital care, Bangkok is fast becoming a destination for medical tourists shopping for more affordable dental check-ups, elective surgery and cosmetic procedures. Pharmacists (chemists) throughout the city can diagnose and treat most minor ailments (Bangkok belly, sinus and skin infections etc). The following hospitals offer 24-hour emergency services, and the numbers below should be contacted if you need an ambulance or immediate medical attention. Most of these hospitals also have daily clinics with English-speaking staff.

Bangkok Christian Hospital (Map pp118-19; ☎ 0 2235 1000-07; 124 Th Silom; Skytrain Sala Daeng, Metro Silom)

BNH (Map pp118-19; ☎ 0 2686 2700; 9 Th Convent, off Th Silom; Skytrain Sala Daeng, Metro Silom)

Bumrungrad Hospital (Map pp122-3; ☎ 0 2667 1000; 33 Soi Nana Neua/3, Th Sukhumvit; Skytrain Ploenchit)

Samitivej Hospital (Map pp122-3; ☎ 0 2711 8000; 133 Soi 49, Th Sukhumvit; Skytrain Phrom Phong)

St Louis Hospital (Map pp118-19; ☎ 0 2675 9300; 215 Th Sathon Tai; Skytrain Surasak)

Rutnin Eye Hospital (Map pp122-3; ☎ 0 2639 3399; 80/1 Soi Asoke/21, Th Sukhumvit; Skytrain Asoke, Metro Sukhumvit) Contact this hospital for urgent eye care.

Money

Regular bank hours in Bangkok are 10am to 4pm, and ATMs are common in all areas of the city. Many Thai banks also have currency-exchange bureaus; there are also exchange desks within the Skytrain stations and within eyeshot of most tourist areas. Go to 7-Eleven shops or other reputable places to break 1000B bills; don't expect a vendor or taxi to be able to make change on a bill 500B or larger.

THE INSIDE SCOOP

Several Bangkok residents, both local and foreign, have taken their experiences to the 'small screen' and maintain blogs and websites about living in Bangkok. Some of the more informative or entertaining include:

- **2Bangkok** (www.2bangkok.com) News sleuth and history buff follows the city headlines from today and yesterday.

- **Absolutely Bangkok** (www.absolutelybangkok.com) Bangkok news, views and links to several other good blogs and sites.

- **Austin Bush Food Blog** (www.austinbushphotography.com/category/foodblog) Written by the author of this chapter, the blog focuses on food culture and eating in Bangkok and elsewhere.

- **Bangkok Jungle** (www.bangkokjungle.com) A blog on the city's live music scene.

- **Gnarly Kitty** (www.gnarlykitty.blogspot.com) Written by a female native of Bangkok, a place where 'there are always things worth ranting about'.

- **Newley Purnell** (www.newley.com) This Bangkok-based American freelance writer comments on everything from local politics to his profound love for *pàt gà·prow* stir-fry.

- **Stickman** (www.stickmanbangkok.com) Formerly associated with naughty Bangkok nightlife, the 'new' Stickman is a more general blog about life, work and love in Bangkok.

BANGKOK

Post

Main post office (Map pp118-19; Th Charoen Krung; ⏰ 8am-8pm Mon-Fri, to 1pm Sat & Sun; river ferry Tha Si Phraya) Services include poste restante and packaging within the main building. Do not send money or valuables via regular mail. Branch post offices throughout the city also offer poste restante and parcel services.

Telephone & Fax

Bangkok's city code (☎ 02) is incorporated into all telephone numbers dialled locally or from outside the city. Public phones for both domestic and international calls are well distributed throughout the city.

Communications Authority of Thailand (CAT; Map pp118-19; ☎ 0 2573 0099; Th Charoen Krung; ⏰ 24hr; river ferry Oriental) Next door to the main post office; offers Home Country Direct service, fax transmittal and phone-card services.

Telephone Organization of Thailand (TOT; Map pp120-1; ☎ 0 2251 1111; Th Ploenchit; Skytrain Chitlom) Long-distance calling services and an English version of Bangkok's *Yellow Pages*.

Toilets

Public toilets in Bangkok are few and far between and your best bet is to head for a shopping centre, hotel or fast-food restaurant. Shopping centres might charge 2B to 5B for a visit; some newer shopping centres have toilets for the disabled. Despite what you'll hear, squat toilets are a dying breed in Bangkok.

Tourist Information

Official tourist offices distribute maps, brochures and advice on sights and activities. Don't confuse these free services with the licensed travel agents that book tours and transport on a commission basis. Often, travel agencies incorporate elements of the official national tourism organisation name (Tourism Authority of Thailand; TAT) into their own to purposefully confuse tourists.

Bangkok Information Center (Map pp114-15; ☎ 0 2225 7612-5; www.bangkoktourist.com; 17/1 Th Phra Athit; ⏰ 9am-7pm; river ferry Tha Phra Athit) City-specific tourism office provides maps, brochures and directions; yellow information booths staffed by student volunteers are located throughout the city.

Tourism Authority of Thailand (TAT; ☎ 1672 for assistance 8am-8pm; www.tourismthailand.org) Head Office (Map pp112-13; ☎ 0 2250 5500; 1600 Th Petchaburi Tat Mai; ⏰ 8.30am-4.30pm; Skytrain City Air Terminal, Metro Phetburi); Banglamphu (Map pp114-15; ☎ 0 2283 1555; cnr Th Ratchadamnoen Nok & Th Chakrapatdipong;

⏰ 8.30am-4.30pm) Opposite the boxing stadium; Suvarnabhumi International Airport (☎ 0 2134 4077; 2nd fl, btwn Gates 2 & 5; ⏰ 8am-4pm).

Travel Agencies

Bangkok is packed with travel agencies where you can book bus and air tickets. Some are reliable, while others are fly-by-night scams issuing bogus tickets or promises of (undelivered) services. Ask for recommendations from fellow travellers before making a major purchase from a travel agent. Generally, it's best to buy bus and train tickets directly from the station rather than via travel agents.

The following are some long-running agencies:

Diethelm Travel (Map p124; ☎ 0 2660 7000; www.diethelmtravel.com; 12th fl, Kian Gwan Bldg II, 140/1 Th Withayu/Wireless Rd; Skytrain Phloenchit)

STA Travel (Map pp118-19; ☎ 0 2236 0262; www.statravel.co.th; 14th fl, Wall Street Tower, 33/70 Th Surawong; Skytrain Sala Daeng, Metro Silom)

Vieng Travel (☎ 0 2326 7191; www.viengtravel.com; Trang Hotel, 12 Soi Lad Krabang)

DANGERS & ANNOYANCES

You are more likely to be charmed rather than coerced out of your money in Bangkok. Practised con artists capitalise on Thailand's famous friendliness and a revolving door of clueless tourists. Bangkok's most heavily touristed areas – Wat Phra Kaew, Wat Pho, Jim Thompson's House, Th Khao San, Erawan Shrine – are favourite hunting grounds for these scallywags. The best prevention is knowledge, so before hitting the ground, be-

COMMON BANGKOK SCAMS

Commit these classic rip-offs to memory and join us in our ongoing crusade to outsmart Bangkok's crafty scam artists. For details on the famous gem scam, see the boxed text on p180.

- **Closed today** Ignore any 'friendly' local who tells you that an attraction is closed for a Buddhist holiday or for cleaning. These are set-ups for trips to a bogus gem sale.

- **Túk-túk rides for 10B** Say goodbye to your day's itinerary if you climb aboard this ubiquitous scam. These alleged 'tours' bypass all the sights and instead cruise to all the fly-by-night gem and tailor shops that pay commissions.

- **Flat-fare taxi ride** Flatly refuse any driver who quotes a flat fare (usually between 100B and 150B for in-town destinations), which will usually be three times more expensive than the reasonable meter rate. Walking beyond the tourist area will usually help in finding an honest driver. If the driver has 'forgotten' to put the meter on, just say, 'Meter, kha/khap'.

- **Tourist buses to the south** On the long journey south, well-organised and connected thieves have hours to comb through your bags, breaking into (and later resealing) locked bags, searching through hiding places and stealing credit cards, electronics and even toiletries. This scam has been running for years but is easy to avoid simply by carrying valuables with you on the bus.

- **Friendly strangers** Be wary of smartly dressed men who approach you asking where you're from and where you're going. Their opening gambit is usually followed with: 'Ah, my son/daughter is studying at university in (your city)' – they seem to have an encyclopaedic knowledge of major universities. As the tourist authorities here pointed out, this sort of behaviour is out of character for Thais and should be treated with suspicion.

come familiar with the more common local scams listed in the boxed text, below.

If you've been scammed, the tourist police can be effective in dealing with some of the 'unethical' business practices and crime. But in general you should enter into every monetary transaction with the understanding that you have no consumer protection or recourse.

SIGHTS
Ko Ratanakosin, Banglamphu & Thonburi
เกาะรัตนโกสินทร์/บางลำพู/ธนบุรี

Welcome to Bangkok's birthplace. The vast city we know today emerged from Ko Ratanakosin, a tiny virtual island ('Ko') made by dredging a canal around Mae Nam Chao Phraya during the late 18th century. Within this area you'll find the glittering temples and palaces that most visitors associate with the city. Ko Ratanakosin's riverfront setting is also home to several museums, markets and universities. All these sights are within walking distance of each other and are best visited early in the morning before the day comes to a boil.

Adjacent Banglamphu suffers from an extreme case of bipolar disorder, encompassing both the most characteristically old-school Bangkok part of town as well as Th Khao San,

a brash, neon-lit decompression zone for international backpackers. Depending on which one you fancy, it's not difficult to escape the other – another of Banglamphu's charms. The bulk of Bangkok's classic buildings are found in this area, as well as lots of authentic Bangkok cuisine and culture.

Directly across the river is Thonburi, which served a brief tenure as the Thai capital after the fall of Ayuthaya. Today the area along the river is easily accessed from Bangkok's cross-river ferries, and there are museums and temples here that are historical complements to those in Ko Ratanakosin.

Despite the abundance of attractions, both areas are still isolated from the more modern forms of public transport. The Chao Phraya River Express is probably the most efficient way of reaching the area, and the *klorng* (canal; also spelt *khlong*) taxi along Khlong Saen Saeb is another convenient option if you're coming from Siam Square or Sukhumvit. The closest Skytrain station is Ratchathewi. If you're planning on doing some extensive exploring in the area, consider borrowing one of the free Green Bangkok Bikes (see the boxed text, opposite) available at eight stations around the district.

(Continued on page 126)

GREATER BANGKOK

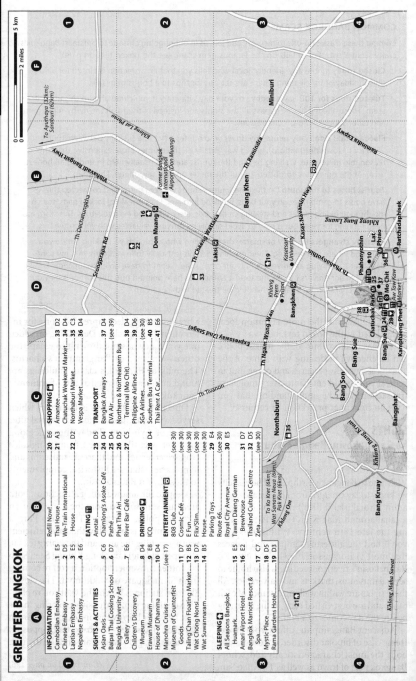

INFORMATION

Cambodian Embassy	1 E5
Chinese Embassy	2 D5
Laotian Embassy	3 E5
Nepalese Embassy	4 E6

SIGHTS & ACTIVITIES

Asian Oasis	5 C6
Baipai Thai Cooking School	6 D7
Bangkok University Art Gallery	7 E6
Children's Discovery Museum	8 D4
Erawan Museum	9 E8
House of Dhamma	10 D4
Manohra Cruises	(see 17)
Museum of Counterfeit Goods	11 D7
Taling Chan Floating Market	12 B5
Wat Chong Nonsi	13 D7
Wat Suwannaram	14 B5

SLEEPING

All Seasons Bangkok Huamark	15 E5
Amari Airport Hotel	16 E2
Bangkok Marriott Resort & Spa	17 C7
Mystic Place	18 D5
Rama Gardens Hotel	19 D3

Refill Now!	20 E6
Thai House	21 A3
We-Train International House	22 D2

EATING

Anotai	23 D5
Chamlong's Asoke Café	24 D4
Pathé	25 D4
Phat Thai Ari	26 D5
River Bar Café	27 C5

DRINKING

ICQ	28 D4

ENTERTAINMENT

808 Club	(see 30)
Cosmic Café	(see 30)
E Fun	(see 30)
Flix/Slim	(see 30)
House	(see 30)
Parking Toys	29 E4
Route 66	(see 30)
Royal City Avenue	30 E5
Tawan Daeng German Brewhouse	31 D7
Thailand Cultural Centre	32 D5
Zeta	(see 30)

SHOPPING

Amantee	33 D2
Chatuchak Weekend Market	34 D4
Nonthaburi Market	35 C3
Vespa Market	36 D4

TRANSPORT

Bangkok Airways	37 D4
EVA Air	(see 39)
Northern & Northeastern Bus Terminal (Mo Chit)	38 D4
Philippine Airlines	39 D6
SGA Airlines	(see 30)
Southern Bus Terminal	40 B5
Thai Rent A Car	41 E6

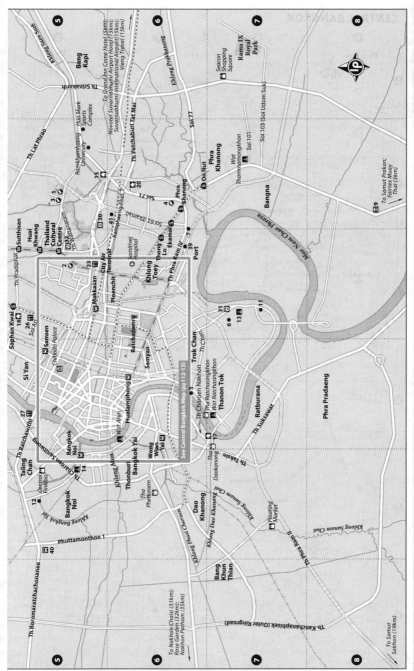

BANGKOK

CENTRAL BANGKOK

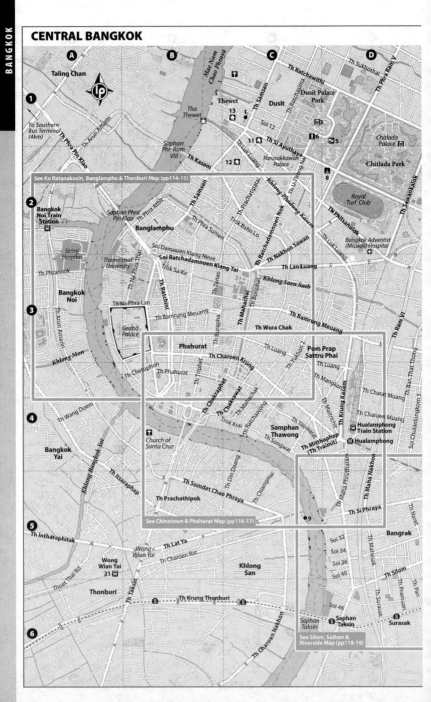

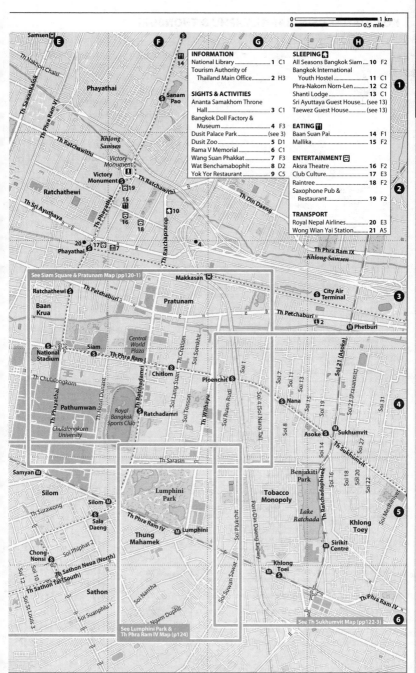

INFORMATION
National Library **1** C1
Tourism Authority of
Thailand Main Office.............. **2** H3

SIGHTS & ACTIVITIES
Ananta Samakhom Throne
Hall.. **3** C1
Bangkok Doll Factory &
Museum................................. **4** F3
Dusit Palace Park.................... (see **3**)
Dusit Zoo.. **5** D1
Rama V Memorial **6** C1
Wang Suan Phakkat **7** F3
Wat Benchamabophit **8** D2
Yok Yor Restaurant **9** C5

SLEEPING
All Seasons Bangkok Siam **10** F2
Bangkok International
Youth Hostel **11** C1
Phra-Nakorn Norn-Len **12** C2
Shanti Lodge **13** C1
Sri Ayuttaya Guest House.... (see **13**)
Taewez Guest House............. (see **13**)

EATING
Baan Suan Pai.................................. **14** F1
Mallika.. **15** F2

ENTERTAINMENT
Aksra Theatre................................. **16** F2
Club Culture..................................... **17** E3
Raintree **18** F2
Saxophone Pub &
Restaurant............................... **19** F2

TRANSPORT
Royal Nepal Airlines..................... **20** E3
Wong Wian Yai Station............... **21** A5

BANGKOK

KO RATANAKOSIN, BANGLAMPHU & THONBURI

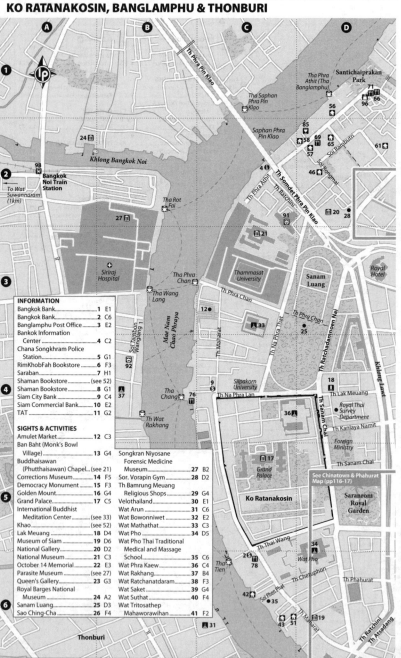

Thonburi

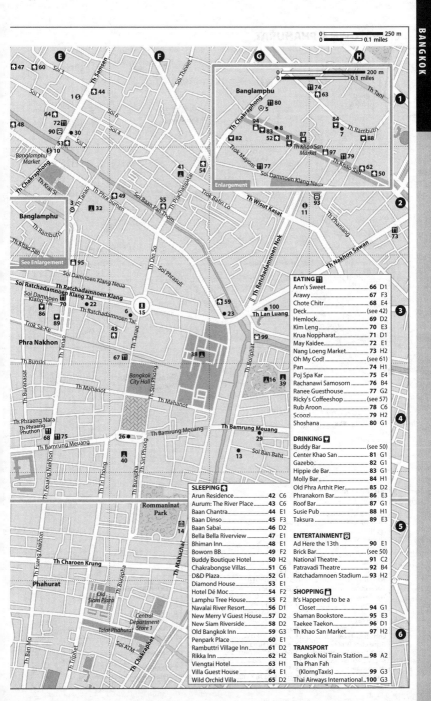

EATING
Ann's Sweet	**66** D1
Arawy	**67** F3
Chote Chitr	**68** E4
Deck	(see 42)
Hemlock	**69** D2
Kim Leng	**70** E3
Krua Nopphanat	**71** D1
May Kaidee	**72** E1
Nang Loeng Market	**73** H2
Oh My Cod!	(see 61)
Pan	**74** H1
Poj Spa Kar	**75** E4
Rachanawi Samosorn	**76** B4
Ranee Guesthouse	**77** G2
Ricky's Coffeeshop	(see 57)
Rub Aroon	**78** C6
Scoozi	**79** H2
Shoshana	**80** G1

DRINKING
Buddy Bar	(see 50)
Center Khao San	**81** G1
Gazebo	**82** G1
Hippie de Bar	**83** G1
Molly Bar	**84** H1
Old Phra Arthit Pier	**85** D2
Phranakorn Bar	**86** E3
Roof Bar	**87** G1
Susie Pub	**88** H1
Taksura	**89** E3

ENTERTAINMENT
Ad Here the 13th	**90** E1
Brick Bar	(see 50)
National Theatre	**91** C2
Patravadi Theatre	**92** B4
Ratchadamnoen Stadium	**93** H2

SHOPPING
It's Happened to be a Closet	**94** G1
Shaman Bookstore	**95** E3
Taekee Taekon	**96** D1
Th Khao San Market	**97** H2

SLEEPING
Arun Residence	**42** C6
Aurum: The River Place	**43** C6
Baan Chantra	**44** E1
Baan Dinso	**45** F3
Baan Sabai	**46** D2
Bella Bella Riverview	**47** E1
Bhiman Inn	**48** E1
Boworn BB	**49** F2
Buddy Boutique Hotel	**50** H2
Chakrabongse Villas	**51** C6
D&D Plaza	**52** G1
Diamond House	**53** E1
Hotel Dé Moc	**54** F2
Lamphu Tree House	**55** F2
Navalai River Resort	**56** D1
New Merry V Guest House	**57** D2
New Siam Riverside	**58** D2
Old Bangkok Inn	**59** G3
Penpark Place	**60** E1
Rambuttri Village Inn	**61** D2
Rikka Inn	**62** H2
Viengtai Hotel	**63** H1
Villa Guest House	**64** E1
Wild Orchid Villa	**65** D2

TRANSPORT
Bangkok Noi Train Station	**98** A2
Tha Phan Fah (KlorngTaxis)	**99** G3
Thai Airways International	**100** G3

CHINATOWN & PHAHURAT

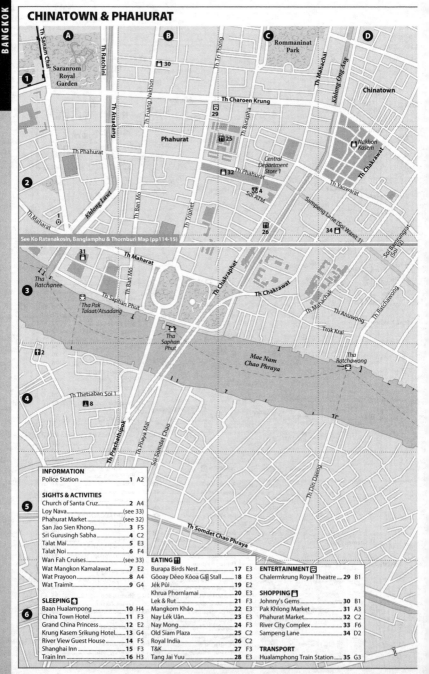

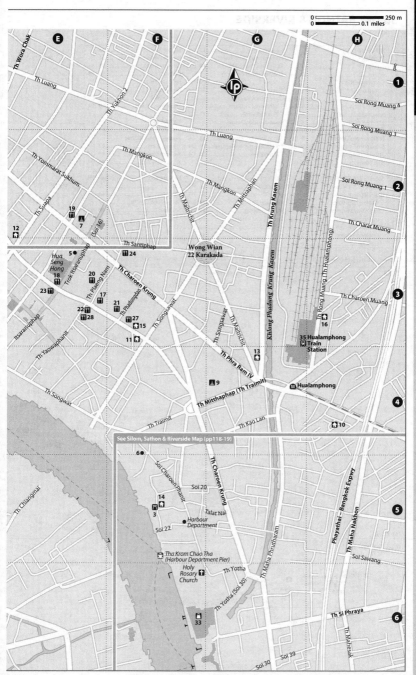

BANGKOK

SILOM, SATHON & RIVERSIDE

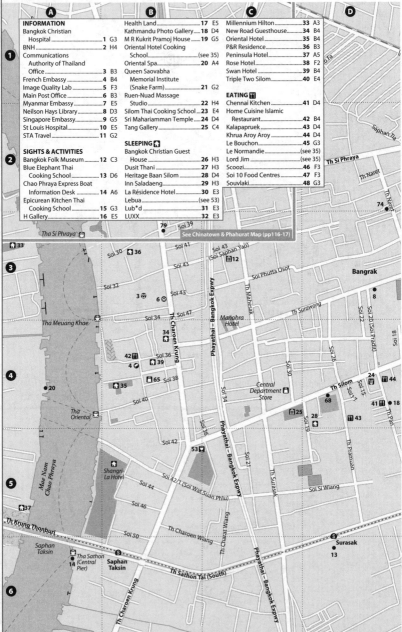

See Chinatown & Phahurat Map (pp116-17)

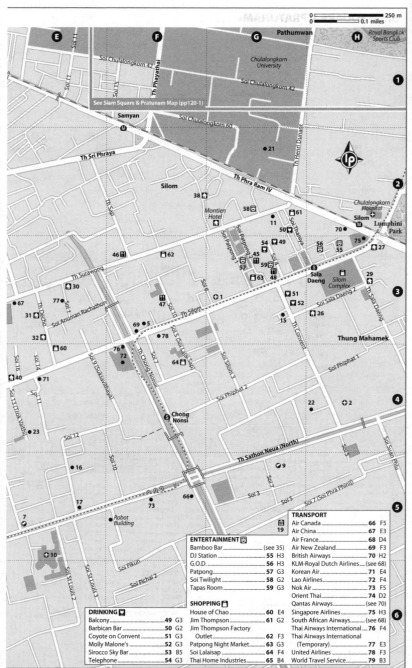

DRINKING 🍷
Balcony.....................................**49** G3
Barbican Bar..........................**50** G2
Coyote on Convent................**51** G3
Molly Malone's.......................**52** G3
Sirocco Sky Bar......................**53** B5
Telephone...............................**54** G3

ENTERTAINMENT 🎭
Bamboo Bar........................(see 35)
DJ Station................................**55** H3
G.O.D.......................................**56** H3
Patpong...................................**57** G3
Soi Twilight............................**58** G3
Tapas Room............................**59** G3

SHOPPING 🛍
House of Chao.........................**60** E4
Jim Thompson.........................**61** G2
Jim Thompson Factory
    Outlet...................................**62** F3
Patpong Night Market..........**63** G3
Soi Lalaisap.............................**64** F4
Thai Home Industries.............**65** B4

TRANSPORT
Air Canada..............................**66** F5
Air China..................................**67** E3
Air France................................**68** D4
Air New Zealand.....................**69** F3
British Airways.......................**70** H2
KLM-Royal Dutch Airlines....(see 68)
Korean Air................................**71** E4
Lao Airlines.............................**72** F4
Nok Air....................................**73** F5
Orient Thai..............................**74** D2
Qantas Airways..................(see 70)
Singapore Airlines..................**75** H3
South African Airways......(see 68)
Thai Airways International....**76** F4
Thai Airways International
    (Temporary)........................**77** E3
United Airlines........................**78** F3
World Travel Service...............**79** B3

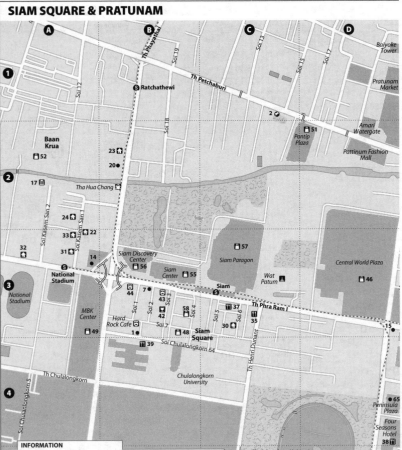

SIAM SQUARE & PRATUNAM

Chulalongkorn University
Intensive Thai Program (400m)

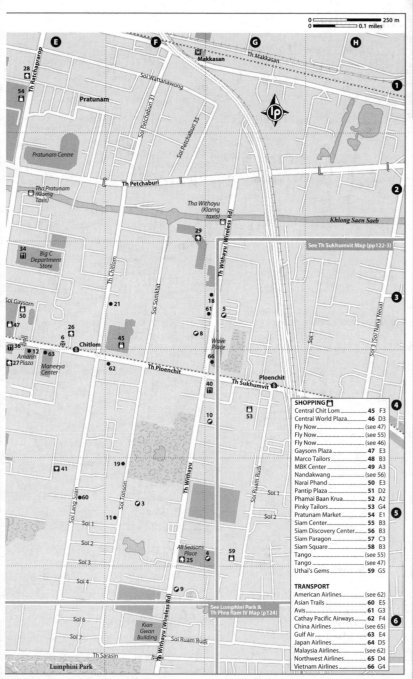

BANGKOK

TH SUKHUMVIT

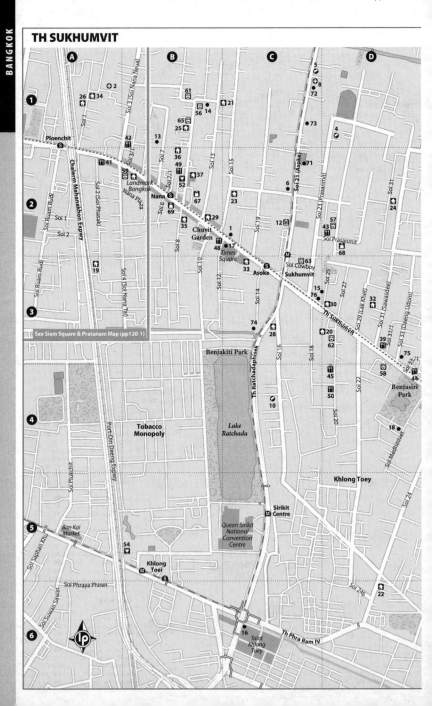

0 — 0.5 km
0 — 0.2 miles

INFORMATION
Asia Books ....(see 66)
Asia Books **1** C2
Bumrungrad Hospital **2** A1
Dasa Book Café **3** E4
Indian Embassy **4** D1
Israeli Embassy **5** C1
Japan Foundation **6** C2
Kinokuniya ....(see 66)
Philippine Embassy **7** E4
Rutnin Eye Hospital **8** C1
Samitivej Hospital **9** F3
Siam Society ....(see 12)
Spanish Embassy **10** C4

SIGHTS & ACTIVITIES
ABC Amazing Bangkok
    Cyclists **11** E4
Ban Kamthieng **12** C2
Buathip Thai Massage **13** B1
Coran Boutique Spa **14** B1
Divana Spa **15** C3
Khlong Toey Market **16** C6
Pro Language **17** C2
Thai Traditional Medical
    Services Society ....(see 14)
Thailand Creative &
    Design Center ....(see 66)
World Fellowship of
    Buddhists **18** D4

SLEEPING 🏠
Atlanta **19** A3
Baan Sukhumvit **20** D3
Citichic **21** C1

Davis **22** D6
Dream Bangkok **23** C2
Eugenia **24** D2
Federal Hotel **25** B1
Golden Palace Hotel **26** A1
HI-Sukhumvit **27** G5
Ma Du Zi **28** C3
Miami Hotel **29** B2
Nana Chart Hotel **30** D3
Napa Place Bed &
    Breakfast **31** F5
Seven **32** D3
Sheraton Grande
    Sukhumvit **33** C3
Soi 1 Guesthouse **34** A1
Stable Lodge **35** B2
Suk 11 ....**36** B2
Swiss Park Hotel **37** B2

EATING 🍴
AH! ....(see 19)
Arirang ....(see 48)
Bed Supperclub ....(see 56)
Bo.lan **38** E5
Duc de Praslin **39** D3
Emporium Food Hall ....(see 66)
Face **40** G6
JW Marriott Buffet **41** A2
Nasser Elmassry **42** B1

Park Food Hall ....(see 66)
Pharani Home Cuisine **43** D2
Ramentei **44** D4
Rang Mahal **45** D4
Scoozi **46** G5
Soi 38 Night Market **47** G5
Sukhumvit Plaza **48** B2
Tapas Café **49** B2
Thonglee **50** D4

DRINKING 🍷
Bull's Head **51** E3
Cheap Charlie's **52** B2
HOBS **53** G3
Rain Dogs **54** B5
Tuba **55** H2

ENTERTAINMENT 🎭
Bed Supperclub **56** B1
Glow **57** D2
Living Room ....(see 33)
Mambo Cabaret **58** D4
Nana Entertainment Plaza **59** B2
Nung-Len **60** H4
Q Bar **61** B1
Scratch Dog **62** D3
SFX Cinema ....(see 66)
Soi Cowboy **63** C3
Tokyo Joe's **64** E4
Twisted Republic **65** B1

SHOPPING 🛍
Emporium Shopping
    Centre **66** E4
Manhattan Custom Tailor **67** B2
Nandakwang **68** D2
Th Sukhumvit Market **69** B2

TRANSPORT
Eastern Bus Terminal
    (Ekamai) **70** H6
Emirates **71** C2
Lufthansa Airlines **72** C1
Myanmar Airways
    International **73** C1
One-Two-Go **74** C3
PB Air **75** D3
Scandinavian Airlines **76** C3

BANGKOK

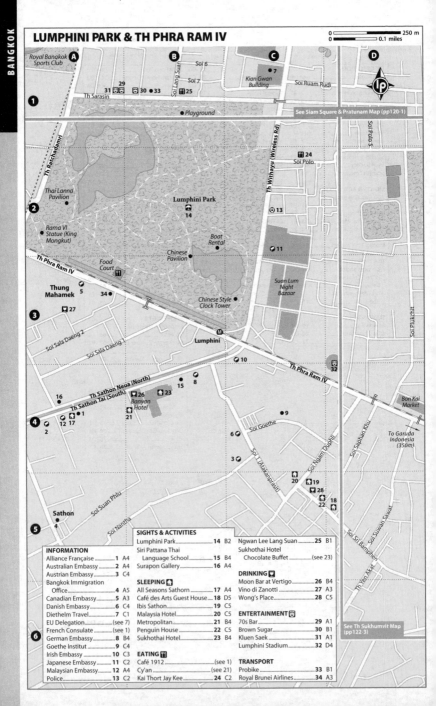

LUMPHINI PARK & TH PHRA RAM IV

BANGKOK TRANSPORT NETWORK

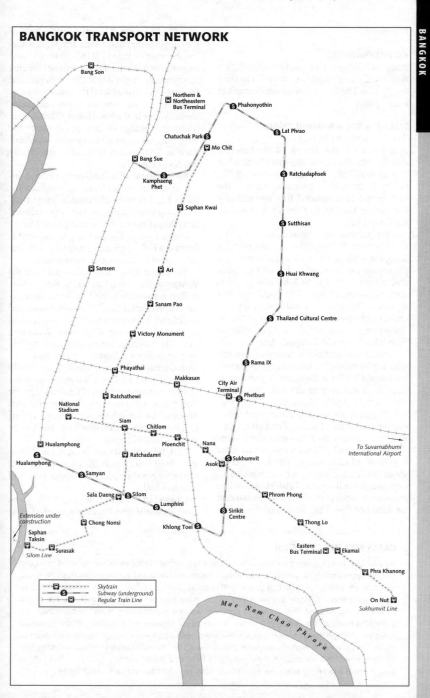

Bang Son

Northern & Northeastern Bus Terminal

Phahonyothin

Chatuchak Park

Lat Phrao

Mo Chit

Bang Sue

Ratchadaphsek

Kamphaeng Phet

Saphan Kwai

Sutthisan

Samsen

Ari

Sanam Pao

Huai Khwang

Victory Monument

Thailand Cultural Centre

Phayathai

Rama IX

Makkasan

Ratchathewi

City Air Terminal

Phetburi

National Stadium

Siam

Chitlom

Ploenchit

Nana

Hualamphong

Ratchadamri

Hualamphong

Samyan

Asok

Sukhumvit

Sala Daeng

Silom

Phrom Phong

Lumphini

Chong Nonsi

Sirikit Centre

Khlong Toei

Thong Lo

Extension under construction

Saphan Taksin

Eastern Bus Terminal

Ekamai

Surasak

Phra Khanong

Silom Line

To Suvarnabhumi International Airport

On Nut

Sukhumvit Line

Skytrain
Subway (underground)
Regular Train Line

Mae Nam Chao Phraya

(Continued from page 109)

KO RATANAKOSIN

Bangkok's biggest and gaudiest tourist sites float regally on this artificial island. The river ferry pier at Tha Chang is the most convenient access point.

Wat Phra Kaew & Grand Palace

วัดพระแก้ว/พระบรมมหาราชวัง

Also known as the Temple of the Emerald Buddha, **Wat Phra Kaew** (Map pp114-15; ☎ 0 2224 1833; admission 350B; ⏰ 8.30am-3.30pm; bus 508, 512, river ferry Tha Chang) is the colloquial name of the vast, fairy-tale compound that also includes the former residence of the Thai monarch, the Grand Palace.

This ground was consecrated in 1782, the first year of Bangkok rule, and is today Bangkok's biggest tourist attraction and a pilgrimage destination for devout Buddhists and nationalists. The 94.5-hectare grounds encompass more than 100 buildings that represent 200 years of royal history and architectural experimentation. Most of the architecture, royal or sacred, can be classified as Ratanakosin (or old-Bangkok style).

Housed in a fantastically decorated *bòht* and guarded by pairs of *yaksha* (mythical giants), the **Emerald Buddha** is the temple's primary attraction. It sits atop an elevated altar, barely visible amid the gilded decorations. The diminutive figure is always cloaked in royal robes, one for each season (hot, cool and rainy). In a solemn ceremony, the king (or in recent years, the crown prince) changes the garments at the beginning of each season. For more details about this sacred statue, see the boxed text, opposite. Recently restored **Buddhist murals** line the interior walls of the *bòht*, and the **murals of the Ramakian** (the Thai version of the Indian epic the *Ramayana*) line the inside walls of the temple compound. Originally painted during the reign of Rama I (1782–1809) and also recently restored, the murals illustrate the epic in its entirety, beginning at the north gate and moving clockwise around the compound.

Except for an anteroom here and there, the buildings of the **Grand Palace** (Phra Borom Maharatchawong) are now put to use by the king only for certain ceremonial occasions, such as Coronation Day (the king mostly resides in Hua Hin).

Borombhiman Hall (eastern end), a French-inspired structure that served as a residence for Rama VI, is occasionally used to house visiting foreign dignitaries. In April 1981 General San Chitpatima used it as headquarters for an attempted coup. The building to the west is **Amarindra Hall**, originally a hall of justice but used today for coronation ceremonies.

The largest of the palace buildings is the **Chakri Mahaprasat**, the Grand Palace Hall. Built in 1882 by British architects using Thai labour, the exterior is a peculiar blend of Italian Renaissance and traditional Thai architecture. It's a style often referred to as *fa·ràng sài chá·dah* (Westerner in a Thai crown) because each wing is topped by a *mon·dòp* – a heavily ornamented spire representing a Thai adaptation of the Hindu *mandapa* (shrine). The tallest *mon·dòp*, in the centre, contains the ashes of Chakri kings; the flanking *mon·dòp* enshrine the ashes of Chakri princes. Thai kings housed their huge harems in the inner palace area, which was guarded by combat-trained female sentries.

Last, from east to west, is the Ratanakosin-style **Dusit Hall**, which initially served as a venue for royal audiences and later as a royal funerary hall.

Guides can be hired at the ticket kiosk; ignore anyone outside. Wat Phra Kaew and the Grand

---

DRESS FOR THE OCCASION

Most of Bangkok's biggest tourist attractions are in fact sacred places, and visitors should dress and behave appropriately. In particular at Wat Phra Kaew and the Grand Palace and in Dusit Park, you won't be allowed to enter unless you're well covered. Shorts, sleeveless shirts or spaghetti-strap tops, capri pants – basically anything that reveals more than your arms (not your shoulders) and head – are not allowed. This applies to men and women. Violators can expect to be shown into a dressing room and issued with a sarong before being allowed in. For walking in the courtyard areas you are supposed to wear shoes with closed heels and toes, although these rules aren't as zealously enforced. Regardless, footwear should always be removed before entering any main *bòht* (chapel) or *wí·hǎhn* (sanctuary). When sitting in front of a Buddha image, tuck your feet behind you to avoid the highly offensive pose of pointing your feet towards a revered figure.

Palace are best reached either by a short walk south from Banglamphu, via Sanam Luang, or by Chao Phraya Express boat to Tha Chang. From the Siam Square area (in front of the MBK Center, Th Phra Ram I), take bus 47.

The admission charge for the complex includes entrance to **Dusit Park** (p138), which includes Vimanmaek Teak Mansion and Abhisek Dusit Throne Hall.

Wat Pho
วัดโพธิ์ (วัดพระเชตุพน)

You'll find significantly fewer tourists here than at Wat Phra Kaew, but **Wat Pho** (Wat Phra Chetuphon; Map pp114-15; ☎ 0 2221 9911; Th Sanamchai; admission 50B; ☺ 8am-5pm; bus 508, 512, river ferry Tha Tien) is our personal fave among Bangkok's biggest temples. In fact, the compound incorporates a host of superlatives: the largest reclining Buddha, the largest collection of Buddha images in Thailand and the country's earliest centre for public education.

Almost too big for its shelter, the genuinely impressive **Reclining Buddha**, 46m long and 15m high, illustrates the passing of the Buddha into nirvana (ie the Buddha's death). The figure is modelled out of plaster around a brick core and finished in gold leaf. Mother-of-pearl inlay ornaments the feet, displaying 108 different auspicious *lák·sà·nà* (characteristics of a Buddha).

The **Buddha images** on display in the other four *wí·hăhn* (sanctuaries) are worth a nod. Particularly beautiful are the Phra Chinnarat and Phra Chinnachai Buddhas, both from Sukhothai, in the west and south chapels. The galleries extending between the four chapels feature no less than 394 gilded Buddha images, many of which display Ayuthaya or Sukhothai features. The remains of Rama I are interred in the base of the presiding Buddha image in the *bòht*.

Wat Pho is also the national headquarters for the teaching and preservation of traditional Thai medicine, including Thai massage, a mandate legislated by Rama III when the tradition was in danger of extinction. The famous massage school has two massage pavilions without air-con located within the temple area and air-con rooms within the training facility outside the temple (p140). Nearby stone inscriptions showing yoga and massage techniques still remain in the temple grounds, serving their original purpose as visual aids.

The rambling grounds of Wat Pho cover 8 hectares, with the major tourist sites occupying the northern side of Th Chetuphon and the monastic facilities found on the southern side.

Amulet Market
ตลาดพระเครื่องวัดมหาธาตุ

This equal parts bizarre and fascinating **market** (Map pp114-15; Th Maharat; ☺ 9am-5pm; river ferry Tha Chang) claims both the sidewalks along Th Maharat and Th Phra Chan, as well as a dense network of covered market stalls near Tha Phra Chan. The trade is based around small talismans carefully prized by collectors, monks, taxi drivers and people in dangerous professions. Potential buyers, often already sporting tens of amulets, can be seen bargaining and flipping through magazines dedicated to the amulets, some of which command astronomical prices.

Also along this strip are handsome shophouses overflowing with family-run herbalmedicine and traditional-massage shops, and additional street vendors selling used books, cassettes and, oddly enough, dentures.

TRAVELS OF THE EMERALD BUDDHA

The Emerald Buddha (Phra Kaew Morakot) holds a prominent position in Thai Buddhism in spite of its size (a mere 66cm) and original material (probably jasper quartz or nephrite jade rather than emerald). In fact, the Emerald Buddha was just another ordinary image, with no illustrious pedigree, until its monumental 'coming out' in 15th-century Chiang Rai. During a fall, the image revealed its luminescent interior, which had been covered with plaster (a common practice to safeguard valuable Buddhas from being stolen). After a few successful stints in various temples throughout northern Thailand, the image was stolen by Laotian invaders in the mid-16th century and remained in that country for 200 years.

In 1778 Thailand's King Taksin waged war against Laos, retrieving the image and mounting it in Thonburi. Later, when the capital moved to Bangkok and General Chakri took the crown, the Emerald Buddha was honoured with one of the country's most magnificent monuments, Wat Phra Kaew.

FARE OR UNFAIR?

If you can read Thai, you'll notice that the entrance fees to many state-run museums, temples, galleries and national parks are significantly cheaper for Thai nationals. Until recently, foreigners generally paid twice as much as the Thais; fair enough, we thought, considering that domestic tax baht fund such important institutions. However, in late 2008 fees were increased significantly, and now foreign visitors pay at least four times as much as domestic visitors. Although museum entrance fees are still generally less than those in the west, a fee of 100B or even 200B may cause some foreign visitors to think twice about visiting a small provincial museum or low-key national park.

On the bright side, if you're in Bangkok and want to visit the Royal Barge Museum, the National Gallery and the National Museum, there's a reduced-price entrance ticket that allows access to all three locales for only 350B (a savings of 150B). The 300B entrance fee for Wat Phra Kaew also allows access to the wide variety of attractions at Dusit Palace Park (p138).

National Museum
พิพิธภัณฑสถานแห่งชาติ

Often touted as Southeast Asia's biggest museum, the **National Museum** (Map pp114-15; ☎ 0 2224 1333; 4 Th Na Phra That; admission 200B; ⏰ 9am-3.30pm Wed-Sun; bus 503, 506, 507, 53, river ferry Tha Chang) is home to an impressive collection of religious sculpture, best appreciated on one the museum's twice weekly guided **tours** (⏰ 9.30am Wed & Thu, in English, German, Japanese & French).

Most of the museum's structures were built in 1782 as the palace of Rama I's viceroy, Prince Wang Na. Rama V turned it into a museum in 1874, and the current museum consists of three permanent exhibitions spread out over several buildings.

The **history wing** has made impressive bounds towards mainstream curatorial aesthetics with a succinct chronology of prehistoric, Sukhothai-, Ayuthaya- and Bangkok-era events and figures. Gems include King Ramakamhaeng's inscribed stone pillar, said to be the oldest record of Thai writing; King Taksin's throne; the Rama V section; and the screening of King Prajadhipok's movie *The Magic Ring*.

The **decorative arts and ethnology exhibit** covers every possible handicraft: traditional musical instruments, ceramics, clothing and textiles, woodcarving, regalia and weaponry. The **archaeology and art history wing** has exhibits ranging from prehistoric to the Bangkok period.

In addition to the main exhibition halls, the **Buddhaisawan (Phutthaisawan) Chapel** includes some well-preserved original murals and one of the country's most revered Buddha images, Phra Phut Sihing. Legend says the image came from Sri Lanka, but art historians attribute it to 13th-century Sukhothai.

Museum of Siam
สถาบันพิพิธภัณฑ์การเรียนรู้แห่งชาติ

This fun new **museum** (Map pp114-15; ☎ 0 2225 2777; Th Maharat; admission free; ⏰ 10am-6pm Tue-Sun; bus 508, 512, river ferry Tha Tien) employs a variety of media to explore the origins and culture of the Thai people. Housed in a Rama III–era palace, the exhibits are superinteractive, well balanced and entertaining; highlights include the informative and engaging narrated videos in each exhibition room, and an interactive Ayuthaya-era battle game. The buzz runs low on steam as you reach the latter exhibits, but it's still a worthwhile destination, particularly for those travelling with children.

Lak Meuang (City Pillar)
ศาลหลักเมือง

Serving as the spiritual keystone of Bangkok, **Lak Meuang** (Map pp114-15; cnr Th Ratchadamnoen Nai & Th Lak Meuang; admission free; ⏰ 6.30am-6.30pm; bus 506, 507, river ferry Tha Chang) is a phallus-shaped wooden pillar erected by Rama I during the founding of the new capital city in 1782. Today the structure shimmers with gold leaf and is housed in a white cruciform sanctuary. Part of an animistic tradition, the pillar embodies the city's guardian spirit (Phra Sayam Thewathirat) and also lends a practical purpose as a marker of the town's crossroads and measuring point for distances between towns.

The pillar was once one of a pair. Its taller counterpart, carved from *chai·yá·préuk* (tree of victory; laburnum wood), was cut down in effigy following the Burmese sacking of Ayuthaya during 1767. Through a series of Buddhist-animist rituals, it is believed that the felling of the tree empowered the Thais to defeat the Burmese in battle. Thus it was considered an especially talismanic choice to mark the founding of the new royal capital. Two metres of the pillar's 4.7m total length are buried in the ground.

If you're lucky, a *lá·kon gâa bon* (commissioned dance) may be in progress. Brilliantly costumed dancers measure out subtle movements as thanks to the guardian spirit for granting a worshipper's wish.

Sanam Luang
สนามหลวง

The royal district's green area is **Sanam Luang** (Royal Field; Map pp114-15; bordered by Th Na Phra That, Th Na Phra Lan, Th Ratchadamnoen Nai, Th Somdet Phra Pin Klao; admission free; 6am-8pm; bus 30, 32, 47, 53, river ferry Tha Chang), which introduces itself to most visitors as a dusty impediment to Wat Phra Kaew and other attractions. The park's more appealing attributes are expressed during its duties as a site for the annual Ploughing Ceremony, in which the king officially initiates the rice-growing season. A large kite competition is also held here during the kite-flying season (mid-February to April). Most recently, the park was the setting for the elaborate cremation ceremony of Princess Galayani Vadhana, the king's older sister. On a daily basis Sanam Luang is home to a large number of Bangkok's homeless population, as well as, at night, streetwalking prostitutes.

National Gallery
หอศิลปแห่งชาติ

The humble **National Gallery** (Map pp114-15; 0 2282 2639; Th Chao Fa; admission 200B; 9am-4pm Wed-Sun; river ferry Tha Phra Athit) belies the country's impressive tradition of fine arts. Decorating the walls of this early Ratanakosin-era building are works of contemporary art, mostly by artists who receive government support. The permanent exhibition is rather dated and dusty, but the temporary exhibitions, held in spacious halls out back, can be good.

BANGLAMPHU

Although slightly less grand than its neighbour, Banglamphu's sights are a window into the Bangkok of yesterday, a city that's largely starting to disappear.

TEMPLE MURALS

Because of the relative wealth of Bangkok, as well as its role as the country's artistic and cultural centre, the artists commissioned to paint the walls of the city's various temples were among the most talented around, and Bangkok's temple paintings are regarded as the finest in Thailand. Some particularly exceptional works:

- **Wat Bowonniwet** (p130) Painted by an artist called In Kong during the reign of Rama II, the murals in the panels of the *ubosot* (chapel) of this temple show Thai depictions of Western life (possibly copied from magazine illustrations) during the early 19th century.

- **Wat Chong Nonsi** (Map pp110-11; Th Nonsi, off Th Phra Ram III; 8am-6pm; access by taxi from Metro Khlong Toei) Dating back to the late Ayuthaya period, Bangkok's earliest surviving temple paintings are faded and missing in parts, but the depictions of everyday Thai life, including bawdy illustrations of a sexual manner, are well worth visiting.

- **Buddhaisawan (Phutthaisawan) Chapel** (opposite) Although construction of this temple located in the National Museum began in 1795, the paintings were probably finished during the reign of Rama III (1824–51). Among other scenes, the graceful murals depict the conception, birth and early life of the Buddha – common topics among Thai temple murals.

- **Wat Suthat** (p130) Almost as impressive in their vast scale as for their quality, the murals at Wat Suthat are among the most awe-inspiring in the country. Gory depictions of Buddhist hell can be found on a pillar directly behind the Buddha statue.

- **Wat Suwannaram** (Map pp110-11; 0 2434 7790; 33 Soi 32, Th Charoen Sanitwong, Khlong Bangkok Noi; 8am-6pm; Khlong taxi from Tha Chang) These paintings inside a late Ayuthaya-era temple in Thonburi contain skilled and vivid depictions of battle scenes and foreigners, including Chinese and Muslim warriors.

- **Wat Tritosathep Mahaworawihan** (Map pp114-15; Th Prachatipatai; bus 12, 19, 56) Although still a work in progress, Chakrabhand Posayakrit's postmodern murals at this temple in Banglamphu have already been recognised as masterworks of Thai Buddhist art.

BANGKOK

Wat Saket & Golden Mount

วัดสระเกศ/ภูเขาทอง

Even if you're wát-ed out, you should take a brisk walk to **Wat Saket** (Map pp114-15; ☎ 0 2223 4561; btwn Th Wora Chak & Th Boriphat; admission to Golden Mount 10B; ☉ 8am-5pm; bus 508, 511, klorng taxi to Tha Phan Fah). Like all worthy summits, the temple's Golden Mount (Phu Khao Thong), which is visible from Th Ratchadamnoen, plays a good game of optical illusion, appearing closer than its real location. Serpentine steps wind through an artificial hill shaded by gnarled trees, some of which are signed in English, and past graves and pictures of wealthy benefactors. At the peak, you'll find a breezy 360-degree view of Bangkok's most photogenic side.

This artificial hill was created when a large stupa, under construction by Rama III, collapsed because the soft soil beneath would not support it. The resulting mud-and-brick hill was left to sprout weeds until Rama IV built a small stupa on its crest. Rama V later added to the structure and housed a Buddha relic from India (given to him by the British government) in the stupa. The concrete walls were added during WWII to prevent the hill from eroding. Every year in November there is a big festival on the grounds of Wat Saket, which includes a candlelit procession up the Golden Mount.

If you're coming from the eastern end of the city, the Golden Mount is a short walk from the *klorng* boats' western terminus at Tha Phan Fah.

Wat Suthat & Sao Ching-Cha

วัดสุทัศน์/เสาชิงช้า

Brahmanism predated the arrival of Buddhism in Thailand and its rituals were eventually integrated into the dominant religion. This **temple** (Map pp114-15; ☎ 0 2224 9845; Th Bamrung Meuang; admission 20B; ☉ 9am-8pm; bus 508, klorng taxi to Tha Phan Fah) is the headquarters of the Brahman priests who perform the Royal Ploughing Ceremony in May. Begun by Rama I and completed in later reigns, Wat Suthat boasts a *wí·hǎhn* with gilded bronze Buddha images (including Phra Si Sakayamuni, one of the largest surviving Sukhothai bronzes) and incredibly expansive *jataka* (stories of the Buddha's previous lives) murals (see the boxed text, p129). The wát also holds the rank of Rachavoramahavihan, the highest royal-temple grade; the ashes of Rama VIII (Ananda Mahidol, the current king's deceased older brother) are contained in the base of the main Buddha image in the *wí·hǎhn*.

Wat Suthat's priests also perform rites at two nearby Hindu shrines: Thewa Sathaan (Deva Sathan), which contains images of Shiva and Ganesh; and the smaller Saan Jao Phitsanu (Vishnu Shrine), dedicated to Vishnu.

The spindly red arch in the front of the temple is **Sao Ching-Cha** (Giant Swing), as much a symbol of Bangkok as Wat Phra Kaew. The swing formerly hosted a spectacular Brahman festival in honour of Shiva, in which participants would swing in ever-higher arcs in an effort to reach a bag of gold suspended from a 15m bamboo pole. Many died trying and the ritual was discontinued during the reign of Rama VII. In 2007 the decaying swing was officially replaced with the current model, made from six specially chosen teak logs from Phrae Province in northern Thailand.

The temple is within walking distance of the *klorng* boats' terminus at Tha Phan Fah.

Other temples

Founded in 1826, **Wat Bowonniwet** (Map pp114-15; cnr Th Phra Sumen & Th Tanao; ☉ 8am-5.30pm; bus 15, 53, river ferry Tha Phra Athit) is the national headquarters for the Thammayut monastic sect. King Mongkut, founder of this minority sect, began a royal tradition by residing here as a monk – in fact, he was the abbot of Wat Bowonniwet for several years. King Bhumibol and Crown Prince Vajiralongkorn, as well as several other males in the royal family, have been temporarily ordained as monks. The *ubosot* (chapel) has some interesting wall murals (see the boxed text, p129) Because of the temple's royal status, visitors should be particularly careful to dress properly for admittance to this wát – no shorts or sleeveless shirts.

Across Th Mahachai from Wat Saket, **Wat Ratchanatdaram** (Map pp114-15; ☎ 0 2224 8807; cnr Th Ratchadamnoen Klang & Th Mahachai; ☉ 9am-5pm; bus 56, 505, klorng taxi to Tha Phan Fah) dates from the mid-19th century and today is home to a well-known market selling Buddhist *prá pim* (magical charm amulets) in all sizes, shapes and styles. The amulets not only feature images of the Buddha, but also famous Thai monks and Indian deities. Buddha images are also for sale.

Th Bamrung Meuang

ถนนบำรุงเมือง

One of the city's earliest thoroughfares (the street was originally an elephant path leading to the royal palace), today the stretches of **Th Bamrung Meuang** (Map pp114-15; bus 508, klorng taxi to Tha

Phan Fah) that extend directly west and east of Wat Suthat form an open-air shopping centre for all manner of religious paraphernalia. In the shops, the contents of which pour out onto the street, you'll see care packages that are typically bought and donated to temples, models of famous monks, monk robes and other devotional items. The large Buddha statues that are wrapped in plastic are particularly photogenic.

Ban Baht (Monk's Bowl Village)
บ้านบาตร

Just when you start to lament the adverse effects of tourism, pay a visit to this **handicraft village** (Map pp114–15; Soi Ban Baht, Th Bamrung Meuang; 10am–6pm; bus 508, klorng taxi to Tha Phan Fah). This is the only surviving village established by Rama I to make the *bàht* (rounded bowls) that the monks carry to receive food alms from faithful Buddhists every morning. Today the average monk relies on a bowl mass-produced in China, but the traditional technique survives in Ban Baht thanks to patronage by tourists.

About half a dozen families still hammer the bowls together from eight separate pieces of steel representing, they say, the eight spokes of the Wheel of Dharma (which symbolise Buddhism's Eightfold Path). The joints are fused in a wood fire with bits of copper, and the bowl is polished and coated with several layers of black lacquer. A typical output is one bowl per day. If you purchase a bowl, the craftsperson will show you the equipment and process used.

Democracy Monument
อนุสาวรีย์ประชาธิปไตย

One of the first striking landmarks you'll notice on your way into Banglamphu is this large Art Deco **monument** (Map pp114–15; Th Ratchadamnoen Klang, Th Din So; bus 44, 511, 512, river ferry Tha Phra Athit) occupying the avenue's traffic circle. It was erected in 1932 to commemorate Thailand's momentous transformation from absolute to constitutional monarchy. Italian artist Corrado Feroci designed the monument and buried 75 cannon balls in its base to signify the year Buddhist Era (BE) 2475 (AD 1932). Before immigrating to Thailand to become the nation's 'father of modern art', Feroci designed monuments for Italian dictator Benito Mussolini. In recent years the monument has become a symbolic spot for public demonstrations, most notably during the antimilitary, prodemocratic protests of 1992.

October 14 Memorial
อนุสาวรีย์ 14 ตุลาคม

This peaceful **amphitheatre** (Map pp114–15; Khok Wua intersection, Th Ratchadamnoen Klang; bus 2, 82, 511, 512) commemorates the civilian demonstrators who were killed on 14 October 1973 (remembered in Thai as *sìp-sèe dù·lah*, the date of the event) by the military during a prodemocracy rally. More than 200,000 people assembled at the Democracy Monument and along Th Ratchadamnoen to protest the arrest of political campaigners and to express their discontent over the continued military dictatorship; more than 70 demonstrators were killed when the tanks met the crowd. The complex is an interesting adaptation of Thai temple architecture for a secular and political purpose. A central *chedi* (stupa) is dedicated to the fallen, and a gallery of historic photographs lines the interior walls.

THONBURI

It's calm enough on the right bank of the Mae Nam Chao Phraya to seem like another province – because it is! The attractions here are relatively few, but *Fàng ton* is a great area for aimless wandering among leafy streets.

Wat Arun
วัดอรุณฯ

Striking **Wat Arun** (Map pp114–15; ☎ 0 2891 1149; Th Arun Amarin; admission 50B; 9am–5pm; river ferry Tha Thai Wang) commands a martial pose as the third point in the holy trinity (along with Wat Phra Kaew and Wat Pho) of Bangkok's early history. After the fall of Ayuthaya, King Taksin ceremoniously clinched control here on the site of a local shrine (formerly known as Wat Jaeng) and established a royal palace and a temple to house the Emerald Buddha. The temple was renamed after the Indian god of dawn (Aruna) and in honour of the literal and symbolic founding of a new Ayuthaya.

It wasn't until the capital and the Emerald Buddha were moved to Bangkok that Wat Arun received its most prominent characteristic: the 82m-high *prang* (Khmer-style tower). The tower's construction was started during the first half of the 19th century by Rama II and later completed by Rama III. Not apparent from a distance are the ornate floral mosaics made from broken, multi-hued Chinese porcelain, a common temple ornamentation in the early Ratanakosin period, when Chinese ships calling at the port of Bangkok used tonnes of old porcelain as ballast.

Also worth an inspection is the interior of the *bòht*. The main Buddha image is said to have been designed by Rama II himself. The murals date from the reign of Rama V; particularly impressive is one that depicts Prince Siddhartha encountering examples of birth, old age, sickness and death outside his palace walls, an experience that led him to abandon the worldly life. The ashes of Rama II are interred in the base of the presiding Buddha image.

Cross-river ferries run over to Wat Arun every few minutes (3B per person) from Tha Tien to Tha Thai Wang.

Sunset views of the temple compound can be caught from across the river at Tha Maharat or from the riverfront warehouses that line the street of the same name. Another great viewpoint is from the elevated patio restaurant at the Deck (p162).

Royal Barges National Museum
พิพิธภัณฑ์เรือพระที่นั่ง

The royal barges are slender, fantastically ornamented vessels used in ceremonial processions along the river. The tradition dates back to the Ayuthaya era, when most travel (for commoners and royalty) was by boat. Today the royal barge procession is an infrequent occurrence, most recently performed in 2006 in honour of the 60th anniversary of the king's ascension to the throne. When not in use, the barges are on display at this Thonburi **museum** (Map pp114-15; ☎ 0 2424 0004; Khlong Bangkok Noi; admission 100B, photo permit 100B; ۞ 9am-5pm; river ferry Tha Saphan Phra Pin Klao).

Suphannahong, the king's personal barge, is the most important of the boats. Made from a single piece of timber, it's the largest dugout in the world. The name means 'Golden Swan', and a huge swan head has been carved into the bow. Lesser barges feature bows that are carved into other Hindu-Buddhist mythological shapes such as *naga* (mythical sea serpent) and *garuda* (Vishnu's bird mount). Historic photos help envision the grand processions in which the largest of the barges would require a rowing crew of 50 men, plus seven umbrella bearers, two helmsmen and two navigators, as well as a flagman, rhythm-keeper and chanter.

The most convenient way to get to the museum is by taking a taxi (ask the driver to go to *reu-a prá têe nâng*) from Tha Saphan Phra Pin Klao. Another alternative is walking from the Bangkok Noi train station (accessible by ferrying to Tha Rot Fai), but the walk is tricky and unpleasant and you'll encounter uninvited guides who will charge for their services. The museum is also an optional stop on long-tail boat trips through Thonburi's canals.

OFFBEAT BANGKOK MUSEUMS

If looking at stuffed tigers and Buddha statues is not doing it for you, then consider a visit to one of these quirky institutions.

▪ **Ancient City** (Muang Boran; Map p189; ☎ 0 2709 1644; www.ancientcity.com; 296/1 Th Sukhumvit, Samut Prakan; adult/child 300/150B; ۞ 8am-5pm) Claiming to be the largest open-air museum in the world, the site covers more than 80 hectares of peaceful countryside littered with 109 scaled-down facsimiles of many of the kingdom's most famous monuments. It's an excellent place to explore by bicycle (daily rental 50B), as it is usually quiet and never crowded. Ancient City lies outside Samut Prakan, which is accessible via air-con bus 511 from the east end of Th Sukhumvit. Upon reaching the bus terminal at Pak Nam, board minibus 36, which passes the entrance to Ancient City.

▪ **Bangkok Folk Museum** (Map pp118-19; ☎ 0 2233 7027; 273 Soi Saphan Yao/43, Th Charoen Krung; admission free; ۞ 10am-4pm Wed-Sun; river ferry Tha Si Phraya) Consisting of three wooden houses, this family-run museum is a window into Bangkok life during the 1950s and '60s. Particularly interesting is the traditional Thai kitchen.

▪ **Corrections Museum** (Map pp114-15; ☎ 0 2226 1706; 436 Th Mahachai; admission free; ۞ 9.30am-4pm Mon-Fri; bus 508, klorng taxi to Tha Phan Fah) Learn about the painful world of Thai-style punishment at what's left of this former jail. Life-sized models re-enact a variety of horrendous executions and punishments, encouraging most visitors to remain law-abiding citizens for the remainder of their stay.

■ **Erawan Museum** (Map pp110-11; ☎ 0 2371 3135; www.erawan-museum.com; Soi 119, Th Sukhumvit; adult/child 150/50B; ☉ 8am-5pm) The centrepiece here is a five-storey sculpture of Erawan, Indra's three-headed elephant mount from Hindu mythology, built by the same benefactor and cultural preserver who built the Ancient City (opposite). Inside the building is a collection of sacred antiques. The museum is 8km from Bangkok's Ekamai bus station and any Samut Prakan–bound bus can drop you off; just tell the driver your destination (Chang Sam Sian).

■ **Museum of Counterfeit Goods** (Map pp110-11; ☎ 0 2653 5555; www.tillekeandgibbins.com/museum /museum.htm; Tilleke & Gibbins, Supalai Grand Tower, 1011 Th Phra Ram III; admission free; ☉ 8am-5pm Mon-Fri by appointment only; access by taxi from Metro Khlong Toei) This private collection displays all the counterfeit booty that has been collected by the law firm Tilleke and Gibbins over the years. Many of the fake items are displayed alongside the genuine ones. Visits by appointment only.

■ **Songkran Niyosane Forensic Medicine Museum & Parasite Museum** (Map pp114-15; ☎ 0 2419 7000; 2nd fl, Forensic Pathology Bldg, Siriraj Hospital, Th Phrannok, Thonburi; admission 40B; ☉ 8.30am-4.30pm Mon-Fri; river ferry Tha Wang Lang) This gory institution contains the various appendages and remnants of famous murders, including the bloodied T-shirt from a victim who was stabbed to death with a dildo. The adjacent Parasite Museum is also worth a visit, much for the same reasons as above. The easiest way to reach the museum is by taking the river-crossing ferry from Tha Chang or Tha Phra Chan. At the exit of the pier, turn right to enter Siriraj Hospital, and follow the signs to the museum.

■ **Thai Human Imagery Museum** (Map p189; ☎ 0 3433 2607; Nakhon Pathom; admission 250B; ☉ 9am-5.30pm Mon-Fri, 8.30am-6pm Sat & Sun) Contains an exhibition of 120 lifelike fibreglass sculptures. A group of Thai artists reportedly spent 10 years studying their subjects and creating the figures, which range from famous Buddhist monks of Thailand to Winston Churchill. The museum is outside town at the Km31 marker on Th Pinklao-Nakhon Chaisi. Any Nakhon Pathom–Bangkok or Salaya bus can drop you off here.

Church of Santa Cruz
โบสถ์ซางตาครู้ส

Dating back to 1913, this Catholic **church** (Map pp116-17; ☎ 0 2466 0347; Th Kuti Jiin; ☉ Sat & Sun; cross-river ferry from Tha Pak Talat/Atsadang) holds relatively little interest unless you visit on a Sunday. But the surrounding neighbourhood, a former Portuguese concession dating back to the Ayuthaya period, is worth a wander for its old-school riverside atmosphere and Portuguese-inspired cakes, *kà·nŏm fa·ràng*.

Chinatown & Phahurat
เยาวราช(สำเพ็ง)/พาหุรัด

Bangkok's Chinatown (called Yaowarat after its main thoroughfare, Th Yaowarat) is the urban explorer's equivalent of the Amazon Basin. Unlike neighbouring Ko Ratanakosin and Banglamphu, the highlights here aren't tidy temples or museums, but rather a complicated web of tiny alleyways, crowded markets and delicious street stalls. And unlike other Chinatowns around the world, Bangkok's is defiantly ungentrified, and getting lost in it is probably the best thing that could happen to you. However, if you do need a guide, you can always refer to our walking tour of the area (see p143).

The neighbourhood dates back to 1782 when Bangkok's Chinese population, many of them labourers hired to build the new capital, were moved here from today's Ko Ratanakosin area by the royal government. Relatively little has changed since then, and you can still catch conversations in various Chinese dialects, buy Chinese herbal cures or taste Chinese dishes not available elsewhere in Thailand. For those specifically interested in the latter, be sure to check out our food-based walking tour of the district (p164).

Getting in and out of Chinatown is hindered by horrendous traffic, and the Chao Phraya Express stop at Ratchawong was previously the easiest way to reach the district. However, the advent of the Metro has put the area a brief walk from Hualamphong station.

At the western edge of Chinatown is a small but thriving Indian district, generally called Phahurat. Here, dozens of Indian-owned shops sell all kinds of fabric and clothes.

BANGKOK

THE CHINESE INFLUENCE

In many ways Bangkok is as much a Chinese city as it is Thai. The presence of the Chinese in Bangkok dates back to before the founding of the city, when Thonburi Si Mahasamut was little more than a Chinese trading outpost on the Chao Phraya River. In the 1780s, during the construction of the new capital under Rama I, Hokkien, Teochiew and Hakka Chinese were hired as coolies and labourers. The Chinese already living in the area were relocated to the districts of Yaowarat and Sampeng, today known as Bangkok's Chinatown.

During the reign of King Rama I, many Chinese began to move up in status and wealth. They controlled many of Bangkok's shops and businesses, and because of increased trading ties with China, were responsible for an immense expansion in Thailand's market economy. Visiting Europeans during the 1820s were astonished by the number of Chinese trading ships in the Chao Phraya River, and some assumed that the Chinese formed the majority of Bangkok's population.

The newfound wealth of certain Chinese trading families created one of Thailand's first elite classes that was not directly related to royalty. Known as *jòw sŏo·a*, these 'merchant lords' eventually obtained additional status by accepting official posts and royal titles, as well as offering their daughters to the royal family. Today it is thought that more than half of the people in Bangkok can claim some Chinese ancestry.

During the reign of King Rama III, the Thai capital began to absorb many elements of Chinese food, design, fashion and literature. The growing ubiquity of Chinese culture, coupled with the tendency of the Chinese men to marry Thai women and assimilate into Thai culture, meant that by the beginning of the 20th century there was relatively little that distinguished many Chinese from their Siamese counterparts.

TALAT MAI
ตลาดใหม่

With nearly two centuries of commerce under its belt, 'New Market' is no longer an entirely accurate name for this **market** (Map pp116-17; Trok Itsaranuphap/Soi 16; river ferry Tha Ratchawong, Metro Hualamphong). Essentially it's a narrow covered alleyway between tall buildings, but even if you're not interested in food the hectic atmosphere and exotic sights and smells culminate in something of a surreal sensory experience. Be sure to get there early, ideally before 8am, and always keep an eye open for the motorcycles that are constantly squeezing through the crowds.

While much of the market centres on cooking ingredients, the section north of Th Charoen Krung (equivalent to Soi 21, Th Charoen Krung) is known for selling incense, paper effigies and ceremonial sweets – the essential elements of a traditional Chinese funeral.

WAT MANGKON KAMALAWAT
วัดมังกรกมลาวาส

Clouds of incense and the sounds of chanting form the backdrop at this Chinese-style Mahayana Buddhist **temple** (Neng Noi Yee; Map pp116-17; Th Charoen Krung; 9am-6pm; Metro Hualamphong, bus 73, 501, 507, river ferry Tha Ratchawong).

Dating back to 1871, it's the largest and most important religious structure in the area, and during the annual Vegetarian Festival (see the boxed text, p163), religious and culinary activities are particularly active here.

WAT TRAIMIT
วัดไตรมิตร

The attraction at **Wat Traimit** (Temple of the Golden Buddha; Map pp116-17; ☎ 0 2225 9775; cnr Th Yaowarat & Th Charoen Krung; admission 20B; 9am-5pm; Metro Hualamphong, bus 53) is undoubtedly the impressive 3m-tall, 5.5-tonne, solid-gold Buddha image, which gleams like, well, gold. Sculpted in the graceful Sukhothai style, the image was 'discovered' some 40 years ago beneath a stucco or plaster exterior, when it fell from a crane while being moved to a new building within the temple compound. It has been theorised that the covering was added to protect it from marauding hordes, either during the late Sukhothai period or later in the Ayuthaya period when the city was under siege by the Burmese. The temple itself is said to date from the early 13th century.

Donations and a constant flow of tourists have proven profitable, and the temple is currently building an immense golden stupa that, when finished, will tower over Chinatown.

TALAT NOI
ตลาดน้อย
Bordered by the river, Th Songwat, Th Charoen Krung and Th Yotha, this ancient neighbourhood is a fascinating jumble of tiny alleys, greasy machine shops and traditional architecture. Located opposite the River View Guest House (p152), **San Jao Sien Khong** (Map pp116-17; admission by donation; ☾ 6am-6pm; river ferry Tha Krom Chao Tha) is one of the city's oldest Chinese shrines, and also one of the best areas to be during the annual Vegtarian Festival (see the boxed text, p163).

PHAHURAT MARKET
ตลาดพาหุรัด
Hidden behind the new and astonishingly out of place India Emporium mall is **Phahurat Market** (Map pp116-17; Th Phahurat & Th Chakraphet; bus 73, river ferry Tha Saphan Phut), an endless bazaar uniting flamboyant Bollywood fabric, photogenic vendors selling *paan* (betel nut for chewing) and several shops stocked with delicious northern Indian–style sweets.

In an alley off Th Chakraphet is **Sri Gurusingh Sabha** (Map pp116-17; Th Phahurat; ☾ 9am-5pm; bus 53, 73, river ferry Tha Saphan Phut), a large Sikh temple reminiscent of a mosque interior, devoted to the worship of the *Guru Granth Sahib*, the 16th-century Sikh holy book, which is itself considered to be a 'living' guru and the last of the religion's 10 great teachers. Reportedly, the temple is the second-largest Sikh temple outside India. Visitors are welcome, but they must remove their shoes.

Silom, Sathon & Riverside
สีลม/สาธร/ริมแม่น้ำเจ้าพระยา
The business district of Th Silom has only a handful of tourist attractions scattered among the corporate hotels, office towers and wining-and-dining restaurants. As you get closer to the river, the area becomes spiced with the sights and smells of its Indian and Muslim residents. Moving north along Th Charoen Krung, the area adjacent to the river was the international mercantile district during Bangkok's shipping heyday. The odd crumbling Victorian building and several of Bangkok's luxury hotels now occupy this neighbourhood of tributary sois.

Traffic is notorious in this part of town, but the Skytrain, subway and Chao Phraya Express provide some transport relief.

SRI MAHARIAMMAN TEMPLE
วัดพระศรีมหาอุมาเทวี(วัดแขกสีลม)
Standing out, even among Bangkok's golden *wát*, this **Hindu temple** (Wat Phra Si Maha Umathewi; Map pp118-19; cnr Th Silom & Th Pan; donations accepted; ☾ 6am-8pm; Skytrain Surasak) virtually leaps off the block. Built in the 1860s by Tamil immigrants in the centre of a still thriving ethnic enclave, the structure is a stacked facade of intertwined, full-colour Hindu deities. In the centre of the main shrine is Jao Mae Maha Umathewi (Uma Devi, also known as Shakti, Shiva's consort); her son Phra Khanthakuman (Subramaniam) is on the right; and on the left is her other son, elephant-headed Phra Phikkhanet (Ganesh). Along the left interior wall sit rows of Shiva, Vishnu and other Hindu deities, as well as a few Buddhas, so that just about any non-Muslim, non-Judaeo-Christian Asian can worship here.

Thais call this temple Wat Khaek – *kàak* is a colloquial expression for people of Indian descent. The literal translation is 'guest', an obvious euphemism for a group of people you don't particularly want as permanent residents; hence most Indians living permanently in Thailand don't appreciate the term.

M R KUKRIT PRAMOJ HOUSE
บ้านหม่อมราชวงศ์คึกฤทธิ์ปราโมช
Author and statesman Mom Ratchawong (M R, an honorary royal title) Kukrit Pramoj once resided in this charming Thai house, now open to the public as a **museum** (Map pp118-19; ☎ 0 2286 8185; Soi Phra Phinij/7, Th Narathiwat Rachananakharin; admission 50B; ☾ 10am-5pm Sat & Sun; Skytrain Chong Nonsi). European-educated but devoutly Thai, M R Kukrit surrounded himself with the best of both worlds: five traditional teak buildings, Thai art, Western books and lots of heady conversations. A guided tour is recommended for a more intimate introduction to the former resident, who authored more than 150 books and served as prime minister of Thailand.

QUEEN SAOVABHA MEMORIAL INSTITUTE (SNAKE FARM)
สถานเสาวภา(สวนงู)
Snake farms tend to gravitate towards carnivalesque rather than humanitarian, except at the **Queen Saovabha Memorial Institute** (Map pp118-19; ☎ 0 2252 0161; cnr Th Phra Ram IV & Th Henri Dunant; adult/child 200/50B; ☾ 9.30am-3.30pm Mon-Fri, to 1pm Sat & Sun; Skytrain Sala Daeng, Metro Silom). Founded in 1923, the snake farm prepares antivenin from venomous snakes – common cobra, king cobra, banded

krait, Malayan pit viper, green pit viper and Russell's viper. This is done by milking the snakes' venom, injecting it into horses, and harvesting and purifying the antivenom that they produce. The antivenoms are then used to treat human victims of snake bites.

The leafy grounds are home to a few caged snakes (and a constant soundtrack of Western rock music), but the bulk of the attractions are found in the Simaseng Building, at the rear of the compound. The ground floor houses several varieties of snakes in glass cages. Daily **milkings** (11am) and **snake-handling performances** (2.30pm Mon-Fri) are held on the 2nd floor.

Siam Square & Pratunam
สยามสแควร์/ประตูน้ำ

Commerce, mainly in the form of multistorey mega-malls, forms the main attraction in this part of town, but there are a couple of sights that don't involve credit cards. Skytrain and the *klorng* taxis provide easy access to most attractions here.

JIM THOMPSON'S HOUSE
บ้านจิมทอมป์สัน

Jim Thompson's House (Map pp120-1; ☎ 0 2216 7368; www.jimthompsonhouse.com; 6 Soi Kasem San 2; adult/child 100/50B; 9am-5pm, compulsory tours in English & French every 10min; Skytrain National Stadium, bus 73, 508, klorng taxi to Tha Ratchathewi) is an unlikely but stunning outpost of Thai architecture and Southeast Asian art.

The leafy compound is the former home of the eponymous American silk entrepreneur and art collector. Born in Delaware in 1906, Thompson briefly served in the Office of Strategic Services (forerunner of the CIA) in Thailand during WWII. Settling in Bangkok after the war, his neighbours' handmade silk caught his eye and piqued his business sense; he sent samples to fashion houses in Milan, London and Paris, gradually building a steady worldwide clientele.

In addition to exquisite Asian art, Thompson also collected parts of various derelict Thai homes in central Thailand and had them reassembled in their current location in 1959. One striking departure from tradition is the way each wall has its exterior side facing the house's interior, thus exposing the wall's bracing system. His small but splendid Asian art collection and his personal belongings are also on display in the main house.

Thompson's story doesn't end with his informal reign as Bangkok's best-adapted foreigner. While out for an afternoon walk in the Cameron Highlands of western Malaysia in 1967, Thompson mysteriously disappeared. That same year his sister was murdered in the USA, fuelling various conspiracy theories. Was it communist spies? Business rivals? Or a man-eating tiger? The most recent theory – for which there is apparently some hard evidence – has it that the silk magnate was accidentally run over by a Malaysian truck driver who hid his remains. *Jim Thompson: The Unsolved Mystery,* by William Warren, is an excellent book on Thompson, his career, residence and subsequent intriguing disappearance.

BAAN KRUA
บ้านครัว

This atmospheric community between Khlong Saen Saep, Th Phayathai and Th Phra Ram I is one of Bangkok's oldest Muslim neighbourhoods, and its skilled silk weavers allegedly inspired Jim Thompson to start selling the stuff abroad (see left). Today production has largely moved elsewhere, but the area retains its Muslim character, and at least one of the original family outfits, **Phamai Baan Krua** (☎ 0 2215 7458; Klorng taxi to Tha Hua Chang), is still weaving silk on old teak looms.

ERAWAN SHRINE
ศาลพระพรหม

A seamless merging of commerce and religion occurs at all hours of the day at this bustling **shrine** (San Phra Phrom; Map pp120-1; cnr Th Ratchadamri & Th Ploenchit; admission free; 8am-7pm; Skytrain Chitlom). Claiming a spare corner of the Grand Hyatt Erawan hotel, the four-headed deity Brahma (Phra Phrom) represents the Hindu god of creation and was originally built to ward off bad luck during the construction of the first Erawan Hotel (see the boxed text, opposite). The shrine was later adopted by the lay community as it gained a reputation for granting wishes.

LINGAM SHRINE AT NAI LERT PARK
Clusters of carved stone and wooden phalli surround a spirit house and **shrine** (Saan Jao Mae Thap Thim; Map pp120-1; Nai Lert Park Hotel, Th Withayu/ Wireless Rd; Skytrain Ploenchit, klorng taxi to Tha Withayu) built by millionaire businessman Nai Lert to honour Jao Mae Thap Thim, a female deity thought to reside in the old banyan tree on the site. Someone who made an offering shortly thereafter had a baby, and the shrine has received a steady stream of worshippers –

AN ELEPHANT'S MEMORY

One of the more clichéd tourist images of Bangkok is that of elaborately dressed classical Thai dancers performing at the Hindu shrine in front of the Grand Hyatt Erawan hotel. As with many things in Thailand, there is great deal hidden behind the serene facade.

The shrine was originally built in 1956 as something of a last-ditch effort to end a string of misfortunes that occurred during the construction of the hotel, at that time known as the Erawan Hotel. After several incidents ranging from injured construction workers to the sinking of ship carrying marble for the hotel, a Brahmin priest was consulted. Since the hotel was to be named after the elephant escort of Indra in Hindu mythology, the priest determined that Erawan required a passenger, and suggested it be that of Lord Brahma. A statue was built, and lo and behold, the misfortunes miraculously ended.

Although the original Erawan Hotel was demolished in 1987, the shrine still exists, and today remains an important place of pilgrimage for Thais, particularly those in need of some material assistance. Those making a wish from the statue should ideally come between 7am and 8am, or 7pm and 8pm, and should offer a specific list of items that includes candles, incense, sugar cane or bananas, all of which are almost exclusively given in multiples of seven. Particularly popular are teak elephants, the money gained through the purchase of which is donated to a charity run by the current hotel, the Grand Hyatt Erawan. And as the tourist brochures depict, it is also possible to charter a classical Thai dance, often done as a way of giving thanks if a wish was granted.

After 40 years of largely benign existence, the Erawan shrine became a point of focus when just after midnight on 21 March 2006, 27-year-old Thanakorn Pakdeepol destroyed the gilded plaster image of Brahma with a hammer. Pakdeepol, who had a history of mental illness and depression, was almost immediately attacked and beaten to death by two Thai rubbish collectors in the vicinity.

Although the government ordered a swift restoration of the statue, the incident became a galvanising omen for the anti-Thaksin movement, which was in full swing at the time. At a political rally the following day, protest leader Sondhi Limthongkul suggested that the prime minister had masterminded the Brahma image's destruction in order to replace the deity with a 'dark force' allied to Thaksin. Rumours spreading through the capital claimed that Thaksin had hired Cambodian shamans to put spells on Pakdeepol so that he would perform the unspeakable deed. In response, Pakdeepol's father was quoted as saying that Sondhi was 'the biggest liar I have ever seen'. Thaksin, when asked to comment on Sondhi's accusations, simply replied: 'That's insane'. A new statue, built using bits of the previous one, was installed a month later, and at press time Thaksin is in exile and has yet to return to Thailand.

mostly young women seeking fertility – ever since. To get here if facing the entrance of the hotel, follow the small concrete pathway to the right which winds down into the bowels of the building beside the car park. The shrine is at the end of the building next to the canal.

Sukhumvit
สุขุมวิท

More time will be spent here eating, drinking and perhaps sleeping (as there is a high concentration of hotels here) rather than sightseeing. The Skytrain is the primary public-transport option.

BAN KAMTHIENG
บ้านคำเที่ยง

An engaging **house museum** (Map pp122-3; ☎ 0 2661 6470; Siam Society, 131 Soi Asoke/21, Th Sukhumvit; adult/child 100/50B; ☻ 9am-5pm Mon-Sat; Skytrain Asoke; Metro Sukhumvit), Ban Kamthieng transports visitors to a northern Thai village complete with informative displays of daily rituals, folk beliefs and everyday household chores, all within the setting of a traditional wooden house. This museum is operated by and shares space with the Siam Society, the publisher of the renowned *Journal of the Siam Society* and a valiant preserver of traditional Thai culture.

KHLONG TOEY MARKET

This wholesale **market** (Map pp122-3; cnr Th Ratchadaphisek & Th Phra Ram IV; ☻ 5-10am; Metro Khlong Toei), one of the city's largest, is inevitably the origin of many of the meals you'll eat during your stay in Bangkok. Get there early, and although some corners of the market can't exactly be described as photogenic, be sure to bring a camera to capture the stacks of durians or cheery fishmongers.

BANGKOK

THAILAND CREATIVE & DESIGN CENTER

Modern design is all the rage in Bangkok and this new **museum** (TCDC; Map pp122-3; ☎ 0 2664 8448; www.tcdc.or.th; 6th fl, Emporium Shopping Centre; Th Sukhumvit; admission free; ⏰ 10.30am-10pm Tue-Sun; Skytrain Phrom Phong) hosts rotating exhibits, houses a cool shop and cafe, and for members has a design library stocked with books, computers and other resources.

Lumphini Park & Th Phra Ram IV
สวนลุมพินี/ถนนพระราม4

The main attraction in this hyper-urban part of town is the city's single largest green zone. The Metro, with stops at Lumphini, Silom and Th Phra Ram IV, is the best way to reach this area.

LUMPHINI PARK
สวนลุมพินี

Named after the Buddha's place of birth in Nepal, **Lumphini Park** (Map p124; Th Phra Ram IV, btwn Th Withayu/Wireless Rd & Th Ratchadamri; admission free; ⏰ 5am-8pm; bus 13, 505, Skytrain Sala Daeng, Metro Lumphini) is the best way to escape Bangkok without leaving town. Shady paths, a large artificial lake and swept lawns temporarily blot out the roaring traffic and hulking concrete towers.

One of the best times to visit the park is before 7am when the air is fresh (well, relatively so for Bangkok) and legions of Thai-Chinese are practising *taijiquan* (t'ai chi). The park reawakens with the evening's cooler temperatures – aerobics classes collectively sweat to a techno soundtrack. Late at night the borders of the park are frequented by streetwalking prostitutes, both male and female.

Central Bangkok
ใจกลางกรุงเทพฯ

Central Bangkok covers a lot of land, but a minimum of visit-worthy sites. The most worthwhile area is Dusit, the royal district of wide streets, monuments and greenery.

WANG SUAN PHAKKAT
วังสวนผักกาด

An overlooked treasure, **Lettuce Farm Palace** (Map pp112-3; ☎ 0 2245 4934; Th Sri Ayuthaya; admission 100B; ⏰ 9am-4pm; Skytrain Phayathai) near Th Ratchaprarop is a collection of five traditional wooden Thai houses that was once the residence of Princess Chumbon of Nakhon Sawan and before that a lettuce farm – hence the name. Within the stilt buildings are displays of art, antiques and

furnishings, and the landscaped grounds are a peaceful oasis complete with ducks, swans and a semi-enclosed garden.

The diminutive **Lacquer Pavilion**, at the back of the complex, dates from the Ayuthaya period and features gold-leaf *jataka* and *Ramayana* murals, as well as scenes from daily Ayuthaya life. The building originally sat in a monastery compound on Mae Nam Chao Phraya, just south of Ayuthaya. Larger residential structures at the front of the complex contain displays of Khmer-style Hindu and Buddhist art, Ban Chiang ceramics and a very interesting collection of historic Buddhas, including a beautiful late U Thong–style image.

WAT BENCHAMABOPHIT
วัดเบญจมบพิตร (วัดเบญฯ)

You might recognise this **temple** (Marble Temple; Map pp112-13; cnr Th Si Ayuthaya & Th Phra Ram V; admission 20B; ⏰ 8am-5.30pm; bus 72, 503) from the back of the 5B coin. Made of white Carrara marble, Wat Ben, as it's colloquially known, was built in the late 19th century under Rama V. The large cruciform *bòht* is a prime example of modern Thai *wát* architecture. The base of the central Buddha image, a copy of Phitsanulok's Phra Phuttha Chinnarat, contains the ashes of Rama V. The courtyard behind the *bòht* exhibits 53 Buddha images (33 originals and 20 copies) representing famous figures and styles from all over Thailand and other Buddhist countries.

DUSIT PALACE PARK
วังสวนดุสิต

Following Rama V's first European tour in 1897 (he was the first Thai monarch to visit the continent), he returned home with visions of European castles swimming in his head and set about transforming these styles into a uniquely Thai expression, today's **Dusit Palace Park** (Map pp112-13; ☎ 0 2628 6300; bounded by Th Ratchawithi, Th U-Thong Nai & Th Ratchasima; adult/child 100/50B or free with Grand Palace ticket; ⏰ 9.30am-4pm; bus 70, 510). The royal palace, throne hall and minor palaces for extended family were all moved here from Ko Ratanakosin, the ancient royal court. Today the current King has yet another home and this complex now holds a house museum and other cultural collections.

Originally constructed on Ko Si Chang in 1868 and moved to the present site in 1910, **Vimanmaek Teak Mansion** contains 81 rooms, halls and anterooms, and is said to be the world's largest golden-teak building, appar-

NEWLEY PURNELL & KHUN JU

An interview with a student of Thai language and a Thai language tutor.

Is it really necessary to be able to speak Thai while in Bangkok? Newley: You can certainly get by without it. But I think it's important to make an effort to learn the local language – it's a sign of respect.

What kind of mistakes do foreigners commonly make when speaking Thai? Khun Ju: A lot of foreigners cannot pronounce the 'ng' and 'ɖ' sounds at the beginning of words, and speak Thai in the wrong tones.

Newley, have you got the tone thing down? I'm getting there! It comes naturally over time, the more you practice words, but it's difficult, to be sure.

Other than pronunciation, what's the hardest thing about learning a language like Thai? Newley: The lack of cognates. This doesn't happen in Thai, of course. So memorising new words can take time.

Which language is harder, Thai or English? Khun Ju: Thai language is harder because of the tones. In Thai, the same word pronounced in different tones can have different meanings.

Newley: Thai grammar is very simple. Verbs aren't conjugated, for example, which makes things a bit easier than learning English.

---

ently built without the use of a single nail. The mansion was the first permanent building on the Dusit Palace grounds, and served as Rama V's residence in the early 1900s. The interior of the mansion contains various personal effects of the king and a treasure trove of early Ratanakosin art objects and antiques. Compulsory tours (in English) leave every half-hour between 9.30am and 3pm, and last about an hour. Free performances of Thai classical dances are staged in a pavilion on the side of the mansion at 10am and 2pm.

The nearby **Ancient Cloth Museum** presents a beautiful collection of traditional silks and cottons that make up the royal cloth collection.

Originally built as a throne hall for Rama V in 1904, the smaller **Abhisek Dusit Throne Hall** is typical of the finer architecture of the era. Victorian-influenced gingerbread architecture and Moorish porticoes blend to create a striking and distinctly Thai exterior. The hall houses an excellent display of regional handiwork crafted by members of the Promotion of Supplementary Occupations & Related Techniques (SUPPORT) foundation, an organisation sponsored by Queen Sirikit.

Near the Th U-Thong Nai entrance, two large stables that once housed three white elephants – animals whose auspicious albinism automatically make them crown property – are now the **Royal Elephant Museum**. One of the structures contains artefacts and photos outlining the importance of elephants in Thai history and explaining their various rankings according to physical characteristics. The second stable

holds a sculptural representation of a living royal white elephant (now kept at the Chitlada Palace, home to the current Thai king). Draped in royal vestments, the statue is more or less treated as a shrine by the visiting Thai public.

Because this is royal property, visitors should wear long pants (no capri pants) or long skirts and shirts with sleeves.

RAMA V MEMORIAL
พระบรมรูปทรงม้า
A bronze **figure** (Map pp112–13; Royal Plaza, Th U-Thong Nai; bus 70, 510) of a military-garbed leader may seem like an unlikely shrine, but Bangkokians are flexible in their expression of religious devotion. Most importantly, the figure is no forgotten general – this is Rama V (King Chulalongkorn; 1868–1910), who is widely credited for steering the country into the modern age and for preserving Thailand's independence from European colonialism. He is also considered a champion of the common person for his abolition of slavery and corvée (the requirement that every citizen be available for state labour when called). His accomplishments are so revered, especially by the middle class, that his statue attracts worshippers (particularly on Tuesdays, the day of his birth), who make offerings of candles, flowers (predominantly pink roses), incense and bottles of whisky. The statue is also the site of a huge celebration on 23 October, the anniversary of the monarch's death.

The domed neoclassical building behind the statue is **Ananta Samakhom Throne Hall**, today a part of Dusit Palace Park (p138), which was built in the early 1900s by Italian architects in the style of European government houses. Used today for ceremonial purposes, the throne hall also hosted the first meeting of the Thai parliament until their meeting place was moved to a facility nearby. Visitors with a ticket from the Dusit Palace Park can explore the architecture of the building and view rotating exhibits.

ACTIVITIES
Traditional Massage
A good massage is the birthright of every Bangkokian, and the joy of every visitor. Correspondingly, massage parlours are everywhere in Bangkok, and they range in quality, depending largely if they offer massage or 'massage'. To avoid the latter, stay clear of the places in the seedier parts of town that advertise via scantily dressed women.

If it's your first time in the hands of a Thai masseur/masseuse, discard any preconceived notions, as many visitors find authentic Thai massage equal parts painful and relaxing. A traditional Thai massage often also involves herbal heat compresses (oil treatments are typically associated with 'sexy' massage).

Depending on the neighbourhood, prices for massages tend to stay fixed: at about 250B for a foot massage and around 500B for a full body massage. Most of the spas listed below also have massage services.

Buathip Thai Massage (Map pp122-3; ☎ 0 2251 2627; 4/13 Soi 5, Th Sukhumvit; 1hr massage 270B, foot 250B; ◷ 10am-midnight; Skytrain Nana) Located in a part of town where massage is typically a euphemism for something else, the experts here are both legitimate and lauded. Buathip is located on a small sub-soi behind the Amari Boulevard Hotel.

Coran Boutique Spa (Map pp122-3; ☎ 0 2651 1588; www.coranbangkok.com; 27/1-2 Soi 13, Th Sukhumvit; 1hr traditional massage 400B; ◷ 11am-10pm; Skytrain Nana) Offers traditional Thai massage by graduates of the adjacent Thai Traditional Medical Services Society, which also offers courses in Thai massage (see p146).

Ruen-Nuad Massage Studio (Map pp118-19; ☎ 0 2632 2662; Th Convent, Th Silom; 1hr traditional massage 350B, foot 350B; ◷ 10am-10pm; Skytrain Sala Daeng, Metro Silom) Set in a refurbished wooden house, this charming place successfully avoids both the tackiness and New Agedness that characterise most Bangkok massage joints. Prices are approachable too.

Wat Pho Thai Traditional Medical and Massage School (Map pp114-15; ☎ 0 2221 2974; Soi Pen Phat, Th Sanamchai; 1hr massage 220B; ◷ 8am-10pm; river ferry

Tha Tien); The primary training ground for the masseuses who are deployed across the country; there are also massage pavilions inside the temple complex (see p127).

Spas
Unless you've spent your entire visit in an air-conditioned bubble (entirely possible in today's Bangkok), at some point you're going to need to rid yourself of the negative effects of the city's urban environment. This can take the form of a simple scrub or can involve multistage treatments involving a customised choice of aromas and oils, a team of staff and possibly even acupuncture needles. There are countless spas in Bangkok now, many of them located in the city's high-end hotels with high-end price tags to match. To round down your choices, visit www.spasinbangkok.com or consider one of the following.

Divana Spa (Map pp122-3; ☎ 0 2261 6784; www.divanaspa.com; 7 Soi 25, Th Sukhumvit; spa treatments from 2500B; Skytrain Asoke, Metro Sukhumvit) Retains a unique Thai touch with a private and soothing setting in a garden house.

Health Land (Map pp118-19; ☎ 0 2637 8883; www.healthlandspa.com; 120 Th Sathon Neua; spa treatments from 850B; ◷ 9am-midnight; Skytrain Chong Nonsi) A winning formula of affordable prices and expert treatments has created a small empire of Health Land centres throughout the city.

Oriental Spa (Map pp118-19; ☎ 0 2659 9000, ext 7440; www.mandarinoriental.com/bangkok/spa; 48 Soi 38, Th Charoen Krung; spa package from 1650B) Regarded as among the premier spas in the world, the Oriental Spa also set the standard for Asian-style spa treatment. After 15 years and a recent renovation, the spa's setting in a wooden house by the Chao Phraya River is better than ever. Depending on where you flew in from, the Jet Lag Massage might be a good option, but all treatments require advance booking.

S Medical Spa (Map pp120-1; ☎ 0 2253 1010; www.smedspa.com; Th Withayu/Wireless Rd; spa treatments from 1000B; Skytrain Ploenchit) Part of the new generation of Bangkok spas merging alternative medicine with relaxation techniques and cosmetic treatments. The centre has a textbook menu of possible treatments, including acupuncture, hydrotherapy, nutritional counselling and exercise programs.

Spa 1930 (Map pp120-1; ☎ 0 2254 8606; www.spa1930.com; Soi Tonson, Th Ploenchit; à la carte from 1200B, packages from 3800B; ◷ 9.30am-9.30pm; Skytrain Chitlom) Rescues relaxers from the contrived spa ambience of New Age music and ingredients you'd rather see at a dinner party. The menu is simple (face, body care and body massage) and all scrubs and massage oils are based on traditional Thai herbal remedies.

Thann Sanctuary (Map pp120-1; ☎ 0 2658 0550; 3rd fl, Gaysorn Plaza, cnr Th Phoenchit & Th Ratchadamri; spa treatments from 900B; ⏱ 10am-10pm; Skytrain Chitlom) An offshoot of the fragrant herbal health products brand next door, this dark day spa offers a variety of treatments for post-shopping therapy. Also at Siam Discovery Center (corner Th Phra Ram I and Th Phayathai, Skytrain National Stadium).

River & Canal Trips

Glimpses of Bangkok's past as the 'Venice of the East' are still possible today, even though the motor vehicle has long since become the city's conveyance of choice. Along the river and the canals is a motley fleet of watercraft, from paddled canoes to rice barges. In these areas many homes, trading houses and temples remain oriented towards life on the water, providing a fascinating glimpse into the past when Thais still considered themselves *jôw nám* (water lords).

The most obvious way to commute between riverside attractions is the **Chao Phraya Express** (Map p186; ☎ 0 2623 6001; www.chaophrayaboat .co.th; tickets 9-32B). The terminus for most northbound boats is Tha Nonthaburi and for most southbound boats it's Tha Sathon (also called Central Pier), near the Saphan Taksin Skytrain station, although some boats run as far south as Wat Ratchasingkhon. See p185 for more information about boat travel.

For an up-close view of the city's famed canals, numerous long-tail boats are available for charter at Tha Chang, Tha Tian and Tha Phra Athit. Most trips spend an hour along the scenic Nonthaburi canals **Khlong Bangkok Noi** and **Khlong Bangkok Yai**, with stops at the Royal Barges National Museum and Wat Arun. Longer trips diverge into **Khlong Mon**, between Bangkok Noi and Bangkok Yai, which offers more typical canal scenery, including orchid farms. It usually costs 1000B for the entire boat for one hour, excluding admission and various mooring fees. Most operators have set tour routes, but if you have a specific destination in mind you can request it.

For dinner cruises along the Chao Phraya River, see p147.

Sports Facilities

If you're dedicated to the cause of athletics in this energy-sucking climate, you need access to an air-conditioned facility. Most membership gyms and top-end hotels have fitness centres and swimming pools. Some hotels offer day-use fees but these policies vary per establishment.

Clark Hatch Physical Fitness Centers (www .clarkhatchthailand.com) is a top-class operation with more than 14 locations throughout the city. All branches have weight machines, aerobics classes, pool, sauna and massage. Other commercial gyms include **California Wow** (www .californiawowx.com), with 13 branches, and **Fitness First** (www.fitnessfirst.co.th), with seven.

These days Bangkok has every imaginable fitness trend: Pilates, kickboxing and even salsa dancing. Most exercise options are centred on the business district on Th Ploenchit or Th Sukhumvit, but there are also studios directly on Th Khao San.

Absolute Yoga (Map pp120-1; ☎ 0 2252 4400; www .absoluteyogabangkok.com; 4th fl, Amarin Plaza, Th Ploenchit; Skytrain Chitlom) offers yoga for the gym rat, not the spiritualist, with classes in hot yoga, Pilates and vinyasa.

Yoga Elements Studio (Map pp120-1; ☎ 0 2655 5671; www.yogaelements.com; 23rd fl, 29 Vanissa Bldg, Th Chitlom; Skytrain Chitlom) teaches classes in vinyasa and ashtanga and offers attractive introductory rates.

One of Bangkok's longest-running sports groups is the **Hash House Harriers** (www.bangkokhhh .com), who pride themselves both on their dedication to running and their ability to subdue dehydration with massive amounts of beer. If you've got commitment issues with either pursuit, start with a simple jog at a local park, like Lumphini (p138) or Sanam Luang (p129). Every imaginable hometown sport – be it softball, ice hockey (yes, really), rugby or biking – attracts a loyal group of expat participants. Most clubs have websites with more information.

WALKING TOURS
Ko Ratanakosin

Most of Bangkok's 'must-see' destinations are found in Ko Ratanakosin, the former royal district, so we've put together a walking tour that links them in the better part of a day (around five hours with stops). It's best to start early to beat the heat and get in before the hordes have descended. Remember to dress modestly (long pants and skirts, shirts with sleeves and closed-toed shoes) in order to gain entry to the temples. Also ignore any strangers who approach you offering advice on sightseeing or shopping.

BANGKOK

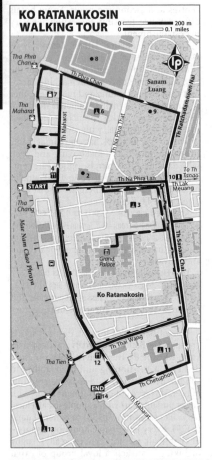

KO RATANAKOSIN WALKING TOUR

0 ——— 200 m
0 ——— 0.1 miles

Tha Phra Chan

Th Phra Chan

Sanam Luang

Tha Maharat

Th Maharat

Th Na Phra That

Th Ratchadamnoen Nai

To Th Tanao

Th Na Phra Lan

Th Lak Meuang

START

Tha Chang

Mae Nam Chao Phraya

Grand Palace

Ko Ratanakosin

Th Sanam Chai

Th Thai Wang

Tha Tien

Th Chetuphon

END

Th Maharat

WALK FACTS

Start Tha Chang
Finish Deck
Distance approximately 5km
Duration three hours

Start at **Tha Chang (1)** and follow Th Na Phra Lan east with a quick diversion to **Silpakorn University (2**; Th Na Phra Lan), Thailand's premier fine-arts university. Originally founded as the School of Fine Arts by Italian artist Corrado Feroci, the university campus includes part of an old palace built for Rama I. Continue east to the main gate into **Wat Phra Kaew & Grand Palace (3**; p126), two of Bangkok's most famous attractions.

Backtrack to Th Maharat and turn right. Staying on the west side of the street, the fourth doorway on the left is **Ah Khung (4**; no roman-script sign; ☎ 0 81775 2540; Th Maharat), a vendor of incredibly refreshing bowls of iced *chŏw gòoay*, grass jelly, your well-deserved first snack stop.

Continue north along Th Maharat, which is a centre of herbal apothecaries and side-walk amulet sellers. Immediately after passing the cat-laden newsstand (you'll know it when you see it), turn left into **Trok Tha Wang (5)**, a narrow alleyway holding a seemingly hidden classic Bangkok neighbourhood. Returning to Th Mahathat, continue moving north. On your right is **Wat Mahathat (6**; p145), one of Thailand's most respected Buddhist universities.

After a block or so, turn left into crowded Trok Mahathat to discover the cramped **amulet market (7**; p127). Follow the alley all the way towards the river to appreciate how extensive the amulet trade is.

As you continue north alongside the river, amulets soon turn to food vendors. The emergence of white-and-black uniforms is a clue that you are approaching **Thammasat University (8**; Th Phra Chan), known for its law and political science departments. The campus was also the site of the bloody October 1976 prodemocracy demonstrations, when Thai students were killed or wounded by the military.

Exiting at Tha Phra Chan, cross Th Maharat and continue east towards **Sanam Luang (9**; p129), the 'Royal Field'. Cross Sanam Luang, being sure to get a pic of the royal skyline at Wat Phra Kaew. Cross Th Ratchadamnoen Nai and go south towards the home of Bangkok's city spirit, **Lak Meuang (10**; p128), which is generally alive with the spectacle of devotion – including burning joss sticks and traditional dancing.

It's time for lunch, and at this point you're only a couple of blocks west of Th Tanao, one of old Bangkok's premier eating areas. Consider an air-conditioned lunch at Poj Spa Kar (p161) or classic Bangkok-style cuisine at Chote Chitr (p161), either of which is just a five-minute walk east along Th Kanlaya Lamit.

Returning at Th Sanamchai, continue south for 500m and turn right onto Th Chetuphon, where you'll enter **Wat Pho (11**; p127), home of the giant reclining Buddha and lots of quiet nooks and crannies.

After a restorative drink or snack at **Rub Aroon** (**12**; p161), head to adjacent Tha Tien to catch the cross-river ferry to Khmer-influenced **Wat Arun** (**13**; p131).

Cross back to Bangkok to end your journey with celebratory drinks at the **Deck** (**14**; p162) – if you're there at the right time, you can catch one of Bangkok's premier sunset views.

Chinatown

This walking tour takes in the hectic markets and main streets of Bangkok's most congested neighbourhood, as well as its lesser-visited riverfront area; it's around three hours, or five with stops.

Take the Metro to **Hualamphong** (**1**). Explore the city's largest train terminal, or proceed directly to Metro exit 1. Emerging on Th Phra Ram IV, cross the *klorng* and turn left into Th Traimit. Continue about 200m until you reach your first stop, **Wat Traimit** (**2**; p134), with its famous golden Buddha statue.

Continuing along Th Traimit, go right at the Chinese gate and cross over to Th Yaowarat, Chinatown's main artery. On the opposite side of the street is a **Kuan Im Shrine** (**3**).

WALK FACTS

Start Hualamphong Metro station
Finish River City Shopping Centre
Distance approximately 5km
Duration three hours

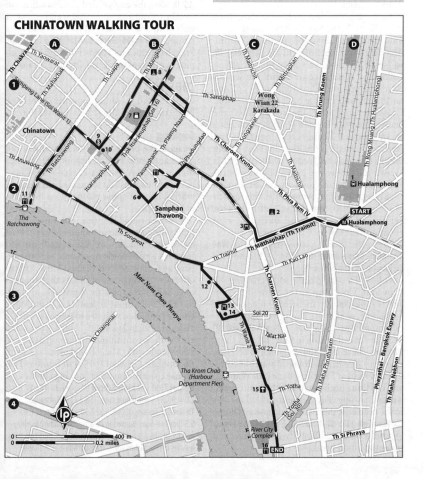

CHINATOWN WALKING TOUR

Dating back to 1902, it is home to an ancient teak statue of the eponymous Buddhist deity, as well as the headquarters of the charitable Thian Fah Foundation.

Continue north along Th Yaowarat until you reach the **Chaloem Buri Intersection (4)**, on the corner of Th Songsawat. The north side of Th Yaowarat is the best place to view the jumble of neon signs that many associate with Bangkok's Chinatown.

Turn left into Th Phadungdao, turning right at the T-intersection. After about 50m you'll see a small Chinese shrine on your right; opposite this you'll see a shopfront cafe invariably populated by old Chinese men. This is **Ia Sae (5**; Th Phat Say), one of the city's oldest coffee houses and your first drink or snack break.

Backtracking along Th Phat Sai, turn down Trok Khao San. Follow this tiny, atmospheric alleyway until you emerge at the first large intersection; this is **Sampeng (6**; Soi Wanit 1), Chinatown's busy market street. Follow the commerce west until the second large intersection. Turn right and continue north until you emerge back at Th Yaowarat. Cross over into Soi 6, the fresh market lane known locally as **Talat Mai (7**; p134). Emerging at Th Charoen Krung, cross the street and continue straight along the alleyway, taking the first right. This section of the market is known for selling the paper offerings burnt at Chinese funerals. Loop around back to Th Charoeng Krung. Moving north, this stretch of Chinese medicine shops, coffin makers, vendors of dry goods and bird nest soup restaurants is classic Chinatown.

Just after Soi 21, turn right into **Wat Mangkon Kamalawat (8**; p134), Chinatown's largest and liveliest temple.

Follow Th Mangkorn south, crossing Th Yaowarat. Continue in the same. direction and two blocks into the street, on either side of the intersection are two of Bangkok's oldest commercial buildings: a **Bangkok Bank (9)** and the venerable **Tang To Kang (10)** gold shop. Both are more than 100 years old, and classic examples of early Ratanakosin architecture.

Turn right at Sampeng Lane (Soi Wanit 1) and continue until you reach the main street, Th Ratchawong. Turn left and walk all the way to the dead end; this is Tha Ratchawong, home to **Wan Fah (11**; ☎ 0 2622 7657; 292 Th Ratchawong; ☽ lunch & dinner), a blissfully air-conditioned potential lunch break.

Backtrack along Th Ratchawong and turn right down Th Songwat. This street holds many of Bangkok's remaining antique buildings. Turn right into Th Phanurangsi, you are now in **Talat Noi (12**; p135). Follow the virtual path of engines and other hardware left into Th Wanit 2 and turn right into Soi Chow Su Kong. Follow this alleyway until you reach **San Jao Jo Sue Kong (13)**, a Chinese shrine. Locate the signs that lead to River View Guest House and follow them until you reach two large banyan trees tied with ribbons and laden with offerings. Follow the garbage-strewn path behind them to **Chao Sua Son's house (14)**, the only remaining traditional Chinese residence in Bangkok.

Making your way back to Th Wanit 2, follow the path south, passing the **Holy Rosary Church (15**; Th Yotha), the city's oldest place of Christian worship. Continue about 200m and end your walk with a well-deserved espresso and *tarte citron* at **Folies (16**; Captain Bush Lane), an open-air French cafe located between River City shopping centre and the Royal Orchid Sheraton.

COURSES

Culture and cooking courses dominate Bangkok's continuing-education syllabus.

Cooking

Imagine the points you'll rack up if you can make authentic Thai dishes for your friends back at home. A visit to a Thai cooking school has become a must-do for many Bangkok itineraries, and for some visitors it's a highlight of their trip.

Courses range in price and value, but a typical half-day course should include at least a basic introduction to Thai ingredients and flavours, and a hands-on chance to both prepare and cook several dishes. Most schools offer a revolving cast of dishes that changes on a daily basis, making it possible to study for a week without repeating a dish. Many courses include a visit to a market, and nearly all lessons include a set of printed recipes and end with a communal lunch consisting of your handiwork. Many Bangkok hotels, from the opulent Oriental (p155) to humble Thai House (p160), also offer cooking courses.

Baipai Thai Cooking School (Map pp110-11; ☎ 0 2294-9029; www.baipai.com; 150/12 Soi Naksuwan, Th Nonsee; lessons 1800B; ☽ 9.30am-1.30pm & 1.30-5.30pm Tue-Sun) Housed in an attractive suburban villa, and taught by a small army of staff, Baipai offers two daily lessons of four dishes each. Transportation is available.

Blue Elephant Thai Cooking School (Map pp118-19; ☎ 0 2673 9353; www.blueelephant.com; 233 Th Sathon Tai; lessons 2800B; ⏰ 8.45am-12.30pm & 1.15-5pm Mon-Sat; Skytrain Surasak) Bangkok's most chi-chi Thai cooking school offers two lessons daily. The morning class squeezes in a visit to a local market, while the afternoon session includes a detailed introduction to Thai ingredients.

Epicurean Kitchen Thai Cooking School (Map pp118-19; ☎ 0 2631 1119; www.thaikitchen.com; 10/2 Th Convent, Th Silom; lessons 2000B; ⏰ 9.30am-1pm Mon-Fri; Skytrain Sala Daeng, Metro Silom) This cramped but classy school offers daily lessons that encompass a whopping eight dishes, as well as a one-hour 'short course' of four dishes.

Khao (Map pp114-15; ☎ 0 89111 0947; khaocooking school@gmail.com; D&D Plaza, 68-70 Th Khao San; lessons 1200B; ⏰ 8.30am-12.30pm & 2.30-6.30pm Mon-Sat) Although it's located smack dab in the middle of Khao San, this new cooking school was started up by an authority on Thai food and features instruction on a wide variety of authentic dishes. Located directly behind D&D Inn.

Silom Thai Cooking School (Map pp118-19; ☎ 0 84726 5669; www.bangkokthaicooking.com; 68 Trok Vaithi/Soi 13, Th Silom; lessons 1000B; ⏰ 9.30am-1pm; Skytrain Chong Nonsi) The facilities are basic but Silom crams a visit to a local market and instruction of six dishes into three and a half hours, making it the best bang for your baht. Transportation available.

Meditation

Although at times Bangkok may seem like the most un-Buddhist place on earth, there are several places where foreigners can practise Theravada Buddhist meditation. For background information on Buddhism, see p65; for temple etiquette, see p45.

House of Dhamma (Map pp110-11; ☎ 0 2511 0439; www.houseofdhamma.com; 26/9 Soi 15, Th Lat Prao; Skytrain Mo Chit, Metro Phahonyothin) This meditation centre in the northern suburbs of Bangkok hosts monthly introduction courses to vipassana meditation as well as weekend retreats in cooperation with the Young Buddhists Association of Thailand.

International Buddhist Meditation Center (Map pp114-15; ☎ 0 2623 5881; www.mcu.ac.th/IBMC; Vipassana Section Room 106, Mahachula Bldg, Wat Mahathat, 3 Th Maharat; bus 47, 53, 503, 508, 512, river ferry Tha Phra Chan) Located at Wat Mahathat, this institute holds regular lectures on Buddhist topics in English, and meditation classes.

Wat Mahathat (Map pp114-15; ☎ 0 2222 6011; 3 Th Maharat; ⏰ 7am-9pm; bus 47, 53, 503, 508, 512, river ferry Tha Phra Chan) Provides daily meditation sessions every three hours starting at 7am and ending at 9pm. Accommodation for long-term meditation is also available; just stop by and fill out an application. Phra Suphe, the monk who runs the centre, speaks flawless English, and there are often Western monks or long-term residents available to interpret.

Wat Rakhang (Map pp114-15; ☎ 0 81622 4507; Soi Wat Rakhang, Thonburi; ⏰ 12.30pm-3.30pm 2nd & 4th Sun every month; river ferry Tha Wat Rakhang) Offers a regular schedule of dhamma and vipassana meditation talks in English.

Additional sources of information include **Dharma Thai** (www.dhammathai.org), which has a rundown on several prominent wát and meditation centres, or speak to the **World Fellowship of Buddhists** (WFB; Map pp122-3; ☎ 0 2661 1284; www.wfb-hq.org; 616 Benjasiri Park, Soi 24, Th Sukhumvit; ⏰ 8.30am-4.30pm Mon-Fri; Skytrain Phrom Phong), which also hosts occasional meditation classes.

Thai Boxing

Training in *moo·ay tai* (also spelt *muay thai*) for foreigners has increased in popularity in the past five years and many camps all over the country are tailoring their programs for English-speaking fighters. The following camps provide instruction in English and accept men and women. Food and accommodation can often be provided for an extra charge. The website www.muaythai.com contains loads of information on training camps.

Fairtex Muay Thai (off Map pp110-11; ☎ 0 2755 3329; www.muaythaifairtex.com; 99/5 Mu 3, Soi Buthamanuson, Th Thaeparak, Bangpli, Samut Prakan; tuition per day 1100B) A popular, long-running camp south of Bangkok.

Muay Thai Institute (Map p189; ☎ 0 2992 0096; www.muaythai-institute.net; Rangsit Stadium, 336/932 Th Prachatipat, Pathum Thani; tuition for 1st level 6400B) Associated with the respected World Muay Thai Council, the institute offers a fundamental course (consisting of three levels of expertise), which can be completed in 120 days, as well as courses for instructors, referees and judges. If you're interested, make an appointment to visit the facility, which is north of Bangkok, and watch the teachers and students at work.

Sor. Vorapin Gym (Map pp114-15; ☎ 0 2282 3551; www.thaiboxings.com; 13 Trok Krasab, Th Chakraphong; tuition per day/month 500/9000B) Specialises in training foreign students of both genders; the gym is sweating distance from Th Khao San and more serious training is held at a gym outside the city.

Thai Language

AAA Thai Language Center (Map pp120-1; ☎ 0 2655 5629; www.aaathai.com; 6th fl, 29 Vanissa Bldg, Th Chitlom; Skytrain Chitlom) Opened by a group of experienced Thai language teachers from other schools, good-value AAA Thai has a loyal following.

American University Alumni Language Centre
(AUA; Map pp120-1; ☎ 0 2252 8170; www.auathai.com; 179 Th Ratchadamri; tuition per hr 102B; Skytrain Ratchadamri) Run by the American University Alumni and one of the largest English-language teaching institutes in the world. There are 10 levels consisting of 200 hours' worth of class time that can be completed within a sliding timescale. The teaching method is based on the natural language acquisition of children, first focusing on listening and comprehension, and then advancing to speaking and reading.

Chulalongkorn University Intensive Thai Program
(Map pp120-1; ☎ 0 2218 4640; www.inter.chula.ac.th; Faculty of Arts, Chulalongkorn University, Th Phayathai; Skytrain Siam) Offers three different levels (basic, intermediate and advanced) of Thai-language coursework with each level lasting five weeks (100 hours of study). Contact the department for tuition, enrolment and accommodation queries.

Pro Language (Map pp122-3; ☎ 0 2250 0072; www.prolanguage.co.th; 10th fl, Times Square Bldg, 246 Th Sukhumvit; Skytrain Asoke) A favourite of expat professionals. Pro Language starts with the basics and increases in difficulty to the advanced level, which involves studying examples of Thai literature. Classes are thematically designed: asking questions, giving opinions, business Thai, and the like.

Siri Pattana Thai Language School (Map p124; ☎ 0 2677 3150; siri_pattanathai@hotmail.com; Bangkok Insurance Bldg, 13 Th Sathon Tai; tuition from 7500B) Located in front of the YWCA building, offers Thai-language courses that cover 30 hours broken into one- or two-hour classes per day, as well as preparation for the *bor hòk* (teaching proficiency exam).

Union Language School (Map pp120-1; ☎ 0 2214 6033; www.unionlanguageschool.com; 7th fl, 328 CCT Office Bldg, Th Phayathai; tuition from 7200B; Skytrain Ratchathewi) Generally recognised as having the best and most rigorous courses (many missionaries study here). Union employs a balance of structure- and communication-oriented methodologies in 80-hour, four-week modules.

Thai Massage

Thai Traditional Medical Services Society (Map pp122-3; ☎ 0 2651 1587; www.school-thaimassage.com; Coran Boutique Spa, 27/1-2 Soi 13, Th Sukhumvit; tuition from 7500B; ☺ 11am-10pm; Skytrain Nana) Authorised by the Thai Ministry of Health, this institute offers scholarship in a variety of massage and holistic cures culminating in certification. Located at Coran Boutique Spa (p140).

Wat Pho Thai Traditional Medical and Massage School (Map pp114-15; ☎ 0 2622 3533; www.watpomassage.com; 392/25-28 Soi Phen Phat; tuition from 6500B; ☺ 8am-6pm; river ferry Tha Tien) Offers basic and advanced courses in traditional massage; basic courses offer 30 hours spread out over five-days and cover either general massage or foot massage. The advanced level spans 60 hours, requires the basic course as a prerequisite, and covers

therapeutic and healing massage. Other advanced courses include oil massage and aromatherapy, and infant and child massage. The school is outside the temple compound in a restored Bangkok shophouse near Tha Tien, and now has branches in northern and eastern Bangkok and Chiang Mai.

BANGKOK FOR CHILDREN

There aren't a whole lot of attractions in Bangkok meant directly to appeal to the little ones, but there's no lack of locals willing to provide attention. The website www.bambiweb.org is a useful resource for parents in Bangkok.

Housing a colourful selection of traditional Thai dolls, both new and antique, is the **Bangkok Doll Factory & Museum** (Map pp112-13; ☎ 0 2245 3008; 85 Soi Ratchataphan/Mo Leng; admission free; ☺ 8am-5pm Mon-Sat). The downside is that it can be really hard to find: approach via Th Si Ayuthaya heading east. Cross under the expressway past the intersection with Th Ratchaprarop and take the soi to the right of the post office. Follow this windy street until you start seeing signs.

Disguising learning as kid's play, most activities at the **Children's Discovery Museum** (Map pp110-11; ☎ 0 2618 6509; www.bkkchildrenmuseum.com; Queen Sirikit Park, Th Kamphaeng Phet 4; adult/child 70/50B; ☺ 9am-5pm Tue-Fri, 10am-6pm Sat & Sun) are geared to early elementary-aged children. There is also a toddler-aged playground at the back of the main building. Opposite Chatuchak Weekend Market.

Although not specifically child-targeted, the Museum of Siam (p128) has lots of interactive exhibits that will appeal to children.

Dusit Zoo (Map pp112-13; ☎ 0 2281 9027; www.zoothailand.org; Th Ratchawithi; adult/child 100/50B; ☺ 8am-6pm Mon-Thu, to 9pm Fri-Sun; bus 18, 510) covers 19 hectares with caged exhibits of more than 300 mammals, 200 reptiles and 800 birds, including relatively rare indigenous species such as banteng, gaur, serow and some rhinoceros. There are shady grounds plus a lake in the centre with paddleboats for hire, a small children's playground, and a Night Zoo (open 6pm to 9pm Friday to Sunday).

A massive underwater world has been re-created at the **Siam Ocean World** (Map pp120-1; ☎ 0 2687 2000; www.siamoceanworld.co.th; basement, Siam Paragon, Th Phra Ram I; adult/child 350/250B; ☺ 10am-7pm; Skytrain Siam) shopping-centre aquarium. Gaze into the glass-enclosed deep-reef zone or view the daily feeding of penguins and sharks.

Lumphini Park (Map p124; Th Phra Ram IV, btwn Th Withayu/Wireless Rd & Th Ratchadamri; admission free; ☺ 5am-8pm; bus 13, 505, Skytrain Sala Daeng, Metro Lumphini) is a trusty ally in the cool hours of the morning and evening for kite-flying (in season) as well as stretching of the legs and lungs. Kids can view lethal snakes become reluctant altruists at the adjacent antivenin-producing Snake Farm (p135).

Join the novice monks and other children as they sprinkle tiny pellets of fish food (which are sold on the pier) into the river at **Tha Thewet** (Map pp112-13; Th Samsen; [hours] 7am-7pm), transforming the muddy river into a brisk boil of flapping bodies.

Near the old Portuguese quarter in Thonburi, **Wat Prayoon** (Map pp116-17; 24 Th Prachathipok, cnr Thetsaban Soi 1; admission free; [hours] 8am-6pm; cross-river ferry from Tha Pak Talaat/Atsadang) is an artificial hill cluttered with miniature shrines and a winding path encircling a turtle pond. Vendors sell cut fruit for feeding to the resident turtles. It's near Memorial Bridge.

MBK Center (p176) and Siam Paragon (p177) both have bowling alleys to keep the older ones occupied. **Krung Sri IMAX** (Map pp120-7; [phone] 0 2129 4631; www.imaxthai.com; Siam Paragon, Th Phra Ram I; adult/child 600/250B) screens special-effects versions of Hollywood action flicks and nature features.

TOURS
Dinner Cruises

Perfect for romancing couples or subdued families, dinner cruises swim along Mae Nam Chao Phraya basking in the twinkling city lights at night, far away from the heat and noise of town. Cruises range from downhome to sophisticated, but the food generally ranges from mediocre to forgettable.

Loy Nava (Map pp116-17; [phone] 0 2437 4932; www.loynava .com; set menu 1618B; [hours] 6-8pm & 8-10pm) Operating since 1970, and quite possibly the original Bangkok dinner cruise, Loy Nava offers two daily excursions, both departing from the River City Complex. Vegetarian menu available.

Manohra Cruises (Map pp110-11; [phone] 0 2477 0770; www.manohracruises.com; Bangkok Marriott Resort & Spa, Thonburi; cocktail/dinner cruise 900/1990B; [hours] cocktail cruise 6-7pm, dinner cruise 7.30-10pm) Commands a fleet of converted teak rice barges that part the waters with regal flair. Boats depart from the Marriott Resort, accessible via a free river shuttle that operates from Tha Sathon (near Skytrain Saphan Taksin).

Wan Fah Cruises (Map pp116-17; [phone] 0 2222 8679; www .wanfah.in.th; cruises 1200B; [hours] 7-9pm) Departing from the River City Complex, Wan Fah runs a buxom wooden boat that floats in style with accompanying Thai music and traditional dance. Dinner options include a standard or seafood set menu and hotel transfer is available.

Yok Yor Restaurant (Map pp112-13; [phone] 0 2439 3477; www.yokyor.co.th; dinner 300-550B plus 140B surcharge;

[hours] 8-10pm) This long-running floating restaurant on the Thonburi side of the river also runs a daily dinner cruise, as well as several boats that can be hired for private functions.

Bang Pa-In & Ayuthaya Cruises

A little faster than the days of sailing ships, river cruises from Bangkok north to the ruins of the former royal capital of Ayuthaya (p195) take in all the romance of the river. Most trips include a guided tour of Ayuthaya's ruins with a stop at the summer palace of Bang Pa In (p204). Normally only one leg of the journey between Bangkok and Ayuthaya is aboard a boat, while the return or departing trip is by bus.

Asian Oasis (Map pp110-11; [phone] 0 2651 9101; www .asian-oasis.com; 2-day trip 9050-14,100B depending on season & direction) Cruise the Chao Phraya River aboard a fleet of restored rice barges with old-world charm and modern conveniences. Trips include either an upstream or downstream journey to/from Ayuthaya with bus transfer in the opposite direction.

Chao Phraya Express Boat (Map pp118-19; [phone] 0 2623 6001; www.chaophrayaboat.co.th; adult/child 1400/1200B) The municipal boat operator offers a once-monthly guided tour to Ayuthaya. For departure date and other details, go to the website or stop by the information desk at Tha Sathon (Skytrain Saphan Taksin).

Manohra Cruises (Map pp110-11; [phone] 0 2477 0770; www.manohracruises.com; Bangkok Marriott Resort & Spa, Thonburi; 3-day trip 64,000B) The nautical equivalent of the *Eastern & Oriental Express* train, the *Mahnora Song* is a restored teak rice barge decorated with antiques, Persian carpets and four luxury sleeping berths. The trip is a three-day, two-night excursion to Ayuthaya, and the package price is all-inclusive except for tax and service. The *Manohra Dream*, an even more luxurious boat for a maximum of two couples, is also available for longer excursions.

Bicycle & Segway Tours

Although some cycling tours tackle the city's urban neighbourhoods, many take advantage of the nearby lush, undeveloped district known as Phra Pradaeng (Map pp110–11), where narrow walkways crisscross irrigation canals that feed small-scale fruit plantations and simple villages.

To tour the sites of old Bangkok by free borrowed bicycle, see the boxed text on p108.

ABC Amazing Bangkok Cyclists (Map pp122-3; [phone] 0 2665 6364; www.realasia.net; 10/5-7 Soi 26, Th Sukhumvit; tours from 1000B; [hours] daily tours depart at 10am or 1pm; Skytrain Phrom Phong) Operating for more than a decade, the bike-based tours here purport to reveal the 'real' Asia by following the elevated walkways of the city's rural canals.

Bangkok Bike Rides (Map pp122-3; ☎ 0 2712 5305; www.bangkokbikerides.com; 14/1-B Soi Phromsi 2, off Soi Phrompong/39, Th Sukhumvit; tours from 1000B) A division of the tour company Spice Roads, offering a variety of tours, both urban and rural.

Thailand Segway Tours (☎ 0 86890 5675; www.thailandsegwaytours.com; 90min tours from 3100B) Not into tropical exertion? Segway offers several tours on the eponymous non-motorised scooter through Bangkok's parks, and to the Ancient City in Samut Prakan (p132).

Velothailand (Map pp114-15; ☎ 0 89201 7782; www.velothailand.com; Soi 2, Th Samsen; tours from 1100B) This small outfit offers unusual programs including a night tour of Thonburi. Bike rentals, repairs and sales are also available at the Banglamphu office.

Walking Tours

Although the pollution and heat are significant obstacles, Bangkok is a fascinating city to explore on foot. If you'd rather do it with an expert guide, **Bangkok Private Tours** (www.bangkokprivatetours.com; full-day walking tour 8000B) conducts customised walking tours of the city, including food-based tours.

FESTIVALS & EVENTS

In addition to the national holidays, there's always something going on in Bangkok. Check the website of **TAT** (www.tourismthailand.org) or the **Bangkok Information Center** (www.bangkoktourist.com) for exact dates. The cultural centres also host various international festivals.

January
Bangkok International Film Festival (www.bangkokfilm.org) Home-grown talent and overseas indies arrive on the silver screens. If you haven't heard, Bangkok is fast becoming a Bollywood and Hong Kong movie hybrid. Held in mid-January.

February/March
Chinese New Year Thai-Chinese celebrate the lunar New Year with a week of housecleaning, lion dances and fireworks. Most festivities centre on Chinatown. Dates vary.

March
Kite-Flying Season During the windy season, colourful kites battle it out over the skies of Sanam Luang and Lumphini Park.

April
Songkran The celebration of the Thai New Year has morphed into a water war with high-powered water guns and water balloons being launched at suspecting and unsuspecting participants. The most intense water battles take place on Th Khao San. Held in mid-April.

May
Royal Ploughing Ceremony His Majesty the King commences rice-planting season with a ceremony at Sanam Luang. Dates vary.
Miss Jumbo Queen Contest With fat trends creeping across the globe, Thailand hosts a beauty pageant for extra-large women (over 80kg) who display the grace of an elephant at Nakhon Pathom's Samphran Elephant Park. Held in early May.

June
International Festival of Music & Dance An extravaganza of arts and culture sponsored by the Thailand Cultural Centre. Held twice a year in June and September.

August
Queen's Birthday The queen's birthday is recognised as Mother's Day throughout the country. In Bangkok, festivities centre on Th Ratchadamnoen and the Grand Palace. Held on 12 August.

September/October
Vegetarian Festival A 10-day Chinese-Buddhist festival wheels out yellow-bannered streetside vendors serving meatless meals. The greatest concentration of vendors is found in Chinatown. Dates vary.

October/November
King Chulalongkorn Day Rama V is honoured on the anniversary of his death at the Royal Plaza in Dusit. Crowds of devotees come to make merit with incense and flower garlands. Held on 23 October.

November
Loi Krathong A beautiful festival where, on the night of the full moon, small lotus-shaped boats made of banana leaf and containing a lit candle are set adrift on Mae Nam Chao Phraya. Held in early November.
Fat Festival Sponsored by FAT 104.5FM radio, Bangkok's indie-est indie bands gather for an annual fest. Held in early November.
Bangkok Pride (www.utopia-asia.com) A week-long festival of parades, parties and awards is organised by the city's gay businesses and organisations. Held in mid-November.

December
King's Birthday Locals celebrate their monarch's birthday with lots of parades and fireworks. Held on 5 December.

SLEEPING

At first glance, deciding where to lay your head in Bangkok appears an insurmountable task; there are countless hotels in virtually every corner of this sprawling city. Making it slightly easier is the fact that where you stay is largely determined by your budget.

Banglamphu and the tourist ghetto of Th Khao San still hold the bulk of Bangkok's budget accommodation, although the downside is that it can be difficult to get to other parts of town. Cheap rooms are also available around lower Sukhumvit, although you'll have to put up with sex tourists and touts. Chinatown also has its share of hotels in this category, with the added bonus of anonymity. And there's a good selection of budget digs on Soi Ngam Duphli, near Th Sathon.

Those willing to spend a bit more can consider staying in 'downtown' Bangkok. Both Th Sukhumvit and Th Silom have heaps of midrange options, often within walking distance of the Skytrain or Metro. The sois opposite the National Stadium, near Siam Square, have some good midrange options, and have the benefit of being close to the Skytrain.

Upper Sukhumvit is home to many of Bangkok's boutique and upscale designer hotels. And the city's most famous hotels are largely found along the riverside near Th Silom.

Ko Ratanakosin & Banglamphu

Ko Ratanakosin, the most touristed area of Bangkok was until relatively recently utterly devoid of lodging options. But with the advent of the boutique hotel craze, a few riverside shophouses are being transformed into charming tourists' nests.

Banglamphu, in particular the neighbourhood that includes the backpacker street of Th Khao San, is ground zero for accommodation in Bangkok. This doesn't necessarily mean it's the only or even best place to stay in town, but prices are generally low, and services such as internet shops, travel agents and beer stalls are available in abundance, making it a convenient base.

In recent years many longstanding Banglamphu guesthouse owners have converted their former hovels into small hotels, leading to an abundance of new, good-value midrangers. Although some see this as the gentrification of Th Khao San, it's added a dimension of accommodation that was previously lacking.

Regardless of your budget, keep in mind that Th Khao San is just one street in a large neighbourhood; there are increasingly attractive options spanning all price levels on outlying streets such as riverside Th Phra Athit,

leafy Soi Rambutri and the residential side streets off Th Samsen.

It would be impossible to list all of Banglamphu's accommodation options in this format; we've chosen a select few that stand out, typically those away from the main strip, which can get pretty noisy. If you've got the time, explore a bit and check out a few guesthouses before making a decision; during the high season (December to February), however, it's probably a wise idea to take the first vacant bed you come across. The best time of day to find a vacancy is around check-out time, 10am or 11am.

BUDGET

The following are just a few of the budget options on and around Th Khao San; just because we haven't included the one you're considering doesn't mean it's no good. If you're having trouble locating a cheapie, other budget options include Soi Rambutri, the sois off Th Samsen, and the alley running parallel between Th Khao San and Th Ratchadamnoen Klang, where you'll find the area's few remaining old-style wooden guesthouses.

our pick **New Merry V Guest House** (Map pp114-15; ☎ 0 2280 3315; 18-20 Th Phra Athit; r 150-700B; bus 53, 506, river ferry Tha Phra Athit; ✖ ▯) The interior of this vast place looks as if it underwent a recent renovation, but it is in fact just exceptionally well maintained. The cheap rooms are as bare as it gets, but are spotless and have ample natural light and the odd view or two. The more expensive rooms, although equipped with amenities, don't represent as good value.

Baan Sabai (Map pp114-15; ☎ 0 2629 1599; baan sabai@hotmail.com; 12 Soi Rongmai; r 190-600B; bus 53, 506, river ferry Tha Phra Athit; ✖ ▯) Truly living up to its name (Comfortable House), this rambling old building holds dozens of plain but comfy rooms, at a variety of prices. There's a palpable old-school atmosphere here, particularly at the fun open-air restaurant/bar area downstairs.

Wild Orchid Villa (Map pp114-15; ☎ 0 2629 0046; www.wild-orchidvilla.com; 8 Soi Chana Songkhram; r 280-950B; bus 53, 506, river ferry Tha Phra Athit; ✖ ▯) The cheapies here are some of the tiniest we've seen anywhere, but all rooms are clean and neat, and come in a bright, friendly package. This place is exceedingly popular, so it's best to book ahead.

Rambuttri Village Inn (Map pp114-15; ☎ 0 2282 9162; www.khaosan-hotels.com; 95 Soi Rambutri; r 290-950B; bus 30, 53, 506, river ferry Tha Phra Athit) If you're

BANGKOK

WHAT TO EXPECT IN BANGKOK

Hotel rooms are generally more expensive in Bangkok than elsewhere in Thailand, but don't fret as there's a huge variety and discounts can be had, making accommodation generally good value overall. We have divided rooms into the following three categories:

Budget under 1000B
Midrange 1000B to 3000B
Top End over 3000B

The prices listed are high-season rack rates, but it's worth noting that significant discounts can be found by booking online. See the boxed text on p158 for recommended sites.

So what do you get for your money? At the **budget** end, the days of 50B beds in Banglamphu are over, but those counting every baht can still get a fan-cooled dorm bed (or a closet-like room) for between 150B and 200B with a shared bathroom. The more you're willing to pay, the more likely you are to get a towel, hot water and air-con. If you require privacy and your own bathroom, paying in the realm of 700B or so can get you a capable, although generally characterless, room.

The biggest mixed bag of all, the **midrange** level starts out with the high-quality guesthouses, then moves into a grey area of mediocrity. Above 1000B, the hotels have all the appearance of a hotel back home – a bellboy, uniformed desk clerks and a well-polished lobby – but without the predictability. If you're on a lower midrange budget, and aren't so keen on aesthetics, some very acceptable rooms can be had for between around 1500B and 2000B. If your budget is near the higher end of the scale, it really pays to book ahead, as online discounts here can be substantial.

Bangkok's growing array of **top-end** hotels typically include amenities such as pool, spa, fitness and business centres and overpriced internet connections. The famous brands generally provide more space, while 'boutique' hotels emphasise ambience. In the top tier rooms start at more than 10,000B, but in most of the luxurious design and boutique hotels, and the vast majority of the international brands, you're looking at about 6000B to 9000B, before hefty online discounting. Keep in mind that the hotels in this category will generally add a 10% service charge plus 7% tax to hotel bills.

willing to subject yourself to the relentless gauntlet of tailors ('Excuse me, suit?'), this newish hotel has an abundance of good-value rooms. A ground-floor courtyard with restaurants and shops makes this a convenient place to stay.

Bella Bella Riverview (Map pp114–15; ☎ 0 2628 8077; 6 Soi 3, Th Samsen; r 300-570B; bus 53, 506, river ferry Tha Phra Athit; ☒ ☐) Wind your way through an atmospheric Bangkok neighbourhood to this gangly guesthouse. River views are slim, and the rooms are bare and largely devoid of amenities, but it's a good choice for those who want to stay near Th Khao San, but not *too* close.

Villa Guest House (Map pp114–15; ☎ 0 2281 7009; 230 Soi 1, Th Samsen; s/d 300/600B; bus 30, 53, 506, river ferry Tha Phra Athit) A quiet older couple have opened their 100-year-old teak house to foreign guests. The 10 fan rooms (all with shared bathrooms) are outfitted with antique furniture, including canopy beds. By the time

this book is published a few additional rooms should also be finished.

Penpark Place (Map pp114–15; ☎ 0 2281 4733; www .penparkplace.com; 22 Soi 3, Th Samsen; s/d 350/400B; bus 53, 506, river ferry Tha Phra Athit; ☒ ☐) This former factory has been turned into a good-value budget hotel. Rooms are little more than a bed and a fan, and only one has an ensuite bathroom, but all are spotless. There's a communal rooftop area, and plans to add even more rooms in the near future.

Boworn BB (Map pp114–15; ☎ 0 2629 1073; www.boworn bb.com; 335 Th Phra Sumen; s/d 600/700B; river ferry to Tha Phra Athit; ☒ ☐) Viewed from the outside, this place looks like a quaint, Banglamphu shophouse. But a peek inside reveals a huge array of mostly bland but tidy rooms. There's an inviting rooftop garden for communal chilling.

Rikka Inn (Map pp114–15; ☎ 0 2282 7511; www .rikkainn.com; 259 Th Khao San; s/d 600-950B; bus 53, 506, river ferry Tha Phra Athit; ☒ ☐ ☒) Boasting tight but attractive rooms, a rooftop pool and a central location, the new Rikka is one of several great-value hotels changing the face of Th Khao San.

Baan Dinso (Map pp114–15; ☎ 0 2622 0560; www .baandinso.com; 113 Trok Sin, Th Dinso; r 942–2000B; bus 53, 506, river ferry Tha Phra Athit; ❀ ▣) Considering that all the bathrooms here are shared, Baan Dinso doesn't rank high on the value scale, but this immaculately refurbished 85-year-old Thai house in a classic Bangkok neighbourhood is among the most unique accommodation experiences in town. The nine rooms are truly homey, and the shared bathrooms are absolutely spotless.

MIDRANGE

This is the fastest growing price bracket in the neighbourhood, and there are some fantastic bargains to be had if you can afford it.

Bhiman Inn (Map pp114–15; ☎ 0 2282 6171; www .bhimaninn.com; 55 Th Phra Sumen; r 1000–1700B; bus 30, 53, 506, river ferry Tha Phra Athit; ❀ ▣ ▣) With an exterior that combines elements of a modern church and a castle, and an interior that relies on copious mirrors and pop-art floor tile patterns, the design concept of this unique hotel is a bit hard to pin down. The rooms are slightly more predictable, although the cheapest are hardly larger than closets. An inviting restaurant and a pool fill out the package.

our pick Lamphu Tree House (Map pp114–15; ☎ 0 2282 0991; www.lamphutreehotel.com; 155 Wanchat Bridge, Th Prachatipatai; r 1200–1800B; klorng taxi to Tha Phah Fah; ❀ ▣ ▣) Despite the name this attractive midranger has its feet firmly on land, and as such represents brilliant value. Rooms are attractive and inviting, and the rooftop bar, pool, internet, restaurant and quiet location ensure that you may never feel the need to leave.

New Siam Riverside (Map pp114–15; ☎ 0 2629 3535; www.newsiam.net; 21 Th Phra Athit; r incl breakfast 1390–2390B; bus 53, 506, river ferry Tha Phra Athit; ❀ ▣ ▣) One of a couple of new places along Th Phra Athit taking advantage of the riverside setting, this hotel has comfortable rooms with tiny bathrooms. But the real value is the amenities (internet, travel agent, restaurant) and the location on one of the city's more pleasant streets.

Hotel Dé Moc (Map pp114–15; ☎ 0 2282 2831; www .hoteldemoc.com; 78 Th Prachatipatai; r incl breakfast 1500–1700B; bus 12, 56; ❀ ▣ ▣) The rooms at this classic hotel are large, with high ceilings and generous windows, but the furnishings could certainly use an update. Complimentary transport to Th Khao San and Wat Phra Kaew, and free bike rental are thoughtful perks.

our pick Diamond House (Map pp114–15; ☎ 0 2629 4008; www.thaidiamondhouse.com; 4 Th Samsen; r 2000–2800, ste 3600; bus 30, 53, 506, river ferry Tha Phra Athit; ❀ ▣) Despite sharing building space with a rather brash Chinese temple, there's no evidence of design conflict at this eccentric, funky hotel. Most rooms are loft style, with beds on raised platforms, and are outfitted with stained glass, dark, lush colours and chic furnishings. There's a lack of windows, and some of the suites aren't that much larger than the cheaper rooms, but a rooftop sunbathing deck and an outdoor Jacuzzi (!) make up for this.

Buddy Boutique Hotel (Map pp114–15; ☎ 0 2629 4477; www.buddylodge.com; 265 Th Khao San; r 2000–2600B; bus 53, 506, river ferry Tha Phra Athit; ❀ ▣ ▣) This gigantic complex, which includes a pool, fitness room and, ahem, a branch of McDonald's, is, as far as we're aware, the most expensive place to stay on Th Khao San. Rooms are evocative of a breezy tropical manor house and outfitted with traditional Thai designs.

Viengtai Hotel (Map pp114–15; ☎ 0 2280 5434; www .viengtai.co.th; 42 Th Rambutri; r 2200–3000B, ste 5200B; bus 53, 506, ferry Tha Phra Athit; ❀ ▣ ▣) Long before Th Khao San was 'discovered', this was an ordinary Chinese-style hotel in a quiet neighbourhood. It now sits comfortably in the midrange with reliable but unstylish rooms. Make advance bookings for cheaper rates.

Baan Chantra (Map pp114–15; ☎ 0 2628 6988; www .baanchantra.com; 120 Th Samsen; r incl breakfast 2700–4000B; bus 30, 53, 506, river ferry Tha Phra Athit; ❀ ▣) This beautiful converted house is without pretensions, preferring to be comfortable and roomy rather than fashionable and pinched. Many of the house's original teak details remain, and the deluxe room boasts a sunny patio.

TOP END

Navalai River Resort (Map pp114–15; ☎ 0 2280 9955; www.navalai.com; 45/1 Th Phra Athit; r incl breakfast 3000–4500B; bus 53, 506, river ferry Tha Phra Athit; ❀ ▣ ▣) The latest thing to go up on breezy Th Phra Athit, this chic hotel has 74 modern rooms, many looking out over the Chao Phraya River. There are attractive Thai design touches throughout, but you might end up spending much of your time checking out the views from the rooftop pool.

Old Bangkok Inn (Map pp114–15; ☎ 0 2629 1787; www.oldbangkokinn.com; 609 Th Phra Sumen; r incl breakfast 3190–6590B; bus 2, 82, 511, 512, klorng taxi to Tha Phan Fah; ❀ ▣) The 10 rooms in this refurbished

BANGKOK

antique shophouse are decadent and sumptuous, combining rich colours and heavy wood furnishings. All have computers for personal use, and some have semi-outdoor bathrooms. The perfect honeymoon hotel.

our pick **Arun Residence** (Map pp114-15; ☎ 0 2221 9158; www.arunresidence.com; 36-38 Soi Pratu Nok Yung, Th Maharat; r/ste incl breakfast 3500/5500B; river ferry Tha Tien; 🛇 🖵) Strategically located across from Wat Arun, this multilevel wooden house on the river boasts much more than just brilliant views. The seven rooms here manage to feel both homey and stylish, some being tall and loftlike, while others cojoin two rooms (the best is the top-floor suite with its own balcony). There are inviting communal areas, including a library, a rooftop bar and the Deck restaurant (p162).

Aurum: The River Place (Map pp114-15; ☎ 0 2622 2248; www.aurum-bangkok.com; 394/27-29 Th Maharat; r incl breakfast 3950-4900B; river ferry Tha Tien; 🛇 🖵) The 12 modern rooms here don't necessarily reflect the grand European exterior of this refurbished shophouse. Nonetheless they're comfortable and well appointed, and most offer fleeting views of the Chao Phraya. Online discounts available.

Chakrabongse Villas (Map pp114-15; ☎ 0 2622 3356; www.thaivillas.com; 396/1 Th Maharat; r incl breakfast 5000-5500B, ste incl breakfast 10,000-25,000B; river ferry Tha Tien; 🛇 🖵 🛱) An occasionally inhabited compound of Thai royalty dating back to 1908, this unique hotel incorporates three sumptuous but cramped rooms and four larger suites and villas. There's a pool, jungle-like gardens and an elevated deck for romantic riverside dining.

Chinatown & Phahurat

Yaowarat, Bangkok's Chinatown, isn't the most hospitable part of town, but for those who wish to stay off the beaten track it's an area where travellers can remain largely anonymous. There's a decent selection of accommodation, much of it just off busy streets, so be sure to assess the noise situation before choosing your room. The area used to be a nightmare to get to, but the Metro stop at Hualamphong has improved things immensely.

Baan Hualampong (Map pp116-17; ☎ 0 2639 8054; www.baanhualampong.com; 336/20 Soi 21, Th Charoen Krung; dm/s 220/290B, d 520-700B; Metro Hualamphong; 🛇 🖵) Repeat visitors rave about the homey setting and warm, personal service at this guesthouse. Located a short walk from Hualamphong station, kitchen and laundry facilities are also available, and there are lots of chill-out areas and computers.

River View Guest House (Map pp116-17; ☎ 0 2234 5429; www.riverviewbkk.com; 768 Soi Phanurangsi, Th Songwat; d 250-950B; river ferry Tha Krom Chao Tha; 🛇) You've probably seen this tall building from the river, but it's a bit harder to find on land. Rooms are basic, suiting the abandoned feel of the place, and only the more expensive rooms on the upper floors have river-view balconies. To get there, heading north on Th Charoen Krung from Th Si Phraya, take a left onto Th Songwat (before the Chinatown Arch), then the second left onto Soi Phanurangsi. You'll start to see signs at this point.

Train Inn (Map pp116-17; ☎ 0 2215 3055; www.thetraininn.com; 428 Th Rong Muang/Hualamphong; r 450-900B; Metro Hualamphong; 🛇 🖵) Located directly behind Hualamphong, the city's main train station, this tidy guesthouse is a good place to base yourself if you've got an early departure or a late arrival. Only the more expensive rooms have attached bathrooms, but free wi-fi and small design touches are available throughout.

Krung Kasem Srikung Hotel (Map pp116-17; ☎ 0 2225 0132; fax 0 2225 4705; 1860 Th Krung Kasem; d 650-700B; Metro Hualamphong; 🛇) The rooms at this old-timer are slightly more hospitable than the exterior (and the neighbourhood) suggest. All have balconies, and those on the upper floors offer great views of Chinatown. Located a brief walk from Hualamphong train station.

China Town Hotel (Map pp116-17; ☎ 0 2225 0204; www.chinatownhotel.co.th; 215 Th Yaowarat; r 1390-1800B, ste 2200-2800B; river ferry Tha Ratchawong; 🛇 🖵) Popular with Chinese tourists, the lobby here plays on the theme suggested by the hotel's name, but the rooms are largely devoid of any design concept. Some suites have recently been remodelled and offer decent value.

our pick **Shanghai Inn** (Map pp116-17; ☎ 0 2221 2121; www.shanghai-inn.com; 479-481 Th Yaowarat; r 2900-4000B; river ferry Tha Ratchawong; 🛇 🖵) Easily the most stylish place to stay in Chinatown, if not in Bangkok. This boutique hotel suggests Shanghai c 1935 via stained glass, an abundance of lamps, bold colours and tongue-in-cheek Chinatown kitsch. There's free wi-fi, and the number of rooms here will have increased 50% by the time this goes to print. If you're willing to splurge, ask for one of the bigger streetside rooms with tall windows that allow more natural light.

Grand China Princess (Map pp116-17; ☎ 0 2224 9977; www.grandchina.com; 528 Th Yaowarat; r 4200-4800B, ste 8400-9000B; river ferry Tha Ratchawong; ※ 🖳 🎨) This characterless but spotless hotel is the conservative choice in Chinatown. Rooms are huge, and those on the top floors offer great views of the city. A rooftop pool and revolving restaurant also take advantage of the sights. Book online for significant discounts.

Silom, Sathon & Riverside

The city's financial district along Th Silom is not the most charming area of town, but it is convenient to nightspots and to the Skytrain and Metro for quick access to modern parts of Bangkok. There's a distinct lack of budget accommodation around Th Silom, but some good-value boutique midrangers can be found on Soi Sala Daeng. Some of Bangkok's most famous top-enders are also located along this stretch of the river; they can be reached via the complimentary hotel ferries at Tha Sathon.

Th Sathon is home to several top-end hotels, but lacks in atmosphere, the primary feature being the vast eponymous road. If you need to stay around this area be sure to see p159 for a few more hotel options around lower Th Sathon.

BUDGET & MIDRANGE

New Road Guesthouse (Map pp118-19; ☎ 0 2630 6994; fax 0 2237 1102; 1216/1 Th Charoen Krung; dm fan/air-con 130/220B, d 280-1500B; river ferry Tha Si Phraya; ※ 🖳) Just far enough from cacophonous Th Charoen Krung (previously known as New Rd) to be quiet, this Danish-run backpacker hostel offers a wide variety of plain but neat rooms. For those on tight budgets, the cheap fan dorms are among the cheapest accommodation in town. The attached JYSK travel agency is reputable.

our pick Lub*d (Map pp118-19; ☎ 0 2634 7999; www .lubd.com; 4 Th Decho; dm/s/d 520/1280/1800B; Skytrain Chong Nonsi; ※ 🖳) The title is a play on the Thai *làp dee*, meaning 'sleep well', but the fun atmosphere at this backpacker hostel might make you want to stay up all night. There are four storeys of dorms (including a ladies-only wing) and a few private rooms, both with and without bathrooms. The communal area, with informative maps painted on the walls, boasts free internet, games and a bar.

P&R Residence (Map pp118-19; ☎ 0 2639 6091-93; pandrresidence@gmail.com; 34 Soi 30, Th Charoen Krung; r 1000-1200B; river ferry Tha Si Phraya; ※) Located on a quiet street near the old Portuguese embassy, there's nothing fancy about the P&R, but its rooms are comfortable and clean and it's very fairly priced for this relatively atmospheric corner of town. Breakfast is 80B extra, and payments are by cash only.

Bangkok Christian Guest House (Map pp118-19; ☎ 0 2233 2206; www.bcgh.org; 123 Soi Sala Daeng 2, Th Convent; s/d 1100/1540B; Skytrain Sala Daeng, Metro Silom; ※ 🖳) This austere guesthouse dates back to 1926, but today resembles any other modern building in Bangkok. Great for families, as some rooms have five beds, and there's a 2nd-floor children's play area and lots of tourist information.

La Résidence Hotel (Map pp118-19; ☎ 0 2233 3301, www.laresidencebangkok.com; 173/8-9 Th Surawong; s/d 1200-2000B, ste 2700B; Skytrain Chong Nonsi; ※ 🖳) La Résidence is a boutique inn with playfully and individually decorated rooms. A standard room is very small and fittingly decorated like a child's bedroom. The next size up is more mature and voluptuous with blood-red walls and modern Thai motifs.

our pick Swan Hotel (Map pp118-19; ☎ 0 2235 9271; www.swanhotelbkk.com; 31 Soi 36, Th Charoen Krung; s/d 1200-1500B; river ferry Tha Oriental; ※ 🖳 🎨) Despite its relatively large size, this classic Bangkok hotel is able to maintain a homey feel. A recent facelift has it looking better than ever, although the room furnishings are still stuck in the 1970s. The inviting pool area is a bit more timeless, and the entire place is virtually spotless. An excellent midrange choice.

Inn Saladaeng (Map pp118-19; ☎ 0 2637 5522; www .theinnsaladaeng.com; 5/12 Soi Sala Daeng; d 1400-1800B; Skytrain Sala Daeng, Metro Silom; ※ 🖳) One of several boutique hotels in the area, the Inn is the newest and most conveniently located. The lobby's bright floral theme carries on into the 38 tight but well-equipped rooms, making up for the lack of windows. Free wi-fi and self-serve breakfast are other perks.

Rose Hotel (Map pp118-19; ☎ 0 2266 8268-72; www .rosehotelbkk.com; 118 Th Surawong; r from 1800B; Skytrain Sala Daeng, Metro Silom; ※ 🖳 🎨) Don't let the unremarkable exterior fool you; a recent renovation has the lobby and rooms of this Vietnam War vet looking quite modern. With a gym, sauna and breakfasts included, it's one of the best deals in town.

Heritage Baan Silom (Map pp118-19; ☎ 0 2236 8388; www.theheritagehotels.com; Baan Silom Shopping Centre, 669 Soi 19, Th Silom; r 2750-3250B; Skytrain Surasak; ※ 🖳) Tucked behind a 'lifestyle arcade' (ie shopping

LATE-NIGHT TOUCHDOWN

A lot of nail-biting anxiety is expended on international flights arriving in Bangkok around midnight. Will there be taxis into town, will there be available rooms, will my family ever hear from me again? Soothe those nagging voices with the knowledge that most international flights arrive late and that Bangkok is an accommodating place. Yes, there are taxis and even an airport bus service (see p183).

If you haven't already made hotel reservations, a good area to look for a bed is lower Sukhumvit; it's right off the airport expressway and hotels around Soi Nana such as the **Swiss Park** (p158) and the **Federal** (p157) are used to lots of late-night traffic, and won't break the bank. Alternatively, you could always go to Th Khao San, which stays up late, is full of hotels and guesthouses, and sees a near-continuous supply of 'fresh-off-the-birds' just like you.

If, for some reason, you can't stray too far from the airport, these places provide a more than adequate roof.

Suvarnabhumi International Airport

Refill Now! The nearest good budget option (see p160).

Grand Inn Come Hotel (off Map pp110–11; ☎ 0 2738 8189-99; www.grandinncome-hotel.com; 99 Moo 6, Th Kingkaew, Bangplee; r from 2000B; ✖ 🖳) Solid midranger 10km from the airport, with airport shuttle and 'lively' karaoke bar.

All Seasons Bangkok Huamark (Map pp110–11; ☎ 0 2308 7888; 5 Soi 15, Th Ramkhamhaeng; r 2040B; ✖ 🖳 🕱) Only 20km from the airport, this midranger has 268 rooms to choose from.

Novotel Suvarnabhumi Airport Hotel (off Map pp110–11; ☎ 0 2131 1111; www.novotel.com; r from 5000B; ✖ 🖳) With 600-plus luxurious rooms in the airport.

Don Muang Airport

We-Train International House (Map pp110–11; ☎ 0 2967 8550-54; www.we-train.co.th; 501/1 Th Dechatungkha, Don Muang; dm 200B, r 800–1100B; ✖ 🕱) Run by the Association for the Promotion of the Status of Women, this place offers good-value rooms a short taxi ride from the airport.

Amari Airport Hotel (Map pp110–11; ☎ 0 2566 1020; www.amari.com; 333 Th Choet Wutthakat; r from 2263B; ✖ 🖳 🕱) Directly opposite Don Muang, this most popular airport hotel also has well-equipped day-use rooms.

Rama Gardens Hotel (Map pp110–11; ☎ 0 2561 0022; www.ramagardenshotel.com; 9/9 Th Vibhavadi Rangsit; r from 4708B; ✖ 🖳 🕱) Tranquil garden setting and very comfortable deluxe wings with deep-soak tubs. Shuttle buses to airport.

---

centre), this wannabe top-ender is a modern interpretation of an English colonial-era mansion. Carefully designed with attractive wood and wicker furnishings, the rooms here are bright and airy, each featuring a different colour theme and custom wall prints.

TOP END

LUXX (Map pp118-19; ☎ 0 2635 8800; www.staywithluxx .com; 6/11 Th Decho; r 3300-6100B; Skytrain Chong Nonsi; ✖ 🖳) Despite their location in a nondescript leafy Bangkok street, the 13 rooms here ooze with a minimalist hipness that wouldn't be out of place in London or New York. Some rooms don't have windows, but rather glass walls that overlook an enclosed courtyard.

Triple Two Silom (Map pp118-19; ☎ 0 2627 2222; www .tripletwosilom.com; 222 Th Silom; r/ste 4800/5500B; Skytrain

Chong Nonsi; ✖ 🖳) Rooms here resemble sleek modern offices – in a good way. But don't worry, with huge bathrooms and inviting-looking beds, you'll be inspired to relax, not work. Guests can use the rooftop garden, but have to go next door to the sister Narai Hotel for the swimming pool and fitness centre.

Millennium Hilton (Map pp118-19; ☎ 0 2442 2000; www.bangkok.hilton.com; 123 Th Charoen Nakorn, Thonburi; r 6800-7300B, ste 12,000-26,000B; hotel shuttle boat from River City & Tha Sathon/Central Pier; ✖ 🖳 🕱) As soon as you enter the dramatic lobby, it's obvious that this is Bangkok's youngest, most modern riverside hotel. Rooms, all of which boast widescreen river views, follow this theme, and are decked out with funky furniture and Thai-themed photos. A glass elevator and an artificial beach are just some of the fun touches.

Lebua (Map pp118–19; ☎ 0 2624 9999; www.lebua .com; State Tower, cnr Th Silom & Th Charoen Krung; d/ste from US$200/300; Skytrain Saphan Taksin; ✆ 🖳 🖭) One of Bangkok's tallest and most distinctive buildings is also a luxury hotel. Suites here are huge, some with two balconies, and if you book online the discounts can be equally large.

Dusit Thani (Map pp118–19; ☎ 0 2200 9000; www .dusit.com; 946 Th Phra Ram IV; r 10,000–17,000B, ste 19,500–79,000B; Skytrain Sala Daeng, Metro Silom; ✆ 🖳 🖭) At one point the tallest building in the country, this venerable luxury hotel is a testament to how much things have changed in Bangkok. Despite the flagrantly 1970s exterior, the rooms, like the lobby, are blandly modern. The hotel's vast ballroom is a popular wedding venue for upper-class locals, and its restaurants are favourite dining destinations for members of the Thai royal family.

Oriental Hotel (Map pp118–19; ☎ 0 2659 9000; www .mandarinoriental.com; 48 Soi Oriental/38, Th Charoen Krung; r incl breakfast US$420–600, ste incl breakfast US$600–3000; hotel shuttle boat from Tha Sathon/Central Pier; ✆ 🖳 🖭) For the true Bangkok experience, a stay at this grand old riverside hotel is a must; see the boxed text on p156 for a brief history. The majority of rooms are located in the modern New Wing, but we prefer the old-world ambiance of the Garden and Authors' Wings. The hotel is home to the city's most longstanding fine dining restaurant, Le Normandie (p164), and across the river in Thonburi the hotel also maintains one of the region's most acclaimed spas (p140) and a cooking school.

our pick **Peninsula Hotel** (Map pp118–19; ☎ 0 2861 2888; www.peninsula.com; 333 Th Charoen Nakhon, Thonburi; r 12,000–15,000B, ste 20,000–120,000B; hotel shuttle boat from Tha Sathon/Central Pier; ✆ 🖳 🖭) After a decade in Bangkok, the Pen still seems to have it all: the location (towering over the river in Thonburi), the rep (it's consistently one of the highest-ranking luxury hotels in the world) and one of the highest levels of service in town. If money is no obstacle, stay on one of the upper floors (there are 38) where you literally have all of Bangkok at your feet.

Siam Square & Pratunam

For centrally located accommodation, there's really no better destination than the area surrounding Siam Square. Home to the intersection of the two Skytrain lines, and only a brief-ish (depending on traffic) taxi ride to Banglamphu, this is about as good as it gets

in ever-expanding Bangkok. The only drawback is that nightlife is nonexistent, but again you're only a short taxi ride to nightspots in Silom or Sukhumvit.

For those on a budget who also need a central location, a low-key backpacker community exists along Soi Kasem San 1 (say 'gà·sǎirm'), across from the National Stadium.

BUDGET & MIDRANGE

Bed & Breakfast Inn (Map pp120–1; ☎ 0 2215 3004; Soi Kasem San 1; s/d incl breakfast 600/700B; Skytrain National Stadium, klorng taxi to Tha Ratchathewi; ✆) This mazelike guesthouse has standard but comfortable rooms. Rates, not surprisingly, include breakfast.

A-One Inn (Map pp120–1; ☎ 0 2215 3029; www .aoneinn.com; 25/13–15 Soi Kasem San 1; d from 650B; Skytrain National Stadium, klorng taxi to Tha Ratchathewi; ✆ 🖳) The lobby is a bit messy here, but a peek into the rooms proves that they are well proportioned and good value. A-One sees a lot of return business.

Wendy House (Map pp120–1; ☎ 0 2214 1149; www .wendyguesthouse.com; 36/2 Soi Kasem San 1; d incl breakfast from 1000B; Skytrain National Stadium, klorng taxi to Tha Ratchathewi; ✆ 🖳) The rooms here are small and basic, but well stocked (TV, fridge) for this price range. There's a cafe downstairs and service is exceedingly friendly.

Reno Hotel (Map pp120–1; ☎ 0 2215 0026; www .renohotel.co.th; 40 Soi Kasem San 1; d 1280–1650B; Skytrain National Stadium, klorng taxi to Tha Ratchathewi; ✆ 🖳 🖭) Only some of the rooms reflect the renovations evident in the lobby and exterior, but the cafe and classic pool of this Vietnam War–era vet still cling to the past.

Golden House (Map pp120–1; ☎ 0 2252 9535; www .goldenhouses.net; 1025/5-9 Th Ploenchit; d 1650B; Skytrain Chitlom; ✆ 🖳) With parquet flooring and built-in wooden furniture, the 27 rooms here are more like modern Thai condos than hotel rooms. The beds are huge, but just like at Thai condos they have the potential to sag. Golden House is located just steps from Skytrain Chitlom; look for the sign that says VIP Guest House.

Indra Regent Hotel (Map pp120–1; ☎ 0 2208 0022–33; www.indrahotel.com; 120/126 Th Ratchaprarop; d from 2720B; Skytrain Chitlom, klorng taxi to Tha Pratunam; ✆ 🖭) This soot-stained '70s-era box doesn't look like much from the outside, but the interior offers one of the better-value stays in this price range. Junior suites are touted as the best buys.

BANGKOK'S GRANDE DAME

The Oriental Hotel started out as a roughshod boarding house for European seafarers in the late 19th century, but was transformed into an aristocratic magnet by Hans Niels Anderson, the founder of the formidable East Asiatic Company (which operated between Bangkok and Copenhagen). He hired an Italian designer to build what is now known as the Authors' Wing, which was the city's most elaborate secular building; all other grand architecture at the time was commissioned by the king.

With a dramatic setting beside Mae Nam Chao Phraya, the hotel has gained its reputation from its famous guests. A Polish-born sailor named Joseph Conrad stayed here in between nautical jobs in 1888. W Somerset Maugham stumbled into the hotel with an advanced case of malaria contracted during his overland journey from Burma. In his feverish state, he heard the German manager arguing with the doctor about how a death in the hotel would hurt business. Maugham's recovery and completion of *Gentleman in the Parlour: A Record of a Journey from Rangoon to Haiphong* contributed to the long-lasting literary appeal of the hotel. Other notable guests have included Noël Coward, Graham Greene, John le Carré, James Michener, Gore Vidal and Barbara Cartland. Some modern-day writers even claim that a stay in the Oriental will overcome writer's block.

To soak up the ambience of old seafaring Bangkok, stop by for a cocktail at the Bamboo Bar or toast the 'swift river' as Noël Coward did from the riverside terrace. For teetotallers, an afternoon brew is served in a frilly Victorian lounge filled with black-and-white photographs of Rama V. To ensure its aristocratic leanings in a less formal age, the hotel enforces a dress code (no shorts, sleeveless shirts or sandals allowed).

Asia Hotel (Map pp120-1; ☎ 0 2215 0808; www .asiahotel.co.th; 296 Th Phayathai; r from 2900B; Skytrain Ratchathewi, klorng taxi to Tha Ratchathewi; ☒ ▣ ⊠) The epitome of an Asian midranger, this huge hotel has plain but large rooms with generous-sized bathrooms. Connoisseurs of kitsch will appreciate the dual presence of Calypso Cabaret (see the boxed text, p173) and an Elvis show. Significant discounts available online.

TOP END

Novotel Bangkok on Siam Square (Map pp120-1; ☎ 0 2255 6888; www.accorhotels-asia.com; Soi 6, Siam Sq; d from 3655B; Skytrain Siam; ☒ ▣ ⊠) For business or leisure, Novotel Siam is conveniently located near the Skytrain and shopping. Rooms are spitting images of corporate class back home, but the deluxe ones are better suited for business purposes.

Nai Lert Park Hotel (Map pp120-1; ☎ 0 2253 0123; www.swissotel.com/bangkok-nailertpark; 2 Th Withayu/ Wireless Rd; d from 5300B; Skytrain Ploenchit, klorng taxi to Tha Withayu; ☒ ▣ ⊠) This hotel has seen a few reincarnations during its 25-year history, but we like the current one; the suites follow the sleek design theme laid out in the lobby, while cheaper rooms follow a more conservative wood-heavy 'classic' theme. Regardless, all are huge and include balconies.

Siam@Siam (Map pp120-1; ☎ 0 2217 3000; www .siamatsiam.com; 865 Th Phra Ram I; r 5700-8400B; Skytrain National Stadium; ☒ ▣ ⊠) The lobby of this new hotel is more amusement park than accommodation, but that's what makes it so fun. A seemingly random mishmash of colours and materials result in a style one could only describe as 'junkyard' – but in a good way, of course. The rooms, which continue the theme, and which are located between the 14th and 25th floors, offer terrific city views, free wi-fi and breakfast. There's also a spa, a rooftop restaurant and a pool on the 8th floor.

Conrad Hotel Bangkok (Map pp120-1; ☎ 0 2690 9999; www.conradhotels.com; 87 Th Withayu/Wireless Rd; d from 7062B; Skytrain Ploenchit; ☒ ▣ ⊠) When built in 2003, the Conrad was one of the first hotels in Bangkok to consciously make an effort to appeal to the young and hip. It has since been surpassed in this area, but still offers attractive accommodation. The interior is decked out in Jim Thompson silks and a vaguely Asian theme. The attached Diplomat Bar is a great place to chill out with a martini and live jazz.

Grand Hyatt Erawan (Map pp120-1; ☎ 0 2254 1234; www.bangkok.hyatt.com; cnr Th Ratchadamri & Th Ploenchit; d from 10,400B; Skytrain Chitlom; ☒ ▣ ⊠) This long-standing luxury staple boasts 380 functional and handsome rooms in the virtual centre of Bangkok's commercial zone. The rooms are seemingly designed for those who wish to work, with inviting and well-positioned desks. For those on holiday (and not constrained by budgets), six new Spa Cottages include a city-view balcony, an attached spa, and complimentary massage and spa services.

Sukhumvit

This seemingly endless urban thoroughfare is Bangkok's unofficial International Zone and also boasts much of the city's accommodation. There's a bit of everything here, from the odd backpacker hostel to sex tourist hovels and five-star luxury. The former two are largely located between Sois 1 and 4, while the latter doesn't begin to appear until you reach Soi 12 or so.

In general, because visitors with larger budgets stay in Sukhumvit, tourist services are more expensive here than in Banglamphu. The trade-off is access to food from virtually every corner of the globe, heaps of nightlife options and easy access to both the Skytrain and subway.

BUDGET

Suk 11 (Map pp122-3; ☎ 0 2253 5927; www.suk11.com; 1/33 Soi 11, Th Sukhumvit; dm/s/d/ste 250/500/750/2000B; Skytrain Nana; ✖ 🖳) Extremely well run and extremely popular, this guesthouse is an oasis of woods and greenery in the urban jungle that is Th Sukhumvit. Although they've somehow managed to stuff nearly 100 rooms in there, you'll still need to book at least two weeks ahead.

HI-Sukhumvit (Map pp122-3; ☎ 0 2391 9338; www.hisukhumvit.com; 23 Soi 38, Th Sukhumvit; dm 300B, s 550-600B, d 800-850B; Skytrain Thong Lo; ✖ 🖳) Located in a quiet residential street a brief walk from the Skytrain, this friendly hostel excels with its neat dorms and accompanying immense bathrooms. There is lots of tourist information, a rooftop deck, laundry and kitchen.

Soi 1 Guesthouse (Map pp122-3; ☎ 0 2655 0604; www.soi1guesthouse.com; 220/7 Soi 1, Th Sukhumvit; dm 350B; Skytrain Ploenchit; ✖ 🖳) Boasting the somewhat intimidating motto 'See the world before it seizes you', this narrow building has four cluttered dorm rooms. When not outside seeing the world, let yourself be 'seized' by the chummy communal area with pool table, TV and computers.

Nana Chart (Map pp122-3; ☎ 0 2259 4900; www.thailandhostel.com; cnr Soi 25, Th Sukhumvit; dm 390B, r 1200-1800B; Skytrain Asoke, Metro Sukhumvit; ✖ 🖳) This tidy, newish backpacker hostel packs 90 plain

but more-than-adequate budget rooms, as well as some of the better dorms around featuring ensuite bathrooms. Restaurants and a travel agency are also located in the compound.

Atlanta (Map pp122-3; ☎ 0 2252 1650/6069; fax 0 2656 8123; 78 Soi Phasak/2, Th Sukhumvit; r 535-650B, ste 1820B; Skytrain Ploenchit; ✖ 🖳) Defiantly antiquated and equally frumpy, this crumbling gem has changed very little since its construction in 1952. The opulent lobby stands in contrast to the simple rooms, but the inviting pool (the country's first hotel pool) and delightful restaurant are incentive enough. The rather fanatical anti-sex-tourist policy may leave Thai friends of either gender waiting outside. **Miami Hotel** (Map pp122-3; ☎ 0 2253 0369; www.thaimiami.com; 2 Soi 13, Th Sukhumvit; s/d 800/1000B; Skytrain Nana; ✖ 🖳) Definitely showing its 40 years, and currently surrounded by the noisy construction of things much grander, the Miami still manages to carry an element of old-school Bangkok charm. Ask for one of the original business cards while they last.

MIDRANGE

Golden Palace Hotel (Map pp122-3; ☎ 0 2252 5115; www.goldenpalacehotel.com; 15 Soi 1, Th Sukhumvit; r 1110-1350B; Skytrain Ploenchit; ✖ 🖳 🖳) The abundance of mirrors in the ground-floor rooms gives this away as a former tryst hotel, but for just a couple of hundred baht more, you can get one of the simple but airy rooms upstairs. A pool, coffee shop and nearby spa ensure that you won't need to go very far to be entertained.

Federal Hotel (Map pp122-3; ☎ 0 2253 0175; www.federalbangkok.com; 27 Soi 11, Th Sukhumvit; r 1200-1500B; Skytrain Nana; ✖ 🖳 🖳) You wouldn't know it from the exterior, but after 40 years 'Club Fed' finally decided to get a makeover. The upstairs rooms are comfortable and almost contemporary, but the rooms at ground level still scream 1967. The real draws are the frangipani-lined pool and time-warped American-style coffee shop.

Stable Lodge (Map pp122-3; ☎ 0 2653 0017; www.stablelodge.com; 39 Soi 8, Th Sukhumvit; r 1495-1695B; Skytrain Nana; ✖ 🖳 🖳) To be honest, we were slightly disappointed that the faux-Tudor theme of the downstairs restaurant didn't carry on into the rooms, but could find no other faults. A recent renovation has given a bit of life to the simple rooms here, and the spacious balconies still offer great city views.

Baan Sukhumvit (Map pp122-3; ☎ 0 2258 5625; www.baansukhumvit.com; 392/38-39 Soi 20, Th Sukhumvit; s/d 1540/1760B; Skytrain Asoke, Metro Sukhumvit; ✖ 🖳) One

BANGKOK

THINKING AHEAD

The rates listed in this chapter are high-season rack rates; ie the highest price a hotel will generally charge for a room. However, there's no reason you should be paying this much, especially if you know ahead of time when you'll be in town. Booking rooms online can lead to savings of at least 20%, and often more, at many of Bangkok's leading hotels. This can be done directly through the hotel websites or via sites such as **Lonely Planet's Hotels & Hostels** (www.lonelyplanet.com), which features thorough reviews from authors and traveller feedback, and a booking facility.

It can also work to your advantage to simply call and book ahead; sometimes hotel desk staff collect commission on walk-ins and are reluctant to discount, something that can be remedied by a pre-emptive phone call and an inquiry about the lowest possible rate.

of three similarly priced hotels located on this small side street off Soi 20, Baan Sukhumvit's 12 rooms exude a homey, cosy atmosphere. A newer branch is located around the corner on Soi 18.

Swiss Park Hotel (Map pp122-3; ☎ 0 2254 0228; 155/23 Soi Chaiyot/11, Th Sukhumvit; r 1900-2350B, ste 3350B; Skytrain Nana; 🞨 🗷) The rooms here are workaday and largely forgettable, but the convenient location and friendly and competent staff make this a good midrange find.

Citichic (Map pp122-3; ☎ 0 2342 3888; www.citichic hotel.com; 34 Soi 13, Th Sukhumvit; r 2700-3000B; Skytrain Nana; 🞨 🖳 🗷) The name and lobby of this stylish midranger ooze self-confidence. And justifiably so; although they are a bit of a tight squeeze, the rooms here come fully equipped with flat-screen TVs and all other amenities – and all of it done with style.

Napa Place Bed & Breakfast (Map pp122-3; ☎ 0 2661 5525; www.napaplace.com; 11/3 Sap 2, Soi 36, Th Sukhumvit; d 2750-4800B; Skytrain Thong Lo; 🞨 🖳) Seemingly hidden in the confines of a typical Bangkok urban compound is what must be the city's homiest accommodation. The 12 expansive rooms here have been decorated with dark woods from the family's former business and light brown cloths from the hands of Thai weavers. The communal areas couldn't be much different from the suburban living room you grew up in.

TOP END

Seven (Map pp122-3; ☎ 0 2662 0951; www.sleepatseven .com; 3/15 Soi Sawasdee/31, Th Sukhumvit; r 3296-6000B; Skytrain Phrom Phong; 🞨 🖳) This tiny hotel somehow manages to be chic and homey, stylish and comfortable, Thai and international all at the same time. Each of the six rooms is decked out in a different colour that corresponds to Thai astrology, and thoughtful amenities abound.

Davis (Map pp122-3; ☎ 0 2260 8000; www.davisbangkok .net; Soi 24, Th Sukhumvit; d from 5000B; 🞨 🖳 🗷) If it's hard to pinpoint the design of this young-feeling hotel it's probably because it seems to have covered all the bases with Chinese-, Japanese-, Myanmar- and Balinese-themed rooms. Domestically speaking, there are also seven Thai-style villas surrounding a pool. It's located way out near Th Phra Ram IV, but there are túk-túks (pronounced dúk dúk; motorised transport) to whisk you to the civilisation of Th Sukhumvit.

our pick **Eugenia** (Map pp122-3; ☎ 0 2259 9017-19; www.theeugenia.com; 267 Soi Sawasdee/31, Th Sukhumvit; r 5800-7200B; Skytrain Asoke, Metro Sukhumvit; 🞨 🖳 🗷) Although Thailand was never anybody's colony, there's no doubt about the design influence of this character-laden hotel. Decked out in antique furniture and an abundance of animal skins, a stay here is like travelling to Burma c 1936. Don't fear though; you won't have to ask the 'boy' to draw you a bath – modern amenities such as flat-screen TVs and free domestic and international calls are also provided (although the baths are beautiful and made of copper). Ask about the vintage-car airport transfers.

Dream Bangkok (Map pp122-3; ☎ 0 2254 8500; www .dreambkk.com; 10 Soi 15, Th Sukhumvit; r from US$200; Skytrain Asoke; 🞨 🖳 🗷) If your idea of interior design involves stuffed tigers, copious mirrors and slick leather, you'll feel at home here. The perfect place for the travelling rock star – real or otherwise – the Dream is Bangkok's most outlandish hotel. The standard rooms are a tight fit, but include ample and quirky amenities such as the Dream signature blue light to aid in sleeping.

Sheraton Grande Sukhumvit (Map pp122-3; ☎ 0 2649 8888; www.sheratongrandesukhumvit.com; 250 Th Sukhumvit; r from 8700B; Skytrain Asoke, Metro Sukhumvit; 🞨 🖳 🗷) This business-oriented hotel offers some of the most spacious rooms in town and fills them with a generous array of amenities. An elevated walkway connecting the hotel to Asoke Skytrain station makes this the convenient choice for those on generous expense accounts.

Ma Du Zi (Map pp122-3; ☎ 0 2615 6400; www.maduzihotel.com; cnr Th Ratchadapisek & Soi 16, Th Sukhumvit; r 17,200-33,000B; Skytrain Asoke, Metro Sukhumvit; ✂ 🖳) The name is Thai for 'come take a look', somewhat of a misnomer for this reservations-only, no walk-ins hotel. If you've gained access, behind the gate you'll find an attractive midsized hotel steeped in dark, chic tones and designs. We fancied the immense bathrooms, with a walk-in tub and minimalist shower. There's no pool, but the rack rate includes everything from airport transfer, breakfast and dinner to domestic and international calls.

Lumphini Park & Th Phra Ram IV

If you were hitting the Asian hippie trail back in the 1970s, you would have laid your love beads at a guesthouse in Soi Ngam Duphli, off Th Phra Ram IV, not too far from Lumphini Park. Despite the decades that have passed, it's still a good area to go to for supercheap accommodation, particularly along Soi Sri Bamphen. And getting there has been made even easier by the Metro stop at Lumphini.

Café des Arts Guest House (Map p124; ☎ 0 2679 8438; 27/39 Soi Sri Bamphen; fan/air-con 350/450B; Metro Lumphini; ✂ 🖳) Run by a French/Thai couple, there's seemingly no cafe (nor art) here, but rather a downstairs Korean barbecue restaurant and eight simple rooms upstairs.

Malaysia Hotel (Map p124; ☎ 0 2679 7127; www.malaysiahotelbkk.com; 54 Soi Ngam Duphli; d 798-998B; Metro Lumphini; ✂ 🖳 🏊) The Malaysia was once Bangkok's most famous budget lodge and even gave shelter to Maureen and Tony Wheeler on their maiden shoestring trip through Southeast Asia. Our sources tell us that the couple stay elsewhere when in Bangkok nowadays, but the Malaysia is still a good choice for the rest of us for its fair prices and frozen-in-time atmosphere.

Penguin House (Map p124; ☎ 0 2679 9991; www.geocities.com/penguinhouses; 27/23 Soi Sri Bamphen; r 800-950B, 2-night minimum; Metro Lumphini; ✂ 🖳) The oddly named Penguin is a breath of fresh air in this area of tired old-timers. Rear rooms will be quieter, and there are a couple of interior rooms that sleep two couples. Weekly and monthly rates are also available.

All Seasons Sathorn (Map p124; ☎ 0 2343 6333; www.allseasons-sathorn.com; 31 Th Sathon Tai; r 1800-2500B; Metro Lumphini; ✂ 🖳) The former King's Hotel has been reborn as this modern attractive choice, right in the middle of the embassy district. The primary colours and bold lines of the design scheme make up for the lack of natural light in some rooms. To see what the hotel (and Th Sathon) used to look like, check out the photos in the dining room.

Ibis Sathon (Map p124; ☎ 0 2659 2888; Soi Ngam Duphli; r incl breakfast 2040B; Metro Lumphini; ✂ 🏊) Business-friendly Ibis delivers comfort and convenience without corporate expense-account prices.

Metropolitan (Map p124; ☎ 0 2625 3333; www.metropolitan.como.bz; 27 Th Sathon Tai, r incl breakfast US$145-185, ste incl breakfast US$210-2000; Metro Lumphini; ✂ 🖳 🏊) The exterior of the former YMCA has changed relatively little, but a peek inside reveals Bangkok's sleekest hotel. Urban minimalism rules here, except where it concerns the size of the two-storey suites. Breakfast is either American or 'organic', and attached Cy'an (p167) is among Bangkok's best upscale restaurants.

Sukhothai Hotel (Map p124; ☎ 0 2344 8888; www.sukhothai.com; 13/3 Th Sathon Tai; r 9500-10,700B, ste 12,900-100,000B; Metro Lumphini; ✂ 🖳 🏊) As the name suggests, this hotel employs brick stupas, courtyards and antique sculptures to create a historical, temple-like atmosphere. The rooms are exquisitely decorated and have hardwood floors and war-room-sized bathrooms.

Central Bangkok

Many of the following hotels lie outside our neat neighbourhood designations, so they often require a little more effort to reach. This also means that they tend to be located in less hectic parts of the city, and are perfect for those who'd rather not stay in the thick of it. Thewet, the district north of Banglamphu near the National Library, is a pleasant backpacker enclave, particularly popular with families and the over-30 crowd. It is a lovely leafy area, but during the rainy season it can be prone to flooding.

Bangkok International Youth Hostel (Map pp112-13; ☎ 0 2282 0950; www.hihostels.com; 25/2 Th Phitsanulok, Dusit; dm 170B, r 600-2400B; bus 16, 509, river ferry Tha Thewet; ✂ 🖳) One of the only options if you want to stay in the quiet Dusit area, this recently refurbished hostel has cheaper rooms in the original building and new but cramped rooms in a tall structure facing Th Phitsanulok. There's a pleasant rooftop balcony and a travel library.

Shanti Lodge (Map pp112-13; ☎ 0 2281 2497; 37 Soi Thewet, Th Si Ayutthaya, Thewet; dm 200B, r 400-2950B; bus 30, 503, river ferry Tha Thewet; 🍴 🖳) This family-run place exudes a peaceful, dharmic aura. It's also a true guesthouse, so there are misplaced baskets of the owners' laundry, an abandoned exercise bike and other 'homey' touches. Walls are bamboo-thin in the cheaper rooms, but there's a huge variety of accommodation; check out a few before making a decision.

Taewez Guest House (Map pp112-13; ☎ 0 2280 8856; 23/12 Th Si Ayutthaya, Thewet; s/d 250/530B; bus 30, 503, river ferry Tha Thewet; 🍴) Popular with French travellers, the cheapest rooms here are plain and share bathrooms, but are good value.

Sri Ayuttaya Guest House (Map pp112-13; ☎ 0 2282 5942; 23/11 Th Si Ayutthaya, Thewet; s 400B, d 600-850B; bus 30, 503, river ferry Tha Thewet; 🍴 🖳) The wood and brick theme here is a nice break from the usual, less permanent-feeling guesthouse design. The rooms, half of which share bathrooms, also feel sturdy and inviting.

Phra-Nakorn Norn-Len (Map pp112-13; ☎ 0 2628 8600; www.phranakorn-nornlen.com; 46 Soi 1, Th Thewet, Thewet; s incl breakfast 1800B, d incl breakfast 2200-2400B; bus 30, 503, river ferry Tha Thewet; 🍴 🖳) Set in an expansive garden compound decorated like the Bangkok of yesteryear, this bright and cheery hotel is an atmospheric if not necessarily great value place to stay. Rooms are simply furnished, but generously decorated with antiques and wall paintings, and there's internet, massage and endless opportunities for peaceful relaxing. Breakfast originates from the hotel's organic rooftop garden.

All Seasons Bangkok Siam (Map pp112-13; ☎ 0 2209 3888; www.accorhotels.com/asia; 97 Th Ratchaprarop; r incl breakfast 2000B; Skytrain Victory Monument, bus 513; 🍴 🖳) Part of a new line-up of business-friendly hotels for modest budgets. Shop the website for plumper discounts.

Greater Bangkok

If you need to stay near one of Bangkok's two airports, check the accommodation options in our boxed text on p154.

Refill Now! (Map pp110-11; ☎ 0 2713 2044; www.refillnow.co.th; 191 Soi Pridi Banhom Yong 42/71, Th Sukhumvit, Phra Khanong; dm/s/d 560/1085/1470B; Skytrain Phra Khanong; 🍴 🖳) Sporting a look that blends the Habitat catalogue and a Kubrick movie, this is the kind of place that might make you think twice about sleeping in a dorm. The spotless white private rooms and dorms have flirtatious pull screens between

each double-bunk; women-only dorms are also available. There's an achingly hip chill-out area, and a massage centre upstairs. If you decide you need to leave, there's a túk-túk (30B per passenger) to Thong Lo and Phra Khanong Skytrain stations.

Thai House (Map pp110-11; ☎ 0 2903 9611; www.thaihouse.co.th; 32/4 Mu 8, Bang Yai, Nonthaburi; s/d 1500/1700B) North of central Bangkok in Nonthaburi is this traditional Thai home surrounded by fruit trees, which has been converted into a guesthouse. Contact the proprietors for transport details. The guesthouse also conducts cooking courses open to non-guests (see p144).

Mystic Place (Map pp110-11; ☎ 0 2270 3344; www.reflections-thai.com; 224/5-9 224/11-18 Th Pradiphat, Th Phahonyothin, Saphan Kwai; r 2250-3250B; Skytrain Saphan Kwai; 🍴 🖳) Now at a new location on noisy Th Pradiphat, this hotel unites 34 rooms, each of which is individually and playfully designed. One of the rooms we checked out combined a chair upholstered with stuffed animals and walls covered with graffiti. Heaps of fun and perpetually popular, so be sure to book ahead.

Bangkok Marriott Resort & Spa (Map pp110-11; ☎ 0 2476 0022; www.marriott.com; 257/1-3 Th Charoen Nakhon, Thonburi; d from 5800B; hotel shuttle boat from Tha Sathon & Tha Oriental; 🍴 🖳 🛥) Located south of the city on the banks of Mae Nam Chao Phraya, 'resort' is in this case at least an accurate moniker for this expansive, relax-oriented hotel. Lest the gardens and pools give the impression you're in another province (well, technically you are), you're easily connected to the rest of Bangkok by a hotel-operated shuttle boat to Saphan Taksin.

EATING

Invariably the safest of Bangkok's infamous carnal pleasures, food is serious business in this city. Attracting hungry visitors from across the globe, Bangkok's eats also draw natives from disparate ends of the city, happy to brave traffic or floods for a bowl of noodles or a plate of rice.

The selection is enormous, with eating places in Bangkok ranging from wheeled carts that set up shop on a daily basis to chic dining rooms in five-star hotels. In our experience the tastiest eats are generally found somewhere in-between, at family-run shophouse restaurants serving a limited repertoire of dishes.

The influences are also vast, and you'll find everything from Thai-Chinese to Thai-

Muslim, not to mention most regional Thai cuisines. And if at some point you do tire of *gŏo·ay dĕe·o* (rice noodles) and curries, Bangkok has an ever-expanding selection of high-quality international restaurants, encompassing everything from hole-in-the-wall French bistros to authentic Japanese ramen houses.

Ko Ratanakosin & Banglamphu

Bangkok's royal district has an abundance of sights but a dearth of restaurants – a pity, considering the potential views.

Despite its proximity to the faux *pàt tai* and tame *đôm yam* of Th Khao San, Banglamphu is one of the city's most legendary eating areas. Decades old restaurants and legendary hawkers line the streets in this leafy corner of Olde Bangkok, and you could easily spend an entire day grazing the southern end of Th Tanao alone.

Although you'd be wisest to get your domestic nosh away from the main drag, the foreign influence on Th Khao San has led to a few import standouts.

THAI

Nang Loeng Market (Map pp114-15; Btw Soi 8-10, Th Nakhon Sawan; ☻ 10am-2pm Mon-Sat; bus 72) Dating back to 1899, this atmospheric market is primarily associated with Thai sweets, but at lunchtime it's also an excellent place to fill up on savouries. Try a bowl of handmade egg noodles at Rung Reuang or the wonderful curries across the way at Ratana.

Chote Chitr (Map pp114-15; ☎ 0 2221 4082; 146 Th Phraeng Phuthon; dishes 30-200B; ☻ lunch & dinner Mon-Sat; bus 15, klorng taxi to Tha Phan Fah) This third-generation shophouse restaurant boasting just six tables is a true Bangkok foodie landmark. The kitchen can be inconsistent, but when they're on, dishes like *mèe gròrp* (crispy fried noodles) and *yam tòoa ploo* (wing-bean salad) are in a class of their own.

Kim Leng (no roman-script sign; Map pp114-15; ☎ 0 2622 2062; 158-160 Th Tanao; dishes 40-100B; ☻ lunch & dinner Mon-Sat; bus 15, klorng taxi to Tha Phan Fah) This tiny family-run restaurant specialises in the dishes of central Thailand. The grumpy owner doesn't speak English, so simply point at whatever looks good from the well-stocked glass case, or refer to the English-language menu.

Pan (Map pp114-15; ☎ 0 83817 4227; Th Rambutri; dishes 50-90B; ☻ 11.30am-10pm; bus 30, 53, 506, river ferry Tha Phra Athit) If you're looking for authentic Thai, but don't want to stray far from Th Khao San, this streetside eatery is your best bet. Simply look for the overflowing tray of raw ingredients, point to whatever looks tasty, and Pan will fry it up for you.

Rub Aroon (Map pp114-15; ☎ 0 2622 2312; 310-312 Th Maharat; dishes 60-95B; ☻ 8am-6pm; river ferry Tha Tien) Strategically located across from Wat Pho, this tastefully restored shophouse is the perfect temple-exploring pit stop. Basic one-plate dishes and refreshing drinks bulk out the menu.

Krua Noppharat (Map pp114-15; ☎ 0 2281 7578; 130-132 Th Phra Athit; dishes 60-100B; ☻ lunch & dinner Mon-Sat; bus 30, 53, 506, river ferry Tha Phra Athit) A few dusty paintings are the only effort at interior design at this family-run standby. Where it concerns flavour, however, Krua Noppharat is willing to expend considerably more energy, and thankfully does not tone down its excellent central- and southern-style Thai fare for foreign diners.

Rachanawi Samosorn (Khun Kung Kitchen; Map pp114-15; ☎ 0 2222 0081; 77 Th Maharat; dishes 70-150B; ☻ 10am-6pm; bus 508, 512, bus 32, 53, river ferry Tha Chang) The restaurant of the Royal Navy Association has one of the few coveted riverfront locations along this stretch of the Chao Phraya. Locals come for the combination of riverfront views and cheap and tasty seafood-based eats. The entrance to the restaurant is near the ATM machines at Tha Chang.

Hemlock (Map pp114-15; ☎ 0 2282 7507; 56 Th Phra Athit; dishes 60-220B; ☻ 4pm-midnight; bus 30, 53, 506, river ferry Tha Phra Athit) Taking full advantage of its cosy shophouse setting, this white-tablecloth local is an excellent intro to Thai food. The vast menu has the usual suspects, but also includes some dishes you'd be hard pressed to find elsewhere, as well as a strong veggie section.

Poj Spa Kar (Map pp114-15; ☎ 0 2222 2686; 443 Th Tanao; dishes 100-200B; ☻ lunch & dinner; bus 15, klorng taxi to Tha Phan Fah) Pronounced *pôht sà·pah kahn*, this is the oldest restaurant in Bangkok, and continues to maintain recipes handed down from a former palace cook. Be sure to order the simple but tasty lemongrass omelette or the deliciously sour/sweet *gaang sôm*, a traditional central Thai soup.

INTERNATIONAL

Shoshana (Map pp114-15; ☎ 0 2282 9948; 88 Th Chakraphong; dishes 30-150B; ☻ 10am-11.30pm; bus 30, 53, 506, river ferry Tha Phra Athit) Although prices have

VEGGING OUT IN BANGKOK

Vegetarianism is a growing trend among urban Thais, but veggie restaurants are still generally few and far between.

Banglamphu has the greatest concentration of vegetarian-friendly restaurants, thanks to the nonmeat-eating *fa·ràng;* these are typically low-scale stir-fry shops that do something akin to what your hippie roommates have cooking in their kitchens. Examples include **May Kaidee** (Map pp114–15; ☎ 0 89137 3173; www.maykaidee.com; 33 Th Samsen; dishes 50B; ☺ lunch & dinner; bus 56, 506, river ferry Tha Phra Athit), which also offers a veggie Thai cooking school, and **Ranee Guesthouse** (Map pp114–15; 77 Trok Mayom; dishes 70–120B; ☺ breakfast, lunch & dinner; bus 56, 506, river ferry Tha Phra Athit).

An indigenous vegetarian movement can be found in the food centres operated by the Santi Asoke community, an ascetic Buddhist sect that practises self-sufficiency through agriculture and strict vegetarian diets. The food centres are operated in conjunction with Bangkok's former governor Chamlong Srimuang, who popularised both the sect and vegetarianism during his corruption-reducing tenure in the 1980s and '90s. **Baan Suan Pai** (Map pp112–13; ☎ 0 2615 2454; Th Phahonyothin; dishes 25B; ☺ lunch & dinner; Skytrain Ari), **Chamlong's Asoke Café** (Map pp110–11; ☎ 0 2272 4282; 580-592 Th Phahonyothin, Chatuchak; dishes 20–30B; ☺ lunch Sat & Sun; Metro Chatuchak Park) and **Arawy** (Map pp114–15; 152 Th Din So, Phra Nakhon; dishes 20–30B; ☺ 7am-8pm; bus 15, klorng taxi to Tha Phan Fah) are all affiliated centres.

Upscale-ish Thai- and Italian-style veggie eats can be found at **Anotai** (Map pp110–11; ☎ 0 2641 5366; 976/17 Soi Rama 9 Hospital, Rama 9; dishes 55–150B; ☺ 10am-9.30pm Thu-Tue; Metro Phra Ram 9), which also has an organic vegetable market.

Indian restaurants, particularly those featuring southern Indian cuisine such as **Chennai Kitchen** (opposite), are also largely veggie.

MBK Food Court (p166) has a delicious vegetarian stall (stall C8) that requires mastery of the Asian queue in order to sneak in an order.

During the vegetarian festival in October, the whole city goes mad for tofu (see the boxed text, opposite). Stalls and restaurants indicate their nonmeat menu with yellow banners; Chinatown has the highest concentration of stalls.

---

gone up slightly since it began back in 1982, Shoshana still puts together a cheap but tasty Israeli meal. Feel safe ordering anything deep-fried – it does an excellent job of it – and don't miss the eggplant dip.

Ricky's Coffeeshop (Map pp114–15; ☎ 0 2629 0509; 18 Th Phra Athit; dishes 50–180B; ☺ 8am-11pm; river ferry Tha Phra Athit) This cosy cafe has moved – a door down – and now serves Mexican food in addition to authentic coffee drinks, hearty breakfasts and baguette sandwiches.

Oh My Cod! (Map pp114–15; ☎ 0 2282 6553; 95d Rambuttri Village Inn, Soi Rambuttri I; dishes 70–200B; ☺ breakfast, lunch & dinner; bus 30, 53, 506, river ferry Tha Phra Athit) Fish and chips, the signature dish here, takes the form of an immense, puffy fillet accompanied by thick-cut chips and peas. Breakfast is served all day, and parched Anglophiles can enjoy a proper cuppa in the sunny courtyard dining area.

Ann's Sweet (Map pp114–15; ☎ 0 86889 1383; 138 Th Phra Athit; dishes 75–150B; ☺ 11.30am-8pm; bus 53, 506, river ferry Tha Phra Athit) Ann, a native of Bangkok and a graduate of the Cordon Bleu cooking

program, makes some of the most authentic Western-style cakes you'll find anywhere in town. Lavazza coffee and iBerry ice creams fill out the tasty menu.

Deck (Map pp114–15; ☎ 0 2221 9158; Arun Residence, 36-38 Soi Pratu Nok Yung, Th Maharat; dishes 170–690B; ☺ lunch & dinner; river ferry Tha Tien) The Deck's claim to fame is its commanding views over Wat Arun, but the restaurant's short but diverse menu, ranging from duck confit to Thai-style pomelo salad, sweetens the pot. After dinner, drinks are served at the hotel's open-air rooftop bar.

Chinatown & Phahurat

When you mention Chinatown, most Bangkokians immediately dream of street food, the best of which we've included in our 'Eats Walk' on p164. The area is also famous as ground zero for the yearly Vegetarian Festival (see the boxed text, opposite). On the western side of the neighbourhood is Bangkok's Little India, the fabric district of Phahurat, filled with small Indian and

Nepali restaurants tucked into the soi off Th Chakraphet.

Old Siam Plaza (Map pp116-17; ground fl, Old Siam Plaza, cnr Th Phahurat & Th Triphet; dishes 15-50B; lunch; river ferry Tha Saphan Phut) Sugar junkies, be sure to include this stop on your Bangkok eating itinerary. The ground floor of this shopping centre is a candyland of traditional Thai sweets and snacks, most made right before your eyes.

Royal India (Map pp116-17; ☎ 0 2221 6565; 392/1 Th Chakraphet; dishes 40-130B; lunch & dinner; river ferry Tha Saphan Phut) Yes, we realise that this legendary hole in the wall has been in every edition of our guide since the beginning, but after all these years it's still the most reliable place to eat in Bangkok's Little India. Try any of the delicious breads or rich curries, and don't forget to finish with a homemade Punjabi sweet.

Tang Jai Yuu (no roman-script sign; Map pp116-17; ☎ 0 2224 2167; 85-89 Th Yaowaphanit; dishes 120-500B; lunch & dinnner; Metro Hualamphong, river ferry Tha Ratchawong) In Bangkok, policemen and big-haired women are usually a tip-off for good eats, not suspicious activity. This longstanding fave is great for a decadent night out, and specialises in Teo Chew and Chinese-Thai specialties with an emphasis on seafood.

Silom, Sathon & Riverside

Th Silom has a bit of everything, from truly old-skool Thai to some of the city's best upscale international dining. The western end of the street, near the Chao Phraya River, is home to several Indian and Thai-Muslim restaurants.

THAI

Soi 10 Food Centres (Map pp118-19; Soi 10, Th Silom; dishes 20-60B; lunch Mon-Fri; Skytrain Sala Daeng, Metro Silom) These two adjacent hangarlike buildings tucked behind Soi 10 are the main lunchtime fuelling stations for this area's office staff. Choices range from southern-style *kôw gaang* (point-and-choose curries ladled over rice) to virtually every form of Thai noodle.

Khrua Aroy Aroy (Map pp118-19; ☎ 0 2635 2365; Th Pan; dishes 30-70B; 6am-6pm; Skytrain Surasak) It can be crowded and hot, but Khrua Aroy Aroy ('Delicious Delicious Kitchen') rarely fails to live up to its lofty name. Stop by for some of Bangkok's richest curries, as well as a revolving menu of daily specials.

Home Cuisine Islamic Restaurant (Map pp118-19; ☎ 0 2234 7911; 196-198 Soi 36, Th Charoen Krung; dishes 45-130B; 11am-10pm Mon-Sat, 6-10pm Sun; river ferry Tha Oriental) This bungalow-style restaurant does tasty Thai-Muslim with an Indian accent. Sit out on the breezy patio and try the rich and sour fish curry, ideally accompanied by a flaky roti or three.

Kalapapruek (Map pp118-19; ☎ 0 2236 4335; 27 Th Pramuan; dishes 60-120B; 8am-6pm; Skytrain Surasak) This venerable Thai eatery has numerous branches and mall spin-offs around town, but we still like the quasi-concealed original branch. The diverse menu spans regional Thai specialties from just about every region, daily specials and, occasionally, seasonal treats as well.

INTERNATIONAL

Chennai Kitchen (Map pp118-19; ☎ 0 2234 1266; 10 Th Pan; dishes 50-150B; 10am-3pm; Skytrain Surasak) This thimble-sized restaurant puts out some of the most solid southern Indian vegetarian around. The arm-length dosais (a crispy southern Indian bread) are always a good choice, but if you're feeling indecisive go for the thali set that seems to incorporate just about everything in the kitchen.

WAVING THE YELLOW FLAG

During the annual Vegetarian Festival in September/October, Bangkok's Chinatown becomes a virtual orgy of nonmeat cuisine. The festivities centre on Chinatown's main street, Th Yaowarat, and the Talat Noi area (see p135), but food shops and stalls all over the city post yellow flags to announce their meat-free status.

Celebrating alongside the ethnic Chinese are Thais who look forward to the special dishes that appear during the festival period. Most restaurants put their normal menus on hold and instead prepare soy-based substitutes for standard Thai dishes like *ðôm yam* and *gaang kĕe·o wăhn*. Even Thai regional cuisines are sold, without the meat, of course. Of the special festival dishes, yellow Hokkien-style noodles appear in stir-fried dishes along with meaty mushrooms and big hunks of vegetables.

Along with abstinence from meat, the 10-day festival is celebrated with special visits to the temple, often requiring worshippers to dress in white.

CHINATOWN EATS WALK

Street food rules in this part of town and many of Chinatown's best kitchens don't require walls or a roof, making the area ideal for a food-based walking tour.

Although many vendors stay open until the wee hours, the more popular stalls tend to sell out quickly, and the best time to feast in this area is from approximately 7pm to 9pm. Avoid Mondays, when most of the city's street vendors stay at home.

Start your walk at the intersection of Th Yaowarat and Th Phadungdao. Moving west, turn right into Th Plaeng Nam. Immediately on your right is **Burapa Birds Nest** (Map pp116–17; ☎ 0 2623 0191; Th Plaeng Nam), as good a place as any to try the very Chinatown dish, birds' nest soup. Directly across from Burapa you'll see a gentleman on the street working three coal-fired stoves. This stall, **Khrua Phornlamai** (ครัวพรละมัย; Map pp116–17; ☎ 0 81823 0397; Th Plaeng Nam), is a great place for greasy but delicious fried faves such as *pàt kêe mow* (wide rice noodles fried with seafood, chillies and Thai basil).

Continue down Th Plaeng Nam and cross Th Charoen Krung. Go straight, staying on the right-hand side for about 50m, until you reach **Nay Mong** (นายหมึ; Map pp116–17; ☎ 0 2623 1890; 539 Th Phlap Phla Chai), a minuscule restaurant renowned for its delicious *hŏy tôrt*, mussels or oysters fried with egg in a sticky batter.

Backtrack to Th Charoen Krung and turn right. Upon reaching Th Mangkorn make a right and immediately on your left-hand side you're bound to see a row of people waiting in line, as well as several more sitting on plastic stools holding plates of rice and curry in their hands. This is **Jék Pûi** (เจ๊กปุ้ย; Map pp116–17; ☎ 0 81850 9960; Th Mangkorn), a stall known for its Chinese-style Thai curries, and also for the fact that it has no tables.

Souvlaki (Map pp118–19; ☎ 0 2632 9967; 114/4 Soi 4, Th Silom; dishes 120–280B; 🕙 lunch & dinner; Skytrain Sala Daeng, Metro Silom) Greek is among Bangkok's most elusive cuisines, and this new eatery has finally brought Hellenic flava to town. The menu runs the predictable gamut of Greek-style fast food and mezze, but also offers interesting daily specials. Warning: serving sizes are truly Olympian.

Scoozi (Map pp118–19; ☎ 0 2234 6999; 174 Th Surawong; dishes 150–350B; 🕙 lunch & dinner; Skytrain Chong Nonsi) Now boasting several locations across Bangkok, we still think the wood-fired pizzas taste best at this, the original branch. However, if you find yourself elsewhere with a dough craving, you can also get your pizza pie on at Th Khao San (Map pp114–15; ☎ 0 2280 5280; 201 Soi Sunset) and Thonglor (Map pp122–3; ☎ 0 2391 5113; Fenix Thonglor, Soi 1, Soi 55/Thong Lor, Th Sukhumvit).

Le Bouchon (Map pp118–19; ☎ 0 2234 9109; Soi 2, Th Patpong; dishes 150–840B; 🕙 noon–3pm & 6pm–midnight; Skytrain Sala Daeng, Metro Lumphini) The Patpong address alone is a tip-off that this is anything but haute cuisine. Instead, this homey bistro is the kind of place where Bangkok's French population comes to forget where they really are. Choose your dishes from the chalkboard menu toted around by the cheery staff, but it'd be a shame to miss the garlicky frogs' legs or savoury foie gras pâté.

Le Normandie (Map pp118–19; ☎ 0 2659 9000; www .mandarinoriental.com; 48 Soi Oriental/38, Th Charoen Krung; dishes 750–3900B; 🕙 lunch & dinner; hotel shuttle boat from Tha Sathon/Central Pier) When it opened in 1962, Le Normandie was Bangkok's only destination for fine dining. Despite the passing of more than four decades, it wouldn't be entirely incorrect to say that little has changed. As the menu, which boasts an entire foie gras section, suggests, this is classic French cuisine, and no fewer than 20 three-starred Michelin chefs have helped to prepare it over the years. To see these influences firsthand, try the degustation menu (4400B), which is also available with a selection of wines (7400B).

Siam Square & Pratunam

If you find yourself hungry in this part of central Bangkok, you're largely at the mercy of shopping-mall food courts and chain restaurants. However, this is still Thailand, and if you can ignore the prefabricated atmosphere, the food can often be quite good. If you don't need air-conditioning, stop by the numerous **food stalls** (Map pp120–1; btwn Sois 5 & 6, Siam Sq; dishes 30–40B; 🕙 10am–2pm; Skytrain Siam) at Siam Square for a quick Thai lunch.

Sanguan Sri (Map pp120–1; ☎ 0 2252 7637; 59/1 Th Withayu/Wireless Rd; dishes 60–150B; 🕙 10am–3pm Mon–Sat; Skytrain Ploenchit) If you don't manage to walk right past it, join the area's hungry office workers at

Head left down Th Charoen Krung again and continue east until you reach Trok Itsaranuphap (Soi 16). This narrow alleyway is also known as **Talat Mai** (ตลาดใหม่; Map pp116–17), and is the area's most famous strip of commerce. Although morning is the best time to visit, if you're not too late you can still get a good idea of the exotic ingredients that make up the area.

At the end of the alley you'll see a gentleman frying noodles with a brass wok and a spoon. He's making **gŏo·ay ōĕeo kôoa galì** (ก๋วยเตี๋ยวคั่วไก่), a simple but delicious dish of rice noodles fried with chicken, egg and garlic oil.

Upon emerging at Th Yaowarat, cross over to the busy market area directly across the street. The first vendor on the right, **Nay Lék Uan** (นายเล็กอ้วน; Map pp116-17; ☎ 0 2224 3450; Soi 11, Th Yaowarat), is among the most popular stalls in Bangkok, and sells *gŏo·ay jáp năm săi*, a thick, intensely peppery broth containing noodles and pork offal. There are several more stalls here, selling everything from *pàt tai* to satay.

Walk east down Th Yaowarat, and on the corner of Th Yaowaphanit and Th Yaowarat you'll see a stall with yellow noodles and barbecued pork. This is **Mangkorn Khâo** (มังกรขาว; Map pp116-17; ☎ 0 2682 2352), a respected vendor of *bà·mèe*, Chinese-style wheat noodles, and delicious wontons.

Keep walking down Th Yaowarat and you'll be back to where you started. By now the two opposing seafood places, **Lek & Rut** (Map pp116-17; ☎ 0 81637 5039) and **T&K** (Map pp116-17; ☎ 0 2223 4519) should be buzzing. You could join the tourists for grilled prawns and fried rice, but hopefully by this point you've had your fill of what Chinatown *really* has to offer.

this old-school Thai eatery. There's a limited English-language menu, but simply pointing to the delicious dishes being consumed around you is probably a better strategy.

Coca Suki (Map pp120-1; ☎ 0 2251 6337; 416/3-8 Th Henri Dunant; dishes 60-200B; ⏰ 11am-11pm; Skytrain Siam) Immensely popular with Thai families, *sù·gêe* takes the form of a bubbling hotpot of broth and the raw ingredients to dip therein. Coca is one of the oldest purveyors of the dish, and the Siam Square branch reflects the brand's efforts to appear more modern. Fans of spice be sure to request the tangy *tŏm yam* broth.

New Light Coffee House (Map pp120-1; ☎ 0 2251 9592; 426/1-4 Siam Sq; dishes 60-200B; ⏰ 8am-11.30pm; Skytrain Siam) Travel back in time to 1960s-era Bangkok at this vintage diner popular with students from nearby Chulalongkorn University. Try old-style Western dishes, all of which come accompanied by a soft roll and green salad, or choose from the extensive Thai menu.

Crystal Jade La Mian Xiao Long Bao (Map pp120-1; ☎ 0 2250 7990; Urban Kitchen, Basement, Erawan Bangkok, 494 Th Ploenchit; dishes 120-300B; ⏰ lunch & dinner; Skytrain Chitlom) The tongue-twistingly long name of this excellent Singaporean chain refers to the restaurant's signature wheat noodles (*la mian*) and the famous Shanghainese steamed dumplings (*xiao long pao*). If you order the hand-

pulled noodles, allow the staff to cut them with kitchen shears, otherwise you'll end up with evidence of your meal on your shirt.

Sukhumvit

This endless ribbon of a road is where to go if you wish to forget you're in Thailand. From Korean to Middle Eastern, just about every cuisine has an outpost here. We've mentioned a few Thai places below, but most domestic eats in this area are more miss than hit, and it's really the place to indulge in the flavours you left at home.

THAI
Soi 38 Night Market (Map pp122-3; Soi 38, Th Sukhumvit; dishes 30-60B; ⏰ 8pm-3am; Skytrain Thong Lo) After a hard night of clubbing, this gathering of basic Thai-Chinese hawker stalls will look like a shimmering oasis. If you're going sober, stick to the knot of 'famous' vendors tucked into an alley on the right-hand side as you enter the street.

Pharani Home Cuisine (Sansab Boat Noodle; Map pp122-3; ☎ 0 2664 4454; Soi Prasanmit/23, Th Sukhumvit; dishes 35-200B; ⏰ 10am-10pm; Skytrain Asoke, Metro Sukhumvit) This cosy Thai restaurant dabbles in a bit of everything, from ox-tongue stew to rice fried with shrimp paste, but the real reason to come is for the rich, meaty 'boat noodles' – so called because they used to be sold from boats plying the *klorngs* of Ayuthaya.

Thonglee (Map pp122-3; ☎ 0 2258 1983; Soi 20, Th Sukhumvit; dishes 40-70B; ⏰ 10am-8pm, closed 3rd Sun of the month; Skytrain Asoke, Metro Sukhumvit) One of the few remaining mom-and-pop Thai places on Sukhumvit, this tiny kitchen offers a few dishes you won't find elsewhere, like *mǒo pàt gà·bì* (pork fried with shrimp paste), and *mèe gròrp* (sweet-and-spicy crispy fried noodles).

Face (Map pp122-3; ☎ 0 2713 6048; 29 Soi 38, Th Sukhumvit; dishes 190-680B; ⏰ 6.30-10pm Mon-Fri, 6.30-11pm Sat & Sun; Skytrain Thong Lo) This handsome dining complex is essentially two very good restaurants in one: Lan Na Thai does some of the best upscale Thai around, while Hazara dabbles in exotic-sounding 'North Indian frontier cuisine'. To make matters even better, Visage, the cafe/bakery next door, prepares some of the best cakes and chocolates in Bangkok.

Bo.lan (Map pp122-3; ☎ 0 2260 2962; www .bolan.co.th; 42 Soi Rongnarong Phichai Songkhram, Soi 26, Th Sukhumvit; set meal 1500B; ⏰ lunch & dinner; Skytrain Phrom Phong) Upscale Thai is usually more garnish than flavour, but this chic new restaurant, started up by two former chefs of London's Michelin-starred Nahm, is the exception. Bo and Dylan (Bo.lan, a play on words that also means 'ancient') take a scholarly approach to Thai cuisine, and perfectly executed set meals featuring full-flavoured regional Thai dishes are the results of this tuition.

INTERNATIONAL

Duc de Praslin (Map pp122-3; ☎ 0 2258 3200; ground fl Fenix Tower, Soi 31/1, Th Sukhumvit; dishes 20-120B; ⏰ 9am-9pm; Skytrain Phrom Phong) Travel from sweaty Bangkok to Olde Europe in one step at this classy cafe-slash-chocolatier. Other than the spot-on bonbons and good coffee, try a hot cocoa, made in front of your eyes by combining steaming milk with shards of rich chocolate.

AH! (Map pp122-3; ☎ 0 2252 6069; Atlanta Hotel, 78 Soi Phasak/2, Th Sukhumvit; dishes 60-150B; ⏰ breakfast, lunch & dinner; Skytrain Ploenchit) The Atlanta Hotel's delightful vintage diner is one of the few places that excels both in atmosphere and cuisine.

FOOD COURT FRENZY

Every Bangkok mall worth its escalators has some sort of food court. In recent years many have gone upscale, and the setting, cuisine and service have also elevated accordingly. The following are some of the better choices.

- **Big C Food Court** (Map pp120-1; ☎ 0 2250 4888; 5th floor, Big C Department Store, 97/11 Th Ratchadamri; ⏰ 9am-10pm; Skytrain Chitlom) Big C's food court is the proletariat of the genre. The food selections here are not going to inspire you to move east, but they are numerous and cheap, and representative of the kind of 'fast food' Thais enjoy eating. To pay you must first exchange your cash for a temporary credit card at one of several counters; your change is refunded at the same desk.

- **Food Loft** (Map pp120-1; 6th floor, Central Chit Lom, 1027 Th Ploenchit; ⏰ 10am-10pm; Skytrain Chitlom) Central Chit Lom pioneered the concept of the upscale food court, and mock-ups of the various Indian, Italian, Singaporean and other international dishes aid in the decision-making process. Upon entering, you'll be given a temporary credit card and will be led to a table. You have to get up again to order, but the dishes will be brought to you. Paying is done on your way out.

- **MBK Food Court** (Map pp120-1; 6th floor, MBK Center, cnr Th Phra Ram I & Th Phayathai; ⏰ 10am-9pm; Skytrain National Stadium) The granddaddy of the genre offers dozens of vendors selling food from virtually every corner of Thailand and beyond. Standouts include an excellent vegetarian food stall (stall C8) and a very decent Isan food vendor (C22).

- **Park Food Hall** (Map pp122-3; 5th floor, Emporium Shopping Centre, 622 Th Sukhumvit, cnr Soi 24; ⏰ 10am-10pm; Skytrain Phrom Phong) Emporium brings together some of the city's best-known international restaurants. The Emporium Food Hall, on the same floor, features cheaper, mostly Chinese/Thai food, and what must be the cheapest meal with a view in town. Paying is done by buying coupons at the windows in the entrance. Be sure to leave these in your pocket until the next day, when it's too late to get a refund – it's an integral part of the food court experience.

Delve back into 1950s-era 'continental' dishes, such as Hungarian goulash or wiener schnitzel, or acclaimed vegetarian Thai.

Boon Tong Kiat Singapore Hainanese Chicken Rice (Map pp122-3; ☎ 0 2390 2508; 440/5 & 396 Soi 55/ Thong Lor, Th Sukhumvit; dishes 60-150B; ☑ lunch & dinner; Skytrain Thong Lo) Order a plate of the restaurant's namesake and bear witness to how a dish can be simultaneously simple and profound. And while you're there you'd be daft not order *rojak*, the spicy/sour fruit 'salad', which here is called 'Singapore Som Tam'.

Nasser Elmassry (Map pp122-3; ☎ 0 2253 5582; 4/6 Soi 3/1, Th Sukhumvit; dishes 80-350B; ☑ 8am-5am; Skytrain Nana) One of several similar Middle Eastern restaurants on Soi 3/1, Nasser Elmassry is easily recognisable by its genuinely impressive floor-to-ceiling stainless-steel 'theme'. Middle Eastern food generally means meat, meat and more meat, but there are also several delicious veggie-based mezze.

Tapas Café (Map pp122-3; ☎ 0 2651 2947; 1/25 Soi 11, Th Sukhumvit; dishes 90-550B; ☑ 11.30am-11.30pm; Skytrain Nana) Vibrant tapas, refreshing sangria and an open, airy atmosphere make this new Spaniard on the block worth the visit. Come before 7pm when tapas are buy-two, get-one-free.

Ramentei (Map pp122-3; ☎ 0 2662 0050; 593/23-24 Soi 33/1, Th Sukhumvit; dishes 120-300B; ☑ lunch & dinner; Skytrain Phrom Phong) Located smack dab in the middle of Bangkok's de facto Japanese district, this workaday ramen joint serves up a variety of authentic noodle dishes for the city's Japanese expat community. *Katsudon* (breaded pork cutlet served over rice) and other basic rice dishes are also available.

Sukhumvit Plaza (Korean Town; Map pp122-3; cnr Soi 12 & Th Sukhumvit; ☑ lunch & dinner; Skytrain Asoke, Metro Sukhumvit) Known around town as 'Korean Town', this multistorey complex is the city's best destination for authentic 'Seoul' food. Local residents swear by Arirang (☎ 0 2653 0177, dishes 120B to 350B) on the 1st floor, although there are slightly cheaper places in the complex as well.

Bed Supperclub (Map pp122-3; ☎ 0 2651 3537; www.bedsupperclub.com; 26 Soi 11, Th Sukhumvit; 3-course à la carte dinner Sun-Thu 1450B, 4-course set dinner Fri & Sat 1850B; ☑ 7.30-10.30pm Sun-Thu, dinner 9pm Fri & Sat; Skytrain Nana) Kiwi chef Paul Hutt and his army of talented Thai chefs are creating the most cutting-edge cuisine in town. Tools and techniques ranging from liquid nitrogen to sous-vide have resulted in creations such as tomato hops-infused broth with

> **DAY OFF**
>
> Fans of street food be forewarned that all of Bangkok's stalls close on Monday for compulsory street cleaning (the results of which are not entirely evident come Tuesday morning). If you happen to be in the city on this day, take advantage of the lull to visit one of the city's upscale hotel restaurants, which virtually never close.

pure haloumi cheese noodle, avocado snow and basil oil. Dinner is à la carte except on Fridays and Saturdays when Hutt does a four-course surprise menu at 9pm sharp.

Lumphini Park & Th Phra Ram IV

Kai Thort Jay Kee (Soi Polo Fried Chicken; Map p124; ☎ 0 2655 8489; 137/1-3 Soi Polo, Th Withayu/Wireless Rd; dishes 30-150B; ☑ breakfast, lunch & dinner; Skytrain Ploenchit, Metro Lumphini) Although the *sôm tam* (spicy green papaya salad), sticky rice and *lâhp* (a Thai-style 'salad' of minced meat) give the impression of a northeastern Thai-style eatery, the restaurant's namesake deep-fried bird is more southern in origin. Regardless, smothered in a thick layer of crispy deep-fried garlic, it is none other than a truly Bangkok experience.

Café 1912 (Map p124; ☎ 0 2679 2056; Alliance Française, 29 Th Sathon Tai; dishes 60-120B; ☑ 7am-7pm Mon-Sat, to 2pm Sun; Metro Lumphini) Part of the French cultural centre, and with food provided by a good local bakery, this cafeteria is a great place to fuel up while on an embassy run. Both French and Thai dishes are available, as well as coffee and delicious cakes and sweets.

Ngwan Lee Lang Suan (Map p124; ☎ 0 2250 0936; cnr Soi Lang Suan & Soi Sarasin; dishes 60-180B; ☑ 10am-2am; Skytrain Ratchadamri) This cavernous food hall is centrally located and open late, making it a perfect post-clubbing destination. It's also a great place to try those dishes you never dare to order elsewhere such as *jàp chài*, Chinese-style stewed veggies, or the delicious *bèt đun*, duck stewed in Chinese spices.

ourpick Cy'an (Map p124; ☎ 0 2625 3333; Metropolitan Hotel, 27 Th Sathon Tai; 9-course set dinner 3100B; ☑ lunch & dinner; Metro Lumphini) The city's best chefs rave about this teal and grey den of gastronomic delight – always a good sign. Combining vibrant Mediterranean and Moroccan flavours, a healthy obsession with the finest seafood, and a stylish and intimate atmosphere, this is one of the best destinations for a splurge.

BANGKOK

HOTEL BUFFET BONANZA

Sunday brunch has become something of a Bangkok institution among resident foreigners, and virtually every large hotel in town puts together decadent buffets on every other day as well. The following choices will leave you with more than simply a distended stomach.

The highly regarded restaurants at the **Four Seasons** (Map pp120-1; ☎ 0 2250 1000; Four Seasons Hotel, 155 Th Ratchadamri; buffet 2350B; ❤ 11.30am-3pm Sun; Skytrain Ratchadamri) set up steam tables for their decadent Sunday brunch buffet – reservations are essential. Even if you can't afford to stay at the Oriental Hotel, you should save up for the riverside seafood buffet at **Lord Jim** (Map pp118-19; ☎ 0 2659 9000; www.mandarinoriental.com; 48 Soi Oriental/38, Th Charoen Krung; buffet 1500B; ❤ noon-2pm Mon-Sat, 11am-3pm Sun; river ferry Tha Oriental).

The award-winning buffet at **JW Marriott** (Map pp122-3; ☎ 0 2656 7700; ground fl, JW Marriott Hotel, 4 Soi Phasak/2, Th Sukhumvit; buffet 1637B; ❤ 11am-3pm Sat & Sun; Skytrain Nana) is likened to Thanksgiving all year-round, and generous options for free-flowing beer or wine are also available. **Rang Mahal** (Map pp122-3; ☎ 0 2261 7100; 26th fl, Rembrandt Hotel, 19 Soi 20, Th Sukhumvit; buffet 848B; ❤ 11am-2.30pm Sun; Skytrain Asok, Metro Sukhumvit), on the top of the Rembrandt Hotel, couples great views with an all-Indian buffet every Sunday. And for those who love the sweet stuff, the **Sukhothai Hotel** (Map p124; ☎ 0 2344 8888; www.sukhothai.com; 13/3 Th Sathon Tai; buffet 790B; ❤ 2-6pm Fri-Sun; Metro Lumphini) offers a unique, entirely cocoa-based chocolate buffet.

Central & Greater Bangkok

Phat Thai Ari (Map pp110-11; ☎ 0 2270 1654; 2/1-2 Soi Ari/7, Th Phahonyothin; dishes 40-95B; ❤ 11am-10pm; Skytrain Ari) One of the city's better-known *pàt tai* shops is just steps away from the Ari Skytrain station. Try the innovative 'noodle-less' version, where long strips of crispy green papaya are substituted for the traditional rice noodles from Chanthaburi.

Pathé (Map pp110-11; ☎ 0 2938 4995; cnr Th Lad Phrao & Th Viphawadee; dishes 40-120B; ❤ 10am-1am; Metro Phahonyothin) The Thai equivalent of a 1950s-era American diner, this popular place combines solid Thai food, a fun atmosphere and a jukebox playing scratched records. Don't miss the deep-fried ice cream.

Mallika (Map pp112-13; ☎ 0 248 0287; 21/36 Th Rang Nam; dishes 70-180B; ❤ 10am-10pm Mon-Sat; Skytrain Victory Monument) A dream come true: authentic regional Thai (southern, in this case), with a legible English menu, good service and tidy setting. The prices are slightly high for a mom-and-pop Thai joint, but you're paying for quality.

River Bar Café (Map pp110-11; ☎ 0 2879 1747; 405/1 Soi Chao Phraya, Th Ratchawithi, Thonburi; dishes 90-240B; ❤ 5pm-midnight; klorng taxi to Tha Krung Thon Bridge pier) Sporting a picture-perfect riverside location, good food and live music, River Bar Café combines all the essentials for a perfect Bangkok night out.

DRINKING

Once infamous as an anything-goes nightlife destination, in recent years Bangkok has been edging towards teetotalism with strict regula-tions limiting the sale of alcohol and increasingly conservative closing times. Regardless, the city still boasts a diverse and fun bar scene, and there are even a few places to go if you find 1am too early to get back on the wagon.

Keep in mind that smoking has been outlawed at all indoor (and some quasi-outdoor) entertainment places since 2008; surprisingly for Thailand, the rule is strictly enforced.

Ko Ratanakosin & Banglamphu

During the day, Th Khao San is dominated by just about everybody but Thais. At night the natives deem it safe to join the crowds, giving the area an entirely different atmosphere. In addition to the main strip, Th Rambutri and Th Phra Athit also draw drinkers and fun seekers from across the city, and the world.

Hippie de Bar (Map pp114-15; ☎ 0 2629 3508; 46 Th Khao San; river ferry Tha Phra Athit) Popular with the domestic crowd, Hippie boasts several levels of fun, both indoor and outdoor. There's food, pool tables and a soundtrack you're unlikely to hear elsewhere in town.

Old Phra Arthit Pier (Map pp114-15; ☎ 0 2282 9202; 23 Th Phra Athit; river ferry Tha Phra Athit) This self-proclaimed 'Gastronobar' consists of an attractive wooden loungelike bar and an open-air deck with fleeting views of the river. As the name apparently suggests, there's food as well.

Taksura (Map pp114-15; ☎ 0 2622 0708; 156/1 Th Tanao; klorng taxi to Tha Phan Fah) There are no signs to lead you to this seemingly abandoned century-old mansion in the heart of old Bangkok, which is all the better, according to the cool uni-artsy crowd who frequent the place. Take a seat outside to soak up the breezes, and go Thai and order some spicy nibbles with your drinks.

Phranakorn Bar (Map pp114-15; ☎ 0 2282 7507; 58/2 Soi Damnoen Klang Tai; klorng taxi to Tha Phan Fah) It must have taken a true visionary to transform this characterless multilevel building into a warm, fun destination for a night out. Students and arty types make Phranakorn Bar a home away from hovel with eclectic decor and changing gallery exhibits.

Bars tend to segregate into foreigner and Thai factions, but you can always reverse that trend. Here are a few popular options:

Buddy Bar (Map pp114-15; Th Khao San; river ferry Tha Phra Athit) Spotless colonial-themed bar for when only air-conditioning will do.

Center Khao San (Map pp114-15; Th Khao San; river ferry Tha Phra Athit) One of many front-row views of the human parade on Th Khao San; the upstairs bar hosts late-night bands.

Molly Bar (Map pp114-15; Th Rambutri; river ferry Tha Phra Athit) Packed on weekends for Thai local bands; more mellow on weekdays with outdoor seating.

Roof Bar (Map pp114-15; Th Khao San; river ferry Tha Phra Athit) Although the live acoustic soundtrack is hit and miss, the views are solid from this elevated pub.

Susie Pub (Map pp114-15; 108/5-9 alley, btwn Th Khao San & Th Rambutri; river ferry Tha Phra Athit) Thai pop and pool tables.

Silom, Sathon & Riverside

Sirocco Sky Bar (Map pp118-19; ☎ 0 2624 9555; The Dome, 1055 Th Silom; Skytrain Saphan Taksin) Bangkok seems to be one of the only places in the world where nobody minds if you slap a bar on top of a skyscraper. Enjoy this liberty while it lasts, and preferably with one of Sky Bar's tasty drink creations. But be sure to dress the part; shorts and sandal wearers have to stay at ground level.

Moon Bar at Vertigo (Map p124; ☎ 0 2679 1200; Banyan Tree Hotel, 21/100 Th Sathon Tai; Metro Lumphini) Also precariously perched on top of a skyscraper, Moon Bar offers a slightly different bird's-eye view of Bangkok. Things can get a bit crowded here come sunset, so be sure to show up a bit early to get the best seats.

Vino di Zanotti (Map p124; ☎ 0 2636 3366; 41 Soi Yommarat; Skytrain Sala Daeng, Metro Silom) A branch of the nearby Italian restaurant of the same name, Vino keeps it casual with live music, a huge wine list and lots of delicious nibbles.

Barbican Bar (Map pp118-19; ☎ 0 2234 3590; 9/4-5 Soi Thaniya, Th Silom; Skytrain Sala Daeng, Metro Silom) Surrounded by massage parlours with teenage prom queens cat-calling at Japanese businessmen, this is a straight-laced yuppie bar where office crews come for some happy-hour drinks and stay until closing time.

Coyote on Convent (Map pp118-19; ☎ 0 2631 2325; 1/2 Th Convent, Th Silom; ☼ 11am-1am; Skytrain Sala Daeng, Metro Silom) Forget the overpriced Tex-Mex cuisine; the real reason to visit Coyote is for its 75+ varieties of margaritas. On Wednesdays from 6pm to 8pm and Saturdays from 10pm to midnight, the icy drinks are distributed free to all women who pass through the door.

Molly Malone's (Map pp118-19; ☎ 0 2266 7160; 1/5-6 Th Convent, Th Silom; ☼ 11-1am; Skytrain Sala Daeng, Metro Silom) A recent makeover has this longstanding local leaning perilously towards Irish kitsch, but it still pulls a fun crowd and the service is friendly and fast.

OUT ALL NIGHT

With most pubs and dance clubs closing around 1am, One Night in Bangkok is not quite what it used to be. Thankfully, there are a few places around town that have gained sufficient 'permission' to stay open until the morning hours.

Off Soi Ngam Duphli, **Wong's Place** (Map p124; 27/3 Soi Sri Bumphen, Th Phra Ram IV; ☼ 8pm until late; Metro Lumphini), a longstanding backpacker bar, is so late-night, it's best not to show up before midnight. Vaguely Middle-Eastern–themed **Gazebo** (Map pp114-15; ☎ 0 2629 0705; 3rd fl, 44 Th Chakraphong; ☼ 7pm-late; river ferry Tha Phra Athit) represents the posh side of Th Khao San. This bar's elevated setting appears to lend it some leniency with the city's strict closing times.

If you can manage to find it, the 'unique' location under a tollway also seems to protect **Rain Dogs** (Map pp122-3; ☎ 0 817206 989; 16 Soi Phrya Phiren, off Soi Sawan Sawat, off Th Phra Ram IV; ☼ 7pm-late; Metro Khlong Toei) from late-night scrutiny by the Men in Brown. Also following the canine theme, **Scratch Dog** (Map pp122-3; ☎ 0 2262 1234; Windsor Suites Hotel, 8-10 Soi 20, Th Sukhumvit; ☼ 8pm-late; Skytrain Asoke, Metro Sukhumvit), a hotel disco, employs a hip-hop theme to propel partiers into the morning hours.

GAY & LESBIAN BANGKOK

Bangkok is so gay it makes San Francisco look like rural Texas. With out-and-open nightspots and annual pride events, the city's homosexual community enjoys an unprecedented amount of tolerance considering attitudes in the rest of the region. It should be mentioned, however, that recent years have seen a sharp rise in HIV and other STDs among gay men in Bangkok; when in town, be sure to play it safe.

Utopia (www.utopia-asia.com) is an online resource for the Southeast Asian gay community, listing Bangkok entertainment venues, news and views, and providing travel services. **Dreaded Ned** (www.dreadedned.com) and **Fridae** (www.fridae.com) also have up to date listings and events. The **Lesbian Guide to Bangkok** (www.bangkoklesbian.com) is the only English-language tracker of the lesbian scene.

Gay women and men are well advised to visit Bangkok in mid-November, when the city's small but fun **Pride Festival** (www.bangkokpride.org) is in full swing. Dinners, cruises, clubbing and contests are the order of the week. For details visit the website.

Bed Supperclub (see p172) hosts a hugely popular 'pink' night on Sundays, and other posh locales often play host to weekend-long 'circuit parties'. Visit **G Circuit** (www.gcircuit.com) to find out when and where the next one is.

All of Soi 2 on Th Silom is lined with dance clubs, such as **DJ Station** (Map pp118-19; ☎ 0 2266 4029; 8/6-8 Soi 2, Th Silom; ☯ 10.30pm-2am; Skytrain Sala Daeng, Metro Silom), where the crowd is a mix of Thai guppies (gay professionals), money boys and a few Westerners. Just half a soi over is **G.O.D.** (Guys on Display; Map pp118-19; ☎ 0 2632 8032; Soi 2/1, Th Silom; cover 280B; ☯ 11.30pm-late; Skytrain Sala Daeng, Metro Silom), which as the name suggests is not averse to a little shirtless dancing. Traipse on over to Soi 4 to find the old-timer conversation bars, such as **Balcony** (Map pp118-19; ☎ 0 2235 5891; 86-88 Soi 4, Th Silom; Skytrain Sala Daeng, Metro Silom) and **Telephone** (Map pp118-19; ☎ 0 2234 3279; 114/11-13 Soi 4, Th Silom; Skytrain Sala Daeng, Metro Silom). The gay men's equivalent of Patpong's go-go bars can be found on nearby Soi Anuman Ratchathon, also known as Soi Twilight.

Th Sarasin, behind Lumphini Park, is lined with more loungey options, such as **70s Bar** (Map p124; ☎ 0 2253 4433; 231/16 Th Sarasin; no cover; ☯ 6pm-1am; Skytrain Ratchadamri), a small dance club that resuscitates the era of disco, and **Kluen Saek** (Map p124; ☎ 0 2254 2962; 297 Th Sarasin; Skytrain Ratchadamri), both part of a strip of formerly 'hetero' bars that are becoming gayer by the day.

Further out of town is a more local scene, where a little Thai will make you feel more welcome. Several of the bars along Th Kamphaeng Phet, including **ICQ** (Map pp110-11; ☎ 0 2272 4775; Th Kamphaeng Phet, Chatuchak; Skytrain Mo Chit, Metro Kamphaeng Phet), are favourites for loud and lushy behaviour.

After all these years, Bangkok finally has something of a lesbian scene. **E Fun** (Map pp110-11; Royal City Ave/RCA, off Phra Ram IX; no cover; ☯ 10pm-2am; Metro Ram IX) and **Zeta** (Map pp110-11; ☎ 0 2203 0994; 29 Royal City Ave/RCA, off Phra Ram IX; no cover; ☯ 10pm-2am; Metro Ram IX) are both easy-going clubs for the girls with a nightly band doing Thai and Western covers. E Fun tends to attract an older crowd, while young tom dees stick to the flashier Zeta.

Siam Square & Pratunam

Diplomat Bar (Map pp120-1; ☎ 0 2690 9999; Conrad Hotel, 87 Th Withayu/Wireless Rd; Skytrain Ploenchit) This is one of the few hotel lounges that the locals make a point of visiting. Choose from an expansive list of innovative martinis and sip to live jazz, played gracefully at conversation level.

To-Sit (Map pp120-1; ☎ 0 2658 4001; Soi 3, Siam Sq, Th Phra Ram 1; Skytrain Siam) To-Sit epitomises everything a Thai university student could wish for on a night out: sappy Thai music and cheap, spicy eats. There are branches all over town, but the Siam Square location has the advantage of being virtually the only option in an area that's buzzing during the day, but dead at night.

Café Trio (Map pp120-1; ☎ 0 2252 6572; 36/11-12 Soi Lang Suan; Skytrain Chitlom) Spend an evening at this cosy jazz bar and you'll go home feeling like a local. Live music is featured on an irregular basis – best to call ahead to find out who and when.

Sukhumvit

Tuba (Map pp122-3; ☎ 0 2622 0708; 30 Ekamai Soi 21, Soi Ekamai/63, Th Sukhumvit; Skytrain Ekamai) Part storage room for over-the-top vintage furniture, part friendly local boozer, this bizarre bar certainly doesn't lack in character. Indulge in a whole bottle for once, and don't miss the delicious chicken wings.

Spring (Map pp122–3; ☎ 0 2392 2747; 199 Soi Promsri 2, Soi Phrompong/39, Th Sukhumvit; Skytrain Phrom Phong) Although not technically a bar, the expansive lawn of this smartly reconverted 1970s-era house is probably the only chance you'll ever have to witness Bangkok's fair and beautiful willingly exposing themselves to the elements.

Cheap Charlie's (Map pp122–3; Soi 11, Th Sukhumvit; ☺ Mon-Sat; Skytrain Nana) There's never enough seating, and the design concept is best classified as 'junkyard', but on most nights this chummy open-air beer corner is a great place to meet everybody, from package tourists to resident English teachers.

Bull's Head (Map pp122–3; ☎ 0 2259 4444; 595/10-11 Soi 33/1, Th Sukhumvit; Skytrain Phrom Phong) Bangkok boasts several English-style pubs, and this is probably the most 'authentic' of the lot. With friendly management and staff, and more events and activities than a summer camp, it's also a good place to meet people, particularly those of the British persuasion.

HOBS (House of Beers; Map pp122–3; ☎ 0 2392 3513; 522/3 Soi 16, Soi Thong Lor/55, Th Sukhumvit; Skytrain Thong Lo) Arguably the word's best brews, Belgian beers have been fleetingly available around Bangkok for a while now, but have found a permanent home at this new pub. Be sure to accompany your beer with a bowl of crispy *frites*, served here Belgian-style with mayonnaise.

ENTERTAINMENT
Shame on you if you find yourself bored in Bangkok. And even more shame if you think the only entertainment options involve the word 'go-go'. Nowadays Bangkok's nightlife is as diverse as that of virtually any modern city – but a lot cheaper. Even if you're usually in bed by 9pm, Bangkok still offers interesting postdinner diversions, from flash cinemas to traditional cultural performances.

Live Music
Music is an essential element of a Thai night out, and just about every pub worth its salted peanuts has a house band of varying quality. For the most part this means perky Thai pop covers or tired international standards (if you've left Bangkok with-

out having heard a live version of 'Hotel California', well, you haven't really been to Bangkok), but an increasing number of places are starting to deviate from the norm with quirky and/or inspired bands and performances. Nightly line-ups at smaller venues can be found online at **Bangkok Gig Guide** (www.bangkokgigguide.com).

Brick Bar (Map pp114–15; ☎ 0 2629 4477; basement, Buddy Lodge, 265 Th Khao San; river ferry Tha Phra Athit) This cavelike pub hosts a nightly revolving cast of live music for an almost exclusively Thai crowd. Come before midnight, wedge yourself into a table a few inches from the horn section, and lose it to Teddy Ska, one of the most energetic live acts in town.

Living Room (Map pp122–3; ☎ 02 649 8888; Level I, Sheraton Grande Sukhumvit, 250 Th Sukhumvit; Skytrain Asoke, Metro Sukhumvit) Don't let looks deceive you; every night this bland hotel lounge transforms into the city's best venue for live jazz. Contact ahead of time to see which sax master or hide hitter is currently in town.

Parking Toys (Map pp110–11; ☎ 0 2907 2228; 17/22 Soi Mayalap, Kaset-Navamin Hwy) Essentially a rambling shed stuffed with vintage furniture, Parking Toys hosts an eclectic revolving cast of fun bands ranging in genre from acoustic/classical ensembles to electro-funk jam acts. To get here, take a taxi heading north from Mo Chit Skytrain station and tell the driver to take you to Th Kaset-Navamin. Immediately upon passing the second stop light on this road, look for the Heineken sign on your left.

Saxophone Pub & Restaurant (Map pp112–13; ☎ 0 2246 5472; 3/8 Th Phayathai; Skytrain Victory Monument) This nightlife staple is the big stage of Bangkok's live music scene. It's a bit too loud for a first date, but the quality and variety of the music makes it a great destination for music-loving buddies on a night out.

Raintree (Map pp112–13; ☎ 0 2245 7230; 116/63-64 Soi Ruam Mit, Th Rang Nam; Skytrain Victory Monument) This atmospheric pub is one of the few remaining places in town to hear 'songs for life', Thai folk music with roots in the communist insurgency of the 1960s and '70s.

Ad Here the 13th (Map pp114–15; 13 Th Samsen; river ferry Tha Phra Athit) Beside Khlong Banglamphu, Ad Here is everything a neighbourhood joint should be: lots of regulars, cold beer and heartwarming tunes delivered by a masterful house band starting at 10pm. Everyone knows each other, so don't be shy about mingling.

Tawan Daeng German Brewhouse (Map pp110-11; ☎ 0 2678 1114; cnr Th Phra Ram III & Th Narathiwat Ratchanakharin) It's Oktoberfest all year round at this hangar-sized music hall. The Thai-German food is tasty, the house-made brews are entirely potable, and the nightly stage shows make singing along a necessity. Music starts at 8.30pm; take a taxi.

Brown Sugar (Map p124; ☎ 0 2250 1825; 231/20 Th Sarasin; Skytrain Ratchadamri) Plant yourself in a corner of this cosy, mazelike pub, and bump to Zao-za-dung, the nine-piece house band. The tables are so close that you can't help but make new friends.

Bamboo Bar (Map pp118-19; ☎ 0 2236 0400; Oriental Hotel, 48 Soi Oriental/38, Th Charoen Krung; river ferry Tha Oriental) The Oriental's Bamboo Bar is famous for its live lounge jazz, which holds court inside a colonial-era cabin of lazy fans, broad-leafed palms and rattan decor.

Dance Clubs

Bangkok's discos are largely fly-by-night outfits, and that really fun club you found on your last trip two years ago is most likely history today. To find out what is going on, check **Dude Sweet** (www.dudesweet.org), organisers of hugely popular monthly parties, and **Bangkok Recorder** (www.bangkokrecorder.com) for rotating theme nights and visiting celeb DJs.

Cover charges for clubs and discos range from 250B to 600B and usually include a drink. Don't even think about showing up before 11pm, and always bring ID. Most clubs close at 2am. You'll see more Thais out on the town at the beginning of the month (pay day) than other times.

Tapas Room (Map pp118-19; ☎ 0 2234 4737; 114/17-18 Soi 4, Th Silom; Skytrain Sala Daeng, Metro Silom) You won't find food here, but the name is an accurate indicator of the Spanish/Moroccan-inspired vibe of this multilevel den. Come Thursday to Saturday when the combination of DJs and live percussion brings the body count to critical level.

Club Culture (Map pp112-13; ☎ 0 89497 8422; Th Sri Ayuthaya; ☻ 7pm-late Wed, Fri & Sat; Skytrain Phayathai) Housed in a unique 40-year-old Thai-style building, Club Culture is the biggest and quirkiest recent arrival on Bangkok's club scene. Come to shake to internationally recognised DJs and the most-touted system in town.

Glow (Map pp122-3; ☎ 0 2261 3007; 96/4-5 Soi 23, Th Sukhumvit; Skytrain Asoke, Metro Sukhumvit) Glow is a small venue with a big reputation. Boasting a huge variety of vodkas and a recently upgraded sound system, the tunes range from hip-hop (Fridays) to electronica (Saturdays), and just about everything in between.

Nung-Len (Map pp122-3; ☎ 0 2711 6564; 217 Soi Ekamai/63; Skytrain Ekamai) Young, loud and Thai, Nung-Len (literally 'sit and chill') is a ridiculously popular sardine tin of live music and uni students on popular Th Ekamai. Make sure you get in before 10pm or you won't get in at all.

Bed Supperclub (Map pp122-3; ☎ 0 2651 3537; www.bedsupperclub.com; 26 Soi 11, Th Sukhumvit; Skytrain Nana) This illuminated tube has been a literal highlight of the Bangkok club scene for a good while now. Arrive early to squeeze in dinner (p167), or if you've only got dancing on your mind, come on Tuesday for the popular hip-hop nights.

Soi 11 is now also home to longstanding **Q Bar** (Map pp122-3; ☎ 0 2252 3274; Soi 11, Th Sukhumvit; Skytrain Nana) and newer **Twisted Republic** (Map pp122-3; ☎ 0 2651 0800; www.twistedrepublic.com; 37 Soi 11, Th Sukhumvit; cover 300B; Skytrain Nana).

Royal City Avenue (RCA; Map pp110-11; off Th Phra Ram IX) is well and truly Club Alley. Formerly a bastion of the teen scene, this Vegas-like strip has finally graduated from high school and at such clubs as the following now hosts partiers of every age.

808 Club (Map pp110-11; www.808bangkok.com) Currently the leader of the pack with big-name DJs and insanely crowded events.

Cosmic Café (Map pp110-11; ☎ 0 2641 5619) Somewhere between a pub and disco, come on Wednesday nights when the DJ spins Thai music from the 1980s.

Flix/Slim (Map pp110-11; ☎ 0 2203 0377) The poshest choice on the strip with big thumping house beats and a more club-jaded clientele.

Route 66 (Map pp110-11; ☎ 0 1440 9666; www.route66club.com) It rocks to a younger beat with hip-hop and R&B to the 'east' and varying shades of house to the 'west'.

Go-Go Bars

All those things your dodgy Uncle Larry told you about Bangkok are true. Although technically illegal, prostitution is fully 'out' in Bangkok, and the influence of organised crime and healthy kickbacks means that it will be a long while before the laws are ever enforced. Yet, despite the image presented by much of the Western media, the underlying atmosphere of Bangkok's red light districts is not one of illicitness and exploitation (although these do inevitably exist), but rather an aura of tackiness and boredom. Stages where ambivalent-looking women perform fabled feats with their genitalia are found at Patpong, and are nowadays largely shows for tourists. Men strictly looking for women (or ladyboys; *gà·teu·i*, also spelt *kàthoey*) have mostly moved to Soi Cowboy or Nana.

Patpong (Map pp118-19; Soi Patpong 1 & 2, Th Silom; Skytrain Sala Daeng, Metro Silom) Possibly one of the most famous red-light districts in the world, but today any 'charm' that the area used to possess has been eroded by modern tourism, and fake Rolexes and Diesel t-shirts are more ubiquitous than flesh. There is, of course, a considerable amount of naughtiness going on, although much of it takes place upstairs and behind closed doors. If you must, before taking a seat at one of Patpong's 'pussy shows', be sure to agree to the price beforehand, otherwise you're likely to receive an astronomical bill.

Soi Cowboy (Map pp122-3; btwn Soi 21 & Soi 23, Th Sukhumvit; Skytrain Asoke, Metro Sukhumvit) This single-lane strip of raunchy bars claims direct lineage to the post-Vietnam War R&R era. A real flesh trade functions amid the flashing neon.

Nana Entertainment Plaza (Map pp122-3; Soi 4/Nana Tai, Th Sukhumvit; Skytrain Nana) Much like Soi Cowboy, this three-storey complex is where the sexpats are separated from the gawking tourists. It's also home to a few ladyboy bars.

Soi Twilight (Soi Pratuchai; Map pp118-19; Soi Pratuchai, Th Surawong; Skytrain Sala Daeng, Metro Silom) Patpong's queer little brother, the shows here range in scope from muscle boy to ladyboy.

Cinemas

Escape the smog and heat at one of the city's high-tech cinemas. All of Hollywood's big releases plus a steady diet of locally bred comedies and horror flicks hit Bangkok's cinemas in a timely fashion. The foreign films are sometimes altered by Thailand's film censors before distribution; this usually involves obscuring nude sequences. Film buffs may prefer the offerings at Bangkok's foreign cultural centres; for contact details, see p106. For the royal treatment, opt for the VIP amenities that only Bangkok would provide (see the boxed text, p174). All movies screened in Thai cinemas are preceded by the Thai royal anthem

and everyone is expected to stand respectfully for its duration.

At the following cinemas, English movies are shown with Thai subtitles rather than being dubbed. The shopping-centre cinemas have plush VIP options, while Lido and Scala are older and artier. House is Bangkok's first 'art-house' theatre. Visit **Movie Seer** (www.movieseer.com) for show times.

EGV Grand (Map pp120-1; ☎ 0 2515 5555; Siam Discovery Center, Th Phra Ram I; Skytrain Siam)

House (Map pp110-11; ☎ 0 2641 5177; www.houserama.com; UMG Bldg, Royal City Ave, near Th Petchaburi; Metro Phetburi)

Lido Cinema (Map pp120-1; ☎ 0 2252 6498; Siam Sq, Th Phra Ram I; Skytrain Siam)

Paragon Cineplex (Map pp120-1; ☎ 0 2515 5555; Siam Paragon, Th Phra Ram I; Skytrain Siam)

Scala Cinema (Map pp120-1; ☎ 0 2251 2861; Siam Sq, Soi 1, Th Phra Ram I; Skytrain Siam)

SF Cinema City (Map pp120-1; ☎ 0 2268 8888; 7th fl, MBK Center, cnr Th Phra Ram I & Th Phayathai; Skytrain National Stadium)

SFX Cinema (Map pp122-3; ☎ 0 2268 8888; 6th fl, Emporium Shopping Centre, Th Sukhumvit; Skytrain Phrom Phong)

Traditional Arts Performances

As Thailand's cultural repository, Bangkok offers an array of dance and theatre performances. For background information about these ancient traditions, see p74 and p77.

Chalermkrung Royal Theatre (Sala Chaloem Krung; Map pp116-17; ☎ 0 2222 0434; www.salachalermkrung.com; cnr Th Charoen Krung & Th Triphet; tickets 1000-2000B; river ferry Tha Saphan Phut) In a Thai Art Deco building

---

GÀ·TEU·I CABARET

Watching men dressed as women perform tacky show tunes has, not surprisingly, become the latest 'must-do' fixture on the Bangkok tourist circuit. Both **Calypso Cabaret** (Map pp120-1; ☎ 0 2653 3960; www.calypsocabaret.com; Asia Hotel, 296 Th Phayathai; tickets 1200B; ☼ show times 8.15pm & 9.45pm; Skytrain Ratchathewi) and **Mambo Cabaret** (Map pp122-3; ☎ 0 2259 5128; Washington Theatre, Th Sukhumvit, btwn Soi 22 & 24; tickets 800B; ☼ show times 8.30pm & 10pm; Skytrain Phrom Phong) host choreographed stage shows featuring Broadway high kicks and lip-synched pop tunes by the most well-endowed dudes you'll find anywhere.

CINEMA STRATEGY

Going to the movies is a big deal in Bangkok. It's unlikely that any other city in the world has anything like EGV's Gold Class, a ticket that grants you entry into a cinema with fewer than 50 seats, and where you're plied with blankets, pillows, foot-warming stockings and, of course, a valet food-and-drink service. There's also Major Cineplex's Emperor Class seat, which for the price of a sticky stool back home entitles you to a sofa-like love seat designed for couples. And if you find Paragon Cineplex's 16 screens and 5000 seats a bit plebeian, you can always apply for Enigma, a members-only theatre.

And despite the heat and humidity on the streets, keep in mind that all of Bangkok's movie theatres pump the air-conditioning with such vigour that a jumper or sweater is an absolute necessity – unless you're going Gold Class, that is.

at the edge of the Chinatown–Phahurat district, this theatre provides a striking venue for kŏhn (masked dance-drama based on stories from the *Ramakian*, the Thai version of the *Ramayana*). When it opened in 1933, the royally funded Chalermkrung was the largest and most modern theatre in Asia. Kŏhn performances last about two hours plus intermission; call for the schedule. The theatre requests that patrons dress respectfully, which means no shorts, tank tops or sandals. Bring along a wrap or long-sleeved shirt in case the air-con is running full blast.

Aksra Theatre (Map pp112-13; ☎ 0 2677 8888, ext 5604; www.aksratheatre.com; King Power Complex, 8/1 Th Rang Nam; tickets 800B; ✆ shows 7pm Tue-Fri, 1pm & 7pm Sat & Sun; Skytrain Victory Monument) The former Joe Louis Puppet Theatre has moved house and is starting a new life here as the Aksra Hoon Lakorn Lek. A variety of performances are now held at this modern theatre, but the highlight are performances of the *Ramakian* by using knee-high puppets requiring three puppeteers to strike humanlike poses.

National Theatre (Map pp114-15; ☎ 0 2224 1352; Th Na Phra That; tickets 50-100B; river ferry Tha Phra Chan) When its seemingly never-ending reconstruction is eventually finished, the National Theatre will host monthly performances of the royal dance traditions of lá·kon (classical dance-drama) and kŏhn. The nearby Bangkok Information Center (p108) can provide an English-language calendar of performances.

Patravadi Theatre (Map pp114-15; ☎ 0 2412 7287; www.patravaditheatre.com; 69/1 Soi Tambon Wanglang 1; tickets 500B; cross-river ferry from Tha Maharat) This open-air theatre is Bangkok's leading promoter of avant-garde dance and drama. The new Studio 9 annexe offers dinner theatre on Friday and Saturday nights. A free river shuttle picks up patrons at Tha Mahathat,

near Silpakorn University; reservations for performances are recommended.

Thailand Cultural Centre (Map pp110-11; ☎ 0 2247 0028; www.thaiculturalcenter.com; Th Ratchadaphisek btwn Th Thiam Ruammit & Th Din Daeng; Metro Thailand Cultural Centre) Occasionally, classical dance performances are held at this venue featuring a concert hall, art gallery and outdoor studios. International dance and theatre groups are also profiled, especially during the International Festival of Music & Dance, held twice a year in June and September. Call for upcoming events as the website doesn't carry an up-to-date schedule.

Dusit Palace Park (p138) also hosts daily classical dance performances at 10am and 2pm.

Thai Boxing

Thai boxing's best of the best fight it out at Bangkok's two boxing stadiums: **Lumphini Stadium** (Sanam Muay Lumphini; Map p124; ☎ 0 2251 4303; Th Phra Ram IV; tickets 3rd/2nd class/ringside 1000/1500/2000B; Metro Lumphini) and **Ratchadamnoen Stadium** (Sanam Muay Ratchadamnoen; Map pp114-15; ☎ 0 2281 4205; Th Ratchadamnoen Nok; tickets 3rd/2nd class/ringside 1000/1500/2000B; bus 70, 503, 509). You'll note that tickets are not cheap, and these prices are exponentially more than what Thais pay. To add insult to injury, the inflated price offers no special service or seating, and at Ratchadamnoen Stadium foreigners are sometimes corralled into an area with an obstructed view. As long as you are mentally prepared for the financial jabs from the promoters, you'll be better prepared to enjoy the real fight.

Ringside puts you right up in the central action but amid a fairly subdued crowd where gambling is prohibited. Second-class seats are filled with backpackers and numbers runners who take the bets from the crowd. Like being in the pit of a stock exchange, hand signals fly between the 2nd- and 3rd-class areas communicating bets and odds. The 3rd-class area is the rowdiest section. Fenced off from the rest of the stadium, most of the die-hard fans follow the match (or their bets) too closely to sit down. If you're lukewarm on watching two men punch and kick each other, then 3rd-class offers the diversion of the crowd.

Fights are held throughout the week, alternating between the two stadiums. Ratchadamnoen hosts the matches on Monday, Wednesday and Thursday at 6pm and on Sunday at 5pm. Lumphini hosts matches on Tuesday, Friday and Saturday at 6pm. Aficionados say the best-matched bouts are reserved for Tuesday nights at Lumphini and Thursday nights at Ratchadamnoen. There is a total of eight to 10 fights of five rounds a piece. The stadiums don't usually fill up until the main events, which usually start around 8pm or 9pm.

There are English-speaking 'staff' standing outside the stadium who will practically tackle you upon arrival. Although there have been a few reports of scamming, most of these assistants help steer visitors to the foreigner ticket windows and hand out a fight roster; they can also be helpful in telling you which fights are the best match-ups between contestants. (Some say that welterweights, between 135lb and 147lb, are the best.) To keep everyone honest, though, remember to purchase tickets from the ticket window, not from a person outside the stadium.

As a prematch warm-up, grab a plate of *gài yâhng* (grilled chicken) and other northeastern dishes from the restaurants surrounding the Ratchadamnoen Stadium.

SHOPPING

Welcome to a true buyer's market. Home to one of the world's largest outdoor markets, numerous giant upscale malls, and sidewalk-clogging bazaars on nearly every street, it's impossible not to be impressed by the amount of commerce in Bangkok. However, despite the apparent scope and variety, Bangkok really only excels in one area when it comes to shopping: cheap stuff. The city is not the place to buy a new Nikon SLR or a (real) Fendi handbag – save those for online warehouses in the US or bargain-basement sales in Hong Kong. Ceramics, dirt-cheap T-shirts, fabric, Asian knick-knackery and

yes, if you can deal with the guilt, pirated software and music – these are the things to stock up on in Bangkok. Other worthwhile purchases include locally made and designed fashion and decor items. See the boxed text on p182 for a few recommended brands.

The difficulty is finding your way around, since the city's intense urban tangle sometimes makes orientation difficult. A good shopping companion is *Nancy Chandler's Map of Bangkok,* with annotations on all sorts of small and out-of-the-way shopping venues and *đà·làht* (markets).

Antiques

Real Thai antiques are rare and costly. Most Bangkok antique shops keep a few authentic pieces for collectors, along with lots of pseudo-antiques or traditionally crafted items that look like antiques. The majority of shop operators are quite candid about what's really old and what isn't.

River City Complex (Map pp116–17; Th Yotha, off Th Charoen Krung; river ferry Tha Si Phraya) Near the Royal Orchid Sheraton Hotel, this multistorey shopping centre is an all-in-one stop for old-world Asiana. Several high-quality art and antique shops occupy the 3rd and 4th floors. Old Maps & Prints offers one-of-a-kind rare maps and illustrations, with a focus on Asia. Although the quality is high, the prices are too, as many wealthy tourists filter in and out. Many stores here close on Sunday.

Ámantee (Map pp110–11; ☎ 0 2982 8694; www.amantee .com; 131/3 Soi 13, Th Chaeng Wattana; ◷ 9am-8pm; access by taxi from Skytrain Mo Chit) Although well outside of the city centre, this 'repository of Oriental and Tibetan art and antiques' is well worth the trip. Consisting of several interconnecting wooden Thai houses holding a variety of classy items, the peaceful compound also boasts a cafe (open 9am to 5pm), accommodation and occasional cultural events. A Thai-language map for taxi drivers can be downloaded at the website.

House of Chao (Map pp118–19; ☎ 0 2635 7188; 9/1 Th Decho; ◷ 9am-7pm; Skytrain Chong Nonsi) This threestorey antique shop, housed, appropriately, in an antique house, has everything necessary to deck out your fantasy colonial-era mansion. Particularly interesting are the various weatherworn doors, doorways, gateways and trellises that can be found in the covered area behind the showroom.

ART ATTACK

Although Bangkok's hyper-urban environment seems to cater to the inner philistine in all of us, the city has a significant but low-key art scene. In recent years, galleries seem to have been opening on a weekly basis, and Bangkok also acts as something of a regional art hub, with works by emerging artists from places like Myanmar and Cambodia. To find out what's happening while you're in town, pick up a free copy of the excellent *BAM!* (Bangkok Art Map). Some of the better galleries:

■ **100 Tonson Gallery** (Map pp120-1; ☎ 0 2684 1527; www.100tonsongallery.com; 100 Soi Tonson, Th Ploenchit; ☼ 11am-7pm Thu-Sun; Skytrain Chitlom) Atmospheric gallery showcasing the work of domestic and international emerging and high-profile painters, sculptors and conceptual artists.

■ **Bangkok Art and Culture Centre** (BACC; Map pp120-1; ☎ 0 2214 6630; www.bacc.or.th; cnr Th Phayathai & Th Phra Ram 1; Skytrain Siam) This brand-new state-owned complex combines art and commerce in a multistorey building smack-dab in the centre of Bangkok.

■ **Bangkok University Art Gallery** (BUG; Map pp110-11; ☎ 0 2350 3500; http://fab.bu.ac.th/buggallery; 3rd fl, Bldg 9, City Campus, Th Phra Ram IV; ☼ 9.30am-7pm Tues-Sat) This spacious new compound is located at what is currently Thailand's most cutting-edge art school. Recent exhibitions have encompassed a variety of media by some of the country's top names, as well as the work of internationally recognised artists.

■ **H Gallery** (Map pp118-19; ☎ 0 1310 4428; www.hgallerybkk.com; 201 Soi 12, Th Sathon; ☼ noon-6pm Wed-Sat; Skytrain Surasak) Leading commercial gallery for emerging Thai abstract painters.

■ **Jamjuree Art Gallery** (Map pp120-1; ☎ 0 2218 3708; Jamjuree Bldg, Chulalongkorn University, Th Phayathai; ☼ 10am-7pm Mon-Fri, noon-6pm Sat & Sun; Skytrain Siam) Modern spiritual themes and brilliantly coloured abstracts from emerging student artists.

■ **Kathmandu Photo Gallery** (Map pp118-19; ☎ 0 2234 6700; www.kathmandu-bkk.com; 87 Th Pan; ☼ 11am-7pm Sun-Fri; Skytrain Surasak) Bangkok's only truly dedicated photography gallery is located in a restored Sino-Portuguese shophouse. The small upstairs gallery plays host to changing exhibitions by local and international artists and photographers.

■ **Queen's Gallery** (Map pp114-15; ☎ 0 2281 5360; www.queengallery.org; 101 Th Ratchadamnoen Klang; admission 20B; ☼ 10am-7pm Tue-Mon; klorng taxi to Tha Phan Fah) This royally funded museum presents five floors of rotating exhibitions of modern and traditionally influenced art.

■ **Surapon Gallery** (Map p124; ☎ 0 2638 0033; www.rama9art.org/gallery/surapon/index.html; Tisco Tower, 1st fl, Th Sathon Neua; Skytrain Sala Daeng, Metro Silom) Unique contemporary Thai art.

■ **Tang Gallery** (Map pp118-19; ☎ 0 2630 1114; basement, Silom Galleria, 919/1 Th Silom; ☼ 11am-7pm Mon-Sat; Skytrain Surasak) Bangkok's primary venue for modern artists from China has also edged its way up to become among the city's top contemporary galleries. Check the posters in the lobby of the Galleria to see what's on.

Department Stores & Shopping Centres

Bangkok may be crowded and polluted, but its department stores are modern oases of order. They're also downright frigid, and Sunday afternoons see a significant part of Bangkok's entire population crowding into the city's indoor malls to escape the heat. By no accident, the Skytrain stations also have shaded walkways delivering passengers directly into nearby stores without ever having to set foot on ground level. Most shopping centres are open from 10am or 11am to 9pm or 10pm.

The selection is surprisingly good at Bangkok's shopping centres, but don't expect any bargains; most imported items cost more than they would elsewhere. Another quirk is that shop assistants follow you around the store from rack to rack. This is the definition of Thai 'service' rather than an indication that they've sniffed you out as a shoplifter. And be sure you're satisfied with an item, as returns are largely unheard of.

MBK Center (Mahboonkhrong; Map pp120-1; ☎ 0 2217 9111; cnr Th Phra Ram I & Th Phayathai; Skytrain National Stadium) This colossal mall has become a tourist destination in its own right. Swedish and other languages can be heard as much as Thai, and on any given weekend half of Bangkok can be found here combing through an inexhaustible range of small stalls and shops. This is the cheapest place to buy contact lenses, mobile phones and accessories, and name-brand knock-offs. It's also one of the better places to stock up on camera gear, both new and used.

Siam Center & Siam Discovery Center (Map pp120-1; cnr Th Phra Ram I & Th Phayathai; Skytrain National Stadium) These linked sister centres feel almost monastic in their hushed hallways compared to frenetic MBK, just across the street. Siam Discovery Center excels in home decor, with the whole 3rd floor devoted to Asian-minimalist styles and jewel-toned fabrics. The attached Siam Center, Thailand's first shopping centre built in 1976, has recently gone under the redesign knife for a younger, hipper look. Youth fashion is its new focus, and several local labels can be found on the 2nd floor.

Siam Paragon (Map pp120-1; ☎ 0 2610 8000; Th Phra Ram I; Skytrain Siam) The biggest, newest and glitziest of Bangkok's shopping malls, Siam Paragon is more of an urban park than shopping centre. Astronomically luxe brands occupy most floors, while the majority of shoppers hang out in the reflecting pool atrium or basement-level food court. The 5th floor is home to Kinokuniya, Thailand's largest English-language bookstore.

Central World Plaza (Map pp120-1; ☎ 0 2635 1111; Th Ratchadamri & Th Phra Ram I; Skytrain Chitlom) After being left behind in the mall race, this behemoth box has gutted itself and transformed from ho-hum shopping mall to extrahuge 'lifestyle' scene. An elevated walkway links the mall to the Skytrain and several other local mega-malls.

Gaysorn Plaza (Map pp120-1; cnr Th Ploenchit & Th Ratchadamri; Skytrain Chitlom) A haute couture catwalk, Gaysorn's spiralling staircases and all-white halls preserve all of fashion's beloved designers in museum-curatorship style. Local fashion leaders occupy the 2nd floor, while the top floor is a stroll through chic home decor.

Central Chit Lom (Map pp120-1; ☎ 0 2655 1444; 1027 Th Ploenchit; Skytrain Chitlom) Generally regarded as the all-round best for quality and selection, Central has 13 branches in Bangkok in addition to this chi-chi flagship. If you're curious about local hooks, look for Thai designers such as Tube and the Thai cosmetic brand Erb.

Emporium Shopping Centre (Map pp122-3; 622 Th Sukhumvit, cnr Soi 24; Skytrain Phrom Phong) You might not have access to the beautiful people's nightlife scene, but you can observe their spending rituals at this temple to red hot and classic cool. Robust expat salaries and trust funds dwindle amid Prada, Miu Miu, Chanel and Thai brands such as Greyhound and Propaganda.

Pantip Plaza (Map pp120-1; 604 Th Petchaburi; Skytrain Ratchathewi) North of Siam Square, this is five storeys of computer and software stores ranging from legit to flea market. Many locals come here to buy 'pirated' software and computer peripherals, but the crowds and touts ('DVD sex?') make it among the more tiring shopping experiences in town.

BARGAINING 101

Many of your purchases in Bangkok will involve an ancient skill that has long been abandoned in the West: bargaining. Contrary to what you'll see on a daily basis on Th Khao San, bargaining (in Thai, *gahn dòr rahkah*) is not a terse exchange of numbers and animosity. Rather, bargaining Thai style is a generally friendly transaction where two people try to agree on a price that is fair to both of them.

The first rule to bargaining is to have a general idea of the price. Ask around at a few vendors to get a rough notion. When you're ready to buy, it's generally a good strategy to start at 50% of the asking price and work up from there. If you're buying several of an item, you have much more leverage to request and receive a lower price. If the seller immediately agrees to your first price you're probably paying too much, but it's bad form to bargain further at this point. In general, keeping a friendly, flexible demeanour throughout the transaction will almost always work in your favour. And remember, only begin bargaining if you're really planning on buying the item. Most importantly, there's simply no point in getting angry or upset over a few baht. The locals, who inevitably have less money than you, never do this.

Fashion & Textiles

In recent years Bangkok has become something of a fashion-conscious and, increasingly, fashion-generating city. Local designers such as senada*, Fly Now and Tango have shown that the city harbours a style scene that can compete on the international catwalk. More affordable looks are exhibited by the city's trendy teens who strut their distinctive 'Bangkok' look in the various shopping areas.

Siam Square (Map pp120-1; btwn Th Phra Ram I & Th Phayathai, Skytrain Siam) This low-slung commercial universe is a network of some 12 soi lined with trendy, fly-by-night boutiques, many of which are the first ventures of young designers. It's a great place to pick up designs you're guaranteed not to find anywhere else, not to mention the best place for urban naturalists to observe Bangkok teens in their natural habitat.

It's Happened to be a Closet (Map pp114-15; ☎ 0 2629 5271; 32 Th Khao San; ☺ 1-11pm; river ferry Tha Phra Athit) Garbled grammar aside, this is a brilliant place to stock up on locally designed and made togs. Bright colours and bold patterns rule and the eclectic shop even features a restaurant and cafe, a hair and nail salon, and private rooms for movie viewing. The forebodingly black complex is located in the same off-street courtyard as Tom Yam Kung restaurant .

Fly Now (Map pp120-1; ☎ 0 2656 1359; 2nd fl, Gaysorn Plaza, cnr Th Ploenchit & Th Ratchadamri; Skytrain Chitlom) A longstanding leader in Bangkok's home-grown fashion scene, Fly Now creates feminine couture that has caught the eyes of several international shows. Also available at Siam Center (p177) and Central World Plaza (p177).

Tango (Map pp120-1; ☎ 0 2656 1047; www.tango .co.th; Gaysorn Plaza, cnr Th Ploenchit & Th Ratchadamri; Skytrain Chitlom) This home-grown brand specialises in funky leather goods, but you may not even recognise the medium under the layers of bright embroidery and chunky jewels. Also available at Siam Center (p177).

Jim Thompson (Map pp118-19; ☎ 0 2632 8100; 9 Th Surawong; ☺ 9am-6pm; Skytrain Sala Daeng, Metro Silom) The surviving business of the international promoter of Thai silk, this, the largest Jim Thompson shop, sells colourful silk handkerchiefs, placemats, wraps and pillow cushions. Just up the road at 149/4-6 Th Surawong (Map pp118–19; ☎ 0 2235 8931) is a factory outlet that sells discontinued patterns at a significant discount.

Handicrafts & Decor

The tourist markets have tons of factory-made pieces that pop up all along the tourist route. The shopping centres sell products with a little better quality at proportionally higher prices, but the independent shops sell the best items all round. See the boxed text on p182 for a few more design-oriented shops.

Thai Home Industries (Map pp118-19; ☎ 0 2234 1736; 35 Soi Oriental, Th Charoen Krung; ☺ 9am-6.30pm Mon-Sat; river ferry Tha Oriental) A visit to this temple-like building, a former monks' quarters, is like discovering an abandoned attic of Asian booty. Despite the odd assortment of items (our last visit revealed items ranging from elegant handmade flatware to wooden model ships) and lack of order, it's heaps more fun than the typically faceless Bangkok handicraft shop.

Narai Phand (Map pp120-1; ☎ 0 2656 0398; www .naraiphand.com; ground fl, President Tower, 973 Th Ploenchit; ☺ 10am-8pm; Skytrain Ploenchit) Souvenir-quality handicrafts are given fixed prices and comfortable air-conditioning at this government-run facility. You won't find anything here that you haven't already seen at all of the tourist street markets, but it is a good stop if you're pressed for time or spooked by haggling.

Nandakwang (Map pp122-3; ☎ 0 2258 1962; 108/2-3 Soi Prasanmit/23, Th Sukhumvit; ☺ 9am-6pm Mon-Sat, 10am-5pm Sun; Skytrain Asoke, Metro Sukhumvit) A Bangkok satellite of a Chiang Mai–based store, Nandakwang sells a fun and handsome mix of cloth, wood and glass products. The cheery hand-embroidered pillows and bags are particularly attractive. There is also a branch in Siam Discovery Center (p177).

Taekee Taekon (Map pp114-15; ☎ 0 2629 1473; 118 Th Phra Athit; ☺ 8.30am-6pm Mon-Sat; river ferry Tha Phra Athit) Representing Thailand's main silk-producing regions, this charming store has a beautiful selection of table runners and wall hangings.

SPEND FRIEND

Gaysorn Plaza (p177) is probably Bangkok's most upscale mall, and the selection of high-end luxury brands must have overwhelmed more than one potential shopper because the shopping centre now offers a **Lifestyle Consultant** (☎ 0 2656 1177) service. Available by appointment, but free of charge, the team consists of two 'experts', a local fashion designer and a makeup artist, whose goal is to guide you to that perfect outfit, shade of mascara or spa treatment.

7-ELEVEN FOREVER

Be extremely wary of any appointment that involves the words 'meet me at 7-Eleven'. According to the company's website there are 3912 branches of 7-Eleven in Thailand alone (there will inevitably be several more by the time this book has gone to print) – more than half the number found in the entire USA. In Bangkok, 7-Elevens are so ubiquitous that it's not uncommon to see two branches staring at each other from across the street.

The first *sewên* (as it's known in Thai) in Thailand was installed in Patpong in 1991. The brand caught on almost immediately, and today Thailand ranks behind only Japan and Taiwan in the total number of branches in Asia. The stores are either owned directly by the company or are franchises, owned and managed by private individuals.

Although the company claims that its stores carry more than 2000 items, the fresh flavours of Thai cuisine are not reflected in the wares of a typical Bangkok 7-Eleven, whose food selections are even junkier than those of its counterparts in the West. Like all shops in Thailand, alcohol is only available from 11am to 2pm and 5pm to 11pm, and branches of 7-Eleven located near hospitals, temples and schools do not sell alcohol or cigarettes at all (but do continue to sell unhealthy snack food).

We love 7-Eleven for the wide selection of drinks, a godsend in sweltering Bangkok. You can conveniently pay most of your bills at the Service Counter, and all manner of phone cards, prophylactics and 'literature' (although, oddly, not most newspapers) are also available. And sometimes the blast of air-conditioning alone is enough reason to stop by. But our single favourite 7-Eleven item must be the dirt-cheap chilled scented towels for wiping away the accumulated grime and sweat before your next appointment.

Alongside silk products, you will also find small examples of celadon pottery and a terrific selection of postcards.

Gems & Jewellery

Although it is common wisdom that Thailand is a bonanza for gems and jewellery, the risk of a rip-off is much greater than finding a bargain. For details on the numerous scams that exist see the boxed text, p180.

Two longstanding and reputable gem vendors:

Johnny's Gems (Map pp116-17; ☎ 0 2224 4065; 199 Th Fuang Nakhon; 🕙 Mon-Sat; river ferry Tha Saphan Phut) A long-time favourite of Bangkok expats, Johnny's Gems is a reliable name in an unreliable business.

Uthai's Gems (Map pp120-1; ☎ 02 253 8582; 28/7 Soi Ruam Rudi; 🕙 Mon-Sat; Skytrain Ploenchit) With 40 years in the business, Uthai's fixed prices and good service, including a money-back guarantee, make him a popular choice among expats.

Markets

Although air-conditioned malls have better PR departments, open-air markets are the true face of commercial Bangkok, and are where you'll find the best bargains.

ALL-PURPOSE MARKETS

Among the largest markets in the world, **Chatuchak Weekend Market** (Talat Nat Jatujak; Map pp110-11; 🕙 9am-6pm Sat & Sun; Skytrain Mo Chit, Metro Chatuchak Park) seems to unite everything buyable, from used vintage sneakers to baby squirrels. JJ, as it's also known, is the ideal place to finally pick up those gifts for people back home, not to mention a pretty item or two for your own home. The market is roughly divided into thematic sections, the best guide to these being *Nancy Chandler's Map of Bangkok*. Because Chatuchak is a Thai institution, food also plays a significant role, and there are numerous drinks and snack vendors, and several good restaurants on the outside edges of the market. Plan to spend a full day, as there's plenty to see, do and buy. But come early, ideally around 9am to 10am, to beat the crowds and the heat.

There is an information centre and a bank with ATMs and foreign-exchange booths at the Chatuchak Park offices, near the northern end of the market's Soi 1, Soi 2 and Soi 3. Schematic maps and toilets are located throughout the market.

There are a few vendors out on weekday mornings, and a daily vegetable, plant and flower market opposite the market's southern side. One section of the latter, known as the Or Tor Kor Market, sells fantastically gargantuan fruit and seafood, and has a decent food court as well.

BANGKOK

Pak Khlong Market (Map pp116-17; Th Chakkaphet & Th Atsadang; 24hr; river ferry Tha Saphan Phut) Every night this market near the Chao Phraya River becomes the city's largest depot for wholesale flowers. Arrive as late as you're willing to stay up, and be sure to take a camera, as the technicolour blur of roses, lotuses and daisies on the move is a sight to behold. During the day, Pak Khlong is a wholesale vegetable market.

Vespa Market (Map pp110-11; cnr Th Ratchadaphisek & Th Lad Phrao, Greater Bangkok; 6pm-midnight Sat; Metro Lat Phrao) Uniting urban cowboys, hip-hoppers, wannabe mods and pissed-off punks, this expansive outdoor market is a virtual melting pot of Bangkok youth subculture. The original emphasis was on vintage vehicles, but quirky T-shirts, used sneakers and modern antiques form the bulk of this fun market.

Nonthaburi Market (Map pp110-11; Tha Nam Non, Nonthaburi; 5am-8am; river ferry Tha Nonthaburi) Located a short walk from Nonthaburi Pier, the northernmost extent of the Chao Phraya Express boats, this is one of the most expansive and atmospheric produce markets in the area. Come early, as most vendors are gone by 9am.

Pratunam Market (Map pp120-1; cnr Th Petchaburi & Th Ratchaprarop; 8am-6pm; klorng taxi to Tha Pratunam) The city's biggest wholesale clothing market, Pratunam is a tight warren of stalls trickling deep into the block. In addition to cheap T-shirts and jeans, luggage, bulk toiletries and souvenirs are also available.

Soi Lalai Sap (Map pp118-19; Soi Lalai Sap/5, Th Silom; 8am-6pm; Skytrain Chong Nonsi) The 'money-melting' street has a number of vendors selling all sorts of cheap clothing, watches and homewares during the day. Regular perusers say that imperfections from name-brand factories often appear in the stacks.

Phahurat Market (Map pp116-17; Th Phahurat & Th Triphet; river ferry Tha Saphan Phut) Across from Old Siam Plaza, the Indian-fabric district prefers boisterous colours, faux fur, neon sparkles and everything you'll need for a Halloween costume or a traditional Thai dance drama. Deeper into the market are cute clothes for kids and good deals on Thai textiles.

Sampeng Lane (Map pp116-17; Sampeng Lane/Soi Wanit 1, Chinatown; river ferry Tha Ratchawong) This wholesale market runs roughly parallel to Th Yaowarat, bisecting the two districts of Chinatown and Phahurat. Pick up the narrow artery from Th Ratchawong and follow it through its many manifestations – handbags, homewares, hair decorations, stickers, Japanese-animation gear, plastic beeping key chains. Unless you're shopping for a grassroots import-export group, Sampeng is more for entertainment than for purchases.

TOURIST MARKETS

The souvenir sellers have an amazing knack for sniffing out what new arrivals want to haul back home – perennial favourites include raunchy T-shirts, *mŏrn kwăhn* (traditional Thai wedge-shaped pillow), CDs and synthetic sarongs. Not all tourist markets are created equal: porn is hard to come by on Th Khao San but plentiful on Th Sukhumvit; and hemp clothing is noticeably absent from Patpong.

Th Sukhumvit Market (Map pp122-3; Th Sukhumvit btwn Soi 2 & 12, 3 & 15; 11am-10.30pm; Skytrain Nana) Knock-offs bags and watches, stacks of skin-flick DVDs, Chinese throwing stars and other questionable gifts for your high-school-aged brother dominate at this market peddling to package and sex tourists.

THE WAR ON THE GEM SCAM

We're begging you, if you aren't a gem trader, then don't buy unset stones in Thailand – period. Countless tourists are sucked into the prolific and well-rehearsed gem scam in which they are taken to a store by a helpful stranger and tricked into buying bulk gems that can supposedly be resold in their home country for 100% profit. The expert con artists (part of a well-organised cartel) seem trustworthy and convince tourists that they need a citizen of the country to circumvent tricky customs regulations. Guess what, the gem world doesn't work like that; and what most tourists end up with are worthless pieces of glass. By the time you sort all this out, the store has closed, changed names and the police can do little to help. Want to know more or want to report a scam? Visit www.2bangkok.com and navigate to the 'Gem Scam' page for five years' worth of tracking the phenomenon, or go to **Thai Gems Scam Group** (www.geocities.com/thaigemsscamgroup) for photos of touts who troll the temples for victims. The tourist police can also help to resolve some purchase disputes, but don't expect miracles.

MARKETING STRATEGY

Open-air markets are the heart and soul of Bangkok-style commerce, but the options can be a bit overwhelming. To help you burn your baht more efficiently, we've put together a brief cheat sheet of the most interesting options.

- **Chatuchak Weekend Market** (p179) Stock up on souvenirs, or invest in a vintage tracksuit – they're all here.

- **Nonthaburi Market** (opposite) The most picturesque fresh market in the area, but get there early, ideally before 7am.

- **Pak Khlong Market** (opposite) Show up late-late for the visual poetry that is the nightly flower market.

- **Pratunam Market** (opposite) Acres of cheap togs, much of it for less than you'd pay for a pair of socks at home.

- **Vespa Market** (opposite) Antique vehicles and urban hipsters unite here every Saturday night.

Th Khao San Market (Map pp114-15; Th Khao San; ⏲ 11am-11pm; river ferry Tha Phra Athit) The main guesthouse strip in Banglamphu is a day-and-night shopping bazaar for serious baht pinchers, with cheap T-shirts, 'bootleg' CDs, wooden elephants, hemp clothing, fisherman pants and other goods that make backpackers go ga-ga.

Patpong Night Market (Map pp118-19; Patpong Soi 1 & 2, Th Silom; ⏲ 7pm-1am; Skytrain Sala Daeng, Metro Silom) Drawing more crowds than the ping-pong shows, this market continues the street's illicit leanings with a deluge of pirated goods, particularly watches and clothing. Bargain with intensity as first-quoted prices tend to be astronomically high.

Tailors

Although Bangkok's diplomatic corps provides a steady clientele for the city's established tailors, the continuous supply of tourists also provides a lot of 'fresh meat' for the less-scrupulous businesses. Common scams range from commission-hungry túk-túk drivers to shoddy workmanship and inferior fabrics. In general, good tailors don't need to call the customer – the customers come to them.

Shirts and trousers can be turned around in 48 hours or less with only one fitting. But no matter what a tailor may tell you, it takes more than one or two fittings to create a good suit, and most reliable tailors will ask for two to five sittings.

Some reputable tailors:

Pinky Tailors (Map pp120-1; ☎ 0 2252 9680; www .pinkytailor.com; 888/40 Mahatun Plaza Arcade, Th Ploenchit; ⏲ 10am-7.30pm Mon-Sat; Skytrain Ploenchit) Custom-made suit jackets have been Mr Pinky's speciality for 35 years. Located behind the Mahatun Building.

Marco Tailors (Map pp120-1; ☎ 0 2251 7633; 430/33 Soi 7, Siam Sq; ⏲ 10am-5pm Mon-Fri; Skytrain Siam) Dealing solely in men's suits, this longstanding and reliable tailor has a wide selection of banker-sensibility wools and cottons.

Manhattan Custom Tailor (Map pp122-3; ☎ 0 2253 0173; 155/9 Soi 11/1, Th Sukhumvit; ⏲ 10am-7pm Mon-Sat; Skytrain Nana) One of an abundance of tailors located around the lower Sukhumvit area, Manhattan gets good reviews.

GETTING THERE & AWAY

Air

Bangkok has two airports. **Suvarnabhumi International Airport** (Map p189; ☎ 0 2723 0000; www .airportthai.com), 30km east of Bangkok, began commercial international and domestic service in September 2006 after several years of delay. The airport's name is pronounced *sù·wan·ná·poom*, and it inherited the airport code (BKK) previously used by the old airport at Don Muang. The unofficial airport website www.bangkokairportonline.com has practical information in English, as well as real-time details of arrivals and departures.

Bangkok's former international and domestic **Don Muang Airport** (Map pp110-11; ☎ 0 2535 1111; www.airportthai.co.th), 25km north of central Bangkok, was retired from commercial service in September 2006, only to be partially reopened five months later to handle overflow from Suvarnabhumi. At the time of writing rumours of the airport's imminent closure had been circulating, but for now it's still serving some domestic flights. The unofficial

---

LOCAL BUYS

Right, so you've got your embroidered elephant, silk runners and one of those croaking wooden frogs, but there are loads of local buys that you might still be proud to be displaying next year.

- **D&O Shop** This open-air gallery is the first retail venture of an organisation created to encourage awareness of Thai design abroad. The items are modern and funky, and give a new breath of life to the concept of Thai design. Available at Gaysorn (p177).

- **Doi Tung/Mae Fah Luang** This royally funded project sells beautiful hand-woven carpets, classy ceramics and Thailand's best domestic coffee beans. Available at Siam Discovery Center (p177).

- **Harnn & Thann** Smell good enough to eat with these botanical-based spa products: lavender massage lotion, rice bran soap and jasmine compresses. Products are all natural, rooted in Thai traditional medicine, and stylish enough to share space with brand-name beauty. Available at Gaysorn (p177).

- **Niwat Cutlery** Born out of the ancient sword-making traditions of Ayuthaya Province, the NV Aranyik company, a family-owned business, produces distinctively Thai stainless-steel cutlery. Available at Gaysorn (p177).

- **Propaganda** Thai designer Chaiyut Plypetch dreamed up this brand's signature character, the devilish Mr P who appears in anatomically correct cartoon lamps and other products. Available at Siam Discovery Center (p177) and Emporium (p177).

---

airport website www.donmuangairportonline .com has real-time details of arrivals and departures.

For hotels near either airport, see the boxed text, p154. For details on getting to and from the airports, see opposite.

AIRLINES

The following carriers service domestic destinations; a few also fly routes to international destinations. For a list of international carriers, see p756.

Air Asia (☎ 0 2515 9999; www.airasia.com; Suvarnabhumi International Airport) Suvarnabhumi to Chiang Mai, Chiang Rai, Hat Yai, Krabi, Nakhon Si Thammarat, Narathiwat, Phuket, Ranong, Surat Thani, Ubon Ratchathani and Udon Thani.

Bangkok Airways (Map pp110-11; ☎ 0 2265 5555; call centre 1771; www.bangkokair.com; 99 Moo 14, Th Viphawadee) Suvarnabhumi to Chiang Mai, Phuket, Ko Samui, Sukhothai and Trat. Branch at Suvarnabhumi International Airport.

Nok Air (Map pp118-19; ☎ 1318; www.nokair.co.th; 17th fl, Rajanakarn Bldg, Th Sathon) This subsidiary of Thai flies from Don Muang to Chiang Mai, Hat Yai, Nakhon Si Thammarat, Phuket, Trang and Udon Thani. Nok Air also operates code-share flights with PB Air from Suvarnabhumi to Buriram, Lampang, Nakhon Phanom, Nan, Roi Et and Sakon Nakhon. Branches at both airports.

One-Two-Go (Map pp122-3; ☎ 0 2229 4260, call centre 1126; www.fly12go.com; 18 Th Ratchadaphisek) Domestic arm of Orient Thai; flies from Don Muang to Chiang Mai,

Chiang Rai, Hat Yai, Nakhon Si Thammarat and Phuket. Branch at Don Muang Airport.

PB Air (Map pp122-3; ☎ 0 2261 0222; www.pbair.com; UBC II Bldg, 591 Soi Daeng Udom/33, Th Sukhumvit) Suvarnabhumi to Buriram, Chumphon, Lampang, Mae Hong Son, Nan, Nakhon Phanom, Roi Et and Sakon Nakhon. Branch at Suvarnabhumi International Airport.

SGA Airlines (Map pp110-11; ☎ 0 2664 6099; www .sga.co.th; 19/18-19 Royal City Ave/RCA, off Th Phra Ram IX) A subsidiary of Nok Air (making the airline a subsidiary of a subsidiary), SGA flies tiny prop planes from Suvarnabhumi to Hua Hin, and from Chiang Mai to Chiang Rai, Mae Hong Son and Pai. Branch at Suvarnabhumi International Airport.

Thai Airways International (THAI; ☎ 0 2356 1111; www.thaiairways.co.th) Silom (Map pp118-19; ☎ 0 2232 8000; temp address ground fl, BUI Building, 175-77 Soi Anuman Rachathon, permanent address 485 Th Silom); Banglamphu (Map pp114-15; ☎ 0 280 0110; 6 Th Lan Luang) Operates domestic air services to many provincial capitals. Branches at both airports.

Bus

Bangkok is the centre for bus services that fan out all over the kingdom. For long-distance journeys to popular tourist destinations, it is advisable to buy tickets directly from the bus companies located at the bus stations, rather than through travel agents in tourist centres such as Th Khao San. See the boxed text p109 for common transport scams to keep an eye open for.

BUS STATIONS

There are three main public bus terminals, two of which are located an inconvenient distance from the centre of the city. Allow an hour to reach all terminals from most parts of Bangkok.

Eastern bus terminal (Ekamai; Map pp122-3; ☎ 0 2391 6846; Soi Ekamai/40, Th Sukhumvit; Skytrain Ekamai) is the departure point for buses to Pattaya, Rayong, Chanthaburi and other points east. Most people call it *sà·tăh·nee èk·gà·mai* (Ekamai station).

Northern & Northeastern bus terminal (Mo Chit; Map pp110-11; ☎ for northern routes 0 2936 2852, ext 311/442, for northeastern routes 0 2936 2852, ext 611/448; Th Kamphaeng Phet) is just north of Chatuchak Park. It's also commonly called *kŏn sòng mŏr chít* (Mo Chit station) – not to be confused with Mor Chit BTS station. Buses depart from here for all northern and northeastern destinations. Buses to Aranya Prathet (near the Cambodian border) also leave from here, not from the Eastern bus terminal as you might expect. To reach the bus station, take Skytrain to Mo Chit and transfer onto city bus 3 or hop on a motorcycle taxi.

The city's new **Southern bus terminal** (Sai Tai Mai; Map pp110-11; ☎ 0 2435 1200; cnr Th Bromaratchachonanee & Th Phuttamonthon 1, Thonburi) lies quite far from the centre of Bangkok. Commonly called *săi dâi mài*, it's among the more pleasant and orderly in the country. Besides serving as the departure point for all buses south of Bangkok, transport to Kanchanaburi and western Thailand also departs from here. To reach the station, take bus 503 from Th Phra Athit, or hop on a river-bound taxi at Th Ratchadamnoen.

Train

Bangkok's **Hualamphong station** (Map pp116-17; ☎ 0 2220 4334, general information & advance booking 1690; www.railway.co.th; Th Phra Ram IV; Metro Hualamphong) is the terminus for the main rail services to the south, north, northeast and east. See p768 for information about train classes and services.

Bookings can be made in person at the advance booking office (just follow the signs; open from 8.30am to 4pm). The other ticket windows are for same-day purchases, mostly 3rd class. From 5am to 8.30am and 4pm to 11pm, advance bookings can also be made at windows 2 to 11. You can obtain a train timetable from the information window. Avoid smiling 'information' staff who try to direct all arrivals to a travel agency in the mezzanine level.

Hualamphong has the following services: shower room, mailing centre, luggage storage, cafes and food courts. To get to the station from Sukhumvit take the Metro to the Hualamphong stop. From western points (Banglamphu, Thewet), take bus 53.

Bangkok Noi station (Map pp114-15; next to Siriraj Hospital, Thonburi) handles infrequent (and overpriced for foreigners) services to Nakhon Pathom, Kanchanaburi and Nam Tok. The station can be reached by river ferry to Tha Rot Fai. Tickets can be bought at the station.

GETTING AROUND

Although Bangkok's rush-hour traffic is the stuff of nightmares, seemingly random acts of *embouteillage* can impede even the shortest trip, any day, any time. If it's an option, going by river, canal or Skytrain is always the best choice; otherwise assume a 45-minute journey for most outings.

To/From the Airport

At the time of writing there were still two functioning airports in Bangkok; the vast majority of flights are relegated to shiny new Suvarnabhumi, but some domestic flights still fly in and out of the old Don Muang Airport. If you need to transfer between the two, pencil in *at least* an hour, as the two airports are at polar opposite ends of town.

The following ground transport options are allowed to leave directly from the airport terminal to in-town destinations: metered taxis, hotel limousines, the airport express bus, private vehicles and private buses. If there are no metered taxis available kerbside or if the line is too long, you can take the airport shuttle to the taxi stand at the public transport centre.

The public transport centre is 3km from the airport terminal and includes a public bus terminal, metered taxi stand, car rental and long-term parking. A free airport shuttle running both an ordinary and express route connects the transport centre with the passenger terminals.

SUVARNABHUMI INTERNATIONAL AIRPORT
Airport Bus

Airport Express runs four useful routes between Suvarnabhumi and Bangkok. They operate from 5am to midnight and cost 150B, meaning a taxi will be a comparable price if there are two of you heading to central Bangkok, but slightly more expensive if you're going to Banglamphu. The Airport Express counter is near entrance 8 on level 1. Routes stop at Skytrain stations, major hotels and other landmarks.

AE-1 to Silom (by expressway) Via Pratunam, Central World Plaza, Ratchadamri Skytrain, Lumphini Park, Th Sala Daeng, Patpong, Plaza Hotel and others, finishing at Sala Daeng Skytrain.

AE-2 to Banglamphu (by expressway) Via Th Petchaburi Soi 30, Democracy Monument, Royal Hotel, Th Phra Athit, Th Phra Sumen and Th Khao San.

AE-3 to Sukhumvit Via Soi 52, Eastern bus terminal, Soi 34, 24, 20, 18, 10, 6, Central Chit Lom, Central World Plaza and Soi Nana.

AE-4 to Hualamphong train station Via Victory Monument, Phayathai Skytrain, Siam Square, MBK and Chulalongkorn University.

Local Transport

With more time and less money, you could take the Skytrain to On Nut (40B), then from near the market entrance opposite Tesco take the BTS minivan (25B, about 40 minutes; look for the yellow BTS 522 Suvarnabhumi on the window) to the airport.

Several other air-con local buses serve the airport's public transport centre, a 3km ride on a free shuttle bus from Suvarnabhumi, charging a flat 35B fare. The most useful routes:

Bus 551 Siam Paragon Via Victory Monument.

Bus 552 Klong Toei Via Sukumvit 101 and On Nut Skytrain.

Buses 554 & 555 Don Muang Airport

Bus 556 Southern bus terminal Via Democracy Monument (for Th Khao San) and Thammasat University.

Intercity buses to destinations east including Pattaya, Rayong and Trat stop at the public transport centre, reached via a free shuttle from the airport.

Minivan

If you are heading to the airport from Banglamphu, the hotels and guesthouses can book you on air-con minivans. These pick up from hotels and guesthouses, and cost about 180B per person (you're better off using the Airport Express bus).

Skytrain

From late 2009 a new Skytrain line will run from downstairs at the airport to a huge new City Air Terminal in central Bangkok, near Soi Asoke/21 and Th Petchaburi. There will be an express service (pink line) that will take 15 minutes, and a local service (red line) taking 27 minutes.

Taxi

As you exit the terminal, ignore the touts and all the yellow signs pointing you to 'official airport taxis' (which cost 700B flat). Instead, walk outside on the arrivals level and join the fast-moving queue for a public taxi. Cabs booked through this desk should always use their meter, but they often try their luck so insist by saying, 'Meter, please'. You must also pay a 50B official airport surcharge and reimburse drivers for any toll charges (usually about 60B); drivers will always ask your permission to use the tollway. Depending on traffic, a taxi to Asoke should cost 200B to 250B, to Silom 300B to 350B and to Banglamphu 350B to 425B. Fares are per vehicle, not per person.

DON MUANG AIRPORT

There are no longer any express airport buses to/from Don Muang.

Bus

Slow, crowded public bus 59 stops on the highway in front of the airport and carries on to Banglamphu, passing Th Khao San and the Democracy Monument; luggage is not allowed. Air-con buses are faster, and you might actually get a seat. Useful air-con routes:

Bus 510 Victory Monument and Southern bus terminal.

Bus 513 Th Sukhumvit and Eastern bus terminal.

Bus 29 Northern bus terminal, Victory Monument, Siam Square and Hualamphong train station.

Taxi

As at Suvarnabhumi, public taxis leave from outside the arrivals hall and there is a 50B airport charge added to the meter fare. A trip to Banglamphu, including airport change and tollway fees, will set you back about 400B. The fare will be slightly less for a trip to Sukhumvit or Silom.

Train

The walkway that crosses from Terminal 1 to the Amari Airport Hotel also provides access to Don Muang train station, which has trains to Hualamphong train station every one to 1½ hours from 4am to 11.30am and then roughly every hour from 2pm to 9.30pm (3rd-class ordinary/express 5/10B, one hour).

Boat

Once the city's dominant form of transport, public boats still survive along the mighty Mae Nam Chao Phraya and on a few interior *klorng*.

RIVER ROUTES

Chao Phraya Express (Map p186; ☎ 0 2623 6001; www .chaophrayaboat.co.th) provides one of the city's most scenic (and efficient) transport options, running passenger boats along Mae Nam Chao Phraya to destinations both south and north of Bangkok. The central pier is known varyingly as Tha Sathon and Saphan Taksin, and connects to the Saphan Taksin Skytrain station, at the southern end of the city. Visitors are most likely to go northwards, to the stops designated with an N prefix.

Tickets range from 13B to 34B and are generally purchased on board the boat, although some larger stations have ticket booths. Either way, hold on to your ticket as proof of purchase.

The company operates express (indicated by an orange, yellow or yellow and green flag), local (without a flag) and tourist boat (larger boat) services. During rush hour, pay close attention to the flag colours to avoid an unwanted journey to a foreign province. See the map on p186 for routes and piers, or ask for one of the maps provided at some of the larger piers.

Local (🕒 6-8.30am & 3-6pm Mon-Fri; 9-13B) The local line (no flag) serves all company piers between Wat Ratchasingkhon, in south-central Bangkok, north to Nonthaburi, stopping frequently.

Tourist (🕒 9.30am-4pm; 19B, one-day pass 150B) The more expensive tourist boat offers heaps of seating and English-language commentary (some of it actually comprehensible); it operates from Tha Sathon to 10 major sightseeing piers, only going as far north as Tha Phra Athit (Banglamphu).

Orange Express (🕒 5.50am-6.40pm Mon-Fri, 6am-6.40pm Sat & Sun; 14B) This, the most frequent line, operates between Wat Ratchasingkhon and Nonthaburi with frequent stops.

Yellow Express (🕒 6.10-8.40am & 3.45-7.30pm Mon-Fri; 19-28B) The yellow express line operates between Ratburana to Nonthaburi with stops at major piers.

Green-Yellow Express (🕒 6.15-8.05am & 4.05-6.05pm Mon-Fri; 11-32B) This rush-hour-only boat takes commuters to the Pakkret Pier, far north of Bangkok.

Blue Express (🕒 7-7.30am & 5.35-6.05pm Mon-Fri; 11-32B) Another rush-hour-only boat takes commuters directly to Nonthaburi.

There are also flat-bottomed cross-river ferries that connect Thonburi and Bangkok. These piers are usually next door to the Chao Phraya Express piers and cost 3B per crossing.

CANAL ROUTES

Over the years boat services along Bangkok and Thonburi's *klorng* have diminished, but with mounting traffic woes there may be plans to revive these water networks. For now, canal taxi boats run along Khlong Saen Saeb (Banglamphu to Ramkhamhaeng) and are an easy way to get from Banglamphu to Jim Thompson's House, the Siam Square shopping centres (get off at Tha Hua Chang for both), and other points further east along Sukhumvit – after a mandatory change of boat at Tha Pratunam. These boats are mostly used by daily commuters and pull into the piers for just a few seconds – jump straight on or you'll be left behind. Fares range from 7B to 20B.

Bus

The city's public bus system is operated by **Bangkok Mass Transit Authority** (☎ 0 2246 4262; www .bmta.co.th); the website is a great source of information on all bus routes. Air-con bus fares typically start at 12B and ordinary (fan) buses start at 7.5B. Smaller privately operated green buses cost 5B.

Most of the bus lines run between 5am and 10pm or 11pm, except for the 'all-night' buses, which run from 3am or 4am to midmorning.

Bangkok Bus Map by Roadway, available at Asia Books (p105), is the most up-to-date route map available. The following bus lines are useful for tourists travelling between Banglamphu and the Siam Square area:

Bus 15 From Tha Phra, on the Thonburi side of the river, to Sanam Luang (accessible to Wat Phra Kaew) with stops at MBK Center (connect to Skytrain) and Th Ratchadamnoen Klang (accessible to Th Khao San).

Bus 47 Khlong Toei Port to Department of Lands, along Th Phahonyothin, in northern Bangkok, with stops along Th Phra Ram IV, MBK Center, Th Ratchadamnoen and Sanam Luang.

Bus 73 Huay Khwang to Saphan Phut (connect to Chao Phraya Express) with stops at MBK Center, Hualamphong (connect to train or Metro) and Chinatown.

Car

For short-term visitors, you will find parking and driving a car in Bangkok more trouble than it is worth. If you need private transport,

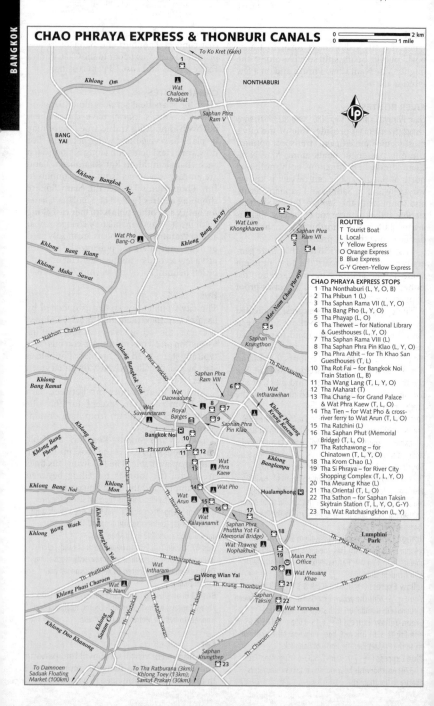

CHAO PHRAYA EXPRESS & THONBURI CANALS

0 —————— 2 km
0 —————— 1 mile

ROUTES
T Tourist Boat
L Local
Y Yellow Express
O Orange Express
B Blue Express
G-Y Green-Yellow Express

CHAO PHRAYA EXPRESS STOPS
1 Tha Nonthaburi (L, Y, O, B)
2 Tha Phibun 1 (L)
3 Tha Saphan Rama VII (L, Y, O)
4 Tha Bang Pho (L, Y, O)
5 Tha Phayap (L, O)
6 Tha Thewet – for National Library
   & Guesthouses (L, Y, O)
7 Tha Saphan Rama VIII (L)
8 Tha Saphan Phra Pin Klao (L, Y, O)
9 Tha Phra Athit – for Th Khao San
   Guesthouses (T, L)
10 Tha Rot Fai – for Bangkok Noi
   Train Station (L, B)
11 Tha Wang Lang (T, L, Y, O)
12 Tha Maharat (T)
13 Tha Chang – for Grand Palace
   & Wat Phra Kaew (T, L, O)
14 Tha Tien – for Wat Pho & cross-
   river ferry to Wat Arun (T, L, O)
15 Tha Ratchini (L)
16 Tha Saphan Phut (Memorial
   Bridge) (T, L, O)
17 Tha Ratchawong – for
   Chinatown (T, L, Y, O)
18 Tha Krom Chao (L)
19 Tha Si Phraya – for River City
   Shopping Complex (T, L, Y, O)
20 Tha Meuang Khae (L)
21 Tha Oriental (T, L, O)
22 Tha Sathon – for Saphan Taksin
   Skytrain Station (T, L, Y, O, G-Y)
23 Tha Wat Ratchasingkhon (L, Y)

consider hiring a car and driver through your hotel or hire a taxi driver that you find trustworthy. One reputable operator is **Julie Taxi** (☎ 0 81846 2014; www.julietaxitour.com), which offers a variety of vehicles and excellent service.

If you're not dissuaded, cars and motorcycles can be rented throughout town, including through such international chains as **Avis** (Map pp120-1; ☎ 0 2255 5300; 2/12 Th Withayu/Wireless Rd) or local chains such as **Thai Rent A Car** (Map pp110-11; ☎ 0 2737 8787; www.thairentacar.com; Th Petchaburi Tat Mai), which has a branch at Suvarnabhumi International Airport. Rates start at around 1000B per day, excluding insurance. An International Driving Permit and passport are required for all rentals.

Metro (MRT)

Bangkok's first subway line opened in 2004 and is operated by the **Metropolitan Rapid Transit Authority** (MRTA; ☎ 0 2624 5200; www.mrta.co.th). Thais call the metro *rót fai fáh dâi din*.

The 20km Blue Line goes from Hualamphong train station to Bang Sue, stopping at 18 stations, including four that link up with the Skytrain, and one that connects with the airport link. Fares cost 15B to 39B; child and concession fares can be bought at ticket windows. The trains run every seven minutes from 6am to midnight, except during peak hours – 6am to 9am and 4.30pm to 7.30pm – when frequency is less than five minutes. The main advantage for visitors is that the Sukhumvit hotel area is now easily connected to Hualamphong train station and Chinatown at one end, and Chatuchak weekend market and the Northern bus terminal at the Bang Sue end.

There are ambitious plans to extend the MRT by more than four times its present length with stabs into northern Bangkok, Samut Prakan and Th Ramkhamhaeng, although if the airport link is anything to judge by, it could be a very long wait indeed.

Motorcycle Taxi

Forming the backdrop of modern Bangkok, teams of cheeky, numbered and vested motorcycle taxi drivers can be found at the end of just about every long street. A ride to the end (*sùt soy*) or mouth (*bàhk soy*) of an average soi usually costs 10B to 15B. Longer journeys should be negotiated in advance, and can range from 20B to 100B.

Helmets are occasionally available upon request, although considering the way some

of these guys drive, any body part is at risk. In particular, keep your legs tucked in – the drivers are used to carrying passengers with shorter legs than those of the average Westerner. Women wearing skirts should sit side-saddle and gather any extra cloth to avoid it catching in the wheel or drive chain.

Skytrain (BTS)

The most comfortable option for travelling in 'new' Bangkok (Silom, Sukhumvit and Siam Square) is the *rót fai fáh* (Skytrain), an elevated rail network that sails over the city's notorious traffic jams. The Skytrain has revolutionised travel in the modern parts of Bangkok. Trips that would have taken an hour now take 15 minutes. Another advantage of the Skytrain is that it offers a pleasant bird's-eye view of the city, allowing glimpses of greenery and historic architecture not visible at street level.

So far two lines have been built by the **Bangkok Mass Transit System Skytrain** (BTS; ☎ 0 2617 7300; www.bts.co.th) – the Sukhumvit and Silom lines.

The Sukhumvit Line terminates in the north of the city at the Mo Chit Skytrain station, next to Chatuchak Park, and follows Th Phayathai south to the Siam interchange station at Th Phra Ram I and then swings east along Th Ploenchit and Th Sukhumvit to terminate at the On Nut station, near Soi 81. Construction has already begun on an extension that will lengthen the line an additional 5.2km, terminating at Soi 107, Th Sukhumvit.

The Silom Line runs from the National Stadium station, near Siam Square, and soon after makes an abrupt turn to the southwest, continuing above Th Ratchadamri, down Th Silom to Th Narathiwat Ratchanakharin, then out Th Sathon until it terminates next to the foot of Saphan Taksin on the banks of Mae Nam Chao Phraya. Construction has already begun on a project to extend this line an additional 2km, crossing over the Mae Nam Chao Phraya and terminating in Thonburi.

Trains run frequently from 6am to midnight along both lines. Fares vary from 10B to 40B, depending on your destination. Most ticket machines accept 5B and 10B coins only, but change is available from the information booths. The staffed booths are also where you buy value-stored tickets. Brochures available at the information booths detail the various commuter and tourist passes.

Taxi

Táak·see mee·dêu (metered taxis) were introduced in Bangkok in 1993 and the current flag fare of 35B is only a slight increase from that time, making us wonder how these guys (and there are a lot of them) earn any money. Although many first-time visitors are hesitant to use them, in general Bangkok's taxis are new and spacious, and the drivers are courteous and helpful, making them an excellent way to get around. Fares to most places within central Bangkok cost 60B to 80B, and freeway tolls – 20B to 45B depending where you start – must be paid by the passenger.

Taxi Radio (☎ 1681; www.taxiradio.co.th) and other 24-hour 'phone-a-cab' services are available for 20B above the metered fare. Taxis are usually plentiful except during peak commute hours, when bars are closing (1am to 2am), or when it is raining and your destination requires sitting in too much traffic.

Taxis that hang around tourist centres typically refuse to use the meter and will quote an exorbitantly high rate. You are more likely to find an honest driver if you walk out to a main thoroughfare.

Túk-Túk

A ride on Thailand's most emblematic three-wheeled vehicle is an experience particularly sought after by new arrivals, but it only takes a few seconds to realise that most foreigners are too tall to see anything beyond the low-slung roof.

Túk-túk drivers also have a knack for smelling crisp bills and can potentially take you and your wallet far beyond your desired destination. In particular, beware of drivers who offer to take you on a sightseeing tour for 10B or 20B – it's a touting scheme designed to pressure you into purchasing overpriced goods. A short trip on a túk-túk should cost at least 40B.

Although it seems unlikely, túk-túk do serve a very useful purpose besides hassling tourists. Locals use the three-wheelers when their destination is closer and cheaper than a metered-taxi flag fall or when gridlock requires a more nimble vehicle. Unfortunately, the recent rise in petrol prices means that túk-túk quotes often start at 100B, sometimes even 200B, making it difficult to negotiate a fair price.

AROUND BANGKOK

If you're itching to get out of the capital city, but don't have a lot of time, consider a day trip to some of the neighbouring towns and provinces. On Bangkok's doorstep are all of Thailand's provincial charms – you don't have to go far to find ancient religious monuments, floating markets, architectural treasures and laid-back fishing villages.

FLOATING MARKETS

ตลาดน้ำ

The photographs of Thailand's floating markets – wooden canoes laden with multicoloured fruits and vegetables, paddled by women wearing indigo-hued clothes and wide-brimmed straw hats – have become an iconic and alluring image for the kingdom. It is also a sentimental piece of history. In the past 20 years, Thailand has modernised, replacing canals with roads, and boats with motorcycles and cars. The floating markets, which were once lively trading posts for produce farmers and local housewives, have crawled ashore.

The most heavily promoted floating market is **Damnoen Saduak** (🕑 7am-4pm Sat & Sun), 104km southwest of Bangkok between Nakhon Pathom and Samut Songkhram. Though little more than a souvenir market catering to tourists, it is one of the most accessible markets from Bangkok and is ideal for those who haven't yet filled their suitcases with touristy gifts. Air-con buses 78 and 996 go direct from the Southern bus terminal in Thonburi to Damnoen Saduak (80B, two hours, every 20 minutes from 6am to 9pm). Most buses will drop tourists off directly at the piers that line Th Sukhaphiban 1, which is the land route to the floating market area. The going rate for boat hire is about 300B per person per hour. A yellow *sŏrng·tăa·ou* (also spelt *săwngthăew;* 5B) does a frequent loop between the floating market and the bus stop in town.

A closer descendant of the original floating markets, **Taling Chan** (Map pp110-11; 🕑 7am-4pm Sat & Sun) offers less of a sales pitch than Damnoen Saduak. On the access road to Khlong Bangkok Noi, Taling Chan looks like any other fresh food market busy with produce vendors from nearby farms. But the twist emerges at the canal where several floating docks serve as informal dining rooms, and the kitchens are canoes tethered to the docks. Many local Thai families

AROUND BANGKOK

come to feast on grilled shrimp and noodles, all produced aboard a bobbing boat. Taling Chan is in Thonburi and can be reached from Bangkok's Th Ratchadamnoen Klang or Th Ratchaprasong via air-con bus 79 (16B, 25 minutes). Long-tail boats from any large Bangkok pier can also be hired for a trip to Taling Chan and the nearby Khlong Chak Phra.

Not technically a swimmer, **Don Wai Market** (Talat Don Wai; 6am-6pm) claims a riverbank location in Nakhon Pathom Province, having originally started out in the early 20th century as a floating market for pomelo and jackfruit growers and traders. Like many tourist attractions geared towards Thais, the main draw here is food, such as fruit, traditional sweets and *bèt páloh* (five-spice stewed duck), which can be consumed onboard large boats that cruise the Nakhon Chaisi River (60B, one hour). The easiest way to reach Don Wai Market is to take a minibus (45B, 35 minutes) from beside Central Pinklao (Map pp110–11) in Thonburi.

The **Amphawa Floating Market** (Talat Náam Amphháwaa; 4-9pm Fri-Sun), about 7km northwest of Samut Songkhram, convenes near Wat Amphawa (see p190). There are other floating markets nearby that meet in the mornings on particular lunar days, including **Tha Kha Floating Market** (7am-noon weekends on 2nd, 7th & 12th day of waxing & waning moons). Tha Kha convenes along an open, breezy *klorng* lined with greenery and old wooden houses.

NAKHON PATHOM
นครปฐม
pop 120,657

Nakhon Pathom is a typical central Thai city, with the Phra Pathom Chedi as a visible link to its claim as the country's oldest settlement. The town's name, which derives from the Pali 'Nagara Pathama' meaning 'First City', appears to lend some legitimacy to this boast.

The modern town is quite sleepy, but it is an easy destination to see everyday Thai ways and practise your newly acquired language skills on a community genuinely appreciative of such efforts.

Sights

In the centre of town, **Phra Pathom Chedi**, rising to 127m, is the tallest Buddhist monument in the world. The original stupa, which is

THE LONG WAY TO AMPHAWA

The quaint canalside village of Amphawa in Samut Songkhram is less than 100km from Bangkok, but if you play your cards right, you can reach the town via a multihour journey involving trains, boats and a short ride in the back of a truck. Why? Because sometimes the journey is just as important as the destination.

Your adventure begins when you take a stab into Thonburi looking for the **Wong Wian Yai train station** (Map pp112–13). Just past the traffic circle (Wong Wian Yai) is a fairly ordinary food market that camouflages the unceremonious terminal of this commuter line, known in English as the Mahachai Shortline. Hop on one of the hourly trains (12B) to Samut Sakhon and you're on your way.

Only 15 minutes out of the station and the city density yields to squatty villages where you can peek into homes, temples and shops, many of which are only arm's length from the tracks. Further on palm trees, small rice fields and marshes filled with giant elephant ears and canna lilies line the route, tamed only briefly by little whistle-stop stations. The backwater farms evaporate quickly as you enter **Samut Sakhon**, a bustling port town several kilometres from the Gulf of Thailand and the end of the first rail segment.

After working your way through what must be one of the most hectic fresh markets in the country, you'll come to a vast harbour clogged with water hyacinth and wooden fishing boats. A few rusty cannons pointing towards the river testify to the town's crumbling fort, built to protect the kingdom from sea invaders. Before the 17th century, the town was known as Tha Jiin (Chinese Pier) because of the large number of Chinese junks that called here. Board the ferry to **Ban Laem** (3B).

Arriving on the opposite side, the Jao Mae Kuan Im Shrine at **Wat Chong Lom** is a 9m-high fountain in the shape of the Mahayana Buddhist Goddess of Mercy. To get here, take a motorcycle taxi (10B) from the pier for the 2km ride to Wat Chong Lom. Conveniently located just beside the shrine is Tha Chalong, a train station with two afternoon departures for your next destination, Samut Songkhram (10B, 1.30pm and 4.40pm).

You'll know you've reached **Samut Songkhram** when it looks like you've crashed into the town's wet market. In fact, the market is held directly on the train tracks, and vendors must frantically scoop up their wares as the daily comes through.

At the mouth of Mae Nam Mae Klong is the province's most famous tourist attraction: a bank of fossilised shells known as **Don Hoi Lot**. The shell bank can really only be seen during the dry season when the river surface has receded to its lowest level (typically April and May), but most visit for the perennial seafood restaurants that have been built at the edge of Don Hoi Lot. To get there you can hop into a *sŏrng·tăa·ou* in front of Somdet Phra Phuttalertla Hospital at the intersection of Th Prasitwatthana and Th Thamnimit; the trip takes about 15 minutes (10B). Or you can charter a boat from the Mae Klong Market pier (*tâh đà·làht mâa glorng*), a scenic journey of around 45 minutes (1000B).

To reach your final destination, charter a boat (1000B) or hop in a *sŏrng·tăa·ou* (9B) near the market for the 10-minute ride to **Amphawa**. This canalside village has become a popular destination among city folk who seek out its quintessentially 'Thai' setting. This urban influx has sparked a few signs of gentrification, but the canals, old wooden buildings, atmospheric cafes and quaint waterborne traffic still retain heaps of charm. On weekends Amphawa puts on a reasonably authentic floating market (p188). Alternatively, visit on a weekday and you'll have the whole town to yourself.

buried within the massive orange-glazed dome, was erected in the early 6th century by Theravada Buddhists of Dvaravati (possibly at the same time as Myanmar's famous Shwedagon stupa). But, in the early 11th century the Khmer king, Suriyavarman I of Angkor, conquered the city and built a Brahman *prang* (Hindi/Khmer-style stupa) over the sanctuary. The Burmese of Bagan, under King Anawrahta, sacked the city in 1057 and the *prang* lay in ruins until Rama

IV (King Mongkut) had it restored in 1860. The temple is best visited on weekends when local families come to make merit.

On the eastern side of the monument, in the *bòht*, is a Dvaravati-style Buddha seated in a European pose similar to the one in Wat Phra Meru in Ayuthaya. It may, in fact, have come from there.

Also of interest are the many examples of Chinese sculpture carved from a greenish stone that came to Thailand as ballast in

Steps from Amphawa's central footbridge is **Wat Amphawan Chetiyaram**, a graceful temple believed to be located at the place of the family home of Rama II, and which features accomplished murals. A short walk from the temple is **King Buddhalertla (Phuttha Loet La) Naphalai Memorial Park** (Km63, Route 35, Samut Songkhram; admission 20B; 🕙 park 9am-6pm daily, museum 9am-6pm Wed-Sun), a museum housed in a collection of traditional central Thai houses set on 1.5 landscaped hectares. Dedicated to Rama II, the museum contains a library of rare Thai books and antiques from early-19th-century Siam.

At night long-tail boats zip through Amphawa's sleeping waters to watch the star-like dance of the *hìng hôy*, fireflies. Several operators lead tours, including **Niphaa** (☎ 0 81422 0726), an experienced and well-equipped outfit located at the mouth of the canal, near the footbridge.

Sleeping & Eating

Amphawa is popular with Bangkok's weekend warriors, and it seems like virtually every other house has opened its doors to tourists in the form of homestays. These can range from little more than a mattress on the floor and a mosquito net to upscale guesthouse-style accommodation.

Baan Song Thai Plai Pong Pang (☎ 0 3475 7333; Amphawa) organises basic homestays and has been recognised for ecotourism excellence. A good middle ground is **Reorn Pae Amphawa** (☎ 0 3475 1333; 139-145 Rim Khlong Amphawa; d 800B; 🍴), a generations-old wooden home with tidy rooms. For something a bit more upscale there's **Baan Ku Pu** (☎ 0 3472 5920; Th Rim Khlong, Amphawa; d 1000B; 🍴), a self-styled 'resort' featuring wooden bungalows, and **Baan Tai Had Resort** (☎ 0 3476 7220; www.baantaihad.com; 1 Moo 2, Th Tai Had, Samut Songkhram; r 1750-5000B; 🍴 🛏), a sleek new riverside resort boasting heaps of activities.

Occupying the imposing ferry building, the seafood **Tarua Restaurant** (☎ 0 3441 1084; Ferry Terminal Bldg, 859 Th Sethakit, Samut Sakhon; dishes 60-200B) offers views over the harbour and an English-language menu.

The open-air seafood restaurant **Khrua Chom Ao** (☎ 0 85190 5677; Samut Sakhon; dishes 60-200B) looks over the gulf and has a loyal local following. It is a brief walk from Wat Chawng Lom, down the road running along the side of the temple opposite the statue of the Chinese goddess Kuan Im.

If you're in town on a weekend, get your eats on at the fun **Amphawa Floating Market** (*dà·làht nám am·pá·wah*; dishes 20-40B; 🕙 4-9pm Fri-Sun), where *pàt tai* and other noodle dishes are served directly from boats.

Getting There & Away

Trains leave Thonburi's Wong Wian Yai station (Map pp112–13) for Samut Sakhon roughly every hour starting at 5.30am. You'll need to leave Thonburi before 8.30am in order to reach Samut Songkhram by train.

Samut Songkhram is the southernmost terminus of the Mahachai Shortline. There are four departures from Ban Laem to Samut Songkhram (10B, one hour, approximately 7.30am, 10.10am, 1.30pm and 4.40pm) and four return trips (6.20am, 9am, 11.30am and 3.30pm).

Between Bangkok and Amphawa, buses run every 40 minutes from Thonburi's Southern bus terminal (Map pp110–11; 72B). There are also regular buses from Samut Sakhon (44B) and Samut Songkhram (65B). Alternatively, you can catch one of several buses to/from Damnoen Saduak (80B) that ply the highway near Amphawa.

the bottom of some 19th-century Chinese junks. Opposite the *bòht* is a **museum** (admission by donation; 🕙 9am-4pm Wed-Sun), with some interesting Dvaravati sculpture and lots of old junk. Within the chedi complex is **Lablae Cave**, an artificial tunnel containing the shrine of several Buddha figures.

The wát surrounding the stupa enjoys the kingdom's highest temple rank, Rachavoramahavihan; it's one of only six temples so honoured in Thailand. King

Rama VI's ashes are interred in the base of the Sukhothai-era Phra Ruang Rochanarit, a large standing Buddha image in the wát's northern *wí·hăhn*.

Southeast of the city stands **Phra Phutthamonthon**, a Sukhothai-style standing Buddha designed by Corrado Feroci. At 15.8m, it is reportedly the world's tallest, and it's surrounded by a 400-hectare landscaped park that contains sculptures representing the major stages in the Buddha's life (eg a

BANGKOK'S ISLAND GETAWAY

Soothe your nerves with a half-day getaway to **Ko Kret**, a car-free island in the middle of Mae Nam Chao Phraya, at Bangkok's northern edge. Actually an artificial island, the result of dredging a canal in a sharp bend in the river, the island is home to one of Thailand's oldest settlements of Mon people, who were the dominant culture in central Thailand between the 6th and 10th centuries AD. The Mon are also skilled potters, and Ko Kret continues the culture's ancient tradition of hand-thrown earthenware, made from local Ko Kret clay.

If you come on a weekday you'll likely have the entire island to yourself. There are a couple of temples worth peeking into and a few places to eat, but the real highlight is taking in the bucolic riverside atmosphere. On weekends things change drastically and Ko Kret is an extremely popular destination for urban Thais. There's heaps more food, drink and things for sale, but with this come the crowds.

The most convenient way to get there is by taxi or bus (33 from Sanam Luang) to Pak Kret, before boarding the cross-river ferry that leaves from Wat Sanam Neua. Alternatively, if you're willing to brave a weekend visit, you can join one of the weekend tours operated by **Chao Phraya Express** (☎ 0 2623 6001; www.chaophrayaboat.co.th; adult/child 300/250B; 🕑 10am-4.45pm Sat & Sun) that depart from Tha Sathon.

6m-high dharma wheel, carved from a single slab of granite).

All Bangkok–Nakhon Pathom buses pass by the access road to the park at Phra Phutthamonthon Sai 4; from there you can walk, hitch or flag down a *sŏrng·tăa·ou* into the park itself. From Nakhon Pathom you can also take a white-and-purple Salaya bus; the stop is on Th Tesa across from the post office.

Don Wai Market, on the banks of Mae Nam Nakhon Chaisi, is another worthwhile destination. See p189 for details on getting there.

Eating

Nakhon Pathom has an excellent market along the road between the train station and Phra Pathom Chedi; its *kôw lăhm* (sticky rice and coconut steamed in a length of bamboo) is reputed to be the best in Thailand. There are many good, inexpensive food vendors and restaurants in this area.

Getting There & Away

Nakhon Pathom is 64km west of Bangkok. The city doesn't have a central bus station, but most transport arrives and departs from near the market and train station.

The most convenient and fastest way to get to Nakhon Pathom is on a *rót đôo* (shared minivan) from Central Pinklao (30B) or the Victory Monument (60B). Vans leave when full, generally from 6am to approximately 6pm.

There are also more frequent trains from Bangkok's Hualamphong station (3rd/2nd/1st class 14/31/60B, one hour) throughout the day. Nakhon Pathom is also on the spur rail line that runs from Thonburi's Bangkok Noi station to Kanchanaburi's Nam Tok station, although because of the route's status as a 'tourist line' the fares are exorbitantly high for foreigners.

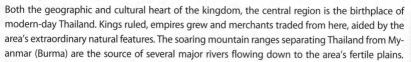

Central Thailand

Both the geographic and cultural heart of the kingdom, the central region is the birthplace of modern-day Thailand. Kings ruled, empires grew and merchants traded from here, aided by the area's extraordinary natural features. The soaring mountain ranges separating Thailand from Myanmar (Burma) are the source of several major rivers flowing down to the area's fertile plains.

As well as being historically important, the region is environmentally significant, with some of the largest protected territories in Southeast Asia. Logging and deforestation have reduced much of the natural landscape, but the majority of terrain is still wild forest, jungle and grassland. Deep within the dense vegetation dwell tigers, elephants and leopards.

Just north of Bangkok is the former Siam royal capital of Ayuthaya, home to fabled palace and temple ruins. Once one of the world's great cities, at its peak it was a major hub for trade, art and culture, but these days the pace is far more genteel. Slightly further north is the small town of Lopburi, where monkeys play and scavenge among the Khmer-style ruins.

Northwest from Bangkok is Kanchanaburi, the country's third-largest province. Its natural beauty makes it a popular destination for Thais and tourists, who come to bathe in waterfalls, trek through jungles and kayak along rivers. War veterans make pilgrimages here to remember those who died in WWII when Japanese forces used prisoners of war to build the 'Death Railway'.

In the mountains of northwest Kanchanaburi are sleepy Thong Pha Phum and Sangkhlaburi. Many ethnic groups live in and around these towns near the border. Few travellers make it this far, but those that do are richly rewarded with a fascinating blend of cultures and beliefs.

HIGHLIGHTS

- Exploring the grassy ruins of **Ayuthaya** (p198), Unesco World Heritage Site and former capital of Siam
- Clambering up the seven-tiered waterfall at **Erawan National Park** (p218)
- Snapping pictures of the mischievous monkeys in **Lopburi** (p207)
- Visiting the WWII memorials in easygoing **Kanchanaburi** (p212)
- Living among the treetops and exploring nature trails in **Thong Pha Phum National Park** (p222)
- Taking a dawn boat along the misty morning waters in sleepy **Sangkhlaburi** (p225)

★ Sangkhlaburi

★ Thong Pha Phum National Park   ★ Lopburi

Erawan
★ National Park   ★ Ayuthaya

★ Kanchanaburi

■ BEST TIME TO VISIT: OCTOBER–DECEMBER   ■ POPULATION: 2.3 MILLION

CENTRAL THAILAND

History

Some of the earliest recorded history in the region is made up of Neolithic stone tools and weapons found at the delta of Mae Nam Khwae Noi and Mae Nam Khwae Yai rivers.

Several empires, including the Dvaravati and Khmer, later used this region as an important base. During the 400-year Ayuthaya period the area flourished and many Western nations established settlements, but none ever subjugated their hosts.

In WWII the Japanese army forced Allied prisoners of war (POWs) and Asian conscripted labourers to build the 'Death Railway' around Kanchanaburi. More than 100,000 workers died during the construction due to disease and the brutal treatment meted out by their captors.

Climate

Central Thailand experiences the country's three seasons in equal measure; Kanchanaburi can be basking in sunshine while torrential rain buffets Sangkhlaburi. It is hot from February to June, rainy from June to October, and cool (relatively speaking) from October to January; one constant is the humidity. Within the region there are some variations. Because of altitude, it can be significantly cooler in Sangkhlaburi and surrounding national parks than in other parts of the region. Ayuthaya and Lopburi sit in a wide-open plain that receives similar amounts of rain and heat as Bangkok.

National Parks

Most of Kanchanaburi Province is covered by forest, grasslands and mountain ranges. These areas are divided up into national parks, the most popular of which are Erawan and Sai Yok. Si Nakharin, Chaloem Ratanakosin, Khao Laem and Thong Pha Phum parks have fewer visitors but all have accommodation and guides available.

Language

The people of central Thailand share a common dialect that is considered 'standard' Thai simply because Bangkok, the seat of power, happens to be in the region. High concentrations of Chinese are found in the cities of the central provinces since this is where a large number of Chinese immigrants started out as farmers and labourers and then later as merchants. Significant numbers of Mon and Karen live in Kanchanaburi Province. Pockets of Lao and Phuan – the descendents of war captives who were forcibly resettled following Thai raids into Laos over the centuries – can be found in the region's three provinces of Ayuthaya, Lopburi and Kanchanaburi.

Getting There & Away
Most people come to central Thailand by bus or train. Buses are quicker, cleaner and usually more comfortable; trains are slower but more scenic and can be more social. Central Thailand is connected to the north and northeast via train. There is a good highway network so it is possible to hire vehicles and travel independently.

Getting Around
Local buses and trains provide a cheap and simple way to get from A to B. In most towns you can catch a private săhm·lór (also spelt *săamláw;* three-wheeled pedicab) or túk-túk (pronounced đúk dúk; motorised transport). These have a set fare for locals which tourists are rarely offered, so it's important to agree a price beforehand. Lopburi can be covered on foot, Ayuthaya requires a bicycle while in Kanchanaburi you'll need private transport or help from tour agencies to visit some of the sites.

AYUTHAYA PROVINCE

AYUTHAYA
พระนครศรีอยุธยา
pop 137,553

Ayuthaya is a former Asian powerhouse that today offers fragmented evidence of its magnificent past.

This former royal capital was a major trading port during the time of the trade winds, when international merchants were regular visitors. Many traders proclaimed Ayuthaya to be the finest city they had ever seen, with towering temples and treasure-laden palaces. After its sacking by an invading army, the city faded as a power and is now remembered as something of a fallen hero.

Today, thanks to major renovation and restoration work, it's possible to envisage

---

AYUTHAYA'S TOP FIVE SITES

- Wat Phra Si Sanphet
- Wat Phanan Choeng
- Wat Chai Wattanaram
- Wat Yai Chai Mongkhon
- Wihaan Mongkhon Bophit

---

just how spectacular the ruins would have looked in their heyday.

Despite the town's popularity among tourists, Ayuthaya remains relatively unspoiled and has its own charm. Away from the grassy ruins, the surrounding countryside is changing from an agricultural to manufacturing base as new factories replace the old rice paddies.

Ayuthaya is a place of great cultural interest and its proximity to Bangkok ensures it is a popular stop-off destination for visitors as part of their journey north.

History
Ayuthaya was the capital of Siam for 417 years, between 1350 and 1767, and had strong links to several European nations. At its peak it controlled an area larger than England and France combined, and was a melting pot of culture, art and trade. Its glorious reign ended in 1767 when the invading Burmese army sacked the city, looting most of its treasures.

Named after Ayodhya (Sanskrit for 'unconquerable'), Prince Rama's city in the Indian epic Ramayana, Ayuthaya emerged as little more than a Khmer outpost to become one of Asia's foremost cities. The first Westerners arrived from Portugal in 1511 and were so astounded by the city's beauty that they named it the 'Venice of the East'.

In 1685 French diplomat Abbe de Choisy wrote that Ayuthaya was a 'large city on an island surrounded by a river three times the size of the Seine, full of French, English, Dutch, Chinese, Japanese and Siamese vessels and an uncountable number of barges, and gilded galleys with 60 oarsmen'.

Ayuthaya had 33 kings, who generally ruled through tolerance rather than violence. Adroit diplomacy ensured no Western power ever took control.

After the Burmese sacked the city there was a period of instability until General Taksin

CENTRAL THAILAND

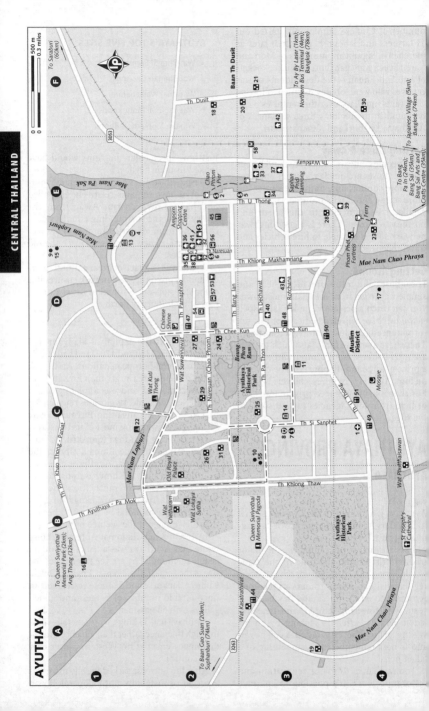

emerged and moved the capital to Bangkok. Ayuthaya continued as a provincial trading town while its ruins continued to crumble or be looted. The Thai Fine Arts Department began restoring the site in the 1950s, and it was designated a Unesco World Heritage Site in 1991.

Orientation

Central Ayuthaya is effectively an island, situated at the confluence of three rivers (Mae Nam Chao Phraya, Mae Nam Pa Sak and Mae Nam Lopburi). Most of the temple ruins are in the northwest quadrant of the island, and most guesthouses and transportation are in the northeast section. Several major ruins are just off the island. A ring road, Th U Thong, hugs the island's perimeter. The train station and long-distance northern bus terminal are off the island in the eastern part of town.

Information

EMERGENCY

Tourist police (☎ emergency 1155; Th Si Sanphet)

INTERNET ACCESS

Several shops on and around Soi 2, Th Naresuan have connections for 30B per hour.

MEDICAL SERVICES

Ayuthaya Hospital (☎ 0 3532 2555, emergency 1669; cnr Th U Thong & Th Si Sanphet) Has an emergency centre and some English-speaking doctors.

MONEY

ATMs are easy to find, especially along Th Naresuan near the Amporn Shopping Centre.

Bank of Ayuthaya (Th U Thong near Th Naresuan)
Kasikorn Bank (Th Naresuan)
Siam City Bank (Th U Thong)
Siam Commercial Bank (Th Naresuan)

POST

Main post office (Th U Thong; ⏲ 8.30am-4.30pm Mon-Fri, 8am-noon Sat & Sun)

TOURIST INFORMATION

Tourism Authority of Thailand (TAT; ☎ 0 3532 2730, 0 3524 6076; 108/22 Th Si Sanphet; ⏲ 8.30am-4.30pm) The tourist office is on the ground floor of the large white government building. Pick up some maps, then go upstairs for the free interactive display about the history of Ayuthaya.

Dangers & Annoyances

The main roads on the island are in good condition, but elsewhere there can be potholes waiting to spoil your day. If cycling, put bags around your body, not in baskets where they can be easy pickings for drive-by thieves.

Be aware that many crossroads don't have traffic lights. Thai road rules therefore apply: if you're bigger and faster, you have right of way.

At night several packs of dogs roam the streets. Avoid eye contact and keep your distance as some will bite if you get too close.

CENTRAL THAILAND

AYUTHAYA THREE-DAY ITINERARY

This three-day itinerary will ensure you get to all the major ruins and also see some of the picturesque countryside just outside the city centre.

Day One
See the Cycling Tour on p201.

Day Two
Take the train to **Bang Pa In Palace** (p204) and then continue on to the **Bang Sai Royal Arts and Crafts Centre** (p204). After lunch, return to Ayuthaya, stopping off on the way at **Wat Phanan Choeng** (opposite).

Day Three
Get off the island and visit **Wat Yai Chai Mongkhon** (p201) and the nearby **Portuguese settlement** (p200). In the afternoon, take a leisurely look around **Baan Th Dusit** (p201), but be sure to return to the island in time for a sunset boat ride (p201) to see the temples at their finest.

Sights

Only a few of the 400 temples built in Ayuthaya now remain, but the headless Buddha images and slumping stone stairways make an ideal place to conjure up images of a once mighty city.

For simpler navigation, we've divided up the sites into 'on the island' and 'off the island' sections. It's easy to get between the sites by bicycle, and hiring a guide for some historical detail is useful.

Most temples are open from 8am to 4pm; the more famous sites charge an entrance fee. A one-day pass for most sites on the island is available for 220B and can be bought at the museums or ruins.

The ruins are symbols of royalty and religion, two fundamental elements of Thai society, and so it is important to show respect (see p45).

ON THE ISLAND

The following sites are in central Ayuthaya, within the boundaries of the river, and can be visited over a day or three.

Wat Phra Si Sanphet

วัดพระศรีสรรเพชญ์

The three dominant *chedi* (stupas) at **Wat Phra Si Sanphet** (admission 50B) make it a must-see location on any temple tour. Built in the late 14th century, this was the largest temple in Ayuthaya and was used by several kings. It once contained a 16m-high standing Buddha (Phra Si Sanphet) covered with 250kg of gold, which was melted down by the Burmese conquerors.

Wihaan Mongkhon Bophit

วิหารมงคลบพิตร

Adjoining Wat Phra Si Sanphet is this sanctuary hall, which houses one of Thailand's biggest bronze Buddhas. This 17m-high figure is also one of the kingdom's most resilient images, having survived both lightning strikes and fire.

In 1955 the Burmese prime minister visited and donated 200,000B to help restore the building, an act of belated atonement for his country's sacking of the city 200 years before.

Wat Phra Mahathat

วัดพระมหาธาตุ

Built in 1374 during the reign of King Borom Rachathirat I, the most famous part of **Wat Phra Mahathat** (admission 50B) is a Buddha head embedded among a tree's maze of roots. Such a blending of nature and religious imagery is auspicious, but no one knows quite how the head ended up there. One theory is that the image was abandoned after the Burmese sacked Ayuthaya, and trees subsequently grew around it. Another idea is that thieves tried to steal the head, but found it was too heavy and so left it at the site. The remaining *prang* (Khmer-style tower) is the other main feature.

Wat Ratburana

วัดราชบูรณะ

Immediately north of Wat Phra Mahathat, this **temple** (Ratcha-burana; admission 50B) has one of the best preserved *prang* in the city. It was built in the 15th century by King Borom Rachathirat II on the cremation site for his two brothers who both died while fighting each other for the throne.

Looters raided the site in 1957 and stole many treasures. Some of the culprits were arrested and a subsequent official excavation of the site uncovered many rare Buddha images in the crypt.

Wat Thammikarat
วัดธรรมิกราช

To the west of Wat Ratburana, this temple is a pleasant place to sit among the ruins. The most prominent feature is a central *chedi* surrounded by *singha* (guardian lion) sculptures. Local people believe that the temple predated the Ayuthaya period, a claim unsupported by architectural evidence.

Wat Suwan Dararam
วัดสุวรรณดาราราม

This temple in the southeast of the island is worth visiting for the different architectural Thai styles. King Rama I designed the exterior of the older-style *uposatha* (a temple's central building, containing Buddha images) while Rama III designed the interior. The slightly bowed line along the temple edge and its relatively plain finish are typical of the period. Next to it is a *wí·hǎhn* (large hall) from Rama IV's reign, resplendent with a glittering external mosaic and internal paintings depicting the life of King Naresuan.

Ayuthaya Historical Study Centre
ศูนย์ศึกษาประวัติศาสตร์อยุธยา

The interesting models in this **centre** (☎ 0 3524 5124; Th Rotchana; adult/student 100/50B; ◷ 9am-4.30pm Mon-Fri, to 5pm Sat & Sun) help give a sense of what life was like in old Ayuthaya. Displays also detail village life and aspects of Thai culture.

Chao Sam Phraya National Museum
พิพิธภัณฑสถานแห่งชาติเจ้าสามพระยา

Most of Ayuthaya's treasures were stolen or melted down long ago. Some pieces did survive though, and are displayed in this **museum** (admission 150B; ◷ 9am-4pm Wed-Sun). Exhibitions include gold treasures from crypts at Wat Phra Mahathat and Wat Ratburana, and an enormous bronze Buddha head from the U Thong period. Several books on Thai art and architecture are for sale at the entrance.

Chantharakasem National Museum
พิพิธภัณฑสถานแห่งชาติจันทรเกษม

The grounds of this national **museum** (Th U Thong; admission 100B; ◷ 9am-4pm Wed-Sun) are actually more interesting than its collection of artefacts, sculptures and ancient weapons. The museum, near the banks of Mae Nam Pasak, is within the grounds of Wang Chan Kasem (Chan Kasem Palace), which was built for King Naresuan by his father in 1577.

Ayuthaya Fighting Show

Behind the elephant 'taxi' stand is the **Ayuthaya Fighting Show** (550B). The 10-strong crew stages 30-minute shows at 10.30am, 11.30am, 1pm, 2pm and 3pm. Their dextrous displays of swords and sticks are a reminder of how wars used to be fought. Each show is quick and slick, and the comic touches are as sharp as the sickles they wave around.

OFF THE ISLAND

On the opposite side of the moat that surrounds central Ayuthaya are several famous temples, as well as ethnic communities that defined the former kingdom's international prestige. You can reach some sites by bicycle, but others will require a motorbike. Evening boat tours around the island are another way to see the highlights (see p201).

Wat Phanan Choeng
วัดพนัญเชิง

This busy, modern **temple** (admission 20B) is a popular place for many Thai-Chinese to make merit or have their fortunes told.

A famous 19m-high Buddha image (Phra Phanan Choeng) sits in the *wí·hǎhn* surrounded by the 84,000 Buddha images that line the walls. A Chinese temple on the grounds ensures there is a constant crackle from exploding firecrackers. Three Buddha images sit in the ordination hall; the central one is a U-Thong image while the flanking ones are Sukhothai style.

Merit making is the main activity here, and many worshippers buy bags of fish which are then ritualistically released into the river.

Wat Phanan Choeng is southeast of the town. The best way to get here from the island is by ferry (5B) from the pier near Phom Phet Fortress. Your bicycle can accompany you on the crossing.

CENTRAL THAILAND

Portuguese Settlement

At the height of Ayuthaya's power up to 40 ethnic groups settled in the city. The Portuguese were first to arrive, followed by the Dutch, British and Japanese. Up to 2000 Portuguese traders and diplomats lived in the area and there were three Catholic churches. A small group of Thai Catholics still live near the site today.

The Portuguese brought guns with them, and this modern weapon helped the Thais defeat the Burmese in 1520. As a result of this victory, the Portuguese were given land on which to build. In 1767 the Burmese invaders burned down the settlement and it wasn't until 1985 that a Portuguese foundation came to restore the village.

Just south of the island, the Portuguese Settlement displays the skeletal remains of 40 Portuguese settlers in an open pit. Look out for the unusual spirit house with figures of St Joseph and St Paul, and a French map which claims the city's waters were once infested with crocodiles. To the west of the Portuguese Settlement is a **Muslim quarter**.

Japanese Village

Another 5km south of the Portuguese Settlement is the **Japanese Village** (adult/child 50/20B; ⏲ 8am-5pm). The Japanese settlement was one of the largest foreign contingents, and many settlers were Christians fleeing persecution in their homelands for more tolerant Ayuthaya. A video presentation sets the scene and a giant electronic image of an oil painting by Dutch artists shows just how glorious the city looked in its heyday. Outside the small exhibition hall is a Japanese-style garden.

Wat Chai Wattanaram

วัดไชยวัฒนาราม

Just 40 years ago this **temple** (admission 50B) was immersed in thick jungle. Today it is one of Ayuthaya's most-photographed sites, thanks to its impressive Khmer-style central *prang*, which stands 35m high. Built in 1630 by King Prasat Thong to honour his mother, the temple is a great place to watch sunsets. The site is west of the island and can be reached on bicycle via a nearby bridge.

Phu Khao Thong

เจดีย์ภูเขาทอง

Clamber up the 79 steps of this *chedi*, also known as Golden Monument, for great

---

WÅT A SIGHT BY NIGHT

If you think the temple ruins look good by day, you should see them at night. Some of Ayuthaya's most impressive ruins take on an ethereal glow after dark, when they are dramatically illuminated.

Wat Ratburana, Wat Chai Wattanaram, Wat Phra Ram and Wat Mahathat are all lit up from 7pm to 9pm. The grounds are closed, but it is still worth strolling past the temples or finding a nearby restaurant to have dinner.

---

views of the city. Originally built by the Burmese during a 15-year occupation, the top section was added later by Thais. The statue at the front is a memorial to the all-conquering King Naresuan, who is surrounded here by a rather surreal collection of fighting cocks. Legend has it that when Naresuan was held as a hostage in Burma his invincible fighting cocks helped to secure his fearsome reputation.

Queen Suriyothai Memorial Park

พระบรมราชานุสาวรีย์สมเด็จพระศรีสุริโยทัย

Close to Phu Khao Thong is this tribute to the warrior queen, near the spot where she died in 1548 while fighting the Burmese. Visit in the early evening, when Thais come to hang out in the vast grounds.

Wat Na Phra Meru

วัดหน้าพระเมรุ

This **temple** (Phra Mehn; admission 20B) was one of only a handful to escape unscathed from the Burmese army's 1767 attack, as it was the invading army's base.

In the *bòht* (central sanctuary) there's an impressive carved wooden ceiling showing the Buddhist heavens. Inside the *wí·hăhn* is a rare green sandstone Buddha from Sri Lanka. It is from the Dvaravati period, making it around 1500 years old. Its prominent facial features and joined eyebrows are typical of the period.

Elephant Kraal

เพนียดคล้องช้าง

Wild elephants were once rounded up and kept in this *krahl* (stockade). Each year the king would look on here as the finest beasts were chosen and either put to work or used as war machines. This restored *krahl*, which has 980 teak logs, is 2km from the centre of town.

Baan Th Dusit
บ้านถนนดุสิต

This group of ruins shows a more rustic side to Ayuthaya. Located just east of the island, the area has picturesque lakes where fishermen while away their time.

Wat Maheyong is a popular weekend meditation retreat in a leafy courtyard near the temple ruins. Slightly farther down the road is **Wat Kudi Dao**, which has been abandoned to nature and is quite atmospheric as a result. **Wat Ayuthaya** is from the early Ayuthaya period and on Wednesday and Saturday evenings plays host to a small market.

Wat Yai Chai Mongkhon
วัดใหญ่ชัยมงคล

The 7m-long reclining Buddha, draped in a long orange robe, is the main feature at this **temple** (admission 20B). King U Thong built the monastery in 1357 to house monks from Sri Lanka. The *chedi* was built later to honour King Naresuan's victory over Burma.

Cycling Tour

Start at the **Ayuthaya Historical Study Centre** (p199) then continue down Th Rotchana to the **TAT office** (p197) and its video presentation. Leaving here, turn left and go over the roundabout. On your right is **Wat Phra Ram**, then make your way to **Wat Phra Si Sanphet** (p198). Walk through here to get to **Wihaan Mongkhon Bophit** (p198), then return to Th Si Sanphet and turn right at the roundabout onto Th Pa Thon. Go over a small wooden bridge and turn right onto Th Khlong Thaw. On the left is the entrance to **Wat Chetharam** and **Wat Lokaya Sutha**. Return to Th Khlong Thaw and head north. Turn right onto Th U Thong and follow the river east before turning left over another small bridge which leads to **Wat Na Phra Meru** (opposite). Return to Th U Thong and go east before turning into Th Chee Kun. Pop into

CYCLING TOUR FACTS

Start Th Rotchana
Finish Th Chee Kun
Distance 10km
Duration four hours

Wat Phra Mahathat (p198) and neighbouring **Wat Ratburana** (p198).

Tours

Informal boat tours (from 200B per hour) can be arranged at the pier near the night market or at guesthouses. Several guesthouses offer night tours of the ruins (200B per person). These tours can be cancelled at the last minute if not enough people sign up.

If you'd like more in-depth coverage of Ayuthaya history, talk to TAT (☎ 0 3524 6076; 108/22 Th Si Sanphet; ☺ 8.30am-4.30pm) about hiring a guide.

A variety of cycling tours are available on and off the island through **Ayutthaya Boat and Travel** (☎ 0 2746 1414; www.ayutthaya-boat.com), off Th Rotchana. Two-day trips around the countryside involve staying overnight with a local family and a canal cruise.

Festivals & Events

In November, the Bang Sai Arts and Crafts Centre (p204) is the place to be for the **Loi Kratong** festival. Hundreds of beautiful lotus-shaped vessels containing candles and incense sticks are set afloat from the riverside. In late January the centre holds its annual fair, complete with traditional fair and dance shows.

The Thailand International **Swan-Boat Races** take place on Mae Nam Chao Phraya at the Bang Sai Arts and Crafts Centre every September.

Sleeping

Backpackers tend to head for Soi 2, Th Naresuan, where there is a modest collection of equally modest guesthouses. Midrange and top-end options can be found along the more scenic riverfront. Look for substantial discounts during the low season (April to November).

BUDGET

Baan Gao Suan (☎ 0 3526 1732; Ko Kert; r 150-250B) Those after that authentic homestay experience can stay with the village chief, who will arrange some hands-on activities. Talk to TAT for details (p197).

Baan Are Gong (☎ 0 3523 5592; siriporntan@yahoo .com.sg; off Th Rotchana; s/d 150/350B; ☒) In the soi opposite the train station is this gorgeous 100-year-old teak guesthouse, run by a Thai-Chinese family. The 4B ferry to the island is just yards away.

HELPING AN OLD FRIEND

Elephants have played an integral part in Thai history, helping to fight wars, build cities and transport kings.

Today their status, and numbers, have diminished and they are often seen walking city streets begging for bananas. There are only 4000 domestic and wild elephants left in Thailand and, as their natural habitat has been reduced and logging is illegal, their main domestic use is now within the tourism industry.

The **Ayuthaya Elephant Palace** (☎ 08 0668 7727; www.elephantstay.com) does its part to raise the profile of the animal, and the mahout. It provides rides for tourists around the city ruins, runs a successful breeding program and holds several innovative promotional activities. Elephants from the *kraal* even featured in Oliver Stone's movie *Alexander* and Jackie Chan's *Around the World in 80 Days*.

Some of the 90 elephants have turned their trunks to art. Their paintings are so impressive that some have been transformed into dresses and featured in a New York fashion show. Even their dung has a purpose – it's made into paper, bookmarks and photo albums.

The elephants displayed their practical value when they helped recover bodies in Phang Nga following the 2004 tsunami, as they were able to reach places rescue machinery could not access.

The centre aims to protect Thailand's remaining elephants by buying sick or abused animals. Some bull elephants that had killed villagers have been retrained and now provide tourist rides around the ruins.

Laithongrien Meepan opened the centre in 1996 after buying his daughter an elephant as a present. He began to understand the importance of the animal within Thai culture and became passionate about restoring its once revered position. Australians Michelle Reedy, a former zoo keeper, and Ewa Narkiewicz run an Elephant Stay program at the site (4000B per day), where visitors learn how to ride, bathe and earn the trust of the animals over several days or weeks.

Keeping an elephant isn't cheap, as they are capable of each munching their way through 150kg of food a day, so elephant taxi rides and the Elephant Stay experience help cover costs. Some of the food comes from a specially designed farm that produces a particular type of nutritious grass, while locals often pop in to donate fruit.

The nonprofit organisation isn't set up for tourists to just walk in, but those that do spend time living with the elephants usually come away with a new-found respect and admiration for Thailand's national animal.

PU Guest House (☎ 0 3525 1213; 20/1 Soi Thaw Kaw Saw; r 180-550B; 🅿 🖵) Bright and cheery, all PU's rooms are comfortable, and some come with satellite TV, minibar and air-con. If you need a Japanese-speaking local, this is a good choice.

Tony's Place (☎ 0 3525 2578; 12/18 Soi 2, Th Naresuan; r 200-500B; 🅿) There's a constant buzz about this place that keeps travellers coming. The rooms offer good value and the service is friendly.

Baan Khun Phra (☎ 0 3524 1978; 48/2 Th U Thong; s/d 250/600B) This charming teak house, built during the reign of King Rama VI, is packed with surprises – where else are you going to find real Thai swords next to your bed? Most rooms have a shared bathroom, while some dorm-style rooms are available.

Sherwood Guest House (☎ 08 6666 0813; 21/25 Th Dechawat; r 280-380B; 🅿 🖵 🎏) The rooms may not be thrilling, but there is a pool and an expat owner who can offer good advice on experiencing the city. Nonguests can also use the pool (adult/child 50/35B).

Chantana Guest House (☎ 0 3532 3200; chantana house@yahoo.com; 12/22 Soi 2, Th Naresuan; r 350-450B; 🅿) With clean, comfortable rooms and helpful staff, the Chantana is a good budget option. Ask for a room with a balcony.

Wieng Fa Hotel (☎ 0 3524 3252; 1/8 Th Rotchana; r 400-500B; 🅿) Retro furniture and an outdoor patio add character to this professionally run hotel.

our pick **Baan Lotus Guest House** (☎ 0 3525 1988; 20 Th Pamaphrao; r 400-600B; 🅿) This charming family-run guesthouse is the pick of the crop.

The teak building is a converted school and sits between a wooded area to the front and a lotus pond to the rear.

MIDRANGE & TOP END

Package tourists tend to occupy most of the midrange and top-end rooms. There are options on and off the island, and while much of the better accommodation may be dated it does come with top riverside views.

Ayothaya Hotel (☎ 0 3523 2855; www.ayothayahotel .com; 12 Soi 2, Th Naresuan; r 650-3500B; ✂ ☐ ☎) In a great location, the Ayothaya would benefit from renovation but has large rooms and friendly staff. Cheaper rooms are in a separate guesthouse to the rear. Look for low-season discounts.

U Thong Hotel (☎ 0 3521 2531; www.uthonginn .com; 210 Th Rotchana; r from 1200B; ✂ ☐ ☎) A good midrange option with great service, extensive facilities and comfortable rooms. A free shuttle bus runs into town.

Krungsri River Hotel (☎ 0 3524 4333; www.krungsri river.com; 27/2 Th Rotchana; r from 1800B; ✂ ☐ ☎) With a scenic river location and large, stylish rooms, this is the plushest pad in town.

River View Place Hotel (☎ 0 3524 1444; 35/5 Th U Thong; r from 2000B; ✂ ☐ ☎) The best of the on-island hotels, the River View Place Hotel has large, comfortable rooms and a raft of amenities.

Eating

Ayuthaya is famed for its sweet Muslim snacks, curries and *nám prík* (spicy dip). Travellers tend to congregate around Soi 2, Th Naresuan, where there's a collection of Western-friendly restaurants to be found. Many riverfront restaurants specialise in seafood and have great views of the temples. The bustling undercover **Chao Phrom Market** (Th Naresuan) has Thai-Chinese and Muslim dishes.

ourpick **Hua Raw Night Market** (Th U Thong) A great evening option, with simple riverfront seating. Along with the usual Thai dishes there are several Muslim food stalls; look for the green star and crescent.

Roti Sai Mai Stalls (Th U Thong; ☀ 10am-8pm) Ayuthaya is famous for the Muslim dessert *roti sai mai*. You make this super-sweet snack yourself by rolling together thin strands of melted palm sugar and then wrapping them inside the roti. Stalls selling this are mainly found opposite Ayuthaya Hospital.

Lung Lek (Th Chee Kun; dishes 30-40B; ☀ 8.30am-4pm) Slurp down delicious noodle soup alongside locals while admiring the view of Wat Ratburana.

Tony's Place (Soi 2, Th Naresuan; dishes 50-180B) Ever-busy, Tony's guesthouse restaurant has a solid Thai/Western menu, including plenty of veggie nibbles.

Baan Watcharachai (off Th Worachate; dishes 75-150B) This charming, peaceful restaurant is found next to Wat Kasatrathirat. Pick a seat on the wooden boat moored outside and tuck in to some *yam plaa dùk fòo* (crispy catfish salad).

Sombat Chao Phraya (Th U Thong; dishes 80-140B; ☀ 10am-9.30pm) A cosy riverside establishment that specialises in sublime seafood.

Baan Khun Phra (☎ 0 3524 1978; dishes 80-140B; 48/2 Th U Thong) Behind the guesthouse of the same name, this restaurant has a pleasant riverside atmosphere and good Thai, Western and vegetarian choices.

Sai Thong (Th U Thong; dishes 80-140B; ☀ 10am-10.30pm) This hugely popular riverside restaurant has an extensive seafood menu and old-school feel.

Rabieng Nam (cnr Th Rotchana & Th Chee Kun; dishes 100-160B; 5pm-midnight) When Thais eat it's as much about fun as it is about food. That's evident here, where improvised karaoke sessions take centre stage as the locals munch on snacks.

Drinking

Ayuthaya isn't much of a night bird, and most backpackers are content to hang around Soi 2, Th Naresuan after dark.

Jazz Bar (Soi 2) Run by four music-loving locals who often break out the drums and double bass.

Spin (cnr Th Naresuan & Th Khlong Makhamriang) Young Thais sip fruit/vodka combos and munch fried snacks at this funky street bar.

Off the island, Ay By Laser (AY) nightclub, near the northern bus terminal, is surrounded by karaoke bars that attracts the city's party crowd.

Getting There & Away

BOAT

Several tour companies run boats along the river to Bangkok; see tours, p201. **Boat Step Travel** (☀ 08 9744 2672, 1500B) runs daily trips, leaving from Ayuthaya at 11.30am and arriving in Bangkok at 4.30pm.

BUS

Ayuthaya has two bus terminals. The long-distance terminal is 5km east of central Ayuthaya and serves destinations north of the city. The provincial bus stop is on Th Naresuan, a short walk from the guesthouse area. Buses from Bangkok arrive two blocks away from the main bus terminal.

Buses to Bangkok's northern terminal (56B, 1½ hours, every 20 minutes) stop by the old Don Muang Airport. If you're coming straight from Suvarnabhumi International Airport, take a bus to Bangkok's northern bus terminal, Mo Chit (p183).

Minivans go to and from Bangkok's Victory Monument (65B, two hours, every hour from 5am to 7pm), and leave Ayuthaya from Th Naresuan, west of the main bus terminal.

Buses to Lopburi (40B, two hours, every 45 minutes) also depart from the terminal on Th Naresuan. If you're heading for Kanchanaburi, you'll need to get a bus to Suphanburi (60B, 1½ hours, every 30 minutes) and then connect to a Kanchanaburi-bound bus for 50B. Large *sŏrng·tăa·ou* (also spelt *săwngthăew;* pick-up trucks) leave for Bang Pa In (25B, 45 minutes) every 20 minutes.

The ticket office for the northern bus terminal is a five-minute walk from the station. Destinations include Sukhothai (291B to 371B, six hours, hourly departures), Chiang Mai (463B to 596B, nine hours, three evening departures), Nan (444B to 571B, eight hours, two morning and three nightly departures) and Phitsanulok (256B to 329, five hours, frequent departures).

TRAIN

The train station is east of central Ayuthaya and is accessible by a quick cross-river ferry (4B).

Trains leave Bangkok's Hualamphong station for Ayuthaya (ordinary/rapid/express 15/20/315B, 1½ hours) throughout the day with more departures between 7am and 11am and 6pm to 10pm. Schedules are available from the information booth at Hualamphong station. To save time, use Bangkok's subway system to go to Bang Sue station, where you can hook up with the state railway line.

From Ayuthaya, you can head north to Chiang Mai (ordinary/rapid/express 586/856/1198B, six departures a day), or northeast to Pak Chong (ordinary/rapid/express 23/73/130B, frequent departures), the nearest station to Khao Yai National Park and Khon Kaen (ordinary/rapid/express 173/265/375B, six hours, four departures a day). *Sŏrng·tăa·ou* from the station to the city centre charge 60B.

Getting Around

Around every corner is a săhm·lór or túk-túk waiting to ask where you're going. The golden rule is to agree a price before you get on. For trips on the island itself, the rate is 30B to 40B.

The main ruins are close together, so the most environmentally friendly way to see them is by bicycle or elephant. Many guesthouses rent bicycles (30B) and motorcycles (200B). You can take brief rides around the temples by elephant (400B to 500B) or by horse and carriage (300B). The elephants stay at a *kraal* on Th Pa Thon.

Long-tail boat tours around the island (from 200B per hour) can be arranged at the pier near the night market or at guesthouses.

AROUND AYUTHAYA

Bang Pa In
บางปะอิน

Bang Pa In Palace (☎ 0 3526 1548; admission 100B; ⏰ 8am-3.30pm) is worth viewing simply for its eclectic mix of architectural styles. The European, Chinese and Thai buildings seem incongruous at first, but reflect the influences of Rama V (King Chulalongkorn, r 1868–1910). King Chula was a progressive leader who studied Western traditions. After returning from Europe he restored the palace, which was first built in the 17th century. Today there is a replica of the Tiber Bridge in Rome, the Chinese-style **Wehut Chamrun**, the Victorian-influenced **Withun Thatsana**, and an elephant-shaped topiary garden.

In 1880, Queen Sunanta drowned during a journey to the palace. Thai law forbade courtiers from touching the queen, and so nobody tried to save her. As a result of the tragedy King Rama V changed the law. A marble obelisk in memory of the queen is in the palace grounds.

Wat Niwet Thamaprawat, to the rear of the palace car park, is the most unlikely of temples. Designed to resemble a cathedral, its Gothic style, stained-glass windows and knights in armour stand in contrast to the Buddha images. Take a free, monk-operated cable car to the other side of the water.

To reach the palace, take a public *sŏrng·tăa·ou* (25B, frequent departures) from the provincial bus stop on Th Naresuan. Once the *sŏrng·tăa·ou* drops you at the Bang Pa In bus station, jump on a motorbike taxi (30B) to the palace, which is 4km away. The alternative is a train from Ayuthaya (3rd class 3B, 30 minutes). The train station is closer to the palace than the bus station, but again you'll need a motorbike taxi (20B) to complete the last leg.

Another 17km southwest of the palace is the **Bang Sai Arts and Crafts Centre** (☎ 0 3536 6252; www.bangsaiarts.com; ☎ 9am-5pm). Opened back in 1984 with support from Queen Sirikit, this 180-hectare site helps preserve traditional Thai handicraft skills. Farmers create products on-site to help provide a supplementary income during the off-season. Visitors can visit workshops where locals carve wood, dye silk or make knives. Jewellery, clothing and textiles can be bought at the Sala Phra Ming Kwan pavilion and in a purpose-built arts and crafts village.

A **Bird Park** (admission 20B) and two giant cylindrical **aquariums** displaying huge freshwater fish from Thailand will keep the younger visitors entertained.

To get to the centre, take a train or *sŏrng·tăa·ou* to Bang Pa In and then hire a motorbike taxi.

LOPBURI PROVINCE

LOPBURI
ลพบุรี

Laid-back Lopburi is a small, charming town where temple ruins sit alongside noodle stalls and street markets.

It's a simple task to stroll between the main sights in a day or two and soak up the history of a town that once played an important role in the Dvaravati, Khmer, Sukhothai and Ayuthaya empires.

Early-morning or evening street markets are great places to wander and experience life in a provincial Thai town. The easygoing pace only shifts a gear when locals chase away Lopburi's most notorious residents – a troop of monkeys. These macaques live among the ruins, but don't be surprised to see their mischievous faces peering into your hotel room either.

The town is famous for its sunflower fields, coconut jelly and rattan furniture, while sugar cane and rice are the main crops.

Most visitors pass through Lopburi, which is approximately 150km north of Bangkok, briefly en route to the north of the country.

History
One of Thailand's oldest cities, Lopburi first came to prominence during the Dvaravati period (6th to 11th centuries).

When the Khmer empire advanced eastwards in the 10th century it had a major influence over the town's architecture and artwork. Many previous buildings were destroyed and so today the town's extant ruins, notably Prang Sam Yot and Wat Phra Si Ratana Mahathat, have strong Khmer features.

Lopburi, then known as Lavo, was a frontier town for the Khmer empire and became an administration and trade hub. The rise of the Sukhothai empire saw a decline in Lopburi's fortunes, but during the Ayuthaya period it was a second capital and hosted many influential foreign dignitaries. These outside influences led to advances in architecture, astronomy and literature.

King Narai fortified the town in the mid-17th century when the Dutch threatened a naval blockade. In 1665 he built a palace in Lopburi, and died there in 1688.

Orientation
Lopburi comes in two parts: the compact old town is on one side of the railway tracks, while on the other is the larger, and distinctly less charming, new town. The old town is walkable and houses all the significant historical sites.

Information
There are several banks in the old part of Lopburi, and a string of internet cafes along Th Na Phra Kan (going rate 20B per hour).
Communications Authority of Thailand (CAT; Th Phra Narai Maharat; ☎ 8.30am-4.30pm)
Hospital (☎ 0 3662 1537-45; Th Ramdecho)
Nature Adventure (☎ 0 3642 7693; kkhumwong@yahoo.com; 15-17 Th Phraya Kamjat) Can organise rock-climbing tours to Khao Chin Lae.
Police (☎ 0 3642 4515; Th Na Phra Kan)
Post office (Th Phra Narai Maharat)
TAT (☎ 0 3642 2768-9; Th Phraya Kamjat; ☎ 8.30am-4.30pm) Pick up a copy of TAT's excellent map here.
Zon Coffee Bar (Th Naresuan) Free wi-fi.

CENTRAL THAILAND

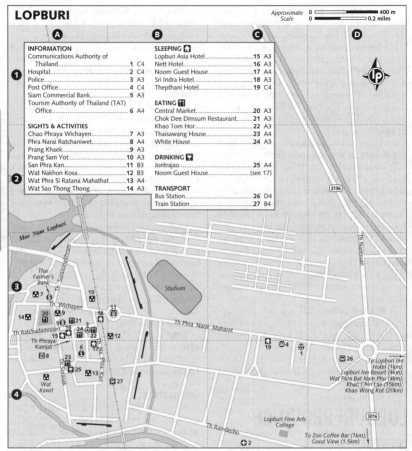

Sights

PHRA NARAI RATCHANIWET

พระนารายณ์ราชนิเวศน์

This **former royal palace** (entrance Th Sorasak; admission 150B; gallery 8.30am-4pm Wed-Sun, palace grounds 7am-5.30pm) is the best place to begin your walking tour of Lopburi's ruins.

The palace grounds house the **Lopburi Museum** (officially called the Somdet Phra Narai National Museum), which has interesting displays explaining the history of the province. The museum is divided among three separate buildings. In the **Phiman Mongkut Pavilion** there are sculptures and art from the Lopburi, Khmer, Dvaravati, U Thong and Ayuthaya periods. The **Chantara Phisan Throne Hall** contains paintings and ar-

tefacts in memory of King Narai, while the European-style **Phra Pratiab Building** has a small display of traditional handicrafts and hunting tools.

French and Italian engineers helped design the palace, which was built between 1665 and 1677. Lopburi was used as a second capital during the reign of Ayuthaya's King Narai. The monarch welcomed foreign dignitaries here and stayed at the palace during hunting vacations.

After King Narai's death in 1688 the palace was abandoned until King Mongkut (Rama IV) ordered its restoration in 1856.

The main entry point for the palace is through **Pratu Phayakkha** gate, off Th Sorasak. To your left, as you walk through the large gate, are what remains of the palace reservoir and the former reception hall where foreign envoys were once greeted.

Ahead of these are the elephant stables and towards the rear of the compound is the **Suttha Sawan** throne hall, where King Narai died. A 150B one-day pass to all the ruins can be bought from here.

WAT PHRA SI RATANA MAHATHAT
วัดพระศรีรัตนมหาธาตุ

Opposite the train station is this 13th-century Khmer **wát** (Th Na Phra Kan; admission 50B; ⏰ 7am-5pm). Once the town's largest monastery, it has been heavily renovated and makes for a great photo opportunity. The central Phra Prang has a bas-relief depicting the life of the Buddha.

PRANG SAM YOT
ปรางค์สามยอด

This **shrine** (Th Wichayen; admission 50B; ⏰ 8am-6pm) is the old town's best-known and most-photographed feature. The three linked towers originally symbolised the Hindu Trimurti of Shiva, Vishnu and Brahma. Now two of them contain ruined Lopburi-style Buddha images. The towers are accessible and offer cool relief from the heat – and the monkeys.

Young guides may offer to show you around and, while their English is minimal, their catapults will keep the monkeys at bay. The monument is the best example of Khmer-Lopburi architecture, and looks especially good at night when it is illuminated.

CHAO PHRAYA WICHAYEN
บ้านวิชาเยนทร์

King Narai built this Thai-European **palace** (Th Wichayen; admission 50B; ⏰ 9am-4pm) as a residence for foreign ambassadors. Greek diplomat and trader Constantine Phaulkon was its most famous resident. Phaulkon's knowledge of European technology helped him gain a place in King Narai's inner circle. However, jealous courtiers disliked his power and riches, and as

---

MONKEY MAYHEM

If you see people running around Lopburi with 2m-long poles and catapults, they haven't all gone mad. These are just some of the methods locals employ in a vain attempt to prevent the monkeys from taking over. The monkeys (a type of macaque) are an essential part of Lopburi's character and in the old town there is simply no avoiding them. Scampering along overhead cables, pounding a passage over corrugated roofs or squabbling over a piece of mango, they are omnipresent.

Their favourite haunts are **San Phra Kan** (Kala Shrine; Th Wichayen) and **Prang Sam Yot** (Th Wichayen). While visiting these places, put bottles of water and anything that may be mistaken for food inside a bag. Any bottles out on display will be considered fair game. The monkeys don't live exclusively in the ruins though; the troop is just as likely to run across your hotel balcony or dangle from a shop's awnings.

While locals may use catapults to keep the simians at bay, the monkeys are never harmed, partly due to the Buddhist belief of preserving all forms of life. In addition, some feel the animals are 'descendants' of the Hindu god Kala and so to injure one would be seriously bad karma. During the last week of November a feast is held at Prang Sam Yot to thank the monkeys for helping to bring prosperity to Lopburi. Each year there is a theme to the food, such as fruit or ice cream. Tables are neatly laid out with all kinds of treats and the monkeys are then free to indulge themselves, for which they need no persuasion. A feeding station has been set up to discourage the monkeys from pilfering tourists' food, and so at 10am and 4pm every day vegetables and fruit are distributed next to the San Phra Kan shrine.

Look out for the burly security officer who zealously guards the shrine's entrance with her police truncheon to prevent any animals from getting inside. One of the strangest sights here is the wild monkeys who watch with bemusement as their cousins are made to perform in a show. Inside a small pavilion the animals jump through hoops of fire and play basketball with coconuts.

Care should be taken when around the monkeys. They may look cute but they are wild animals, and wherever there is a sweet baby monkey, you can bet a protective mother is not far behind. Take a look at the arms of the young guides who offer to show you around for proof that the monkeys can, and sometimes do, bite.

Narai lay dying, Phaulkon was arrested and beheaded. The palace is across the street and northeast of Wat Sao Thong Thong.

PRANG KHAEK
ปรางค์แขก

This 11th-century tower is on a triangular piece of land bordered by Th Wichayen to the north. The structure has Khmer-style brickwork and may have once been a temple to the Hindu god Shiva.

OTHER RUINS

Just along from the railway station is **Wat Nakhon Kosa** (Th Na Phra Kan). Built in the 12th century, it may have originally been a Hindu shrine. The main *chedi* was built during the Dvararati period, while the *wí·hǎhn* was added later by King Narai. To the rear is a collection of headless Buddha images.

Northwest of the palace centre, **Wat Sao Thong Thong** (Th Wichayen) is remarkable only for its unusual Gothic-style windows, which were added by King Narai so it could be used as a Christian chapel. The grounds may have once served as a residence for Persian ambassadors.

Wat Phra Bat Nam Phu
วัดพระบาทน้ำพุ

Monks at this temple care for HIV/AIDS patients and are involved in several outreach projects. Set beside mist-covered mountains and verdant fields, the temple offers a tranquil setting for its patients. The Buddhist philosophy that death is merely a part of life and not something to fear is particularly evident in the 'Life Museum'. This displays the preserved bodies of men, women and children who have succumbed to the disease. Sculptures using bone resin are also on display. It is possible to spend time volunteering at the temple, but visitors should remember that this is a home for patients, not a tourist attraction, so respect and sensitivity are essential. The temple is 4km off Th Phahol Yothin.

BAT CAVES

Out of town there are several caves and scenic spots. The best of these is the bat cave at **Khao Wong Kot**, 20km northwest of Lopburi. At sunset thousands of bats emerge for their nocturnal hunt. The cave can be reached by taking a train (5B) north from Lopburi to Nong Sai Khao station and then catching a motorbike taxi. The last train back to Lopburi departs at 4.45pm.

Activities
ROCK CLIMBING

Nearby Khao Chin Lae has more than 40 climbing routes, meaning there is a way up for just about anyone. Those who conquer the mountain are rewarded with views of Lopburi's famous sunflower fields (providing they come between November and January when the flowers are in bloom). If you want to just see the sunflowers, take the bus from Lopburi to Ban Muang (18B) and ask the driver to stop at Khao Chin Lae.

Festivals & Events

For three days in mid-February the **King Narai Festival** (www.thailandgrandfestival.com) is held at the Phra Narai Ratchaniwet. Locals don traditional clothes and stage a colourful parade that leads to the former palace. Highlights include a demonstration of *lá·kon ling* (a traditional drama performed by monkeys).

The real macaques take centre stage during the last week of November for their very own **Monkey Festival** (see the boxed text, p207). Thousands gather to watch the simians devour their banquet.

Sleeping

Options in Lopburi are limited to basic budget rooms with fading paint. Staying in the old town means you will be close to the historic ruins, and also the monkeys. If you prefer not to have monkeys scurrying around outside your window, choose a hotel away from Prang Sam Yot. There are midrange options in the new town but you'll need transport.

BUDGET

It's almost impossible to have anything but a budget room in Lopburi. The rooms may be dated, but in the old town they're close to everything.

Noom Guest House (☎ 0 3642 7693; kkhumwong@yahoo.com; Th Phraya Kamjat; r 150-300B) Bamboo-roofed bungalows facing a leafy garden make this one of the more pleasant places to stay. Upstairs rooms have shared bathrooms.

Sri Indra Hotel (☎ 0 3641 1261; Th Na Phra Kan; r 200-300B; 🖵) Opposite the train station, the Sri Indra has views of the San Phra Kan shrine, neat rooms and great service.

Lopburi Asia Hotel (☎ 0 3661 8894; cnr Th Sorasak & Th Phraya Kamjat; s/d from 250/450B; 🐱) The rooms need work but they do come with TV, air-con and hot water. Ask to see a few different options before picking one.

Nett Hotel (☎ 0 3641 1738; 17/1-2 Th Ratchadamnoen; r 300-500B; 🐱) In the heart of the old town, the Nett's renovated rooms still offer the best value in town.

Thepthani Hotel (☎ 0 3641 1029; Th Phra Narai Maharat; r 400B; 🐱) Just outside the old town, the Theptani is run by the Rajabhat University's tourism and hospitality department. Rooms are reasonable and bathrooms are immaculate. Blue buses running between the old and new town will stop here for 10B.

MIDRANGE & TOP END

Lopburi Inn Hotel (☎ 0 3641 2300; www.lopburiinn hotel.com; 28/9 Th Phra Narai Maharat; r 700-950B; 🐱 🖥) Just in case you haven't had enough of monkeys, there's a 3m-bronze one waiting to greet you, along with dozens of smaller simian statues. The top rooms come with enormous bathrooms.

Lopburi Inn Resort (☎ 0 3642 0777; www.lopburiinn resort.com; 144 Tambon Tha Sala; r 950-1350B; 🐱 🖥) The monkey theme continues unabashed at the Lopburi Inn Hotel's sister site. Being 5km out of town isn't ideal, but it is the fanciest place in town.

Eating & Drinking

Streets in the old town are packed with food stalls offering all manner of snacks. On Wednesdays a market fills Th Phraya Kamjat, while every evening other stalls do business in Th Na Phra Kan.

Khao Tom Hor (cnr Th Na Phra Kan & Th Ratchadamnoen, dishes 30-80B) Locals fill this feeding station every night. The Thai-Chinese menu includes the excellent *plaa salid tôrd* (deep-fried salted fish) and *pàd gàprow gài* (chicken with kaprao leaf).

Thaisawang House (Th Sorasak; dishes 60-100B; 🕐 8.30am-8pm) This simple Thai-Vietnamese restaurant serves up some of the biggest portions in town. Especially good is the iced lemon tea and steamed pancakes. Be sure to check out the 'shrine' surrounded by toy action figures behind the counter.

Central Market (off Th Ratchadamnoen & Th Surasongkhram; 🕐 6am-5pm) Stroll and snack amid the dozens of stalls. Try out the *kôw đom*

mùd (rice wrapped in coconut leaves), *đa·go peu·ak* (taro custard with coconut milk), or *gài tôrt* (fried chicken). In the centre of the market is a vegetarian pavilion.

White House (Th Phraya Kamjat; dishes 80-200B; 🕐 5-10pm) This colonial-looking restaurant offers reasonable Thai-Chinese dishes, and while you're eating you can grill the amiable Khun Piak for travel tips.

Chok Dee Dimsum Restaurant (Th Ratchadamnoen, dishes 16-22B; 🕐 8.30am-10pm) Meat dumplings and steamed pork balls are among the tiny but tempting dishes here. The waiters who herald the arrival of every dish with a little cry give this place a cheery feel.

The new town has a few restaurants and bars, mainly along Th Naresuan. Of these, **Good View** (Th Naresuan; dishes 80-150B; 🕐 5pm-1am) is the best bet. This three-tiered, country-style bar has a wide range of seafood.

When it comes to drinking, options in the old town are limited to **Noom Guest House** (Th Phraya Kamjat), where expats can be found cradling their Changs and Leos, or around the corner there is **Jontrajao** (no roman-script sign; Th Sorasak), a popular venue for locals with its Karabao-style house band. There's no English sign, so look for the giant 'Benmore' advert on the roof.

Getting There & Away

BUS

Lopburi's **bus station** (Th Naresuan) is nearly 2km away from the old town. Buses run to Ayuthaya (32B, two hours, every 30 minutes), Bangkok's northern bus terminal (120B, three hours, every 40 minutes) and Nakhon Ratchasima (Khorat; 136B, 3½ hours, hourly). For Ayuthaya, head to stand 21. Motorbike taxis from the station to the old town cost 30B.

If you are heading to Kanchanaburi, leave from stand 13 and get off at Suphanburi (65B, three hours, every 90 minutes). From there you can catch a local bus to Kanchanaburi for 50B. Other nearby destinations include Singburi and Ang Thong.

TRAIN

The **train station** (Th Na Phra Kan) is within walking distance of the old town and its guesthouses.

Trains heading south towards Ayuthaya (ordinary/rapid/express 13/20/310B) and Bangkok's Hualamphong station (ordinary/rapid/express 28/50/344B) leave roughly every hour up until 2.50pm, followed by a handful of early-evening departures. Express trains take about three hours, ordinary trains 4½ hours. If heading for Bangkok, save time by disembarking at Bangkok's Bang Sue station and take the nearby subway to the city centre.

Trains heading north from Lopburi stop at Phitsanulok (ordinary/rapid/express 49/99/393B). Departures are regular, although there are none between 3pm and 8pm. If you're not stopping long, you can store luggage at the station for 10B per bag.

Getting Around

Sŏrng·tăa·ou and city buses run along Th Wichayen and Th Phra Narai Maharat between the old and new towns for 10B per

passenger; săhm·lór will go anywhere in the old town for 30B.

KANCHANABURI PROVINCE

Kanchanaburi may be one of Thailand's largest provinces, but it is also one of the least developed. This is largely thanks to the vast mountain ranges that separate the kingdom from Myanmar, and the fertile fields that produce rice, sugar cane and tapioca.

Most visitors head to the provincial capital for a few days, visiting the WWII memorials and going on trekking tours. Outside of

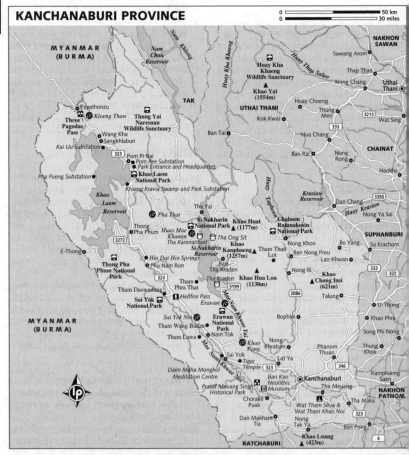

KANCHANABURI PROVINCE

the main town there are cascading waterfalls, caves and forests within easy reach. To the north of the province several national parks are home to reclusive tigers, elephants and gibbons, attracting increasing numbers of visitors who are keen to get closer to nature.

The town of Kanchanaburi is the best place to book tours and has the greatest choice of accommodation and activities. Head out to the northwest and you'll discover rarely visited towns and ethnic groups which have escaped the harsh regime in neighbouring Burma. It's easy to spend longer than planned in these frontier towns, where the pace of life is as slow as the fishing boats that drift across the rivers. Areas such as this help dispel the myth that there is nowhere left in Thailand untainted by tourism and development.

KANCHANABURI
กาญจนบุรี
pop 63,112

The natural beauty of Kanchanaburi attracts tourists looking for an alternative to the bustle of Bangkok, 130km away. Many city dwellers head here for the weekend, often boarding flashy karaoke boats and belting out songs that momentarily shatter the serenity.

Sitting in the slightly elevated valley of Mae Nam Mae Klong, the town is surrounded by fields filled with tapioca, sugar cane and corn. Waterfalls, rivers and jungle to the north and northwest provide some of the finest scenery the kingdom can offer. Limestone hills contain caves packed with stalactites, stalagmites and glittering crystal formations. The caves are also the spiritual home for animist worship and contain many Buddhist images.

During WWII the town experienced darker times. Japanese forces used Allied prisoners of war and conscripted Southeast Asian labourers to build a rail route to Myanmar. The harrowing story was told in Pierre Boulle's book *The Bridge Over the River Kwai* and in the 1957 movie that was based on it. The bridge in question is in Kanchanaburi and several cemeteries and museums around the town pay tribute to the fallen. Roads in the guesthouse area are named after countries that were involved in the conflict.

History

Rama I established Kanchanaburi as a first line of defence against the Burmese along an old invasion route through the Three Pagodas Pass on the Thailand-Myanmar border.

During WWII the Japanese used Allied POWs to build the infamous 'Death Railway' along this same route, from Mae Nam Khwae Noi to the pass. Thousands of prisoners died as a result of brutal treatment by their captors. During the construction of the Death Railway, a Dutch prisoner of war, HR van Heekeren, uncovered Neolithic remains. After the war was over, a Thai-Danish team retraced Van Heekeren's discovery and concluded that the area is a major Neolithic burial site. Archaeological evidence suggests it may have been inhabited 10,000 years ago.

Orientation

Kanchanaburi has a mini version of Bangkok's Th Khao San concentrated along Th Mae Nam Khwae, within walking distance of the train station. Most accommodation is built beside or floating on the river. The commercial strip of the town follows Th Saengchuto. The in-town attractions are too spread out to cover on foot, so you'll want a bicycle or motorbike to get around.

Information

EMERGENCY
Tourist police (☎ 0 3451 2668/2795; Th Saengchuto)

INTERNET ACCESS
Internet cafes can be found along Th Mae Nam Khwae for 30B per hour.

MEDICAL SERVICES
Thanakarn Hospital (☎ 0 3462 2366, emergency 0 3462 2811; Th Saengchuto) Near the junction of Th Chukkadon, this hospital is best equipped for foreign visitors.

MONEY
Several major Thai banks can be found on Th Saengchuto near the market and the bus terminal.

AS Mixed Travel (☎ 0 3451 2017; Apple's Guesthouse, 3/17 Th Chaokunen) Foreign-exchange service available outside of bank hours.

Bangkok Bank (Th U Thong) Located near Kanakan Mall.

Krung Thai Bank (Th Saengchuto) Near the Death Railway Bridge.

Thai Military Bank (Th Saengchuto) Near the bus station.

POST
Main post office (Th Saengchuto; ☯ 8.30am-4.30pm Mon-Fri, 9am-noon Sat & Sun)

CENTRAL THAILAND

TELEPHONE

Many private shops along Th Mae Nam Khwae offer long-distance calls.

CAT (off Th Saengchuto; ☼ 8.30am-4.30pm Mon-Fri) This office has an international telephone service.

TOURIST INFORMATION

TAT (☎ 0 3451 1200; Th Saengchuto; ☼ 8.30am-4.30pm) Provides free maps of the town and province, along with advice on what to do and where to stay.

Sights

One-day package trips to the waterfalls and war sights are a good way to see the main attractions but don't give you much time to savour them. All the popular destinations are easy to reach, so an alternative is to use the bus and rail networks and travel independently.

The war museums and most caves can be seen in two days. A few more days can then be spent exploring the other sights, via train or bus. Many parks and caves have a 200B entry fee for foreigners, which works as a one-day pass for all similar locations.

THAILAND-BURMA RAILWAY CENTRE

ศูนย์รถไฟไทย–พม่า

This informative **museum** (☎ 0 3451 0067; www.tbrc online.com; 73 Th Chaokunen; adult/child 100/50B; ☼ 9am-5pm) is the ideal place to begin your look at Kanchanaburi's role in WWII. The museum's nine galleries use images, artefacts and models to explain the history of the railway, how the POWs were treated and what happened to the railway once it was complete. A video from survivors is particularly poignant and ensures that the deaths remain a tragedy, not merely a statistic.

ALLIED WAR CEMETERY

สุสานทหารสัมพันธมิตรดอนรัก

Across the street from the museum is the **Allied War Cemetery** (Th Saengchuto; ☼ 8am-6pm), which is immaculately maintained by the War Graves Commission. Of the 6982 prisoners of war buried here, nearly half were British. The rest came mainly from Australia and the Netherlands. It is estimated that at least 100,000 people died while working on the railway, the majority being labourers from nearby Asian countries. For those looking for the graves of a loved one, a small office to the side of the cemetery has lists of names and their locations in the cemetery.

DEATH RAILWAY BRIDGE (BRIDGE OVER THE RIVER KWAI)

สะพานข้ามแม่น้ำแคว

This 300m **railway bridge** (Th Mae Nam Khwae) is one huge tourist trap. Avoid the hawkers and walk, carefully, along the wooden and metal slats. The centre of the bridge was destroyed by Allied bombs in 1945 so today only the outer curved spans are original. Once you make it to the other side there are some cafes and greenery by the waterfront.

Construction material came from a dismantled bridge in Java. The first version, completed in 1943, was wooden and was later replaced by a steel bridge. During the last week of November and first week of December a nightly sound-and-light show marks the Allied attack on the 'Death Railway' in 1945. Rooms are hard to come by when this show takes place, so book ahead if you want to witness the spectacle.

The bridge spans Mae Nam Khwae Yai, which is 2.5km from the centre of Kanchanaburi. This means it is walkable from Th Mae Nam Khwae or you can jump on a northbound *sŏrng·tăa·ou* (10B) along Th Saengchuto.

WWII MUSEUM

พิพิธภัณฑ์สงครามโลกครั้งที่สอง

One of the most bizarre sites around, this **museum** (admission 40B; ☼ 8am-6.30pm) has to be admired simply for squeezing so many randomly connected things into one place.

The museum is divided into two buildings. Along the front of the smaller building are life-size sculptures of figures connected with WWII, including Churchill, Hitler, Hirohito and Einstein. Inside is a display of Japanese wagons used to transport prisoners, old photographs and unconvincing waxwork models of POWs. Notes about the area's history are painted on the walls, but the translations sometimes go badly awry, with unfortunate and unintentionally comic results. One sign about the victims of an Allied bombing raid reads: 'the bodies lay higgledy-piggledy beneath the bridge'. Another says simply: 'England was pushed into the sea by Dunkirk'.

The larger building resembles a Chinese temple and is far more opulent, or garish, depending on your viewpoint. Inside there are displays of ancient Thai weaponry and colourful portraits of each Thai king.

KANCHANABURI

0 ———— 500 m
0 ———— 0.3 miles

CENTRAL THAILAND

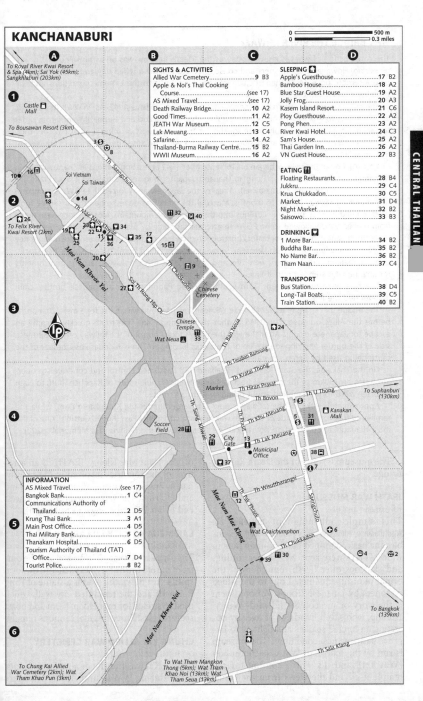

SIGHTS & ACTIVITIES
Allied War Cemetery...........................**9** B3
Apple & Noi's Thai Cooking
  Course......................................(see 17)
AS Mixed Travel............................(see 17)
Death Railway Bridge......................**10** A2
Good Times..................................**11** A2
JEATH War Museum.......................**12** C5
Lak Meuang..................................**13** C4
Safarine.......................................**14** A2
Thailand-Burma Railway Centre......**15** B2
WWII Museum...............................**16** A2

SLEEPING
Apple's Guesthouse........................**17** B2
Bamboo House...............................**18** A2
Blue Star Guest House.....................**19** A2
Jolly Frog.....................................**20** A3
Kasem Island Resort.......................**21** C6
Ploy Guesthouse............................**22** A2
Pong Phen....................................**23** A2
River Kwai Hotel............................**24** C3
Sam's House.................................**25** A2
Thai Garden Inn............................**26** A2
VN Guest House.............................**27** B3

EATING
Floating Restaurants.......................**28** B4
Jukkru..**29** C4
Krua Chukkadon............................**30** C5
Market..**31** D4
Night Market................................**32** B2
Saisowo......................................**33** B3

DRINKING
1 More Bar...................................**34** B2
Buddha Bar..................................**35** B2
No Name Bar.................................**36** B2
Tham Naan...................................**37** C4

TRANSPORT
Bus Station...................................**38** D4
Long-Tail Boats.............................**39** C5
Train Station.................................**40** B2

To Royal River Kwai Resort
& Spa (4km); Sai Yok (45km);
Sangkhlaburi (203km)

Castle
Mall

To Bousawan Resort (3km)

Soi Vietnam
Soi Taiwan

To Felix River
Kwai Resort (2km)

Th Saengchuto

Th Mae Nam Khwae

Th Chaokhunen

Th Rong Hip Oi

Chinese
Cemetery

Chinese
Temple

Wat Neua

Th Ban Neua

Th Tesban Banrung

Th Kratai Thong

Th Hiran Prasat

Market

Th Bovon

Th Khu Meuang

Th Pak Phraek

Th Lak Meuang

Th U Thong

To Suphanburi
(130km)

Kanakan
Mall

Soccer
Field

City
Gate

Municipal
Office

Th Song Khwae

Mae Nam Khwae Yai

Mae Nam Mae Klong

Wat Chaichumphon

Th Wisuttharangsi

Th Sangchuto

Th Chukkadon

To Bangkok
(139km)

INFORMATION
AS Mixed Travel............................(see 17)
Bangkok Bank...............................**1** C4
Communications Authority of
  Thailand....................................**2** D5
Krung Thai Bank............................**3** A1
Main Post Office............................**4** D5
Thai Military Bank..........................**5** C4
Thanakarn Hospital........................**6** D5
Tourism Authority of Thailand (TAT)
  Office.......................................**7** D4
Tourist Police................................**8** B2

Mae Nam Khwae Noi

To Chung Kai Allied
War Cemetery (2km); Wat
Tham Khao Pun (3km)

To Wat Tham Mangkon
Thong (5km); Wat Tham
Khao Noi (13km); Wat
Tham Seua (13km)

Th Sala Klang

WHY BRIDGE THE RIVER KHWAE?

The construction of what is known today as the 'Death Railway' was an astonishing feat of engineering. However, the prisoners and conscripted workers who toiled day and night to build it paid a terrible price. More than 100,000 labourers died due to the extreme conditions and the brutality of their captors.

The railway was built during the Japanese occupation of Thailand (1942–43) in WWII. Its strategic objective was to link 415km of rugged terrain between Thailand and Burma (Myanmar) in order to secure an alternative supply route for the Japanese conquest of other west Asian countries. Some considered the project impossible but the track was completed despite a lack of equipment and appalling conditions.

Construction of the railway began on 16 September 1942 at existing stations at Thanbyuzayat in Myanmar and Nong Pladuk (Ban Pong) in Thailand. Japanese engineers estimated it would take five years to link Thailand and Burma by rail. In reality, the Japanese army forced the POWs to complete the 1m-gauge railway in just 16 months. Much of the work was done by hand with simple tools used to build bridges and carve cuttings into the sides of the mountains. Most bridges were made from timber, which allowed some POWs to attempt sabotage by placing termite nests nearby.

As the Japanese demand for faster construction grew, so conditions worsened. The meagre rice supplies were often laced with kerosene, a by-product of Allied bombing raids over rice stocks. Cholera, malaria and dysentery were rife, and Japanese guards employed barbaric punishments for anyone who stepped out of line.

The rails were finally joined 37km south of Three Pagodas Pass; a Japanese brothel train inaugurated the line.

The bridge that spans Mae Nam Khwae Yai near Kanchanaburi was in use for a mere 20 months before the Allies bombed it in 1945. Rather than a supply line, the route quickly became an escape for Japanese troops. After the war the British took control of the railway on the Burmese side of the border and ripped up 4km of the tracks leading to Three Pagodas Pass for fear of the route being used by Karen separatists.

On the Thai side, the State Railway of Thailand (SRT) assumed control and continues to operate trains on 130km of the original track between Nong Pladuk, south of Kanchanaburi, to Nam Tok. See p218 for information about riding this historic route.

Approximately 40km of the railway is now submerged under the Khao Laem Dam, while the remaining track on either side of the dam was dismantled. Hellfire Pass (Konyu Cutting), one of the most demanding construction points, can be seen today at the Hellfire Pass Memorial (p220).

The museum is south of the Death Railway Bridge.

JEATH WAR MUSEUM
พิพิธภัณฑ์สงคราม

This simple but poignant **museum** (Th Wisuttharangsi; admission 30B; ⏰ 8.30am-6pm) resembles the basic, cramped bamboo-*atap* huts in which POWs were kept. Newspaper cuttings and sketches offer harsh reminders of the brutal punishments meted out to the Allied prisoners by Japanese troops. Among them is the story of surgeon Sir Edward 'Weary' Dunlop, who saved hundreds of lives by operating on injured soldiers and fighting to improve basic medical conditions. The museum is run by the monks of Wat Chaichumphon (Wat Tai), and it's worth coming for the temple itself and the views from the banks of Mae Nam Mae Klong. 'JEATH' is an acronym of the countries involved in the railway: Japan, England, Australia/America, Thailand and Holland. The war museum is at the west end of Th Wisuttharangsi (Visutrangsi).

LAK MEUANG (CITY PILLAR)
ศาลหลักเมือง

The **city pillar** (lák meuang; Th Lak Meuang) is at the centre of the old town and gives shelter to the local spirits. Just down the road is a statue of King Rama III and the renovated city wall, which used to stretch for more than 400m and boast six fortresses. Three original cannons remain.

CHUNG KAI ALLIED WAR CEMETERY
สุสานสัมพันธมิตรช่องไก่

Chung Kai was the site of a major prisoner camp during WWII, and Allied prisoners built their own hospital and church close to here. Today relatively few people come to see this remote cemetery, which is the final resting place of 1700 soldiers. Most graves have short, touching epitaphs for the Dutch, British, French and Australian soldiers buried here.

The cemetery is 4km south of central Kanchanaburi across Mae Nam Khwae Noi and can be easily reached by bicycle or motorcycle.

WAT THAM KHAO PUN
วัดถ้ำเขาปูน

Continue past the Chung Kai Allied War Cemetery and go over a railway crossing to find this **temple** (admission 20B; ⏱ 6am-6.30pm), which has a collection of nine different caves. The first, and biggest cave, is home to a reclining Buddha, while the others have some particularly unusual features, including a fig tree's roots that hang all the way down into the cave, a crystallised column and a rock formation said to resemble a mermaid from the literature of Thai poet Sunthorn Phu. The exact origins of the temple are a mystery, though it is known that King Rama V visited here in 1870.

The caves have a somewhat ignominious history. It is rumoured that the Japanese used some of the caves to torture POWs during WWII. In 1995 a British tourist was murdered here by a drug-addicted monk.

WAT THAM SEUA & WAT THAM KHAO NOI
วัดถ้ำเสือ/วัดถ้ำเขาน้อย

These neighbouring hilltop monasteries have magnificent views of verdant fields and mountains. Wat Tham Khao Noi (Little Hill Cave Monastery) has an intricately designed Chinese-style pagoda while across the way, Wat Tham Seua (Tiger Cave Monastery) has several styles of chedi and an 18m-tall Buddha covered in a golden mosaic. In front of the image a conveyor belt has small silver trays on which 1B donations are made. You can walk to the top of the temples or take the easy option and go by cable car (10B).

The temples are around 14km south of the town centre. If you have a motorbike, take the right fork of the highway when you reach Tha Meuang, turn right across the Kheuan Meuang (City Dam) and right again on the other side of the river. By bicycle, you can avoid taking the highway by using back roads along the river. Follow Th Pak Phraek in Kanchanaburi southeast and cross the bridge towards Wat

Tham Mangkon Thong, then turn left on the other side and follow the road parallel to the river. After about 14km, you'll see the Kheuan Meuang dam up ahead – at this point you should start looking for the hilltop pagodas on your right. Buses (10B) leave from Kanchanaburi bus station to Ratchaburi every 20 minutes. Get off at Tha Meuang Hospital and hire a motorbike taxi (40B).

Activities
THAI COOKING

If you don't know your *sôm·đam* from your *đôm yam* then **Apple & Noi's Thai Cooking Course** (☎ 0 3451 2017; Apple's Guesthouse, Th Chaokunen; 1250B) can assist. The one-day Thai cookery course begins at the local market and ends, five dishes later, at the dining table.

TREKKING & CYCLING

Tour companies sell elephant rides, waterfall excursions and rafting tours, but there are many other activities to try.

For those with more time, and stamina, cycling tours, canoeing and jungle trekking can all be booked from Kanchanaburi. Some of the main roads offer stunning routes and are best enjoyed by bike, while going off-road provides access to waterfalls and caves that few get to see. Several trips stay overnight in a Mon or Karen village and involve a combination of rafting, trekking and elephant rides.

For those with less time, the countryside close to Kanchanaburi is replete with wonderful vistas and a bicycle is an ideal way to see them. One particularly scenic route lies immediately behind the backpacker guesthouses. From the northern end of Th Mae Nam Khwae, cross Sutjai Bridge and bear right. Explore Baan Thamakham and Baan Hua Hin, where lemongrass, corn, tapioca and teak trees soak up the sun while in the

---

DON'T BE A BUFFALO

The Bridge on the River Kwai movie made the waterway famous, and also ensured a generation grew up pronouncing it incorrectly. You should talk about the River Khwae (sounds like 'square' without the 's') and not Kwai (sounds like 'why'). Get it wrong and you'll be talking about the River Buffalo, which the Thais always find very amusing.

CENTRAL THAILAND

SINGING THE KARAOKE BLUES

The rivers running through Kanchanaburi look to be among the most peaceful places you could hope to find. They are generally quiet and tranquil, but come nightfall the karaoke/disco boats pump up the volume and serenity is forced to take a back seat.

Every weekend, Bangkokians and many Asian tourists are bussed in and taken onboard karaoke boats. The commotion used to make guesthouses along Soi Rong Hip Oi very unappealing, but now the all-nighters have stopped and they are just a temporary nuisance as they go by.

---

distance mist-covered mountains serve as a breathtaking backdrop.

Some package tours are cancelled if not enough people sign up, so check before booking. The following agencies are reputable:

AS Mixed Travel (☎ 0 3451 2017; www.applenoi -kanchanaburi.com; Apple's Guesthouse, Th Chaokunen) A well-organised company with longevity. Trips can be tailor-made to suit travellers' preferences, and pockets.

Good Times (☎ 0 3462 4441; www.good-times-travel .com; 63/1 Tha Mae Nam Khwae) All the standard day trips are available, as well as adventure packages to more remote areas. Cycling tours can be arranged from here.

KAYAKING

Paddling down the river in a canoe or kayak is a great way to get around. The French-managed **Safarine** (☎ 0 3462 5567; www.safarine .com; Th Mae Nam Khwae) arranges one- or two-day trips tailored to suit the customer.

Sleeping

Along a 1km stretch of Th Mae Nam Khwae there are numerous guesthouses offering simple rooms, usually with riverfront views. Across the river there are midrange and top-end resorts that come with all the bells and whistles you'd expect. The former backpacker mainstay along Soi Th Rong Hip Oi is much quieter these days due to the occasional karaoke cacophony from passing boats, but the disturbances are less frequent than before and there are budget guesthouses available here.

Along Th Saengchuto there are several midrange guesthouses, but the rooms nearer the river are cheaper and have far more character. Check out **Kanchanaburi Info** (www .kanchanaburi-info.com) for more choices.

BUDGET

The best deals in town can be found along the fast-growing Th Mae Nam Khwae strip. Rooms are basic but often come with great river views. During the peak season, and especially December, it's wise to call ahead to book a room with a view.

Jolly Frog (☎ 0 3451 4579; 28 Soi China; s 70B, d 150-290B; 🏊) It may lack a few of life's finer things, like towels and flushing toilets, but the backpackers who roll in from Th Khao San don't seem to mind.

Blue Star Guest House (☎ 0 3451 2161; 241 Th Mae Nam Khwae; r 150-650B; 🏊) Accommodation here ranges from backpacker simplicity to comfy rooms with air-con and TV. The mangled-looking wood on the riverfront bungalows is impressive.

Pong Phen (☎ 0 3451 2981; www.pongphen.com; Th Mae Nam Khwae; r 150-900B; 🏊 ⚓) Comfortable rooms, a good restaurant and a pool make Pong Phen stand out from the rest. Most rooms are centred on the pool rather than the river.

Bamboo House (☎ 0 3462 4470; 3-5 Soi Vietnam, Th Mae Nam Khwae; r 200-500B; 🏊) Set a little way from the main action, the river raft rooms and spacious garden give the place a genuine away-from-it-all vibe.

Apple's Guesthouse (☎ 0 3451 2017; www.applenoi -kanchanaburi.com; 3/17 Th Chaokunen; r with fan/air-con 450/650B; 🏊 ⚓) Apple and Noi's new guesthouse comes with the same hospitality and expertise as their old one. Noi's one-day Thai cooking courses (see p215) are popular.

VN Guest House (☎ 0 3451 4082; www.vnguesthouse .net; 44 Soi Th Rong Hip Oi; r 250-450B; 🏊) Away from the main strip, these simple raft-house rooms have some of the best views of the river, but you may have to put up with the odd passing karaoke boat.

Sam's House (☎ 0 3451 5956; www.samsguesthouse .com; Th Mae Nam Khwae; d 450-600B; 🏊) Bright and airy from reception to terrace, rooms are basic but come with some of the finest views of the lotus-covered water. Fan rooms are particularly good value.

MIDRANGE

Many midrange places offer discounts during the low season (April to November), but reservations should be made in advance.

Ploy Guesthouse (☎ 0 3451 5804; www.ploygh .com; 79/2 Th Mae Nam Kwai; r 600-950B; 🏊) Stylish and chic, this guesthouse stands head and shoulders above its budget-style neighbours. Outside bathrooms and a pleasant rooftop terrace are great extra touches.

Thai Garden Inn (☎ 08 5819 1686; www.thaigardeninn.com; 74/11 M4 Baan Tamakahm; r 650-850B; 🅿 🖭) Set just behind bustling Th Mae Nam Khwae is this peaceful 11-bungalow resort. Rooms are tastefully furnished with natural materials, while the upstairs restaurant is the place to be come sunset.

Kasem Island Resort (☎ 0 3451 3359, in Bangkok 0 2255 3604; r 800-1600B; 🅿 🖭) Located on an island in Mae Nam Mae Klong, here you can sit by your balcony and dip your toes in the water. Terraces and pavilions make great places from which to view the surrounding scenery. A free shuttle boat runs to and from Th Chaichumphon.

Bousawan Resort (☎ 0 3451 4324; off Th Mae Nam Khwae; r 1000B; 🅿) This gorgeous Thai-style resort with bungalows and raft rooms set among spacious grounds is a little removed from the main area, so transport is required.

TOP END

Although the following places fall into the top-end category, they do vary in quality. Most resorts are north of the bridge on either side of the river. Shop the online booking services for discounts.

River Kwai Hotel (☎ 0 3451 3348; www.riverkwai.co.th; 284/3-16 Th Saengchuto; r from 1500B; 🅿 🖭) The best option for those wanting to stay in the centre of town, but the rooms are unremarkable. The hotel includes 'Glitzy', the only nightclub in town.

Royal River Kwai Resort & Spa (☎ 0 3465 3297; 88 Kanchanaburi-Saiyok Rd; r from 2450B; 🅿 🖭) Beautiful grounds and chic rooms make this a splendid resort. The spa, with riverfront rooms, has a range of health treatments.

Felix River Kwai Resort (☎ 0 3455 1000; www.felixhotels.com; r from 3500B; 🅿 🖭) Kanchanaburi's granddaddy of resorts is starting to show its age but it remains a luxurious option with all manner of facilities.

Eating

Food options are numerous in Kanchanaburi. The **night market** (Th Saengchuto; 🕑 Thu-Tue) near the train station has a busy food section offering satays, shakes and even sandwiches. Food stalls light up the roadside close to the River Kwai Hotel on Th Saengchuto, while down by Th Song Khwae there are some good-quality floating restaurants, which are usually full of package-company tourists. Th Mae Nam Khwae has many Western-style restaurants. The **market** (Th Saengchuto) near the bus station is well known for its excellent *hǒy tôrt* (fried mussels in an egg batter).

Saisowo (no roman-script sign; Th Chaokunen; dishes 20-30B; 🕑 8am-4pm) A long-running noodle emporium with some of the finest *gǒo·ay đěe·o mǒo* for miles around.

Krua Chukkadon (no roman-script sign; Th Chukkadon; dishes 40-100B) This simple floating restaurant near the JEATH War Museum has a limited menu, but what it does, it does well. There's a bilingual menu and monolingual, though thoroughly charming, staff.

Jukkru (no roman-script sign; Th Song Khwae; dishes 50-120B) It lacks the glamour of the floating restaurants opposite, but Jukkru compensates with superb Thai cuisine. There is an unusually large vegetarian selection for a Thai restaurant. Look for the blue tables and chairs outside.

Drinking

Tourists tend to sip their beers along Th Mae Nam Khwae, which has several bars including the backpackers' retreat Buddha Bar and 1 More Bar; there are pool tables and even prostitutes towards the busier southern end. Thais meanwhile head to Th Song Khwae, which has a handful of restaurants and bars.

No Name Bar (Th Mae Nam Khwae) You have to admire any bar that has the logo 'Get shit-faced on a shoestring' emblazoned on its wall. The irreverent theme continues inside, along with a solid supply of snacks, veggie dishes and cocktails.

Tham Naan (Th Song Khwae) Live Thai band and a relaxed country theme. Whisky lovers will appreciate the variety of choices.

Getting There & Away

BUS

Kanchanaburi's **bus station** (☎ 0 3451 5907; Th Saengchuto) is to the south of the town. The following destinations are served: Bangkok's southern bus terminal (112B, three hours, every 20 minutes between 3.30am and 8pm), Bangkok's northern bus terminal (2nd/1st class 108/139B, three hours, every hour between 6.30am and 6pm), Nakhon Pathom (50B, two hours, every 15 minutes between 4am and 6.30pm) taking the old Bangkok route and departing from platform 14, Sangkhlaburi (2nd/1st class 174/273B, four hours, frequent between 7.30am and 4.30pm) and Suphanburi (50B, two hours, every 20 minutes between 4.50am and 6pm), from where you can connect to Ayuthaya and Lopburi.

If you're going south, head for Ratchaburi (50B, two hours, frequent departures) and change to a Hua Hin- or Phetchaburi-bound bus. If you're heading north, the quickest option is to head back to Bangkok's northern bus terminal and find a ride there.

TRAIN

Kanchanaburi's train station is around 2km northwest of the bus station. Kanchanaburi is on the Bangkok Noi–Nam Tok rail line, which includes a portion of the historic 'Death Railway' built by WWII POWs during the Japanese occupation of Thailand. The SRT promotes this as a historic route, and so charges foreigners 100B for any one-way journey along the line, no matter how short the distance. Coming from Bangkok Noi station (located in Thonburi), 100B isn't a bad price, but for short trips in Kanchanaburi it's extremely steep.

The most historic part of the journey begins north of Kanchanaburi as the train crosses the Death Railway Bridge and terminates at Nam Tok station. Ordinary trains leave Thonburi's Bangkok Noi station at 7.44am and 1.55pm for Kanchanaburi. Trains do the return trip leaving Kanchanaburi at 7.19am and 2.44pm. The journey takes three hours.

Trains along the historic section of the rail line leave Kanchanaburi heading north to Nam Tok at 5.57am, 10.50am and 4.19pm. Return trains depart from Nam Tok at 5.20am, 12.50pm and 3.15pm. The trip takes about two hours. From Nam Tok train station it's possible to walk to Sai Yok Noi waterfall, or you can flag down one of the frequent Sangkhlaburi–Kanchanaburi buses.

The SRT runs a daily **tourist train** (☎ 0 3451 1285) from Kanchanaburi to Nam Tok (one way 300B). This is the same train that carries the 100B passengers, but if you want to pay the extra you'll be rewarded with a certificate and a snack.

Getting Around

Trips from the bus station to the guesthouse area will cost 50B on a sǎhm·lór and 30B on a motorcycle taxi. Public sǒrng·tǎa·ou run up

and down Th Saengchuto for 10B per passenger (get off at the cemetery if you want the guesthouse area). The train station is within walking distance of the guesthouse area.

Motorcycles can be rented at guesthouses and shops along Th Mae Nam Khwae for 150B a day. Bicycle rentals cost 50B.

The river ferry that crosses Mae Nam Mae Klong costs 5B per person for a one-way trip.

Long-tail boats offer 1½-hour trips to various attractions by the riverside. Prices start at 700B but are negotiable, depending on how many are in a group. The boats leave from the pier off Th Chukkadon or from the JEATH War Museum.

AROUND KANCHANABURI

Step outside the provincial town and you'll be greeted by a patchwork of streams, rivers and waterfalls.

Thailand's largest area of protected forest offers opportunities to explore caves filled with glistening crystals, trek through untamed jungle and visit remote villages. It's possible to see some of the highlights on one-day outings from Kanchanaburi, but generally speaking the further northwest you go, the better it gets.

Those that make it up to Thong Pha Phum and Sangkhlaburi are able to experience life in truly unspoiled towns where life drifts along at a relaxed pace. They are also ideal bases from which to explore nearby national parks.

The following sites are organised geographically along the major access highways to make it easier to visit via public transport.

The waterfalls outside of Kanchanaburi are best visited during the rainy season from June to October or in November and December, when water levels are at their peak.

Erawan National Park

อุทยานแห่งชาติเอราวัณ

The seven-tiered waterfall at this 550-sq-km **park** (☎ 0 3457 4222; admission 200B; ☼ 8am-4pm, levels 1-2 to 5pm) is the best-known attraction, but there are several other natural features worth seeking out.

The waterfall's top tier is named due its resemblance to Erawan, the three-headed elephant of Hindu mythology. Walking to the first three tiers is simple work, but after that good walking shoes and some endurance are needed to complete the 1.5km hike. Levels two and four are particularly impressive, but be wary of monkeys who may snatch belongings while you're taking a dip.

Tham Phra That boasts a large variety of limestone formations. Guides with paraffin lamps lead visitors through the unlit cave, pointing out the translucent rocks, glittering crystals and bat-covered caverns. Geologists find the caves interesting due to a clearly visible fault line. You'll need your own transport to reach the cave, which is 12km northwest of the park entrance, or you can try and negotiate a ride with park staff. The approach road is a dirt track and there's a stiff walk up to the cave entrance. Another 5km north is the enormous and extremely scenic **Si Nakharin Reservoir**.

Around 80% of Erawan is forest, and many of the park's various trees can be seen along three nature trails, which range from 1km to 2km. Birdwatchers try to spy hornbills, woodpeckers and parakeets from the camping areas and observation trails. **Park bungalows** (☎ 0 2562 0760; www.dnp.go.th; camping 90-150B, bungalows 800-5000B) sleep between two and 52 people.

Buses from Kanchanaburi stop by the entrance of the Erawan waterfall (55B, 1½ hours, peak every hour from 8am to 5.20pm, off peak noon, 2pm and 4pm). The last bus back to Kanchanaburi is at 4pm. Within the park, you can rent bicycles for 20B to 40B per day.

Prasat Meuang Singh Historical Park

อุทยานประวัติศาสตร์ปราสาทเมืองสิงห์

This **historical park** (☎ 0 3459 1122; admission 40B; ◷ 8am-5pm) preserves the remains of a 13th-century Khmer outpost that may have been a relay point for trade along Mae Nam Khwae Noi. The restored ruins show a Bayon style of architecture and cover 73.6 hectares. They were declared a historical park under the administration of the Fine Arts Department in 1987.

All the park's shrines are constructed of laterite bricks and are situated in a huge grassy compound surrounded by layers of laterite ramparts. Sections of the ramparts show seven additional layers of earthen walls, suggesting cosmological symbolism in the city plan. Evidence of a sophisticated water system has also been discovered amid the ramparts and moats.

The town encompasses four groups of ruins, although only two groups have been excavated and are visible. The principal shrine, **Prasat Meuang Singh**, is in the centre of the park and faces east (the cardinal direction

---

> **TURNING OVER THE WRONG LEAF**
>
> The tapioca fields around Kanchanaburi occasionally get special attention from travellers. Tour guides report seeing visitors surreptitiously picking leaves and stuffing them into their bags. The guides then have to patiently explain that while the leaves may closely resemble a marijuana plant, they are just plain old tapioca.

---

of most Angkor temples). Walls surrounding the shrine have gates in each of the cardinal directions; the ponds and ditches around it represent the continents and oceans. A reproduction of a sculpture of Avalokitesvara stands on the inside of the northern wall and establishes Meuang Singh as a Mahayana Buddhist centre. The original is in the National Museum in Bangkok. Inside the main *prang* is a reproduction of a sculpture of Prajnaparamita, the goddess of wisdom in Mahayana Buddhism.

To the northeast of the main temple are the remains of a smaller **shrine** whose original contents and purpose are unknown. Near the main entrance to the complex at the north gate is a small **exhibition hall** that contains various sculptures of Mahayana Buddhist deities and stucco decorations, most of which are reproductions.

Prasat Meuang Singh is 40km west of Kanchanaburi and is best reached by private transport. Trains heading from Kanchanaburi to Nam Tok stop nearby at Tha Kilen station (100B; see opposite for train departure times). From here it's a 1km walk to the entrance, but it's best having some form of transport as the grounds are large.

Ban Kao Neolithic Museum

พิพิธภัณฑ์บ้านเก่ายุคหิน

During WWII a Dutch POW named HR van Heekeren unearthed a collection of ancient stone tools in Ban Kao, around 7km from Meuang Singh. After the war the former archaeologist returned and much of what he helped to excavate is now displayed in this **museum** (admission 50B; ◷ 9am-4pm Wed-Sun).

The Thai-Danish project led the excavation and concluded that the area was an important Neolithic burial site, dating back around 5000 years.

Fairly uninspiring displays detail the geology and geography of the province, while

CENTRAL THAILAND

the most intriguing feature is a collection of hollowed-out tree trunks that may have once been boats, or coffins.

Ban Kao is best reached by private transport. The train heading north of Kanchanaburi to Nam Tok stops 6km away at Tha Kilen stop (100B; see p218 for train departure times). There might be motorcycle taxis available at the train station for the remaining 3km trip to the museum.

Daen Maha Mongkol Meditation Centre
แดนมหามงคล

If you've ever dreamt of a world without TV, telephones and email, then this **meditation centre** (⏲ 5am-6pm) could be the answer. Founded in 1986, the retreat is well known among locals. Tamara, an English woman who has lived here for several years, can help with the two-hour meditation classes, which take place at 4am and 6pm. It's worth dropping by to drink in the serene atmosphere of the centre, which is set among beautifully maintained grounds. Cross the teak bridge over Mae Nam Khwae Noi to get in, and first pay respects before the wooden Buddha image in the meditation pavilion.

About 300 people stay at the centre, 200 of them permanently. Most are nuns, but there is a separate area for men. There is no charge for visiting or even staying at the centre, but donations are appreciated. Basic accommodation is available for those who want to immerse themselves in life here. White shirts and trousers are provided free at the entrance and should be worn.

The centre is off Hwy 323, 12km from the Tiger Temple, and is well signposted. By train, get off at Maha Mongkol station.

Tiger Temple
(Wat Luang Ta Bua Yanna Sampanno)
วัดหลวงตาบัวญาณสัมปันโน

Kanchanaburi's most expensive tourist attraction is also its most controversial. This **monastery** (☎ 0 3453 1557; admission 500B; ⏲ 12.30-3.30pm) affords incredible photo opportunities for visitors to get up close and personal with the big cats. Some of the temple's 30 tigers pose for pictures in a canyon while visitors are shepherded in and out in quick succession.

Despite the endless queues, the attraction has long been a source of controversy. Some ask why the tigers are so docile and others question the increasingly high entry fees. Abbot Phra Chan, who established the site

in 1994, told Lonely Planet that the tigers are never drugged and are healthy, but he declined to comment on the reasons for the increased admission charges. One explanation given for the tigers' placid manners is that they eat and are exercised immediately before their public appearances, and that they only come out during the hottest part of the day, when they would normally be inactive.

Work on an 'island' enclosure is under way but it will be some time yet before the 20 million baht project is complete. The opportunity to get so close to such awesome animals is rare, but we would encourage potential visitors to do their own research before deciding whether to go. If you do go, avoid wearing 'hot' colours, such as red or orange, which could excite the tigers.

The temple is 38km from Kanchanaburi on Hwy 323. You can take the Kanchanaburi–Sangkhlaburi public bus to the temple turnoff, from where it's a 2km walk to the entrance. Most travellers book an afternoon tour with a travel company.

Allegations about tiger trading, poor treatment of the animals and a lack of progress in developing the site (despite the rising entry fees) have been made, and denied by the temple. Visit www.careforthewild.org to see the UK conservation group's report on the temple.

Sai Yok Noi Waterfall
น้ำตกไทรโยค

If you want to see how Thais enjoy themselves, there is no better place than this waterfall, which is part of Sai Yok National Park (opposite). Thais flock here at weekends to sit on mats, munch *sôm·đam* (spicy green papaya salad) and watch the water tumble over the sloping rocks. Teenagers clamber up the rocks while younger children paddle in the shallow pools below.

The waterfall is 60km northwest from Kanchanaburi on Hwy 323 and easily reached by using the Sangkhlaburi–Kanchanaburi bus (45B, one hour, frequent departures); tell your driver you're going to *nám đòk sai yôhk nóy*. The last bus back is at 5pm. Nam Tok train station is 2km away (100B; see p218 for train departure times).

Hellfire Pass Memorial
ช่องเขาขาด

This **museum** (www.dva.gov.au/commem/oawg/thailand .htm; admission by donation; ⏲ 9am-4pm) is a joint

Thai-Australian project that remembers the tragedy of the 'Death Railway' in a simple and dignified manner. The museum doesn't have many artefacts, simply because there was so little equipment for prisoners to use, but it does use displays and video clips of survivors to outline events. A 4km-long walking trail (which takes three hours round trip) runs along the original railbed.

Close to the start of the trail, the most famous cutting is **Hellfire Pass** (known locally as Konyu Cutting). The area earned its name following the three-month 'Speedo' construction period where shifts of 500 prisoners worked 16 to 18 hours a day. The glow from burning torches cast eerie shadows of the Japanese guards and on the gaunt prisoners' faces, so that the scene was said to resemble Dante's *Inferno*.

Poor hygiene, a lack of medical equipment and the brutal treatment of prisoners claimed the lives of around 15,000 Allied prisoners of war. A further 100,000 civilian labourers from Southeast Asian countries also died.

The walk along the track includes stunning views of Khwae Noi Valley towards Myanmar and the **Pack of Cards** bridge, which earned its name after collapsing three times.

A walking trail map and audio guide are available. The museum is 80km northwest of Kanchanaburi on Hwy 323 and can be reached by Sangkhlaburi–Kanchanaburi bus (50B, 1½ hours, frequent departures). The last bus back to Kanchanaburi passes here at 4.30pm.

National Parks

Northern Kanchanaburi has a collection of **national parks** (☎ 0 2562 0760; www.dnp.go.th) that are home to cascading waterfalls, thick jungle and an array of wildlife. They form part of the Western Forest Complex, one of Asia's largest protected areas.

Entry to the parks is 200B for foreigners. Bungalows and camping facilities are available at most sites, but it is important to book ahead.

Park headquarters have free booklets and maps, and guides can be hired for 200B to 300B. The temperature range here can be between 8°C and 45°C, depending on the time of year, so bring appropriate clothing.

Some tour companies in Kanchanaburi can arrange guided tours of the parks; see p215.

SAI YOK NATIONAL PARK
อุทยานแห่งชาติไทรโยค

The 1400-sq-km **Sai Yok National Park** (☎ 0 3451 6163; www.dnp.go.th; admission 200B) is easy to reach and has several waterfalls, caves and some particularly rare animals.

The park was the setting for the famous Russian-roulette scenes in the 1978 movie *The Deer Hunter*. Notable wildlife here includes elephants, barking deer, wreathed hornbills, gibbons and red, white and blue queen crabs, first discovered here in 1983.

Near the main entrance are limestone caves, remains of a bridge on the 'Death Railway' and Japanese cooking stoves (little more than piles of bricks). The park is well signposted and free leaflets provide information about hiking trails and how to hire canoes, rafts or bicycles. A cycling route is available to the Kitti's hog-nosed bat cave, where the eponymous creature, the smallest mammal in the world, was first found in 1973.

Near the visitors centre is Nam Tok Sai Yok Yai (Sai Yok Yai waterfall), which is more of a creek than a waterfall. It empties into Mae Nam Khwae Noi near a suspension bridge.

Forestry department **bungalows** (☎ 0 2562 0760; 800-2100B) are available and sleep up to six. Several raft guesthouses near the suspension bridge offer fantastic views. One of the prettiest is **Saiyok View Raft** (☎ 08 1857 2284; r 800B), which has rooms with private bathrooms that look out onto the river. There are floating restaurants nearby and rows of food stalls near the visitors centre.

The entrance to the park is about 100km northwest of Kanchanaburi and 5km from Hwy 323. You can take the Sangkhlaburi–Kanchanaburi bus (60B, two hours, frequent departures) to the turn-off and hire a motorcycle taxi to reach the entrance. Tell the driver that you want *nám dòk sai yôhk yài*. The last bus back to Kanchanaburi passes at about 4.30pm.

Around 18km south of Sai Yok Noi is **Lawa Cave** (admission 200B), a 500m-long cave with five large caverns and imposing stalactites and stalagmites. To get here, private transport is best, or you can take the train to Nam Tok station and try to find a motorcycle taxi.

Long-tail boats near the suspension bridge can be hired for sightseeing trips along the river, and also to **Tham Daowadung** cave. It's wise to take a guide and torch with you before entering Tham Daowadung. Chartering a long-tail costs about 800B per hour, but rates are negotiable.

THONG PHA PHUM NATIONAL PARK

อุทยานแห่งชาติทองผาภูมิ

This **park** (☎ 0 1382 0359; Thong Pha Phum district) includes the Jorgrading waterfall and simple but breathtaking accommodation in **tree houses** (☎ 0 2562 0760; www.dnp.go.th; r600-1200B).

The 62km ride from Thong Pha Phum to the park is along a meandering but well-made road that is shaded by soaring hillside trees. The main Jorgrading Waterfall is 5km from the entrance.

Another 8km along Hwy 3272 is the frontier village of **E-Thong**, where 80% of the population is Burmese. In the centre of this village, **E-Thong Homestay** (☎ 08 7169 0394; r600-800B) can help with trips out. If things get too quiet in this remote frontier village, there is always the family karaoke machine.

KHAO LAEM NATIONAL PARK

อุทยานแห่งชาติเขาแหลม

With the mighty Khao Laem reservoir at its heart, this 1497-sq-km **park** (☎ 0 3453 2099; Thong Pha Phum district) is one of the country's most picturesque. The park headquarters are 28km south of Sangkhlaburi.

More than 260 species of wildlife have been recorded at the park, including gibbons, deer and wild boar. Ornithologists flock to **Kroeng Kravia Swamp** to view the birdlife, which includes Asian fairy bluebirds and green-billed malkohas. To reach the swamp, go to the Kroeng Kravia substation, 45km south of Sangkhlaburi.

The reservoir is surrounded by several waterfalls and huge limestone mountains. **Kra Teng Jeng** waterfall begins 400m from the park entrance and has a shaded trail leading towards the main falls; a guide is required to complete the 4km walk. Approximately 12km south from the park entrance is the 15m-high **Dai Chong Thong** waterfall.

Around 1km north from the park entrance is **Pom Pee substation** (☎ 0 2562 0760; www .dnp.go.th; r from 900B) with camping and bungalows; the main park only offers camping facilities. From here you can hire long-tail boats to cross the reservoir to Pha Pueng or Kai Uu substations, or head back to the Mon settlement of Wang Kha. Prices vary, but a boat with eight people would cost 2000B.

The **Lake Safari** (www.insideasia.travel; adult/child 15,400/10,780B) houseboat leaves from Khao Laem National Park on a leisurely four-day trip to Sangkhlaburi. It's also possible to privately hire the houseboat.

SI NAKHARIN NATIONAL PARK

อุทยานแห่งชาติศรีนครินทร์

The 1500-sq-km **park** (☎ 0 3451 6667; Si Sawat district) is dominated by the Si Nakharin Reservoir. The seven-tiered **Huay Mae Khamin** waterfall, close to the park entrance, is regarded as one of Thailand's most beautiful falls. Flowing from limestone mountains, its waters drop seven levels along a route stretching more than 2km.

Camping and bungalows (☎ 0 2562 0760; www.dnp.go.th; r 150-600B, bungalows 900-2700B) are available.

Facilities at the park headquarters are good, but getting there can be tricky. The 40km dirt track leading to Si Nakharin requires a four-wheel drive. Another option is the car ferry, which crosses the reservoir between Tha Ong Sit in the east and Tha Kamnantuet in the west. The ferry runs from 6am to 8pm and leaves once it is full, or you can charter it for 300B per vehicle. After the 45-minute crossing, the park entrance is 7km from Tha Kamnantuet. It's also possible to charter a speedboat on the east side from Tha Kradan pier (about 1500B).

CHALOEM RATANAKOSIN NATIONAL PARK

อุทยานแห่งชาติเฉลิมรัตนโกสินทร์

This relatively small **park** (☎ 0 3451 9606; Nong Preu district) has two main features: the caves of **Tham Than Lot Noi** and **Tham Than Lot Yai**. The former is fairly unremarkable but leads through to a pleasant 2.5km nature trail. At the end of the trail is Tham Than Lot Yai, an enormous cave with jagged stalactites.

At the **Slider Waterfall** it's possible to aquaplane 20m from top to bottom during the rainy season, something Thai children do with great aplomb.

Wildlife here includes Asian koels, long-tailed cuckoos famed for their apparent fear of heights: they rarely go above 10m. Tigers, leopards, gibbons and elephants live deep in the dry evergreen forests.

Sleeping options include **bungalows** (☎ 0 2562 0760; www.dnp.go.th; tents 300-500B, r 700-2700B) and there is a restaurant on-site. Another option is to stay nearby with a Karen family at the **Khao Lek Homestay** (☎ 08 7110 8445; per person 150B).

Most visitors arrive at this 59-sq-km park by private transport along Hwy 3086. One bus a day (75B, three hours, 7.45am) makes the 97km journey from Kanchanaburi to Dahn Chang. Ask to get off at Muang Tow, which is 2km from the park. Buses depart from Muang Tow for Kanchanaburi at 6.20am, 8.15am and 12.25pm.

THONG PHA PHUM
ทอง ผาภูมิ

Surrounded by cloud-capped mountains and dense forests, this tiny town is a great place to sample a quieter way of life. Thong Pha Phum acts as a stop-off point for those heading north to Sangkhlaburi, and also as an access point for nearby natural attractions.

The town is simple to navigate as there is just one main street, and at its heart is the marketplace. Mae Nam Khwae Noi runs parallel to the east of the town. Facilities are somewhat sparse, although there are two banks and a handful of guesthouses.

The market is a good place to go for an early-morning mingle, where the food ranges from sugary snacks to noodles. At night the hilltop **temple** is illuminated and casts a golden glow over a town that has already gone to bed. To reach the temple during the day, follow the riverfront road towards the main highway, cross a footbridge and then walk up.

South of Thong Pha Phum town is **Hin Dat Hot Springs** (admission 40B; ⊙ 6am-10pm). If the effects of the two geothermal pools aren't enough, there is a massage pavilion nearby. You can soak in the pools or brave the adjacent fast-running stream. The *bòr nám rórn* (hot springs) are accessible via the Sangkhlaburi–Kanchanaburi bus on Hwy 323 (Km105 marker) and are 1km from the main road.

Along the same road as the hot springs is **Nam Tok Pha That** (admission 200B), a pretty multi-level waterfall that doesn't get many visitors. There are areas where bathing is possible, but be wary of the slippery stones.

Kheuan Khao Laem, known locally as Vachiralongkorn Dam, is 9km northwest of the town. Among those who enjoy the views from the top of the dam is a troop of monkeys.

Sleeping & Eating

There are several guesthouses along the main road, and some hotels near the dam.

Som Jainuk Hotel (☎ 0 3459 9001; 29/10 Mu 1; r 200-500B; ⊠) Close to the market, this hotel has

simple fan rooms or comfortable stone-walled bungalows with balconies. Ask for June, who can offer invaluable travel advice.

Barn Cha Daan (☎ 0 3459 9035; Mu 1; r 450B; ⊠ ⊟) Near the main entrance to town, with split-level rooms set among a wooded courtyard. Rooms include TV, hot water and air-con.

Ban Suan (☎ 0 3459 98412; off Hwy 3272; r 650-1200B; ⊠) Outside of town, Ban Suan has great views of the dam, good facilities and an English-speaking manager, something of a rarity in these parts.

Restaurants around town reflect the large Burmese and ethnic communities who live here: the large metal pots full of tempting curries are typically Mon. The three-tiered Krua Tom Nam restaurant behind the market has views of the river. A few restaurants near the town's main entrance offer local dishes, but usually at night you'll see more cats than people.

Getting There & Away

Air-con buses leave from opposite Siam City Bank on the main road. Tickets are sold at the back of the **Krua Ngobah** (☎ 0 3459 9377) restaurant. Buses to Bangkok's northern terminal (202B, five hours, every 90 minutes) depart until 3.40pm, while buses to Sangkhlaburi (67B, 1½ hours, four times a day) also leave from here. Local buses leave from the market.

Getting Around

A good option is to negotiate with the motorbike taxi drivers at the market, as they will rent their bikes out for around 300B a day, depending on your bartering skills. *Sŏrng·tăa·ou* run up and down the main road and should cost no more than 10B for rides within town.

SANGKHLABURI
สังขละบุรี
pop 47,147

For most travellers Sangkhlaburi is the end of the line, but for many residents it marks the start of a new journey. Few places in Thailand have such a blend of ethnic identities, with Burmese, Karen, Mon, Thai and some Lao each calling this home. Many cross the Burmese border driven by economic need or through fear of oppression. The result is a melange of cultures, beliefs and even languages.

HELPING TO NURTURE NATURE

Covering 6200 sq km, **Thung Yai Naresuan** and **Huay Kha Khaeng Wildlife Sanctuary** form the largest mainland conservation area in Southeast Asia. Designated a Unesco World Heritage Site in 1991, the sanctuaries host an incredible range of fauna and flora.

Set in the northeastern corner of Kanchanaburi and sprawling into neighbouring provinces, the sanctuaries are largely a mountainous wilderness with rivers and streams separating the grassy lowlands and valleys.

In the past 50 years the amount of natural forest cover in Thailand has been drastically reduced but burgeoning environmental consciousness has seen more conservation and less destruction. The sanctuaries are protected areas, not national parks, so visitors require prior permission to get in. Despite this, some unwelcome visitors do still gain access to carry out illegal logging or hunt wildlife.

The sanctuaries are one of the last natural habitats for around 700 tigers, although a recent report suggested the area could sustain up to 2000 of the animals, if they were effectively protected. The **Western Forest Conservation Club** (WFCC; www.thungyai.org) monitors tiger activity. Sharing space with the tigers is a wide variety of wildlife; at the last count there were 400 types of birds, 96 reptiles and 120 mammals, including leopards, gaur, bears and maybe even Javan rhinoceroses. Living within the sanctuaries are 34 internationally threatened species. Reports suggest that one of the most sought-after animals around the Three Pagodas Pass area is the Gan monkey, highly valued for its supposed medicinal benefits.

Thung Yai Naresuan (meaning large field) takes its name from its enormous central grassland plain and the fact that King Naresuan once used the area as a temporary army base. Among the more unusual features are limestone sink holes, some of which are 2km long and 30m deep. Archaeologists believe the area has remains from the Pleistocene period, but for now these remain hidden away as no major research has been undertaken.

Huay Kha Khaeng has slightly more amenities and camping sites, though there are no restaurants or bungalows. During the rainy season flooding is common, so it's important to check the local situation before heading out. The park includes the **Khao Hin Daeng** nature study route, which can be reached by private transport via Uthai Thani by following Hwy 333, then Hwy 3438. The 6km study route has a pleasant viewpoint at Pong Thian and it's often possible to spot a great number of birds along this stretch.

There are two camping areas within Huay Kha Khaeng: Cyber Ranger Station and Huay Mae Dee. Cyber Ranger Station is 7km from the main office and has several waterfalls and valleys within trekking distance. The 37km off-road track to Huay Mae Dee passes by a Karen village and is set within thick forest. Thai-speaking guides can be hired from both sites. Camping sites (per tent 30B) are available, but you'll need to bring all your own equipment.

The main office is best reached by private transport. The closest buses or trains run is to Lan Sak, from where it's a 35km drive to the office.

Sanctuaries such as these are valuable because they are untouched and so tourism is not encouraged. The few hundred visitors that do come each year usually take part in scientific field trips. Anyone else wanting to enter should first get consent from the Royal Thai Forestry department.

Sangkhlaburi is a remote town that overlooks the enormous Kheuan Khao Laem (Khao Laem Reservoir), and owes its existence to the waters. It was founded after an old village, near the confluence of the three rivers that feed the dam, was flooded.

Several NGOs in town help the ethnic communities survive and fight for what few rights they have. As a result, there is a constant need for volunteers (see opposite).

The town comes to life on **Mon National Day**, celebrated during the last week of July.

Information

For money matters go to Siam Commercial Bank (ATM), near the market. Internet shops are also near the market and charge 25B per hour. There is an international phone in front of the post office on the main street.

Sights & Activities
WANG KHA
วังคา

Across what is reputedly Thailand's longest **wooden bridge** (Saphan Mon) sits this Mon settlement. The village relocated here after the dam's construction flooded the original settlement. Burma's constant conflicts pushed many Mon into Thailand and now Wang Kha has its own unmistakable character. Children play a form of cricket in the street, women smoke enormous cheroots and many wear traditional white face powder. The times are definitely changing though; there's also an internet cafe.

A **day market** in the centre of the village has pots of delicious Mon curry. North of the market is **Wat Wang Wiwekaram** (Wat Mon), the spiritual centre of the Mon people in Thailand. The temple has two complexes that are 600m apart. To the right of the T-junction is the multiroofed *wí·hǎhn* with heavy, carved wooden doors and marble banisters. To the left of the T-junction is the **Chedi Luang Phaw Uttama**; this was constructed in a similar style to that of the Mahabodhi *chedi* in Bodhgaya, India. At night the 6kg of gold that covers it is illuminated. Men may climb the few short steps to the top; women may not. In the same courtyard are an ageing *chedi* and a handicrafts market.

The temple is famous for being the home of a highly respected monk, Luang Phaw Uttama. Born in Burma in 1910, he fled to Thailand in 1949 to escape the civil war and was a cornerstone of the Mon community. He helped secure this area after the Mon village's previous location was submerged by the construction of the dam. In 2006 he died aged 97 at Bangkok's Srirat Hospital and his medical bills were covered by the queen.

KHAO LAEM RESERVOIR
เขื่อนเขาแหลม

This enormous lake was formed when the **Vachiralongkorn Dam** (known locally as Khao Laem Dam) was constructed across Mae Nam Khwae Noi in 1983. The lake submerged an entire village at the confluence of the Khwae Noi, Ranti and Sangkhalia Rivers. In the dry season it's still possible to see the spires of the village's **Wat Sam Prasop** protruding from the lake.

Canoes, long-tail boats and, sadly, jet-skies, can be found on the lake. Early morning here is a magical time, when mist and the sounds of nature envelope the water. Guesthouses can arrange trips out onto the water.

Volunteering
The large orange building overlooking the town is **Baan Unrak** (House of Joy; www.baanunrak.org), which cares for orphaned or abandoned children from ethnic groups. Since 1991 the home has grown in line with demand and now 140 children live there. As well as the children's home, Baan Unrak runs a weaving centre to help provide an income for local women, helps single mothers struggling to raise their children, and works with HIV/AIDS patients. Most of the children at Baan Unrak are Karen and all follow the home's neo-humanist philosophy of vegetarianism, universal love and meditation.

Due to the large refugee numbers in Sangkhlaburi there is great demand for such services, and volunteers are always needed. The home usually only accepts helpers for six months or longer, but visitors are welcome. The children stage yoga performances at the home every Wednesday at 6pm.

For short-term commitments, consider lending your English-language skills and elbow grease to the remote **Hilltribe Learning Centre** (via P Guest House; ☎ 0 3459 5061); see p50.

Sleeping
Burmese Inn (☎ 0 3459 5146; www.sangkhlaburi.com; 52/3 Mu 3; r 120-800B; 🛜) The cheapest place in town, and with good reason. Rooms range from the single, flimsy kind that cling to the hillside, or larger bungalows.

P Guest House (☎ 0 3459 5061; www.pguesthouse .com; 8/1 Mu 1; r 252-909; 🛜) With English-speaking staff and rooms with fabulous lake views, P Guest House is a safe choice. Fan-rooms are plain and have shared bathrooms. Trips can be arranged from here, along with motorbike, bicycle and canoe hire.

Samprasob Resort (☎ 0 3459 5050; www.samprasob .com; 122 Mu 3; r 600-3000B; 🛜) For a touch more comfort, this elegant resort has everything from compact double rooms to two-storey houses for the larger Thai groups that visit at weekends. Breakfast is included.

Eating
Guesthouses tend to be the favourite eating venues, thanks largely to their scenic waterfront locations. As with most Thai towns, the market offers the greatest variety of food. Be sure to sample some of the delicious Thai and Burmese curries (20B).

CENTRAL THAILAND

WHO ARE THE MON?

The Mon people have a proud history. As well as introducing Theravada Buddhism to the region, their Dvaravati kingdom covered much of the central plains of Thailand and Burma between the 6th and 11th centuries.

Today, many Mon have fled the oppressive regime in Burma and live as refugees around Sangkhlaburi. Less than a million people speak the Mon language and they face a fight to preserve their heritage, beliefs and independence.

For centuries there has been conflict between the Burmese and the Mon. The British exploited this tension during its colonisation of Burma by promising the Mon independence in return for their support. Once Burma achieved independence in 1948, the Mon launched a campaign for self-determination but protests were swiftly crushed, with Mon leaders killed and their villages razed. In 1974 a semi-autonomous state, Monland, was created and a ceasefire was declared in 1996, but clashes continue to this day.

Many Mon escape the violence by crossing the border into Thailand, predominantly around Sangkhlaburi. Of the town's 47,000 residents, 23,800 are from ethnic groups. Thailand does little more than tolerate their presence. The Mon are given Thai ID cards, although these paradoxically declare that the holder has almost no rights. Travel is restricted and there are checkpoints all around Sangkhlaburi and Three Pagodas Pass. Many Mon and Karen live in these areas, most working for 100B a day or less. They fear being fined, deported or even attacked and so often have a self-imposed curfew.

One breakthrough did occur in 2006 when the Thai government granted citizenship to 2000 Mon children in Sangkhlaburi who had been born in the kingdom.

In 2008 Burma's violent crackdown against protestors and the Nagris cyclone disaster created a fresh wave of people looking to flee the country. The Mon people in Burma continue to suffer and reports of rape, beatings and arrests are common. They are stuck between a country where they are repressed and a country where they have few rights. Because of this, there are fears their once proud traditions and culture could eventually become completely assimilated and lost forever.

Baan Unrak Bakery (snacks 25-90B) Vegetarians will love this meatless cafe, which has excellent pastries and Thai dishes. The cheese and red bean doughnut is nothing short of spectacular. The bakery is part of the Baan Unrak organisation (see p225).

Shopping

Visitors interested in Karen weaving should spend time at the small store at the Baan Unrak Bakery or the shop outside P Guest House; the products are made by the Baan Unrak women's cooperative.

Getting There & Away

Right across from the market is a bare patch of land that serves as Sangkhlaburi's bus station. Ordinary bus 8203 leaves Sangkhlaburi for Kanchanaburi (130B) at 6.45am, 8.15am, 9.45am and 1.15pm, and takes five hours. Air-con buses depart for Bangkok's northern terminal (1st/2nd class 333/259B) at 7.30am, 9am, 10.30am and 2.30pm on the four-hour journey south. These buses also stop at Sai Yok and Kanchanaburi. To the rear of the market is a minivan office where you can book tickets to Kanchanaburi (180B, three times a day). Stops include Thong Pha Phum (80B). A motorbike taxi to guesthouses will cost around 15B.

The distance between Kanchanaburi and Sangkhlaburi is about 230km. From Thong Pha Phum to Sangkhlaburi it's 74km.

AROUND SANGKHLABURI
Three Pagodas Pass
ด่านเจดีย์สามองค์

This frontier town may be within Thailand's borders but there's a distinct Burmese flavour to it. The pagodas (Phrá Jedii Săam Ong) after which the town is named are unremarkable, and the main reason many come here is to gain a day pass into secretive Myanmar.

On the other side of the border is the town of Payathonzu, which has a **souvenir market** and a few **teahouses**. It's important to check with locals before coming, as the Myanmar government habitually shuts its side of the border due to fighting between Burmese military and ethnic armies.

If there is no way through, the **market** on the Thai side is full of traders selling Burmese whisky, jewellery, cigars and bizarre health treatments involving goats' heads. At the entrance to one noodle restaurant is a time capsule which was buried in 1995 by Allied POWs to mark the 50th anniversary of the 'Death Railway'. If you're passing this way on 20 April 2045 you can see it being opened.

Should the border be open, foreigners can obtain a day pass, but it's not possible to gain a visa extension. You will need to temporarily surrender your passport and provide a passport photo to the Thai immigration office. At the Myanmar immigration office, a copy of the photo page of your passport and a passport photo is needed, plus 500B or US$10. When you return to Thailand, you will receive your passport back. There is a small photocopy shop near the Thai immigration office.

These days things seem peaceful enough, but Karen and Mon rebels used to fight the Burmese army for control of the pass. Any taxes the rebels could raise from smuggled goods helped fund their resistance movements. Even today the pass is said to be an important drug smuggling route, especially for amphetamines.

At the time of writing the border had been closed for more than a year.

Getting There & Away

Sǒrng·tǎa·ou leave from Sangkhlaburi's bus station (40B) every 45 minutes between 6.40am and 5.20pm. The 28km journey north takes around 40 minutes.

The border is a short walk from the *sǒrng·tǎa·ou* stop in Three Pagodas Pass.

CENTRAL THAILAND

Southeastern Thailand

There's nothing moderate about southeastern Thailand. Catering to holidaying hedonists and laid-back hippies, the region represents the many attractions of Thailand – in their extremes.

First there's Pattaya, a testosterone-fuelled, heavy-breathing resort town, where skirts are short and heels high. It's reinventing itself as a family place, but Pattaya still sweats a buzzy late-night aphrodisiac. At the other end of the region, in geography and intensity, is Mu Ko Chang National Marine Park, where islands rise from waters the colour of blue skies and are just as clear.

And then there's everything in between.

The razzle-dazzle of jewels lures dealers to Chanthaburi's gem markets. Equally alluring are Ko Samet's aquamarine waters and white beaches, which once earned it a name that translates to 'Vast Jewel Isle', and on weekends you can watch – or join – Bangkok locals as they make a different kind of trade: weekday anxieties for weekend amusements.

More subdued but no less attractive are the region's subtle hints of Old Siam: teak houses and pier buildings scattered along the coast. Si Racha's pier-front looks across the cargo ship–studded water to Ko Si Chang, a quiet island with hillside temples often overlooked by weekend Bangkok escapees. Trat Province, with its riverside ambience and excellent budget lodgings, invites backpackers en route to Mu Ko Chang and Cambodia to ease off the travellers' accelerator.

Finally, several national parks round out the offerings. In the northern area around Prachinburi, white-water rafting and mountain biking are on offer, while in the smaller parks near the coast, day trips to tiered waterfalls offer shady respite from the buzz of towns and traffic.

HIGHLIGHTS

- Taking in the temples and shrines of **Ko Si Chang** (p232) from the back of a souped-up túk-túk
- Transitioning from wild to mild in **Pattaya** (p234), with its cabaret- and club-filled nightlife and its amusement-park, family-oriented day life
- Navigating the footpaths from beach to beach and bungalow to bungalow along the eastern coast of **Ko Samet** (p245)
- Swinging in a hammock while contemplating another lazy beach day on mellow **Ko Mak** (p269)
- Embarking on a sweaty jungle trek (and cooling waterfall swim) on mountainous **Ko Chang** (p261)

★ Ko Si Chang
★ Pattaya
★ Ko Samet
Ko Chang ★
★ Ko Mak

- BEST TIME TO VISIT: NOVEMBER–MAY
- POPULATION: 3.6 MILLION

SOUTHEASTERN THAILAND

Climate
Southeastern Thailand experiences a three-season, monsoonal climate: a relatively cool dry season in November and December is followed by a hot dry season stretching from January to May. A hot wet season follows from June to October.

During the wet season, Ko Samet stays unusually dry and is the region's most 'monsoon proof' island.

National Parks
The islands of Ko Samet (p245) and Ko Chang (p258) fall within national parks (Khao Laem Ya/Mu Ko Samet National Park and Mu Ko Chang National Marine Park, respectively) and are the region's biggest drawcards after Pattaya. Ko Chang is covered in dense, unspoilt forest, and while the island's coastline is developing fast, the interior is still rugged and untouched.

Khao Chamao/Khao Wong (p244), Khao Khitchakut (p255) and Nam Tok Phlio (p255) National Parks hold fewer surprises, but are worth a visit for a break from the coastal buzz.

Getting There & Away
For the majority of travellers, a trip into, and then through, southeastern Thailand is an eastward progression from Bangkok to Hat Lek on the Cambodian border. Air-con buses link the capital with all major towns, and there are flights from Phuket and Ko Samui to Pattaya, and from Bangkok to Trat. A once-daily train service links Bangkok with Pattaya.

If you are coming from northeast Thailand, regular air-con bus services travel to Rayong and Pattaya from Khorat and Ubon Ratchathani.

Getting Around
Getting around southeastern Thailand is straightforward, with good bus links and steady minivan services between all main attractions. Hourly ferries run to the region's main islands throughout the year, although services to the outlying islands of the Ko Chang archipelago are reduced during the wet season.

CHONBURI PROVINCE

SI RACHA
ศรีราชา
pop 141,400
Si Racha is a jumble of fishing-village roots and immigrant implants. A labyrinth of rickety piers and pontoons testifies to its Old Siam history, while the glitter and glam of sushi restaurants and karaoke bars highlight the Japanese and Korean immigrants of the present. Down on the seafront you're just as likely to see fishermen mending their nets in a tropical twilight as you are a crowd of hundreds aerobicising as one colour-coordinated unit. Though ships waiting to dock at Si Racha's modern port stud the near horizon, they're far enough away not to spoil the illusion of days gone by.

Si Racha is home to the famous *nám prík sěe rah·chah* (spicy sauce), a perfect complement to the town's excellent seafood.

Information
Coffee Terrace (94 Th Si Racha Nakorn 1; noon-11pm) Coffee (45B) and internet (25B per hour).
Krung Thai Bank (cnr Th Surasak 1 & Th Jermjompol)
Post office (Th Jermjompol) A few blocks north of the Krung Thai Bank.
Samitivej Sriracha Hospital (0 3832 4111; Th Jermjompol, Soi 8) Regarded as Si Racha's best.

Sights
Working-class Si Racha's attractions are limited, but the shambling ambience of the waterfront piers is worth a second glance, and **Ko Loi**, a small rocky island connected to the mainland by a long jetty at the northern end of Si Racha's waterfront, is fun to explore. Here you'll find a **Thai-Chinese Buddhist temple** (daylight), a low-key festival atmosphere, food stalls, and a couple of giant ponds with turtles of every size, from tiny hatchlings to seen-it-all-before seniors. Just south of Ko Loi jetty is the **Health Park**, where you can spot – or join – fitness-conscious individuals walking off a meal. Just a little inland is **Night Square**, where an evening market sets up – it's not too exciting but it's a good landmark to get your bearings.

Sleeping
The most authentic (read: basic) places to stay are the wooden hotels on the piers. A couple of better hotels are located inland.

Siriwatana Hotel (0 3831 1037; 35 Th Jermjompol; s/d 160/200B) This wooden hotel sits above the sea – in fact, you can look straight through the squat toilet's hole to the ocean. It's simple, but the basic rooms are cheap.

Samchai (0 3831 1800; Soi 10; r 300-450B;) The Samchai has a similar ambience, though it feels a bit like a port: cement floors with yellow lines wind through the large complex. When we visited a few of the rooms were getting a facelift with new floors and paint (both

SOUTHEASTERN THAILAND

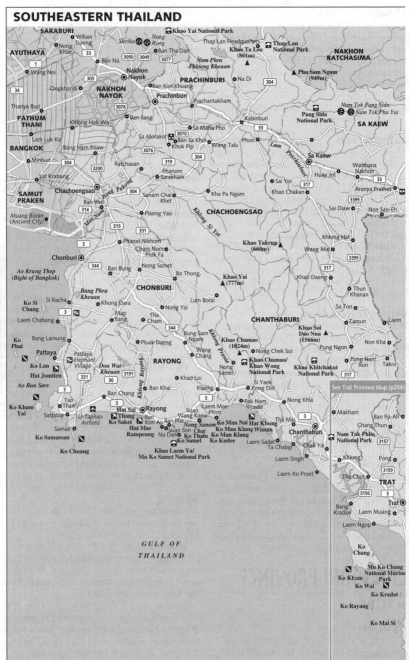

turquoise). The highest price should secure you air-con and a hot-water shower.

Seaview Sriracha Hotel (☎ 0 3831 9000; 50-54 Th Jermjompol; r 890-1150B; ✷ ▯) Lovely rooms are large and comfortable, and some have delicious views of the sea and piers. Rooms facing the street can be a tad noisy, but Si Racha is not Times Square, and a gentle hush settles relatively early.

City Hotel (☎ 0 3832 2700; www.citysriracha.com; 6/126 Th Sukhumvit; r from 2300B; ✷ ▯ ▣) Si Racha's fanciest hotel comes with wi-fi internet, a swimming pool and a gym. Service is slick but friendly, and the slightly austere rooms are softened with a veneer of Asian decor, and marble sinks.

Eating & Drinking

Si Racha is famous for seafood, and a sprawling night market kicks off around 5pm on Th Si Racha Nakorn 3.

Picha Bakery (☎ 0 3832 4796; cnr Th Jermjompol & Th Surasak 1; coffee 40B, snacks 20-40B; ☯ breakfast, lunch & dinner) Baked goodies, excellent coffee and spotless air-con surroundings make this a convenient haven from Si Racha's busy streets. The iced coffee is especially good.

Lahp Ubon (Southeast of Night Square; dishes 20-80B; ☯ breakfast, lunch & dinner) An Isan place with yummy *nám đòk mŏo* (spicy pork salad). The menu doesn't offer English (and neither does the sign out front), but thankfully it has pictures so just point to whatever looks good.

Moom Aroy (dishes 100-350B; ☯ lunch & dinner) Across from Samitivej Hospital, its name means 'delicious corner', and we have to agree. With soft lighting, tiered seating and views of the pier and squid rigs, this large restaurant is one of the best places to eat in Si Racha. Turn left at the hospital and look for the tank with the 2m fish out front. There's no roman script sign.

Pop (Th Jermjompol; dishes 60-220B; ☯ 5-11pm) More like 'Rock', this waterfront beer-hall-meets-music-club boasts a menu ranging from salty snacks to full meals.

Other recommendations:

Seafood stalls (Ko Loi jetty; dishes 40-160B; ☯ lunch & dinner) Perched on the Ko Loi jetty, these humble spots specialise in fresh seafood. There is no English menu but it's all good.

Getting There & Around

Frequent buses travelling to Si Racha depart from both Bangkok's Eastern (Ekamai) and Northern (Mo Chit) Stations from 5am to 9pm

SOUTHEASTERN THAILAND

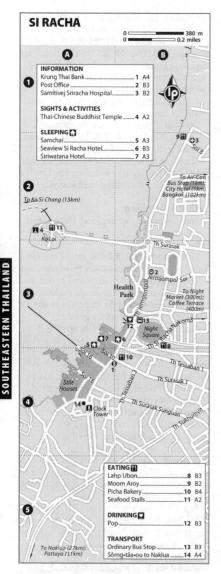

SI RACHA

0 _____ 380 m
0 _____ 0.2 miles

INFORMATION
Krung Thai Bank..........................**1** A4
Post Office..................................**2** B3
Samitivej Sriracha Hospital..........**3** B2

SIGHTS & ACTIVITIES
Thai-Chinese Buddhist Temple......**4** A2

SLEEPING
Samchai.....................................**5** A3
Seaview Si Racha Hotel................**6** B3
Siriwatana Hotel.........................**7** A3

To Ko Si Chang (13km)
Ko Loi

To Air-Con
Bus Stop (1km);
City Hotel (1km);
Bangkok (102km)

Th Surasak

Health
Park

Jermjompol Soi 1

To Night
Market (300m);
Coffee Terrace
(400m)

Night
Square

Th Si Racha Nakorn

Th Tessaban

Th Tessaban 1

Th Surasak 1

Th Surasak Sunguan

Stilt
Houses

Clock
Tower

Th Sukhumvit

To Naklua (27km);
Pattaya (31km)

EATING
Lahp Ubon....................................**8** B3
Moom Aroy...................................**9** B2
Picha Bakery................................**10** B4
Seafood Stalls..............................**11** A2

DRINKING
Pop...**12** B3

TRANSPORT
Ordinary Bus Stop.......................**13** B3
Sŏrng·tăa·ou to Naklua.................**14** A4

SOUTHEASTERN THAILAND

(ordinary/air-con 73/94B, 1¾ hours). Ordinary direct buses stop on the waterfront, but through buses and air-con buses stop on Th Sukhumvit (Hwy 3), near the Laemthong Apartments, and from there túk-túks (motorised three-wheeled pedicab) go to the pier (40B). There are also buses to and from Suvarnabhumi Airport, 10 times a day from 6am to 6.40pm (85B).

There is one train from Bangkok bound for Pattaya per day. It leaves Hualamphong at 6.55am and returns from Si Racha at 2.50pm (3rd class 25B to 35B, three hours).

White sŏrng·tăa·ou (small pick-up trucks) to Naklua (north Pattaya) depart from the clock tower throughout the day (25B, 30 minutes). In Naklua catch another sŏrng·tăa·ou (10B to 20B) to central Pattaya. Local buses (40B, 30 minutes) run to Pattaya from near the Laemthong Apartments on Th Sukhumvit.

Boat services to Ko Si Chang leave from the end of Ko Loi jetty (p234), and you can easily get around town via motorcycle taxi or túk-túk for about 30B to 40B.

KO SI CHANG
เกาะสีชัง
pop 4500
With a fishing-village atmosphere, gentle hills studded with Chinese and Thai temples, and beachfront reminders of a stately royal palace, Ko Si Chang is practically the anti-Thai island. No sweeping sandy beaches, no coconut groves – and no hoards of tourists.

Enrich your mind through meditation in the limestone caves of the Tham Yai Phrik Vipassana Monastery and exercise your body by paddling a kayak to nearby Bat Island, where there's good snorkelling.

On weekdays you'll have this gentle footfall on the Thai tourist trail all to yourself, but things liven up at the weekend when Bangkok holidaymakers arrive.

Orientation & Information
The island's one small settlement faces the mainland and is the terminus for the ferry. A bumpy road network links the village with all the other sights.
Kasikornbank (99/12 Th Atsadang) Has an ATM and exchange facilities.
Post office (Th Atsadang) Near the pier.
www.koh-sichang.com An excellent source of local information.

Sights & Activities
The Buddhist **Tham Yai Phrik Vipassana Monastery** (☎ 08 5388 0059, 0 3821 6104; ☉ dawn to dusk) is built around several meditation caves running into the island's central limestone ridge, and offers fine views from its hilltop chedi (stupa). Monks and mâa chee (nuns) from across Thailand come to take advantage of the caves' peaceful environment, and foreign-

monastic life are also welcomed. Studying at the monastery is free of charge (phone ahead to make sure there's room and bring your passport), but you'll be expected to follow the monastery's strict code of conduct. Whether you visit for an hour, or stay a month, leave an appropriate donation (roughly equivalent to basic food and lodging if staying a few days) with the monk or nun who shows you around. Your tour will likely be extensive, and if you have any interest in Buddhism it will be well worth your time.

The western side of the island has some OK swimming spots. **Hat Tham Phang** (Fallen Cave Beach) in the southwest has simple facilities with deckchair and umbrella rental. A beach area along the coast by Hat Tha Wang Palace (below) is popular with locals, and the island's best swimming is at **Hat Sai Kaew** to the south.

At the western end of the island (2km from the pier), you can visit **Hat Tha Wang Palace** (Th Chakra Pong; admission free; 9am-5pm). The carefully managed lawns are a prime picnic spot for visitors from Bangkok, who share the gardens with foraging white squirrels. The palace was once used by Rama V (King Chulalongkorn) over the summer months, but was abandoned when the French briefly occupied the island in 1893. The main throne hall – a magnificent golden teak structure known as Vimanmek Teak Mansion – was moved to Bangkok in 1910 (p138). The Fine Arts Department has since restored the remaining palace buildings.

Overlooking Hat Tha Wang is a large white stupa that holds **Wat Atsadang Nimit** (daylight), a small, consecrated chamber where Rama V used to meditate. The unique Buddha image inside was fashioned more than 50 years ago by a local monk. Nearby is a stone outcrop wrapped in holy cloth, called Bell Rock because it rings like a bell when struck.

Near Wat Atsadang Nimit a large limestone cave, **Tham Saowapha** (admission free; daylight), plunges deep into the island. Have a peek inside if you've got a torch.

Just before you reach the palace is the **Cholatassathan Museum** (admission by donation; 9am-5pm Tue-Sun) run by the Aquatic Resources Research Institute. The displays are small but there are a few interesting ones on the marine life in the area.

The most imposing sight on the island is the ornate **San Jao Phaw Khao Yai Chinese Temple**

(daylight). During Chinese New Year in February, the island is overrun with Chinese visitors from the mainland. This is one of Thailand's most interesting Chinese temples, with shrine caves, multiple levels and a good view of the ocean. It's east of the town, high on a hill overlooking the sea.

Several locals run **snorkelling trips** to Koh Khang Khao (Bat Island) off Ko Si Chang's southern tip. A boat for 10 people will cost around 2500B. Ask at Pan & David Restaurant (p234) or the Tiewpai-Park Resort (p234).

Sea kayaks are available for rent (150B per hour) on Hat Tham Phang. A nice paddle is down the coast to Koh Khang Khao, which is also a good spot for snorkelling. Recharge at the **Si Chang Healing House** (0 3821 6467; 167 Mu 3 Th Makham Thaew; 8am-6pm Thu-Tue), which offers massage and beauty treatments (400B to 800B) in a garden labyrinth opposite Pan & David Restaurant.

Sleeping

Rim Talay (0 3821 6237; 38/3 Mu 2 Th Devavongse; r 500-800B, houseboats 1000-1500B;) Behind the Pan & David Restaurant, this waterside spot has simple but clean air-con rooms, and a selection of colourful Thai fishing boats that have been transformed into mini-apartments sleeping up to five people.

Sripitsanu (0 3821 6034; 38/3 Moo 2 Th Devavongse; r 550-1000B;) The simple rooms are just that, but they all come with dazzling views of the water and you can hear the sea sloshing onto the rocks below you. A couple of air-con rooms are built into the hillside and plastered with shells – both inside and out.

Sichang View Resort (0 3821 6210; r 600-1400B;) You'll need transport to make this your island base, but the rooms are spacious and the landscaping is smooth, with lots of stone. It's a relaxing getaway, and sunset is special. The hotel's restaurant features a clifftop setting and excellent seafood from 180B to 300B. To get here, follow the road up the hill past the Chinese temple; after 1.5km the resort is on your right.

Sichang Palace (0 3821 6276; Th Atsadang 81; r 1200-1400B;) The lobby features an ostentatious display of wooden furniture and carvings, but the modern rooms are sun-dappled (gold wallpaper adds to the hue) and come with balconies. You'll pay an extra 200B for a sea view, and non-guests can use the hotel pool for 50B.

Other recommendations:

Tampang Beach Resort (☎ 0 3821 6179; r from 450B; 🔀) The staff don't speak much English, but the beach-front location is excellent. Rooms are simple.

Tiewpai-Park Resort (☎ 0 3821 6084; tom_tiewpai@hotmail.com; Th Atsadang; r 200-850B; 🔀) Spread throughout a quiet glade, this central option has super-basic rooms with shared bath right up to multi-family digs. It's close to the pier and good for local information and snorkelling trips.

Eating

The town has several small restaurants, with simply prepared seafood your best bet.

our pick Pan & David Restaurant (☎ 0 3821 6629; 167 Mu 3 Th Makham Thaew; dishes 40-260B; 🕙 breakfast, lunch & dinner, Wed-Mon) With free-range chicken, homemade ice cream (we thoroughly enjoyed the maple-pecan), French-pressed coffee, a wine list and excellent Thai dishes, the menu can't go wrong. Phoning ahead for a booking is recommended.

Getting There & Away

Boats to Ko Si Chang leave hourly from 7am to 8pm from the Ko Loi jetty in Si Racha (60B). From Ko Si Chang boats shuttle back hourly from 6am to 6pm. Boats leave promptly. A túk-túk to the ferry from Si Racha's waterfront hotels is 30B.

Getting Around

Ko Si Chang's túk-túks are big and bad and they'll take you anywhere for 40B to 60B. Island tours are available for around 300B: you might need to haggle. Motorbikes are available to rent from Tiewpai-Park Resort for 250B per day. You can also rent bicycles for around 120B to 150B per day at several places along Th Atsadang.

PATTAYA

พัทยา

pop 117,000

A sex-crazed and sweaty testament to profitable pleasure-seeking, Pattaya has lured tourists for almost four decades, and it's showing no sign of slowing down. As past visitors move on to more genteel Thai resorts, first-time travellers from Russia and Eastern Europe now air their new passports with a fling in Asia's first and foremost Sin City.

The cast may be evolving, but the scenery and soundtrack remain the same. The gorgeous half-moon of Pattaya Bay swoops around the headland to (slightly) more refined Hat Jomtien, and sea breezes whip up a heady cocktail of suntan lotion, fast food and jet-ski fumes. Wide-eyed package tourists jostle with Indian tailors, ruddy-faced middle-aged Western men, and beachfront fruit and seafood vendors. Thumping beats, cruising 'baht buses' and the commercial hubbub provide an irresistible symphony. After dark the tourists' eyes open even wider with a stroll past Pattaya's infamous go-go bars amid the sex tourism hub of Walking St.

Pattaya's a stay-up-late kind of town, but wake up earlier than most and there are activities galore to redress your daytime/nighttime balance. Hit the dive shops then head out to explore the city's offshore reefs and wrecks, or get some fresh air on world-class golf courses. And if you're here with the family, the kids (and mum and dad) will find plenty to do to make it a real holiday.

The town's wicked essence remains defiantly intact, but around the fringes it's softening and becoming more inclusive. If you welcome this town with a dash of confidence and a pinch of adventure, Pattaya's sun-kissed pursuit of happiness might prove irresistible.

History

US GIs kick-started Pattaya's dramatic transformation from quiet fishing village into throbbing tourist mecca when they ventured down the coast in search of fun and frolics from their base in Nakhon Ratchasima. That was 1959. During the Vietnam War, the flow became a flood as troops on leave arrived to soak up Pattaya's cocktail of sun, sand and sex. Package – and sex – tourists followed, and Southeastern Thailand's golden goose grew fat on the seemingly bottomless pot of dollars pouring into the local economy.

More recently Pattaya is striving to reposition itself as a 'family friendly' destination, and while the grit, glitz and seedy glamour remain, the 'town that sex built' is now offering more attractions that won't have the kids asking awkward questions.

Orientation

Curving around Ao Pattaya (Pattaya Bay), Hat Pattaya (Pattaya Beach) is the city's showcase stretch of sand. Th Hat Pattaya (known colloquially as Beach Rd) runs along the waterfront and is lined with hotels, shopping centres and

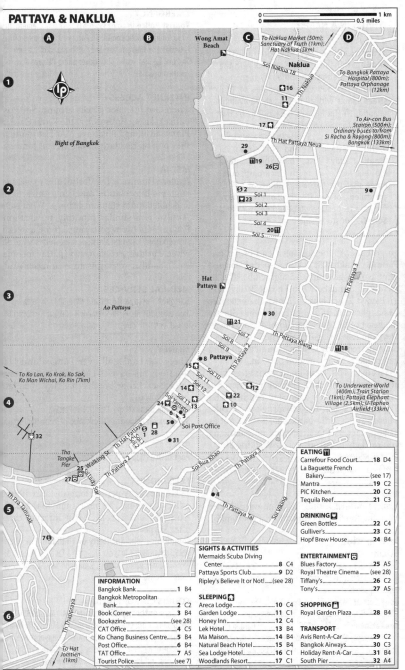

PATTAYA & NAKLUA

SOUTHEASTERN THAILAND

INFORMATION

Bangkok Bank	**1** B4
Bangkok Metropolitan Bank	**2** C2
Book Corner	**3** B4
Bookazine	(see 28)
CAT Office	**4** C5
Ko Chang Business Centre	**5** B4
Post Office	**6** B4
TAT Office	**7** A5
Tourist Police	(see 7)

SIGHTS & ACTIVITIES

Mermaids Scuba Diving Center	**8** C4
Pattaya Sports Club	**9** D2
Ripley's Believe It or Not!	(see 28)

SLEEPING

Areca Lodge	**10** C4
Garden Lodge	**11** C1
Honey Inn	**12** C4
Lek Hotel	**13** B4
Ma Maison	**14** B4
Natural Beach Hotel	**15** B4
Sea Lodge Hotel	**16** C1
Woodlands Resort	**17** C1

EATING

Carrefour Food Court	**18** D4
La Baguette French Bakery	(see 17)
Mantra	**19** C2
PIC Kitchen	**20** C2
Tequila Reef	**21** C3

DRINKING

Green Bottles	**22** C4
Gulliver's	**23** C2
Hopf Brew House	**24** B4

ENTERTAINMENT

Blues Factory	**25** A5
Royal Theatre Cinema	(see 28)
Tiffany's	**26** C2
Tony's	**27** A5

SHOPPING

Royal Garden Plaza	**28** B4

TRANSPORT

Avis Rent-A-Car	**29** C2
Bangkok Airways	**30** C3
Holiday Rent-A-Car	**31** B4
South Pier	**32** A4

WHAT'S IN A NAME?

Given Pattaya's international appeal, some of the streets are known by both their Thai and English names. We have stuck with the Thai names, although some city maps use the English equivalent. Examples of Thai street names with their English equivalent include: Th Hat Pattaya (Beach Rd), Th Hat Jomtien (Jomtien Beach Rd), Th Hat Pattaya Neua (North Pattaya Rd), Th Pattaya Klang (Central Pattaya Rd) and Th Pattaya Tai (South Pattaya Rd). To further confuse matters, while all maps (including ours) agree that the two alleys south of Soi 13 are called Soi Yamato and Soi Post Office, they are respectively labelled Soi 13/1 and Soi 13/2 on street signs.

---

go-go bars. At the southern end of Th Hat Pattaya, Walking St is a semi-pedestrianised jumble of restaurants and nightclubs. The alleyways running between Th Hat Pattaya and Th Pattaya 2 each have their own character: Soi 13 has pleasant, midrange hotels while Soi 3 is the heart of the gay area, dubbed 'Boyztown'. Development is ongoing with new places popping up frequently – shop around a little and you're likely to find a good bargain.

Head to Hat Jomtien, a 6km stretch of attractive beach and cleaner water, for a mellower scene. It's only 5km south of Hat Pattaya, or a 20B to 40B sŏrng·tăa·ou ride. There's still a girlie-bar scene, but it's not as in your face as the street-side pole-dancing you're likely to encounter on Walking St.

Hat Naklua, a smaller beach 1km north of Pattaya, is also quiet(er).

MAPS
Explore Pattaya, a local magazine available free from the tourist office, includes a good map.

Information
BOOKSHOPS
Book Lovers (Map p238; Soi 3; ⏲ 10am-6pm Mon-Sat) Has a good selection of used, reasonably priced English and German paperbacks.

Book Corner (Map p235; Soi Post Office; ⏲ 10am-10pm) English-language fiction and travel guides.

Bookazine (Pattaya Map p235; 1st fl, Royal Garden Plaza, Th Hat Pattaya; ⏲ 11am-11pm; Hat Jomtien Map p238; Th Hat Jomtien, ⏲ 11am-11pm) Travel books, literature and magazines.

EMERGENCY
Tourist Police (Map p235; ☎ 0 3842 9371, emergenc 1155; tourist@police.go.th; Th Pattaya 2) The head office is beside the Tourism Authority of Thailand office on Th Phra Tamnak with police boxes along Pattaya and Jomtien beaches.

INTERNET ACCESS
There are internet places around Soi Pos Office (aka Soi Praisani), at the Royal Garde Plaza and along Th Pattaya 2. At Hat Jomtien they pop up regularly along Th Hat Jomtien

MEDIA
Explore Pattaya, a free fortnightly magazine contains information on events, attraction and hotel and restaurant listings. *What's O Pattaya* is a similar monthly publication *Pattaya Mail* (www.pattayamail.com), a weekl newspaper, covers Pattaya's famed social ill while *Pattaya People* (www.pattayapeople com), another weekly, is an even racier read

MEDICAL SERVICES
Bangkok Pattaya Hospital (☎ 0 3842 9999; www .bph.co.th; 301 Mu 6, Th Sukhumvit, Naklua; ⏲ 24hr) Fo first-class health care.

MONEY
There are banks all over Pattaya and Ha Jomtien; all have ATMs and most hav foreign-exchange booths that stay open lat (usually 8pm).
Bangkok Bank (Map p235; Th Hat Pattaya)
Bangkok Metropolitan Bank (Map p235; Th Hat Pattaya

POST
Post office (Map p235; Soi 13/2)

TELEPHONE
There are many private long-distance phon offices, charging 12B per minute to the USA Australia and Europe. Most internet cafe offer Skype.
Communications Authority of Thailand (CAT; Map p235; ☎ 0 3842 5301; cnr Th Pattaya Tai & Th Pattaya 3; ⏲ 8.30am-4.30pm Mon-Fri, 9am-noon Sat) Southeast of central Pattaya.

TOURIST INFORMATION
Tourism Authority of Thailand (TAT; Map p235; ☎ 0 3842 8750; tatchon@tat.or.th; 609 Mu 10, Th Phra Tamnak; ⏲ 8.30am-4.30pm) Located at the northwestern edge of Rama IX Park. The helpful staff have many brochures, including the excellent *Bigmap Pattaya*.

TRAVEL AGENCIES

Travel agencies all over town offer activities and accommodation around Thailand.
Ko Chang Business Centre (Map p235; ☎ 0 3871 0145; Soi Post Office; ☺ 9am-midnight) Specialises in trips to Ko Chang and Ko Samet, but does it all.

Dangers & Annoyances

Remember sex tourism is a booming industry in Pattaya and large sections of the city are chock full of go-go bars and strip clubs. This seedier side of Pattaya is hard to avoid, especially at night, and if you are travelling with young children prepare yourself for some awkward questions.

Late-night Pattaya can get a little wild, and though it's not necessarily dangerous, we witnessed more than one brawl between drunken Westerners. If you find yourself caught in the middle of an uncomfortable situation, walk away (or, in our case, push the button on the *sŏrng·tăa·ou* and get off). The police are prompt.

Sights & Activities

BEACHES

Hat Pattaya is the city's showcase stretch of sand, sporting sunbathers, souvenir sellers, and buzzing jet skis and speedboats. The sand is reasonably clean and the water is calm. If you get bored there's good shopping over the road.

Hat Jomtien, about 1km south of Pattaya, stretches for 6km and is quieter than its northern neighbour. It's a better base for backpackers: you're relatively removed from Pattaya's sex scene but still just a short *sŏrng·tăa·ou* ride away from the really wild nightlife. At the northern end of the beach, **Hat Dongtan** is a hub for gay travellers.

Hat Naklua, a smaller beach north of Pattaya, is quiet and a good choice for families.

The islands of **Ko Lan**, **Ko Krok** and **Ko Sak** are around 7km offshore and have some popular beaches – especially **Hat Ta Waen** on Ko Lan. Boats leave Pattaya's South Pier (Map p235) every two hours between 8am and 4.30pm (30B). The last boat back from Ko Lan is at 5pm. A daytrip including viewing from a glass-bottom boat costs around 150B.

WATER SPORTS

Though not home to Thailand's best dive sites, Pattaya's proximity to Bangkok makes it a popular spot to get some underwater action. However, overfishing and heavy boat traffic mean the sites closest to Pattaya can be barren, with poor visibility. Nearby Ko Lan, Ko Sak and Ko Krok are good for beginners, while accomplished divers may prefer the outer islands of **Ko Man Wichai** and **Ko Rin**, which have better visibility and marine life. In most places expect 3m to 9m of visibility under good conditions, or in more remote sites 5m to 12m.

Further south, the **shipwrecks** *Petchburi Bremen*, off Sattahip, and *Hardeep*, off Samae, have created artificial reefs. The scuttled Thai navy vessel HMS *Khram* sits in 30m of water

SOUTHEASTERN THAILAND

PATTAYA VICE

Pattaya's notoriety for sex tourism revolves around the agglomeration of discos, outdoor 'beer bars' and go-go clubs making up Pattaya's red-light district at the southern end of the beach. Known as 'the village', the area attracts a large number of prostitutes, including *gà·teu·i* (transvestites), who pose as female hookers and ply their trade among the droves of *fa·ràng* (Western) sex tourists. There is also a prominent gay sex-for-sale scene in Pattaya, especially at nearby Hat Dongtan. This activity is obvious to any visitor, but less overt is the shadowy child-sex trade, although sadly it is not uncommon to see Western men walking with young Thai boys and girls. See p51 for more information on stopping child-sex tourism in Thailand.

Traditionally the sex scene was focussed around Walking St, but every year a batch of new beer bars opens. A sign at the entrance to Walking St proclaims 'International Meeting Place', and they're not kidding. White prostitutes come from Romania and Moldova (favourites with male Asian sex tourists), and black male prostitutes from Nigeria (primarily servicing female sex tourists from Japan) can all be had in Pattaya. Globalisation is all too evident with the growing influence of organised crime cartels from as far away as Russia.

Of course, prostitution is just as illegal here as elsewhere in Thailand. But with millions of baht swilling around from money laundering, drug trafficking and diamond trading, let's just say enforcement of the laws is cyclic at best.

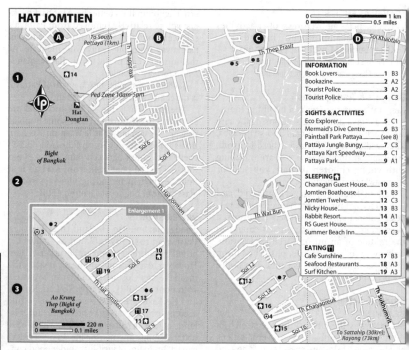

HAT JOMTIEN

off Ko Phai, and many operators offer excursions around the sunken hulk.

One of the best dive sites is an old US navy ammunition dump called **Samaesan Hole**, south of Pattaya, near Sattahip. This advanced dive goes down to 87m and has a gentle slope covered with coral where you can see barracuda and large rays. Visibility here is up to 20m on a good day.

A two-dive excursion to most sites averages around 3000B. Snorkellers may tag along for 600B to 1000B. Full PADI certification (three to four days) costs between 12,000B and 15,000B.

Mermaids Scuba Diving Center (www.mermaid dive.com; Hat Jomtien Map p238; ☎ 0 3823 2219; Soi White House, Hat Jomtien; Pattaya Map p235; ☎ 0 3871 0726; Siam Bayview Hotel, Th Hat Pattaya) is popular, with four locations between Hat Naklua, Hat Pattaya, and Hat Jomtien. They offer a boatload of options, from a single-day trip to full PADI instructor certification.

Pattaya and Jomtien have some of the best water-sports facilities in Thailand with **waterskiing** for 200B per hour, **parasailing** for 250B to 350B for about 10 to 15 minutes, and **windsurf-**

ing for 300B to 400B an hour. Hat Jomtien is the best for windsurfing because you're less likely to run into parasails or jet skis.

SANCTUARY OF TRUTH
This surreal **experience** (☎ 0 3836 7229; www.sanctuary oftruth.com; 206/2 Mu 5 Th Naklua; admission 500B; ⏰ 8am-6pm) begins with a horse-and-buggy ride and ends in a magnificent cathedral built entirely of wood – no nails or screws here. Give yourself time to marvel at the ornate carvings.

SPORTS
Pattaya offers many sports including **bowling**, **lawn bowls**, **snooker**, **archery**, **target shooting**, **softball**, **horse riding** and **tennis**. Most are available at the **Pattaya Sports Club** (Map p235; ☎ 0 3836 1167; www.pattayasports.org; 3/197 Th Pattaya 3) or can be organised by hotels. Golf packages can be booked through the **East Coast Travel & Golf Organisation** (☎ 0 3830 0927; www.pattayagolfpackage.com).

VOLUNTEERING
At the **Pattaya Orphanage** (☎ 0 3824 1373; volunteer@ redemptorists.or.th) volunteers are needed to care for more than 50 children under the age of

three, to teach English to older children and to work in a drop-in centre for street kids. The well-run orphanage is an uplifting balance to the Sin City streets of Pattaya. Volunteers are expected to commit to at least six months, but shorter stays are considered on a case-by-case basis. Food and accommodation are provided.

Sleeping

BUDGET

Pattaya offers a huge number of sleeping options. Weekends and holidays get crowded and many budget options fill up, but on quieter weekdays many hotels and guesthouses offer discounts. Hat Jomtien is the best place for lower-priced rooms.

Pattaya

The cheapest guesthouses are in south Pattaya, along Th Pattaya 2, the street parallel to Th Hat Pattaya. Most are clustered near Sois 6, 10, 11 and 12.

Honey Inn (Map p235; ☎ 0 3842 9133; 529/2 Soi 11, Th Pattaya 2; r 600-800B; 🔀 🖳) Clean rooms with a good little cafe downstairs, and you're quite close to Pattaya's nightlife without being right in its lap.

Hat Jomtien

Explore the area around Sois 3 and 4 for good-value budget guesthouses.

Chanagan Guest House (Map p238; ☎ 08 9834 3561; Soi 6, Th Hat Jomtien; r 500B; 🔀) Big rooms at the right price: they come with cable, hot water and air-con. The soi is fairly quiet at night and you're metres from the beach and good eating.

RS Guest House (Map p238; ☎ 0 3823 1867; Th Hat Jomtien; r from 650B; 🔀) With small but clean rooms and a lovely little two-tiered swimming pool, RS Guest House is a good-value haven

---

PATTAYA FOR CHILDREN

Ripley's Believe It or Not! (Map p235; ☎ 0 3871 0294; 2nd fl, Royal Garden Plaza, Th Pattaya 2; adult/child 380/195B; 🕒 11am-11pm) puts a Disney-esque spin on the world's oddities and includes high-tech theme rides.

Budding Michael Schumachers (and petrolhead dads) should head to **Pattaya Kart Speedway** (Map p238; www.easygokart.net; ☎ 0 3842 2044; 248/2 Th Thep Prasit, Soi 9; 🕒 9am-6.30pm), where you can race go-karts around an impressive 800m loop. Prices start at 300B for 10 minutes in a 10HP kart. There's a down'n'dirty off-road circuit and the littlest ones will enjoy the 'baby karts' on a 400m beginners' track.

At nearby **Paintball Park Pattaya** (Map p238; ☎ 0 3830 0608; 248/10 Mu 12, Th Thep Prasit; 50 bullets starting at 400B; 🕒 9am-6pm) older kids can vent their frustration at being on holiday with their uncool parents.

Of course, if the kids don't behave then you can threaten them with the 50m jump at **Pattaya Jungle Bungy** (Map p238; ☎ 08 6378 3880; www.thaibungy.com; Mu 12, Th Hat Jomtien; jumps 1800B; 🕒 9am-6pm).

Pattaya Park (Map p238; ☎ 0 3836 4129; www.pattayapark.com; 345 Th Hat Jomtien; adult/child 100/50B; 🕒 9am-6pm) has three different ways to exit the 55-storey tower in its water park. Once the kids (and Mum and Dad) have recovered, get them all excited again on the roller coaster and dodgems in the venue's Funnyland Amusement Park.

Escape the heat and sun at **Underwater World** (☎ 0 3875 6879; Th Sukhumvit; adult/child 450/250B; 🕒 9am-6pm) with acrylic tunnels making up a walk-through aquarium. It's 200m past the Tesco-Lotus shopping centre on the main road south.

The **Pattaya Elephant Village** (☎ 0 3824 9853; www.elephant-village-pattaya.com) is a non-profit sanctuary for former working elephants. There's a 2.30pm elephant show (adult/child 500/400B), which demonstrates training techniques, and one-hour (adult/child 900/700B) and 3½-hour (adult/child 1900/1300B) elephant treks. The elephant village is 7km off Th Sukhumvit.

You can spend from a half day to four weeks working with mahouts and their elephants, in rehabilitation after being forced to work in the city, at the Elephant Mahout Project run by **Eco Explorer** (Map p238; ☎ 08 4561 8873; www.theelephantmahoutproject.com; 217/7 Soi 15, Th Thep Prasit; per half-day incl lunch €27). An average day includes an early start to bathe and feed the elephants, followed by training to develop your own skills as a mahout.

---

away from the bright lights at the southern end of Hat Jomtien. Two breakfasts are included in the room rate.

MIDRANGE

Pattaya has many midrange hotels, with competition keeping standards high and prices (relatively) low. Hotels tend to age fast in Pattaya, so watch out for the latest openings, which may be offering special deals.

Pattaya

Natural Beach Hotel (Map p235; ☎ 0 3842 9239; natural beach@excite.com; 216 Mu 10, Soi 11; r 750-950B; ☒ ☒) Infused with a low-key relaxed ambience that's nicely at odds with the surrounding hubbub of Pattaya, the Natural Beach delivers a pretty garden, a shady swimming pool and tidy rooms with an unintentional 1970s retro feel.

Lek Hotel (Map p235; ☎ 0 3842 5552; lek_hotel@hot mail.com; 284/5 Th Pattaya 2; r 850-1200B; ☒ ☒) It's about time for the Lek to replace the bright red carpet in its hallways – and the bright blue carpet in its rooms – but it's still popular with return visitors, who come back for the central location and good-value breakfast (110B). Ask for a quieter room away from the street.

Ma Maison (Map p235; ☎ 0 3871 0433; www.mamaison -hotel.com/e_index; Soi 13; r 1180-1480B; ☒ ☒ ☒) Sip your pastis around *la piscine* (swimming pool) at this very French low-rise oasis. The French management can be a bit snooty to non-French speakers, but it's nothing a lounge by the pool can't allay. You can also hitch your laptop to the hotel's wi-fi network.

Areca Lodge (Map p235; ☎ 0 3841 0123; www.areca lodge.com; 198/23 Mu 9, Soi 13, Th Pattaya 2; r incl breakfast 2000B; ☒ ☒ ☒) With stylish rooms and two swimming pools, this place almost gatecrashes into the top-end category. No one has told the owners though, and from February through November, rooms run at a much lower price of 1300B – one of Pattaya's better bargains.

Naklua

Garden Lodge (Map p235; Th Naklua; ☎ 0 3842 9109; fax 0 3842 1221; r 850-1300B; ☒ ☒ ☒) Escape the hype and hustle of Pattaya in one of the town's best-value midrange options. There's no skimping on the garden atmosphere with fish ponds and leafy pavilions, and the tour desk at reception offers a raft of day trips.

Sea Lodge Hotel (Map p235; ☎ 0 3842 5128; 170/1 Moo 5 Soi 18/2, Th Naklua; r from 1000B; ☒ ☒ ☒) If Garden Lodge is full, pop over to the Sea Lodge, which offers a similar (though toned-down) setting and clean bungalows.

Hat Jomtien

Head to the southern end of the beach for a quieter and more family-friendly atmosphere. It's popular with Thai tourists, who come for fresh seafood on weekends.

Nicky House (Map p238; ☎ 0 3823 2000; 75/2-3 Moo 12, Th Hat Jomtien; r 650-950B; ☒ ☒) A new hotel with friendly staff and a good internet cafe downstairs. Make sure to get a room with a window; some have only peepholes.

Summer Beach Inn (Map p238; ☎ 0 3823 1777; Th Hat Jomtien; r 650-1500B; ☒) A brand-new building with floor-to-ceiling windows makes this hotel good value. The cheapest rooms are in the old building, and some have a lingering cigarette smell. Do a sniff test before deciding.

Jomtien Twelve (Map p238; ☎ 0 3875 6865; 240/13 Soi 12, Th Hat Jomtien; r 1100-1500B; ☒) The lobby promises urbane designer delights, but the rooms are slightly less impressive (though they come with breakfast). It's popular with weekending Bangkok professionals.

Jomtien Boathouse (Map p238; ☎ 0 3875 6143; www .jomtien-boathouse.com; 380/5-6 Th Hat Jomtien; r 1200-1400B; ☒) Rooms are shipshape if not super-exciting. Sea-view rooms have balconies and a surprisingly low amount of road noise. The restaurant downstairs is nautically themed and quite popular.

TOP END

Pattaya is popular with package tourists and convention goers, so there are plenty of top-end options. Rooms are often cheaper when booked through a Bangkok travel agency or via the internet. There are plenty of standard high-rise resorts, but the following three offer something different.

Naklua

Woodlands Resort (Map p235; ☎ 0 3842 1707; www .woodland-resort.com; 164/1 Th Naklua; r incl breakfast 2900-7600B; ☒ ☒ ☒) Low key but sophisticated, Woodlands Resort is set around tropical gardens with two swimming pools, and is good for families. The rooms are light and airy with teak furniture, and include high-speed internet, along with CD and DVD players. Several restaurants cater to your cravings.

Hat Jomtien

Rabbit Resort (Map p238; ☎ 0 3830 3303; www.rabbit resort.com; Dongtan Beach, Hat Jomtien; r 6900-7500B, villas up to 4 people 13,500-15,000B; 🕲 💻 🖭) Rabbit Resort has stunning bungalows and villas set in beach-front forest at the northern end of Jomtien. Furnishings showcase Thai design and art, and the sign in reception advertises 'soft mattress available'. Bathrooms are especially stylish with accents of river stone and granite.

Eating

Western food rules the roost in Pattaya, and while there are plenty of Thai restaurants, the taste of authentic Thailand is sometimes lacking. Whether you want schnitzel, samosas or smorgasbord, you'll find it amid the many eateries.

In between sois 6 and 7 along Th Hat Jomtien are some good seafood restaurants; you can also head to south Pattaya around Walking St for more of these.

Carrefour Food Court (Map p235; Th Pattaya Klang; 🕲 11am-10pm) In the absence of a decent night market, head to the food court under the Carrefour supermarket. The Thai food is authentically spicy and dishes start from just 30B.

Surf Kitchen (Map p238; ☎ 0 3823 1710; Th Hat Jomtien; dishes 80-180B; 🕲 breakfast, lunch & dinner) This lively restaurant is at the top of relaxed dining options on Jomtien Beach. The Thai food is authentic in all the right places and the talented kitchen staff are skilled at Western food as well.

Cafe Sunshine (Map p238; Th Hat Jomtien; dishes 100-300B; 🕲 breakfast, lunch & dinner) In a shady garden, Cafe Sunshine is especially recommended for breakfast, and if you time it right you'll still be there when happy hour kicks off at a ridiculously early 10am.

PIC Kitchen (Map p235; ☎ 0 3842 8374; 10 Soi 5, Th Pattaya 2; dishes 110-290B; 🕲 lunch & dinner) This teak-lined place is polished and atmospheric, with cushions and low wooden tables, and an extensive wine and cocktail list. Excellent Thai food is the main draw, and live jazz bubbles away downstairs every night from 8pm at the Jazz Pit. It's a great place to relax.

La Baguette French Bakery (Map p235; ☎ 0 3842 1707; 164/1 Th Naklua; crêpes from 120B; 🕲 breakfast, lunch & dinner; 💻) Part of the Woodlands Resort, this cool, sleek cafe has yummy pastries, good espresso, and even better crêpes. You can also link into its wi-fi network.

Tequila Reef (Map p235; ☎ 0 3841 4035; Soi 7, Th Hat Pattaya; dishes 220-310B; 🕲 lunch & dinner) Mexican cantina meets Californian surf shack in this buzzy restaurant that dispenses Pattaya's best margaritas. It's popular with the lads from the United States Navy who probably know a thing or two about a good burrito.

Mantra (Map p235; ☎ 0 3842 9591; Th Hat Pattaya; dishes 240-800B; 🕲 dinner Mon-Sat, brunch & dinner Sun; 🕲) Ceilings several stories high and staff that memorise your name: Mantra is fun even if you can only afford a classy cocktail. The bar is swathed in raw silk and the expansive dining room is cloaked in dark wood. The menu combines Japanese, Thai and Indian flavours, and there's a big cocktail list and more than 20 wines by the glass.

Drinking

Despite the profusion of noisy, identikit beer bars, go-go bars and nightclubs in this town, there are still some good places for a no-strings-attached drink.

Hopf Brew House (Map p235; ☎ 0 3871 0650; Th Hat Pattaya 219; 🕲 3pm-1am Sun-Fri, 4pm-2am Sat; 🕲) Moodily authentic in dark wood, the Hopf Brew House is a haven for middle-aged beer aficionados and splurging Scandinavian backpackers. A very drinkable pilsner and a wheat beer are brewed on site, and you can smell the hops when you walk in. Huge wood-fired pizzas and only slightly smaller schnitzels are recommended to soak up the liquid hospitality.

Gulliver's (Map p235; ☎ 0 3871 0641; Th Hat Pattaya; 🕲 11.30am-2am; 🕲 💻) The classy ornamental pool outside belies the laid-back sports-bar vibe inside. At the northern end of Pattaya, cavernous Gulliver's has free wi-fi internet and a big Thai and Western menu. Before 7pm, take advantage of happy hour with discounted beer and cocktails.

Green Bottles (Map p235; ☎ 0 3842 9675; 216/6-20 Th Pattaya 2; 🕲 11am-2am; 🕲) Charmingly cosy and retro (you can even request your favourite songs from the band), Green Bottles has been on the scene since 1988 and is one of Pattaya's more traditional pubs. The dim lights mean it's good for easing into another night's carousing with an early evening hair of the dog.

Entertainment

Merry-making in Pattaya, aside from the sex scene, means everything from hanging out in a video bar to dancing all night in a south

Pattaya disco. The best place to start is Th Hat Pattaya. At its southern end, this main drag becomes Walking St, a semi-pedestrianised area with bars and clubs for every predilection. Nearby 'Pattaya Land' encompasses Soi 1, 2 and 3 and is packed with go-go bars. The many gay bars on Soi 3 are announced by a sign reading 'Boyztown'. Around Hat Dongtan at the northern end of Hat Jomtien there is another burgeoning gay scene.

CLUBS & CABARETS

Tony's (Map p235; ☎ 0 3842 5795; www.tonydisco.com; 139/15 Walking St; admission free; ⌚ 8.30pm-2.30am; ⊠) You'll either love or hate this supernova monument to nocturnal nirvana. A pumping neon-saturated disco complete with white plastic benches, karaoke and pool tables blend with a good-value buffet, strong cocktails and live music.

Tiffany's (Map p235; ☎ 0 3842 1700; www.tiffany -show.co.th; 464 Mu 9, Th Pattaya 2; admission 500-800B; ⌚ from 6pm; ⊠) Established in 1974, Pattaya's leading transvestite cabaret is a remarkably chaste affair, oozing old-school showbiz charm and covering the globe in a fast-paced show lasting 75 minutes. The absolutely fabulous parade of sequins, satin and surprises begins at 6pm, 7.30pm and 9pm.

Blues Factory (Map p235; ☎ 0 3830 0180; www .thebluesfactorypattaya.com; Soi Lucky Star; admission free; ⌚ from 8.30pm; ⊠) Off Walking St, Pattaya's best venue for no-nonsense live music features at least two bands every night, and a hassle-free atmosphere just metres from the heavier hype of its close neighbours.

CINEMAS

Royal Theatre Cinema (Map p235; ☎ 0 3842 8057; shop C30, 2nd fl, Royal Garden Plaza, Th Pattaya 2; admission 200B) Get away from the stall holders selling fake designer gear by escaping into the latest make-believe offering from Hollywood.

Shopping

Thanon Hat Pattaya is lined with stalls selling everything from dodgy DVDs and counterfeit CDs to T-shirts and jewellery. For more serious shopping, head to the **Royal Garden Plaza** (Map p235; Th Pattaya 2; ⌚ 11am-11pm).

Getting There & Away

AIR

Bangkok Airways (Map p235; ☎ 0 3841 2382; www .bangkokair.com; 179/85-212, Mu 5, Th Pattaya 2; ⌚ 8.30am-4.30pm Mon-Fri, to noon Sat) links **U-Taphao airfield** (☎ 0 3824 5599) about 33km south of Pattaya, with Ko Samui and Phuket (one way from 3200B, daily).

BUS

There are air-con buses to Pattaya from Bangkok's Eastern (Ekamai) and Northern (Mo Chit) bus terminals (100B to 140B, two hours, every half-hour from 6am to 9pm). From Pattaya, buses to Ekamai run every half-hour from 9.30am to 11pm, and to Mo Chit from 4.30pm to 9pm. In Pattaya the air-con bus station is on Th Hat Pattaya Neua, near the intersection with Th Sukhumvit. Once you reach the main Pattaya bus terminal, waiting red *sŏrng·tǎa·ou* will take you to the main beach road for 30B to 40B per person. Note that buses travelling from Ekamai to Hat Jomtien are often 2nd class; it's often faster to take the 1st class bus to north Pattaya and hop a *sŏrng·tǎa·ou* to Hat Jomtien.

Several hotels and travel agencies run minibuses to addresses within Bangkok, or east to Ko Samet and Ko Chang – the fares start at about 200B. Try Ko Chang Business Centre (p237) or ask at your hotel.

A direct bus service runs from Bangkok's Suvarnabhumi Airport to Pattaya and Hat Jomtien (120B to 150B, two hours).

From Si Racha, you can grab a public bus on Th Sukhumvit to Pattaya (60B, 30 minutes) – in Pattaya, they stop near the corner of Th Sukhumvit and Th Pattaya Neua. From here, you can flag down buses to Rayong (80B to 90B, 1½ hours).

You can also catch a white *sŏrng·tǎa·ou* from the Naklua market to Si Racha (25B, 30 minutes), and then to continue to Ko Si Chang, catch another *sŏrng·tǎa·ou* from where you're dropped off at the clock tower (see p231).

TRAIN

One train per day travels between Pattaya and Bangkok's Hualamphong station (3rd class 40B, 3¾ hours). It leaves Bangkok at 6.55am on Monday to Friday. The return train departs from Pattaya at 2.20pm.

Schedules for this service can change, so it's wise to check the latest times at **Pattaya train station** (☎ 0 3842 9285), off Th Sukhumvit just north of Th Hat Pattaya Neua, before travelling.

Getting Around

CAR & MOTORCYCLE

Avis Rent-A-Car (Map p235; ☎ 0 3836 1628; www.avisthai land.com; Th Hat Pattaya Neua; ❤ 8am-9pm) has offices at the Dusit Thani Resort.

Holiday Rent-A-Car (Map p235; ☎ 0 3842 6203; www .pattayacar-rent.com; TTh Pattaya 2; ❤ 9am-5pm) Located opposite Royal Garden Plaza this cheaper local company also offers full insurance. Prices for a 1500cc Toyota Vios start at 1250B per day. Discounts are offered for longer periods.

Local travel agents offer Suzuki jeeps from around 1000B per day, but expect to pay through the nose if you have an accident.

Motorcycles cost 150B to 250B per day for a 100cc machine; a 125cc to 150cc will cost around 350B, and you'll see 750cc to 1000cc machines for hire for 500B to 1000B. There are motorcycle hire places along Th Hat Pattaya and Th Pattaya 2.

SŎRNG·TĂA·OU

Locally known as 'baht buses', *sŏrng·tăa·ou* cruise Th Hat Pattaya and Th Pattaya 2 frequently – just hop on, and when you get out pay 10B anywhere between Naklua and south Pattaya, or 40B for as far as south Jomtien. Price lists posted in the vehicles state the maximum drivers can charge for any given journey.

Readers have complained about having taken the 10B *sŏrng·tăa·ou* with local passengers and then having been charged a higher 'charter' price of 20B to 50B. Establish the correct fare in advance. Also don't board a *sŏrng·tăa·ou* that is waiting empty at the side of the road, as the driver may insist you have 'chartered' the entire vehicle.

RAYONG PROVINCE

From Pattaya, most travellers fast-forward down the coast to the weekday calm and occasional weekend chaos of Ko Samet. The little port of Ban Phe is the jumping-off point for the island, but occasionally you might need to change buses in Rayong. If you're definitely bound for Samet, it doesn't make much sense to hang around the mainland beaches, but if you do venture to the other strips of sand and small islands in the vicinity, you'll probably be the only Western visitor.

For information about travelling to and from Rayong and Ban Phe, see p250.

RAYONG

ระยอง

pop 106,700

The dusty strip of banks, markets and motorcycle dealerships that makes up Rayong holds few surprises. You're most likely to be here for its location as a major transport interchange, but if you do arrive too late to secure an onward connection for a boat to Ko Samet, there are a couple of OK hotels.

Information

Krung Thai Bank (144/53-55 Th Sukhumvit) One of several banks along Rayong's main drag, Th Sukhumvit, with exchange services and ATMs.

Tourism Authority of Thailand (TAT) (☎ 0 3865 5420; tatyong@tat.or.th; 153/4 Th Sukhumvit; ❤ 8.30am-4.30pm) 7km east of Rayong on Hwy 3; a worthwhile stop if you have your own transport.

Sleeping & Eating

For cheap food, head to the market near the Thetsabanteung cinema or the restaurants and noodle shops along Th Taksin Maharat, just south of Wat Lum Mahachaichumphon. The food stalls around the bus station are a good choice as well.

Rayong President Hotel (☎ 0 3861 1307; Th Sukhumvit; r incl breakfast from 550B; ❤ ▯) There's not much English spoken, but it's friendly as well as quiet at night. From the bus station, cross to the other side of Th Sukhumvit. The hotel is down a side street that starts next to the Siam Commercial Bank; look for the sign.

Getting There & Around

Air-con buses to Rayong (132B, 2½ hours, every 30 minutes) leave Bangkok's Eastern (Ekamai) bus terminal from 4am to 10pm. You can also get to the Northern (Mo Chit) and Southern terminals from Rayong – buses aren't as frequent but the prices and times are similar. Buses to Chanthaburi from Rayong bus station cost 80B and take about 2½ hours. From Pattaya to Rayong, flag down a southbound bus near the corner of Th Sukhumvit and Th Pattaya Neua (ordinary/air-con 60/80B, 1½ hours). Blue *sŏrng·tăa·ou* from Rayong bus station to Ban Phe cost 25B and it's a straightforward ride.

BAN PHE

บ้านเพ

The little port of Ban Phe is only on the map thanks to its role as a launch pad for nearby Ko Samet. However the busy seafood markets near the ferry terminal are worth a peek, and there are a few beaches nearby that are blissfully quiet during the week and make a nice detour.

Check email and make international calls at **Tan Tan Cafe** (☎ 08 1925 6713; Soi 2; per min 1B; ⏰ 7.30am-7pm), down a lane opposite the ferry terminal. There's an ATM outside the 7-Eleven store across from Christie's Guesthouse. Opposite the pier, **Blue Sky Books** (☎ 0 3865 1885; Soi 1; ⏰ 10am-7pm) has a good range of English-language titles, arranged by genre by a true bibliophile. The array of old Lonely Planet titles is positively archaeological.

The **post office** (Th Ban Phe), east of the Ban Phe pier, also has a Western Union for monetary emergencies.

Sleeping

There are several hotels in Ban Phe in close proximity to the pier.

Hotel Diamond (☎ 0 3865 1826; fax 0 3865 1757; 286/12 Mu 2; r 350-500B; ❄) The rooms aren't the cleanest, but they're nothing the seasoned budget traveller can't handle. Turn left out of the ferry terminal and go 150m down the main road. It's fine for one night if you miss the last ferry.

Christie's Guesthouse (☎ 0 3865 1976; fax 0 3865 2103; 280/92 Soi 1; r from 500B; ❄ ❄) With good rooms and a popular restaurant/bar downstairs, Christie's is the most comfortable place near the pier. There's also a good pizzeria and second-hand bookshop next door to keep you occupied while you wait for the ferry.

M@c Garden (☎ 0 3865 1150; 280/153 Th Ban Phe Mu 2; r 700B; ❄ 🖳) A friendly new hotel that has beautiful teak bungalows (1200B) and smaller rooms that, though plain, are clean and new. Walk another 50m past the Hotel Diamond.

You can also rent tidy air-con rooms at **Tan Tan Cafe** (☎ 08 1925 6713; Soi 2; 500B).

Eating

Christie's Bar and Restaurant (☎ 0 3865 1976; 280/92 Soi 1; ⏰ breakfast, lunch & dinner) With funky tunes and friendly staff, Christie's is where you'll meet other travellers waiting for the ferry. Buy a takeaway baguette sandwich before you board the boat. At night, the bar becomes the regular drinking hole for expats in town teaching English.

Getting There & Away

There are two air-con bus stations in Ban Phe that have buses to Bangkok's Eastern (Ekamai) bus terminal. Fifty metres west of Ban Phe pier, buses depart four times a day starting in the afternoon at 12.30pm; they leave Bangkok as many times in the mornings beginning at 7am (138B, 2½ hours). Slower but more frequent buses depart across from Nuan Tip pier, 100m east of Ban Phe pier. These buses leave Ekamai hourly from 5am to 8.30pm and return from 4am to 7pm (167B, four hours).

Slightly more simple, but also more expensive, are the tourist minivans that run to and from Ban Phe and other traveller destinations: Pattaya (200B per person); Victory Monument or Th Khao San in Bangkok (300B to 450B per person); and the Laem Ngop pier, the departure point for Ko Chang (300B per person). These can be booked through guesthouses on Ko Samet, the travel agencies near the 7-Eleven opposite the ferry terminal in Ban Phe, or through travel agencies in Pattaya.

For information about boats to and from Ko Samet see p250.

AROUND RAYONG & BAN PHE
Khao Chamao/Khao Wong National Park

อุทยานแห่งชาติเขาชะเมา–เขาวง

Although less than 85 sq km, **Khao Chamao/Khao Wong National Park** (☎ 0 3889 4378; reserve@dnp.go.th; admission 200B; ⏰ 8.30am-4.30pm) is well known for its limestone mountains, high cliffs, caves, dense forest and waterfalls. Secreted in the rugged landscape are tigers, wild elephants and bears. The headquarters has eating facilities and a small store, as well as visitor information and accommodation. The park is inland from Ban Phe, 17km north of the Km274 marker off Hwy 3. You'll need your own transport to get to the park; a taxi from Ban Phe will cost around 1500B.

You can stay at a campsite (50B per person) or rent a two-person bungalow (600B to 800B). To book go to www.dnp.go.th or phone ☎ 0 2562 0760.

Islands & Beaches

Ko Man Klang, **Ko Kudee** and **Ko Man Nok**, along with **Ko Man Nai** to the west, are part of **Khao Laem Ya/Mu Ko Samet National Park** (☎ 0 3865 3034; reserve@dnp.go.th; admission adult/child 200/100B; ⏰ 8.30am-4.30pm). This official status hasn't kept away all development, only moderated it. Ko Kudee has a small, pretty sandy stretch, clear water for decent snorkelling and a nice little hiking trail. Ko Man Nai is home to the **Rayong Turtle Conservation Centre** (☎ 0 3861 6096; ⏰ 9am-4pm), which is a breeding place for endangered sea turtles and has a small visitor centre. The best way to visit is to join a boat tour from Ko Samet (p246).

You can also volunteer to work at the centre through **Starfish Ventures** (www.starfishventures .co.uk; 4 weeks incl accommodation £900). Activities include monitoring the progress of the turtles, releasing young turtles into the ocean and explaining the project to tourists on day trips from Ko Samet. Accommodation is in a fishing village, and every day you'll go to work in a speedboat across to Ko Man Mai. It's pretty leisurely – you'll be expected to work from 8am to 1pm four days a week – and in your downtime there are good beaches nearby to explore.

Ko Saket, a small island near Rayong, is a 20-minute boat ride from the beach of Hat Sai Thong (turn south off Hwy 3 at the Km208 marker).

Suan Son (Pine Park), 5km further down the highway from Ban Phe, is a popular place for Thai picnickers.

Suan Wang Kaew is 11km east of Ban Phe and has more beaches. **Ko Thalu**, across from Suan Wang Kaew, has decent diving, a nice beach and a woodsy walking trail up to a viewpoint.

Other resort areas along the Rayong coast include **Laem Mae Phim** and **Hat Sai Thong**. **Hat Mae Rampeung**, a 10km strip of sand between Ban Taphong and Ban Kon Ao (11km east of Rayong), is also part of Khao Laem Ya/Mu Ko Samet National Park. There are relatively frequent *sŏrng·tăa·ou* to all these beaches, leaving from the eastern edge of Ban Phe. At the weekend, these areas are busy with weekending Thais, but during the week you'll have them to yourself. Laem Mae Phim has the best range of options for eating and sleeping.

Sleeping

Ko Man Klang and Ko Man Nok offer upmarket accommodation packages that include boat transport from the mainland and all meals. These can only be arranged by phone in advance.

Mun Nork Island Resort (Bangkok office ☎ 0 2860 3025; www.munnorkislandresort.com; packages per person 3990-4390B; ❄) On Ko Man Nok, this classy resort has one-night, two-day packages in a variety of villas. The island is 15km off Pak Nam Prasae (53km east of Ban Phe).

Raya Island Resort (Bangkok office ☎ 0 2316 6717; 1-night, 2-day package per person 1400-2500B; ❄ ▣) This comfortable place has 15 bungalows and plenty of hush. It is 8km off Laem Mae Phim (27km east of Ban Phe), on Ko Man Klang.

Getting There & Away

Public transport to the pier departure points for Ko Man Klang and Ko Man Nok can be arranged in Ban Phe. On weekends and holidays there may be *sŏrng·tăa·ou* out to the piers; otherwise charter a vehicle from the market for around 100B one way – arrange a pick-up for your return.

KO SAMET

เกาะเสม็ด

What happens when an island blessed with 14 white-sand beaches is just half a day's travel from a Southeast Asian super city? If it's pretty Ko Samet it becomes a weekend and holiday getaway for the good people of Bangkok – locals and expats alike. Toss in the fact that the island is unusually dry (it misses the worst impact of the monsoons) and you've got the geographic equivalent of Miss Popularity. Arrive on a weekend and you may be hit with rate hikes of up to 100%, and you could be ducking for cover from volleyballs and banana boats on certain beaches.

During the week the island relaxes and you're more likely to discover what attracted the original backpackers a few short decades ago.

Ostensibly Ko Samet is a national park, but along the developed northeast coast it's hard to see where your 200B park entrance fee is being invested. You'll probably encounter garbage along the trails and beaches, always a disheartening experience. The island's ecosystem is overtaxed and it is vital that visitors play their part by conserving water and being mindful of rubbish.

If you're willing to venture further south, there are some undeniably gorgeous bays where development is still low-key and where a relaxed traveller vibe still exists.

History

Ko Samet won a place in Thai literature when classical Thai poet Sunthorn Phu set part of his epic *Phra Aphaimani* here. The story follows the travails of a prince exiled to an undersea kingdom ruled by a lovesick female giant. A mermaid aids the prince in his escape to Ko Samet, where he defeats the giant by playing a magic flute. Formerly Ko Kaew Phitsadan or 'Vast Jewel Isle' – a reference to the abundant white sand – this island became known as Ko Samet or 'Cajeput Isle' after the cajeput tree that grows in abundance here, and which is highly valued for its essential oil and as firewood throughout Southeast Asia. Locally, the samet tree has also been used in boat building.

Orientation

Ko Samet is vaguely T-shaped. The best beaches (and most developed) are located on the island's eastern shore. A few upmarket hotels are on the west coast, clustered around pretty Ao Prao. Na Dan, the island's biggest village and the terminus for the Ban Phe ferry, is on the north coast, facing the mainland. A few low-key sleeping options can be found on the north coast; it's nice and quiet but the beaches are not that great.

Information

Ko Samet is a national park and the entrance fee (adult/child 200/100B) is collected at the main National Parks office – your *sŏrng·tăa·ou* from the pier will stop at the gates. Hold on to your ticket for later inspections.

There are several ATMs on Ko Samet. One is at the pier and another two are near the National Parks main office.

There are internet cafes on the road from Na Dan to Hat Sai Kaew; the best is Miss You Cafe (p250).

Around the island you can check your email at Jep's Bungalows (p248) and Naga Bungalows (p248) in Ao Hin Khok, and at a couple of spots along Ao Wong Deuan. All charge a steep 2B per minute.

A satellite phone for making international calls is located outside the National Parks main office visitors centre.

Ko Samet Health Centre (☎ 0 3861 1123; ✆ 8.30am-9pm Mon-Fri, 8.30am-4.30pm Sat & Sun) On the main road between Na Dan and Hat Sai Kaew. On-call mobile numbers are posted for after-hours emergencies.

National Parks main office (btwn Na Dan & Hat Sai Kaew) Also has another office on Ao Wong Deuan.

Police station (☎ 1155) On the main road between Na Dan and Hat Sai Kaew. There's a substation on Ao Wong Deuan.

Post office Naga Bungalows in Ao Hin Khok acts as the island's post office; it also loans and sells second-hand books.

Samed Travel Service (☎ 08 1664 8563; ✆ 8.30am-5pm) Opposite the ferry terminal; makes transport (including railway) and accommodation bookings.

Dangers & Annoyances

Ko Samet has been malarial in the past, and while the health centre now claims to have the problem under control, the island is infested with mosquitoes. Cover up and use buckets of repellent.

Take care on the road leading away from the beach past Sea Breeze Bungalows in Ao Phai, as travellers have reported being robbed in this area.

We've also had reports of boat scams on the mainland, in which travellers are sold a speedboat ticket for around 800B per person. Refer to p250 for prices and timetables, but note that a speedboat going one way should cost anywhere from 1500 to 2500B *total,* no matter how many passengers.

Activities

Sailboards, boogie boards, inner tubes and snorkelling equipment can all be rented on the beaches at Hat Sai Kaew, Ao Hin Khok and Ao Phai. Dive operators run trips to nearby sites; the best diving is at Hin Pholeung, halfway between Ko Samet and Ko Chang. This isolated spot is well away from destructive boat traffic and has two towering underwater rock pinnacles with excellent visibility (up to 30m). Here you can spot large pelagics like manta rays, barracuda, sharks and, if you're lucky, whale sharks.

Two reputable dive operations on the island are **Ploy Scuba Diving** (☎ 0 3864 4212; www .ployscuba.com) in Hat Sai Kaew, and **Ao Prao Divers** (☎ 0 3864 4100-3; aopraodivers@hotmail.com), based at Saikaew Villa and the Ao Prao Resort.

Naga Bungalows (p248) offers *moo·ay tai* (also spelt *muay thai*) lessons in its beachside boxing ring. One program caters specifically to women and is quite popular.

Tours

Jimmy's Tours (☎ 08 9832 1627) runs tours around Ko Samet and the neighbouring islands. A six-hour boat tour (10am to 4pm) of the neighbouring islets, including the Rayong Turtle Conservation Centre (p245) on Ko Man Nai, costs 1500B per person (minimum group size of 10 people).

Sleeping

Ko Samet was originally a backpacker idyll, but accommodation is inching up the price chain, and it seems that the majority of the old backpacker shacks are either being razed

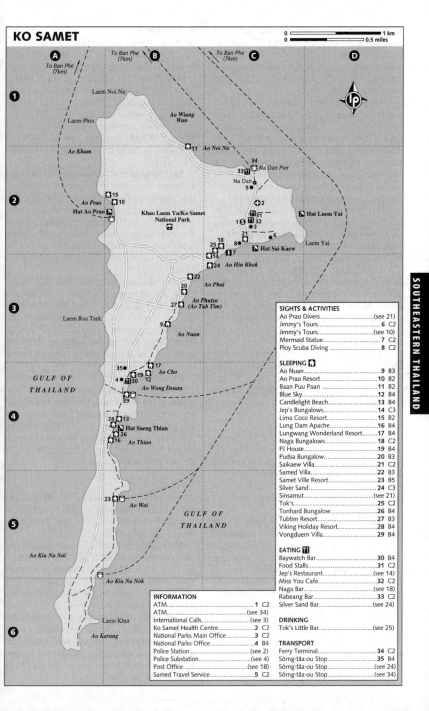

KO SAMET

SOUTHEASTERN THAILAND

SIGHTS & ACTIVITIES

Ao Prao Divers	(see 21)
Jimmy's Tours	**6** C2
Jimmy's Tours	(see 10)
Mermaid Statue	**7** C2
Ploy Scuba Diving	**8** C2

SLEEPING

Ao Nuan	**9** B3
Ao Prao Resort	**10** B2
Baan Puu Paan	**11** B2
Blue Sky	**12** B4
Candlelight Beach	**13** B4
Jep's Bungalows	**14** C3
Lima Coco Resort	**15** B2
Lung Dam Apache	**16** B4
Lungwang Wonderland Resort	**17** B4
Naga Bungalows	**18** C2
PJ House	**19** B4
Pudsa Bungalow	**20** B3
Saikaew Villa	**21** C2
Samed Villa	**22** B3
Samet Ville Resort	**23** B5
Silver Sand	**24** C3
Sinsamut	(see 21)
Tok's	**25** C2
Tonhard Bungalow	**26** B4
Tubtim Resort	**27** B3
Viking Holiday Resort	**28** B4
Vongduern Villa	**29** B4

EATING

Baywatch Bar	**30** B4
Food Stalls	**31** C2
Jep's Restaurant	(see 14)
Miss You Cafe	**32** C2
Naga Bar	(see 18)
Rabeang Bar	**33** C2
Silver Sand Bar	(see 24)

DRINKING

Tok's Little Bar	(see 25)

TRANSPORT

Ferry Terminal	**34** C2
Sŏrng·tǎa·ou Stop	**35** B4
Sŏrng·tǎa·ou Stop	(see 24)
Sŏrng·tǎa·ou Stop	(see 34)

INFORMATION

ATM	**1** C2
ATM	(see 34)
International Calls	(see 3)
Ko Samet Health Centre	**2** C2
National Parks Main Office	**3** C2
National Parks Office	**4** B4
Police Station	(see 2)
Police Substation	(see 4)
Post Office	(see 18)
Samed Travel Service	**5** C2

Map labels: To Ban Phe (7km); Laem Noi Na; Ao Wiang Wan; Laem Phra; Ao Kham; Ao Noi Na; Na Dan Pier; Na Dan; Hat Laem Yai; Khao Laem Ya/Ko Samet National Park; Laem Yai; Ao Prao; Hat Ao Prao; Hat Sai Kaew; Ao Hin Khok; Ao Phai; Ao Phutsa (Ao Tub Tim); Laem Rua Taek; Ao Nuan; GULF OF THAILAND; Ao Cho; Ao Wong Deuan; Hat Saeng Thian; Ao Thian; Ao Wai; GULF OF THAILAND; Ao Kiu Na Nai; Ao Kiu Na Nok; Laem Khut; Ao Karang

or surrounded by midrange and high-end bungalows. A lot of resorts offer all three options, the reason for the wide price variance under many listings. A simple hut is usually around 350B, while an air-con bungalow goes for at least 1200B.

We quote standard weekday rates, which may (it's all about supply and demand) as much as double in price during weekends and holidays. If you do turn up at the weekend, make sure you ask for the reduced weekly rate on the Monday – this reduction is often conveniently forgotten. If you come during the week, always ask for a discount. Most bungalows now provide 24-hour electricity and running water.

In the past many places did not take forward bookings, but this is changing and more places now have websites and email addresses. Note that for some of the more simple places, even if they have phones, they still may not take – or honour – bookings. Be prepared to be flexible, because your chosen accommodation may still operate on a first-come-first-served basis. Offices and touts in Ban Phe offering reservations often inflate prices.

EAST COAST

The two most developed beaches are Hat Sai Kaew and Ao Wong Deuan. Most other beaches are still comparatively quiet, but expansion is ongoing. Accommodation is listed from north to south.

Hat Sai Kaew

Known as 'Diamond Sand', this is the island's biggest and busiest beach. The sand here is white and relatively clean, though the seafront is lined with hotels, bars and restaurants. It's a favourite for Thais from Bangkok, and at the weekends expect a cacophony of jet skis and karaoke.

Saikaew Villa (☎ 0 3864 4144; r 500-1550B; 🕸) Big rooms or small rooms, fan or air-con, Saikaew Villa conjures up a wide range of accommodation options amid a manicured space that (almost) goes too far with the holiday-camp atmosphere. Don't expect much privacy, but do expect food, drinks and activities all on tap.

Sinsamut (☎ 0 3864 4207; www.sinsamut-kohsamed .com; r 800-1300B; 🕸) Bright, light and colourful (but slightly shabby) rooms come with brick walls and the bathrooms have gravel floors with stepping stones. Fan rooms have cold-water showers, while air-con rooms come with TVs, hot water and refrigerators.

Ao Hin Khok

At the southern end of Hat Sai Kaew, statues of the prince and the mermaid from Sunthorn Phu's epic (see p245) gaze lovingly into each other's eyes. Ao Hin Khok begins here: it's a pretty stretch of sand, lined with trees and boulders. This is the island's traditional backpacker hub, and while the ambience is slowly moving towards the upmarket, there's still loads of energy from independent travellers to make it a fun spot – especially after dark.

Naga Bungalows (☎ 0 3864 4035; r 350-600B; 🖵) At Naga, Ko Samet's backpacker spirit lives on. Simple fan bungalows are set into a forested hillside, and movies are shown every night in the outstanding restaurant. Expat Sue runs the post office, library and charity (ask how you can be involved), and is an excellent source of information about the island.

Tok's (☎ 0 3864 4072; r 300-1200B; 🕸) Same, same, but different (there are some air-con rooms at Tok's). You'll need a torch after dark to negotiate the steep hillside to the simple bungalows – especially if you've been taking part in Tok's regular drinking games. Some snazzy new bungalows were being built when we visited.

Jep's Bungalows (☎ 0 3864 4112; www.jepbungalow .com; r 600-2600B; 🕸 🖵) Spearheading the evolution of Ao Hin Khok, the long established Jep's offers rooms ranging from dingy fan bungalows to air-con rooms with satellite TV. Despite the changes, a backpacker spirit lingers with nightly movies and barbecues in the seafront restaurant.

Ao Phai

Around the next headland Ao Phai is another shallow bay with a wide beach, but it can get crowded during the day. After dark, there's fun aplenty.

Silver Sand (☎ 08 6530 2147; www.silversandresort .com; s 300-800B; d 1200-2000B; 🕸) The manicured gardens are a bit much, though thankfully the bungalows are equally attended to. The after-hours action in the Silver Sands bar can be a tad more disorderly.

Samed Villa (☎ 0 3864 4094; www.samedvilla.com; r 1800-4000B; 🕸) A Swiss-run place, and it shows. Everything is spick and span, and the architects allocated a substantial budget to make the inside of some of the rooms as flash as the outside.

Ao Phutsa

Also known as Ao Tub Tim, this small and secluded beach is popular with return travellers and Bangkok expats.

Tubtim Resort (☎ 0 3864 4025; www.tubtimresort .com; r 600-1500B; 🔀) A range of bungalows, from fan-cooled to fab, fill a garden that's edging slowly towards jungle status. The cheapest huts have some gaps in the floorboards – bring a mosquito coil.

Pudsa Bungalow (☎ 0 3864 4030; r 600-1500B; 🔀) The nicer bungalows near the beach are trimmed with driftwood, but unfortunately are right beside the main footpath from Ao Phai to Ao Phutsa. You might have to put up with overhearing inane alcohol-fuelled conversations late at night. An OK backup if Tubtim is full.

Ao Nuan

This tiny beach is the most secluded place to stay without having to go to the far south of the island.

Ao Nuan (r 700-1500B) The best place for chillaxin' on Ko Samet. Here, simple wooden bungalows are hidden among vegetation. A funky gazebo/bar/restaurant has books and good beats, and there's a community atmosphere. No phone means no reservations, so just walk on over. Bring along your mozzie repellent.

Ao Cho

A five-minute walk from Ao Nuan, Ao Cho has a decent strip of sand though it's dominated by a large resort.

Lungwang Wonderland Resort (☎ 0 3864 4162; www.samedlungwang.com, in Thai; r 500-3000B; 🔀) The grounds could use some TLC and the air-con rooms are overpriced, but the simple bungalows are good – they're decked out in cheerful colours and bright, mismatched tiles. Kayak rentals are 200B per hour.

Ao Wong Deuan

This crescent-shaped bay has a good nightlife and a chilled after-dark vibe, but your daytime soundtrack may be jet skis and speedboats. Ferries (70B each way) run to and from Ban Phe, with increased services at the weekend.

PJ House (☎ 0 3864 4182; r 500B; 🔀) Next to Baywatch Bar, this small place is pretty basic but 500B scores you an air-con room. There's a pool table downstairs dominated by the local 10-year-old sharks.

Blue Sky (☎ 08 1509 0547; r 600-800B; 🔀) One of the last budget spots on Ao Wong Deuan, Blue Sky has simple bungalows set on a rocky headland. The restaurant does tasty things with seafood.

Vongduern Villa (☎ 0 3864 4260; www.vongduern villa.com; r 1200-3000B; 🔀) Sprawling along the bay's southern edge, Vongduern's bungalows are either near the beach or higher on the cliff top for better views. The Beach Front Bar is a sociable spot for sundowner cocktails, but romantic couples may prefer the subdued ambience of the Rock Front Restaurant.

Ao Thian

Better known by its English name, Candlelight Beach, Ao Thian has stretches of sand with rocky outcrops. To get here, catch a ferry to Ao Wong Deuan and walk south over the headland. It's also a quick walk from here to the west side of the island – look for the marked trail near Tonhard Bungalow.

Candlelight Beach (☎ 08 1762 9387; r 700-1200B; 🔀) On the beach, these fan and air-con bungalows have a natural, woody ambience.

Lung Dam Apache (☎ 08 1659 8056; r 800-1200B; 🔀) These quirky bungalows look like they've been thrown together from marine debris. Some have enclosed verandas and wraparound windows.

Tonhard Bungalow (☎ 08 1435 8900; r 700-1500B; 🔀) On a wooded and sandy part of the beach, this place is quiet, friendly and somewhat private. Most bungalows differ from each other. At the southern end of Candlelight.

Viking Holiday Resort (☎ 0 3864 4353; r from 2000B; 🔀) Rooms are large and luxurious, and there's only nine of them so book ahead.

Ao Wai

The southern reaches of the island are still practically untouched, with only a couple of hotels spread over as many kilometres of coastline. Lovely Ao Wai is about 1km from Ao Thian, but can be reached from Ban Phe by chartered speedboat (1500B for two people).

Samet Ville Resort (☎ 0 3865 1682; www.sametville resort.com; r incl breakfast 2000-5300B; 🔀) Under a forest canopy, it's a case of 'spot the sky' at the very secluded Samet Ville. It's a romantic spot, but if you do have a fight with your loved one, take advantage of the water sports on offer and cool off in separate kayaks for the day. At dusk, patch things up over cocktails and

SOUTHEASTERN THAILAND

subdued beats in the beachfront bar. There is a huge range of different fan and air-con rooms for all budgets.

WEST & NORTH COASTS
Ao Prao

West-facing Ao Prao gets fabulous sunsets and offers a smattering of chic hotels for the posh set. Speedboat transfers from the mainland are included (of course).

Lima Coco Resort (☎ 0 2938 1811; www.limacoco.com; r 2600-7000B; ⊠) Whitewashed rooms could go either way: Mediterranean or bland. No matter what, they're bright and a little different from the norm.

Ao Prao Resort (☎ 0 2437 7849; www.samedresorts .com; r from 6300B; ⊠ ⊡) This resort opened in the 1990s as the island's first luxury accommodation. It's holding its age well, with private bungalows cascading down a hill to the gorgeous beach. High ceilings create a spacious ambience and there is an excellent restaurant.

Ao Noi Na

Northwest of Na Dan, the beach at Ao Noi Na is only average, but there is a refreshing solitude with a couple of good places to stay.

Baan Puu Paan (☎ 0 3864 4095; r 700-1200B; ⊠) This English-run spot has a couple of stand-alone huts above the ocean at the end of a pier. Bring a fat book – it's a good place to get away.

Eating & Drinking

Most places to stay have restaurants that moonlight as bars at sunset. The food won't blow you away, but it's OK value, with Thai and Western favourites for around 80B to 130B. For the greatest choice check out Hat Sai Kaew, Ao Hin Khok, Ao Phai and Ao Wong Deuan, but hotels on the remote stretches make sure you won't go to bed hungry. Look for nightly beach barbecues, particularly along Ao Hin Khok and Ao Phai.

Drinking-wise, many places offer nightly 'toss a coin' promotions. Basically heads or tails decides if you end up paying for your drink or not. Ao Wong Deuan is slightly more upmarket, but not much.

For seriously cheap eats, check out the food stalls that set up in the late afternoon on the road between Na Dan and Hat Sai Kaew.

Rabeang Bar (Na Dan; dishes 30-100B; ☯ breakfast, lunch & dinner) Right by the ferry terminal, this over-the-water spot has good waiting-for-the-next-boat-to-the-mainland kind of food.

Miss You Cafe (coffee 40-90B; ☯ breakfast, lunch & dinner; ⊠ ⊡) Located beside the National Parks main office, this spot has 13 different kinds of coffee, and almost as many variations on cake and ice cream. Have a latte as you hitch your laptop to the wi-fi network.

Jep's Restaurant (☎ 0 3864 4112; Ao Hin Khok; dishes 40-150B; ☯ breakfast, lunch & dinner) With Thai, Indian, Mexican, Japanese and European food, you should find something you like at this sand-between-the-toes spot that also does regular beach barbecues.

Naga Bar (☎ 0 3864 4035; Ao Hin Khok; dishes 60-150B) Has a huge menu with Thai set meals (so you can taste everything), meat pies, real coffee and fresh-baked goods. There's a bar across the road next to the *moo·ay tai* ring (where you can duke out who pays for the next round).

Silver Sand Bar (☎ 0 6530 2417; Ao Phai; dishes 60-180B; ☯ breakfast, lunch & dinner) As well as a regular menu, Silver Sand offers fresh crêpes (sweet and savoury), a juice bar and nightly movies. Once the movies end, the action progresses (regresses?) to cocktail buckets and fire shows on the beach. There is even a burger bar to appease the midnight munchies.

Baywatch Bar (☎ 08 1826 7834; Ao Wong Deuan; kebabs 190-290B; ☯ breakfast, lunch & dinner) There's chill-out platforms and Asian umbrellas, and beanbag chairs on the sand after dark. The cocktails are strong and it's a fun evening crowd.

Tok's Little Bar (☎ 0 3864 4072; Ao Hin Khok) With sticks-and-straw decor, a few locals who fancy themselves as ladykillers, and nightly drinking games, you won't mistake this place for a sophisticated cocktail bar. Food is also available (60B to 150B).

Getting There & Away

Ferries (one way/return 50/100B, 40 minutes) depart hourly between 7am and 5pm from Ban Phe's Saphan Nuan Tip pier – opposite the 7-Eleven, where the buses and *sŏrng·tăa·ou* stop. Tickets can be bought from a small **tourist information centre** (☎ 0 3889 6155; ☯ 7am-5pm) on the pier itself. Ferries return to Ban Phe from the pier in Na Dan hourly from 7am to 5pm – buy your ticket at the pier. Despite what you may be told, you don't need to buy a round-trip ticket.

From Ban Phe, two scheduled ferries (9am and noon) also make the run to Ao Wong Deuan (one way/return 70/110B, one hour). They make the trip in reverse at 8.30am and noon. In the high season boats run to other bays if enough people show an interest. Alternatively, you can charter a speedboat to any of the island's beaches. They are quite expensive (1200B to Na Dan or 1600B to Ao Wai), but they take up to 10 passengers for this price, so it's worthwhile if you're travelling in a group.

Ignore the touts that congregate around the ferry terminal as they charge inflated prices for boat tickets and will hassle you into pre-booking expensive accommodation – just go straight to the ticket office. There have been complaints of boat scams from Ban Phe; see p246.

To get off Ko Samet in a hurry, charter a speedboat. Ask at your hotel, or call **Jimmy's Tours** (☎ 08 9832 1627). Prices start at 1200B from Na Dan.

Getting Around
Ko Samet's small size makes it a great place to explore on foot. A network of dirt roads connects the western beach and most of the southern bays, while walking trails snake over the boulders and headlands that separate beaches all the way to the southernmost tip.

It's only a 15-minute walk from Na Dan to Hat Sai Kaew, but if you are carting luggage or want to go further, grass-green *sŏrng·tăa·ou* meet arriving boats at the pier and provide drop-offs down the island. Set fares for transport from Na Dan are posted on a tree in front of Na Dan harbour. Nobody takes them that seriously, but you shouldn't have to pay much more than 20B to 50B. If drivers don't have enough people to fill the vehicle, they either won't go or they will charge passengers 200B to 500B to charter the whole vehicle. *Sŏrng·tăa·ou* also congregate at Silver Sand and behind the beach on Ao Wong Deuan.

You can rent motorcycles nearly everywhere along the northern half of the island. Expect to pay about 300B per day or an hourly rate of 100B. The dirt roads are rough and quite hilly – you may want to walk. At any rate, make sure to test the brakes before you decide.

CHANTHABURI PROVINCE

CHANTHABURI
จันทบุรี
pop 86,400
The so-called 'City of the Moon' is proof that all that glitters is not gold. Here, gemstones

do the sparkling, and if traders get the deal right, the glimmer infuses their pockets with healthy profits. Buyers from across Southeast Asia come to Chanthaburi to deal in sapphires and rubies, and from Friday to Sunday the city is bustling and cosmopolitan. On other days the city breathes out, and a diverse history including French, Chinese and Vietnamese influences echoes around the quiet riverside lanes to provide a calming remedy to the push and shove of its more mercantile face.

History
The city's Vietnamese community began arriving in the 19th century when Christian refugees escaped religious and political persecution in Cochin China (southern Vietnam). A second wave followed in the 1920s and 1940s, fleeing French rule, and a third arrived after the 1975 communist takeover of southern Vietnam.

From 1893 to 1905, while negotiating with the Siamese over the borders for Laos and Cambodia, the French occupied Chanthaburi, stamping their own identity on the town as well.

Orientation
Th Si Chan, or 'Gems Rd', runs parallel to the river and is Chanthaburi's commercial heart. Around this thoroughfare is where you'll find famed gem shops. The bus station and King Taksin Park are about 800m west.

Information
Banks with change facilities and ATMs can be found across town.
Bank of Ayudhya (Th Khwang)
Chanthaburi Bangkok Hospital (☎ 0 3935 1467; Th Tha Luang; ☺ 6am-9pm) Part of the Bangkok group; handles emergencies.
Om.com (134 Th Si Chan; per hr 10B; ☺ 9am-10pm) Possibly the cheapest internet in Thailand.

Sights & Activities
Peering through magnifying glasses in **gem shops** along Th Si Chan and Th Thetsaban 4, the city's gem dealers are Chanthaburi's living, breathing highlight. All day Friday and Saturday, and on Sunday morning, the surrounding streets are overflowing with the banter and intrigue of the hard sell. You'll be offered the 'deal of a lifetime', but walk away unless you really know what you're doing. This is strictly a spectator sport – great deals

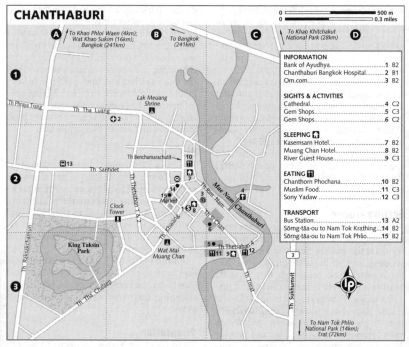

CHANTHABURI

can be clinched by the savvy, but amateurs are likely to go home with a bagful of worthless rocks. You're better off filling up at the food stalls surrounding the commercial bustle; there'll be more guarantee of satisfaction. If you really feel the urge to buy, plenty of air-con gem shops offer pricier but less risky deals.

The Vietnamese and French have left an indelible stamp on Chanthaburi. Creaking **shophouses** run alongside the river on Th Rim Nam and garish **Chinese temples** punctuate the town. The French-style **cathedral** (daylight), across a footbridge from Th Rim Nam, is the architectural highlight. A small missionary chapel was built here in 1711, but after undergoing four reconstructions between 1712 and 1906 (the last by the French), the structure is now the largest building of its kind in Thailand.

King Taksin Park (24 hr) is the town's main oasis and is filled with picnicking families. Judging by some of the expressions on show, that includes a few who have lost out on the gem market. It's a pleasant spot for a quiet, thoughtful stroll.

Four kilometres north of town off Rte 3249 is **Khao Phloi Waen** (Ring-Sapphire Mountain; admission free; daylight hr), which is only 150m high but features a Sri Lankan–style *chedi* on top, built during the reign of Rama IV. Tunnels dug into the side of the hill were once gem-mining shafts.

Wat Khao Sukim doubles as a local meditation centre and is 16km north of Chanthaburi, off Rte 3322. The **museum** (donation appreciated) on the *wát* (temple) grounds contains valuable items donated to the temple, including jade carvings, ceramics and antique furniture, as well as resin figures of some of Thailand's most revered monks.

Festivals

During early December every year there is a **gem festival**, when Chanthaburi gets very crowded. Highlights of the festival include jewellery shows and a gem-design competition. In the first week of June each year, Chanthaburi's annual **fruit festival** is a good opportunity to sample the region's superb produce, especially rambutans, mangosteens and the ever-pungent durian.

SOUTHEASTERN THAILAND

Sleeping

Accommodation can get very busy. Try and book ahead, especially from Friday to Sunday when the gem traders are in town.

River Guest House (☎ 0 3932 8211; 3/5-8 Th Si Chan; r incl breakfast 150-350B; 🕸 💻) Painted in shades of soft taupe and beige, Chanthaburi's real gems are the clean rooms and relaxed sitting area by the river at this friendly place. There's a fair bit of highway noise, but air-con should drown it out. The cheapest rooms share baths.

Muang Chan Hotel (☎ 0 3932 1073; fax 0 3932 7244; 257-259 Th Si Chan; r 250-600B; 🕸) A bit dingy – the toothpaste-green walls could use a touch-up – but perfectly friendly. An OK back-up if River Guest House is full.

Kasemsarn Hotel (☎ 0 3931 1100; kasemsarnhotel @yahoo.com; Th Benchamarachutit 98/1; r 1300-1500B; 🕸) Leaves cascade down from the outdoor hallways, and the staff are very attentive. The rooms are large, and with discounts of up to 45% during the week it can be a good-value option.

Eating

To try the famous Chanthaburi *gŏo·ay đĕe·o sên jan* (noodles), head for the Chinese-Vietnamese part of town along Mae Nam Chanthaburi where you'll see variations on the basic rice-noodle theme, including delicious crab with fried noodles. Fruit harvested locally is famous throughout Thailand. Get to the market early for the best selection.

Muslim Food (☎ 08 1353 5174; 19/5 Th Thetsaban 4; dishes 25-50B; 🕙 9.30am-9pm) This tiny place has excellent paratha, biriani, curries and chai tea.

Sony Yadaw (Th Si Chan; dishes 30-100B; 🕙 breakfast, lunch & dinner) Many Indian and Sri Lankan gem dealers come to Chanthaburi to trade, and this tiny hole-in-the-wall vegetarian restaurant is their home away from home. Luckily the friendly Indian owner will also sell you a Heineken, so you don't have to be too healthy and righteous.

Chanthorn Phochana (☎ 0 3931 2339; 102/5-8 Th Benchamarachutit; dishes 30-120B; 🕙 breakfast, lunch & dinner) A dazzling array of Thai and Chinese meals includes such specialities as stir-fried papaya and local mangosteen wine. Try the Vietnamese spring rolls, and buy a bag of local durian chips (tastier than you think) for your next bus ride.

Getting There & Away

Buses operate between Chanthaburi and Bangkok's Eastern (Ekamai) bus station (200B, 4½ hours) every half hour from 4.30am

to 11:30pm. From Bangkok's Northern (Mo Chit) bus terminal, buses begin running at 6am and run frequently until 8.45pm. Buses also travel to Rayong (80B, 2½ hours, five daily) and Trat (55B to 70B, 1½ hours, hourly). If you're heading to Ko Chang, you can ride all the way to Laem Ngop.

It's also possible to catch a through-bus north to Sa Kaew and then east to Aranya Prathet (if you do need to change buses in Sa Kaew, the ones heading east are frequent) on the Thailand–Cambodia border (150B, 4½ hours). From this crossing you can take a share taxi from Poipet on the Cambodian side of the border to Siem Reap (near Angkor Wat).

Motorbike taxis around town cost 20B to 30B. *Sŏrng·tăa·ou* departing for various destinations, such as the national parks (see p255), stop in the market.

TRAT PROVINCE

In Trat Province, gem trading is a favoured method of putting rice on the table – unsurprisingly, *đà·làht ploy* (gem markets) abound. A by-product of this gem mining has been the destruction of vast tracts of land, as the topsoil is stripped away, leaving hectares of red-orange mud.

But there's plenty more to fire your imagination. Before you head to the beaches of rugged Ko Chang or its more delicate and subdued island neighbours, linger in the traditional riverside ambience of Trat. If you're in no hurry to travel east to Cambodia, then relax on the expansive beaches that run lazily down the coast to the border. Hat Sai Si Ngoen, Hat Sai Kaew, Hat Thap Thim and Hat Ban Cheun are all worth a look.

TRAT

ตราด

pop 20,100

For too many travellers, all they see of Trat is the shiny new bus station before they are shunted onto a *sŏrng·tăa·ou* to the Ko Chang ferry, or a minibus east to the Cambodian border at Hat Lek.

But if you linger for at least a night, the town's relaxed appeal takes hold. Meandering pedestrian alleys are lined with century-old teak houses filled with traveller-friendly guesthouses and restaurants, and you'll spend longer than you realise at the bustling markets.

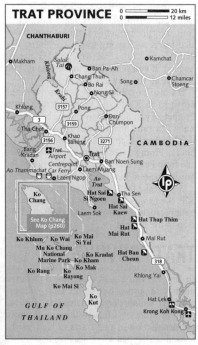

TRAT PROVINCE

If you're heading to Ko Chang, ignore the touts at the bus station advising you to hurry to catch the 'last ferry' to the island, otherwise you can expect the cost of your *sŏrng·tăa·ou* to the pier to be inflated. With Trat's guesthouses such good value, you're better off staying at least one night (don't miss the night market) and continuing your journey in the morning.

Orientation & Information

Trat's new bus station is around 1.5km north of the centre of town. A *sŏrng·tăa·ou* or motorbike taxi to the guesthouse area will cost around 30B to 40B.

Th Sukhumvit runs through town, though it's often referred to as Th Ratanuson.

Bangkok Trat Hospital (☎ 0 3953 2735; Th Sukhumvit; ☺ 24hr) Best health care in the region. It's 400m north of the town centre.

Koh Chang TT Travel (☎ 0 3953 1420; 109 Th Sukhumvit; ☺ 8am-5pm)

Krung Thai Bank (Th Sukhumvit) Has an ATM and currency-exchange facilities.

Police station (☎ 1155; cnr Th Santisuk & Th Wiwatthana) Located a short walk from Trat's centre.

Post office (Th Tha Reua Jang) East of Trat's commercial centre.

Sawadee@Cafe Net (☎ 0 3952 0075; Th Lak Meuang; per min 1B; ☺ 10am-10pm) Internet and Skype are both available.

Telephone office (Th Tha Reua Jang) Located near the post office.

Tratosphere Books (23 Soi Rimklong; ☺ 8am-10pm) Has second-hand titles in English and pretty much every other language. Owner Serge is a good source of information about Ko Kut, Ko Wai and Ko Mak.

Sights

Wat Plai Khlong (Wat Bupharam; ☺ 9am-5pm) offers a quiet (during the week) retreat from the bustle of central Trat. Several of the wooden buildings date to the late-Ayuthaya period, including the *wí·hähn* (large hall), bell tower and *gù·dì* (monks' quarters). The *wí·hähn* contains sacred relics and Buddha images dating from the Ayuthaya period and earlier. It is 2km west of the centre.

Trat is overpopulated with markets. The indoor market beneath the municipal shopping centre off Th Sukhumvit, the old day market off Th Tat Mai, and another nearby day market are all worth a look. The latter becomes an excellent night market in the evening.

The city is also famous for its *nám·man lĕu·ang* (yellow oil), a herb-infused liquid touted as a remedy for everything from arthritis to stomach upsets. It's produced by a resident, Mae Ang-Ki (Somthawin Pasananon), using a secret pharmaceutical recipe that has been handed down through her Chinese-Thai family for generations. It's said if you leave Trat without a couple of bottles of *nám·man lĕu·ang*, then you really haven't been to Trat. Put a couple of drops on your palms, rub them together and take a good whiff. It's also great for aches and pains, insect bites and pimples, and is available at pharmacies across town as well as Tratosphere Books (see above).

A **walkway** follows the river at the southern edge of the old town. It provides a good perspective of life along the river, but unfortunately has been constructed in ugly concrete.

About 5km outside town towards Tha Dan Kao is a **mangrove forest** that has a nice raised walkway meandering through it. Arrive at sunset for a firefly show.

In the opposite direction, behind Wat Plai Khlong, is a small **lake**. While it's not exactly stunning, it has pretty sunsets, a couple of restaurants, and you can loop around the lake on a pleasant bike ride. Enquire at your guesthouse or Cool Corner (p256) about bike rentals.

Sleeping

Trat has many cheap hotels housed in traditional wooden buildings on and around Th Thana Charoen. You'll find it hard to spend more even if you want to. Guesthouse owners in Trat are becoming increasingly competitive and you may be met by a scrum at the bus station. There have been reports of travellers being offered air-con rooms, but then having to accept cheaper, more budget accommodation once they were delivered to the guesthouse. Ask the touts to ring their guesthouse for you, and try and speak to reception to get an assurance that the room type being offered is actually available.

Garden Guest House (☎ 0 3952 1018; 87/1 Th Sukhumvit; r 120B) Don't be put off by the young Thai boxers lifting weights out front; the rooms are in back, quiet and testosterone-free. Of the eight rooms, only one has a private bath (200B). It's across Th Sukhumvit from the old town.

Ban Jaidee Guest House (☎ 0 3952 0678; 6 Th Chaimongkol; r 150-200B) This relaxed Thai-style home has simple rooms with shared bathrooms, and the whole place is finished with paintings and wooden objects made by one of the artistically inclined owners. It's very popular and booking ahead is essential.

Residang Guest House (☎ 0 3953 0103; www .trat-guesthouse.com; 87/1-2 Th Thana Charoen; r 260-500B; ☒) Big beds with thick mattresses and good bathrooms with hot showers – what more do you need? Fan rooms come with breezes and balconies, some of which overlook the river.

Other recommendations:

Sawadee (☎ 0 3951 2392; sawadee_trat@yahoo.com; 90 Th Lak Meuang; r 100-300B) Simple, but fastidiously clean, fan rooms with shared bathroom.

Pop Guest House (☎ 0 3951 1152; popson1958@ hotmail.com; 1/1 Th Thana Charoen; r 100-500B; ☒ ☐) Pop has rooms spread throughout the neighbourhood. When we visited, a new place was almost complete along the river a few km from town. Though the owners are friendly, at times they might be too friendly: readers have complained about getting the hard sell from them and from local touts at the bus station.

NATIONAL PARKS NEAR CHANTHABURI

Two small national parks are easily reached from Chanthaburi, and make good day trips. Both are malarial, so take the usual precautions.

Khao Khitchakut National Park (☎ 0 3945 2074; reserve@dnp.go.th; admission 400B; ☿ 8.30am-4.30pm) is 28km northeast of town off Rte 3249. Though it's one of Thailand's smallest national parks (59 sq km), it's bordered by the Khao Soi Dao Wildlife Sanctuary (itself bordered by another wildlife sanctuary), and is said to harbour herds of wild elephants.

The watery cascade of **Nam Tok Krathing** is Khao Khitchakut's main attraction. Thirteen tiers tumble from a high hill, visible from the road. A trail follows the numbered falls, climbs up past turquoise plunge pools (hint: numbers 1, 7 and 8 are best for swimming), and gets very steep after number 9.

Park **accommodation** (☎ 0 2562 0760; reserve@dnp.go.th) is available in a grassy lakeside campsite (50B per person) or in a two-person bungalow (600B per room). Phone or book online.

To get to Khao Khitchakut, take a *sŏrng·tăa·ou* from next to the post office, near the northern side of the market in Chanthaburi (35B, 45 minutes). The *sŏrng·tăa·ou* stops 1km from the park headquarters on Rte 3249, from which point you'll have to walk. Returning transport is a bit thin – expect to wait up to an hour.

Nam Tok Phlio National Park (☎ 0 3943 4528; reserve@dnp.go.th; admission 400B; ☿ 8.30am-4.30pm), off Hwy 3, is 14km to the southeast of Chanthaburi and is much more popular, as evidenced by the food stalls lining the road to the entrance. A pleasant, 1km nature trail loops around the waterfalls, which writhe with soro brook carp. Also on display are the mossy Phra Nang Ruar Lom stupa (c 1876) and Along Khon *chedi* (c 1881).

Accommodation is available in a campsite (site 10B, plus 50B per person) or in a six-person bungalow (1800B per room). Book online or phone **park reservations** (☎ 0 2562 0760; www.dnp.go.th).

To get to the park, catch a *sŏrng·tăa·ou* from the northern side of the market in Chanthaburi to the park entrance (30B, 30 minutes). You'll get dropped off about 1km from the entrance.

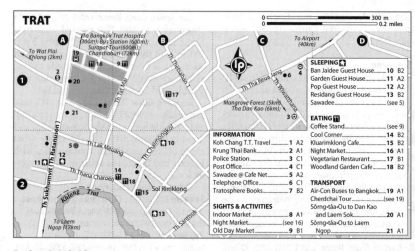

TRAT

INFORMATION	
Koh Chang T.T. Travel	1 A2
Krung Thai Bank	2 A1
Police Station	3 C1
Post Office	4 C1
Sawadee @ Cafe Net	5 A2
Telephone Office	6 C1
Tratosphere Books	7 B2

SIGHTS & ACTIVITIES	
Indoor Market	8 A1
Night Market	(see 16)
Old Day Market	9 B1

SLEEPING	
Ban Jaidee Guest House	10 B2
Garden Guest House	11 A2
Pop Guest House	12 A2
Residang Guest House	13 B2
Sawadee	(see 5)

EATING	
Coffee Stand	(see 9)
Cool Corner	14 B2
Kluarimklong Cafe	15 B2
Night Market	16 A1
Vegetarian Restaurant	17 B1
Woodland Garden Cafe	18 B2

TRANSPORT	
Air-Con Buses to Bangkok	19 A1
Cherdchai Tour	(see 19)
Sŏrng·tǎa·Ou to Dan Kao and Laem Sok	20 A1
Sŏrng·tǎa·Ou to Laem Ngop	21 A1

Eating & Drinking

With all the markets in Trat, you're usually only going to be mere metres from something tasty. The indoor market beneath the shopping centre has a food section, with cheap noodle and rice dishes from morning to evening. Grab a cheap breakfast at the ancient coffee stand in the old day market on Th Tat Mai.

The night market (confidently advertised as 'Food Safety Street'), is the best place for cheap eats. During the day, an unnamed **vegetarian restaurant** (dishes 20B; ☼ 6am-11am) east of the night market offers tasty vegetarian food at knockdown prices from the crack of dawn. It closes as soon as the food is gone – usually well before midday.

Cool Corner (☎ 08 4159 2030; 49-51 Th Thana Charoen; dishes 50-150B; ☼ breakfast, lunch & dinner) Though it's no longer on the corner since the original building burned down in 2008, the hip artist/owner (see opposite) still serves up great vibes, phat beats and darn good mango lassies.

Kluarimklong Cafe (☎ 0 3952 4919; Soi Rimklong; dishes 70-90B; ☼ breakfast, lunch & dinner; ❄) The winning combination here is delicious Thai food served in modern surroundings. The dishes are surprisingly affordable given the slick decor.

Other recommendation:

Woodland Garden Cafe (53 Th Thana Charoen; ☼ 6pm-midnight) Your best bet for cocktails and cold beers. When we visited the owner had just remodelled and was about ready to roll out a new French menu.

Getting There & Away

AIR

Bangkok Airways (☎ Trat Airport 0 3952 5767; in Bangkok 0 2265 5555; www.bangkokair.com) flies three times a day to and from Trat and Bangkok (one way/return 2575/5150B). The airport is 40km from town; minibuses and taxis meet flights. In the high season booking ahead is recommended.

BUS

Cherdchai Tour (☎ 0 3951 1062; Th Sukhumvit; ☼ 6am-11.30pm) runs hourly services (less frequent during off-peak season) from Trat's bus station to Bangkok's Eastern (Ekamai) and Northern (Mo Chit) stations, both 5½ hours, with fares 223B to 260B. Buses from Bangkok to Trat depart with the same frequency. Note that most Mo Chit buses also stop at Bangkok's Suvarnabhumi Airport, so if you're leaving Thailand you don't need to double back to Bangkok. At the bus station, **Suparat Tour** (☎ 0 3951 1481) also offers services to Ekamai and Mo Chit; fares are 257B to 266B. Cherdchai and Suparat's air-con Bangkok bus services also stop in Chanthaburi (55B to 70B, 1¼ hours). Ordinary government buses make the run to and from Bangkok's Eastern bus terminal for 200B, departing on an hourly basis.

Direct minibuses from Trat to Hat Lek (120B, one hour) leave every 45 minutes from the bus station. Sŏrng·tǎa·ou (50B) also trundle from the bus station to Hat Lek, but you will have to wait for enough people to show up.

Sŏrng·tăa·ou for Laem Ngop and Centrepoint Pier (40B to 60B) leave Trat from a stand on Th Sukhumvit, in front of the pharmacy (don't get confused with the ones a block north near the market – you'll end up chartering your own), and also from the bus station. They depart regularly throughout the day, but after dark you will have to charter one (250B to 300B).

Getting Around
Motorbike taxis around town should cost around 20B.

AROUND TRAT
Laem Ngop
แหลมงอบ

Laem Ngop is the jumping-off point for Ko Chang (see p266). TAT (☎ 0 3959 7259; tattrat@tat .or.th; 100 Mu 1, Th Trat-Laem Ngop; ☩ 8.30am-4.30pm) has an information office right near the pier. Further north on the road to Trat there is an **immigration office** (☎ 0 3959 7261; Th Trat-Laem Ngop; ☩ 8.30am-noon & 1-4.30pm Mon-Fri), where you can apply for visa extensions.

Between the two, **Kasikornbank** (Th Trat-Laem Ngop) has an exchange counter.

See opposite for transport information to Laem Ngop.

SLEEPING & EATING
There's usually no reason to stay here, as there are regular boats to Ko Chang during the day and Trat is only 20km away. If you do get stuck, try **Laem Ngop Inn** (☎ 0 3959 7044; s/d 300/600B; ☒), with a choice of simple air-con and fan rooms. It's a five- to seven-minute walk along the road to Trat.

Near the pier in Laem Ngop are several seafood eateries with views of the sea and islands.

Beaches
The sliver of Trat Province that extends southeast along the Cambodian border is fringed by several Gulf of Thailand beaches. **Hat Sai Si Ngoen** (Silver Sand Beach) lies just north of the Km41 marker off Hwy 3. It's good for sunsets and swimming, if the water is calm. Nearby, at the Km42 marker, is **Hat Sai Kaew** (Crystal Sand Beach) and at the Km48 marker, **Hat Thap Thim** (also known as Hat Lan); they're OK for a walk along the water's edge or a picnic in the shade of casuarina and eucalyptus trees. The only place for accommodation here is the **Sun Sapha Kachat Thai** (Thai Red Cross; ☎ 0 3950 1015; r 800B), which has comfortable bungalows with all the usual amenities and a restaurant.

There is accommodation at **Hat Ban Cheun**, a long stretch of clean sand near the Km63 marker. The 6km road that leads to the beach passes a defunct Cambodian refugee camp. There are casuarina and eucalyptus trees, a small restaurant and basic bungalows (300B) set on swampy land behind the beach.

HAT LEK TO CAMBODIA
The small Thai border outpost of Hat Lek is the southernmost part on the Trat mainland. There's not much here apart from a

---

MORN LAPKEON

As a writer, artist, traveller and cafe owner, Samorm 'Morn' Lapkeon brings a bit of Bangkok hip to small-town Trat. Partial to colourful headbands and baggy shorts, and often spotted riding a silver collapsible bike around town, Morn looks much younger than her 37 years. However, she runs Cool Corner Cafe (opposite) with a degree of sophistication and flair that makes obvious her life experience.

Morn was born and raised in Ayuthaya and earned a degree in Communication and Art from Bangkok University. She worked for a while in the casting departments for movie productions, but when an economic slowdown caused the loss of her job she headed to Trat. 'I had friends who ran a guesthouse here,' she explains, 'so I came to visit, but I liked it so much I stayed.' Enticed by the city's 'small size, good food, friendly people,' and proximity to Bangkok, Morn decided to open Cool Corner.

When asked why she opened a cafe that caters to travellers, Morn cites her love of learning English – and, though it's hard to believe, admits to once being very shy about speaking to foreigners – as well as her own enjoyment of travel. 'We can share our experiences,' she says. 'Travellers come to see my life, but then tell me about places like Europe and India. It makes me want to travel, to see *their* lives.'

small market just before the border crossing, and loads of touts to guide you through border protocols.

Motorcycle and automobile taxis are available from Hat Lek into Cambodia for 50B to 60B. There is accommodation on the island of Krong Koh Kong in Cambodia, but little to keep you there. If you plan to continue further, you can embark on a four-hour boat ride (US$15) to Sihanoukville. There is only one boat per day to Sihanoukville and it leaves at 8am, so if you don't get across the border early you'll have to spend a night on Krong Koh Kong. Basically, if you want to get from Trat to Sihanoukville in one day on the boat, you should be on the 6am minibus to Hat Lek and at the border with passport in hand as soon as it opens at 7am. From Krong Koh Kong, there are also minibuses that go to Sihanoukville (550B) and Phnom Penh (650B); both leave at 9am.

Cambodian tourist visas (1200B) are available at the border (bring a passport photo), but you should check with the Cambodian embassy in Bangkok before heading out there. Despite Cambodian tourist visas costing US$20 at other borders, payment is only accepted in baht at this border. If you try and debate the issue, be prepared for a frustrating time.

If you are going into Cambodia for a day trip, you can use the opportunity to renew your Thai visa, but do note that visas at land borders have been shortened to 15 days. See p754 for more information. This border crossing closes at 8pm.

See p256 for transport information to Hat Lek.

KO CHANG

อุทยานแห่งชาติเกาะช้าง

With steep, jungle-covered peaks erupting from the sea and ringed with swirls of white-sand beaches, verdant Ko Chang is in many ways the ideal tropical island. Others agree. Earmarked as the 'next Phuket' a few short years ago, Ko Chang's soundtrack is the beat and whine of hammers and power saws. Development has transformed great swathes of the island's west coast and expansion is now beginning to stud other more isolated areas of Thailand's second-largest island.

But escape to Ko Chang's mountainous interior and you'll find a lost world of rugged waterfalls and impenetrable jungle filled with a Noah's ark of wildlife, including stumptailed macaques, small Indian civets and reticulated pythons. Emerge from the forest and you'll reach isolated lookouts that gaze down on beaches just made for wannabe Crusoes. Thus, if your time on other Thai islands has included just a few too many days lying on the beach, on Ko Chang you can get nicely active and brush off any holiday cobwebs.

After all that honest exercise, recharge in an increasingly cosmopolitan range of bars and restaurants, and relax in accommodation that stretches from basic beach bungalows to luxury five-star resorts. Each of Ko Chang's beaches has a different style, from the family-friendly ambience of Hat Sai Khao and Hat Kai Mook, to the perfect party vibe of Hat Tha Nam (Lonely Beach). And while it's true that finding a pristine stretch of sand on Ko Chang is becoming more difficult, with a bit of time and travellers' get-up-and-go it's still possible.

After Ko Chang, move on to the other nearby islands of the Mu Ko Chang National Marine Park. You'll find less to do on gorgeous islands like Ko Kut, Ko Mak and Ko Wai, but after a few days of combining Ko Chang's catalogue of outdoor pursuits with late-night cocktails and beachside barbecues, you'll probably need a rest anyway.

Orientation

The **national park** (☎ 0 3955 5080; reserve@dnp.go.th; entry fee 200B; ⏰ 8am-5pm) is divided into four units, with offices at Ban Khlong Son, Tha Than Mayom, Ban Salak Phet, and just west of Nam Tok Khlong Plu. Entry fees are collected at any one of the four park offices. Keep your receipt as rangers may demand payment from visitors who don't have one.

Only the western coast has been developed for significant tourism and 75% of the island remains untouched rainforest. The sealed road down the west coast is a measure of Ko Chang's ongoing development. A few years ago it only reached Hat Tha Nam; at the moment it extends to Bang Bao, but plans to circle the island are in the pipeline.

The northern Hat Sai Khao is the longest beach strip and packs in the most accommodation, bars and restaurants per kilometre. Just south, Hat Kai Mook is a quieter alternative with good-value, family-oriented places to stay. Ao Khlong Prao sits around a rocky headland from Hat Kai Mook and focuses on more upmarket digs, while Hat Kaibae, further south, is transitioning between a laid-back beach setting and a bustling tourist centre.

The fast developing Lonely Beach needs a new English name, and is the island's centre for nightlife for younger travellers. However, there are still quieter bays with relatively deserted beaches just north and south of Lonely Beach's nocturnal fun. Bang Bao is a small fishing settlement in the far south with several places to stay, good seafood restaurants and a busy pier with dive shops, boat transport companies and souvenir shops. Development is impending though, and a luxury condo complex was being built when we visited.

The east coast is largely undeveloped with only a few low-key resorts. Hat Yao is one of the island's best, though a few new bungalow operations are drawing attention to this once-isolated stretch. Ao Salak Phet in the southeast of the island has a fishing village atmosphere and features good seafood restaurants, with a few quiet places to stay perched above the water.

Information
EMERGENCY
Police station (☎ 0 3958 6191; Ban Dan Mai)
Tourist Police office (☎ 0 3957 7255, emergency 1155) Based north of Ban Khlong Prao. Also has smaller police boxes in Hat Sai Khao and Hat Kaibae.

INTERNET ACCESS
Internet access is easy to find all the way down the west coast. Expect to pay up to 2B per minute.
BW Cafe (Hat Sai Khao; free wi-fi; ☯ 9am-late) Tucked off the road in the middle of Hat Sai Khao. Fresh baked goods and a nice happy hour from 6pm to 9pm.
Earthlink (Hat Sai Khao; per min 1B; ☯ 10am-11pm) For cool coffees and Skype at the northern end of Hat Sai Khao.
iSite (Ban Khlong Prao; www.i-sitekohchang.com; per min 2B; ☯ 9.30am-9.30pm) Has Skype, wi-fi, a travel agency and decent coffee.

MEDICAL SERVICES
Bang Bao Health Centre (☎ 0 3955 8088; Ban Bang Bao; ☯ 8.30am-6pm) For the basics.
Ko Chang Hospital (☎ 0 3952 1657; Ban Dan Mai) Just south of the main ferry terminal.
Ko Chang International Clinic (☎ 0 1863 3609, 0 3955 1151; Hat Sai Khao; ☯ 24hr) Related to the Bangkok Hospital Group and can handle most minor emergencies. Has an ambulance.

MONEY
There are banks with ATMs and exchange facilities along Hat Sai Khao, and ATMs at all the west coast beaches.

POST
Ko Chang post office (☎ 0 3955 1240; Hat Sai Khao)
At the far southern end of Hat Sai Khao.

TOURIST INFORMATION
The nearest tourist office is in Laem Ngop (p257). The free magazine *Koh Chang, Trat & the Eastern Islands* (www.whitesandsthailand. com) is widely available on the island and is packed with useful listings and tips. Its website is an excellent resource for pre-trip planning. It also publishes a 'Koh Chang Restaurants and Bars' guide.

The comprehensive website www.iamkoh chang.com is a labour of love from an irreverent Brit living on the island. His 'KC Essentials A-Z' section is jam-packed with opinion and information.

Dangers & Annoyances
The western beaches are often posted with warnings about dangerous rip tides and undercurrents during the monsoon (May to September). If a beach has such a warning, don't go in above your knees. Hat Tha Nam, Hat Sai Khao and Ao Khlong Prao have suffered several fatalities.

The police conduct regular drug raids on the island's accommodation. If you get caught with narcotics, you could face heavy fines or imprisonment.

Although the island's ring road is now sealed, parts of the route are very steep with several hairpin turns. The southeastern end of the island is especially bad, with many parts of the road washed out. Don't ride a motorbike unless you're experienced.

Smaller speedboats buck and kick like an angry mule, even on relatively calm water. If you're heading to or from the smaller islands and you're susceptible to motion sickness, take some meds beforehand and try to sit at the back of the boat.

Activities
COURSES
The **Koh Chang Thai Cookery School** (☎ 08 1940 0649; Ao Khlong Prao) at the Blue Lagoon Resort offers fun cookery courses for those wanting to re-create their favourite tastes once they

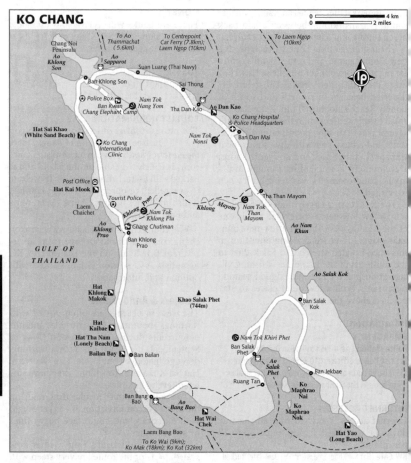

KO CHANG

0 — 4 km
0 — 2 miles

To Ao Thammachat (5.6km)
To Centrepoint Car Ferry (7.8km); Laem Ngop (10km)
To Laem Ngop (10km)

Chang Noi Peninsula
Ao Khlong Son
Ao Sapparot
Suan Luang (Thai Navy)
Ban Khlong Son
Sai Thong
Police Box
Ban Kwan Chang Elephant Camp
Nam Tok Nang Yom
Tha Dan Kao
Ao Dan Kao
Ko Chang Hospital & Police Headquarters
Hat Sai Khao (White Sand Beach)
Ko Chang International Clinic
Nam Tok Nonsi
Ban Dan Mai
Post Office
Hat Kai Mook
Tourist Police
Khlong Prao
Nam Tok Khlong Plu
Khlong Mayom
Nam Tok Than Mayom
Tha Than Mayom
Laem Chaichet
Ao Khlong Prao
Chang Chutiman
Ban Khlong Prao
Ao Nam Khun

GULF OF THAILAND

Ao Salak Kok
Hat Khlong Makok
Khao Salak Phet (744m)
Ban Salak Kok
Hat Kaibae
Hat Tha Nam (Lonely Beach)
Nam Tok Khiri Phet
Ban Salak Phet
Bailan Bay
Ban Bailan
Ao Salak Phet
Ban Jekbae
Ruang Tan
Ko Maphrao Nai
Ban Bang Bao
Ao Bang Bao
Ko Maphrao Nok
Hat Wai Chek
Hat Yao (Long Beach)
Laem Bang Bao
To Ko Wai (9km); Ko Mak (18km); Ko Kut (32km)

SOUTHEASTERN THAILAND

get home. Five-hour courses cost 1000B and you can expect to learn four recipes per visit. Book ahead.

KaTi (☎ 08 1903 0408; Ban Khlong Prao; class per person 1300B) also offers culinary classes, with a mother and daughter team demonstrating family recipes. Classes are Monday to Saturday from 10am to 3pm. You'll also need to book ahead.

Jungle Way (☎ 08 9223 4795; www.jungleway .com) offers tuition in the subtle art of reiki (Japanese healing). An eight-hour course held in a relaxed forest setting costs 5000B. Jungle Way also hosts numerous yoga and massage retreats; check the website for specific dates.

If you wish to learn a new discipline in a lagoon-side setting, head to **Baan Zen** (☎ 08 6530 9354; www.baanzen.com) on the lagoon at Ao Khlong Prao. In a breezy pavilion beside the water, courses are held in yoga and natural healing techniques (weekend course 4000B, three-day course 5500B).

DIVING & SNORKELLING

The seamounts off the southern tip of the island stretch between Ko Chang and Ko Kut, offering a new frontier of diving opportunities in Thailand. **Hin Luk Bat** and **Hin Lap** – rocky, coral-encrusted seamounts with depths of around 18m to 20m – are havens for schooling fish. Both **Hin Phrai Nam** and **Hin Gadeng** (between Ko Wai and Ko Rang) are formed by spectacular rock pinnacles and have coral visible to around 28m. Southwest of Ao Salak

Phet, reef-fringed **Ko Wai** features a good variety of colourful hard and soft corals at depths of 6m to 15m.

By far the best diving, however, is around **Ko Rang**. Protected from fishing by its marine park status, this place has some of the most pristine coral in Thailand. Visibility here is much better than near Ko Chang and averages between 10m and 20m. In the area, **Ko Yak** and **Ko Laun** are both shallow dives perfect for both beginners and advanced divers. These two small rocky islands can be circumnavigated and have lots of coral, schooling fish, puffer fish, morays, barracuda, rays and the occasional turtle. On the eastern side of Ko Rang, **Hin Kuak Maa** (also known as Three Finger Reef) is probably the top dive and is home to a coral-encrusted wall sloping from 2m to 14m and attracting swarms of marine life.

Diving trips typically include two dives with all guiding, transport, equipment and food, and cost around 3500B. PADI Open Water certification costs 11,500B per person.

Many dive shops close during the off season (June to September) as visibility and sea conditions can be poor. The following are some of the more popular outlets:

BB Divers (☎ 0 3955 8040; www.bbdivers.com) Based at Bang Bao, though it has another office at Hat Tha Nam.

Scuba Evolution (☎ 08 7926 4973; www.scuba-evolution.com) This newer business has three offices: Hat Sai Khao, Hat Kaibae and Hat Tha Nam. The instructors come highly recommended.

ELEPHANT TREKKING

There are several elephant camps on Ko Chang where you can get up close and personal with former working elephants. Of these, the award-winning (2007 TAT eco-awards for community involvement) **Ban Kwan Chang Elephant Camp** (☎ 08 1919 3995; changtone@yahoo.com; ☷ 8.30am-5pm), near Ban Khlong Son, is the best. In a beautiful setting the owner stresses the importance of seeing elephants in the wild, and he delivers informative and educational programs. A one-hour 'experience', involving feeding, bathing and an elephant ride, costs 900B; a 40-minute ride costs 500B.

Chang Chutiman (☎ 08 9939 6676; Ban Khlong Prao; ☷ 8am-5pm) offers a similar deal in a less dramatic setting. A one-hour ride costs 500B; two hours 900B. Kids under five ride free. The camp is in Ban Khlong Prao, opposite Blue Lagoon Resort.

> ### COVER UP ON KO CHANG
>
> Nudity and topless sunbathing are forbidden by law in Mu Ko Chang National Marine Park; this includes all beaches on Ko Chang, Ko Kut, Ko Mak, etc.

Transfers are included in these prices, but make sure you book in advance. Most places to stay can arrange these elephant treks with a day's notice.

HIKING

A combination of steep terrain and year-round streams creates a wealth of scenic waterfalls on Ko Chang. A series of three falls along the stream of Khlong Mayom in the interior of the island, **Nam Tok Than Mayom** (park fee 200B; ☷ 8am-5pm) can be reached via Tha Than Mayom or Ban Dan Mai on the east coast. The view from the top is superb and nearby there are inscribed stones bearing the initials of Rama V, Rama VI and Rama VII.

Nam Tok Khlong Plu (park fee 200B; ☷ 8am-5pm), another impressive (and popular) fall, is easily accessible from Ao Khlong Prao on the western coast. Set amid striking jungle scenery, the three-tiered fall is quickly reached by walking 600m along a well-marked, lush, jungle path. There's a pool to cool off in after your mini-adventure.

Nam Tok Khiri Phet is a small waterfall about 2km from Ban Salak Phet on the southeastern coast. A 15-minute walk takes you to a small, deep, plunge pool at the base of a small chute. It's usually quieter than many of the larger falls.

At the southeastern end of Ao Bang Bao, around the headland that leads to Ao Salak Phet, is a beautiful and secluded beach, **Hat Wai Chek**. Don't try hiking all the way from Bang Bao to Ao Salak Phet unless you're an experienced tropical hiker with moderate orienteering skills – there are a lot of hills and many interconnecting, unmarked trails. If you don't get lost, this rewarding hike will take four to six hours. Should you decide to attempt it, carry enough food and water for an overnight stay. If you do get lost, following any stream will usually take you either to a village or to the sea. Then you can follow the coast or ask directions.

SOUTHEASTERN THAILAND

The ranger stations around the island aren't very useful for solo trekkers, but you can arrange guides at **Evolution Tour** (☎ 0 3955 7078; www .evolutiontour.com; Khlong Prao). Lek from **Jungle Way** (☎ 08 9223 4795; www.jungleway.com) runs one-day (800B) and two-day (950B) treks into the island's interior. The one-day Chang Noi peninsula trek in the island's north is recommended if you're after some serious exercise. **Salak Phet Kayak Station** (☎ 08 7834 9489) guides overnight treks (one night 1500B) to the highest point on Ko Chang, the 744m Khao Salak Phet, from where it's possible to view both sunrise and sunset. You can choose to sleep in a tent or under the stars. Independent guide Mr Tan (☎ 08 9645 2019) leads equally intense treks from the west side of the island, often on trails he's cut himself. Hikes range from a half-day (600B) to a full day with elephant trekking (1300B). Birdwatchers should contact the **Trekkers of Koh Chang** (☎ 08 1578 7513) who run one-day and two-day trips (1000B to 2000B) into the national park.

KAYAKING

The **Salak Kok Kayak Station** (☎ 08 1919 3995; Ban Salak Kok), in a traditional stilt village in the island's southeast, hires kayaks for viewing the mangrove-forested bay. Kayak rental for one hour costs 100B and a 90-minute guided tour is 200B. It also runs a three-hour 'dinner cruise' (1200B per person) where you're guided through the mangroves at sunset while dining on home-cooked food.

Nearby a raised concrete walkway wends its way through the mangroves. It's not the most attractive construction, but it does immerse you in this fascinating ecosystem.

Many guesthouses rent out kayaks; prices generally run from 100B per hour and 300B to 500B per day.

OTHER ACTIVITIES

Some of the guesthouses at Hat Sai Khao, Hat Kai Mook and Hat Kaibae rent out inflatable beach rafts, sailboards, masks and snorkels, and boogie boards. Mountain bikes can be rented for 150B per day at several places on the island, most of which are located at Hat Sai Khao and Hat Kaibae. You can also organise day trips (200B to 1000B) and overnight trips (1500B to 2000B) to nearby islands from most accommodation places.

Bailan Herbal Sauna (☎ 08 6252 4744; Ban Bailan; ☽ 4-8pm) has a round earthen sauna set amid lush greenery where you can get healthy with different herbal concoctions for 200B. Bailan also offers Lao massage (350B) and facial treatments (40B to 60B) with locally harvested ingredients. Cool down afterwards in the juice bar.

Regarded by some as the best massage on the island, **Sima Massage** (☎ 08 1489 5171; Ao Khlong Prao; massage per hr 250B; ☽ 8am-10pm) is where the locals head when they need to nurse sports injuries or work out some stress. Male and female masseurs are on hand, and other treatments are offered: try the After Sun Body Treatment (600B) to soothe your skin after a day (or five) on the beach. It's on the road next to KaTi cooking school.

VOLUNTEERING

You'll probably notice fewer stray animals on Ko Chang compared to other places in Thailand. This is due to the efforts of the **Koh Chang Animal Foundation** (☎ 08 9042 2347; www .kohchanganimalfoundation.org; Ban Khlong Son), established in 2000 by American Lisa McAlonie. The foundation is funded entirely by donations, offers free-of-charge vet services to the people of Ko Chang, and provides refuge and treatment for stray animals around the island. Volunteer visits by travelling vets and veterinarian nurses are particularly appreciated, but the foundation also welcomes day visits from anyone who wants to donate a bit of TLC to help bathe and socialise abused animals.

Sleeping

More snazzy sleeping options are opening up every year. Rustic backpacker bungalows are far from gone, however, and the resulting mix of accommodation should please all tastes. Most development has been limited to the west coast, where you will find nearly all the sleeping and eating facilities. Ko Chang is also seeing a growth in package tourists from Europe, and remains very popular with Thai visitors on weekends and public holidays.

A few places close down during the wet season (April to October), during which time boats will usually go only as far as Ao Sapparot and Tha Dan Kao. Note that the surf further south along the east coast can be impassable during heavy rains.

The following are high season prices; expect discounts of up to 40% from April to October. Many places now offer websites and email addresses; consider booking ahead during peak season (November to March), weekends and major holidays, as the island fills up quickly.

Accommodation is listed in regions from north to south.

BAN KHLONG SON

At the northern tip of the island is the largest village, Ban Khlong Son, which has a network of piers at the mouth of the *klorng* (canal; also spelt *khlong*), a *wát*, a school, several noodle shops, a health clinic and an ATM.

Jungle Way (☎ 08 9223 4795; www.jungleway.com; r 200-400B) Stilted bungalows and a funky restaurant with a wildlife-viewing platform are tucked into the jungle near the Ban Kwan Chang Elephant Camp. You're nowhere near the beach, but there's trekking on offer (opposite), and the staff are fun and friendly.

HAT SAI KHAO

The long beach at Hat Sai Khao is not the island's best, but a wide range of eating and sleeping options, and a lively nightlife keep it popular. Over the last few years, more package tourists are staying here, keeping the prices of accommodation higher than elsewhere on the island.

There's a backpacker enclave on the north side of the beach; to get there you'll need to walk. Turn at the 7-Eleven in front of the KC Grande. When you reach the beach, turn right and walk for about half a kilometre. You'll know when you're there.

Independent Bo's (☎ 0 3955 1165; r 250-500B) A colourful place that clambers up the jungled hillside, Bo's is what the Swiss Family Robinson would've built if the family were on acid. All bungalows are funky and unique, and very clean. The cheapest rooms are 'way, way' up in the jungle.

Rock Sand Beach Resort (☎ 0 8712 0044; r 400-1500B;) Just past Bo's, Rock Sand takes budget accommodation up a notch. Simple fan bungalows share bathrooms, while the highest-priced air-con rooms look out over the sea. It's also family friendly with a kids' play area. The restaurant is popular and hovers over the clear blue water.

Logan's Place (☎ 0 3955 1451; r from 1500B;) Cool and crisp Scandinavian decor and service features in this Swedish-run boutique hotel found across the road from the beach. Unfortunately, a Wild West themed bar resides downstairs – mechanical bull included.

Cookies Hotel (☎ 0 3955 1056; www.fly.to/cookies hotel; r 2000-3500B;) Cookies has progressed from backpacker huts to two grand buildings straddling the main beach road. You'll pay about half as much again on the beach side, but the rooms in the low-slung building are nicer than across the road. The beachside section has a pool and bar.

KC Grande Resort (☎ 0 3955 1199; www.kcresortkoh chang.com; r 3000-6300B;) What was once an original backpacker setting has gone completely upmarket. Unfortunately, the original rustic charm of this spot has been diluted and the atmosphere is now a bit like a holiday camp. Welcome to the future of Ko Chang.

Next door to Bo's Independent and Rock Sand, Pan's Bungalows and Star Beach Bungalows offer rickety ambience at a similar cost.

HAT KAI MOOK

Laid-back Hat Kai Mook (Pearl Beach) is a quieter alternative to Hat Sai Khao and features mostly midrange accommodation. Most places are on the small, rocky beach and away from the busy main road.

Saffron on the Sea (☎ 0 3955 1253; r 1200-1800B;) Owned by an arty escapee from the hectic streets of Bangkok, this friendly boutique guesthouse has a deliciously bohemian ambience. Individually designed huts are painted warm colours, and the grounds are landscaped with rattan furniture and local flora. There's no real beach, but that makes the setting intimate and quiet.

Penny's Bungalow Resort (☎ 08 1595 9750; www .penny-thailand.com; r incl breakfast 1600-3500B;) To make room for the pool, the bungalows are a bit close together, but this is still a well run and quiet option a short ride from the brighter lights of Hat Sai Khao. It's family friendly, with plus-sized bungalows to comfortably store the whole brood.

Remark Cottage (☎ 0 3955 1261; www.remarkcottage .com; r 2000-3500B;) An overgrown garden conceals 15 Balinese-style bungalows that look simple at first, but are actually accented with interesting design details. Relax in the wooden spa pool or treat yourself with a course of shower spray therapy. Green and serene.

AO KHLONG PRAO

About 4km south of Hat Sai Khao, Ao Khlong Prao is developing as the island's luxury hub, but a few affordable places remain.

Tiger Huts (☎ 08 1762 3710; r 300-600B) In a sparkly sea of upmarket resorts, Tiger Huts clings firmly to the low-budget market. Forty unadorned thatch huts line a strip of sandy beach and come in two models: shared bath or private bath. They're simple, but (relatively) cheap.

ourpick **Blue Lagoon Resort** (☎ 08 1940 0649; r 600-1000B; ✹) Whitewashed bungalows with private decks and softly striped curtains sit right above a calm lagoon, and further back two-story air-con bungalows stand in a shady grove. A wooden walkway leads to the beach and there's even a hand-pulled raft across the water. This exceedingly friendly resort also runs a Thai cooking class (p259).

Aana (☎ 0 3955 1539; www.aanaresort.com; r from 7000B; ✹ ▣ ▤) Private villas perch prettily above the forest and Khlong Prao. With round walls and crisp decor, the Aana throws away the rule book for tropical resort design, and comes up with something fresh and unique. The rooms are effortlessly romantic and a few come with personal jacuzzis. This is one of the island's best.

HAT KAIBAE

South of the lagoon, Hat Kaibae is an expanding scene of midrange places and former backpacker spots moving upmarket. In the high season there are bad traffic jams (especially at weekends) as cars and bikes squeeze past on the narrow main road.

Kaibae Beach (☎ 0 3955 7142; r 700-2000B; ✹) Popular with holidaying Thais, Kaibae Beach has simple wooden fan bungalows and concrete (but well-designed) air-con ones. A large open-air restaurant fires up nightly barbecues.

KB Resort (☎ 0 1862 8103; www.kbresort.com; r 1150-2600B; ✹ ▣ ▤) An old backpacker stomping ground, KB Resort has gone upmarket and family friendly with a tot-sized waterslide and a teeny playground filled with wooden toys. Decor and design are very nice, but everything is a tad overpriced.

Garden Resort (☎ 0 3955 7260; www.gardenresortkoh chang.com; r 2200B; ✹ ▣ ▤) In a quiet location off the busy main road, Garden Resort has individually decorated bungalows, in-room internet access and arty touches such as bamboo piping in the sinks and showers. You can tell the owner had fun designing the place – look for the massive cement feet sticking out of the fountain.

HAT THA NAM (LONELY BEACH) & BAILAN BAY

South from Hat Kaibae is Hat Tha Nam – more commonly known as Lonely Beach. A backpacker fave, it's moving upmarket with flashier resorts moving in and a pumping nightlife scene flourishing in the tiny village. If you're looking for peace and quiet you're in the wrong place. Just south, Bailan Bay is still nicely low-key.

Paradise Cottages (☎ 08 5831 4228; Hat Tha Nam; r 300-500B; ▣) There's no real beach out front and the thatch huts are simple affairs with cold-water showers, but Paradise lives up to its name with a hip yet relaxing chill-out area. Individual dining pavilions are decked out with lazy-day hammocks and sea views, while a sleek fountain adds class. Cool beats further separate Paradise from the usual Jack Johnson/Bob Marley beach soundtrack, and the crowd tends to be a mellow one.

P & Nico Guest House (☎ 08 4362 6673; Hat Tha Nam; r 400-800B) Small tidy huts decorated in summertime blue and yellow are across the road from the beach, but well placed for bars and restaurants.

Magic Garden (☎ 08 3756 8827; www.magicgarden resort.com; Hat Tha Nam; r 500-750B; ▣) Mix Thai island style with an Ibiza groove and add a touch of the Burning Man festival. The Magic Garden's not for everyone, but this place is perfect for sociable 21st-century neo-hippies. Two-story round bungalows resemble tree houses; the smaller huts are your basic backpacker model. All have en suite bathrooms with hot showers.

Siam Beach Resort (☎ 08 9161 6664; www.siam beachkohchang.com; Hat Tha Nam; r 1000-2500B; ✹ ▣ ▤) The spacious, though somewhat tatty, air-con huts that gaze down on the water are the cheapest accommodation here. Fan and air-con bungalows cluster on the beach, and there are also new 'deluxe' air-con rooms right on the water. If you're really counting your baht, the same outfit runs Siam Huts just down the coast with simple, ramshackle huts (500B to 700B), complete with backpackers swinging in hammocks from the small verandas.

Mangrove (☎ 08 1949 7888; Bailan Bay; r 1000B) Here's proof that not all bungalows are created equal. Cascading down a hill to a private beach and an architecturally designed restaurant, the bungalows are round and spacious, with skylights and accordion doors that open to the views. Open-air, Bali-style attached bathrooms complete this laid-back, jungle paradise.

White House (☎ 08 1409 8307; www.whitehousekoh chang.com; Bailan Bay; r 1200-1500B; ⌘ 🔊) Bright white bungalows surround a small pool at this mid-sized beachfront resort. The beds are size XL but the best feature is the sunken bathrooms, decked out with clean white tiles. Less-expensive hotel-type rooms are set back from the beach and pool, but have less restaurant noise.

Warapura Resort (☎ 08 9122 9888; Hat Tha Nam; r incl breakfast 1500-3500B; ⌘ 🔊) Bringing Hat Tha Nam up a notch (but on a contained scale), these sculpted concrete bungalows are whitewashed and bright. All have open porches, and a few are seafront. A sleek dining area has eating pavilions with traditional Thai tables as well as a few hammocks, and a pool is being built when we visited. The faux-wood floors at reception sort of kill the vibe, but it's still a posh spot.

BAN BANG BAO

Though any trace of the original fishing village has been obliterated by dive shops, guesthouses and seafood restaurants, Bang Bao is still picturesque and charming to visit. The village teeters on stilts above the water, and is beautiful in the late afternoon sun. Some good accommodation options and the early-evening retreat of day-trippers makes a night or two here appealing, especially if you're headed to smaller islands south of Ko Chang.

Bang Bao Cliff Cottage (☎ 08 5904 6706; www.cliff-cottage.com; r 300B) Partially hidden on a verdant hillside above the Nirvana resort are a few dozen thatch huts that are nicely spaced out. Most have good views of the small cove down the hill, and a couple offer spectacular vistas. There's easy-access snorkelling down below.

Ocean Blue (☎ 08 1889 2348; www.oceanbluethailand com; r 700B) Simple fan rooms line a long, polished-wood hallway at this traditional pier house. Toilets are the bucket variety, and showers are cold, but the rooms are clean and you can hear the ocean slosh beneath you. The young crew running the place are quirky and funny.

Bang Bao Sea Hut (☎ 08 1285 0570; r 2000B; ⌘) With individual bungalows extending into Bang Bao harbour, this is one of Ko Chang's most enchanting places to stay. Each elegant thatched roof 'hut' (actually much flasher than it sounds) is surrounded by a private deck, with wooden shutters opening to the sea breeze.

Nisa Cabana Resort (☎ 0 3955 8161; www.nisacabana kohchang.com; r 4650-13,500B; ⌘ 🖳 🔊) Brand new and waiting for the posh set to arrive, Nisa has luxurious bungalows hidden in a jungle where no trees were unnecessarily felled. Quiet, privacy and seclusion are the themes, yet the sleek Asian architecture allows for plenty of light in the rooms. There isn't a beach, but a tiered infinity pool looks over the Gulf.

Nirvana (☎ 0 3955 8061; www.nirvanakohchang.com; r 5900-9900B; ⌘) Ko Chang's premium resort is hidden away on a quiet peninsula, and almost impossible to spot among rambling vegetation. 'Balinese' was the initial design brief, but each bungalow is furnished slightly differently in muted earth tones with subtle Asian accents.

EAST COAST

This part of the island can feel isolated with most resorts catering to Thai customers. A few stand-out options do exist though. Transport is limited.

A road now runs from just south of Judo Resort to Hat Yao (Long Beach), a quiet, pristine slip of sand with minimal development. Though the road has brought some development to the area, it was still poorly maintained and in bad shape when we visited. We don't recommend trying to drive a motorbike there unless you don't mind walking it for long stretches.

Treehouse Lodge (☎ 08 1847 8215; www.tree-house .org; Hat Yao; r 300B) The original Treehouse Lodge moved here from Hat Tha Nam, and yet another opening is scheduled on Ko Pha Ngan in 2009. Nevertheless, the new owners are keeping the name, and the vibe, going. A true backpacker paradise, travellers often stay longer than they planned. Basic huts (which share super-basic bathrooms) chill along a hillside, looking down to a softly sanded slice of beach.

Salak Phet Homestay (☎ 08 1294 1650; Ban Salak Phet; r incl meals 300B) One of several pier house stays on the island, Salak Phet's sees fewer tourists than, say, Bang Bao, and is all the more authentic for it. Accommodation consists of a bedroll on the floor of a small room, and shared, basic baths. You'll dine with the family, and meals usually include fresh seafood. The **Salak Phet Kayak Station** (☎ 08 7834 9489) can help arrange the stay for you.

Zion Guest House (☎ 08 4947 8179; yann.espinosa@ yahoo.fr; Hat Yao; r 300-400B) Just past the Treehouse Lodge is Zion, run by the wonderfully chill Yann (rhymes with 'yawn'). Though there are about a dozen en suite huts now, he has plans to expand accommodation on this beachfront locale. If the Treehouse isn't mellow enough for you, head down here.

Amber Sands (☎ 0 3958 6177; www.funkyhut-thailand.com; Ao Dan Kao; r 1600-1850B; 🕱 ▢ 🖳) The former Funky Hut Resort is under new ownership and is decidedly less funky and certainly more comfortable than its predecessors. Sporting a full facelift and some pleasant landscaping, the invitingly roomy bungalows still smell of fresh paint and are good value. Warm hosts Cheryl and Julian can pick you up from the ferry if you contact them in advance.

Eating & Drinking

Virtually all of the island's accommodation options have attached restaurants, but a few specialist restaurant scenes are also developing.

HAT SAI KHAO

Hat Sai Khao has the highest concentration of eateries.

Thor's Palace (☎ 08 1927 2502; mains 70-170B; 🕑 breakfast, lunch & dinner) The deliciously camp Thor serves up excellent food and terrific beats amid gorgeous surroundings dotted with mementos of his globetrotting. This shrine to Thor's innate good taste has fantastic views of Hat Sai Khao, but is only open in the high season.

Tonsai (☎ 08 9895 7229; dishes 40-150B; 🕑 lunch & dinner) Settle down on the funky cushions in this tree house/restaurant built in a sturdy banyan tree (*đôn sai* in Thai). There's a good selection of Thai and Western eats amid a nicely relaxed ambience. Make an afternoon of it.

Oodie's Place (☎ 0 3955 1193; pizza 170-260B; 🕑 lunch & dinner) Local musician Oodie runs a nicely diverse operation with excellent French food, tasty Thai specialities and live music from 10pm.

Invito (☎ 0 3955 1326; dishes 250-550B; 🕑 lunch & dinner) Probably the best place to splash out on the island, Invito is pricey and authentic. Wood-fired pizzas and hand-made pasta are the signature dishes and there's a full wine cellar. Be sure to finish your meal with Italian coffee and moist tiramisu. It's at the southern end of Hat Sai Khao.

AO KHLONG PRAO

With a couple of cooking schools and a laidback crowd, Khlong Prao has some decent dining options.

Blue Lagoon Resort (☎ 08 1940 0649; dishes 60-220B) 🕑 breakfast, lunch & dinner) With a cooking schoo on the premises, you know the food has to be good. Even better are the private eating pavilions perched over the lagoon and joined by wooden walkways. The service is friendly and dishes are creatively presented.

KaTi (☎ 08 1903 0408; dishes 60-120B; 🕑 lunch & dinner) Another Thai cooking school, another safe bet. The Thai food is what you'd expect from someone who teaches how to cook it, and your request for 'Thai spicy' will be respected. Also on the menu are a variety of unique smoothies, including lychee, lemon and peppermint It's on the main road 50m across from the entrance to Blue Lagoon Resort.

Barracuda Bar (☎ 08 1448 2187; dishes 70-150B 🕑 breakfast, lunch & dinner) A small place that is consistently good and popular with local ex pats. The prices are a little high since most o the guests come from nearby resorts, but it' not *too* overpriced. The few beachfront tables are where it's at.

HAT KAIBAE

Hat Kaibae is also developing a good bar and restaurant scene. At the time of writing, the always-evolving area included a French restaurant, a Muslim vegetarian eatery and a good Indian curry house. See what else you can discover.

Kharma (☎ 08 1663 3286; 🕑 breakfast, lunch & dinner Eclectic music, a wide-ranging menu featuring Thai, Mexican and vegetarian food, and a few inflated blowfish are all good reasons to head to this gay-friendly spot. The cocktails aren't to be sneezed at either.

BAN BANG BAO

A handful of excellent seafood restaurants line the pier in Bang Bao.

Ruan Thai (☎ 08 7000 162; dishes 80-300B; 🕑 lunch & dinner) The seafood is a little pricey, but it' about as fresh as it gets (note your future din ner swimming around as you walk in) and the portions are large. The doting service i beyond excellent – they'll even help you crack your crabs.

Near Ruan Thai, Chow Talay and the Bay offer similar food.

Getting There & Away

Three piers in Laem Ngop serve Ko Chang the main one, at the end of the road from Trat, is Tha Laem Ngop (also called Tha Krom

Luang Chumporn or Naval Battle Monument pier); another 4km northwest of Laem Ngop is Tha Ko Chang Centrepoint; while Tha Thammachat is located at Ao Thammachat, further west of Laem Ngop.

During the high season, Tha Laem Ngop is the main pier to many of the Ko Chang National Marine Park islands. There is a passenger (back-packer) ferry that runs a rusty fishing boat to Ko Chang hourly (100B, one hour), but it's often overcrowded and not the safest option.

From Tha Ko Chang Centrepoint, there are hourly ferries to and from Ko Chang's Tha Dan Kao from 6am until 7pm daily (one way/return 80/160B, 45 minutes). This is also a vehicle ferry – cars and motorbikes can ride it free with every paying passenger. This is a faster, cheaper and safer option than the backpacker ferry and will drop you off closer to the main beaches. A *sŏrng·tăa·ou* from Trat to Tha Ko Chang Centrepoint costs around 60B per person, though be wary of drivers who don't want to take you straight to the pier. Some will stop and have you buy a ticket at a travel agency, which is slightly more expensive than buying it at the pier.

Another way to get to Ko Chang is via the hourly vehicle ferry from Tha Thammachat. This ferry arrives at Ao Sapparot on Ko Chang (per person/car 60/120B, 30 minutes) and may be the only boat running during rough seas.

Getting Around

BOAT

Charter trips to nearby islands cost around 500B to 900B for a half day, or 1200B to 2000B for a full day. Make sure that the charter in-cludes all 'user fees' for the islands – some-times boat operators demand 200B on top of the charter fee for 'using' the beach.

At the southern end of Ko Chang, you can charter a long-tail boat or fishing boat between Hat Kaibae and Ao Bang Bao for 2000B, or around 250B per person if you can manage to fill a boat. Similar charters are also available between Ao Bang Bao and Ao Salak Phet.

Boat rides up Khlong Prao to the falls cost around 50B per person and can be arranged through most bungalows.

CAR & MOTORCYCLE

Bungalow operations along the west coast charge 200B to 300B per day for motorbike hire. Elsewhere on the island, rental bikes are scarce. Ko Chang's hilly and winding roads are quite dangerous and are best left to rela-tively experienced riders, as there have been a number of fatal accidents involving Western tourists. Jeeps can be hired for around 2000B per day in the high season.

SŎRNG·TĂA·OU

The *sŏrng·tăa·ou* meeting the boats at Tha Dan Kao and Ao Sapparot charge 60B per per-son to Hat Sai Khao, 70B to Ban Khlong Prao, 80B to Hat Kaibae and 100B to Hat Tha Nam along the west coast. You may need to negoti-ate. There are irregular *sŏrng·tăa·ou* to Bang Bao, but expect to pay around 120B to 150B. Between Tha Dan Kao and Ban Salak Phet, the local price is 50B per person, although tourists may be charged more.

AROUND KO CHANG

There are some dazzling smaller islands in Mu Ko Chang National Marine Park, some uninhabited but many welcoming tourists with open arms to postcard-perfect beaches. Getting to these islands is still expensive, but becoming more straightforward every year. Costs for transport, food and accommodation remain relatively high compared to Ko Chang and Ko Samet.

Visiting the islands is easier in the high season, and during the May-to-September low season many boats stop running and bunga-low operations wind down. On weekends and holidays during the high season, vacationing Thais fill the resorts on Ko Kut, Ko Wai and Ko Mak, but during the week the ambience is very laid-back.

In Trat, Serge at Tratosphere Books (p254) is a reliable source for up-to-date information on accommodation and transport to and from the islands.

Ko Kut

A rough tangle of jungle and gritty roads, Ko Kut is half as big as Ko Chang and the fourth largest island in Thailand. The water is clear, the palms are shady, and the beaches are top-notch; there's nothing in the form of nightlife or even dining, really, but those are the reasons for visiting.

ORIENTATION & INFORMATION

There are no banks or ATMs, though major resorts can exchange money. A small **hospi-tal** (☎ 0 3952 5748; ⏰ 8.30am-4.30pm) can handle

SOUTHEASTERN THAILAND

minor emergencies and is located inland at Ban Khlong Hin Dam. The **police station** (☎ 0 3952 5741) is nearby. Internet access is still a bit spotty, though many resorts have at least something going.

Beaches with gorgeous aquamarine water are along the western side at Hat Taphao, Hat Khlong Chao, Ao Bang Bao and Hat Khlong Yai Ki. A sealed road links Ban Khlong Hin Dam, the island's main village on the west coast, with Ao Khlong Chao further south, and with piered fishing village Bang Ao Salat on the northeastern shore. Just south from Ao Khlong Chao the road disintegrates into a bumpy dirt track, eventually petering out into a single track only suitable for motorcycles. Other villages on the island include Ban Ta Poi, Ban Laem Kluai and Ban Lak Uan.

ACTIVITIES

With its gin-clear waters and quiet coves, Ko Kut's surrounds are great for **snorkelling** and **kayaking**. Most resorts have equipment on offer.

Two waterfalls on the island make good short hiking destinations. The larger and more popular **Nam Tok Khlong Chao** is wide and pretty with a massive plunge pool. Expect to share it with dozens of other visitors, especially on weekends. It's a quick jungle walk to the base, or you can kayak up Khlong Chao. Further north is **Nam Tok Khlong Yai Ki**, which is smaller but also has a large pool to cool off in.

Koh Kood Ngamkho Resort (below) rents mountain bikes (per day 150B), and **bicycling** is a pleasant, if not rather dusty, way to tour the hilly island.

SLEEPING

Ko Kut lacks decent transport infrastructure, and most resorts cater to package tourists. Therefore, it's difficult to arrive and shop around for rooms, though the following all take walk-in bookings. You'd be wise to phone ahead though, especially since most speedboat operators will deliver you to your guesthouse's pier.

Koh Kood Ngamkho Resort (☎ 08 1825 7076; www.kohkood-ngamkho.com; Ao Ngam Kho; hut/bungalow 300/650B) Shady huts perch on a forested hillside on pretty Ao Ngam Kho (north of Bang Bao). 'Uncle Joe' runs a great setup that's the best budget option around – though the quarters are rustic, they're made fun with colourful tiles and mosaics. Super-simple huts hold only a mattress and mosquito net; they're snug and a step above camping.

Mangrove Bungalows (☎ 08 5279 0278; www.kohkoodmangrove.com; Ban Khlong Chao; r 600-1200B; ⊠) Away from the beach but lounging pleasantly along mangrove-smothered Khlong Chao this place has brand-new bungalows sporting polished wood floors and hot-water showers. A restaurant hangs out above the canal, and kayaks are on offer for heading upriver.

Dusita (☎ 08 1523 7369; Ao Ngam Kho; r 700-1200B; ⊠) With a sandy beach, leafy surroundings and pavilions and restaurants open to the sea breeze, the bungalows (both fan and air con) at Dusita are good value. Weekends are especially busy in the high season.

Siam Beach (☎ 08 1945 5789; Ao Bang Bao; r 800-1500B; ⊠ 💻) Sub-simple fan huts with mattresses on the floor and more expensive air-con bungalows sit on the best part of Ao Bang Bao' beach. A few have nice sea views, but the huts are overpriced.

Koh Kood Resort & Spa (☎ 08 1829 7751; www.kohkoodholiday.com; Ao Bang Bao; r incl breakfast 1000-1800B; ⊠) If you don't choose the air-con option, these roomy, jungle-clad bungalows with whitewashed outdoor showers are a good deal. Though there's no 'spa' to speak of, there are plenty of opportunities for relaxing – each bungalow has a massive veranda, while inside floor-to-ceiling windows let in sea breeze through wispy curtains. Don't confuse it with 'Ko Kut Resort & Spa,' on a different part of the island.

Beach Natural Resort (☎ 08 6999 9420, Bangkok 0 222 9969; www.thebeachkohkood.com; Ao Bang Bao; r incl breakfast 1200-2600B; ⊠ 💻) Balinese-style bungalows sit among loads of vegetation on a quiet cove that's great for kayaking. The customer service is beyond Thai-friendly, and the restaurant is the best on the beach. Chill-out pavilions beckon above the sand. Thais pack this place for karaoke-fuelled fun at the weekend, so try and come on a weekday for a quieter experience.

Shantaa (☎ 08 1817 9648; www.shantaakohkood.com; Hat Khlong Yai Ki; r incl breakfast 5000B; ⊠) Stylish bungalows top a sunny cliff at what is probably the classiest spot on the island. The whole place is luxurious but the best feature is the bathrooms. Stepping stones lead into a private garden, complete with two leafy outdoor showers or a soaking tub, and herbal toiletries complete the experience. Other amenities include stereos, king-sized beds, a private beach and a welcome lack of TVs.

GETTING THERE & AROUND

As the islands become more popular, transport options have expanded. Following is a summary of what's available; the range and frequency of boats increases during the high season. During the low season, transport to the islands can be nonexistent.

From Ko Chang, **Bang Bao Boats** (☎ 08 7054 4300) runs a 'fast ferry' twice a day in the high season between Bang Bao and the other islands. It departs Ko Kut at 9am and arrives at Bang Bao at 11am (900B). In reverse, the boat leaves from Ko Chang at noon. Alternatively, the 'wooden' (slow) boat to Ko Chang leaves Ko Kut at 9am (700B, five hours). A reverse-direction boat also departs from Bang Bao at 9am for Ko Kut.

Siriwite Speedboat (☎ 08 6126 7860) departs from Tha Laem Sok, 22km (approximately 45 minutes) southeast of Trat. It has a daily departure at 1pm for Ko Kut (600B, 1¼ hours). In the reverse direction, boats leave Ko Kut at 9.30am and 1pm. **Ninmungkorn Express Boat** (☎ 08 6126 7860; Laem Sok) runs a service from the same pier, departing from Ko Kut at 10am and from the mainland at noon (350B, 2¼ hours). Share taxis to and from Laem Sok are included in ticket prices.

Speedboat Dan Kao departs Tha Dan Kao, 5km east of Trat (not to be confused with Ko Chang's Tha Dan Kao), at 9am daily during the high season (550B, 1¼ hours). It departs Ko Kut for the mainland at 1pm.

On-island transport is thin on the ground, and you're better off renting a motorbike or mountain bike (see opposite). Motorbikes are widely available on Ko Kut, with prices ranging from 300B to 500B for 24 hours.

Ko Mak

Pretty little Ko Mak is only 16 sq km and doesn't have the jungled peaks and valleys of Ko Chang or Ko Kut, but its small size and lack of drama just means it has a lot more chill. Palm-fringed beaches are bathed by gently lapping water – it's almost a tropical-paradise cliché. Rainforest covers 30% of the island while coconut and rubber plantations take up another 60%, and few roads are sealed.

ORIENTATION & INFORMATION

There are no banks or ATMs on the island, so stock up on cash before visiting. The main pier is at Ao Nid, on the eastern side of the island, and a small village sits inland from there. A network of roads, most not sealed, links the beaches.

Ball's Cafe (☎ 08 1925 6591; Ao Nid Pier; per min 1B; ⏰ 9am-6pm) Has internet access and can help arrange accommodation and tours.

Ko Mak Health Centre (☎ 08 9403 5986; on cross-island road near Ao Nid Pier; ⏰ 8.30am-4.30pm) Can handle basic first-aid emergencies and illnesses.

Police (☎ 0 3952 5741) Near the health centre.

ACTIVITIES

With an array of dirt roads curving across the island as well as mellow terrain, Ko Mak has good opportunities for **mountain biking**. Near the health centre, **Chan Chao** (☎ 08 9728 0703) rents sturdy bikes (50/150B per hour/day) and has routes mapped out. Many guesthouses also rent bikes.

Snorkelling and **diving trips** can be arranged through most guesthouses, though **Kok Mak Divers** (☎ 08 3297 7724), on the road behind Island Huts, has a good reputation and is actively involved in coral development projects. Snorkelling, lunch and transport costs 650B, while a dive trip is 2300B.

SLEEPING & EATING

Ko Mak has some charming non-resorts (especially along Ao Khao) that offer a glimpse of slow-paced, Thai-island life. We have listed high season prices – expect discounts of up to 50% in the low season at the places that remain open.

The whole island, including accommodation operators, shows up to meet the daily boat from the mainland. Don't worry, they'll find you.

Island Huts (☎ 08 7139 5537; Ao Khao; huts 300-350B) Colourful wood huts with lazy hammocks and a small slice of semi-private beach make this budget spot pleasant, if you don't mind the fairly unforgiving mattresses.

Buri Huts (☎ 08 9752 5285; www.kohmakburihut.com; Baan Lang; r 500-1300B; ❄️ 🖥️) On the eastern side of the island, Buri has African-style huts that perch cheerfully on a tiered bluff above the water. The cheapest huts are thatch-roofed, while the concrete ones are topped with perky blue cones. An earth-coloured pool is surrounded by lounge chairs, though signs directing you to the resort promise 'no sand flies' on the beach.

Monkey Island (☎ 08 9501 6030; www.monkeyislandkohmak.com; Ao Khao; r 600-3000B; ❄️ 🖥️ 🍴) All budgets are catered for at what is probably the best backpacker accommodation on the island. Earthen or wood thatched-roof bungalows come in three models: Baboon, Chimpanzee and Gorilla. The former have shared bath, whilst the latter have open-air en suite bathrooms and spacious decks. All have fun design touches – when's the last time you saw purple sheets? One bar and one restaurant liven up the nights on sleepy Ko Mak, while a swimming pool the size of an iPod is fun for the kids.

Baan Koh Maak (☎ 0 3952 4028; www.baan-koh-mak.com; Ao Khao; r 700-1400B; 🏊) Competing for most stylish flashpacker digs on the island, Baan Koh Maak's bungalows are bright and funky. The white picket fences give it a fairy-tale Thai suburbia feel, but the neon green and fuchsia paint add a rebellious bit of psychedelia. The mattresses are softer than the usual low- to mid-range variety. The property also operates Koh Mak Cottages, with simple fan bungalows (550B), next door.

Ko Mak Coco-Cape (☎ 08 1937 9024; www.kohmakcococape.com; r 1000-4500B; 🏊 🍴) Owned by a couple of Bangkok architects (and it shows), this sprawling place is kind of Ko Med with its crisply whitewashed walls in the flashier bungalows and villas. The cheapest options are bamboo huts that totter over tide pools; these start at 1000B for a shared bath and fan. A compact swimming beach is just minutes away.

Makathanee Resort (☎ 08 7600 00374; www.makathanee.com; Ao Khao; r 2500-3000B; 🏊 🖥 🍴) Floor-to-ceiling windows open to sea views in these plush bungalows, which have deliciously soft mattresses and lots of breathing room. Though it shouldn't ruin the views any, the proximity of the new hotel that was being built directly behind the grounds when we visited was a bit of a buzz-kill.

Food Garden (Ao Khao; dishes 30-80B; 🕓 4pm-10pm) Across the road from Monkey Island, Food Garden is just that – a fenced in area filled with tables and surrounded by food stalls. A server will take your order so you don't need to peruse each stall (unless, of course, you want to). We recommend the *hŏy tôrt* – fried mussels with a side of sweet chilli sauce (50B). It's delish.

GETTING THERE & AROUND

Several speedboat companies run frequent trips between Ko Mak and the mainland; the best way to book them is through your guesthouse. Panan Speedboat leaves from the Ko Mak Resort pier on the northwest side of the island at 8am and 1pm, and departs Tha Laem Ngop at 10am and 4pm (450B, one hour). Leelawadee Speedboat has departures outside Makathanee Resort at 8am, 10.30am and noon; and Laem Ngop at 10.30am, 2pm and 3pm (450B, 1¼ hours).

A slow ferry (via Ko Wai) leaves Ko Mak's Ao Nid Pier at 8am for Tha Laem Ngop, and leaves the mainland to go back at 3pm (300B, three hours).

All boats passing from the mainland and Ko Chang to Ko Kut will stop at Ko Mak. Examples include Bang Bao Boat's speedboat, which leaves Ko Chang's southern town Bang Bao at noon (550B, one hour), and wooden boat, which leaves Ko Chang at 9am (400B, two hours); and Siriwite Speedboat, which departs Tha Laem Ngop at 1pm (450B, one hour). See p269 for more information on speedboats. Expect to pay 200B to 400B for transport between Ko Kut and Ko Mak.

Once on the island, you can pedal your way around (see p269), or it's small enough to explore by foot if you're so inclined. Motorbikes go for 60B to 80B per hour or 300B to 450B per day.

Other Islands

A few other small islands offer seclusion, azure waters and overnight accommodation. Most speedboats make stops at these points upon request.

KO WAI

Ko Wai is teensy and somewhat primitive, but endowed with excellent coral reefs. There are now several places to lay your head, all along the northern side of the island. Expect to share the bulk of your afternoons with day-trippers but have the remainder of your time in peace.

Ao Yai Ma (☎ 08 1841 3011; r 200-350B) A cheap and simple place to call it a night. The pricier huts have private baths.

Ko Wai Paradise (r 300B) A popular place with simple wooden bungalows on the beach. You'll likely have to share the coral out front with hoards of snorkelling day-trippers.

Good Feeling (☎ 08 8503 3410; r 300B) Your basic thatch huts with shared bath.

Grand Mer (r 400B) Six huts on a quiet smile of beach, with a small restaurant. It's on the northeastern side of the island.

Ko Wai Pakarang (☎ 08 4113 8946; www.kohwaipakarang.com; r 800-2500B; 🏊 🖥) The concrete aircon bungalows are as flash as it gets on Ko Wai. There's also a half-hearted coral information centre and turtle hatchery, as well as a restaurant/bar.

KO KHAM

Just northwest of Ko Mak, this tiny island is recommended for underwater explorations. Like Ko Wai, Ko Kham sees a lot of day-trippers bobbing around in the water. There is only one place to overnight here: **Ko Kham Resort** (☎ 08 1393 1229; r 400-2000B), which is tiny, simple and a tad overpriced. Speedboats (70B) zip across from Ko Mak Resort, and other boats will stop upon request. You can also kayak across from Ao Suan Yai on Koh Mak.

KO RAYANG

Rayang Island Resort (☎ 0 3950 1000; www.rayang -island.com; r 2400-3360B) Another tiny island off Ko Mak and another tiny resort. The Rayang Island Resort has fifteen refurbished one- and two-bedroom bungalows. There are no day-trippers, so it's wonderfully quiet. If you do want to be noisy, you can rent the whole island for €500 per day. If you're sleeping here transport is included, otherwise a speedboat will cost 150B.

PRACHINBURI & SA KAEW PROVINCES

The town of Prachinburi is worth a look for its interesting hospital, and the area is a good base from which to explore the southern stretches of the Khao Yai National Park (p467). Also in the region, along the length of the southern escarpment of the Khorat Plateau, are the contiguous Thap Lan and Pang Sida National Parks.

The rural areas of Prachinburi and Sa Kaew Provinces are peppered with many small Dvaravati and Khmer ruins. Sa Kaew means 'Jewel Pool', a reference to various Mon-Khmer reservoirs in the area. Not much more than loose collections of laterite blocks, most are of little interest to the casual visitor; keep going east on Rte 33 to Cambodia and see the real deal at Angkor Wat.

PRACHINBURI

In Prachinburi the **Chaophraya Abhaibhubejhr Hospital** (☎ 0 3721 3610; www.adhaibhubejhr.org; 32/7 Moo 12, Th Prachin-Ahuson) is renowned across Thailand for using traditional medicine to develop herbal remedies. The hospital's shop (open 8.30am to 8.30pm) sells affordable health and beauty products. The soaps, including galangal and mangosteen variants, are excellent, and the safflower herbal tea is recommended for lowering cholesterol. Buy these authentic products before your local Body Shop or Starbucks launches the mass-market versions.

Attached to the hospital is a serene massage room (massage per hour 160B) where masseuses take your blood pressure before they begin. Next door is a baroque edifice built by the hospital's founder, Siamese governor Chao Phraya Abhaibhubejhr. It's now a museum of herbal medicine. A túk-túk to the hospital from Prachinburi's bus station is 40B, and from the train station is 60B.

Getting There & Away

Buses leave for Prachinburi (95B to 115B) from Bangkok's Northern (Mo Chit) bus terminal. Four trains a day (two to three hours; 42B to 110B) travel from Bangkok's Hualamphong station to Prachinburi.

AROUND PRACHINBURI

There are a number of Dvaravati and Angkor laterite foundations in the area around town. Southeast of Prachinburi via Rtes 319 and 3070, in the village of Ban Sa Khoi (between Khok Pip and Sa Maha Pho on Rte 3070), is the Angkor-period **Sa Morakot** (Emerald Pool; admission free; ⌚ daylight). This was an important Khmer reservoir during the reign of Angkor's Jayavarman VII. Original lateriteblock sluices, along with assorted *săir·mah* (boundary stones), *naga* (a mythical serpent-like being with magical powers) sculptures, pedestals and a sandstone lingam can still be seen here. Water from this reservoir is considered sacred and has been used in Thai coronation ceremonies. You'll need private transport to get here.

Further west on Rte 33, the town of Nakhon Nayok is a popular getaway for Thais from Bangkok keen on outdoor adventure, especially year-round rafting. **Sarika Adventure Point** (☎ 0 3732 8432; Nakhon Nayok) runs combination trips featuring rafting on the nearby Tha Dan dam and mountain biking (one day 1800B). There's also abseiling on offer (one day 1500B). Sarika is 11km from town near the intersection of Rte 3049 and Rte 3050. Outdoors enthusiasts can also rock climb and trek; contact the **Tourism Authority of Thailand** (☎ 0 3731 2284; 182/88 Suwannason Rd) in Nakhon

Nayok for routes and bookings. Weekends see more companies running trips.

To the north of Prachinburi, Rte 3077 leads to the southern entrance of **Khao Yai National Park** (p467). The Palm Garden Lodge (below) runs daytrips (1700B per person) from Ban Kon Khuang to Khao Yai; the lodge is only 7km from the park entrance.

Sleeping

In Nakhon Nayok, Thai tourists pack the family-run bungalows along Soi Suan Lung Nai off Rte 3029 on weekends, but on weekdays these establishments are very quiet. There are misty views of nearby mountains and a network of pretty streams. Most places hire mountain bikes and kayaks. Not much English is spoken and there's no public transport, but a taxi from the Nakhon Nayok bus station can be found for around 200B.

Near the quieter, southern border of the national park, the village of Ban Kon Khuang on Rte 33 includes some good accommodation and is close to the park entrance.

Mai Ked Homestay (☎ 08 1458 9531; Nakhon Nayok; s from 100B) This friendly home is on a small farm, with a dozen different types of fruit trees as well as a fish pond. Breakfast, lunch and dinner cost an extra 50B, 80B and 100B, respectively. Beds are mattresses on the floor in a shared room. The **Tourism Authority of Thailand** (☎ 0 3731 2284) in Nakhon Nayok can assist with booking, as not much English is spoken.

Palm Garden Lodge (☎ 08 9989 4470; www.palmgalo .com; Moo 10, Ban Kon Khuang, Prachinburi; r 400-650B, bungalow 1200B; 🐾) Set in a leafy garden and featuring fan and air-con rooms, the Palm Garden Lodge is run by a friendly family. The food's exceptional and they've got loads of ideas for seeing the area. Motorcycles are available (250B per day) and they can arrange transport to Prachinburi's excellent night market and the Chao Phraya Abhaibhubejhr hospital (around 300B). Be sure to say hi to the pet iguana.

Getting There & Around

Frequent buses run to Nakhon Nayok (75B to 95B) from Bangkok's Northern (Mo Chit) bus terminal. Buses along Rte 33 to Aranya Prathet from Mo Chit stop in Ban Kon Khuang on request. **Palm Garden Lodge** (www.palmgalo.com) can arrange private transport and also hires out motorcycles (250B per day).

The area has excellent roads and is good to explore with a private car.

THAP LAN & PANG SIDA NATIONAL PARKS

At 2235 sq km, the **Thap Lan National Park** (☎ 0 3721 9408; reserve@dnp.go.th; 400B; ⏰ 8am-5pm) is Thailand's second-largest national park. Well known as a habitat for the abundant and gracefully impressive *dôn lahn* (talipot palm), the park is also home to elephants, tigers, gaur, sambar, barking deer, palm civets, hornbills and gibbons. It is hoped that the kouprey, a rare species of primitive cattle, still lives here, though it's been more than 30 years since the last official sighting. Illegal logging has damaged the park, but tree-planting programs are redressing the imbalance.

Facilities are minimal. To explore the interior contact the rangers at **park headquarters** (☎ 0 3721 9408) in Thap Lan village. They can arrange a tour of the park and provide camping permits (50B per person). There are also three six-bed bungalows (1500B) available – book through the Thap Lan National Park email address.

There is no public transport to the park entrance, which is 32km north of Kabinburi via Rte 304 (the road to Nakhon Ratchasima).

Approximately 30km southeast of Thap Lan close to Sa Kaew, **Pang Sida National Park** (☎ 0 3724 6100; reserve@dnp.go.th; 200B; ⏰ 8am-5pm) is smaller and hillier than Thap Lan. There are several scenic waterfalls, including Nam Tok Pang Sida and Nam Tok Na Pha Yai near the park headquarters, and the more difficult to reach Suan Man Suan Thong and Nam Tok Daeng Makha. From the bus terminal at Sa Kaew, you can catch a minibus to the park for 50B.

ARANYA PRATHET

อรัญประเทศ

pop 15,800

The border town of Aranya Prathet (aka Aran) has long been a magnet for refugees fleeing the turbulent chapters of Cambodia's roller-coaster 20th century. Displaced Cambodians flooded into the area after the Khmer Rouge takeover of 1975 and the subsequent Vietnamese invasion of 1979. Random skirmishes between Khmer Rouge guerrillas and the Phnom Penh government continued until 1998, but now the area is safe and is the most used border crossing for trips between Thailand and Angkor Wat in Cambodia.

A crackdown on gambling in Phnom Penh has caused a glut of casinos to be built in

Poipet. Most cater to Thais from Bangkok, and the contrast between visiting Thais and poor Khmers pushing rudimentary handcarts is startling.

Parts of this area are still heavily mined – don't stray from marked roads and paths.

Sights

The large border market of **Talat Rong Kluea**, at the northern edge of town, attracts a rag-tag crowd of Cambodians who cross the border to trade with the more affluent Thais. Gems, handicrafts and textiles were traditionally sold, but the emphasis is now on second-hand gear from developed countries. It's mainly thrift-store tat, but if you're after knockoff Converse, Prada or Gucci, or taekwondo gear formerly used by the South Korean national team, it's definitely worth a browse. Hire a bike (20B) to explore the maze of over 3000 shops. If you're not buying, it's still fascinating to observe the steady stream of Cambodians crossing the border with huge hand-pulled carts piled high with market goods.

Sleeping & Eating

Simple rooms for rent (from 200B to 300B) are available near the turn-off to the market just before the border. Look for the Pepsi sign in Thai.

Market Hotel (☎ 0 3723 2302; 105/30-32 Th Rat Uthit; r 250-400B; ✵ ☐) Service is a little lacking here, but it's a backpacker-friendly spot.

Ban Ratanatam (r 350B) Simple air-con rooms are just up the road from Talat Rong Kluea. No English is spoken. Look for the internet gaming cafe and food stalls.

Aran Mermed Hotel (☎ 0 3722 3655; fax 0 3722 3666; 33 Th Tanawithi; r/ste 1200/2500B; ✵) With air-con and spacious and comfy rooms in a shiny high-rise, you almost forget you're in a Thai border town. The Aran Mermed is tucked right behind the bus station.

Across from Kasikorn Bank in Talat Rong Kluea, a sign that simply advertises Coffee Steak Internet serves just that – on a shady wooden deck under red umbrellas.

Around the market there are many cheap food stalls.

Getting There & Around

Ordinary buses from Bangkok's Northern (Mo Chit) bus station to Aranya Prathet (125B, five hours) leave on an hourly basis from 5.30am to 4.30pm; air-con buses (215B, 4¼ hours) leave hourly from 5.30am to 10.30am, and from noon to 5pm. If you're travelling to Northeastern Thailand there are regular buses from Aranya Prathet to Khorat (200B, five hours). There's also a direct bus service from Bangkok's Suvarnabhumi airport to the border with Cambodia (190B, four hours).

Two trains per day (5.55am and 1.05pm) depart Bangkok's Hualamphong station for Aranya Prathet (3rd-class only, 48B, six hours).

From the bus station, a local bus (15B) goes to Talat Rong Kluea, from where you can walk to the border. The train station is near the bus station and a túk-túk from either the border or the market is 60B to 80B. Motorbike taxis cost about half as much as túk-túks and will also take you to the market.

Border Crossing (Cambodia)

The border to Cambodia is open daily from 7am to 8pm. First proceed through the Thai immigration office and then cross the border by foot to the Cambodian immigration office. You'll need a photo and 1200B (or US$25). You can also pre-arrange a Cambodian visa in Bangkok at the Cambodian embassy. A tourist shuttle bus outside the Cambodian immigration office delivers passengers free of charge to Poipet's taxi stand, where onward transport can be arranged. At the time of writing the road from Poipet was finally on its way to being in reasonable shape. Travel time has been cut in half and it's now only a two-hour trip to Siem Reap. See Lonely Planet's *Cambodia* guidebook for more information.

Note that this border gets very busy at weekends when Thais are crossing to the casinos in Poipet. Border officials suggest you get there early to avoid delays.

Chiang Mai Province

The mist-shrouded mountains of Chiang Mai Province have long enticed visitors to explore this southern slice of the great Himalayan mountain range. Initially drawn north by tales of elephants and vine-filled jungles, visitors are pleasantly distracted by the gateway city of Chiang Mai, a laid-back cultural capital. Further piquing the imagination are the minority tribes who live among the high-altitude valleys, struggling to maintain their ethnically independent identities.

The province straddles one of Asia's great crossroads – a southern spur of the Silk Road – fusing commerce and culture between points further north and west in modern-day China, Laos and Myanmar. Ancient caravan traders dealt in opium, silks and timber. Today, only silk remains a legal commodity and the horse-drawn conveyances are merely historical legends. Instead the province has adapted to the expectations of a modern marketplace. Chiang Mai is among Thailand's largest cities, though it retains the charm of a small town, and it functions as the north's principal hub for tourism, transport, education and cross-border commerce.

Outside of the provincial capital, Chiang Mai Province boasts more natural forest cover than any other province in the north. In addition, two of Thailand's highest mountain peaks are in the province: Doi Inthanon (2565m) and Doi Chiang Dao (2195m). Cycling, hiking, elephant trekking, birdwatching and river rafting attract those interested in the province's natural surrounds.

CHIANG MAI PROVINCE

HIGHLIGHTS

- Touring the sacred temples of **Wat Phra Singh** (p282), **Wat Chedi Luang** (p282) and **Wat Chiang Man** (p283)
- Making merry at Chiang Mai's **Saturday Walking Street** (p291) and **Sunday Walking Street** (p287)
- Learning how to whip up a Thai feast with a **cooking course** (p300)
- Embarking on the popular pilgrimage to **Wat Phra That Doi Suthep** (p296)
- Escaping to the country with a weekend trip to **Chiang Dao** (p327)

Chiang Dao ★

Wat Phra That
Doi Suthep ★
★ Chiang Mai

- BEST TIME TO VISIT: NOVEMBER–FEBRUARY:
- POPULATION: 1.65 MILLION

Climate

Most visitors will find the weather in Chiang Mai province to be most enjoyable during the cool season, roughly from November to February, when temperatures are mild and rain is scarce. The landscape is still green from the previous months' rains and the temperatures can be cool enough to warrant a jacket at night, particularly at higher elevations.

During the hot season, from March until June, Chiang Mai often experiences a 'fire season', when a thick haze forms over the city, a combination of dust and smoke from the burning off of nearby rice fields. Temperatures can be brutal and the once green forests become dry and brown. You'll find some relief from the heat at the higher elevations of Chiang Dao and Doi Inthanon.

The annual monsoons, usually lasting from June to October, are generally lighter in Chiang Mai than in central or southern Thailand. The outer areas of Chiang Mai city can flood when rains are unusually heavy but it shouldn't present an impediment to your travel plans.

Getting There & Away

Chiang Mai International Airport is an important regional airport receiving domestic and international flights. Chiang Mai city serves as the road transport hub for all of northern Thailand. The northern rail line terminates in Chiang Mai.

Getting Around

Buses and *sŏrng·tăa·ou* run frequently to towns and villages around Chiang Mai Province from Chiang Mai's Chang Pheuak bus terminal. Private transport is also available for independent touring.

CHIANG MAI

เชียงใหม่

pop 174,000

Snuggled into the foothills of northern Thailand, Chiang Mai is a sanctuary of sorts with a refreshing combination of city accoutrements and country sensibilities. It is a city of artisans and craftspeople, of university professors and students, of idealists and culture hounds – creating a disposition that is laid-back, creative and reverential.

Life is easier here than in the urban grid of Bangkok, making it possible to cast off the workaday blues in pursuit of long-delayed dreams, a popular fantasy among Thais from other provinces.

The city is often lauded for its enduring Lanna characteristics; for the quaint, walled quarter filled with temples; and for the surrounding mountains with their legendary, mystical attributes. The sacredness of the city is evidenced by nearly 300 temples (121 of which are within the municipality), a number that rivals Bangkok, the country's religious and monarchical centre.

But Chiang Mai isn't a pickled city, preserved to the point of inauthenticity. In reality, it is dynamic and modern without having lost its down-to-earth charm. Sure there's traffic, pollution and ugly concrete buildings that detract from the old-timers' stories of an old-fashioned village filled with bicycles, but the conveniences of Western-style grocery stores, widespread wi-fi and an internationally savvy tourism industry always comes with trade-offs. Adding to the modern mix of the city, the university students keep Chiang Mai looking youthful in indie fashions. The population of expats is relatively small and most do a better job of integrating (and learning to speak Thai) than their counterparts in Bangkok. This makes it easier for the average visitor to peek more closely into the average Thai life without bumping into cultural barriers. Plus Chiang Mai Thais have a noteworthy sense of humour that eases awkward exchanges.

So enough praises, what can you do in Chiang Mai? First, be glad you aren't suffocating in Bangkok and then be a culture geek for a few days: do a cooking course, go temple spotting, shop for local handicrafts or explore some of the nearby natural attractions. Before you know it, a week will have slipped by before you even start to get itchy feet.

HISTORY

Though modern-day borders slice the region's history into its own national allegiance, Chiang Mai and Thailand's other northern provinces share more of their early development with the Shan state of present-day Myanmar, neighbouring parts of Laos and even the southern mountains of China than with Bangkok and Thailand's central plains. For more information about the history and language of the region, see p337.

CHIANG MAI PROVINCE

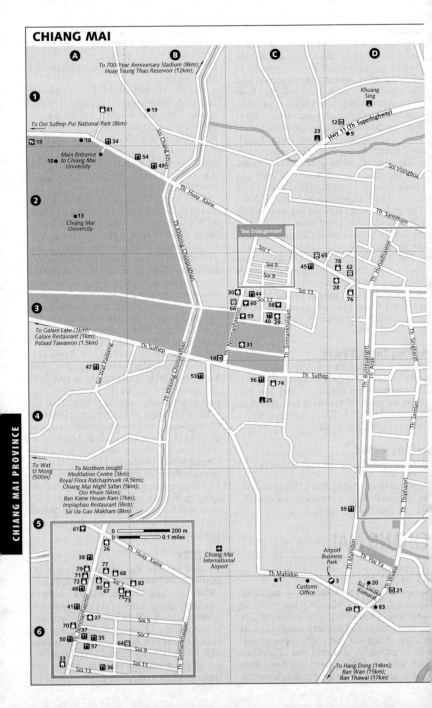

CHIANG MAI

A   B   C   D

To 700-Year Anniversary Stadium (8km);
Huay Teung Thao Reservoir (12km);

Khuang Sing

81   19   12   9   23

To Doi Suthep-Pui National Park (8km)

15   18   34   Hwy 11 (Th Superhighway)

Sa Chang Khian

54   49   Soi Viangbua

10   Main Entrance to Chiang Mai University

Th Huay Kaew   Th Santitham

13   Chiang Mai University

Th Klong Choprathan

See Enlargement

Soi 7   65   78   62

Soi 5   45   28   76

Soi 9

Soi 13

30   44   Soi 17

60   58

66   59   40   29

Th Kimmahaemin

Th Sirimankhalajan

Th Hutsadisewi

31

To Galare Lake (1km);
Galare Restaurant (1km);
Palaad Tawanron (1.5km);

Th Suthep   14   Th Suthep

47   Soi Wat Padaeng   53   56   74   Th Bunrueangrit   Th Arak

25   Th Samlan

To Wat U Mong (500m)

To Northern Insight
Meditation Centre (3km);
Royal Flora Ratchaphruek (4.5km);
Chiang Mai Night Safari (5km);
Doi Kham (6km);
Ban Kaew Heuan Kam (7km);
Implaphao Restaurant (8km);
Sai Ua Gao Makham (8km);

Th Thiphanet

55

61   0 —— 200 m
26   0 —— 0.1 miles

38   Th Huay Kaew   Chiang Mai International Airport

79   77   Airport Business Park

71   68   Th Mahidon   Th Mahidon

72   80   Soi 1   82

48   67   1   Customs Office   3   Soi Siwaka Komarat   20   21

75   73   69   83

41   Th Wualai

27   Soi 5   To Hang Dong (14km);
Ban Wan (15km);
Ban Thawai (17km);

70   37   Soi 7

50   35   64   Soi 9

33   57

36   Soi 11   Soi 13

CHIANG MAI PROVINCE

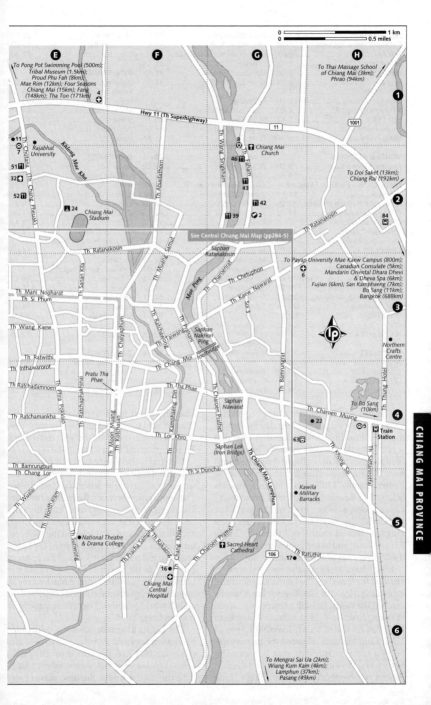

The history and culture of the region has been primarily shaped by tribes classified under the Tai ethno-linguistic group that migrated south from the Yunnan area of China to the mountainous belt of Southeast Asia. The dominant Tai kingdom of this region was known as Lanna (literally 'Million Rice Fields'), which is believed to have originated near present-day Chiang Saen, a border town on the west bank of the Mekong River. In the 13th century, the kingdom moved southwards through Chiang Rai and Fang, and to Lamphun, which was then the Mon capital of Hariphunchai.

King Phaya Mengrai (also spelt Mangrai) is credited for founding the Lanna kingdom and expanding it into the Ping River valley. Once he reached the valley, he built a temporary capital at Wiang Kum Kam. (The ruins at Wiang Kum Kam can be visited today, see p290.) Around 1296, King Mengrai relocated the Lanna capital to a more picturesque spot between Doi Suthep and the Ping River and named the auspicious city Nopburi Si Nakhon Ping Chiang Mai (shortened to Chiang Mai, meaning the 'New Walled City'). Traces of the original 1296 earthen ramparts can still be seen today along Th Kamphaeng Din in Chiang Mai.

Mengrai is also remembered by history as a skilled diplomat who formed alliances with potential rivals in nearby Sukhothai and Phayao. The cooperation between these three northern kingdoms, as well as geographic impediments, contributed to the region's successful resistance of the Mongol expansion in the 13th century. In the 14th and 15th centuries, the Lanna kingdom expanded as far south as Kamphaeng Phet and as far north as Luang Prabang in Laos. During this time, Chiang Mai became an important religious and cultural centre and the eighth world synod of Theravada Buddhism was held here in 1477.

The Lanna kingdom was soon confronted by challenges from Ayuthaya, the powerful city-state that had flourished in Thailand's central plains and that would later consolidate the region under Siamese control and help shape the broader 'Thai' identity. But it was the Burmese who would overtake the city and the kingdom in 1556, an occupation that lasted 200 years.

The fall of Ayuthaya in 1767 to the Burmese marked another turning point in Chiang Mai's history. The defeated Thai army reunited under Phraya Taksin south of Ayuthaya in present-day Bangkok and began a campaign to push out the occupying Burmese forces. Chao Kavila, a chieftain (known as *jôw meu·ang*) from nearby Lampang principality, helped 'liberate' northern Thailand from Burmese control, which led to the eventual integration of the Lanna kingdom into the now-expanding Thai kingdom based in Bangkok.

Under Kavila, Chiang Mai became an important regional trade centre. In 1800 Kavila built the monumental brick walls around Chiang Mai's inner city and expanded the city in southerly and easterly directions, establishing a river port at the end of what is today Th Tha Phae (*tha phae* means 'raft pier'). Many of the later Shan- and Burmese-style temples were built by wealthy teak merchants who emigrated from Burma during this period. Labour was needed to reconstruct the war-ravaged city and many workers from the Shan state and other outside regions were brought to Chiang Mai under the practice of corvée (involuntary service to the state).

There were many political and technological factors that ultimately lead to the demise of an independent Lanna state. The Bangkok-based government designated Chiang Mai as an administrative unit in 1892 during the expansion of colonial rule in neighbouring Burma and Laos. The completion of the northern railway to Chiang Mai in 1921 finally linked the north with central Thailand. In 1927, King Rama VII and Queen Rambaibani rode into the city at the head of an 84-elephant caravan, becoming the first central Thai monarchs to visit the north. In 1933, Chiang Mai officially became a province of Siam.

During the 20th century, Chiang Mai was an important centre for handcrafted pottery, weaving, silverwork and woodcarving. But by the mid-1960s tourism had replaced commercial trade as Chiang Mai's number-one revenue source. Throughout the decades, the national government has helped to modernise Chiang Mai by sponsoring educational and infrastructure projects as well as working to eradicate opium production in the province's highlands. In 2001, then prime minister and Chiang Mai native Thaksin Shinawatra sought to make Chiang Mai one of the nation's primary centres of information technology by expanding the airport and building super-highways. Thaksin envisioned doubling the size and wealth of the city and encouraging the building of five-star hotels so as to attract international meetings and high-end tourists.

The political demise of the Thaksin administration by the military coup of 2006 and the ongoing political stand-off in Bangkok has dampened the initial enthusiasm for Chiang Mai's grand makeover. The global economic downturn in 2008 has also added more uncertainty. But the city still plans to build an international convention and exhibition centre, slotted for completion at the end of 2009, and hoteliers feel confident that the city can position itself as an important conference destination.

ORIENTATION

In stark contrast to Bangkok, Chiang Mai is a very manageable city to navigate. Many residents scoot around town on motorbikes, covering nominal distances between their respective homes, jobs and playgrounds.

Most visitors base themselves in the old city. The majority of backpacker accommodation occupies the sois that connect to Th Moon Muang along the eastern edges of the old city, while the famous temples are spread out along Th Ratchadamnoen. The old city is easily navigated on foot or by bike.

Chiang Mai's newer parts follow main roads that generally bisect the city into the four cardinal points. Sometimes directions are given in relation to the various gates that allow traffic passage into and out of the old walled city.

The easternmost gate is Pratu Tha Phae, which leads to Th Tha Phae, another tourist area. Th Tha Phae leads to Mae Nam Ping (the Ping River) and the famous Talat Warorot. Nearby is the Chiang Mai Night Bazaar. The eastern riverbank (in this chapter under Riverside) has a lively restaurant and nightlife scene. Further east is the train station and the long-distance bus station.

Pratu Suan Dok exits the western moat and allows access to Th Suthep and Th Huay Kaew, two busy thoroughfares connecting the old city to the leafy environs of Chiang Mai University and Doi Suthep further west. The centre of Chiang Mai's uni scene is Th Nimmanhaemin.

CARAVANS OF NORTHERN THAILAND

Dating from at least the 15th century, Chinese-Muslim caravans from Yunnan Province (China) used Chiang Mai as a 'back door' for commodities transported between China and the Indian Ocean bound for international seagoing trade.

The principal means of transport for the Yunnanese caravaneers were ponies and mules, an animal-husbandry tradition adopted during the Mongol invasions of Yunnan in the 13th century. Astride their strange beasts of burden, the foreigners were nicknamed *jeen hor* (galloping Chinese) by the Thais.

Exports along the southern routes included silk, opium, tea, dried fruit, lacquerware, musk, ponies and mules, while northward the caravans brought gold, copper, cotton, edible birds' nests, betel nut, tobacco and ivory. By the end of the 19th century many artisans from China, northern Burma and Laos had settled in the area to produce crafts for the steady flow of regional trade. The city's original transhipment point for such trade movements was a market district known as Ban Haw, just a stone's throw from today's night bazaar (p321).

The northern gate is Pratu Chang Pheuak and Th Chang Pheuak passes the provincial bus station (Chang Pheuak station). The southern gate is Pratu Chiang Mai. The outskirts of the city are partially circumnavigated by three concentric ring roads that branch off Rte 121 (also known as the *klorng* road). The innermost ring road is called Th Superhighway.

Maps

A copy of Nancy Chandler's *Map of Chiang Mai*, available in bookshops, is a worthwhile investment. It shows the main points of interest, shopping venues and oddities that you will be pleased to stumble upon. *Groovy Map Chiang Mai Map'n'Guide*, also in bookshops, adds Thai script and more nightspots.

INFORMATION

Bookshops

Chiang Mai's 'bookshop alley' is concentrated on Th Chang Moi Kao. Most are open from 9am to 9pm.

Backstreet Books (Map pp284–5; ☎ 0 5387 4143; 2/8 Th Chang Moi Kao) In a rambling shop next to Gecko Books.

Book Zone (Map pp284–5; ☎ 0 5325 2418; Th Tha Phae) Directly opposite Wat Mahawan; new travel guides and travel literature, plus contemporary fiction.

Gecko Books (Map pp284–5; ☎ 0 5387 4066; Th Chang Moi Kao) A Chiang Mai chain, Gecko Books has several branches, including Th Ratchamankha and Th Loi Kroh; includes new and used books sheathed in annoying plastic wrap.

Lost Book Shop (Map pp284–5; ☎ 0 5320 6656; 34/3 Th Ratchamankha) Second-hand books free of plastic wrap for easy browsing; same owner as Backstreet Books.

On the Road Books (Map pp284–5; ☎ 0 5341 8169; 38/1 Th Ratwithi) A long-running second-hand shop with a small selection of good-quality reads.

Suriwong Book Centre (Map pp284–5; ☎ 0 5328 1052; 54 Th Si Donchai) A Chiang Mai institution carrying mainly Thai titles with a small but sturdy English-language section of Thai and Southeast Asian non-fiction.

Cultural Centres

Alliance Française (Map pp284–5; ☎ 0 5327 5277; 138 Th Charoen Prathet) French films subtitled in English are screened at 8pm on Friday.

American University Alumni (AUA; Map pp284–5; ☎ 0 5327 8407, 0 5327 7951; 73 Th Ratchadamnoen) Has a small English-language library and offers popular Thai language courses (see p301).

British Council (Map pp284–5; ☎ 0 5324 2103; 198 Th Bamrungrat) Small English-language library and offers the services of an honorary consul.

Payap University (☎ 0 5324 1255, ext 7242; http://ic.payap.ac.th; Th Superhighway, Mae Kaew campus) Hosts Thursday night lectures in English (called Payap Presents), discussing a variety of Southeast Asia topics.

Emergency

Tourist police (Map pp276–7; ☎ 0 5324 7318, 24-hr emergency 1155; Th Faham; ◷ 6am–midnight) Has a volunteer staff of foreign nationals who speak a variety of languages; some volunteers are posted at the Sunday Walking Street.

Internet Access

Most of the guesthouses in Chiang Mai have free internet access, including wi-fi. You'll also find plenty of internet centres along Th Tha Phae, Moon Muang and Ratchamankha.

Internet Resources & Media

1 Stop Chiang Mai (www.1stopchiangmai.com) Website covering city attractions with an emphasis on day trips and outdoor activities.

Chiang Mai 101 Quarterly magazine offering a guide-book-style introduction to Chiang Mai and surrounding attractions.

Chiangmai Mail (www.chiangmai-mail.com) Weekly English-language newspaper covering local and regional news and politics.

City Now (www.city-now.com) Fortnightly listing of events and workshops published by *City Life* magazine.

Citylife (www.chiangmainews.com) Lifestyle magazine profiling restaurants, local culture, politics and people.

Guidelines (www.guidelineschiangmai.com) Monthly advertorial magazine that features respectable historical essays on the north.

Irrawaddy News Magazine (www.irrawaddy.org) A well-respected journal covering news in Myanmar, northern Thailand and other parts of Southeast Asia.

Medical Services

Chiang Mai Ram Hospital (Map pp284-5; ☎ 0 5322 4861; www.chiangmairam.com; 8 Th Bunreuangrit) The most modern hospital in town; recommended by most expats.

Lanna Hospital (Map pp276-7; ☎ 0 5335 7234; Th Superhighway) One of the better hospitals in town and less expensive than Chiang Mai Ram.

Malaria Centre (Map pp284-5; ☎ 0 5322 1529; 18 Th Bunreuangrit) Offers blood checks for malaria.

Mungkala Traditional Medicine Clinic (Map pp284-5; ☎ 0 5327 8494; 21-27 Th Ratchamankha; ☼ 9am-12.30pm, 2.30-7pm) Government-licensed clinic using acupuncture, massage and Chinese herbal remedies.

McCormick Hospital (Map pp276-7; ☎ 0 5326 2200; 133 Th Kaew Nawarat) Former missionary hospital; good for minor treatments.

Money

All major Thai banks have several branches and ATMs throughout Chiang Mai; many of them along Th Tha Phae.

Western Union (Map pp276-7; ☎ 0 5322 4979) Send or receive money by wire; counters at Central Airport Plaza, Kad Suan Kaew Shopping Centre, Th Huay Kaew and also available at any post office.

Post

Main post office (Map pp276-7; ☎ 0 5324 1070; Th Charoen Muang; ☼ 8.30am-4.30pm Mon-Fri, 9am-noon Sat & Sun) Other convenient branches: Th Singharat/Samlan, Th Mahidon at Chiang Mai International Airport, Th Charoen Prathet, Th Phra Pokklao, Th Chotana and Chiang Mai University.

Telephone

Many internet cafes are outfitted with head-sets so that customers can use Skype. There are also some direct-dial shops in the tourist sections of Chiang Mai and numerous phone-card booths in shops and bars around town.

Communications Authority of Thailand (CAT; Map pp276-7; ☎ 0 5324 1070; Th Charoen Muang; ☼ 24hr) Out of the way, by the main post office.

Tourist Information

Tourism Authority of Thailand (TAT; Map pp284-5; ☎ 0 5324 8604; tatchmai@tat.or.th; Th Chiang Mai-Lamphun; ☼ 8.30am-4.30pm) English-speaking staff provide maps and recommendations for tour guides; TAT doesn't make hotel reservations.

DANGERS & ANNOYANCES

Compared to Bangkok, Chiang Mai is a breeze for tourists. The hassles from the *sŏrng·tăa·ou* and túk-túk drivers are minimal. See Getting There & Away (p322) for guidelines on reasonable transport rates from the bus and train stations.

Beware of bus or minivan services from Th Khao San in Bangkok that advertise a free night's accommodation in Chiang Mai if you buy a Bangkok to Chiang Mai ticket. What usually happens on arrival is that the 'free' guesthouse demands you sign up for hill treks immediately. The better guesthouses don't play this game. Theft can also be a problem on the buses that originate in Bangkok's Th Khao San.

Many less expensive guesthouses in Chiang Mai will sometimes evict guests who don't engage trekking tours. Most places are pretty forthcoming with their policies on this and will usually offer rooms to non-trekking guests for a limited period.

SIGHTS
Old City

Chiang Mai's historic quarter is tightly bound by old ways with a semi-gloss of modernity. The two-lane roads are now traversed by cars and motorcycles instead of bicycles and horse-drawn carriages, but the slow-moving pace of non-motorised travel still sets the communal clock. The buildings are human-scaled and reserve the highest elevation for the temple stupas that peak out over the rooftops. These temples were built with teak money and reflect the aesthetics of an ancient trade dependent on the forest: subdued colours of red earth artfully festooned with gold leaf. Small bells decorating the eaves tinkle in the morning wind before the motorcycle engines awake. With its many temples, it is easier to save your mortal soul than to accomplish more earthly errands like buying toiletries.

The narrow footpaths see a regular flow of temple-spotters as well as orange-robed monks (sidewalk space should be ceded to the boys and men of the cloth and women should step into the street to avoid an accidental brush), and off the main roads are meandering lanes through residential neighbourhoods filled with gardens and fragrant flowers.

All roads eventually lead to the old city wall, in some parts preserved or rebuilt and in other parts so worn and rounded by time that it looks more like a sunbathing lizard. The one-way roads that circumnavigate the moat are a jolt of big-city energy packed with speeding machines belching blue smoke.

WAT PHRA SINGH
วัดพระสิงห์

Chiang Mai's most visited temple, **Wat Phra Singh** (Map pp284–5; ☎ 0 5381 4164; Th Singharat; donations appreciated) owes its fame to the fact that it houses the city's most revered Buddha image, Phra Singh (Lion Buddha), and it has a fine collection of classic Lanna art and architecture.

Despite Phra Singh's exalted status, very little is actually known about the image. Legend says that it originally came from Sri Lanka, but it is not particularly Sinhalese in style. It is, in fact, considered one of the most beautiful examples of Lanna religious art thanks to its thick human-like features and lotus-shaped topknot. It does, however, have the usual travel itinerary of a famous Buddha, having been moved from Sukhothai, Ayuthaya, Chiang Rai and Luang Prabang either to elude looters or as a prized piece of booty. Because there are two nearly identical images in Nakhon Si Thammarat and Bangkok, no one knows if this is the real one, nor can anyone document its place of origin. Regardless, this Phra Singh image came to reside here in around the 1360s and today is a fixture in the religious ceremonies of the Songkran festival.

Phra Singh is housed in Wihan Lai Kham, a small chapel to the rear of the temple grounds next to the *chedi*. The exterior chapel displays the Lanna characteristics of a three-tiered roofline and carved gables. Inside, the temple

features sumptuous *lai-krahm* (gold pattern) stencilling on its interior back wall. On the north wall, a worn mural depicts the Thai fairy tale 'Sangthong', about an exiled prince who was hidden by his mother in a conch shell. A small figure above one of the windows is thought to be a self-portrait of the artist, an ethnic Chinese painter. The scene on the south wall depicts the popular northern Thai story of a divine golden swan, Suwannahong.

Wat Phra Singh's main *chedi* displays classic Lanna style with its octagonal base. It was built by King Pa Yo in 1345 in honour of his father. Closer to the entrance is the main *wí·hǎhn*, which houses a bigger but less important Buddha known as Thong Thip. This temple has royal associations, indicated by the garuda (the royal symbol) displayed on the front of the main *wí·hǎhn*.

Near the entrance is a small scripture library sitting atop a raised platform beautifully ornamented with Lanna-style features, including glass mosaics decorating the gables, ornate woodcarving details and sonorous bells attached to the eaves.

WAT CHEDI LUANG
วัดเจดีย์หลวง

Another venerable stop on the temple trail, **Wat Chedi Luang** (Map pp284–5; ☎ 0 5327 8595; Th Phra Pokklao; donations appreciated) is built around a partially ruined Lanna-style *chedi* dating from 1441 that was believed to be one of the tallest structures in ancient Chiang Mai. Stories say it was damaged by either a 16th-century earthquake or by the cannon fire of King Taksin in 1775 during the recapture of Chiang Mai from the Burmese. The famed Phra Kaew (Emerald Buddha), now held in Bangkok's Wat Phra Kaew (p126), sat in the eastern niche here in 1475. Today there is a jade replica sitting in its place, financed by the Thai king and carved in 1995 to celebrate the 600th anniversary of the *chedi* (according to some reckonings), and the 700th anniversary of the city.

A restoration of the *chedi* was financed by Unesco and the Japanese government. Despite their good intentions, the restoration work is easily spotted: new porticoes and *naga* (mythical serpent) guardians and new Buddha images in three of the four directional niches. On the southern side of the monument, five elephant sculptures in the pediment can be seen. Four are cement restorations; only the one on the far right – without ears and trunk –

is original brick and stucco. The restoration efforts also stopped short of creating a new spire, since no one knows for sure how the original superstructure looked.

Wat Chedi Luang's other prominent attraction is the *làk meu·ang* (city pillar, believed to house the city's guardian deity) enshrined in a small building to the left of the compound's main entrance. In May the building is opened to the public for merit-making. It is believed that Chiang Mai's liberator, Chao Kawila, brought the city pillar here in the hopes of future protection (mainly from the Burmese). The nearby trees were considered good luck symbols for the safety of the city as long as they were never cut down.

In the main *wí·hǎhn* is the standing Buddha, known as Phra Chao Attarot, flanked by two disciples both renowned for meditation and mysticism.

In the far rear of the grounds are two new chapels, built within the last decade in neo-Lanna style with pretty gold stencilling and thick wooden columns. Such new displays of wealth are unusual in historic temples like this. The first chapel contains a wax statue of Ajahn Mun Bhooretaḍo, a former abbot of Wat Chedi Luang and one of the founders of the Thai forest tradition of meditation. The chapel next door is made of rosewood and teak and contains glass-enclosed relics as well as a wax figure of Luang Ta Maha Bua, who collected donations to buy gold reserves for the national bank during the Asian currency crisis of 1997 and was a disciple of Ajahn Mun Bhooretaḍo.

Have a chat to the monks while you are here (see boxed text, p288).

WAT PHAN TAO
วัดพันเถา

Near Wat Chedi Luang, **Wat Phan Tao** (Map pp284-5; ☎ 0 5381 4689; Th Phra Pokklao; donations appreciated) contains a beautiful old teak *wí·hǎhn* that was once a royal residence and is today one of the unsung treasures of Chiang Mai. Constructed entirely of moulded teak panels fitted together and supported by 28 gargantuan teak pillars, the *wí·hǎhn* features *naga* bargeboards inset with coloured mirror mosaic. On display inside are old temple bells, some ceramics, a few old northern-style gilded wooden Buddhas, and antique cabinets stacked with old palm-leaf manuscripts. The front panel of the building displays a mirrored mosaic of a peacock

standing over a dog, representing the astrological year of the former royal resident's birth, making this temple a necessary pilgrimage site for those born in the year of the dog.

WAT CHIANG MAN
วัดเชียงมั่น

Considered to be the oldest *wát* in the city, **Wat Chiang Man** (Map pp284-5; ☎ 0 5337 5368; Th Ratchaphakhinai; donations appreciated), is believed to have been established by the city's founder, Phaya Mengrai. The *wát* features typical northern Thai temple architecture.

Two important Buddha images are kept in a glass cabinet inside the smaller sanctuary to the right of the main chapel. Phra Sila is a marble bas-relief Buddha that stands about 30cm high and reportedly came from Sri Lanka or India 2500 years ago, but since no Buddha images were produced anywhere before around 2000 years ago, it must have arrived later. The well-known Phra Sae Tang Khamani, a crystal seated-Buddha image, was shuttled back and forth between Thailand and Laos like the Emerald Buddha. It's thought to have come from Lavo (Lopburi) 1800 years ago and stands just 10cm high. The chapel housing the venerated images is open between 9am and 5pm.

Inside the larger chapel are red-and-gold stencilled murals completed in 1996 to celebrate the 700th anniversary of the founding of the city. The murals depict scenes from the life of Chiang Mai's founding father, Phaya Mengrai. Going clockwise from the front door, the scenes depict Mengrai's birth, his rule of Chiang Rai and its winding river and his expansion into the walled city of Lamphun. Another panel shows him hunting on Doi Suthep and being directed by the gods to build his new city. The final panel shows his death from a lightning bolt.

In front of the *bòht* (ordination hall), a stone slab, engraved in 1581, bears the earliest known reference to the city's 1296 founding.

CHIANG MAI CITY ARTS & CULTURAL CENTRE
หอศิลปวัฒนธรรมเชียงใหม่

The **Chiang Mai City Arts & Cultural Centre** (Map pp284-5; ☎ 0 5321 7793; www.chiangmaicitymuseum .org; Th Ratwithi; adult/child 90/40B; 8.30am-5.30pm Tue-Sun) offers a fine primer on Chiang Mai history. The 1st floor is comfortably

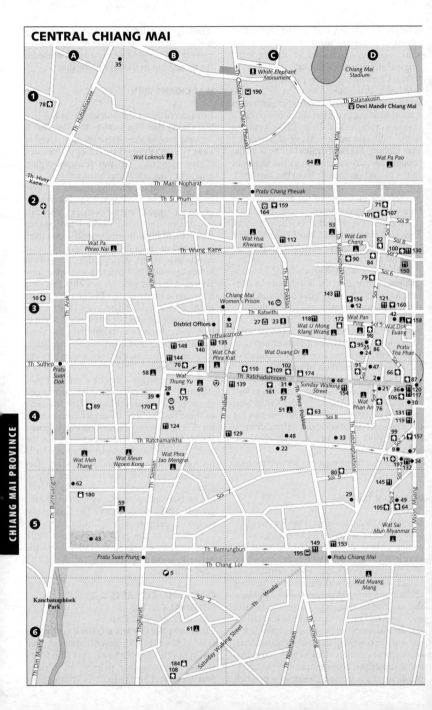

CENTRAL CHIANG MAI

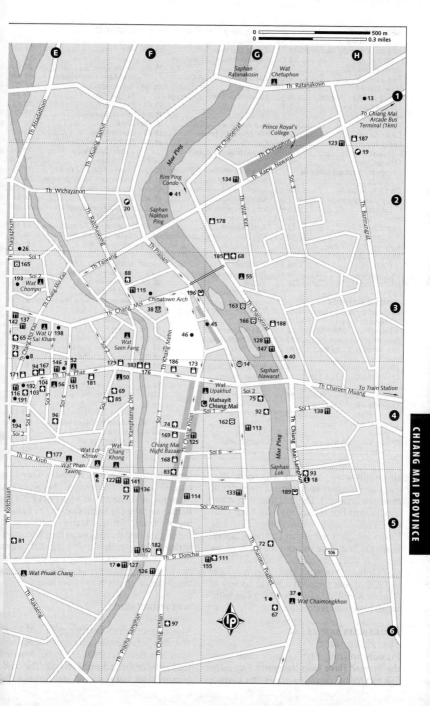

air-conditioned and has engaging displays on religious and cultural elements of northern Thailand. The 2nd floor is not air-conditioned but the rooms have been converted into historic settings: there's an early Lanna village, a temple and a train display. From the 2nd floor you can see more of the beauty of this post-colonial building, Chiang Mai's former Provincial Hall, originally built in 1924. It was awarded a Royal Society of Siamese Architects award in 1999 for its faithful architectural restoration.

ANUSAWARI SAM KASAT
อนุสาวรีย์สามกษัตริย์

Proudly wearing 14th-century royal garb, the bronze **Three Kings Monument** (Map pp284-5; Th Phra Pokklao) commemorates the alliance forged between the three northern Thai-Lao kings (Phaya Ngam Meuang of Phayao, Phaya Mengrai of Chiang Mai and Phaya Khun Ramkhamhaeng of Sukhothai) in the founding of Chiang Mai. The statues mark one of the city's spiritual centres and have become a shrine to local residents, who regularly leave offerings of flowers, incense and candles at the bronze feet in return for blessings from the powerful spirits of the three kings.

WAT PHUAK HONG
วัดพวกหงส์

This neighbourhood **wát** (Map pp284-5; ☎ 0 532 8864; off Th Samlan; donations appreciated; located be hind Suan Buak Hat (Buak Hat Park), contain the locally revered Chedi Si Pheuak. The *ched* is more than 100 years old and features the

CHIANG MAI PROVINCE

'stacked spheres' style seen only here and at Wat Ku Tao, and most likely influenced by Thai Lü *chedi* in China's Xishuangbanna (also spelled Sipsongpanna) district, Yunnan.

SUNDAY WALKING STREET
ถนนเดินวันอาทิตย์

A unique shopping experience, the **Sunday Walking Street** (pp284–5; Th Ratchadamnoen; ☾ 4pm–midnight Sun) offers better-than-average products and a good dose of provincial culture. It is also a reminder of an itinerant merchant tradition of the ancient Chinese caravans. Arrive early when Th Ratchadamnoen is first blocked off to vehicle traffic to watch the vendors unpack their swollen packs and neatly arrange their product displays. The first sale of the night might be followed by a small ritual or prayer in hopes that more business will follow.

Vendors line Th Ratchadamnoen all the way from the square in front of Pratu Tha Pae to Wat Phra Singh and stretching a few blocks down both sides of Th Phra Pokklao. Many of the products are handmade in and around Chiang Mai, including the cotton scarves, leather sandals and wood carvings. Chiang Mai lets down its hippie hair at this market with lots of ethnic chic accessories, undyed cotton T-shirts and 'save the planet' canvas tote bags.

The temples along the way host food stalls selling northern Thai cuisine and other shopping-stamina boosts. Near the grounds of Wat Chedi Luang on Th Phra Pokklao, look for earthenware bowls containing rich concoctions of *kôw soy*.

We prefer the less crowded time that precedes the playing of the national anthem at 6pm, but after dark has its attractions as well: buskers stake out small spots of the pedestrian path to serenade the crowd with old-fashioned favourites and new-fangled hits. When you tire of shopping, grab a massage chair where

---

MONK CHAT

You can go to a million spots in Thailand and be blissfully ignorant, but come to Chiang Mai to learn something. To aid in this pursuit, some of the temples in town offer a 'monk chat', where a resident monk or novice fields questions from foreigners. This simple exchange gives them a chance to practise their English while answering questions about daily routines, Buddhist teachings or even how monks stay wrapped up in their robes. Remember that it is respectful to dress modestly: cover your shoulders and knees. Women should take care not to touch the monks or their belongings or to pass anything directly to them.

Wat Suan Dok (Map pp276-7; ☎ 0 5380 8411-3; Th Suthep; ⏰ 5-7pm Mon, Wed & Fri) has a dedicated room for foreigners to interact with the monastic students. To find the room, enter the wát from the main entrance and walk 100m or so into the temple grounds.

Wat Chedi Luang (Map pp284-5; ☎ 0 5327 8595; Th Phra Pokklao; ⏰ 1-6pm Mon-Fri) and **Wat Sisuphan** (Map pp284-5; ☎ 0 5320 0332; 100 Th Wualai; ⏰ 5.30-7pm Tue, Thu & Sat) both have monk chat tables on certain days.

---

customers are stretched and pulled into angular lumps of dough.

If you're not in town on Sunday, check out the **Saturday Walking Street** (p291) on Th Wualai.

East of the Old City & Riverside

Passing through Pratu Tha Phae leads to a standard-issue commercial neighbourhood of two-storey concrete shophouses and busy multi-laned roads. Th Tha Phae is the main tourist drag filled with interesting craft shops and a few heritage-style buildings once belonging to British and Burmese teak merchants. It is much more functional here than the old city with everyday shops selling plastic and paint as well as the nearly derelict shops specialising in dust and gossip. South of Talat Warorot, on Th Chang Khlan, is the Chiang Mai Night Bazaar (p321). The meandering Mae Ping is another historical attraction and the eastern riverside neighbourhood makes an interesting cycling tour.

WAT CHETAWAN, WAT MAHAWAN & WAT BUPPARAM

วัดเชตวัน/วัดมหาวัน/วัดบุปผาราม

These three wáts along Th Tha Phae feature highly ornate wí·hǎhn and chedi designed by Shan and Burmese artisans. Financed by Burmese teak merchants who immigrated to Chiang Mai a century or more ago, evidence of Shan/Burmese influence is easily seen in the abundant peacock symbol (a solar symbol common in Burmese and Shan temple architecture) and the Mandalay-style standing Buddhas found in wall niches.

TALAT WAROROT

ตลาดวโรรส

Following Th Chang Moi towards the river you'll discover a beehive of activity around Chiang Mai's oldest and most famous marketplace, **Talat Warorot** (Map pp276-7; cnr Th Chang Moi & Th Praisani; ⏰ 6am-5pm). In many ways it looks like any other market, except more dilapidated and more crowded, but this unassuming place is a surviving remnant of Chiang Mai's early mercantile history. Its placement beside the river isn't for scenic value but for historical necessity: the waterway was an important thoroughfare collecting goods from the countryside and shipping them south to Bangkok. In northern Thai dialect, the market is known as gàht lŏo·ang (northern Thai for 'great market').

Technically there are two multi-storey buildings that comprise the market, but so much activity surrounds these enclosures and spreads into the neighbouring area that it is hard to define Talat Warorot's specific boundaries. Outside the market buildings are fruit and vegetable vendors selling highland varieties that are considered exotic to central Thais. Parked nearby are an extinct species in Bangkok, sǎhm·lór drivers who shuttle home produce-burdened shoppers.

If you push your way through the thick barrier of vendor stalls, you'll find the interior market selling pickled products, pre-made curries and packaged kâap mŏo (pork rinds). There are a number of basic food stalls on the ground floor of the main hall serving popular daytime noodle dishes. It's an especially good market for cheap clothes, fabrics and cooking implements, as well as inexpensive cosmetics and handicrafts.

Facing the river, **Talat Tonlamyai** (Map pp284-5; Th Praisani; 24 hr) is the city's main fresh flower market, locally called *gàht dòrk mái*. The arm-width bundles of asters, roses and coreopsis are ripened in the cooler climate of the surrounding highlands and are brought to market at night to avoid the wilting daytime heat. Varieties, like pussy willow, which need even colder tempera-tures, are grown by hill-tribe villages perched at higher altitudes. Then there are the voluptu-ous tropical flowers, like jasmine, orchids and lotus buds that flourish in the heat. The flowers are sold wholesale for delivery to Bangkok and other provincial centres as well as arranged into funeral wreaths or sold in smaller quantities to merit-making Thais and households. The flower market is always busy but even more so during citywide festivals, like Loi Krathong and, of course, the Flower Festival.

West of the market, along Th Chang Moi is the city's small **Chinatown**, most obviously marked by a flamboyant Chinese-style arch and the typical two-storey shophouses of Southeast Asia's mercantile districts. Most stores are family-owned businesses selling bulk household products and yellow-gold jewellery. There are also the old apothecaries smelling of tree bark and dried herbs. The area is also home to two Chinese temples and clan houses and hosts an annual Chinese New Year parade. A small population of Sikhs also live in this area and specialise in selling bolts of fabric. They worship at the nearby **Namdhari Sikh Temple** (Map pp284-5; Th Ratchawong), catering to the Namdhari sect of Sikhism.

MAE PING & WAT KETKARAM
แม่ปิง/วัดเกตการาม

In ancient times, Thai cities were intimately tied to the waterways for basic survival and transportation. The fundamental role of rivers in everyday life often elevated them from thoroughfares and faucets to revered entities honoured by such annual festivals as Loi Krathong. Chiang Mai's exalted river is the **Mae Ping** (Map pp284-5), which starts in the mountains of Chiang Dao and winds through the highlands to the fertile Mae Sa Valley, the commercial hub of Chiang Mai and through the Ping Valley, the larg-est fertile valley in the northern provinces. In Nakhon Sawan, the river joins the Chao Phraya River, which flows all the way to Bangkok and the Gulf of Thailand. Along its 569km run, the river feeds a vast agricul-tural system of rice paddies, coffee planta-tions, *lam yai* orchards, strawberry fields and flower gardens.

The Mae Ping also fed Chiang Mai's role as a thriving trading centre in the early 19th century. It was a much busier and a more powerful river in those days but still subject to seasonal water fluctuations. To accommo-date the dry season's low water levels, boats had shallow bottoms and a tall forked tail, often called a 'scorpion's tail', which allowed for greater stability and buoyancy. Today the scorpion-tailed boats live on in the tourist-oriented river trips (see p291). You can also enjoy the scenery from the riverside restau-rants (p313) that sit on the east bank.

CHIANG MAI PROVINCE

WORKING OFF THE RICE GUT

Chiang Mai doesn't have a central park like Bangkok but it does have a few green spaces where the locals go in the evenings to exercise without working up a sweat – a Thai speciality.

Suan Buak Hat (Map pp284-5; Th Bamrungburi) is the old city's only park with a well-maintained running track where you can do laps around the shuffling Thais. There's also a fish pond, a vendor selling fish food and a small playground.

The area around Chiang Mai University has loads of green space, including the wooded exercise course at **Huay Kaew Fitness Park** (Map pp276-7; Th Huay Kaew) and nearby **Ang Kaew reservoir**. For city views head to **Galare Lake** (off Th Suthep); it isn't much of a workout but the students like this spot because no one seems to mind an open container.

Carving out a slice of civilization at the southern base of Doi Suthep, **Royal Flora Ratchaphruek** (off Rte 121/Th Klorng Chonprathan; admission free; sunrise-sunset) first opened in 2006 as a 65-hectare garden exposition in honour of the king's 60th anniversary on the throne. In 2008, the landscaped grounds opened to the public, but are only useable during the cool hours of the day because of the lack of shade. The same access road leads to **Doi Kham**, a popular jogging route that winds past Brahmin cows to the summit. You'll want to have your own wheels to reach this area as a taxi ride would be expensive.

A community of Chinese traders and Western missionaries populated the eastern riverbank directly across from Talat Warorot. Today the neighbourhood is called Wat Ket, the nickname of the nearby temple, **Wat Ketkaram** (Map pp284-5; ☎ 0 5326 2605; Th Charoenrat). The temple was built in the 15th century and houses an eclectic museum of attic-like treasures. Th Charoenrat is still lined with relics from those early days, like the missionary hospitals and the old Chinese shophouses that now support restaurants and antique stores. If Th Charoenrat had footpaths, this area would rival the old city for its ancient ambience and tourist appeal. But speeding traffic claims the narrow space between buildings. Instead, dive deeper into the neighbourhood along one of the little lanes off Th Charoenrat and behind the temple.

Further south is **Talat San Pakoy** (Map pp276-7; off Th Charoen Muang), a low-key municipal market that offers all manner of goods and sees few tourists. San Pakoy opens around 4am and does a brisk trade until around 10am. Nearby is a little soi completely canopied by towering trees; the residents have built their ramshackle houses around the thick tree trunks because they don't own the land, instead renting it from the government, sometimes for as low as 900B a year.

WIANG KUM KAM
เวียงกุมกาม

These **excavated ruins** (⏰ 8am-5pm) offer an easy trip into the country. Climb aboard one of the horse-drawn carriages (200B) and relax into the mellow pace of an old-fashioned conveyance. The driver typically passes pleasantries with the locals who live among the old ruins, which are mainly half-buried brick foundations spread out over 3 sq km. The actual ruins are of more historical importance than spectacle but it is the peaceful surrounding village that completes the attraction.

Wiang Kum Kam was the earliest historical settlement in the Chiang Mai area and was established by the Mon as a satellite town for the Hariphunchai kingdom. It was occupied by Phaya Mengrai in 1286 and used as the Lanna capital for 10 years before the construction of Chiang Mai. The city was abandoned in the 16th century due to massive flooding when the Mae Ping changed its course. Only the four-sided Mon-style *chedi*

of Wat Chedi Si Liam and the layered brick pediments of Wat Kan Thom (its Mon name; in Thai the temple was known as Wat Chang Kham) are left. Chedi Si Liam is said to have been inspired by the similar *chedi* at Wat Kukut in Lamphun.

Over 1300 inscribed stone slabs, bricks, bells and *chedi* have been excavated at the site. The most important archaeological discovery has been a four-piece inscribed stone slab, now on display in the Chiang Mai National Museum. The early 11th-century inscriptions on this slab indicate that the Thai script predates King Ramkhamhaeng's famous Sukhothai inscription (introduced in 1293) by 100 or more years.

Another way to reach Wiang Kum Kam is to hire a bicycle; follow Th Chiang Mai-Lamphun (Rte 106) southeast for approximately 3km and look for a sign to the ruins on the right. From this junction it's another 2km. You could also hire a túk-túk or red *sŏrng·tăa·ou* for around 100B (one way). If you've got your own transport, Wiang Kum Kam is on the way to Lamphun to complete a thematic day of sightseeing.

South of the Old City
The southern part of the city is a mix of quaint antique districts and impersonal modern spaces. In olden times, the settlements outside of the city walls were usually the domain of foreigners. Some came willingly, like the Chinese merchants and the Western missionaries who settled on the eastern bank of the river, while others were forced from their homelands to help rebuild the destroyed city after the end of the Burmese occupation. Roughly 200 years ago the Tai Khoen people from what is known today as Kengtung in the Shan state of Myanmar were captured by the Siamese-Lanna army and resettled in this area. The Tai Khoen, who were silver- and blacksmiths, stonemasons and other skilled craftspeople, provided technical artistry to the great reconstruction efforts.

Today Th Wualai is renowned for its silver shops and is often filled with the tapping sound of a decorative pattern being imprinted on to a plate of silver (or, more often, aluminium). One of the best ways to observe Th Wualai is to come at the start of the Saturday Walking Street when traffic is blocked off for pedestrians.

RIVER CRUISES

The Mae Ping is rural and rustic in most parts with grassy banks and small stilted houses crouching alongside. There are several day and evening boat tours that explore this waterway.

Scorpion Tailed River Cruise (Map pp284-5; ☎ 08 1960 9308, 0 5324 5888; www.scorpiontailed.com; Th Charoenrat; fare 500B) focuses on the history of the river using traditional-style craft, known as scorpion-tailed boats. Informative cruises (five daily) last one to 1½ hours. They depart from Wat Srikhong pier near Rim Ping Condo and stop for a snack at the affiliated Scorpion Tailed Boat Village.

Mae Ping River Cruises (Map pp284-5; ☎ 0 5327 4822; www.maepingrivercruise.com; Wat Chaimongkhon, Th Charoen Prathet) offers daytime cruises (450B, two hours) in roofed long-tail boats. The boats stop at a small farm for fruit snacks after touring the countryside. The Thai dinner cruise (550B, two hours, daily at 7pm) offers a set menu.

Riverside Bar & Restaurant (p313) also has a post-dinner cruise.

SATURDAY WALKING STREET
ถนนเดินวันเสาร์

The **Saturday Walking Street** (pp284-5; Th Wualai; ☽ 4pm-midnight Sat) is developing a reputation of having more authentic handicrafts and being less commercial than the Sunday Walking Street. This might be a bit of an exaggeration as most vendors work both markets without exclusion. But the atmospheric old neighbourhood with its silver shops and old ladies wrapped up in Thai silk does impart a time-warp feeling.

WAT SISUPHAN
วัดศรีสุพรรณ

This **wát** (Map pp284-5; ☎ 0 5320 0332; Soi 2, Th Wualai; donations appreciated) was founded in 1502, but little remains of the original structures except for some teak pillars and roof beams in the wí·hăhn. The murals inside show an interesting mix of Taoist, Zen and Theravada Buddhist elements. The ubosòht next door was undergoing a renovation at the time of writing, and is allegedly the only silver ordination hall in Thailand (although technically they were using a mix of aluminium, compounded silver and pure silver). The temple hosts a monk chat and meditation instruction (see p288). Wat Sisuphan is one of the few wáts in Chiang Mai where you can see the Poy Luang (also known as Poy Sang Long) Festival, a Shan-style group ordination of young boys as Buddhist novices, in late March.

SBUN-NGA TEXTILE MUSEUM
พิพิธภัณฑ์ผ้าโบราณสบันงา

A surprisingly wonderful museum, **Sbun-Nga Textile Museum** (Map pp276-7; ☎ 0 5320 0655; www.sbun-nga.com; Chiang Mai Cultural Centre, 185/20 Th Wualai; admission 100B; ☽ 10.30am-6.30pm Thu-Tue) displays northern Thai textiles along with ethno-cultural information about the different tribes that are categorised as Lanna: Tai Lue, Tai Kaun, Tai Yai and Tai Yuan. The different patterns and colours used by each group is an evocative way to tell the story of the people who populated Chiang Mai and northern Thailand. There are also some displays of Tai Lao fabrics.

Textiles range from everyday sarongs to opulent royal garments, including the Lanna- and-Burmese-patterned dress of Princess Dararasmi (consort of King Rama V) and the bejewelled coronation costume of a Tai Yai prince. There is recorded English audio information as well as well-signed descriptions. The collection is a result of 20 years of work by the owner Akarat Nakkabunlung.

West of the Old City

Th Huay Kaew is the main thoroughfare to the western reaches of the city and it becomes more interesting as it enters the gravitational pull of Chiang Mai University (referred to in Thai by its initials 'Mor Chor'). Indie students crowd into cute boutique cafes, scoot around on vintage Vespas and waste all their book money on weekend carousing. Th Nimmanhaemin is the city's most stylish avenue, a cross between Bangkok's Siam Square and Banglamphu. It is a busy multi-lane road with a number of small residential lane offshoots, where 1970s garden houses have been converted to style-conscious commercial concerns, mainly nightlife. But true to Chiang Mai's low-key personality, rarely is an establishment so over-designed as to achieve exclusivity.

WAT SUAN DOK
วัดสวนดอก

Built on a former flower garden in 1373, this **temple** (Map pp276-7; ☎ 0 5327 8967; Th Suthep; donations appreciated) is not as architecturally interesting as the temples in the old city but it does have a very powerful photographic attribute: the temple's collection of whitewashed *chedi* sit in the foreground while the blue peaks of Doi Suthep and Doi Pui loom in the background. Photographers often arrive in the early morning to capture the juxtaposition when the mountains are still wrapped in mist.

Wat Suan Dok is also spiritually united with the temple that sits upon Doi Suthep thanks to an auspicious relic brought to Chiang Mai by Phra Sumana Thera, a visiting monk from Sukhothai. (In fact this temple was built for his visit by Phaya Keu Na, the sixth Lanna king). According to legend, the relic miraculously duplicated itself: one piece was enshrined in the temple's large central *chedi* (recently wrapped in gold sheet), while the other was used as a 'guide' for the founding of Wat Doi Suthep (see p296 for the full story). This main *chedi* is a textbook example of the Lanna period that began to be influenced by Sukhothai. The other *chedi* on the grounds contain the ashes of various members of the Lanna royal family.

The large, open-sided preaching hall was rebuilt in 1932 by Khruba Siwichai, a prominent Lanna monk responsible for the construction of the road to Wat Doi Suthep and other improvements. The hall is often filled with Thai meditators.

Further into the property is a small *bòht* that contains a 500-year-old bronze Buddha image, known as Phra Chao Kao Tu, which was originally intended for Wat Phra Singh but was too heavy to be moved. There are also vivid *jataka* (Buddha's past-life stories) murals.

Today Wat Suan Dok is home to a large population of resident monks and novices, many of them students at the monastery's Mahachulalongkorn Buddhist University. Foreigners often come to Wat Suan Dok for the popular monk chat (see p288) and the English-language meditation retreats.

CHIANG MAI UNIVERSITY (CMU)
มหาวิทยาลัยเชียงใหม่

The city's principal public **university** (Map pp276-7; ☎ 0 5384 4821; Th Huay Kaew) was established in 1964, making it the first Thai university to be set up outside of Bangkok. Today the university is considered the most well-respected centre for higher education in the north and boasts 107 departments, 26,800 students and 2165 lecturers. Scholastically CMU doesn't compare overall to such notable Bangkok universities as Silpakorn, Chulalongkorn or Thammasat, but it has earned special respect for its faculties of engineering and medical technology; the education was good enough for one-term Bangkok governor Apirak Kosayothin, one of the university's notable graduates.

The main campus occupies a 2.9 sq km wedge of land about 2km west of the city centre that has preserved much of its original forest character. Architecturally the campus buildings are soot-stained boxes, but the verdant environment achieves a distinctively Thai version of an idyllic collegiate setting. There are two main entrances into the campus on Th Suthep and Th Huay Kaew. When giving directions, Thais often refer to the university area on Th Suthep as '*lăng mor*' (behind the university) and on Th Huay Kaew as '*nâh mor*' (in front of the university). Near both entrances are small night bazaars selling cheap food and clothes for cash-strapped students.

One way to savour the academic atmosphere is at **Chiang Mai University Art Museum** (Map pp276-7; ☎ 0 5394 4833; Th Nimmanhaemin; admission free 9am-5pm Tue-Sun), near the intersection of Th Suthep and Th Klorng Chonprathan. The museum displays temporary exhibitions of contemporary Thai and international art. There's no permanent collection and the visiting shows can be of uneven quality. If you need a pit stop after the museum, check out Din Dee Teahouse, a little earthen hut on the museum grounds known for its herbal brews.

CHIANG MAI ZOO
สวนสัตว์/แหล่งเพาะพันธุ์ไม้ป่าเขตร้อนเชียงใหม่

At the foot of Doi Suthep, the **Chiang Mai Zoo** (Map pp276-7; ☎ 0 5335 8116; www.chiangmaizoo.com; Th Huay Kaew; adult/child 100/50B; 8am-6pm, ticket booth closes at 5pm) occupies a lush park setting that is often crowded with Thai families and school groups. The zoo boasts a fairly comprehensive assortment of animals plus two special attractions (pandas and an aquarium) that require separate admission fees.

The panda exhibit (admission adult/child 100/50B) features adorable Chuang-Chuang and Lin-Hui, who live in a specially designed air-conditioned building and are relative star among Chiang Mai school children. Hoping to boost tourism to the zoo, the new 600 million baht aquarium (adult/child 450/350B) reportedly has Asia's longest viewing tunnel (measuring 113m) and replicates the water environments of Thailand, from the northern rivers to the mangrove swamps and coastal oceans, as well as the Amazon basin.

If you get here early enough, it is an easy walk to visit most of the interesting exhibits lions, giraffes, tigers and birds – near the entrance. Except for the elephant and orang-utan, most of the animals seem better off than their counterparts in other Third World zoos. You can also walk to see the pandas, but the aquarium is a little too far to go on foot. Open-sided buses (adult/child 20/10B) and an elevated tram (adult/child 100/50B) are available to take you around the zoo, but there is a lot of waiting for the next car to arrive. The bus or tram ticket is good for your entire visit but hold on to the ticket in case you're asked for proof of purchase. If you're visiting with small children, it is a good idea to bring a stroller.

The zoo also has a parking garage that costs 10B for motorcycles and bicycles and 50B for cars or trucks.

WAT U MONG
วัดอุโมงค์

If you've never visited a **forest wát** (☎ 0 5327 3990; Soi Wat U Mong, Th Khlong Chonprathan; donations appreciated), you should make the trek to this temple. Not only does it offer a secluded sylvan setting, considered an important component for meditation in the forest wát tradition, it is also famous for its interconnecting tunnels built underneath the main *chedi* terrace.

The temple was first used during Phaya Mengrai's rule in the 14th century. The brick-lined tunnels were allegedly fashioned around 1380 for the clairvoyant monk Thera Jan. The monastery was abandoned at a later date and wasn't reactivated until a local Thai prince sponsored a restoration in the late 1940s. The since-deceased Ajan Buddhadasa Bhikkhu, a well-known monk and teacher at southern Thailand's Wat Suanmok, sent a number of monks to re-establish a monastic community at U Mong in the 1960s.

A marvellously grisly image of the fasting Buddha – ribs, veins and all – can be seen in the grounds on top of the tunnel hill, along with a very large and highly venerated *chedi*. Also on the grounds is a small artificial lake, surrounded by *gù·đì* (monastic cottages).

Resident foreign monks give dhamma talks in English on Sunday afternoon at 3pm by the lake.

Wat U Mong is accessible from a series of small lanes off Th Suthep near Chiang Mai University. Once you reach the university, keep an eye out for signs pointing the way. Note that there is another temple named Wat U Mong in Chiang Mai. To make sure a *sŏrng·tăa·ou* or túk-túk driver understands you want this one ask for 'Wat U Mong Thera Jan'.

CHIANG MAI NIGHT SAFARI
เชียงใหม่ไนท์ซาฟารี

The slick **Night Safari** (☎ 0 5399 9050; www.chiangmainightsafari.com; Rte 121/Th Klorng Chonprathan; ⏰ 1pm-midnight Mon-Fri, 10am-midnight Sat & Sun) was one of former prime minister Thaksin Shinawatra's mega-projects, intended to upgrade Chiang Mai's image to appeal to the business-class tourist.

The attraction is open during the day but the real action happens at night during the 'Predator Prowl' and 'Savannah Safari' (admission adult/child 500/300B), when an open-sided bus transports visitors through the parkland. The English-language tram leaves at 7.45pm and 9.30pm and the tour takes about two hours. The night safari differs from the Chiang Mai Zoo in that some animals – like wildebeests, giraffes, white rhinoceroses and zebras – are allowed to roam and often come right up to the bus. In the 'Predator Prowl' section, the tigers, lions, Asiatic black bears and crocodiles are kept at a safe distance by deep trenches.

During the day you can visit the Jaguar Trail (admission adult/child 100/50B) that encircles Swan lake, a 1.2km walk where over 50 species (ranging from rabbits to cranes) are generally not in cages, except of course the trail's namesake animal.

The Night Safari is about 12km from central Chiang Mai and a *sŏrng·tăa·ou* should cost about 100B. You can also book this through a tour agency that handles hotel transfer. When it was built, it caused much controversy because of its primary location on 1.3 million sq km of Doi Suthep National Park land, and the consequential (and as yet unassessed) environmental impact it may have.

North of the Old City

Sights north of the old city through Pratu Chang Pheuak (the 'white elephant gate', a reference to the elephant who carried the sacred relic to Doi Suthep) are less of a tourist draw, which is a draw in itself for some. These sights tend to be too far spread out to visit on foot; it is advisable to hire your own transport.

WAT CHIANG YEUN
วัดเชียงยืน

Another unique local temple is 16th-century **Wat Chiang Yeun** (Map pp284-5; Th Mani Nopharat), just northeast of Pratu Chang Pheuak. Besides the large northern-style *chedi* here, the main attraction is an old Burmese colonial-style gate and pavilion on the eastern side of the school grounds attached to the *wát*. This area of Chiang Mai was historically settled by Shan people and the shops still maintain that ethnic identity, catering to Shan and Burmese temple-goers with such products as pickled tea leaves (*mêe·ang* in Thai) and Shan-style noodles.

WAT KU TAO
วัดกู่เต้า

North of the moat, **Wat Ku Tao** (Map pp276-7; ☎ 0 5321 1842; Soi 6, Th Chang Pheuak) dates from 1613 and has a unique *chedi* that looks like a pile of diminishing spheres, a Tai Lü design common in Yunnan, China. The *chedi* is said to contain the ashes of Tharawadi Min, a son of the Burmese king Bayinnaung, ruler of Lanna from 1578 to 1607.

WAT JET YOT
วัดเจ็ดยอด

Dedicated temple-spotters are the prime candidates for **Wat Jet Yot** (Map pp276-7; ☎ 0 5322 1947; Th Superhighway). It was built to host the eighth World Buddhist Council in 1477, a momentous occasion for the Lanna capital. To the back of the temple compound are the ruins of the old *wí·hǎhn*, which was supposed to be a replica of the Mahabodhi Temple in Bodhgaya, India, but the proportions don't match up. Some scholars assume that the blueprint for the temple must have come from a small votive tablet depicting the Mahabodhi in distorted perspective.

Although much of the decorative stucco work is gone, you can still count the *jèt yôrt* (seven spires) that represent the seven weeks Buddha was supposed to have spent in Bodhgaya after his enlightenment. Of the original stucco relief, a few intact Bodhisattva (Buddhist saints, usually associated with Mahayana Buddhism) depictions remain on the outer walls.

There's an adjacent *chedi* of undetermined age and a very glossy *wí·hǎhn* near the entrance that contains fairly modern murals depicting ordinary life in the age of automobiles.

CHIANG MAI NATIONAL MUSEUM
พิพิธภัณฑสถานแห่งชาติเชียงใหม่

Operated by the Fine Arts Department and established in 1973, the **Chiang Mai National Museum** (Map pp276-7; ☎ 0 5322 1308; www.thailandmuseum.com; off Th Superhighway; admission 100B; 9am-4pm Wed-Sun) functions as the primary caretaker of Lanna artefacts and as the curator of northern Thailand's history. This museum is a nice complement to the municipally run Chiang Mai City Arts & Cultural Centre (p283) because you'll find more art and artefacts here and the scope of the exhibits reaches beyond the city limits. Other national museums that display important artefacts from the north are located in Lamphun, Chiang Saen and Nan – all operate under the auspices of the Chiang Mai National Museum.

The best curated section of the museum is the Lanna art section, which displays a selection of Buddha images in all styles, and explains the different periods and influences.

TRIBAL MUSEUM
พิพิธภัณฑ์ชาวเขา

Overlooking a lake in Suan Ratchamangkhala on the northern outskirts of the city, this octagonal **museum** (☎ 0 5321 0872; off Th Chang Pheuak; admission free; 9am-4pm Mon-Fri) houses a collection of handicrafts, costumes, jewellery, ornaments, household utensils, agricultural tools, musical instruments and ceremonial paraphernalia. There are also informative displays showing the cultural features and background of each of the major hill tribes in Thailand; an exhibition on activities carried out by the Thai royal family on behalf of the hill tribes; and various bits of research and development sponsored by governmental and non-governmental agencies. Video shows run from 10am to 2pm (20B to 50B). The museum is closed on public holidays.

HUAY TEUNG THAO RESERVOIR
อ่างเก็บน้ำห้วยตึงเฒ่า

Thais love lounging by the water and this sizeable **reservoir** (admission 20B; ☒ 8am-sunset), at the northwestern foot of Doi Suthep-Pui park, has become more than just a piece of infrastructure. The banks are dotted with floating bamboo huts (10B per person) where Thais come to snack on fried bugs (another reservoir pastime), share a bottle of whisky and perfect the art of relaxation. Should the day get hot, you can have a dip from your personal dock. Fishing is permitted if you'd like to try your luck at hooking lunch.

There are a couple of small restaurants nearby that prepare the local speciality of *gûng dên* (dancing shrimp), freshwater shrimp served live in a piquant sauce of lime juice and *prík lâhp* (a northern Thai blend of spicy herbs and chillies).

The reservoir is about 12km northwest of the city. Travelling by car or motorcycle you can reach Huay Teung Thao by driving 10km north on Rte 107 (follow signs towards Mae Rim), then west 2km past an army camp to the reservoir. Cyclists would do best to pedal to the reservoir via Th Klorng Chonprathan (also known as the *klorng* road), which has a dirt frontage road. From the northwestern corner of the moat, the bicycle ride takes about an hour.

Doi Suthep-Pui National Park
อุทยานแห่งชาติดอยสุเทพ–ปุย

Chiang Mai's sacred peaks, Doi Suthep (1676m) and Doi Pui (1685m) loom over the city like guardian spirits and were used by the city's founders as a divine compass in locating an auspicious position. Suthep was named after the hermit Sudeva, who lived on the mountain's slopes for many years, and is the site of Chiang Mai's holy temple Wat Phra That Doi Suthep.

Portions of the mountains form a 265 sq km **national park** (☎ 0 5321 0244; adult/child under 14 yr 200/100B; ☒ 8am-sunset) that contains a mix of wilderness, hill-tribe villages and tourist attractions, including Wat Phra That Doi Suthep. Despite human encroachment, the park is still an excellent forest playground for city dwellers. Most people stick to the main road, visiting the temple, the winter palace and one of the touristy Hmong villages, altogether bypassing the forested interior.

The eastern side of the mountain stays green and cool almost year-round. The mountain ascends from the humid lowlands into the cool (and sometimes even cold) cloud belt with moss growing on the curbs and mist wafting across the road. Thriving in the diverse climate are more than 300 bird species and nearly 2000 species of ferns and flowering plants. During the rainy season, butterflies bloom as abundantly as the flowers.

There are hiking and mountain-biking trails as well as camping, birdwatching and waterfall spotting. One of the most scenic waterfalls is **Nam Tok Monthathon** (the park admission fee is collected here), 2.5km off the paved road to Doi Suthep. Pools beneath the falls hold water year-round, although swimming is best during or just after the annual monsoon. Close to the base of the mountain, **Nam Tok Wang Bua Bahn** is free, and full of frolicking locals, although it is more of a series of rapids than a falls.

You can hike through the park independently, but the lack of transport and trail information can be an impediment. For off-road mountain biking, the park has technical single-track trails that were old hunting and transport routes used by hill-tribe villagers. The routes are never crowded and provide hours of downhill. Because the trails aren't well-marked it is advisable to join a guided mountain-biking tour; see Activities on p298 for more information.

The park fee is collected at some of the park's waterfalls. There is no park fee charged to visit the attractions along the main road, though the attractions have their own admission prices.

Accommodation (www.dnp.go.th; camping 60-90B, bungalows 500-300B) in the national park includes smart bungalows, about 1km north of the temple by the park headquarters and the Doi Pui campground, near the mountain summit.

The park is about 16km northwest of central Chiang Mai and is accessible via shared *sŏrng·tǎa·ou* that leave from the main entrance of Chiang Mai University on Th Huay Kaew. One-way fares start at 40B and increase from there depending on the destination within the park and the number of passengers. You can also charter a *sŏrng·tǎa·ou* for about 600B or rent a motorcycle for much less. *Sŏrng·tǎa·ou* also depart from Pratu Chang Pheuak and the Chiang Mai Zoo. Cyclists can also make the

13km ascent to the temple – preferably either early in the morning or in the late evening when traffic is diminished.

WAT PHRA THAT DOI SUTHEP
วัดดอยสุเทพ

One of the north's most sacred temples, **Wat Suthep** (admission 30B) sits majestically atop Doi Suthep's summit. Thai pilgrims flock here to make merit to the Buddhist relic enshrined in the picturesque golden *chedi*. The temple also offers an interesting collection of Lanna art and architecture, and has fine city views if the clouds cooperate.

The temple was first established in 1383 under King Keu Naone and enjoys a fantastically mystical birth story. A visiting monk from Sukhothai instructed the Lanna king to take the twin of a miraculous relic (enshrined at Wat Suan Dok) to the mountain and establish a temple. The relic was mounted on the back of a white elephant, which was allowed to wander until it 'chose' a site on which a *wát* could be built to enshrine it. The elephant stopped and died at a spot on Doi Suthep, 13km west of Chiang Mai, where the temple was built in the Year of the Goat.

At the main road, near the tram entrance is a shrine to Kruba Siwichai, a highly venerated Lanna monk from the early 20th century. He is often recognised as something akin to a patron saint for northern Thais and worked to reconstruct and revitalise many dilapidated temples in the region. He also raised funds in order to build a road from Chiang Mai city to Wat Suthep.

The temple is reached by a strenuous *naga*-balustrade staircase of 306 steps, a feature that incorporates aspects of meditation with a cardio workout. (For the less fit, there's a tram for 20B.) You'll first reach an open-air terrace filled with important statues and shrines documenting the history of the temple. Near a signed jackfruit tree is a shrine to Sudeva, the hermit who lived on the mountain, and nearby is a statue of the white elephant who carried the relic up the mountain slope. Follow the walkway around in the clockwise direction to reach a viewpoint and a small sanctuary dedicated to the king who established the temple. The building is guarded by two *mom*, mythical figures with the characteristics of a lion, chameleon and fish.

A second set of stairs leads to the main cloister and the temple's famously photo-graphed gold-plated *chedi*, topped by a five-tiered umbrella erected in honour of the city's independence from Burma and its union with Thailand. In the case of Wat Suthep, it is the *chedi* (and the sacred Buddha relic enshrined inside) not a resident Buddha image that attracts the majority of worshippers. The *chedi* has many Lanna-style characteristics, including the gate around its base, the redented square pedestal and the octagonally shaped bell tower. Flanking the *chedi* are several *wí·hǎhn* containing Lanna-style Buddhas with their distinctive fat facial and body features, two upturned footpads, shortened chest bands and lotus-shaped topknot.

Within the monastery compound, the International Buddhism Center conducts a variety of religious outreach programs for visitors; see Courses (p300) for more information.

PHRA TAMNAK PHU PHING
พระตำหนักภูพิงค์

About 4km beyond the temple is **Phra Tamnak Phu Phing** (Phu Phing Palace; admission 50B; 8.30am-11.30am & 1-3.30pm), a winter palace for the royal family surrounded by gardens that are open to the public. It closes if the royal family is visiting, but these days the royals don't visit often. The gardens specialise in cool-weather flowers, like roses, which are exotic to Thais but a little anaemic for Westerners. More interesting is the water reservoir brought to life by dancing fountains moving in sync to musical compositions by the king. The nearby fern garden is also a pleasant stroll. Though not a must, the gardens are good for 'nature sightseers' who like their forests to have paved footpaths.

HMONG VILLAGES
หมู่บ้านชาวม้ง

The road that passes the palace splits off to the left, stopping at the peak of Doi Pui. From there, a road proceeds for a couple of kilometres to **Ban Doi Pui**, a Hmong hill-tribe village. Don't expect much evidence of village life here though – it is basically a tourist market selling Hmong crafts and souvenirs. There is a tiny **museum** (admission 10B) giving some information about hill tribes and opium production.

A more interesting Hmong village is **Ban Kun Chang Kian**, north of the Doi Pui campground. Instead of going left on the road past the palace head right. The road is paved just past the campground and then for the last 500m or so it is a bumpy dirt track. To save wear and tear, you can park at the campground's visitor centre and walk from there to enjoy the ridgeline and the pink flowering trees (called '*pá·yah sĕua krôhng*' in Thai). You'll find a basic village-run coffee house surrounded by coffee plants that are harvested in January. Nearby is basic accommodation (from 600B) with fantastic views.

WALKING TOUR
Old City Temple Tour

No visit to Chiang Mai is complete without spending a sweaty day temple-spotting. This walking tour takes you to the old city's most famous temples (you should devote another day to Wat Suthep, opposite). Start early before the day gets hot so that you can see the everyday uses of a temple: the comings and goings of monks, the prayer rituals of merit-makers and spotting which meditators are really asleep. Remember to dress modestly (covering shoulders and knees), take off your shoes when you enter a building and sit in the 'mermaid' position (with your legs tucked behind you) while you are observing the interior of a sanctuary.

Starting with the best, **Wat Phra Singh** (1; p282) is home to the city's most revered Buddha image (Phra Singh) and is an excellent example of Lanna architecture. Trot down Th Ratchadamnoen and turn right on Th Phra Pokklao to **Wat Chedi Luang** (2; p282), another venerable temple. If you're starting to wonder what Buddhism is all about, go and have a chat with the monks at the north side of the *chedi*. Backtrack to charming **Wat Phan Tao** (3; p283), a teak temple that is more photogenic than venerated. If it isn't too hot, squeeze in one more temple by turning right on Th Ratchadamnoen and left on Th Ratchaphakhinai to **Wat Chiang Man** (4; p283), the oldest *wát* in the city.

So much merit-making works up the appetite, but you're a little far from the city's main rice breaks. Instead you can use this opportunity to indulge your wheat tooth by turning right on Th Wiang Kaew and taking another right on Th Phra Pokklao to reach **Amazing Sandwich** (5; p311), a popular expat antidote to rice. Head south on Th Phra Pokklao and turn right at Th Ratwithi where you can nod to the **Anusawari Sam Kasat** (6; p286), the

CHIANG MAI WALKING TOUR

Three Kings Monument, on your way to the informative and air-conditioned **Chiang Mai City Arts & Cultural Centre** (7; p283).

If your feet are aching, carry on along Th Ratwithi until you reach Chiang Mai Women's Prison, where you'll find the **Chiang Mai Women's Prison Massage Centre** (8; p302). Don't attempt to enter the prison itself (unless you have something to confess!) but go to the building on the south side of the road with the 'Prison Shop' sign.

ACTIVITIES

Chiang Mai is truly new millennial with its selection of adventure tours. The surrounding mountains, rivers and byways now boast a new wave of adrenaline sports that have begun to eclipse the traditional trekking tour. If you're more of a do-gooder than a go-getter, consider volunteering at one of Chiang Mai's many NGO-run English-language schools; see p49.

Canopy Tours

Flight of the Gibbon (☎ 08 9970 5511; www.treetopasia. com; Mae Kampong; tours from 2000B) is a new adventure outfit in Chiang Mai operating a zipline

THE FRESHMEN MARCH

At the start of every academic year in July, the freshman class from Chiang Mai University makes the annual pilgrimage on foot to Wat Suthep. It is a long-time tradition that fills the winding mountain road with close to 10,000 exuberant students and faculty members. The purpose of the trek is to introduce the new students to the spirit of the city, believed to reside in the mountain, and to make merit to the revered Buddha relic at Wat Suthep. But it is also a chance for the students to introduce themselves to each other and make friends that might last a lifetime.

through the forest canopy some 1300m above sea level. Nearly 2km of wire with 18 staging platforms follow the ridgeline and mimic the branch-to-branch route a gibbon might take down the mountain. You can also tack on a waterfall hike or an overnight at a homestay in Mae Kampong (see p332), a pretty high-altitude village an hour's drive east from Chiang Mai.

The company has some ambitious conservation goals, including donating 10% of its profit to forest restoration projects at the zipline site and working to develop a healthy habitat for a small population of macaque monkeys.

Cycling, Mountain Biking & Motorcycling

The countryside and mountains surrounding Chiang Mai are exceptional for two-wheeled outings. The city's closest green space, Doi Suthep (p296) is gaining its own fame for off-road mountain biking. For motorcyclists and long-distance cyclists, the Mae Sa–Samoeng loop (p326) is the closest and most stunning escape into the mountains. Chiang Mai is also an easy town to scoot around on a bicycle or a motorcycle; see Getting Around (p324) for tips on hiring your own two-wheeled chariot.

Chiang Mai Mountain Biking (Map pp284-5; ☎ 08 1024 7046; www.mountainbikingchiangmai.com; 1 Th Samlan; tours from 1450-1550B) offers a variety of guided mountain biking (as well as hike-and-bike) tours through Doi Suthep for all levels.

Click and Travel (☎ 0 5328 1553; www.clickandtravel online.com; tours 950-1300B) specialises in half-day and full-day bicycle tours of Chiang Mai. It is a pedal-powered (and family friendly) cultural

trip, visiting temples and attractions outside of the city centre. Hotel transfer is included in the price; make arrangements online or via phone.

Contact Travel (Map pp276-7; ☎ 0 5320 4665; www .activethailand.com; 420/3 Th Chang Khlan; one-day tours 1800-2000B, multi-day tours from 12,500B) leads multi-day, long-distance mountain biking tours through northern Thailand, mainly from Chiang Mai to Chiang Dao or Chiang Rai travelling small country lanes with some off-road riding.

Golden Triangle Rider (www.gt-rider.com) provides motorcycle touring suggestions, tips on motorcycle rentals and publishes detailed topographical road maps of the popular routes to the Golden Triangle, Mae Hong Son and Samoeng (and Mae Sa Valley).

Elephant Tours

Chiang Mai is one of Thailand's most famous destinations for elephant 'encounters'. In the past, most elephant attractions were circus-like sideshows. But within the past 10 years, there has been a new sensitivity towards the quality of life for Thailand's emblematic animal, resulting in a diversification of attractions towards nature preserves and mahout-training schools.

Elephant Nature Park (Map pp284-5; booking office: ☎ 0 5320 8246; www.elephantnaturepark.org; 1 Soi 1, Th Ratchamankha; full-day tour 2500B) Khun Lek (Sangduen Chailert) has won numerous awards for her elephant sanctuary in the Mae Taeng valley, 60km (1½-hour drive) from Chiang Mai. The forested area provides a semi-wild environment for the elephants that have been rescued from abusive situations or retired from a lifetime of work. There are 22 adult elephants and four babies. Visitors can help wash the elephants and watch the herd but there is no show or riding. Group tours are limited to 25 people and the tour price includes hotel transfers. Khun Lek also operates a pachyderm medical program and invites volunteers to help her with her work.

Patara Elephant Farm (☎ 08 1992 2551; www .pataraelephantfarm.com; full-day tour 5800B) More expensive and more hands-on, Patara's farm has a slightly different focus than the Elephant Nature Park. The first mission is to combat the declining numbers of elephants in Thailand through a breeding program and to develop a safe tourism model. The six resident elephants are 'adopted' by the guests for the day. Activities with your elephant include feeding, bathing, learning basic mahout commands and riding to a waterfall. Tours are limited to six people and the fee includes hotel transfers. The farm is a 30-minute drive south of Chiang Mai in the Hang Dong area.

Rock Climbing & Abseiling

Rock climbers head to Crazy Horse Buttress, an impressive set of limestone cliffs located behind Tham Meuang On, near Sankamphaeng 45km east of Chiang Mai. While the scenery isn't as stunning as Krabi's seaside cliffs, the ascents reward with pastoral views. The following companies offer introductory climbing courses for beginners and advanced training for multi-pitch climbs; trips include guides, gear, hotel transfers and lunch.

Chiang Mai Rock Climbing Adventures (Map pp284-5; ☎ 0 6911 1470; www.thailandclimbing.com; 55/3 Th Ratchaphakhinai; climbing course 1800-6600B) bolted and now maintains many of the climbing routes at Crazy Horse Buttress, and the expat owner publishes a guide to rock climbing in northern Thailand. If you prefer subterranean cliffs, they also lead caving trips in the same area. The office on Th Ratchaphakhinai has gear sales and rental, a partner-finding service and a bouldering wall for practice sessions.

Peak (☎ 0 5380 0567; www.thepeakadventure.com; climbing course 1500-2500B) teaches introductory and advanced rock-climbing courses at Crazy Horse Buttress. The Peak also leads a variety of soft adventure trips, including abseiling down Nam Tok Wachiratan at Doi Inthanon (p334), as well as trekking, white-water rafting and a jungle survival cooking course.

Trekking

Thousands of visitors trek into the hills of northern Thailand each year hoping to see fantastic mountain scenery, interact with primitive cultures and ride elephants. Most come with an Indiana Jones sense of adventure but leave with disappointment: the actual walk through the jungle lasted less than an hour, the hill-tribe villagers were disinterested in the lowlanders and the other trekkers were boring.

Most companies operating out of Chiang Mai offer the same type of tour: a one-hour mini-bus ride to Mae Taeng or Mae Wang (depending on the duration of the trip), a brief hike to an elephant camp, an hour elephant ride to a waterfall, another hour rafting down a river and an overnight in or near a hill-tribe village. The day goes by pretty quickly and then you've got to entertain yourself among strangers from sunset to bedtime, without the usual social lubricants.

The best reports we've heard have been from people who bonded with their fellow trekkers. The group dynamic can often turn an otherwise standard trip into a great experience. In general we've also heard that the interaction with the hill-tribe villagers is often exaggerated by the booking agent.

Chiang Mai is not the only base for hill-tribe treks but it is the most accessible. Most guesthouses in Chiang Mai act as booking agents in exchange for a commission, which in turn subsidises the cheap room rates. One-day treks usually cost around 1500B, while multi-day treks (three days and two nights) cost 2500B. Both prices include transport, guide and lunch; in the case of overnight trips, the price also includes lodging.

For general tips on choosing a trekking company and places to go trekking, see p740.

White-Water Rafting

The Mae Taeng River is north of Chiang Mai and carves a path through the Doi Chiang Dao National Park and the Huai Nam Dang National Park. The river is a wild and frothy white-water ride for nine months of the year (roughly from July to March), a surprisingly long season in this monsoonal climate. The 10km rafting route travels through grade II to grade IV, and some grade V, rapids. In one particularly thrilling stretch, the river drops almost 60m in about 1.5km. Following a heavy rain, especially in September, the river can become so swollen and ferocious that drownings do occur. When choosing a white-water outfitter, ask about their safety standards and training. If the answer seems hurried or vague, then shop around for a more reputable operator.

Siam River Adventures (Map pp284-5; ☎ 08 9515 1917; www.siamrivers.com; Kona Cafe, 17 Th Ratwithi; tours from 1800B) has the best safety reputation. The guides have Swiftwater Rescue training and additional staff are located at dangerous parts of the river with throw ropes. Trips can be combined with elephant trekking and village overnights. They also operate kayak trips.

CHIANG MAI PROVINCE

Yoga & Fitness

700-Year Anniversary Stadium (☎ 0 5311 2301; Th Klorng Chonprathan) Modern sports complex with Olympic-sized swimming pool.

Anantasiri Tennis Courts (Map pp276-7; off Th Superhighway; ◷ 6am-8pm daily) The best public tennis facility in Chiang Mai.

Anodard Hotel (Map pp284-5; ☎ 0 5327 0755; 57-59 Th Ratchamankha) In-town hotel with pool open to non-guests for a day-use fee.

Chiang Mai Yoga Sala (Map pp284-5; ☎ 0 5320 8452; www.cmyogasala.com; 48 Th Ratchamankha; classes 250-300B) Beginner hatha and Mysore-style practice in the morning, mixed level hatha classes in the evening.

Gymkhana Club (Map pp276-7; ☎ 0 5324 1035; Th Ratuthit) Scenic sports and social club with squash and tennis courts, golf and driving range open to non-members for a day-use fee.

Pong Pot Swimming Pool (☎ 0 5321 2812; 73/22 Soi 4, Th Chotana) Public swimming pool.

Top North Guest House (Map pp284-5; ☎ 0 5327 8900; 15 Soi 2, Th Moon Muang) Hotel pool open to non-guests for a day-use fee.

Top North Hotel (Map pp284-5; ☎ 0 5327 9623; 41 Th Moon Muang) Hotel pool open to non-guests for a day-use fee.

Yoga Studio (Map pp284-5; ☎ 08 6192 7375; www.yoga-chiangmai.com; 65/1 Th Arak; classes 250B) Drop-in morning classes held four times a week. The studio also hosts a meditation session on Thursday evening.

COURSES
Buddhist Meditation

The following temples offer *vipassana* meditation courses and retreats to English-language speakers. Participants should dress in modest white clothes, which can typically be purchased from the temple. Following Buddhist precepts, there is no set fee but donations are appreciated. Peruse the various websites for course descriptions and daily routines.

International Buddhism Center (IBC; ☎ 0 5329 5012; www.fivethousandyears.org; Wat Phra That Doi Suthep) is headquartered within the temple grounds on Doi Suthep. They offer beginner to advanced meditation retreats, lasting from three to 21 days.

Northern Insight Meditation Centre (☎ 0 5327 8620; Wat Ram Poeng) is located 4km south of Chiang Mai and offers an intensive 26-day or longer course. Days start at 4am and meals are taken in silence. The formal name for Wat Ram Poeng is Wat Tapotaram.

Wat Sisuphan (Map pp284-5; ☎ 0 5320 0332; 100 Th Wualai; 7-9pm Tue, Thu & Sat) offers a two-hour introduction to meditation using the four postures: standing, walking, sitting and lying down.

Wat Suan Dok (Map pp276-7; ☎ 0 5380 8411 ext 114; www.monkchat.net; Th Suthep) offers a two-day meditation retreat every Tuesday to Wednesday. At the end of each month, the temple extends the retreat to a three-day period (Tuesday to Thursday). Participants should register in advance and meet at Wat Suan Dok for transfer to the meditation centre, 15km northeast of Chiang Mai. Check the website for cancellation notices.

Cooking

Courses in Thai cuisine are another staple of Chiang Mai's vacation learning scene. Dozens of schools offer cooking classes, typically costing 900B a day, either at an in-town location, like an atmospheric old house, or out of town in a garden or farm setting. Classes are usually offered five or more times a week and the menu might vary each day. Students will learn about Thai culinary herbs and spices, tour a local market and prepare a set menu. Of course, you also get to eat the Thai food and travel home with a recipe booklet.

Asia Scenic Thai Cooking (Map pp284-5; ☎ 0 5341 8657; www.asiascenic.com; 31 Soi 5, Th Ratchadamnoen) is a place run by Khun Gayray who speaks great English and has done some backpacking herself.

Baan Thai (Map pp284-5; ☎ 0 5335 7339; www.baanthaicookery.com; 11 Soi 5, Th Ratchadamnoen) has an in-town location where you can select which dishes to prepare; their 'intensive' courses include a menu of northern Thai specialities.

Chiang Mai Thai Cookery School (Map pp284-5; ☎ 0 5320 6388; www.thaicookeryschool.com; booking office, 47/2 Th Moon Muang) is one of Chiang Mai's first cooking schools and holds classes in a rural setting outside of Chiang Mai. The school also has a 'masterclass' with a northern Thai menu.

Gap's Thai Culinary Art School (Map pp284-5; ☎ 0 5327 8140; www.gaps-house.com; 3 Soi 4, Th Ratchadamnoen) is affiliated with the guesthouse Gap's House (where you can make your booking) and holds its classes out of town at the owner's house.

Thai Farm Cooking School (Map pp284-5; ☎ 08 717 9285, 08 1288 5989; www.thaifarmcooking.com; booking office, 2/2 Soi 5, Th Ratchadamnoen) teaches cooking classes at its organic farm, located 17km outside of Chiang Mai.

Language & Culture

Being a university town, Chiang Mai fosters continuing education opportunities in Thai language and culture.

American University Alumni (AUA; Map pp284-5; ☎ 0 5327 8407, 0 5327 7951; www.learnthaiinchiangmai .com; 73 Th Ratchadamnoen; group course 4200B) conducts six-week Thai courses that work on mastering tones, small talk and basic reading and writing. Classes meet for 2¼ hours, Monday to Friday. Private instruction is also available.

Chiang Mai Thai Language Center (Map pp284-5; ☎ 0 5327 7810; www.thaicultureholidays.com; 131 Th Ratchadamnoen; group course 3000B) has a more flexible class schedule and offers courses for beginners to advanced learners, as well as private classes, business Thai and northern Thai dialect lessons. As part of the course it is possible to stay in a village homestay just north of Chiang Mai. Classes run for three weeks.

Chiang Mai University (Map pp276-7; ☎ 0 5394 1000; www.cmu.ac.th; Th Huay Kaew) offers a one-year certificate program in Thai as a foreign language through the **faculty of education** (International Relations Section; ☎ 0 5394 4274; fax 0 5322 1283; kuku_cmu@hotmail.com; per semester from 42,000B). The program is offered as an exchange through CMU's sister universities as well as for interested foreigners. The program covers all levels in Thai conversation, reading and writing, as well as Thai culture, and is to be completed in two successive semesters with approximately 10 hours of coursework per week.

Payap University (Map pp276-7; http://ic.payap.ac.th; Kaew Nawarat Campus, Th Kaew Nawarat) is a private university founded by the Church of Christ of Thailand and offers an Academic Thai course through the **foreign languages department** (☎ 0 5324 1255, ext 7220) that covers all levels in 60/120-hour modules (7500B/19,700B). Payap also offers a **Thai and Southeast Asian Studies Certificate Program** (☎ 0 5385 1478, ext 7227; http://thaistudies.payap.ac.th), for one to two semesters that includes coursework on Thai language, history and culture and contemporary issues in Southeast Asia.

Thai Boxing

Lanna Muay Thai Boxing Camp (Kiatbusaba; Map pp276-7; ☎ 0 5389 2102; www.lannamuaythai.com; 64/1 Soi Chang Khian, Th Huay Kaew; fees per day/month 400/8000B) offers *moo·ay tai* (Thai boxing, also spelt *muay thai*) instruction to foreigners and Thais.

Several Lanna students have won stadium bouts, including the famous transvestite boxer Parinya Kiatbusaba.

Traditional Massage

The following are government accredited programs that will provide students with the fundamentals to practise Thai massage professionally. Some schools are also recognised as continuing education options by international bodywork organisations.

Bangkok's Wat Pho massage school established the Chiang Mai branch of **Chetawan Thai Traditional Massage School** (Map pp276-7; ☎ 0 5341 0360; www.watpomassage.com; 7/1-2 Soi Samud Lanna, Th Pracha Uthit; courses from 6500B), outside of town near Rajabhat University.

Khun Lek of **Lek Chaiya** (Map pp284-5; ☎ 0 5327 8325; www.nervetouch.com; 25-29 Th Ratchadamnoen; course from 5200B) learned *jàp sên* (literally 'nerve touch'), a northern Thai massage technique akin to acupressure, from her mother and became a well-known practitioner before retiring and passing the business and the technique on to her son. Courses last from three to five days and cover about 50% of a traditional Thai massage course with the remainder dedicated to the nerve-touch technique and herbal therapies. To experience *jàp sên*, stop in for a massage either from an assistant (500B) or from Lek's son Jack (950B).

A former instructor at the Old Medicine Hospital has developed his own curriculum at **International Training Massage School** (Map pp284-5; ☎ 0 5321 8632; 17/6-7 Th Morakot; www.itmthaimassage. com; 3500-5000B), using northern-style massage techniques. Each of the four training levels includes 30 hours of instruction, culminating in a fifth teacher training level. There are also shorter foot reflexology, massage and spa treatment courses.

The curriculum at **Old Medicine Hospital** (OMH; Map pp276-7; ☎ 0 5327 5085, 0 5320 1663; www.thai massageschool.ac.th; 78/1 Soi Siwaka Komarat, Th Wualai; courses 2500-5000B) is very traditional, with a northern-Thai slant, and was one of the first to develop massage training for foreigners. There are two 10-day massage courses a month, as well as shorter foot and oil massage courses. Classes tend to be large from December to February, but smaller the rest of the year.

Northeast of town, **Thai Massage School of Chiang Mai** (TMC; ☎ 0 5385 4330; www.tmcschool.com; 203/6 Th Chiang Mai-Mae Jo; courses 7000-7500B) has a

PAMPERING & PUMMELLING

While there are a few truly exceptional spas in Chiang Mai, the city excels in a more modest category: old-fashioned Thai massage. The massage parlour might be just a few mattresses on the floor, but the practitioner can bend, stretch and pummel knotted bodies into jelly without New Age gimmicks.

Many of the temples in the old city have a massage *sǎh·lah* (often spelt as *sala*) on the grounds, continuing an ancient tradition of the monasteries being a repository for traditional knowledge and healing. All of the massage schools (see p300) also offer massage sessions to those who'd rather be prostrate than be proselytised.

Chiang Mai Women's Prison Massage Centre (Map pp284-5; ☎ 08 1706 1041; 100 Th Ratwithi; ☸ 8.30am-4.30pm; 150-200B) offers fantastic full body and foot massages performed by inmates at the women's prison as a part of their rehabilitation training program. Despite their incarceration, the ladies aren't career criminals but eager to turn their lives around with the job skills they've developed behind bars; those working in the massage centre are due for release within six months. The money earned from these treatments goes directly to the prisoners for use after their release. Other rehabilitation initiatives include teaching sewing and cake baking – the results of which you'll find in the same building.

Ban Hom Samunphrai (☎ 0 5381 7362; www.homprang.com; 93/2 Moo 12; treatments 500-800B) is a unique time capsule of old folk ways, 9km from Chiang Mai near the McKean Institute. Maw Hom ('Herbal Doctor') is a licensed herb practitioner and massage therapist, but learned most of her craft from her grandmother, a midwife and herbalist living near the Burmese border. She runs a traditional herbal steam bath recreating what was once a common feature of rural villages. Traditional Thai massage is also available and can be combined with a steam bath for an upcountry 'spa' session. Call for directions.

solid, government-licensed massage curriculum. There are three foundation levels and an intensive teacher-training program. There's also a one-day Thai yoga program.

If you're just curious about massage and don't want to make a serious commitment, you might also consider the following 'home grown' alternatives.

Thai Healing Arts Association at Wat Si Koet (Map pp284-5; ☎ 0 4042 2452; Th Ratchadamnoen; courses 3000-6000B) On the temple grounds, Khun Nek teaches three- to 10-day courses on body and foot massage.

Ban Nit (Map pp284-5; ☎ 08 1035 2103; Soi 2, Th Chaiyaphum; courses 1000-4000B) The long-time teacher, Khun Nit, has retired at the ripe age of 76, but her daughter Noy now teaches the informal classes; stop in for a visit to see if the family suits your style.

FESTIVALS & EVENTS

Chiang Mai is famous for the Flower Festival, Songkran and Loi Krathong; make your travelling arrangements far in advance during these periods.

Chiang Mai Red Cross and Winter Fair (late December to early January) This 10-day festival is held behind the Chiang Mai City Arts & Cultural Centre and assumes a country-fair atmosphere, with food booths purveying northern Thai cuisine and cultural displays.

Flower Festival (early February) This agricultural celebration (called *têt·sà·gahn mái dòrk mái brà·dàp)* is held over a three-day period and includes displays of flower arrangements, cultural performances and beauty pageants. The festival highlight is the parade that starts at Saphan Nawarat, travelling down Th Tha Phae and then all the way to Suan Buak Hat.

Chiang Mai Chinese New Year (February) The city's Chinatown heralds its cultural new year with a spotlight on Chinese food and cultural displays.

Songkran (mid-April) The traditional Thai New Year is celebrated in Chiang Mai with an enthusiasm that borders on pandemonium. Thousands of revellers line up along all sides of the moat to have a ready supply of ammunition. It is virtually impossible to stay dry during the five days of this festival.

Intakin Festival (mid-May) Held at Wat Chedi Luang, this religious festival (known as *ngahn tam bun sǒw in·tá·gin)* is centred around the *làk meu·ang* (city pillar) and propitiates the city's guardian deity to ensure that the annual monsoon will arrive on time.

Loi Krathong (late October to early November) Chiang Mai's riverbanks are alive with people floating the small lotus-shaped boats honouring the spirit of the river. In Chiang Mai this festival is also known as Yi Peng, and some *kon meu·ang* (people of northern Thailand) celebrate by launching cylindrical hot-air balloons, lighting up the night skies with hundreds of pinpoints of fire.

SLEEPING

Chiang Mai is kind to the thrifty traveller: there are heaps of competing guesthouses, and resulting low rates. A new crop of concept/boutique hotels have recently filled in

Thai Massage Conservation Club (Map pp284–5; ☎ 0 5390 4452; 99 Th Ratchamankha; massage 150B) We're not sure why it's the case, but Chiang Mai's massage world likes to form their own clubs complete with banners and overly ornate names. This particular massage group employs all blind masseuses, who are considered to be expert practitioners because of their heightened sense of touch.

Dheva Spa (☎ 0 5388 8888; www.mandarinoriental.com/hotel; Mandarin Oriental Dhara Dhevi, 51/4 Th Chiang Mai-San Kamphaeng; treatments from 3400B) The grandest spa in all of Chiang Mai is an architectural treasure, built to look like the ancient Burmese palace located at Mandalay. It is also a cheaper passport into the exclusive and stunning grounds of the luxurious Mandarin Oriental Dhara Dhevi resort than a night's stay there would be. Try the *tok sen* massage, an old Lanna technique that uses a wooden gavel to tap on pressure points. Now you'll know how a piece of carved wood feels.

RarinJinda Wellness Spa Resort (Map pp284–5; ☎ 0 5330 3030; www.rarinjinda.com; 14 Th Charoenrat; treatments from 1500B) This health retreat boasts one of Chiang Mai's largest hydrotherapy pools as well as Vichy shower and sauna (both steam and infrared). Their spa packages are surprisingly affordable for the usual menu of body polishes, massage and even a few zingers like Tibetan sound therapy.

Oasis Spa (Map pp284–5; ☎ 0 5381 5000; www.chiangmaioasis.com; 4 Th Samlan; treatments 1900-2500B; ✆ 10am-10pm) A tranquil garden setting navigated by elevated walkways hosts private villas for single or couples treatments. If you've spa-ed elsewhere in Thailand, the Oasis will be a familiar friend, offering scrubs, wraps, massage and ayurvedic treatments.

the anaemic midrange to top end to capitalise on the hopes of the city becoming a more upmarket destination. Many cultural students come to Chiang Mai for long-term stays and most places offer weekly and monthly discounts or a flat monthly rate with additional electricity and water usage fees.

There are basically two kinds of budget accommodation: converted family homes and multi-storey apartment buildings. The old houses typically have the best atmosphere but the least privacy, while the apartment blocks have solid quirkless rooms. In both, the furnishings are basic – a bed and a few sticks of furniture. Most guesthouses make their money from trekking commissions, which in turn subsidises the low room rates. When checking in, most places will ask if you're planning on trekking and might limit your stay to three nights if you opt out.

Straddling the budget and midrange category, you will find the classic Thai-Chinese hotel: a multi-storey building that must have seemed sophisticated in the 1980s. Most are showing their age but there is a slight retro appeal. Several 'flashpacker' hotels offer excellent value for a tad more baht. Most will have grown-up expectations like stylish and quiet rooms, but they skimp on the services, such as bellhops and concierges, to keep the tariffs low. In this category, you

can expect daily room cleaning, air-con, fridge and cable TV. In most cases, rates include breakfast.

Many budget and midrange places have bicycle and motorcycle rentals as well as free internet and wi-fi. If you phone ahead, some will collect you from the train or bus terminal for free to avoid paying a commission to a driver.

The top-end range is dominated mainly by huge corporate-style hotels, some of which are international chains. The more interesting ones are the intimate boutique hotels that tend to marry antique Lanna elements with modern amenities. At the summit of the scale are the destination resorts that have recreated a village setting complete with rice fields and historic architecture on the outskirts of town. Most top-end hotels include breakfast in the rates but charge for internet access. A few still offer smoking floors.

For midrange and top-end hotels, always check online for discounts especially during the low season.

Old City

There are so many guesthouses in the residential sois off Th Moon Muang, especially in Soi 7 and Soi 9, that a Chiang Mai friend recently dubbed it Th Khao Muang ('*kôw meuang*' is

CHIANG MAI PROVINCE

> ## WHAT TO EXPECT IN CHIANG MAI
>
> ■ Budget (under 1000B)
> ■ Midrange (1001B to 3000B)
> ▢ Top End (over 3000B)

northern Thai for 'sticky rice', a reference to Bangkok's popular Th Khao San, which means 'uncooked rice'). There are also a few guesthouses in the southeastern corner of the old city off Th Ratchamankha and in the lower numbered sois off Th Moon Muang.

BUDGET
Julie Guesthouse (Map pp284–5; ☎ 0 5327 4355; www .julieguesthouse.com; 7 Soi 5, Th Phra Pokklao; dm 70B, r 100–300B) Part hostel, part guesthouse, Julie has cornered the young backpackers' social scene. The garden cafe is full of enthusiastic first-timers swapping tips and tales. In the evenings, folks retire to the covered roof terrace strung up with hammocks.

Malak Guest House (Map pp284–5; ☎ 0 5322 4648; malakguesthouse@hotmail.com; 25 Soi 2, Th Ratwithi; r 180–250B; 🖳) Newly refurbished apartment building has all the backpackers flocking inside for its crisp clean rooms with private bath.

Lamchang House (Map pp284–5; ☎ 0 5321 0586; Soi 7, Th Moon Muang; r 200B) One of Chiang Mai's cheapest, this old wooden house has basic fan rooms with shared bath. The downstairs rooms are a little dark but there's a pleasant front-yard garden and attached restaurant.

Supreme House (Map pp284–5; ☎ 0 5322 2480; 44/1 Soi 9, Th Moon Muang; r 200–300B) This nondescript three-storey building is run by Mr Gordon, a backpacker who turned into a life-term expat. The atmosphere is relaxed, the clientele devoted and there's a small library on the ground floor.

Jonadda Guest House (Map pp284–5; ☎ 0 5322 7281; 23/1 Soi 2, Th Ratwithi; r 250–450B; 🗶) Run by an Aussie-Thai couple, this multi-storey building has spotless but basic rooms. There is a pleasant ground-floor cafe filled with trekking information.

Smile House 1 (Map pp284–5; ☎ 0 5320 8661; www .smileguesthouse.com; 5 Soi 2, Th Ratchamankha; r 250–700B; 🗶 🖳) A little backpacker village flourishes around an old Thai house, which has basic shared-bath rooms. Next door is a grubby multi-storey building that might make you migrate elsewhere. The one-storey buildings

that flank the pool are much nicer and popular with families. The atmosphere is friendly and the staff gets rave reviews. The owner confirmed that the old house once served as the 'safe house' of Kun Sa, the infamous Shan-Chinese opium warlord.

Siri Guesthouse (Map pp284–5; ☎ 0 5332 6550; Soi 5 Th Moon Muang; s/d 250/300B) This mellow place offers fairly stylish rooms considering the price. Some rooms can be a little dark but are still comfortable and clean.

Thapae Gate Lodge (Map pp284–5; ☎ 0 5320 7134; www.thapaegatelodge.com; 38/7 Soi 2, Th Moon Muang; s 250–350B, d 300–400B; 🗶 🖳) Across the street from All in 1, this multi-storey building has clean and cheap rooms with small terraces and a friendly owner who speaks good English.

Awanahouse (Map pp284–5; ☎ 0 5341 9005; www .awanahouse.com; 7 Soi 1, Th Ratchadamnoen; r 300–900B; 🗶 🖳 🗶) What started out as a small guesthouse has grown into a standard multi-storey apartment building on a quiet soi. Awana has large and bright rooms, some with balconies, TV and fridge. The cheapest rooms have fan and shared bath. The lap pool is good for a plunge but not for sunbathing. The top floor has been converted into a chill-out space with city views and a pool table.

Rendezvous Guest House (Map pp284–5; ☎ 0 5321 3763; rendezvousgh@hotmail.com; 3/1 Soi 5, Th Ratchadamnoen; r 350–500B; 🗶) An adequate wallflower of a place, this three-storey guesthouse has clean and cheap rooms. The primary difference in price is if you opt for fan or air-con. Some rooms have spiffier tiles and all have TV, safety box and fridge. Rates include breakfast.

Safe House Court (Map pp284–5; ☎ 0 5341 8955; www .safehousecourt.com; 178 Th Ratchaphakhinai; r 350–550B; 🗶) This apartment-court building is in the middle of the old city and has no-nonsense lodgings. The rooms at the front of the building will get a lot of street noise, while the back end will get monk noise from the nearby temple.

Gap's House (Map pp284–5; ☎ 0 5327 8140; www.gaps -house.com; 3 Soi 4, Th Ratchadamnoen; r 350–800B; 🗶 🖳) A quirky little gem, Gap's House has Thai-style wooden rooms planted in a thick jungle garden cluttered with statuary, cabinets of trinkets and a *săh·lah* (open-air pavilion, often spelt as *sala*). Some rooms have antiquey furnishings but are a tad musty with thin walls. The cheaper, sturdier concrete rooms are more basic. Bring your mozzie spray. Gap's is also famous for its Thai cooking course (p300) and nightly vegetarian buffet.

All In 1 (Map pp284-5; ☎ 0 53207133; www.allin1gh.com; 31 Soi 2, Th Moon Muang; r 400-500B; ✖ ⬜) Formerly named Baan Manee, this apartment building has received a makeover and boasts clean rooms with cable TV. Soi 2 tends to attract an older male clientele and the nearby Mandalay disco isn't a good sleeping companion.

RCN Court (Map pp284-5; ☎ 0 5341 8280-2; www .rcnguesthouse.com; 35 Soi 7, Th Moon Muang; r 450-500B; ✖ ⬜) This basic place is well known for its affordable monthly rates (from 6300B) and quiet central location. The rooms are nothing special but have cable TV and fridge. At the time of writing, the 2nd floor was getting a makeover. There is an outdoor kitchen for guests, a small front patio and a fitness room.

Tri Gong Residence (Map pp284-5; ☎ 0 5321 4754; www.trigong.com; 8 Soi 1, Th Si Phum; r 700-1000B; ✖ ⬜) Guesthouses often have humble beginnings: Kun Adam was sitting in his garden one day when a traveller asked for a room and now he's a stay-at-home boss ushering foreigners into a comfortable home away from home. Built around a courtyard, the large rooms have better-than-average furniture, cable TV and fridge. There is also a common kitchen, free coffee corner and the enthusiastic proprietor.

Mini Cost (Map pp284-5; ☎ 0 5341 8787; www.mini costcm.com; 19-19/4 Soi 1, Th Ratchadamnoen; s 550B; d 750-1050B; ✖ ⬜) This apartment-style spot has modern rooms with easy chairs, calming colours and a few touches of Thai-style decor. The cheapest rooms have shared bath and occupy the top floor. Except for the new construction projects, Soi 1 is a quiet and easy escape from all the tourist action on Th Moon Muang.

Montri Hotel (Map pp284-5; ☎ 0 5321 1069/70; 2-6 Th Ratchadamnoen; r 850B; ✖) A classic Thai-Chinese hotel, the Montri might need a little Botox work on the beds but the spacious rooms are filled with light. It is centrally located on the busy corner of Th Moon Muang and Th Ratchadamnoen. A renovation was still in progess at the time of writing.

MIDRANGE

Top North Hotel (Map pp284-5; ☎ 0 5327 9623; www.top northgroup.com; 41 Th Moon Muang; r 800-1200B; ✖ ⬛) Close to Pratu Tha Phae, this old-fashioned high-rise has a central location among Th Moon Muang's tourist services. The centrepiece pool is the main attraction for budget-minded water-lovers. Otherwise the rooms are a tad tatty.

ourpick Sri Pat Guest House (Map pp284-5; ☎ 0 5321 8716; www.sri-patguesthouse.com; 16 Soi 7, Th Moon Muang; r 1000B; ✖) Some flashpacker hotels can be convenient and comfortable but a tad too cookie-cutter. Sri Pat has just the right dose of personality. Rooms have sunny outlooks, celadon-coloured tiles, folksy cotton drapes and balconies. Skip the fan rooms though, as your money will go further elsewhere.

3 Sis (Map pp284-5; ☎ 0 5327 3243; www.3sisbed andbreakfast.com; 1 Soi 8, Th Phra Pokklao; r 1350-1650B; ✖ ⬜) Get all the comfort of a hotel without all the fuss at this new flashpacker place. Rooms in the primary building (the 'vacation lodge') have spacious beds, clean white walls, fridge and cable TV. The adjoining building (aka 'B&B') has smaller carpeted rooms that might not stand up to the rainy season.

Charcoa House (Map pp284-5; ☎ 0 5321 2681; www .charcoa.com; 4 Soi 1, Th Si Phum; r 1400-3500B; ✖ ⬜) Popping up in the backpacker neighbourhood, this new boutique hotel is reminiscent of a petit four, a pretty confection in miniature. The 10 rooms rely on an imported heritage style with exposed timbers and whitewashed walls but they are smaller than small. The attached bakery and restaurant is well known among Chiang Mai's hi-so Thais.

Buri Gallery (Map pp284-5; ☎ 0 5341 6500; 102 Th Ratchadamnoen; r 1600-2000B; ✖ ⬜) A glorified guesthouse, Buri Gallery occupies a converted teak building decorated with Lanna handicrafts. Most of the ground-floor rooms don't have windows and the walls are too thin to block out noise. The upstairs deluxe rooms are quieter and have small terraces and in-room internet-enabled computers. Though the rates are a tad high, the staff provide the kind of services you'd find at fully fledged hotels.

TOP END

Villa Duang Champa (Map pp284-5; ☎ 0 5332 7199; www .duangchampa.com; 82 Th Ratchadamnoen; r 2800-3800B; ✖ ⬜) Victorian architecture meets modern minimalism in this mini boutique hotel. With only 10 rooms, Duang Champa occupies a colonial-style building with rooms so sparse they're almost bare, save for the mattresses suited for ageing backs and the modern electronic toys. The top floor deluxe rooms have views of Doi Suthep.

U Chiang Mai (Map pp284-5; ☎ 0 5332 7000; www .uchiangmai.com; 70 Th Ratchadamnoen; r from 4500B; ✕ ☐ ☒) Golf clubs and briefcases are shuttled in and out of this corporate-friendly hotel, a rare find in the heart of the old city. The rooms are situated around a central infinity pool and have lavender-and-black colour schemes that are contemporary without being cutting edge. Superior rooms have shower only (no bathtubs). The hotel has a 24-hour checkout policy: you leave at the same time you arrived.

Tamarind Village (Map pp284-5; ☎ 0 5341 8896-9; www.tamarindvillage.com; 50/1 Th Ratchadamnoen; r 6000-18,000B; ✕ ☐ ☒) Considered to be one of the first of the 'Lanna revival' hotels, Tamarind Village has recreated the quiet spaces of a temple with galleried buildings and garden courtyards on the grounds of an old tamarind orchard. The bamboo-shrouded walkway and whitewashed perimeter wall shut out the distracting modern world. Cultural and religious activities at the nearby temple are an added bonus. Internet is available in the common spaces only.

Rachamankha (Map pp284-5; ☎ 0 5390 4111; www .rachamankha.com; 6 Th Ratchamankha; r 7000-9,500B; ✕ ☐ ☒) The encore effort by architect Ong-ard Satrabhandu to Tamarind Village, Rachamankha imitates an ancient monastery in Lampang. Considering the reputation, the rooms aren't opulent and the superiors are quite small. The deluxe rooms are more generous with four-poster beds and bathrooms that double the living space. The highlight of the hotel is the library, a light-strewn room smelling of polished wood and musty paper.

East of the Old City

Traffic is more intense outside of the old city and the roar of engines often detracts from Chiang Mai's low-key ambience. While it isn't as quaint as the old city, Th Tha Phae is just as convenient for sightseeing and nightlife and even closer to the night bazaar. More upmarket visitors will also like the convergence of stylish lodging next door to ordinary Thai life – musty old houses, commuting motorbikes, and housewives selling coffee and noodles.

Corporate hotels with business centres and conference capacity occupy the area near the Chiang Mai Night Bazaar. The surrounding businesses cater to conservative travellers. Previously, Chiang Mai filled the corporate niche with home-grown hotels while the international chains could hardly find this backwater on a map. But multinational brands have now staked out massive claims in this area in preparation of Chiang Mai becoming a new conference destination.

BUDGET

Daret's House (Map pp284-5; ☎ 0 5323 5440; 4/5 Th Chaiyaphum; r 150-160B) A long-time backpackers fave with stacks of basic, well-worn rooms. Daret's looks like many of Th Khao San's backpacker flops. But because this is Lanna-land, Kun Daret is an amiable guy often found in the cafe with his pet bird. You pay more for the luxury of hot water.

Tawan Guesthouse (Map pp284-5; ☎ 0 5320 8077; Soi 6, Th Tha Phae; r 240-500B) This simple guesthouse stands out from the pack with its stunning garden filled with fountains and *kòi* ponds all woven together by the flowering vines of bougainvillea and a big shade tree with hair-like tendrils. Rooms are nothing special: some occupy an old wooden house while others are in a flimsy bamboo hut, where noise will be a factor. Everything was clean but the staff were a little grumpy about showing us a room (maybe our timing was bad).

Sarah Guest House (Map pp284-5; ☎ 0 5320 8271; http://sarahgh.hypermart.net; 20 Soi 4, Th Tha Phae; s 240-400B, d 300-450B; ✕ ☐) A long-running backpacker spot, Sarah's sits in a quiet garden and is run by the original English owner. There are only 12 simple rooms, which have chunky wood furniture and large bathrooms, and the option of fan or air-con.

New Mitrapap Hotel (Map pp284-5; ☎ 0 5325 1262, fax 0 5325 1260; 94/96 Th Ratchawong; r from 330B; ✕) Near Talat Warorot, New Mitrapap is a bit of a time warp both for its prices and its classic Thai-Chinese hotel decor. The air-con rooms are good value with TV and mini-fridge. The hotel is built around a central atrium and skylight making the hallways bright and sunny.

Roong Ruang Hotel (Map pp284-5; ☎ 0 5323 4746; fax 0 5325 2409; roongruanghotel@yahoo.com; 398 Th Tha Phae; r 400-800B; ✕ ☐) With a prime location near Pratu Tha Phae, Roong Ruang is a great deal for an older-style hotel. It doesn't look like much from the outside but the interior courtyard is cocooned from traffic noise and the 2nd-floor rooms have pleasant sitting areas on the shared terrace. The more expensive rooms have air-con, while the cheaper rooms have fan.

Lai-Thai Guesthouse (Map pp284–5; ☎ 0 5327 1725; www.laithai.com; 111/4-5 Th Kotchasan; r 440–750B; ❄ 🖳) This three-storey apartment-court building is outfitted in northern Thai decor, transforming an otherwise institutional setting into ethno-chic. The rooms are comfortable if a little cramped, with cable TV and mini-fridge. The cheapest rooms are on the top floor and share a bathroom. This property comes at a decent price for a place with a pool, but the location is right beside a busy, traffic-filled street.

Thapae Boutique House (Map pp284–5; ☎ 0 5328 5295, www.thapaeboutiquehouse.com; 4 Soi 5, Th Tha Phae; r from 750B; ❄ 🖳) Smart and stylish Thapae Boutique House delivers all the flashpacker standards: a plum bed, bamboo-themed decor, cute bathrooms and breezy outdoor sitting areas.

Baan Kaew Guest House (Map pp284–5; ☎ 0 5327 1606; www.baankaew-guesthouse.com; 142 Th Charoen Prathet; r 800B; ❄) Hiding away from the tourist crowds in a genteel part of the city, Baan Kaew is the type of place that Chiang Mai veterans might call home for an extended stay. The two-storey apartment building is set back from the road behind the owner's own residence. The rooms are well maintained but rather bland and have mini-fridges and outdoor seating areas. The manager speaks English and enjoys a good chat about world politics.

MIDRANGE & TOP END

Amora (Map pp284–5; ☎ 0 5325 1531; www.amorahotels.com; 22 Th Chaiyaphum; r 1900–2200B; ❄ 🖳) Think of it as Chiang Mai's Best Western: adequate rooms, adequate beds and hotel-issue decor. Amora's best features are the pool and the big drinkable view of Doi Suthep from the rooms. Rates include breakfast but there's a usage charge for internet.

Imperial Mae Ping Hotel (Map pp284–5; ☎ 0 5328 3900; www.imperialhotels.com; 153 Th Si Donchai; r from 4000B; ❄ 🖳) Of the big boxy hotels near the night bazaar, Imperial Mae Ping has the best combination of Asian quirks and modern fashion. Renovations are creeping through the hotel floor by floor, and at the time of writing the superior rooms had just been nicely modernised. Starting at the 5th floor, there are grand views of Doi Suthep. Floors are segregated into smoking and non-smoking.

our pick **Banthai Village** (Map pp284–5; ☎ 0 5325 2789; www.banthaivillage.com; 19 Soi 3, Th Tha Phae; r from 4500B; ❄ 🖳) The stylised rice village is a popular concept for Chiang Mai's new bou-tique hotels, but Banthai's version gets a few things right: the rooms are big enough to walk around in without bumping into hard modern corners. With only 33 rooms, it also strikes the right balance between intimacy and privacy. Rooms occupy several Lanna-style terraced rowhouses with generously sized beds and glass-fronted bathrooms with mini soak-tubs.

Yaang Come Village (Map pp284–5; ☎ 0 5323 7222; www.yaangcome.com; 90/3 Th Si Donchai; r 6000–9000B; ❄ 🖳) A clever twist on the Lanna re-production hotel is this homage to a Tai Lue village, based on the owner's travels to the Yunnan region of China. The hotel recre-ates architectural and cultural elements of the highlands village, including the shrine-like water well near the entrance of the property and the steep rooflines of the hotel buildings. Rooms are large and tastefully decorated with murals, textiles and teak furniture. Winding paths and a manicured garden lead to the pool and restaurant.

Le Meridien Chiang Mai (Map pp284–5; ☎ 0 5325 2666; www.starwoodhotels.com; 108 Th Chang Khlan; r from 6000B; ❄ 🖳) Scheduled to open a month after the research of this book, Le Meridien is one of three international chains to migrate to the night bazaar area (described on its website as the city's central business district) to capi-talise on the promotion of Chiang Mai as a convention centre.

Manathai (Map pp284–5; ☎ 0 5328 1666; www.manathai.com; 39/9 Soi 3, Th Tha Phae; r 7000–16,000B; ❄ 🖳) Boutique Manathai merges Lanna and colonial elements to create a secluded village around a central swimming pool. The rooms are tightly packed with teak furniture, black-and-white photographs and contemporary bathrooms. Although professional and suited for the sophisti-cated traveller, the intimate atmosphere seems a tad claustrophobic considering its romantic ambitions.

Shangri-La Hotel (Map pp284–5; ☎ 0 5325 3888; www.shangri-la.com/chiangmai; 89/8 Th Chang Khlan; r from 7000B; ❄ 🖳) This massive corporate tower looks as if it were airlifted from a much big-ger megalopolis. It isn't Chiang Mai's most charming hotel, but it was built to address the city's lack of meeting space. The rooms are standard for the chain and the grounds include a huge pool and tennis courts. There's free wi-fi in the lobby but the rooms only have broadband for a charge.

CHIANG MAI PROVINCE

DusitD2 Chiang Mai (Map pp284-5; ☎ 0 5399 9999; www.dusit.com; 100 Th Chang Khlan; r 8000B; ❄ 🖳 🖩) An anomaly in Chiang Mai, D2 is the hotel version of an urban hipster fuelled by funky cocktails and pulsing lounge music. The lobby is a chic chill-out space with orange sherbet palette and moulded furnishings. The rooms are more functional than fashionable. There's a top-floor fitness room with a view of Doi Suthep and the hotel restaurant and bar have new-millennium attitude.

Riverside

Riverside House (Map pp284-5; ☎ 0 5324 1860; www .riversidehousechiangmai.com; 101 Th Chiang Mai-Lamphun; r 500-900B; ❄ 🖳) Next door to the Tourism Authority of Thailand, this quiet and friendly place has great cheap rooms arranged around a pretty garden. All rooms have cable TV and include a continental breakfast. The 700B rooms might get some street noise and there's a new 900B wing being constructed deeper into the property.

our pick **Galare Guest House** (Map pp284-5; ☎ 0 5381 8887; www.galare.com; 7/1 Soi 2, Th Charoen Prathet; r 1100B; ❄) With an affordable riverside setting, Galare is a repeat visitor's favourite. Although the rooms don't have river views, they are spacious, if a tad dated, and open on to a wide shared veranda. There's a small parking lot and it's walking distance to the night bazaar.

River View Lodge (Map pp284-5; ☎ 0 5327 1109; www.riverviewlodgch.com; 25 Soi 4, Th Charoen Prathet; r 1500-2200B; ❄ 🖩) The River View Lodge has got an edge on charm, with cabinets stuffed full of antiques and trinkets, a two-level garden overlooking Mae Ping and a good-size pool. The rooms are rather plain, but still bright and breezy with a view of the river. This property also boasts a parking lot and is within walking distance of the night bazaar.

Baan Orapin (Map pp284-5; ☎ 0 5324 3677; 150 Th Charoenrat; r from 2400B; ❄ 🖳 🖩) It's a family affair at Baan Orapin, a pretty garden compound anchored by a stately teak house, which has been in the family since 1914. Guest residences (a total of 15 rooms) are in separate and modern buildings spread throughout the property. The rooms are spacious and contemporary with a sense of privacy.

Chedi (Map pp284-5; ☎ 0 5325 3333; www.ghmhotels .com; 123 Th Charoen Prathet; r 16,200-24,000B; ❄ 🖳 🖩) Chiang Mai's most ambitious homage to modernism, the Chedi has transformed the former British Consulate into a minimalist

sculpture with bento-box glass-fronted rooms and restrained Zen-like grounds. The club suites have more amenities (complimentary mini-bar, laundry and airport transfer) than the compact deluxe rooms. Despite its riverfront location, only the top floor and the corner rooms have water views. It's all very sleek and stylish, but for the price we'd rather stay on New York's Central Park.

West of the Old City

Several Thai-style business hotels are clustered on Th Huay Kaew near Kad Suan Kaew shopping centre. The sois off Th Nimmanhaemin have sprouted some new 'guest-tels' (a cross between a guesthouse and a hotel). Prices tend to be a little higher here than in the backpacker areas but you're closer to Chiang Mai University.

Uniserv-International Center Hostel (Map pp276-7; ☎ 0 5394 2881; off Th Nimmanhaemin; r 500-800B; ❄ 🖳) Looking for a place to stay close to the university? You can't get much closer than this hostel, which shares space with CMU's busy International Center. The rooms are straightforward concrete blocks all with TV and fridge. Rates include breakfast and monthly rates are available.

Baan Say-La (Map pp276-7; ☎ 08 1930 0187; www .baansaylaguesthouse.com; Soi 5, Th Nimmanhaemin; r 500-950B; ❄) The same owners as Yesterday the Village run this bohemian-chic guesthouse. Rooms have four-poster beds, rattan furnishing and cable TV. Black-and-white photography decorates the walls, and the shared seating areas have large easy chairs. The 500B rooms have shared bathrooms. Downside is that it is behind the 'Fine Thanks' live music bar, so some rooms may be noisy.

International Hotel Chiangmai (Map pp284-5; ☎ 0 5322 1819; www.ymcachiangmai.org; 11 Soi Sermsak, Th Hutsadisawee; r 600-900B; ❄ 🖳 🖩) Quite possibly the ugliest building in a country where the competition is fierce, this local branch of the YMCA redeems itself with some excellent bargains for rooms with a view of Doi Suthep, and a pool. Skip their overpriced dorm beds. The residential neighbourhood of flower gardens and single-family homes is another plus and the hotel is conveniently located between the university and the old city.

Pann Malee Home (Map pp284-5; ☎ 0 5328 9147; www.pannmalee.com; off Soi 17, Th Nimmanhaemin; r 1000B; ❄) This converted townhouse has four rooms that feel as if an arty Thai friend has let you crash at her house. In a way you are. The owner decorated each room to reflect the personalities of her family members.

our pick **Pingnakorn Hotel** (Map pp284-5; ☎ 0 5335 7755; www.pingnakorn.com; 4 Soi 12, Th Nimmanhaemin; r 1500-3000B; ⊠ 🖵) Mainly an extended-stay residence, this multi-storey tower at the far end of the soi has smart and breezy apartment-style rooms with all the amenities. Monthly rates start at 10,000B plus water and electricity charges. Rates include breakfast.

Yesterday the Village (Map pp284-5; ☎ 0 5321 3809; 24 Th Nimmanhaemin; www.yesterday.co.th; r from 2000B; ⊠ 🖵) The new breed of lodging, Yesterday does a quick trip backwards to the near past. The common spaces of the converted apartment building are artistically decorated with vintage prints, old phonographs and the soon-to-be-extinct tube televisions. The deluxe rooms have more panache than the superiors but both are spare. There aren't a lot of midrange options on Th Nimmanhaemin but this one is a tad self-inflated.

Chiang Mai Orchid Hotel (Map pp276-7; ☎ 0 5322 2091; www.chiangmaiorchid.com; 23 Th Huay Kaew; r from 2000B; ⊠ 🖵 🕾) Classy in a time-capsule way, Chiang Mai Orchid is oriented towards business travellers and package tourists and has a central city location. The recently renovated rooms were a lot more appealing. They also have smoking and non-smoking floors. There's a fitness room and a business centre and it is next to Kad Suan Kaew shopping centre.

Amari Rincome Hotel (Map pp276-7; ☎ 0 5322 1130; www.amari.com; 1 Th Nimmanhaemin; r 2700-6600B; ⊠ 🖵 🕾) This reliable business hotel close to the university is tastefully decorated in a heritage style with a few remodels sporting more modern decor.

Elsewhere

Viangbua Mansion (Map pp276-7; ☎ 0 5341 1202; www .viangbua.com; 3/1 Soi Viangbua, Th Chang Pheuak; r from 900B; ⊠ 🖵) North of Pratu Chang Pheuak, this multi-storey hotel doesn't have the best location for sightseers but it has plenty of amenities for long-term guests. The rooms have contemporary furnishings, wardrobe, fridge, small lounge, cable TV and wi-fi; some also have a kitchen. There's also a gym, restaurant and coffee shop. Weekly/monthly rates start at 5600/12,000B.

our pick **Tri Yaan Na Ros** (Map pp284-5; ☎ 0 5327 3174; www.triyaannaros.com; 156 Th Wualai; r from 3600B; ⊠ 🕾) A honeymoon candidate of superb qualifications, this pint-size boutique hotel creates a romantically antique world with its artfully restored house, galleried chambers and narrow walkways leading to various sitting areas. The friendly owner is usually on site and her architect son has his offices above the hotel's restaurant.

Four Seasons Chiang Mai (☎ 0 5329 8181; www .fourseasons.com; Th Mae Rim-Samoeng Kao; r from 19,000B; ⊠ 🖵 🕾) Chiang Mai's first premier destination resort features vaulted pavilion suites and residences spread amid eight hectares of landscaped gardens and rice terraces worked by water buffalo. The resort is north of the city in the forested foothills and includes all the necessary self-contained distractions: cooking school, award-winning spa, swimming pool and tennis courts.

Mandarin Oriental Dhara Dhevi (☎ 0 5388 8888; www.mandarinoriental.com; 51/4 Th Chiang Mai-San Kamphaeng; r from 20,000B; ⊠ 🖵 🕾) Almost a kingdom unto itself, the Dhara Dhevi is an amazing resort destination that has recreated a miniature Lanna village with footpaths through walled residence compounds surrounding terraced rice fields. So much architectural history has been reproduced here that the resort fancies itself a cultural attraction, offering guided tours to guests as well as craft demos. The rooms are of course aristocratic and the grounds host many wedding parties. There's also a slightly cheaper and less imposing colonial wing.

EATING

Chiang Mai's restaurant scene is surprisingly down to earth and wholesome. Modest family-run establishments and open-air food courts dominate the city's hot dining spots. Plus there are loads of vegetarian restaurants, ranging from backpacker cafes to religious society outreaches. You can also explore the local markets and small shopfronts for the regional speciality of *kôw soy*, (sometimes written as *khao soi*) a curried noodle dish claiming Shan-Yunnanese heritage. It's usually accompanied with pickled vegetables and a thick red chilli sauce. For more information on northern Thai specialities, see p346.

For fine dining Chiang Mai is still a little provincial. The hotel restaurants dominate the splash-out options but there are a few independent upmarket eateries that attract the expats and expense accounts.

Old City

THAI

There is a cluster of made-to-order shops (*ráhn ah·hǎhn đahm sàng*), along from the police station on Th Ratchadamnoen, which do a brisk lunch business. Residents pick up *gàp kôw* (pre-made food served with rice) from evening vendors lining the stretch of Th Samlan south of Th Ratchadamnoen.

ourpick Tien Sieng Vegetarian Restaurant (Map pp284–5; ☎ 0 5320 6056; Th Phra Pokklao; dishes 20B; ◷ 6.30am-5pm) This Buddhist society–affiliated restaurant serves a variety of pre-made vegetarian dishes over rice. Technically the dishes are *jair*, meaning they don't contain meat, garlic or onions, but they're still tasty and for 20B you get a choice of two dishes.

Mangsawirat Kangreuanjam (Map pp284–5; Th Inthawarorot; dishes 20-35B; ◷ 8am-2pm) Look for the difficult-to-see English sign that reads 'Vegetarian Food'. The cooks put out several pots of fresh, 100% Thai vegetarian dishes daily.

Bang Moey Kaafae (Map pp284–5; Th Ratwithi; dishes 25-30B; ◷ 9am-3pm Mon-Fri) Noodle-heads will find an unusual addition to their lunchtime pastime: ambience. Instead of the tables-and-tiles decor of most noodle shops, this spot occupies an old wooden house with antique metal advertisements adorning the front.

Pak Do Restaurant (Map pp284–5; Th Samlan; dishes 25-30B; ◷ 7am-early afternoon) Across the street from Wat Phra Singh, this morning curry shop displays its dishes in big metal bowls out front. To do as the Thais, you can lift the lid to survey the contents. If your stomach has developed a hankering for rice in the morning, you'll be glad you peeked into the pots.

Kow Soy Siri Soy (Map pp284–5; ☎ 0 5321 0944; Th Inthawarorot; dishes 30-35B; ◷ 7am-3pm Mon-Fri) This simple shop prepares a rich and hearty broth for its *kôw soy*, served with or without chicken. It also serves the popular *kôw man gài* (chicken and rice) dish.

Nayok Fa (Map pp284–5; Th Ratchaphakhinai; dishes 30-35B; ◷ 10am-6pm) This ma-and-pa place cooks up fresh food in the massive woks out front. Try *pàt see·éw* (stir-fried wide noodles with a choice of beef, pork or chicken) or the suckling pig and rice.

Sailomyoy (Map pp284–5; Th Ratchadamnoen; dishes 30-80B) The Thai equivalent of a greasy spoon, this simple place serves all-day breakfasts, should your days be your nights, as well as basic Thai dishes. It isn't the pinnacle of cuisine but it i cheap and conveniently located near Prat Tha Phae.

Si Phen Restaurant (Map pp284–5; ☎ 0 5331 5328 103 Th Inthawarorot; dishes 40-80B; ◷ 9am-5pm) Thi inexpensive stopover near Wat Phra Singl specialises in northern- and northeastern style dishes, including *sôm·đam* (spicy greer papaya salad).

AUM Vegetarian Food (Map pp284–5; ☎ 0 5327 8315 66 Th Moon Muang; dishes 50-140B; ◷ 8am-5pm) Fee healthier and less anxious with a full belly of AUM's health-friendly meals. There's organic coffee from Laos, seasonal juices and a range of all-veggie Thai-style stir-fries. The restaurant is friendly with an attached second hand bookshop and an additional eating area with floor cushions and low tables.

Heuan Phen (Map pp284–5; ☎ 0 5327 7103; 112 Tl Ratchamankha; dishes 60-150B; ◷ 8am-3pm & 5-10pm At this well-known restaurant everything i on display, from the northern Thai food to the groups of culinary visitors and the antique cluttered dining room. Chiang Mai local might sniff at the quality, but for newbies the ambience and the dishes are a treat. Daytime meals are served in a large canteen out front.

Rachamankha (Map pp284–5; ☎ 0 5390 4111 Rachamankha Hotel, 6 Th Ratchamankha; dishes 250 1100B) Tucked away behind Wat Phra Singh in the sumptuous grounds of the boutique hotel of the same name, one dines at the Rachamankha to enjoy the crisp white lin ens and antique atmosphere as much as the food. The menu is Thai-centred, along wit hints of Myanmar, Yunnan and Europe the periphery. Do yourself a favour though and skip the one-dish noodle meals, which by definition, should be eaten at a roadsid wok for around 30B.

INTERNATIONAL

Bierstube (Map pp284–5; ☎ 0 5327 8869; 33/6 Th Moo Muang; dishes 50-130B; ◷ 7am-midnight) This cos wooden place is the restaurant version o an old German uncle. It has been cookin up German comfort fare for so many year that its age can be measured by the regulars expanding waistlines. In Bangkok such dino saurs would be shunned, but here in Chiang Mai this is considered family.

Pum Pui Italian Restaurant (Map pp284–5; ☎ 0 532 8209; 24 Soi 2, Th Moon Muang; dishes 60-180B; ◷ 11am 11pm) A charming 'date' restaurant, Pum Pu romances its guests with a garden setting and

CHIANG MAI PROVINCE

moderately priced dishes. The menu covers the usual Italian suspects, from antipasto to digestives and leaves room in the budget for some fine Italian beverages.

Chiangmai Saloon (Map pp284–5; ☎ 0 6161 0690; Th Ratwithi; dishes 80–300B) Welcome to the Wild West, Thai style, where a gunslinger, or more accurately a backpack slinger, can fill up on a real meal of meat – mainly burgers and steaks – before conquering some hill-tribe villages and taming wild elephants. The original branch is on Th Loi Kroh.

Amazing Sandwich (Map pp284–5; 252/3 Th Phra Pokklao; dishes 90–150B; 8.30am–8.30pm) A self-described island in a sea of rice, Amazing Sandwich delivers the bread to the wheat-deprived. Expats rank the make-your-own sandwiches right up there with sliced bread.

Ginger Kafe (Map pp284–5; ☎ 0 5341 9011; 199 Th Moon Muang; dishes 90–200B; 10am–11pm) Within the same grounds as the House, Ginger Kafe is a smart place for the local debutantes and LWLs (ladies who lunch). The sunny dining room is dressed up in proper manorhouse prints and the chefs entertain the palate with well-educated international and Thai dishes.

Juicy 4U (Map pp284–5; ☎ 0 5327 8715; 5 Th Ratchamankha; dishes 95–135B; 8.30am–5.30pm) This cute cafe serves hangover-fighting juices, make-your-own vegetarian sandwiches and standard Thai dishes. Bring along some reading material as the kitchen can be very slow.

our pick Jerusalem Falafel (Map pp284–5; ☎ 0 5327 0208; 35/3 Th Moon Muang; dishes 100–280B) You might yawn at the thought of yet another Middle Eastern restaurant in a backpacker ghetto but let us sing the praises of this exotic import. The restaurant is a lively place to assemble with friends and nosh on a meze platter of falafel, shashlik, hummus and tabouli. Yoghurt, halloumi and feta cheese are home-made here.

House (Map pp284–5; ☎ 0 5341 9011; 199 Th Moon Muang; dishes 200–800B; 6pm–11pm) This restaurant occupies a mid-20th-century house (it once belonged to an exiled Burmese prince) that's now outfitted with colonial accoutrements. The House menu is a pan-Pacific affair, combining imported lamb and salmon with local spices and cooking techniques. If you're commitment shy about dinner, stop in and enjoy a few tapas dishes at the outdoor Moroccan-themed bar.

East of the Old City
THAI
Chiang Mai's small Chinatown, along Th Chang Moi, is a tasty quarter to investigate early in the morning. On Th Khang Mehn, you'll find kà·nŏm jeen and other noodle dishes. An alley next to the Top Charoen Optical shop, wakes up early thanks to a popular nám đow·hôo (soy milk) stall, serving warm soy milk accompanied with Chinese-style deep-fried doughnuts.

Kuaytiaw Kai Tun Coke (Map pp284–5; Th Kamphaeng Din; dishes 30–50B; 8am–4pm Mon-Sat) This small food shop, directly opposite the main entrance to the Imperial Mae Ping Hotel, prepares a unique version of gŏoay đĕeo gài đŭn yah jeen. Here the chicken is marinated in Coca-Cola and spices overnight, then steamed and served with rice noodles. It's actually quite good and has become famous as far away as Bangkok.

Aomngurn (Map pp284–5; ☎ 0 5323 3675; Th Ratchawong; dishes 30–100B) Next to the New Mitrapap Hotel, this humble spot is an easy escape from Talat Warorot's chaos and crowds. It specialises in Thai-Chinese dishes as well as grilled chicken and zesty yam (Thai-style salads).

Ratana's Kitchen (Map pp284–5; ☎ 0 5387 4173; 320-322 Th Tha Phae; dishes 30–150B) For all the talk of Chiang Mai having cool temperatures, it still gets hot by midday. Jump out of the oven and into Ratana's kitchen. It isn't a culinary legend but the dishes and prices are sensible and it's got a prime spot near Pratu Tha Phae for wilting tourists.

Galare Food Centre (Map pp284–5; Galare Night Bazaar, Th Chang Khlan; dishes 50–80B; 6pm–midnight) A classic food court, the Galare Food Centre offers a stress-free version of a night market. You buy coupons at the front desk, select a ready-made dish from one of the vendors and eat in a clean, traffic-free environment. There's also nightly entertainment, including Thai classical dancing.

Taste From Heaven (Map pp284–5; ☎ 0 5320 8803; 237-239 Th Tha Phae; dishes 60–100B) Eat like an elephant at this vegetarian restaurant benefiting the Elephant Nature Park (p298).

Just Khao Soy (Map pp284–5; ☎ 0 5381 8641; 108/2 Th Charoen Prathet; dishes 100B) This is the gourmet version of kôw soy. Served on a wooden artist's palette you can create your own noodle broth with several condiments, including coconut milk to thicken it at will. Two different noodle

---

THE LEGAL STIMULANT: CHIANG MAI'S CAFE CULTURE

Chiang Mai's creative and sociable temperament has eagerly adopted the global phenomenon of cafe culture, largely supplied by local coffee chains and home-grown Arabica beans. The proliferation of these coffee dens has been a boon to the royally sponsored agricultural projects that have worked for nearly 30 years to wean the highland hill-tribe villagers away from opium production and into coffee cultivation.

Often credited for introducing Chiang Mai to cafe culture is the unassuming **Libernard Cafe** (Map pp284-5; ☎ 0 5323 4877; 36 Th Chaiyaphum; ☾ 8am-5pm Tue-Sun), run by Pong who roasts her own beans daily, making different adjustments based on the day's climate conditions. She makes a smooth latte, hardly needing to be spiked with sugar.

At the other end of the caffeine scale is **Black Canyon Coffee** (Map pp284-5; ☎ 0 5327 0793; 1-3 Th Ratchadamnoen), with a high energy 'see-and-be-seen' location in front of Pratu Tha Phae that is always packed with people watchers. It is a local chain with multiple branches in the city.

Almost an attraction in its own right, Soi Kaafae (Coffee Lane on Soi 9, Th Nimmanhaemin) is populated by two bustling coffee shops and lots of laptop-tapping Thais. On one side of the street is **Wawee Coffee** (Map pp276-7; ☎ 0 5326 0125; Soi 9, Th Nimmanhaemin), a local chain that originally started at Mae Sa Elephant Camp and has since expanded to the point of Starbucks saturation. (There's also a Wawee on Th Ratchadamnoen in the old city.) Across the street is **94° Coffee** (☎ 0 5321 0234; Soi 9, Th Nimmanhaemin).

For coffee drinkers who fancy saving the world, **Lanna Cafe** (Map pp276-7; Th Huay Kaew; ☾ 8am-5pm Mon-Sat) is an NGO-run cafe that brews and sells fairtrade hill-tribe coffee.

The mountains of the north also produce Assam tea served in the Victorian-era **Tea House** (Th Tha Phae; ☾ 9.30-6pm), which shares space with Siam Celadon. The **House of Thai Coffee** (☎ 0 5327 7810; 131-133 Th Ratchadamnoen) is a fairly non-descript foreigner cafe with an eclectic tea menu, featuring northern Thai teas that have medicinal properties.

---

shapes are offered: Chiang Mai style and Mae Salong style.

Dalaabaa Bar & Restaurant (Map pp284-5; ☎ 0 5324 2491; 113 Th Bamrungrat; dishes 110-350B; ☾ 6pm-midnight) One of Chiang Mai's first urbane eateries, Dalaabaa has aged gracefully into a stylish old friend with subdued lighting washing over orange and red silks that decorate a glass-encased dining room. The Thai menu is artful and affordable considering the sophistication factor.

Antique House (Map pp284-5; ☎ 0 5327 6810; 71 Th Charoen Prathet; dishes 130-260B; ☾ 11am-midnight) A postcard setting for out-of-town visitors, Antique House is a quaint two-storey teak house and garden filled with wooden antiques and mellow nightly music. The menu is mainly northern Thai with all the central Thai classics, but the dishes are just window dressing for the Thai-style ambience.

Whole Earth Restaurant (Map pp284-5; ☎ 0 5328 2463; 88 Th Si Donchai; dishes 130-300B; ☾ 11am-10pm) This confectionery-coloured teak house wears a garden stole of hanging vines, *kòi* ponds and orchids growing in the crooks of tree limbs. It is the sort of place you might take your mum for her birthday – where the staff will treat her like royalty and the dishes seem exotic (Thai Indian and vegetarian) without being demanding.

Anusan Night Market (Map pp284-5; Anusan Night Bazaar, Th Chang Khlan; dishes 200-350B; ☾ 6pm-midnight) Further south of Galare Food Centre, Anusan is a buzzing food market best known for its Thai-Chinese seafood restaurants. Stalls surround a large cluster of tables where each 'restaurant' has a section allocated with its own waiters. Nearby are other stand-alone restaurants, some of which have their own prawn holding ponds acting as centrepieces for their menu speciality. The prices are higher than they ought to be but these are special-occasion splash-out restaurants for Thais.

INTERNATIONAL

Libernard Cafe (Map pp284-5; ☎ 0 5323 4877; 36 Th Chaiyaphum; dishes 50-110B; ☾ 8am-5pm Tue-Sun) A low-key cafe, Libernard serves fresh Arabica coffee grown in Thailand. The usual backpacker menu is rescued from derision with such care that the banana pancake actually becomes a tasty recommendation. Try also the *gaang mát·sà·màn* (Muslim-style curry). Pong does everything herself, which means service is a little slow, but comes with a smile.

Tianzi Tea House (Map pp284-5; ☎ 0 5344 9539; Th Kamphaeng Din; dishes 60-120B; ☒ 10am-10pm) Such hard-core health food is usually found in dirt-floor hippy shacks, but Tianzi has adopted the ascetic's meal to an aesthetic surrounding. Pretty open-air *săh·lah*, decorated with flowers and dappled with sunlight, host a range of organic and macrobiotic dishes, such as Yunnanese tofu cheese, beetroot soup and herbal coffees.

Art Cafe (Map pp284-5; ☎ 0 5320 6365; cnr Th Tha Phae & Th Kotchasan; dishes 60-150B) A classic holiday-land restaurant, Art Cafe could just as easily appear in an ageing beach resort back home. The menu aims to please with Thai, Italian, Mexican and American dishes. It is particularly good for breakfasts; the hours and location are both convenient and it gives your stomach a break from being adventurous.

Mike's Burgers (Map pp284-5; cnr Th Chaiyaphum & Th Chang Moi; dishes from 130B; ☒ 6pm-3am) A little bit of Coney Island has been transplanted into Chiang Mai at this replica American burger stand. From the worn red vinyl stools, barely a barrier away from the moat-road traffic, watch the fry-cook flip burgers, or swivel 90 degrees for a view of Doi Suthep. There are other branches on Th Nimmanhaemin and near the night bazaar.

Giorgio Italian Restaurant (Map pp284-5; ☎ 0 5381 8236; 2/6 Th Pracha Samphan; dishes 150-300B; ☒ 11.30am-2pm & 6-10.30pm Mon-Sat) With a trattoria setting near the night bazaar, this well-loved Italian restaurant features all the favourites from the boot-shaped peninsula. During the high season, dinner is also served on Sunday.

Moxie (Map pp284-5; ☎ 0 5399 9999; DusitD2 Chiang Mai, 100 Th Chang Khlan; dishes 150-400B; ☒ 6.30am-1am) This achingly hip restaurant in the DusitD2

hotel offers Chiang Mai a glimpse at what a more hyperactive metropolis would look like. The dining room is suited up in a clean geometric puzzle of orange, cream and dark wood. The dishes are edible sculptures of Thai, Japanese and Italian components.

Favola (Map pp284-5; ☎ 0 5325 3299; Le Meridien, 108 Th Chang Khlan; dishes 280-650B; ☒ 11am-11pm) Le Meridien's showcase Italian restaurant features a flamboyant chef who has transformed mama's cooking into a high-tech affair using molecular gastronomy techniques to prepare foams, infused oils and savoury ice creams. Hints of vanilla and pumpkin oil add dramatic character to fettuccini, but the best bets are the surprisingly affordable pizzas with wood oven–crisped crusts.

Good Health Store (Map pp284-5; ☎ 0 5320 6888; Th Si Donchai; ☒ 10am-6pm) Next to Suriwong Book Centre, this health-food store sells mainly chemical-free products, like whole grains, honey and nuts, as well as herbal remedies. They also sell fairtrade hill-tribe coffee.

Riverside

The area east of the river boasts two distinct culinary attractions. North of Saphan Nawarat (Nawarat Bridge) is a cluster of riverside restaurants that dish up dinner and entertainment with a view. Most are best visited on weekends when the locals celebrate a few days of rest. *Sŏrng·tăa·ou* and túk-túk drivers who sit outside of the restaurants typically ask for a flat and inflated fare of 100B to return to the old city after dark.

Further north, past Saphan Nakhon Ping, is Th Faham, known as Chiang Mai's *kôw soy* ghetto. Situated here are **Khao Soi Lam Duan** (Map pp276-7; Th Faham; dishes 35-60B), which also serves *kà·nŏm rang pêung* (literally bee-hive pastry – a coconut-flavoured waffle),

CHIANG MAI PROVINCE

SOI BAN HAW

A remnant from the days when Chiang Mai was a detour on the Silk Road is the Thai-Muslim community along Soi 1 off Th Chang Khlan, near Chiang Mai Night Bazaar. The 100-year-old **Matsayit Chiang Mai** (Map pp284-5; Soi 1, Th Charoen Prathet), also known as Ban Haw Mosque, was founded by *jeen hor* ('galloping Chinese'), the Thai expression for Yunnanese caravan traders. Within the past two centuries, the city's Muslim community has also grown to include ethnic Yunnanese Muslims escaping unrest in neighbouring Laos and Burma.

There are also a number of simple restaurants and vendors selling Thai-Muslim curries, *kôw soy* (curried chicken and noodles), *kôw mòk gài* (chicken biriani), and *néu·a òp hŏrm* ('fragrant' dried beef), a speciality of Chiang Mai's Yunnanese Muslim community. An evening food vendor does delicious *roh·đee* (Indian flat bread).

Khao Soi Samoe Jai (Map pp276-7; Th Faham; dishes 25-65B) and **Khao Soi Ban Faham** (Map pp276-7; Th Faham; dishes 30-55B). *Kôw soy* foodies sometimes spend the day sampling a bowl at each place to select their favourite. Also in the vicinity, near Prince Royal's College, is **Khao Soi Prince** (Map pp284-5; Th Kaew Nawarat; dishes 20-35B; ⏰ 9am-3pm).

Love at First Bite (Map pp284-5; ☎ 0 5324 2731; 28 Soi 1, Th Chiang Mai-Lamphun; pastries 40-80B; ⏰ 10.30am-6pm) Tucked deep into a residential soi on the east bank of the river, this famous dessert shop is filled with middle-class, cake-confident Thais. Don't be surprised to see folks posing in front of the dessert display case for a souvenir photo – the bakery's cheesecakes are famous among food bloggers.

Riverside Bar & Restaurant (Map pp284-5; ☎ 0 5324 3239; Th Charoenrat; dishes 90-200B; ⏰ 10am-1am) This rambling set of wooden buildings has been the most consistently popular riverside place for over 20 years. The food – Thai, Western and vegetarian – is just a minor attraction to the good-times ambience. The clientele is a mix of Thais and *fa·ràng*, lured into a singalong by the classic-rock band. There's inside and outside dining, as well as a spiffy new overflow building across the street. Some veterans opt to dine on the docked boat (90B surcharge) before the nightly 8pm river cruise.

Huan Soontaree (Map pp276-7; ☎ 0 5325 2445; 46/2 Th Wang Singkham; dishes 100-150B; ⏰ 5pm-1am) Visiting Thais from Bangkok make the pilgrimage to this rustic restaurant built on the west bank of the river, partly for the food but mainly for the owner, Soontaree Vechanont, a famous northern singer popular in the 1970s. She performs at the restaurant on weekends while other local musicians perform during the week. The menu is a pleasant blend of northern, northeastern and central Thai specialities.

Good View (Map pp284-5; ☎ 0 5324 1866; 13 Th Charoenrat; dishes 100-200B; ⏰ 10am-1am) Next door to the Riverside, Good View lives up to its name with open-air seating in a contemporary setting. The formula is similar to the Riverside, except the menu focuses more on Thai food and the nightly music covers a broader genre range.

Mahanaga (Map pp276-7; ☎ 0 5326 1112; 431 Th Charoenrat/Faham; dishes 250-600B; ⏰ 5.30pm-midnight) The Chiang Mai branch of a Bangkok-based fusion restaurant, Mahanaga is all style and romance with flickering candles, traditional Lanna-style buildings and tall trees. The menu features citified Thai food: classic recipes using high-end, imported meats, such as New Zealand lamb in yellow curry.

West of the Old City

THAI

The area west of Wat Suan Dok on Th Suthep has several popular vegetarian *(ah·hǎhn jair)* restaurants, indicated by yellow banners, as well as a carnivore's friend, a crispy pork *(mǒo gròrp)* restaurant. Dining becomes more contemporary on Th Nimmanhaemin but the busiest place is the grilled pork *(mǒo 'bĭng)* restaurant, near the corner of Soi 9, that is open only in the evening.

Milk Garden (Suan Nom; Map pp276-7; ☎ 0 5381 1680; Th Huay Kaew; dishes 15-90B; ⏰ 11am-9pm) The backbone of the Western culinary tradition, bread is merely a fanciful dessert in Thailand, often toasted and drowned in sweetened condensed milk. It is normally served from vendor stalls, but milk shops, like this arty hangout, often pop up wherever there are students. Drinks and other snackable dishes are also served.

Kanom Jeen Nimman (Map pp276-7; Th Nimmanhaemin; dishes 25-30B) You don't have to trek out to a morning market to blast your senses with the intense flavours of *kà·nǒm jeen* (white rice noodles served with curry). This open-air shop along the main road saves you the commute.

Khun Churn (Map pp276-7; ☎ 0 5322 4124; Soi 17, Th Nimmanhaemin; dishes 50-70B) You might think that vegetarian means rustic, but Khun Churn has kept up with the times with its 21st-century minimalist dining space. The main attraction is the extensive daily buffet (80B) as well as à la carte fruit drinks, crispy rice with coconut dip or pomelo salad. It's closed on the 16th of each month.

Hong Tauw Inn (Map pp276-7; ☎ 0 5322 8333; 95/17-18 Nantawan Arcade, Th Nimmanhaemin; dishes 50-150B; ⏰ 11am-11pm) Decked out in an old-fashioned costume of aged pendulum clocks and antiques, this intimate restaurant is a starter course on Lanna cuisine, including the banana-flower salad.

100% Isan Restaurant (Map pp276-7; Th Huay Kaew; dishes 60-200B; ⏰ 5-11pm) Directly in front of CMU's main gate, this fluorescent-lit shop does a bumping business of northeastern standards: *sôm·đam, kôw něe-o* and *gài yâhng*. From the looks of it, everyone who leaves the university gets hungry when they hear the mortar-and-pestle music of *sôm·đam*.

Ban Kaew Heuan Kam (☎ 0 5381 1616; 96/8 Th Klorng Chonprathran; dishes 65-185B; 🕙 5-10pm) Outside of town on the *klorng* road, this pretty teak building is a thoroughly Thai affair (even the menu is written in Thai) and it's a lovely spot to invite a Thai speaker to dinner. Without a translator, the first two pages of the menu are mainly northern Thai dishes (such as #1008 frog salad, #1014 steamed chicken in pandanus leaf, #2003 Burmese-style curry and #2012 fish curry with forest vegetables).

Implaphao Restaurant (☎ 0 5380 6603; Rte 121; dishes 80-160B) Dining by the water is an appetising feature for Thais and this barn-like restaurant lures in the supping parties for *blah pŏw* (broiled fish stuffed with aromatic herbs) and *dôm yam gûng*. It isn't the easiest restaurant to reach since it is 10km southwest of Chiang Mai, across from Talat Mae Huay, but it is an undiluted Thai experience.

Dong (Map pp276-7; ☎ 0 5322 2207; Soi 13, Th Nimmanhaemin; dishes 90-200B; 🕙 11am-3pm) Northern Thai food for northern Thai people, Dong nails the Lanna specialities – *nám prík nùm*, *lâhp kôo·a* and *gaang hang·lair* – in a gewgaw-free setting, an incredible demonstration of restraint considering Chiang Mai's obsession with wooden knick-knacks. But the service is so slow you'll wonder if they had to trek to Burma to fetch the dishes.

Galare Restaurant (☎ 0 5381 1041; 65 Th Suthep; dishes 90-200B; 🕙 5-11pm) Out on the outskirts of Chiang Mai, Galare is a terraced open-air restaurant nestled by a small lake and a green park that overlooks the city. A carpet of flowers fills in the spaces between the wooden picnic tables. The menu is mainly northern Thai, and though it's not spectacular you'll hardly notice more than the tranquil setting.

Palaad Tawanron (☎ 0 5321 6039; Th Suthep; dishes 90-350B; 🕙 11.30am-midnight) Set in the woods near Doi Suthep, this restaurant draws in Thais and foreigners alike for the Thai food and the spectacular views over twinkly Chiang Mai. To truly eat like a Thai you should order a centrepiece of grilled fish adorned with smaller Northern Thai curries and salads. Entry is via the rear gate to Chiang Mai Zoo.

INTERNATIONAL

I-Berry (Map pp276-7; ☎ 0 5389 5181; sub soi off Soi 17, Th Nimmanhaemin; dishes from 50B) A Bangkok-based ice-cream store has churned a pretty wooden lot into a hip phenomenon. Students and locals flock here with cameras in tow hoping to run into the famous owner, comedian Udom Taepanich (nicknamed 'Nose'). If he's not around they'll settle for the huge yellow sculpture out front said to mimic the star's signature feature (his big nose). The ice cream is pretty good, but watching Chiang Mai's celebrity worship is even better.

Tsunami (☎ 08 7189 9338; Th Huay Kaew; dishes 60-180B; 🕙 5.30-11.30pm) CMU students are really into Kyoto-style ramen and sushi stalls, which have sprung up all along Th Huay Kaew. The most famous is Tsunami, which always has a wait even during *bit teum* (semester break). If you can't get a seat head further north to Na Mor Sushi, which is unsigned but recognisable by the big wok out front.

Smoothie Blues (Map pp276-7; Th Nimmanhaemin; dishes 90-140B; 🕙 7.30am-9pm) Talk about expat HQ, this health-food cafe is an escapee from a yuppie neighbourhood in any Western city. Despite the geographic dislocation, the cafe is known for its breakfasts, as well as its sandwiches, baguettes and namesake drink.

Mi Casa (Map pp276-7; ☎ 0 5381 0088; Soi Wat Padaeng, Th Suthep; dishes 200-500B; 🕙 11am-2pm & 6-10pm) A Mediterranean crash course is available at this vivacious restaurant located behind Chiang Mai University. The chef is from northern Spain and invites Chiang Mai's fresh produce and imported ingredients to tango with him in the kitchen, preparing tapas standards and artful entrees.

Elsewhere

Chiang Mai reveals its Chinese heritage with its devotion to pork products, most obvious in the northern Thai speciality of *sâi òo·a* (pork sausage). Good quality *sâi òo·a* should be zesty and spicy with discernible flavours of lemongrass, ginger and turmeric. Two famous sausage makers are **Mengrai Sai Ua** (Th Chiang Mai-Lamphun), near the Holiday Inn on the east bank of the river, and **Sai Ua Gao Makham** (Rte 121), a small stall in Talat Mae Huay (Mae Huay market), which is a few kilometres south of the Night Safari on the way to Hang Dong.

Vegetarian Centre of Chiang Mai (Map pp276-7; ☎ 0 5327 1262; 14 Th Mahidol; dishes 15-30B; 🕙 6am-2pm Mon-Fri) Sponsored by the Asoke Foundation, an ascetic Buddhist movement, this restaurant serves inexpensive cafeteria-style veg. The society's founder was a leader of the PAD anti-government movement and the restaurant was closed at the time of writing due to the demonstrations in Bangkok.

CHIANG MAI PROVINCE

Spirit House (Map pp276-7; ☎ 08 4803 4366; Soi Viangbua, Th Chang Pheuak; dishes 100-200B) Sometimes the most charming restaurants are just display cases for an eccentric personality. This antique-filled dining room is the creative outlet for the American owner who's a master of many trades, from antique dealer to classical musician. A former chef in New Orleans, he's a self-described 'nut about food' and builds the daily menu around what looks interesting at the market. The restaurant hosts monthly classical concerts and many of the city's music professors and students hang out here. In the low season, the restaurant is open 5.30pm to 10.30pm.

Fujian (☎ 0 5388 8888; Mandarin Oriental Dhara Dhevi Hotel, Th Chiang Mai-San Kamphaeng; dishes from 400B; ◷ 11.30am-2.30pm & 6.30-10.30pm) Thais traditionally celebrate a special occasion with a trip to a Chinese restaurant. And Chiang Mai is especially well-endowed with celebratory fare thanks to this sumptuous setting at the Dhara Dhevi hotel. Top-flight dim sum fills the lunch menu while Cantonese and Sichuan classics are served family-style on fine bone china.

DRINKING

There are three types of watering holes in Chiang Mai: the backpacker bars on Th Moon Muang and Th Ratwithi, the student bars and clubs on Th Nimmanhaemin, and the riverside restaurants for live music. Chiang Mai is much more monogamous about nighttime encounters than Bangkok: the beloved bars have been around forever and are rarely the newest tap on the block. Another plus is that Thais in Chiang Mai aren't shy or snobby about hanging out with foreigners, so you're likely to find more mixed spots here than in Bangkok.

On Th Ratwithi near the intersection of Th Ratchaphakhinai is a parking lot filled with squatty bars with twinkling fairy lights and thundering sound systems. We've heard that this little piece of heaven is going to be torn down, but that's all the details we could find. Bob Marley–homage bars are fully represented here thanks to Babylon (Map pp284–5) and Heaven Beach (Map pp284–5), while Cafe del Sol (Map pp284–5) has garnered a steady crowd with its cheap cocktail menu.

Writer's Club & Wine Bar (Map pp284-5; ☎ 08 1928 2066; 141/3 Th Ratchadamnoen) Run by an ex-foreign correspondent, this unassuming traveller

hangout hosts an informal Friday night gathering of Chiang Mai's reporters and writers. There's also English pub grub to help anchor a liquid meal.

UN Irish Pub (Map pp284-5; ☎ 0 5321 4554; 24/1 Th Ratwithi) A standard-issue backpacker joint, this two-storey bar and restaurant is an old favourite for its Thursday quiz night and match nights. There's nothing particularly Irish here other than an interest in drinking.

John's Place (Place on the Corner; Map pp284-5; Th Moon Muang) Another old-school spot, John's dominates the triangular wedge of Th Ratchamankha and Soi 2 with neon and beer bellies. Climb the stairs past the faded posters of Thai scenery to the roof deck where you and your drinking buddies can howl at the moon and take turns playing 'beer nórng' (a variation of the Thai tradition in which the youngest in the group is in charge of keeping everyone's drinks filled).

Pinte Blues Pub (Map pp284-5; 33/6 Th Moon Muang) This place deserves some sort of award for staying in business so long (more than 20 years) while serving only espresso and beer, and for sticking to a blues-music format the whole time. It is easy to walk by and not notice it, so you'll have to use your ears as your guide.

Kafe (Map pp284-5; Th Moon Muang) A cosy bar snuggled in beside Soi 5, Kafe is often crowded with Thais and backpackers when every other place is empty. It offers a simple formula: cheap cold beer and efficient service.

Khan-Asa (Map pp284-5; ☎ 08 1681 0037; 84 Th Si Phum) Too lazy to cab it over to Th Nimmanhaemin, but need a break from the backpacker trail? This arty spot is mainly known for its Thai food, which is cheap enough not to put a dent in your beer budget. The soundtrack is light years beyond Chiang Mai's strange fascination with Phil Collins and Jack Johnson.

Pub (Map pp276-7; ☎ 0 5321 1550; 189 Th Huay Kaew) In an old Tudor-style cottage set well off the road, this venerable Chiang Mai institution semi-successfully calls up the atmosphere of an English country pub. The Friday-evening happy hour assembles all the old expats who claim to have arrived in the city on the back of elephants.

Drunken Flower (Map pp276-7; ☎ 0 5389 4210; 28/3 Soi 17, Th Nimmanhaemin) Though this old standard has changed locations, it has carried across its loyal cast of characters, a mix of CMU bohemians and NGO expats. The closet-

---

MARKET MEALS

Market mavens will love Chiang Mai's covered food and grocery centres, which offer everything from morning noodles to daytime snacking and evening supping. To impress a Thai friend, pick up a bag of *man gâa·ou*, a roasted acorn-like nut harvested at the end of the rainy season.

Talat Somphet (Map pp284-5; Soi 6, Th Moon Muang; 6am-6pm) North of the Th Ratwithi intersection, this day market sells all the fixings for a Thai feast, including takeaway curries, sweets and fruit. Many of the cooking schools do their market tours here. Unfortunately, the market's proximity to the tourist area has encouraged the fruit sellers to be creative with their prices.

Talat Pratu Chiang Mai (Map pp284-5; Th Bamrungburi; 4am-noon & 6pm-midnight) In the early morning, this market is Chiang Mai's communal larder, selling foodstuffs and ready-made dishes. If you want to make merit to the monks, come early and find the woman who sells pre-assembled food donations (20B); she'll explain the ritual to you. Things quiet down by lunchtime, but the burners are re-ignited for a large and popular night market that sets up across the road.

Talat Thanin (Map pp276-7; off Th Chang Pheuak; 5am-early evening) Market aficionados would be impressed by this efficient and clean covered market, one of the tidiest we've seen in Thailand. The meat vendors are segregated into their own glass-enclosed area preventing an accidental tour by sensitive stomachs. The fruit and vegetable section is a beautiful display of tropical bounty. In the prepared food section you'll find Chiang Mai's recent food trends: sushi and *fahin salad* (a Thai-style salad bar with 1950s options, like tapioca and jello). Continue deeper to the covered food centre for made-to-order noodles and stir-fries.

Talat Warorot (Map pp284-5; Th Chang Moi; 6am-5pm) Thanks to the Great Market's cheap prices on household goods, there should be enough money for a bowl of noodles, served in the interior building's main hall. A night market sets up after dark for cheap riverside dining.

Talat Ton Phayom (Map pp276-7; Th Suthep) This place acts as both a local market and a souvenir stop for Thais visiting from other provinces. Take a look at the packaged food area to see the kinds of edible gifts (like bags of *kâap mŏo* and *sâi òo·a*) that make a visit to Chiang Mai complete. Because CMU students make up a good portion of the clientele, prices tend to be low.

---

sized bar invokes an antique mood where the shaggy-headed students might have drunk and noshed away their haircut money.

Mix Bar (Map pp284-5; ☎ 0 5399 9999; DusitD2 Chiang Mai, 100 Th Chang Khlan) Looking for a night out on a town that is more cosmopolitan than Chiang Mai? Chart a course to DusitD2 hotel's slinky cocktail bar, a swish elixir after roving the night market. The last weekend of the month hosts gay-friendly rainbow parties.

NimMahn Bar (Map pp276-7; Th Nimmanhaemin) This open-air bar used to be the warm-up spot for the Warm-Up club (p318), but it has recently morphed into the smoking room now that the butts have been kicked out of the air-conditioned clubs.

Glass Onion (Map pp276-7; ☎ 0 5321 8479; Rooms Boutique Mall, Th Nimmanhaemin) Tucked away at the far end of the walking mall is this small lounge bar outfitted in '60s-style mod fashions. While the barely legals try to blow their eardrums out at Nimmanhaemin's dance clubs, this is the domain of grown-ups desiring cocktails and conversation. The bar also enjoys a gay-friendly reputation.

ENTERTAINMENT
Live Music

Riverside Bar & Restaurant (Map pp284-5; ☎ 0 5324 3239; 9-11 Th Charoenrat) In a twinkly setting on Mae Ping, Riverside is a one of the longest-running live-music venues in Chiang Mai. The cover bands made up of ageing Thai hippies stake out centre stage and fill the room with all the singalong tunes from the classic-rock vault. It is the perfect antidote for electronica overload.

Good View (Map pp284-5; ☎ 0 5324 1866; 13 Th Charoenrat) If the Riverside is too rustic for you, go next door to Good View, which features a more modern interpretation of cover tunes.

Le Brasserie (Map pp284-5; ☎ 0 5324 1665; 37 Th Charoenrat; 11.15pm-1am) North of the riverside restaurants, Le Brasserie is a popular late-night spot filled with devotees of local guitarist Took. Rock and blues from all the dead legends fill the set. Food service is available inside the bar or out the back by the river.

Tha Chang Gallery (Map pp284-5; Th Charoenrat) Next door to the Gallery restaurant, this tiny music venue has great live jazz and blues nights. It was closed for renovation at the time of writing.

North Gate Jazz Co-Op (Map pp284-5; Th Si Phum) This tight little jazz club packs in more musicians than patrons, especially for its Tuesday open-mic night.

Sudsanan (Map pp276-7; ☎ 08 5038 0764; Th Huay Kaew) Down a driveway diagonally opposite Kad Suan Kaew, this warmly lit wooden house is filled with a lot of local soul. Long-haired Thais and expats (who know how to use a squat toilet) come here to applaud the adept acoustic performances that jog from samba to *pleng pêu·a chee·wít* (songs for life). Be prepared for some bowed heads and sniffles during particularly tear-jerking songs.

Clubs

Warm-Up (Map pp276-7; ☎ 0 5340 0676; 40 Th Nimmanhaemin) The perennial favourite of the dance-floor divas, Warm-Up aims to please with a little bit for everybody, including an interior courtyard filled with seating for dancers who need a breather. Off to the sides are various enclosed boxes dedicated to different DJ genres, from lounge and break beats to rock. Young hipsters arrive in their coolest duds: tight jeans, spiked wolf hair-dos, sparkly shirt dresses and pointy heels. But ever youthful *fa·ràng* join the crowd as well. Warm-Up occasionally hosts nationally known Thai bands.

Monkey Club (Map pp276-7; ☎ 0 5322 6997; Soi 9, Th Nimmanhaemin) Merging dinner with dancing, Monkey Club attracts a tribe of affluent Thai students and a few expats who might migrate from the garden seats to the glassed-in, all-white bar and club. It is an alternative to Warm-Up for the social butterflies.

Discovery (Map pp276-7; ☎ 0 5340 4708; 12 Th Huay Kaew) You don't have to be hip to have fun at this disco. It is big, loud and totally cheesy – the perfect recipe for joining the massive blob of gyrating bodies. Discovery is across the street from Kad Suan Kaew.

Bubbles (Map pp284-5; Pornping Tower Hotel, Th Charoen Prathet). A tad sleazy but Bubbles still mysteriously wins the affections of the prowlers and the ravers alike. The dance floor heaves with a mix of mainly tourists and some pros.

Spicy (Map pp284-5; Th Chaiyaphum; ☽ 9pm-5am) Near Pratu Tha Phae, people pile into Spicy when everything else has closed for the night. Not the most salubrious place, it transforms from super-seedy to after-party cool around 2am. There's also a nearby cocktail van that distracts some late-night zombies.

Cinemas

Major Cineplex (Map pp276-7; ☎ 0 5328 3939; Central Airport Plaza, 2 Th Mahidol; tickets 80-160B) and **Vista Movie Theatre** (Map pp276-7; Kad Suan Kaew Shopping Centre, Th Huay Kaew; tickets 70-90B) show mediocre Hollywood flicks and the latest Thai teenage movies.

Chiang Mai University Art & Culture Center (Map pp276-7; Faculty of Media Art & Design; admission free; ☽ 6.30pm Sun) Feed your art-flick hunger at the university's weekly showings of foreign films, often showcasing a certain theme; screenings are in the main auditorium. Admission is free.

Thai Boxing

Thapae Boxing Stadium (Map pp284-5; ☎ 08 6187 7655; Th Moon Muang; admission 400B; ☽ 9pm Thu) Right in the heart of the backpacker scene, this stadium caters to foreign audiences complete with a cabaret.

Kawila Boxing Stadium (Map pp276-7; off Th Charoen Muang; admission 600B; ☽ 8pm Wed & Fri) Near Talat San Pakoy, this is the locals' stadium for *moo·ay tai* (also spelt as *muay thai*).

SHOPPING

Chiang Mai is Thailand's handicraft centre, ringed by small cottage factories and workshops. It is also a trading crossroads, much like Bali or Kathmandu, where antiques and textiles migrate from small villages in Laos, southern China, Myanmar and Vietnam. Some 20 years ago, old hill-tribe art and textiles were sold directly by villagers at ordinary markets in and around Chiang Mai, but today much of the old treasures have passed into the hands of dealers. The antiques world has also experienced a demographic shift. Most of the Thai antiques now reside in private collections, while old furnishings from Burma have replaced the retail stockpiles.

There are several shopping corridors throughout the city: the Chiang Mai Night Bazaar (p321), east of the old city; Saturday Walking Street on Th Wualai (p291); and Sunday Walking Street on Th Ratchadamnoen (p287). East of the old city on Th Tha Phae is the place to go for hill-tribe crafts. Th Chang Moi Kao is the city's bookshop row (see Information, p280). Th Nimmanhaemin, west of the old city near Chiang Mai University, has a handful of contemporary boutiques haunted by trend-conscious Thais.

Handicraft villages lie just outside of the city to the south and to the east. Hang Dong (p333) is widely regarded as the area's furniture capital. San Kampaeng and Bo Sang (p332) are the places to go for everything else.

Old City

Mengrai Kilns (Map pp284-5; ☎ 0 5327 2063; www.mengraikilns.com; 79/2 Th Arak) In the southwestern corner of the inner moat, Mengrai Kilns are particularly focused on keeping the old Thai celadon-pottery traditions alive.

HQ Paper Maker (Map pp284-5; ☎ 0 5381 4717; www.hqartgallery.com; 3/31 Th Samlan) Mainly an art paper retailer, this small shop sells handmade mulberry paper *(săh)*, another Chiang Mai handcrafted speciality. There's a variety of colours and designs, including sheets printed with the northern Thai alphabet. Also on display are paintings and woodcuts by Chiang Mai artists using this rough-textured paper.

Herb Basics (Map pp284-5; ☎ 0 5341 8289; Th Ratchadamnoen; 9am-6pm Mon-Sat, 2-9pm Sun) All of these good-smelling products – such as herbal lip balm, soap and shampoo – were made in Chiang Mai.

East of the Old City

Most stores along Th Tha Phae open at 9am.

Elements (Red Ruby; Map pp284-5; ☎ 0 5325 1750; 400-402 Th Tha Phae) Located next to Roong Ruang Hotel, Elements stocks embroidered bags, a diverse collection of fun jewellery and other trinkets.

Angel (Map pp284-5; ☎ 0 5323 2651; 370 Th Tha Phae; 10am-6pm) Original and modern silver designs decorate this shop further bolstering Thailand's reputation for fine silver jewellery.

Nova (Map pp284-5; ☎ 0 5327 3058; www.nova-collection.com; 201 Th Tha Phae; 9am-8.30pm Mon-Sat, 12.30-8.30pm Sun) For contemporary jewellery, this studio hand-makes high-quality rings, pendants and earrings using silver, gold and precious stones. Pieces can be custom made and are pretty enough to wed with.

Lost Heavens (Map pp284-5; ☎ 0 5325 1557; 228-234 Th Tha Phae; 10am-6pm) This store specialises in museum-quality tribal arts, including textiles, carpets and antiques, as well as ritual artefacts from the Yao (also known as Mien) tribe.

Kesorn (Map pp284-5; ☎ 0 5387 4325; 154-156 Th Tha Phae) A collector's best friend, this cluttered shop has been trading old stuff for years. They specialise mainly in hill-tribe textiles, beads and crafts, but lately the owner has become interested in the cloth version of the protective tattoos *(sàk yan)* that contain zodiac- and numerology-based spells.

Sun Gallery (Map pp284-5; ☎ 0 5387 4028; 86-88 Th Tha Phae) Na Chanok Siemmai (nicknamed 'Sun') runs this friendly art gallery, where you can poke around without being a heavyweight collector. He displays his own pieces as well as his friends' works, ranging from abstract to 3D collages. And if you're a miniature aficionado, there are also photo postcards.

Siam Celadon (Map pp284-5; 0 5324 3518; 158 Th Tha Pae) This established company sells its fine collection of cracked-glazed celadon ceramics in a lovely teak building. Enjoy the Victorian-era structure and its dainty fretwork longer with a proper English tea at the attached Tea House Siam Celadon (p312).

Gong's Shop (Map pp284-5; ☎ 0 5323 3235; Th Wichayanon) You can never have too many wrinkly cotton dresses in this tropical climate and with sizings to fit the Western gals, Gong's selection won't make you feel like a giant.

Under the Bo (Map pp284-5; ☎ 0 5381 8831; Chiang Mai Night Bazaar Bldg, Th Chang Khlan) This decor shop carries many unique pieces of tribal art, including furniture, bronze and wood figures, woodcarvings and weavings. There's another shop out on the road to Hang Dong in the Kad Farang shopping mall.

KukWan Gallery (Map pp284-5; ☎ 0 5320 6747; 37 Th Loi Kroh) Set slightly back from the road, this charming teak building houses natural cotton and silk by the metre. It's a great place to shop for gifts, with scarves, bedspreads and tablecloths available in subtle colours.

Pantip Plaza (Map pp284-5; Th Chang Khlan) Near the night bazaar, this shiny shopping centre is a more legitimate version than its grey-market counterpart in Bangkok. Mainly licensed suppliers of electronic hardware, such as computers and cameras, fill the space without a single bootleg software vendor in sight.

Riverside

La Luna Gallery (Map pp284-5; ☎ 0 5330 6678; www.lalunagallery.com; 190 Th Charoenrat) In the old shophouse row on the east bank of the river, this professional gallery picks a fine bouquet of emerging Southeast Asian artists. Many canvases have a social commentary angle and give the viewer a window into the different artistic styles in the region. A more portable piece is the art calendar featuring a different painting and artist biography for every month.

CREATING AN ARTISTIC SPACE

'Don't expect much from The Land. There isn't much to see,' Ajahn Kamin Lertchaiprasert warned me as we sped along the *klorng* road to the piece of land that has hosted a uniquely Thai artistic experiment since 1998. Indeed it is just a small rice paddy tended full-time by a local farmer and his two water buffaloes. There is no electricity or running water. There is no exhibition space or great artistic monument, only a few open-sided huts on stilts and a *săh·lah* with a wave-shaped floor. But output isn't the point of the project.

'The space is not a gallery or a classroom,' Ajahn Kamin wrote in 2005 after completing that year's One Year Project, the title of The Land's periodic collaborative residency program. Every two or three years, international participants come to live on The Land, where there are workshops on meditation and artistic discussions. Some visiting artists have initiated architectural projects on the property. Some permanent pieces are still usable, others are now just trash heaps. 'It is an experiment of life. The artists can do what they want at The Land,' said Ajahn Kamin. Afterwards, the artists who do create works inspired by The Land organise a travelling exhibition with shows in Chiang Mai and Bangkok galleries.

'My co-founder and I started this as an experiment in three things: natural farming, *vipassana* meditation and artistic collaboration,' he explained. 'No one owns The Land. I helped give life to it but now it has its own life.' As his own career has taken off, Ajahn Kamin has passed much of the management of The Land to a group of his former Chiang Mai University students. 'They work together to take care of it. There isn't one person who is the leader,' he explains yet another fundamental component to The Land, the Buddhist ideal of suppressing the ego.

In many ways, The Land is an artistic version of a Thai temple: it is open to the public and people come to work together – be it through meditation, exchanging ideas or donating creative energy and projects to the physical space. 'So the point of the project is the process not the product?' I asked him. 'You talk like an artist,' he replied in true Thai complimentary fashion.

Vila Cini (Map pp284-5; ☎ 0 5324 6246; www.vilacini.com; 30-34 Th Charoenrat) Villa Cini sells high-end, handmade silks and cotton textiles that are reminiscent of the Jim Thompson brand. Perhaps the real draw is the store's atmospheric setting: a beautiful teak house with marble floors and a narrow, rickety staircase that leads to a galleried courtyard.

Sop Moei Arts (☎ 0 5332 8143; www.sopmoeiarts.com; 150/10 Th Charoenrat) Lots of shops sell hill-tribe crafts, but this one has put a modern makeover on the traditional crafts of the Pwo Karen, a tribal group living in Mae Hong Son Province. The shop's directors began working with the village through a health program some 30 years ago, but have since harnessed the craft traditions of textile weaving and basketry as an economic-development project (over 60% of the net income returns to the village and any profits go into a scholarship fund).

Thai Tribal Crafts (Map pp284-5; ☎ 0 5324 1043; 208 Th Bamrungrat) Peruse the ornate needlework of the various hill tribes at this tribal-owned store near the McCormick Hospital. It operates by the principals of a fairtrade organisation.

South of the Old City

Just south of Pratu Chiang Mai, historic Th Wualai is known for its silver shops (Map pp284–5).

Central Airport Plaza (Map pp276-7; Th Mahidon) Anchored by a Robinson department store and, compared to Kad Suan Kaew (below), this mall is more upmarket with more international brands and a more affluent clientele. The Northern Village complex on the 2nd floor sells high-quality souvenirs with set prices. Silks and ready-made clothes are good buys.

West of the Old City

Close to Chiang Mai University, Th Nimmanhaemin is often referred to as the trendy part of town. It has several malls filled with closet-sized clothing and gift boutiques. Don't miss the home-grown art and decor shops lining Soi 1 off Th Nimmanhaemin and its art and design festival every December. The stores on this lane open around 10am or 11am.

Kad Suan Kaew Shopping Centre (Map pp276-7; Th Huay Kaew; 🕑 10am-9.30pm) Kad Suan Kaew offers retail therapy with air-con comfort. The anchor tenant is the Bangkok-based Central Department and there's a Tops Marketplace for buying foreign-friendly foods. Mobile phones and accessories are on the top floor while clothing boutiques occupy the ground floor. Students hang out here in the evenings and lots of small-time vendors set up outside the mall on Thursday and Friday.

Hill-Tribe Products Promotion Centre (Map pp276–7; ☎ 0 5327 7743; 21/17 Th Suthep) This royally sponsored project sells handmade hill-tribe crafts and touristy souvenirs. The embroidered dolls and small change purses make nice gifts for little girls. All the profits from sales go to hill-tribe welfare programs.

Sipsong Panna (Map pp276–7; ☎ 0 5321 6096; Nantawan Arcade, 6/19 Th Nimmanhaemin) Opposite the Amari Rincome Hotel, this upmarket shop is the place for jewellery collected in Thailand, Laos, Myanmar and southwestern China.

Srisanpanmai (Map pp276–7; ☎ 0 5389 4717; 6 Soi 1, Th Nimmanhaemin) If a trip to the Sbun-Nga Textile Museum (p291) has gotten you all wrapped up in silks, come to this knowledgeable textile shop where the display cases show a visual textbook of Lanna textiles. From the technicolour rainbow patterns of Burma to the wide-hem panel style of Chiang Mai, Srisanpanmai specialises in silks made in the old tradition.

Adorn with Studio Naenna (Map pp276–7; ☎ 0 5389 5136; 22 Soi 1, Th Nimmanhaemin) The pensive colours of the mountains have been woven into these naturally dyed silks and cottons, part of a village weaving project pioneered by Patricia Cheeseman, an expert and author on Thai-Lao textiles. This is the in-town shop, but you can see the production process at the studio (below).

Studio Naenna (Map pp276–7; ☎ 0 5322 6042; www .studio-naenna.com; 138/8 Soi Chang Khian, Th Huay Kaew) If you liked what you saw at Adorn with Studio Naenna, then head out of town to the main gallery of this textile cooperative.

Shinawatra (Map pp276–7; ☎ 0 5322 1638; www .shinawatrathaisilk.co.th; 16 Th Huay Kaew) This venerable family-owned silk shop was already a household name before the owners' nephew, Thaksin Shinawatra, became the controversial prime minister. The colours and styles are a little dowdy for foreign tastes, but reconsider their selection should you happen to be elected mayor of Chiang Mai.

Classic Model (Map pp276–7; ☎ 0 5321 6810; 95/22 Th Nimmanhaemin) Bold geometric patterns define this clothing brand from fashion designer Sumate Phunkaew, a native of Nan Province. Certainly, the boy-from-the-province success story is heartwarming, but the clothes have a high frump factor. If you flip through the racks with enough concentration though you might find some suitable 'teacher' wear.

Koland (Map pp276–7; ☎ 0 5321 4715; Soi 1, Th Nimmanhaemin) The hippest store on the block sells a mix of locally made ceramics and kitsch art from China.

Kachama (Map pp276–7; ☎ 0 5321 8495; www.ka chama.com; Soi 1, Th Nimmanhaemin) If you're planning on hanging textiles instead of wearing them, visit this upmarket textile studio featuring the artist's traditionally inspired weavings.

Gongdee Gallery (Map pp276–7; ☎ 0 5322 2230; 30 Soi 1, Th Nimmanhaemin) With one of the largest showrooms on the block, Gongdee is the soi's primary incubator for young artistic talent. There's a mix of home decor, furniture and paintings. Keep an eye out for the Byzantine icon–like Buddhas and altars painted by Chiang Mai artist Barinya.

COMMERCE AFTER DARK

Chiang Mai Night Bazaar (Map pp284–5; Th Chang Khlan; ☺ 7pm-midnight) is one of the city's main night-time attractions, especially for families, and is the modern legacy of the original Yunnanese trading caravans that stopped here along the ancient trade route between Simao (in China) and Mawlamyaing (on Myanmar's Gulf of Martaban coast). Today the night bazaar sells the usual tourist souvenirs, like what you'll find at Bangkok's street markets. In true market fashion, vendors form a gauntlet along the footpath of Th Chang Khlan from Th Tha Phae to Th Loi Kroh. In between are dedicated shopping buildings: the Chiang Mai Night Bazaar Building is filled mainly with antique and handicraft stores. Across the street is the Galare Night Bazaar selling upmarket clothes and home decor. Behind the collection of shops is the Galare Food Centre (p311). The Anusan Market is less claustrophobic and filled with tables of vendors selling knitted caps, carved soaps and other cottage-industry goods. Deeper into the market is the Anusan Food Centre (p312). The quality and bargains aren't especially impressive, but the allure is the variety and concentration of stuff and the dexterity and patience it takes to trawl through it all.

SHOPPING FOR A CAUSE

Chiang Mai is Thailand's conscience in part because the city is the de facto caretaker of struggling immigrants from Burma and hill-tribe villagers who lack the proper citizenship to get an education, good paying jobs and medical care. This close proximity to poverty prods the average resident out of complacency and into action, resulting in a myriad of non-governmental organisations that help develop legitimate sources of income.

Dor Dek Gallery (Map pp284-5; ☎ 08 9859 6683; Th Samlan) sells the craft projects of street children employed by the Volunteers for Children Development Foundation. This private organisation runs an orphanage and work-training program for displaced children. The profits from sales are divided among the child artist, the program's educational fund and future supply purchases.

Or what about something novel, like a gift that doesn't need to be carried home? At **Freedom Wheel Chairs Workshop** (Map pp284-5; ☎ 0 5321 3941; www.freedomwheelchairs.org; 133/1 Th Ratchaphakhinai) you can purchase a wheelchair (9500B) that will be donated to a disabled person who cannot afford such an expense. Run by a Thai survivor of polio and her husband, the workshop purchases and customises wheelchairs and mobility aids for needy recipients.

Would you rather treat yourself to something pretty with a social-justice hook? Adorn with Studio Naenna (p321) is the in-town showroom of a village weaving project that gives young women in the Chom Thong district of Chiang Mai a viable economic income without having to leave their families and migrate to the city for work. It also preserves traditional weaving techniques and aims for a softer environmental footprint through the use of natural fibres and dyes.

Other handicraft outlets for village-weaving projects include Kukwan Gallery (p319), Sop Moei Arts (p320), Thai Tribal Crafts (p320) and the Hill-Tribe Products Promotion Centre (p321).

Suriyam Chandra (Map pp276-7; ☎ 0 5322 7480; www.suriyanchandra.com; Soi 1, Th Nimmanhaemin) The artist of the same name has crafted cute terracotta figurines of full-figured Thai ladies, in the tradition of Colombian artist Fernando Botero.

Aka (Map pp276-7; ☎ 0 5389 4425; www.aka-aka.com; Soi 1, Th Nimmanhaemin) Thai furniture and decorative arts designer Eakrit Pradissuwana has created a contemporary look for modern Asia-philes. The furniture is slick and minimalist but distinctively 'Eastern' in character.

Chabaa (Map pp276-7; www.atchabaa.com; Nimman Promenade, 14/32 Th Nimmanhaemin) If Putumayo put out clothes instead of music, you'd have Chabaa, which specialises in global ethno-chic. You'll find brightly coloured embroidered tops and skirts plus big-statement jewellery.

Ginger (Map pp276-7; ☎ 0 5321 5635; 6/21 Th Nimmanhaemin) For something more night-on-the-townish, check out the shimmery dresses, sparkly mules, fabulous jewellery and colourful accessories. Not cheap though; the 3rd-floor is the sale room.

GETTING THERE & AWAY
Air
Regularly scheduled flights arrive into and depart from **Chiang Mai International Airport** (Map pp276-7; ☎ 0 5327 0222), which is 3km south of the centre of the old city. Unless otherwise noted the following airlines use the Suvarnabhumi Airport for travel from and to Bangkok.

Air Asia (☎ 0 2515 9999; www.airasia.com) Flies to Bangkok (1660B, six daily) and Kuala Lumpur (from 4000B, one daily).

Bangkok Airways (☎ 0 2265 5556; www.bangkokair.com) Flies to Bangkok (3400B; two daily) and continues to Samui (7300B).

China Airlines (☎ 0 5320 1268; www.china-airlines.com) Flies to Taipei (12,000B, two per week).

Lao Airlines (☎ 0 5322 3401; www.laoairlines.com) Flies to Vientiane (8400B, two daily) and Luang Prabang (5600B, one daily).

Nok Air (☎ 1318; www.nokair.com) Flies to Bangkok Don Muang (2440B, four to five daily); note that Nok Air is a subsidiary of THAI; it also operates a code-share flight from Chiang Mai to Pai (660B, one daily) and Mae Hong Son (1090B, one daily) with SGA.

One-Two-Go (☎ 1141, ext 1126; www.fly12go.com) Flies to Bangkok's Don Muang (1950B, three daily).

Siam GA (SGA; ☎ 0 5328 0444; www.sga.co.th) Flies to Pai (660B, one daily) and Mae Hong Son (1090B, one daily); these are code-share flights with Nok Air.

Silk Air (☎ 0 5390 4985; www.silkair.com) Flies to Singapore (16,000B, one daily).

Thai Airways International (THAI; ☎ 0 5321 1044/7; www.thaiair.com) Flies to Bangkok (1700B); there are two daily flights to Don Muang Airport and eight to Suvarnabhumi Airport. Also flies to Mae Hong Son (1300B, three daily).

Bus

Chiang Mai's long-distance terminal is known as **Arcade Bus Terminal** (Map pp276-7; ☎ 0 5324 2664; Th Kaew Nawarat) and is about 3km from the old city. From the town centre, a túk-túk or chartered *sŏrng·tăa·ou* should cost 40B to 60B.

From Chiang Mai's Arcade bus terminal, Bangkok-bound buses leave about every hour between 7am to 10.30am and again between 7pm to 9pm. Green Bus Thailand is the biggest company at the Arcade terminal; it serves Chiang Rai with hourly departures from 7am to 4pm. Mae Sai, Mae Sot and Chiang Saen buses leave twice a day. Other routes include Phayao to Chiang Khong with frequent departures between 6.30am to 5.30pm; Lampang, Phrae and Nan with hourly departures between 6.30am to 6.30pm.

The ticket counters that serve Pai, Mae Hong Son and Mae Sariang are beyond the main terminal. For Udon Thani there are five departures from noon to 8pm.

Do note that from Bangkok, the most reliable companies use Bangkok's Northern and Northeastern bus terminal (Mo Chit). It is not advisable to go north with a bus company that leaves from Bangkok's tourist centres, like Th Khao San. These invariably over-promise and under-deliver. The most egregious example occurred in November 2008 when the driver and staff of a Bangkok–Chiang Mai bus contracted by a Khao San Rd travel agent stole up to 150,000B worth of valuables from the passengers and then abandoned the bus and the riders outside of Ayuthaya.

For buses to destinations within Chiang Mai Province, use the **Chang Pheuak Bus Terminal** (Map pp284-5; ☎ 0 5321 1586; Th Chang Pheuak), which is north of the old city. You should be able to get a *sŏrng·tăa·ou* to Chang Pheuak terminal for 20B. Destinations served by the Chang Pheuak terminal include Chiang Dao (50B, 1½ hours, every 30 minutes), Chom Thong (41B, two hours, every 20 minutes), Fang (105B, three hours, every 30 minutes), Hang Dong (15B, 30 minutes, every 20 minutes) and Tha Ton (115B, every two hours, four hours).

There is also a *sŏrng·tăa·ou* stop on Th Praisani between Talat Warorot and Mae Ping serving nearby towns, like Lamphun, Bo Sang, San Kamphaeng and Mae Rim. *Sŏrng·tăa·ou* and buses also park on the east side of the river near Saphan Lek and make the trip to Lamphun, Lampang and Chiang Rai (via an older and slower road).

Train

Chiang Mai's **train station** (Map pp276-7; ☎ 0 5324 5364, 0 5324 7462; Th Charoen Muang) is about 2.5km east of the old city. The train station has an ATM, a left-luggage room (10B per piece) and an advance-booking counter at the regular ticket window (open 24 hours). For information on schedules and fares contact the station or the **State Railway of Thailand** (☎ free hotline 1690; www.railway.co.th; ☺ 24 hr).

All Chiang Mai–bound trains originate from Bangkok's Hualamphong station. At the time of writing there were six daily departures from Bangkok to Chiang Mai (and the same number in the opposite direction) and the journey took between 12 and 15 hours. Note in the fares below that we've indicated seats in air-con cars; if there is no designation this means that the seats are in fan-cooled cars.

Rapid trains leave Bangkok at 2.30pm arriving at 5.10am the next day. Fares are 391/231B for 2nd-/3rd-class seats and 541/491B for lower/upper sleeping berths in the 2nd-class cars.

Express trains leave Bangkok at 10pm and arrive in Chiang Mai at 12.45pm the following afternoon. Fares are 431/271B for 2nd-/3rd-class seats, 541B for 2nd-class air-con seats, 581/531B for lower/upper sleeping berths in 2nd-class cars, and 821/751B for lower/upper sleeping berths for a 2nd-class air-con cars.

Sprinter (special express diesel) trains leave Bangkok at 8.30am and 7.20pm arriving in Chiang Mai at 8.30pm and 7.40am, respectively. Fares are 611B for 2nd-class air-con seat.

Special Express trains leave at 6pm and 7.20pm, arriving the next day at 7.15am and 9.45am. Fares are 1253B for a 1st-class air-con sleeper and 881/791B for lower/upper 2nd-class air-con sleeper.

Trains from Chiang Mai to Bangkok include the following services: express (departing 2.50pm, arriving 5.10am), special express (departing 4.30pm and 5.50pm, arriving 5.30am and 7am, respectively), sprinter (departing 9pm and 8.45am, arriving 9.10am and 8.25pm) and rapid (departing 6.45am, arriving 9.10pm).

Sleeping berths are increasingly hard to reserve without booking well in advance; tour groups sometimes book entire cars and available spots get even more scarce during holidays like Songkran (mid-April), Chulalongkorn Day (October) and Chinese New Year (late February to early March). See the Transport chapter (p768) for information about advance bookings.

GETTING AROUND
To/From Airport
There is only one licensed airport taxi service charging a flat 150B fare. Public bus number 6 (15B) goes from the airport to points west en route to Chiang Mai University; it isn't a convenient option if you're staying in the old city. Many guesthouses and hotels also provide airport transfers.

From any point within the city, you can charter a túk-túk or red sǒrng·tǎa·ou to the airport for 60B or 70B.

Bicycle
Cycling is a good way to get around Chiang Mai. Rickety cruiser bikes with a fixed gear can be rented for around 50B a day from some guesthouses or from various places along the east moat. Brakes on the older models wouldn't stop you from a dead halt. **Chiang Mai Mountain Biking** (Map pp284-5; ☎ 0 5381 4207; Th Samlan; ☺ 8am-5pm) rents well-maintained mountain bikes and city bikes for the day.

If you want to buy a bike or you need repairs, your best bet is Canadian-owned **Top Gear Bike Shop** (Map pp284-5; ☎ 0 5323 3450; 173 Th Chang Moi), near Soi 2.

Bus
After much protracted talk, and studies concerning a public mass transit to alleviate Chiang Mai's traffic congestion, a bus system finally emerged and then retracted shortly thereafter. The city service uses white air-con buses that run from 6am to 9pm daily and cost 15B. The transit authority claims that there are three surviving bus lines but the described routes did not match our experience. We did successfully take a No 6 bus from the Arcade bus terminal

to the Chang Pheuak bus terminal via the Superhighway (Rte 11), so the bus is a reliable option between the two terminals if nothing else.

Car & Truck
Private transport is available from rental agencies throughout the city, mainly along Th Moon Muang. Be sure that the vehicle you rent has insurance (liability) coverage, which usually includes a 5000B excess. This does not cover personal injury and medical payments of anyone injured in a traffic accident. Ask to take a look at the terms of the insurance policy so you're clear on what is and isn't included.

Two of the most well-regarded agencies are **North Wheels** (Map pp284-5; ☎ 0 5387 4478; www.northwheels.com; 70/4-8 Th Chaiyaphum) and **Journey** (Map pp284-5; ☎ 0 5320 8787; www.journeycnx.com; 283 Th Tha Phae). Both offer hotel pick-up and delivery, 24-hour emergency road service, and comprehensive insurance. Journey even has baby seats available.

The following are standard rental rates per day: Toyota Vios (1200B) and Toyota Sportrider (1800B). Weekly and monthly rates are available and petrol is not included in the price. Most agencies around town have similar rates; what varies is the quality of the vehicle.

The good-value and highly recommended **Alternative Travel** (☎ 08 1784 4856, 08 9632 6556; noree9000@hotmail.com) offers customised tours, with English-speaking drivers, in Toyota sedans, 4WD trucks or vans (1500B to 2000B a day, plus petrol). Contact Winai to discuss car or itinerary options.

Other car-rental agencies in town:
Budget Car Rental (Map pp276-7; ☎ 0 5320 2871; 201/2 Th Mahidol) Across from Central Airport Plaza.
National Car Rental (Map pp276-7; ☎ 0 5321 0118; Amari Rincome Hotel, 1 Th Nimmanhaemin)

Motorcycle
One of the most popular options for getting about on your own is to rent a motorcycle. Agencies along Th Moon Muang and even some guesthouses rent Honda Dream 100cc step-through manual/automatic bikes for about 150/200B a day. The Honda or Yamaha 125cc to 150cc rent for 250B a day. A few places rent 400cc motorcycles (600B to 900B).

BUS DESTINATIONS FROM CHIANG MAI'S ARCADE TERMINAL

Destination	Class	Fare (B)	Duration (hr)
Bangkok	1st class	596	9½
	VIP	695	
Chiang Khong	2nd class	239	6½
	1st class	308	
Chiang Rai	fan	110	3-4
	2nd class	150	
	1st class	190	
	VIP	295	
Chiang Saen	fan	126	3½-4
	1st class	220	
Khon Kaen	1st class	578	12
Khorat	1st class	643	12
	VIP	750	
Lampang	fan	37	2
	2nd class	71	
	1st class	105	
Lamphun	fan	20	1
Mae Hong Son	fan	150	7-8
	2nd class	210	
Mae Sai	2nd class	188	5
	1st class	241	
	VIP	375	

Destination	Class	Fare (B)	Duration (hr)
Mae Sariang	fan	106	4-5
	2nd class	191	
Mae Sot	2nd class	280	6-6½
	1st class	347	
Nan	2nd class	235	6
	1st class	302	
	VIP	578	
Pai	fan	84	4
	2nd class	118	
Phayao	fan	97	2½-3
	2nd class	107	
	1st class	164	
Phrae	2nd class	155	3½-4
	1st class	200	
	VIP	310	
Phitsanulok	2nd class	155	5-6
	1st class	306	
	VIP	350	
Sukhothai	2nd class	249	5-6
	1st class	320	
Udon Thani	1st class	601	12
	VIP	801	

Most agencies offer motorcycle insurance for around 50B a day; ask what this insurance coverage actually includes. Some policies will cover free repairs if the bike breaks down, but will charge a 1500B excess in case of accident and a 10,000B excess if the motorbike is stolen.

If you're renting a motorcycle for touring the countryside around Chiang Mai, check out the tips and routes at **Golden Triangle Rider** (www.gt-rider.com).

Among the more established and more reliable outlets:

Dang Bike Hire (Map pp284-5; ☎ 0 5327 1524; 23 Th Kotchasan)

Mr Mechanic (Map pp284-5; ☎ 0 5321 4708; 4 Soi 5, Th Moon Muang) There are also two other branches in the old city.

Pop Rent-A-Car (Map pp284-5; ☎ 0 5327 6014; Th Kotchasan, near Soi 2)

Tony's Big Bikes (Map pp284-5; ☎ 0 5320 7124; 17 Th Rachamankha) Rents well-maintained 125cc to 400cc motorbikes that all have license plates. Also offers riding lessons, can give touring advice and repairs motorcycles.

Metered Taxi

Fares start at 40B for the first 2km, plus 5B for each additional kilometre. However, it is very rare to see a metered taxi to flag down in Chiang Mai. Call **Taxi Meter** (☎ 0 5327 1242/9291) for a pick-up.

Sŏrng·tăa·ou, Túk-Túk & Săhm·lór

Chiang Mai residents who don't have their own wheels rely on the red sŏrng·tăa·ou (also called 'rót daang') or túk-túk.

The sŏrng·tăa·ou are shared taxis: you can flag them down, tell them your destination and if they are going that way they'll nod. If they shake their heads, it is because they aren't going in that direction. Along the way they might pick up other passengers if the stops are en route. Short trips should cost 20B per person and longer trips should cost 40B per person. A ride from Pratu Tha Phae to the night bazaar should be 20B, while a ride from Wat Phra Singh to the night bazaar should be 40B. By and large you hopefully shouldn't have a problem with sŏrng·tăa·ou drivers being too greedy about fares. Most quote honest prices and it seems to be something of a tradition for the drivers to scoot around town in the evenings and on weekends with their wives in the front seat for company.

Túk-túks work only on a charter basis and are about 20B per trip more expensive than *sŏrng·tăa·ou*. We felt lucky when we could get a fare for 40B to 60B. In entertainment areas at night most túk-túk drivers will ask for an optimistic 100B.

Chiang Mai still has a few sǎhm·lór (pedicabs), typically parked at Talat Warorot. Sǎhm·lór cost around 20B to 30B for most trips.

NORTHERN CHIANG MAI PROVINCE

North of Chiang Mai the province becomes mountainous and rugged as it bumps against Myanmar's frontier. Among the highlights are the beautiful Mae Sa Valley and the forested peaks around Chiang Dao.

MAE SA VALLEY & SAMOENG
น้ำตกแม่สา/สะเมิง

One of the easiest mountain escapes, the Mae Sa–Samoeng loop travels from the lowland's concrete expanse into the highlands' forested frontier. The 100km route makes a good day trip with private transport or a country getaway with an overnight in Samoeng. **Golden Triangle Rider** (www.gt-rider.com) publishes a detailed map of the area.

Head north of Chiang Mai on Rte 107 (Th Chang Pheuak) toward Mae Rim, then left onto Rte 1096. The road becomes more rural but there's a steady supply of tour-bus attractions: orchid farms, butterfly parks, snake farms, you name it.

Only 6km from the Mae Rim turn-off, **Nam Tok Mae Sa** (entrance adult/child 100/50B) is part of the Doi Suthep-Pui National Park. The cascade is a picturesque spot to picnic or tramp around in the woods for a bit and it is a favourite weekend getaway for locals.

The road starts to climb and twist after the waterfall entrance. Catch your breath at the **Maesa Elephant Camp** (☎ 0 5320 6247; www.maesaele phantcamp.com; Rte 1096; admission adult/child 120/80B), one of the route's better elephant attractions where the animals seem happy and treated

well. One hour shows (8am and 9.40am daily, plus 1.30pm during high season) feature the usual circus-like antics. If you arrive between shows, you can hang out on the pretty grounds, feeding the elephants sugar cane and bananas or go on an elephant trek into the jungle (for two people, 30 minutes/one hour 800/1200B).

Two kilometres past the elephant camp is the **Queen Sirikit Botanic Gardens** (☎ 0 5384 1000; www.qsbg.org; Rte 1096; admission adult/child 40/10B; ☀ 8.30am-5pm), featuring a shorn mountainside displaying 227 hectares of various exotic and local flora for conservation and research purposes. The highlight of the collection is the glasshouse complex sitting near the mountain peak. Take the provided bus (30B) or your own car (100B) to get around the whole facility. Motorbikes are not allowed in the gardens.

After the botanic gardens the road climbs up into the fertile **Mae Sa Valley**, once a high-altitude basin for growing opium poppies. Now the valley's hill-tribe farmers have re-seeded their terraced fields with sweet peppers, cabbage, flowers and fruits – which are then sold to the royal agriculture projects under the Doi Kham label. The royal project at the Hmong village of Nong Hoi sits some 1200m above sea level and is accessible by a turn-off road in the village of Pong Yeang.

Sitting at the western wedge of the valley is a sign of things to come: **Proud Phu Fah** (☎ 0 5387 9389; www.proudphufah.com; Km17, Rte 1096; r 4500-7000B; ☒ 🖳 ☒) is a small boutique hotel with creature-comfort villas designed to give the illusion of sleeping amid the great outdoors. The open-air restaurant serves healthy Thai food (dishes 90B to 150B) with a panoramic view of the valley.

After Proud Phu Fah, the road swings around the mountain ridge and starts to rise and dip until it reaches the conifer zone. Beyond, the landscape unfolds in a cascade of mountains. Eventually the road spirals down into **Samoeng**, a pretty Thai village. If you want to stay overnight, try the simple **Samoeng Resort** (☎ 0 5348 7074; www.samoengresort.com; Rte 6033; r 500-400B; ☒), about 2.5km outside the village with 15 solid bungalows in a garden setting.

Getting There & Away
Only part of the route is accessible via public transport. *Sŏrng·tăa·ou* go to Samoeng (70B, 2¾ hours, two morning departures) from the

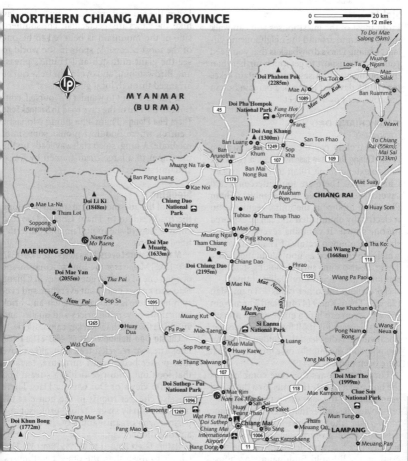

NORTHERN CHIANG MAI PROVINCE

Chang Pheuak bus terminal in Chiang Mai. In Samoeng, the vehicles stop near the market, across from Samoeng Hospital.

CHIANG DAO
เชียงดาว

Pai without the party, Chiang Dao is an easy escape for families and 30-something travellers looking for mountain scenery and northern rural ambience. The star attraction is Doi Chiang Dao, allegedly Thailand's highest limestone mountain. It is a thickly forested peak with a revered cave shrine burrowed into the base, and trails popular for birders and trekkers.

Chiang Dao town isn't much but a dusty crossroads that hosts a colourful **Tuesday morning market** (7am-12am), when hill tribes come to sell their wares. The more charming part of town is 5km west along the road that leads to Tham Chiang Dao (Chiang Dao Cave). The surrounding village and guesthouses are smack up against the mountain.

From the main four-way junction at Chiang Dao, those with their own wheels can head eastwards to visit Lahu, Lisu and Akha villages, which are all within 15km. Roughly 13.5km east from Rte 107 is the Lisu village of Lisu Huay Ko, where rustic accommodation is available. Without independent transportation, you can arrange hill-tribe treks through the guesthouses at Chiang Dao.

Sights

From most of the guesthouses you can walk to the cave and around the neighbouring village. Chiang Dao's drawback is that you need your own transport to get much further than that. Some guesthouses rent mountain bikes for 100B a day, not much of a bargain but an improvement over two feet.

THAM CHIANG DAO

ถ้ำเชียงดาว

In the heat of the day, the coolest place in town is the **Chiang Dao Cave** (admission 20B), a complex said to extend some 10km to 14km into Doi Chiang Dao. There are four interconnected caverns that are open to the public. Tham Phra Non (360m) is the initial segment and is electrically illuminated and can be explored on one's own. It contains several religious shrines, a common feature of Thailand's caves, which are regarded as holy meditation sites. There are also some surreal-looking stalactites reminiscent of a Salvador Dali painting.

To explore the other caves – Tham Mah (735m), Tham Kaew (474m) and Tham Nam (660m) – you can hire a guide with a pressurised gas lantern for 100B for up to five people. Local village ladies lead the guided tours and can point out the interior cave formations that have been named.

Local legend says this cave complex was the home of a *reu·sĕe* (hermit) for a thousand years and that the sage was on such intimate terms with the deities that he convinced some *tair·wá·dah* (the Buddhist equivalent of angels) to create seven magic wonders inside the caverns: a stream flowing from the pedestal of a solid-gold Buddha; a storehouse of divine textiles; a mystical lake; a city of *naga* (mythical serpents); a sacred immortal elephant; and the hermit's tomb. Such fantastical wonders are said to be much deeper inside the mountain, beyond the last of the illuminated caverns.

There is a temple complex outside the cavern, and a stream with huge carp and catfish you can feed. Vendors by the parking lot sell medicinal roots and herbs harvested in the nearby forests.

DOI CHIANG DAO

ดอยเชียงดาว

Part of the Doi Chiang Dao National Park, Doi Chiang Dao (also called Doi Luang) pokes into the heavens at 2195m above sea level. From the summit, reachable by a two-day hike, the views are spectacular. The southern side of the mountain is believed to be one of the most accessible spots in the world to see the giant nuthatch and Hume's pheasant. Birdwatching and overnight treks can be arranged through local guesthouses.

If you just want to wander by yourself, continue to the end of the cave road to **Samnak Song Tham Pha Plong** (Tham Pha Plong Monastic Centre), where Buddhist monks sometimes meditate. A long, steep stairway leads up the mountain to a large *chedi* framed by forest and limestone cliffs.

Sleeping

Many of the guesthouses are spread out along the road leading to Tham Chiang Dao and enjoy a view of the mountain and butterfly-filled gardens.

Malee's Nature Lovers Bungalows (☎ 0 1961 8387; r 300-1200B) Malee is something of a maven: she opened one of the first guesthouses in Chiang Dao and knows just about everyone and everything. There is a range of thatch-and-brick bungalows of varying prices and quality and an old-fashioned backpacker camaraderie.

Chiang Dao Rainbow (☎ 08 4803 8116; r 380-750B) The two recycled teak bungalows have four-poster beds, smart furniture, terraces that look out onto rice fields, a stream and dramatic views of Doi Chiang Dao. There are also cheaper rooms in the house at the back. It is run by an ex-Oxford professor and partner who organise tours of the area with an educational bent.

Nature Guest House (☎ 08 9955 9074; r 500-700B) Closer to town than the other guesthouses, this quiet place is set in a neat garden with mountain views. The A-frame wooden bungalows with terraces are simple yet stylish.

Chiang Dao Nest (☎ 08 6017 1985; www.chiangdao .com; r 695-995B; 🖳 🖭) The Nest is the epicentre of Chiang Dao's traveller scene. Its large garden setting contains basic A-frame bungalows and a convivial atmosphere thanks to the English-Thai owners. Book early as they are often full. Even if you don't stay here, pop over for a meal at the award-winning restaurant.

Chiang Dao Nest 2 (☎ 0 5345 6242; www.chiangdao .com; r 695-995B; 🖳) The overflow site for Chiang Dao Nest, this is a cluster of five bungalows about 600m past the cave turn-off on the left side of the road. The restaurant at Chiang Dao Nest 2 focuses on Thai cuisine.

Other recommended places:

Hobby Hut (☎ 08 0034 4153; r 250B) A new homestay project close to town; meals with the family are 55/85B for lunch/dinner.

Chiang Dao Hut (☎ 08 7208 1269; www.chiangdaohut .com; r 580B) Two wooden bungalows close to the road.

Eating

Chiang Dao has a lovely assortment of farm-fresh produce – mostly chemical free – thanks to the nearby royal agriculture projects.

Mon & Kurt Restaurant (dishes 40-280B) A fixture in Chiang Dao, this Thai-Western restaurant was on a one-year hiatus at the time of writing and will reportedly re-open in 2009.

Chiang Dao Rainbow (☎ 08 4803 8116; dishes 50-230B) This highly recommended restaurant offers two menus – northern Thai and Greek/Mediterranean. Its Shan pork stew and banana-flower salad are favourites. There are plenty of vegetarian options, too.

Baan Krating Chiang Dao (☎ 0 5345 5577; Km63, Rte 107; dishes 60-130B) Located 9km south of Chiang Dao on Rte 107, this resort is a good place to stop en route for a meal. The restaurant overlooks manicured gardens, pomelo trees and a stream. Dishes are standard Thai fare as well as Western sandwich options.

our pick **Chiang Dao Nest** (☎ 0 6017 1985; www .chiangdao.com; dishes 300-500B) A fusion restaurant that makes Bangkok look parochial, the Nest's restaurant serves sophisticated European food in a relaxed garden setting. Wicha, the owner and chef, received her culinary training in the UK and creates a menu that reflects the seasons and the best of the local produce. There's a kids' menu and Sunday afternoons look a lot like an after-church gathering. The evenings are more subdued.

There is a daily food market off the main street through Chiang Dao. The Tuesday morning market is the most colourful, with hill tribes bringing wares to sell.

Getting There & Around

Chiang Dao is 72km north of Chiang Mai along Rte 107. Buses to Chiang Dao (50B, 1½ hours, every 30 minutes) leave from Chiang Mai's Chang Pheuak terminal. The buses arrive and depart from Chiang Dao's new bus station but it is advisable to hop off in front of the pub to catch a *sŏrng·tăa·ou* to your guesthouse. Most drivers charge 150B to deliver passengers to guesthouses on the cave road. Buses also travel to Fang (60B).

DOI ANG KHANG

ดอยอ่างขาง

Way off in the northern corner of the province, this high-altitude peak is often dubbed Thailand's 'Little Switzerland', for its cool climate and mountain scenery. The namesake mountain sits 1300m above sea level and supports the cultivation of many species of temperate flowers, fruits and vegetables that are considered exotic in Thailand and were introduced as substitutions for opium. But it is the sensation of winter that draws many Thais here, especially in January when they might spot frost or even a dusting of snow and get the rare opportunity to bundle up in heavy jackets and hats. For winter veterans, Doi Ang Khang borders Myanmar and offers the illusion of peeping over the border into that country's vast frontier.

The Tourism Authority of Thailand in Chiang Mai has a basic map of Doi Ang Khang outlining cycling routes and treks to hill-tribe villages, many of whom participate in royal agriculture projects. Another source of information on Doi Ang Khang is the eco-friendly Angkhang Nature Resort (see below), which arranges cycling, mule riding and trekking to hill-tribe villages.

The main way to the summit is via Rte 1249, but a more scenic back road is Rte 1178, which winds along a ridge to the mountain's western slopes. The village of **Ban Luang** is an interesting stopover for Yunnanese atmosphere. Nineteen kilometres south of the park's turn-off on Rte 107, you can make a 12km detour west to visit **Ban Mai Nong Bua**, a Kuomintang (KMT) village with an old-fashioned Yunnanese feel.

Near the summit of Doi Ang Khang and the Yunnanese village of **Ban Khum**, there are several places to stay.

Part of the Amari Hotel Group, **Angkhang Nature Resort** (☎ 0 5345 0110; www.amari.com/ang khang; 1/1 Mu 5, Ban Khum, Tambon Mae Ngan, Fang; r from 4000B; 🖳 🛜) is an unexpectedly plush hotel featuring large bungalows spread out over a slope. The attractive lobby boasts stone fireplaces to complete the winter-lodge atmosphere. The on-site restaurant uses locally grown organic produce. Mr Macku, who runs the resort, is a great source of information on the area and arranges lots of outdoor activities.

Naha Guest House (☎ 0 5345 0008; Ban Khum; bungalows from 2500B) has large five- and eight-person bungalows with shared hot-water shower and toilet.

At the base of the slope are a couple of open-air restaurants serving a variety of dishes with an emphasis on Thai and Yunnanese Muslim cuisine.

Getting There & Away

Doi Ang Khang is about 20km before Fang on the turn-off for Rte 1249. The summit is about 25km from the highway. It is possible to get to Doi Ang Khang via public transport, but travelling to points along the mountain will be difficult. You can catch a bus heading to Fang (105B, three hours, every 30 minutes) from Chiang Mai's Chang Pheuak terminal. Tell the driver that you want to get off at the Rte 1249 turn-off, about 20km south of Fang. From there you can take a *sŏrng·tăa·ou* to Ban Khum (1500B chartered), which is near the summit and has accommodation options.

FANG & THA TON

ฝาง/ท่าตอน

For most people Fang is just a road marker on the way to Tha Ton, the launching point for river trips to Chiang Rai. If you do hang around town, there are some quiet backstreets lined with little shops in wooden buildings and the Shan/Burmese-style **Wat Jong Paen** (near the New Wiang Kaew Hotel), which has an impressive stacked-roof *wí·hǎhn*. The city of Fang was originally founded by Phaya Mengrai in the 13th century, although the locale dates back at least 1000 years as a stop for *jeen hor* caravans. Being so close to Myanmar, the surrounding district is an 'underground' conduit for *yah bâh* (methamphetamine).

Along the main street in Fang there are banks offering currency exchange and ATMs.

Tha Ton sits along a pretty bend of the Mae Nam Kok, which is lined by a few riverside restaurants and the boat launch for river trips to Chiang Rai.

In Tha Ton, there is a **tourist police office** (☎ 1155; ☿ 8.30am-4.30pm) near the bridge on the boat-dock side.

Sights & Activities

Doi Pha Hompok National Park (☎ 08 6430 9748; admission adult/child 200/100B) has a hot springs complex *bòr nám rórn* (*bor náam hórn* in northern Thai) that lies about 10km west of Fang at Ban Meuang Chom, near the agricultural station, off Rte 107 at the end of Rte 5054 (the park is sometimes referred to as Doi Fang or Mae Fang National Park). On weekends there are frequent *sŏrng·tăa·ou* carrying Thai picnickers from Fang to the hot springs. Also around midday, tour groups from Chiang Mai and Chiang Rai crowd the pools.

Within 20km of Fang and Tha Ton you can visit **local villages**, inhabited by Palaung (a Karennic tribe that arrived from Myanmar around 16 years ago), Black Lahu, Akha and Yunnanese, on foot, mountain bike or motorcycle. Treks and rafting trips can be arranged through any of Tha Ton's guesthouses or hotels.

In Tha Ton, **Wat Tha Ton** (☎ 0 5345 9309; www .wat-thaton.org) climbs up the side of a wooded hill. There are nine different levels punctuated by shrines, Buddha statues and a *chedi*. Each level affords stunning views of the mountainous valley towards Myanmar and the plains of Tha Ton. From the base to the ninth level, it is about 3km or a 30-minute walk. The short walk to the first level has a statue of Kuan Yin, the Chinese goddess of compassion; the international liaison monk has his office here too. The temple also offers seven-day, silent *vipassana* meditation retreats. Visit the website to check dates and to book. There's also a herbal medical centre with traditional massage, acupuncture and public saunas.

From Tha Ton you can make a half-day, long-tail **boat trip** (☎ 0 5345 9427; 350B; departs 12.30pm) to Chiang Rai. The regular passenger boat takes up to 12 travellers. The trip is a bit of a tourist trap these days as the passengers are all tourists, and the villages along the way sell cola and souvenirs. The best time to go is at the end of the rainy season in November when the river level is high. The travel time down river depends on river conditions and the skill of the pilot, taking anywhere from three to five hours. You could actually make the boat trip in a day from Chiang Mai, catching a bus back from Chiang Rai as soon as you arrive, but it's better to stay overnight in Tha Ton so that you aren't rushed.

Some travellers take the boat to Chiang Rai in two or three stages, stopping first in Mae Salak (90B), a large Lahu village, or Ban Ruammit (300B), a Karen village. Both are well touristed, but you can get off the path by joining a **hill-tribe trek** from here to other Shan, Thai and hill-tribe villages or longer treks south of Mae Salak to Wawi, a large multi-ethnic community of *jeen hor*, Lahu Lisu, Akha, Shan, Karen, Mien and Thai peo les. The Wawi area has dozens of hill-tribe villages of various ethnicities, including the largest Akha community in Thailand (Saen Charoen) and the oldest Lisu settlement (Doi Chang). Another alternative is to trek south from Mae Salak all the way to the town of Mae Suay, where you can catch a bus on to Chiang Rai or back to Chiang Mai.

You can also make the trip (much more slowly) upriver from Chiang Rai – this is possible despite the rapids. The boats are also available for charter hire (2500B, six people).

Sleeping

Most visitors who do stay overnight prefer to stay in Tha Ton.

Thaton Garden Riverside (☎ 0 5345 9286; r 300-00B) Next to Thaton Chalet by the bridge, this spick-and-span place has Tha Ton's best choice of air-con and fan rooms. It's worth paying the extra baht for the air-con room as you get a river terrace. There is also a restaurant overlooking the river.

Apple Guest House (☎ 0 5337 3144; r 350-600B) Conveniently located opposite the boat landing, the rooms in this two-storey building are spacious and well equipped. There's a restaurant on the ground floor.

Garden Home (☎ 0 5337 3015; r 380-1500B) A tranquil place along the river, about 150m from the bridge, with thatch-roofed bungalows spaced among lychee trees and bougainvillea. There are also a few stone bungalows, and three larger, more luxurious bungalows on the river with small verandas, TV and fridge. From the bridge, turn left at the Thaton River View Hotel sign.

Baan Suan Riverside Resort (☎ 0 5337 3214; fax 0 5337 3215; r 700-1500B; 🏊) Although the grounds are beautifully landscaped, this hotel is slightly overpriced. There are small cement air-con bungalows with terraces set back from the river and a couple of large air-con wooden bungalows with terraces right on the river.

ourpick Thaton River View Hotel (☎ 0 5337 3173; fax 0 5345 9288; r 1400B; 🏊) Further upstream, this quiet resort has 33 rooms facing Mae Nam Kok, joined by wooden walkways lined with frangipani trees. The rooms are stylishly decorated and enjoy a forested view. The restaurant at the hotel is considered one of the best in the area.

Thaton Chalet (☎ 0 5337 3155/7; www.thatonchalet.com; 1400-2200B; 🏊) A bit more institutional, this four-storey hotel next to the bridge has slightly dated rooms. The hotel features a pleasant beer garden right on the river, as well as an indoor restaurant.

Maekok River Village Resort (☎ 0 5345 9355; www.maekok-river-village-resort.com; r 2600-4300B; 💻 🏊) On the boat-dock side, downstream along the river, this sprawling affair offers four-bed family rooms as well as two-bed poolside rooms. It is best known, however, as an outdoor education venue, hosting annual visits from international research teams. There is a variety of tour activities available including trekking, rafting, mountain biking and caving.

Eating
FANG

The food stalls on the main street market are good places to eat. There is also a few restaurants serving Yunnanese specialities such as *kôw soy*, *man·toh* (mantou in Mandarin; steamed buns) and *kôw mòk gài*, plus *gŏo·ay dĕe·o* (rice noodles) and other standards.

THA TON

Most of the top-end hotels have riverside restaurants. There is a row of basic **Thai/Chinese restaurants** (dishes 25-35B) by the boat dock, and the **Coffee Cup** (dishes 60-90B; ⏰ 7.30am-4.30pm) – a funky looking place that sells good breakfasts and sandwiches, as well as iced and hot coffee and tea.

Getting There & Away
BUS & SŎRNG·TĂA·OU

Buses to Fang (105B, three hours, every 30 minutes) leave from the Chang Pheuak bus terminal in Chiang Mai. Air-con minivans make the trip to Fang (150B, three hours, every 30 minutes), leaving from behind the Chang Pheuak bus terminal on the corner of Soi Sanan Kila.

From Fang it's about 23km to Tha Ton (25B). Yellow *sŏrng·tăa·ou* leave from the market for the 40-minute trip from 5.30am to 5pm.

The river isn't the only way to get to points north of Tha Ton. The road trip along the mountain ridge to the village of Mae Salong in Chiang Rai Province is one of our favourite routes in Thailand. Yellow *sŏrng·tăa·ou* leave from the northern side of the river in Tha Ton to Mae Salong (70B, 1½ hours, every two hours between 8am and 12.30pm).

CHIANG MAI PROVINCE

To get to Mai Sai (70B to 90B) or Chiang Rai (95B to 105B) directly, take the afternoon bus from the bridge.

If you're heading west to Mae Hong Son Province, it's not necessary to dip all the way south to Chiang Mai before continuing on. At Mae Malai, the junction of Rte 107 (the Chiang Mai–Fang highway) and Rte 1095, you can pick up a bus to Pai for 65B; if you're coming from Pai, be sure to get off at this junction to catch a bus north to Fang.

MOTORCYCLE
Motorcycle trekkers can travel between Tha Ton and Doi Mae Salong, 48km northeast, over a fully paved but sometimes treacherous mountain road. There are a couple of Lisu and Akha villages on the way. The 27km or so between the village of Muang Ngam and Doi Mae Salong are very steep and winding – take care, especially in the rainy season. When conditions are good, the trip can be done in 1½ hours.

SOUTHERN CHIANG MAI PROVINCE

To the immediate south of Chiang Mai is the Ping Valley, a fertile agricultural plain that has also grown some noteworthy handicraft villages. Further to the southwest is Thailand's highest peak, Doi Inthanon.

BO SANG & SAN KAMPHAENG
บ่อสร้าง/สันกำแพง
Southeast of Chiang Mai is Bo Sang, known throughout the country as the 'umbrella village'. It is mainly a tourist market filled with craft shops selling painted umbrellas (often produced elsewhere), fans, silverware, statuary, celadon pottery and lacquerware. You'll find many of the same items at the Chiang Mai Night Bazaar but there's a greater concentration and variety here.

In late January the Bo Sang Umbrella Festival (*têt-sà-gahn rôm*) features a colourful umbrella procession during the day and a night-time lantern procession. Although it sounds touristy, this festival is actually a very Thai affair; a highlight are the many northern-Thai music ensembles that perform in shopfronts along Bo Sang's main street.

Further down Rte 1006 is San Kamphaeng, known for its cotton and silk weaving shops. The main street is lined with textile showrooms while the actual weaving is done in small factories down side streets. You can take a peek if you like.

Getting There & Away
White *sŏrng·tăa·ou* to Bo Sang (20B) and San Kamphaeng (20B) leave Chiang Mai frequently during the day from the *sŏrng·tăa·ou* stop on Th Praisani near Talat Warorot. Bo Sang is 10km from Chiang Mai and San Kamphaeng is 14km.

MAE KAMPONG
แม่กำปอง
If you plough across the Ping Valley on Rte 1317 past the rice fields and cow pastures to Mae On district, the road begins to narrow and climb into the forested hills of Mae Kampong, an area that has recently started to entice visitors for a day or overnight excursion because of its interesting combination of nature and cultural activities. Most visitors are first introduced to the area on daytrips with **Flight of the Gibbons** (p297), a zipline canopy tour.

Sitting at an altitude of about 1300m, **Ban Mae Kampong** is a Thai village that produces *mêeang* (pickled tea leaves), the northern Thai equivalent of betel nut. Most villagers make their living in this small-scale industry and head out into the forest to collect the tea leaves. In the early mornings the pickers stop by the local temple where the monk has prepared a restorative brew of medicinal herbs. The village itself is a gravity-defying collection of maze-like huts hugging the steep hillside. Flowers bow in the cool breezes and the jungle insects screech at each other. Several families participate in a **homestay program** (☎ 0 5322 9526; per person 980B) that includes three meals and basic lodging.

The narrow road through the village summits the hill and winds down into **Chae Son National Park** (see p349), where you'll find waterfalls and hot springs.

If the natural solitude is appealing, stay awhile at one of the nature lodges south of the village. **Tharnthong Lodge** (☎ 0 5393 9472; www .tharnthonglodges.com; r 1200–4000B) is bisected by a pebble-strewn stream crossed by a wooden bridge to the six houses dotting the property. If you don't need a bed, stop by the restau-

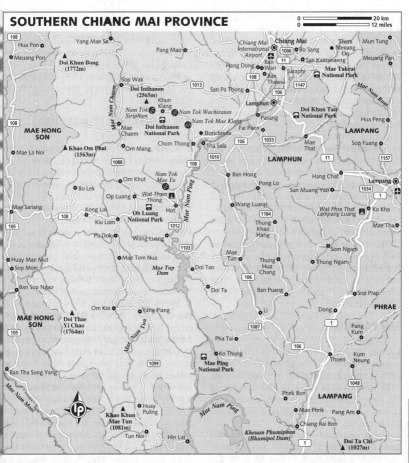

rant to enjoy the affordable Thai food (dishes 70B to 180B). Closer to the village is **John's House Bed & Breakfast** (☎ 0 9813 2559; www.john-housethailand.com; r 1500B), built on stilts across a deep ravine.

Mae Kampong is 48km east of Chiang Mai and can be reached by following Rte 1317 toward San Kamphaeng. At the T-junction at Ban Huay Kaew, turn right towards the signs for Ban Mae Kampong.

HANG DONG, BAN WAN & BAN THAWAI
หางดง/บ้านวัน/บ้านถวาย

Just 15km south of Chiang Mai is a veritable 'furniture highway' where stores and workshops specialise in decorative arts, woodcarving, antiques and contemporary furniture.

The shops along Rte 108 in Hang Dong are impossible to explore on foot and still a bit of a pain in a car. The high-end **Gàht Farang** (Rte 108) walking mall has attempted to remedy the problem of access, but it may never be filled to capacity. North of Hang Dong centre, near Amarin Place, **Siam Lanna Art** (☎ 0 5382 3419; Rte 108) is an eccentric stop for junk aficionados. We're told it is a great spot for browsing, but impossible to buy from as no one knows the prices.

A greater concentration of stores can be found in Ban Wan on Th Thakhilek, the first left turn after Talat Hang Dong. A cluster of stores near the intersection sells antique reproductions using new wood; in times past they used salvaged teak but most of that is now gone. Further down the road is **Chili Antiques & Arts** (☎ 0 5343 3281; 125 Th Thakhilek), a massive showroom of bronze and wooden Buddhas, sculptures, wood carvings and fine decor. Across the street is **Jirakarn Antique** (☎ 0 5344 1615; 137 Th Thakhilek), an old-fashioned junk shop selling salvaged teak. **Crossroads Asia** (☎ 0 5343 4650; Chaiyo Plaza, 214/7 Th Thakhilek) is the Pier One of Thailand, selling ethnic art and antiques from across Asia.

Continue toward the right fork in the road to **Ban Thawai Tourism Village**, which is a pedestrian-friendly market with 3km of shops selling all sorts of home decor. Past Zone 5 is Sriboonmuang's workshop, an example of what made Ban Thawai famous in the first place. In the factory's covered sheds, workers sand and polish small armies of wooden elephants, hobby horses and dolls.

Many of the shops here deal in wholesale as well as retail, and shipping can be arranged. It is advisable to come with private transport, but you can catch a *sŏrng·tăa·ou* from Pratu Chiang Mai to Hang Dong (10B) and to Ban Thawai (15B).

SAN PA THONG
สันป่าตอง

Further south on Rte 108, this overgrown village is home to a huge and lively water buffalo and cattle **market** (☼ 5.30am-11am Sat), held weekly next door to the Temple of the Sleeping Buddha. The mechanical machines, namely motorcycles, now outnumber the livestock.

On the outskirts of San Pa Thong, **Kao Mai Lanna Resort Hotel** (☎ 0 5383 4470; www.kaomailanna .com; Km29, Th Chiang Mai-Hot; r 2500-3500B; ☒ ☒) is almost reason enough to travel this far. The resort has turned many of the property's abandoned tobacco-curing sheds into characterful and comfortable lodgings amid a lush garden setting. This used to be one of many northern Thai tobacco farms supplying the international cigarette market before China supplanted the local growers. The resort also arranges tours to the nearby handicraft villages (which are truly villages instead of souvenir markets). Even if you don't stay here, the outdoor restaurant serves superb Thai food.

Back behind the resort is a scenic village filled with *lam yai* orchards and old ladies cycling about. Deeper into the narrow lanes is **Pee Goon's Saa House** (☎ 08 4613 8450), a small cottage industry employing about 100 villagers in the process of making craft paper from mulberry bark. Pi Goon can show you the process; bring along someone who speaks Thai if you're curious.

You can catch a bus or *sŏrng·tăa·ou* to San Pa Thong from the bus queue near Pratu Chiang Mai.

DOI INTHANON NATIONAL PARK
อุทยานแห่งชาติดอยอินทนนท์

Thailand's highest peak is Doi Inthanon (often abbreviated as Doi In), which measures 2565m above sea level, an impressive altitude for the kingdom, but a tad diminutive compared to its cousins in the Himalayan range. The 1000 sq km **national park** (☎ 0 5328 6730; adult/child 200/100B, car/motorbike 30/20B; ☼ 8am-sunset) surrounding the peak has hiking trails, waterfalls and two monumental stupas erected in honour of the king and queen. It is a popular day trip from Chiang Mai for tourists and locals, especially during the New Year's holiday when there's the rarely seen phenomenon of frost.

There are eight waterfalls that dive off the mountain. **Nam Tok Mae Klang** (at Km8) is the largest and the easiest to get to. **Nam Tok Wachiratan** (at Km20.8) is another popular stop with food vendors at its base and a huge frothy mane that plummets 50m. If you'd rather be a part of the cascade, try abseiling with the Peak (p299). **Nam Tok Siriphum** (at Km30) looks like a river of silver from the vantage point of Ban Mong Khun Klang, a Hmong village. In February the village builds and races wooden carts down a steep incline. Along the road to the top are terraced rice fields and covered greenhouses tended by Hmong and Karen tribespeople.

About 3km before the summit of Doi Inthanon, **Phra Mahathat Naphamethanidon** and **Nophamethanidon** at Km41-42 (admission 20B) are two *chedi* built by the Royal Thai Air Force to commemorate the king's and queen's 60th birthdays in 1989 and 1992, respectively. In the base of the octagonal *chedi* is a hall containing a stone Buddha image.

The whole point of the park is to get as high as you can to see life in a colder climate. At the summit is a sightseeing extravaganza. Thais relish bundling up in hats and jackets and posing for pictures among conifers and rhododendrons. Almost at the exact summit is a *chedi* dedicated to one of the last Lanna kings (Inthawichayanon) and beyond is the

Ang Ka Trail, a 360m platform walkway through a moss-festooned bog.

The views from Doi Inthanon are best in the cool dry season from November to February. But don't expect a rewarding view from the summit, as for most of the year a mist, formed by the condensation of warm humid air below, hangs around the top of the mountain creating an eerie effect. You can expect the air to be quite chilly towards the top, so take a jacket or sweater.

The park is one of the top destinations in Southeast Asia for naturalists and birdwatchers. The mist-shrouded upper slopes produce abundant orchids, lichens, mosses and epiphytes, while supporting nearly 400 bird species, more than any other habitat in Thailand. The mountain is also home to Assamese macaques, Phayre's leaf monkeys, and a selection of other rare and not-so-rare monkeys and gibbons as well as the more common Indian civet, barking deer and giant flying squirrel – around 75 mammal species in all. Most of the park's bird species are found between 1500m and 2000m; the best birdwatching season is from February to April, and the best spots are the *beung* (bogs) near the top.

Park accommodation is available in comfortable bungalows (from 1000B) located next to the information centre and a restaurant at Km31. There is also camping (60B to 90B) in front of the information centre or at Nam Tok Mae Pan. Make reservations online at www.dnp.go.th.

Getting There & Away

Although most visitors come with private transport or on a tour from Chiang Mai, you can reach the park via public transport. Buses leave from Chang Pheuak terminal and yellow *sŏrng·tăa·ou* leave from Pratu Chiang Mai for Chom Thong (61B), 58km from Chiang Mai and the closest town to the park. Some buses go directly to the park's entrance gate near Nam Tok Mae Klang and some are bound for Hot and will drop you off in Chom Thong.

From Chom Thong there are regular *sŏrng·tăa·ou* to the park's entrance gate at Nam Tok Mae Klang (30B), about 8km north. *Sŏrng·tăa·ou* from Mae Klang to the summit of Doi Inthanon (80B) leave almost hourly until late afternoon.

Instead of backtracking to Chiang Mai, you can go to Hot, where you can get buses west to Mae Sariang or Mae Hong Son, a time-saving measure if you're leaving the park after an overnight stay.

CHIANG MAI PROVINCE

Northern Thailand

Northern Thailand's 'mountainous' reputation may cause residents of Montana or Nepal to chuckle, but it's the fertile river valleys between these glorified hills that served as the original homeland of the Thai people, and thus the birthplace of much of what is associated with Thai culture. The mountains may not be large, but their impact and significance are immense.

Despite the centuries that have passed since early Tai tribes from southern China are thought to have settled here, northern Thailand continues to cling to its roots, and for many Thais the area still maintains an aura of the 'real' Thailand. The dialect and food of the northern Thais are among the more conservative and unchanged, and traditions here continue to run deep.

In addition to the Thai majority, the north is the most ethnically diverse part of the country, with well-known hill tribes such as Hmong and Akha, to lesser known groups such as the unique Chinese community of Mae Salong and Mae Hong Son's small Muslim communities.

Put all this together and it's clear that these old hills are the perfect destination for seeking out a special cultural experience. Exploring a Buddhist temple in Phrae, volunteering at a refugee clinic in Tak, or sampling a dish at Lampang's evening market; northern Thailand's attractions are generally low-key but eminently rewarding. And for those seeking something more vigorous, the region's geography and climate ensure that there is also ample opportunity for more active pursuits such as rafting in Nan, visiting a Phitsanulok national park or a road trip to Phayao.

HIGHLIGHTS

- Exploring one of the region's numerous and diverse national parks, such as Phitsanulok's historical **Phu Hin Rong Kla National Park** (p395) or Mae Hong Song's rugged **Salawin National Park** (p454)
- Hiking and rafting in Um Phang, where the end of the road leads to **Nam Tok Thilawsu** (p418), Thailand's biggest, most beautiful waterfall
- Learning to be a mahout (elephant caretaker) at Lampang's **Elephant Conservation Center** (p348)
- Getting off the beaten path to the little-visited but atmospheric northern cities such as **Phayao** (p375)
- Cycling around the awesome ruins of Thailand's 'golden age' at **Sukhothai** (p398) and **Si Satchanalai-Chaliang Historical Parks** (p404)
- Renting a vehicle and driving the legendary **Mae Hong Son Loop** (p426) or the extraordinary drive from **Chiang Khong** to **Phayao** (p376)

★ Chiang Khong

★ Mae Hong Son Province

★ Phayao

★ Elephant Conservation Center

★ Salawin National Park

★ Phu Hin Rong Kla National Park

★ Si Satchanalai-Chaliang Historical Park

★ Sukhothai Historical Park

★ Nam Tok Thilawsu

- BEST TIME TO VISIT: NOVEMBER–MARCH
- POPULATION: 7.8 MILLION

History

Northern Thailand's history has been characterised by the shifting powers of various independent principalities. One of the most significant early cultural influences in the north was the Mon kingdom of Hariphunchai (modern Lamphun), which held sway from the late 8th century until the 13th century. Hariphunchai art and Buddha images are particularly distinctive, and many good examples can be found at the Hariphunchai National Museum in Lamphun.

The Thais, who are thought to have migrated down from China since around the 7th century, united various principalities in the 13th century – this resulted in the creation of Sukhothai and the taking of Hariphunchai from the Mon. In 1238 Sukhothai declared itself an independent kingdom under King Si Intharathit and quickly expanded its sphere of influence. Because of this, and the influence the kingdom had on modern Thai art and culture, Sukhothai is considered by Thais to be the first true Thai kingdom. In 1296 King Mengrai established Chiang Mai after conquering the influential Mon kingdom of Hariphunchai.

Later, Chiang Mai, in an alliance with Sukhothai in the 14th and 15th centuries, became a part of the larger kingdom of Lan Na Thai (Million Thai Rice Fields), popularly referred to as Lanna. This extended as far south as Kamphaeng Phet and as far north as Luang Prabang in Laos. The golden age of Lanna was in the 15th century. For a short time the Sukhothai capital was moved to Phitsanulok (1448–86), and Chiang Mai became an important religious and cultural centre. However, many Thai alliances declined in the 16th century. This weakness led to the Burmese capturing Chiang Mai in 1556 and their control of Lanna for the next two centuries. The Thais regrouped after the Burmese took Ayuthaya in 1767, and under King Kawila, Chiang Mai was recaptured in 1774 and the Burmese were pushed north.

In the late 19th century Rama V of Bangkok made efforts to integrate the northern region with the centre to ward off the colonial threat. The completion of the northern railway to Chiang Mai in 1921 strengthened those links until the northern provinces finally became part of the kingdom of Siam in this early period of the 20th century.

Climate

The mountains in northern Thailand influence the climate. It can get quite cold in the highland town of Mae Hong Son and rain pockets can get stuck in the ranges of Tak Province. The central-plains areas around Sukhothai are less variable.

National Parks

Travellers who make it to one of northern Thailand's national parks usually consider it a highlight of their trip. In a region where the elevation reaches as high as 2000m, the north is home to some of Thailand's rarest geography and wildlife. Chae Son (p349) is known for its waterfalls and hot springs. Doi Luang (p349) and Thung Salaeng Luang (p396) were designated for wildlife protection, while Phu Hin Rong Kla (p395) is of interest for its ties to Thailand's Communist Party. Other parks in the north include Salawin National Park (p454), with its rocky river, and Doi Phu Kha (see p388) with its 2000m peaks. All of the national parks in this section are worth the extra effort if you love nature and want some peace and quiet.

Language

Thailand's regional dialects vary greatly and can even be unintelligible to native speakers of Thai not familiar with the vernacular being spoken. *Găm méuang*, the northern Thai dialect, is no exception and, in addition to an entirely different set of tones to master, possesses a wealth of vocabulary specific to the north. The northern dialect also has a slower rhythm than Thailand's three other main dialects, an attribute reflected in the relaxed, easy-going manner of the people who speak it.

Northern Thai also has its own writing system, based on an old Mon script that was originally used only for Buddhist scripture. The script became so popular during the Lanna period that it was exported for use by the Thai Lü in China, the Khün in the eastern Shan State and other Thai-Kadai–speaking groups living between Lanna and China. Although few northerners nowadays can read the northern Thai script – often referred to as 'Lanna script' – it is occasionally used in signage to add a northern Thai cultural flavour.

The Language chapter covers only the central Thai dialect; for some useful northern Thai words and phrases, see boxed text, p339.

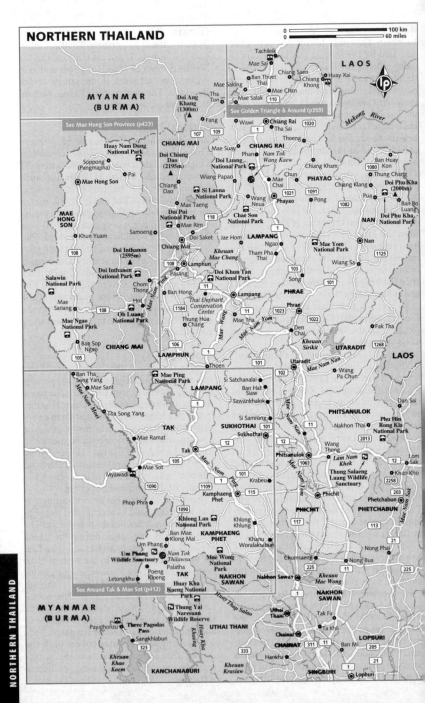

NORTHERN THAILAND

0 —————— 100 km
0 —————— 60 miles

LAOS

MYANMAR (BURMA)

See Mae Hong Son Province (p423)

See Golden Triangle & Around (p359)

Mekong River

See Around Tak & Mae Sot (p412)

MYANMAR (BURMA)

LAOS

NORTHERN THAILAND

Getting There & Away

Some travellers make stops in this region to break up the 700km-trip between Bangkok and Chiang Mai. Others only use Chiang Mai as a jumping off point for other destinations – both are good strategies. Going by train is probably the most comfortable way to get up north, although there's only one northern line and getting there is comparatively quite slow. For those in a hurry, there are now airports in almost every large city in northern Thailand. And of course, just about everywhere in the region is accessible by bus (or minivan), except the communities along the Myanmar (Burma) border where the *sŏrng·tăa·ou* (pick-up truck, also spelt *săwngthăew*) is typically the transport of choice.

Getting Around

Public transport to most places in northern Thailand is plentiful and reliable, if occasionally somewhat slow. Car rental is available at most urban centres. If you know how to ride a motorcycle, you can rent one. If you don't know how to ride one it's easy to learn and you'll be glad you did. For details on motorcycle touring in the north, see the boxed text on p340.

LAMPHUN PROVINCE

LAMPHUN

ลำพูน

pop 56,800

Essentially a culture stop for Chiang Mai sightseers, this provincial capital sits quietly along the banks of the Mae Kuang, a tributary of the Mae Ping, without much fanfare regarding its superlative as one of Thailand's oldest cities. The old fortress wall and ancient temples are surviving examples of Lamphun's former life as the northernmost outpost of the ancient Mon Dvaravati kingdom then known as Hariphunchai (AD 750–1281). For a period, the city was ruled by Chama Thewi, a Mon queen who has earned legendary status among Thailand's constellation of historic rulers.

The 26km ride between Chiang Mai and Lamphun is one of the city's primary attractions. It's along a beautiful country road, parts of which are canopied by tall dipterocarp trees.

Sights

WAT PHRA THAT HARIPHUNCHAI

วัดพระธาตุหริภุญชัย

This **temple** (Th Inthayongyot; admission 20B) enjoys an exalted status because it dates back to the Mon

---

EASY RIDER

One of the increasingly popular ways of exploring northern Thailand is from the saddle of a rented motorcycle. Despite the obvious risks of driving in Thailand, motorcycle touring is one of the best ways to explore the countryside at your own pace, and provides the opportunity to leave the beaten track at any moment.

Unless you're specifically intending to go off-road or plan on crossing unpaved roads during the wet season, it's highly unlikely you'll need one of the large dirt bikes you'll see for rent in Chiang Mai. The automatic transmission 110-150cc scooter-like motorcycles found across Thailand are fast and powerful enough for most roads. If you want something a bit larger and more comfortable on those long straightaways, an alternative is the 200cc Honda Phantom, a Thai-made chopper wannabe.

Rental prices in Chiang Mai start at about 150B per day for a 125cc Honda Wave/Dream, all the way to 1200B per day for a Honda CB1000. For general renting information and safety considerations, see p766.

A good introduction to motorcycle touring in northern Thailand is the 100km Samoeng loop, which can be tackled in half a day. The route extends north from Chiang Mai and follows Rtes 107, 1096 and 1269, passing through excellent scenery and ample curves, providing a taste of what a longer ride up north will be like. The 470km Chiang Rai loop, which passes through scenic Fang and Tha Ton along Rtes 107, 1089 and 118, is another popular ride that can be broken up with a stay in Chiang Rai. The classic northern route is the Mae Hong Son loop (p426), a 950km ride that begins in Chiang Mai and takes in Rte 1095's 1864 curves with possible stays in Pai, Mae Hong Son and Mae Sariang, before looping back to Chiang Mai via Rte 108. And a lesser known but equally fun ride is to follow Rtes 1155 and 1093 from Chiang Khong in Chiang Rai province to the little-visited city of Phayao (p376), a day trip that passes through some of the most dramatic mountain scenery in the country.

The best source of information on motorcycle travelling in the north, not to mention publishers of a series of terrific motorcycle touring–based maps, is **Golden Triangle Rider** (GT Rider; www .gt-rider.com). Their website includes heaps of information on renting bikes (including recommended hire shops in Chiang Mai and Chiang Rai) and bike insurance, plus a variety of suggested tours with maps and an interactive forum.

period, having been built on the site of Queen Chama Thewi's palace in 1044 (1108 or 1157 according to some datings). It lay derelict until Khru Ba Sriwichai, a famous northern Thai monk, made renovations in the 1930s. It boasts some interesting architecture, a couple of fine Buddha images and two old *chedi* (stupas) in the original Hariphunchai style. The tallest of the ancient *chedi*, Chedi Suwan is a narrow brick spire dating from 1418 that sits 21m high. The newer *chedi*, 46m-high Phra Maha That Chedi, is regarded as a textbook example of 15th-century Lanna architecture with its square pedestal rising to a rounded bell shape.

Behind the temple is **Kad Khau Moon Tha Singh**, a small souvenir market on a covered bridge selling local OTOP (One Tambon, One Product) items such as dried *lam yai* (longan) and silk.

HARIPHUNCHAI NATIONAL MUSEUM
พิพิธภัณฑสถานแห่งชาติลำพูน

Across the street from Wat Phra That Hariphunchai is the informative **Hariphunchai**

National Museum (☎ 0 5351 1186; Th Inthayongyot; admission 100B; ☺ 9am-4pm Wed-Sun). Run by the national Fine Arts Department, this museum has a collection of Mon and Lanna artefacts and Buddhas from the Dvaravati kingdom, as well as a stone inscription gallery with Mon and Thai Lanna scripts. The curator's passion for the museum and Lamphun's heritage is infectious. The temporary exhibitions are also interesting, focusing on more contemporary subjects like the settlement of the Yong in Lamphun. There is a small bookshop with some English titles.

WAT CHAMA THEWI
วัดจามเทวี

A more unusual Hariphunchai *chedi* can be seen at Wat Chama Thewi (popularly called Wat Kukut) and dates to around the 13th century. Known as Chedi Suwan Chang Kot, it has been restored many times since then, so it is now a mixture of several schools of architecture but is widely regarded as one of the most recent examples of Dvaravati architecture.

The stepped profile bears a remarkable resemblance to the 12th-century Satmahal Prasada at Polonnaruwa in Sri Lanka. Each side of the *chedi* has five rows of three Buddha figures, diminishing in size on each higher level. The standing Buddhas, although made recently, are in Dvaravati style.

The temple is bout 1.5km from Wat Phra That Hariphunchai; you can take a motorcycle taxi (30B) from in front of the museum.

Festivals

During the second week of August, Lamphun hosts the annual **Lam Yai Festival**, spotlighting its primary agricultural product. The festival features floats made of fruit and, of course, a Miss Lam Yai contest. **Songkran** (mid-April) is a milder, more traditional affair in Lamphun should Chiang Mai's water fight be too wet and wild.

Sleeping & Eating

You're unlikely to stay overnight as Lamphun is so close to Chiang Mai. But in a pinch, try **Si Lamphun Hotel** (☎ 0 5351 1176; Soi 5, Th Inthayongyot; s/d 200/300B), south of Wat Phra That, or **Supamit Court** (☎ 0 5353 4865; fax 0 5353 4355; Th Chama Thewi; s/d 250-600B; ✿), opposite Wat Chama Thewi.

There is a string of decent **noodle and rice shops** (Th Inthayongyot) south of Wat Phra That on the main street.

Getting There & Away

Blue *sŏrng·tăa·ou* and white buses to Lamphun (20B, every 30 minutes) leave Chiang Mai from a stop on Th Praisani in front of Talat Warorot and from another stop on the east side of the river on Th Chiang Mai-Lamphun, just south of the Tourist Authority of Thailand (TAT). Transport also leaves from Chiang Mai's Chang Pheuak terminal. Both can drop you off on Th Inthayongyot at the stop in front of the national museum and Wat Phra That Hariphunchai.

Transport returns to Chiang Mai from the stop in front of the national museum or from Lamphun bus terminal on Th Sanam.

AROUND LAMPHUN
Pasang
ป่าซาง

The province's cotton-weaving village, Pasang (not to be confused with Bo Sang) is southwest of Lamphun on Rte 106. It's not really a shopping destination, but there are busy looms in the residential workshops.

The village's **Wat Chang Khao Noi Neua**, off Rte 106 towards the southern end of town, features an impressive gilded Lanna-style *chedi*.

You'll find a few **cotton shops** near the main market in town, opposite Wat Pasang Ngam. A few vendors in the market also sell cotton textiles and souvenirs. The town celebrates its weaving tradition in December with an annual fair and exhibition.

A *sŏrng·tăa·ou* will take you from Lamphun to Pasang for 15B. If you're heading south to Tak Province using your own vehicle, traffic is generally lighter along Rte 106 to Thoen than on Hwy 11 to Lampang; and a winding 10km section of the road north of Thoen is particularly scenic. Both highways intersect Hwy 1 south, which leads directly to Tak's capital.

Wat Phra Phutthabaht Tak Phah
วัดพระพุทธบาทตากผ้า

Regionally famous, this hillside temple belongs to the popular Mahanikai sect and is a shrine to one of the north's most renowned monks, Luang Pu Phromma. It's about 9km south of Pasang or 20km south of Lamphun off Rte 106 in Tambon Ma-Kok (follow Rte 1133 1km east). It contains a lifelike resin figure of the deceased monk sitting in meditation.

Behind the spacious grounds are a park and a steep hill mounted by a *chedi*. The *wát* is named after a Buddha footprint (*prá pút·tá·bàht*) shrine in the middle of the lower temple grounds and another spot where Buddha supposedly dried his robes (*đàhk pâh*).

A *sŏrng·tăa·ou* from Lamphun to the *wát* costs 30B.

Doi Khun Tan National Park
อุทยานแห่งชาติดอยขุนตาล

Not worth a special trip, but if you're in the area check out this 225-sq-km **park** (☎ 0 5354 6335; admission 200B), which straddles the mountains between Lamphun and Lampang provinces. It ranges in elevation from 350m at the bamboo forest lowlands to 1363m at the pine-studded summit of Doi Khun Tan. Wildflowers, including orchids, ginger and lilies, are abundant. At the park headquarters there are maps of well-marked trails that range from short walks around the headquarters' vicinity to trails covering the mountain's

NORTHERN THAILAND

WHAT TO EXPECT IN NORTHERN THAILAND

We list high-season rack rates in this book. See the boxed text on p150 for more details on the different sleeping categories.

- Budget (under 600B)
- Midrange (600B to 1500B)
- Top End (over 1500B)

---

four peaks; there's also a trail to **Nam Tok Tat Moei** (7km round trip). Intersecting the mountain slopes is Thailand's longest train tunnel (1352m), which opened in 1921 after six years of manual labour by thousands of Lao workers (several of whom are said to have been killed by tigers).

Bungalows (☎ 0 2562 0760; www.dnp.go.th; bungalows 1500-2700B) are available near the park headquarters. There is a restaurant by the bungalows. The park is very popular on cool-season weekends.

This park is unique in that the main access is from the Khun Tan train station (2nd/3rd class 33/15B, 1½ hours, five daily). The last train back to Chiang Mai leaves at 1.35pm. Once at the Khun Tan station, cross the tracks and follow a steep, marked path 1.3km to the park headquarters. By car take the Chiang Mai–Lampang highway to the Mae Tha turn-off then follow the signs along a steep unpaved road for 18km.

LAMPANG PROVINCE

LAMPANG
ลำปาง
pop 148,199

Boasting lumbering elephants, the elegant mansions of former lumber barons and impressive (and in many cases, lumber-based) Lanna-era temples, Lampang seems to unite every northern Thai cliché – but in a good way. Despite all this, the city sees relatively few visitors, giving it more of an 'undiscovered' feel than some of the more touristed destinations in the north.

History
Although Lampang Province was inhabited as far back as the 7th century in the Dvaravati period, legend has it that Lampang city was founded by the son of Hariphunchai's Queen Chama Thewi, and played an important part in the history of the Hariphunchai Kingdom (8th to 13th centuries).

Like Chiang Mai, Phrae and other older northern cities, modern Lampang was built as a walled rectangle alongside a river (in this case Mae Wang). At the end of the 19th and beginning of the 20th century Lampang, along with nearby Phrae, became an important centre for the domestic and international teak trade. A large British-owned timber company brought in Burmese supervisors familiar with the teak industry in Burma to train Burmese and Thai loggers in the area. These well-paid supervisors, along with independent Burmese teak merchants who plied their trade in Lampang, sponsored the construction of more than a dozen impressive temples in the city, a legacy that lives on in several of Lampang's most impressive wáts.

Information
There are many banks with ATMs along Th Boonyawat, especially near Wat Suan Dok.

M@cnet (Th Chatchai; per hr 15B; ☺ 9am-10pm) Internet access.

Monkey Jump (Th Talat Kao; per hr 15B; ☺ 9am-10pm) Internet access.

Post office (Th Pa Kham; ☺ 8.30am-4.30pm Mon-Fri, 9am-noon Sat)

Tourist information office (☎ 0 5423 7237 ext 4103; Th Thakhrao Noi; ☺ 8am-noon & 1-4.30pm Mon-Fri) Locally run, with a decent map of the area and details about local sights.

Sights
WAT PHRA KAEW DON TAO
วัดพระแก้วดอนเต้า
From 1436 to 1468, this **wát** (admission 20B; ☺ 7am-6pm) was among four in northern Thailand to previously house the Emerald Buddha (now in Bangkok's Wat Phra Kaew, see p126). The main *chedi* shows Hariphunchai influence, while the adjacent *mon·dòp* (the small square, spired building in a wát) was built in 1909. The *mon·dòp*, decorated with glass mosaic in typical Burmese style, contains a Mandalay-style Buddha image. A display of Lanna artefacts (mostly religious paraphernalia and woodwork) can be viewed in the wát's **Lanna Museum** (admission by donation; ☺ 7am-6pm).

NORTHERN THAILAND

LAMPANG

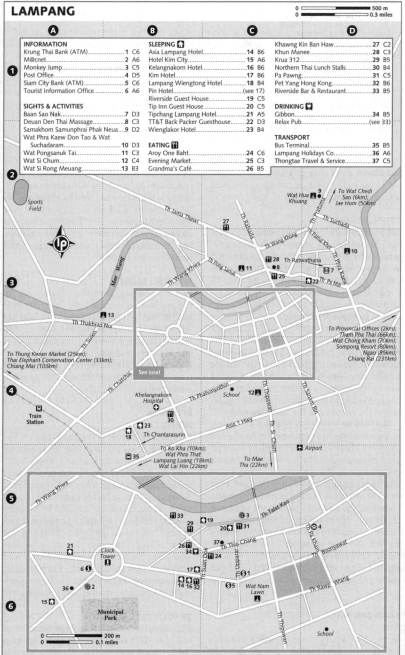

0 ━━━━━ 500 m
0 ━━━━━ 0.3 miles

INFORMATION
Krung Thai Bank (ATM)..................... 1 C6
M@cnet... 2 A6
Monkey Jump... 3 C5
Post Office.. 4 D5
Siam City Bank (ATM)........................ 5 C6
Tourist Information Office............... 6 A6

SIGHTS & ACTIVITIES
Baan Sao Nak... 7 D3
Deuan Den Thai Massage.................. 8 C3
Samakhom Samunphrai Phak Neua..9 D2
Wat Phra Kaew Don Tao & Wat
   Suchadaram................................... 10 D3
Wat Pongsanuk Tai............................ 11 C3
Wat Si Chum.. 12 C4
Wat Si Rong Meuang......................... 13 B3

SLEEPING 🏠
Asia Lampang Hotel.......................... 14 B6
Hotel Kim City.................................... 15 A6
Kelangnakorn Hotel.......................... 16 B6
Kim Hotel... 17 B6
Lampang Wiengtong Hotel............ 18 B4
Pin Hotel..(see 17)
Riverside Guest House..................... 19 C5
Tip Inn Guest House......................... 20 C5
Tipchang Lampang Hotel............... 21 A5
TT&T Back Packer Guesthouse...... 22 D3
Wienglakor Hotel.............................. 23 B4

EATING 🍴
Aroy One Baht.................................... 24 C6
Evening Market................................. 25 C3
Grandma's Café.................................. 26 B5

Khawng Kin Ban Haw........................ 27 C2
Khun Manee.. 28 C3
Krua 312... 29 B5
Northern Thai Lunch Stalls............ 30 B4
Pa Pawng.. 31 C5
Pet Yang Hong Kong........................ 32 B6
Riverside Bar & Restaurant............. 33 B5

DRINKING 🍸
Gibbon... 34 B5
Relax Pub..(see 33)

TRANSPORT
Bus Terminal....................................... 35 B5
Lampang Holidays Co....................... 36 A6
Thongtae Travel & Service.............. 37 C5

NORTHERN THAILAND

USE YOUR MELON

Diminutive Wat Suchadaram, located at Wat Phra Kaew Don Tao, is said to be located on the former melon patch (*dorn ɗôw*) of Mae (Mother) Suchada, a pious local woman. It is said that during a time of famine, a monk appeared and was given an unusually shaped melon by Mae Suchada. Upon opening the melon, the monk found a large green gem inside, and with the help of Mae Suchada, as well as the divine intervention of Indra, the gem was shaped into a Buddha image. Villagers suspected the collaboration between the monk and Mae Suchada of being a bit too friendly, and in a fit of rage, beheaded Suchada. Upon realising their mistake later (the beheading led to yet another famine), a temple was built in the woman's honour. Today, the emerald Buddha image is held at Wat Phra That Lampang Luang.

Adjacent to the temple complex, pretty **Wat Suchadaram** dates back to 1809 and is named after Mae Suchada, the central figure in a local legend (see boxed text, above).

OTHER TEMPLES

Wat Si Rong Meuang and **Wat Si Chum** are two wáts built in the late 19th century by Burmese artisans. Both have temple buildings constructed in the Burmese 'layered' style, with tin roofs gabled by intricate woodcarvings. Wat Si Rong Meuang has a display with detailed information in English about the history and artistic merits of the temple.

Despite having lost much of its character in a recent renovation, the *mon·dòp* at **Wat Pongsanuk Tai** is still one of the few remaining local examples of original Lanna-style temple architecture, which emphasised open-sided wooden buildings. To get an idea of what it was like previously, look at the carved wooden gateway at the entrance to the north stairway.

Wat Chedi Sao (☎ 0 5432 0233), about 6km north of town towards Jae Hom, is named for the *sow* (northern Thai for 20) whitewashed Lanna-style *chedi* on its grounds. But the wát's real treasure is a solid-gold, 15th-century seated Buddha on display in a glassed-in **pavilion** (⏰ 8am-5pm), built over a square pond. The image is said to contain a piece of the Buddha's skull in its head and an ancient Pali-inscribed golden palm leaf in its chest; precious stones decorate the image's hairline and robe. A farmer reportedly found the figure next to the ruins of nearby Wat Khu Kao in 1983. Monks stationed at Wat Chedi Sao make and sell herbal medicines; the popular *yah mòrng* is similar to tiger balm.

BAAN SAO NAK

บ้านเสานัก

In the old Wiang Neua (North City) section of town, **Baan Sao Nak** (☎ 0 5422 7653; 85 Th

Ratwathana; admission 50B; ⏰ 10am-5pm) was built in 1895 in the traditional Lanna style. A huge teak house supported by 116 square teak pillars, it was once owned by a local *kun·yĭng* (a title equivalent to 'Lady' in England); it now serves as a local museum. The entire house is furnished with Burmese and Thai antiques, but the real treasure is the structure itself and its manicured garden.

WALKING STREET

Perhaps wanting to emulate the success of Chiang Mai's street markets, Lampang now has its own along the charming **Th Talat Kao** (also known as Kat Korng Ta). Dotted with old shophouses showcasing English, Chinese and Burmese architectural styles, the street is closed to traffic on Saturday and Sunday from 4pm to 10pm and fills up with souvenir, handicraft and food stalls.

Activities

HORSE CARTS

Lampang is known throughout Thailand as Meuang Rot Mah (Horse Cart City) because it's the only town in Thailand where horse carts are still found, although nowadays they are exclusively used for tourists. You can't miss the brightly coloured horse carts that drip with nylon flowers, and are handled by Stetson-wearing drivers. A 15-minute horse-cart tour around town costs 150B; for 200B you can get a half-hour tour that goes along the Mae Wang. For 300B a one-hour tour stops at Wat Phra Kaew Don Tao and Wat Si Rong Meuang. Horse carts can be found near the larger hotels and just east of the market on Th Boonyawat.

TRADITIONAL MASSAGE

The **Samakhom Samunphrai Phak Neua** (☎ 08 9758 2396; 149 Th Pratuma; massage per hr 200B, sauna 100B; ⏰ 8am-7.30pm), next to Wat Hua Khuang in the Wiang Neua area, offers traditional northern-Thai massage and herbal saunas. Slightly closer to downtown, **Deuan Den Thai Massage** (☎ 08 7305 9838; 41/1 Th Phai Mai; ☺ 10am-7pm) offers traditional massage and other basic spa services.

Sleeping
BUDGET

Tip Inn Guest House (☎ 0 5422 1821; 143 Th Talat Kao; r 150-350B; ✖) Although the cheapies are little more than a bed in a box, Tip Inn is a homey alternative to the city's overwhelmingly characterless budget hotels. It's also the only accommodation to be located smack-dab in the middle of historic Th Talat Kao.

TT&T Back Packer Guesthouse (☎ 0 5422 1303; 82 Th Pa Mai; r 200-350B; ✖) Proceed directly to the newer building in the back that offers fleeting glances of the Mae Wang. Bathrooms are shared here, but this is made up for by the attractive and comfortable chill-out area downstairs. A good bargain find.

Kim Hotel (☎ 0 5421 7721; 168 Th Boonyawat; s/d 250/350B; ✖) Although they are significantly in need of a dose of character, the rooms here are clean, comfortable and have TV. If full, proceed directly across the street to the virtually identical Kelangnakorn Hotel (☎ 0 5421 6137; 719-720 Th Suan Dok; s/d 230/290B; ✖).

our pick Riverside Guest House (☎ 0 5422 7005; www.theriversidelampang.com; 286 Th Talat Kao; r 300-800B; ✖) Although still within budget range, this leafy compound of refurbished wooden houses is by far the most pleasant place to stay in Lampang. Try to score one of the two upstairs rooms in the main structure that feature vast balconies overlooking the Mae Wang. Shaded tables for chatting or eating abound, and motorcycle rental and other tourist amenities are available.

Hotel Kim City (☎ 0 5431 0238-40; 274/1 Th Chatchai; r incl breakfast 400-900, ste 1100B) You'll probably be led to the ground-floor cheapies, but do yourself a favour and request a room upstairs to avoid the mustiness. Small groups travelling on a budget will be happy to find an abundance of huge triple rooms.

Asia Lampang Hotel (☎ 0 5422 7844; www.asialampang .com; 229 Th Boonyawat; r 490-550B; ✖) The cheaper rooms on the ground floor are starkly plain and a bit dark, but for a tiny bit more go up a couple of floors where the wood-panelled rooms represent decent value.

Pin Hotel (☎ 0 5422 1509; 8 Th Suan Dok; r 500-950; ✖ ▭) Spotless, spacious and secluded, the rooms here come decked out with cable TV, minibar and large bathrooms. A travel agent is attached and books domestic and international flights. An excellent choice.

MIDRANGE & TOP END

Lampang Wiengtong Hotel (☎ 0 5422 5801/2; www .lampangwiengthonghotel.com; 138/109 Th Phahonyothin; r 600-1200, ste 2500B; ✖ ▭) Not surprisingly, Lampang's largest hotel also boasts some of the largest rooms we've seen anywhere. The bad news is that little if any effort is made at making them pleasant to the eye. The budget rooms, on the other hand, are cramped and boast the tiniest bathtubs we've seen outside of Tokyo.

Tipchang Lampang Hotel (☎ 0 5422 6501; www .tipchanghotel.com; 54/22 Th Thakhrao Noi; r incl breakfast 700-1400B, ste 1500-2000B; ✖ ▭ ▨) Large and imposing from the outside, but in need of an update of its 'vintage' 1970s-style rooms. A pool and the view from the top floors justify a stay at this wannabe top ender.

Wienglakor Hotel (☎ 0 5431 6430-5; www.wienglakor .com; 138/35 Th Phahonyothin; r 900-2400, ste 2500B; ✖ ▭) If you're going to go upscale, this is Lampang's best choice. The lobby is tastefully decorated in a teak and northern Thai temple theme, a design that continues into the rooms. Deluxe rooms feature an added sitting area and walk-in closet, and the hotel's attractive outdoor dining area with carp pond is a nice touch.

Eating

For a relatively small town, Lampang boasts a pretty strong repertoire of restaurants, ranging from northern Thai to Western fare, and a few things in between.

Lampang is known for its addictive *kôw đaan*, deep-fried rice cakes drizzled with palm sugar, the making of which can be observed at **Khun Manee** (☎ 0 5431 2272; 35 Th Ratsada).

Pa Pawng (☎ 08 5706 7748; 125 Th Talat Kao; dishes 20-30B; ☺ 7am-10pm Sat & Sun) If you happen to be in town on a weekend, be sure to stop by this popular local haunt serving *kà·nŏm jeen* (fresh rice noodles topped with various curries). You can't miss it (simply look for a row of bubbling curries in earthenware pots), and ordering is a snap (simply point to whatever looks good). Auntie Pawng's speciality is *kà·nŏm jeen nám ngée·o*, a delicious northern-style broth of pork and tomato.

NORTHERN NOSH

Much like the language, Thailand's food seems to take a slightly different form every time you cross a provincial border. The cuisine of Thailand's northern provinces is no exception and is indicative of the region's seasonal and relatively cool climate, not to mention a love for pork, veggies and all things deep-fried. Traditionally, the residents of Thailand's north ate almost exclusively *kôw něe·o*, sticky rice, known in the local dialect as *kôw nêung*. Coconut milk rarely makes its way into the northern kitchen, and northern Thai cuisine is probably the least spicy of Thailand's regional schools of cooking, often relying on bitter or bitter/hot flavours instead.

Paradoxically (and unfortunately), it can be quite difficult to find authentic local food outside of Chiang Mai and the other large cities in Northern Thailand. There are relatively few restaurants serving northern-style dishes, and the vast majority of authentic local food is sold from stalls in 'to go' bags. However, if you manage to come across a local restaurant, some must-try dishes include:

■ *Gaang hang·lair* – Burmese in origin (*hang* is a corruption of the Burmese *hin*, meaning curry), this rich pork curry is often seen at festivals and ceremonies.

■ *Kâap mŏo* – deep-fried pork crackling is a common – and delicious – side dish in northern Thailand.

■ *Kôw gân jîn* – banana leaf packets of rice mixed with blood that are steamed and served with garlic oil.

■ *Kôw soy* – this popular curry-based noodle dish is most likely Burmese in origin, and was probably introduced to northern Thailand by travelling Chinese merchants.

■ *Ka·nŏm jeen nám ngée·o* – fresh rice noodles served with a spaghetti-like pork- and tomato-based broth.

■ *Lâhp kôo·a* – literally 'fried *lâhp*', this dish takes the famous Thai minced-meat 'salad' and fries it with a mixture of local bitter/hot dried spices and herbs.

■ *Lôo* – raw blood mixed with a curry paste and served over deep-fried intestines and crispy noodles – the most hardcore northern dish of all.

■ *Năam* – fermented raw pork, a sour delicacy that tastes much better than it sounds.

■ *Nám prík nùm* – green chillies, shallots and garlic that are grilled then mashed into a paste served with sticky rice, parboiled veggies and deep-fried pork crackling.

■ *Nám prík òrng* – a chili dip of Shan origin made from tomatoes and minced pork – a northern Thai bolognese of sorts.

■ *Sâi òo·a* – a grilled pork sausage supplemented with copious fresh herbs.

■ *Ŧam sôm oh* – the northern Thai version of *sôm·đam* substitutes pomelo for green papaya.

■ *Đôm yam* – the northern Thai version of this Thai staple is flavoured with some of the same bitter/spicy dried spices featured in *lâhp kôoa*.

our pick Aroy One Baht (☎ 08 970 0944; cnr Th Suan Dok & Th Talat Kao; dishes 20-90B; ☽ 4pm-midnight) Some nights it can seem like just about everybody in Lampang has gathered at this rambling wooden house, and understandably so; the food is delicious and embarrassingly cheap, the service lightning fast, and the setting in a wooden house-cum-balcony-cum-garden heaps of fun.

Pet Yang Hong Kong (Th Boonyawat; dishes 25-60B; ☽ 8am-6pm) This is the best spot for roast duck with rice (or noodles). It's opposite Kim Hotel, near several other rice and noodle joints.

Grandma's Café (☎ 0 5432 2792; 361 Th Thip Chang; dishes 30-40B; ☽ 10am-9pm) Well-worn teak chairs and doily window shades suggest grandma's influence, but we doubt she had any role in the slate greys and minimalist feel of this trendy coffee shop. Regardless, stop by for decent java and a menu of rice dishes that rarely exceeds the 30B barrier.

Krua 312 (Th Thip Chang; dishes 30-60B; ☽ 10am-9pm) Set in a charming wooden shophouse and surrounded by black-and-white pictures of Lampang and the king, this tiny, simple restaurant serves good curries, noodle and rice dishes.

Riverside Bar & Restaurant (☎ 0 5422 1861; 328 Th Thip Chang; dishes 45-225B; ☺ 11am-midnight) This wooden shack that appears to be on the verge of tumbling into the Mae Wang is extremely popular with visiting and resident foreigners. Live music, a full bar and an expansive menu of local and Western dishes bring in the crowds, and you'd be wise to plan your visit around the homemade pizza nights (Tuesday, Thursday, Saturday and Sunday).

Khawng Kin Ban Haw (72 Th Jama Thewi; dishes 50-110B; ☺ lunch & dinner) Located just outside the centre of town but worth the trip, this local favourite is most popular after dark when a bottle of whisky is regarded as a typical side dish. This is a good place to try northern Thai staples such as *gaang kaa gòp* (a herb-laden soup with frog) or *lâhp kôo·a* (*lâhp* that has been stir-fried with local spices).

Self-caterers or those interested in local eats will want to check out Lampang's **evening market** (Th Ratsada; ☺ 4-8pm) where steaming baskets of sticky rice and dozens of sides to dip it in are on daily display. Cheap and authentic northern Thai food can also be found at the few **lunch stalls** (Th Phahonyothin; dishes 20-30B; ☺ 10am-2pm) that operate directly opposite Khelangnakorn Hospital.

Drinking

The strip of Th Thip Chang near Riverside Bar & Restaurant (above) is Lampang's nightlife district, and includes a few friendly open-air restaurant/pubs such as **Relax Pub** (Th Thip Chang; dishes 50-150B; ☺ 6pm-midnight) and the curiously named **Gibbon** (Th Thip Chang; ☺ 7pm-midnight).

Getting There & Away

AIR

Several agents around town, such as **Lampang Holidays Co** (☎ 0 5431 0403; 260/17 Th Chatchai; ☺ 9am-7pm) can arrange air tickets, saving you the trouble of a trip to the airport.

Nok Air (☎ nationwide call centre 1318; www.nokair .co.th; Lampang airport) and **PB Air** (☎ 0 5422 6238, Bangkok ☎ 0 2261 0220; www.pbair.com; Lampang airport) conduct code-share daily flights between Lampang and Bangkok (3025B, one hour, three times daily).

BUS

The bus terminal in Lampang is some way out of town, at the corner of Asia 1 Hwy and Th Chantarasurin – 15B by shared *sŏrng·tăa·ou*.

There are frequent buses to Chiang Mai (ordinary/2nd class air-con/1st class/VIP 56/76/97/150B, two hours, every 45 minutes from 6am to 4pm) and Phrae (2nd class/1st class/VIP 88/113/175B, two hours).

To Chiang Rai, there are three daily departures (162B, four hours, 6.30am, 9am and 3pm). There are also relatively frequent buses to Nan (2nd class air-con/1st class/VIP 169/218/335B, four hours) and Phitsanulok (2nd class air-con/1st class/VIP 176/227/265B, four hours). Buses to other destinations in northern Thailand generally depart from 8am to 6pm.

To Bangkok, most buses depart around 8pm (2nd class air-con/1st class/VIP 399/513/710B, eight to nine hours). **Thongtae Travel & Service** (☎ 0 5432 2813; 250/2 Th Thip Chang; ☺ 9am-7pm) can arrange bus tickets to Bangkok.

TRAIN

Lampang's historic **train station** (☎ 0 5421 7024; Th Phahonyothin) dates back to 1916 and is located a fair hike from most accommodation.

The train is a relatively slow but comfortable way to get to/from Chiang Mai (3rd/2nd class 23/50B, two to three hours, six times daily), and there are several trains every day that stop in Lampang en route to/from Bangkok (3rd class fan 256B, 2nd class air-con/fan 574/394B, 2nd class fan sleeper upper/lower 494/544B, 2nd class air-con sleeper upper/lower 754/844B, 1st class sleeper 1272B, 12 hours, six times daily), the majority reaching the city between 5pm and 11pm. To check the most up-to-date timetables and prices in advance call the **State Railway of Thailand** (☎ free 24hr hotline 1690; www.railway.co.th) or look at their website.

AROUND LAMPANG
Wat Phra That Lampang Luang

วัดพระธาตุลำปางหลวง

This ancient temple compound houses several interesting religious structures, including what is arguably the most beautiful wooden Lanna temple in northern Thailand, the open-sided **Wihan Luang**. Dating back to 1476, and thought to be the oldest standing wooden structure in the country, the impressive *wí·hăhn* features a triple-tiered wooden roof supported by immense teak pillars and early 19th-century *jataka* murals (stories of the Buddha's previous lives) painted on wooden panels around the inside upper perimeter. A huge, gilded *mon·dòp* in the back of the *wí·hǎhn* contains a Buddha image cast in 1563.

The small and simple **Wihan Ton Kaew**, to the north of the main *wí·hǎhn*, was built in 1476.

The tall Lanna-style *chedi* behind the main *wí·hǎhn*, raised in 1449 and restored in 1496, is 45m high.

The *wí·hǎhn* to the north of the *chedi*, **Wihan Nam Taem**, was built in the early 16th century and, amazingly, still contains traces of the original murals, making them among the oldest in the country.

Wihan Phra Phut (admission 20B), which is south of the main *chedi*, dates back to the 13th century and is the oldest structure in the compound.

Unfortunately, only men are allowed to see a camera obscura image of the *wí·hǎhn* and *chedi* in the **Haw Phra Phutthabaht**, a small white building behind the *chedi*. The image is projected (upside down) onto a white cloth, and clearly depicts the colours of the structures.

The lintel over the entrance to the compound features an impressive dragon relief – once common in northern Thai temples but rarely seen these days. This gate supposedly dates to the 15th century.

In the arboretum outside the southern gate of the *wát*, there are now three **museums**. One displays mostly festival paraphernalia and some Buddha figures. Another, called 'House of the Emerald Buddha', contains a miscellany of coins, banknotes, Buddha figures, silver betel-nut cases, lacquerware and other ethnographic artefacts, along with three small, heavily gold-leafed Buddhas placed on an altar behind an enormous repoussé silver bowl. The third, a fine, small museum, features shelves of Buddha figures, lacquered boxes, manuscripts and ceramics, all well labelled in Thai and English.

Wat Phra That Lampang Luang is 18km southwest of Lampang in Ko Kha. To get there by public transport from Lampang, flag an eastbound *sǒrng·tǎa·ou* (20B) on Th Rawp Wiang. From the Ko Kha *sǒrng·tǎa·ou* stop, it's a 3km chartered motorcycle taxi ride to the temple (40B). Minibuses outside the temple go back to the city for 30B.

If you're driving or cycling from Lampang, head south on the Asia 1 Hwy and take the Ko Kha exit, then follow the road over a bridge and bear right. Follow the signs and continue for 3km over another bridge until you see the temple on the left.

If you've got your own transport, you might also consider a visit to beautiful **Wat Lai Hin**, also in Ko Kha. If coming from Ko Kha, the temple is located about 6km down a road that turns off 1km before reaching Wat Phra That Lampang Luang. Built by artists from Chiang Tung, Myanmar, the tiny temple is one of the most characteristics Lanna temples around, and was an influence on the design of the Mandarin-Oriental Dhara Dhevi Hotel in Chiang Mai, not to mention a set for the 2001 Thai blockbuster, *Suriyothai*.

Thai Elephant Conservation Center & Around
ศูนย์อนุรักษ์ช้างไทย

Located in Amphoe Hang Chat, 33km from Lampang, this unique **facility** (TECC; ☎ 0 5424 7875; www.changthai.com; child/adult incl shuttle bus 30/70B; 🕙 elephant bathing 9.45am & 1.15pm, public shows 10am, 11am & 1.30pm) promotes the role of the Asian elephant in ecotourism, and also provides medical treatment and care for sick elephants from all over Thailand. For more information on the plight of Thailand's elephants, see p53.

The elephant show at this 122-hectare centre is less touristy and more educational than most, focusing on how elephants work with logs, as well as the usual painting of pictures and playing oversized xylophones. There is an exhibit on the history and culture of elephants, an elephant art gallery, an elephant graveyard, and oh yes, **elephant rides** (15/30/60 min 100/400/800B; 🕙 8am-3.30pm) through the surrounding forest.

Accommodation at the centre is available in the form of activity-packed homestays (see boxed text, opposite) with mahouts in basic huts, or in bungalows at the **Chang Thai Resort** (☎ 08 618 1545; bungalows 1/2 bedroom 1000/1500B). There are three restaurants on the centre grounds.

All proceeds from the entrance fee and souvenir shops go to the elephant hospital on site, which cares for old, abandoned and sick elephants from all over Thailand, as well as working for the preservation of elephants by various research and breeding programs.

Nearby, but not affiliated with the TECC is the **FAE's Elephant Hospital** (Friends of the Asian Elephant; ☎ 08 1914 6113; www.elephant-soraida.com; 🕙 suggested visiting hr 8am-1pm), which claims to be the first

---

MAHOUT TRAINING

For those keen on delving deeper into pachyderm culture, the TECC's **Mahout Training School** (☎ 0 5424 7875; www.thaielephant.org; 1/2/3/6/10 days 3500/8000/12,000/20,000/35,000B) offers an array of scholarships ranging in duration from one day to one month, all with the aim of making you a bona-fide *kwahn cháhng* (elephant caretaker) or mahout

The popular one-day course involves learning a few simple commands for leading an elephant, experimenting with dung paper, riding an elephant in the jungle and a tour of the elephant hospital. A more involved three-day, two-night **homestay** (☎ 0 5424 7875; 2/3 days 5800/8500B) program includes all meals, a night's lodging in a well-equipped wood-and-bamboo bungalow and another night at a jungle camp, plus a general introduction to elephant care and training.

Packages are for two people or more and all food and accommodation is provided. Long-term courses are often booked far in advance, so call ahead.

---

of its kind in the world. Although visitors are appreciated and provided for, keep in mind that this is a functioning medical facility, and there are no guided tours and certainly no elephant art. Donations are greatly appreciated. In June 2008 the centre reached another first when it successfully provided an elephant with a prosthetic leg.

Both facilities can be reached by Chiang Mai–bound bus or *sŏrng·tăa·ou* (25B) from Lampang's main bus terminal. Let the driver know where you are headed and get off at the Km37 marker. The centre is 1.5km from the highway, and shuttle buses will take you inside. Alternatively, you can hire a blue *sŏrng·tăa·ou* for 350B to 500B at the bus terminal.

If you have your own transport, on the way to the elephant camp, 25km from Lampang, is the **Thung Kwian market**. Very popular with Thais, this market is a crash course in northern Thai food and handicraft, offering everything from *rót dòo·an* (deep-fried worms, a northern speciality), to the distinctive rooster bowls made in Lampang.

Other Attractions

North and east of Lampang are the cotton-weaving villages of **Jae Hom** and **Mae Tha**. You can wander around and find looms in action; there are also plenty of shops along the main roads.

Ngao district, 85km north of Lampang, has developed something approaching a buzz for its numerous low-key attractions, although most of these would be quite inconvenient to visit without a private vehicle. **Tham Pha Thai** (Pha Thai Cave) and the national park of the same name are located 20km south of Ngao. Besides the usual cave

formations, Tham Pha Thai contains a large Buddha image. **Wat Chong Kham**, 15km south of Ngao, features a Burmese-style wooden *wí·hăhn* with a seven-tiered roof. The temple is also home to the largest Buddhist school in northern Thailand, and dozens of young monks and novices can be seen studying in outdoor classrooms during the daytime. **Wat Mon Sai Non**, just south of the turn-off to Ngao, is located on a hill and offers views of the surrounding area. Ngao town features an aged suspension bridge. The only accommodation in the area is the self-proclaimed 'karaoke' resort **Sompong Resort** (☎ 08 1746 5270; Asia 1 Hwy; r 500B), located about 3km south of the turn-off to Ngao.

Lampang is well endowed with waterfalls. Three are found within Amphoe Wang Neua, roughly 120km north of the provincial capital: **Wang Kaew**, **Wang Thong** and **Than Thong** (Jampa Thong). Wang Kaew is the largest, with 110 tiers. Near the summit is a Mien hill-tribe village. This area became part of the 1172-sq-km **Doi Luang National Park** (☎ 0 5316 3363; Tambon Mae Yen, Amphoe Phan, Chiang Rai; admission 200B) in 1990; animals protected by the park include serows, barking deer, pangolins and pig-tailed macaques.

In Amphoe Meuang Pan, about halfway between Wang Neua and Lampang, is another waterfall, **Nam Tok Jae Sawn**, part of the 593-sq-km **Chae Son National Park** (☎ 0 5422 9000; Tambon Jae Son, Amphoe Muang Ban, Lampang; admission 200B). Elevations in the park reach above 2000m. Jae Sawn has six drops, each with its own pool; close to the falls are nine hot springs. Small huts house circular baths, recessed into the floor and lined with clay tiles, that are continuously filled with water direct from the spring. For 20B you can take a 20-minute soak, preceded and followed by an invigorating cold-water shower.

Camping is permitted in both Chae Son and Doi Luang national parks. Chae Son has a visitors centre, 12 bungalows for hire and a restaurant, but food must be ordered in advance of your visit. Several privately run food/snack stalls provide sustenance as well. For further information, and to book accommodation, contact the **Royal Forest Department** (☎ 0 2562 0760; www.dnp .go.th).

CHIANG RAI PROVINCE

Chiang Rai, Thailand's northernmost province, has a bit of everything: the mountains in the far east of the province are among the most dramatic in the country, the lowland Mekong River floodplains to the northeast are not unlike those one would find much further south in Isan, and the province shares borders with Myanmar and Laos, allowing relatively easy access to China.

In terms of people, it's also among Thailand's most ethnically diverse provinces, and is home to a significant minority of hill tribes, Shan and other Tai groups, and relatively recent Chinese immigrants.

CHIANG RAI

เชียงราย

pop 61,188

Chiang Rai province has such a diversity of attractions, that its capital city is often overlooked. If you take the time to know it, Chiang Rai is a small but delightful city with a relaxed atmosphere, good value accommodation and some tasty eats. It's also the ideal base from which to plan excursions to the more remote corners of the province.

Founded by Phaya Mengrai in 1262 as part of the Lao-Thai Lanna kingdom, Chiang Rai didn't become a Siamese territory till 1786, then a province in 1910.

Information
BOOKSHOPS
Gare Garon (869/18 Th Phahonyothin; ☺ 10am-10pm) Mainly new books with a smattering of overpriced used ones; also sells coffee, tea and some handicrafts.
Orn's Bookshop (☎ 08 1022 0318; ☺ 8am-8pm) By far the best used bookshop in Chiang Rai, this place is run by the eccentric and discerning Peter. His superb collection of books spans many languages.

EMERGENCY
Tourist Police (☎ 0 5374 0249; Th Phahonyothin; ☺ 24hrs) English is spoken and police are on stand-by 24 hours a day.

INTERNET ACCESS
Internet access is readily available around town and costs around 30B per hour. It's especially abundant around the night market.
Connect Café (☎ 0 5374 0688; 868/10 Th Phahonyothin; ☺ 10.30am-10.30pm) This colourful, funky internet cafe serves homemade brownies and good coffee while you're typing away. It has an overseas call service, burns digital photos onto CDs, sells books and maps, and plays chilled-out music.

MEDICAL SERVICES
Overbrook Hospital (☎ 0 5371 1366; www.overbrook hospital.com; Th Singkhlai) English is spoken in this modern hospital.

MONEY
There is an abundance of banks and ATMs on both Th Phahonyothin and Th Thanalai.

POST
Main post office (Th Utarakit; ☺ 8.30am-4.30pm Mon-Fri, 9am-noon Sat, Sun & holidays) South of Wat Phra Singh.

TELEPHONE
Many internet places offer international call services, including Connect Café (above).
Communications Authority of Thailand office (CAT; cnr Th Ratchadat Damrong & Th Ngam Meuang; ☺ 7am-11pm Mon-Fri) Offers international telephone, internet and fax services.

TOURIST INFORMATION
Tourism Authority of Thailand office (TAT; ☎ 0 5374 4674, 0 5371 1433; tatchrai@tat.or.th; Th Singkhlai; ☺ 8.30am-4.30pm) English is limited, but staff here do their best to give advice, and can provide a small selection of maps and brochures.

Sights
WAT PHRA KAEW
วัดพระแก้ว
Originally called Wat Pa Yia (Bamboo Forest Monastery) in local dialect, this is the city's most revered Buddhist temple. Legend has it that in 1434 lightning struck the temple's octagonal *chedi*, which fell apart to reveal the Phra Kaew Morakot, or Emerald Buddha (actually made of jade). After a long journey that included a long stopover in Vientiane, Laos

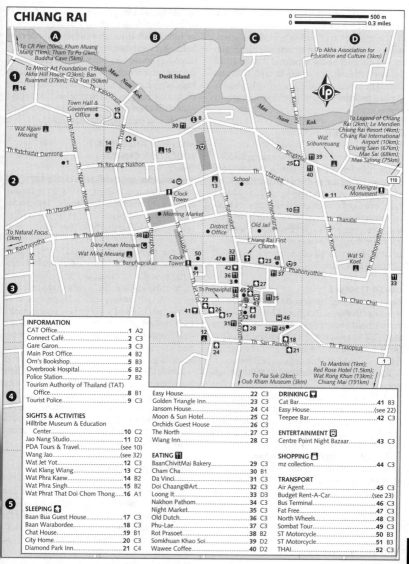

CHIANG RAI

To CR Pier (50m); Khum Muang
Mang (1km); Tham Tu Pu (2km);
Buddha Cave (5km)

To Mirror Art Foundation (15km);
Akha Hill House (23km); Ban
Ruammit (37km); Tha Ton (50km)

To Akha Association for
Education and Culture (3km)

Dusit Island

Mae Nam Kok

Mae Nam Kwy

To Legend of Chiang
Rai (2km); Le Meridien
Chiang Rai Resort (4km);
Chiang Rai International
Airport (10km);
Chiang Saen (67km);
Mae Sai (68km);
Mae Salong (75km)

To Natural Focus
(3km)

To Mantrini (1km);
Red Rose Hotel (1.5km);
Wat Rong Khun (13km);
Chiang Mai (191km)

To Paa Suk (2km);
Oub Kham Museum (3km)

INFORMATION

CAT Office	1 A2
Connect Café	2 C3
Gare Garon	3 C3
Main Post Office	4 B2
Orn's Bookshop	5 B3
Overbrook Hospital	6 B2
Police Station	7 B2
Tourism Authority of Thailand (TAT) Office	8 B1
Tourist Police	9 C3

SIGHTS & ACTIVITIES

Hilltribe Museum & Education Center	10 C2
Jao Nang Studio	11 D2
PDA Tours & Travel	(see 10)
Wang Jao	(see 32)
Wat Jet Yot	12 C3
Wat Klang Wiang	13 C2
Wat Phra Kaew	14 B2
Wat Phra Singh	15 B2
Wat Phrat That Doi Chom Thong	16 A1

SLEEPING

Baan Bua Guest House	17 C3
Baan Warabordee	18 C3
Chat House	19 B1
City Home	20 C3
Diamond Park Inn	21 C4

Easy House	22 C3
Golden Triangle Inn	23 C3
Jansom House	24 C4
Moon & Sun Hotel	25 C2
Orchids Guest House	26 C3
The North	27 C3
Wiang Inn	28 C3

EATING

BaanChivitMai Bakery	29 C3
Cham Cha	30 B1
Da Vinci	31 C3
Doi Chaang@Art	32 C3
Loong It	33 D3
Nakhon Pathom	34 C3
Night Market	35 C3
Old Dutch	36 C3
Phu-Lae	37 C3
Rot Prasoet	38 B2
Somkhuan Khao Soi	39 D2
Wawee Coffee	40 D2

DRINKING

Cat Bar	41 B3
Easy House	(see 22)
Teepee Bar	42 C3

ENTERTAINMENT

Centre Point Night Bazaar	43 C3

SHOPPING

mz collection	44 C3

TRANSPORT

Air Agent	45 C3
Budget Rent-A-Car	(see 23)
Bus Terminal	46 C3
Fat Free	47 C3
North Wheels	48 C3
Sombat Tour	49 C3
ST Motorcycle	50 B3
ST Motorcycle	51 B3
THAI	52 C3

(see boxed text, p127), this national talisman
is now ensconced in the temple of the same
name in Bangkok.

In 1990 Chiang Rai commissioned a
Chinese artist to sculpt a new image from
Canadian jade. Named the Phra Yok Chiang
Rai (Chiang Rai Jade Buddha), it was inten-
tionally a very close but not exact replica of the
Phra Kaew Morakot in Bangkok, with dimen-
sions of 48.3cm across the base and 65.9cm in
height, just 0.1cm shorter than the original.
The image is housed in the impressive Haw
Phra Yoke, the walls of which are decorated
with beautiful modern murals, some depict-
ing the journey of the original Phra Kaew
Morakot, as well as the elaborate ceremony

NORTHERN THAILAND

that saw the current image arrive at its new home in Chiang Rai.

The main prayer hall is a medium-sized, well-preserved wooden structure with unique carved doors. The *chedi* behind it dates from the late 14th century and is in typical Lanna style. The adjacent two-storey wooden building is a **museum** (9am-5pm) housing various Lanna artefacts.

WAT PHRA SINGH
วัดพระสิงห์

Housing yet another copy of a famous Buddha image, this temple was built in the late 14th century during the reign of Chiang Rai's King Mahaphrom. A sister temple to Chiang Mai's Wat Phra Singh, its original buildings are typical northern Thai–style wood structures with low, sweeping roofs. The impressive wooden doors are thought to have been carved by local artists. The main *wí·hăhn* houses a copy of Chiang Mai's Phra Singh Buddha.

OTHER TEMPLES

The seven-spired *chedi* at **Wat Jet Yot** (Th Jet Yot) is similar to that of its Chiang Mai namesake, but without stucco ornamentation. Of more aesthetic interest is the wooden ceiling of the front veranda of the main *wí·hăhn*, which features a unique Thai astrological fresco.

Wat Klang Wiang (cnr Th Ratanaket & Th Utarakit) appears thoroughly modern, but dates back at least 500 years. Extensive remodelling in the early '90s has left several structures in the temple with a unique 'modern Lanna' style, but the elegant *hŏr drai* (manuscript depository) appears to retain its original form.

The hilltop **Wat Phra That Doi Chom Thong** has partial views of the river and gets an occasional river breeze. The Lanna-style *chedi* here most likely dates from the 14th to 16th centuries, and may cover an earlier Mon *chedi* inside. King Mengrai, Chiang Rai's founder, first surveyed the site for the city from this peak.

OUB KHAM MUSEUM
พิพิธภัณฑ์อูบคำ

This privately-owned **museum** (0 5371 3349; www.oubkhammuseum.com; 81/1 Military Front Rd; admission adult/child 300/100B; 8am-5pm) houses an impressive collection of paraphernalia from virtually every corner of the former Lanna kingdom. The items, some of which truly are one of a kind, range from a monkey bone food taster used by Lanna royalty to an impressive carved

throne from Chiang Tung, Myanmar. Guided tours (available in English) are obligatory, and include a walk through a gilded artificial cave holding several Buddha statues, complete with disco lights and fake torches! The grounds of the museum are equally kitschy, and include a huge golden *naga* (mythical serpent-like being with magical powers) statue and countless waterfalls and fountains. Truly an equal parts bizarre and enlightening experience.

HILLTRIBE MUSEUM & EDUCATION CENTER
พิพิธภัณฑ์และศูนย์การศึกษาชาวเขา

This **museum and handicrafts centre** (0 5374 0088; www.pda.or.th/chiangrai; 3rd fl, 620/1 Th Thanalai; admission 50B; 8.30am-6pm Mon-Fri, 10am-6pm Sat & Sun) is a good place to visit before undertaking any hill tribe trek. The centre, run by the nonprofit Population & Community Development Association (PDA), is underwhelming in its visual presentation, but contains a wealth of information on Thailand's various tribes and the issues that surround them. A visit begins with a 20-minute slide show on Thailand's hill tribes, and exhibits include typical clothing for six major tribes, examples of bamboo usage, folk implements and other anthropological objects. The curator is passionate about his museum, and will talk about the different hill tribes, their histories, recent trends and the community projects that the museum helps fund. The PDA also runs highly recommended treks (see opposite). There's a gift shop and a branch of Bangkok's Cabbages & Condoms restaurant is on the premises.

THAM TU PU & BUDDHA CAVE
ถ้ำตูปู/ถ้ำพระ

If you follow Th Winitchaikul across the bridge to the northern side of Mae Nam Kok, you'll come to a turn-off for both Tham Tu Pu and the Buddha Cave. Follow the road 1km, then turn off onto a dirt path 200m to the base of a limestone cliff where there is a steep set of stairs leading to a main chamber holding a dusty Buddha statue; this is Tham Tu Pu. Continue along the same road for 3km more and you'll reach Buddha Cave, a cavern by the Mae Nam Kok containing a tiny but active Buddhist temple, a lone monk and several cats. The temple was one of several destinations on a visit to the region by King Rama V in the early 20th century.

Neither attraction is particularly amazing on its own, but the surrounding country is beautiful and would make an ideal destination for a lazy bike ride. Bikes can be rented at Fat Free (p357).

Activities
TREKKING
More than 30 travel agencies, guesthouses and hotels offer trekking trips, typically in the Doi Tung, Doi Mae Salong and Chiang Khong areas. Many of the local travel agencies merely act as brokers for guides associated with one of the local guesthouses, so it may be cheaper to book directly through a guesthouse. As elsewhere in northern Thailand, you're more assured of a quality experience if you use a TAT-licensed guide.

Trek pricing depends on the number of days and participants, and the type of activities. Rates range from 950B per person per day in a group of six or more to 2300B per person per day for two people. Generally everything from accommodation to transport and food is included in this price.

For details on rules and taboos when visiting a hill tribe village, see p47.

The following agencies have a reputation for operating responsible treks and cultural tours, and in some cases profits from the treks go directly to community-development projects:.

Akha Hill House (☎ 08 9997 5505; www.akhahill .com) Wholly owned and managed by Akha tribespeople, this outfit does one- to seven-day treks. They begin with a long-tail boat up the river, before trekking to and around their Akha Hill House about 23km from Chiang Rai, at a height of 1500m. Profits from the guesthouses and their activities go back into the hill community and its school.

Mirror Art Foundation (☎ 0 5373 7412-3; www .mirrorartgroup.org; 106 Moo 1, Ban Huay Khom, Tambon Mae Yao) This nonprofit NGO does many admirable hill-tribe projects, ranging from educational workshops to Thai citizenship advocacy. Trekking with this group encourages real interaction with the villagers.

Natural Focus (☎ 08 5888 6869; www.naturalfocus -cbt.com; 129/1 Mu 4, Th Pa-Ngiw, Soi 4, Rop Wiang) Formerly a project of the Hill Area and Community Development Foundation (www.hadf.org), this now private company offers tours ranging from one to 15 days that concentrate on nature and hill-tribe living.

PDA Tours & Travel (☎ 0 5374 0088; crpdatour@ hotmail.com; 620/1 Th Thanalai, Hilltribe Museum & Education Center; 620/1 Th Thanalai) Culturally sensitive treks are ed by Population & Community Development Association–

trained hill-tribe members. One- to three-day treks are available and profits go back into community projects that include HIV/AIDS education, mobile health clinics, education scholarships and the establishment of village-owned banks.

From Chiang Rai's pier, boats can take you upriver as far as Tha Ton (see p356). An hour's boat ride east from Chiang Rai is **Ban Ruammit**, which is a fair-sized Karen village. From here you can trek on your own to Lahu, Mien, Akha and Lisu villages – all of them within a day's walk. Another popular area for do-it-yourself trekkers is **Wawi**, south of the river town of Mae Salak near the end of the river route.

MASSAGE
Wang Jao (☎ 08 9787 0123; 542 Th Ratanaket; massage 600B; 9am-6pm Mon-Sat, 1-6pm Sun) Located in the same compound as Doi Chaang@Art, this spa emphasises traditional Thai treatments and massage. Five-day courses in Thai massage are also available.

LANNA PORTRAITS
Dress up like a member of Lanna royalty and have your portrait taken for posterity – a must-do activity for Thai visitors to Chiang Mai and Chiang Rai. **Jao Nang Studio** (☎ 0 5371 7111; 645/7 Th Utarakit; 10am-7pm) has a huge array of costumes and backdrops. The adjacent shop also sells a variety of traditional northern-style clothing and other local items.

Sleeping
Chiang Rai has a good selection of accommodation, and prices seemed to have climbed little since the last edition, making the town good value. The two main areas for accommodation are in the centre, clustered around Th Jet Yot and off Th Phahonyothin.

BUDGET
our pick **Easy House** (☎ 0 5360 0963; 869/163-4 Th Premaviphat; r 170B) The simple but inviting rooms here represent the city's most attractive choice for those on a budget. The shared bathrooms are spotless, the staff friendly and helpful, and downstairs is a convivial restaurant/pub. It's also centrally located.

Baan Bua Guest House (☎ 0 5371 8880; www.baan buaguesthouse.com; 879/2 Th Jet Yot; r 200-350B;) This quiet guesthouse consists of a strip of 17 bright green rooms surrounding an inviting garden. The guide who does the tours has been with them for a decade.

City Home (☎ 0 5360 0155; 868 Th Phahonyothin; r 250-400B; ✷ ▯) Down a tiny soi, smack in the middle of town, this quiet four-storey hotel has 17 large rooms. Air-con rooms have wooden floors and cable TV, and are well furnished. A couple of shared-bathroom fan-cooled rooms are downstairs, but are somewhat musty smelling.

Jansom House (☎ 0 5371 4552; 897/2 Th Jet Yot; r 450B; ✷ ▯) This three-storey hotel offers spotless, spacious rooms set around a small courtyard filled with plants. You normally wouldn't expect frills at this price, but amazingly rooms here are equipped with cable TV, well-designed bathrooms and tiled floors. An excellent value.

Orchids Guest House (☎ 0 5371 8361; www.orchids guesthouse.com; 1012/3 Th Jet Yot; r 450B; ✷ ▯) This collection of spotless rooms in a residential compound looks even younger than its scant two years. Various services are available here, including internet and airport transfer (250B).

The North (☎ 0 5371 9873; www.thenorth.co.th; 612/100-101 Sirikon Market; r 450-650; ✷ ▯) Located steps away from the bus station, this new hotel has provided the drab market area with a bit of colour. The 18 rooms here combine both Thai and modern design, and the more expensive ones open to inviting chill-out areas. A friendly, family atmosphere fills out the package.

our pick **Baan Warabordee** (☎ 0 5375 4488; 59/1 Th San Pannat; r 500-700B; ✷ ▯) A delightful small hotel has been made from this modern three-storey Thai villa. Rooms are decked out in dark woods and light, hand-woven cloths. The owners are friendly and can help with local advice. The hotel is nearly at the end of residential street Th San Pannat.

MIDRANGE

Moon & Sun Hotel (☎ 0 5371 9279; www.moonandsun hotel.com; 632 Th Singkhlai; r 800-1000B, ste 1100B; ✷ ▯) Bright and sparkling clean, this little hotel offers large modern rooms. Some come with four-poster beds, all come with desk, cable TV and refrigerator. Suites have a separate, spacious sitting area.

Golden Triangle Inn (☎ 0 5371 1339; www.golden chiangrai.com; 590 Th Phahonyothin; r incl breakfast 800B; ✷) Resembling an expansive Thai home (including the occasional lived-in untidiness

this can involve), the 39 rooms here have tile or wood floors and wooden furniture. The compound includes a restaurant, a Budget car-rental office and an efficient travel agency. It's a popular place so book in advance.

Diamond Park Inn (☎ 0 5375 4960; www.diamond parkinn.com; 74/6 Moo 18, Th San Pannat; r incl breakfast 900-1050B, ste incl breakfast 1500B; ✷ ▯) Aggressive marketing strategy aside ('When ever you are at Chiang Rai. Stay at The Diamond Park Inn'), this new hotel is a terrific midrange choice. Rooms are large and attractive, with modern furniture and beds on an elevated platform. The more expensive rooms have tubs, wide balconies, and are big enough to feel slightly empty.

our pick **Red Rose Hotel** (☎ 0 5375 6888; www .redrosehotel.com; 14 Th Prachasanti; r incl breakfast 900-1050B, ste incl breakfast from 1600B; ✷ ▯) Think Disneyland on acid; the Red Rose is by far northern Thailand's wackiest place to stay. The owner was inspired by US-style amusement parks, and rooms here feature themes such as UFO, Jungle House and Love Boat (we suggest the Thai Boxing room, complete with ringside bed and punching bags). Fun communal areas with equipment ranging from table tennis to a pool table make the Red Rose perfect for families or for adults who haven't grown up yet.

TOP END

Mantrini (☎ 0 5360 1555-9; www.mantrini.com; 292 Moo 13, Robwiang on the Superhighway; r 2880-3290B, ste 9700B; ✷ ▯ ☢) This is the place to stay if design is your most important consideration. Rooms are delightfully chic, some boasting bathrooms with super-inviting recessed tubs. A highlight is the two 'Sweet Rooms', which are decked out in a faux-Victorian motif that somehow successfully combines disparate decorative items such as an African mask and a rocking horse. The hotel is located about 2km outside the city centre but operates a shuttle downtown.

Wiang Inn (☎ 0 5371 1533; www.wianginn.com; 893 Th Phahonyothin; r 3296-3422B; ✷ ▯ ☢) The large, modern lobby sets the stage for this centrally located, business-class hotel. The rooms are well maintained and have a few Thai touches, although the cheaper rooms only have double beds. Low season rates differ significantly.

our pick **Legend of Chiang Rai** (☎ 0 5391 0400; www .thelegend-chiangrai.com; 124/15 Moo 21, Th Kohloy; r 3900-5900B, villa 8100B; ✷ ▯ ☢) One of the few hotels in town to take advantage of a river location, this upscale resort feels like a traditional Lanna village. Rooms feel romantic and luxuriously understated with furniture in calming creams and rattan. Each has a pleasant outdoor sitting area, frosted glass for increased privacy and a cool, outdoor lake bathroom with an oversized shower; villas have a small private pool. The riverside infinity pool and spa are the icing on the comfort-filled cake.

Le Meridien Chiang Rai Resort (☎ 0 5360 3333; www.lemeridien.com; 221/2 Moo 20, Th Kwaewai; r 6800-9800B, ste 15,500B; 🕸 🖳 🖭) Chiang Rai's newest upscale digs is located about 2km outside of the city centre on a beautiful stretch of the Kok River. Rooms are immense and decked out in greys, whites and blacks, and the compound includes two restaurants and an infinity pool, in addition to the usual amenities of a hotel this price.

Eating

The night market has a decent collection of food stalls offering snacks and meals, from deep-fried won tons to fresh fish. Choose a dish and sit at the nearby tables, or step inside one of several restaurants on and off Th Phahonyothin by the night market.

Paa Suk (no roman-script sign; ☎ 0 5375 2471; Th Sankhongnoi; dishes 10-25B; 🕙 8am-3pm Mon-Sat) This immensely popular third-generation restaurant specialises in the local dish *kà·nǒm jeen nám ngée·o*, a thin broth of pork or beef and tomatoes served over fresh rice noodles. The restaurant is located just past the first stop light on Th Sankhongnoi (the street is called Th Sathan Phayaban where it intersects with Th Phahonyothin) roughly opposite HI Saban-nga.

Somkhuan Khao Soi (no roman-script sign; Th Singkhlai; dishes 25B; 🕙 8am-3pm Mon-Fri) Friendly Mr Somkhuan sells Chiang Rai's tastiest *kôw soy*, a curry noodle dish, from a basic street stall under two giant trees.

Rot Prasoet (Muslim food; Th Itsaraphap; dishes 25-50B; 🕙 7am-8pm) This Thai-Muslim restaurant next to the mosque on Th Itsaraphap dishes up delicious Thai-Muslim favourites, including *kôw nòk gài*, the Thai version of chicken biryani.

our pick Loong It (Local Food; Th Wat Phranorn; dishes 40-60B; 🕙 8am-3pm) To eat like a local, look no further than this rustic but delicious northern-style food shack. There's an English-language menu on the wall, but don't miss the sublime *làhp gài*, minced chicken fried with herbs and topped with crispy deep-fried shallots and garlic. The restaurant is on Th Phranorn near the intersection with the Superhighway; look for a sign that says 'Local Food'.

Cham Cha (Th Singkhlai; dishes 35-100B; 🕙 7am-4pm Mon-Sat) This casual little hole-in-the-wall is good for breakfast or lunch. It has all the usual Thai and Chinese dishes, along with a few Isan dishes that are not on the English menu, such as *lâhp* (spicy minced-meat salad) and *sôm·đam* (spicy green papaya salad), plus ice cream.

Nakhon Pathom (no roman-script sign; Th Phahonyothin; dishes 40-60B; 🕙 8am-3pm) Named after a central-Thailand city, Nakhon Pathom is very popular for inexpensive *kôw man gài* (chicken rice) and *gŏo·ay đĕe·o ʾbèt yâhng* (roast duck with rice noodles).

Old Dutch (541 Th Phahonyothin; dishes 50-1000B; 🕙 8am-midnight) This cosy, foreigner-friendly restaurant is a good choice for those not quite ready for the city's more authentic Thai offerings. A variety of cuisines are available, not to mention exceedingly cheap draught beer.

Phu-Lae (☎ 0 5360 0500; 612/6 Th Phahonyothin; dishes 60-150B; 🕙 lunch & dinner) This air-conditioned restaurant is exceedingly popular among Thai tourists for its yummy northern Thai dishes. Oddly, this is the only section of the extensive menu that hasn't been translated into English, but you can still point-and-choose from the glass case out front. Recommended local dishes include the *gaang hang·lair*, pork belly in a rich Burmese-style curry, here served with pickled garlic, and *saï òo·a*, herb-packed sausages.

Da Vinci (☎ 0 5375 2535; 879/4-5 Th Phahonyothin; mains 125-300B; 🕙 noon-11pm) This slightly pricey, smart restaurant serves a variety of Italian dishes, but most come for the pizzas fired in a wood-burning oven.

Drinking & Entertainment

Th Jet Yot is the liveliest area for bars. A dodgy girly bar centre is at the end of Th Jet Yot on an L-shaped lane that leads to Th Banphaprakan.

Teepee Bar (Th Phahonyothin; 🕙 6.30pm-midnight) A hang-out for backpackers and Thai hippies, the Teepee is a good place to exchange information.

Cat Bar (1013/1 Th Jet Yot; 🕙 5pm-1am) Kind service, the coldest beer we've encountered in Thailand, and a Bob Dylan soundtrack make this the best among the strip of bars

CAFE CULTURE, CHIANG RAI STYLE

For such a relatively small town, Chiang Rai has an abundance of high-quality, Western-style cafes. This is largely due to the fact that many of Thailand's best coffee beans are grown in the more remote corners of the province. Some of the more interesting choices include the following.

■ **BaanChivitMai Bakery** (☎ 08 1764 7020; www.baanchivitmai.com; Th Prasopsuk; ⌚ 7am-9pm Mon-Sat, 2-9pm Sun) In addition to a very well prepared cup of local joe, you can snack on amazingly authentic Swedish-style sweets at this popular bakery. Profits go to BaanChivit-Mai, an organisation that runs homes and education projects for vulnerable, orphaned or AIDS-affected children.

■ **Doi Chaang@Art** (☎ 0 5375 2918; 542/2 Th Rattanakhet; ⌚ 7am-10pm) Doi Chaang is the leading brand among Chiang Rai coffees, and its beans are now sold as far abroad as Canada and Europe. In addition to sublime coffee, tasty sweets are available, and located next door is Doi Soong Cha, a small tea-tasting gallery featuring Chinese-style teas also grown in Chiang Rai.

■ **Wawee Coffee** (cnr Th Singkhlai & Th Si Koet; ⌚ 7am-10pm) Another local brand done well, this expansive, modern cafe serves a variety of creative coffee drinks using Chiang Rai beans. Between sips you can check your email on one of the widescreen iMacs, or read a paper that you can buy from the attached newsstand.

along Th Jet Yot. There's also a pool table and live music nightly at 10.30pm.

Easy House (☎ 0 5360 0963; Th Premaviphat; ⌚ 11am-midnight) On the corner of Th Jet Yot and Th Premaviphat, the ground floor of this backpacker hostel serves beer and food on chunky wooden tables and chairs.

Centre Point Night Bazaar (off Th Phahonyothin) Free northern Thai music and ladyboy dance performances are staged nightly.

Shopping

Adjacent to the bus station off Th Phahonyothin is Chiang Rai's **night market** (⌚ 6-11pm). On a much smaller scale than Chiang Mai's, it is nevertheless a decent place to find an assortment of handicrafts. On entering the night market from Th Phahonyothin you'll see **mz collection** (☎ 0 5375 0145; www.mzcollection.net; 426/68 Kok Kalair) on the right-hand side. This shop has unusual handmade silver and semiprecious stone jewellery. Each piece is unique so don't expect bargain basement prices.

If you're around on a Saturday evening be sure not to miss the **Kaat Jiang Hai Ramleuk** (⌚ 4-10pm), an expansive street market focusing on all things Chiang Rai, from handicrafts to local dishes. The market spans Th Thanalai from the Hilltribe Museum to the morning market.

Getting There & Away

AIR

Chiang Rai Airport (☎ 0 5379 8000) is 8km north of the city. Taxis run into town from the airport for 200B. Out to the airport you can get a túk-túk for approximately 250B. The terminal has restaurants, a money exchange, a post office (open 7am to 7pm) and car-rental booths.

In town, **Air Agent** (☎ 0 5374 0445; 863/3 Th Phahonyothin; ⌚ 8am-10pm) can book domestic and international flights in advance. Alternatively, book online or go directly to the websites or airport offices listed below.

Air Asia (☎ 0 5379 3545/8275; www.airasia.com; Chiang Rai Airport) Flies between Bangkok and Chiang Rai (from 1800B, 1¼ hours, three times daily).

Nok Air (☎ nationwide call centre 1318; www.nokair .co.th; Chiang Rai Airport) With its subsidiary **SGA Airlines** (☎ 0 5379 8244; www.sga.co.th), operates propeller-powered flights between Chiang Rai and Chiang Mai (from 1690B, 40 minutes, twice daily).

One-Two-Go (☎ nationwide call centre 1126; www .fly12go.com; Chiang Rai Airport) Flies between Bangkok's Don Muang airport and Chiang Rai (from 2100B, 1¼ hours, once daily).

THAI city centre (☎ 0 5371 1179; www.thaiair.com; 870 Th Phahonyothin; ⌚ 8am-5pm Mon-Fri); airport office (☎ 0 5379 8202/3; ⌚ 8am-8pm) Flights to/from Bangkok (3745B, 1¼ hours, three times daily).

BOAT

Another way to reach Chiang Rai is by boat on Mae Nam Kok from Tha Ton (see p330).

For boats heading upriver, go to **CR Pier** (☎ 0 5375 0009) in the northwest corner of town. Passenger boats embark daily at 10.30am, otherwise you can charter an entire boat to Ban Ruammit for 700B or all the way to Tha Ton for 2500B at the pier.

BUS

Chiang Rai's bus terminal is in the centre of town. The **Green Bus** (☎ 114 ext 8000; www.green busthailand.com) desk offers several useful lines, including hourly departures for Chiang Mai and Chiang Khong. To Bangkok, **Sombat Tour** (☎ 0 5371 4971; Th Prasopsuk) has an office across from the bus terminal.

Check the table on p358 for information on bus fares and journeys duration from Chiang Rai.

Getting Around

A sǎhm·lór (three-wheeled pedicab) ride anywhere in central Chiang Rai should cost around 40B. Túk-túk often charge twice that. Shared sǒrng·tǎa·ou cost 15B per person.

Bicycles rental can be arranged at **Fat Free** (☎ 0 5375 2532; 542/2 Th Banphaprakan; per day city/mountain bike 80/250B; ⏰ 9am-8pm). Motorcycles can be hired at **ST Motorcycle** (☎ 0 5371 3652; Th Banphaprakan; per day Yamaha TTR motorcycles less than 115cc 150-300B, less than 250cc 700-1000B; ⏰ 8am-6pm), which has another outlet on Th Wat Jet Yot – they take good care of their bikes. Many guesthouses also rent out motorcycles and bikes.

Several small agencies near the night market rent out a variety of cars (800B to 1200B a day), with and without driver.

The following companies have good reputations but charge a little more.

Avis Rent-A-Car (☎ 0 5379 3827; www.avisthailand .com; Chiang Rai Airport)

Budget Rent-A-Car (☎ 0 5374 0442/3; www.budget .co.th; 590 Th Phahonyothin) At Golden Triangle Inn.

National Car Rental (☎ 0 5379 3683; Chiang Rai Airport)

North Wheels (☎ 0 5374 0585; www.northwheels .com; 591 Th Phahonyothin; ⏰ 8am-7pm)

AROUND CHIANG RAI

WAT RONG KHUN
วัดร่องขุ่น

Thirteen kilometres south of Chiang Rai is the unusual and popular **Wat Rong Khun** (☎ 0 5367 3579), aka the 'White Wat'. Whereas most temples have centuries of history, this one's construction began in 1997 by noted Thai painter-turned-architect Chalermchai Kositpipat.

Seen from a distance, the temple appears to be made of glittering porcelain; a closer look reveals that the look is due to a combination of whitewash and clear-mirrored chips. Walk over a bridge and sculpture of reaching arms (symbolising desire) to enter the sanctity of the wát where instead of the traditional Buddha life scenarios, the artist has painted contemporary scenes representing samsara (the realm of rebirth and delusion). Images such as a plane smashing into the Twin Towers and, oddly enough, Keanu Reeves as Neo from *The Matrix*, dominate the one finished wall of this work in progress. If you like what you see, an adjacent gallery sells reproductions of Chalermchai Kositpipat's rather New Age–looking works.

To get to the temple, hop on one of the regular buses that run from Chiang Rai to Chiang Mai and ask to get off at Wat Rong Khun (15B).

NORTHERN THAILAND TO YUNNAN, CHINA

If you're in Chiang Rai Province and have already arranged a visa for visiting China, there are a couple of ways to travel from Thailand to China's Yunnan Province, a route that ties together the Golden Triangle and Yunnan's Xishuangbanna district (called Sipsongpanna in Thailand) in southwest China. The Thai, Shan and Lao people all consider Xishuangbanna to be a cultural homeland.

The Mekong River is the most direct way. It is possible to take a passenger boat from Chiang Saen in Thailand directly to Jinghong in China, a trip of about 15 hours when the water is high enough. For details see p369.

It's also relatively straightforward to travel via Laos. From Chiang Khong, cross the Mekong River to the Lao town of Huay Xai, where you can board one of three weekly buses that go directly to the Xishuangbanna town of Mengla via the Lao border town of Boten. From Mengla it's then a four-hour bus ride to Jinghong, the capital of Xishuangbanna district, or an overnight bus ride to Kunming. For details see p375.

From Mae Sai, also in Chiang Rai, it was previously possible to go to China via Mong La, in Myanmar, but this border has been closed since 2005.

BUSES FROM CHIANG RAI

Destination	Bus	Fare (B)	Duration (hr)	Destination	Bus	Fare (B)	Duration (hr)
Bangkok	air-con	546	12	Khorat	air-con	508	13
	1st class	706	11		1st class	653	12
	VIP	733-1035	11		VIP	767	12
Ban Huay Khrai (for Doi Tung)	ordinary	28	¾	Lampang	air-con	162	5
				Mae Sai	ordinary	39	1½
Basang	ordinary	20	¾	Mae Sot	air-con	270	12
Chiang Khong	ordinary	70	2		1st class	347	12
Chiang Mai	ordinary	106	4	Nan	air-con	188	6
	1st class	191	3	Phayao	ordinary	49	2
	VIP	295	3		air-con	69	1½
Chiang Saen	ordinary	38	1½		1st class	88	1½
Fang	ordinary	95	2½	Phitsanulok	1st class	367	7
Khon Kaen	air-con	462	12		VIP	428	7
	1st class	594	12	Phrae	1st class	218	4

MAE SALONG (SANTIKHIRI)

แม่สลอง(สันติคีรี)

pop 25,428

For a taste of China without crossing any international borders, head to this atmospheric village perched on the back hills of Chiang Rai. Although Mae Salong is now thoroughly on the beaten track, its hilltop setting, Chinese residents, and abundance of hill tribes and tea plantations converge in a unique destination not unlike a small town in southern China's Yunnan Province. It's a great place to kick back for a couple of days, and the surrounding area is ripe for exploration.

For an explanation of the town's unusual ethnic background, see boxed text, p360.

Information

There is an ATM at the Thai Military Bank opposite Khumnaiphol Resort.

Sights

A tiny but interesting **morning market** convenes from 6am to 8am at the T-intersection near Shin Sane Guest House. The market attracts town residents and tribespeople from the surrounding districts. An **all-day market** forms at the southern end of town, and unites vendors selling hill-tribe handicrafts, shops selling tea and a few basic restaurants.

To soak up the great views from **Wat Santakhiri** go past the market and ascend 718 steps (or drive if you have a car). The wát is of the Mahayana tradition and Chinese in style.

Past the Khumnaiphol Resort and further up the hill is a **viewpoint** with some teashops and a famous Kuomintang (KMT) general's **tomb**. It is sometimes guarded by a soldier who will describe (in Thai or Yunnanese) the history of the KMT in the area. In the same vein and south of the turn-off to the tomb is the **Chinese Martyr's Memorial Museum**, an elaborate Chinese-style building that is more memorial than museum.

Across from Mae Salong Villa at the north end of town is the **Agro Tourism Guide Center**, a source of local information that unfortunately appears to only sporadically open, generally during the tourist season (November to January).

Trekking

Shin Sane Guest House has a free map showing approximate routes to Akha, Lisu, Mien, Lahu and Shan villages in the area. Nearby Akha and Lisu villages are less than half a day's walk away.

The best hikes are north of Mae Salong between Ban Thoet Thai and the Myanmar border. Ask first about political conditions before heading off in this direction; Shan and Wa armies competing for control over this section of the Thailand–Myanmar border do occasionally clash in the area. A steady trade in methamphetamine and, to a lesser extent, heroin, flows across the border via several conduit villages.

Shin Sane Guest House (opposite) arranges four-hour **horseback treks** to four nearby vil lages for 500B per day. You could also trek the 4km to an Akha village on your own. A basic guesthouse there offers rooms and meals.

Sleeping

Since the road from Mae Salong to Tha Ton opened, fewer visitors are opting to stay overnight in Mae Salong. The resulting surplus of accommodation often makes prices negotiable, except during the high season (November to January).

Shin Sane Guest House (☎ 0 5376 5026; 32/3 Th Mae Salong; s/d from 50/100B, bungalows 300B; 💻) Although Mae Salong's first hotel is starting to show its 40 years, it still remains an atmospheric place to stay. The rooms are bare but spacious with shared bathrooms. The bungalows are much more comfortable and have private bathrooms and cable TV. Trekking details are available, including a good map, and there are motorcycles for rent.

ourpick **Little Home Guesthouse** (☎ 0 5376 5389; www.maesalonglittlehome.com; 31 Moo 1, Th Mae Salong; s/d from 50/100B, bungalows 600B; 💻) Located next door to Shin Sane, this delightful wooden house holds a few basic but cosy rooms and a handful of sparkling new bungalows out back. An attached restaurant does local dishes. The owner is extremely friendly and has put together one of the more accurate maps of the area.

Saeng A Roon Hotel (☎ 0 5376 5029; 25/3 Moo 1, Th Mae Salong; r 300-500B; 💥 💻) Next to the teashop of the same name, this new hotel has friendly staff, spacious tiled-floor rooms and great views of the hills. The cheaper rooms share spick-and-span hot-water bathrooms.

Mae Salong Central Hills Hotel (☎ 0 5376 5113; 18/1 Moo 1, Th Mae Salong; r 500B) Situated directly across from the 7-Eleven, this large hotel offers two floors of characterless but comfortable rooms. There's a restaurant upstairs (open primarily during the tourist season) and a teashop on the premises.

Maesalong Mountain Home (☎ 08 4611 9508; www.maesalongmountainhome.com; bungalows 800-1500B) Located down a dirt road 1km east of the town centre (signs say 'Maesalong Farmstay'), this is a great choice if you've got your own wheels. The nine new bungalows here are located in the middle of a working farm and are bright and airy, with huge bathrooms. Another bonus is its location near a tea farm with

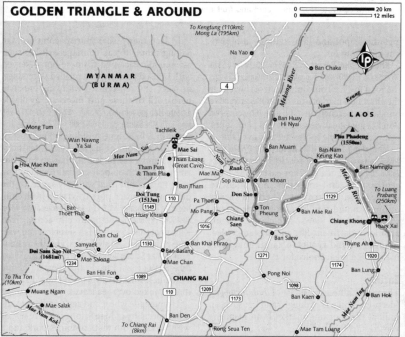

HOME AWAY FROM HOME

Mae Salong was originally settled by the 93rd Regiment of the Kuomintang (KMT), who'd fled to Myanmar from China after the 1949 Chinese revolution. The renegades were forced to leave Myanmar in 1961 when the Yangon government decided it wouldn't allow the KMT to remain legally in northern Myanmar. Crossing into northern Thailand with their pony caravans, the ex-soldiers and their families settled into mountain villages and re-created a society like the one they'd left behind in Yunnan.

After the Thai government granted the KMT refugee status in the 1960s, efforts were made to incorporate the Yunnanese KMT and their families into the Thai nation. Until the late 1980s they didn't have much success. Many ex-KMT persisted in involving themselves in the Golden Triangle opium trade in a three-way partnership with opium warlord Khun Sa and the Shan United Army (SUA). Because of the rough, mountainous terrain and lack of sealed roads, the outside world was rather cut off from the goings-on in Mae Salong, so the Yunnanese were able to ignore attempts by the Thai authorities to suppress opium activity and tame the region.

Infamous Khun Sa made his home in nearby Ban Hin Taek (now Ban Thoet Thai; opposite) until the early 1980s when he was finally routed by the Thai military. Khun Sa's retreat to Myanmar seemed to signal a change in local attitudes and the Thai government finally began making progress in its pacification of Mae Salong and the surrounding area.

In a further effort to separate the area from its old image as an opium fiefdom, the Thai government officially changed the name of the village from Mae Salong to Santikhiri (Hill of Peace). Until the 1980s packhorses were used to move goods up the mountain to Mae Salong, but today the 36km road from Basang (near Mae Chan) is paved and well travelled. But despite the advances in infrastructure, the town is unlike any other in Thailand. The Yunnanese dialect of Chinese still remains the lingua franca, residents tend to watch Chinese, rather than Thai, TV, and you'll find more Chinese than Thai food.

In an attempt to quash opium activity, and the more recent threat of *yah bâh* (methamphetamine) trafficking, the Thai government has created crop-substitution programs to encourage hill tribes to cultivate tea, coffee, corn and fruit trees.

gigantic teapot and lion statues – a bizarre but fun photo op.

Khumnaiphol Resort (☎ 0 5376 5001/4; fax 0 5376 5004; 58 Mu 1; r 600-900B, bungalows 1200-4000B; ⚹) On the road to Tha Ton, 1km south of town near the afternoon market, this resort has attractive bungalows perched on a hillside. The covered porches give great views of the tea plantations below. Hotel-style rooms are also available.

Maesalong Flower Hills Resort (☎ 0 5376 5496; www.maesalongflowerhills.com; r 1500B, bungalows 2000-2500B; ⚹ ⚛) Located 2km east of the town centre, you can't miss this monument to flower-based landscaping. There's a variety of modern and tidy bungalow-style rooms, some with great views. The cheaper rooms are more apartment-like and are fan-cooled. A huge pool and a couple of larger bungalows make this a great choice for families.

Eating

The very Chinese breakfast of *ฺbah·tôrng·gŏh* (deep-fried fingers of dough) and hot soybean milk at the morning market is an inspiring way to start the day.

In fact, many Thai tourists come to Mae Salong simply to eat Yunnanese dishes such as *màn·tŏh* (steamed Chinese buns) served with braised pork leg and pickled vegetables, or black chicken braised with Chinese-style herbs. All of these and more are available at **Sue Hai** (no roman-script sign; ☎ 08 9429 4212; 288 Moo 1, Th Mae Salong; dishes 60-150B; ☯ 7am-9pm), located in a light blue building 100m west of Sweet Maesalong. This family-run teashop-cum–Yunnanese restaurant has an English-language menu of local specialities including local mushroom fried with soy sauce, or the delicious air-dried pork fried with fresh chili. **Nong Im Phochana** (☎ 0 5376 5309; Th Mae Salong; dishes 60-150B; ☯ lunch & dinner), directly across from Khumnaiphol Resort, has a similar menu with an emphasis on local veggies, and the restaurant at **Mae Salong Villa** (☎ 0 5376 5114; Th Mae Salong; dishes 60-150) is said to do the most authentic Yunnanese food in town, including a delicious duck smoked over tea leaves.

Homemade wheat and egg noodles are another speciality of Mae Salong, and are served with a local broth that combines pork and a spicy chili paste. They're available at several places in town.

Countless teahouses sell locally grown teas (mostly oolong and jasmine) and offer complimentary tastings. If you require a considerably higher degree of caffeine, stop by **Sweet Maesalong** (☎ 08 1855 4000; 41/3 Moo 1, Th Mae Salong; dishes 45-90B; ☽ 8am-8pm) a cosy modern cafe with an extensive menu of coffee drinks using local beans. Baked snacks and simple dishes are also available.

Getting There & Away

Mae Salong is accessible via two routes. The original road, Rte 1130, winds west from Ban Basang. Newer Rte 1234 approaches from the south, allowing easier access from Chiang Mai. The older route is more spectacular.

To get to Mae Salong by bus, take a Mae Sai bus from Chiang Rai to Ban Basang (20B, 30 minutes, every 15 minutes from 6am to 4pm). From Ban Basang, *sŏrng·tăa·ou* head up the mountain to Mae Salong (60B, one hour). To get back to Basang, *sŏrng·tăa·ou* park near the 7-Eleven. *Sŏrng·tăa·ou* stop running at around 5pm but you can charter one in either direction for about 500B.

You can also reach Mae Salong by road from Tha Ton (see p330).

BAN THOET THAI & AROUND

บ้านเทิดไทย

Those with an interest in Khun Sa history (see boxed text, opposite) can make a side trip to this Yunnanese-Shan village, formerly known as Ban Hin Taek (Broken Stone Village), 12km off the road between Ban Basang and Mae Salong.

Today, many of Ban Thoet Thai's 3000 residents – a mix of Shan, Yunnanese, Akha, Lisu and Hmong – claim to have fond memories of the man once hunted (but never captured) by heroin-consuming countries. The warlord's former camp headquarters, a simple collection of wood and brick buildings on a hillside overlooking the village, has been turned into a free rustic **museum**. There are no set opening hours, and admission is free so you simply have to turn up and ask one of the caretakers to open the exhibition room for you.

Inside, the walls are hung with maps of the Shan states and Mong Tai (the name the Shan use for the independent nation they hope to establish in the future) homelands, a photograph of the former Kengtung (East Shan

State) palace and a few political posters. It's not much considering Khun Sa's six years (1976–82) in the area and, of course, there is no mention of opium.

A busy **morning market**, part of which was once used to store the Shan United Army arsenal, trades in products from Thailand, Myanmar and China. Khun Sa was also responsible for the construction of **Wat Phra That Ka Kham**, a Shan-style monastery near his former camp.

Accommodation and food are available at **Rimtaan Guest House** (☎ 0 5373 0209; 15 Moo 1, Thoet Thai; r 300-800B), a collection of tidy bungalows set in a garden near a rushing stream.

If you're in the area in mid-November/December and have your own transport, it's worth continuing the 30km toward the Myanmar border to **Hua Mae Kham**, a picturesque hillside village where *dòrk booa torng*, a local flower, blooms in abundance. Along the way you'll pass hill tribe villages and rice fields in stream-fed mountain valleys.

MAE SAI

แม่สาย

pop 21,816

At first glance, Thailand's northernmost town, Mae Sai, appears to be little more than a large open-air market. But the city can be used as a starting point for exploring the Golden Triangle, Doi Tung and Mae Salong, and its position across from Myanmar also makes it a stepping off point for those wishing to explore some of the more remote parts of Shan State.

Because occasional fighting within Myanmar or disputes between the Thai and Myanmar governments can lead to the border being closed temporarily, it's always a good idea to check the current situation before travelling to Mae Sai.

Information

Immigration (☎ 0 5373 3261; ☽ 6.30am-6.30pm) At the entrance to the border bridge.

Internet Café (per hr 40B) Behind the Wang Thong Hotel by its car park.

Nino House (☎ 08 6911 4964; Soi 2, Th Phahonyothin; ☽ 9am-10pm) Located just off Soi 2, this cafe/restaurant has free wi-fi if you have your own laptop.

Overbrook Clinic (☎ 0 5373 4422; 20/7 Th Phahonyothin; ☽ 9am-3pm) Connected to the modern hospital in Chiang Rai, this small clinic on the main road has doctors who can speak English.

Tourist police (☎ 115) They have a booth in front of the border crossing before immigration.

NORTHERN THAILAND

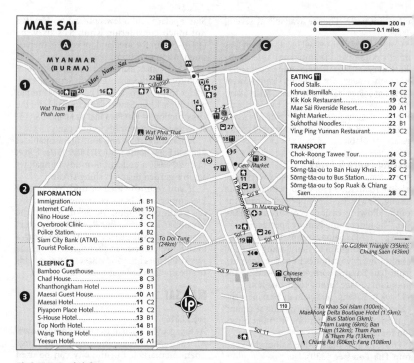

MAE SAI

Sights & Activities

Take the steps up the hill near the border to **Wat Phra That Doi Wao**, west of the main street, for superb views over Mae Sai and Myanmar. This wát was reportedly constructed in memory of a couple of thousand Burmese soldiers who died fighting the KMT here in 1965 (you'll hear differing stories around town, including a version wherein the KMT are the heroes).

Sleeping

BUDGET & MIDRANGE

Chad House (☎ 0 5373 2054; off Soi 11, Th Phahonyothin; d 80-120B, bungalows 250B) The rooms here are about as basic as it gets, but it's a friendly, comfortable choice if you're on a budget. There are a couple of bungalows with private cold-water bathrooms. Look for the sign on the left when coming into town.

Bamboo Guesthouse (☎ 08 6916 1895; 135/3 Th Sailomjoi; r 150-200B) The rooms here are truly basic, but cool and comfortable. Cheaper rooms have shared bathrooms, and some rooms are decorated with giant Burmese-themed posters.

Maesai Hotel (☎ 0 5373 1462; 125/5 Th Phahonyothir r with fan/AC 250/400B) Located in a green buildin, just off Th Phahonyothin, fan rooms here are decent value and have beds on an elevated concrete pedestal. More expensive air-co rooms have flimsy beds and cheap furniture

Yeesun Hotel (☎ 0 5373 3455; 816/13 Th Sailomjoi r 400B; 🕸) This four-storey family-run hote has great value if rather characterless rooms Rooms are large and include comfortable fur niture and beds.

Maesai Guest House (☎ 0 5373 2021; 688 T Wiengpangkam; bungalows s 200-300B, d 400-600B Located at the end of the narrow lane tha stretches behind Mai Sai Riverside Resort this collection of A-frame bungalows range from simple rooms with shared cold wate showers, to bungalows on the river with ter races and private bathrooms. There is a riv erside restaurant on site serving Thai and Western dishes.

Top North Hotel (☎ 0 5373 1955; 306 Th Phahonyothin d 400-600B, tr 900B; 🕸 🖵) A five-minute walk to the bridge to Myanmar, this older hotel ha spacious rooms and friendly staff. Some o the rooms look newer than others and have

NORTHERN THAILAND

cable TV; choose the ones at the back of the building to avoid street noise.

S-House Hotel (☎ 0 5373 3811; s_house43234@yahoo .com; 384 Th Sailomjoi; r 500-600B; ✷) At the end of the covered part of Th Sailomjoi, away from the border crossing, this hotel has spacious rooms with balconies overlooking the hills.

our pick **Khanthongkham Hotel** (☎ 0 5373 4222; 7 Th Phahonyothin; r 950B, ste 1190-1390B; ✷) This brand new hotel features huge rooms that have been tastefully decorated in light woods and brown textiles. Suites are exceptionally vast, and like all rooms, also have flat-screen TVs and truly user-friendly–looking bathrooms. A downside is that many rooms don't have windows.

Maekhong Delta Boutique Hotel (☎ 0 5364 2517; www.maekhongtravel.com; 230/5-6 Th Phahonyothin; r 900-1500B; ✷) It's an odd name, considering that the Mekong delta is way down in Vietnam. Odder too that the rooms here are somehow reminiscent of a ski lodge. Regardless, the rooms are both cosy and comfortable, albeit a bit far from the centre of town. Popular with groups, a full-scale travel agency is located next door.

Piyaporn Place Hotel (☎ 0 5373 4511-3; www.piya porn-place.com; 77/1 Th Phahonyothin; r 1000B; ✷ 🖳) On the main road by Soi 7, this seven-storey hotel is good value. The large, contemporary-styled rooms have wooden floors, a small sofa and the usual four/five-star amenities like bath, cable TV and minibar. There is a conference room and a smart, stylish restaurant serving Thai and European food.

Wang Thong Hotel (☎ 053733389-95; www.wangthong -maesai.com; 299 Th Phahonyothin; r 1200B, ste 4500B; ✷ 🖳 🖳) The nine-storey Wang Thong is a comfortable choice and great for its convenient location by the border crossing. The rooms are nothing special but they're spacious and come with amenities you'd expect at this price. In addition to the pool there is a pub, disco and a popular restaurant. Discounts are available in low season.

Eating

A decent night market unfolds every evening along Th Phahonyothin.

Khao Soi Islam (no roman-script sign; ☎ 0 5373 3026; 140 Th Phahonyothin; dishes 25-30B; ✷ 7am-5pm) This friendly Muslim restaurant serves the usual beef and chicken versions of the eponymous noodle dish; for something a bit different try ba̓h·ba̓h soy, kôw soy served with thick noodles made from brown rice. They do sev-

eral other Muslim dishes as well, and dining entertainment involves listening to the staff converse in a mixture of Chinese, northern Thai, central Thai and Burmese.

Khrua Bismillah (no roman-script sign; ☎ 08 1530 8198; Soi 4, Th Phahonyothin; dishes 25-40B; ✷ 6am-6pm) Run by Burmese Muslims, this tiny restaurant does an excellent biryani, not to mention virtually everything else Muslim, from roti to samosa. There's no English sign, simply look for the green halal sign.

Sukhothai Noodles (no roman-script sign; ☎ 08 1530 1997; 399/9 Th Sailomjoi; dishes 30-40B; ✷ 7am-2pm) This open-air restaurant serves the namesake noodles from Sukhothai, as well as satay and a few other basic dishes. A picture menu shows the varieties of noodles available, and the pictures on the wall are of the owner's daughter. Look for the busy pink restaurant opposite S-House Hotel.

Kik Kok Restaurant (Th Phahonyothin; dishes 30-120B; ✷ 6am-8pm) This restaurant prepares a huge selection of Thai dishes and has an English menu. It's a good dinner option if you'd rather not eat on the street.

Mae Sai Riverside Resort (☎ 0 5373 2630; Th Wiengpangkam; dishes 40-139B) Recommended for its Thai dishes, like the tasty lemon-grass fried fish, this restaurant has a great location looking out over the river to Myanmar.

Ying Ping Yunnan Restaurant (☎ 0 5373 2213; 132/3 Soi 6, Th Phahonyothin; dishes 100-300B) For a special night out, head to this banquet-style Chinese restaurant. The menu here features a variety of exotic-sounding dishes you're unlikely to find elsewhere, as well as humble Yunnan-style noodle soup.

Shopping

Commerce is ubiquitous in Mae Sai, although most of the offerings are of little interest to travellers. One interesting commodity is gems, and dealers from as far away as Chanthaburi frequent the gem market that is opposite the police station. A walk down Soi 6 will reveal several open-air gem dealers diligently counting hundreds of tiny semi-precious stones on the side of the street.

Getting There & Away

On the main Th Phahonyothin road, by Soi 8, is a sign saying 'bus stop'. From here sörng·tăa·ou run to Sop Ruak (45B, every 40 minutes from 9am to 2pm), terminating in Chiang Saen (50B).

For Doi Tung take one of the *sŏrng·tăa·ou* that park by Soi 10 to Ban Huay Khrai (25B), then another *sŏrng·tăa·ou* to Doi Tung (60B, one hour).

Mae Sai's government **bus station** (☎ 0 5364 437) is 4km south of the frontier immigration office, or a 15B shared *sŏrng·tăa·ou* ride from the corner of Th Phahonyothin and Soi 2.

There are numerous buses to Chiang Rai (ordinary 38B, 1½ hours, 5.45am to 6pm). Hop on any of these buses for Mae Chan (30B, 30 minutes).

There are buses to Chiang Mai (1st class air-con/VIP 241/375B, four to five hours) with 1st-class departures at 6.45am, 9.45am and 2.30pm, and VIP departures at 8.15am and 3.30pm; as well as a direct bus from Mae Sai to Fang (91B, two hours, 7am), one to Tha Ton (51B, 1½ hours, 7am), and two to Mae Sot (2nd-class air-con/1st class 442/569B, 12 hours, 6.15am and 6.45am).

Further abroad, there are buses to Nakhon Ratchasima (2nd class air-con/1st class/VIP 582/749/874B, 15 hours, six times daily) and Bangkok (2nd class air-con/1st class/VIP 554/713/1105B, 13 hours, from 4pm to 5.45pm).

Chok-Roong Tawee Tour (no roman-script sign; ☎ 0 5364 0123) For the same prices as at the bus station you can buy tickets in advance here. There is no sign in English so look for the large red 'International Telephone' sign.

Getting Around

Sŏrng·tăa·ou around town are 15B shared. Motorcycle taxis cost 20B to 30B.

Honda Dreams can be rented at **Pornchai** (☎ 0 5373 1136; 4/7 Th Phahonyothin) for 150B a day.

AROUND MAE SAI
Caves

There are a few interesting cave networks just south of Mae Sai. **Tham Luang**, 6km south of Mae Sai off Rte 110, extends into the hills for at least a couple of kilometres, possibly more. The first kilometre is fairly easy-going, but after that you have to do some climbing over piles of rocks to get further in. At this point the roof formations become more fantastic and tiny crystals make them change colour according to the angle of the light. For 40B you can borrow a gas lantern from the caretakers in front of the cave or you can take someone along as a guide (for which there's no fixed

fee; just give them whatever you feel they deserve). Apparently, guides sometimes have better things to do during the week. Charter a *sŏrng·tăa·ou* or rent a bike in Mae Sai to get to Tham Luang.

Another 7km south, at Ban Tham, **Tham Pum** and **Tham Pla** have freshwater lakes inside. Bring a torch to explore the caves as there are no lights. Another attraction here is the unique cakelike *chedi* in front of the cave entrance. It's a very large, multitiered structure stylistically different from any other in Thailand.

There is a police checkpoint at Ban Tham so bring some ID. To get to any of these caves rent a motorbike or charter a *sŏrng·tăa·ou* to the turn-off on Rte 110 at Ban Tham; from there it is a 1km walk down to the caves.

Doi Tung & Around
ดอยตุ๋ง

About halfway between Mae Chan and Mae Sai on Rte 110 is the turn-off (west) for **Doi Tung**. The name means 'Flag Peak', from the northern Thai word for flag (*đung*). King Achutarat of Chiang Saen ordered a giant flag to be flown from the peak to mark the spot where two *chedi* were constructed in AD 911; the *chedi* are still there, a pilgrimage site for Thai, Shan and Chinese Buddhists.

But the main attraction at Doi Tung is getting there. The 'easy' way is via Rte 1149 which is mostly paved to the peak of Doi Tung. But it's winding, steep and narrow so if you're driving or riding a motorcycle take it slowly.

On the theory that local hill tribes would be so honoured by a royal presence that they would stop cultivating opium, the late Princess Mother (the king's mother) built the **Doi Tung Royal Villa** (☎ 0 5376 7011; www.doitung .org; admission 70B; ☉ 6.30am-5pm), a summer palace on the slopes of Doi Tung near Pa Klua Reservoir, which is now open to the public as a museum. The royal initiative also provided education on new agricultural methods to stop slash and burn practices. Opium has now been replaced by crops such as coffee, macadamia nuts and various fruits. The rest of the property including the **Mae Fah Luang Garden** and **Mae Fah Luang Arboretum** (admission 80B; ☉ 7am-5pm), is also open to the public. There is also a top-end hotel (see opposite), a restaurant, coffee kiosk and Doi Tung craft shop up here. Near the parking lot, the **Doi Tung Bazaar** is a small open-air market with local agricultural products, prepared food and hill-tribe handicrafts. This entire complex is popular with bus tour groups.

At the peak, 1800m above sea level, **Wat Phra That Doi Tung** is built around the twin Lanna-style *chedi*. The *chedi* were renovated by Chiang Mai monk Khruba Siwichai, famous for his prodigious building projects, early in the 20th century. Pilgrims bang on the usual row of temple bells to gain merit. Although the wát isn't that impressive, the forested setting will make the trip worthwhile. From the walled edge of the temple you can get an aerial view of the snaky road you've just climbed. A walking path next to the wát leads to a spring and there are other short walking trails in the vicinity.

A bit below the peak is the smaller **Wat Noi Doi Tung**, where food and beverages are available from vendors.

SLEEPING & EATING

If you want to spend the night, **Ban Ton Nam 31** (☎ 0 5376 7003; www.doitung.org; Doi Tung Development Project, Mae Fah Luang District; r incl breakfast 2500-3000B; ✷ 🖳) consists of 46 comfortable rooms that formerly served as the living quarters of the Princess Mother's staff. The more expensive rooms have better views. A self-service **restaurant** (dishes 80-250B; ✷ 7am-9pm) offers meals made with local produce, and there's also a Doi Tung cafe.

GETTING THERE & AWAY

Buses from Mae Chan or Mae Sai (15B) and *sŏrng·tăa·ou* from Mae Sai (25B) go to Ban Huay Khrai, the turn-off for Doi Tung. From there *sŏrng·tăa·ou* are available to Doi Tung (60B, one hour).

Alternatively, if you've got your own wheels, you can travel between Doi Tung and Mae Sai along an even more challenging, 24km, sealed but narrow and windy road. From Doi Tung Royal Villa simply follow the signs to Wat Phrathat Doi Tung. The road hugs the Thai-Burma border behind the large limestone mountains you may have seen from Rte 110, and emerges at Soi 7 in Mae Sai. There are at least three military checkpoints along the way, so be sure to bring ID.

If you want to do a full loop from Mae Sai, ride/drive via Rte 110 south of Mae Sai, then Rte 1149 up to Doi Tung. Once you've had a look around the summit, return to Mae Sai via aforementioned roads; this means you'll be travelling downhill much of the way.

If you're coming from Mae Salong, Rte 1338 weaves from steep hills to a lush valley, before climbing again to Rte 1149 and Doi Tung. The road is fully sealed and in good shape, although it can be quite steep and windy in parts.

Cross-Border Trips to Tachileik & Beyond

Foreigners are ordinarily permitted to cross the bridge over the Nam Sai into Tachileik. On occasion the border may close temporarily for security reasons, so be prepared for possible disappointment if the political situation between Thailand and Myanmar deteriorates again.

The Thai immigration office is officially open from 6.30am to 6.30pm. After taking care of the usual formalities, cross the bridge and head to the Myanmar immigration office. Here you pay $10 or 500B and your picture is taken for a temporary ID card that allows you to stay in town for 14 days; your passport will be kept at the office. On your return to Thailand, the Thai immigration office at the bridge will give you a new 15-day tourist visa (see p754).

There is little to do in **Tachileik** apart from sample Burmese food and shop – the prices are about the same as on the Thai side and everyone accepts baht. There's an interesting morning market and it can be fun to hang about in the teashops.

If going further afield than Tachileik (you're limited to Kengtung and Mong La), proceed directly to Myanmar Travel & Tours, next to the immigration booth. You'll need to pay the same $10/500B fee, and will also need three passport-sized photos and a copy of your passport. You'll be asked to state how far you wish to travel and will be given a temporary ID card; this card is stamped at every checkpoint along the route. This same office also gives out free rough maps of Kengtung and Mong La.

KENGTUNG

Kengtung (called Chiang Tung by the Thais and usually spelt Kyaingtong by the Burmese), 163km north, is a sleepy but historic capital for the Shan State's Khün culture. The Khün speak a northern Thai language related to Shan and Thai Lü, and use a writing script similar to the ancient Lanna script. It's a bit over halfway between the Thai and Chinese borders. Built around a small lake and dotted with ageing **Buddhist temples** and crumbling British **colonial architecture**, it's a much more scenic town than Tachileik and one of the most interesting towns in Myanmar's entire Shan State.

Harry's Trekking House (☎ 21418; 132 Mai Yang Rd; r US$5-15) is the best choice for budget travellers. The guesthouse is about 1km north of the lake in Kanaburoy village. Guests have a choice of simple wooden rooms at the back or smarter doubles with TV in the annexe. All sorts of treks can be arranged and you can rent motorcycles for US$10 per day. **New Sam Yweat Guest House** (☎ 21643; 21 Airport Rd; s/d from US$8/16) is near the pond on the airport road, and was built to cater to visiting tour groups. **Princess Hotel** (☎ 21319; kengtung@mail4u.com.mm; s US$20-25, d US$28-35; 🕸) has a great location near the market, and the rooms have TV, air-con, fridge and phone.

MONG LA

About 85km north of Kengtung, Mong La (Mengla) straddles the border between Myanmar and China. Until recently, the town was Myanmar's answer to Las Vegas, with dozens of casinos, luxury hotels and hostess bars catering to a steady stream of 'vice tourists' crossing the border from Yunnan. The bubble burst in 2005 when the Chinese government banned its citizens from visiting Mong La to prevent the laundering of millions of yuan by Chinese crime syndicates. The ban also extends to foreigners, and Mong La is no longer a legal border crossing into China.

Since the closure of the big casinos, the main sights in town are the huge and busy **central market** and the towering **Shwedagon Pagoda**, which offers great views over the town and Chinese border post. Nearby is a **Drug Eradication Museum** (free admission; 🕑 daylight hr).

There are several modern hotels in Mong La, none accustomed to dealing with English-speaking tourists. Try the business-like **Haung Faun Hotel** (r 60 yuan) beside the market or the flashy-looking **Powerlong Hotel** (r 150 yuan) by the river.

The best place to eat is the central market – there are dozens of stalls here.

For a complete description of Kengtung and Mong La, see Lonely Planet's *Myanmar (Burma)* guidebook.

Getting There & Away

From Tachileik there are two daily air-con bus departures to Kengtung (5000 kyat, four hours, 9am and 1pm). During the day there are also shared taxis (front/back seat 500/700B, three hours) and *sŏrng·tǎa·ou* (3000 kyat, four hours). A motorcycle taxi ride to the bus station costs 20B.

From Kengtung there are buses and taxis to Mong La (bus/shared taxi 7000/12,000 kyat, three to four hours), but remember that you'll need to have arranged permission beforehand in Tachileik.

CHIANG SAEN

เชียงแสน

pop 10,807

The dictionary definition of a sleepy river town, Chiang Saen was the site of a Thai kingdom thought to date back to as early as the 7th century. Scattered throughout the modern town are the ruins of the former empire – surviving architecture includes several *chedi* Buddha images, *wí·hǎhn* pillars and earthen city ramparts. Chiang Saen later became loosely affiliated with various northern Thai kingdoms, as well as 18th-century Myanmar, and never became a Siamese possession until the 1880s.

Today huge river barges from China moor at Chiang Saen, carrying fruit, engine parts and all manner of other imports, keeping the old China–Siam trade route open. Despite this trade, and despite commercialisation of the nearby Sop Ruak, the town hasn't changed too much over the last decade, and because of this is a pleasanter base than the latter .

Only locals are allowed to cross the Mekong River into the Lao town of Ton Pheung, but foreigners who already hold a Chinese visa can use the town as a base for river trips to Jinghong in China's Yunnan Province (see p369).

Information

Chiang Saen's immigration office has two branches: the main office on the southwest corner of the town's main intersection, and a smaller one next to the Mekong River pier (for crossings to Ton Pheung).

Chiang Saen Hospital (☎ 0 5377 7017–7035) This government hospital is just south of Wat Pa Sak. Staff speak little English. The best hospital nearby is in Chiang Rai (see p350).

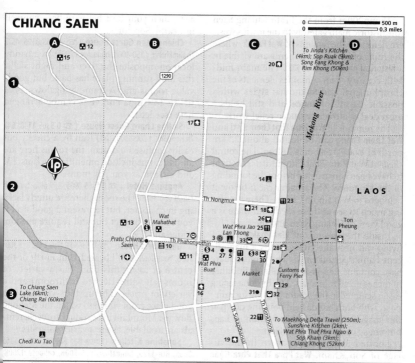

CHIANG SAEN

To Jinda's Kitchen
(4km); Sop Ruak (9km);
Song Fang Khong &
Rim Khong (50km)

Mekong River

LAOS

Ton
Pheung

To Chiang Saen
Lake (6km);
Chiang Rai (60km)

Chedi Ku Tao

Customs &
Ferry Pier

To Maekhong Delta Travel (250m);
Sunshine Kitchen (2km);
Wat Phra That Phra Ngao &
Sop Kham (3km);
Chiang Khong (52km)

INFORMATION	
Chiang Saen Hospital	1 B3
Immigration Office	2 C3
Internet	3 C2
Krung Thai Bank (ATM)	4 C3
Main Immigration Office	5 C3
Police	6 C2
Post Office	7 B2
Siam Commercial Bank (ATM)	8 C3
Visitors Centre	9 B2

SIGHTS & ACTIVITIES	
Chiang Saen National Museum	10 B3
Wat Chedi Luang	11 B3
Wat Chom Chang	12 A1
Wat Pa Sak	13 B2

Wat Phakhaopan	14 C2
Wat Phra That Chom Kitti	15 A1

SLEEPING	
Angsuna Hotel	16 B3
Chengsan Golden Land Resort	17 B1
Chiang Saen Guest House	18 C2
Chiang Saen River Hill Hotel	19 C3
Gin's Guest House	20 C1
Sa Nae Charn Guest House	21 C2

EATING	
Ah Ying	22 C3
Evening Food Vendors	23 C2
Food Stalls	24 C3
Kiaw Siang Hai	25 C2

DRINKING	
2 be 1	26 C2

TRANSPORT	
Angpao	
Chiangsean Tour	27 C3
Boats to Sop Ruak & Chiang	
Khong	28 C3
Boats to Sop Ruak & Chiang	
Khong	29 C3
Bus Stop	30 C3
Chiang Saen Tour and Travel	31 C3
Sombat Tour	(see 4)
Sŏrng·tăa·ou to Chiang Khong	32 C3
Sŏrng·tăa·ou to Sop Ruak & Mae	
Sai	33 C2

Internet (Th Phahonyothin; per hr 20B; ☺ 10am-8pm)
There are two internet shops, located across from each
other, a block east of Wat Chedi Luang.

Post office (Th Phahonyothin; ☺ 8.30am-4.30pm Mon-
Sat) Located roughly across from Wat Chedi Luang.

Siam Commercial Bank (Th Phahonyothin) On the
main street leading from the highway to the Mekong River.
Has an ATM and currency exchange.

Visitors centre (Th Phahonyothin; ☺ 8.30am-4.30pm
Mon-Sat) Has a good relief display showing the major ruin
sites as well as photos of various *chedi* before, during and
after restoration.

Sights & Activities

Near the town entrance, the **Chiang Saen
National Museum** (☎ 0 5377 7102; 702 Th Phahonyothin;
admission 100B; ☺ 8.30am-4.30pm Wed-Sun) is a great
source of local information considering its
relatively small size.

Behind the museum to the east are the ruins
of **Wat Chedi Luang**, which features an 18m octagonal *chedi* in the classic Chiang Saen or Lanna
style. Archaeologists argue about its exact construction date but agree it dates to some time
between the 12th and 14th centuries.

About 200m from the Pratu Chiang Saen (the historic main gateway to the town's western flank) are the remains of **Wat Pa Sak**, where the ruins of seven monuments are visible in a **historical park** (admission 50B). The main mid-14th-century *chedi* combines elements of the Hariphunchai and Sukhothai styles with a possible Bagan influence, and still holds a great deal of attractive stucco relief work.

The remains of **Wat Phra That Chom Kitti** and **Wat Chom Chang** can be found about 2.5km north of Wat Pa Sak on a hilltop. The round *chedi* of Wat Phra That Chom Kitti is thought to have been constructed before the founding of the kingdom. The smaller *chedi* below it belonged to Wat Chom Chang. There is nothing much to see at these *chedi*, but there is a good view of Chiang Saen and the river.

Inside the grounds of **Wat Phakhaopan**, a living *wát* near the river, stands a magnificent Lanna-period *chedi*. The large, square base contains Lanna-style walking Buddhas in niches on all four sides. The Buddha facing east is sculpted in the *mudra* ('calling for rain') pose, with both hands held pointing down at the image's sides – a pose common in Laos but not so common in Thailand.

Located 3km south of town in the village of Sop Kham, **Wat Phra That Phra Ngao** contains a large prayer hall built to cover a partially excavated Chiang Saen–era Buddha statue. The walls of the brick building are partially covered by stucco relief murals that have been painted, giving the surface the impression of polished wood or copper. A beautiful golden teak *hŏr drai* (manuscript depository) is currently being built, and a steep road leads to a hilltop pagoda and temple with views over the area.

MEKONG RIVER TRIPS

Six-passenger speedboats leaving from the waterfront jet to Sop Ruak (per boat one way/return 500/600B, 35 minutes), or all the way to Chiang Khong (per boat one-way only 2000B, 1½ hours).

If you've already arranged a visa, it's also possible to take a passenger boat to Jinghong, in China's Yunnan Province. For details see opposite.

Sleeping

Chiang Saen lacks in quality accommodation, particularly of the upscale type. If you require a higher level of service and stand-

ards, then your best bet is to base yourself in nearby Sop Ruak.

Chiang Saen Guest House (☎ 0 5365 0196; 45/2 Th Rimkhong; r 150-300B, bungalows 200B) In a handy location opposite the river and night stalls, this long-running place has basic but good-value rooms and A-frame bungalows. Boat tickets to China and visas can be arranged here (see left).

Sa Nae Charn Guest House (☎ 0 5365 1138; 641 Th Nongmut; r 200-450B; ⊠) Run by a cheeky but easily-confused old man, the rooms here are all basic, but include amenities such as TV and air-con as you pay more.

Angsuna Hotel (☎ 0 5365 0955; 359 Moo 3; r with fan/AC 250/350B) The rooms here are utterly lacking in character, but represent a good deal if you're on a budget but still require air-con, fridge and TV.

Gin's Guest House (☎ 0 5365 0847; 71 Mu 8; r 300-700B, bungalows 200B) Located 1km north of the centre of town, this place has a variety of rooms (all with attached bathroom) and a variety of prices. The upstairs veranda is a good place from which to watch the Mekong flow by. Mountain bike and motorcycle rentals are available, as are a variety of tours.

Sunshine Kitchen (Khrua Ban Rot Fai; ☎ 0 5365 0605; Rte 1129; bungalows 600-800B, caboose 1200B; ⊠) Named after the riverfront restaurant that also shares this compound, lodging here takes the form of three bamboo bungalows and, of all things, an authentic train caboose. The bungalows are basic, while the fully refurbished caboose appears to be a comfortable and, in this case, stationary place to sleep. The owner is friendly and speaks English.

Chengsan Golden Land Resort (☎ 0 5365 1100; www.chengsanresort.com; 663 Moo 2; r 800B, bungalows 1200-2000B; ⊠ ⊠) Choose from large well-equipped rooms in a two-storey building or several attractive wooden bungalows surrounding a garden and a covered swimming pool. There is another branch with 10 similarly priced bungalows in the village of Sop Kham, 3km south along the Mekong.

Chiang Saen River Hill Hotel (☎ 0 5365 0826; www.chiangsaenriverhill.net; 714 Th Sukapibansai 2; r incl breakfast 1200B; ⊠) Although the pink exterior and floor tiles don't exactly compliment the northern Thai furnishing touches, this is still probably the best place in town. Rooms are large, and equipped with TV, fridge and a small area for relaxing.

Eating & Drinking

Cheap noodle and rice dishes are available at food stalls in and near the market on the river road and along the main road through town from the highway, near the bus stop. Evening food vendors set up at the latter location and stay open till around midnight.

our pick **Jinda's Kitchen** (no roman-script sign; ☎ 08 6654 3116; Rte 1290; dishes 20-50B; ☺ 7am-8pm) This cosy roadside restaurant has been serving up local dishes for more than 50 years. Try the famous northern noodle dishes *kôw soy* or *kà·nŏm jeen nám ngèe·o*, or choose a curry or homemade sausage from the English-language menu. Jinda's Kitchen is located roughly halfway between Chiang Saen and Sop Ruak, near Km31; look for the Pepsi sign.

Ah Ying (no roman-script sign; ☎ 08 9655 3468; 778/1 Th Rimkhong; dishes 25-60B; ☺ 7am-10pm) This tiny family-run restaurant specialises in delicious hand-pulled noodles. Topped with a spicy minced pork mixture, they're a great breakfast. There's no English sign; simply look for the Chinese cooks busy stretching and flinging lengths of dough.

Evening food vendors (dishes 30-60B; ☺ 4-11pm) During the dry months these vendors sell sticky rice, green papaya salad, grilled chicken, dried squid and other fun foods for people to eat while sitting on mats along the river bank in front of Chiang Saen Guest House – a very pleasant way to spend an evening. Local specialities include fish or chicken barbecued inside thick joints of bamboo, eaten with sticky rice and *sôm·đam* (green papaya salad).

Kiaw Siang Hai (no roman-script sign; 44 Th Rimkhong; dishes 60-120B; ☺ 6.30am-8.30pm) Serving the workers of Chinese boats that dock at Chiang Saen, this authentic Chinese restaurant prepares a huge menu of dishes in addition to the namesake noodle and wonton dishes. Try the spicy Szechuan-style fried tofu, or one of the Chinese herbal soups.

2 be 1 (☺ 6pm-1am) By the river, this funky bar with inside and outside seating, has colourful lamps and plays house music.

Nearby in Sop Ruak, **Song Fang Khong** (dishes 40-100B; ☺ 11am-11pm) and **Rim Khong** (dishes 35-100B; ☺ 11am-11pm) are two *sŏo·an ah·hăhn* food garden-style) riverside restaurants, off the river road from Chiang Saen. Both offer extensive menus of Thai, Chinese and Isan food. Bring your Thai-language skills.

Getting There & Away

Blue *sŏrng·tăa·ou* that travel to Sop Ruak (20B) and Mae Sai (50B) wait at the eastern end of Th Phahonyothin during daylight hours. The green *sŏrng·tăa·ou* bound for Chiang Khong (100B) park on Th Rimkhong, south of the riverside immigration office.

Chiang Saen has no proper bus terminal, rather there is a covered bus shelter at the eastern end of Th Phahonyothin where buses pick up and drop off passengers. From this stop there are frequent buses between Chiang Rai and Chiang Saen (35B, 1½ hours, 5.30am to 5.30pm). If you're going to Chiang Mai (ordinary/air-con 126/227B, five hours, 7.15am/9am) be sure to ask for the *săi mài* (new route); the *săi gòw* (old route) meanders through Lamphun, Lampang and Phayao, taking between seven and nine hours. Alternatively, you can take a bus first to Chiang Rai then change to a Chiang Mai bus (about 4½ hours).

To Bangkok, **Sombat Tour** (☎ 08 1595 4616; Th Phahonyothin) offers approximately 10 seats in a daily VIP bus (990B, 12 hours, 5pm), departing from a small office adjacent to Krung Thai Bank. Space is limited, so book ahead.

CHINA

Although it was once possible to travel by cargo ship from Chiang Saen to Jinghong in China, now it's only permitted via passenger boat through **Maekhong Delta Travel** (☎ 0 5364 2517; www.maekhongtravel.com; 230/5-6 Th Phaholyothin, Mae Sai; one way 820 yuan/4000B; ☺ 8am-5pm). A bare-bones Chiang Saen office of this Mae Sai–based outfit is located at the southern end of Th Rimkhong, approximately 250m south of the large boat pier. To do this trip you must already have your visa for China (quicker to arrange from Chiang Mai or Bangkok). The people at Chiang Saen Guest House (opposite) can book you a ticket and help you get a visa for China. It takes two to three days to get the visa. If you already have the latter, you can buy tickets directly from Maekhong Delta, or more conveniently through **Chiang Saen Tour and Travel** (☎ 0 5377 7051; manthana2425@yahoo.com; 64 Th Rimkhong; ☺ 10am-8pm).

The trip from Chiang Saen to Jinghong takes 15 hours when conditions are good. During drier months the going is slower, as rocks and shallows can hamper the way. When this is the case a night's stay in Guanlei is included. Boats depart from Chiang Saen on Monday, Wednesday and Saturday at 5am.

LAOS

Although boats do travel from Chiang Saen to Laos, the closest crossing open to foreigners is in Chiang Khong (see p375).

Getting Around

Motorbike taxis and sǎhm·lór will do short trips around town for 20B. They congregate near and across from the bus stop.

A good way to see the Chiang Saen–Mae Sai area is on two wheels. Mountain bikes (per day 50B) and motorcycles (per day 200B) can be rented at Gin's Guest House (p368) and **Angpao Chiangsean Tour** (☎ 0 5365 0143; www.angpao-r3a.com; Th Phahonyothin; ☼ 9am-8pm). The latter can also provide a vehicle with driver, and conducts a variety of local tours.

AROUND CHIANG SAEN
Sop Ruak
สบรวก

The borders of Myanmar, Thailand and Laos meet at Sop Ruak, the official 'centre' of the Golden Triangle, at the confluence of Nam Ruak and the Mekong River.

In historical terms, 'Golden Triangle' actually refers to a much larger geographic area, stretching thousands of square kilometres into Myanmar, Laos and Thailand, within which the opium trade was prevalent. Nevertheless hoteliers and tour operators have been quick to cash in on the name by referring to the tiny village of Sop Ruak as 'the Golden Triangle', conjuring up images of illicit adventure, exotic border areas and opium caravans.

But that's all history, and today the only caravan you're likely to see is the endless parade of huge buses carrying package tourists. The opium is now fully relegated to museums, and even the once-beautiful natural setting has largely been obscured by ATMs, countless stalls selling tourist tat, and the loud announcements from the various temples.

On the good side, the two opium-related museums, the House of Opium (right) and Hall of Opium (right), are both worth a visit, and a boat trip is an enjoyable way to pass an hour. But the only reason to consider a stay here is if you've already booked a room in one of the area's outstanding luxury hotels.

SIGHTS & ACTIVITIES

The first sight you'll inevitably see in Sop Ruak is **Phra Chiang Saen Si Phaendin** (☼ 7am-9pm), a giant Buddha statue financed by a Thai-Chinese foundation. The statue straddles a boat-like platform, and visitors here are encouraged to donate by rolling coins from an elevated platform behind the statue.

The **House of Opium** (Baan Phin; ☎ 0 5378 4060; www.houseofopium.com; admission 50B; ☼ 7am-8pm), a small museum with historical displays pertaining to opium culture, is worth a peek. Exhibits include all the various implements used in the planting, harvest, use and trade of the *Papaver somniferum* resin, including pipes, weights, scales and so on, plus photos and maps with labels in English. The museum is at the southeastern end of Sop Ruak, virtually across from Phra Chiang Saen Si Phaendin.

Next to the House of Opium are some steps up to **Wat Phra That Pu Khao**, from where you get the best viewpoint of the Mekong meeting of Laos, Myanmar and Thailand.

On the Burmese side of the river junction stands the **Golden Triangle Paradise Resort** (☎ 053 652 111; r 3500-400B, ste 7000B), a huge hotel and casino financed by Thai and Japanese business partners who have leased nearly 480 hectares from the Myanmar government. The casino is open 24 hours, but visits can only be arranged from 8am to 6pm, when immigration posts are open. Only two currencies – baht and dollars – are accepted at the hotel and casino.

One kilometre south of Sop Ruak on a plot of about 40 hectares opposite the Anantara Golden Triangle Resort & Spa, the Mah Fah Luang Foundation has established the 5600-sq-m **Hall of Opium** (☎ 0 5378 4444; www.golde trianglepark.com; Mu 1 Baan Sobruak; admission 300B ☼ 10am-3.30pm). The goal of this impressive facility is to become the world's leading exhibit and research facility for the study of opiate use around the world. This multimedia exhibition includes a fascinating history of opium, and examines the effects of abuse on individuals and society. Well balanced and worth seeing.

For **Mekong River Cruises** (1hr cruise max 5 people per boat 400B), local long-tail boat trips can be arranged through several local agents or at the various piers. The typical trip involves a circuit around a large island and upriver for a view of the Burmese casino hotel. There's a fee of 700B (500B to the Burmese side, 200B to the Thais) to go onto the casino island for the day (they'll stamp you in and out at the same time).

You can also arrange to stop off at a Lao village on the large river island of **Don Sao**, roughly halfway between Sop Ruak and Chiang Saen. The Lao immigration booth here is happy to allow day visitors onto the island without a Lao visa. A 20B arrival tax is collected from each visitor. There's not a lot to see, but there's an official post office where you can mail letters or postcards with a Laos PDR postmark, a few shops selling T-shirts and Lao handicrafts, and the Sala Beer Lao, where you can quaff Beer Lao and munch on Lao snacks.

SLEEPING & EATING

The only reason to stay in or around Sop Ruak is to take advantage of some of northern Thailand's best upscale lodgings. Those on a budget are advised to go to Chiang Saen. There are several tourist-oriented restaurants overlooking the Mekong River.

Greater Mekong Lodge (☎ 0 5378 4450; www .maefahluang.org; s/d 1600/1800B; ✷ ▣) Part of the Hall of Opium compound, this hotel has 28 well-equipped rooms with cable TV in the cavernous, stark main building. But for the same price, the 13 elevated bungalows are the better choice.

Imperial Golden Triangle Resort (☎ 0 5378 4001/5; www.imperialhotels.com; 222 Ban Sop Ruak; r 4708-5290B; ✷ ▣ ✷) Another first-class option, this huge hotel is located a brief walk from all of Sop Ruak's tourist services. Rooms include balconies with impressive river views.

our pick Anantara Golden Triangle Resort & Spa (☎ 0 5378 4084; www.anantara.com; r/ste from 10,900/15,200B; ✷ ▣ ✷) This award-winning resort takes up a large patch of beautifully landscaped ground directly opposite the Hall of Opium (opposite). The rooms combine Thai and international themes, and all have balconies looking over the Mekong. A Jacuzzi, squash and tennis courts, gym, sauna, library, medical clinic and spa round out the luxury amenities. Special attractions include the King's Cup Elephant Polo Tournament (held in March) and one- to three-day mahout-training packages.

our pick Four Seasons Tented Camp (☎ 0 5391 0200; www.fourseasons.com; minimum 3-night stay 220,000B; ✷ ▣ ✷) If you can fit it into your schedule (and budget), this safari-inspired 'tented camp' is among the most truly unique accommodation experiences in Thailand. Located at a secluded spot of riverside jungle outside Sop Ruak, a brief boat ride is necessary to reach the vast compound of 15 hillside tents. The tents are luxurious and decked out in colonial-era safari paraphernalia, the focus of which is an

incredibly inviting copper and resin bathtub. There's no TV or iPod dock, rather guests are encouraged to take in the natural setting (tip: tent 15 looks over an elephant bathing area) and take part in daily activities, which range from mahout training to spa treatment. A minimum stay of at least three nights is required, and the fee covers every aspect of the stay, from airport pick up to food and drink.

GETTING THERE & AWAY

There are frequent *sŏrng·tǎa·ou* between Chiang Saen and Sop Ruak (20B, every 20 minutes from 7am to 5pm). It's an easy bicycle ride of 9km from Chiang Saen to Sop Ruak.

CHIANG KHONG

เชียงของ

pop 12,311

More remote yet livelier than its neighbour Chiang Saen, Chiang Khong is historically an important market town for local hill tribes and for trade with northern Laos. At one time the city was part of a small *meuang* (city-state) called Juon, founded in AD 701 by King Mahathai. Over the centuries Juon paid tribute to Chiang Rai, then Chiang Saen and finally Nan before being occupied by the Siamese in the 1880s. The territory of Chiang Khong extended all the way to Yunnan Province in China until the French turned much of the Mekong River's northern bank into French Indochina in 1893.

Today the riverside town is a popular traveller's gateway into Laos. From Huay Xai, on the opposite side of the Mekong, it's a two-day slow boat trip to Luang Prabang. And for those who have set their sights even further, Huay Xai is only an eight-hour bus ride from Boten, a legal border crossing to and from China – see p375 for more information.

Information

Si Ayuthaya, Kasikornbank and Siam Commercial Bank have branches in town with ATMs and foreign-exchange services.

Easy Trip (☎ 0 5365 5174, 0 8997 7246; www.discovery laos.com; 63/2 Moo 1, Th Sai Klang; ⏰ 8am-8pm) This very professional travel agency organises boats and buses to Laos (see p375), as well as minibuses to Chiang Mai (250B) and Pai (450B). Flights in Thailand and to Laos can be booked here. Many guesthouses in Chiang Khong also offer similar services.

Internet (Th Sai Klang; per hr 30B; ⏰ 10am-10pm) On the main street roughly across from Bamboo Mexican House (p374).

Sights

Chiang Khong has a few northern Thai-style wát of minor interest. **Wat Luang**, on the main road, was once one of the most important temples in Chiang Rai Province and features a *chedi* dating from the 13th century, which was restored in 1881.

On a hill overlooking the town and the river is a **Nationalist Chinese Soldiers Cemetery**, where more than 200 KMT soldiers are buried. The grave mounds are angled on the hill so that they face China. A shrine containing old photos of KMT soldiers-in-arms stands at the top of the hill.

The nearby village of **Ban Hat Khrai** is famous as being one of the few places where *blah bèuk* (giant Mekong catfish) are still occasionally caught. During the *blah bèuk* season, late-April to June, you may catch the small fishing boats coming and going from **Tha Pla Beuk**, about 1.5km south of Chiang Khong on the Mekong; the turn-off is near Km137. For more information on this fish, see the boxed text, p374.

Sleeping

The vast majority of accommodation in Chiang Khong is geared towards the budget market.

OUR PICK Baanrimtaling (☎ 0 5379 1613; maleewan _th@yahoo.com; 99/4 Moo 3, Baan Sop Som; dm 80B, r 160-350B, bungalows 450B; 🖳) The rooms here are pretty run-of-the-mill for this price range, and the location isn't exactly ideal, but the home-like atmosphere and gentle service may have you staying a bit longer than you planned. Great river views certainly don't hurt, and extras like free wi-fi, a Thai-style herbal sauna and Thai cooking lessons seal the deal.

Baan-Fai Guest House (☎ 0 5379 1394; 108 Moo 8, Th Sai Klang; r 100-200B) The eight rooms here are located in an attractive wooden Thai home; unfortunately the rooms don't quite live up to the exterior. They're clean though, and represent a decent choice if funds are running low.

Boom House (☎ 0 5365 5136; www.boomhouse resort.com; 406/1 Moo 1, Th Sai Klang; r 150-350B; 😂) This multilevel place has a variety of plain but tidy rooms, the more expensive of which have air-con, TV and fridge. There is a pleasant restaurant right on the riverbank.

Reuan Thai Sophaphan (☎ 0 5379 1023; suka tungka@gmail.com; 83 Moo 8, Th Sai Klang; r 300-600B; 🖳) This guesthouse/resort/homestay (the terms are used both interchangeably and gratuitously) is a beautiful, multifloor teak building with heaps of character. The rooms can be slightly dark, however, and none take full advantage of the river views. Discounts are available, and cheaper rooms can be found at an equally rambling compound of wooden buildings across the street that are run by the same people.

Ban Tammila (☎ 0 5379 1234; baantammila@hotmail .com; 113 Mu 8 Th Sai Klang; bungalows 350/450B, r 350B) Although the exterior looks a bit ragged, the stylish rooms and well-designed bungalows here are neat and decorated in warm colours. This relaxing place can also organise bicycle trips.

PP Home (Baan Pak Pon; ☎ 0 5365 5092; baanpakpon@ hotmail.com; 177/Moo 2; r 350-500B; 🖳) One of a dwindling number of accommodation still owned by locals, this attractive wooden house features large rooms with wood panelling, each with a private balcony looking over the river.

Chiangkhong River View Hotel (☎ 0 5379 1375; www.chiangkhong.com/riverviewhotel.htm; 141 Moo 12; r 500B; 😂) At the southern end of town, this tall building holds several virtually identical tiny rooms, all with air-con, TV and fridge. Locally owned, and a good value.

Portside Hotel (☎ 0 5365 5238; portsidehotel@hot mail.com; 546 Moo 1, Th Sai Klang; r 600B; 😂 🖳) This new, smart hotel features two floors of tidy but slightly cramped rooms. There are no river views, but a communal rooftop area makes up for this. Free wi-fi and other services are also available.

Namkhong Riverside Hotel (☎ 0 5379 1796; 174-176 Th Sai Klang; r incl breakfast 800-1000B; 😂 🖳) Perhaps the first sign that things are (slowly) moving upscale in Chiang Khong, this modern three-storey hotel holds heaps of clean, neat rooms, most with private balconies overlooking the river. The cheaper rooms are at ground level, and all rooms suffer from the noise pollution of nightly karaoke parties.

OUR PICK Rai Saeng Arun (☎ 0 5391 8255; www .raisaengarun.com; 2 Moo 3, Ban Phakub; bungalows incl breakfast 3000-3750B; 😂 🖳) Located 22km from Chiang Khong on the quiet rural road that leads to Chiang Saen, this resort brings together 14 bungalows in an attractive, natural setting. Some are perched on a hillside, while others are near stream-bordered rice fields and three are at the edge of the Mekong River. All are stylish and comfortable, feature balconies and open-air showers, and

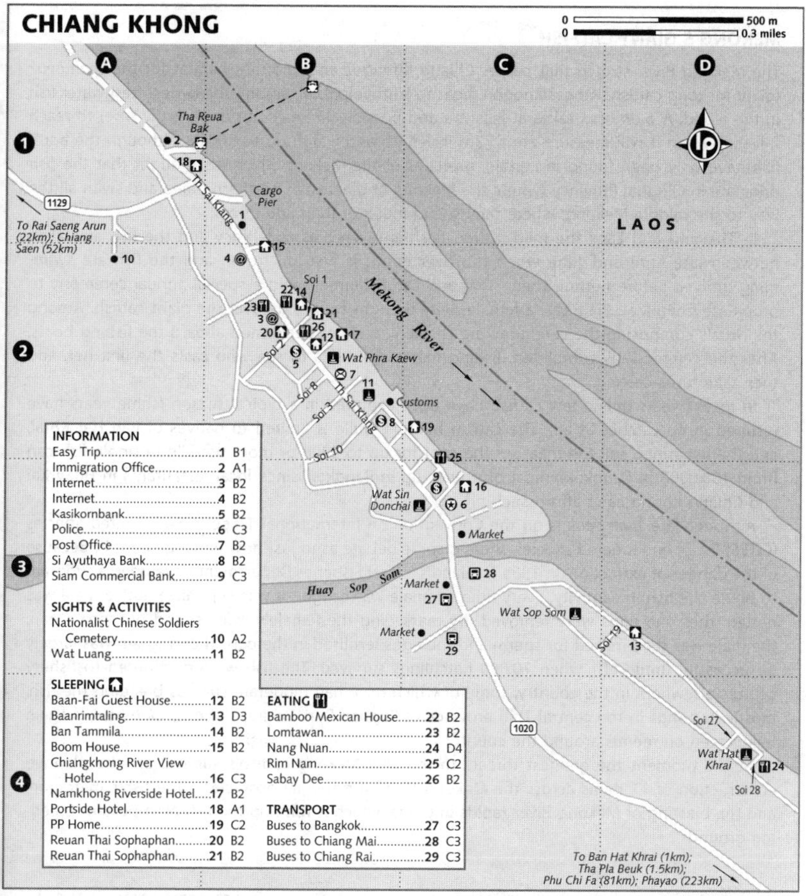
CHIANG KHONG
0 500 m
0 0.3 miles
LAOS
Mekong River
Tha Reua Bak
Cargo Pier
Th Sai Klang
To Rai Saeng Arun (22km); Chiang Saen (52km)
1129
Soi 1
Soi 2
Soi 8
Soi 3
Soi 10
Wat Phra Kaew
Customs
Wat Sin Donchai
Market
Huay Sop Som
Wat Sop Som
Soi 19
1020
Soi 27
Wat Hat Khrai
Soi 28
To Ban Hat Khrai (1km); Tha Pla Beuk (1.5km); Phu Chi Fa (81km); Phayao (223km)
INFORMATION
Easy Trip 1 B1
Immigration Office 2 A1
Internet 3 B2
Internet 4 B2
Kasikornbank 5 B2
Police 6 C3
Post Office 7 B2
Si Ayuthaya Bank 8 B2
Siam Commercial Bank 9 C3
SIGHTS & ACTIVITIES
Nationalist Chinese Soldiers Cemetery 10 A2
Wat Luang 11 B2
SLEEPING
Baan-Fai Guest House 12 B2
Baanrimtaling 13 D3
Ban Tammila 14 B2
Boom House 15 B2
Chiangkhong River View Hotel 16 C3
Namkhong Riverside Hotel 17 B2
Portside Hotel 18 A1
PP Home 19 C2
Reuan Thai Sophaphan 20 B2
Reuan Thai Sophaphan 21 B2
EATING
Bamboo Mexican House 22 B2
Lomtawan 23 B2
Nang Nuan 24 D4
Rim Nam 25 C2
Sabay Dee 26 B2
TRANSPORT
Buses to Bangkok 27 C3
Buses to Chiang Mai 28 C3
Buses to Chiang Rai 29 C3

are connected by bridged walkways over rice fields. The restaurant looks over the Mekong and serves dishes using vegetables and herbs from the resort's organic farm. Considerable discounts are available during the low season.

Eating

our pick Sabay Dee (no roman-script sign; ☎ 08 3594 0676; Th Sai Klang; dishes 15-20B; 4-7pm) Stick around long enough, and it seems like just about everybody in Chiang Khong stops by this family-run cart for a bag of curry or chili dip to take home. For those of us who don't live here, the owners are more than happy to provide dishes and seating. Prepared by natives of Chiang Khong, you're at the mercy of whatever local dishes they've made that day, but if you're lucky you'll get to try the delicious *gaang hŏoa Ђlee,* banana flower soup, or a spicy northern-style *lâhp* made from pork, buffalo or fish (raw or cooked – your call). Regardless, make it an early dinner, as choices become slimmer the darker it gets. Sabay Dee has no English sign, but is located directly adjacent to the soi that leads to Baan-Fai Guest House.

Rim Nam (dishes 30-90B; 11am-9pm) On a narrow road down beside the river, is this simple indoor-outdoor restaurant that overlooks the Mekong. The bilingual menu is much shorter than the Thai menu; *yam* (spicy salads) are the house specialities, but the kitchen can whip up almost anything.

MEKONG'S GIANT CATFISH

The Mekong River stretch that passes Chiang Khong is an important habitat for the *blah bèuk* (giant Mekong catfish, Pangasianodon gigas to ichthyologists), among the largest freshwater fish in the world. A *blah bèuk* takes at least six and possibly 12 years (no-one's really sure) to reach full size, when it will measure 2m to 3m in length and weigh up to 300kg. Although the adult fish have only been found in certain stretches of the Mekong River, it's thought that the fish originate in Qinghai Province (where the Mekong originates) in northern China and swim all the way to the middle Mekong, where they spend much of their adult lives.

In Thailand and Laos the mild-tasting flesh is revered as a delicacy and the fish are taken between late-April and June when the river depth is just 3m to 4m and the fish are swimming upriver. Before netting them, Thai and Lao fishermen hold a special annual ceremony to propitiate Chao Mae Pla Beuk, a female deity thought to preside over the giant catfish. Among the rituals comprising the ceremony are chicken sacrifices performed aboard the fishing boats. After the ceremony is completed, fishing teams draw lots to see who casts the first net, and then take turns casting.

In recent years only a few catfish have been captured in a typical season (some years have resulted in no catches at all). The catfish hunters' guild is limited to natives of Ban Hat Khrai, and the fishermen sell the meat on the spot for up to 500B or more per kilo (a single fish can bring 100,000B in Bangkok); most of it ends up in Bangkok, since local restaurants in Huay Xai and Chiang Khong can't afford such prices.

Although the *blah bèuk* is on the Convention on International Trade in Endangered Species (CITES) list of endangered species, there is some debate as to just how endangered it is. Because of the danger of extinction, in 1983 Thailand's Inland Fisheries Department developed a program to breed the fish in captivity. Every time a female was caught, it was kept alive until a male was netted, then the eggs were removed (by massaging the female's ovaries) and put into a pan; the male was then milked for sperm and the eggs fertilised in the pan. The program was largely unsuccessful until 2001 when 70,000 hatchlings survived. The fish were distributed to fishery centres elsewhere in the country, some of which have had moderate success breeding the fish, mostly in ponds in the central Thai province of Suphan Buri. Because of this, *blah bèuk* is again being seen on menus around the country.

At the moment the greatest threats to the wild Mekong catfish's survival are the planned construction of 11 dams across the Mekong River, a potential obstacle to the fish's migration, and the blasting of Mekong River rapids in China, which is robbing the fish of important breeding grounds.

Nang Nuan (☎ 0 5365 5567; Ban Hat Khrai; dishes 30-150B; ⏱ 9am-midnight) The menu here boasts that the restaurant is 'At the first great catfish's reproduction place', but it isn't all about the captivating locality; they also do some tasty food. Freshwater fish from the Mekong is the emphasis here, and it's prepared in a variety of ways, as the extensive English-language menu describes. A few local dishes are available too.

Bamboo Mexican House (☎ 0 5379 1621; 1 Moo 8, Th Sai Klang; dishes 30-180B; ⏱ 7am-8pm) Run by the manager of a now-defunct guesthouse, the chef of this tiny restaurant/bakery learned to make Mexican dishes from her American and Mexican guests. To be honest, though, we never got past the delicious homemade breads and cakes. Opens early, and boxed lunches can be assembled for the boat ride.

Lomtawan (☎ 0 5365 5740; 354 Moo 8, Th Sai Klang; dishes 60-180B; ⏱ lunch & dinner) If you don't require river views, this cosy, candlelit home is a great dinner option. The English-language menu is extensive and includes daring options such as green curry with salmon. Stay late, and the soundtrack becomes live and the place gradually transforms into an intimate bar.

Getting There & Away

There are frequent buses to Chiang Rai (70B 2½ hours, every hour from 4am to 5pm) there are also frequent buses going to/from Chiang Saen.

There are a few morning buses to Chiang Mai (2nd class air-con/VIP 225/290B, 6am to 11am).

To Bangkok (2nd class air-con/1st class/ VIP 529/680/794B, 12 hours, 3.30pm), arrive at the bus stop at least 30 minutes early, or buy tickets in advance from the office or from Easy Trip (see p371).

Boats taking up to 10 passengers can be chartered up the Mekong River from Chiang Khong to Chiang Saen for around 2000B. Boat crews can be contacted at the pier for ferries to Laos.

BORDER CROSSING (LAOS)

Long-tail boats to Huay Xai, Laos (40B, from 8am to 6pm), leave frequently from Tha Reua Bak, a pier at the northern end of Chiang Khong.

Foreigners can purchase a 30-day visa for Laos upon arrival in Huay Xai for US$30 to $42, depending on nationality. There is an extra US$1 or 50B charge after 4pm and on weekends. Be sure to get an exit stamp from Thai officials before heading to Laos. Travellers who forget to do this find themselves in uncomfortable situations later on. On your return to Thailand, immigration will stamp your passport with a new 15-day visa (see p754).

Once on the Lao side you can continue by road to Luang Nam Tha and Udomxai, or by boat down the Mekong River to Luang Prabang. If you're bound for the capital, **Lao Airlines** (☎ 211026, 211494; www.laoairlines.com) has flights from Huay Xai to Vientiane three times a week for US$94.

If time is on your side, the daily slow boat (900B, 10am) to Luang Prabang takes two days, including a night in the village of Pak Beng. Avoid the noisy fast boats (1450B, six to seven hours) that ply the Huay Xai to Luang Prabang route, as there have been reports of bad accidents. Booking tickets through an agent like Easy Trip (p371) costs slightly more, but they arrange tickets for you, provide transport from your guesthouse and across the Mekong River, and provide a boxed lunch for the boat ride.

BORDER CROSSING (CHINA)

If you already hold a Chinese visa, it's now also possible to go more or less directly to China from Chiang Khong. After obtaining a 30-day Laos visa-on-arrival in Huay Xai, simply board one of three weekly buses that go directly to the Xishuangbanna town of Mengla (700B, eight hours, 8am Monday, Wednesday and Friday) via the Lao border town of Boten. From Mengla it's a five-hour bus ride to Jinghong, the capital of Xishuangbanna district, or an overnight bus to Kunming.

Getting Around

A sǎhm·lór from the bus station to Tha Reua Bak, the border crossing to Laos, costs 30B.

Mountain bikes can be rented from Ban Tammila (p372) and Easy Trip (p371).

PHAYAO PROVINCE

PHAYAO

พะเยา

pop 19,118

Few people, including many Thais, are aware of this quiet but attractive northern city. Perhaps in an overzealous effort to remedy this, a tourist brochure we came across described Phayao as 'The Vienna of South East Asia'. Although this is just *slightly* stretching the truth, Phayao is certainly one of the more pleasant towns in northern Thailand. Its setting on Kwan Phayao, a vast wetland, gives the town a back-to-nature feel that's utterly lacking in most Thai cities, and the tree-lined streets, temples and old wooden houses of 'downtown' Phayao provide a pleasing old-school Thai touch.

The little-visited town is the perfect place to break up your journey to/from Chiang Rai, or as a bookend to our suggested driving trip from Chiang Khong (see boxed text, p376)

Information

Internet@Cafe (Th Pratu Khlong; per hr 20B; ☼ 10am-10pm) Other shops offering internet access dot Th Don Sanam.

Krungsri Bank (Th Phasart; ☼ 8.30am-3.30pm) Located near the city pillar, this bank has a foreign exchange desk.

Post office (Th Don Sanam; ☼ 8.30am-4.30pm Mon-Fri, 9am-noon Sat & Sun)

Sights & Activities

KWAN PHAYAO

กว๊านพะเยา

This vast body of water is the largest swamp in northern Thailand and a symbol of Phayao. Although naturally occurring, the water level is artificially controlled, otherwise the wetlands would tend to go dry outside of the wet season. Framed by mountains, the swamp is in fact

---

DETOUR: THE LONG WAY TO PHAYAO

If you're in Chiang Khong and happen to have your own wheels, we have an excellent suggestion for a drive. Rtes 1155 and 1093 are among Thailand's most dramatic land routes, hugging steep mountainsides along the Thai–Lao border and passing waterfalls, incredible vistas and national parks. If you need a destination you can continue all the way to Phayao, a little-visited province and town with ample accommodation and good food.

From Chiang Khong, the trip is as straightforward as heading south on Rte 1020 and following the signs to Phu Chi Fa, a national park near the Lao border. For Thailand, the signs are surprisingly clear, but a good companion is the Golden Triangle Rider's *Golden Triangle* map.

At the mountaintop village of Doi Pha Tang, you can take a quick detour to Pratu Siam, at 1653m, one of Thailand's most impressive viewpoints. There is basic lodging and food here.

Rte 1093 narrows and becomes markedly less populated as you approach Phu Chi Fa, a mountaintop that offers high-altitude views into Laos. There are a few different ways to approach the peak, the most popular being via Ban Rom Fah Thai. There is a variety of accommodation and some basic restaurants on either side of Phu Chi Fa.

Upon passing Phu Chi Fa, stay on Rte 1093 and follow the signs to Ban Huak. This is a picturesque village in Phayao province, 2km from the Lao border. There's a border market on the 10th and 30th of every month, homestay-style accommodation in the town, and nearby Nam Tok Phu Sang is a unique waterfall of thermally heated water.

From Ban Huak, follow signs to Chiang Kham, then take Rte 1021 to Chun, from where it's a straight shot to Phayao (via Dok Kham Tai), itself another worthwhile destination (p375).

If you do the drive in one go, allow at least six hours, including stops for taking photos, coffee and a meal.

---

more scenic than the name suggests, and is the setting for what must be among the most beautiful sunsets in Thailand. Rowing crews can be seen practising in the evenings, and there's a pier at the southern end of Th Chai Kwan where there are **boat rides** (20B) to what remains of **Wat Tiloke Aram**, a submerged 500-year-old temple. There are ambitious plans to rebuild the temple, one of many submerged religious structures in Kwan Phayao. In addition to lost Buddhist artefacts, there are at least 50 types of fish native to these waters, and there's a small **fish breeding area** where for 5B you can feed the fish.

WAT SRI KHOM KHAM
วัดศรีโคมคำ

Phayao's most important temple is thought to date back to 1491, but its present structure was finished in 1923. The immense prayer hall holds the Phra Jao Ton Luang, the largest Chiang Saen–era Buddha statue in the country. Standing 18m high, legend has it that the construction of the statue took more than 30 years. It's not the most beautiful or well-proportioned Buddha image in Thailand, but it certainly is impressive. The ordination hall that is elevated over Kwan Phayao features graceful modern wall paintings. Also located on the grounds of the wát is a Buddhist sculpture garden, which includes gory, larger-than-life depictions of Buddhist hell.

Next door to the temple is the **Phayao Cultural Exhibition Hall** (☎ 0 5441 0058; admission 40B; ⏲ 8.30am-5pm Mon-Sat), a two-storey museum packed with artefacts and a good amount of information on local history and culture in English. Standout items include a unique 'black' Buddha statue, and a fossil of two embracing crabs labelled 'Wonder Lover'.

Other Attractions

Just off Rte 1 opposite the turn-off to Phayao, **Wat Li** features a small **museum** (admission by donation; ⏲ 9am-3pm) with a decent variety of items from the Chiang Saen previous eras. **Wat Phra That Jom Thong** is an attractive *chedi* on a wooded hilltop 3km from the centre of town.

Sleeping

Tharn Thong Hotel (☎ 0 5443 1302; 56-59 Th Don Sanam; d 150-350B; ❄ 🖵) Stark fan-cooled rooms are available in the main building, while more comfortable air-con rooms can be found in the complex behind it.

Wattana Hotel (✆ 0 5443 1203; 69 Th Don Sanam; fan/air-con 150/280B; ❄) Next to the Tharn Thong, Wattana offers a nearly identical package, but the rooms aren't quite as tidy as its neighbour's.

Phuthong Place (☎ 0 5441 0505; 335 Moo 3, Th Pratu Khlong; r 500B; ❄ 🖳) The rooms at Phuthong are large, spotless and comfortable, making the place excellent value. It's also just a short walk from the night market along Th Rob Wiang.

Phayao Northern Lake Hotel (☎ 0 5441 1123; 15/7 Th Rob Wiang; r 400-600B; ❄ 🖳) This large hotel, a short walk from the bus terminal, offers slightly aged but comfortable rooms. The cheaper rooms are rather small, but they're well equipped.

Gateway Hotel (☎ 0 5441 1333; 7/36 Soi 2, Th Pratu Khlong; d 800B, ste 1800B; ❄ 🖳 📺) Despite being the city's most upmarket hotel, the rooms here are a bit on the tired side, although the 'sea view' rooms on the upper floors do boast great views of Kwan Phayao.

Eating & Drinking

For such a small town, Phayao has an amazing abundance of food, much of it quite good. During the day, dozens of vendors sell similar repertoires of grilled fish and papaya salad along the northern end of Th Chai Kwan. Kaat Boran, a largely food-based night market, sets up every evening from 6pm to 10pm around the King Ngam Muang monument. Another incredibly extensive night market convenes along the north side of Th Rob Wiang every evening.

There are literally dozens of lakefront restaurants along Kwan Phayao, beginning at Th Kwan and extending all the way to the public park. Of these, **Chuechan** (no roman-script sign; ☎ 0 5448 4670; Th Chai Kwan; dishes 60-120B; ❄ 10am-10.30pm) has received the most acclaim from the various Thai food authorities. The lengthy menu, which has both pictures and English, spans dishes you won't find elsewhere, such as stuffed pig leg or sour fish fried with egg. There's no English sign, but the restaurant is the tallest building on this stretch of Th Chai Kwan.

Khao Soi Saeng Phian (no roman-script sign; Th Tha Kwan; dishes 25-40B; ❄ 9am-3pm) One of the better bowls of *kôw soy* in this neck of the north is available at this family-run restaurant. *Kà·nŏm jeen nám ngée·o* and various other noodle dishes are also available. Fans of northern-style noodles will be happy to know that there are at least four other shops boasting similar menus within a block radius of the intersection of Th Kwan and Th Ratchawong.

Miracle Coffee (☎ 08 4047 7375; cnr Th Chai Kwan & Th Ratchawong; dishes 25-60B; ❄ 9am-midnight) During the day this lakefront shop is a casual cafe. Come dark, it transforms into a lively bar popular among locals.

Laap Kai Tawan Daeng (no roman-script sign; ☎ 08 1033 2089; 37/2 Th Phasart; dishes 49-79B; ❄ 11am-midnight) The speciality here is delicious northern-style *lâhp gài*, minced chicken mixed with crispy deep-fried herbs. The restaurant is most fun in the evenings when it becomes a typical upcountry pub, complete with live music. Look for the large rooster out front.

Tem Im (no roman-script sign; cnr Th Harinsut & Th Pratu Khlong; per person 89B; ❄ 6-11pm) Extremely popular with locals, this open-air restaurant is a type of do-it-yourself, all-you-can-eat barbeque. Simply load up on whatever raw ingredients you fancy, then grill them over coals at your table. Not a dish to be enjoyed alone, *mŏo gà·tá* is best eaten with lots of friends and even more beer.

Getting There & Away

Phayao's bus station is quite busy, primarily because the city lies on the main north–south highway.

There are frequent buses to Chiang Rai (ordinary/2nd class air-con/1st class/VIP 49/88/103/119B, two hours, every 40 minutes from 7am to 5pm) and two to Nan (2nd class air-con 139B, four hours, 8am and 1.30pm). To Chiang Mai (2nd class air-con/1st class 127/164B, three hours, every 40 minutes from 7.30am to 5.30pm), be sure to ask for the *săi mài* (new route); departures along the *săi gòw* (old route) are cheaper (ordinary/2nd class air-con/VIP 73/102/239B, five hours, but take a longer, circuitous route.

To Bangkok, there are a few morning and a few afternoon buses that depart from Phayao (2nd class air-con/1st class/VIP 461/592/920B, 11 hours), but it's also possible to hop on one of the 40 or so buses that pass through the station from points further north.

PHRAE PROVINCE

Phrae is a rural, mountainous province most often associated with teak. Despite a nationwide ban on logging, there's not a whole lot of the hardwood left, and the little that does exist is under threat (see boxed text, p379).

PHRAE
แพร่
pop 17,971

Walking around the old city of Phrae one is struck by similarities with the historical Lao city of Luang Prabang: ample greenery, traditional wood buildings and scenic temples dominate the scenery, and monks form a significant part of the traffic. The city's residents must be among the friendliest folks in Thailand, and Phrae's location on the banks of the Mae Nam Yom and its ancient wall invite comparisons with Chiang Mai. Despite all this, Phrae is a little-visited city and a great destination for those who require little more than a few low-key attractions, good local food and cheery company.

Information

CAT office (Th Charoen Meuang; ☽ 8am-8pm) Attached to the main post office. Long-distance calls can be made and you can use a T-card to access the internet.

Government Savings Bank (Th Rong Saw; ☽ 8.30am-3.30pm Mon-Fri) The ATM is next to the police station.

Krung Thai Bank (Th Charoen Meuang; ☽ 8.30am-3.30pm Mon-Fri) Foreign-exchange service and ATM.

Modern (Th Charoen Meuang; per hr 20B; ☽ 10am-10pm) An internet/online games shop located near Pratu Chai.

Nok Bin (☎ 08 9433 3285; www.nokbinphrae.th.gs; 24 Th Wichairacha; ☽ 10am-6pm) Khun Kung, a local journalist, and her husband have created two cheery cafes that also function as informal information centres for visitors. The couple prints a tourist map of Phrae that is updated regularly and can also arrange bicycle or motorcycle rental. The second, smaller branch of Nok Bin is near Pratu Chai, at the entrance to the old city.

Phrae Hospital (☎ 0 5452 2444) Just east of Th Chaw Hae, southeast of town.

Post office (Th Charoen Meuang; ☽ 8.30am-4.30pm Mon-Fri, 9am-noon Sat)

Sights

WAT LUANG
วัดหลวง

This is the oldest wát in Phrae, probably dating from the founding of the city in the 12th or 13th century. **Phra That Luang Chang Kham**, the large octagonal Lanna-style *chedi*, sits on a square base with elephants supporting it on all four sides. As is sometimes seen in Phrae and Nan, the *chedi* is occasionally swathed in Thai Lü fabric.

The veranda of the main *wí·hǎhn* is in the classic Luang Prabang–Lan Xang style but has unfortunately been bricked in with later-

ite. Opposite the front of the *wí·hǎhn* is **Pratu Khong**, part of the city's original entrance gate. No longer used as a gate, it now contains a statue of Chao Pu, an early Lanna ruler.

Also on the temple grounds is a **museum** displaying temple antiques, ceramics and religious art dating from the Lanna, Nan, Bago and Mon periods. A 16th-century, Phrae-made sitting Buddha on the 2nd floor is particularly exquisite. There are also some 19th-century photos with English labels on display, including some gruesome shots of a beheading. The museum is usually open weekends only, but the monks will sometimes open it on weekdays on request.

WAT PHRA NON
วัดพระนอน

Located west of Wat Luang is a 300-year-old *wát* named after its highly revered reclining *prá norn* (reclining Buddha image). The *bòht* (central sanctuary) was built around 200 years ago and has an impressive roof with a separate, two-tiered portico and gilded, carved, wooden facade with Ramayana scenes. The *wí·hǎhn* behind the *bòht* contains the Buddha image, swathed in Thai Lü cloth with bead and foil decoration.

WAT JOM SAWAN
วัดจอมสวรรค์

Outside the old city on Th Ban Mai, this temple was built by local Shan in the late 19th and early 20th centuries, and shows Shan and Burmese influences throughout. On our most recent visit the temple was in the process of being refurbished and was looking better than ever, although the interior was not yet finished. An adjacent copper-crowned *chedi* has lost most of its stucco to reveal the artful brickwork beneath.

OTHER TEMPLES

Across from the post office within the old city, **Wat Phra Baht Ming Meuang** combines two formerly separate temple compounds (one of which contains a museum that is sporadically open), a Buddhist school, an old *chedi*, an unusual octagonal drum tower made entirely of teak and the highly revered Phra Kosai, which closely resembles the Phra Chinnarat in Phitsanulok. Just outside the northeastern corner of the moat, **Wat Sa Bo Kaew** is a Shan-Burmese–style temple similar to Wat Jom Sawan.

THE DANCING TIGER

Kaeng Sua Ten (Dancing Tiger Rapids) are a series of rocky outcrops along the Mae Nam Yom, in Phrae's Song district. Part of Mae Yom National Park, the rapids are wild and beautiful, and are also the site of one of the more long-standing environmental conflicts in Thailand.

Since the early 1980s, the Thai government has repeatedly announced plans to build a dam across the Mae Nam Yom at Kaeng Sua Ten. Villagers in Tambon Sa-lab, the closest settlement to Kaeng Sua Ten, have vocally, and occasionally violently, objected to the plan. They claim that the dam would irrevocably alter their traditional lifestyle, forcing an estimated 2700 families to move away from their homes, and flood 3200 hectares of land, some of which include Thailand's last remaining natural stands of golden teak.

Many elsewhere in Phrae and northern Thailand would like to see the dam built, as it is claimed that it will help control rampant flooding of the Mae Yom during the wet season and manage water during frequent droughts. Politicians in Bangkok claim that the dam will provide additional power for the country and irrigation for farmers in provinces south of Phrae. And perhaps most significantly, dam building has been an important part of the king's rural development policy for several decades, and as recently as 1995, the monarch publicly pushed for the dam to be built.

In reality, the government's reasons for proposing the dam have inconsistently fluctuated between a need for power and irrigation, relying on whichever argument is more popular at the time. At one point the World Bank declined to fund the project, stating that the government's environmental impact assessment was incomplete. And many opponents have pointed out that the proposed site for the dam lies directly on a fault line.

In 2008 Samak Sundaravej became the most recent prime minister to revive plans to build the dam. When confronted with concerns of the dam's potential environmental impact, Samak claimed that there were no teak trees and only 'three stupid peacocks' left in the area (the comments were made on World Environment Day, and Samak also claimed that the dam would reduce the effects of global warming). Villagers in Sa-lab reacted to the comments by burning an effigy of Samak and 'ordaining' several golden teak trees near Kaeng Sua Ten with orange monastic robes, a method of environmental protest that makes the trees 'sacred' and thus less likely to be cut down.

For now the project is at a stalemate, but this is largely due to political instability rather than any change in government policy. What is certain is that plans to build a dam at Kaeng Sua Ten have caused many to question the concept of development in Thailand, and will continue to embody the struggle between poor rural Thais, who have little say in the development of their own environment, and the often authoritarian rule of the Bangkok-based central Thai government.

VONGBURI HOUSE
บ้านวงศ์บุรี

The two-storey teak house of the last prince of Phrae has been converted into a private **museum** (☎ 0 5462 0153; 50 Th Kham Leu; admission 30B; ✉ 8am-5pm). It was constructed between 1897 and 1907 for Luang Phongphibun and his wife Chao Sunantha, who once held a profitable teak concession in the city. Elaborate carvings on gables, eaves, balconies and above doors and windows are in good condition. Inside, many of the house's 20 rooms display late-19th-century teak antiques, documents (including early-20th-century slave concessions), photos and other artefacts from the bygone teak-dynasty era. Most are labelled in English as well as Thai.

PRATUBJAI HOUSE
บ้านประทับใจ

On the outskirts of the town is **Pratubjai House** (Impressive House; ☎ 0 5451 1282; admission 40B; ✉ 8am-5pm), a large northern Thai–style teak house that was built using more than 130 teak logs, each over 300 years old. Opened in 1985, the house took four years to build, using timber taken from nine old rural houses. The interior pillars are ornately carved. The house is also filled with souvenir vendors and is rather tackily decorated, so don't take the moniker 'impressive' too seriously.

NORTHERN THAILAND

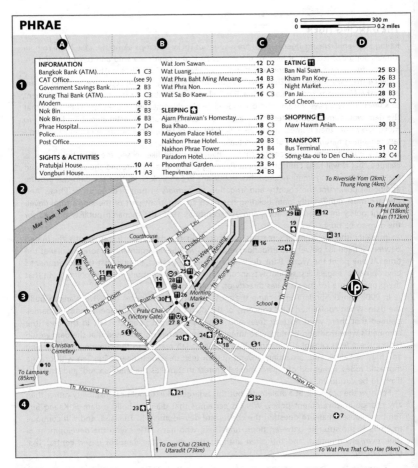

PHRAE

0 — 300 m
0 — 0.2 miles

INFORMATION
Bangkok Bank (ATM)......................**1** C3
CAT Office.....................................(see 9)
Government Savings Bank.............**2** B3
Krung Thai Bank (ATM)..................**3** C3
Modern..**4** B3
Nok Bin...**5** B3
Nok Bin...**6** B3
Phrae Hospital...............................**7** D4
Police...**8** B3
Post Office.....................................**9** B3

SIGHTS & ACTIVITIES
Pratubjai House..............................**10** A4
Vongburi House..............................**11** A3

Wat Jom Sawan..............................**12** D2
Wat Luang.....................................**13** A3
Wat Phra Baht Ming Meuang..........**14** B3
Wat Phra Non.................................**15** A3
Wat Sa Bo Kaew.............................**16** C3

SLEEPING
Ajarn Phraiwan's Homestay............**17** B3
Bua Khao.......................................**18** C3
Maeyom Palace Hotel.....................**19** C2
Nakhon Phrae Hotel.......................**20** B3
Nakhon Phrae Tower.......................**21** B4
Paradorn Hotel...............................**22** C3
Phoomthai Garden..........................**23** B4
Thepviman.....................................**24** B3

EATING
Ban Nai Suan..................................**25** B3
Kham Pan Koey...............................**26** B3
Night Market...................................**27** B3
Pan Jai...**28** B3
Sod Cheon.....................................**29** C2

SHOPPING
Maw Hawm Anian...........................**30** B3

TRANSPORT
Bus Terminal..................................**31** D2
Sŏrng·tǎa·ou to Den Chai................**32** C4

Sleeping
BUDGET

Thepviman (☎ 0 1595 0153; 76-78 Charoen Meuang; r 100-170B) These very basic rooms with cold-water showers, some of which come with Western toilets, are a reasonable choice for baht-pinching travellers.

Ajarn Phraiwan's Homestay (☎ 08 1764 8447; 1 Th Weera; r 150B) This enterprising local language teacher has opened up her vast wooden house to foreign guests. The six rooms are simply furnished and share a bathroom. There's no sign here; simply look for the vegetarian restaurant that she also runs.

Nakhon Phrae Hotel (☎ 0 5451 1122; fax 0 5452 1937; 29 Th Ratsadamnoen; r 290-400B; 🕸 🖵) Being the closest accommodation to the old city has

made this large hotel the most popular, but not necessarily the best budget option. Rooms definitely look their age and have tiny bathrooms, but are mostly clean and comfortable.

Bua Khao (☎ 0 5451 1372; 8 Soi 1, Th Charoen Meuang; r 350-600B; 🕸) Tucked just off the main road, this teak monstrosity has mostly tiny rooms, but heaps of character. Service is great and there's an inviting communal area (involving even more wood) on the ground floor.

Paradorn Hotel (☎ 0 5451 1177; www.phrae-paradorn .th.gs; 177 Th Yantarakitkoson; r 360-650B, ste 800B; 🕸 🖵) Probably the best budget option in town, you can't miss this place with its Burmese-style facade. The fan-cooled rooms have private balconies, and all rates include a simple

NORTHERN THAILAND

breakfast. The hotel is on both sides of Th Yantarakitkoson, and there's also a museum dedicated to the Free Thai movement.

MIDRANGE & TOP END

our pick **Phoomthai Garden** (☎ 0 5462 7359; svoaph@ yahoo.com; 31 Th Sasiboot; r incl breakfast 700-900B, bungalows & ste incl breakfast 1200B; 🕸 💻) Although it's a bit of a hike from the old town, this hotel is the best all-around choice in town. The rooms are modern and comfortable, and all have balconies overlooking the hotel's attractive garden. There are even a few wooden bungalows with huge bathrooms and inviting tubs.

Nakhon Phrae Tower (☎ 0 5452 1321; nakornphrae@ yahoo.com; 3 Th Meuang Hit; s/d incl breakfast 700/900B, ste incl breakfast 2100-2500B; 🕸 💻) A large business-class hotel, this sister to the Nakhon Phrae lies a bit further from the old city.

Maeyom Palace Hotel (☎ 0 5452 1029-35; wcc phrae@hotmail.com; 181/6 Th Yantarakitkoson; r incl breakfast 900-2000B, ste incl breakfast 3500-4000B; 🕸 💻 🌊) Opposite the bus terminal, Phrae's top-end option has all the modern amenities: carpeted rooms with cable TV, sofa and minibar, and the city's only hotel pool. Discounts of up to 30% are typical in the low season.

Eating & Drinking

A small but fun night market convenes just outside the Pratu Chai (Victory Gate) intersection every evening. The vendor in front of the Chinese shrine makes tasty *sôm·dam*, tiny but tasty bowls of *kà·nŏm jeen nám ngée·o* (rice noodle dishes) and dishes of *kôw sôm*, a northern dish of rice cooked with tomatoes.

our pick **Pan Jai** (no roman-script sign; ☎ 0 5462 0727; 2 Th Weera; dishes 20-40B; 🕒 7am-4pm) This open-air place combines everything we like in a restaurant; delicious local eats, attractive setting, good service and low prices. The emphasis is on *kà·nŏm jeen*, fresh rice noodles served with various curries and herbs, but there are a couple of different kinds of noodle soups, a variety of rice dishes and more. Everything's on display, so simply point to whatever looks tastiest.

Kham Pan Koey (no roman-script sign; cnr Th Rawp Meuang & Th Charoen Meuang; dishes 25-40B; 🕒 10am-10pm) This recently refurbished shophouse across from Pratu Chai serves a bit of everything, from *sôm·dam* to rice and noodle dishes. Ice cream and an arsenal of drinks are also there to help beat the heat.

Ban Nai Suan (Route Beat; Th Weera; dishes 30-40B; 🕒 11am-midnight) During the day, this 'house in the garden' serves up a short menu of local dishes. At night, the venue changes to Route Beat, and a Thai menu is served to the sounds of live music.

Sod Cheon (Th Yantarakitkoson; dishes 30-90B; 🕒 11am-4am) On the crossroads, 50m north of the Maeyom Palace Hotel, is this simple but very popular Chinese/Thai restaurant. Choose from the big pots of Chinese-style soups or go for your usual Thai dishes. Good for late night eats. The menu is in Thai only.

There are several restaurants serving local dishes along Rte 1022 as one approaches Wat Phra That Cho Hae (p382).

Shopping

Phrae is known for the distinctive *sêua môr hôrm*, the indigo-dyed cotton farmer's shirt seen all over Thailand. The cloth is made in Ban Thung Hong, just outside the city. A good place to buy *môr hôrm* in town is **Maw Hawm Anian** (no roman-script sign; 36 Th Charoen Muang; 🕒 7am-8.30pm), a shop about 60m from the southeastern gate (Pratu Chai) into the old city.

Getting There & Away

BUS

Unlike most cities in Thailand, Phrae's bus terminal is conveniently located within walking distance of a few accommodation choices.

Come afternoon, there are frequent buses to Den Chai (15B, 30 minutes, every hour from 3.30pm to 7pm). *Sŏrng·tăa·ou* also travel to Den Chai (40B, from 6am to 6pm), departing from next to the vocational college. From Den Chai you can catch the northern train line.

There are frequent buses to Nan (ordinary/2nd class air-con/1st class/VIP 65/88/112/174B, two hours, every hour from 7am to 8.30pm). Buses to Chiang Mai (2nd class air-con/1st class/VIP 147/189/294B, four hours) pass through Lampang and Lamphun on their way to the city. Buses that stop in Chiang Rai (2nd class air-con/1st class/VIP 160/205/239B, four hours, every hour from 7am to 4pm) often continue on to Mae Sai (2nd class air-con/1st class/VIP 196/252/294B, five hours).

There are also several buses to Bangkok (2nd class air-con/1st class/VIP 340/437/680B, eight hours), leaving from 9.15am to noon and from 6.30pm to 10.30pm.

NORTHERN THAILAND

TRAIN

Den Chai train station (☎ 0 5461 3260) is 23km from Phrae. There are frequent blue *sŏrng·tăa·ou* and red buses between Phrae and the station (30B to 40B).

There are eight trains that stop in Den Chai on the way to Bangkok (3rd class fan 256B, 2nd class air-con/fan 574/394B, 2nd class fan sleeper upper/lower 494/544B, 2nd class air-con sleeper upper/lower 754/844B, 1st class sleeper 1272B, 12 hours), most passing the station between 5.30pm and 11pm. To check the most up-to-date timetables and prices in advance call the **State Railway of Thailand** (☎ free 24hr hotline 1690; www.railway.co.th) or look at their website.

Getting Around

A *săhm·lór* anywhere in the old town costs 30B; further afield to somewhere like Pratubjai House it can cost up to 60B. Motorcycle taxis are available at the bus terminal; a trip from here to, say, Pratu Chai should cost around 40B.

Shared *sŏrng·tăa·ou* ply a few of the roads (mainly Th Yantarakitkoson) and cost 10B to 20B, depending on the distance.

AROUND PHRAE
Wat Phra That Cho Hae
วัดพระธาตุช่อแฮ

On a hill about 9km southeast of town off Rte 1022, this *wát* is famous for its 33m-high gilded *chedi*. Cho Hae is the name of the cloth that worshippers wrap around the *chedi* – it's a type of satin thought to have originated in Xishuangbanna (Sipsongpanna, literally '12,000 Rice Fields' in northern Thai), China. Like Chiang Mai's Wat Doi Suthep, this is an important pilgrimage site for Thais living in the north. Tiered *naga* stairs lead to the temple compound.

The interior of the *bòht* is rather tackily decorated with a gilded wooden ceiling, rococo pillars and walls with lotus-bud mosaics. The **Phra Jao Than Jai** Buddha image here, which is similar in appearance to the Phra Chinnarat in Phitsanulok, is reputed to impart fertility to women who make offerings to it.

The scenery along the road leading to the *wát* is picturesque and there is also an abundance of restaurants serving local dishes. *Sŏrng·tăa·ou* between Phrae and Phra That Cho Hae (30B) are frequent.

Phae Meuang Phi
แพะเมืองผี

The name Phae Meuang Phi means 'Ghost-Land', a reference to this strange geological phenomenon approximately 18km northeast of Phrae off Rte 101. Erosion has created bizarre pillars of soil and rock that look like giant fungi. The area has been made a provincial park; a few walking trails and viewpoints are recent additions. There are picnic pavilions in the park and food vendors selling *gài yâhng* (grilled, spiced chicken), *sôm·đam* and sticky rice near the entrance.

Getting to Phae Meuang Phi by public transport is complicated; talk to Khun Kung at Nok Bin (p378) for details.

NAN PROVINCE

Tucked into Thailand's northeastern corner, Nan is a remote province to be explored for its natural beauty. Nan's unique ethnic groups are another highlight and differ significantly from those in other northern provinces. Outside the Mae Nam Nan valley, the predominant hill tribes are Mien, with smaller numbers of Hmong, and dispersed throughout Nan are four lesser-known groups seldom seen outside this province: the Thai Lü, Mrabri, Htin and Khamu.

It's now also possible for foreign travellers holding a Lao visa to cross into Laos at the village of Ban Huay Kon, 140km north of Nan. For details see p389.

NAN
น่าน
pop 20,413

Due to its remote location, Nan is not the kind of destination most travellers are going to stumble upon. And its largely featureless downtown isn't going to inspire many postcards home. But if you've taken the time to get here, you'll be rewarded by a city rich in both culture and history. Many of Nan's residents are Thai Lü, the ancestors of immigrants from Xishuangbanna, in southern China. This cultural legacy is seen in the city's art and architecture, particularly in its exquisite temples. A Lanna influence on the town can also be seen in the remains of the old city wall and several early *wát*.

History

For centuries Nan was an isolated, in-dependent kingdom with few ties to the outside world. Ample evidence of prehistoric habitation exists, but it wasn't until several small *meuang* consolidated to form Nanthaburi in the mid-14th century that the city became a power to contend with. Towards the end of the 14th century Nan became one of the nine northern Thai-Lao principalities that comprised Lan Na Thai. The city-state flourished throughout the 15th century under the name Chiang Klang (Middle City), a reference to its position approximately midway between Chiang Mai (New City) and Chiang Thong (Golden City, which is today's Luang Prabang). The Burmese took control of the kingdom in 1558 and transferred many of the inhabitants to Burma as slaves; the city was all but abandoned until western Thailand was wrested from the Burmese in 1786. The local dynasty then regained local sovereignty and it remained semi-autonomous until 1931, when Nan finally (and reluctantly) accepted full Bangkok sponsorship.

Information

Bangkok Bank (Th Sumonthewarat) Near the Nan Fah and Dhevaraj hotels. Operates foreign-exchange services and has ATMs.

CAT office (Main post office, Th Mahawong; 7am-10pm) Has a Home Country Direct Phone.

Kan Internet (Th Mahayot; per hr 15B; 9am-10pm) Other places offering internet services are available around town for about 20B per hour.

Kasikornbank (Th Sumonthewarat) Near Bangkok Bank and offering the same services.

Main post office (Th Mahawong; 8.30am-4.30pm Mon-Fri, 9am-noon Sat, Sun & holidays) In the centre of town.

Siam Commercial Bank (Th Anantaworarittidet) ATM and foreign-exchange service.

Tourist Information centre (0 5471 0216; Th Pha Kong; 8am-5pm) New centre, complete with coffee shop. Opposite Wat Phumin. Fhu Travel is also a good source of information (p385).

Sights

WAT PHUMIN

วัดภูมินทร

Nan's most famous temple is celebrated for its exquisite murals that were executed during the late 19th century by a Thai Lü artist called Thit Buaphan. For an insight into the historical significance of the murals, see boxed text, p385.

The exterior of the temple takes the form of a cruciform *bòht* that was constructed in 1596 and restored during the reign of Chao Anantavorapitthidet (1867–74). The *bòht* exemplifies the work of Thai Lü architects, and the ornate altar sitting in the centre of the *bòht* has four sides, with four Sukhothai-style sitting Buddhas in *mahn wí-chai* ('victory over Mara' – with one hand touching the ground) posture, facing in each direction.

NAN NATIONAL MUSEUM

พิพิธภัณฑสถานแห่งชาติน่าน

Housed in the 1903-vintage palace of Nan's last two feudal lords, this **museum** (0 5477 2777; Th Pha Kong; admission 100B; 9am-4pm) first opened its doors in 1973. In terms of collection and content, it's one of the country's better provincial museums, and has English labels for most items.

The ground floor has ethnological exhibits covering the various ethnic groups found in the province. Among the items on display are silverwork, textiles, folk utensils and tribal costumes. On the 2nd floor are exhibits on Nan history, archaeology, local architecture, royal regalia, weapons, ceramics and religious art. Of the latter, the museum's collection of Buddha images includes some rare Lanna styles as well as the floppy-eared local styles. Also on display on the 2nd floor is a rare 'black' elephant tusk said to have been presented to a Nan lord over 300 years ago by the Khün ruler of Chiang Tung (Kengtung).

WAT PHRA THAT CHAE HAENG

วัดพระธาตุแช่แห้ง

Two kilometres past the bridge that spans Mae Nam Nan, heading southeast out of town, this temple dating from 1355 is the most sacred *wát* in Nan Province. It's set in a square, walled enclosure on top of a hill with a view of Nan and the valley. The Thai Lü–influenced *bòht* features a triple-tiered roof with carved wooden eaves and dragon reliefs over the doors. A gilded Lanna-style *chedi* sits on a large square base next to the *bòht*; visit late in the day and the structure practically glows in the afternoon light.

WAT PHRA THAT CHANG KHAM

วัดพระธาตุช้างค้ำ

This is the second-most important **temple** (Th Pha Kong) in the city after Wat Phra That Chae

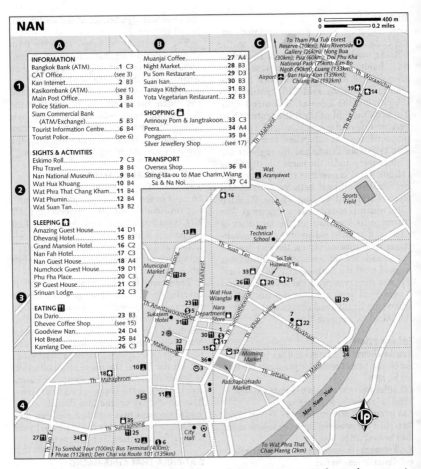

NAN

0 — 400 m
0 — 0.2 miles

INFORMATION
Bangkok Bank (ATM)...................**1** C3
CAT Office.............................(see 3)
Kan Internet...........................**2** B3
Kasikornbank (ATM)................(see 1)
Main Post Office....................**3** B4
Police Station........................**4** B4
Siam Commercial Bank
(ATM/Exchange).................**5** B3
Tourist Information Centre.......**6** B4
Tourist Police......................(see 6)

SIGHTS & ACTIVITIES
Eskimo Roll..........................**7** C3
Fhu Travel............................**8** B4
Nan National Museum.............**9** B4
Wat Hua Khuang...................**10** B4
Wat Phra That Chang Kham....**11** B4
Wat Phumin..........................**12** B4
Wat Suan Tan.......................**13** B2

SLEEPING
Amazing Guest House.............**14** D1
Dhevaraj Hotel......................**15** B3
Grand Mansion Hotel.............**16** C2
Nan Fah Hotel......................**17** C3
Nan Guest House..................**18** A4
Numchock Guest House..........**19** D1
Phu Fha Place......................**20** C3
SP Guest House....................**21** C3
Srinuan Lodge......................**22** C3

EATING
Da Dario.............................**23** B3
Dhevee Coffee Shop.............(see 15)
Goodview Nan.....................**24** D4
Hot Bread...........................**25** B4
Kamlang Dee.......................**26** C3

Muanjai Coffee....................**27** A4
Night Market.......................**28** B3
Pu Som Restaurant...............**29** D3
Suan Isan...........................**30** B3
Tanaya Kitchen....................**31** B3
Yota Vegetarian Restaurant....**32** B3

SHOPPING
Amnouy Porn & Jangtrakoon...**33** C3
Peera.................................**34** A4
Pongparn............................**35** B4
Silver Jewellery Shop............(see 17)

TRANSPORT
Oversea Shop......................**36** B4
Sǒrng·tǎa·ou to Mae Charim, Wiang
Sa & Na Noi.....................**37** C4

To Tham Pha Tub Forest
Reserve (10km); Nan Riverside
Gallery (26km); Pua (60km); Doi Phu Kha
National Park (75km); Nong Bua
(30km); Ban Bo
Ngob (90km); Luang (133km);
Ban Huay Kon (139km);
Chiang Rai (192km)
Airport

Wat Aranyawat

Sports Field

Wat Hua Wiangtai

Municipal Market

Nara Department Store

Sukasem Hotel

Morning Market

Ratchaphatsadu Market

City Hall

To Sombat Tour (100m); Bus Terminal (400m);
Phrae (112km); Den Chai via Route 101 (135km)

To Wat Phra That
Chae Haeng (2km)

Haeng. The founding date is unknown, but the main *wí·hăhn*, reconstructed in 1458, has a huge seated Buddha image and faint murals that have been partially recovered. (Sometime in the mid-20th century an abbot reportedly ordered the murals to be whitewashed because he thought they were distracting worshippers from concentrating on his sermons!)

Also in the *wí·hăhn* is a set of Lanna-period scrolls inscribed (in Lanna script) not only with the usual Buddhist scriptures but with the history, law and astrology of the time. A *tam·mâht* (a 'dhamma seat' used by monks when teaching) sits to one side.

The *chedi* behind the *wí·hăhn* dates to the 14th century, probably around the same time as the temple was founded. It features

elephant supports similar to those seen in Sukhothai and Si Satchanalai.

Next to the *chedi* is a small, undistinguished *bòht* from the same era. Wat Chang Kham's current abbot tells an interesting story involving the *bòht* and a Buddha image that was once kept inside. According to the abbot, in 1955 art historian AB Griswold offered to purchase the 145cm-tall Buddha inside the small *bòht*. The image appeared to be a crude Sukhothai-style walking Buddha moulded of plaster. After agreeing to pay the abbot 25,000B for the image, Griswold began removing the image from the *bòht* – but as he did it fell and the plaster around the statue broke away to reveal an original Sukhothai Buddha of pure gold underneath. Needless to say, the abbot made

Griswold give it back, much to the latter's chagrin. Did Griswold suspect what lay beneath the plaster? The abbot refuses to say. The image is now kept behind a glass partition in the *hŏr đrai* (Tripitaka library) adjacent to the *wí-hăhn*, the largest of its type in Thailand.

OTHER TEMPLES

Wat Hua Khuang, located diagonally opposite Wat Phra That Chang Kham features a distinctive Lanna/Lan Xang–style *chedi* with four Buddha niches, an attractive wooden *hŏr đrai* and a noteworthy *bôht* with a Luang Prabang–style carved wooden veranda. Inside is a carved wooden ceiling and a huge *naga* altar. The temple's founding date is unknown, but stylistic cues suggest this may be one of the city's oldest *wát*.

Reportedly established in 1456, **Wat Suan Tan** (Th Suan Tan) features an interesting 15th-century *chedi* that combines *prang* (Hindu/Khmerstyle *chedi*) and lotus-bud motifs of obvious Sukhothai influence. The heavily restored *wí-hăhn* contains an early Sukhothai-style bronze sitting Buddha.

Activities

TREKKING & RAFTING

Nan has nothing like the organised trekking industry found in Chiang Rai and Chiang Mai, and most visitors, particularly Thais, opt to float rather than walk. White-water rafting along Mae Nam Wa, in northern Nan, is only possible when the water level is high (September to January), and is said to be best during the early part of the rainy season. The rapids span from level I to IV, and pass through intact jungle and remote villages.

Eskimo Roll (☎ 08 3902 6111; www.kayakraft.com; 40/1 Th Norkham; 2 days & 1 night per person 3900B, 3 days & 2 nights per person 4500B), run by the amicable Mr Boy, conducts two- to three-day, all-inclusive, rafting and/or kayaking trips.

Fhu Travel (☎ 0 5471 0636, 08 1287 7209; www .fhutravel.com; 453/4 Th Sumonthewarat; 2-person min, per person 'soft' trek 1 day 1200–1500B, 2 days & 1 night 2700B, 3 days & 2 nights 3500B) offers treks to Mabri, Hmong, Mien, Thai Lü and Htin villages, and can also arrange elephant trekking, cycling tours and city tours. The operators have been leading tours for more than 20 years.

THE MURALS OF WAT PHUMIN

Wat Phumin is northern Thailand's Sistine Chapel, and the images on its walls are now found on everything from knick-knacks at Chiang Mai's night bazaar to postcards sold in Bangkok. However, despite the happy scenes depicted, the murals were executed during a period that saw the end of Nan as a semi-independent kingdom. This resulted in several examples of political and social commentary manifesting themselves in the murals, a rarity in Thai religious art.

The murals commissioned by Jao Suliyaphong, the last king of Nan, include the *Khaddhana Jataka*, a relatively obscure story of one of the Buddha's lives that, according to Thai historian David K Wyatt in his excellent book, *Reading Thai Murals*, has never been illustrated elsewhere in the Buddhist world. The story, which is on the left side of the temple's northern wall, depicts an orphan in search of his parents. Wyatt argues that this particular tale was chosen as a metaphor for the kingdom of Nan, which also had been abandoned by a succession of 'parents', the Thai kingdoms of Sukhothai, Chiang Mai and Ayuthaya. At roughly the same time as the murals were painted, Nan was fully incorporated into Siam by King Rama V, and much of its territory was allotted to France. Apparent discontent with this decision can be seen in a scene on the west wall that shows two male monkeys attempting to copulate against a background that, not coincidentally according to Wyatt, resembles the French flag.

The murals are also valuable purely for their artistic beauty, something that is even more remarkable if one steps back and considers the limited palette of colours that the artist, Thit Buaphan, had to work with. The paintings are also fascinating for their fly-on-the-wall depictions of local life in Nan during the end of the 19th century. A depiction of three members of a hill tribe on the west wall includes such details as a man's immense goitre and a barking dog, suggesting this group's place as outsiders. Multiple depictions of a man wearing a feminine shawl, often seen performing traditionally female-only duties, are among the earliest depictions of a *gà·teu·i* (transsexual). And in what must be one of the art world's most superfluous cameos, the artist painted himself on the west wall, flirting with a woman. Considering that the murals took Thit Buaphan more than 20 years to complete, we'll allow him this excess.

Sleeping

Amazing Guest House (☎ 0 5471 0893; 23/7 Th Rat Amnuay; s/d 120/350B; ✷) This intimate place is a bit like staying with your long-lost Thai grandparents. All rooms have wooden floors, clean beds and shared hot-water showers. Rooms in concrete rooms out the back have en-suite bathrooms. Bicycles and motorbikes can be rented here, and free pick-up from the bus station is available.

Numchock Guest House (☎ 08 1998 1855; 37 Th Rat Amnuay; r with fan/air-con 200/300B; ✷) Also on Th Rat Amnuay, across from Amazing Guest House, another local family has turned part of its tidy residential compound into an inviting guesthouse. Rooms are well equipped, but a long walk from the centre of town.

Nan Guest House (☎ 0 5477 1849; 57/16 Th Mahaphrom; r 170-250B; ✷ ⬛) In a quiet residential area a short walk from most of Nan's famous temples, this well-maintained place has spotless spacious rooms, most with en-suite hot-water bathrooms. The Australian owner also organises tours, has an international call service and rents out mountain bikes.

Grand Mansion Hotel (no roman-script sign; ☎ 0 5475 0514; 71/1 Th Mahayot; r 230-500B; ✷ ⬛) This long two-storey building holds 71 rooms around an interior courtyard. They're largely featureless, but include ample amenities, and some have balconies. There's no English sign, so look for the tall wooden gateway on Th Mahayot after Wat Suan Tan; the hotel is about 100m off the road.

SP Guest House (☎ 0 5477 4897; Soi Tok Huawiang Tai; r with fan/air-con 300/400B; ✷) This small guesthouse boasts a homey feel. There are six large, well-equipped bedrooms and bathrooms, with wooden or tiled floors. All come with hot water and cable TV, and a choice of fan or air-con. Eight new rooms were being built at the time of writing.

ourpick Phu Fha Place (☎ 0 5471 0222; 237/8 Th Sumonthewarat; r 350B; ✷ ⬛) This brand new family-run hotel is by far the best deal in town, if not in this part of northern Thailand. The huge rooms have been decorated with attractive teak furniture, including the kind of puffy inviting beds you'd normally find at places that charge 10 times this much. Bathrooms are also big enough to get lost in, and like the rooms, are outfitted with attractive tiles. The only downside is that there are no windows to let in natural light.

Nan Fah Hotel (☎ 0 5471 0284; fax 0 5475 1087; 438-440 Th Sumonthewarat; s/d/tr 350/600/700B; ✷) This 80-year-old all-wooden hotel feels like a rooming house, with neat, large rooms. They all come with cable TV, fridge and hot-water showers. There's a good restaurant attached, and bicycles, motorbikes and pick-ups can be rented here.

Srinuan Lodge (no roman-script sign; ☎ 0 5471 0174; 40 Th Norkham; r/ste 400/300B; ✷) This two-storey brick structure holds 25 rooms decked out in *faux rustique*–style with logs, bamboo and local textiles. Despite the design theme, the rooms look comfortable, and are about as close as you'll get to sleeping near the Mae Nam Nan.

Dhevaraj Hotel (☎ 0 5471 0078; 466 Th Sumonthewarat; r incl breakfast 600-1200B; ste incl breakfast 3500B; ✷ ⬛ ⬛) From the outside, this hotel looks like a featureless box, but a peek inside reveals clean, modern rooms with all the amenities you'd expect at this price. Paradoxically, the cheaper rooms appear a bit nicer, with lots of natural light and attractive wicker furniture.

Eating & Drinking

Despite its other charms, Nan has one of the least inspiring dining scenes in northern Thailand.

Yota Vegetarian Restaurant (Th Mahawong; dishes 10-35B; ⏱ 7am-3pm) Run by the friendliest lady in town who will not let you leave hungry, this is perhaps the best deal in Nan. It's popular and once the food is gone after lunch, that's it for the day.

Kamlang Dee (no roman-script sign; Th Sumonthewarat; dishes 15-30B; ⏱ 11am-7.30pm) This tiny, colourful restaurant is known for its *sôm·đam tôrt*, deep-fried *sôm·đam*. It's an equal parts crunchy and refreshing snack. They also do great fruit smoothies and other basic dishes.

Hot Bread (☎ 08 9635 9375; 38/1-2 Th Suriyaphong; dishes 20-80B; ⏱ 7am-8pm) This cheery, foreigner-friendly restaurant does breakfasts and coffee, as well as a lengthy menu with heaps of veggie options. The attached noodle shop sells *kâo soy* and other noodle dishes until 5pm.

ourpick Pu Som Restaurant (no roman-script sign; ☎ 08 1675 3795; 203/1 Th Mano; dishes 30-70B; ⏱ 11am-midnight) Like a misplaced Texas barnhouse, this popular local restaurant is decked out in cowboy hats, cow skulls, gun holsters, and a plethora of images of the Marlboro Man. Fittingly, the emphasis here is on beef, served in the local style as *lâhp*, or as *néu·a nêung*, steamed over herbs and served with an incredibly delicious galangal dip. The menu here is only in Thai, but the enthusiastic staff will do all they can to help.

Tanaya Kitchen (☎ 0 5471 0930; 75/23-24 Th Anantaworarittidet; dishes 30-80B; ♥ 7am-9.30pm) Neat and tidy, with a creative selection of dishes made without MSG, and a variety of vegetarian (and nonvegetarian) options, Tanaya is a good choice for any diet. It caters to a mostly tourist clientele.

Suan Isan (☎ 0 5477 2913; Th Sumonthewarat; dishes 30-90B; ♥ 11am-11pm) For Isan food, this semi-outdoor spot is 200m up the lane off Th Sumonthewarat past the Bangkok Bank.

Muanjai Coffee (☎ 08 9636 3970; 19/3 Th Jao Fa; dishes 35-45B; ♥ 7am-7.30pm) With its modern decor and militant self-service policy, this cafe is the Starbucks of Nan. They do good coffee, and even have a fireplace for those cold northern winters.

Goodview Nan (☎ 08 1675 3795; 203/1 Th Mano; dishes 35-150B; ♥ 11am-midnight) One of the few places in town to take advantage of the views over the Mae Nam Nan, this place works equally well as a dinner date or a riverside pub. There's an English-language menu and at night, a live music soundtrack.

Dhevee Coffee Shop (☎ 0 5471 0094; Dhevaraj Hotel, 466 Th Sumonthewarat; dishes 40-140B; ♥ 6am-2am) Modest, clean and reliable, Dhevaraj Hotel's restaurant does good buffets (lunch buffet 69B), has a huge menu and is open when many other places are closed.

Da Dario (☎ 08 7184 5436; Th Mahayot; dishes 40-160B; ♥ 9am-5pm) This Italian restaurant makes great breakfasts, delicious pizza and pasta, as well as other Western treats and some Thai dishes. Prices are reasonable, service is excellent, the atmosphere is homey and the food attracts a cadre of regulars.

The night market, on Th Pha Kong, provides a few decent food stall offerings.

Shopping

Nan is a great place to pick up some souvenirs, and good buys include local textiles, especially the Thai Lü weaving styles. Typical Thai Lü fabrics feature red and black designs on white cotton in floral, geometric and animal designs. A favourite is the *lai nám lǎi* (flowing-water design) that shows stepped patterns representing streams, rivers and waterfalls. Local Hmong appliqué and Mien embroidery are of excellent

quality. Htin grass-and-bamboo baskets and mats are worth a look, too. Good shops for textiles are Amnouy Porn and Jangtrakoon, next to each other on Th Sumonthewarat; there are several other similar shops along the same stretch of road. **Pongparn** (☎ 0 5475 7334; www.pongparn.com; 10/4 Th Suriyaphong; ♥ 8am-7pm), a short walk from Wat Phumin, offers a variety of local textiles and handicrafts in one location. And just up the road, **Peera** (☎ 0 5475 7007; 26 Th Suriyaphong; ♥ 8am-7pm) offers high-quality local textiles, mostly women's skirts and blouses. There's also a silver shop attached to Nan Fah Hotel (opposite).

Getting There & Away

AIR

Nok Air (☎ nationwide call centre 1318; www.nokair .co.th) and **PB Air** (☎ 0 5477 1729; www.pbair.com; Nan Airport) operate a code-share flight between Nan and Bangkok's Suvarnabhumi (3440B, 1⅓ hours, once daily).

BUS

From Nan all buses, including privately run buses, leave from the bus terminal at the southwestern edge of town. A motorcycle taxi from the station to the centre of town costs 25B.

To get to the border crossing at Ban Huay Kon, you'll need to take a bus to Ngob (85B, 2½ hours); buses leave once every hour during the day. For details on getting to the border, see p389.

If you're connecting to the train station at Den Chai in Phrae, there are buses on a nearly hourly basis during the day (ordinary/2nd class air-con 71/99B, three hours).

The most convenient route to Chiang Mai is via Phrae and Lampang (2nd class air-con/ 1st class/VIP 221/284/442B, five hours), with departures leaving on a regular basis during the day. To Chiang Rai, there are two daily departures (2nd class air-con 176B, five hours, 9am and 9.30am).

There are numerous buses to Bangkok (2nd class air-con/1st class/VIP 414/523/829B, 10 to 11 hours, from 8am to 9am and 6.45pm to 7.30pm). The private **Sombat Tour** (☎ 0 5471 1078) buses to Bangkok can be found on the road leading to the bus terminal.

SŎRNG·TĂA·OU

Pick-ups to districts in the northern part of the province (Tha Wang Pha, Pua, Phah Tup) leave from the bus terminal. Southbound *sŏrng·tăa·ou* (for Mae Charim, Wiang Sa, Na Noi) depart from the car park opposite Ratchaphatsadu Market on Th Jettabut.

TRAIN
The northern railway makes a stop in Den Chai, a three-hour bus ride from Nan. See p382 for more Den Chai train details.

Getting Around
Săhm·lór around town cost 20B to 30B.

Oversea Shop (☎ 0 5471 0258; 488 Th Sumonthewarat; bicycles per day 50-80B, motorcycles per day 180-200B; 8.30am-5.30pm) rents out better bicycles and motorcycles than other places in town. It can also handle repairs.

AROUND NAN
Tham Phah Tup Forest Reserve
ถ้ำผาตูบ
This limestone cave complex is about 10km north of Nan and is part of a relatively new wildlife reserve. Some 17 **caves** have been counted, of which nine are easily located by means of established (but unmarked) trails.

From Nan you can catch a *sŏrng·tăa·ou* bound for Pua or Thung Chang; it will stop at the turn-off to the caves for 30B. The vehicles leave from the bus station.

Nan Riverside Gallery
Twenty kilometres north of Nan on Rte 1080, this private **art gallery** (☎ 0 5479 8046; www.nanart gallery.com; Km20, Rte 1080; admission 20B; 9am-5pm Wed-Sun) exhibits contemporary Nan-influenced art in a peaceful setting. Established in 2004 by Nan artist Winai Prabipoo, the two-storey building holds the more interesting temporary exhibitions downstairs – sculpture, ceramics and drawings – as well as a permanent painting collection upstairs – which seems to be mainly inspired by the Wat Phumin murals. The unusual building is a light-filled converted rice barn with an arrow-shaped turret. The shop and cafe have seats right on the Mae Nam Nan and the beautiful manicured gardens are nice to wander around. From Nan, take a northbound bus (20B) or a *sŏrng·tăa·ou* (30B) to the gallery.

Nong Bua
หนองบัว
This neat and tidy Thai Lü village near the town of Tha Wang Pha, approximately 30km north of Nan, is famous for Lü-style **Wat Nong**

Bua. Featuring a typical two-tiered roof and carved wooden portico, the *bòht* design is simple yet striking – note the carved *naga* heads at the roof corners. Inside the *bòht* are some noteworthy *jataka* murals thought to have been painted by Thit Buaphan, the same mural artist whose work can be seen at Wat Phumin. Be sure to leave at the altar a donation for temple upkeep and for its restoration.

There is a model Thai Lü house directly behind the *wát* where weaving is done and you can buy attractive local textiles.

To get there, northbound buses and *sŏrng·tăa·ou* (35B) to Tha Wang Pha leave from the bus terminal. Get off at Samyaek Longbom, a three-way intersection before Tha Wang Pha, and walk west to a bridge over Mae Nam Nan and turn left. Continue until you reach another small bridge, after which Wat Nong Bua will be on your right. It's 3km from the highway to the *wát*.

Doi Phu Kha National Park
อุทยานแห่งชาติดอยภูคา
This **national park** (☎ 0 5470 1000; admission 200B) is centred on 2000m-high Doi Phu Kha, the province's highest peak, in Amphoe Pua and Amphoe Bo Kleua in northeastern Nan (about 75km from Nan). There are several Htin, Mien, Hmong and Thai Lü **villages** in the park and vicinity, as well as a couple of **caves** and **waterfalls**, and endless opportunities for forest **walks**. The park headquarters has a basic map and staff can arrange a local guide for walks or more extended excursions around the area, as well as rafting on the Nam Wa. The park is often cold in the cool season and especially wet in the wet season.

The park offers a variety of **bungalows** (☎ 0 2562 0760; www.dnp.go.th; 2-7 people 300-2500B), and there is a nearby restaurant and basic shop.

To reach the national park by public transport you must first take a bus or *sŏrng·tăa·ou* north of Nan to Pua (50B), and then cross the highway to pick up one of the few daily *sŏrng·tăa·ou* that pass the park headquarters (40B, 30 minutes, 7.30am, 9.30am, 11.30am and 2pm).

Ban Bo Luang
บ้านบ่อหลวง
pop 4000
Ban Bo Luang (also known as Ban Bo Kleua, or Salt Well Village) is a picturesque Htin village southeast of the Doi Phu Kha National Park

where the long-standing occupation has been the extraction of salt from local salt wells. It's easy to find the main community salt wells, more or less in the centre of the village.

If you have your own transport, the village is a good base for exploring the nearby national parks, Doi Phu Kha and **Khun Nan National Park** (☎ 08 4483 7240; admission free). The latter is located a few kilometres north of Ban Bo Kleua, and has a 2km walk from the visitor centre that ends in a viewpoint looking over local villages and nearby Laos.

Phu Fah (☎ 0 5471 0610; Tambon Phu Fah), a development program established by Princess Sirindhorn, is located approximately 15km south of Ban Bo Luang. The expansive grounds include tea plantations and other agricultural projects. There's a gift shop with local goods, as well as accommodation (☎ 08 9557 5734; dorms 100B, doubles 600B to 800B) and a restaurant.

Accommodation in Ban Bor Luang is available at **Boklua View** (☎ 08 1809 6392; www .bokluaview.com; Ban Bo Luang; bungalows 1500-1650B), a new, attractive and well-run hillside resort overlooking the village and the Nam Mang that runs through it. The resort has its own garden and serves good food (be sure to try Chef Toun's chicken deep-fried with northern Thai spices).

There are a few small restaurants serving basic dishes in Ban Bo Luang.

To reach Ban Bo Luang from Nan, take a bus or *sŏrng·tǎa·ou* north of Nan to Pua (50B), cross the highway to take the *sŏrng·tǎa·ou* that terminate in the village (80B, one hour, 7.30am, 9.30am, 11.30am and 2pm).

Ban Huay Kon

Located 140km north of Nan, Ban Huay Kon is a very quiet village in the mountains near the Lao border. There's a fun **border market** on Saturday mornings, but most will come here because of the town's recent status as an international border crossing to Laos. A sign near the border boasts that it's only 35km to the Lao town of Hongsa, 152km to Luang Prabang (90km by boat), 295km to the Chinese town of Mengla, and 406km to Dien Bien Phu in Vietnam.

To get to Ban Huay Kon, you'll need to hop on a bus from Nan to Ngob (85B, 2½ hours, once every hour during the day). From there you'll need to transfer to either the morning or afternoon *sŏrng·tǎa·ou* that goes the 30km

further uphill to Ban Huay Kon (50B, one hour, twice daily).

BORDER CROSSING (LAOS)

To cross at Ban Huay Kon you must have arranged a Lao visa ahead of time. If you have this, the **Thai immigration booth** (☎ 0 5469 3530; ☑ 8am-5pm), 3km from Ban Huay Kon, will allow you to cross over to the Lao immigration booth and on to the Lao village of Meuang Ngoen, where you can find sporadic transport to points abroad.

There's basic bungalow-style accommodation between the village and the border. Ask in the village for details.

PHITSANULOK PROVINCE

PHITSANULOK

พิษณุโลก

pop 80,254

Phitsanulok sees relatively few independent travellers, but a fair amount of package tourists, perhaps because the city is a convenient base from which to explore the attractions of historical Sukhothai, Si Satchanalai and Kamphaeng Phet. Due to large parts of the town being burned down by a massive fire in 1957, Phitsanulok's architecture is pretty nondescript. Yet this vibrant and extremely friendly city boasts some interesting sites and museums, chief of which is Wat Phra Si Ratana Mahathat, which contains one of Thailand's most revered Buddha images. And those willing to forge their own path can also use the city as a base to visit the nearby national parks and wildlife sanctuaries of Thung Salaeng Luang (p396) and Phu Hin Rong Kla (p395), the former strategic headquarters of the Communist Party of Thailand (CPT).

Information

Shops offering internet access dot the streets around the railway station, near Topland Plaza and on the western bank of the river near Saphan Ekathotsarot. Several banks in town offer foreign-exchange services and ATMs. There are also several ATMs inside the Wat Phra Si Ratana Mahathat compound.

CAT office (Th Phuttha Bucha; ☑ 7am-11pm) At the post office. Offers phone and internet services.

Krung Thai Bank (35 Th Naresuan; ⊗ to 8pm) An after-hours exchange window.

Main post office (Th Phuttha Bucha; ⊗ 8.30am-4.30pm Mon-Fri, 9am-noon Sat & Sun)

TAT office (☎ 0 5525 2742/2743; tatphlok@tat.or.th; 209/7-8 Th Borom Trailokanat; ⊗ 8.30am-4.30pm) Off Th Borom Trailokanat, with helpful staff who hand out free maps of the town and a walking-tour sheet. It also runs a sightseeing tram (see p395). This is the official information office for Sukhothai and Phetchabun provinces as well. If you plan to do the trip from Phitsanulok to Lom Sak, ask for the 'Green Route' map of Hwy 12, which marks several national parks, waterfalls and resorts along the way.

Tourist police (☎ 1155; Th Ekathotsarot) Located 300m north of Topland Plaza.

Sights

WAT PHRA SI RATANA MAHATHAT

วัดพระศรีรัตนมหาธาตุ

The full name of this temple is Wat Phra Si Ratana Mahathat, but the locals call it Wat Phra Si or Wat Yai. The main *wí·hǎhn* appears small from the outside, but houses the Phra Phuttha Chinnarat, one of Thailand's most revered and copied Buddha images. This famous bronze statue is probably second in importance only to the Emerald Buddha in Bangkok's Wat Phra Kaew.

The story goes that construction of this wát was commissioned under the reign of King Li Thai in 1357. When it was completed, King Li Thai wanted it to contain three high-quality bronze images, so he sent for well-known sculptors from Si Satchanalai, Chiang Saen and Hariphunchai (Lamphun), as well as five Brahman priests. The first two castings worked well, but the third required three attempts before it was decreed the best of all. Legend has it that a white-robed sage appeared from nowhere to assist in the final casting, then disappeared. This last image was named the Chinnarat (Victorious King) Buddha and it became the centrepiece in the *wí·hǎhn*. The other two images, Phra Chinnasi and Phra Si Satsada, were later moved to the royal temple of Wat Bowonniwet in Bangkok.

The image was cast in the late Sukhothai style, but what makes it strikingly unique is the flamelike halo around the head and torso that turns up at the bottom to become dragon-serpent heads on either side of the image. The head of this Buddha is a little wider than standard Sukhothai, giving the statue a very solid feel.

Another sanctuary to one side has been converted into a free **museum** (⊗ 9am-5.30pm Wed-Sun), displaying antique Buddha images, ceramics and other historic artefacts.

Despite the holiness of the temple, endless loud broadcasts asking for donations, Thai musicians, a strip of vendors hawking everything from herbs to lottery tickets, several ATM machines, and hundreds of visitors all contribute to a relentlessly hectic atmosphere. Come early (ideally before 7am) if you're looking for quiet contemplation or simply wish to take photos, and regardless of the time be sure to dress appropriately – no shorts or sleeveless tops.

Near Wat Yai, on the same side of the river, is another temple of the same period – **Wat Nang Phaya**.

FOLK MUSEUM, BUDDHA-CASTING FOUNDRY & BIRD GARDEN

พิพิธภัณฑ์พื้นบ้านนายทวี/โรงหล่อพระ/สวนนก

A nationally acclaimed expert on Thai folkways, a former military cartographer and Buddha statue caster, and apparent bird aficionado, Sergeant Major Thawee Buranakhet has taken from his diverse experiences and interests to create three very worthwhile attractions in Phitsanulok.

The **Sergeant Major Thawee Folk Museum** (26/43 Th Wisut Kasat; child/adult 20/50B; ⊗ 8.30am-4.30pm Tue-Sun) displays a remarkable collection of tools, textiles and photographs from Phitsanulok Province. This fascinating museum is spread throughout five traditional-style Thai buildings with well-groomed gardens, and the displays are all accompanied by informative and legible English descriptions. Those interested in cooking will find much of interest in the display of a traditional Thai kitchen and the various traps used to catch game. Male visitors will be undoubtedly disturbed by a display that describes traditional bull castration – a process that apparently involves no sharp tools. To get here take bus 8.

Across the street and also belonging to Dr Thawee is a small **Buddha Casting Foundry** (⊗ 8am-5pm) where bronze Buddha images of all sizes are cast. Visitors are welcome to watch and there are even detailed photo exhibits demonstrating the lost-wax method of metal casting. Some of the larger images take a year or more to complete. There is a small gift shop at the foundry where you can purchase bronze images of various sizes.

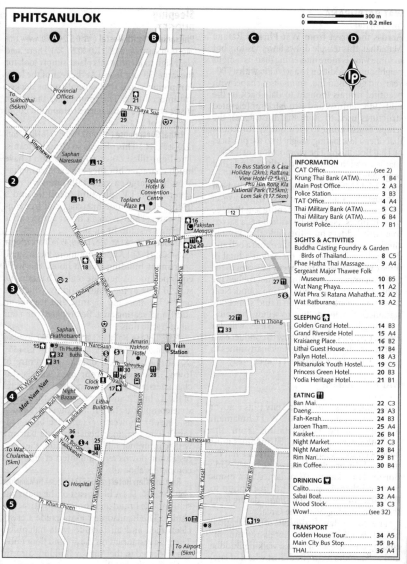

PHITSANULOK

In addition to the bronze foundry, there is also a display of fighting cocks, which are bred and sold all over the country. (The official English name for this part of the facility is 'The Centre of Conservative Folk Cock'.)

Attached to the foundry is Dr Thawee's latest project, **Garden Birds of Thailand** (☎ 0 5521 2540; child/adult 20/50B; ☺ 8.30am-5pm). This collection of aviaries contains indigenous Thai birds including some endangered species, like the very pretty pink-chested jamu fruit-dove, and the prehistoric-looking helmeted hornbill. Unfortunately, the cages are generally rather small and don't reflect the birds' natural environments.

WAT RATBURANA
วัดราชบูรณะ

Across the street from Wat Phra Si Ratana Mahathat, this temple draws fewer visitors but in some ways is more interesting than its famous neighbour. In addition to a *wí·hähn* with a 700-year-old gold Buddha, an *ùbohsòt* chapel with beautiful murals thought to date back to the mid-19th century, and two *hör drai* (elevated structures used to store Buddhist texts), the temple is also home to a few quirky attractions that offer a fascinating insight into the practices of Thai Buddhism. The most obvious of these is a large wooden boat decked with garlands that originally served to transport King Rama V on an official visit to Phitsanulok. Today the boat is thought to grant wishes to those who make an offering and crawl under its entire length three or nine times. Next to the *wí·hähn* is a sacred tree with ladders on either side that visitors climb up, leave an offering, then ring a bell and descend, again repeating the action a total of three or nine times. And directly adjacent to the tree is an immense gong that, when rubbed the right way, creates a unique ringing sound. Near each of these attractions you'll find somebody stationed who, in addition to selling the coins, incense and flowers used in offerings, will also instruct visitors in exactly how to conduct each particular ritual, including how many times to pass, what to offer, and what prayer to say.

WAT CHULAMANI
วัดจุฬามณี

Five kilometres south of the city (bus 5 down Th Borom Trailokanat, 5B), Wat Chulamani harbours some ruins dating from the Sukhothai period. The original buildings must have been impressive, judging from what remains of the ornate Khmer-style tower. King Borom Trailokanat was ordained as a monk here and there is an old Thai inscription to that effect on the ruined *wí·hähn*, dating from the reign of King Narai the Great.

The tower has little left of its original height, but Khmer-style lintels remain, including one with a Sukhothai walking Buddha and a *dhammacakka* (Buddhist wheel of law) in the background.

Activities
MASSAGE

Relaxation takes an entirely new form at **Phae Hatha Thai Massage** (☎ 0 5524 3389; Th Wangchan; massage per hr with fan/AC 120/150B; ❦ 9am-10pm), a Thai massage centre housed on a floating raft.

Sleeping
BUDGET

Phitsanulok Youth Hostel (☎ 0 5524 2060; www.tyha .org; 38 Th Sanam Bin; d 120, r 200-400B; ✷) There's no clear sign to identify this place; simply look for the large '38' out front. At the rear of the leafy compound you'll find several rooms decked out in aged teak. The rooms have their own rustic charm, but the entire compound could use a bit of TLC.

Lithai Guest House (☎ 0 5521 9626; 73 Th Phayalithai; r 220-460B; ✷) This place is so clean it gleams. The light-filled 60 or so rooms don't have much character but they are excellent value. Most have large en-suite bathrooms with hot water, cable TV, plentiful furniture and a fridge. Rates include breakfast and free bottled water. There is an air ticket agent, coffee shop and restaurant on site.

Kraisaeng Place (☎ 0 5521 0509; 45 Th Thammabucha; r 350-450B; ✷ ▯) Appearing more like a small apartment building than a hotel, the well-equipped rooms here are a good bargain. Be sure to look at the double rooms, which for only a bit more are gigantic and feature an additional seating area. Be prepared for a fair bit of traffic noise.

our pick Casa Holiday (☎ 0 5530 4340; www.my casaholiday.com; 305/2 Th Phichaisongkhram; r 380-650B; ✷ ▯) Located 2km outside the centre of town, if you've got your own wheels this character-laden place is a no-brainer. Several of the 42 bright and airy rooms in the ranch-style complex feature fun design extras such as outdoor showers or 'Japanese beds' (futons). The top floor boasts a wide balcony with communal tables and chairs, there's a restaurant downstairs, and internet-equipped computers abound.

Rattana View Hotel (☎ 0 5522 1999; 847 Th Mitraphap; r 450-790B; ✷ ▯) A block east of the main bus station, this brand-new hotel is an attractive choice. The handsome rooms exude a crisp, clean feel, and all include wide balconies. There's a restaurant on the ground floor and a spa is located in the Amway Building directly in front of the hotel.

Princess Green Hotel (☎ 0 5530 4988; www.princess green.com; 8 Th Phra Ong Dam; r 490B; ✷ ▯) This 28-room hotel has spacious, tidy rooms that are well furnished and have cable TV and minibar. The only downside here is the hotel's proximity to the town mosque, making early morning wake-up calls a potential issue for some.

MIDRANGE & TOP END

Golden Grand Hotel (☎ 0 5521 0234; www.goldengrand hotel.com; 66 Th Thammabucha; r 790-950B; ✖ ▯) Mint green went out of style a long time ago, but this is about the only fault we can find with the Golden Grand. The rooms are so tidy we're wondering if they've ever even been slept in, and friendly staff and great views of the city from the upper floors are even more incentive to stay here.

Pailyn Hotel (☎ 0 5525 2411; 38 Th Borom Trailokanat; s/d/ste incl breakfast 900/1000/3500B; ✖) The conveniently located, 13-storey Pailyn has an enormous lobby with an unfortunate looking catfish squashed in a tank. The rooms are spacious, have cable TV and minibar, and are well decorated apart from very loud batik panels above the beds. Some have great river views. There are restaurants and lounges downstairs, and the staff members are professional and helpful.

Grand Riverside Hotel (☎ 0 5524 8333; www.tgrhotel .com; 59 Th Phra Ruang; r 1500-1800B, ste 3000B; ✖ ▯ ✖) Overlooking the Mae Nam Nan from its west bank, this towering hotel offers all the amenities you'd expect in a relatively new, top-end hotel. Deluxe rooms offer an additional sitting area and river views. There's a restaurant and spa, and by the time you read this, a pool and fitness centre as well.

Yodia Heritage Hotel (☎ 08 1613 8496; www.yodia heritage.com; Th Phuttha Bucha; r 3750-6000B, ste 15,000B; ✖ ▯ ✖) Although still under construction at the time of research, when finished this boutique hotel will undoubtedly take the crown as Phitsanulok's most upscale accommodation. Located near a quiet stretch of the Mae Nam Nan, but still conveniently close to the centre, the 21 rooms here will follow several different design themes, all luxurious.

Eating

Phitsanulok takes its cuisine seriously. The city is particularly obsessive about night markets, and there are no fewer than three dotted in various locations around town. The most well known, Phitsanulok's **Night Bazaar** (dishes 40-80B; ✖ 5pm-3am), focuses mainly on clothing, but a few riverfront restaurants specialise in *pàk bûng loy fáh* (literally 'floating-in-the-sky morning glory vine'), where the cook fires up a batch of *pàk bûng* in the wok and then flings it through the air to a waiting server who catches it on a plate. If you're lucky, you'll be here when a tour group is trying to catch the flying vegetables, but is actually dropping *pàk bûng* all over the place. Another **night market** (dishes 20-40B; ✖ 5pm-midnight) lines either side of Th Phra Ong Dam north of Th U Thong. A famous vendor here sells a variety of deep-fried insects.

Another dish associated with Phitsanulok is *gŏoay-dĕe-o hôy kăh* (literally, 'legs-hanging' noodles). The name comes from the way customers sit on the floor facing the river, with their legs dangling below. **Rim Nan** (☎ 08 1379 3172; 5/4 Th Phaya Sua; dishes 20-35B; ✖ 9am-4pm), north of Wat Phra Si Ratana Mahathat, is one of a few similar restaurants along Th Phutta Bucha that offer noodles and 'alternative' seating. The restaurant has an English menu with photos; try the *bà-mèe nám*, yellow egg and wheat noodles with pork broth.

Fah-Kerah (786 Th Phra Ong Dam; dishes 5-20B; ✖ 6am-2pm) There are several Thai-Muslim cafes near the mosque on Th Phra Ong Dam, and this is a popular one. Thick *roh-dee* is served up with *gaang mát-sà-màn* (Muslim curry), fresh yogurt is made daily and the *roh-dee gaang* (*roh-dee* served with a small bowl of curry) is a steal at 20B.

Jaroen Tham (Vegetarian Food; Th Sithamatraipidok; dishes 15-20B; ✖ 8am-3pm) Around the corner from the TAT office, this simple place serves a choice of vegetarian dishes paired with husky brown rice. Look for a sign saying 'Vegetarian Food'.

Rin Coffee (☎ 0 5525 2848; 20 Th Salreuthai; dishes 20-85B; ✖ 7.30am-9pm Mon-Fri, 9.30am-9pm Sat & Sun) This light-filled, glass-fronted cafe is popular with young Thais. Whole menu pages are dedicated to various green tea, coffee and chocolate drink concoctions. Sit in the brightly coloured seats or perch at the bar and sample the ice cream, hearty breakfasts, waffles, sandwiches or salads.

Karaket (☎ 0 5525 8193; Th Phayalithai; dishes 25-40B; ✖ 1-8pm) Opposite Lithai Guest House, this simple restaurant has a variety of Thai curries, soups and stir-fries on display. Simply point to whatever looks good. On the walls, there are interesting pictures of Phitsanulok before the 1957 fire.

Daeng (☎ 0 5522 5127; Th Borom Trailokanat; dishes 40-120B; ✖ lunch & dinner) Across from Pailyn Hotel, this small shop is part of a popular chain of Thai/Vietnamese food that originated in Nong Khai. Be sure to order the restaurant's signature dish, *năam neu-ang*, grilled pork balls served with fresh herbs and rice paper sheets to wrap it all up in.

our pick **Ban Mai** (☎ 08 6925 5018; 93/30 Th U Thong; dishes 70-140B; ◷ 11am-2pm & 5-10pm) Dinner at this local favourite is like a meal at your grandparents'; opinionated conversation resounds, frumpy furniture abounds, and an overfed Siamese cat appears to rule the dining room. Don't expect home cooking though; Ban Mai specialises in unusual, but perfectly executed dishes that aren't easily found elsewhere, like the *gaang pèt 'bèt yâhng*, a curry of smoked duck, or *yam đà·krái*, lemon grass 'salad'.

For snacks and self-catering, there's a huge supermarket in the basement of the Topland Shopping Plaza, and a very busy **night market** (dishes 20-60B; ◷ 4-8pm) just south of the train station that features mostly take-away items. One particularly popular dish is *kôw nĕe·o hòr*, tiny banana-leaf parcels of sticky rice with various toppings; there are two vendors opposite each other near the Th Ekathotsarot entrance to the market.

Drinking & Entertainment

A few floating pubs can be found along the strip of Th Wangchan directly in front of the Grand Riverside Hotel including **Sabai Boat** (Th Wangchan; dishes 40-140B; ◷ 11am-11pm) and **Wow!** (Th Wangchan; dishes 50-150B; ◷ 5pm-midnight), both proffering food as well as drink. **Calito** (☎ 08 1953 2629; 84/1 Th Wangchan; dishes 70-100B; ◷ 6pm-midnight), located on firm ground, has an extensive menu of Thai eats and cold draught beer.

Wood Stock (☎ 08 1785 1958; 148/22-23 Th Wisut Kasat; dishes 35-70B; ◷ 5pm-midnight) combines funky '60s and '70s-era furniture, live music, and a brief and cheap menu of *gàp glâam* (Thai-style nibbles). Staff are very friendly, and although English is limited, they'll do their best.

Getting There & Away

AIR

Phitsanulok's **airport** (☎ 0 5530 1002) is 5km south of town.

THAI (☎ 0 5524 2971-2; 209/26-28 Th Borom Trailokanat) operates flights between Phitsanulok and Bangkok (3185B, 55 minutes, twice daily). Tickets can also be booked at the travel agent attached to Lithai Guest House (p392).

Golden House Tour (☎ 0 5525 9973; 55/37 Th Borom Trailokanat) has a board at the airport indicating its mini-van service from the airport to hotels (150B per person). Túk-túk go to the airport from town for 150B.

BUS

Transport options out of Phitsanulok are good, as it's a junction for bus routes both north and northeast. Phitsanulok's bus station is 2km east of town on Hwy 12.

There are buses directly to Sukhothai (ordinary 45B, one hour, every half-hour from 7am to 5pm), or you can hop on any bus bound for Chiang Rai (2nd class air-con/1st class/VIP 286/367/428B, five hours). There are frequent buses to Lampang (2nd class air-con/1st class/VIP 176/227/265B, four hours), Nan (2nd class air-con/1st class 197/254B, two hours) and Phrae (2nd class air-con/1st class/VIP 130/167/195B, three hours). Buses to Kamphaeng Phet (2nd class air-con/1st class 60/81B, three hours) and Chiang Mai (2nd class air-con/1st class/VIP 241/310/361B, six hours) depart every hour during the day. There are also buses to Tak (2nd class air-con 101B, three hours) and several minivans bound for Mae Sot (176B, four hours).

To Isan, there are buses to Nakhon Ratchasima (2nd class air-con/1st class/VIP 280/360/420B, six hours) and Khon Kaen (2nd class air-con/1st class 231/297B, seven hours).

There's no lack of buses to Bangkok (2nd class/1st class air-con/VIP 246/317/490B, six hours, every hour from 8am to 11.30pm), with VIP buses departing at 10pm.

TRAIN

Phitsanulok's train station is within walking distance of ample accommodation and offers a left-luggage service. The station is a significant train terminal, and virtually every northbound and southbound train stops here. There are 10 trains to Bangkok (3rd class fan 219B, 2nd class fan/air-con 309/449B, 2nd class fan sleeper upper/lower 409/459B, 2nd class air-con sleeper upper/lower 629/699B, 1st class sleeper 1064B, six hours) departing at virtually all times of day and night; to check the most up-to-date timetables and prices in advance call the **State Railway of Thailand** (☎ free 24hr hotline 1690; www.railway.co.th) or look at their website.

Getting Around

Rides on the town's Darth Vader–like *sǎhm·lór* start at 60B. Outside the train station there's a sign indicating *túk-túk* prices for different destinations around town.

Ordinary city buses cost 8B to 11B and there are several routes, making it easy to get just about anywhere by bus. The main bus stop for city buses is next to the Asia Hotel, on Th Ekathotsarot, and there is a chart describing the various bus routes in English.

Run by the TAT, the Phitsanulok Tour Tramway (PTT) is a quick way to see many sights. The ride takes around 45 minutes, with the first departing at 9am and the last at 3pm. The tram (child/adult 20/30B) leaves from Wat Yai and stops at 15 sights before returning to the same temple.

Budget (☎ 0 5530 1020; www.budget.co.th) and **Avis** (☎ 0 5524 2060; www.avisthailand.com) have car-rental offices at the airport. They charge from 1350B per day.

PHU HIN RONG KLA NATIONAL PARK

อุทยานแห่งชาติภูหินร่องกล้า

Between 1967 and 1982, the mountain that is known as Phu Hin Rong Kla served as the strategic headquarters for the Communist Party of Thailand (CPT) and its tactical arm, the People's Liberation Army of Thailand (PLAT). The remote, easily defended summit was perfect for an insurgent army. China's Yunnan Province is only 300km away and it was here that CPT cadres received their training in revolutionary tactics. (This was until the 1979 split between the Chinese and Vietnamese communists, when the CPT sided with Vietnam.)

For nearly 20 years the area around Phu Hin Rong Kla served as a battlefield for Thai troops and the communists. In 1972 the Thai government launched an unsuccessful major offensive against the PLAT. The CPT camp at Phu Hin Rong Kla became especially active after the Thai military killed hundreds of students in Bangkok during the October 1976 student-worker uprising. Many students subsequently fled here to join the CPT, setting up a hospital and a school of political and military tactics. By 1978 the PLAT ranks here had swelled to 4000. In 1980 and 1981 the Thai armed forces tried again and were able to recapture some parts of CPT territory. But the decisive blow to the CPT came in 1982, when the government declared an amnesty for all the students who had joined the communists after 1976. The departure of most of the students broke the spine of the movement, which had become dependent on their membership. A final military push in late 1982 resulted in the surrender of the PLAT, and Phu Hin Rong Kla was declared a national park in 1984.

Orientation & Information

The **park** (☎ 0 5523 3527; admission 200B; 8.30am-5pm) covers about 307 sq km of rugged mountains and forest, much of it covered by rocks and wildflowers. The elevation at park headquarters is about 1000m, so the area is refreshingly cool even in the hot season. The main attractions don't tend to stray too far from the main road through the park and include the remains of the CPT stronghold – a rustic meeting hall, the school of political and military tactics – and the CPT administration building. Across the road from the school is a water wheel designed by exiled engineering students.

Sights & Activities

A 1km trail leads to **Pha Chu Thong** (Flag Raising Cliff, sometimes called Red Flag Cliff), where the communists would raise the red flag to announce a military victory. Also in this area is an **air-raid shelter**, a **lookout** and the remains of the main **CPT headquarters** – the most inaccessible point in the territory before a road was constructed by the Thai government. The buildings in the park are made out of wood and bamboo and have no plumbing or electricity – a testament to how primitive the living conditions were.

There is a small **museum** at the park headquarters that displays relics from CPT days, although there's not a whole lot of English explanation. At the end of the road into the park is a small **White Hmong village**.

If you're not interested in the history of Phu Hin Rong Kla, there are **waterfalls, hiking trails** and **scenic views**, as well as some interesting rock formations – jutting boulders called **Lan Hin Pum**, and an area of deep rocky crevices where PLAT troops would hide during air raids, called **Lan Hin Taek**. Ask at the **Visitor Centre** (8.30am-4.30pm) for maps.

Phu Hin Rong Kla can become quite crowded on weekends and holidays; schedule a more peaceful visit for midweek.

Sleeping & Eating

Golden House Tour (☎ 0 5525 9973; 55/37 Th Trailokanat; 8am-6.30pm) near the TAT office in Phitsanulok can help book accommodation.

Thailand's Royal Forest Department (☎ 0 2562 0760; www.dnp.go.th; tent site 30B, 2-8 person tent 150-600B, bungalows 800-2400B) Bungalows for two to eight people, in three different zones of the park, can be rented from this organisation. You can also pitch a tent or rent one. Sleeping bags (30B) and pillows (10B) and a sleeping pad (20B) are available.

Near the camping ground and bungalows are restaurants and food vendors. The best are Duang Jai Cafeteria – try its famous carrot *sôm·đam* – and Rang Thong.

Getting There & Away

The park headquarters is about 125km from Phitsanulok. To get here, first take an early bus to Nakhon Thai (ordinary/air-con 53/73B, two hours, hourly from 6am to 6pm). From there you can charter a *sŏrng·tăa·ou* to the park (approximately 500B to 800B) from near the market. From Phitsanulok, Golden House Tour (see p395) charges 1700B for car and driver; petrol is extra. This is a delightful trip if you're on a motorcycle since there's not much traffic along the way, but a strong engine is necessary to conquer the hills to Phu Hin Rong Kla.

PHITSANULOK TO LOM SAK

พิษณุโลก/หล่มสัก

Hwy 12 between Phitsanulok and Lom Sak is known as the 'Green Route', and runs along the scenic, rapid-studded Lam Nam Khek. Off this route are waterfalls, resorts, and the Phu Hin Rong Kla (p395) and Thung Salaeng Luang (right) national parks. The sites tend to be more popular on weekends and holidays.

Any of the resorts along Hwy 12 can organise white-water rafting trips on the Lam Nam Khek along the section with the most rapids, which corresponds more or less to between Km45 and Km52 of Hwy 12.

The Phitsanulok TAT office (p390) distributes a 'Green Route' map of the attractions along this 130km stretch of road. You may want to bypass the first two waterfalls, Nam Tok Sakhunothayan (at the Km33 marker) and Kaeng Song (at the Km45 marker), which on weekends can get overwhelmed with visitors. The third, Kaeng Sopha at the Km72 marker, is a larger area of small falls and rapids where you can walk from rock formation to rock formation – there are more or fewer rocks depending on the rains. Food vendors provide inexpensive *sôm·đam* and *gài yâhng* (papaya salad and grilled chicken). In between the Kaeng Song and Kaeng Sopha waterfalls, turning off at Km49, is the Dharma Abha Vipassana Meditation Center (☎ 08 1646 4695; www.dhamma.org/en/schedules/schabha.htm), which does regular 10-day meditation retreats.

Further east along the road is the 1262-sq-km Thung Salaeng Luang National Park (☎ 0 5526 8019; admission 200B; ◷ 8am-5pm), one of Thailand's largest and most important wildlife sanctuaries. Thung Salaeng Luang encompasses vast meadows, evergreen and dipterocarp forests, limestone hills and numerous streams. From November to December the meadows bloom with carpets of wild flowers, and the best place to see wildlife is on these meadows and around the ponds and salt licks. There are over 190 bird species confirmed in the park, most significant of which for birdwatchers is the Siamese fireback pheasant. Thung Salaeng Luang was also once home to the PLAT. The entrance is at the Km80 marker, where the park headquarters here has information on walks and accommodation.

If you have your own wheels, you can turn south at the Km100 marker onto Rte 2196 and head for Khao Kho (Khow Khor), another mountain lair used by the CPT during the 1970s. About 1.5km from the summit of Khao Kho, you must turn onto the very steep Rte 2323. At the summit, 30km from the highway, stands a tall obelisk erected in memory of the Thai soldiers killed during the suppression of the communist insurgency. Gun emplacements and sandbagged lookout posts perched on the summit have been left intact as historical reminders. On a clear day, the 360-degree view from the summit is wonderful.

If you've made the side trip to Khao Kho you can choose either to return to the Phitsanulok–Lom Sak highway, or take Rte 2258, off Rte 2196, until it terminates at Rte 203. On Rte 203 you can continue north to Lom Sak or south to Phetchabun. On Rte 2258, about 4km from Rte 2196, you'll pass Khao Kho Palace. One of the smaller royal palaces in Thailand, it's a fairly uninteresting, modern set of structures but has quite a nice rose garden. If you've come all the way to Khao Kho you may as well take a look.

Sleeping & Eating

Thung Salaeng Luang National Park (☎ 0 2562 0760; www.dnp.go.th; tent site 30B, 2-8 person tent 150-600B, bungalows 1000-5000B) In the park there are 15 well-equipped wooden bungalows that accommodate four to 10 people. Bungalows are available near the headquarters by the Km80 entrance or in two other park zones. It's also possible to pitch a tent. There's a restaurant and food vendors in the park.

Rainforest Resort (☎ 0 5529 3085-6; www.rainforest thailand.com; Km42; 2-6 person cottages 1600-4500B; ❄) There are several resorts just off Hwy 12 and this is by far the best of the lot. Consisting of a jungled hillside of delightful cottages alongside Mae Nam Khek, the resort also includes an indoor-outdoor restaurant with an interesting Thai food menu.

Another good choice is **Wang Thara Health Resort & Spa** (☎ 0 5529 3411-4; www.wanathara.com; Km46, Hwy 12; r 1600-3800B; ❄), a slightly aged but still attractive resort with the added bonus of a reasonably priced spa. Budget accommodation can be found near Kaeng Song, around Km45, including **Ban Kiang Num** (☎ 0 5529 3441; www.bankiangnum.9nha.com; Km45, Hwy 12; r 600-1000B), which offers large but basic rooms with vast balconies overlooking Song Rapids.

Several restaurants are located on the banks of the Nam Khek, most taking full advantage of the views and breezes. **Ran Rim Kaeng** (☎ 0 5529 3370; Km45, Hwy 12; dishes 70-120B; ⏲ 11am-10pm) is known for its spicy dishes and is popular with locals. Look for the yellow building at Km45 near Kaeng Song. A few clicks up the road at Km42, **Ran Thin Thai Lan Lanthom** (☎ 08 3219 2822; Km42, Hwy 12; dishes 30-90B; ⏲ 7am-7pm) serves up excellent coffee, yummy homemade cookies and custard apple ice cream, not to mention an acclaimed menu of Thai dishes. Look for the sign advertising 'Doi Tung' coffee.

Getting There & Away

For more freedom it's best to do this route with your own wheels. Buses between Phitsanulok and Lom Sak cost 50B for ordinary and 70B for air-con, each way. During daylight hours it's possible to flag down another bus to continue your journey, but after 4pm it gets a little chancy.

SUKHOTHAI PROVINCE

SUKHOTHAI

สุโขทัย

pop 17,510

The Sukhothai (Rising of Happiness) Kingdom flourished from the mid-13th century to the late 14th century. This period is often viewed as the 'golden age' of Thai civilisation – the religious art and architecture of the era are considered to be the most classic of Thai styles. The remains of the kingdom, today known as the *meuang gòw* (old city), feature around 45 sq km of partially rebuilt ruins, which are one of the most visited ancient sites in Thailand.

Located 12km east of the historical park on the Mae Nam Yom, the market town of New Sukhothai is not particularly interesting. Yet its friendly and relaxed atmosphere, good transport links and attractive accommodation make it a good base from which to explore the old city ruins.

History

Sukhothai is typically regarded as the first capital of Siam, although this is not entirely accurate (see boxed text, p400). The area was previously the site of a Khmer empire until 1238, when two Thai rulers, Pho Khun Pha Muang and Pho Khun Bang Klang Hao, decided to unite and form a new Thai kingdom.

Sukhothai's dynasty lasted 200 years and spanned nine kings. The most famous was King Ramkhamhaeng, who reigned from 1275 to 1317 and is credited with developing the first Thai script – his inscriptions are also considered the first Thai literature. Ramkhamhaeng eventually expanded his kingdom to include an area even larger than that of present-day Thailand. But a few kings later in 1438, Sukhothai was absorbed by Ayuthaya. See Sukhothai Historical Park for more information (p398).

Information

There are banks with ATMs scattered all around the central part of New Sukhothai, and now a few in Old Sukhothai as well. Internet is easy to find in New Sukhothai, and is available at many guesthouses. Sukhothai's best sources of tourist information are the guesthouses, especially Ban Thai (p401).

CAT office (Map p398; Th Nikhon Kasem; ⏲ 7am-10pm) Attached to the post office and offers international phone services.

Police station (Map p398; ☎ 0 5561 1010) In New Sukhothai.

Post office (Map p398;Th Nikhon Kasem; ⏲ 8.30am-noon Mon-Fri, 1-4.30pm Sat & Sun, 9am-noon holidays)

Sukhothai Hospital (Map p398; ☎ 0 5561 0280; Th Jarot Withithong)

Tourist police (Map p399; Sukhothai Historical Park) Call 1155 for emergencies or go to the tourist police station opposite the Ramkhamhaeng National Museum.

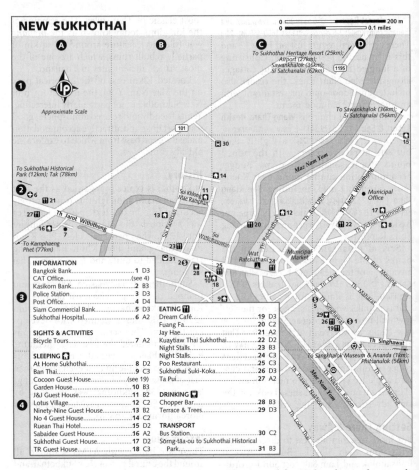

NEW SUKHOTHAI

INFORMATION
Bangkok Bank	1	D3
CAT Office	(see 4)	
Kasikorn Bank	2	B3
Police Station	3	D3
Post Office	4	D4
Siam Commercial Bank	5	D3
Sukhothai Hospital	6	A2

SIGHTS & ACTIVITIES
Bicycle Tours	7	A2

SLEEPING
At Home Sukhothai	8	D2
Ban Thai	9	C3
Cocoon Guest House	(see 19)	
Garden House	10	B3
J&J Guest House	11	B2
Lotus Village	12	C2
Ninety-Nine Guest House	13	B2
No 4 Guest House	14	C2
Ruean Thai Hotel	15	D2
Sabaidee Guest House	16	A2
Sukhothai Guest House	17	D2
TR Guest House	18	C3

EATING
Dream Café	19	D3
Fuang Fa	20	C2
Jay Hae	21	A2
Kuaytiaw Thai Sukhothai	22	D2
Night Stalls	23	B3
Night Stalls	24	C3
Poo Restaurant	25	C3
Sukhothai Suki-Koka	26	D3
Ta Pui	27	A2

DRINKING
Chopper Bar	28	B3
Terrace & Trees	29	D3

TRANSPORT
Bus Station	30	C2
Sŏrng·tăa·ou to Sukhothai Historical Park	31	B3

Sights

SUKHOTHAI HISTORICAL PARK

อุทยานประวัติศาสตร์สุโขทัย

The **Sukhothai ruins** (Map p398; admission 100-350B, plus per bicycle/motorcycle/car 10/20/50B; 6am-6pm) are one of Thailand's most impressive World Heritage Sites. The park includes remains of 21 historical sites and four large ponds within the old walls, with an additional 70 sites within a 5km radius.

The ruins are divided into five zones – central, north, south, east and west – each of which has a 100B admission fee. For 350B you can buy a single ticket that allows entry to all the Sukhothai sites, plus Sawanworanayok Museum (p406), Ramkhamhaeng National Museum (opposite) and the Si Satchanalai and Chaliang (p404). The ticket is good for 30 days, but in theory only allows a single visit to each site.

The architecture of Sukhothai temples is most typified by the classic lotus-bud *chedi*, featuring a conical spire topping a square-sided structure on a three-tiered base. Some sites exhibit other rich architectural forms introduced and modified during the period, such as bell-shaped Sinhalese and double-tiered Srivijaya *chedi*.

Despite the popularity of the park, it's quite expansive, and solitary exploration is usually possible. Some of the most impressive ruins are outside the city walls, so a bicycle or motorcycle is essential to fully appreciate everything. See p404 for details on the best way to tour the park.

NORTHERN THAILAND

Ramkhamhaeng National Museum
พิพิธภัณฑสถานแห่งชาติรามคำแหง

A good starting point for exploring the historical park ruins is **Ramkhamhaeng National Museum** (Map p399; ☎ 0 5561 2167; admission 150B; ⏰ 9am-4pm). A replica of the famous Ramkhamhaeng inscription, said to be the earliest example of Thai writing, is kept here among an impressive collection of the Sukhothai artefacts.

Wat Mahathat
วัดมหาธาตุ

Completed in the 13th century, the largest wát in Sukhothai is surrounded by brick walls (206m long and 200m wide) and a moat that is believed to represent the outer wall of the universe and the cosmic ocean. The *chedi* spires feature the famous lotus-bud motif, and some of the original stately Buddha figures still sit among the ruined columns of the old *wí·hăhn*. There are 198 *chedi* within the monastery walls – a lot to explore in what many consider was once the spiritual and administrative centre of the old capital.

Wat Si Chum
วัดศรีชุม

This wát is northwest of the old city and contains an impressive *mon·dòp* with a 15m, brick-and-stucco seated Buddha. This Buddha's elegant, tapered fingers are much photographed. Archaeologists theorise that this image is the 'Phra Atchana' mentioned in the famous Ramkhamhaeng inscription. A passage in the *mon·dòp* wall that leads to the top has been blocked so that it's no longer possible to view the *jataka* inscriptions that line the tunnel ceiling.

Wat Saphan Hin
วัดสะพานหิน

Four kilometres to the west of the old city walls in the west zone, Wat Saphan Hin is on the crest of a hill that rises about 200m above the plain. The name of the wát, which means 'stone bridge', is a reference to the slate path and staircase that leads up to the temple, which are still in place. The site gives a good view of the Sukhothai ruins to the southeast and the mountains to the north and south.

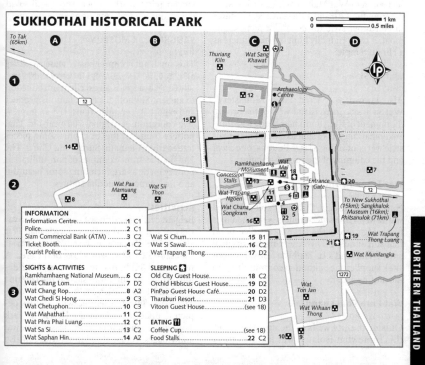

NORTHERN THAILAND

THE FIRST?

The establishment of Sukhothai in 1238 is often described as the formation of the first Thai kingdom. But the kingdom of Chiang Saen (see p366) had already been established 500 years earlier, and at the time of Sukhothai's founding, other Thai kingdoms such as Lanna, Phayao and Chiang Saen also existed. Sukhothai's profound influence on the art, language, literature and religion of modern Thai society, not to mention the immense size of the kingdom at its peak in the early 13th century, are doubtlessly reasons for the proliferation of this convenient, but technically incorrect, historical fact.

All that remains of the original temple are a few *chedi* and the ruined *wí·hǎhn*, consisting of two rows of laterite columns flanking a 12.5m-high standing Buddha image on a brick terrace.

Wat Si Sawai
วัดศรีสวาย
Just south of Wat Mahathat, this shrine (dating from the 12th and 13th centuries) features three Khmer-style towers and a picturesque moat. It was originally built by the Khmers as a Hindu temple.

Wat Sa Si
วัดสระศรี
Also known as 'Sacred Pond Monastery', Wat Sa Si sits on an island west of the bronze monument of King Ramkhamhaeng (the third Sukhothai king). It's a simple, classic Sukhothai-style *wát* containing a large Buddha, one *chedi* and the columns of the ruined *wí·hǎhn*.

Wat Trapang Thong
วัดตระพังทอง
Next to the museum, this small, still-inhabited *wát* with its fine stucco reliefs is reached by a footbridge across the large lotus-filled pond that surrounds it. This reservoir, the original site of Thailand's **Loi Krathong** festival (opposite), supplies the Sukhothai community with most of its water.

Wat Phra Phai Luang
วัดพระพายหลวง
Outside the city walls in the northern zone, this somewhat isolated *wát* features three

12th-century Khmer-style towers, bigger than those at Wat Si Sawai. This may have been the centre of Sukhothai when it was ruled by the Khmers of Angkor prior to the 13th century.

Wat Chang Lom
วัดช้างล้อม
Off Hwy 12 in the east zone, Wat Chang Lom (Elephant Circled Monastery) is about 1km east of the main park entrance. A large bell-shaped *chedi* is supported by 36 elephants sculpted into its base.

Wat Chetupon
วัดเชตุพน
Located 2km south of the city walls, this temple once held a four-sided *mon·dòp* featuring the four classic poses of the Buddha (sitting, reclining, standing and walking). The graceful lines of the walking Buddha can still be made out today.

Wat Chedi Si Hong
วัดเจดีย์สี่ห้อง
Directly across from Wat Chetupon, the main chedi here has retained much of its original stucco relief work, which show still vivid depictions of elephants, lions and humans.

SANGKHALOK MUSEUM
พิพิธภัณฑ์สังคโลก
This small but comprehensive **museum** (off Map p398; ☎ 0 5561 4333; 203/2 Mu 3 Th Muangkao; child/adult 50/100B; ☺ 8am-5pm) is an excellent introduction to ancient Sukhothai's most famous product and export, its ceramics. It displays an impressive collection of original 700-year-old Thai pottery found in the area, plus some pieces traded from Vietnam, Burma and China. The 2nd floor features examples of non-utilitarian pottery made as art, including some beautiful and rare ceramic Buddha statues.

Activities
Belgian cycling enthusiast Ronny offers a variety of fun and educational **bicycle tours** (Map p398; ☎ 0 5561 2519; www.geocities.com/cycling_sukhothai; half-/full day 550/650B, sunset tour 250B) of the area. A resident of Sukhothai for 15 years, his rides follow themed itineraries such as the Dharma & Karma Tour, which includes a visit to bizarre Wat Tawet, a temple with statues depicting Buddhist hell, or the Historical Park Tour, which includes stops at lesser seen *wát* and villages. Personalised itineraries can also

be arranged. Ronny is based near Sabaidee Guest House (right), and he also offers free transport for customers.

Festivals

The **Loi Krathong** festival in November is celebrated for five days in historical Sukhothai, and the city is one of the most popular destinations in Thailand to celebrate the holiday. In addition to the magical floating lights, there are fireworks, folk-dance performances and a light-and-sound production.

Sleeping

Most accommodation is still in New Sukhothai, and is dominated by budget options. There are an increasing number of options near the park, many of them in the upscale bracket. Prices tend to go up during the Loi Krathong festival.

BUDGET

Sukhothai offers a strong selection of budget rooms. Cheap and clean shared-bathroom accommodation abounds, and virtually every place seems to offer a few bungalows as well. Several guesthouses offer free pick-up from the bus station, and many also rent bicycles and motorcycles.

New Sukhothai

Garden House (☎ 0 5561 1395; tuigardenhouse@yahoo .com; 11/1 Th Prawet Nakhon; r 150-200B, bungalows 300-350B; ✍ ▯) The main structure at this popular guesthouse complex can get a bit hectic, so be sure to check out the relatively isolated bungalows out back. The restaurant, which also serves as the communal area, screens movies nightly.

No 4 Guest House (☎ 0 5561 0165; no4guesthouse@ yahoo.co.th; 140/4 Soi Khlong Mae Ramphan; s/d 200/300B) From the outside, No 4 appears a bit rundown, but a closer look reveals a shady garden featuring several bungalows not without their own charm. Close by the Ninety-Nine Guest House (☎ 0 5561 1315; 234/6 Soi Panitsan; singles/doubles 120/150B) is managed by the same people. Ninety-nine's rooms are in a two-storey teak house surrounded by gardens. Both places run cookery courses.

Ban Thai (☎ 0 5561 0163; banthai_guesthouse@yahoo .com; 38 Th Prawet Nakhon; r with shared bathroom 200B, bungalows 300-500B; ✍ ▯) Centred around an inviting garden, this mish-mash of rooms and tiny bungalows is among the more popular

budget places in town. None of the accommodation is particularly remarkable in itself, but the combination of friendly atmosphere and low prices culminate in a winner.

Sabaidee Guest House (☎ 0 5561 6303, 08 9988 3589; www.sabaidee-guesthouse.com; 81/7 Mu 1 Tambol Banklouy; r 200-600B; ✍ ▯) Having graduated from homestay status, this cheery guesthouse has followed the route of much of Sukhothai's budget accommodation and now boasts five attractive bungalows. Cheaper accommodation is still available in the main house, not to mention perks such as free bicycles and transport from the bus station.

TR Guest House (☎ 0 5561 1663; www.sukhothaibudget guesthouse.com; 27/5 Th Prawet Nakhon; r 250-400B, bungalows 400B; ✍ ▯) The rooms here are basic but extremely tidy, and there are four spacious bungalows out back for those needing leg room. A cosy terrace provides even more incentive. An excellent budget choice.

J&J Guest House (☎ 0 5562 0095; www.jj-guesthouse .com; 122 Soi Mae Ramphan; r 300-500B, bungalows 700-800B; ✍ ▯ ▯) Hardly a leaf is out of place at this expansive resort-like guesthouse. A smorgasbord of bungalows and spacious rooms spans just about every budget, and homemade bread and the swimming pool make the decision even easier.

Sukhothai Guest House (☎ 0 5561 0453; www.suk hothaiguesthouse.net; 68 Th Vichien Chamnong; r 350-750B; ✍ ▯) This long-running guesthouse has 12 bungalows with terraces packed into a shaded garden. The communal area is filled with an eclectic mix of bric-a-brac and the owners are friendly and very helpful.

Cocoon Guest House (☎ 0 5561 2081; 86/1 Th Singhawat; r 500B; ✍) The four simple rooms at the back of Dream Café are down a path and set in a junglelike garden. By the time you read this several other rooms in an attractive wooden building should be completed.

ourpick At Home Sukhothai (☎ 0 5561 0172; www.athomesukhothai.com; 184/1 Th Vichien Chamnong; r 500-750B; ✍ ▯) Located in the 50-year-old childhood home of the proprietor, the attractive structure could easily pass as a newborn after recent renovations. Combining original wooden furnishings with new, the results blend seamlessly, and the simple but comfortable rooms really do feel like home. There's a lotus pond out back, and virtually every other service, from food to Thai massage, in front. Ask to look at the owner's family photo album that shows what the house used to look like.

Sukhothai Historical Park

The following places are across from the historical park. Both rent out bicycles.

Old City Guest House (☎ 0 5569 7515; 28/7 Mu 3; r 150-400B; 🌀) This vast complex features heaps of rooms at a variety of styles and budgets; ask to see a few before you make a decision. A good choice if you want to stay close to the historic park; unfortunately there isn't a garden area for relaxing.

Vitoon Guest House (☎ 0 5569 7045; 49 Mu 3; r 300-500B; 🌀 🖳) Rooms at Vitoon are comfortable but cluttered compared to its neighbour Old City.

PinPao Guest House Café (☎ 0 5563 3284; orchid_hibiscus_guest_house@hotmail.com; Hwy 12; r 500B) Affiliated with the Orchid Hibiscus Guest House (below), this is a large building with 10 of the most gaily coloured rooms we've seen anywhere, although many lack windows and can be rather dark. The guesthouse is on Hwy 12, directly opposite the turn-off to Rte 1272.

MIDRANGE
New Sukhothai

our pick **Ruean Thai Hotel** (☎ 0 5561 2444; www.rueanthaihotel.com; 181/20 Soi Pracha Ruammit, Th Jarot Withithong; rooms 1350-3200B; 🌀 🖳 🖀) At first glance, you may mistake this eye-catching complex for a temple or museum. The rooms on the upper level are very Thai, and feature worn teak furnishings and heaps of character. Poolside rooms are slightly more modern, and there's a concrete building with simple air-con rooms out the back. Service is both friendly and flawless. Call for free pick-up from the bus station.

Sukhothai Historical Park

Lotus Village (☎ 0 5562 1484; www.lotus-village.com; 170 Th Ratchathani; r 790-1540B; 🌀 🖳) Village is an apt label for this peaceful compound of elevated wooden bungalows. Smaller rooms in an attractive wooden building are also available, and an attractive Burmese/Indian design theme runs through the entire place. An on-site spa offers a variety of services.

Orchid Hibiscus Guest House (☎ 0 5563 3284; orchid _hibiscus_guest_house@hotmail.com; 407/2 Rte 1272; r 800B, bungalows 1200B; 🌀 🖀) This collection of rooms and bungalows is set in relaxing, manicured grounds with a swimming pool as a centrepiece. Rooms are spotless and fun, featuring various design details and accents.

The guesthouse is on Rte 1272 about 600m off Hwy 12 – the turn-off is between Km48 and Km49 markers.

TOP END

our pick **Tharaburi Resort** (Map p399; ☎ 0 5569 7132; www.tharaburiresort.com; 321/3 Moo 3, Rte 1272; r 1200-4200B, ste 5000-6500B; 🌀 🖳 🖀) Near the historical park, this boutique hotel features three main structures divided up into 20 individually and beautifully styled rooms and suites. Some are themed (Moroccan, Japanese, Chinese) and this is done with fine antiques, lush silks and exquisite attention to detail. The cheaper rooms are simpler, the suites feel like a small home, and there are also two-floor family rooms. Definitely the most stylish hotel in Sukhothai.

Ananda (off Map p398; ☎ 0 5562 2428-30; www.ananda sukhothai.com; 10 Moo 4, Th Muangkao; r 2500-3100B; 🌀 🖳) The label 'Museum Gallery Hotel' may cause some to wonder what actually goes on here, but this architecturally striking hotel is straightforwardly attractive. Resembling something of a suburban church with Sukhothai influences, the 32 rooms combine dark woods and earth-coloured silks, and the hotel also houses a spa and antique shop. About 2km outside the centre of town, Ananda is directly next door to the excellent Sangkhalok Museum (p400).

Sukhothai Heritage Resort (off Map p398; ☎ 0 5564 7564-574; www.sukhothaiheritage.com; 999 Moo 2; r 3500-4500B, ste 10,000B; 🌀 🖳 🖀) Owned by Bangkok Airways and located near their airport, this new resort is now the area's most upscale accommodation. A virtual continuation of the historical park, the low-lying brick and peak-roofed structures are interspersed by calming lotus-filled ponds, culminating in a temple-like environment. The rooms take you back to the secular world with large flat-screen TVs and modern furniture.

Eating

Sukhothai's signature dish is *gŏo·ay dĕe·o sù·kŏh·tai*, 'Sukhothai-style noodles', featuring a slightly sweet broth with different types of pork, ground peanuts and thinly sliced green beans. There are several places in town to try the dish, including **Kuaytiaw Thai Sukhothai** (Map p398; Th Jarot Withithong; dishes 20-30B; ⏰ 9am-8pm), about 200m south of the turn-off for Ruean Thai Hotel. For many visiting Thais, you haven't been to Sukhothai if you haven't tried the noodles at **Jay Hae** (Map p398; ☎ 0 5561 1901; Th Jarot Withithong; dishes 25-40B; ⏱ 7am-4pm), an extremely popular restaurant that also serves *pàt tai* and tasty coffee drinks. Across the street and consisting of little more than a brick floor with a tin roof over it, **Ta Pui** (Map p398; Th Jarot Withithong; dishes 20-30B; ⏱ 7am-3pm) claims to be the first shop in Sukhothai to have sold the famous noodle dish.

Poo Restaurant (Map p398; ☎ 0 5561 1735; 24/3 Th Jarot Withithong; dishes 25-80B; ⏱ breakfast, lunch & dinner) Deceptively simple, this restaurant offers a diverse menu of breakfasts, hearty sandwiches and even a few Thai dishes. A good source of information, this is also the place to rent motorbikes in town.

Sukhothai Suki-Koka (Map p398; Th Singhawat; dishes 30-90B; ⏱ 10am-11pm) Specialising in Thai-style sukiyaki, this bright, homey place is popular for lunch. It serves plenty of Thai dishes but also does sandwiches and pasta.

Coffee Cup (Map p399; Mu 3, Old Sukhothai; dishes 30-150B; ⏱ 7am-10pm) If you're staying in the old city or are an early riser, come here for breakfast; the coffee is strong and the bread is fresh. It also serves a variety of snacks and a whopping good hamburger. Internet service is 30B per hour. There's also Coffee Cup 2, just a few doors down, which has a bar inside.

Fuang Fa (Map p398; ☎ 08 1284 8262; 107/2 Th Khuhasuwan; dishes 60-120B; ⏱ lunch & dinner) Pretend you're a local in the know and stop by this riverside restaurant specialising in Sukhothai's abundant and delicious freshwater fish. Try the *Ьlah néua òrn tôrt grà·teeam*, small freshwater fish deep-fried with garlic and served with ripe starfruit, or any of the numerous and delicious *đôm yam*–style soups. The English-language menu is limited, so be sure to ask about recommended dishes.

ourpick Dream Café (Map p398; ☎ 0 5561 2081; 86/1 Th Singhawat; dishes 80-150B; ⏱ lunch & dinner) A meal at Dream Café is like dining in a museum or an antique shop. Eclectic but tasteful furnishings and knick-knackery abound, staff are equal parts competent and friendly, and most importantly of all, the food is good. The helpful menu lays down the basics of Thai food, explaining what to order and how to eat it. Try one of the well-executed *yam* (Thai-style 'salads'), or one of the dishes that feature freshwater fish, a local speciality.

Don't miss New Sukhothai's numerous night stalls. Most are accustomed to accommodating foreigners and even have bilingual,

written menus. On Tuesday nights, there are more lively night stalls in the square opposite Poo Restaurant. Near the ticket kiosk in the historical park, there is a collection of food stalls and simple open-air restaurants.

Drinking

Chopper Bar (Map p398; Th Prawet Nakhon; ⏱ 5-12.30pm) Travellers and locals congregate from dusk till hangover for food, drinks, live music and flirtation at this place, within spitting distance from Sukhothai's tiny guesthouse strip.

Terrace & Trees (Map p398; Th Singhawat; ⏱ 5-12.30pm) Directly behind the Sawasdipong Hotel, this new bar/restaurant features live music of varying quality and is one of the trendier places in town to put back a few.

Getting There & Away

AIR

Sukhothai's airport is 27km from town off Rte 1195, about 11km from Sawankhalok. It's privately owned by Bangkok Airways and is a beautifully designed small airport using tropical architecture to its best advantage. **Bangkok Airways** (☎ 0 5564 7224; www.bangkokair.com) operates a daily flight from Bangkok (2870B, 70 minutes, once daily). There is a minivan service (120B) between the airport and Sukhothai.

BUS

Sukhothai's bus station is located almost 1km northwest of the centre of town on Rte 101. Within Sukhothai province, there are frequent buses to Sawankhalok (ordinary/ 2nd class air-con/1st class 21/29/38B, 45 minutes, every hour from 6am to 6pm) and Si Satchanalai (ordinary/2nd class air-con/1st class 37/52/67B, one hour, every hour from 6am to 6pm). The 9am bus to Chiang Rai is a good choice if you're bound for Sawankhalok.

To other points in northern Thailand, there are buses to Phitsanulok (ordinary/2nd class air-con/1st class 32/42/58B, one hour, every half-hour from 7am to 5pm), Tak (ordinary/ 2nd class air-con/1st class 43/60/77B, 1½ hours, every 40 minutes from 7am to 5pm) and Kamphaeng Phet (ordinary/2nd class air-con/1st class 44/62/79B, 1½ hours, every 40 minutes from 7am to 5pm), Phrae (2nd class air-con 132B, three hours, four times daily), Nan (2nd class air-con 210B, four hours) and Lampang (2nd class air-con/1st class 185/238B, four hours).

NORTHERN THAILAND

There are frequent buses to Chiang Mai (2nd class air-con/1st class 249/320B, 5½ hours, 7am to 2am), which travel via Tak, and less frequent to Chiang Rai (2nd class air-con 284B, nine hours, four times daily). There are also eight 12-seat minivans to Mae Sot (136B, three hours, eight departures from 8.15am to 4.15pm).

There are a couple of buses every evening bound for Khon Kaen (2nd class air-con/1st class 267/344B, seven hours).

Sukhothai is also easily connected to Bangkok (2nd class air-con/1st class/VIP 291/374/435B, six to seven hours, every half-hour from 8am to 11pm).

Getting Around

A ride by săhm·lór around New Sukhothai should cost no more than 40B. Sŏrng·tăa·ou run frequently from 6.30am to 6pm between New Sukhothai and Sukhothai Historical Park (20B, 30 minutes), leaving from Th Jarot Withithong near Poo Restaurant (p403). The sign is on the north side of the street, but sŏrng·tăa·ou actually leave from the south side.

The best way to get around the historical park is by bicycle, which can be rented at shops outside the park entrance for 30B per day. Don't rent the first beater bikes you see at the bus stop in the old city as the better bikes tend to be found at shops around the corner, closer to the park entrance. The park operates a tram service through the old city for 20B per person, although departures are infrequent.

Transport from the bus terminal into the centre of New Sukhothai costs 60B in a chartered vehicle, or 10B per person in a shared sŏrng·tăa·ou. Motorbike taxis charge 40B. If going directly to Old Sukhothai, sŏrng·tăa·ou charge 100B and motorcycle taxis 120B.

Motorbikes can be rented at Poo Restaurant (p403) and many guesthouses in New Sukhothai.

AROUND SUKHOTHAI
Si Satchanalai-Chaliang Historical Park
อุทยานประวัติศาสตร์ศรีสัชนาลัย/ชะเลียง

If you have the time, don't skip this portion of the Sukhothai World Heritage Site. Bring your imagination and sense of adventure and you're sure to love this more rustic collection of truly impressive ruins.

Set among the hills, the 13th- to 15th-century ruins of the old cities of Si Satchanalai

and Chaliang, about 50km north of Sukhothai, are in the same basic style as those in the Sukhothai Historical Park, but the setting is more peaceful and almost seems untouched. The **park** (admission 220B or free if you have the 350B inclusive ticket from Sukhothai, usable for 30 days, plus per bike/motorbike/car 10/30/50B; ⏰ 8.30am-5pm) covers roughly 720 hectares and is surrounded by a 12m-wide moat. Chaliang, 1km southeast, is an older city site (dating to the 11th century), though its two temples date to the 14th century. Those listed below represent only the more distinctive of the numerous Si Satchanalai ruins.

An **information centre** (⏰ 8.30am-5pm) at the park distributes free park maps and has a small exhibit outlining the history and major attractions. There are bicycles to rent (20B) near the entrance gate to the park that are slightly better than those rented where the bus stops on the main road. A tram can also be taken around the park (20B).

The nearby towns of Ban Hat Siaw (p406) and Sawankhalok (p407) are the main supply centres for the area.

WAT CHANG LOM
วัดช้างล้อม

This fine temple, marking the centre of the old city of Si Satchanalai, has elephants surrounding a bell-shaped *chedi* that is somewhat better preserved than its counterpart in Sukhothai. An inscription says the temple was built by King Ramkhamhaeng between 1285 and 1291.

WAT KHAO PHANOM PHLOENG
วัดเขาพนมเพลิง

On the hill overlooking Wat Chang Lom to the right are the remains of Wat Khao Phanom Phloeng, including a *chedi*, a large seated Buddha and stone columns that once supported the roof of the *wí·hăhn*. From this hill you can make out the general design of the once-great city. The slightly higher hill west of Phanom Phloeng is capped by a large Sukhothai-style *chedi* – all that remains of Wat Khao Suwan Khiri.

WAT CHEDI JET THAEW
วัดเจดีย์เจ็ดแถว

Next to Wat Chang Lom, these ruins contain seven rows of *chedi*, the largest of which is a copy of one at Wat Mahathat in Sukhothai. An interesting brick-and-plaster *wí·hăhn* features barred windows designed to look like

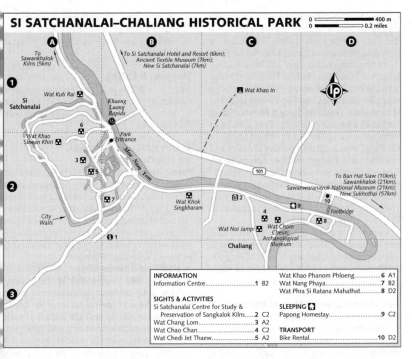

SI SATCHANALAI–CHALIANG HISTORICAL PARK

INFORMATION	
Information Centre	**1** B2

SIGHTS & ACTIVITIES	
Si Satchanalai Centre for Study & Preservation of Sangkalok Kilns	**2** C2
Wat Chang Lom	**3** A2
Wat Chao Chan	**4** C2
Wat Chedi Jet Thaew	**5** A2
Wat Khao Phanom Phloeng	**6** A1
Wat Nang Phaya	**7** B2
Wat Phra Si Ratana Mahathat	**8** D2

SLEEPING	
Papong Homestay	**9** C2

TRANSPORT	
Bike Rental	**10** D2

lathed wood (an ancient Indian technique used all over Southeast Asia). A *prasat* (small ornate building with a cruciform ground plan and needlelike spire) and *chedi* are stacked on the roof.

WAT NANG PHAYA
วัดนางพญา

South of Wat Chang Lom and Wat Chedi Jet Thaew, this *chedi* is Sinhalese in style and was built in the 15th or 16th century, a bit later than the other monuments at Si Satchanalai. Stucco reliefs on the large laterite *wí·hǎhn* in front of the *chedi* – now sheltered by a tin roof – date from the Ayuthaya period when Si Satchanalai was known as Sawankhalok. Goldsmiths in the district still craft a design known as *nahng pá·yah*, modelled after these reliefs.

WAT PHRA SI RATANA MAHATHAT
วัดพระศรีรัตนมหาธาตุ

These ruins at Chaliang consist of a large laterite *chedi* (dating back to 1448–88) between two *wí·hǎhn*. One of the *wí·hǎhn* holds a large seated Sukhothai Buddha image, a smaller standing image and a bas-relief of the famous walking Buddha, exemplary of the flowing, boneless Sukhothai style. The other *wí·hǎhn* contains some less distinguished images.

There's a separate 10B admission for Wat Phra Si Ratana Mahathat.

WAT CHAO CHAN
วัดเจ้าจันทร์

These *wát* ruins are about 500m west of Wat Phra Si Ratana Mahathat in Chaliang. The central attraction is a large Khmer-style tower similar to later towers built in Lopburi and probably constructed during the reign of Khmer King Jayavarman VII (1181–1217). The tower has been restored and is in fairly good shape. The roofless *wí·hǎhn* on the right contains the laterite outlines of a large standing Buddha that has all but melted away from exposure and weathering.

SAWANKHALOK KILNS
เตาเผาสังคโลก

The Sukhothai–Si Satchanalai area was once famous for its beautiful pottery, much of which was exported to countries throughout Asia. In

NORTHERN THAILAND

China – the biggest importer of Thai pottery during the Sukhothai and Ayuthaya periods – the pieces came to be called 'Sangkalok', a mispronunciation of Sawankhalok.

At one time, more than 200 huge pottery kilns lined the banks of Mae Nam Yom in the area around Si Satchanalai. Several have been carefully excavated and can be viewed at the **Si Satchanalai Centre for Study & Preservation of Sangkalok Kilns** (admission 100B). Two groups of kilns are open to the public: a kiln centre in Chaliang with excavated pottery samples and one kiln; and a larger outdoor Sawankhalok Kilns site 5km northwest of the Si Satchanalai ruins. The exhibits are interesting despite the lack of English labels. These sites are easily visited by bicycle. Admission is included in the 220B all-inclusive ticket.

Ceramics are still made in the area, and several open-air shops can be found around the kiln centre in Chaliang. One local ceramic artist even continues to fire his pieces in an underground wood-burning oven.

Sawanworanayok National Museum

พิพิธภัณฑสถานแห่งชาติสวรรควรนายก

In Sawankhalok town, near Wat Sawankhalam on the western river bank, this state-sponsored **museum** (☎ 0 5564 1571; 69 Th Phracharat; admission 50B; ☉ 9am-4pm) houses an impressive collection of 12th- to 15th-century artefacts. The ground floor focuses on the area's ceramic legacy, while the 2nd floor features several beautiful bronze and stone Sukhothai-era Buddha statues.

Ban Hat Siaw

บ้านหาดเสี้ยว
pop 7299

This small town south of Si Satchanalai is a possible base from which to explore the ruins, and is home to the Thai Phuan (also known as Lao Phuan), a Tai tribal group that emigrated from Xieng Khuang Province in Laos about 100 years ago.

The local Thai Phuan are famous for **hand-woven textiles**, particularly the *pâh sîn đeen jòk* (brocade-bordered skirts), which have patterns of horizontal stripes bordered by thickly patterned brocade. The men's *pá'h ká·máh* (short sarong) from Hat Siaw, typically in dark plaids, are also highly regarded. Vintage Hat Siaw textiles, ranging from 80 to 200 years old, can be seen at the **Ancient Textile Museum** (☎ 0 5536 0058; admission free; ☉ 7am-6pm) opposite the market at the northern end of town.

Another Thai Phuan custom is the use of **elephant-back** processions in local monastic ordinations; these usually take place in early April.

Sleeping & Eating

There's very little in terms of accommodation or food near the park. A better alternative is to be based out of nearby Sawankhalok or Ban Hat Siaw.

SI SATCHANALAI-CHALIANG HISTORICAL PARK

Papong Homestay (☎ 0 5563 1557, 08 7313 4782; r 500B; Chaliang; ⬚) These three rooms in the large home of a friendly local are a minute's walk from Wat Phra Si Ratana Mahathat at Chaliang. All rooms include en-suite bathrooms and are tidy and comfortable. The only thing lacking is food, which is best obtained near the entrance of the park, ideally before 6pm.

Si Satchanalai Hotel and Resort (☎ 0 5567 2666; 247 Moo 2, Rte 101; r 400B, bungalow 1200B; ⬚) Resembling neither hotel nor resort, nonetheless this is virtually the only formal accommodation to be based relatively near the historical park. Rooms are featureless but tidy, and the expansive bungalows would be great for families. It's approximately 6km north of the park on the west side of Rte 101.

BAN HAT SIAW

Although there's only one place to stay here, there are several restaurants in this town, making it a logical base if you want to stay more or less near the historical park.

Hotel 59 (☎ 0 5567 1024; r 200-500B; ⬚) With about as much character as the name suggests, this is definitely not somewhere you're going to write home about, but it works if you want to stay relatively close to the historical park. It's at the northern end of town, just down the turn-off to Utaradit.

Kulap (no roman-script sign; ☎ 0 5567 1151; 473 Moo 2, Rte 101; dishes 50-100B) Located at the far north end of town on the left-hand side, this tired-looking restaurant serves some truly excellent Thai food that has earned it a reputation among both visitors and locals. Spice addicts will love the *gaang ʼbàh* ('jungle curry'), served with your choice of local fish, boar, frog or shrimp. For something more savoury try *ʼboo lǒn*, a mild 'dip' of crab, minced pork, coconut milk and fresh herbs, served with fresh vegetables.

Sawankhalok
สวรรคโลก
pop 18,840

This small town about 20km south of the historical park has some overnight options, including the **Saengsin Hotel** (☎ 0 5564 1259/1424; 2 Th Thetsaban Damri 3; s/d from 220/360B; 🕸), about 1km south of the train station on the main street that runs through Sawankhalok. It has clean, comfortable rooms and a coffee shop. A couple of other options also line the main drag.

This isn't a big town for eating; most food places sell noodles or curries and not much else. Sawankhalok's night market assembles every evening along its main streets.

Getting There & Away
BUS

Si Satchanalai-Chaliang Historical Park is off Rte 101 between Sawankhalok and new Si Satchanalai. From New Sukhothai, take a Si Satchanalai bus (38B, two hours) and ask to get off at 'meuang gòw' (old city). Alternatively, catch the 9am bus to Chiang Rai, which costs the same but makes fewer stops. The last bus back to New Sukhothai leaves at 4.30pm.

There are two places along the left side of the highway where you can get off the bus and reach the ruins in the park; both involve crossing Mae Nam Yom. The first, mentioned above, leads to a footbridge over Mae Nam Yom to Wat Phra Si Ratana Mahathat at Chaliang; the second crossing is about 2km further northwest just past two hills and leads directly into the Si Satchanalai ruins.

TRAIN

Sawankhalok's original train station is one of the local sights. King Rama VI built a 60km railway spur from Ban Dara (a small town on the main northern trunk) to Sawankhalok just so that he could visit the ruins. Amazingly, there's a daily special express from Bangkok to Sawankhalok (482B, seven hours, 10.50am). The train heads back to Bangkok at 7.40pm, arriving in the city at 3.30am. You can also take this train to Phitsanulok (50B). It's a 'Sprinter' – 2nd class air-con and no sleepers. The fare includes dinner and breakfast.

Getting Around

You can rent bicycles (per day 20B) from a shop at the gateway to Wat Phra Si Ratana Mahathat as well as near the food stalls at the entrance to the historical park.

KAMPHAENG PHET PROVINCE

KAMPHAENG PHET
กำแพงเพชร
pop 30,114

Located halfway between Bangkok and Chiang Mai, Kamphaeng Phet literally means 'Diamond Wall', a reference to the apparent strength of this formerly walled city's protective barrier. This level of security was necessary, as the city previously helped to protect the Sukhothai and later Ayuthaya kingdoms against attacks from Burma or Lanna. Parts of the wall can still be seen today, and the impressive ruins of several religious structures also remain. The modern city stretches along a shallow section of the Mae Nam Ping and is one of Thailand's pleasanter provincial capitals.

Information

Most of the major banks also have branches with ATMs along the main streets near the river and on Th Charoensuk. There are a couple of internet cafes in town on Th Thesa and Th Ratchadamnoen, otherwise try the main post office.

Main post office (Th Thesa) Just south of the old city. Has internet.
Police station (☎ 0 5571 1199, emergency 1155)
Tourist Information Centre (🕘 8am-4.30pm) Across from the National Museum; has some maps and pamphlets. There is another more history-focused centre at the group of ruins north of the city wall.

Sights
KAMPHAENG PHET HISTORICAL PARK
อุทยานประวัติศาสตร์กำแพงเพชร

A Unesco World Heritage Site, this **park** (☎ 0 5571 1921; inclusive admission 100-150B, bicycle/motorbike/săhm-lór/car 10/20/30/50B; 🕘 8am-5pm) features the ruins of structures dating back to the 14th century, roughly the same time as the better-known kingdom of Sukhothai. Kamphaeng Phet's Buddhist monuments continued to be built until the Ayuthaya period, nearly 200 years later, and thus possess elements of both Sukhothai and Ayuthaya styles, resulting in a school of Buddhist art quite unlike anywhere else in Thailand.

The park is divided into two distinct parts; an inclusive ticket allows entry to both areas. The old city (admission 100B) is surrounded by a wall (the 'Diamond Gate' of the city's name) and was formerly inhabited by monks of the *gamavasi* ('living in the community') sect. This area is dominated by **Wat Phra Kaew**, which used to be adjacent to the royal palace (now in ruins). It's not nearly as well restored as Sukhothai, but it's smaller, more intimate and less visited. Weather-corroded Buddha statues have assumed slender, porous forms that remind some visitors of the sculptures of Alberto Giacometti. About 100m southeast of Wat Phra Kaew is **Wat Phra That**, distinguished by a large round-based *chedi* surrounded by columns.

The majority of Kamphaeng Phet's ruins are found a few hundred metres north of the city walls in an area previously home to monks of the *arani* ('living in forests') sect. An inclusive ticket purchased at the old city also allows entrance here, and there is an excellent **visitor centre** (admission 100B; ☉ 8.30am-4.30pm) at the entrance. There are more than 40 temple compounds in this area, including **Wat Phra Si Iriyabot**, which has the shattered remains of standing, sitting, walking and reclining Buddha images all sculpted in the classic Sukhothai style.

Northwest of here, **Wat Chang Rawp** (Elephant-Encircled Temple) is just that – a temple with an elephant-buttressed wall. Several other temple ruins – most of them not much more than flat brick foundations, with the occasional weather-worn Buddha image – can be found in the same general vicinity.

OTHER TEMLPES

Across Mae Nam Ping are the neglected ruins of **Wat Phra Borommathat**, in an area that was settled long before Kamphaeng Phet's heyday, although visible remains are postclassical Sukhothai. The compound has a few small *chedi* and one large *chedi* of the late Sukhothai period which is now crowned with a Burmese-style umbrella added early in the 20th century.

Wat Khu Yang contains a handsome wooden *hŏr drai* dating back to the 19th century.

KAMPHAENG PHET NATIONAL MUSEUM
พิพิธภัณฑสถานแห่งชาติกำแพงเพชร
The **national museum** (☎ 0 5571 1570; Th Pindramri; admission 100B; ☉ 9am-noon & 1-4pm Wed-Sun) has the

usual survey of Thai art periods downstairs. Upstairs there is a collection of artefacts from the Kamphaeng Phet area including an immense Shiva statue that is the largest bronze Hindu sculpture in the country. The image was formerly located at the nearby **San Phra Isuan** (Shiva Shrine) until a tourist stole the idol's hands and head in 1886 (they were later returned). Today a replica stands in its place.

KAMPHAENG PHET REGIONAL MUSEUM
พิพิธภัณฑ์เฉลิมพระเกียรติกำแพงเพชร
The **regional museum** (☎ 0 5572 2341; Th Pindramri; admission 10B; ☉ 9am-4pm) is a series of Thai-style wooden structures on stilts set among nicely landscaped grounds. There are three main buildings in the museum featuring displays ranging from history and prehistory to the various ethnic groups that inhabit the province.

PHRA RUANG HOT SPRINGS
บ่อน้ำร้อนพระร่วง
Located 20km outside Kamphaeng Phet along the road to Sukhothai, this complex of natural **hot springs** (☉ 8.30am-4pm) is the Thai version of a rural health retreat. The reputedly therapeutic hot waters have been diverged into seven private bathing rooms (50B), and there's also an outdoor foot pool and several places offering traditional Thai massage. There is no public transport to the hot springs, but transport can be arranged at Three J Guest House (below).

Sleeping

Gor Choke Chai (☎ 0 5571 1247; 19-43 Soi 8, Th Ratchadamnoen 1; r 260-320B; ✖ ▢) This egg carton–like building is a good budget choice with its smallish but tidy rooms. Popular with Thai businessmen, it's conveniently located in the centre of the new town.

Three J Guest House (☎ 0 5571 3129; threejguest@ hotmail.com; 79 Th Rachavitee; r 300-600B; ✖ ▢) This pleasant collection of bungalows in a pretty garden has a very hospitable and friendly host. Pathways lead to clean log bungalows with terraces. The cheapest ones share a clean bathroom and the more expensive have aircon. There's heaps of local information, bicycles and motorcycles are available for rent, and the owner can also arrange visits to his country resort near Klong Wang Chao National Park.

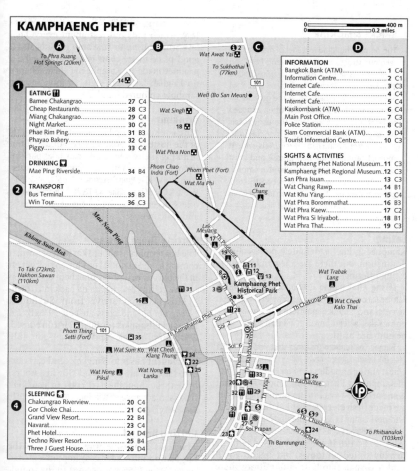

KAMPHAENG PHET

Navarat (☎ 0 5571 1211; 2 Soi Prapan; r 400-500B, ste 950B; ❄) Like many provincial Thai hotels, the Navarat has changed little, if at all, since its apparent construction in the early '70s. Despite this, it's a clean, cosy place and some rooms have nice views.

Phet Hotel (☎ 0 5571 2810-5; www.phethotel.com; 189 Soi Pracha Hansa; r 500-650B; ❄ 🖳 🖳) Near the morning market, this comfortable hotel features spacious, well-maintained, modern rooms with views over Kamphaeng Phet. There is a small pool, a restaurant and bar. Look for the sign on the top of the building. The street-side sign is only in Thai script.

Chakungrao Riverview (☎ 0 5571 4900-8; www .chankungraoriverview.com; 149 Th Thesa; r 1000-1200B, ste 5000B; ❄ 🖳) Kamphaeng Phet's posh-

est digs has some nice rooms despite its unremarkable facade. Rooms are tastefully decked out in dark woods and forest green and feature balconies with river or city views. Suites are huge and available at a considerable discount.

There are also literally dozens of Thai-style riverside 'resorts' at Nakhon Chum, along the east bank of the Mae Nam Ping. **Grand View Resort** (☎ 0 5572 1104; 34/4 Moo 2, Nakhon Chum; r 290-390; ❄), the first one you'll come to on the left-hand side, is similar to many others in quality and price. **Techno River Resort** (☎ 0 5579 9800; 27/27 Moo 2, Nakhon Chum; r 450-1200B; ❄) is the poshest of the lot, and offers a huge variety of clean, though generally characterless rooms.

NORTHERN THAILAND

BRICKS & MORTAR

The primary building material of many of the religious structures of Kamphaeng Phet and Sukhothai is laterite (*sì-lah laang* in Thai), a clay-like substance found over much of Southeast Asia. When still in the ground, laterite is soft and pliable, but when exposed to light and air, it hardens. The early locals discovered this, and shaped the clay into bricks before drying it in the sun. As is evident today, laterite is extremely porous and must be coated with plaster to give it a smooth look. The new and helpful 'Reconstructed' placards near most ruins give an idea of what the structures originally looked like.

Eating

Kamphaeng Phet is definitely not a culinary destination, but there are a few mildly interesting offerings.

Miang Chakangrao (☎ 0 5571 1124; 273 Th Ratchadamnoen) sells a huge variety of local sweets and snacks, particularly the shop's namesake, a fermented tea salad eaten with peanut-rice brittle.

Bamee Chakangrao (no roman-script sign; ☎ 0 5571 2446; Th Ratchadamnoen; dishes 25-30B; ☾ 8.30am-3pm) Thin wheat and egg noodles *(bà·mèe)* are a speciality of Kamphaeng Phet, and this famous restaurant is one of the best places to try them. The noodles are made fresh every day behind the restaurant, and pork satay is also available.

Phayao Bakery (Th Thesa 1; dishes 45-120B; ☾ breakfast, lunch & dinner) It may look closed with its heavily tinted windows, but inside you'll find a casual, family-friendly atmosphere with real coffee, a variety of baked goods and ice cream. Air-conditioned, it's a great place to escape from the heat.

Piggy (no roman-script sign; Th Ratchadamnoen; per person 70B; ☾ 5-10pm) *Mŏo gà·tá*, pork grilled over a hotpot, is one of the more popular dishes in these parts. Simply choose your ingredients from the buffet, then grill your meats, adding your veggies and other ingredients to the broth. There's no English sign, but Piggy is found on the corner and usually boasts several grilling customers.

A busy night market sets up every evening near the river just north of the Navarat Hotel. There are also some cheap restaurants near the roundabout near the main bridge over the Mae Nam Ping, including the exceedingly popular **Kamphaeng Phet Phochana** (no

roman-script sign; ☎ 0 5571 3035; dishes 25-50B; ☾ 6am-1am), which puts out just about every Thai fave from *pàt tai* to *kŏw man gài*. It's also a good place to try *chŏw góoay*, grass jelly, a product made in Kamphaeng Phet. There's no English-language sign, so look for the rainbow-coloured facade.

Drinking

Much of Kampaeng Phet's 'entertainment' is of the hostess/karaoke variety. For a night of drinking the whole family can take part in, try one of the various riverfront restaurants-cum-pubs. **Mae Ping Riverside** (☎ 0 5572 2455; 050/1 Moo 2, Nakhon Chum; dishes 40-120B; ☾ lunch & dinner) offers decent eats, draught beer, live music and cool breezes.

Getting There & Away

The bus terminal is about 1km west of town. If coming from Sukhothai or Phitsanulok get off in the old city or at the roundabout on Th Tesa to save getting a *sŏrng·tăa·ou* back into town.

Most visitors arrive from Sukhothai (*sŏrng·tăa·ou*/2nd class air-con 50/62B, 1½ hours), Phitsanulok (ordinary/air-con 60/84B, 2½ hours) or Tak (2nd class air-con 48B, 1½ hours).

Frequent buses to Bangkok (2nd class air-con/1st class air-con 244/308B, five hours) leave throughout the day. You can also book tickets in advance at **Win Tour** (☎ 0 5571 3971; Th Kamphaeng Phet).

Getting Around

The least expensive way to get from the bus station into town is to hop on a shared *sŏrng·tăa·ou* (15B per person) to the roundabout across the river. From there take a *sähm·lór* anywhere in town for 20B to 30B. Motorcycle taxis from the bus station to most hotels downtown cost 40B.

It is worth renting a bicycle or motorbike to explore areas outside of the old city – Three J Guest House (p408) has both for rent (per day bicycle/motorcycle 50/200B).

TAK PROVINCE

Tak is a wild and mountainous province. Its proximity to Myanmar has resulted in a complex history and unique cultural mix.

The majority of Tak is forested and mountainous and is an excellent destination for those wanting to trek. There are Hmong, Musoe (Lahu), Lisu and White and Red Karen settlements throughout the west and north. In the 1970s many of these mountains were a hotbed of communist guerrilla activity. Since the 1980s the former leader of the local CPT movement has been involved in resort-hotel development and most of Tak is open to outsiders, but the area still has an untamed feeling about it.

Western Tak in particular has always been in distinct contrast with other parts of Thailand because of strong Karen and Burmese cultural influences. The Thailand–Myanmar border districts of Mae Ramat, Tha Song Yang and Mae Sot are dotted with refugee camps, an outcome of fire fights between the Karen National Union (KNU) and the Myanmar government. At the time of writing there were more than 121,000 registered Burmese refugees in Tak Province alone.

There's little of interest in the eponymous provincial capital, and in recent years, transport to other parts of the province has improved greatly, allowing travellers to circumvent the city altogether. However, if you happen to be in the area, you can visit **Wat Phra Borommathat** in Ban Tak, 25km upstream along Mae Nam Tak from Tak. The wát is the original site of a Thai *chedi* that, according to legend, was constructed during the reign of King Ramkhamhaeng (1275–1317) to celebrate his elephant-back victory over King Sam Chon, ruler of an independent kingdom once based at or near Mae Sot. The wát's main feature is a large, slender, gilded *chedi* in the Shan style surrounded by numerous smaller but similar *chedi*. Many Thais flock to the temple each week in the belief that the *chedi* can somehow reveal to them the winning lottery numbers for the week.

Approximately 45km north of Tak via Rte 1 and then 17km west (between the Km463 and Km464 markers), via the road to Sam Ngao, is **Kheuan Phumiphon** (Bhumibol Dam), which impounds Mae Nam Ping at a height of 154m, making it the tallest dam in Southeast Asia. The shores and islands of the reservoir are a favourite picnic spot for local Thais.

MAE SOT
แม่สอด
pop 41,158
Despite its remote location and relatively small size, Mae Sot is among the most culturally diverse cities in Thailand. Walking

down the streets of the town, you'll see a fascinating ethnic mixture – Burmese men in their *longyi* (sarongs), Hmong and Karen women in traditional hill-tribe dress, bearded Muslims, Thai army rangers and foreign NGO workers. Burmese and Karen are spoken more than Thai, shop signs along the streets are in Thai, Burmese and Chinese, and most of the temple architecture in Mae Sot is Burmese. Mae Sot has also become the most important jade and gem centre along the border, with most of the trade controlled by Chinese and Indian immigrants from Myanmar.

Although there aren't many formal sites to see in Mae Sot, and most tourists just come for a visa run, many end up staying longer than expected. A vibrant market, several good restaurants and a fun nightlife scene have become attractions in their own right.

Information
Several centrally located banks have ATMs. International phone services can be found at Bai Fern restaurant (p416) and Se. Southeast Express Tours. There is no official tourist information or TAT office in Mae Sot, but good sources of information are Ban Thai Guest House (p415) and Khrua Canadian (p416); the latter prints a map of the area and has a chart of current bus times and fares.
Se. Southeast Express Tours (522/3 Th Intharakhiri; per hr 20B) There are a few other internet cafes west of this one.
Tourist police (☎ 1155; 738/1 Th Intharakhiri) Has an office east of the centre of town and at the market by the Friendship Bridge.

Sights & Activities
BORDER MARKET & MYAWADI
ตลาดริมเมย/เมียวดี
There is an expansive covered **market** alongside the Mae Nam Moei on the Thai side that legally sells a mixture of workaday Burmese goods and cheap Chinese electronics.

However the real reason most come here is to cross to Myawadi in Myanmar (Burma). Immigration procedures are taken care of at the **Thai immigration booth** (☎ 0 5556 3000; 6.30am-6.30pm) at the Friendship Bridge, although if you have any problems there's another immigration office in the nearby Mae Moei Shopping Bazaar. It takes a few minutes to finish all the paperwork to leave Thailand officially, and then you're free to walk across the arched 420m Friendship Bridge.

NORTHERN THAILAND

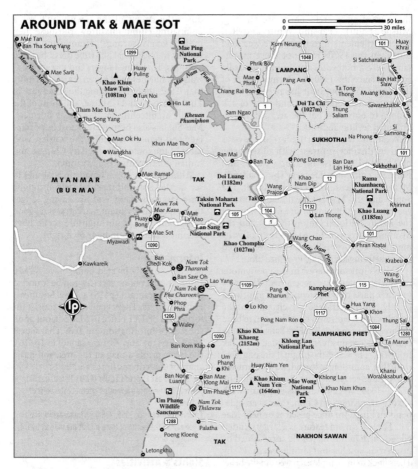

AROUND TAK & MAE SOT

At the other end of the bridge is the **Myanmar immigration booth**, where you'll fill out permits for a one-day stay, pay a fee of US$10 or 500B and leave your passport as a deposit. Then you're free to wander around Myawadi as long as you're back at the bridge by 5.30pm Myanmar time (which is a half-hour behind Thai time) to pick up your passport and check out with immigration. On your return to Thailand, the Thai immigration office at the bridge will give you a new 15-day visa (p754).

Before going to the Friendship Bridge, ask about the border situation in Mae Sot. Sporadic relations between Myanmar and Thailand can sometimes cause the border to close for a few days. If the border is closed and

your 30-day visa has run out, it is possible to get a one-day extension for free at the immigration office. For each day's extension after that it costs 500B.

Myawadi is a fairly typical Burmese town, with a number of monasteries, schools, shops and so on. The most important temple is **Shwe Muay Wan**, a traditional bell-shaped *chedi* gilded with many kilos of gold and topped by more than 1600 precious and semiprecious gems. Another noted Buddhist temple is **Myikyaungon**, called Wat Don Jarakhe in Thai and named for its crocodile-shaped sanctuary. A hollow *chedi* at Myikyaungon contains four marble Mandalay-style Buddhas around a central pillar, while niches in the surrounding wall are filled with Buddhas in other styles, including several bronze Sukhothai-style Buddhas. Myawadi's 1000-year-old earthen city walls, probably erected by the area's original Mon inhabitants, can be seen along the southern side of town.

Sŏrng·tăa·ou frequently go to the border (15B, frequent departures from 6.30am to 5.30pm), 6km west of Mae Sot: ask for Rim Moei (Edge of the Moei). The last sŏrng·tăa·ou going back to Mae Sot leaves Rim Moei at 5.30pm.

HERBAL SAUNA

Wat Mani has separate herbal **sauna** (admission 20B; ☾ 3-7pm) facilities for men and women. The sauna is towards the back of the monastery grounds, past the monks' gù·dì (living quarters).

COOKERY COURSE

Held at Borderline shop (p416), this **course** (☎ 0 5554 6584; borderlineshop@yahoo.com; 674/14 Th Intharakhiri; 450B per person, 3 people min; lessons ☾ 8am-1pm) teaches Shan, Burmese and Karen dishes, and includes a trip to the market, food and drink preparation, a cookbook, and sharing the results in the adjoining cafe.

Tours

Several guesthouses arrange tours of the surrounding area. The staff working at the Khrua Canadian restaurant (p416) keep pretty good tabs on the different tours and are a good source of information. If you're thinking of going to Um Phang, it's probably a good idea to book directly from there, as relatively few outfits seem to have offices in Mae Sot. See p420 for other tour options out of Um Phang.

The following are the longest-running and most reliable.

Mae Sot Conservation Tour (☎ 0 5553 2818; mae sotco@hotmail.com; 415/17 Th Tang Kim Chiang; 1-day tour per person 1500B) Runs educational tours to Karen villages surrounding Mae Sot.

Max One Tour (☎ 0 5554 2942; www.maxonetour .com; Mae Sot Sq, Th Intharakhiri; 3-day trek per person 5550B) This company conducts adventure-centric tours, mostly based around the Um Phang area.

Se. Southeast Express (☎ 0 5554 7048; 522/3 Th Intharakhiri; 3-day tour per person 6500B) Does the usual three- to four-day tours to Um Phang and around, as well as one-day tours around Mae Sot.

BURMESE REFUGEES & MIGRANTS

Burmese refugees first crossed into Thailand in 1984, when the Burmese army penetrated the ethnic Karen state and established bases near the Thai-Burma border, from where they launched forced relocation campaigns of the indigenous populations. Large numbers of civilian ethnic minority populations, students and pro-democracy advocates were forced into Thailand following the suppression of pro-democracy demonstrations in 1988 and the overturned 1990 elections. Today, refugees continue to cross the border to escape from ongoing fighting and persecution in eastern Burma.

According to the UNHCR, 121,383 registered Burmese live in nine refugee camps scattered along the border. In these camps the Thai government allows international organisations to provide humanitarian assistance, including health care and schooling.

Many who flee Burma are not permitted to be registered refugees if not running from active fighting, and there are also tens of thousands of undocumented refugees, many of them also living in camps. Those who cross the border because of politically induced economic hardship or human rights violations often become migrant workers, with a precarious political and legal status. Approximately two million Burmese migrant workers and their families live in Thailand – often at way below subsistence levels – performing farm, factory, fishery, construction and domestic work. They are extremely vulnerable to exploitation by employers and deportation by officials, and frequently lack access to basic educational and health services.

It is possible for migrant workers from the region to be legally registered, obtain non-Thai identification cards and be issued work permits once employment is secured. Thai government policy also grants migrants and registered workers access to a national health insurance scheme, and allows migrant children a right to basic education. But the legal status of most Burmese immigrants makes them avoid Thai institutions. For now, international organisations and NGOs are providing many of these services. To lend a hand see p48 for the various volunteer opportunities in northern Thailand. To find out more about the refugees and migrants, as well as the situation in Burma, useful sites are www.burmanet.org and www.irrawaddy.org.

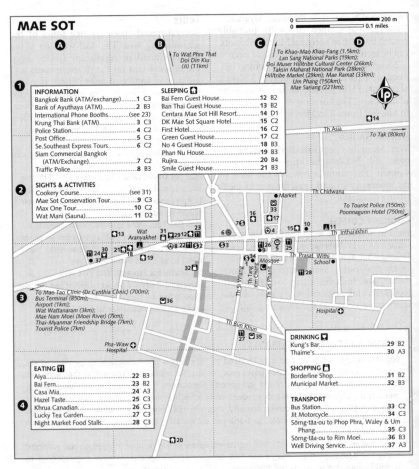

MAE SOT

Map labels:
To Wat Phra That Doi Din Kiu (Ji) (11km)
To Khao-Mao Khao-Fang (1.5km); Lan Sang National Parks (19km); Doi Muser Hilltribe Cultural Center (26km); Taksin Maharat National Park (28km); Hilltribe Market (29km); Mae Ramat (33km); Um Phang (150km); Mae Sariang (221km);
Th Asia
To Tak (80km)
Th Chidwana
Th Intharakhiri
To Tourist Police (150m); Poonnagunn Hotel (750m)
Market
Wat Aranyakhet
Mosque
Th Prasat Withi
School
Th Si Wiang
Th Tang Kim Chiang
Th Sri Phanit
To Mao Tao Clinic (Dr Cynthia Clinic) (700m); Bus Terminal (850m); Airport (1km); Wat Wattanaram (3km); Mae Nam Moei (Moei River) (7km); Thai-Myanmar Friendship Bridge (7km); Tourist Police (7km)
Pha-Waw Hospital
Th Bun Khun
Hospital

Festivals & Events

A big **Thai-Burmese gem fair** is held in April. Around this time Thai and Burmese boxers meet for a **Thai-boxing competition**, held somewhere outside town in the traditional style. Five-round matches are fought in a circular ring; the first four rounds last three minutes, the fifth has no time limit. With their hands bound in hemp, boxers fight till first blood or knockout. You'll have to ask around to find the changing venue for the annual slugfest.

Sleeping

BUDGET

Many places in Mae Sot fit in the budget range and cater for NGO workers that are staying longer-term.

Green Guest House (☎ 0 5553 3207; krit.sana@hotmail.com; 406/8 sub-soi off Th Intarahakhiri; dm 100B, r 150-250B) Run by a teacher and her husband, this peaceful, friendly guesthouse offers a variety of good-sized rooms with TV and decent furniture. It's great value, centrally located and has a pretty garden.

Smile Guest House (☎ 08 5129 9293; smilemaesot@gmail.com; 738 Th Intarahakhiri; r 100-300B; 🚫 🖵) A variety of basic but clean rooms in a large wooden home. The cheaper rooms share bathrooms and long-term stays can be arranged.

Bai Fern Guesthouse (☎ 0 5553 1349; www.bai-fern.com; Th Intharakhiri; r 150-300; 🚫 🖵) Set just off the road in a large house, the rooms here are tidy, but plain. All have well-equipped shared bathrooms. The service is very friendly with the use of a kitchen, fridge, wireless internet and TV in the communal area.

DK Mae Sot Square Hotel (Duang Kamol Hotel; ☎ 0 5554 2648; 298/2 Th Intharakhiri; r with fan or air-con 250-450B; ✆ 🖳) If the beds, towels and sheets here were upgraded, it would be a fantastic budget deal. Until then the large rooms in this three-storey hotel are average, but conveniently located.

Phan Nu House (☎ 08 1972 4467; 563/3 Th Intharakhiri; r 250-500B; ✆ 🖳) This new place unites 19 large rooms in a residential compound just off the street. Most are equipped with air-con, TV, fridge and hot water, making them a good deal.

ourpick Ban Thai Guest House (☎ 0 5553 1590; banthai_mth@hotmail.com; 740 Th Intharakhiri; r 250-950B; ✆ 🖳) This tiny neighbourhood of five converted Thai houses down a hibiscus-lined alley has spacious, very stylish wooden rooms with Thai-style furniture, axe lounging pillows and Thai textiles. The cheaper rooms have plentiful shared bathrooms; the more expensive have en suite bathrooms, large terraces and some come with a lounge/office. Shared sitting areas have cable TV, DVDs and free wireless internet. There are bicycles and motorbikes to rent and a laundry service. The place is popular with long-stay NGO workers, so booking ahead is a good idea.

First Hotel (☎ 0 5553 1233; fax 0 5553 1340; 44 Th Intharakhiri; r with fan/air-con 270/450B; ✆) This is among the more bizarre hotels we've encountered in our research for this book. From the outside the First appears abandoned, or worse. However, the inside reveals a fantasy of teak, with elaborate carvings ranging from gargoyles to mermaids covering virtually every surface. The rooms are huge, floored in marble, feature even more teak carvings, and appear quite comfortable.

MIDRANGE & TOP END

Rujira (☎ 0 5554 4969; rujira_tom@hotmail.com; 3/18 Th Buakjoon; r incl breakfast 350-1000B; ✆ 🖳) This great value place has spacious, apartment-like rooms with lots of homey touches. There's also a pleasant communal feeling, with lots of shaded outdoor seating, a restaurant and a cute coffee shop. The only downside is that it's a long walk to the town centre. Call for pick-up from the bus station (100B).

Poonnagunn Hotel (☎ 0 5553 4732; www.poonnagunn.com; 10/3 Th Intharakhiri; r incl breakfast 1200-1500B; ✆ 🖳) This is the kind of hotel you wish you could take with you everywhere; rooms are new and large and tastefully decked out with attractive furnishings, and include a small veranda. The hotel is located about 750m east of town. A 20% discount is generally available.

Centara Mae Sot Hill Resort (☎ 0 5553 2601; www.centarahotelsresort.com; 100 Th Asia; r incl breakfast 1800-2000B, ste incl breakfast 3000-3500B; ✆ 🖳 ⚖) For this price range, the rooms here look a bit tired. But if you don't mind staying outside of the city centre, and require facilities such as a pool, tennis courts, good restaurant, disco and a bar, it's your only choice.

Eating

Mae Sot is a virtual culinary crossroads with a diversity of cuisines not seen in most other Thai towns. For a fun breakfast head to the area directly south of the mosque where several buzzing Muslim restaurants serve sweet tea, roti and *nanbya*, tandoor-style bread. The town's vibrant day market is the place to try Burmese dishes such as *mohinga*, the country's unofficial national dish, or Burmese-style curries served over rice. Mae Sot's night market features mostly Thai/Chinese-style dishes.

Lucky Tea Garden (Th Bun Khun; dishes 10-50B; ⏲ 5.30am-9pm) For the authentic Burmese teashop experience without crossing over to Myawadi, visit this friendly cafe equipped with sweet tea, tasty snacks, and of course, bad Burmese pop music. Or come with an empty stomach and try one of the better biryanis in town.

Hazel Taste (Th Intharakhiri; dishes 20-60B; ⏲ 8am-9pm) This modern, air-conditioned cafe offers a huge selection of great coffee drinks, tasty sweets and internet.

Casa Mia (☎ 08 7204 4701; Th Don Kaew; dishes 30-180B; ⏲ 8am-10pm) Tucked down a side street, this simple restaurant serves the cheapest homemade pasta dishes you'll find anywhere. And better yet, they're right tasty. They also do Thai and Burmese, and some exceptional desserts, including a wicked banoffee pie.

Aiya (☎ 0 5553 0102; 533 Th Intharakhiri; dishes 45-80B; ⏲ 10am-10pm) Opposite Bai Fern Guest House, Aiya is a simple place that serves good Burmese food, which is particularly strong on vegetarian options. They do a mean Burmese tea-leaf salad, or you could try any item from the 'One Dream One World Menu', of which 20% of the cost is donated to the eponymous NGO. There's live music some nights.

Khrua Canadian (☎ 0 5553 4659; 3 Th Sri Phanit; dishes 40-280B; ☺ 7am-9pm) This is the place to go if you want to forget you're in Asia for one meal. Dave, the Canadian, brews his own coffee and also offers homemade bagels, deli meats and cheeses, in addition to a huge breakfast menu. The servings are large, the menu is varied, and when you finally remember you're in Thailand again, local information is also available.

Bai Fern (☎ 0 5553 3343; Th Intharakhiri; dishes 50-350B; ☺ 8am-10pm) The cosy, wood-furnished Bai Fern has a pleasant atmosphere and is popular all day long. The Thai food here comes recommended, and there are steaks, salads and Burmese curries too. Or just stop by for the good coffee and cake and a look at the paper.

ourpick **Khao-Mao Khao-Fang** (no roman-script sign; ☎ 0 5553 2483; 382 Mu 5, Mae Pa; dishes 80-220B; ☺ 11am-10pm) Like dining in a gentrified jungle, this place, designed by a Thai botanist, replaces chandeliers with hanging vines, orchids and lots of running water. It also has one of the more interesting Thai menus you'll find anywhere, with dishes featuring local ingredients such as fish from the Mae Nam Moei or local herbs and veggies. Try one of the several delicious-sounding yam (Thai-style spicy salads), featuring ingredients ranging from white turmeric to local mushrooms. The restaurant is north of town between the Km1 and Km2 markers on the road to Mae Ramat.

Drinking & Entertainment

Mae Sot has a lively nightlife that heats up at the weekends. The strip of Th Intharakhiri that runs west from Wat Aranyakhet is where most bars, including those below, are located.

Kung's Bar (Th Intharakhiri) Popular with the NGO set, this fun bar is decked out with murals and an odd combination of antiques and kitsch. A huge and detailed drink menu will appeal to those who don't be beer.

Thaime's (☎ 08 9649 9994; Th Intharakhiri; ☺ 3pm-midnight) The only not-for-profit bar we've ever encountered, this place is exceedingly casual and has a brief snack menu. Profits from your fun go to a school for migrant children. The bar sometimes accepts volunteer help, so call ahead for details.

Shopping

Mae Sot's **municipal market** is among the largest and most vibrant we've encountered anywhere in Thailand. In addition to the usual Thai wet market veggies and dry goods, there's heaps of exotic stuff from Myanmar, including Burmese bookshops, sticks of thanaka (the source of the yellow powder you see on most faces), bags of pickled tea leaves, bizarre cosmetics from across the border and velvet thong slippers from Mandalay. Unlike most markets in Thailand it doesn't require a 6am wake-up call and is up and running pretty much all day. It's also a great place to try authentic Burmese food.

Mae Sot is most famous for its gems trade, and is the most important jade and gem centre along the border. Check out the hustle and bustle among the glittering treasures in the shops and stalls along Th Prasat Withi, just east of the market. If looking to buy be prepared to bargain hard.

Borderline Shop (☎ 0 5554 6584; borderlinecollective .org; 674/14 Th Intharakhiri; ☺ 10am-6pm Tue-Sun) Selling arts and craft items made by refugee women, the profits of this shop go back into a women's collective and a child-assistance foundation. All of the products, such as bags, clothes and household items, have labels on them so you know where the money is going. Upstairs a gallery sells paintings, and a cookery course (see p413) and an outdoor 'tea garden' are also here.

Getting There & Away

Orange sŏrng·tăa·ou to Mae Sariang (200B, six hours, five departures from 6am to noon) depart from the old bus station near the centre of town. Blue sŏrng·tăa·ou to Um Phang (120B, four hours, every hour from 7.30am to 3.30pm) leave from an office on Th Bun Khun. Sŏrng·tăa·ou to Rim Moei (15B, 15 minutes, 6am to 5.30pm) also leave from a spot nearby on Th Bun Khun.

All buses now leave from the bus station 850m west of the town centre on Th Intharakhiri. There are frequent minivans to Tak (56B, every half-hour from 7am to 6pm), as well as to Sukhothai (140B, six departures from 7am to 2.30pm) and Phitsanulok (176B, six departures from 7am to 2.30pm).

The **Green Bus** (☎ 114 ext 8000; www.greenbusthailand.com) runs two daily departures to Mae Sai (2nd class air-con/1st class 388/499B, 12 hours, 6am and 8am), with stops in Lampang (2nd class air-con/1st class 181/232B, four hours), Chiang Mai (2nd class air-con/1st class 237/304B, six hours) and Chiang Rai (2nd class air-con/1st class 354/455B, 10 hours).

There are now also daily departures to Mukdahan (1st class 675B, 12 hours, 6pm) and Laem Ngob (1st class 750B, 15 hours, 5pm) in Trat province.

There are several daily departures to Bangkok (2nd class air-con/1st class/VIP 328/421/655B, eight hours, 11 departures from 8am to 9.45pm).

Getting Around

Most of Mae Sot can be seen on foot. Regular *sŏrng·tăa·ou* serve surrounding communities including Moei (15B). Motorcycle taxis and săhm·lór charge 20B for trips around town.

Several tourism-related business around town rent out vehicles. Ban Thai Guest House (p415) rents out motorbikes. Cars and vans can be hired at Bai Fern restaurant (opposite). And bicycles are available for rent at Borderline (opposite), which also includes a suggested tour of the area.

Jit Motorcycle (☎ 0 5553 2099; 127/4-6 Th Prasat Withi; motorcycles per day 150B) rents out motorcycles.

Well Driving Service (☎ 0 5554 4844; wdeacha@yahoo .com; 764/7 Th Intharakhiri; car hire per day 1200-1500B, with driver per day 1800-2500B) offers a variety of vehicles for rent, both with and without driver.

AROUND MAE SOT
Doi Muser Hilltribe Cultural Center
ศูนย์พัฒนาและสงเคราะห์ชาวเขาดอยมูเซอ

At the top of the mountain on the road to Tak is this **research and cultural centre** (☎ 0 5551 2131, 0 5551 3614; Km26, Th Tak-Mae Sot; bungalows 200-700B) where you can visit for the day, or spend the night. Here they grow and sell crops such as tea, coffee, fruits and flowers. Call ahead to find out about seeing a cultural performance. The temperature can go as low as 4°C in the winter. During November and December, *boo·a torng* (a kind of wild sunflower) blossom around the centre.

Just up the road, at Km29, is the huge roadside **hill-tribe market** featuring a variety of agricultural products, in addition to hill-tribe handicrafts.

Taksin Maharat & Lan Sang National Parks
อุทยานแห่งชาติตากสินมหาราช/ลานสาง

These small national parks receive a steady trickle of visitors on weekends and holidays, but they are almost empty during the week.

Taksin Maharat National Park (☎ 0 5551 1429; admission 200B) covers 149 sq km; the entrance is

2km from the Km26 marker on Rte 105. The most outstanding features here are the 30m, nine-tiered waterfall **Nam Tok Mae Ya Pa** and a record-holding *dà·bàhk*, a dipterocarp that is 50m tall, 16m in circumference and 700 years old. Birdwatching is said to be particularly good here; known resident and migratory species include tiger shrikes, forest wagtails and Chinese pond herons.

Nineteen kilometres before Tak, **Lan Sang National Park** (☎ 0 5551 9278; admission 200B) preserves a 104-sq-km area of rugged, 1000m-high granite peaks – part of the Tenasserim Range. A network of **trails** leads to several **waterfalls**, including the park's 40m-high namesake.

Taksin Maharat National Park offers **utilitarian rooms** (1000-2400B) that sleep between four and 10 people and a **camping ground** (tent sites 100B). Lan Sang National Park rents rustic **bungalows** (400-4000B) that can accommodate two to 32 people. Two-person **tents** (100B) are also available. Food service can be arranged in both parks. For further information, and to book accommodation, contact the **Royal Forest Department** (☎ 0 2562 0760; www.dnp .go.th).

The best way to reach the parks is by private car, but the bus from Mae Sot to Tak will drop you off on the road where you can easily walk to the park entrance. By car take Rte 1103 3km south of Rte 105.

UM PHANG & AROUND
อุ้มผาง

Rte 1090 goes south from Mae Sot to Um Phang, 150km away. This stretch of road used to be called the 'Death Highway' because of the guerrilla activity in the area that hindered highway development. Those days ended in the 1980s, but lives are still lost because of brake failure or treacherous turns on this steep, winding road through incredible mountain scenery.

Along the way there are short hikes off the highway to two waterfalls, **Nam Tok Thararak** (26km from Mae Sot) and **Nam Tok Pha Charoen** (41km). Nam Tok Thararak streams over limestone cliffs and calcified rocks with a rough texture that makes climbing the falls easy. It's been made into a park of sorts, with benches right in the stream at the base of the falls for cooling off and a couple of outhouse toilets nearby; on weekends food vendors set up here.

Just beyond Ban Rom Klao 4 – roughly midway between Mae Sot and Um Phang – is

Um Piam, a very large Karen and Burmese refugee village with around 20,000 refugees that were moved here from camps around Rim Moei. There are also several Hmong villages in the area.

Sitting at the junction of Mae Nam Klong and Huay Um Phang, **Um Phang** is an overgrown village populated mostly by Karen. Many Karen villages in this area are very traditional, and elephants are a common sight, especially in **Palatha**, a traditional Karen village 25km south of Um Phang. *Yaeng* (elephant saddles) and other tack used for elephant wrangling are a common sight on the verandas of the houses in this village.

An interesting hike can be done that follows the footpaths northeast of the village through rice fields and along Huay Um Phang to a few smaller Karen villages. At the border where Amphoe Um Phang meets Myanmar, near the Thai-Karen villages of Ban Nong Luang and Ban Huay, is a Karen refugee village inhabited by more than 500 Karen who originally hailed from Htikabler village on the other side of border.

South of Um Phang, towards Sangkhlaburi in Kanchanaburi province, **Um Phang Wildlife Sanctuary** is a Unesco World Heritage Site. One of its most popular attractions is Nam Tok Thilawsu (below), the largest waterfall in Thailand. Um Phang Wildlife Sanctuary links with the Thung Yai Naresuan National Park and Huay Kha Kaeng Wildlife Sanctuary (another Unesco World Heritage Site), as well as Khlong Lan and Mae Wong national parks to form Thailand's largest wildlife corridor and one of the largest intact natural forests in Southeast Asia.

Information

There are now two ATMs in Um Phang, although it's still probably a good idea to bring cash. **Internet** (per hr 20B) is available at a large cafe on the way to Ban Palatha. There's a post office, which has a couple of long-distance phones. There's a police station and a small branch of the **TAT** (☎ 0 5556 1338; 8.30am-5pm) across from the school, along the road leading to Mae Sot.

Sights & Activities
NAM TOK THILAWSU
น้ำตกทีลอซู

This **waterfall** is Thailand's largest, measuring an estimated 200m high and up to 400m wide during the rainy season. Thais, particularly fanatical about such things, consider Nam Tok Thilawsu to be the most beautiful waterfall in the country. There's a shallow cave behind the falls and several levels of pools suitable for swimming. The best time to visit is after the rainy season (November and December) when the 200m to 400m limestone cliffs alongside the Mae Nam Klong are streaming with water and Nam Tok Thilawsu is at its best.

The falls are near the headquarters of the **Um Phang Wildlife Sanctuary** (☎ 0 5557 7318; admission 200B), a distance of about 50km from Um Phang. The 2km path between the headquarters and falls has been transformed into a self-guided nature tour, with the addition of well-conceived educational plaques. Surrounding the falls on both sides of the river are Thailand's thickest stands of natural forest, and the hiking in the vicinity of Nam Tok Thilawsu can be superb. The forest here is said to contain more than 1300 varieties of palm; giant bamboo and strangler figs are also commonplace.

You can **camp** (50-100B) at the sanctuary headquarters at any time of year, although it's best to book ahead from November to January, when the falls are a particularly popular destination for Thais. This is also the only time of year when food is generally available at the headquarters, and if you visit at any other time you'll have to bring your own.

The vast majority of people visit the falls as part of an organised tour, but it's also possible to go independently. If you've got your own wheels, take the turn-off to Rte 1167 just north of Um Phang. After 12km, turn left at the police checkpoint onto Rte 1288. Continue 6km until you reach the sanctuary checkpoint, where you're expected to pay the entry fee. It's another 30km along a rough road to the sanctuary headquarters.

If you're without transport, it's easy to book a truck just about anywhere in Um Phang (round trip 1400B to 1600B). Alternatively, you can take a Poeng Kloeng–bound *sŏrng·tăa·ou* to the sanctuary checkpoint (30B, every hour from 6.30am to 3.30pm), and organise transport from there, although it's not always certain that trucks will be waiting. Another option is to get a ride south of Um Phang towards Ban Palatha and get off at Km19; there's a jungle path to the falls via **Mo**

POLAMAT, 30

How long have you been a working with elephants? Since I was 12. I started by helping out and feeding. When I was 15 or 16 I really started working with the elephants by taking tourists to the waterfalls and things like that.

Are the elephants in Ban Palatha still used for work? Nowadays elephants are only used for tourists. Sometimes we use elephants to move firewood, but not for logging or other hard work.

How many elephants do you work with? I look after one elephant, a male. My dad was the first to take care of this elephant. When he was too old, I took over.

Tell me about your elephant. He is called Plona. In Karen this means 'torn ear', which is how he was born. He is about 23 years old now. This is not old; he's a strong adult.

Is it hard looking after elephants? You have to be careful with the males, especially when they're ready to mate. They're just like people, sometimes they're grumpy.

How do you communicate with your elephant? I use Karen. Some elephants also understand Thai, it depends on how they've been trained.

How many elephants are there in Ban Palatha? There are about 30 elephants here. We have the most elephants in Um Phang District.

Do your children want to work with elephants? My son is only nine and he told me he wants to be a mahout. But when he grows up, who knows? He may change his mind.

Polamat is a mahout from Ban Palatha, Um Phang District, Tak

Phado village. It's said to take about four hours, but we wouldn't advise taking this unmarked trail without a guide who knows the area.

AROUND NAM TOK THILAWSU

From Ban Mae Klong Mai, just a few kilometres north of Um Phang via the highway to Mae Sot, Rte 1167 heads southwest along the Thai–Myanmar border. Along the way is the extensive cave system of **Tham Ta Khu Bi**, which in Karen apparently means 'Flat Mango'. There are no guides here, so be sure to bring your own torch.

After 12km, turn left onto Rte 1288, which leads to the checkpoint for Um Phang Wildlife Sanctuary. Past this point the road deteriorates in quality, yet continues more than 70km, terminating in **Poeng Kloeng** – a Karen, Burmese, Indo-Burmese, Talaku and Thai trading village where buffalo carts are more common than motorcycles. The picturesque setting among spiky peaks and cliffs is worth the trip even if you go no further. From the *sŏrng·tăa·ou* station in Um Phang there are frequent *sŏrng·tăa·ou* to Poeng Kloeng (100B, 3½ hours, every hour from 6.30am to 3.30pm).

Four hours' walk from Poeng Kloeng along a rough track (passable by 4WD in the dry season), near the Myanmar border on the banks of Mae Nam Suriya next to Sam Rom mountain, is the village of **Letongkhu**. According to what little anthropological information is available, the villagers, although for the most part Karen in language, belong to the Lagu or Talaku sect, said to represent a form of Buddhism mixed with shamanism and animism. Letongkhu is one of only six such villages in Thailand; there are reportedly around 30 more in Myanmar. Each village has a spiritual and temporal leader called a *pu chaik* (whom the Thais call *reu·sĕe* – 'rishi', or 'sage') who wears his hair long – usually tied in a topknot – and dresses in white, yellow or brown robes, depending on the subsect.

Evangelistic Christian missionaries have infiltrated the area and have tried to convert the Talaku, thus making the Talaku sensitive to outside visitation. The village is also located in a 'sensitive' border area and foreign travellers are said to have been turned away upon arrival. Local authorities suggest contacting the **Um Phang Border Police** (☎ 0 5556 1008) beforehand to request permission. If you do visit Letongkhu, take care not to enter any village structures without permission or invitation. Likewise, do not take photographs without permission. If you treat the villagers with respect then you shouldn't have a problem.

Sangkhlaburi (p223) is 90km or a four-to five-day trek from Poeng Kloeng. The route to Sangkhlaburi has several branches; the main route crosses over the border into Myanmar for some distance before crossing back into Thailand.

Because of the overall sensitive nature of this border area and the very real potential for

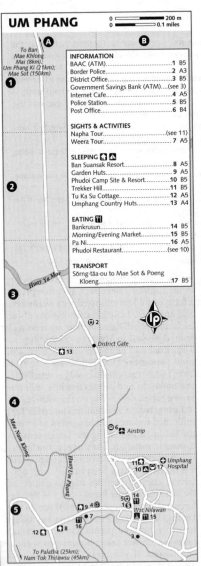

UM PHANG

0 — 200 m
0 — 0.1 miles

To Ban
Mae Khlong
Mai (8km);
Um Phang Ki (21km);
Mae Sot (150km)

Huay Ya Mae

District Gate

Airstrip

Umphang Hospital

Mae Nam Klong

Huay Um Phang

Wat Nilawan

To Palatha (25km);
Nam Tok Thilawsu (45km)

TREKKING & RAFTING

Several of the guesthouses in Um Phang can arrange combination trekking and rafting trips in the area. A typical three-day, two-night trip costs from 3000B to 4500B per person (four or more people), and includes rafting, an elephant ride, food and a guide service. The majority involve trips to Nam Tok Thilawsu and beyond, and longer or shorter trips, and trips to other local destinations, may also be arranged.

Rafting trips range from one-day excursions along the Mae Klong from Um Phang to Nam Tok Thilawsu, to three-days trips from Palatha to Nam Tok Thi Lo Re. Most rafting is only possible between November and May.

Um Phang Khi is a 'new' area for rafting, northeast of Um Phang. Officially there are 47 (some rafting companies claim 67) sets of rapids rated at class III (moderate) and class IV (difficult) during the height of the rainy season. The rafting season for Um Phang Khi is short – August to October only – as at other times of the year the water level isn't high enough. Rafting trips arranged in Um Phang typically cost 3500B for a two-night, three-day program.

The companies below have English-speaking guides.

Napha Tour (☎ 0 5556 1287; www.naphatour.com; Th Pravitpaiwan; 3-day trek per person 4500B) This outfit offers a variety of programs and English-speaking guides.

Trekker Hill (☎ 0 5556 1090; 620 Th Pravitpaiwan; 3-day trek per person 3500-4000B) This highly recommended outfit has the greatest number of English-speaking guides and offers a variety of treks running from one day to four.

Tu Ka Su Cottage (☎ 0 5556 1295; 40 Moo 6) Contact this resort for excellent tours, although at research time they only had two English-speaking guides.

Weera Tour (no roman-script sign; ☎ 0 5556 1368) Located just off the main road, this company arranges excellent tours, although the number of English-speaking guides is limited.

Sleeping

Most places in Um Phang cater to large groups of Thai visitors, so individual foreign travellers are met with a bit of confusion. Likewise, many of the rooms in town are designed for four or more people, and singles or couples can usually negotiate lower rates, especially in the wet season.

Phudoi Camp Site & Resort (☎ 0 5556 1049; www .phudoi.com; 637 Th Pravitpaiwan; tent 150B; r 400B; 🖵) Primarily catering to its prebooked tour cli-

becoming lost, ill or injured, a guide is highly recommended for any sojourn south of Um Phang. If you speak Thai, you may be able to arrange a guide for this route in Poeng Kloeng. Otherwise, a few trekking agencies in Mae Sot (p413) and Um Phang have previously arranged such trips with advance notice. The best time of year to do the trek is October to January.

NORTHERN THAILAND

ents, Phudoi has bungalows set on a well-landscaped hillside near the village centre. The log cabin-style bungalows are spacious and have verandas. There's also a camping area and a restaurant with the same name (right).

Garden Huts (Boonyaporn Garden Hut; ☎ 0 5556 1093; www.boonyapornresort.com; 8/1 Mu 6; r 200-1500B) Operated by a sweet older couple, this collection of bungalows of varying degrees of comfort and size fronts the river. It features pleasant sitting areas and a well-cared-for garden.

Trekker Hill (☎ 0 5556 1090; 620 Th Pravitpaiwan; r 300B) This rustic collection of huts on a steep hillside has hot water and views of the valley and Um Phang. The restaurant serves three meals a day and also has satellite TV.

Ban Suansak Resort (☎ 0 5556 1169, 08 9839 5308; r 500-1500B) Just outside the city on the road to Palatha, this 'resort' has 13 rooms in a new two-storey building and three bungalows that can sleep from three to 10 people. The beds look pretty thin, but the place is spotless and has its own restaurant.

Umphang Country Huts (☎ 0 5556 1079; www.umphangcountryhut.com; r 500-1500B) Off the highway 1.5km before Um Phang, these huts enjoy a wooded hilly setting. Some of the rooms in the middle price range have two levels and balconies looking over a stream. The cheapest rooms have cold-water bathrooms.

our pick **Tu Ka Su Cottage** (☎ 0 5556 1295; www.tukasu.net; 40 Moo 6; r 600-1800B; 🖳) This is the cleanest and best-run accommodation in Um Phang. The attractive collection of brick-and-stone, multiroom cottages is surrounded by flower and exotic fruit gardens. All bathrooms have hot-water showers with an outdoor feel. The cheaper bungalows are also vast and comfortable, and terrific value. The owner is a great source of local information and free wi-fi is available throughout.

Eating
Um Phang has several simple restaurants, morning and evening markets and a couple of small shops.

Bankrusun (dishes 20-35B; 🕑 6.30am-8.30pm) Owned by a Thai musician, this souvenir shop/cafe offers good coffee, drinks and basic breakfasts.

Pa Ni (no roman-script sign; ☎ 08 9676 3721; 🕑 7am-9pm) Has a brief English-language menu, which includes a couple of veggie options (the Thai menu is much more expansive). It's gener-

ally considered the best kitchen in town. The restaurant is just across the bridge on the road leading out to Ban Palatha.

Phudoi Restaurant (☎ 0 5556 1049; dishes 30-70B; 🕑 8am-10pm) When open, this restaurant has decent food. There's a bilingual menu and it's often the only place open past 9pm.

Getting There & Away
There are frequent *sŏrng·tăa·ou* to Um Phang from Mae Sot (120B, four hours, every hour from 7.30am to 3.30pm), stopping for lunch at windy **Ban Rom Klao 4** on the way.

MAE SOT TO MAE SARIANG
แม่สอด/แม่สะเรียง
Route 105 runs north along the Myanmar border from Mae Sot all the way to Mae Sariang (226km) in Mae Hong Son Province. The winding, paved road passes through the small communities of **Mae Ramat, Mae Sarit, Ban Tha Song Yang** and **Ban Sop Ngao** (Mae Ngao). The thick forest in these parts still has a few stands of teak and the Karen villages continue to use the occasional work elephant.

Nam Tok Mae Kasa, between the Km13 and Km14 markers, is an attractive waterfall fronting a cave. There's also a hot spring in the nearby village of Mae Kasa.

In Mae Ramat, don't miss **Wat Don Kaew**, behind the district office, which houses a large Mandalay-style marble Buddha.

At Km58, after a series of roadblocks, you'll pass the immense refugee village of **Mae La** where it's estimated that 60,000 Burmese refugees live. The village is at least 3km long and takes a couple of minutes to drive past, bringing home the significant refugee problem that Thailand faces.

There are extensive limestone caverns at **Tham Mae Usu**, at Km94 near Ban Tha Song Yang (there's another village of the same name further north). From the highway it's a 2km walk to Tham Mae Usu; note that it's closed in the rainy season, when the river running through the cave seals off the mouth.

At the northern end of Tak province, you'll reach **Ban Tha Song Yang**, a Karen village attractively set at the edge of limestone cliffs by the Mae Nam Moei. This is the last significant settlement in Tak before you begin climbing uphill and into the dense jungle and mountains of Mae Ngao National Park, in Mae Hong Son.

Ban Sop Ngao, little more than a roadside village that is home to the park headquarters, is the first town you'll come to in Mae Hong Son. From there it's another 40km to Mae Sariang (p451), where there's ample food and accommodation.

Sleeping & Eating

There aren't too many places to stay and eat along this route. The most convenient base is Tha Song Yang (the town near Km90 – not the village of the same name at the northern edge of Tak province), as there are a few restaurants in town. Mae Sarit, slightly further north, also has basic accommodation and food.

Thasongyang Hill Resort (☎ 0 5558 9088; www .thasongyanghill.9nha.com; Km85, Rte 105, Ban Tha Song Yang; r 200-800B) North of Tha Song Yang, accommodation here takes the form of large modern rooms in a long building, or attractive bungalows in a flower-lined garden. There are a couple of similar hotels in the area, but this place is the nicest.

Per-Pon Resort (☎ 08 1774 5624; 110 Moo 2, Mae Salit; bungalows 300B) Just south of Mae Salit, this place has a few rustic bungalows looking over the Mae Nam Moei.

Krua Ban Tai (Th Si Wattana, Ban Tha Song Yang; dishes 20-50B; ☻ 8am-9pm) This is a two-storey wooden restaurant in the centre of Ban Tha Song Yang, around the corner from the main market.

Getting There & Away

Sŏrng·tǎa·ou to Mae Sariang (200B, six hours, five departures from 6am to noon) depart from Mae Sot's old bus station, close to downtown.

MAE HONG SON PROVINCE

Accessible only by incredibly windy mountain roads or a dodgy flight to the provincial capital, this is Thailand's most remote province. Although it's undergone a tourist miniboom over the past decade, with many resorts opening in the area around the capital, few visitors seem to make it much further than Pai.

MAE HONG SON

แม่ฮ่องสอน
pop 6,023
Mae Hong Son, with its remote setting and surrounding mountains, fits many travellers'

preconceived notion of how a northern Thai city should be. A palpable Burmese influence and an edgy border town feel don't dispel this image, and best of all, there's hardly a túk-túk or tout to be seen. This doesn't mean Mae Hong Son is uncharted territory; the tour groups have been coming here for years, but the city's potential as a base for activities, from spa treatment to trekking, ensures that your visit can be quite unlike anyone else's.

Mae Hong Son is best visited between November and March when the town is at its most beautiful. During the rainy season (June to October) travel to the more remote corners of the province can be difficult because there are few paved roads. During the hot season, the Mae Pai valley fills with smoke from slash-and-burn agriculture. The only problem with going in the cool season is that the nights are downright cold – you'll need at least one thick sweater and a good pair of socks for mornings and evenings, and a sleeping bag or several blankets.

History

Mae Hong Son has been isolated from Thailand geographically, culturally and politically for most of its short existence. The city was founded as an elephant training centre in the early 19th century, and remained little more than this until 1856, when fighting in Burma caused thousands of Shan to pour into the area. In the years following, Mae Hong Son prospered as a centre for logging and remained an independent kingdom until 1900, when King Rama V incorporated the area into the Thai kingdom.

Information

Most of the banks at the southern end of Th Khunlum Praphat have ATMs. Foreign-exchange services are available at Bangkok Bank, Kasikornbank and Bank of Ayudhya.

International telephone service is available at the CAT office, which is attached to the post office – hours are the same. There's a Lenso International Phonecard telephone outside the entrance to the post office.

A few internet shops can be found around the southern end of Th Khunlum Praphat.

Mae Hong Son Internet (88 Th Khunlum Praphat; per hr 30B; ☻ 8am-10pm)

Main post office (Th Khunlum Praphat; ☻ 8.30am-4.30pm Mon-Fri, closed holidays) Towards the southern end of Th Khunlum Praphat.

Srisangwal Hospital (☎ 0 5361 1378; Th Singhanat Bamrung) A full-service facility that includes an emergency room.

TAT office (☎ 0 5361 2982; www.travelmaehongson .org; Th Khumlum Praphat; ⏲ 8.30am-4.30pm Mon-Fri) In an old two-storey wooden building opposite the post office, with helpful staff. Tourist brochures and maps can be picked up here.

Tourism Information centre (☎ 0 5361 4010; Th Khunlumpraphat; ⏲ 8.30am-midnight) Offers basic tourism information and internet access (per hr 50B).

Tourist police (☎ 0 5361 1812, emergency 1155; Th Singhanat Bamrung; ⏲ 8.30am-4.30pm)

Sights

With their bright colours, whitewashed stupas and glittering zinc fretwork, Mae Hong Son's Burmese- and Shan-style temples will have you scratching your head wondering just which country you're in anyway.

WAT PHRA THAT DOI KONG MU
วัดพระธาตุดอยกองมู

Climb the hill west of town, Doi Kong Mu (1500m), to visit this Shan-built *wát*, also known as Wat Plai Doi. The view of the sea of fog that collects in the valley each morning is impressive; at other times of the day you get a view of the town. Two Shan *chedi*, erected in 1860 and 1874, enshrine the ashes of monks from Myanmar's Shan state. Around the back of the *wát* you can see a tall, slender, standing Buddha and catch views west of the ridge.

WAT JONG KHAM & WAT JONG KLANG
วัดจองคำ/วัดจองกลาง

Wat Jong Kham was built nearly 200 years ago by Thai Yai (Shan) people, who make up about half of the population of Mae Hong Son Province. Wat Jong Klang houses 100-year-old glass *jataka* paintings and a **museum** (admission by donation; ⏲ 8am-6pm) with 150-year-old wooden dolls from Mandalay that depict some of the more gruesome aspects of the wheel of life. Wat Jong Klang has several areas that women are forbidden to enter – not unusual for Burmese-Shan Buddhist temples.

The temples are lit at night and reflected in Jong Kham Lake – a popular photo op for visitors.

WAT HUA WIANG
วัดหัวเวียง

This **wát** (Th Phanit Wattana), east of Th Khunlum Praphat, is recognised for its *bòht* boasting an

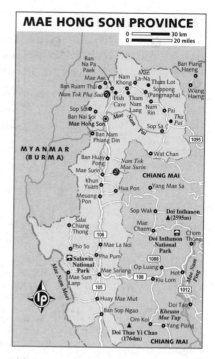

elaborate tiered wooden roof and a revered bronze Buddha statue from Mandalay.

OTHER TEMPLES

Other notable temples include **Wat Kam Kor**, known for its unique covered walkway, and **Wat Phra Non**, home to the largest reclining Buddha in town.

Activities
TREKKING & RAFTING

Mae Hong Son's location at the edge of mountainous jungle makes it an excellent base for treks into the countryside. Trekking here is not quite the large-scale industry it is elsewhere, and visitors willing to get their boots muddy can expect to find relatively untouched nature and isolated villages. Trekking trips can be arranged at several guesthouses and travel agencies.

Long-tail boat trips on the nearby Mae Pai are gaining popularity, and the same guesthouses and trekking agencies that organise treks from Mae Hong Son can arrange river excursions. The most common trip sets off from **Tha Pong Daeng**, 4km southwest of Mae

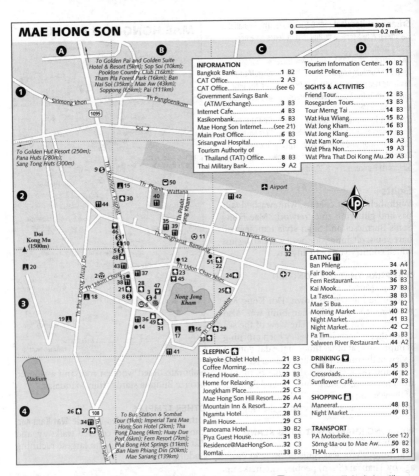

MAE HONG SON

0 ————— 300 m
0 ————— 0.2 miles

INFORMATION

Bangkok Bank	**1** B2
CAT Office	**2** A3
CAT Office	(see 6)
Government Savings Bank (ATM/Exchange)	**3** B3
Internet Cafe	**4** B3
Kasikornbank	**5** B3
Mae Hong Son Internet	(see 21)
Main Post Office	**6** B3
Srisangwal Hospital	**7** C3
Tourism Authority of Thailand (TAT) Office	**8** B3
Thai Military Bank	**9** A2
Tourism Information Center	**10** B2
Tourist Police	**11** B2

SIGHTS & ACTIVITIES

Friend Tour	**12** B3
Rosegarden Tours	**13** B3
Tour Merng Tai	**14** B3
Wat Hua Wiang	**15** B2
Wat Jong Kham	**16** B3
Wat Jong Klang	**17** B3
Wat Kam Kor	**18** A3
Wat Phra Non	**19** A3
Wat Phra That Doi Kong Mu	**20** A3

EATING

Ban Phleng	**34** A4
Fair Book	**35** B2
Fern Restaurant	**36** B3
Kai Mook	**37** B3
La Tasca	**38** B3
Mae Si Bua	**39** B2
Morning Market	**40** B2
Night Market	**41** B3
Night Market	**42** C2
Pa Tim	**43** B3
Salween River Restaurant	**44** A2

SLEEPING

Baiyoke Chalet Hotel	**21** B3
Coffee Morning	**22** C3
Friend House	**23** B3
Home for Relaxing	**24** C3
Jongkham Place	**25** C3
Mae Hong Son Hill Resort	**26** A4
Mountain Inn & Resort	**27** A4
Ngamta Hotel	**28** B3
Palm House	**29** C3
Panorama Hotel	**30** B2
Piya Guest House	**31** B3
Residence@MaeHongSon	**32** C3
Romtai	**33** B3

DRINKING

Chilli Bar	**45** B3
Crossroads	**46** B2
Sunflower Café	**47** B3

SHOPPING

Maneerat	**48** B3
Night Market	**49** B3

TRANSPORT

PA Motorbike	(see 12)
Sŏrng·tǎa·ou to Mae Aw	**50** B2
THAI	**51** B3

Hong Son, or **Huay Due Port** at Ban Huay Deua, 2km further. Boats travel 15km downstream to the 'long-neck' village of **Huay Pu Keng** followed by a stop at the border town of **Ban Nam Phiang Din**, 20km from the pier, before returning. It takes approximately 1½ hours to reach Ban Nam Phiang Din and costs 900B from Huay Due, 800B from Tha Pong Daeng.

Another popular route conducts bamboo rafts between **Thung Kong Moo** (10km northwest of town) and the village of **Soppong** to the west (not to be confused with the larger Shan trading village of the same name to the east).

The prices quoted here are for two people; as with elsewhere in Thailand, the per day rates drop significantly with a larger group and a longer trek.

Friend Tour (☎ 0 5361 1647; 21 Th Pradit Jong Kham; trek per person per day 700-900B) With nearly 20 years experience, this recommended outfit offers trekking, elephant riding and rafting, as well as day tours.

Nature Walks (☎ 0 5361 1040, 08 9552 6899; www .trekkingthailand.com; natural_walks@yahoo.com) Although the treks here cost more than elsewhere, John, a native of Mae Hong Son, is the best guide in town. Treks here range from day long nature walks (1000B) to multiday journeys across the province (per person per day 2500B). John can also arrange custom nature-based tours, such as the orchid-viewing tours he conducts from March to May. John has no office; email and phone are the only ways to get in touch with him.

Rosegarden Tours (☎ 0 5361 1577; www.rosegarden -tours.com; 86/4 Th Khunlum Praphat; tour per person per day 1500B) English- and French-speaking guides focus on cultural tours.

Tour Merng Tai (☎ 0 5361 1979; www.maehongson4u .com; 89 Th Khunlum Praphat; tours per person per day 1450B) This outfit mostly does city-based van tours, but can also arrange treks.

MUD SPA

Pooklon Country Club (☎ 0 5328 2579; www.pook lon.com; Ban Mae Sanga; ☺ 8am-6.30pm) is touted as Thailand's only mud treatment spa. Discovered by a team of geologists in 1995, the mud here is pasteurised and blended with herbs before being employed in various treatments (facial 100B). There's thermal mineral water for soaking (60B), massage (per hour 200B), or cheapskates can soak their feet for free out front. The attached 'country club' includes a driving range and accommodation.

Pooklon is 16km north of Mae Hong Son in Mok Champae district. If you haven't got your own wheels, you can take the daily Mae Aw-bound *sŏrng·tăa·ou* (see p439), but this means you might have to find your own way back.

Festivals & Events

Poi Sang Long Festival (March) Wat Jong Klang and Wat Jong Kham are the focal point of this festival, where young Shan boys are ordained as novice monks in the ceremony known as *bòuat lôok gâaou*. As part of the Shan custom, the boys are dressed in ornate costumes (rather than simple white robes) and wear flower headdresses and facial make-up.

Jong Para Festival (October) Another important local event, it is held towards the end of the Buddhist Rains Retreat – three days before the full moon of the 11th lunar month, so it varies from year to year. The festival begins with local Shan bringing offerings to monks in the temples in a procession marked by the carrying of models of castles on poles. An important part of the festival is the folk theatre and dance, which is performed on the *wát* grounds, some of it unique to northwest Thailand.

Loi Krathong (November) During this national holiday – usually celebrated by floating *grà·tong* (small lotus floats) on the nearest pond, lake or river – Mae Hong Son residents launch balloons called *grà·tong sà·wăn* (heaven *grà·tong*) from Doi Kong Mu.

Sleeping

Mae Hong Son generally lacks in inspiring accommodation, although there are a couple of standout midrange options. Because it's a tourist town, accommodation prices fluctuate with the seasons, and outside of the high season (November to January) it's worth pursuing a discount.

BUDGET

Friend House (☎ 0 5362 0119; 20 Th Pradit Jong Kham; r 150-400B) Superclean rooms run from the ultra basic that share hot-water bathrooms to larger en-suite rooms. Set in a teak and concrete house, the upstairs rooms have a view of the lake. Breakfast is available and there is a laundry service.

Home For Relaxing (☎ 0 5362 0313; 26/1 Th Chamnan Sathit; r 200B) Run by a friendly young couple from Chiang Mai, the three rooms here are in a cosy wooden house near Nong Jong Kham.

Palm House (☎ 0 5361 4022; 22/1 Th Chamnansathit; r 300-600B; ☒) Resembling an apartment complex in the suburban US, this two-storey cement building offers several characterless but clean rooms with TV, hot water and fan/aircon. The helpful owner speaks English and can arrange transport when he's not napping.

Coffee Morning (☎ 0 5361 234; 78 Th Singhanat Bamrung; r 400-600B) This old wooden house unites an attractive cafe-and-bookshop and four basic but cosy rooms. Considering that bathrooms are shared, the high-season rates aren't exactly a deal, but free internet and the fun cafe atmosphere make up for this somewhat.

Panorama Hotel (☎ 0 5361 1757; www.panorama.8m .com; 51 Th Khunlum Praphat; r 400-1200B; ☒ ⌨) Popular with tour groups, this large, long-standing hotel features a cluttered lobby and several plain, well-worn rooms. The location is quite convenient though.

Romtai (☎ 0 5361 2437; Th Chumnanatit; r 500-900B, bungalows 1200B; ☒) Behind the lakeside temples, this place has a huge variety of accommodation, ranging from spacious, clean rooms to bungalows looking over a lush garden with fishponds.

Mae Hong Son Hill Resort (☎ 0 5361 2475; 106/2 Th Khunlum Praphat; bungalows with fan/air-con 500/600B; ☒) Although it doesn't look like much at first, this quiet spot offers 24 well-kept bungalows, each with woven bamboo walls, a bit of furniture, hot showers and a private veranda. It's a friendly, family-run place.

MIDRANGE

Piya Guest House (☎ 0 5361 1260; piyaguesthouse@ hotmail.com; 1/1 Th Khunlum Praphat; bungalows 600B; ☒) Although the bungalows and the garden they're set in appear a bit tired, the rooms have wooden floors, air-con and hot showers, and are well furnished and of a decent size. There is a pleasant lake view from the restaurant.

DETOUR: THE MAE HONG SON LOOP

One of the most popular motorcycle riding tours in northern Thailand is the circuitous route that begins in Chiang Mai and passes through the length of Mae Hong Son province before looping back to the city – a round trip of nearly 1000km.

The Mae Hong Son loop really begins 34km north of Chiang Mai when you turn onto Rte 1095 and lean into the first of its 1864 bends. It's slow going, and you start climbing almost immediately; however, the good thing about this route is that potential overnight stops are frequent – many of the towns with good accommodation and food are less than 70km apart – giving riders ample chance to reclaim the blood flow to their bottoms. Convenient overnight stops include Pai, 130km from Chiang Mai, Soppong, another 40km up the road, and Mae Hong Son, 65km from Soppong.

Upon reaching Khun Yuam, 70km south of Mae Hong Son, you can opt to take Rte 1263 to Mae Chaem, before continuing back to Chiang Mai via Doi Inthanon, the country's highest peak, or you can continue south to Mae Sariang and follow Rte 108 all the way back to Chiang Mai via Hot, although the distances between towns here are greater and best done on a more powerful and more comfortable motorcycle.

An excellent driving companion is Golden Triangle Rider's *Mae Hong Son Loop Guide Map*, available at most bookshops in Chiang Mai. The map shows accurate distances between locations along the loop, as well as potential side trips and other helpful information.

Pana Huts (☎ 0 5361 4331; www.panahuts.com; 293/9 Moo 11 Th Makhasanti; r & bungalows 700-750B) Set in a wooded area outside of town, the five slightly overpriced bamboo huts all have hot-water bathrooms and terraces. The communal area feels appropriately rustic, with its thatched teak leaf roof, wooden benches and enclosed campfire for chilly nights.

Golden Hut Resort (☎ 0 5361 4294; www.golden hut.com; 253 Moo 11 Th Makhasanti; r & bungalows 700-1800B; ❖) Outside of town near Sang Tong Huts, this Thai-style 'resort' compound combines faux-Roman pillars and concrete pandas with a variety of bungalows and rooms. Unabashedly corny, but comfortable and quiet.

our pick **Sang Tong Huts** (☎ 0 5362 0680; www .sangtonghuts.com; Th Makhasanti; r 700B, bungalows 800-3000B; ❖) This popular set of bungalows in a wooded area outside of town is one of the more character-filled places to stay. There's a huge variety of bungalows, all of them spacious and well designed. And the tasty baked goods and a pool make up for the distance from the centre of town. It's popular among repeat visitors to Mae Hong Son, so it pays to book ahead.

Jongkham Place (☎ 0 5361 4294; 4/2 Th Udom Chao Nites; bungalows 800B, ste 2000B; ❖) This new family-run place by the lake has four attractive wooden bungalows and one penthouse-like suite. All accommodation includes TV, fridge and air-con.

our pick **Residence@MaeHongSon** (☎ 0 5361 4100; www.theresidence-mhs.com; 41/4 Th Nives Pisarn; r 900-1400B; ❖ 🖵) One of the more recent places to go up, this cheery yellow building houses eight stylish and inviting rooms. Teak furnishings abound, and lots of windows ensure ample natural light. There's also a sunny communal rooftop area, a friendly English-speaking owner, and bicycles provided free of charge.

Baiyoke Chalet Hotel (☎ 0 5361 3132; trv1864@ hotmail.com; 90 Th Khunlum Praphat; r incl breakfast 1280-1600B; ❖ 🖵) The rooms at this long-standing midranger aren't quite as nice as the attractive wooden lobby, but it's still a decent, convenient choice. Some of the more expensive rooms are quite large and have been remodelled and represent a good deal. The restaurant/lounge downstairs can get quite loud, so request a room away from the street or on an upper level. Low-season rates are 50% less.

TOP END

Southwest of town, a few kilometres towards Ban Huay Deua and Ban Tha Pong Daeng on the river, are several 'resorts', which in the Thai sense of the term means any hotel near a rural or semirural area. Discounts of up to 40% are common in the low season and online discounts can be found any time of year.

Ngamta Hotel (☎ 0 5361 2794; Th Khunlum Praphat; r 1500-1800B; ❖) The rooms at the new three-storey hotel are charged at the top-end bracket but are more midrange in amenities and style

Nonetheless, they're centrally located and offer fleeting views of the lake and temples. Discounts available in the off-season.

Golden Pai and Golden Suite Hotel & Resort (☎ 0 5306 1114; www.goldenpaihotel.com; 285 Moo 1 Ban Pang Moo; r & bungalows 1500-2500B; ❄ ▯ ▣) At the edge of the quiet Shan village of Ban Pang Moo, 5km out of town off the road to Pai, this compound features a mish-mash of tidy bungalows and duplexes. Rooms are spotless, large, and tastefully decorated with textiles and have outside seating areas. The restaurant makes the most of the Pai River location.

Mountain Inn & Resort (☎ 0 5361 1802; www .mhsmountaininn.com; 112/2 Th Khunlum Praphat; r incl breakfast 2400-2800B; ste incl breakfast 4500B; ❄ ▯) This hotel has clean, cosy rooms with Thai decorative touches. There is a pretty courtyard garden with small ponds, benches and parasols. Standard rooms are a better deal than deluxe as you get a terrace overlooking the garden. All have cable TV.

ourpick Fern Resort (☎ 0 5368 6110; www.fernresort .info; 64 Moo 10 Tambon Pha Bong; bungalows 2500-3500B; ❄ ▯ ▣) This long-standing eco-friendly resort is one of the more pleasant places to stay in northern Thailand. The 40 Shan-style wooden bungalows are set among tiered rice paddies and streams and feature stylishly decorated interiors. Nearby nature trails lead to the adjacent Mae Surin National Park, and to encourage community-based tourism, most of the employees come from local villages. The resort is 7km south of town, and free pick-up is available from the airport and bus terminal, and regular shuttles run to/from town stopping at the Fern Restaurant (p428).

Imperial Tara Mae Hong Son Hotel (☎ 0 5368 4444-9; www.imperialhotels.com/taramaehongson; 149 Mu 8; r incl breakfast 4472B, ste incl breakfast 5885-7768B; ❄ ▯ ▣) Rooms in this upmarket, 104-room hotel all have wooden floors and are tastefully decorated. French windows that open onto a terrace make a change from the standard business hotel layout. Facilities include a sauna, swimming pool and fitness centre.

Eating

Mae Hong Son's morning market is a fascinating place to have breakfast. Several vendors at the north end of the market sell unusual dishes such as *tòo·a òon*, a Burmese noodle dish supplemented with thick gram porridge and deep-fried bits of vegetables, gram flour cakes and tofu. Other vendors along the same strip sell a local version of *kà·nǒm jeen nám ngée·o*, often topped with *kahng pòrng*, a Shan snack of battered and deep-fried vegetables.

The city also has two good night markets; the one near the airport offers mostly take-away northern Thai-style food while the market near Nong Jong Kham has more generic Thai food and some tables and chairs.

Fair Book (no roman-script sign; Th Nives Pisarn; dishes 20-30B; ☺ 6am-4pm) Although atmosphere is nonexistent, this place has real coffee and the best selection of English-language newspapers, making it our favourite place to catch up with the outside world. They also do good Thai-style breakfasts.

Mae Si Bua (☎ 0 5361 2471; 51 Th Singhanat Bamrung; dishes 20-30B; ☺ 8.30am-6.30pm) Like the Shan grandma you never had, Auntie Bua prepares more than a dozen different Shan curries, soups and dips on a daily basis. Try her delicious *gaang hang·lair*, an incredibly rich curry of pork belly with a flavour not unlike American-style barbecue sauce.

Pa Tim (Th Khunlum Praphat; dishes 25-80B; ☺ 9am-10pm) Everyone loves this place for its extensive variety of well-priced Thai and Chinese options.

ourpick Ban Phleng (Local northern Thai food; ☎ 0 5361 2522; 108 Th Khunlum Praphat; dishes 30-60B; ☺ 7am-11pm) Just south of town and taking up both sides of the road, this popular restaurant is a virtual crash course in authentic northern Thai and local Shan food. Come at lunch, when as many as a dozen different dishes are on display; simply point to what looks interesting or refer to the English-language menu. There's a branch in Pai (p446) as well.

Salween River Restaurant (☎ 0 5361 2050; Th Singhanat Bamrung; dishes 50-160B; ☺ 7am-midnight) The menu here spans just about everything, ranging from excellent organic hill-tribe coffee to baked goods, local-style Shan specialities and imaginative Western dishes. The menu is also very strong on vegetarian options. The owners are very friendly and a good source of information.

Fern Restaurant (Th Khunlum Praphat; dishes 60-120B; ☺ 10.30am-midnight) The Fern is probably Mae Hong Son's most upscale restaurant, but remember, this is Mae Hong Son. Nonetheless, service is professional and the food is good. The expansive menu covers Thai, local and even Spanish dishes. There is live lounge music some nights.

Kai Mook (☎ 0 5361 2285; 23 Th Udom Chao Nites; dishes 60-170B; ☯ 10am-2pm & 5pm-midnight) This open-air restaurant just off the main street combines a lengthy menu with a fun atmosphere. Try dishes such as *dôm yam* made with fish from the Mae Nam Pai, or wild boar fried with curry paste.

La Tasca (☎ 0 5361 1344; Th Khunlum Praphat; dishes 69-189B; ☯ 10am-10pm) This cosy place has been serving homemade pasta, pizza and calzone for as long as we can remember and is one of the few places in town to serve relatively authentic Western food.

Drinking

Crossroads (☎ 0 5362 0221; 61 Th Khunlum Praphat; 8am-midnight) Where else in Mae Hong Son can you have your beer served by a Thai bartender who speaks fluent Spanish, while chatting with a Shan trekking guide who used to live in Belgium? This friendly bar/restaurant is a crossroads in every sense, from its location at one of Mae Hong Son's main intersections to its clientele that ranges from wet-behind-the-ears backpackers to hardened locals. Oh, and there's steak.

Sunflower Café (☎ 0 5362 0549; Th Pradit Jong Kham; ☯ 7am-midnight) This open-air place combines draught beer, live lounge music and views of the lake. Sunflower also does meals (35B to 180B) and runs tours.

Chilli Bar (Th Pradit Jong Kham; ☯ 7am-1am) Loud blues and a pool table dominate the scene at this friendly pub. The available food (30B to 80B), from bar snacks to sandwiches, is chalked up on boards.

Shopping

From October to February the walkway around the Jong Kham Lake becomes a lively **night market** (☯ 5-10pm).

A few well-stocked souvenir shops can be found near the southern end of Th Khunlum Praphat, including **Maneerat** (☎ 0 5361 2213; 80 Th Khunlum Praphat; ☯ 8am-9pm), which features an extensive array of Shan and Burmese clothing, as well as Burmese lacquerware boxes.

Getting There & Away
AIR
For many people the time saved flying from Chiang Mai to Mae Hong Son versus bus travel is worth the extra baht.

Nok Air (☎ nationwide call centre 1318; www.nokair .co.th; Mae Hong Son airport) and its subsidiary, **SGA**

Airlines (☎ 0 5379 8244; www.sga.co.th; Mae Hong Son airport), conduct a code-share flight to/from Chiang Mai (1800B, 35 minutes, once daily).

THAI (☎ 0 5361 2220; www.thaiair.com; 71 Th Singhanat Bamrung; ☯ 8.30am-5.30pm Mon-Fri) also fly to/from Chiang Mai (1365B, 35 minutes, twice daily), from where they have connections to Bangkok (3600B).

BUS
Mae Hong Son's bus station has been moved 1km outside the city and **Prempracha Tour** (☎ 0 5368 4100) conduct bus services within the province, including south to Khun Yuam (ordinary/air-con 70/110B, two hours, 6am, 8am, 10.30am, 8pm and 9pm) with a stop in Mae Sariang (ordinary/air-con 100/180B, four hours) before culminating in Chiang Mai (ordinary/air-con 187/337B, eight hours).

Going north, buses stop in Soppong (ordinary/air-con 60/80B, two hours, 8am, 10.30am and 12.30pm) and Pai (ordinary/air-con 80/100B, three hours) before culminating in Chiang Mai (ordinary/air-con 143/210B, eight hours). Relatively frequent minivans also ply this route, stopping in Soppong (150B, 1½ hours, frequent departures from 7am to 2pm) and Pai (150B, two hours) before reaching Chiang Mai (250B, six hours).

Sombat Tour (☎ 0 5361 3211), located at the new bus station, run buses to Bangkok (1st-class 718B, 15 hours, 2pm and 3pm).

Getting Around
The centre of Mae Hong Son can easily be covered on foot, and it is one of the few towns in Thailand that doesn't seem to have a motorcycle taxi at every corner. However some can be found at the bus station and near the entrance to the morning market and charge 20B to 30B for trips within town; to Doi Kong Mu it costs 100B return. There are also a few túk-túk in town most are at the bus stop and charge 40B per trip and 80B to/from the airport or new bus station.

Because most of Mae Hong Son's attractions are outside of town, renting a vehicle is a good option here.

PA Motorbike (☎ 0 5361 1647; 21 Th Pradit Jong Kham), opposite Friend House, rents motor bikes (150B to 200B per day), cars and jeeps (1000B to 2500B per day).

(Continued on page 432)

THE CHARISMATIC KINGDOM

Thailand's iconic Buddhas and beaches lure the culture vultures and the sun soakers. But Thailand abhors monotony and breaks up the sea and temple fatigue with a diversity of attractions along with a dynamic culture on display in ordinary marketplaces, during national festivals or at plastic tables over steaming bowls of noodles.

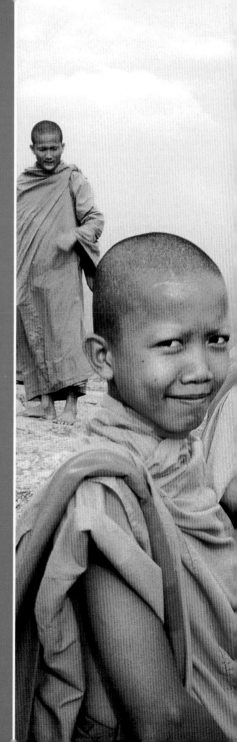

Beaches & Islands

Known the world over for sun and fun, Thailand's beaches come in two varieties: the high-end beach resort and the rustic 'village' island, a distinction that has blurred towards the upmarket. Regardless, each burns bright in traveller lore, enticing visitors to come on beach-hopping binges.

① Ko Phi-Phi

Phi-Phi (p692) is heartbreakingly beautiful, with flowing ribbons of cerulean sea massaging the craggy forested cliffs of the twin islands. It's a famous resort playground for the well-to-do but backpackers can sneak into a few budget crevices.

② Phuket

A city by the sea, Phuket (p649) pioneered Thailand's position in sun-worshipping circles. The island has all the mod-cons (an airport and bridge connections) for time-crunched travellers seeking 21st-century rest and recreation.

③ Ko Samui

Eager to please, Samui (p575) is a civilised beach-resort island for the vacationing masses, who can fly in and out with hardly a care for cultural adaptation. But beyond the Chaweng crowds are sleepy spits reminiscent of Samui's old moniker, 'Coconut Island'.

④ Ko Pha-Ngan

Be a hammock hanger at this bohemian beach retreat (p595) that's still far away enough from modern towers to be idyllic. In one corner are the sloppy Full Moon parties, while the rest of the island remains peaceful and drowsy from sun-soaked days.

⑤ Ko Adang

Deep in the southern reaches of the Andaman, this small island (p726) is known by most as merely a snorkelling spot, but wilderness seekers can pitch a tent or rent a longhouse to commune with nature.

⑥ Ko Tao

The dive-master's island, Ko Tao (p610) is the cheapest spot around to strap on a tank and explore the deep. Little 'Turtle Island' doesn't have star-power sand but it does have scenic rocky coves filled with brightly coloured fish.

⑦ Krabi

Sand and sea are not Krabi's (p681) claim to fame. The limestone mountains that protrude out of the ocean are all the bait this coastal peninsula needs for novice and veteran rock climbers looking for a vertical scramble with stunning views.

⑧ Ko Lanta

The west coast of Lanta (p698) is a long expanse of sand once famous for its sleepy, hippie demeanour, now a rarity amongst the Andaman beaches. Times and tides have washed ashore a party scene but quiet spots can still be found.

⑨ Khao Lak

One of the few mainland beaches, Khao Lak (p640) survived a beating from the 2004 tsunami and has since recovered its favoured reputation amongst accomplished divers. Popular live-aboards set off for the famous Surin and Similan dive sites.

⑩ Surin & Similan Islands National Marine Parks

Explore above and below the water at these two Andaman reserves (p644 & p645), famous for clear seas, whale sharks and coral gardens. Live-aboard trips set out from the mainland, giving their crews plenty of time to explore the far-flung islands.

Heavenly Aspirations

Religion permeates Thailand like a constantly burning joss stick. Historic empires built great monuments and replicas of heaven amongst the celestially governed rice fields. The glittering Buddhist temples are the modern-day repositories of divine rulers, while more humble household shrines honour the mid-level managers of the spirit world.

❶ Bangkok
Bangkok (p103) is the seat of the government, the monarch and of the Buddhist religion, claiming the country's most exalted Buddha image at Wat Phra Kaew and several royally associated temples of architectural beauty and significance.

❷ Ayuthaya
The fabled fallen kingdom, Ayuthaya (p195) was a golden capital ruling Thailand's central plains and beyond. Today only the brick and stucco ruins remain, punctuated by headless Buddhas still meditating through the trials of history and the weight of gravity.

❸ Sukhothai
One of the original Thai kingdoms, Sukhothai's ancient ruins (p397) survived with fewer battle scars than Ayuthaya and inhabit a quiet, car-free historic park, creating an idyllic setting for contemplating the past.

❹ Chiang Mai
Chiang Mai (p275) is deeply rooted in spiritual traditions. It was founded beside a mythical mountain now bearing a holy relic and the old city is decorated with antique temples more akin to those found in Myanmar than the central plains of Thailand.

❺ Lopburi
The imposing monuments of the Khmer empire reside amidst the provincial business of Lopburi (p205), one of Thailand's oldest cities. The most intact ruin is best known for its resident troop of macaques, who eclipse the temple's architectural merits.

❻ Phimai
Nearly 100 years older than Angkor Wat in Cambodia, Prasat Phimai (p465) is a stunning example of the Angkor kingdom's obsession with monument building and is one of Thailand's finest surviving temples from this era.

❼ Phanom Rung
Facing east towards the Angkor capital, this hilltop sanctuary (p470) commands an authoritative view of what was once the kingdom's western frontier. The temple's Hindu reliefs and elaborate *naga*-punctuated avenue are hallmarks of Angkor's artistic apex.

❽ Nong Khai
Breaking the 'spiritual spaces' mould, Nong Khai's Sala Kaew Ku Sculpture Park (p509) is a three-dimensional journey through Hindu-Buddhist mythology built by a Laotian immigrant whose life story has taken on mythic elements.

Outdoor Adventures

From the mountains in the north to the rainforests of the south, a variety of adventures allow visitors to trek, crawl and be carried through Thailand's jungles. Monkeys and birds inhabit the canopy, while elephants and mahouts part the brush with their tourist cargo.

1 Kanchanaburi

Western Thailand is a scenic landscape of dragon-scaled limestone mountains bejewelled with silvery waterfalls and rushing rivers. Kayak the famous River Kwai (p216), explore the forest aboard an elephant, or soak away your aches in nearby hot springs.

2 Chiang Mai

No other urban centre in Thailand is so close to so many outdoor adventures as Chiang Mai (p275). Mountain-bike down Doi Suthep, hike to hill-tribe villages, visit an elephant sanctuary, or rappel down a thundering waterfall.

3 Chiang Rai

Loads of trekking companies will haul you off to hill-tribe villages but few provide as much economic benefit to these communities as the eco-minded companies in Chiang Rai (p350).

4 Mae Hong Son Province

So far northwest, this province (p422) is nearly in Myanmar, and the remoteness is more obvious after the gruelling bus ride through altitude-climbing switchbacks. Treks plunge into the wilderness to visit subsisting hill-tribe villages and white-water trips brave the rapids.

5 Khao Yai National Park

A vast monsoon forest blankets Khao Yai (literally 'big mountain'; p467) and beyond, catapulting this park into World Heritage status. Nature in all its glory is the primary draw but the show stealers are the day-tripping Thais.

6 Khao Sok National Park

A deep and dark jungle hugs the midsection of southern Thailand. This ancient rainforest (p639) is filled with long sweaty hikes, postcard views and riverside camping.

7 Elephant Centres & Mahout Training

Thailand's beloved pachyderm is no longer an unemployed beast of burden. Centres in Lampang, Pattaya and Chiang Mai teach tourists how to be mahouts, and the Elephant Nature Park (p298), outside Chiang Mai, allows domesticated elephants to return to the herd.

Thai Cuisine

Complex and confident, Thai food is one of the globe's most accomplished cuisines. And it is even better in its native setting, where fresh and abundant ingredients are celebrated with near-constant adoration. Thais surround themselves with food, from simple snacks to multi-course meals.

① Curries

The soup that eats like a meal, Thai curry (p85) is pungent, fiery and colourful. Each region does its own variation and many visitors could earn a degree in curry appreciation from their intensive fieldwork.

② Isan Specialties

The northeastern region is famous for the tri-umvirate dishes (p458) of sôm·đam (papaya salad), gài yâhng (grilled chicken) and kôw něe·o (sticky rice) – the fuel for the country's construction crews.

③ Thai Fruits

Meet bananas that don't taste like chalk, pineapples that balance sweet and sour, and edible oddities that look like medieval armour or Velcro tennis balls. Thailand's fruits (p87) are luscious, bountiful and often monopolise whole meals.

(Continued from page 428)

AROUND MAE HONG SON
Pha Bong Hot Springs

บ่อน้ำร้อนผาบ่อง

Eleven kilometres south of the capital in the Shan village of Pha Bong is this public park with **hot springs** (private bath/bathing room 50/400B; 8am-sunset). You can take a private bath or rent a room, and there's also massage (per hour 150B). The springs can be reached on any southbound bus.

THAM PLA FOREST PARK

อุทยานแห่งชาติถ้ำปลา

This **park** (admission free; 6am-6pm), 16km north of Mae Hong Son, is centred around Tham Pla, or **Fish Cave**, a water-filled cavern where hundreds of soro brook carp thrive. The fish grow up to 1m long and are found only in the provinces of Mae Hong Son, Ranong, Chiang Mai, Rayong, Chanthaburi and Kanchanaburi. The fish eat vegetables and insects, although the locals believe them to be vegetarian and feed them only fruit and vegetables, which can be purchased at the park entrance.

A 450m path leads from the park entrance to a suspension bridge that crosses a stream and continues to the cave. A **statue** of a Hindu *rishi* called Nara, said to protect the holy fish from danger, stands nearby. It's a bit anticlimactic, but the park grounds are a bucolic, shady place to hang out; food and picnic tables are available.

Buses to Pai pass by, but renting a motorcycle is the best way to get here.

Long-Necked Kayan Villages

หมู่บ้านกะเหรี่ยงคอยาว

These villages are Mae Hong Son's most touted — and most controversial — tourist attraction. The 'long-necked' moniker stems from the habit of some Kayan (sometimes also referred to as Padaung, a Shan term) women of wearing heavy brass coils around their necks. The coils depress the collarbone and rib cage, which makes their necks look unnaturally stretched. A common myth claims if the coils are removed, the women's necks will fall over and the women will suffocate. In fact the women attach and remove the coils at will and there is no evidence that this deformation impairs their health at all.

Nobody knows for sure how the coil custom got started. One theory is that it was meant

to make the women unattractive to men from other tribes. Another story says it was so tigers wouldn't carry the women off by their throats; most likely it is probably nothing more than a simple fashion accessory. Until relatively recently the custom was largely dying out, but money from tourism, and quite possibly the influence of local authorities eager to cash in on the Kayan, have reinvigorated it.

Regardless of the origin, the villages are now on every group tour's itinerary, and have become a significant tourist draw for Mae Hong Son. The villages are often derided as human zoos, and there are certainly elements of this, but we find them more like bizarre rural markets, with the women earning much of their money by selling tacky souvenirs and drinks. The Kayan we've talked to claim to be happy with their current situation, but the stateless position they share with all Burmese refugees is nothing to be envied, and these formerly independent farmers are now reliant on aid and tourists to survive.

If you want to see any of the three Kayan settlements in Mae Hong Son, any travel agency in Mae Hong Son can arrange a tour. The most-touted Kayan village is **Kayan Tayar**, near the Shan village of Ban Nai Soi, 35km northwest of Mae Hong Son. It collects an entry fee from non-Thais of 250B per person. Another 'long-necked' community is based at **Huay Pu Keng** and is included on long-tail boat tours departing from Huay Due Pier and Tha Pong Daeng; see p423 for details on costs and how to get there. It's possible to visit Huay Pu Keng independently and even stay overnight in the village. See www.huaypukeng.com for details.

Mae Aw & Around

แม่ออ

A worthwhile day trip from the provincial capital is to Mae Aw, an atmospheric Chinese outpost right at the Myanmar border, 43km north of Mae Hong Son.

The road to Mae Aw is a beautiful route that passes through tidy riverside Shan communities such as **Mok Champae** before suddenly climbing and winding through impressive mountain scenery. Stops can be made at **Pha Sua Waterfall**, about 5km up the mountain, or **Pang Tong Summer Palace**, a rarely used royal compound a few kilometres past the waterfall.

For an interesting detour, at Ban Na Pa Paek take a left and continue 6km to the Shan village of **Ban Ruam Thai**. There are several basic

NORTHERN THAILAND

PUE-LEH, 78

How did you come to Thailand? We walked here. It took 10 days, I think. It was so long ago I can't remember.

How long have you been in Thailand? I've lived here for 20 years.

Have you ever been anywhere else in Thailand? No, I've never been anywhere else. I can't speak Thai so I can't go anywhere!

Is living in Thailand better than living in Burma? It's better being here than in Burma. The Burmese soldiers took things from us, money and rice.

Would you go back to Burma if you had the chance? Burma has changed. I don't think I could go back.

What do you think of tourists? I like them. They take pictures and buy things, that helps us.

Don't you get tired of being photographed? No, not tired, just embarrassed because I'm so old, not beautiful any longer, and I can't speak with the tourists in English!

Do you speak any English? A little bit. Sometimes.

Pue-Leh is a 'long-necked' Kayan in Ban Kayan Tayar, Mae Hong Son

---

places to stay and eat here, and the road ends 500m further at **Pang Ung**, a peaceful mountain reservoir surrounded by pines that is immensely popular among Thai day-trippers in search of a domestic Switzerland.

Drive back to Ban Na Pa Paek the way you came. From there it is 6km further north past hills holding tea and coffee plantations to Mae Aw. The modern Thai name for the town is Ban Rak Thai (Thai-Loving Village) and the town was established by Yunnanese KMT fighters who fled from communist rule in 1949. The town sits on the edge of a large reservoir and the faces and signs are very Chinese. The main industry here has become tea, and there are numerous places to taste the local brew, as well as several restaurants serving Yunnanese cuisine.

There's a brief dirt road to the border crossing, but it's not advisable to do any unaccompanied trekking here, as the area is an infamous drug route.

SLEEPING & EATING

Ban Din Guest House (☎ 08 4854 9397; Mae Aw/Ban Rak Thai; r 300-750B) This place and other similar outfits ringing Mae Aw's reservoir offer basic accommodation in adobe-style bungalows.

Guest House and Home Stay (☎ 0 5307 0589, 08 3571 6668; Ban Ruam Thai; r 400-1500B) The first guesthouse in Ban Ruam Thai (there are now numerous 'homestays' offering accommodation from 200B to 400B), this place consists of several simple bamboo huts positioned on a slope surrounded by coffee plants, tea plants and fruit trees. Even if not staying, stop here for a brew; the owner is passionate about coffee,

and there is a roasting room where visitors can roast and grind their own beans.

Riverside Guest House (☎ 0 5306 1574, 08 6117 9623; Mok Champae; r 750B) Located outside the small town of Mok Champae, just before ascending the mountains to Mae Aw, accommodation here takes the form of four attractive bungalows by a rushing stream. There's a restaurant run by the same people in the town, about 1km away.

Tha Law Sue Rak Thai Resort (☎ 08 9557 2258; Mae Aw; dm 200B, r 600-1200B) At the edge of the reservoir as you enter Mae Aw, this place is quite plush and has large bamboo huts at the water's edge, some of which have their own terraces. There is a restaurant attached serving Yunnanese dishes.

Jingmeay Restaurant (☎ 08 9985 5794; Mae Aw/Ban Rak Thai; dishes 20-180B; ☺ 7am-7pm) This place, 500m into Mae Aw, in the central market area, serves Yunnanese dishes, including excellent noodle soup and a delicious 'Young tea leafs salad'.

Gee Lee Restaurant (☎ 0 5307 2301; Mae Aw/Ban Rak Thai; dishes 40-250B; ☺ 8am-7pm) This was one of the first places in Mae Aw to serve the town's Yunnanese-style Chinese dishes to visitors. Stewed pork leg and stir-fried local veggies are the specialities here. It's at the corner of the lake, just before the intersection that leads to the centre of the village.

GETTING THERE & AWAY

There are two daily *sŏrng·tǎa·ou* that head toward Mae Aw: one that stops in Ban Ruam Thai before terminating in Mae Aw (80B, 9.30am) and another that only goes as far as Ban Ruam Thai (70B, 3.30pm). Both depart from Mae Hong Son's municipal market only when full, which can sometimes be a couple of hours after the scheduled departure time. Because of this, it's probably worth getting a group of people together and chartering a vehicle; any tour agency in Mae Hong Son will arrange a vehicle for around 1300B.

Alternatively, the route also makes a brilliant motorcycle ride – just make sure you have enough petrol, as the only station is in Ban Na Pa Paek, at the end of a very long climb.

PAI

ปาย

pop 2284

Spend enough time in northern Thailand and eventually you'll hear rumours that Pai is the Khao San Rd of northern Thailand. Although this is definitely a stretch, in recent years the small town has started to resemble a Thai island getaway – without the beaches. Guesthouses appear to outnumber private residences in the 'downtown' area, the internet is never more than a few steps away and the nights buzz with the sound of live music and partying.

However, unlike the islands, Pai (pronounced more like the English 'bye' not 'pie') is now just as popular among Thais as foreigners. During the peak of the cool season, thousands of Thais from Bangkok crowd the town, making parts of it feel more like Chatuchak Weekend market than a remote valley town in Mae Hong Son. Traffic jams aren't unusual during this time of year, and accommodation becomes so scarce that many are forced to rough it in tents.

Despite all this, the town's popularity has yet to impact its setting in a nearly picture-perfect mountain valley. There's heaps of quiet accommodation outside the main drag, a host of natural, lazy activities to keep visitors entertained, a vibrant art and music scene, and the town's Shan roots can still be seen in its temples, quiet back streets and fun afternoon market.

Information

There are plenty of places around town, especially at the eastern end of Th Chaisongkhram, that offer internet services (20B to 30B per hour).

Pai Post (www.paipost.com) is the free local English language monthly newspaper. It cov-

ers cultural events, travel destinations, political pieces, and some restaurant and bar openings, and can be picked up around town. The *Pai Events Planner* (PEP) is a free monthly map that covers much of the same ground.

In addition to the two we list below, several exchange booths and ATMs can be found along Th Rangsiyanon and Th Chaisongkhram.

Bank of Ayudhaya (Th Rangsiyanon; 9am-8pm) ATM and foreign-exchange service.

Krung Thai Bank (Th Rangsiyanon) ATM and foreign-exchange service.

Siam Books (☎ 0 5369 9075; Th Chaisongkhram) Boasts the town's largest selection of new and used books.

Tourist information booth (☎ 0 5369 9935; 8.30am-4.30pm) This small booth near the District Office is staffed with officials who speak basic English and who can provide a simple map of the area.

Sights & Activities

Many of Pai's sights are found just outside the city centre and in the surrounding areas.

WAT PHRA THAT MAE YEN

วัดพระธาตุแม่เย็น

This temple sits atop a hill and has good views overlooking the valley. Walk 1km east from the main intersection in town, across a stream and through a village, to get to the stairs (353 steps) that lead to the top. Or take the 400m sealed road that follows a different route to the top.

AROUND PAI

Northwest of town, the road that leads to the town hospital extends several kilometres to a Shan temple, a KMT village and a waterfall. The temple, **Wat Nam Hoo**, is about 2km from Pai and houses a sacred Buddha image said to have once emitted holy water from its head. The place is popular with visiting Thais and there's a small market on the grounds. Approximately 2km further, the atmospheric KMT village of **Ban Santichon** boasts a small market, Yunnanese **adobe-style accommodation** (☎ 08 1024 3982) and a delicious Yunnanese restaurant (see p445). **Nam Tok Mo Paeng**, the waterfall, has a couple of pools that are suitable for swimming and are best just after the rainy season, October to early December. There are Lahu and Lisu villages in the immediate area. The waterfall is a total of 8km from Pai – a long walk indeed, but suitable for a bike ride or short motorcycle trip. Motorcycle and bike

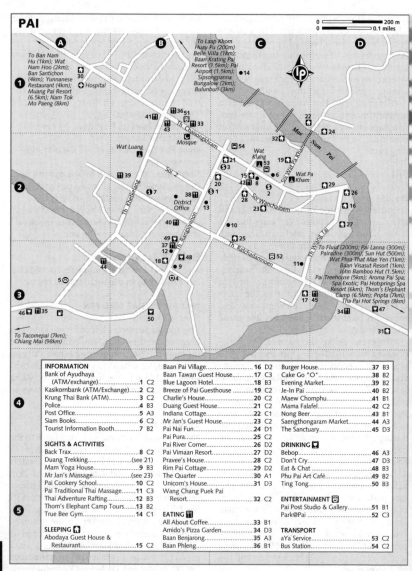

PAI

rentals are available at several guesthouses, as well as at aYa Service (p447).

Across Mae Nam Pai and 7km southeast of town via a paved road is **Tha Pai Hot Springs** (admission 200B; ⏰ 7am-6pm), a well-kept local park 1km from the road. A scenic stream flows through the park; the stream mixes with the hot springs in places to make pleasant bath-

ing areas. There are also small public bathing houses into which hot spring water is piped. The water is also diverted to a couple of nearby spas; see below for details.

TREKKING & RAFTING

Most guesthouses in town can provide information on local trekking and a few offer guided treks for as little as 700B per day if there are no rafts or elephants involved. Among the more established local agencies are **Back-Trax** (☎ 0 5369 9739; backtraxinpai@yahoo .com; Th Chaisongkhram) and **Duang Trekking** (Duang Guest House; ☎ 0 5369 9101; 8 Th Rangsiyanon).

Rafting along the Mae Nam Pai during the wet season is also a popular activity. Back-Trax offers rafting options, but **Thai Adventure Rafting** (☎ 0 5369 9111; www.thairafting .com; Th Rangsiyanon) is generally considered the most professional outfit. It leads two-day white-water rafting trips in sturdy rubber rafts, from Pai to Mae Hong Son for 2500B per person including food, rafting equipment, camping gear, dry bags and insurance. On the way, rafters visit a waterfall, a fossil reef and hot springs; one night is spent at the company's permanent riverside camp. One-day trips are also available for 1500B on slightly easier rapids. The main rafting season typically runs from mid-June to mid-February.

ELEPHANT RIDING
The road that leads to Tha Pai Hot Springs now boasts several elephant camps. The most established of these, and with an office in town, is **Thom's Pai Elephant Camp** (☎ 0 5369 9286; www.thomelephant.com; Th Rangsiyanon; elephant rides per person 500-1200B). You can choose between riding bareback or in a seat, and some rides include swimming with the elephants – a barrel of laughs on a bouncing elephant in the river. Rides include a soak in the hot-spring-fed tubs afterwards. Thom's can also arrange a variety of trips, including bamboo or rubber rafting, hill-tribe village stays or any combination of the aforementioned for about 1000B per person per day.

MASSAGE & SPA TREATMENTS
There are plenty of traditional Thai massage places around town charging around 150B an hour. Reiki, crystal healing acupuncture, reflexology and other non-indigenous methods of healing are also available; keep your eyes open for signs or refer to the *Pai Post* or the *Pai Events Planner*. Some of the more established outfits follow.

Pai Traditional Thai Massage (PTTM; ☎ 0 5369 9121; 68/3 Soi 1, Th Wiang Tai; massage per 1/1½/2hr 180/270/350B, sauna per visit 80B, 3-day massage course 2500B; ⏰ 9am-9pm) This established and locally-owned outfit offers very good northern-Thai massage, as well as a sauna where you can steam yourself

in *sà·mǔn·prai* (medicinal herbs). Three-day massage courses begin every Monday and Friday and last three hours per day. The friendly couple that do the massages and teach the course are accredited and are graduates of Chiang Mai's Old Medicine Hospital.

Mr Jan's Massage (Mr Jan's Bungalows; Soi Wanchaloem 18; per hr 150B) For those into the rougher stuff, this place employs a harder Shan-Burmese massage technique.

A few local businesses near Tha Pai Hot Springs have taken advantage of the healing thermal waters. **Aroma Pai Spa** (☎ 08 7187 0791; 110 Moo 2, Ban Mae Hi; thermal water soak 50B, spa treatments from 850B; ⏰ 7.30am-9pm) offers soaks in private rooms and a communal pool, as well as a variety of spa treatments. Next door, **Spa Exotic** (☎ 0 5306 5722; www.spaexotic.com; 86 Moo 2, Ban Mae Hi) goes a step further and channels the hot water into its bungalow bathrooms; nonguests can soak for 100B, or combine this with a Thai massage for 300B. **Pai Hotsprings Spa Resort** (☎ 0 1951 2784; www.thapaispa.com; Ban Mae Hi; 1hr massage 300B, thermal water soak 50B) is a resort-style hotel that also offers massages and thermal water soaks.

SPORTS FACILITIES
Fluid (Ban Mae Yen; admission 60B; ⏰ 9am-6pm) is a pool/gym complex just outside of town, roughly across from Sun Hut. There's a herbal steam room (per hour 80B) and yoga lessons are offered (10am Monday, Wednesday and Friday).

Courses
COOKING
Pai Cookery School (☎ 08 1706 3799; Soi Wanchaloem; courses per day 750-1000B) With nearly a decade of experience, this outfit offers a choice of three courses spanning several different dishes. The course typically involves a trip to the market for ingredients, learning how to make five meals, getting a free recipe book and, of course, eating your creations at the end. One- to three-day courses are available.

Many guesthouses also offer cooking courses.

THAI BOXING
True Bee Gym (☎ 08 4704 4833; www.truebee.com; Ban Mae Hi; tuition per half-day/day 250/400B) offers scholarship in Thai boxing just across the Nam Pai. Lessons are held twice daily (8am to 10.30am and 4pm to 6.30pm).

YOGA

Mam Yoga House (☎ 08 9954 4981; Th Rangsiyanon; 1-day course 200-550B) Just north of the police station, Mam offers Hatha Yoga classes and courses in small groups.

Sleeping

Pai used to be an exceedingly inexpensive place to stay and we still recall the days of the 50B riverside bungalow. But the 2005 flood demolished most of the truly cheap places, most of which have been replaced by upper-budget or midrange choices. There are still some cheap places outside of the centre of town, which is where you should base yourself if you're coming to Pai with preconceived notions of an idyllic, rural stay.

The fastest growing bracket at the moment is the top end, with most new hotels being built a few kilometres outside the centre of town. Many of these are run by people from Bangkok and are generally targeted towards domestic, rather than foreign, tourists.

Keep in mind that prices fluctuate immensely in Pai, and nearly all the midrange and top-end accommodation cut their prices, sometimes by as much as 60%, during the off season.

During the height of the Thai tourist season (December to January), tents are available in abundance for about 100B.

IN TOWN

Budget

Duang Guest House (☎ 0 5369 9101; 8 Th Rangsiyanon; r & bungalows 150-500B) Apparently one of the first guesthouses in Pai, the rooms here are bare and look their age, but there's a reliable trekking agency, a decent restaurant and a convenient central location.

Mr Jan's Guest House (☎ 0 5369 9554; Soi Wanchaloem 18; r 200-400B) Owned by a native of Pai, the rooms here are set around a medicinal herb garden, although they can be plain and somewhat dark. Massages and herbal saunas are available in high season.

Charlie's House (☎ 0 5369 9039; Th Rangsiyanon; r 200-600B; 🔀) This long-standing and locally run place offers a range of options in a suburban compound. Despite a recent paint job, the rooms are still a bit musty, although there's no more central place if that's what you're looking for.

Breeze of Pai Guesthouse (☎ 08 1998 4597; helen davis2@yahoo.co.uk; Soi Wat Pa Kham; r 400-800B) This well-groomed compound near the river consists of nine attractive and spacious rooms and six large A-frame bungalows fitted out in contemporary Thai style, with hot-water bathrooms and hammocks. It's close to the action without the noise pollution, and the friendly English owner can provide good local advice.

Abodaya Guest House & Restaurant (☎ 0 5369 9041; Th Chaisongkhram; r 500-600B) The rooms at this guesthouse are behind the restaurant of the same name. They're modern, clean and have some cosy touches and are a good deal, with cable TV, hot-water showers and a central location.

Pravee's House (☎ 0 5369 9368; Soi Wanchaloem; r with fan/air-con 500/600B; 🔀) Tucked in a shady corner, this compound offers basic but clean rooms with some decent furnishings and small verandas. There is a small garden out front.

Baan Tawan Guest House (☎ 0 5369 8116/7; www .baantawan-pai.com; 117 Mu 4, Th Wiang Tai; r 500-1500B; 🔀 🖳) The older, more charming, more expensive, riverside two-storey bungalows made with salvaged teak are the reason to stay here, but there are also spacious rooms in a large two-storey building. Motorcycles and inner tubes (for floating down the river) are available for rent.

Midrange

Pai Pura (☎ 08 1891 1771; Th Ratchadamnoen; r 600-1200B; 🔀) Although the rooms don't follow the rather decadent external design theme of stones, fountains and bricks, they're still a good value. A highlight is the herbal sauna and adjacent dipping pool.

Pai Nai Fun (☎ 08 9123 5042; www.painaifun.com; Ban Mae Hi; bungalows incl breakfast 800-1800B) and the adjacent Indiana Cottage (☎ 08 1952 3340; www.indiana-cottage.com; Ban Mae Hi; bungalows 1200B) offer similar accommodation just across the river. The former is a bit tidier and the more expensive bungalows have TV. A couple of other similar bungalow operations can be found along this stretch of the river.

Blue Lagoon Hotel (☎ 0 5369 9998; Th Rangsiyanon; r 900-1500B; 🔊) This two-storey suburban-feel hotel, complete with pool and tropical plants, is more Las Vegas than Pai. It's a good choice for those who don't require a bungalow, and who need creature comforts such as TV and fridge. Large rooms are available for travelling families.

our pick **Baan Pai Village** (☎ 0 5369 8152; www.baan paivillage.com; Th Wiang Tai; bungalows 1000-1600B; 🔀 🖳) This well-maintained place has a collection of

TROUBLE IN PAIRADISE?

In September 2005, a series of mudslides and floods devastated Pai, wiping away entire guesthouse complexes and destroying the city's bridges. In a few short days it seemed that the town's tourism infrastructure, which had been growing steadily since the 1980s, would suffer a major, if not permanent, setback.

It certainly didn't take long to recover. The next year it's estimated that 367,869 tourists visited Pai. Many were foreign tourists, drawn to the town's cheap accommodation and reputation as a peaceful, natural destination. But in 2006, for the first time, the majority of visitors were Thai, largely inspired by the Thai love flicks *Rak Jang* and *Happy Birthday*, both of which were filmed in the town.

Despite its immense popularity, Pai has largely been able to remain a positive example of tourism development in Thailand. Unlike elsewhere in the country, the residents of Pai have maintained a significant role in the development of their town. Natural and cultural conservation have long been fundamental aspects of Pai's tourism sector. And the town has been able to remain loyal to its rural roots, which form the basis of a lively art and music scene that leave most visitors with an overwhelmingly positive impression.

Tourism has also brought prosperity to the formerly isolated farming community. Land in desirable parts of the town is said to sell for as much as US$65,000 an acre, and many locals are now employed in various tourist service–related jobs, or supplement their income by selling handicrafts. Roads and other infrastructure have improved, and in 2007, Pai's commercial airport commenced flights. And the general consensus among residents is that they welcome the tourists and the income they bring.

On the other hand, the huge influx of visitors to Pai has also resulted in a host of new problems. The town is beginning to experience difficulties in dealing with increasing amounts of rubbish and sewage. Locals complain of being kept awake by the sound of live music and partying. Drug use is widespread. And the city's police force has garnered considerable negative press where it concerns tourists and tourism, ranging from a brief crackdown on so-called 'illegal dancing' in the city's bars, to the controversial shooting death of a Canadian tourist in early 2008.

In some ways the 2005 floods have been something of a wake-up call for the residents of Pai. Closing times at the town's bars are now strictly enforced, wastewater treatment is in the process of being made mandatory, and a new dump is being considered. But if Pai continues to maintain its current level of popularity, it remains to be seen whether or not the town can maintain the same level of responsible development that made it such an attractive destination to begin with.

wooden bungalows set among winding pathways. Beautifully designed, each bungalow has floor-to-ceiling sliding windows, large, quite plush bathrooms, rattan mats and axe cushions for relaxing, plus spacious terraces to enjoy the garden. There are also several cheaper, but simpler, riverside bungalows under the name Baan Pai Riverside.

Wang Chang Puek Pai Resort (☎ 0 5369 9796; www .wangchangpuek.com; bungalows with fan/air-con 1200/2500B; ❉ 🖳) This newish place boasts some of the more attractive midrange riverside bungalows in town. Rooms are spacious and attractive, and have wide balconies that encourage lazy riverside relaxing. The fan bungalows differ little from their air-con sisters and represent excellent value.

Top End

our pick **Rim Pai Cottage** (☎ 0 5369 9133; www.rim paicottage.com; Th Chaisongkhram; bungalows incl breakfast 1500-5000B; ❉ 🖳) The homelike bungalows here are spread out along a secluded and beautifully wooded section of the Nam Pai. The interiors have a romantic feel with their mosquito nets and Thai decorating details, and the open bathrooms are particularly nice. There are countless cosy riverside corners to relax at, and a palpable village-like feel about the whole place. Rim Pai is an excellent deal in low season when the prices drop dramatically.

Pai River Corner (☎ 0 5369 9049; www.pairiver corner.com; Th Chaisongkhram; r incl breakfast 3270-6540B; ❉ 🖳 🕿) Boasting accommodation that is 'Natural, Fresh, Private', the nine rooms here include beautiful Thai furniture, gorgeous colours and lots of deluxe details. Definitely the place for the design-conscious, all rooms have river-facing balconies and some have lounges and interior spa pools. Discounts are available in low season.

Pai Vimaan Resort (☎ 0 5369 9403; wwww.paivimaan.com; Th Wiang Tai; r 3500-4500, ste 10,000B; 🛏 🖵) This is the most expensive place to stay in 'downtown' Pai, although there are other options with more character. The duplex bungalows are bright and airy, with the top-floor ones allowing great views of the river. There are also rooms in the main wooden structure.

The Quarter (☎ 0 5369 9423; www.thequarterhotel.com; 245 Moo 1 Th Chaisongkhram; r 4800B; 🛏 🖵 🖭) With more in common with Ko Samui than Pai, this modern resort is the town's most self-consciously stylish place to stay. The 36 rooms face a central pool and are simultaneously minimalist and well equipped. The hotel is next door to Pai Hospital.

OUT OF TOWN
Southeast of town are a number of places to stay along the road that leads to the hot springs, not very far from Wat Phra That Mae Yen.

Budget
Tacomepai (☎ 08 6112 3504; Ban Teen That; bungalows 150-300B) For the ultimate Pai experience, base yourself at this rather eccentric compound, 7km south of town along Rte 1095. Consisting of eight truly rustic bungalows spread out over a semi-wooded hillside, the place is run by Sandot, an enthusiastic local who encourages his guests to take part in events such as local festivals and crop harvests. It may not be the most comfortable or most well-organised place to stay, but you're bound to collect some memories.

Unicorn's House (☎ 0 5369 8068; Wiang Tai; bungalows 250-350B) This is one of the few remaining places still offering cheap and basic bamboo-based accommodation. The compound of 30 stilt-raised bungalows feels something like a remote hill-tribe village, but is within walking distance of downtown. Unicorn is located just across the permanent bridge east of town, and there's also a branch with more expensive, but cramped bungalows on Th Ratchadamnoen.

John Bamboo Hut (☎ 08 1764 4427; www.johnbamboohut.9ha.com; Ban Mae Hi; bungalows 400-2500B) Offers a variety of basic but comfortable bungalows. Some are found in the shade of the eponymous bamboo trees, while others, including a family-sized house, are found on a hill looking over the valley.

Baan Visasut Resort (☎ 08 3568 7979; Th Rangsiyanon; bungalows 450-550B) Next door to John Bamboo Hut, this place has five slightly dark, but cosy bungalows in a shady compound.

Sun Hut (☎ 0 5369 9730; www.thesunhut.com; 28/1 Ban Mae Yen; r 350-1350B) Located in a jungle-like setting with a stream running through it, this is one of the more unique places in the area. Bungalows are nicely spaced apart and more expensive ones have porches and lots of charm. Service is friendly and gentle, there's an organic garden, a vegetarian restaurant, and an attractive communal area with hammocks and napping guests.

Midrange
Pairadise (☎ 0 5369 8065; www.pairadise.com; 98 Mu 1, Ban Mae Hi; bungalows 850-1350B) Popular with the Western yoga-and-meditation set, this tidy resort looks over the Pai Valley from atop a ridge just outside town. The bungalows are stylish, spacious and include gold leaf lotus murals, beautiful rustic bathrooms and terraces with hammocks. All surround a waterfall-fed pond that is suitable for swimming. Next door, Pai Lanna (☎ 08 9691 3367; www.pailanna.com; 169 Mu 1, Ban Mae Yen; bungalows including breakfast 900B) offers a similar, although somewhat more basic setup.

ourpick Sipsongpanna Bungalow (☎ 0 5369 8259, 08 1881 7631; 60 Mu 5, Ban Juang, Wiang Neua; bungalows 1000-2500B) This fun place boasts a chilled-out atmosphere that feels authentically local rather than contrived. The adobe-style riverside bungalows are rustic and a bit quirky with a mix of bright colours, beds on elevated platforms and sliding-glass doors opening to wide balconies. There are also still a few original wooden bungalows, although these are being phased out. There is a vegetarian cafe and Thai vegetarian cooking lessons are available.

ourpick Pai Treehouse (☎ 08 1911 3640; www.paitreehouse.com; 90 Moo 2 Mae Hi; bungalows 1000-5500B; 🖵) It's every child's fantasy hotel: wooden bungalows suspended from a giant old tree. Even if you can't score one of the three elusive treehouse rooms (they're popular), there are several other attractive bungalows, many near the river. On the vast grounds you'll also find elephants and floating decks on the Mae Nam Pai, all culminating in a family-friendly atmosphere. The resort is 6km from Pai, just before Tha Pai Hot Springs.

Spa Exotic Home (☎ 0 5306 5722; www.spaexotic.com; 86 Moo 2 Mae Hi; bungalows incl breakfast 1400-1800B; 🌊) All of the charming bungalows here sit around a beautifully landscaped garden. A highlight is that each has a private tub in partially open-air bathrooms for enjoying the on-site thermal spring water. Service is conscientious and the overall atmosphere is relaxing. Discounts of 35% are available from March to September.

Top End

our pick **Bulunburi** (☎ 0 5336 5440; www.blunburi.com; 28 Moo 5 Ban Pong; bungalows 1800-2800B; 🌊) Set in a tiny secluded valley of rice fields and streams, the seductively bucolic location is as much a reason to stay here as the attractive accommodation. The compound's most apparent structure, the cone-like open-air lobby, is decorated with attractive murals and boasts a central fireplace. The bungalows mostly continue the tasteful design theme established in the lobby, and are large, well equipped and stylish.

Baan Krating Pai Resort (☎ 0 5369 8255, www .baankrating.com; 119 Th Wiang Nua; bungalows 2500-3100B, ste 6000B; 🌊 🛱) These bungalows on stilts are all beautifully decorated with white linen, rattan and teak, and have large windows overlooking manicured gardens or rice paddies. The nearby restaurant serves its home-grown jasmine rice with tasty Thai dishes.

our pick **Pripta** (☎ 0 5306 5750; www.pripta.com; 90 Moo 3 Mae Hi; r 4800-6800B; 🌊 🖥) One of the more recent arrivals, this hillside compound features eight chic white bungalows perched at the edge of the Pai Valley. Rooms are huge, with tall ceilings, and feature outdoor tubs with water supplied by the nearby hot springs. The furnishings and interior design don't always reach the level established by the exterior, but it's still among the more style-conscious places around. It's about 7km from Pai, between Tha Pai Hot Springs and Rte 1095.

Eating

Pai has a pretty good range of restaurants for such a small town, but the foreign offerings are generally more miss than hit.

During the day, there's takeaway food at **Saengthongaram market** (Th Khetkalang). For tasty take-home local eats, try the **evening market** (gàht láang; Th Ratchadamnoen) that unfolds every afternoon from about 3pm to sunset. And every night several vendors sell a variety of food along Th Chaisongkhram and Th Rangsiyanon, including all manner of food and drink sold from stalls and refurbished VW vans.

Maew Chomphu (no roman-script sign; cnr Th Khetkalang & Th Chaisongkhram; dishes 20-50B; 🕑 7am-9pm) Head to this corner restaurant for a tasty Asian-style breakfast. Go for dim sum or try kài gà·tá, two eggs cooked in a tiny wok with Vietnamese sausage.

Cake Go "O" (Th Rangsiyanon; dishes 20-70B; 🕑 8am-8pm) This Muslim-run bakery serves decent baked treats (try the oatmeal scones), coffee and light meals. There are a couple of other Muslim bakeries in town, although the others don't have quite as many entertaining sign-posted house rules.

Je-In Pai (Pure Vegetarian Food; Th Ratchadamnoen; dishes 25-80B; 🕑 10am-8pm) Opposite the District Office, this simple open-air place serves tasty and cheap vegan and vegetarian Thai food. During lunch, choose from the dishes in the metal trays out front. There's good fruit and soy milk shakes too.

our pick **Yunnanese Restaurant** (no roman-script sign; ☎ 08 1024 3982; Ban Santichon; dishes 25-200B; 🕑 8am-10pm) This open air-place in the Chinese village of Ban Santichon serves the traditional dishes of the town's Yunnanese residents. Standouts include màntŏ (steamed buns), here fried until crispy and seved with pork leg stewed with Chinese herbs. There are several dishes using unique local crops and other dishes involving exotic ingredients such as black chicken. Or you could always go for the excellent noodles, made by hand and topped with a delicious mixture of minced pork, garlic and sesame. The restaurant is in an open-air adobe building behind the giant rock in Ban Santichon, about 4km west of Pai.

Nong Beer (☎ 0 5369 9103; cnr Th Khetkalang & Th Chaisongkhram; dishes 30-60B; 🕑 10am-10pm) The atmosphere at this extremely popular place is akin to a food court (you have to exchange cash for tickets, and everything is self-serve), but it's a good place for cheap and authentic Thai eats ranging from khâw soy to curries ladled over rice. Open until they run out of food – usually about 9pm.

our pick **Baan Phleng** (Local Northern Thai food; cnr Th Khetkalang & Th Chaisongkhram; dishes 30-60B; 🕑 10am-10pm) A branch of the excellent Mae Hong Son restaurant of the same name, this popular place does a mix of northern Thai and Mae Hong Son–specific dishes. To go truly local, try the 'fern salad Maehongson style', tender ferns par-boiled and mixed with a dressing combining sesame oil, dried chili and garlic, or 'pork and tomato chili paste', the Shan dish known locally as *nám prík òrng*. There's an English-language menu with photos if you feel you're treading in unfamiliar waters.

our pick **Laap Khom Huay Pu** (no roman-script sign; ☎ 0 5369 9126; Ban Huay Pu; dishes 35-60B; ⏰ 9am-10pm) Escape the dreadlocks and tofu crowd and get your meat at this unabashedly carnivorous local eatery. The house special, and the dish you must order, is *lâhp kôoa*, minced meat (beef or pork) fried with local herbs and spices. Accompanied by a basket of sticky rice, a plate of bitter herbs and a cold Singha, it's the best meal in Pai. The restaurant is about 1km north of town, on the first street just past the turn-off to Belle Villa and Baan Krating.

All About Coffee (☎ 0 5369 9429; Th Chaisongkhram; dishes 45-75B; ⏰ 8.30am-6.30pm) This tiny wooden place was probably the first business to do the cutesy 'bohemian' style that now dominates much of Pai. Come here for eye-opening coffee drinks and the best French toast in town. Yummy open sandwiches are made with homemade bread.

Burger House (☎ 0 5369 9093; Th Rangsiyanon; dishes 50-240B; ⏰ 9am-9pm) If you are hankering after a big juicy burger this is the place to come. Try the super-high Barbarian Burger with its two quarter pounders, two cheeses and special sauce. Or if you need a fortifying breakfast, go for the Truck Driver Special, which will probably take most of the morning to get through.

Mama Falafel (Soi Wanchaloem; dishes 60-90B; ⏰ 11am-8pm) Since 2002 this friendly native of Pai has been cooking up tasty felafel, hummus, schnitzel and other Jewish/Israeli faves. Come on Friday and Saturday when she does hamin, the Jewish stew, accompanied by challah bread.

Baan Benjarong (☎ 0 5369 8010; Th Rangsiyanon; dishes 60-150B; ⏰ lunch & dinner) This converted house serving central Thai dishes is where the locals come for a 'nice' Thai meal. Dishes like stewed, salted crabs in coconut milk, and spicy banana flower salad are delectable. Out the back are tables with views of the rice paddies.

The Sanctuary (☎ 0 5369 8150; 115/1 Moo 4 Th Wiang Tai; dishes 80-290B) The local/organic dishes at this new-agey quasi-veggie restaurant are rather expensive by local standards, but the cakes and coffee are tasty, and the free wi-fi and, yes, free yoga lessons (10.30am Tuesday, Thursday

and Saturday) are a good deal. There's also a variety of live music on most nights.

Amido's Pizza Garden (Th Ratchadamnoen; dishes 80-320B; ⏰ dinner) Considering how far Pai is from Naples, we reckon they do a pretty damn good pizza here. If you're willing to book ahead of time, they also do special set meals for groups, such as a goat leg feast or paella. It's just across the permanent bridge over Mae Nam Pai.

Drinking & Entertainment

Pai boasts a small but happening live-music scene.

Bebop (Th Rangsiyanon; ⏰ 6pm-1am) This legendary box is popular with travellers and has live music nightly (from about 9.30pm), playing blues, R&B and rock.

Park@Pai (Th Ratchadamnoen; ⏰ 6pm-midnight) Parking Toys (p171), one of Bangkok's best live-music pubs, has opened a branch in Pai. Rock to visiting bands while seated on funky furniture and snacking on their excellent food (it'd be a crime to miss their fantastic 'hot & sour crispy chicken salad').

Ting Tong (Th Rangsiyanon; ⏰ 7pm-1am) A sprawling compound of bamboo decks, concrete platforms, hidden tables and towering trees, this is one of the larger bars in town. Reggae/dub defines but doesn't rule the play list, and there's occasional live music. Ting Tong is just outside the town centre on the road to Chiang Mai.

Phu Pai Art Café (Th Rangsiyanon; ⏰ 5pm-midnight) This attractive wooden house is another highlight of Pai's live music scene. The amps turn on at 8pm, and on our visit we enjoyed some very good live acoustic guitar music.

Pai Post Studio & Gallery (Th Chaisongkhram; ⏰ 7.30-midnight) This white wooden building is home to Pai's English-language rag, and the front is a white space for photography. But every night, after the computers are turned off, a fun mixture of live music (mostly rock/jazz) and performance (a ventriloquist, at last check) takes over.

Don't Cry (Th Ratchadamnoen; ⏰ 6pm-late) Located just across the river, this is the kind of reggae bar you thought you left behind on Ko Phangan. Soporifically chilled out and open (albeit quietly) until the last guy goes home.

Eat & Chat (Th Rangsiyanon; ⏰ 6pm-midnight) For a couple of beers and a chat at conversation, rather than shouting-over-the-guitar-solo level, head to this low-key place across from the Blue Lagoon Hotel. Music ranges from jazz to Sinatra, there's live acoustic most nights, and as the name suggests, there's food as well.

Getting There & Away
AIR
Pai's airport is around 2km north of town along Rte 1095.

SGA Airlines (☎ nationwide call centre 0 2264 6099, 0 5369 8207; www.sga.co.th; Pai airport), a subsidiary of Nok Air, operates propeller-powered flights between Pai and Chiang Mai (from 1930B, 30 minutes, twice daily).

BUS
From Pai it's easy to get to Soppong (ordinary/ air-con/minivan 40/80/100, 1½ hours, 8.30am to 2pm) and Mae Hong Son (ordinary/air- con/minivan 80/100/150B).

A couple of ordinary buses depart from Pai's bus station for Chiang Mai (112B, four hours, 8.30am and 10.30am). Buses and mini- vans originating in Mae Hong Son also stop in Pai (ordinary/air-con/minivan 80/100/150B, three hours).

Book your ticket in advance at **aYa Service** (☎ 0 5369 9940; 22/1 Moo 3 Th Chaisongkhram); it runs hourly air-con minivan buses to Chiang Mai (150B, three hours, from 7.30am to 4.30pm), as well as less frequent departures to Chiang Rai (550B, five hours), Mae Sai (700B, six hours) and Chiang Khong (750B, 10 hours).

Getting Around
Most of Pai is accessible on foot. Motorcycle taxis wait at the taxi stand across from the bus station. Fares are 40B to Ban Santichon and 70B to Nam Tok Mo Paeng.

For local excursions you can rent bicycles or motorcycles at several locations around town including **aYa Service** (☎ 0 5369 9940; Th Chaisongkhram; bikes per 24hr 100cc 80B, larger 100-700B). There are a couple of similar places in the immediate vicinity.

SOPPONG & AROUND
สบปอง

Soppong (also sometimes known as Pangmapha, actually the name of the entire district) is a small market village a couple of hours northwest of Pai and about 70km from Mae Hong Son. There's not much to see in town, but the surrounding area is defined by dense forests, rushing rivers and dramatic limestone outcrops and is *the* place in north- ern Thailand for **caving**. The best source of information on caving and trekking in the area is the owner of Cave Lodge (p449) in nearby Tham Lot, the most accessible cave in the area.

There are also several Shan, Lisu, Karen and Lahu **villages** that can easily be visited on foot.

Soppong and Tham Lot have become popular destinations for minivan tours from Pai and Mae Hong Son, although few people stay overnight.

If you're here on Tuesday morning, check out the town's rustic **market**.

Information
Soppong's police station is 1.5km west of the town. The town's only ATM is found there.

Activities
TREKKING & RAFTING
Cave Lodge (p449) near Tham Lot, 9km from Soppong, has experienced local guides and arranges recommended kayaking, trekking and caving trips in the area.

The new outfit **Poodoi Namfaa Tour & Trekking** (☎ 08 9048 2886) can arrange various outdoor pursuits, all led by local Musoe, Lisu and Karen guides. The emphasis is on two-day rafting trips along the Nam Khong and Nam Pai rivers (1500B per person, at least four peo- ple). Two-day treks start at 800B per person (at least two people). The office is at the far western edge of town.

Sleeping & Eating
All accommodation, most of which is found along Soppong's main road, is clearly marked by signs. There's little in the way of food in Soppong, but virtually every guesthouse has a restaurant attached.

Rim Doi (☎ 08 9952 8870; r & bungalows 200-600B) About 2km from Soppong, along the road to Tham Lot, this place unites bamboo huts and more permanent-feeling rooms on a grassy hillside. Rooms are large and comfortably furnished.

Lisu Hill Tribe Homestay (☎ 08 9998 4886, 08 5721 1575; www.lisuhilltribe.com; r incl meals 300B) Run by an American and his Lisu wife, this place of- fers activity-based accommodation in Nong Thong, a Lisu village within walking distance of Soppong. Various craft and culture classes ranging from Lisu music to meditation can be arranged for an additional 700B; check out the website for options. Call ahead for pick-up from the town's bus station (20B).

Lemon Hill Guest House (☎ 0 5361 7039, 0 5361 7213; r & bungalows 300-1500B; 🖳) Due to its location across from the town bus stop, this guesthouse is probably the most popular place in town, although it must be said that there are nicer places to stay. There's a mish-mash of accommodation ranging from rooms to bungalows – check out a few before coming to a decision. The restaurant overlooking the river serves tasty food using its homegrown organic veggies.

our pick Soppong River Inn (☎ 0 5361 7107; www.soppong.com; bungalows 300B; r 700-1200B; 🖳) Combining five rooms in a rambling riverside structure and a handful of free-standing bungalows, this is the most attractive place in Soppong. Set among lush gardens with winding paths, the rooms have heaps of character and are all slightly different. The River Rim Cottage is our fave, as it has a private balcony situated right over the river. All guests have access to the shared balcony overlooking a small gorge. Soppong River Inn is at the western edge of town, within walking distance from the bus station.

our pick Little Eden Guesthouse (☎ 0 5361 7054; www.littleeden-guesthouse.com; r & bungalows 450-2000B; 🖳) The nine A-frame bungalows around a pleasant, grass-decked pool are well kept with hot-water showers. Yet, it's the beautiful two-storey 'houses' that make this place special. Perfect for families or a group of friends, they are stylishly decorated, have living rooms, interesting nooks and crannies, and terraces with hammocks. The owner can speak Thai, English, Danish and German and organises all sorts of activities in the area.

Baan Café (☎ 0 5361 7081; khunjui@yahoo.com; r 600B; bungalows 1200B) At the edge of town near the bridge, this place combines spotless rooms and house-like bungalows in a park-like setting by the Nam Lang. The bungalows include fireplaces, have balconies looking over the river and are terrific value. Baan Café is also one of the better restaurants in town and serves locally grown coffee.

Northern Hill Guest House (☎ 0 5361 7081; khunjui@yahoo.com; r & bungalows 600-1500B) This place combines several cramped but tidy bungalows on a hill looking over Soppong. Some rooms include TV and fridge. Northern Hill is at the eastern extent of town, opposite the turn-off to Tham Lot.

Hillside Cottage (☎ 0 5361 7107; www.sopponghills .com; r & bungalows 900-1200B) Directly opposite Soppong River Inn, Hillside consists of several tidy, but slightly overpriced, rooms and bungalows on a manicured hill. Take-away northern Thai food is available outside the gate every evening.

Baankeawmora (Coffee Cottage; ☎ 0 5361 7078; dishes 40-160B; ☺ 8am-6pm) Good food and real coffee can be had at this cute wooden house along the road to Tham Lot. Early morning breakfasts and late dinners can be arranged in advance.

Border (☎ 0 5361 7102; ☺ noon-midnight) Next to Lemon Hill and run by an English and Thai couple, this formerly bare-bones beer shack has expanded to serving coffee and food. There's free wi-fi and it's also the place to find out about what's going on around Soppong.

Tham Lot
ถ้ำลอด

About 9km north of Soppong is Tham Lot (pronounced *tâm lôrt* and also known as *tâm nám lôrt*), a large limestone cave with impressive stalagmites and 'coffin caves' (see boxed text, opposite), and a wide stream running through it. Along with Tham Nam Lang further west, it's one of the largest known caves in Thailand. The total length of the cave is 1600m and for 600m the stream runs through it.

At the **Nature Education Centre** (☺ 8am-5.30pm) and entrance, you must hire a gas lantern and guide for 150B (one guide leads one to four people) to take you through the caverns; visitors are not permitted to tour the caves alone. Tham Lot is a good example of community-based tourism as all of the guides at the cave are from local Shan villages.

Apart from the main chamber, there are also three side chambers – Column Cavern, Doll Cave and Coffin Cave – that can be reached by ladders. It takes around two hours to explore the whole thing. Depending on the time of year it is necessary to take a bamboo raft for some or all of the journey through the caves. Access to parts of the cave may be limited between August and October because of water levels.

From the entrance to the exit and taking in the Column Cavern, Doll Cave and Coffin Cave, the rafts (up to four adults) cost 400B return, or 300B one way. If going one way you can walk back from outside of

THE CAVES OF PANGMAPHA

The 900-sq-km area of Pangmapha district is famous for its high concentration of cave systems, where over 200 have been found. Apart from Tham Lot, one of its most famous is Tham Nam Lang, which is 20km northwest of Soppong near Ban Nam Khong. It's 8.5km long and said to be one of the largest caves in the world in terms of volume.

Many of the caves are essentially underground river systems, some of which boast waterfalls, lakes and 'beaches'. *Cryptotora thamicola,* an eyeless, waterfall-climbing troglobitic fish that forms its own genus, is found in only two caves in the world, both of which are in Pangmapha, Thailand. Other caves contain little or no life, due to an abundance of noxious gases or very little oxygen.

More than 85 of the district's 200 limestone caverns are known to contain ancient teak coffins carved from solid teak logs. Up to 9m long, the coffins are typically suspended on wooden scaffolds inside the caves. The coffins have been carbon-dated and shown to be between 1200 and 2200 years old. The ends are usually carved and Thai archaeologists have identified at least 50 different design schemes. Pottery remains found in coffin caves are on display in the Nature Education Centre (opposite) at Tham Lot.

The local Shans know these burial caves as *tâm pĕe* (spirit caves), or *tâm pĕe maan* (coffin caves). It is not known who made them or why they were placed in caves, but as most caves have fewer than 10 coffins it indicates that not everyone was accorded such an elaborate burial. Similar coffins have been found in karst areas west of Bangkok and also in Borneo, China and the Philippines, but the highest concentration of coffin caves from this period is in Pangmapha.

The easiest coffin caves to visit are found just past Pangmapha Hospital, 2km west of Soppong, and the coffin caves in Tham Lot, 9km from Soppong. Several caves that scientists are investigating at the moment are off-limits to the public, but John Spies at Cave Lodge (below) may know which caves are possible to explore. His book, *Wild Times,* is also a great informal guide to the area's caves.

---

the cave (20 minutes), only possible during the dry season. In the dry season it may be possible to wade to the Doll Cave and then take a raft through to the exit (300B return, 200B one way). Try to be at the exit at sunset when hundreds of thousands of swifts pour into Tham Lot and cling to their bedtime stalagmites.

SLEEPING & EATING

our pick **Cave Lodge** (☎ 0 5361 7203; www.cavelodge .com; dm 90-120B, r 250B, bungalows 300-2000B) Open since 1986, this is one of the more legendary places to stay in northern Thailand (and probably the first guesthouse in Mae Hong Son). Run by the unofficial expert on the area, John Spies, the 11 bungalows here are basic but unique and varied. The setting on a wooded hillside above the Nam Lang is beautiful and options for adventure abound. Choose from caving and kayaking trips, guided or unguided treks (good maps are available) or just hang out in the beautiful communal area. The traditional Shan herbal sauna is an experience and the custom ovens

bake bread and other treats. Tham Lot is a short walk away.

A row of **outdoor restaurants** (dishes 15-40B; ❤ 9am-6pm) outside the Tham Lot park entrance offers simple Thai fare.

Mae La-Na

แม่ละนา

Set in an incredibly picturesque mountain valley 6km off Rte 1095, this tiny Shan village feels like a lost corner of the world. The most famous local attraction is **Tham Mae La-Na**, a 12km-long cavern with a stream running through it. Although local guides are willing to take people inside, in reality the cave lacks the appropriate infrastructure to support visitors, who run a serious risk of permanently damaging delicate cave formations and disturbing the habitat of sensitive cave fish. A better bet is to check out the nearby **Tham Pakarang** (Coral Cave) and **Tham Phet** (Diamond Cave), both of which feature good wall formations. Guides (100B) can be found during the day at the *sǎh·lah* (often spelt as *sala*; open-sided, covered meeting hall) and at the main village shop. Some of the caves may not be accessible during the rainy season.

Mae La-Na is also a good base for some inspiring **walks**. Some of Mae Hong Son's most beautiful scenery is within a day's ramble, and there are several Red and Black Lahu villages nearby. It's also possible to walk a 20km half-loop all the way from Mae La-Na to Tham Lot and Soppong, staying overnight in Red Lahu villages along the way. Khun Ampha at Maelana Garden Home (below) can provide a basic map and advice. Experienced riders can do this route on a sturdy dirt bike – but not alone or during the rainy season.

The Mae La-Na junction is 13km west of Soppong. Infrequent *sŏrng·tăa·ou* from the highway to the village cost 30B per person – mornings are your best bet. Along the way you'll pass the Black Lahu village of Jabo, which also boasts a coffin cave.

SLEEPING & EATING
Maelana Garden Home (☎ 0 5304 0016, 08 706 6021; r 200-500B) At the edge of town towards Tham Mae La-Na, this attractive farm-like compound combines two wooden houses and a few A-frame bamboo bungalows. The rooms are basic but clean and comfy. Authentic Shan meals can be prepared (80B per person), and the lady who runs it speaks a bit of English and is a good source of information. Call ahead or ask for Khun Ampha at the village shop/petrol station.

A dozen homes in Mae La-Na have collaborated to form a **homestay program** (per person per night 100B) where the money goes back into a community fund. Meals can be prepared for 70B per person. Enquire at the sporadically staffed wooden house at the entrance to town.

Ban Nam Rin
บ้านน้ำริน
At this Lisu village 9km south of Soppong towards Pai, you can stay at **Lisu Lodge** (☎ 08 3582 4496, 08 3054 8497; lisulodge@gmail.com; r 150-600B), a quiet place set in beautiful mountain scenery with a garden filled with fruit trees. Choices range from simple, shared bathroom A-frames to wood and stone bungalows with lovely recycled teak furniture, tasteful Thai styling and terraces. A family bungalow is available too. The German

owner can give information on nearby hill-tribe villages to visit, plus he makes a wicked mulberry liqueur.

Getting There & Around
Buses and minivans between Pai and Mae Hong Son stop in Soppong and there are six a day in either direction. The trip between Pai and Soppong (ordinary/air-con/minivan 40/80/100B) takes one hour to 1½ or two hours. For details on getting to/from Mae Hong Son see p428.

Motorcycle taxis stationed at the bus stop in Soppong will take passengers to Tham Lot or the Cave Lodge for 70B per person; private pick-up trucks will take you and up to five other people for 300B.

Khun Yuam
ขุนยวม
pop 6823
About halfway between Mae Sariang and Mae Hong Son, where all northbound buses make their halfway stop, is the quiet hillside town of Khun Yuam. This little-visited town is a nice break from more 'experienced' destinations nearby. There are a couple of places to stay and a few notable sights.

At the northern end of town, a collection of rusted military trucks marks the **Thai-Japan Friendship Memorial Hall** (admission 50B; ☼ 8am-4pm). Here weapons, military equipment, personal possessions and fascinating black-and-white photographs document the period when the Japanese occupied Khun Yuam in the closing weeks of the war with Burma. After they had recovered, some of the Japanese soldiers stayed in Khun Yuam and married. The last Japanese soldier who settled in the area died in 2000.

About 6km to the west of Khun Yuam, the atmospheric **Wat To Phae** sits alongside a country stream and boasts a Mon-style *chedi* and an immaculate Burmese-style *wí·hǎhn*. Inside the latter, take a look at the large, 150-year-old Burmese *kalaga* (embroidered and sequined tapestry) that's kept behind curtains to one side of the main altar. The tapestry depicts a scene from the *Vessantara Jataka* and local devotees believe one accrues merit simply by viewing it.

On the slopes of Doi Mae U Khaw, 25km from Khun Yuam via Rte 1263, is the Hmong village of **Ban Mae U Khaw**. During late November the area blooms with scenic

NORTHERN THAILAND

Mexican sunflowers, known locally as *dòrk booa torng*. This event is incredibly popular among Thais and accommodation in the town is booked out. Continue another 25km along the same route and you'll reach the 100m **Nam Tok Mae Surin** (admission 200B; part of the Mae Surin National Park), reportedly Thailand's highest cataract.

There are a couple of banks with ATMs along the main strip in Khun Yuam, and a few sleeping options. There are also a few homestay options in Ban To Phae, a traditional and picturesque Shan village 6km west of Khun Yuam.

Ban Farang (☎ 0 5362 2086; janny5alisa@hotmail .com; 499 Th Ratburana; dm 100B; bungalows 600-1400B; 🖳) is off the main road towards the north end of town (look for the signs near the bus stop). The tidy bungalows are set on a wooded hillside. The cheaper fan bungalows are plain and dark but have a terrace. The more expensive ones come with air-con, fridge, cable TV and a terrace. Herbal massage is available and the restaurant on site is reasonable.

When finished, the two duplex buildings of **Khun Yuam Resort** (☎ 08 9432 1032; www.khunyuam resort.multiply.com; 139 Moo 1 Ban To Phae; 1200-2000B; 🖳), looking over a valley, will have the best views in the area. For now, the existing rooms are large, but featureless and rather overpriced.

On the main road through the town centre, **Mithkhoonyoum Hotel** (☎ 0 5369 1057; 61 Rte 108; r 150-550; 🖳) has simple, clean rooms, some with en-suite bathrooms.

In Khun Yuam you'll find a collection of modest rice and noodle shops along the east side, or Rte 108, towards the southern end of town. Most of these close by 5pm or 6pm.

Buses stop regularly at Khun Yuam (ordinary/air-con 67/110B, two hours) on their runs between Mae Sariang and Mae Hong Song.

MAE SARIANG
แม่สะเรียง
pop 10,012

Little-visited Mae Sariang is gaining a low-key buzz for its attractive riverside setting and potential as a launching pad for sustainable tourism and trekking opportunities. There are several hill-tribe settlements nearby, particularly around Mae La Noi, 30km north of the city, and the area south of Mae Sariang is largely mountainous jungle encompassing both Salawin and Mae Ngao National Parks.

Information
Mae Sariang has several banks with ATMs and an **immigration office** (☎ 0 5368 1339; Route 108) that will extend your visa by a couple of days if you're in a pinch and on your way to the border. It's opposite the petrol station on the road to Mae Hong Son. **Internet** (per hr 20B) is available next to River House Hotel.

Sights & Activities
There are few formal sights in Mae Sariang. Two adjacent Burmese-Shan temples, **Wat Jong Sung** and **Wat Si Bunruang**, just off Mae Sariang's main street, are definitely worth a visit if you have time. Built in 1896, Wat Jong Sung is the more interesting of the two temples and has slender, Shan-style *chedi* and wooden monastic buildings.

The area surrounding Mae Sariang is probably one of the country's best for **trekking** and **tours**. This is not only due to the area's natural beauty and cultural diversity, but also because of a new breed of responsible, sustainable and community-based touring and trekking outfits.

Dragon Sabaii Tours (☎ 08 9956 9897, 08 7190 4469; www.thailandhilltribeholidays.com; Th Mongkolchai; 1-day tour per group of 4 people 1800B) emphasises eco- and cultural tourism primarily in the Mae La Noi area just north of Mae Sariang. This new outfit offers a variety of tours aimed at giving a genuine introduction to the local way of life and hill-tribe culture. Activities range from non-intrusive tours of hill-tribe villages, to homestays, 'volunteerism', and cooking and farming with hill tribes, all of which are designed to benefit local communities directly.

Mae Sariang Man, as the owner of **Mae Sariang Tours** (☎ 08 2032 4790; www.maesariang travel.multiply.com; Th Laeng Phanit; 1-day trek 1200B plus expenses) prefers to be known, is an experienced trekker who leads environmentally-conscious and community-based treks and rafting trips in the jungles and national parks surrounding his native city. To ensure that the communities receive what they deserve, trekkers can opt to pay all expenses outside of the guide fee directly to the villagers themselves.

The ex-teacher running **Kanchana Tour** (☎ 08 1952 2167; www.orchidhomestay.com; half-day cycling tour 600B, one-day tour 1000B) offers half- and full-day cycling tours around Mae Sariang, as well as other tours ranging from boat trips along the

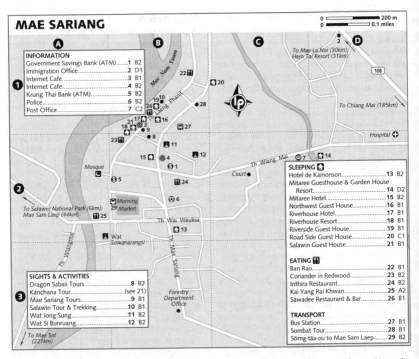

MAE SARIANG

0   200 m
0   0.1 miles

INFORMATION
Government Savings Bank (ATM)......1 B2
Immigration Office.............................2 D1
Internet Cafe.....................................3 B1
Internet Cafe.....................................4 B2
Krung Thai Bank (ATM)....................5 B2
Police..6 B2
Post Office..7 C2

To Mae La Noi (30km);
Hern Tai Resort (31km)

108

To Chiang Mai (185km)

Hospital

SLEEPING
Hotel de Kamonson.........................13 B2
Mitaree Guesthouse & Garden House
  Resort...14 D2
Mitaree Hotel..................................15 B2
Northwest Guest House...................16 B1
Riverhouse Hotel.............................17 B1
Riverhouse Resort...........................18 B1
Riverside Guest House.....................19 B1
Road Side Guest House....................20 C1
Salawin Guest House.......................21 B1

EATING
Ban Rao...22 B1
Coriander in Redwood.....................23 B2
Inthira Restaurant...........................24 B2
Kai Yang Rai Khwan.........................25 A2
Sawadee Restaurant & Bar..............26 B1

TRANSPORT
Bus Station......................................27 B1
Sombat Tour....................................28 B1
Sŏrng-tǎa-ou to Mae Sam Laep......29 B2

Mosque

Morning Market

Wat Sowarangsi

Court

Forestry Department Office

To Salawin National Park (6km);
Mae Sam Laep (44km)

To Mae Sot (221km)

SIGHTS & ACTIVITIES
Dragon Sabaii Tours..........................8 B2
Kanchana Tour...........................(see 21)
Mae Sariang Tours.............................9 B1
Salawin Tour & Trekking.................10 B1
Wat Jong Sung.................................11 B2
Wat Si Bunruang..............................12 B2

Mae Nam Salawin, to visits to local hill tribes. She also offers homestay-style accommodation at her home, 2km from the town centre. You can often find her at Salawin Guest House (opposite).

Mr Salawin and his brothers have been leading tours in the area for 16 years. Their trips at **Salawin Tour & Trekking** (☎ 08 2181 2303; Th Laeng Phanit; 1-/3-day trek 1300/2500B) typically involve activities such as elephant riding, rafting and hiking. They keep an 'office' next to Riverside Guest House, and can communicate in English.

Sleeping

Road Side Guest House (☎ 0 5368 2713; road-sidegh@ hotmail.com; 44 Th Mae Sariang; r 200B) Playing on a theme of cowboys and Indians, the six rooms at this new guesthouse are correspondingly rustic, but clean and comfortable. The owner, an experienced trekking guide, leads various tours of the area.

Northwest Guest House (☎ 0 5368 1956; www .northwestgh.blogspot.com; 81 Moo 12, Th Laeng Phanit; r 200-400B) The rooms in this cosy wooden house are simple (think mattress on the floor) but

get natural light and are a good size. To make up for it, the guesthouse offers a huge variety of services, ranging from motorcycle rental to laundry service.

Mitaree Guesthouse and Garden House Resort (☎ 0 5368 1109; www.mitareehotel.com; 24 Th Wiang Mai; r 150-4000, bungalows 600-800B; ✷) Located by the post office and owned by the same people who run Mitaree Hotel, it has a mish-mash of nicer rooms and bungalows, all with hot water, air-con and cable TV.

Mitaree Hotel (☎ 0 5368 1110; www.mitareehotel .com; 256 Moo 2, Th Mae Sariang; r 250-480B; ✷) This is Mae Sariang's oldest hostelry. It has rooms in the old wooden wing or rooms with hot-water shower in the new wing.

Riverside Guest House (☎ 0 5368 1188; 85 Th Laeng Phanit; r 250-550B; ✷) This friendly, ramshackle guesthouse keeps growing and improving. Some rooms feel cramped but most share large terraces with great views of a turn in the river and the valley beyond.

Hotel de Kamonson (☎ 0 5368 1524; Th Mae Sariang; r 350-700B; ✷) Despite the pretentious quasi-French name, this multistorey hotel has clean rooms but zero character. Some rooms lack natural light, so look at a few before making a decision. Limited English (and even less French) is spoken.

Salawin Guest House (☎ 0 5368 1490; 2 Th Laeng Phanit; r 400-480B; 🐾 🖵) The beds are hard and the towels are thin, but the graciousness extended by the lovely older couple who run this place make it worth it. Rooms are clean with large hot-water bathrooms, there's internet and it's very conveniently located.

Hern Tai Resort (☎ 0 5368 9033; www.herntai.com; 420 Moo 1, Ban Mae La Noi; r 400-800B, bungalows 1000B) Set in the middle of scenic rice fields in Ban Mae La Noi, 25km north of Mae Sariang, this place combines a unique setting and attractive accommodation. There are large rooms in a wooden Shan-style building and two expansive bungalows. To get here, take the turn-off just after the viewpoint/coffee shop at the southern end of town.

our pick **Riverhouse Hotel** (☎ 0 5362 1201; www .riverhousehotels.com; 77 Th Laeng Phanit; r incl breakfast 1000-1300B; 🐾 🖵) The combination of nostalgia-inducing teak and stylish decor makes this riverside hotel the best spot in town. Air-conditioned 2nd-floor rooms have huge verandas overlooking the river, as well as floor-to-ceiling windows. Downstairs, fan rooms are also riverside and have hammocks outside and there's a good restaurant.

Located virtually next door, and run by the same people, **Riverhouse Resort** (☎ 0 5368 3066; www.riverhousehotels.com; Th Laeng Phanit; r incl breakfast 1800-2800B; 🐾 🖵) is similar but lacks its sister's charm. Ask for a river view room as the townside ones are the same price. Both places have good restaurants.

Eating & Drinking

Ban Rao (☎ 0 5368 1743; Th Laeng Phanit; dishes 30-140B; 🕒 5-10pm) For an authentic Thai dinner minus the spice, head to this homey riverside restaurant. The English-language menu touches on just about everything, from familiar curries to the more exotic *yam sôm oh*, a Thai-style salad of pomelo.

Inthira Restaurant (☎ 0 5368 1529; Th Wiang Mai; dishes 30-150B; 🕒 8am-10pm) Probably the town's best restaurant, this place features a strong menu of dishes using unique ingredients such as locally-grown shiitake mushrooms and fish from the Mae Nam Moei. Everything's tasty, the prices are low and the setting cosy and informal.

Kai Yang Rai Khwan (dishes 30-180B; 🕒 10am-5pm) Head here for the Isan trinity of grilled chicken, papaya salad and sticky rice. This simple place is at the foot of the bridge crossing.

Sawadee Restaurant & Bar (Th Laeng Phanit; dishes 40-150B; 🕒 8am-midnight) Like a beachside bar, this is a great place to recline with a beer and watch the water (in this case the Mae Nam Yuam). There's a lengthy menu with lots of options for vegetarians.

Coriander in Redwood (Th Laeng Phanit; dishes 40-180B; 🕒 noon-10pm) The city's poshest restaurant, this attractive wooden structure makes a big deal of its steaks, but we'd suggest sticking with Thai dishes such as the various *nám prík* (chili-based dips). There's also ice cream and iced coffee drinks for an afternoon cooler.

Getting There & Around

There are several *sŏrng·tǎa·ou* to Mae Sot (200B, six hours, seven departures from 6.30am to 12.30pm), departing from the bus station when full.

Located at the bus station, **Prempracha Tour** (☎ 0 5368 1347) conducts buses between Mae Sariang and Mae Hong Song (ordinary/aircon 100/180B, four hours, five departures from 7am to 5.30pm), with a stop midway in Khun Yuam (ordinary/air-con 70/110B, two hours). There are also buses to Chiang Mai (ordinary/air-con 100/180B, four hours, five departures from 7am to 3pm).

With an office just north of the bus station, **Sombat Tour** (☎ 0 5368 1532; Th Mae Sariang) handles buses to Bangkok (2nd-class air-con/1st-class 508/653B, 14 hours, four departures from 4pm to 7pm).

Motorcycles are available for rent at Sawadee Restaurant & Bar (p453) and Northwest Guest House (p452).

Destinations anywhere in town are 20B by motorcycle taxi.

AROUND MAE SARIANG
Salawin National Park & Mae Sam Laep
อุทยานแห่งชาติสาละวิน/แม่สามแลบ

This **national park** (☎ 0 5307 1429; admission 100B) covers 722 sq km of protected land in Mae Sariang and Sop Moei districts. The park is heavily forested in teak, Asian redwood and cherrywood, and is home to the second-largest teak tree in Thailand. There are numerous hiking trails, and it's also possible to travel by boat along the Mae Nam Salawin to the park's outstation at Tha Ta Fang. The main headquarters are 6km from Mae Sariang and have bungalow-style accommodation (300B to 1200B), which can be booked via the **Royal Forest Department** (☎ 0 2562 0760; www.dnp .go.th).

The riverside trading village of **Mae Sam Laep** is nearly at the end of a 50km winding mountain road from Mae Sariang, within the park boundaries. Populated by Burmese refugees, many of whom are Muslims, the town has a raw, border-town feel and is a launching point for boat trips along the Mae Nam Salawin. The trips pass through untouched jungle, unusual rock formations along the river and, occasionally, mount illegal forays into Myanmar.

From the pier at Mae Sam Laep it's possible to charter boats south to Huay Mae Ti (700B), the Karen village of Ban Pu Tha (1200B) and Sop Moei (1300B, two hours), 25km from Mae Sam Laep; and north to the Salawin National Park station at Tha Ta Fang (1200B, 1½ hours), 18km north of Mae Sam Laep, as well as Ban Mae Sakeup (2000B) and the Sop Ngae Wildlife Sanctuary (2500B). There are passenger boats as well, but departures are infrequent and, unless you speak Thai, difficult to negotiate.

There are frequent *sŏrng·tăa·ou* from Mae Sariang to Mae Sam Laep (70B, 10 departures from 6.30am to 5pm), departing from Th Laeng Phanit near the morning market.

Northeastern Thailand

For most travellers, and many Thais, the northeast is Thailand's forgotten backyard. Isan (*ee·sähn*), the collective name for the 19 provinces that make up the northeast, offers a glimpse of the Thailand of old: rice fields run to the horizon, water buffaloes wade in muddy ponds, silk weaving remains a cottage industry, pedal-rickshaw drivers pull passengers down city streets, and, even for those people who've had to seek work in the city, the village lifestyle prevails. This colossal corner of the country continues to live life on its own terms: slowly, steadily, and with a profound respect for heritage and history.

If you spend even just a little time here you'll start to find as many differences as similarities to the rest of the country. The language, food and culture are more Lao than Thai, with hearty helpings of Khmer and Vietnamese thrown into the melting pot.

And spend time here you should. If you have a penchant for authentic experiences, it will surely be satisfied: Angkor temple ruins pepper the region, superb national parks protect some of the wildest corners of the country, sleepy villages host some of Thailand's wildest celebrations and the scenery along parts of the Mekong is often nothing short of stunning. Thailand's tourist trail is at its bumpiest here (English is rarely spoken), but the fantastic attractions and daily interactions could just end up being highlights of your trip.

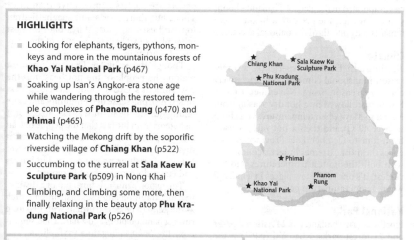

HIGHLIGHTS

- Looking for elephants, tigers, pythons, monkeys and more in the mountainous forests of **Khao Yai National Park** (p467)

- Soaking up Isan's Angkor-era stone age while wandering through the restored temple complexes of **Phanom Rung** (p470) and **Phimai** (p465)

- Watching the Mekong drift by the soporific riverside village of **Chiang Khan** (p522)

- Succumbing to the surreal at **Sala Kaew Ku Sculpture Park** (p509) in Nong Khai

- Climbing, and climbing some more, then finally relaxing in the beauty atop **Phu Kradung National Park** (p526)

★ Chiang Khan   ★ Sala Kaew Ku Sculpture Park
★ Phu Kradung National Park

★ Phimai

★ Khao Yai National Park   ★ Phanom Rung

- BEST TIME TO VISIT: NOVEMBER–FEBRUARY
- POPULATION: 22 MILLION

History

The social history of this enigmatic region stretches back at least 4000 years, to the hazy days when the ancient Ban Chiang culture started tilling the fields with bronze tools.

Thais employ the term *ee·săhn* (Isan) to classify the region *(pâhk ee·săhn)*, the people *(kon ee·săhn)* and food *(ah hăhn ee·săhn)* of northeastern Thailand. The name comes from Isana, the Sanskrit name for the early Mon-Khmer kingdom that flourished in what's now northeastern Thailand and Cambodia. After the 9th century, the Khmer empire held sway over these parts and erected many of the fabulous temple complexes that pepper the region today.

Until the arrival of Europeans, Isan remained largely autonomous from the early Thai kingdoms. But as the French staked out the borders of colonial Laos, Thailand was forced to define its own northeastern boundaries. Slowly, but surely, Isan fell under the mantle of broader Thailand.

Long Thailand's poorest area, the northeast soon became a hotbed of communist activity. Ho Chi Minh spent 1928 to 1929 proselytising in the area, and in the 1940s a number of Indochinese Communist Party leaders fled to Isan from Laos and helped bolster Thailand's Communist Party. From the 1960s until an amnesty in 1982, guerrilla activity was rife in Isan, especially in the provinces of Buriram, Loei, Ubon Ratchathani, Nakhon Phanom and Sakon Nakhon. But growing urbanisation drew many peasants to the cities and the various insurgencies evaporated in the glare of Thailand's boom years. However, the per capita income here remains only one-third the national average.

Climate

Northeastern Thailand experiences a three-season monsoonal climate, with a relatively cool dry season from November to late February, followed by a hot dry season from March to May (when temperatures can climb to over 40°C) and then a hot rainy season from June to October. Loei Province experiences the most extreme climactic conditions, with both the hottest temperatures and the coldest; it's one of the few places in Thailand where temperatures dip below zero.

National Parks

Northeastern Thailand has 24 national parks and 21 forest parks. Khao Yai (p467) is the most impressive, covering much of the largest intact monsoon forest in mainland Asia. Other highlights include Phu Kradung (p526), for its wildlife watching and high-altitude hiking; Phu Chong Nayoi (p489), one of Thailand's remotest corners; and Phu Wiang (p500), a must for dinosaur lovers.

Language & Culture

Isan language and culture are melting pots of Thai, Lao and Khmer influences. The Khmers left behind Angkor Wat–like monuments across much of the region, particularly in Buriram, Surin and Si Saket Provinces, while Lao-style temples (most notably Wat Phra That Phanom) are as common as Thai designs. The Isan language, still a more common first language than Thai, is very similar to Lao. In fact, there are probably more people of Lao heritage in Isan than in all of Laos. Many villages in the far south still maintain Khmer as their primary tongue.

The people of Isan are known by other Thais for their friendliness, work ethic and sense of humour: flip through radio stations and you'll surely hear DJs laughing at their own jokes. Respect and hospitality towards guests is a cornerstone of Isan life and most villagers, plus plenty of city folk, still pride themselves on taking care of others before themselves. The best food is usually reserved for monks and guests, and if you get invited to a village home your hosts will almost certainly kill one of their chickens to feed you (vegetarians should speak up early). Isan people are far less conservative than most Thais, but short shorts and spaghetti-strap tops will earn far more stares than in most other places in Thailand because of the scarcity of tourists here.

Though this is by far Thailand's poorest region, the people of the northeast top the government's Gross Domestic Happiness Index. A strong sense of community and close family ties are the main reasons cited, but it also stems from the fact that the people of Isan seek happiness from the inside, not from what they own. In the villages you can almost never tell who is rich or poor, because big homes and fancy clothes garner little respect.

The region's music is born out of a distinctive folk tradition and uses instruments such as the *kaan* (a reed instrument with two long rows of bamboo pipes and a hardwood soundbox), the *bohng·lahng* (like a xylophone) and the *pin* (a small three-stringed lute played

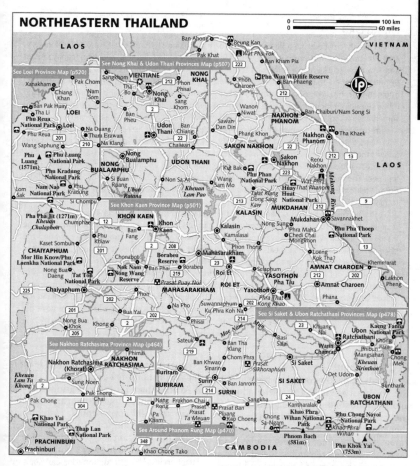

NORTHEASTERN THAILAND

with a large plectrum). The most popular song form is the *lôok tûng* (literally, children of the fields), which is far more rhythmic than the classical styles of central Thailand.

Thailand's best silk comes from the northeast, particularly from Khon Kaen, Surin, Chaiyaphum and Nakhon Ratchasima. Cotton fabrics from Loei, Nakhon Phanom and Udon Thani are also highly regarded. The defining style uses *mát·mèe* methods (see boxed text, p493) in which threads are tie-dyed before weaving. Most large stores stock some fabrics naturally dyed using plant materials, an old process being revived across Isan. Prices for fabrics can be 20% to 30% cheaper (maybe 50% for less-common fabric styles) in the weaving villages than in Bangkok

shops. Another handicraft speciality of the northeast is *mŏrn kwăhn* (literally, axe pillow), a stiff triangle-shaped pillow used as an arm support while sitting on the floor. Sticky-rice baskets also make good souvenirs.

Getting There & Away

The main train and bus lines in the northeast run between Bangkok and Nong Khai, and between Bangkok and Ubon Ratchathani, though buses link even small towns directly to Bangkok at least once a day. The northeast can also be reached from northern Thailand by bus through Phitsanulok, with Khon Kaen as the gateway. Several cities are also connected to Bangkok by air, though the number of flights is limited.

EATING ISAN

Isan's culinary creations are a blend of Lao and Thai cooking styles that make use of local ingredients. The holy trinity of northeastern cuisine – *gài yâhng* (grilled chicken), *sôm·đam* (papaya salad) and *kôw nĕe·o* (sticky rice) – is integral to the culture. Also essential are chillies, as well as a fistful of potent peppers that find their way into most dishes, especially *lâhp* (a super spicy meat salad originating from Laos). *Gaang aòrm* has little in common with typical Thai curries as it uses *b̃lah ráh* (a popular fermented fish sauce that looks like rotten mud) instead of coconut and sugar. It is sometimes served with glass noodles, but even then it is still meant to be eaten with rice.

Fish dominates Isan menus with *b̃lah dùk* (catfish), *b̃lah chôrn* (striped snake-head) and *b̃lah boo* (sand goby) among the most popular options. These are mostly caught in the Mekong and a few other large rivers. Fish that families catch themselves are usually small (sometimes so tiny they're eaten bones and all) because they come from streams and rice paddies, as do crabs, frogs and eels. The most famous fish associated with the northeast is *b̃lah bèuk* (giant Mekong catfish), but it's seldom eaten here because it's expensive. Fish farming, however, is slowly bringing it back to menus.

To both Westerners and other Thais, nothing stands out in Isan cuisine like insects. Even as recently as the 1970s insects composed a large part of the typical family's diet, though it became a fading tradition when the government promoted chicken and pig farming, thus lowering the prices of these now popular meats. While the younger generation doesn't eat bugs all that often anymore, insects are still very common as snacks and chilli-sauce ingredients. You might see purple lights shining out in the countryside; these are for catching giant water bugs, which, along with crickets, grasshoppers, cicadas, *nŏrn mái pài* (bamboo worms) and more, are sold in most night markets. In fact, there's still enough of a demand that imports come from Cambodia. Thailand has no shortage of silkworm larvae, which, after they're popped into the boiling water to remove the silk threads from the cocoon, are popped into the mouth for a literal taste explosion – try one when you visit a weaving village and you'll see what we mean.

Getting Around

If you have time on your side, travelling in the northeast is rarely a problem: all large and medium-sized towns are linked to even the smallest villages by public transport, though in the remotest corners it may only run a couple of times a day. If you're short on time, however, remember that distances are large in this part of Thailand and buses are often slow. Consequently, if you plan to visit remote sites, a hire car or motorcycle will save a great many headaches while also letting you get a closer look at the region.

NAKHON RATCHASIMA PROVINCE

Most visitors to Khorat, the original and still most commonly used name for Thailand's largest province, are here to jump into the jungle at Khao Yai, Thailand's oldest national park and newest World Heritage Site. Its large size and healthy ecosystems make it one of the best wildlife-watching sites in Southeast Asia and one of the most rewarding destinations in Thailand.

While Khao Yai is the soaring pinnacle of the province's tourist industry, silk and stone are solid cornerstones. Fashionistas should hit the shops in Pak Thong Chai, home of the region's silk-weaving industry and a town known for staying on top of the latest styles. History aficionados can soak up the stone remains of the region's Angkor-period heyday. Khmer temples still pepper the province and, while most have been reduced to amorphous piles of rubble, the restored complex of Prasat Phimai provides an evocative glimpse of times past.

Khorat city offers little as a destination, but with a solid selection of hotels and the northeast's biggest and broadest dining scene, it makes a good base during your Isan sojourn.

NAKHON RATCHASIMA (KHORAT)

นครราชสีมา(โคราช)

pop 215,000

Khorat city doesn't wear its heart on its sleeve. Only those sporting a hefty set of rose-tinted specs will be reaching for their camera as they step off the bus in the brash gateway to the northeast. A bumper dose of urban hubbub reflects the city's growing affluence, and Khorat's onetime historic charm has been largely smothered under a duvet of homogenous development.

Khorat is a city that grows on you. Distinctly Isan, with a strong sense of regional identity, this busy centre is at its best in its quieter nooks (inside the east side of the historic moat, for example), where Thai life, largely untouched by the country's booming tourist industry, goes on in its own uncompromising way.

Information

EMERGENCY & MEDICAL SERVICES
Bangkok Hospital (☎ 0 4426 2000; Th Mittaphap)
Tourist police (☎ 0 4434 1777; Th Chang Pheuak) Opposite Bus Terminal 2.

INTERNET ACCESS
Walk two or three blocks and you're bound to pass an internet cafe. **Net Guru** (Th Phoklang; per hr 15B; 🕑 8.30am-midnight) has longer hours than most.

MONEY
Bangkok Bank (Th Jomsurangyat; 🕑 10am-8pm) At Klang Plaza 2 shopping centre. Changes cash only.
Siam Commercial Bank (Th Mittaphap; 🕑 10.30am-8pm) Located on the 2nd floor of the Mall. It changes travellers cheques.

POST
Post office (Th Jomsurangyat; 🕑 8.30am-4.30pm Mon-Fri, to noon Sat & holidays) Has a stamp museum.

TOURIST INFORMATION
Tourism Authority of Thailand (TAT; ☎ 0 4421 3666; 2102-2104 Th Mittaphap; 🕑 8.30am-4.30pm) Covers Khorat and Chaiyaphum Provinces.

Sights & Activities

MAHA WIRAWONG NATIONAL MUSEUM
พิพิธภัณฑสถานแห่งชาติมหาวีรวงศ์
Despite an interesting collection of Khmer and Ayuthaya-period artefacts, including stone and bronze Buddhas, woodcarvings from an ancient temple and various domestic utensils, chances are you'll have this interesting little **museum** (☎ 0 4424 2958; Th Ratchadamnoen; admission 50B; 🕑 9am-4.30pm Wed-Sun) to yourself. It's hidden away in the grounds of Wat Sutthachinda.

THAO SURANARI MEMORIAL
อนุสาวรีย์ท้าวสุรนารี
Thao Suranari is something of a Wonder Woman in these parts. As the wife of the city's assistant governor, she rose to notoriety in 1826, during the reign of Rama III, when she led a ragtag army of locals to victory against the ravaging Vientiane forces of Chao Anuwong. Some scholars suggest the legend was concocted to instil a sense of Thai-ness in the ethnic-Lao people of the province, but locals and visiting Thais still flock to her shrine on Th Ratchadamnoen in adoring droves; she is also known as Ya Mo (Grandma Mo). People burn incense and leave offerings of flowers and food; those whose supplications have been honoured hire troupes to perform *pleng koh·râht* (the traditional Khorat folk song) on a stage across the street.

Just north of her shrine, in the little white building, is a sort of **Thao Suranari museum** (Th Chumphon; admission free; 🕑 9am-6pm Tue-Sun), which has a cool diorama and even cooler sculpted mural of the famous battle.

OTHER SIGHTS & ACTIVITIES
Smack behind the Thao Suranari memorial is a small section of the city wall, including the **Chumphon Gate**, which is the only old gate left standing (the other three are recent rebuilds). It was erected in 1656, by French technicians, on the orders of Ayuthaya King Narai.

When the abbot of **Wat Pa-Yap** (Th Phonsaen; 🕑 8am-6pm) learned that blasting for a quarry in Saraburi Province was destroying a beautiful cave, he rescued pieces of it and plastered the stalactites, stalagmites and other incredible rocks all over a room below his residence, creating a shrine like no other.

Thao Suranari and her husband founded **Wat Salaloi** (Th Thao Sura, Soi 1; 🕑 daylight hr) in 1827. Her ashes were interred here after her death and many people hire singers to

---

WHAT TO EXPECT IN NORTHEASTERN THAILAND

There are few guesthouses in the northeast, so most budget rooms are in Chinese-style concrete-box hotels, and many of these properties mix both older budget rooms and dowdy but decent midrange options. When available, top-end properties usually offer excellent value.

NORTHEASTERN THAILAND

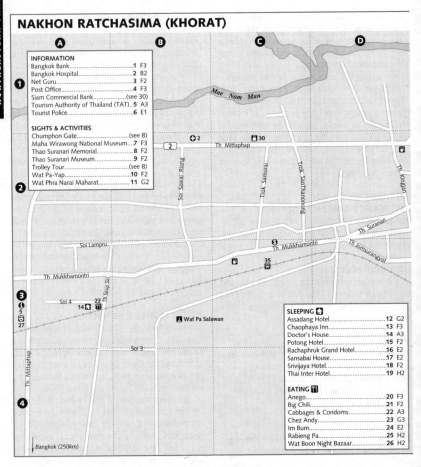

NAKHON RATCHASIMA (KHORAT)

INFORMATION
Bangkok Bank	1 F3
Bangkok Hospital	2 B2
Net Guru	3 F2
Post Office	4 F3
Siam Commercial Bank	(see 30)
Tourism Authority of Thailand (TAT)	5 A3
Tourist Police	6 E1

SIGHTS & ACTIVITIES
Chumphon Gate	(see 8)
Maha Wirawong National Museum	7 F3
Thao Suranari Memorial	8 F2
Thao Suranari Museum	9 F2
Trolley Tour	(see 8)
Wat Pa-Yap	10 F2
Wat Phra Narai Maharat	11 G2

SLEEPING
Assadang Hotel	12 G2
Chaophaya Inn	13 F3
Doctor's House	14 A3
Potong Hotel	15 F2
Rachaphruk Grand Hotel	16 E2
Sansabai House	17 E2
Srivijaya Hotel	18 F2
Thai Inter Hotel	19 H2

EATING
Anego	20 F3
Big Chili	21 F2
Cabbages & Condoms	22 A3
Chez Andy	23 G3
Im Bum	24 E2
Rabieng Pa	25 H2
Wat Boon Night Bazaar	26 H2

Bangkok (250km)

---

perform here for her spirit. The award-winning *bòht*, built in 1967, resembles a Chinese junk and, along with several other buildings, is decorated with Dan Kwian pottery (see p463). A small statue of the heroine sits praying in the pond in front of the *bòht*.

Wat Salaloi and Wat Pa-Yap are both stops on the 90-minute **trolley tour** (per person 20B; 9am-4.30pm) that runs around the moat. It departs from the Thao Suranari Memorial after 10 tickets have been sold.

Wat Phra Narai Maharat (Th Chomphon; 8am-8pm) is of interest because of the very holy Khmer sandstone sculpture of Phra Narai (Vishnu) that was unearthed on the temple grounds. Follow the signs with red arrows back to the southeast corner till you hear Indian music.

Festivals

Khorat explodes into life during the **Thao Suranari Festival**, when the city celebrates Thao Suranari's victory over the Lao (see p459). It's held annually from 23 March to 3 April and features parades, theatre and folk song.

Sleeping
BUDGET

Potong Hotel (☎ 0 4425 1962; 652 Th Ratchadamnoen; s 190B, d 240-350B;) Potong trades the Doctor's House's homey vibe for an unbeatable location. These are some of the cheapest rooms in the city, with good reason. They make the pass list, but just barely.

Doctor's House (☎ 08 5632 3396; 78 Soi 4, Th Seup Siri; r 200-350B;) The only lodging in town where

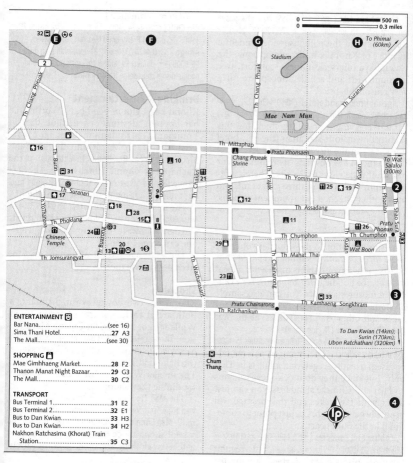

guests bearing rucksacks are the norm, this homestay has seven simple but clean rooms with shared bathrooms in an old wooden house. There are plenty of bars and restaurants out here, but with a 10pm lockup you won't get to explore many of them. Bikes (50B) and motorcycles (200B) are available for hire.

ourpick Sansabai House (☎ 0 4425 5144; 335 Th Suranari; r 270-500B; ❄) Walk into the welcoming lobby and you half expect the posted prices to be a bait-and-switch ploy. But no, all rooms are bright and spotless and come with good mattresses, mini-fridges and little balconies.

Srivijaya Hotel (☎ 0 4424 2194; 9-11 Th Buarong; r 400-500B; ❄ 🖥) The Srivijaya is far too ordinary to justify the 'boutique hotel' label it's given

itself. Nevertheless, the comfy, spic-and-span rooms guarantee a good night's sleep.

Assadang Hotel (☎ 0 4424 2514; 315 Th Assadang; r 400-500B; ❄) There's no escaping the fact that this is just an old concrete box with small rooms, but a two-toned paint job and various little decorations (not to mention the little dumbwaiter for your luggage) make for a nice change from the usual. The owner is very friendly.

MIDRANGE & TOP END

Thai Inter Hotel (☎ 0 4424 7700; www.thaiinterhotel .com; 344/2 Th Yommarat; r 550-650B; ❄ 🖥) This little hotel opened in 2008. It tries to be hip, and it pretty much pulls it off – patching together an odd mix of styles. It's got a convenient location near many good restaurants and bars.

Chaophaya Inn (☎ 0 4426 0555; www.chaophaya inn.com; 62/1 Th Jomsurangyat; r 500-1000B; ✷ ▯) Rising beyond the jailhouse vibes endemic in most of Khorat's midrange options, the Chaophaya offers cleanliness, comfort, free in-room wi-fi and a little atmosphere for a very reasonable price.

Rachaphruk Grand Hotel (☎ 0 4426 1222; www .rachaphruk.com; Th Mittaphap; r 1200-1500B; ✷ ▯ ▯) 'Grand' is laying it on a little thick, but this slightly dowdy four-star affair (the only hotel in its class in the city centre) is a decent bet if you fancy a few business-style comforts, or just want wide views of the city. There's a fitness centre with a sauna, three restaurants and many other attached entertainment options. Plus, the staff dress like cowboys.

Eating

One speciality not to miss during your stay is *pàt mèe koh·râht*. It's similar to *pát tai*, but boasts more flavour and is made with a local style of rice noodle (*mèe koh·râht*). It's available at most restaurants. You can also sample it, along with deep-fried crickets, pork sausages and other Isan specialities, at the **Wat Boon Night Bazaar** (Th Chomphon).

Im Bum (☎ 08 1725 6008; Th Buarong; dishes 25-130B; ✻ breakfast & lunch) The menu at this wood-encased, friendly, vegetarian affair is in Thai only. But since they do mock-meat versions of Thai and Chinese standards, you can just order your favourites and the message will probably get through. Or, just point to something in the buffet cart.

Cabbages & Condoms (☎ 0 4425 3760; 86/1 Th Seup Siri; dishes 35-200B; ✻ lunch & dinner) This regular favourite offers a leafy terrace, a wine list (something of a rarity in this part of Thailand) and plenty of newspaper clippings celebrating the work of the nonprofit Population & Community Development Association, towards which all proceeds go.

ourpick Rabieng-Pa (☎ 0 4424 3137; 284 Th Yommarat; dishes 45-220B; ✻ dinner) The leafiest and loveliest restaurant on this stretch of Th Yommarat (and arguably all of Khorat) is also one of the most low key. The picture menu makes ordering the tasty Thai food risk free.

Chez Andy (☎ 0 4428 9556; Th Manat; dishes 80-1250B; ✻ lunch & dinner Mon-Sat) Khorat's archetypal expat haunt, this Swiss-managed place (appropriately housed in a red-and-white villa set back off the road) has a global menu with fondue, steak and fried rice available.

Also recommended:

Big Chili (☎ 0 4424 7469; 158/8 Th Chakkri; dishes 70-350B; ✻ dinner) Pretty good Mexican, for Thailand.

Anego (☎ 0 4426 0530; 62/1 Th Jomsurangyat; dishes 50-600B; ✻ dinner) For authentic Japanese sushi and noodle dishes, plus some Italian pastas.

Drinking & Entertainment

Khorat has a glut of good bars. Worthwhile bar-hopping destinations include the Th Yommarat/Th Kudan junction, Th Mahat Thai east of Th Manat and the Th Seup Siri/Soi 3 area. **Bar Nana** (Th Mittaphap) at the Rachaphruk Grand Hotel has the hottest dance floor downtown – it closes at 2am and isn't really hopping until close to midnight.

The top-tier **Sima Thani Hotel** (☎ 0 4421 3100; Th Mittaphap) often hosts *ʼbohng·lahng* Isan music and dance shows for tour groups, though anyone can come to watch.

The Mall has a mini-waterpark and the city's best movie theatre.

Shopping

Khorat has two downtown night markets. Both are at their best from 6pm to 10pm. While it's got nothing on Chiang Mai's version, **Thanon Manat Night Bazaar** (Th Manat) is fun to stroll. It's mostly clothes and accessories (no handicrafts) and draws a youthful crowd. The smaller Wat Boon Night Bazaar is better for dining than shopping.

The **Mall** (Th Mittaphap; ✻ 10.30am-9.30pm Mon-Fri, from 10am Sat & Sun) is Isan's largest and glossiest mall. **Mae Gimhhaeng Market** (Th Suranari) is an old school shopping centre full of food vendors with a few clothing and other stalls for variety.

Getting There & Away

BUS

Khorat has two bus terminals. **Terminal 1** (☎ 0 4424 2899; Th Burin) in the city centre serves Bangkok and towns within the province. Buses to other destinations, plus more for Bangkok, use **Terminal 2** (☎ 0 4425 6006) off Hwy 2.

You never have to wait long for a bus to Bangkok (ordinary/2nd class/1st class/VIP 75/154/189/198B, three hours) since buses from most cities in Isan pass through Khorat on their way to the capital.

TRAIN

Eleven daily trains leave Khorat **train station** (☎ 0 4424 2044) for Bangkok (3rd/2nd/1st class 50/115/230B) taking four to six hours –

in other words, much longer than the bus. There are also seven trains (3rd/2nd class air-con 58/423B, four to six hours) to/from Ubon Ratchathani.

Getting Around

There are fixed *sŏrng·tăa·ou* (small pick-up trucks used as buses/taxis; also spelt as *săwngthăew*) routes through the city, but even locals complain about how difficult it is to figure them out because of the dizzying array of numbers and colours representing the many destinations. Most pass down Th Suranari near Mae Gimhhaeng Market, so if you want to go somewhere just head there and ask around; someone will put you on the right one. The pink-and-white *sŏrng·tăa·ou* 17 is the best of several that will take you from downtown to Bus Terminal 2 *(bor kŏr sŏr sŏrng)*. The white *sŏrng·tăa·ou* 1 with green and yellow stripes will take you near Doctor's House (nobody knows this place, so ask for *tà nŏn sèup sì rì*) and the yellow *sŏrng·tăa·ou* 1 with white and green stripes goes to the tourism office.

Túk-túk (pronounced '*dúk dúk*') and motorcycle taxis cost between 30B and 70B to most places around town, and there are metered taxis waiting for passengers at Bus Terminal 2. Several shops on the eastern half of Th Suranari near Bus Terminal 1 rent out motorcycles.

AROUND NAKHON RATCHASIMA

Dan Kwian

ด่านเกวียน

Even if you think you have no interest in ceramics, you should pay Dan Kwian a visit. Just a quick trip out of Khorat, this village has been producing pottery for hundreds of years and its creations are famous for their rough texture and rust-like hue. Only kaolin sourced from this district produces such results. Myriad shops line the highway and some are as much art gallery as shop. It's not all pots, though. Clay is fired into all kinds of objects, from jewellery and wind chimes to reproductions of ancient Khmer sandstone sculpture.

Originally the village was a bullock-cart stop for traders on their way to markets in old Khorat (*dàhn gwee an* means 'bullock-cart checkpoint'). The ramshackle private **Kwian Museum** (☎ 08 7877 0680; admission 50B; ☼ 8am-5pm), at the north end of the strip, displays a vari-

BUSES TO/FROM KHORAT			
Destination	Class	Fare (B)	Duration (hr)
Chaiyaphum	ordinary	56	2
	2nd	78	
	1st	101	
Chiang Mai	1st	560	13
	VIP	653	
Khon Kaen	2nd	129	3
	1st	187	
Loei	2nd	260	6
	1st	321	
Nang Rong	2nd	70	2
	1st	85	
Nong Khai	2nd	225	6
	1st	270	
Pattaya	1st	290	5
	VIP	310-410	
Surin	2nd	120	4
	1st	178	
Ubon Ratchathani	2nd	203	7
	1st	269	

ety of old carts from around Isan, as well as some farming implements and examples of old-style pottery.

To get here from Khorat, hop on a bus (14B, 30 minutes) from near the south city gate, the east gate or Terminal 2.

Ban Prasat

บ้านปราสาท

About 3000 years ago, a primitive agricultural/ceramic culture put down roots at Ban Prasat, near the banks of Mae Nam Than Prasat. It survived for nearly 500 years, planting rice, domesticating animals, fashioning coloured pottery, weaving cloth and, in later years, forging tools out of bronze. The secrets of this early civilisation were finally revealed during extensive archaeological digs completed in 1991. Three of the **excavation pits** (admission free; ☼ 24hr), with skeletons and pottery left *in situ*, are on display in the village. A small **museum** (admission free; ☼ 8am-4.30pm Wed-Sun) houses some of the more interesting discoveries and explains what life was like in those days.

Many families are part of an award-winning **homestay** (☎ 08 1725 0791; per person incl 2 meals 400B) program where villagers put up visitors in their homes and show them daily activities

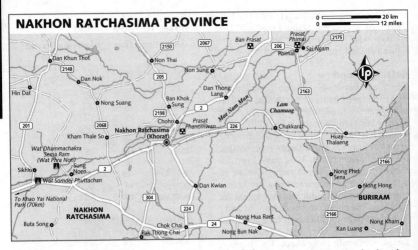

NORTHEASTERN THAILAND

like basketry and farming. Reservations should be made at least a day in advance.

GETTING THERE & AWAY

Ban Prasat is 45km northeast of Khorat, off Hwy 2, and buses (ordinary/2nd class 28/35B, 45 minutes) heading to Phimai will drop you off. Motorcycle taxis waiting at the highway will zip you around to all the sites, including a bit of sightseeing time, for 50B.

Sandstone Reclining Buddha Image

พระพุทธไสยาสน์หินทราย

Housed inside **Wat Dhammachakra Sema Ram** (☼ daylight hr), which locals call Wat Phra Non (Sleeping Buddha Temple), is Thailand's oldest reclining Buddha. Dating back to the 7th or 8th century BC, the 13.3m-long Dvaravati-style image is unique in that it hasn't been covered with a layer of stucco and a coat of whitewash. It actually looks as old as it is. The crude but appealing image is protected from the elements by a huge roof. On display nearby is a stone rendition of the Buddhist Wheel of Law that is thought to pre-date the Buddha image.

The temple is 40km southwest of Khorat in Sung Noen, on the railway line to Bangkok (although only three local trains stop here). From Khorat the train costs 6B, and takes 40 minutes. It can also be reached by bus (21B, 30 minutes) from either terminal in Khorat. From Sung Noen you'll have to hire a motorcycle taxi for the final 4.5km to the wát. Expect to pay about 100B for the return trip.

The large Mueang Sema Historical Site, which you pass on the way to the reclining Buddha, has just a few foundations and the remains of a moat. It's only really of interest to archaeologists and picnickers.

Pak Thong Chai

ปักธงชัย

Amphoe Pak Thong Chai became one of Thailand's most famous silk-weaving centres when Jim Thompson started buying silk here (for more on Thompson, see p136). Today there are around 10 mechanised silk factories in the district and thousands of families still work hand-looms at home in every village in the district. Pak Thong Chai is known for turning out new fashions, but some shops stock traditional styles, like *mát·mèe*, from other provinces.

Because Pak Thong Chai is a fairly large town, it's not nearly as fun a place to visit as other Isan silk centres like Chonabot (p499) or Ban Tha Sawang (p476), but **Macchada** (☎ 0 4444 1684; ☼ 8am-5pm), at the southern end of the main road through town, where you can watch weavers working, is worth seeking out if you do come here. There are large highway signs directing you to the Silk Cultural Centre, but it's been closed for years.

Pak Thong Chai is 30km south of Khorat on Rte 304. Buses (23B, 40 minutes) leave from Terminal 1 every half-hour.

Phimai
พิมาย

The otherwise mundane little town of Phimai has one of Thailand's finest surviving Khmer temple complexes right at its heart. Reminiscent of Cambodia's Angkor Wat, Prasat Phimai once stood on an important trade route linking the Khmer capital of Angkor with the northern reaches of the realm. Peppered with ruins and surrounded by ragged sections of the ancient town wall, modern-day Phimai still offers a little taste of that historic heyday.

There's almost nothing to do here once you've wandered the ruins, but if you prefer the quiet life you'll probably enjoy a night or two here. However, those with discerning tastes will probably want to daytrip it out of Khorat.

SIGHTS

Phimai Historical Park
อุทยานประวัติศาสตร์พิมาย

Started by Khmer King Jayavarman V (AD 968–1001) during the late 10th century and finished by King Suriyavarman I (AD 1002–49) in the early 11th century, this Hindu-Mahayana Buddhist temple projects a majesty that transcends its size. Although pre-dating Angkor Wat by a century or so, **Prasat Phimai** (☎ 0 4447 1568; Th Anantajinda; admission 100B; ⏰ 7.30am-6pm) nevertheless shares a number of design features with its more famous cousin, not least the roof of its 28m-tall main shrine. However, unlike most Khmer temples, this one faces south. It may well be wishful thinking, but tourist brochures

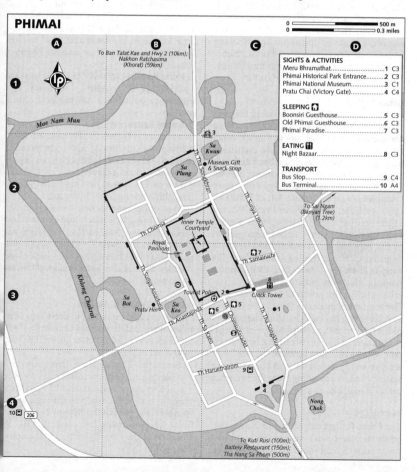

PHIMAI

0 —————— 500 m
0 —————— 0.3 miles

SIGHTS & ACTIVITIES	
Meru Bhramathat.................................1	C3
Phimai Historical Park Entrance.........2	C3
Phimai National Museum.....................3	C1
Pratu Chai (Victory Gate)...................4	C4

SLEEPING 🏠	
Boonsiri Guesthouse............................5	C3
Old Phimai Guesthouse........................6	C3
Phimai Paradise..................................7	C3

EATING 🍴	
Night Bazaar.......................................8	C3

TRANSPORT	
Bus Stop...9	C4
Bus Terminal.....................................10	A4

To Ban Talat Kae and Hwy 2 (10km);
Nakhon Ratchasima (Khorat) (59km)

Mae Nam Mun

Sa Kwan
Sa Plung
Museum Gift & Snack Shop
Th Tha Songkhran
Th Chomsa
Inner Temple Courtyard
Royal Pavilions
Th Suriya Asadon
Th Suriya Uthai
Th Samairuchi
Tourist Police
Clock Tower
Khlong Chakrai
Sa Bot
Pratu Hin
Sa Keo
Th Anantajinda
Th Sa Keo
Th Chomsudasat
Th Tha Songkhran
To Sai Ngam (Banyan Tree) (1.2km)

Th Haruethalrom

Nong Chok

To Kuti Rusi (100m);
Baitey Restaurant (150m);
Tha Nang Sa Phom (500m)

claim it might have been the model for Angkor Wat.

Unlike so many of northeastern Thailand's Khmer temples, Prasat Phimai has been elegantly reconstructed by the Fine Arts Department and is one of the most complete monuments on the circuit. A free brochure provides a good overview of the complex, and English-speaking guides offer free (tips expected) tours.

Phimai National Museum
พิพิธภัณฑสถานแห่งชาติพิมาย
Situated on the banks of Sa Kwan, a 12th-century Khmer reservoir, this **museum** (☎ 0 4447 1167; Th Tha Songkhran; admission 100B; 9am-4pm Wed-Sun) houses a fine collection of Khmer sculptures from Phimai, Phanom Rung and other ruins, as well as ceramics from nearby Ban Prasat. The museum's most prized possession, a stone sculpture of Angkor King Jayavarman VII, comes from Prasat Phimai and looks very much like a sitting Buddha. There are also displays on Isan culture.

Other Sights
A number of very minor historic features (all free) sit in and around Phimai. **Meru Bhramathat** (Th Tha Songkhran) is a brick *chedi* (stupa) dating back to the late Ayuthaya period. Its name is derived from a folk tale that refers to it as the cremation site of King Bhramathat. Most of the city walls have crumbled away, but what's left of **Pratu Chai** (Victory Gate), which faces Prasat Phimai at the southern end of the city, is a good indication of how they once looked. South of the gate you can see **Kuti Rusi** (Hermit's Quarters), once a healing station, and **Tha Nang Sa Phom** (daylight hr), a 13th-century landing platform constructed out of laterite now on the grounds of the Fine Arts Department compound.

A bit east of town is Thailand's largest and oldest banyan tree, a 350-plus-year-old megaflorum spread over an island in a large reservoir. The locals call it **Sai Ngam** (Beautiful Banyan; admission free; daylight hr), and the extensive system of roots cascading from the branches makes it look like a small forest.

FESTIVALS
The **Phimai Festival**, staged in mid-November, celebrates the town's history, with cultural performances, light shows and longboat races.

A smaller version of the light show is held on the last Saturday of the month from October to April.

SLEEPING & EATING
Old Phimai Guesthouse (☎ 0 4447 1918; www.phimai gh.com; 214/14 Th Chomsudasadet; dm 90B, s 150-350B, d 180-450B;   ) The backpacker vibe prevails in this historic wooden house tucked away down a quiet soi. The friendly hosts are a great source of information about Phimai and also run reasonably priced day trips to Phanom Rung.

Boonsiri Guesthouse (☎ 08 9424 9942; www.boonsiri .net; 228 Th Chomsudasadet; dm 150B, r 400-500B;   ) From the front there doesn't seem to be a whole lot to this hotel, but there are plenty of good-for-the-price rooms behind the scenes. Standards are high (the dorms have lockers) and the rooms are big and airy. There's a nice little lounge in the back and wi-fi reaches some of the rooms. They also do Phanom Rung excursions.

Phimai Paradise (☎ 0 4428 7565; 100/2 Th Samairuchi; r 400-500B;   ) Nothing too fancy, but this newly built block has the best rooms in town.

Baiteiy Restaurant (☎ 0 4428 7103; Th Phimai-Chumpuang; dishes 45-200B; breakfast, lunch & dinner) Appropriately decorated with some pseudo-Khmer carvings, this pleasant outdoor eatery, about 500m south of Pratu Chai (Victory Gate), does a decent spread of Thai-Isan-Chinese fare, plus a few international staples.

Most of the vendors next to Sai Ngam are open for breakfast, lunch and dinner, and serve Thai and Isan basics, including *pàt phimai*, which is basically similar to *pàt mèe koh râht* (p462) but always uses handmade noodles. Phimai also has a small **night bazaar** (Th Anantajinda; 4-10pm).

GETTING THERE & AWAY
Phimai has a bus station, but there's no need to use it since all buses pass near Pratu Chai, the clock tower and the museum on their way in and out of town.

Buses for Phimai leave from Khorat's Bus Terminal 2 (ordinary/2nd class 45/50B, 1¼ hours) every half-hour until 7pm. Few buses to northern cities pass through town, so it's easiest to take the Khorat bus to Ban Talat Kae (ordinary/2nd class 10/13B, 15 minutes) at the Hwy 2 junction and catch a connection there.

GETTING AROUND

Phimai is small enough to stroll, but to see more of the town and its environs (eg Sai Ngam) you can hire bicycles from Old Phimai (20/80B per hour/day) and Boonsiri (20/100B per hour/day) guesthouses.

KHAO YAI NATIONAL PARK

อุทยานแห่งชาติเขาใหญ่

Up there on the podium with some of the world's greatest parks, **Khao Yai** (☎ 08 1877 3127; admission 400B) is Thailand's oldest and most visited reserve. Covering 2168 sq km, Khao Yai incorporates one of the largest intact monsoon forests remaining in mainland Asia, which is why it was named a Unesco World Heritage Site (as part of the Dong Phayayen–Khao Yai Forest Complex). The mostly English-speaking staff at the **visitor centre** (☯ 8am-8pm) are very friendly and helpful.

Rising to 1351m at the summit of Khao Rom, the park's terrain covers five vegetation zones: evergreen rainforest (100m to 400m); semi-evergreen rainforest (400m to 900m); mixed deciduous forest (northern slopes at 400m to 600m); hill evergreen forest (over 1000m); and savannah and secondary-growth forest in areas where agriculture and logging occurred before it was protected. Many orchids bloom from the middle of June through the end of July (one of the few benefits of rainy-season visits).

Some 300 elephants tramp the park's boundaries. Other mammals recorded include barking deer, gaur, bears, tigers, leopards, otters, various gibbons and macaques and some rather large pythons. Khao Yai also has one of Thailand's largest populations of hornbills, including the great hornbill (*nók gòk* or *nók gah·hang*), king of the bird kingdom, as well as the wreathed hornbill (*nók grahm cháhng*; literally, 'elephant-jaw bird'), Indian pied hornbill (*nók kàak*) and brown hornbill (*nók ngêuak sěe nám đahn*). Over 200 bird species make the park their home, with some 315 having been recorded is sighted.

There are two primary entrances to the park. The first is the northern entrance through Nakhon Ratchasima Province, with most travellers passing through the town of Pak Chong (see p469 for transport information). The southern entrance is in Prachinburi Province (see p272), which is closer to Bangkok, but less popular.

Sights & Activities

The easiest attraction to reach, other than the **roadside overlooks** (Pha Diew Die, on the way to the radar station, is the highest), is **Nam Tok Kong Kaew**, a small waterfall right behind the visitor centre. **Nam Tok Haew Narok**, whose three levels combine to form a 150m drop, is the biggest waterfall and is just a 1km walk from the road in the far south of the park. But the beauty award goes to 25m **Nam Tok Haew Suwat**, which scooped a starring role in Danny Boyle's film *The Beach*. You can swim in the pool at the bottom. Though easily reached by car, this forest-encased jewel is best reached via Trail 1 (8km), a somewhat challenging path (you sometimes have to detour around fallen trees) that connects it and other waterfalls to the visitor centre. There's a good chance of seeing gibbons and hornbills, and it's probably the best footpath for spotting elephants, though encounters are unlikely (the roads are better for this).

It's 5.4km from the visitor centre to **Nong Phak Chi observation tower**, along Trail 5. This tower (there's another one closer to the visitor centre) overlooks a little lake and a salt lick, and is one of the best wildlife-spotting spots in the park. This is the most likely place you'll see a tiger, but you have to be very lucky (like lottery-winner lucky) to do so. Trail 9 (3km) is a seldom-used path to this tower, but it's the better bet for spotting animals on your way. The shortest route to the tower, ideal for getting there at dawn or dusk (the best wildlife-watching times), is a 1km path along a creek bed, starting near the Km35 pillar.

Most other hiking trails (some of them formed by the movement of wildlife) aren't as well trodden, so guides are recommended. No matter what trail you take, you should wear boots and long trousers. Some of the paths get a little rough, and during the rainy season leeches are a problem – mosquito repellent also helps keep them away. The staff at the visitor centre give hiking advice (especially important in the rainy season), and **bikes** (per hr 50B) can also be hired there. Rangers, if they're available, will guide trail walks. Prices are negotiable.

Outside the park, about 3km from the northern gate, is a **bat cave** that begins disgorging millions of rare wrinkle-lipped bats around 5.30pm.

Many of the hotels and resorts around Khao Yai offer **park tours** and this is really the

BEYOND THE FOREST

The greater Khao Yai region is a very popular escape for Bangkokians, and for many of them the national park is beside the point. The roads approaching Khao Yai are lined with enough sweet-corn stands, BB gun shooting ranges, outlet malls and other tourist traps for families to stay busy all weekend without ever thinking about nature. Several of these attractions are pretty good.

By far the most popular stop is **Farm Chokchai** (☎ 0 4432 8485; www.farmchokchai.com; Mittraphap Hwy, Km159; ⏰ 8.30am-8pm Mon-Fri, from 7.30am Sat & Sun), a 3200-hectare dairy farm overflowing with cowboy kitsch. The expanding empire now includes an ice-cream parlour, steakhouse, souvenir shop and safari-style tented camp (weekday/weekend 3735/4270B per adult). **Tours** (2½hr tour 235/250B; ⏰ 10am-2pm Tue-Fri, 9am-3.40pm Sat & Sun) visit the milking parlour, a petting zoo and a cowboy show.

Thailand is the pioneer of 'New Latitude Wines'. Although the country's first vintage came from Chateau de Loei (p525), the Khao Yai area is now the epicentre of this increasingly respectable industry, with over a dozen wineries in the area. Two of the leaders, **Khao Yai Winery** (☎ 0 3622 6416; www.khaoyaiwinery.com; ⏰ 9am-8pm Sun-Thu, to 10pm Fri & Sat), which corked its first bottle in 1998, and **GranMonte** (☎ 0 3622 7334; www.granmonte.com; ⏰ 11am-8pm), which got in the game three years later, lie along Pansuk-Kudkla Rd, the direct route from Bangkok to Khao Yai (exit Km144). Both are scenically set and offer tours (book in advance), tastings and classy restaurants, the latter serving Western food only. They're 22.5km and 16km respectively from the park gate.

Life Park (☎ 0 4429 7668; Th Thanarat, Km19.5; per activity 160-500B), right near the park gate at the Greenery Resort, is one of several area adventure parks. It's got go-karts, rock climbing, paintball, pony rides and much more.

ideal way to visit. Khao Yai Garden Lodge (right) and Greenleaf Guesthouse (right) have long earned widespread praise for their trips, as has **Wildlife Safari** (☎ 0 4431 2922; www.khaoyaiwildlife.com), although it is inconveniently located 2km north of Pak Chong. The typical day-long program (1100B to 1300B) includes some easy walks looking for wildlife and a visit to Haew Suwat waterfall, and returns after dark, when you have a good chance of meeting elephants on the road. You can also arrange **night safaris** (spotlighting drives) at the visitor centre. Lunch, snacks, water and, in the rainy season, 'leech socks' (gaiters) are always included, but sometimes the park entry fee is not, so do some comparison shopping. Half-day trips (300B to 500B) typically stay outside the park to visit a cave temple and watch the bats disgorge. Birdwatching, camping, trekking and other speciality tours are also available.

Sleeping & Eating

There are at least a hundred places to stay on the roads leading to the park and plenty more in the not-so-pleasant gateway city of Pak Chong. For budget lodging, touts at the train station and bus stops are helpful (if in doubt, call the hotel yourself; most have English-speaking staff), since the best places for visit-

ing the park are south of town along Rte 2090 (Th Thanarat) and they'll get you a free ride there. At the top end, expect off-season (May to October) discounts of 30%, and a fee as high as 500B for transfer to/from Pak Chong.

ourpick Greenleaf Guesthouse (☎ 0 4436 5024; www.greenleaftour.com; Th Thanarat, Km7.5; r 200-300B) Step past the slightly chaotic common areas and you'll be surprised by the great-value rooms (all with private bathrooms) at the back of this long-running place. These are just about the only budget beds outside Pak Chong.

Khao Yai Garden Lodge (☎ 0 4436 5178; www.khaoyai-gardenlodge.com; Th Thanarat, Km7; r 350-2600B, f 3800-6800B; 🕸 🖳 🖭) This friendly and funky place offers a very different experience from the big, fancy resorts up the road. Rooms have individual character (except the 350B shared bathroom ones) and are spread out around a lush garden. It's a bit worn, but still good value by area standards. There's free wi-fi in the lounge.

Juldis (☎ 0 4429 7297; www.juldiskhaoyai.com; Th Thanarat, Km17; r 1760-4800B, bungalows 4800-7200B; 🕸 🖳 🖭) This plush place is one of the Khao Yai area originals, but it's kept up with the times with a 2008 renovation. It's classier than most of the competition at these rates, which in these parts means the karaoke crooning aren't likely to drift into your room at night. It offers tennis courts, spa treatments and pleasant gardens.

Kirimaya (☎ 0 4442 6000; www.kirimaya.com; Rte 3052; r 7600-14,300B; pool villas 15,400B; tented villas 22,200B; ✗ 🖳 🗷) The first impression of this luxury resort-spa is usually either 'Wow!' or stunned silence. Step 'through' the wooden front doors and you're greeted by a towering stilted restaurant and other Thai-Bali fusion buildings, all rising from a lotus- and reed-filled pond and backed by the mountains. Rooms have bamboo furniture, balconies and all the mod cons. We're not too keen on having an 18-hole golf course on the edge of the park (even one designed by Jack Nicklaus), but there's no denying this place is special. It's 7km east of the park gate.

The best setting for sleeping is, of course, in the park itself. There are two **campsites** (per person with own tent 30B, 2-4-person tents 150-250B) and a variety of **rooms and bungalows** (☎ 0 2562 0760; www.dnp.go.th/parkreserve; 2-8 people 800-3500B).

Each of the lodges listed above serves food, and there are many lovely garden restaurants along Th Thanarat. The park itself has restaurants at all the busy locations, including the visitor centre, campsites and some waterfalls. Even the campsite ones close early (around 7pm) though, so plan ahead.

Getting There & Away

Just about all buses between Bangkok (2nd/1st class 108/139B, two hours) and Khorat (2nd/1st class 59/74B, one hour) stop in Pak Chong. You can also get to Pak Chong by train from Bangkok and Khorat, but it's slower than the bus, especially if coming from Bangkok. Ayuthaya, on the other hand, has no direct bus service, so the train (3rd class 173B, 2nd class 203–333B; two hours), of which there are 11 daily, is the best option.

Sŏrng·tăa·ou travel the 30km from Pak Chong down Th Thanarat to the park's northern gate (40B, 45 minutes), every half-hour from 6am to 5pm, from in front of the 7-Eleven store near the deer statue. It's about 500m west of the ordinary bus terminal, but note that most buses stop at their own company offices at various points on the main road.

It's another 14km to the visitor centre, and park guards are used to talking drivers into hauling *fa·ràng* (foreigners of European descent) up there. Some also do a side business

hiring motorcycles out for about 500B per day. Some motorcycle shops on Pak Chong's main road do rentals for around 300B to 400B, though you'll probably have to do your negotiations without the use of English.

BURIRAM PROVINCE

Buriram is not a province for urban exploration. Despite hanging on to half of its historic moat, Meuang Buriram, the provincial capital and only large town, is a tough sell as a tourist destination. Buriram Province is a place to come for a look at the past. The countryside is chock-a-block with tradition and peppered with over 50 Khmer ruins (out of 259 in the whole country).

The crowning glory is Phanom Rung, a beautifully restored Khmer temple complex straddling the summit of an extinct volcano. The most spectacular Angkor-era monument in Thailand, Phanom Rung is well worth the journey and should impress even those suffering acute temple overload.

NANG RONG

นางรอง

pop 20,300

This workaday city is even more forgettable than Buriram, 45km to the north, but it's the most convenient base for visiting Phanom Rung. A full range of services and a good selection of hotels at least make it a friendly and comfortable base. The town has ambitions of becoming a capital city, and you'll see signs for Nang Rong Province, but for the foreseeable future these are nothing but dreams.

Sleeping & Eating

our pick **Honey Inn** (☎ 0 4462 2825; www.honeyinn .com; 8/1 Soi Si Kun; r 200-400B; ✗ 🖳) This welcoming guesthouse, 1km from the bus station, is run by a knowledgeable retired English teacher. The rooms are simple but bright and travel tips get shared around the dinner table. Motorcycle hire, guided tours and food (with advance notice) are all available at good prices. To find it, walk north from the bus station, cross the main road and head east until you see the sign; or take a túk-túk for 30B.

our pick **P California Inter Hostel** (☎ 0 4462 2214; www.nangronghomestay.com; 59/9 Th Sangkakrit; r 250-700B; ✗ 🖳) Another friendly, helpful, English-speaking place, this one is on the east side of

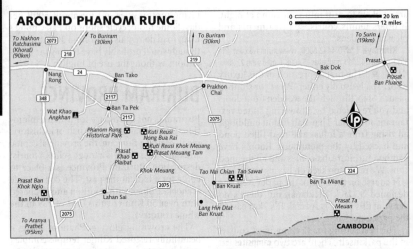

AROUND PHANOM RUNG

town. The California is somewhat shinier than the Honey Inn, although some of the rooms are a little more cramped. Khun Wicha, who is a wealth of knowledge about the area, also hires bikes and motorcycles and leads tours.

Cabbages & Condoms (☎ 0 4465 7145; Hwy 24; r 240-1500B; 🕳 🖭) The cheapest (shared bathroom) rooms at this Population & Community Development Association–run resort, which is set in a garden and ringed by several little lakes, are pretty limp. But move up the price scale (where you get large rooms with stone floors) and this is a pleasant place to stay. The restaurant is also very good. There's a clothing and shoe (including Nike) factory on site, opened to bring work normally found in the city to the villages. It's 6.5km west of town.

Phob Suk (no roman-script sign; ☎ 0 4463 1619; Hwy 24; dishes 50-360B; 🕑 breakfast, lunch & dinner) Nang Rong has the usual assortment of street stalls and simple restaurants, many serving the city's famous *kǎh mǒo* (pork-rump roast), but for something nicer head out to this place by the bus station. The picture menu presents the typical mix of Thai, Isan and Chinese and you can eat inside or in the noisy garden. Wi-fi is free and there's a playground for the kids.

There are also some restaurants and simple food stalls at Phanom Rung.

Getting There & Away

Nang Rong's **bus terminal** (☎ 0 4463 1517) is on the west side of town. See Phanom Rung Historical Park (following) for transport details.

PHANOM RUNG HISTORICAL PARK

อุทยานประวัติศาสตร์เขาพนมรุ้ง

Phanom Rung (Big Mountain; ☎ 0 4478 2715; admission 100B; 🕑 6am-6pm) has a knock-me-dead location. Crowning the summit of a spent volcano, this sanctuary sits a good 70 storeys above the paddy fields below. To the southeast you can clearly see Cambodia's Dongrek Mountains, and it's in this direction that the capital of the Angkor Empire once lay. The Phanom Rung temple complex is the largest and best restored Khmer monument in Thailand. It took 17 years to complete the restoration.

The Phanom Rung temple was erected between the 10th and 13th centuries, the bulk of it during the reign of King Suriyavarman II (r AD 1113–50), which by all accounts was the apex of Angkor architecture. The complex faces east, towards the original Angkor capital. If you can, plan your visit for one of the four times when the sun shines through all 15 sanctuary doorways. The correct solar alignment happens during sunrise on 3 to 5 April and 8 to 10 September and sunset on 5 to 7 March and 5 to 7 October (one day earlier in leap years). The park extends its hours during this event. Locals celebrate the **Climbing Khao Phanom Rung Festival** around the April alignment with sound-and-light shows and dance-dramas performed in the temple complex. Camping is allowed during this time.

Below the main sanctuary, after the long row of gift shops, an **Information Centre** (admission free; 🕑 9am-4.30pm) houses artefacts found at the site and displays about both the construc-

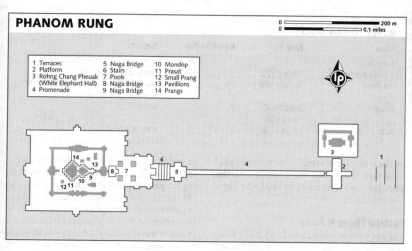

PHANOM RUNG

1 Terraces	5 Naga Bridge	10 Mondòp
2 Platform	6 Stairs	11 Prasat
3 Rohng Chang Pheuak	7 Pools	12 Small Prang
(White Elephant Hall)	8 Naga Bridge	13 Pavillions
4 Promenade	9 Naga Bridge	14 Prangs

tion and restoration. You can pick up a free informative brochure or arrange a guide (fees are negotiable) here.

Design

One of the most remarkable design aspects of Phanom Rung is the promenade leading to the main gate. It's the best surviving example in Thailand. It begins on a slope 400m east of the main tower, with three earthen **terraces**. Next comes a cruciform base for what may have been a wooden pavilion. To the right of this is a stone hall known locally as **Rohng Chang Pheuak** (White Elephant Hall) where royalty bathed and changed clothes before entering the temple complex. Flower garlands to be used as offerings in the temple may also have been handed out here. After you step down from the pavilion area, you'll come to a 160m **promenade** paved with laterite and sandstone blocks, and flanked by sandstone pillars with early Angkor style (AD 1100–80) lotus-bud tops. The promenade ends at the first and largest of three **naga bridges**. The first is flanked by 16 five-headed *naga* (mythical serpentlike beings with magical powers) in the classic Angkor style. In fact, these figures are identical to those found at Angkor Wat.

After passing this bridge and climbing the **stairs** you come to the magnificent east gallery leading into the main sanctuary. The central **bràh-sàht** (building with a cruciform ground plan and needle-like spire) has a gallery on each of its four sides and the entrance to each gallery is itself a smaller version of the main tower.

The **galleries** have curvilinear roofs and false-balustrade windows. Once inside the temple walls, have a look at each of the galleries and the **gopura** (entrance pavilion), paying particular attention to the lintels over the porticoes. The craftsmanship at Phanom Rung represents the pinnacle of Khmer artistic achievement, on par with the reliefs at Angkor Wat in Cambodia.

Sculpture

The Phanom Rung complex was originally constructed as a Hindu monument and exhibits iconography related to the worship of Vishnu and Shiva. Excellent sculptures of both Vaishnava and Shaiva deities can be seen in the lintels or pediments over the doorways to the central monuments and in various other key points on the sanctuary exterior. On the east portico of the **mon·dòp** (square, spired building) is a Nataraja (Dancing Shiva), which is late Baphuan or early Angkor style, while on the south entrance are the remains of Shiva and Uma riding their bull mount, Nandi. The central cell of the **bràh·sàht** contains a Shivalingam (phallus image).

Several sculpted images of Vishnu and his incarnations, Rama and Krishna, decorate various other lintels and cornices. Probably the most beautiful is the **Phra Narai lintel**, a relief depicting a reclining Vishnu (Narayana) in the Hindu creation myth. Growing from his navel is a lotus that branches into several blossoms, on one of which sits the creator god, Brahma. On either side of Vishnu are heads of Kala, the god of time and death. He is asleep

BUSES TO BAN TAKO

From	Fare (B)	Duration (hr)	Departs
Bangkok (Gitjagaan Tours)	1st class 275B	5	hourly until 5.30pm
Pak Chong	1st class 140B	2½	hourly 10am-8.30pm from the Shell petrol station on east side of town
Khorat	2nd class 70B 1st class 85B	2	hourly
Surin	1st class 65B	2	every half-hour

on the milky sea of eternity, here represented by a *naga*. This lintel sits above the **eastern gate** (the main entrance) beneath the Shiva Nataraja relief.

Getting There & Away

The easiest way to the ruins from Nang Rong is to arrange a ride from your hotel (expect to pay about 800B). Otherwise, *sŏrng·tăa·ou* (20B, 45 minutes) leave every half-hour from the old market on the east end of town, for Laan Jod Rod Kheun Khao Phanom Rung, a parking area at the foot of the mountain used by some tour buses. From here there are many *sŏrng·tăa·ou* waiting to shuttle tourists the rest of the way. They charge 40B per person, though on weekdays you may have to wait quite a while for the 15 passengers needed before departing. A motorcycle taxi from here should cost around 100B, including waiting time while you tour the ruins. Another option is the Nang Rong–Chanthaburi bus (20B, 30 minutes), which passes through Ban Ta Pek hourly. Then a motorcycle taxi from Ban Ta Pek will probably cost 150B, or you can charter a *sŏrng·tăa·ou* for 500B.

Those coming from further abroad should get a bus (see the table above for details) to Ban Tako, a well-marked turn-off about 14km east of Nang Rong. Here you can wait for one of the buses or *sŏrng·tăa·ou* (10B) from Nang Rong and then continue as described previously, or just take a motorcycle taxi (300B return) all the way to Phanom Rung.

AROUND PHANOM RUNG
Prasat Meuang Tam
ปราสาทเมืองต่ำ

In the little village of Khok Meuang, the restored Khmer temple of **Prasat Meuang Tam** (Lower City; admission 100B; 7am-6pm) is an ideal bolt-on to any visit to Phanom Rung, which is only 8km to the northwest. Dating back to the late 10th

or early 11th century and sponsored by King Jayavarman V, this is Isan's third most interesting temple complex (after Phanom Rung and Phimai; fourth if you count Khao Phra Wihan) in terms of size, atmosphere and the quality of restoration work. The whole complex (once a shrine to Shiva) is surrounded by laterite walls, within which are four lotus-filled reservoirs, each guarded by whimsical five-headed *naga*.

Sandstone galleries and *gopura*, the latter exquisitely carved, surround five *prang* (Khmer-style tower on temples). The principal *prang* could not be rebuilt and the remaining towers, being brick, aren't nearly as tall or as imposing as the sandstone *prang* at Phanom Rung. However, they do hold some superb lintels, including one depicting Shiva and his consort Uma riding the sacred bull, Nandi. The temple's plan is based on the same design as that of Angkor Wat: the *prang* stand for the five peaks of Mt Meru, the mythical abode of the Hindu gods, and Barai Meuang Tam (a 510m-by-1090m reservoir across the road) represents the surrounding ocean.

Begin your visit in the small **information centre** (admission free; 8am-4.30pm). You can also enquire here about the village's **homestay** (08 1068 6898; per person 150B, with meals 300B) program.

Any motorcycle-taxi driver will add Meuang Tam onto a trip to Phanom Rung for about 100B.

Other Khmer Ruins

For those with an insatiable appetite for Khmer ruins, the area around Phanom Rung offers a smorgasbord of lesser-known sites that, taken together, create a picture of the crucial role this region once played in the Khmer empire. Even history buffs will likely find these places of only minor interest, but driving through this rice-growing region offers an unvarnished look at village life and will surely be an enlightening trip. Note that many roads around here are in terrible shape and signage is somewhat erratic.

All of the following sites, restored or stabilised to some degree by the Fine Arts Department, are free of charge and open during daylight hours.

Kuti Reusi Nong Bua Rai sits between Phanom Rung and Meuang Tam, and **Kuti Reusi Khok Meuang** is just northwest of Prasat Meuang Tam, opposite Barai Meuang Tam. So you might as well stop if you're heading this way.

Little of **Prasat Khao Plaibat** is left standing. But the adventure of finding it, along with cool views of both Phanom Rung and the Dangrek Mountains on the Cambodian border, make it worth seeking out. The seldom-used trail starts at Wat Khao Plaibat, about 4km from Prasat Meuang Tam. Walk around the gate next to the giant Buddha image, veer right at the *gù·dì* (monks' quarters) and slip through the barbed-wire fence. From here follow the strips of orange cloth tied to trees. The walk up the hill should take less than 30 minutes if you don't get lost along the way, though it's likely you will.

Prasat Ban Khok Ngio, 3km before Ban Pakham, is the only one of these sites that can conveniently be reached by public transport; any *sörng·tǎa·ou* heading south from Nang Rong will drop you off.

Archaeologists assume that much of the rock used to build these ancient structures came from the widely scattered **Lang Hin Dtat Ban Kruat** (Ban Kruat Quarry). It's actually more interesting for its beauty and serenity than its history. Stand in front of the big rock at the entrance to hear a bizarre echo effect from the little waterfall.

Also near Ban Kruat are **Tao Sawai** and **Tao Nai Chian**, two kilns that supplied pottery to much of the Khmer empire between the 10th and 12th centuries. Today they're little more than piles of dirt with roofs over them.

You can easily tack on **Prasat Ta Meuan** (p476), a secluded Khmer complex on the Thai–Cambodian border. Although it lies in Surin Province, it is more conveniently visited from this region. It's 55km from Phanom Rung.

Wat Khao Angkhan
วัดเขาอังคาร

Although this peaceful temple atop an extinct volcano has an ancient past, as evidenced by the 8th or 9th century Dvaravati sandstone boundary markers, it's the modern constructions that

make **Wat Khao Angkhan** (☯ daylight hr) worth a visit. The *bòht* and several other flamboyant buildings were erected in 1982 in an unusual nouveau-Khmer style that sort of hearkens back to the age of empire. Inside the *bòht*, the *jataka* (stories of the Buddha's previous lives) murals, painted by Burmese artists, have English captions. The *wát* also hosts a Chinese-style pagoda, a 29m reclining Buddha and beautiful views of the surrounding mountains and forest.

The temple is about 20km from Nang Rong or Phanom Rung, and there's no public transport. The route is pretty well signposted, but you'll have to ask directions at some junctions. A motorcycle taxi from Ban Ta Pek could cost as little as 200B, and 300B from Nang Rong.

SURIN & SI SAKET PROVINCES

Surin and Si Saket Provinces are dotted with Angkor-era Khmer ruins. Most are now looking rather tatty, but for those with a history habit many are worth the effort to reach. In particular, Prasat Ta Meuan is very evocative and Khao Phra Wihan ranks among the northeast's best attractions, despite the Cambodian government's refusal to renovate it. The Khmer influence comes not only from the past, but also the present. Over one-third of the population of these two closely related provinces is ethnically Khmer and this remains the principal language in many villages.

Besides the temples, Surin Province is home to Ban Tha Klang elephant village and some famous craft centres, while Si Saket holds two of Thailand's most unusual temples. The region's towns are rather less interesting, although Surin makes a comfortable base and each November provides the backdrop for the raucous Annual Elephant Round-up.

SURIN
สุรินทร์
pop 41,200

Surin doesn't have much to say for itself until November, when the provincial capital explodes into life for the **Surin Elephant Round-up**. Hosting giant scrums of pachyderm (you've never seen so many well-dressed tuskers), the city celebrates for 10 days. However, the massive crowds come on just the last weekend for the main event, which features 300 elephants showing their skills and taking part in a battle re-enactment. Tickets start at 40B, but VIP seats (which get you closest to the action, English commentary and guaranteed shade) start at 500B. Arguably the festival's best event is the elephant buffet on the Friday before the big show.

Information

Most of Thailand's big banks have branches on Th Thesaban south of the train station, which is also where the post office is found.

Microsys (Th Sirirat; internet per hr 15B; ☼ 24hr) Across from Thong Tarin Hotel.

OTOP (☎ 0 4451 4447; Th Jit Bamrung; ☼ 9am-7.30pm) Across from City Hall, this shop has the broadest selection of crafts, plus a city-specific tourist office.

Ruampaet Hospital (☎ 0 4451 3192; Th Thesaban 1)

Tourism Authority of Thailand (TAT; ☎ 0 4451 4447; tatsurin@tat.or.th; 355/3-6 Th Thesaban 1; ☼ 8.30am-4.30pm) Across from the hospital.

Sights & Activities

As has been the case ever since the **Surin National Museum** (☎ 0 4451 3358) was constructed a decade ago, the best guess anyone can give for when it will open is 'next year'. Displays focus on Surin's ethnic groups (including the Suai, the region's renowned elephant herders) and the province's Khmer ruins. It's 5km south of town on Rte 214 and if you drop by they'll probably let you in.

The **Surin Agriculture Service Centre** (☎ 0 4451 1393; Hwy 226; admission free; ☼ 8am-4.30pm Mon-Fri), a sericulture research centre 4km west of town, is the easiest place around to see the entire silk-making process, from larva to loom.

Surin is well set up for those looking to give something back during their trip. **Starfish Ventures** (☎ 08 1723 1403; www.starfishvolunteers.com) runs over a dozen volunteer projects ranging from nursing to English teaching to home building. The work is done in surrounding villages, but volunteers get private rooms in the city. June Niampan, a former Starfish employee, has recently started **LemonGrass** (☎ 08 1977 5300; www.lemongrass-volunteering.com), which offers English-teaching placements in Surin.

Tours

Pirom, at Pirom-Aree's House (right), offers a wide range of tours, from a half day in Ban Tha Klang and the craft villages (per person 1400B with four people) to a three-day Isan immersion experience (per person per day 2400B with four people). Tours to all the well-known Khmer temples (and many others) are also available. Prices are very high but the tours are good.

Saren Travel (☎ 0 4452 0174; 202/1-4 Th Thesaban 2; ☼ 8.30am-6pm Mon-Sat) offers customised day tours in and around Surin Province from 1600B.

Sleeping

Hotels fill up fast during the Elephant Round-up and prices skyrocket, so book as far in advance as you can.

our pick Pirom-Aree's House (☎ 0 4451 5140; Soi Arunee, Th Thungpo; s/d 120/200B) The location for this long-time budget favourite, 1km west of the city, is inconvenient but very peaceful. Simple wooden rooms (all with shared bathroom) in two new houses and a shady garden overlook a rice paddy. Aree cooks some pretty good food and Pirom is one of the best sources of information on the region you'll meet.

New Hotel (☎ 0 4451 1341; 6-8 Th Tanasan; s 160-330B; d 180-440B; ✖) This place, right smack outside the train station, is so old the name's almost ironic, but it's clean and convenient. Take a room in the front half of the building and you'll get a real sit-down toilet.

Kritsada Grand Palace (☎ 0 4471 3997; Th Suriyarat; r 400-450B; ✖ 🖳) Sitting on a quiet side street behind city hall, this newly opened property is a bit hard to find, but that makes for a very quiet downtown location. Rooms are rather plain, but good value. Wi-fi in the lobby only.

Treehouse Resort (☎ 08 9948 4181; sboonyoi@gmail .com; Hwy 226; r 350-1000B; ✖) This peculiar place, under slow-mo construction since 1998, is a combination of Gilligan's Island and your grandparents' dishevelled basement. If this sounds good to you, you'll love it. It's 3km from downtown, right on Surin's outskirts. Khun Boonyai, the cheerful owner and creator, prefers that you book a day in advance; in return, he'll pick you up in town for free when you arrive.

Maneerote Hotel (☎ 0 4453 9477; www.maneerote hotel.com; 11/1 Soi Poytango Th Krung Si Nai; r 650-750B; ✖ 🖳) This newish hotel west of the markets is a shiny, solid three-star, though it's a little out of the way. It has a few nice decorative touches, and wi-fi spreads throughout the building and is free in the lobby.

Surin Majestic Hotel (☎ 0 4471 3980; 99 Th Jit Bamrung; r 900-1200B, ste 1800-4500B; ✖ 🖳 ▨) The city's top digs sits alongside the bus terminal in the heart of town. The rooms are nothing special, but good for the price (the junior suites are actually a very good deal) and the hotel has plenty of extras, like a fitness centre. There's wi-fi in the lobby only.

Eating & Drinking

Petmanee 2 (no roman-script sign; ☎ 08 4451 6024; Th Murasart; dishes 20-60B; ⌚ lunch) This simple spot south of Ruampaet Hospital and next to Wat Salaloi (look for the chicken grill in front) is Surin's most famous purveyor of *sôm·đam* and *gài yâhng*. The *súʔ nòr mái* (bamboo shoot salad) is good too. There's no English, spoken or written, but the food is so good it's worth stumbling through an order. The smaller original is around the corner.

Surin Chai Kit (no roman-script sign; 297-299 Th Tanasan; dishes 25-60B; ⌚ breakfast & lunch) This no-frills spot whips up a tasty breakfast; try a plate of pan-eggs and Isan sausages. The owner wears a welcoming permagrin and gives *fa·ràng* customers a handy city map. It's a short walk south of the train station, past the fountain.

Larn Chang (☎ 0 4451 2869; 199 Th Siphathai Saman; dishes 35-200B; ⌚ dinner) Tasty and low-priced Thai and Isan dishes are served in and around an old wooden house overlooking a surviving stretch of the city moat. The moat is now known as Sǔan Rak (Love Park) and couples come here to hold hands at night. The food and the setting are lovely; unfortunately the service isn't always. It's a longish walk south of the centre, on the east side of the park.

Sumrub Tornkruang (☎ 0 4451 5015; off Th Jit Bamrung; dishes 65-250B; ⌚ lunch & dinner) This unexpected place, tucked away behind the bus station, is classy in a totally Thai way. Prices are reasonable for the properly prepared Thai (and some Isan) food.

Farang Connection (☎ 0 4451 1509; off Th Jit Bamrung; dishes 50-750B; ⌚ breakfast, lunch & dinner) Also behind the bus station, this aptly named, British-owned place meets many travellers' needs. The menu is a thick list of foreign favourites like chicken tikka masala, Wiener schnitzel and BLTs, and the liquor list is just as global. The Thai food is pretty good too. There's an internet cafe upstairs and a small book exchange in the pub across the road. Wi-fi is free.

Coffee More (Th Tanasan; cappuccino 25B; ⌚ breakfast, lunch & dinner) This bright modern place just south of the train station has some of the best coffees in town, plus ice cream and other snacks.

Surin's principal **night market** (Th Krung Si Nai; ⌚ 5-10pm) is a block south of the fountain. Just to the west, by the clock tower, vendors fronting the municipal market serve until at least 2am. Both markets whip up an excellent selection of Thai and Isan dishes, including, as always, fried insects.

Surin's surprisingly wild nightlife is centred on Soi Kola and Th Sirirat around the Thong Tarin Hotel.

Getting There & Away

BUS

From Surin's **bus terminal** (☎ 0 4451 1756; Th Jit Bamrung) buses head to/from Si Saket (ordinary 60B, 1½ hours, hourly), Ubon Ratchathani (2nd/1st class 144/212B, three hours, hourly), Roi Et (2nd class 98B, three hours, hourly), Khorat (2nd/1st class 120/178B, four hours, every half-hour), Chiang Mai (2nd class/32-seat VIP 698/893B, 14 hours, six daily) and Pattaya (2nd class/32-seat VIP 412/584B, eight hours, hourly). Most of the frequent buses going to Bangkok (2nd/1st class 345/399B, seven hours) also use Surin's bus terminal, including **999 VIP** (☎ 0 4451 5344), which has a 24-seat VIP service (530B, 9.30pm).

Because of the casino, there's a lot of minibus (65B, 1½ hours, every half-hour) traffic from the bus terminal to the Cambodian border crossing (open 7am to 8pm) at Chong Chom, where visas are available on the spot (see p754 for details). There's little transport on the Cambodian side. A seat in a car will cost 500B for the four-hour drive to Siem Reap, but if you arrive late you may have to pay 2500B for the whole vehicle.

TRAIN

Surin is on the Bangkok–Ubon line and there are 10 daily services to both destinations. A 3rd-/2nd-class seat to Ubon (three hours) starts at 81/150B. To Bangkok (seven to nine hours) 3rd-/2nd-/1st-class sleeper prices begin at 183/389/1149B. Call **Surin Station** (☎ 0 4451 1295) for more information.

Getting Around

Surin is a very convenient city for travellers; virtually everything you'll want or need is within a few blocks of the bus and train stations. If you don't want to walk, túk-túk charge around 30B to 40B for a trip within the centre.

Pirom-Aree's House, Saren Travel and Farang Connection all hire cars, plus the latter has motorcycles.

AROUND SURIN
Ban Tha Klang
บ้านตากลาง

To see Surin's elephants during the low season, visit the **Elephant Study Centre** (☎ 0 4414 5050; admission free; ☺ 9.30am-4.30pm) in Ban Tha Klang, about 50km north of Surin. A little museum discusses elephants and elephant training, and some of the performers at the annual festival live here in traditional Suai homes sheltering elephants and humans together.

There are daily one-hour **talent shows** (donations expected; ☺ 10am & 2pm, not during the festival) with painting and basketball among the many tusker tricks. The elephants bathe in the river after the second show. If you'd like to spend some quality time with the elephants, you can work alongside a mahout for 1000B per person. Book in advance. The village hosts an **Elephant Parade** around May's full moon, with all the pachyderms brightly painted as part of the new monks' ordination ceremony.

Ban Tha Klang's **homestay** (☎ 08 1879 5026; per person 350B) program includes three meals and some elephant time.

Sŏrng·tăa·ou run from Surin's bus terminal (45B, two hours, hourly) with the last one returning at 4pm. If you're driving, take Rte 214 north for 40km and follow the 'Elephant Village' signs down Rte 3027.

Craft Villages

There are many silk-weaving villages in easy striking distance of Surin town. The province's distinct fabrics – principally *pâh hoh,* a tightly woven *mát·mèe* – have a Khmer influence. They use only natural dyes and the most delicate silk fibres from the insides of the cocoons. Surin silks aren't readily available in other parts of Thailand (though they're becoming easier to find in Bangkok), and prices can be over 50% cheaper.

By far the most famous weaving centre is Ban Tha Sawang, where **Chansoma** (☎ 08 1726 0397; ☺ 8am-5pm) makes exquisite brocade fabrics (*pâh yók torng*) incorporating threads coated in silver and gold. The weaving process is mighty impressive. Four women, including one sitting a floor below the others, work the loom simultaneously and can produce no more than 4cm a day. Many of the finished products are destined for the royal court, but you can custom order your own if you can afford at least 30,000B per metre. Dozens of other nearby shops selling more typical silks serve the masses of Thai tourists disgorged by a steady stream of tour buses. The village is just 8km west of the city via Rte 4026, but finding it can be tough on your own since English-language signage is scattershot. *Sŏrng·tăa·ou* (17B, 20 minutes) run regularly from Surin's market, and a túk-túk should cost about 100B.

Ban Khwao Sinarin and **Ban Chok**, next-door neighbours 18km north of Surin via Rtes 214 and 3036, are known for silk and silver respectively. However, these days you can buy both in each village. One of the silk specialities is *yók dòrk*, a much simpler brocade style than what's made in Ban Tha Sawang, but that still requires up to 35 foot pedals on the looms. Khun Manee, who runs **Phra Dab Suk** (☎ 08 9865 8720) on the main drag, takes visitors out to see silk being woven for 100B per person; you must call in advance. The silver standout is *brà keuam*, a Cambodian style of bead brought to Thailand by Ban Chok's ancestors many centuries ago. **Ban Chok Silver Co-operative** (Glùm Krèung Ngeum Bâhn Chôhk; ☎ 08 1309 4352), south of the main road, creates unique silver jewellery. *Sŏrng·tăa·ou* go from Surin (25B, 1½ hours) to Ban Khwao Sinarin hourly.

The residents of **Ban Buthom** (14km out of Surin on Rte 226 on the way to Sikhoraphum) weave sturdy, unlacquered rattan baskets, including some rather flat ones that pack well.

Prasat Ta Meuan
ปราสาทตาเมือน

The most atmospheric (and most difficult to reach) of Surin's Khmer ruins is a series of three sites known collectively as **Prasat Ta Meuan** (admission free; ☺ daylight hr), in Tambon Ta Miang on the Cambodian border. It lines the ancient route linking Angkor Wat to Phimai.

The first site, **Prasat Ta Meuan** proper, was built in the Jayavarman VII period (AD 1181–1210) as a rest stop for pilgrims. It's a fairly small monument with a two-door, 10-window sanctuary constructed of laterite blocks; only one sculpted sandstone lintel remains.

Just 300m south, **Prasat Ta Meuan Toht**, which was the chapel for a 'healing station', is a bit larger. Also built by Jayavarman VII, the ruins consist of a *gopura, mon·dòp* and main *prang*, all surrounded by a laterite wall.

Nearly 1km further south, next to the army base at the end of the road, is the largest site, **Prasat Ta Meuan Thom**. This site pre-dates the other two by as much as two centuries. Despite a somewhat haphazard reconstruction, this one nearly justifies the effort it takes to get here. Three *prang* and a large hall are built of sandstone blocks on a laterite base. Several smaller buildings also still stand inside the wall. Many carvings encase the principal *prang*, although the best were pried or blasted away and sold to unscrupulous Thai dealers by the Khmer Rouge who occupied the site in the 1980s. A stairway on the southern end drops to Cambodian territory. Landmines and undetonated hand grenades still litter the thick jungle surrounding the complex; heed the 'danger' signs.

The sites begin 10.3km south of Ban Ta Miang on Rte 224, 23km east of Ban Kruat via a winding road used by far more cows than cars. You need your own transport to get here, and a visit is usually more convenient from Phanom Rung Historical Park (p473) than from Surin town.

Other Khmer Temple Ruins

The southern reaches of Surin Province, along the Cambodian border, harbour several minor Angkor-period ruins. The 11th-century **Prasat Ban Pluang** (admission 30B; 7.30am-6pm) is 33km south of Surin. It's just a solitary sandstone *prang* with most of its top gone, but some wonderful carvings (including a lintel above the entrance with the Hindu god Indra riding his elephant, Airavata) make it worth a stop. A U-shaped moat rings the *prang*. The site sits 600m off Rte 214; the turn-off is 2.5km south of Hwy 24. Any vehicle bound for Kap Choeng or the border can drop you nearby (25B, 30 minutes).

A larger Khmer site is seen 30km northeast of town at **Prasat Sikhoraphum** (admission 50B; 8-5pm), in the town of the same name. Built in the 12th century, Sikhoraphum features five brick *prang*, the tallest of which reaches 32m. Two *prang* still hold their tops, including the central one whose doorways are decorated with stone carvings of Hindu deities, following the Angkor Wat style. There's a sound-and-light show here during the Elephant Round-up. Sikhoraphum can be reached by bus (25B, one hour) or train (7B, 30 minutes) from Surin town.

If driving out here, you may as well take a 400m detour off Rte 226 for a peep at **Prasat Muang Thi** (admission free; daylight hr), 15km from Surin. The three remaining brick *prang* are in sad shape (one looks like it's ready to topple), but they're so small they're actually kind of cute.

The ruined **Prasat Phumpon** (admission free; daylight hr) in Amphoe Sangkha, dating from the 7th or 8th century, is the oldest Khmer *brah·sàht* in Thailand. However, that's its only claim to fame and you'll likely be disappointed by this simple brick *prang* if you're expecting something magnificent. Amphoe Sangkha is 9km south of Hwy 24 on Rte 2124; veer right through the village at the fork in the road.

SI SAKET

ศรีสะเกษ
pop 42,800

There's not a whole lot to do in the humdrum town of Si Saket, but if you're headed to the Angkor-era temple complex of Khao Phra Wihan, you may pass through.

Si Saket is centred on its train station. The bus terminal is about 2km south on Th Kuang Heng. Banks and internet cafes are widely scattered, with the former lying mostly south of the tracks in the more commercial half of the city. Staff at the **Si Saket Tourism Coordination Centre** (0 4561 1283; cnr Th Lak Muang & Th Thepa; 8.30am-4.30pm Mon-Fri) are enthusiastic about their province; pity they don't have more to promote.

The city's principal (and pretty much only) attraction is **Tak Khun Ampai Panich** (0 4561 2637; cnr Th Ubon & Th Wijitnakorn; 9am-8pm), a very pretty wood-and-stucco shophouse built in 1925. It now houses an OTOP Center selling locally produced silks and crafts. Upstairs is a little museum in the making with a few antiques. It's about a 10-minute walk southwest of the train station.

Sleeping & Eating

Si Saket Hotel (0 4561 2582; 384/85 Th Si Saket; r 150-250B;) Just a stone's throw north of the train station, Si Saket is a bit rough, but right for the price. Even the cheapest rooms have cable TV; that money would have been better spent on quality mattresses.

Phrompiman Hotel (0 4561 2677; 849/1 Th Lak Meuang; r 400-990B;) This hotel, just west of the train station, offers good value,

NORTHEASTERN THAILAND

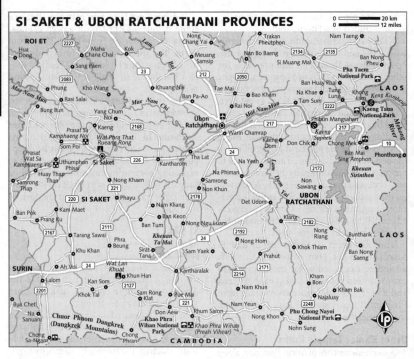

SI SAKET & UBON RATCHATHANI PROVINCES

especially if you step up to Superior level (650B), which is why it's sometimes full. Among its many on-site facilities are a travel agency, bar, snooker club, minimart and two restaurants.

There are some simple restaurants just north of the train station, but most of the city's culinary razzmatazz is in the great **night market** (⏱ 4-11pm) that convenes immediately to the south. For something more special, try **Sisaket** (☎ 08 1593 2330; Th Thepa 1; dishes 20-100B; ⏱ dinner), a nice garden spot with thatched-roofed tables. Their speciality is steamed fish with chilli paste. The menu's in Thai only, but the staff speak some English. A túk-túk from the centre should cost 40B to 50B; if the driver doesn't know the restaurant, tell them 'Nòrng Utai'.

Getting There & Away

From Bangkok there are frequent departures to/from Si Saket (2nd/1st class 329/434B, 8½ hours) stopping at either the **bus terminal** (☎ 0 4561 2523) or on Th Si Saket just north of the train station. There are also buses to/from Ubon Ratchathani (ordinary/2nd class

40/59B, 1¼ hours) and Surin (ordinary 60B, 1½ hours, hourly). **999 VIP** (☎ 0 4561 2523) has a 24-seat VIP service (685B) to Bangkok at 7.40pm.

There are 10 daily trains from **Si Saket Station** (☎ 0 4561 1525) to Bangkok (3rd/2nd class 197/311B, eight to 11 hours) including an overnight express service (1st-class air-con sleeper 1236B, 11 hours) departing Bangkok at 8.30pm and departing Si Saket at 7.30pm. A 3rd/2nd-class train to Ubon Ratchathani (one hour) costs as little as 13/29B.

The Thai–Cambodian border at Chong Sa–Ngam is open, and visas (see p754 for details) are available here, but there's no public transport.

AROUND SI SAKET
Khao Phra Wihan National Park
อุทยานแห่งชาติเขาพระวิหาร
KHAO PHRA WIHAN
เขาพระวิหาร

Just inside Cambodia, and all but inaccessible from that side of the border, Khao Phra Wihan (Preah Vihear in Khmer) is one of the region's great Angkor-period monuments. Straddling a 600m-high cliff on the brow of the Dangrek (Dong Rek) escarpment and accessed via a series of steep stepped *naga* approaches, the large temple complex towers over the plains of Cambodia, offering dreamy views and some beautiful and evocative ruins.

Claimed by both countries because of a misdrawn French map, the temple was finally awarded to Cambodia in a 1962 World Court ruling. Thailand's bruised pride never healed. In June 2008, as the Cambodian government sought Unesco World Heritage status, a border dispute flared and eventually led to deadly clashes between the nations' armies. Because of this unresolved situation, the temple complex is closed to visitors and may remain closed for quite some time.

Though there has long been talk of building a cable car to the temple from the Cambodian side (possibly associated with a casino complex) the only practical access (when the temple is open) remains through the **national park** (☎ 0 4581 8021; admission 200B, car fee 30B). A visitor centre marks the path into Cambodia and up to the temple (last entry 4pm), about 1km away. On the Thai side you have to pay 5B for a border pass (passports aren't necessary, but bring it anyway in case things change) and just after the border the Cambodian authorities collect their 200B fee (total cost 405B).

Khao Phra Wihan itself was constructed over three centuries under a succession of Khmer kings, beginning with Rajendravarman II in the mid-10th century and ending with Suryavarman II in the early 12th century. It was the latter who also commanded the construction of Angkor Wat. The hill itself was sacred to Khmer Hindus for at least 500 years before the completion of the temple complex, however, and there were smaller brick monuments on the site prior to its construction.

The temple complex is only semirestored and the Cambodians appear to have little interest in completing the job any time soon, which makes one wish the World Court had sided with the Thais. During Khmer Rouge occupation, which lasted until Pol Pot's death in 1998, the site suffered from the pilfering of artefacts, lintels and other carvings, although some of this smuggled art has been intercepted and may eventually be returned to the site.

One *naga* balustrade of around 30m is still intact. The first two *gopura* have all but fallen down and many of the buildings are roofless, but abundant examples of stone carving are intact and visible. The doorways to the third *gopura* have been nicely preserved and one (the inner door facing south) is surmounted by a well-executed carved stone lintel depicting Shiva and his consort Uma sitting on Nandi (Shiva's bull) under the shade of a symmetrised tree. A Vishnu creation lintel is also visible on the second *gopura;* in contrast to the famous Phanom Rung lintel depicting the same subject, this one shows Vishnu climbing the churning stick rather than reclining on the ocean below.

The main *Ɓrah·sàht* tower in the final court at the summit needs major restoration before the viewer can get a true idea of its former magnificence. Many of the stone carvings from the *Ɓrah·sàht* are missing, while others lie buried in nearby rubble. The galleries surrounding the *Ɓrah·sàht* have fared better and have even kept their arched roofs.

The area around the temple witnessed heavy fighting between Khmer Rouge guerrillas and the Phnom Penh government, and landmines and artillery pieces still litter the surrounding forest, so heed the skull-and-crossbones signs around the temple, even when the locals don't.

OTHER SIGHTS

The 130-sq-km national park (still open to visitors) contains a number of sights that are worth a peep before (or after) tramping over the border to Khao Phra Wihan itself. Near the **visitor centre** (🕑 7am-5pm), which includes some interesting exhibits on the temple's history, the **Pha Mo-E-Daeng** cliff features some fabulous views and the oldest bas-relief in Thailand. The carving depicts three figures, sitting below a roughly cut pig (which might represent Vishnu), whose identities are an enigma to archaeologists and art historians. Although they give the general impression of representing deities, angels or kings, the iconography corresponds to no known figures in Thai, Mon or Khmer mythology. Stylistically the relief appears to date back to the Koh Ker (AD 921–45) period of Khmer art, when King Jayavarman IV ruled from his capital at Koh Ker. Across the parking lot is **Nam Tok Khun Si**, a waterfall flowing over a cave large enough to hold an orchestra. There's usually only water in the stream from late June to October, and you should visit with a park ranger because it's assumed landmines are buried in the area.

SLEEPING & EATING

The park has four **bungalows** (☎ 0 2562 0760; www
.dnp.go.th/parkreserve; 4-6 people 600-2000B) well away
from the visitor centre, and a **campsite** (per person
with own tent 30B; 2-10-person tent hire 150-600B). There
were once many restaurants across from the
visitor centre, and vendors in the ruins themselves sold drinks and snacks.

The nearest town with accommodation is
Kantharalak. It's not a bad place to lay your
head if you're leaving the ruins late in the day
or intending to visit them early in the morning. The rooms are rather dull, but the **SB
Hotel** (☎ 0 4566 3103; 136 Th Anan Ta Pak Dee; r 250-550B;
🅿 🖳) is clean and friendly; and the coffee
shop/internet cafe out front makes it a good
base. It's in the heart of the city, and a túk-túk
from the bus station should cost 20B.

GETTING THERE & AWAY

Route 221 leads 95km south from Si Saket
to Phum Saron (10km before the temple) via
Kantharalak. First take a bus from Surin to
Kantharalak (45B, 1½ hours) and then catch
a sŏrng·tǎa·ou to Phum Saron (35B, 40 minutes); both depart about every half-hour until
3pm. From Phum Saron you'll have to hire a
motorcycle taxi to the park; figure on 200B
return with a couple of hours waiting time. A
truck may cost 400B. Drivers in Phum Saron
are well aware that visitors who have already
come this far are unlikely to turn back and so
they hold all the cards in bargaining. Hitching
to the park is possible, but could take a long
time (especially on weekdays).

You can also catch a bus from Ubon
Ratchathani to Kantharalak (50B, 1½ hours,
every half-hour).

Other Khmer Ruins

Thirty kilometres west of Si Saket via Rte 226
in Amphoe Uthumphon Phisai, **Prasat Wat Sa
Kamphaeng Yai** (admission free; 🕑 daylight hr), built as
a shrine to Shiva, features four 11th-century
prang and two *wí·hǎhn* (large hall in a Thai temple, usually open to laity). The *prang* (including
the main one, which was built of sandstone but
restored with brick) have lost their tops, but
many lintels and other carvings remain. The
ruined sanctuary can be found on the grounds
of Wat Sa Kamphaeng Yai, the *prasat*'s modern
successor. Buses from Si Saket (20B, 30 minutes) and Surin (55B, 1½ hours) can drop you
right nearby; the train is faster and cheaper but
the station is a couple of kilometres away.

About 8km west of Si Saket on the way
to Kamphaeng Yai (on the north side of the
highway in a temple with no sign in English)
is **Prasat Sa Kamphaeng Noi** (admission free; 🕑 daylight
hr). Like many other Khmer ruins in the area,
Angkor King Jayavarman VII made it a healing station. It had sat as a jumbled pile of
rubble for ages, but is finally being re-erected.
Still, it's very modest.

Temples

Officially it's Wat Pa Maha Chedi Kaeo, but
these days nearly everyone calls it **Wat Lan
Khuat** (🕑 daylight hr), the 'Million Bottle Temple'.
In 1982 the abbot dreamt of a *bràh·sàht* in
heaven made entirely of glass. Realising that
glass symbolised the need for clarity of purpose in one's life, he decided to replicate the
idea as best as he could on earth by covering nearly every surface of every building of
his current temple with glass bottles. He also
figured the idea would save the community
lots of money on paint. The more you look
around, the less the name seems like an exaggeration. He took the theme one step further
by using bottle caps to create much of the
adornment. It's in Khun Han, 11km south of
Hwy 24 via Rte 2111. Turn west at the roundabout in the centre of town.

Wat Phra That Rueang Rong (🕑 daylight hr) is
another unusual temple. A previous abbot,
lamenting the loss of the old ways, built the
bòht like an oxcart being pulled by two giant
cows. He also created a **museum** (admission free;
🕑 7.30am-5pm), with old tools, musical instruments and the like from the province's four
cultures: Lao, Khmer, Suai and Yer. Concrete
statues of people on the grounds wear
traditional clothes, while oversized animals
offer life lessons (lead a bad life and you
might come back as a gorilla the next time
around). The *wát* is 7km north of town;
take *sŏrng·tǎa·ou* 2 (12B, 20 minutes) from
in front of the train station.

UBON RATCHATHANI PROVINCE

This varied province, famous across
Thailand for its forest temples, pushes down
into the jungle-clad intersection of Thailand,
Laos and Cambodia. To bolster the region's
tourist profile, TAT has labelled its south-

ern reaches the 'Emerald Triangle' in recognition of its magnificent green landscapes, and drawing obvious parallels with northern Thailand's 'Golden Triangle'. Despite having plenty to entertain the rustic rover, the hoped-for hordes of visitors have failed to arrive.

Phu Chong Nayoi and Pha Taem National Parks are two of Thailand's most remote corners, and Ubon remains one of the region's more charming cities.

History
Ubon's Mae Nam Mun and Mae Nam Chi river basins were centres for Dvaravati and Khmer cultures many centuries ago. Following the decline of the Khmer empires, the area was settled by groups of Lao in the late 18th century, and they founded the capital city. By the early Ratanakosin era it had become part of *monthon* Ubon, a southeastern Isan satellite state extending across what are now Surin, Si Saket and Ubon Provinces, as well as parts of southern Laos. Champasak, Laos, was the *monthon* capital. Today the Lao influence in the province dominates over the Khmer.

UBON RATCHATHANI
อุบลราชธานี
pop 115,000
Survive the usual knot of choked access roads and Ubon will reveal an altogether more attractive face. Racked up against Mae Nam Mun, Thailand's second-longest river, the southern portions of the city have a sluggish character rarely found in the region's big conurbations. Temples pepper the city, the urban push-and-shove is easily escaped and, despite the quick-time march of modernisation, a deep sense of Isan identity lives on. Few cities in Thailand reward aimless wandering as richly as Ubon.

A US air base during the Vietnam era, 21st-century Ubon is primarily a financial, educational and agricultural market centre for eastern Isan. The nearby Thai–Lao border crossing at Chong Mek guarantees a small but steady stream of travellers.

Orientation & Information
Most of the activity in Ubon takes place to the north of Mae Nam Mun and east of the main north–south thoroughfare, Th Chayangkun/Th Uparat. Ubon's historic heart is down by the river, below Th Si Narong. Although there aren't many old wooden shophouses left, Th Yutthaphan has several fine examples. The train station is south of the river in Warin Chamrap.

EMERGENCY & MEDICAL SERVICES
Tourist police (☎ 0 4524 5505; Th Suriyat) A block behind the regular police station.
Ubonrak Thonburi Hospital (☎ 0 4526 0285; Th Phalorangrit) Has a 24-hour casualty department.

INTERNET ACCESS
Ubon isn't exactly flush with internet cafes, but you don't have to look too hard to find them.
Blink (105-107 Th Yutthaphan; internet per hr 15B; ☻ 9am-10pm) Around the corner from TAT.

MONEY
Banks that are open normal business hours are found around the city centre and along Th Chayangkun. The following are open later and change both cash and travellers cheques.
Krung Thai Bank (Th Ratchathani; ☻ 10am-7pm) Inside Ying Charoen Park shopping centre.
Siam Commercial Bank (Tesco-Lotus, Th Chayangkun; ☻ 10.30am-8pm) At Tesco-Lotus department store.

POST
Main post office (Th Luang; ☻ 8.30am-4.30pm Mon-Fri, 9am-noon Sat, Sun & holidays)

TOURIST INFORMATION
Tourism Authority of Thailand (TAT; ☎ 0 4524 3770; www.tatubon.org; 264/1 Th Kheuan Thani; ☻ 8.30am-4.30pm) Has helpful staff.

TRAVEL AGENCIES
Sakda Travel World (☎ 0 4525 4333; www.sakdatour .com; Th Phalorangrit; ☻ 9am-6pm Mon-Sat) Sells plane tickets, hires out cars and leads tours.

Sights & Activities
UBON NATIONAL MUSEUM
พิพิธภัณฑสถานแห่งชาติอุบลราชธานี
Don't miss the informative **Ubon National Museum** (☎ 0 4525 5071; Th Kheuan Thani; admission 100B; ☻ 9am-4pm Wed-Sun). Occupying the former city hall, this is the spot to swot up on background information before venturing out into the wider province. And there's plenty on show, from Buddhist ordination-precinct stones from the Dvaravati period and a 2500-year-old Dong

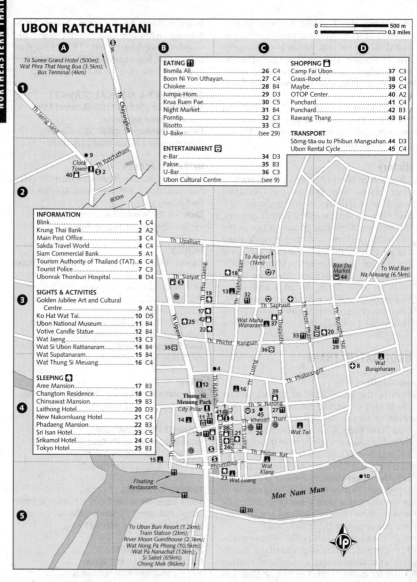

UBON RATCHATHANI

EATING
Bismila Ali	26	C4
Boon Ni Yon Uthayan	27	C4
Chiokee	28	B4
Jumpa-Hom	29	D3
Krua Ruen Pae	30	C5
Night Market	31	B4
Porntip	32	C3
Risotto	33	C3
U-Bake	(see 29)	

ENTERTAINMENT
e-Bar	34	D3
Pakse	35	B3
U-Bar	36	C3
Ubon Cultural Centre	(see 9)	

SHOPPING
Camp Fai Ubon	37	C3
Grass-Root	38	C4
Maybe	39	A2
OTOP Center	40	A2
Punchard	41	C4
Punchard	42	B3
Rawang Thang	43	B4

TRANSPORT
Sŏrng·tăa·ou to Phibun Mangsahan	44	D3
Ubon Rental Cycle	45	C4

INFORMATION
Blink	1	C4
Krung Thai Bank	2	A2
Main Post Office	3	C4
Sakda Travel World	4	C4
Siam Commercial Bank	5	A1
Tourism Authority of Thailand (TAT)	6	C4
Tourist Police	7	C3
Ubonrak Thonburi Hospital	8	D4

SIGHTS & ACTIVITIES
Golden Jubilee Art and Cultural Centre	9	A2
Ko Hat Wat Tai	10	D5
Ubon National Museum	11	B4
Votive Candle Statue	12	B4
Wat Jaeng	13	C3
Wat Si Ubon Rattanaram	14	B4
Wat Supatanaram	15	B4
Wat Thung Si Meuang	16	C4

SLEEPING
Aree Mansion	17	B3
Changtom Residence	18	C3
Chinsawat Mansion	19	B3
Laithong Hotel	20	D3
New Nakornluang Hotel	21	C4
Phadaeng Mansion	22	B3
Sri Isan Hotel	23	C5
Srikamol Hotel	24	C4
Tokyo Hotel	25	B3

Son bronze drum to Ubon textiles and betel-nut sets. The museum's most prized possession is a 9th-century Ardhanarisvara, a composite statue combining Shiva and his consort Uma into one being; one of just two ever found in Thailand.

The museum is on the edge of Thung Si Meuang Park, the centrepiece of which is a huge concrete replica of an elaborate **votive candle** representing Ubon's annual Candle Parade (see p484).

GOLDEN JUBILEE ART & CULTURAL CENTRE
ศูนย์วัฒนธรรมอุบลฯ

There is a **museum** (☎ 0 4535 2000; Th Jaeng Sanit; admission free; 8.30am-4.30pm) in the lower level of this striking contemporary Isan-design tower at Rajabhat University. It's more scattershot than the National Museum, but there are some interesting cultural displays, particularly of houses and handicrafts. There's also a whole lot of wax sculpture.

WAT THUNG SI MEUANG
วัดทุ่งศรีเมือง

Wat Thung Si Meuang (Th Luang; ☻ daylight hr) was built during the reign of Rama III (1824–51) and has a classic *hŏr đrai* (Tripitaka hall) in excellent shape. Like many *hŏr đrai*, it rests on tall, angled stilts in the middle of a small pond, surrounded by water, to protect the precious scriptures (written on palm-leaf paper) from termites. It's kept open, so you can look around inside. Alongside it, the interior of the little *bòht* is painted with 200-year-old murals depicting the life and culture of the day.

WAT SI UBON RATTANARAM
วัดศรีอุบลรัตนาราม

The *bòht* at **Wat Si Ubon Rattanaram** (Th Uparat; ☻ daylight hr) resembles Bangkok's Wat Benchamabophit, but it's the 7cm-tall Topaz Buddha inside that most people come to see. Phra Kaew Butsarakham was reportedly brought here from Vientiane at Ubon's founding and is the city's holiest possession. It sits behind glass high up the back wall, all but out of sight. There are sometimes binoculars available to get a closer look, and the image directly in front of the largest Buddha is a copy.

The temple has turned a beautiful old wooden *săh·lah* (open-sided, covered meeting hall or resting place, often spelt sala) into a **museum** (admission free; ☻ 9am-4pm) of religious items. The highlight is the collection of 18th-century *đoô prá đrai·ʰidòk*, gorgeous boxes used for storing sacred palm-leaf texts. If you can understand Thai, someone will demonstrate the process used to paint the designs with real gold.

WAT PHRA THAT NONG BUA
วัดพระธาตุหนองบัว

The richly adorned 55m *chedi* at **Wat Phra That Nong Bua** (Th Thammawithi; ☻ daylight hr) closely resembles the Mahabodhi stupa in Bodhgaya, India. Two groups of four niches on each side of the four-sided *chedi* contain Buddhas standing in stylised Gupta or Dvaravati closed-robe poses. It's the only square stupa in Ubon Province (unless you count the older one it was built over, or the four similar but smaller ones on the corners). The elaborate *jataka* reliefs on the outside were getting a renovation during our last visit. It's on the outskirts of town; take *sŏrng·tăa·ou* 10.

WAT BAN NA MEUANG
วัดบ้านนาเมือง

Also known as Wat Sa Prasan Suk, **Wat Ban Na Meuang** (☻ daylight hr) stands out from other temples in many ways. Most famously, the *bòht* sits on a boat: a ceramic encrusted replica of King Rama IX's royal barge *Suphannahong*, complete with a sculpted crew. The *wí·hăhn* also has a boat-shaped base (this time the prince's personal craft), and this one is surrounded by an actual pond. These were not just artistic endeavours. The water represents our desires and the boats represent staying above them. Finally, to reach all of these, you must pass under an immense statue of Airavata, Hindu god Indra's three-headed elephant mount. The commissioner of these creations, Luang Pu Boon Mi, died in 2001 and his body (not to be confused with the lifelike wax statue) is on display in the *săh·lah* next to the boat *bòht*. The temple is 4km northwest of town, 1km off the ring road; *sŏrng·tăa·ou* 8 passes it.

WAT JAENG
วัดแจ้ง

Founded around the time of the city's founding, **Wat Jaeng** (Th Nakhon Baan; ☻ daylight hr) has an adorable Lan Xang-style *bòht*. There are large eave brackets on the side and the carved wooden facade depicts Airavata and two mythical lions.

WAT SUPATANARAM
วัดสุปัฏนาราม

Called **Wat Supat** (Th Supat; ☻ daylight hr) for short, the unique *bòht* at this riverside temple, built between 1920 and 1936, features a Thai roof, European arches and a Khmer base. And, in contrast to other temple structures of the region, it's made entirely of stone, like the early Khmer stone *ʰrah·sàht*. Hanging nearby is a wooden bell, reputed to be the largest in Thailand.

KO HAT WAT TAI
เกาะหาดวัดใต้

Picnicking families flock to this island in Mae Nam Mun during the hot, dry months of February to May when beaches rise along its

NORTHEASTERN THAILAND

shore. A makeshift bamboo bridge connects it to the northern shore and floating restaurants set up shop.

WARIN CHAMRAP DISTRICT TEMPLES

The famous monk and meditation master Luang Pu Cha, a former disciple of Luang Pu Man known for his simple and direct teaching method, was quite a name in these parts. During his life he founded the following two well-known forest monasteries and many more around the world.

Wat Nong Pa Phong
วัดหนองป่าพง

Peaceful **Wat Nong Pa Phong** (☽ daylight hr) is known for its quiet discipline and daily routine of work and meditation. Dozens of Westerners have lived here over recent decades, and several still do. The wát features the golden *chedi* where Luang Pu Cha's relics are interred and a three-storey **museum** (admission free; ☽ 8am-4.30pm) displaying an odd assortment of items, from Luang Pu Ajahn Cha's worldly possessions to world currencies to a foetus in a jar. The temple is about 10km past the river. *Sŏrng·tăa·ou* 3 gets you within 2km; a motorcycle taxi (if one is available) should cost 20B.

Wat Pa Nanachat
วัดป่านานาชาติบุ่งหวาย

Wat Pa Nanachat (www.watpahnanachat.org; Ban Bung Wai; ☽ daylight hr) is a Western-oriented wát, opened in 1975 specifically for non-Thais, and English is the primary language. Those with previous meditation experience are welcome to apply (write to the Guest Monk, Wat Pa Nanachat, Ban Bung Wai, Amphoe Warin Chamrap, Ubon Ratchathani 34310) to stay here. Guests must follow all temple rules including eating just one meal a day, rising at 3am and shaving heads and eyebrows.

There's nothing really to see here, but visitors are welcome to drop by. A senior monk is available to answer questions most days after the 8am meal and someone will likely be around until 11am. A *sŏrng·tăa·ou* from Warin Market or any Si Saket bus can drop you on Hwy 226, about 500m from the entrance. The wát is in the forest behind the rice fields.

Festivals

Ubon's famous **Candle Parade** (Hae Tian) began during the reign of King Rama V when the governor decided the city's rocket festival was too

dangerous. The original simple designs have since grown to gigantic, elaborately carved wax sculptures. It's a part of Khao Phansaa, a Buddhist holiday marking the commencement of *wan òrk pan·săh*, the Rains Retreat (Buddhist Lent) in July. The rest of the year you can see the candles at most temples (where they're kept until they're melted down for the next parade) and at the OTOP Center (p486). The festival is very popular with Thai tourists and the city's hotels are booked out long in advance.

Sleeping
BUDGET

River Moon Guesthouse (☎ 0 4528 6093; 21 Th Sisaket 2; s 120B, d 150-180B) Every year it gets tougher and tougher to recommend this crumbling old place, but it still sees a trickle of travellers wanting something out of the ordinary. The rustic rooms, 300m from the train station, are in old railway workers quarters and facilities are shared.

New Nakornluang Hotel (☎ 0 4525 4768; 84-88 Th Yutthaphan; r 170-320B; ✸) Unlike River Moon, which is run down with character, this definitely-not-new place is simply a dive. But, if you want to spend as little as possible and still be in the city centre, it's clean enough.

Tokyo Hotel (☎ 0 4524 1262; 360 Th Uparat; r 200-600B; ✸ 🖵) Besides being a popular though dour midranger, the Tokyo is a long-standing budget favourite. The pricier rooms are in a new tower while the humble air-con and fan affairs (all with cold-water showers) are in the old. The free wi-fi sometimes creeps across to rooms in the old building.

Aree Mansion (☎ 0 4526 5518; 208-212 Th Pha Daeng; r 250-350B; ✸ 🖵) The clear pick of the pack for shoestring travellers can't hide its age, but it deserves credit for trying. The bright, newly painted rooms are big and clean and even the cheap fan versions come with hot water, fridge and free wireless.

Changtom Residence (☎ 0 4526 5525; 216 Th Suriyat; r 400B; ✸ 🖵) Not only does this mid-sized place have clean, comfortable rooms, but the friendly English-speaking owner will pick you up for free when you arrive in town.

Phadaeng Mansion (☎ 0 4525 4600; 126 Th Pha Daeng; r 400-500B; ✸ 🖵) The copies of classic paintings on the walls don't make this new (opened in 2008) place classy, though they're a nice touch. Rooms are boxy, but they're good and have little balconies. And free wi-fi reaches them all.

Chinsawat Mansion (☎ 0 4524 1179; 164/4 Th Saphasit; r 450B; 🅿 💻) Minus the Monets, Chinsawat isn't much different from Phadaeng, only it somehow manages to exude a homey feeling, which isn't a common feat for the typical mansion hotel. Also like Phadaeng, the rooms have little balconies, but here there isn't much to look at from them.

Srikamol Hotel (☎ 0 4524 6088; 26 Th Ubonsak; r 450-600B; 🅿) Unlike the previously listed places in this price range, Srikamol has been around the block. From the chandelier in the lobby to the tile floors, there are still signs from its time as one of Ubon's best; though those days are way behind it. It's not better than the others, but if you like it old-school, you'll like this one.

MIDRANGE

our pick **Sri Isan Hotel** (☎ 0 4526 1011; www.sriisanhotel .com; 62 Th Ratchabut; r 650-1400B; 🅿 💻) The exception to the rule of Ubon's typical uninspired midrangers, this bright, cheerful place is full of natural light, which streams down through the atrium and gives the lobby an open, airy feel. The rooms are small and the decor is a little twee (a knitted toilet-roll cover wouldn't be out of place) but standards are high and an orchid comes gratis on every pillow. They'll pick you up at the train station or airport for free, but charge 100B from the bus station.

Ubon Buri Resort (☎ 0 4526 6777; www.ubonburihotel .com; Th Srimongkol; r 1140-1330B, bungalows 1500B, ste 3000B; 🅿 💻 🏊) This bona fide, self-contained resort is the place to come if you're planning on staying in Ubon without really *being* in Ubon. With rooms and bungalows set in acres of gardens on a little branch of the Mun River, Isan folk-art styling and tip-top staff, it's as good as Ubon's pricier top-enders, though the wi-fi doesn't reach most of the rooms.

TOP END

Laithong Hotel (☎ 0 4526 4271; www.laithonghotel .net; 50 Th Phichit Rangsan; r 1300-1900B, ste 3300B; 🅿 💻 🏊) The rooms should, perhaps, be a bit swankier at these prices, but the attentive staff simply cannot be improved upon. It has all the usual 'executive' facilities, a Japanese restaurant and the odd token nod to traditional Isan design. There's a 3rd-floor outdoor swimming pool.

Sunee Grand Hotel (☎ 0 4535 2900; www.suneegrand hotel.com; Th Chayangkun; r 2800-3600B, ste 4800-25,000B; 🅿 💻 🏊) One of the few hotels in Isan that could hold its own in Bangkok, the Sunee Grand is a stunner; and far less expensive than its peers in the capital. The owners, who opened the hotel in 2008, appear to have nailed it in all regards, from the stylish light fixtures to the at-a-snap service. There's a large business centre, a piano player in the lobby and an adjacent shopping mall, plus a rooftop waterpark and bowling alley were under construction at the time of writing.

Eating

Night Market (🕐 4pm-1am) It's still rather small, but Ubon has improved its night market in recent years.

Boon Ni Yon Uthayan (☎ 0 4524 0950; Th Si Narong; per plate 10-15B; 🕐 breakfast & lunch Tue-Sun) Run by the ascetic Sisa Asoka group, this restaurant has an impressive vegetarian buffet under a giant roof. Most of the food is grown organically just outside the city.

Porntip (☎ 08 9720 8101; Th Saphasit; dishes 20-100B, ½ chickens 60-80B; 🕐 9am-6pm) It looks like a tornado whipped through this no-frills spot, but the chefs cook up a storm of their own. This relocated restaurant, formerly Gai Yang Wat Jaeng, is considered by many to be Ubon's premier purveyor of *gài yâhng*, *sôm·đam*, sausages and other Isan food.

Chiokee (☎ 0 4525 4017; 307-317 Th Kheuan Thani; dishes 25-160B; 🕐 6am-7pm) Offering a slightly incongruous blend of East (dark-wood styling and a decorative Chinese shrine) and West (Heinz ketchup and white tablecloths), this popular (especially for breakfast) spot whips up a wide range of dishes, from eel sour-and-spicy soup to hamburgers.

Bismila Ali (☎ 08 6871 5852; 177 Th Kheuan Thani; dishes 30-100B; 🕐 7am-9pm) This little hole in the wall serves both Indian and Thai-Muslim (try the 'fish three taste': red tilapia cooked in chilli sauce) food. Unless you just snatch a roti from the cart out front, your food won't come fast but it'll be done right.

our pick **Krua Ruen Pae** (no roman-script sign; ☎ 0 4532 4342; dishes 40-300B; 🕐 lunch & dinner) One of several floating restaurants on the Mun River, Krua Ruen Pae serves up tasty Thai and Isan food and a relaxed atmosphere. The *đôm kàh gài* (spicy chicken curry with galangal in coconut milk) is lovely. If driving here, exit to the west and then go under the bridge.

U-Bake (☎ 0 4526 5671; 49/3 Th Phichit Rangsan; chocolate cake 60B; 🕐 lunch & dinner) There are many good bakeries in town, but only U-Bake gets to share space with lovely Jumpa-Hom.

Risotto (☎ 08 1879 1869; Th Phichit Rangsan; dishes 80-300B; ☺ lunch & dinner) The dining room can't quite pull off an Italian vibe, but the kitchen offers a dash of *la dolce vita*. The menu has a full roster of pasta, plus salmon steak and one of the best pizzas in Isan.

Jumpa-Hom (☎ 0 4526 0398; 49/3 Th Phichit Rangsan; dishes 55-1500B; ☺ dinner) One of the classiest places in town, Jumpa-Hom serves pricey but good Thai, Isan, Chinese and Western cuisine on a gorgeous water-and-plant–filled wooden deck. The dining room is lovely too and has a choice of chairs or cushions for floor seating.

Drinking & Entertainment

Ubon has no nightlife district; the few happening places are spread out across town.

U-Bar (☎ 0 4526 5141; 97/8-10 Th Phichit Rangsan; ☺ 7pm-1am) While other clubs have come and gone over the years, this place has long remained at the top of the heap for the college crowd, partly because DJs from Bangkok sometimes take the stage. If you go, try a Blue Kamikaze, served out of a sinister-looking slush machine behind the bar.

e-Bar (Th Phichit Rangsan; ☺ 7pm-1am) A newer club going head to head with U-Bar, only with more glitz and more dancing. Their special promotions and regular visits from Bangkok bands have made it very popular.

Pakse (no roman-script sign; Th Uparat; ☺ 6pm-12.30am) More of a pub than a club, only with very loud music, this large place has oodles of cosy character, a pool table and a full menu. It's not flashy, just cool.

Golden Jubilee Art & Cultural Centre (☎ 0 4535 2000; Th Jaeng Sanit) There are sometimes Isan music and dance performances here.

Shopping

The speciality of Ubon Province is natural-dyed, hand-woven cotton, and you'll find a fantastic assortment of clothing, bags and fabric here. First stop should be **Camp Fai Ubon** (☎ 0 4524 1821; 189 Th Thepyothi; ☺ 8am-5pm), which is signed as Peaceland. Smaller, but also good is **Grass-Root** (☎ 0 4524 1272; 87 Th Yutthaphan; ☺ 9am-5pm). Although it features less natural-dyed fabric, **Maybe** (☎ 0 4525 4452; 124 Th Si Narong; ☺ 8am-7pm) is another good clothing shop with reasonable prices.

There's also some Ubon cotton at **Punchard** (☎ 0 4526 5751; 156 Th Pha Daeng; ☺ 9am-8pm), a large all-rounder handicrafts shop with a pricey but great selection. There is also a **Punchard branch** (☎ 0 4524 3433) on Th Ratchabut that is mostly a home-decor centre. The new, and still half-empty, **OTOP Center** (Th Jaeng Sanit; ☺ 8.30am-5pm) also has a varied shopping selection.

In a completely different vein from the above shops, **Rawang Thang** (☎ 08 1700 7013; 301 Th Kheuan Thani; ☺ 9am-9pm Mon-Sat) sells fun and funky T-shirts, postcards, picture frames and assorted bric-a-brac, most created by the friendly husband-and-wife owners. They can fill you in on all things Ubon and are considering opening a riverside guesthouse.

Getting There & Away

AIR

THAI (www.thaiairways.com) has two daily flights to/from Bangkok (one-way 2020B), while **Air Asia** (www.airasia.com) has one (1400B).

BUS

Ubon's **bus terminal** (☎ 0 4531 6085) is north of the town; take *sŏrng·tăa·ou* 2, 3 or 10 to the centre.

Buses link Ubon with Bangkok (2nd/1st class 396/473B, eight hours) frequently in the morning and evening, plus a few around midday. **999 VIP** (☎ 0 4531 4299; 24-seat VIP 724B; ☺ 6.30pm & 7.30pm) has the slickest service, but **Nakhonchai Air** (☎ 0 4526 9777; 32-seat VIP 595B; ☺ 10 daily) is also very good. The former also has direct service to Pakse, Laos (1st class 200B, 9.30am and 2pm, three hours) while the latter also goes straight to Rayong (2nd class/32-seat VIP 427/641B, 14 hours, 11 daily) and Chiang Mai (2nd class/32-seat VIP 595/893B, 17 hours, six daily). Other fares to/from Ubon are in the table, opposite.

Phibun (35B, 1½ hours, every 20 minutes) and Khong Jiam (80B, three hours, 10am) buses stop briefly at the Warin Market across the river after leaving the terminal, but you may not get a seat if you board there.

TRAIN

The **train station** (☎ 0 4532 1588) is in Warin Chamrap; take *sŏrng·tăa·ou* 2 from Ubon. The overnight express train leaves Bangkok nightly at 8.30pm, arriving in Ubon at 7.25am the next day, while the Bangkok-bound service heads west at 6.30pm arriving at 5.50am. Fares for 3rd-class seat/2nd-class air-con seat/2nd-class fan sleeper/1st-class air-con sleeper are 245/551/471/1180B. Six other trains also make the run throughout the day, taking just as long except the 5.45am (from Bangkok)

2.50pm (from Ubon) special express service, which takes 8½ hours. Trains also stop in Si Saket, Surin and Khorat (3rd-/2nd-class air-con 58/423B, four to six hours).

Getting Around

Numbered *sŏrng·tăa·ou* (10B) run throughout town. The free city map that TAT hands out marks the routes, most of which pass near its office. A normal túk-túk trip will cost at least 40B.

Ubon Rental Cycle (☎ 0 4524 4708; 115 Th Si Narong; ☽ 8.30am-6pm Mon-Sat) has a few bikes for hire at 100B per day.

AROUND UBON RATCHATHANI PROVINCE

Ban Pa-Ao
บ้านผาอ่าว

Northwest of Ubon on Hwy 23, Ban Pa-Ao is a silk-weaving village, but it's best known for producing brass and bronze items using the lost-wax casting method. It's the only place in Thailand where the entire process is still done by hand. You can watch workers creating bells, bowls and other items at **Soon Thorng Leuang Ban Pa-Ao** (☽ 8am-5pm) cooperative on the far side of the village. There's also a silk-weaving co-op on the way into town.

Ban Pa-Ao's **homestay** (☎ 08 1076 1249; per person incl 2 meals 300B) program offers the chance to try your hand at both of the town's trades, though little English is spoken.

Ban Pa-Ao is 3.5km off the highway. Buses to/from Yasothon pass the turn-off, and a motorcycle taxi from the highway should cost 20B.

Phibun Mangsahan
อำเภอพิบูลมังสาหาร

Visitors often stop in the dusty town of Phibun Mangsahan to see a set of rapids called **Kaeng Sapheu**, just downstream of the Mun River bridge. The rocky islets make 'Python Rapids' rise between February and May, but the shady park here makes a pleasant stop year-round. It's got a Chinese temple, several simple restaurants – most serving *tòrt năng gòp* (deep-fried frog skins) – and a long line of souvenir shops. Many fishermen work here and they'll take you on short boat trips (200B per hour) in little long-tails to visit island temples. Ask at *'dăaw'* restaurant if you'd rather ride a bigger boat (500B per hour or 2000B for the day), which can hold 20 people.

BUSES TO/FROM UBON		
Destination	**Fare (B)**	**Duration (hr)**
Khon Kaen	ordinary 137	5
	2nd class 212	
	1st class 247	
Khorat	2nd class 203	7
	1st class 269	
Mukdahan	ordinary 85	3½
	2nd class 119	
	1st class 144	
Roi Et	ordinary 82	3
	2nd class 113	
	1st class 148	
Sakon Nakhon	ordinary 125	5
	2nd class 175	
	1st class 225	
Si Saket	ordinary 40	1¼
	2nd class 59	
Surin	2nd class 144	3
	1st class 212	
Yasothon	ordinary 50	1½
	2nd class 70	
	1st class 90	

Phibun Mangsahan has an **immigration office** (☎ 0 4544 1108; ☽ 8.30am-4.30pm Mon-Fri), where visa extensions are available. It's 1km south of the bridge on the way to Chong Mek.

The villages just over the bridge, as you drive east to Khong Jiam along Rte 2222, are famed for forging iron and bronze gongs, both for temples and classical Thai-music ensembles. You can watch the gong makers hammering the flat metal discs and tempering them in rustic fires at many roadside workshops. Small gongs start at around 500B and the 2m monsters fetch as much as 200,000B. People make drums and cymbals around here too.

SLEEPING & EATING

In the centre of town, midway between the bus stop and the bridge, **Phiboonkit Hotel** (☎ 0 4520 4872; 65/1-3 Th Phiboon; r 200-350B; ☒) is your usual, slightly chaotic, budget hotel.

Tom Reung Ruang (no roman-script sign; 135 Th Luang; ☽ breakfast & lunch), a ramshackle shop right at the bridge, is famous for *sah·lah·bow* (Chinese buns) and *năng jip* (small pork-filled wraps). Thais visiting Pha Taem National Park and Khong Jiam usually stop here to stock up on these items (5B each), and countless shops in town and on the highway have piggy-backed on their success.

GETTING THERE & AWAY

Phibun's bus park is behind the market. There are ordinary buses (35B, 1½ hours) every 20 minutes to Ubon's bus station, and *sŏrng·tăa·ou* (35B, 1½ hours) every half-hour to Talat Ban Du (Ban Du Market) near the city centre. There are also *sŏrng·tăa·ou* to Chong Mek (35B, one hour) every 20 minutes.

Kaeng Tana National Park

อุทยานแห่งชาติแก่งตะนะ

Five kilometres before Khong Jiam you can cross the Pak Mun dam to little **Kaeng Tana National Park** (☎ 0 4540 6887; admission 100B). After circling thickly forested Don Tana (Tana Island), linked to the mainland by a small suspension bridge, the Mun River roils through its beautiful namesake rapids, which lie underwater during the rainy season. The 1.5km clifftop trail to **Lan Pha Phueng** viewpoint is serene and there are canoes for hire (per hour 100B). Five kilometres south of the **visitor centre** (☒ 8am-4.30pm) is **Nam Tok Tad Ton**, a wide waterfall just a 300m walk from the road. There's a **campsite** (per person with own tent 30B, 3-/8-person tent hire 150/225B) and four **bungalows** (☎ 0 2562 0760; www.dnp.go.th/park reserve; 5/10 people 1000/2000B). The simple restaurant opens during the day only.

By road, the park is 14km from Khong Jiam. There's no public transport, but boats in town will take you upriver and drop you at the park for 800B, if the water levels permit. They'll even wait a few hours for you to stroll around before bringing you back.

Khong Jiam

โขงเจียม

Khong Jiam sits on a picturesque peninsula at the confluence of the Mekong and Mun Rivers – which the Thais call Mae Nam Song Si (Two-Colour River) after the contrasting currents formed at the junction. In the rainy season the multicoloured merger is visible from the shore, but the rest of the year you'll need to go out in a boat to see it properly; or, in April, just before the rains begin, you can walk out. A large boat with a sunshade that can carry 10 people costs 350B, while you'll pay 200B in a tiny boat that holds two. The big boats can also take you to Kaeng Tana (800B) or Pha Taem (1200B) National Parks.

Fishermen here use huge conical traps that look much like the fish traps appearing in the 3000-year-old murals at Pha Taem. *Naga*

fireballs (see the boxed text, p514) began appearing here in 2005.

Thais can cross the Mekong to Laos here, but foreigners cannot. The **immigration office** (☎ 0 4535 1084; 12/1 Th Kaewpradit; ☒ 8.30am-4.30pm) does, however, give visa extensions.

SLEEPING & EATING

Khong Jiam doesn't get many *fa·ràng* visitors, but it's popular with Thais, so there's an abundance of lodging choices.

Apple Guesthouse (☎ 0 4535 1160; 267 Th Kaewpradit; r 150-300B; ☒ ☐) Down a tiny little alley, the worn-out Apple has wooden buildings with concrete rooms below. It's pretty basic but clean, and it's the cheapest place in town.

Bon Pak Mongkhon Resort (☎ 0 4535 1352; www .mongkhon.com; 595 Th Kaewpradit; r 200-800B; ☒ ☐) From the simple fan rooms to the four cute wooden cottages, this place near the highway has friendly owners and lots of character, making it a great choice for any budget.

Khong Jiam Homestay (☎ 08 1977 2825; r 300B) Talk about yin and yang, these six wood-and-thatch cottages sit in a patch of forest right next to the Tohsang Resort, and have mattresses on the floors and roofless (but private) bathrooms. There's no food, but you can cook over a fire, or splash out and eat next door at Tohsang. It's often empty, but sometimes full with groups from Bangkok, so you may want to call before coming out here. A túk-túk from town should cost about 50B.

Baansuanrimnam Resort (☎ 08 7460 0100; www .baansuan.th.gs; 505 Th Rimmoon; r 700-1000B; ☒) This quiet, shady spot sits at the end of a little row of resorts along the Mun River. It has comfortable bungalows, with the most expensive featuring terraces looking at the water through a line of trees. To get there, turn right at the school just before the temple.

Tohsang Khong Jiam Resort (☎ 0 4535 1174; www .tohsang.com; r 2350-3890B, villas 3500-14,800B; ☒ ☐ ☒) The glitz and gloss at this large resort-spa are somewhat incongruous for this stretch of rural Thailand, but it holds all the aces in the posh-accommodation stakes, and the prices for the rooms are fair for what you get. Ask for a 3rd-floor room for the best views. It's 3.5km out of town on the south bank of the river.

There are several simple restaurants near the Mae Nam Song Si, including two pricey ones floating on the Mekong.

GETTING THERE & AWAY

All transport in town stops at the highway junction. There's only one bus from Ubon (80B, three hours, 10am) each day. It returns at 1pm. If you miss it, go to Phibun Mangsahan (p487) first and continue by *sörng·tǎa·ou* (35B, one hour, every 1½ hours) from the parking area next to the bridge, which is about 1km (20B by túk-túk) from the Phibun bus park.

Both Apple and Mongkhon guesthouses hire out bicycles (100B per day) and motorcycles (200B per day).

Pha Taem National Park

อุทยานแห่งชาติผาแต้ม

Up the Mekong from Khong Jiam is a long cliff named Pha Taem, the centrepiece of **Pha Taem National Park** (☎ 0 4531 8026; admission 200B). From the top you get an amazing bird's-eye view of Laos, and can see the first sunset in Thailand. Down below, reached via a trail, the cliff features prehistoric rock paintings that are at least 3000 years old. Mural subjects include fish traps, *blah bèuk* (giant Mekong catfish), elephants, human hands and geometric designs. The second viewing platform fronts the most impressive pictographs. A clifftop **visitor centre** (☯ 8am-5pm) contains exhibits pertaining to the paintings and local geology.

Nam Tok Soi Sawan, a 25m-tall waterfall flowing from June to October, is another popular spot. It's a 19km drive from the visitor centre and then a 500m walk, or you can hike (with a ranger) for 9km along the top of the cliff. What the park calls **Thailand's largest flower field** (blooming brightest in December) lies just beyond the falls. The far north of the park, where roads are really bad, holds many more waterfalls and wonderful views. **Pa Cha Na Dai** cliff also serves Thailand's first sunrise and amazing **Nam Tok Saeng Chan** flows through a hole cut into the overhanging rock. Scattered across the 340-sq-km park are several areas with **Sao Chaliang**, mushroom-shaped stone formations similar to those found in Mukdahan's Phu Pha Thoep National Park.

Pha Taem has **campsites** (per person with own tent 30B, tent hire 150-225B), **cabins** (4 people 300B) and five **bungalows** (☎ 0 2562 0760; www.dnp.go.th/park reserve; 6-person bungalow with fan 1200B, 5-person with air-con 2000B). Vendors sell snacks and fast food near the visitor centre.

Pha Taem is 18km from Khong Jiam via Rte 2112. There's no public transport, so the best way to get there is to hire a motorcycle in Khong Jiam (150B to 200B).

Chong Mek

ช่องเม็ก

South of Khong Jiam, at the end of Rte 217, is the small border town of Chong Mek, the only place in Thailand where *fa·ràng* can cross into Laos by land (that is, you don't have to cross a river). The southern Lao capital of Pakse is about 45 minutes by road from Vangtao, the village on the Lao side of the border, where you can buy a 30-day visa (see p754 for details) on the spot. The crossing is largely hassle free – buses crossing here wait for passengers to complete the paperwork – though some Lao officials still try to extract a 50B 'stamping fee'.

The opening of the bridge in Mukdahan has reduced traffic on this route and stolen much of the bustle from the Chong Mek market, which used to be a big hit with Thai tourists.

If you get here after hours, the **Nonthaveth & Ounchith Guesthouse** (☎ 0 4547 6144; r 200-400B; ✪) is clean and friendly, though a little overpriced.

Buses from Ubon (2nd /1st class 80/100B, 1½ hours) are infrequent, so you may want to first get to Phibun Mangsahan and then take a *sörng·tǎa·ou* (35B, one hour, every 20 minutes until 5pm) from there. If you're in a hurry, there are also three morning and two late-afternoon buses direct to/from Bangkok (2nd class/32-seat VIP 421/632B). There's no public transport between Chong Mek and Khong Jiam; either go through Phibun or hire a túk-túk for about 350B.

For continuing on to Pakse, it's easy to catch a ride on the Lao side.

Phu Chong Nayoi National Park

อุทยานแห่งชาติภูจองนายอย

Sitting at the heart of the 'Emerald Triangle' is the little-known **Phu Chong Nayoi National Park** (☎ 0 4541 1515; admission 200B), one of Thailand's wildest parks and healthiest forests. Resident fauna includes Malayan sun bears, barking deer, gibbons, black hornbills and endangered white-winged ducks. Elephants and tigers spend most of their time in Laos, but often make their way over the border into the park.

The park's primary attraction is **Nam Tok Huay Luang**, which plunges 40m over a cliff in two parallel streams. A short trail leads to the top, and you can walk down 274 steps to the bottom. Another 170m downstream is little **Nam Tok Jum Jim**, also a pretty picture. You can swim below both, though they dry up around March. Rangers love taking visitors on short bamboo-raft trips (price negotiable) above the falls, where they insist you might see a python. Unfortunately, water levels are often too high or too low to allow the trip, especially from February to April. At the far end of the 687-sq-km park, from atop **Phu Hin Dang**, there are superb views of the surrounding countryside, which looks much like the view from Pha Taem cliff, p489, but with jungle instead of the Mekong at the bottom of the valley. It's a 50km drive from the main park entrance and then a 2km hike.

Stargazing is superb here, so consider spending the night. There are three **bungalows** (☎ 0 2562 0760; www.dnp.go.th/parkreserve; 4-/6-person bungalow 600/1200B) plus a **campsite** (per person with own tent 30B; tent hire 150-300B). A couple of restaurants operate on weekends and holidays only, but park staff will cook for overnight guests with advance notice. Snacks and drinks are available daily.

Getting There & Away
From Ubon catch one of the three morning buses to the town of Najaluay (60B, 3½ hours). From Najaluay, túk-túk can be hired for about 300B for the 20km return journey to Nam Tok Huai Luang with a short wait.

CHAIYAPHUM PROVINCE

Travelling through Chaiyaphum Province, you're almost as likely to run into a tiger as a foreign tourist; and this is not a province with lots of tigers. Despite its position at the heart of the country, it's a remote region and remains something of a mystery, even to Thais. Famous for its fields of flowers (but not a whole lot else), Chaiyaphum has several sights worth a peep, but its primary appeals are the peace and quiet and sense of straying off the beaten track.

History
In the late 18th century a Lao court official brought 200 Lao from Vientiane to settle this area, which had been abandoned by the Khmers some 500 years earlier. The community paid tribute to Vientiane but also cultivated relations with Bangkok and Champasak. When Prince Anou (from Vientiane) declared war on Siam in the early 19th century, the Lao ruler of Chaiyaphum, Jao Pho Phraya Lae, wisely switched allegiance to Bangkok, knowing that Anou's armies didn't stand a chance against the more powerful Siamese. Although Jao Pho Phraya Lae lost his life in battle in 1806, the Siamese eventually sacked Vientiane and ruled most of western Laos until the coming of the French near the end of the 19th century. Today a statue of Jao Pho Phraya Lae (renamed Phraya Phakdi Chumphon by the Thais) stands at the entrance to the capital city.

CHAIYAPHUM
ชัยภูมิ
pop 55,500
Chaiyaphum is a bit of a nowhere town. It is a base for visiting the surrounding attractions, all just a short hop outside the city, rather than a destination in itself. Fashionistas should head west to the silk village of Ban Khwao and the outdoorsy should hit the mountains. There are several national parks in the area, of which Tat Ton is the star.

Information
Bangkok Bank (1st fl, Tesco-Lotus; Th Sanambin; ☺ 10am-8pm) The city centre's only late-opening bank; exchanges cash only.
Pat Pat (☎ 0 4483 0037; Th Tantawan; internet per hr 15B; ☺ 11am-10pm) Friendly internet cafe and coffee shop. Owner Pan is a good source of information about Chaiyaphum.

Sights
PRANG KU
ปรางค์กู่
This Khmer *prang*, on Th Bannakan just east of the city, was constructed during the reign of the final Angkor king, Jayavarman VII (1181–1219). It was built as a place of worship, at a 'healing station' on the Angkor temple route between the Angkor capital in Cambodia and Prasat Singh in Kanchanaburi Province. The Buddha figure inside the *ku* (small *chedi*) purportedly hails from the

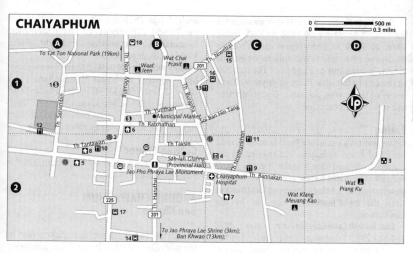

Dvaravati period (6th to 10th centuries). However, the *prang* is poorly preserved and not much to look at. As this is the top ancient site in the province, it's not surprising that history buffs don't flock to Chaiyaphum.

TAMNAK KEOW
ตำหนักเขียว

Built in 1950 as the governor's residence and now restored as a museum, **Tamnak Keow** (Green Hall; ☎ 0 4481 1574; Th Burapha; admission free) has hohum displays of old *mát·mèe* cloth and photos from King Rama IX's 1955 visit. It's open by appointment only; it's hardly worth the effort.

Festivals

Chaiyaphum residents celebrate two nine-day festivals yearly in honour of Jao Pho Phraya Lae (see opposite for more on him). The Jao Pho Phraya Lae Fair starts on 12 January, the date of his death, and takes place at *sǎh·lah glahng* (provincial hall), near his statue. Activities in late April or early May during the Jao Pho Phraya Lae Elephant Offering Ceremony are focused on a lakeside shrine erected where he

was killed, about 3km southwest of the centre off the road to Ban Khwao. Both events feature music and an elephant parade.

Sleeping

Ratanasiri Hotel (no roman-script sign; ☎ 0 4482 1258; 667/19 Th Non Meuang; r 200-500B; ❄) This dowdy giant is a great choice for those on a budget. But if you're planning on spending in the 500B range, then definitely head for Tonkoon, because rooms at Ratanasiri generally get bigger rather than better as the price rises. Smiling staff make up for the lack of atmosphere.

Tonkoon Hotel (☎ 0 4481 7881; 379 Th Bannakan; r 500B; ❄ 💻) Rooms rather resemble a college dorm; nevertheless, this spic-and-span 'mansion' standard hotel is the clear choice at this price. Free wi-fi extends throughout.

Deeprom Hotel (☎ 0 4482 2222; 339/9 Th Bannakan; r 800-900B; ste 1800B; ❄ 💻) With its crazy colour scheme and bold boast (the name means 'good at everything'), this new (opened 2008) hotel demands attention. Rooms are a little less flashy, but good for the price and also have free wi-fi.

Siam River Resort (☎ 0 4481 1999; www.siamriver resort.com; Th Bannakan; r 890-1500B, ste 2000B, cottage 3500B; ✷ ⬚ ⬚) Chaiyaphum doesn't cater to droves of tourists, but this incongruous resort, hidden out of earshot of the hubbub of the city (what little there is, anyway) hosts many of those who do come. Guests get free use of wi-fi and bicycles.

Eating

Chaiyaphum's signature food is *mahm* (sour beef and liver) sausages, but they're an acquired taste and don't make it onto many menus. The **Night Bazaar** (⏲ 4-11pm) west of downtown is a better foraging destination than the **night market** (⏲ 5pm-1am) by the bus station.

Chor Ra Gah Lahb Gory (no roman-script sign; ☎ 08 7246 7951; 299/21 Th Bannakan; dishes 25-60B; ⏲ breakfast, lunch & dinner) With its concrete floor, corrugated metal roof and old-time foods – like the namesake *gôry* (raw beef with lemon, chilli, fish sauce and extra blood) – this no-nonsense Isan eatery takes diners back to the village. The partial picture menu gets you through the language barrier.

Jae Hai Tek (no roman-script sign; ☎ 08 6914 0439; Th Tantawan; dishes 30-40B; ⏲ breakfast, lunch & dinner) This is a simple, friendly, all-vegetarian affair. It serves a range of Thai and Chinese standards, using mock meats to make chicken, cuttlefish (*blah mèuk*) and other dishes. Order from the pictures taped to the side of the glass case.

Lady Restaurant (☎ 0 4482 1404; Th Nonthankhon; dishes 30-180B; ⏲ dinner) One of several garden restaurants in this part of town, Lady serves some exquisite Thai food. Unfortunately, there's no English menu, but you can't go wrong with *dôm yam gài bâhn* (Isan-style spicy and sour soup with free-range chicken), *blah tábtim râht prík* (deep-fried red tilapia with sweet-and-sour chilli sauce) or *pàt gà rèe gûng* (shrimp with Indian curry sauce).

Getting There & Away

Khon Kaen (ordinary/2nd class 58B/90, 2½ hours, hourly) and Khorat (ordinary/1st class 56/101B, two hours, every half-hour) buses leave from Chaiyaphum's **bus terminal** (☎ 0 4481 1344). So do some 2nd-class buses for Bangkok (2nd class 196B, five hours, every half-hour in the morning and every two hours in the afternoon). However, there are more departures for Bangkok with **Air Chaiyaphum** (☎ 0 4481 1556) and **Air Loei** (☎ 0 4481 1446). They each charge 252B for 1st class and 294B for the 32-seat VIP service, and have their own terminals. Air Loei also has a midnight 24-seat VIP (392B) departure.

Nakhonchai Air (☎ 0 4481 2522) has six evening-only services to Ubon Ratchathani (2nd class/32-seat VIP 234/347B, seven hours) and Chiang Mai (2nd class/32-seat VIP 377/716B, 11 hours), also from its own terminal. Buy tickets behind the orange gate.

Getting Around

A túk-túk should cost no more than 30B for any destination in town.

AROUND CHAIYAPHUM
Ban Khwao
บ้านเขว้า

Most visitors to Chaiyaphum make a stop in the silk village of Ban Khwao, 13km southwest of town on Rte 225, where some 50 shops sell fabric and clothing. The town is known for its *mát·mèe* designs (and its low prices due to the material being rather thin). However, these days embroidery is all the rage and most families in town have sewing machines under their homes rather than looms.

The **Silk Development Centre** (no roman-script sign; ☎ 0 4489 1409; admission free; ⏲ 8.30am-4.30pm) by the market has a few displays about silk making, and arranges free tours. If you've never observed the process, from the cultivation of mulberry trees and propagation of silkworms to the dyeing and weaving of silk thread, you're in for an interesting time. Advanced reservations are required.

Sörng·tăa·ou to Ban Khwao (17B, 30 minutes, every 20 minutes) park in front of Pat Pat internet cafe in Chaiyaphum.

Tat Ton National Park
อุทยานแห่งชาติตาดโตน

The best known of Chaiyaphum's natural reserves, **Tat Ton National Park** (☎ 0 4485 3333; admission 200B) is a scenic little spot on the edge of the Laenkha mountain range, 23km north of the city. Covering 218 sq km, Tat Ton is best known for its photogenic namesake waterfall, which is only 6m tall but stretches to 50m wide during the May to October rainy season. Some people think it's more beautiful from January to April, because the water is clearer then. On weekdays when school is in session, you'll probably be the only sightseer at the park's smaller waterfalls. **Tat Fah** is the

MÁT·MÈE

Thanks to growing interest from both Thais and foreigners, the once-fading Isan tradition of *mát·mèe* has undergone a major revival and is now one of Thailand's best-known weaving styles. Similar to Indonesian *ikat*, *mát·mèe* is a tie-dye process (*mát* is 'tie' and *mèe* is 'strands') that results in a geometric pattern repeatedly turning back on itself as it runs up the fabric. No matter what the design, every *mát·mèe* fabric has an ever-so-slight blur to it, which, more than anything else, makes it so distinct.

To start, the weavers string their thread (either silk or cotton) tightly across a wooden frame sized exactly as wide as the finished fabric will be. Almost always working from memory, the weavers then tie plastic (traditionally the skin of banana plant stalks was used) around bunches of strands in their desired design. The frame is then dipped in the dye (usually a chemical colour, though natural sources such as flowers and tree bark are regaining popularity), which grips the exposed thread but leaves the wrapped sections clean. The wrapping and dipping continues for multiple rounds, which results in intricate, complex patterns that come to life on the loom. The more you see of the process, the more you realise how amazing it is that the finished product turns out so beautifully.

Most of the patterns, handed down from mother to daughter, are abstract representations of natural objects such as trees and birds, but increasingly designers are working with weaving groups to create modern patterns, which invariably fetch higher prices. On the other hand, a thin silk with a simple pattern that can be turned out quite fast, might cost as little as 100B per metre.

next most beautiful and functions as a 20m waterslide during the rainy season.

The park has **campsites** (per person with own tent 30B, 3-/5-person tent hire 320/525B) and 15 **bungalows** (☎ 0 2562 0760; www.dnp.go.th/parkreserve; 2-14 people 600-3500B), most along the river near Nam Tok Tat Ton, plus a restaurant and snack shops.

Sŏrng·tăa·ou (30B, one hour, every half-hour) from Chaiyaphum pass the park entrance road (a hilly 1.5km walk from the falls; the park guards will get you a ride if you wait), but after 9.30am they rarely return along this route. You can continue north to Ban Tah Hin Ngin and loop around from there, but it is faster just to hitch a ride back to town, which is quite easy to do.

Mor Hin Khow
มอหินขาว

Promoted as the 'Stonehenge of Thailand', **Mor Hin Khow** (small hill with white rocks; ☎ 04481 0902; admission free) is the most popular part of **Phu Laenkha National Park**. It comprises a line of five natural stone pinnacles, **Grun Sao Hin**, with tapered bottoms that rise to 15m. Between these and the sunset-perfect **Pha Hua Nak** (Naga-head Cliff), another 2.5km up the mountain, are three more fields of less dramatic, but still oddly sculpted, rocks.

Most of the well-signposted route, 21km northwest of Tat Ton National Park, is on smooth new roads, but it's dirt for the last

5.5km. You can camp for free amidst the rocks. Toilets and showers are available at the little visitor centre, but bring your own food. There's no public transport.

KHON KAEN PROVINCE

Khon Kaen Province, the gateway to Isan if you're arriving from Chiang Mai or elsewhere in Northern Thailand, serves up an interesting mix of old and new. Farming and textiles still dominate life in the countryside, while things are booming in Khon Kaen city, which makes for a lively stopover if you fancy a quick slug of metropolitan living.

KHON KAEN
ขอนแก่น
pop 145,300

Khon Kaen is the darling of Isan's economic boom time. The skyline rises high, neon illuminates the night and a bumper crop of bars and restaurants entertains an expanding middle class. As the site of the northeast's largest university and an important hub for all things commercial and financial, the city is youthful, educated and on the move.

It's growing faster than most other Isan towns, which has brought some pretty heavy traffic and resulted in a sterile concrete veneer over most of the centre. There may be times when it takes the elephants trudging down

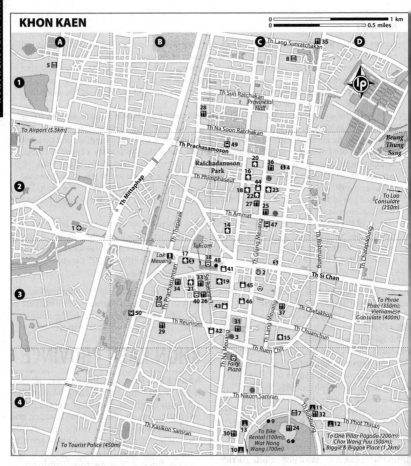

KHON KAEN

0 — 1 km
0 — 0.5 miles

the busy streets to remind you that you're in Thailand. But Isan's idiosyncratic appeal is still here, you just have to work a little harder these days to uncover it.

History

According to one of several theories, the city got its name from Phra That Kham Kaen (Tamarind Heartwood Reliquary), a revered *chedi* in the village of Ban Kham, 30km to the northeast. Legend says that early in the last millennium a contingent of monks carrying Buddha relics to Phra That Phanom (in today's Nakhon Phanom Province) camped next to a dead tamarind tree that miraculously came to life after they spent the night. By the time they reached That Phanom there was no more

room for relics, so the monks retraced their path. When they saw the revitalised tree they decided to erect their own *tâht* (four-sided curvilinear Buddha reliquary) there. A town developed nearby, but was abandoned several times. In 1789 a Suwannaphum ruler founded a city at the current site, which he named Kham Kaen after the *chedi*. Over the years the name morphed to Khon Kaen (Heartwood).

Orientation & Information

Khon Kaen has two tourist centres. The original lies along Th Glang Meuang, between the bus stations, and has many budget and midrange hotels. The upmarket choices and the main nightlife district are a quick hop southwest. There are good eats in both places. Further south, Beung Kaen Nakhon lake, which is a good place to browse for restaurants, is growing as a night-time destination, but is fun at any time of the day.

CONSULATES

Laos (☎ 0 4324 2857; 171/102-103 Th Prachasamoson; ☼ 8am-noon & 1-4pm Mon-Fri) Normal turnaround for visas is three days, but for an extra 200B you can get immediate service. It only accepts baht, and at a poor exchange rate.
Vietnam (☎ 0 4324 1586; Th Chatapadung; ☼ 8.30-11.30am & 2-4pm Mon-Fri) Visas ready next day.

EMERGENCY SERVICES

Khon Kaen Ram Hospital (☎ 0 4333 3800; Th Si Chan) Provides 24-hour emergency care.
Tourist police (☎ 0 4322 6195; Th Mittaphap) Next to HomePro.

INTERNET ACCESS

Finding an internet cafe in Khon Kaen isn't too tough. There are several near the hotels on Th Glang Meuang, or try **S-Force** (Th Na Meuang; per hr 17B; ☼ 9am-10pm).

MONEY

There are banks with exchange and ATM facilities all over Khon Kaen. **Siam Commercial Bank** (Th Si Chan; ☼ 10.30am-8pm) inside Tukcom shopping centre keeps extended hours.

POST

Main post office (Th Glang Meuang; ☼ 8.30am-4.30pm Mon-Fri, 9am-noon Sat, Sun & holidays)

TOURIST INFORMATION

Tourism Authority of Thailand (TAT; ☎ 0 4324 4498; 15/5 Th Prachasamoson; ☼ 8.30am-4.30pm) Distributes maps of the city and can answer queries on Khon Kaen and the surrounding provinces.

TRAVEL AGENCIES

KK Stawan (☎ 08 9715 6137; kkstawan@yahoo.com; 18/8 Th Phimphaseut; ☼ 9am-8pm Mon-Fri) At First Choice guesthouse.

Sights

Although it doesn't seem like it at first look, there's more to do in Khon Kaen than shop for souvenirs and dive into the nightlife.

BEUNG KAEN NAKHON
บึงแก่นนคร

This 100-hectare lake is the most pleasant place in town to spend some time. It is lined with eateries and walkways and there are quite a few interesting places to visit around its shore. If you don't want to walk, you can hire bikes (20B per hour per seat) at the lakeside market or, better still, down along the west side where there are some two- and three-seater rides.

Down at the south end of the lake is Khon Kaen's one must-see, **Phra Mahathat Kaen Nakhon** (☼ 6am-5pm), a gorgeous nine-storey *chedi* at the heart of **Wat Nong Wang** (Th Robbung; ☼ daylight hr). Inside you'll find enlightening murals depicting Khon Kaen history, various historical displays and a staircase to the top.

NORTHEASTERN THAILAND

Head north along the shore and you'll pass the **Mhesak Spirit House** (Th Robbung), a Khmer-style *prang* dedicated to the Hindu god Indra, and **Wat That** (Th Robbung; ☿ daylight hr), which has a soaring *bòht* and *chedi*.

Across from Wat That, right on the northern shore, is a **lakeside market** with food and shopping stalls. Most don't open until the late afternoon, but during the day (in addition to bike hire) there are paddleboats and canoes (30B per half-hour) and an abundance of paint-your-own pottery stalls. Just east of the market is the Khon Kaen City Museum, and across the street is **Wat Jeen Beung Kaen Nakhon** (Th Robbung; ☿ daylight hr), Khon Kaen's biggest and most beautiful Chinese temple.

Around the corner, just off the lake is the peaceful, tree-filled **Wat Pho Ban Nontan** (Th Phot Thisan; ☿ daylight hr). It pre-dates the city and has a *săh·lah* like no other temple building in Thailand. The ground floor is covered with ingeniously sculpted trees, animals, and village scenes of people acting out old Isan proverbs. Back to the lake and a little further down the shore you'll find a replica of Hanoi's **One Pillar Pagoda**, built by Khon Kaen's Vietnamese community.

MUSEUMS

The **Khon Kaen National Museum** (☎ 0 4324 6170; Th Lang Sunratchakan; admission 100B; ☿ 9am-4pm Wed-Sun) has an interesting collection of artefacts dating from prehistoric times to the present. The collection includes Ban Chiang painted pottery; and a Dvaravati *săir·mah* (temple boundary marker) from Kalasin, depicting Princess Pimpa washing Lord Buddha's feet with her hair.

The National Museum's household and agricultural displays shed light on what you'll see out in the countryside. But for a more in-depth introduction to Isan, visit the excellent **Khon Kaen City Museum** (Hong Moon Mung; ☎ 0 4327 1173; Th Robbung; admission 90B; ☿ 9am-5pm Mon-Sat), which has dioramas and displays going back to the Jurassic period.

The focus of the **Art & Culture University Museum** (☎ 0 4333 2780; admission free; ☿ 10am-7pm) at Khon Kaen University is the art gallery, which features both student and professional exhibitions. The Educational Museum has informative exhibits about Isan history and culture, but, despite a few touch-screen displays in English, you won't get much out of it unless you read Thai.

Festivals

The **Silk Fair** and the **Phuk Siaw Festival** are held simultaneously over 12 days starting in late November. Centred on the *săh·lah glahng*, the festival celebrates and seeks to preserve the tradition of *pòok sèe·o* (friend bonding), a ritual union of friends during which *fâi pòok kăn* (sacred thread) are tied around one's wrists. More than just a symbolic act, the friends gain a standing on par with siblings in each other's families. Other activities include parades, Isan music and lots of shopping.

Sleeping

BUDGET

First Choice (☎ 08 1546 2085; firstchoicekhonkaen@ lycos.com; 18/8 Th Phimphaseut; r 150-200B; ▢) This friendly little spot is the city's proto-backpacker hostel, with no-frills, shared-bathroom quarters upstairs and a traveller-friendly eatery below. Plane tickets, massage and travel advice are all available.

Saen Samran Hotel (☎ 0 4323 9611; 55-59 Th Glang Meuang; s 170-200B, d 250B; ▢) The city's oldest hotel is also its most charismatic, with the wooden front holding onto its once-upon-a-time glory. The rooms are scrubbed spotless and are nice for a night or two. They also have wi-fi.

Roma Hotel (☎ 0 4333 4444; 50/2 Th Glang Meuang; s 230-500B, d 250-500B, ste 800B; ✖ ▢) The Roma's air-con rooms are good value, spotless and comfy. The fan rooms are…well, good value and comfy. The 'suites' have some unexpected style, but it's just lipstick on a pig. Unfortunately, the hotel has some noisy neighbours, so you might get an early wake-up call.

Grand Leo Hotel (☎ 0 4332 7745; 62-62/1 Th Si Chan; r 380-480B; ✖) This humdrum place, around the corner from the nightlife district, is functional albeit a little frumpy. The rooms promise a good night's sleep no matter what hour you stumble back.

Charoenchit House (☎ 0 4322 7300; www.chouse khonkaen.com; 20/11 Th Chuanchun; r 400-500B; ✖ ▢) Viewed from the outside, you don't expect to find much to get excited about inside these two stark white towers. But checkerboard-tiled floors, decorative headboards and free wi-fi give the rooms a fair amount of va-va-voom for the price. It's not the most convenient location, but the lake and the nightlife district are walkable distances.

Chaipat Hotel (☎ 0 4333 3055; 106/3 Soi Na Meuang; r 400-600B; ❄ ▯) Set back off Th Na Meuang, this older-but-reasonable place features marble floors, in-room wi-fi and a lot of furnishings in the little rooms.

MIDRANGE

Biggie & Biggoe Place (☎ 0 4332 2999; Th Robbung; r 650-850B; ❄ ▯) If you're in Khon Kaen to relax rather than live it up, this midsize hotel at the foot of the lake is a good bet. Rooms are rather bland, but as it was built in 2005 there are none of the irritating quirks so common in older hotels. Wi-fi is free and the restaurant is excellent.

our pick Piman Garden (☎ 0 4333 4111; www.piman garden.com; 6/110 Th Glang Meuang; r 650-950B; ste 1200B; ❄ ▯) Set back off the road around a lovely garden, Piman offers serenity and privacy despite its city centre location. The attractive rooms all come with safes, fridges and free wi-fi, plus most have balconies or porches.

Khon Kaen Hotel (☎ 0 4333 3222; 43/2 Th Phimphaseut; s 650B, d 700-1200B; ❄ ▯) This older, seven-storey place is looking rather sorry for itself on the outside and in the hallways. But with the odd nod to traditional decor in the recently renovated rooms, it bags a few points for atmosphere. With a balcony and free wi-fi, rooms are definitely above average for this class.

TOP END

Kosa Hotel (☎ 0 4332 0320; www.kosahotel.com; 250-252 Th Si Chan; s 1900-2300B, d 2100-2500B, ste s/d 3300/5500B; ❄ ▯ ❄) Less glitzy than its neighbour, the Pullman, this good-value place (25% discounts are pretty much always available) is a great top-end choice. It offers excellent facilities and slick service.

Pullman Raja Orchid (☎ 0 4332 2155; www.pullman hotels.com; 9/9 Th Prachasumran; r 3180-3950B; ste 6300B; ❄ ▯ ❄) A stunning lobby sets the tone for one of Isan's best hotels. This international-standard Accor-run place in the heart of the city has plenty of razzle-dazzle, well-equipped rooms, a spa and gym and even its own microbrews. It also offers discounted rates most of the time.

Eating & Drinking

For cheap eats, the city's main **night market** (Th Reunrom; ☾ 5pm-midnight) is a good one, plus many cheap **food stalls** (Th Glang Meuang; ☾ lunch & dinner) open up between Th Ammat and the

Roma Hotel and stay open very late. There are also food vendors in the unnamed **lakeside market** (☾ dinner) in the park at the top of Beung Kaen Nakhon, though people come here for the atmosphere, not the cuisine.

Gai Yang Rabeab (no roman-script sign; ☎ 0 4324 3413; 391/5 Th Theparak; dishes 20-150B; whole chickens 110-130B; ☾ lunch) Many locals believe Khon Kaen Province makes Thailand's best *gài yâhng* and this simple joint, serving an all-Isan menu, gets the most nods as best of the best in the city.

our pick Dee Dee (☎ 08 5006 3922; 348/25 Soi Reunrom 1; dishes 30-60B; ☾ breakfast, lunch & dinner) Though it may look like just a humble food-to-order shop, Khun Jaang works wonders with a wok and the food is extraordinary – truly some of the best in Thailand. She is co-creator of a new Thai dish called *pàt tim* (egg noodles stir-fried with red curry paste).

Tawantong (☎ 0 4333 0389; 227/129 Th Lang Sunratchakan; dishes 40B; ☾ breakfast & lunch) This large, all-veggie, health-food buffet sits across from the National Museum. The food is so good it also gets many carnivorous diners.

our pick Turm-Rom (☎ 0 4322 1752; 4/5 Th Chetakhon; dishes 35-129B; ☾ dinner) This superb place combines one of the best kitchens in town with a quiet, covered garden to create something of a gourmet pub. It's the kind of place where people tend to stick around long into the night. The menu focuses on curries, spicy seafood and salads (*yam*). The *hòr mòk tá·lair* (seafood curry served in a coconut) is especially good, but in our many visits we've never had a dud dish.

Plapanoy (no roman-script sign; ☎ 0 4322 4694; Th Robbung; dishes 40-200B; ☾ lunch & dinner) This large alfresco spot near Beung Kaen Nakhon is where locals bring out-of-town guests to sample genuine Isan food. Fish is the speciality and the menu has English.

First Choice (☎ 08 1546 2085; 18/8 Th Phimphaseut; dishes 40-250B; ☾ breakfast, lunch & dinner) An unusual thing for Thailand: a traveller-focused guesthouse serving Thai food good enough that Thai people sometimes eat here. Eat inside or on a little terrace surrounded by potted plants.

Restaurant Didine (☎ 08 7189 3864; Th Prachasumran; dishes 45-250B; ☾ dinner) This place is as much a bar as a restaurant, as the three-page drinks list and free pool table attest. The French chef-owner whips up some swanky *fa·ràng* food, like red snapper with saffron, that belies the simple surrounds, plus there's pub grub and Thai standards. He also takes a shot at Italian and Indian food, but with far less success.

Bualuang Restaurant (☎ 0 4322 2504; Th Rop Buengkaen Nakhon; dishes 55-800B; ☯ lunch & dinner) Ask a local out for dinner and they'll probably want to go here. Perched on a pier over Beung Kaen Nakhon, it serves up a typical spread of Thai and Chinese dishes in a largely alfresco setting. Prices are high, but the food is good.

Chor Wang Puu (no roman-script sign; ☎ 0 4332 1178; Th Robbung; dishes 80-350B; ☯ lunch & dinner) This wood-and-thatch place resembles a fishing village and, in fact, they farm fish and frogs in the ponds over which the dining areas sit. Naturally, fish features prominently on the Thai, Isan and Chinese menu. It's a beautiful spot at night, and you might even catch a little sunset view way back behind the lake. The little playground helps make it a family favourite.

Khon Kaen's youthful population has spawned many good coffee shops. Our favourites are **Hom Krun** (☎ 0 4327 0547; Th Reunrom; dishes 35-129B; ☯ 9am-midnight, no coffee after 7pm), with its shady patio and full kitchen; and stylish **Mud** (☎ 0 4332 2131; 280/5 Th Glang Meuang; cappuccino 50B, dishes 60-140B; ☯ 10am-10pm), where most of the coffees, teas, juices, sandwiches and salads are organic. Both have free wi-fi.

Also recommended:

Chokdee (☎ 0 4324; 2252; Th Glang Meuang; dishes 16-22B; ☯ 24hr) A branch of the national chain, this dim-sum shop sits next to the air-con bus station.

Trajit (no roman-script sign; ☎ 0 4324 3610; 1/2 Th Glang Meuang; dishes 25-40B; ☯ breakfast & lunch) Serves Nang Rong–style *kǎa mǒo* (pork rump roast) in a cute, crumbling, piece-of-history shophouse.

Kosa Coffee Shop (☎ 0 4332 0320; 250-252 Th Si Chan; dishes 60-400B; ☯ breakfast, lunch & dinner) Serves an excellent lunch buffet (229B) and the beer garden out the front is nice at night.

Pomodoro (☎ 0 4327 0464; off Th Prachasumran; dishes 130-280B; ☯ dinner) The best Italian in town, bar none.

Entertainment

Khon Kaen's exuberant nightlife is centred on Th Prachasumran, where clubs and bars run wild to mild. Most get going around 10pm. The anchor is **Rad Complex** (☎ 0 4322 5987; Th Prachasumran; ☯ 9pm-2am), a multifaceted place with live music, DJs, karaoke, 'coyote' dancers and an alfresco restaurant. Nearby, **U-Bar** (☎ 0 4332 0434; off Th Prachasumran; ☯ 8pm-

2am), almost exclusively the domain of Khon Kaen University students, is classier, but just as loud. Both sometimes book good bands from Bangkok.

Kosa Bowl (Th Si Chan; per game 50-65B; ☯ noon-midnight) has 30 lanes atop Tukcom shopping centre.

Shopping

With an excellent selection of shops, Khon Kaen is the best place to buy Isan handicrafts.

Prathamakhan (☎ 0 4322 4080; 79/2-3 Th Reunrom; ☯ 9am-8pm) By far the largest selection in town, this well-known, reasonably priced shop has both textiles and handicrafts and makes a good one-stop shop. Don't miss the knick-knack and handicraft display at the back.

Phrae Phan (☎ 0 4333 7216; 131/193 Th Chatapadung; ☯ 8am-6pm) Run by the Handicraft Centre for Northeastern Women's Development, this out-of-the-way store has a superb selection of natural-dyed, hand-woven silk and cotton, which is produced in nearby villages. Prices are very low.

Sueb San (no roman-script sign; ☎ 0 4334 4072; 16 Th Glang Meuang; ☯ 8am-6.30pm) More accessible than Phrae Phan, this store also stocks natural-dyed fabrics, plus some atypical Isan souvenirs.

Rin Thai Silk (☎ 0 4322 0705; 412 Th Na Meuang; ☯ 8am-6.30pm) Locals, especially brides-to-be, looking for top-quality silk shop here.

Khon Kaen OTOP Center (☎ 0 4332 0320; off Th Si Chan; ☯ 9.30am-8.30pm) This large handicrafts store is most convenient to the top-end hotels, but it's predictably pricey.

Naem Laplae (no roman-script sign; ☎ 0 4323 6537; 32 Th Glang Meuang; ☯ 6am-9.30pm Mon-Thu, to 10pm Fri-Sun) You can follow the pungent aromas to this old-school Isan food store (if you've got a cold, look out for the bright yellow-and-red shopfront), one of several in this area. This and the others sell everything from sweets to sausages, most notably *gun chee-ang* (red pork sausages).

The most enjoyable souvenir-shopping is looking for the handful of people selling traditional baskets and wooden items, hidden away within the fresh food and household-goods stalls in **Talat Bobae** (Th Glang Meuang). **Talat Banglamphu** (Th Glang Meuang), immediately to the north, has more food and a second-hand clothing bonanza.

Getting There & Away

AIR

THAI (☎ 0 4322 7701; www.thaiairways.com; Pullman Raja Orchid, 9/9 Th Prachasumran; ☺ 8am-5pm Mon-Fri) operates three daily flights between Bangkok and Khon Kaen (one way 2805B, 55 minutes).

Khon Kaen Airport (☎ 0 4324 6345) is just west of the city off Hwy 12. The Pullman and Kosa hotels have airport shuttles meeting every flight. Those not staying at either hotel can use them for 80B and 70B respectively.

BUS

Khon Kaen is a busy transport hub and you can ride directly to nearly all cities in Isan and many beyond. The **Ordinary Bus Terminal** (☎ 0 4333 3388; Th Prachasamoson) and the **Air-con Bus Terminal** (☎ 0 4323 9910; Th Glang Meuang) are central and convenient. The Air-con Terminal should be called the 'first-class and VIP bus terminal', since second-class air-con buses (and even a few first-class) use the Ordinary Terminal.

For nearly all cities other than Bangkok, departures are more frequent from the ordinary terminal. Options are listed in the table, p500. For the Vientiane bus, officially you need to already have a Lao visa, but they'll sometimes sell you a ticket if you promise to get off at the bridge and continue on your own from there.

TRAIN

Khon Kaen is on the Bangkok–Nong Khai line. Express trains leave from Bangkok for **Khon Kaen station** (☎ 0 4322 1112) at 8.20am, 6.30pm and 8pm, arriving about eight hours later. Bangkok-bound express trains leave Khon Kaen at 8.39am, 8.11pm and 9.05pm. The fares to Bangkok are 227/399/1168B for a 3rd-class seat/2nd-class seat/1st-class sleeper.

Getting Around

A regular, colour-coded *sŏrng·tăa·ou* system plies the city for 8B per ride. Some of the handiest are *sŏrng·tăa·ou* 8 (light blue), which runs along Th Glang Meuang past Wat Nong Wang and also west to the university; *sŏrng·tăa·ou* 10 (light blue), which runs past the Lao and Vietnamese consulates; *sŏrng·tăa·ou* 11 (white), which will take you from the train station to the Air-con Bus Terminal, just a short walk to the budget hotels; and *sŏrng·tăa·ou* 21 (orange), which will

take you to the National Museum from Th Glang Meuang.

Túk-túk drivers will want 40B to 60B for a medium-length trip around town.

There are many car-hire outlets around the Pullman and Kosa hotels; **Narujee** (☎ 0 4322 4220; off Th Si Chan; ☺ 7am-5pm), which charges 1500B for a car with driver, is a reliable choice.

AROUND KHON KAEN
Chonabot
ชนบท

This small town located 55km southwest of Khon Kaen is one of Thailand's most successful silk villages. It's known for producing top-quality *mát·mèe*. The **Sala Mai Thai** (Thai Silk Pavilion; no roman-script sign; ☎ 0 4328 6160; admission free; ☺ 8am-5pm Mon-Fri, from 9am Sat & Sun) is a silk-weaving museum on the campus of Khon Kaen Industrial & Community Education College where you can learn about the entire silk-making process, and even take a turn at a loom. Besides showing the simple wooden contraptions devised to spin, tie, weave and dry silk, there's an exhibition hall upstairs that catalogues traditional *mát·mèe* patterns and a couple of typical northeastern wooden houses. It's 1km west of town on Rte 229. The pavilion sells silk too, but most people buy from the myriad shops on **Th Sribunreung**, aka Silk Rd.

Buses bound for Nakhon Sawan, departing from Khon Kaen's ordinary bus terminal, will drop you in Chonabot (2nd/1st class 44/53B, one hour, six daily). Or take just about any south-bound bus (2nd/1st class 34/43B, one hour) or train (9B, 30 minutes, 7.50am, 1.50pm and 3.50pm) to Ban Phai, where you can get a *sŏrng·tăa·ou* to Chonabot (10B, 20 minutes, every half-hour).

Prasat Puay Noi
ปราสาทเปือยน้อย

The 12th-century **Prasat Puay Noi** (admission free; ☺ daylight hr) is the largest and most interesting Khmer ruin in northern Isan, though it can't compete with even some of the not-so-famous ruins further south. About the size of Buriram's Prasat Meuang Tam, but far less intact, the east-facing monument comprises a large central sandstone sanctuary surmounted by a partially collapsed *prang* and surrounded by laterite walls with two major gates. It has some good lintels left.

BUSES FROM KHON KAEN

Destination	Cost (B)	Duration (hr)	Frequency
From the Ordinary Terminal			
Chaiyaphum	ordinary 58 2nd class 90	2½	hourly
Khorat	2nd class 129 1st class 187	3	every ½ hour
Loei	2nd class 141	2½	every ½ hour
Mukdahan	2nd class 155	4½	every ½ hour
Nakhon Phanom	2nd class 227	5	6 daily
Nong Khai	2nd class 120	3½	hourly
Phitsanulok	2nd class 223 1st class 280	5	hourly
Roi Et	2nd class 80	2	every 20 minutes
Udon Thani	2nd class 83	2	every 20 minutes
From the Air-con Terminal			
Bangkok	1st class 383 32-seat VIP 414 24-seat VIP 585	6½	at least hourly between 8am and midnight
Chiang Mai	1st class 570	12	8pm & 9pm
Khorat	1st class 187	3	every hour
Nong Khai	1st class 157	3½	3 daily
Suvarnabhumi Airport	1st class 335	6½	10.30pm
Ubon Ratchathani	1st class 247	5	4 daily
Udon Thani	1st class 104	2½	hourly
Vientiane	1st class 180	4	7.45am, 1.30pm & 3.15pm

GETTING THERE & AWAY

By public transport from Khon Kaen, catch a bus (2nd/1st class 34/43B, one hour) or the 7.50am local train (9B, 30 minutes) to Ban Phai, then a *sŏrng·tăa·ou* to Puay Noi (30B, 30 minutes). The last *sŏrng·tăa·ou* back to Ban Phai leaves at 2pm.

If you have your own wheels, head 40km south from Khon Kaen on Hwy 2 to Ban Phai, then east on Hwy 23 (signposted to Borabu) for 11km to Rte 2301. Follow it and Rte 2297 for 24km southeast through a scenic tableau of rice fields to Ban Puay Noi.

Phu Wiang National Park

อุทยานแห่งชาติภูเวียง

Uranium miners discovered a giant patella bone in this region in 1976. Palaeontologists then unearthed a fossilised 15m-long herbivore later named *Phuwianggosaurus sirindhornae* (after Her Royal Majesty, Princess Sirindhorn). Dinosaur fever followed (explaining the epidemic of model dinosaurs in Khon Kaen), more remains were uncovered and **Phu Wiang National Park** (☎ 0 4335 8073; admission 400B) was born.

Enclosed **excavation sites** (☾ 8.30am-4.30pm) – including one with a partial skeleton of *Siamotyrannus isanensis*, an early ancestor of *Tyrannosaurus rex* – can be easily reached by trails from the visitor centre or nearby parking areas. Park guides (some speak a little English) offer free tours of the bone sites if you call in advance. Those who want to explore further (best done by car or mountain bike) will find dinosaur footprints, waterfalls and prehistoric cave paintings.

The **Phu Wiang Museum** (☎ 0 4343 8204; admission free; ☾ 9am-5pm), 5km before the park, has geology and palaeontology displays, including full-size models of the dinosaur species that once lived in the area. Kids will love it.

The park has one six-person **bungalow** (☎ 0 2562 0760; www.dnp.go.th/parkreserve; 1200B) and a **campsite** (per person with own tent 30B, 3-/6-person tent hire 225/450B). Simple food is available.

GETTING THERE & AWAY

The park entrance is 90km west of Khon Kaen. Buses from Khon Kaen's ordinary bus terminal stop in Phu Wiang town (ordinary/

2nd class 35/47B, 1½ hours, every half-hour). It's best to get off downtown (not at the bus terminal) where you can hire a túk-túk (one way/return 200/400B) or motorbike taxi (one way/return 150/350B) for the remaining 19km to the park entrance. If you only pay for a one-way trip you'll risk not being able to get a ride back, and hitching is tough.

Nam Nao National Park

อุทยานแห่งชาตินำหนาว

One of Thailand's most beautiful and valuable nature preserves, **Nam Nao National Park** (☎ 0 5681 0724; admission 400B) covers nearly 1000 sq km at an average elevation of 800m, across the border of Chaiyaphum and Phetchabun Provinces, just beyond Khon Kaen Province. Although it covers remote territory (this remained a People's Liberation Army of Thailand stronghold until the early 1980s) Hwy 12 makes access easy. Temperatures are fairly cool year-round, especially nights and mornings, and frost occasionally occurs in December and January.

Marked by the sandstone hills of the Phetchabun mountains, the park also fea-

tures dense, mixed evergreen and deciduous forest on mountains and hills, open dipterocarp pine-oak forest on plateaus and hills and dense bamboo mountain forest with wild banana stands in river valleys, plus scattered savannah on the plains. Three rivers are sourced here: the Chi, Saphung and Phrom. A fair system of trails branches out from the visitor centre to several scenic viewpoints, and the park also features waterfalls and caves, some of which are easily reached by car along the highway. Nam Nao's highest peak, **Phu Pha Jit**, reaches a height of 1271m. You used to be able to camp on the summit, but the trail is temporarily closed.

The 1560-sq-km **Phu Khiaw Wildlife Sanctuary** lies adjacent to the park, so wildlife is abundant. However, the animals here are more timid than at nearby Phu Kradung National Park, and so are spotted less often. Elephants and tigers are rarely seen but still reside here, as do Malayan sun bears, banteng (wild cattle), Asian jackals, barking deer, gibbons, pangolins and flying squirrels. Over 200 species of bird, including parrots and hornbills, fly through the forest.

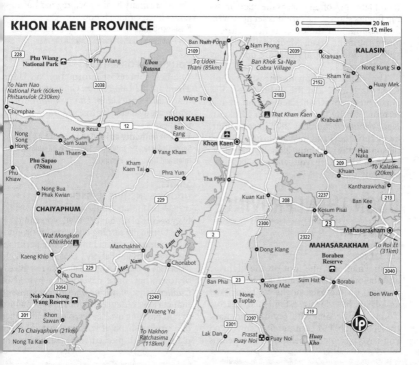

There's a variety of **bungalows** (☎ 0 2562 0760; www.dnp.go.th/parkreserve; bungalows 1000-5000B) that hold up to 30 people, plus a **campsite** (per person with own tent 30B, 2-6 person tent hire 100-300B) and some simple restaurants next to the visitor centre.

Buses between Khon Kaen (90B, 2½ hours, hourly) and Phitsanulok travel through the park. The visitor centre is a 1.5km walk from the highway.

Ban Khok Sa-Nga Cobra Village
โครงการอนุรักษ์งูจงอาง

The self-styled 'King Cobra Village' of Ban Khok Sa-Nga has a thing about snakes. Locals rear hundreds of the reptiles, and most families have some in boxes under their houses. The strange custom began in 1951 when a travelling herb farmer, Ken Yongla, began putting on snake shows to attract customers. His plan was a success, and the art of breeding and training snakes has been nurtured ever since. Today two groups, each calling themselves the King Cobra Club of Thailand, put on **snake shows** (donations expected; ☽ 8am-5pm) where handlers taunt snakes and tempt fate; they often lose, as the many missing fingers show. One group is set up at Wat Si Thamma and the other is just before it along the main road. Medicinal herbs are still sold and other animals are on display in pitiful cages.

The village is 50km northeast of Khon Kaen via Hwy 2 and Rte 2039. Take a Kra Nuan bus from Khon Kaen's ordinary bus terminal to the turn-off for Ban Khok Sa-Nga (ordinary/2nd class 28/35B, one hour, every half-hour) and then a túk-túk (20B per person) for the remaining 2km. If you're driving from Khon Kaen, you can't miss it as there are many signs.

UDON THANI PROVINCE

UDON THANI
อุดรธานี
pop 227,200

Udon Thani has one foot on the highway and the other off the beaten track. The city boomed on the back of the Vietnam War as US air bases were established nearby. Today it's become the region's primary transport hub and commercial centre, and you have to dig deep behind its prosperous concrete veneer to find any flashes of its past. Because it lacks the urban chutzpah of Khon Kaen and the touristy appeal of Nong Khai, which is an equally convenient base for visiting the wonderful surrounding attractions, Udon sees relatively few foreign travellers other than a large number of sex tourists.

Information
Aek Udon International Hospital (☎ 0 4234 2555; 555/5 Th Pho Si) Has a 24-hour casualty department.
Fuzzy Ken's (☎ 08 6011 4627; Th Prajak Silpakorn; ☽ 9am-midnight Mon-Sat) Has one of the best used-book shops in Isan.
MT Coffee (300/4 Th Prajak Silpakorn; per hr 30B; ☽ 9am-9pm) Expensive but fast internet connection and pleasant surrounds.
On Time (☎ 0 4224 7792; 539/72 Th Sai Uthit; ☽ 8am-5pm Mon-Sat, to 2pm Sun) One of many travel agencies on this corner.
Post office (Th Wattananuwong; ☽ 8.30am-4.30pm Mon-Fri, 9am-noon Sat, Sun & holidays)
Tourist police (☎ 0 4221 1291; Th Naresuan)

MONEY
There are many banks open regular business hours lined along Th Pho Si.
Kasikornbank (Charoensri Complex, Th Teekathanont; ☽ 11am-8pm) One of several banks in the mall.

TOURIST INFORMATION
The best sources of information on Udon Thani are the *Udon Thani Guide* (www.udon map.com) and *Udon Thani Map*, both of which are available for free at *fa·ràng*-focused businesses.
Tourism Authority of Thailand (TAT; ☎ 0 4232 5406; Th Thesa; ☽ 8.30am-4.30pm) Has information on Udon and Nong Khai Provinces.

Sights
UDORN SUNSHINE NURSERY
สวนกล้วยไม้หอมอุดรซันไชน์

Ever seen a plant dance? Well, you can do it here. Originally earning notoriety for producing the first ever orchid made into a perfume, the **Udorn Sunshine Nursery** (☎ 08 5747 4144; 127 Th Udorn-Nong Samrong; ☽ 8am-5pm), just northwest of town, has since developed a hybrid of *Codariocalyx motorius ohashi leguminosae* that curiously 'dances' to music. The mature gyrant has long oval leaves, plus smaller ones of a similar shape. If you sing or talk to the plant in a high-pitched voice (saxophone or violin works even better), a few of the smaller leaves will shift back and forth. This is no hype; we've seen it for ourselves, although it's much more of a waltz than a jig. The plants are most active from November to February, the cool season, and from 7am to 9.30am and 4.30pm to 6.30pm.

The plants aren't for sale. You can, however, buy Udorn Dancing Tea, made from the plant, along with the more famous Miss Udorn Sunshine orchids and perfumes. The nursery's newest product is Udorn Toob Moob Maeng Kaeng, a perfume derived from brown stink bugs.

To get here, go under the Ban Nongsamrong sign on Rte 2024, then after 150m follow the Udorn Sunshine Fragrant Orchid sign. *Sŏrng·tăa·ou* 5 and 16 pass here, and the Yellow Bus will get you nearby. A túk-túk from Udon's city centre should cost about 80B.

WAT JIIN SANJAO PU-YA
ศาลเจ้าปู่ย่า

The garish **Sanjao Pu-Ya** (Th Nittayo; ☼ daylight hr) on the southern shore of Nong Bua is a particularly large Chinese temple that attests to the wealth of the local Thai-Chinese merchant class. At its heart, the **Pu-Ya Shrine** houses small images of the god and goddess of mercy.

For 10 days during December's **Thung Si Meuang Fair**, which features dragon dancing (on 1, 5 and 10 December) and Isan cultural performances, Pu (Grandpa) and Ya (Grandma) are moved to a temporary temple in the northwest corner of City Field in a grand procession.

UDON THANI PROVINCIAL MUSEUM
พิพิธภัณฑ์เมืองอุดรธานี

Filling a 1920s colonial-style building that used to be a girls' school, **Udon Thani Provincial Museum** (☎ 0 4224 5976; Th Pho Si; admission free; ☼ 8.30am-4pm Mon-Fri, from 8am Sat & Sun) has an interesting catch-all collection spanning geology to handicrafts.

Sleeping

Puttarag Hotel (☎ 0 4224 7032; 380/15 Th Prajak Silpakorn; r 160B) This cold-water flophouse is right in the thick of Udon's nightlife. The wood floors lend a hint of history, but mostly it's just old.

Top Mansion (☎ 0 4234 5015; topmansion@yahoo .com; 35/3 Th Sampanthamit; r 350-490B; ✷ ▢) Mix the quality, location and well-appointed rooms and this newish tower gives the biggest bang

for your baht in Udon. Wi-fi isn't free, but it does reach the rooms.

City Lodge (☎ 0 4222 4439; thecitylodge@yahoo.com; 83/14-15 Th Wattananuwong; r 600-1000B; ✷ ▢) This British-owned property is a good example of the new breed of small hotels in this area that deliver more value and style than the big boys. The already bright and colourful rooms are cheered up even more with wicker furniture and free wi-fi.

Charoensri Grand Royal Hotel (☎ 0 4234 3555; www.charoensrigrand.com; Th Teekathanont; s 1300-1900B, d 1400-2000B, ste 2400-36,000B; ✷ ▢ ☒) This has long been the town's glossiest top-ender. The rooms are small but immaculate, the facilities are top-notch (including a fitness centre and spa) and the staff are on the ball. Its large adjoining shopping mall, Charoensri Complex, is the hub of the city.

Eating & Drinking

They're nothing near Chiang Mai quality, but Udon's Centre Point, Precha and **UD Bazar Night Markets** (Th Prajak Silpakorn; ☼ 4-11pm), in front of the train station, offer an impressive spread. Besides dining you can shop for clothes, watch football on the big screen or listen to a live band.

A bevy of massage and paint-your-own pottery stands joins the small food shops on the sunset-watching side of Nong Prajak Park to form the **Nong Prajak Night Market** (Th Thesa; ☼ 5.30am-10pm). It has proven so popular that it now runs all day, but it's still busiest at night.

Kwan Jit (no roman-script sign; ☎ 08 6367 7565; Th Adunyadet; dishes 39-89B; ☼ dinner) If you're looking for something mellow, this peculiar 1960s-themed pub will satisfy. The music is classic Thai folk songs, played quiet enough that you can chat, and the food is mostly Isan style. But there's no English on the menu.

Maeya (no roman-script sign; ☎ 0 4222 3889; 79/81 Th Ratchaphatsadu; dishes 40-260B; ☼ lunch & dinner) One part Thai restaurant and three parts English tearoom, this labyrinth has waiters dressed in black tie and a menu stretching from sandwiches to wild boar in red-curry sauce. Their translations are a little cryptic; the 'rice with spit in sauce' is really 'rice with liver in sauce'.

ourpick Rabiang Phatchanee (☎ 0 4224 1515; 53/1 Th Suphakit Janya; dishes 40-350B; ☼ lunch & dinner) On the lake's east shore, this classy place whips up a fabulous array of local dishes (including

UDON THANI

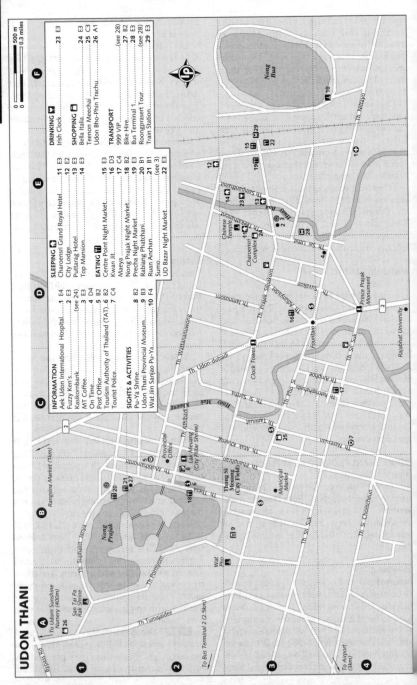

0   500 m
0   0.3 miles

many you've probably never tried before, like spicy appendix salad) and serves them on the shady deck or in air-conditioned dining rooms.

Irish Clock (☎ 0 4224 7450; 19/5-6 Th Sampanthamit; dishes 60-350B; ⏰ breakfast, lunch & dinner) This wood-trimmed, Guinness-infused pub is an island of class in a sea of pick-up joints. The menu has both Thai and fa·ràng food, plus there are hotel rooms upstairs and free wi-fi.

Also recommended:

Ruan Anchan (no roman-script sign; per bottle 10B; ⏰ dinner) Not all juice is created equal, and this highly recommended lakeside stand proves it.

Bella Italia (☎ 0 4234 3134; Charoensri Complex, Th Teekathanont; dishes 80-700B; ⏰ lunch & dinner) As close to Italy and as fancy as you'll get in Udon.

Sumo (☎ 0 4222 4542; 300/6-8 Th Prajak Silpakorn; dishes 39-1800B; ⏰ lunch & dinner) A good choice for Japanese.

Shopping

Teenon Meechai (☎ 0 4222 2838; 206-208 Th Pho Si; ⏰ 2-5pm Mon-Sat) This souvenir shop has so much quirky style you'll forget you're a tourist.

Udon Bho-Phin Trachu (no roman-script sign; ☎ 0 4224 5618; Th Porniyom; ⏰ 7am-6.30pm) There's a great selection of silk and cotton, including some natural-dyed fabrics, at this large spot northwest of Nong Prajak Lake. Look for the sign with the wooden roof.

Getting There & Away

AIR

THAI (www.thaiairways.com), **Nok Air** (www.nokair .com) and **Air Asia** (www.airasia.com) each fly twice daily to Bangkok (one hour). Fares average 2200B one way, but with promotions are often much lower. **Lao Airlines** (www.laoairlines.com) flies on Friday and Sunday to Luang Prabang for 2600B one way.

The Charoensri Grand offers an airport shuttle for 30B per person.

BUS

For most destinations, including Bangkok (2nd/1st class 321/412B, eight hours, every half-hour), buses use the downtown **Bus Terminal 1** (☎ 0 4222 2916; Th Sai Uthit) or the street in front of it. Other destinations include Khorat (2nd/1st class 207/248B, 4½ hours, every half-hour), Sakon Nakhon (ordinary/1st-class 73/148B, 3½ hours, every half-hour), Khon Kaen (2nd/1st class 83/104B, 2½ hours, every 15 minutes), Pattaya (2nd/1st class

419/470B, 10 hours, 10 daily), Suvarnabhumi International Airport (418B, eight hours, 9pm) and Vientiane (80B, two hours, six daily; you must already have a Lao visa). **999 VIP** (☎ 0 4222 1489) and **Roongprasert Tour** (☎ 0 4234 3616) operate 24-seat VIP buses (641B) to Bangkok leaving around 9pm in the evening, plus Roongprasert also goes at 10am.

Bus Terminal 2 (☎ 0 4224 7788), on the Ring Rd west of the city (take sŏrng·tăa·ou 6, 7 or 15 or the Yellow Bus), serves western destinations including Loei (ordinary/1st class 70/113B, three hours, every half-hour) and Chiang Mai (2nd class/32-seat VIP 438/657B, 12 hours, five daily).

For Nong Khai (ordinary/1st class 25/47B, one hour, every 45 minutes) you can use either terminal, but the most frequent departures are from Rangsina Market, reached by the White bus or sŏrng·tăa·ou 6.

TRAIN

Udon Thani is on the Bangkok–Nong Khai line. Express trains leave Bangkok at 8.20am, 6.30pm and 8pm arriving at **Udon station** (☎ 0 4222 2061) about 10 to 11 hours later. In the reverse direction, departures are at 6.54am, 6.40pm and 7.20pm. The fares to Bangkok are 245/369/1277B for a 3rd-class seat/2nd-class seat/1st-class sleeper.

Getting Around

Sŏrng·tăa·ou (8B) run regular routes across town. There are also two city buses (8B), the Yellow and the White. The former runs up and down Th Pho Si–Nittayo and the latter tracks Hwy 2. The free Udon Thani Map shows the routes. Short túk-túk (called skylab here) trips start at 40B and it's 200B to the airport.

There are many car-hire outlets around Charoensri Complex. A bike-hire outlet in Nong Prajak Park has one-, two- and three-seaters for 20B to 50B per day.

AROUND UDON THANI
Ban Chiang
บ้านเชียง

This town, 50km east of Udon, was once an important centre of the ancient Ban Chiang civilisation, an agricultural society that thrived in northeastern Thailand for thousands of years. Archaeological digs here have uncovered a treasure trove of artefacts dating back to 3600 BC that overturned the prevailing theory that Southeast Asia was a cultural backwater compared to China and India at the time.

What's now one of Southeast Asia's most important archaeological sites was discovered quite accidentally in 1966. Stephen Young, an anthropology student from Harvard, tripped while walking through the area and found the rim of a buried pot right under his nose. Looking around he noticed many more and speculated that this might be a burial site. He was right. The first serious excavations took place in 1974–75 and they uncovered over a million pottery pieces, as well as 126 human skeletons. Researchers later uncovered the earliest evidence of farming and the manufacture of metal tools (they began working bronze c 2000 BC) in the region. Seven layers of civilisation have been excavated here; the famous burnt-ochre swirl-design pottery comes from the third and fourth layers. The area was declared a Unesco World Heritage Site in 1992.

The excellent, recently expanded **Ban Chiang National Museum** (☎ 0 4220 8340; admission 150B; 8.30am-4.30pm) exhibits a wealth of pottery from all Ban Chiang periods, plus myriad metal objects including spearheads, sickles, fish hooks, ladles, neck rings and bangles. The displays (with English labels) offer excellent insight into the region's distant past and how its mysteries were unravelled. There is an original **burial ground excavation pit** (admission incl in museum ticket; 8.30am-6pm), with a cluster of 52 individual burial sites dating to 300 BC, 1km east at Wat Pho Si Nai. It shows how bodies were buried with (infants were placed inside) pottery.

The **University of Pennsylvania Museum of Archaeology & Anthropology** (www.museum.upenn .edu) has good information about Ban Chiang on its website. From the home page, type Ban Chiang into the search engine.

Rice cultivation remains the town's primary livelihood, but souvenir selling is now a close second. Many area villages make handicrafts such as basketry and clothes sewn with a distinctive rough cotton fabric called *fâi sên yài* (big thread fabric). These and more can be bought from shops facing the museum. Walk down the road facing the museum to find a pottery workshop; you'll pass a cotton-weaving co-op on the way into town. Locals also attempt to sell Ban Chiang artefacts, both real and fake, but the former aren't allowed out of the country and the latter may create hassles at the airport, so don't buy them.

The town **visitor centre** (8am-4pm Mon-Fri) near the museum hires out bikes for 20B per day and can arrange **homestay** accommodation.

SLEEPING & EATING

Lakeside Sunrise Guesthouse (☎ 0 4220 8167; r 200B;) On the west side of the lake, within easy striking distance of the museum, this homey, nicely landscaped place is reason enough to spend the night in town. Clean, shared facilities are downstairs, while the wooden upper floor boasts a spacious verandah. The joyful owner, an encyclopaedia of Ban Chiang knowledge, speaks English and hires out bikes and motorcycles.

There are several simple restaurants across from the national museum entrance.

GETTING THERE & AWAY

The direct *sŏrng·tǎa·ou* service from Udon became a casualty of high petrol prices, but it's worth checking if it has resumed. Otherwise, take a bus bound for Sakon Nakhon or Nakhon Phanom and get off at Ban Nong Mek (35B, one hour) where a túk-túk or motorcycle taxi will charge 60B per person for the 10-minute ride to Ban Chiang.

Phu Phrabat Historical Park

อุทยานประวัติศาสตร์ภูพระบาท

Steeped in mythical intrigue and peppered with bizarre rock formations, **Phu Phrabat Historical Park** (☎ 0 4225 1350; admission 100B; 8.30am-4.30pm) is one of the region's highlights. The formations are a collection of balanced rocks, spires and whale-sized boulders with several shrines and wáts built in and around them. Prehistoric paintings in several grottoes feature wild animals, humans and cryptic symbols. There are also some small but sophisticated rock carvings of Buddha images dating back to when the Mon and, later, Khmer ruled this area. A climb beyond the rock formations to **Pha Sa Dej**, at the edge of the escarpment, ends with dramatic views of the valley below and the mountains of Laos beyond. A well-marked web of trails meanders past these sites and you can see all of them in about an hour; but it's worth spending several.

Most of the bizarre rock formations to be found here feature in an enchanting local legend about a king (Phaya Kong Phan), his stunningly beautiful daughter (Nang Usa), a hermit (the Rishi Chantra) and a love-struck prince (Tao Baros) from another kingdom. The most striking rock formation, **Hoh Nang·**

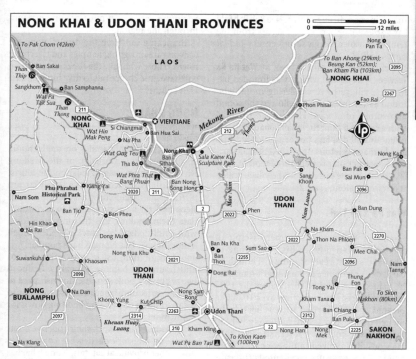

NONG KHAI & UDON THANI PROVINCES

Usa, an overturned boot-shaped outcrop with a shrine built into it, is said to be the tower where the beautiful princess was forced to live by her overprotective father. Many of these rock formations are signposted with names in Thai and English alluding to the legend, but, unless you're familiar with it, they'll make little sense. There's a short version in the museum, but if you're staying at the Mut Mee Garden Guesthouse in Nong Khai (p512), you can read the entire tale.

If you wish to camp, the charge is 20B per small tent and 50B for a big one; or you can rent tents for 50B to 200B. There are also three bungalows with a cost of 600B for up to five people and double that for up to 12.

Not too far from the entrance is **Wat Phra That Phra Phutthabaht Bua Bok**, with its name-sake Lao-style *chedi* covering a Buddha footprint. It also has some odd temple buildings in the general mood of those in the park.

GETTING THERE & AWAY
The park is 70km from Udon Thani and Nong Khai, near the small town of Ban Pheu, and can be visited as a day trip from either city.

From Udon's Rangsina Market, Ban Pheu is a 30B, 1½-hour bus or *sǒrng·tǎa·ou* ride; it's 45B and two hours from Nong Khai's bus station. In Ban Pheu a motorcycle taxi to the park costs about 80B to 100B. Túk-túk are also available, but they have a hard time with the hills.

The vehicles from Udon continue to Ban Tiu, the village at the base of the hill, where a motorcycle taxi should cost 40B for the final 4km, but there are very few of them available.

If you're using public transport, you should plan on leaving the park by 3.30pm.

Ban Na Kha
บ้านนาข่า

This cotton-weaving village, 16km north of Udon right on Hwy 2, is renowned for *kít*-pattern fabrics. *Kít* is a geometric diamond-grid minimal weft brocade traditionally used in pillows and other decorative items, but now commonly worked into clothing. It's a dying tradition since women can make more money working in the farm fields for a day than they can weaving these complicated designs. Dozens of shops line the highway and the main road through town. **Maa Bah Pah Fahi** (☎ 0 4220 6104; ◷ 7am-5.30pm), across from the temple entrance, hangs some century-old *kít* on its walls.

Before leaving, take a peek at **Wat Na Ka Taewee** (◷ daylight hr), which was founded before the village by a wandering monk who found a hole from which bellowed the sound and smoke of a *naga*. He plugged the hole with a rock and built the small *bòht* over it. An open-air hall displays pottery, gold Buddhas and human skeletons unearthed during various construction projects at the temple.

Udon's White bus runs to the village; catch it anywhere along Hwy 2.

Wat Pa Ban Tad
วัดป่าบ้านตาด

Luang Ta Maha Bua, a former disciple of Luang Pu Man now in his 90s, is one of Thailand's most revered monks. Though he earned his reverence as a meditation master, he gained universal celebrity after the 1997 economic crisis by collecting over 10,000kg of gold (people turned in jewellery to be melted down) and US$10 million in baht to help pay the country's international debts. He's heavily involved in other charity work and in 2005 made unprecedented criticisms of Thaksin, the now-fugitive prime minister. Over 250 monks and *mâa chee* (nuns), all taking ascetic vows in addition to the regular 227 precepts, live and meditate at **Wat Pa Ban Tad** (◷ daylight hr), a humble forest wát 16km south of Udon, including about a dozen Westerners.

Hundreds come every morning to hear Luang Ta Maha Bua's simple, direct talks on Buddhism, and thousands more listen via a nationally broadcast radio program (103.25FM in Udon) or at www.luan gta.com.

NONG KHAI PROVINCE

Occupying a narrow, 320km-long sweep along the banks of the Mekong, Nong Khai Province is a beautiful, intriguing region. The capital, Nong Khai, is where the Friendship Bridge (only the second bridge to span the Mekong; the first was in China) crosses into Laos, and this has made the town one of northeastern Thailand's most popular destinations. But long before the river was spanned, the surreal Sala Kaew Ku

Sculpture Park was a must-see on any jaunt through the region.

Branching out from the capital along the Mekong are intriguing temples and riverfront towns. Those who take the time to reach them will have little choice but to dive into genuine Isan culture.

NONG KHAI
หนองคาย
pop 61,500

Lady Luck certainly smiles on the location, spread out along the edge of the Mekong River. As a major staging post on the tourist trail north, Nong Khai hosts a steady stream of travellers. A clutch of excellent places to sleep and eat have sprung up to accommodate them, making this the only Isan town with a full-fledged backpacker scene – albeit a modest one. But Nong Khai's popularity is about more than just its proximity to Laos and bounty of banana pancakes. Seduced by its dreamy pink sunsets, sluggish pace of life and surrounding attractions, many who mean to stay a day end up bedding down for many more.

Developers have stuck their concrete boots into the city's historic districts but, compared to most other provincial capitals, Nong Khai has managed to keep at least one foot firmly rooted in the past. Cut through with a sprinkling of French colonial villas and a starburst of wáts, time appears to flow a little more slowly here.

History
Crammed between nations, Nong Khai is both a historic and physical bridgehead between Thailand and Laos. Nong Khai once fell within the boundaries of the Vientiane (Wiang Chan) kingdom, which itself vacillated between independence and tribute to either Lan Xang (1353–1694) or Siam (late 18th century until 1893). In 1827 Rama III gave a Thai lord, Thao Suwothamma, the rights to establish Meuang Nong Khai at the present city site, which he chose because the surrounding swamps (*nong*) would aid in the city's defence. In 1891, under Rama V, Nong Khai became the capital of *monthon* Lao Phuan, an early Isan satellite state that included what are now Udon, Loei, Khon Kaen, Sakon Nakhon, Nakhon Phanom and Nong Khai Provinces, as well as Vientiane.

The area came under several attacks by *jeen hor* (Yunnanese) marauders in the late

19th century. The Prap Haw Monument (*bràhp hor* means 'defeat of the Haw') in front of the former provincial office (now used as a community college) commemorates Thai-Lao victories over Haw invaders in 1886. When western Laos was partitioned off from Thailand by the French in 1893, the *monthon* capital was moved to Udon, leaving Nong Khai to fade into a provincial backwater.

The opening of the US$30 million, 1174m-long Saphan Mittaphap Thai-Lao (Thai-Lao Friendship Bridge) on 8 April 1994 marked the beginning of a new era of development for Nong Khai as a regional trade and transport centre. The skyline has been creeping slowly upwards ever since.

Orientation & Information

Nong Khai runs narrow along the Mekong River, and most of the hotels and restaurants are on or near the water in the western half of the centre of town. The bus terminal lies a semi-long walk away to the east while the train station and Friendship Bridge are about 3km back to the west.

BOOKSHOPS

Hornbill Bookshop (☎ 0 4246 0272; off Th Kaew Worawut; ❂ 10am-7pm Mon-Sat) Buys, sells and trades English-language books. It's the best English-language bookstore in Isan.

EMERGENCY & MEDICAL SERVICES

Nong Khai Hospital (☎ 0 4241 1504; Th Meechai)
Tourist police (☎ 0 4246 0186; Th Prajak) Next to the *naga* fountain.

IMMIGRATION

Immigration Office (☎ 0 4242 3963; ❂ 8.30am-noon & 1-4.30pm Mon-Fri) South of the Friendship Bridge. Offers Thai visa extensions.

INTERNET ACCESS

Coffee Net (Soi Thepbunterng; per hr 30B; ❂ 10am-midnight) Free coffee and tea while you surf.
Oxy.Net (569/2 Th Meechai; per hr 20B; ❂ 9am-10pm)

MONEY

Siam Commercial Bank (Hwy 2, Big Jieng Mall; ❂ 10.30am-8pm) Has your foreign exchange needs covered after normal business hours.

POST

Main post office (Th Meechai; ❂ 8.30am-4.30pm Mon-Fri, 9am-noon Sat, Sun & holidays)

TOURIST INFORMATION

Tourism Authority of Thailand (TAT; ☎ 0 4242 1326; Hwy 2; ❂ 8.30am-4.30pm Mon-Fri) Inconveniently located outside of town.

TRAVEL AGENCIES

Go Thasadej (☎ 08 1592 0164; www.gothasadej.com; Mekong Promenade; ❂ 10am-7pm) One of the most reliable, all-round travel agents in Thailand.

Sights & Activities

SALA KAEW KU SCULPTURE PARK

ศาลาแก้วกู่

One of Thailand's most enigmatic attractions, **Sala Kaew Ku Sculpture Park** (admission 20B; ❂ 8am-6pm) is a surreal, sculptural journey into the mind of a mystic shaman. Built over a period of 20 years by Luang Pu Boun Leua Sourirat, who died in 1996, the park features a weird and wonderful array of gigantic sculptures ablaze with Hindu-Buddhist imagery.

As he tells his own story, Luang Pu (a Lao national) tumbled into a hole as a child and met an ascetic named Kaewkoo. Kaewkoo introduced him to the manifold mysteries of the underworld and set him on course to become a Brahmanic yogi-priest-shaman. Shaking up his own unique blend of Hindu and Buddhist philosophy, mythology and iconography, Luang Pu developed a large following in northeastern Thailand, which was his adopted home following the 1975 communist takeover in Laos, where he had been working on a similar project.

The park is a smorgasbord of bizarre cement statues of Shiva, Vishnu, Buddha and every other Hindu and Buddhist deity imaginable (as well as numerous secular figures), all supposedly cast by unskilled artists under Luang Pu's direction. Some of the sculptures are quite amusing. If you're travelling with kids, they'll enjoy the serene and stately elephant wading though a pack of anthropomorphic dogs. The tallest sculpture, a Buddha seated on a coiled *naga* with a spectacular multiheaded hood, is 25m high. Also of interest is the Wheel of Life, which you enter through a giant mouth. It boils Luang Pu's philosophies down to a single, slightly baffling image. An explanation is available on the Mut Mee Garden Guesthouse website, www.mut mee.com.

The main shrine building, almost as bizarre as the sculpture park, is full of framed pictures

NORTHEASTERN THAILAND

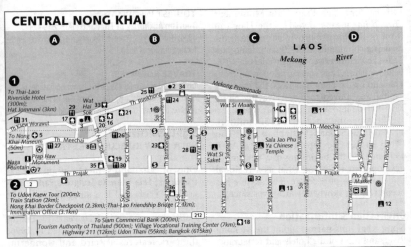

CENTRAL NONG KHAI

of Hindu and Buddhist deities, temple donors and Luang Pu at various ages, plus smaller bronze and wooden figures of every description and provenance – guaranteed to throw an art historian into a state of disorientation. Luang Pu's corpse lies under a glass dome ringed by flashing lights in the upper room.

To get to Sala Kaew Ku, board a bus heading to Phon Phisai or any other eastern destination and ask to get off at Wat Khaek (10B), as the park is also known; it's about a five-minute walk from the highway. Chartered túk-túk cost 150B return with a one-hour wait – don't pay up front, or it may turn into a one-way fare. Or you can reach it by bike in about 30 minutes; Mut Mee Garden Guesthouse distributes handy maps if you want to take the scenic route.

WAT PHO CHAI
วัดโพธิ์ชัย

Luang Pho Phra Sai, a large Lan Xang–era Buddha, awash with gold, bronze and precious stones, sits at the hub of **Wat Pho Chai** (Th Phochai; 6am-7pm). The head of the image is pure gold, the body is bronze and the *ùt-sà-nít* (flame-shaped head ornament on a Buddha) is set with rubies. The altar on which the image sits features gilded wooden carvings and mosaics, while the ceiling bears wooden rosettes in the late-Ayuthaya style.

This was one of three similar statues, and the murals in the *bòht* depict their travels from the interior of Laos to the banks of the Mekong, where they were put on rafts. A storm sent one of the statues to the bottom of the river where it

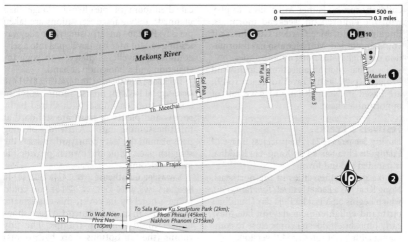

remains today. It was never recovered because, according to one monk at the temple, the *naga* like having it. The third statue, Phra Soem, is at Wat Patum Wanaram in Bangkok.

WAT NOEN PHRA NAO
วัดเนินพระเนาว์

A forest wát on the south side of town, **Wat Noen Phra Nao** (daylight hr) boasts a *vipassana* (insight meditation) centre on pleasant, tree-shaded grounds. It serves as a spiritual retreat for those facing personal crises (Westerners included, if they're serious about meditation).

Some extremely ornate temple architecture, including perhaps the most rococo bell tower we've ever seen, stands in contrast to the usual ascetic tone of forest monasteries. There's a Chinese cemetery here, and some of the statuary wouldn't be out of place at Sala Kaew Ku.

WAT LAM DUAN
วัดลำดวน

You can easily pick **Wat Lam Duan** (Th Rimkhong; daylight hr) out of the skyline because an immense Buddha image sits on top of the *bòht*. You're welcome to climb up (shoes off) and gaze over the Mekong with it.

WAT TUNG SAWANG
วัดทุ่งสว่าง

The *bòht* at **Wat Tung Sawang** (Soi Silpakhom; daylight hr) is one of the city's smallest, but the artistic flair put into the decoration makes it one of the most attractive. Nine Buddhist and Hindu sculptures sit on fanciful pedestals alongside it.

PHRA THAT NONG KHAI
พระธาตุหนองคาย

Also known as Phra That Klang Nam (Holy Reliquary in the Middle of the River), this ruined Lao *chedi* is submerged in the middle of the Mekong and can only be seen in the dry season when the waters lower about 13m. The *chedi* was gobbled up by the meandering Mekong in the middle of the 18th century, and it toppled over in 1847. When the waters drop low enough in the dry season, coloured flags are fastened to it. **Phra That La Nong**, a replica erected on land, glows brightly at night.

MUSEUMS

Recently renovated and opened as a museum, the 1926 French Colonial **Governor's Mansion Museum** (Th Meechai; admission free; 8.30am-6pm) has more shine outside than in. It looks lovely lit up at dusk.

The little **Nong Khai Museum** (0 4241 3658; Th Meechai; admission free; 9am-4pm Mon-Fri), in the old (1929) city hall has little more than photographs, but the price is right.

VOLUNTEERING

While volunteer opportunities usually require a fairly long commitment, you can do a lot of good in just a couple of hours by stopping at one of the **Sarnelli House** (www.sarnelli orphanage.org) orphanages for HIV-positive children, run by Father Mike Shea, to play with the children on weekend mornings. Enquire at Mut Mee Garden Guesthouse if you're interested. Mut Mee also has information on English-teaching opportunities.

Two Thai-wide organisations, Open Mind Projects (p49) and Travel to Teach (p49), are based in Nong Khai and have lots of opportunities here.

Festivals & Events

During **Songkran** (p21) the priceless image of Luang Pu Phra Sai, a Lan Xang–era Buddha, is paraded around town.

Like many other cities in the northeast, Nong Khai has a **Rocket Festival** *(Bun Bâng Fai)*, which begins on Visakha Puja day (Buddha's birth and enlightenment day) in late May/early June, but it doesn't come close to competing with Yasothon's (p542) version.

At the end of Buddhist Lent *(Okk Paan Saa)* in late October/early November, there's a large **Rowing Festival** featuring longboat races on the Mekong. It corresponds with the October full moon, which is when **naga fireballs** (see the boxed text, p514) can be seen.

One particularly fun event is Nong Kai's version of the **Chinese Dragon Festival**, held over 10 days in late October and early November, with dragon dancing, acrobatics, Chinese opera and lots of firecrackers. It's quite possibly the world's loudest festival.

The **Anou Savari Festival** on 5 March marks the end of the Haw rebellions and boasts the city's biggest street fair.

Sleeping

BUDGET

Catering to the steady flow of backpackers heading across the border, Nong Khai's budget offerings are some of the best in the region. In fact, the pricier rooms at many of these guesthouses are some of the best midrange rooms available.

our pick Mut Mee Garden Guesthouse (☎ 0 4246 0717; www.mutmee.com; off Th Kaew Worawut; dm 100B; r 140-750B; 😂) Occupying a sleepy stretch of the Mekong, Nong Khai's budget old-timer has a garden so relaxing it's intoxicating, and most nights it's packed with travellers. A huge variety of rooms are clustered around a thatched-roof restaurant where the owner, Julian, holds court with his grip of local legend and his passion for all things Isan. Because nobody will ever be required to va-

cate their room (people often stay longer than planned), only a few reservations are taken per day. Perhaps unsurprisingly, the alleyway leading to Mut Mee has developed into a self-contained travellers' village with yoga instruction and a bookshop at hand.

Rimkhong Guesthouse (☎ 0 4246 0625; 815/1-4 Th Rimkhong; s/d 140/200B) Sparse rooms, some in a shaky wooden house, with shared bathrooms and plenty of hush are standard at this unassuming outfit. A friendly old dog pads around the leafy courtyard and sets the sluggish pace, while the owners provide the warm welcome.

Sawasdee Guesthouse (☎ 0 4241 2502; 402 Th Meechai; s 140B, d 200-450B; 😂 💻) If you could judge a hotel by its cover, this charismatic guesthouse in an old Franco-Chinese shophouse would come up trumps. The tidy rooms (the fan options share bathrooms) lack the old-school veneer of the exterior and lobby, but at least you'll sleep well in the knowledge that you're bedded down in a little piece of living history. There's free in-room wi-fi.

E-San Guesthouse (☎ 08 6242 1860; 538 Th Khun Muang; r 150-450B; 😂) Just off the river in a small, beautifully restored wooden house with a long verandah, this is a very peaceful and atmospheric place to stay. The air-con rooms (the only ones with private bathrooms) are in a separate modern building.

Ruan Thai Guesthouse (☎ 0 4241 2519; 1126/2 Th Rimkhong; r 200-400B, f 1000B; 😂 💻) Once little more than a small private home, this pleasant spot has grown with the boom time, boasting a good variety of good-quality rooms from simple shared-bathroom basics in the back to a family room in a little wooden cottage. Factor in the tangle of flower-filled garden greenery and the free wi-fi, and it's a winner.

Jumemalee Guesthouse (☎ 08 5010 2540; 419/1 Th Khun Muang; r 250B) Also in an old wooden house, Jumemalee is less lovely (and subsequently more authentically Thai) than its neighbour the E-San. Rooms here have private bathrooms. The family runs the business to honour the wishes of their parents that the house never be sold. Check in at the modern house at the back.

Khiang Khong Guesthouse (☎ 0 4242 2870; 541 Th Rimkhong; r 300-400B; 😂 💻) Rooms in this newly built concrete block sparkle and shine, and you can lament the lack of history with river views from the 3rd-floor terrace or your private balcony. There's free in-room (the signal is pretty weak in the back of the building) wi-fi.

Thai Nongkhai Guesthouse (☎ 0 4241 3155; www.thainongkhai.com; 1169 Th Banthoengjit; r 400-500B, ❌ 🖳) The seven gleaming new rooms (the four pricier units are detached bungalows) in this backyard set-up are fairly humdrum, but the owners make it kind of homey. The wi-fi is free.

Thai-Laos Riverside Hotel (☎ 0 4246 0263; 51 Th Kaew Worawut; r 500-700B; ❌) Upkeep is lagging at this dowdy tour-bus favourite, but if you don't mind a few tears in the carpets, you'll get good views. The 700B rooms have their own little balconies on the riverfront face of the building, but all look at the water. And if you're into tacky hotel clubs, you'll find three of them here.

MIDRANGE & TOP END

Pantawee Hotel (☎ 0 4241 1568; www.pantawee.com; 1049 Th Hai Sok; s 600-900B, d 700-1000B, q 1400-2200B; ❌ 🖳 🖳) The efficiently run Pantawee is almost a village unto itself, with various lodging blocks plus a spa, travel agency and 24-hour restaurant. The rooms are reasonably priced (a tad on the high side for Nong Khai) and come with DVD players and internet-connected PCs. Free wi-fi flows throughout, including the flower-filled garden lounges.

Nong Khai Grand (☎ 0 4242 0033; www.nongkhaigrand.com; Hwy 212; r 1290-1700B, ste 2700-3700B; ❌ 🖳 🖳) Tops in town, this slick, modern place is starting to show its age, but still has plenty of sparkle. A big hit with passing suits, 'executive' standards are maintained throughout. Swanky suites (usually available at 40% discount) are on offer for those after the Midas touch, but even the standard rooms are large and well-appointed.

Eating

For quick, colourful eats swing by the **Hospital Food Court** (no roman-script sign; Th Meechai; ❤ breakfast, lunch & dinner) where about a dozen cooks whip up the standards, or visit the **night market** (Th Prajak; ❤ 4-11pm) between Soi Cheunjit and Th Hai Sok. During the day, grilled fish reigns supreme at the lunch-only **riverside restaurants** (Th Rimkhong) tucked behind Tha Sadet Market.

Khrua Sukapap Kwan Im (☎ 0 4246 0184; Soi Wat Nak; dishes 30B; ❤ breakfast & lunch) The owners of this simple little vegetarian place make a mumsy fuss over fa·ràng diners. The food is

Thai and Chinese standards (from a buffet counter and an English-language menu) plus some excellent juices.

Darika Bakery (☎ 0 4242 0079; 668-669 Th Meechai; dishes 30-60B; ❤ breakfast & lunch) If you're an early riser, this spartan English-speaking outfit will be waiting for you from 5am with hearty egg-and-toast breakfasts, banana pancakes, Vietnamese-style baguette sandwiches and more.

Nung-Len Coffee Bar (☎ 08 3662 7686; 1801/2 Th Kaew Worawut; dishes 35-180B; ❤ breakfast, lunch & dinner) One of the friendliest places in Nong Khai, this petite place has good java and juices plus an eclectic menu of Thai and fa·ràng food, and even a few fusions of the two, like spaghetti fried chilli with chicken.

Daeng Namnuang (☎ 0 4241 1961; 526 Th Rimkhong; dishes 35-180B; ❤ breakfast, lunch & dinner) This Vietnamese place has grown into an Isan institution and hordes of out-of-towners head home with car boots and carry-on bags (there's an outlet at Udon Thani's airport) stuffed with Vietnamese năam neu·ang (pork spring rolls). The kitchen operates as much like a factory as a restaurant; the food really is superb nonetheless.

Mut Mee Garden Guesthouse (☎ 0 4246 0717; off Th Kaew Worawut; dishes 40-130B; ❤ breakfast, lunch & dinner) Mut Mee's food is very popular, especially the breakfasts, but keep in mind that the Thai dishes are toned down to European tastes. But whether you like it hot or not, you simply cannot beat this riverside location, and there's a good selection of vegetarian dishes, like mushroom lâhp (a super-spicy meat salad originating from Laos).

Nagarina (☎ 0 4241 2211; dishes 40-250B; ❤ lunch & dinner) There's no paucity of peppers in the kitchen of Mut Mee's floating restaurant, which sits below the guesthouse. It specialises in seafood and often features some unusual species from the Mekong. There's a sunset cruise (100B, around 5pm) most nights.

Rom Luang (☎ 08 7853 7136; 45/10 Th Prajak; dishes 40-150B; ❤ dinner) Though the menu is mainly Thai, most of the Yellow Umbrella's best-known dishes, like sausages and kor mŏo yâhng (grilled pork neck), are Isan specialities. The handmade tables and chairs add flair, and the grills stay smoking until 5am.

Café Thasadej (☎ 0 4242 3921; 387/3 Soi Thepbunterng; dishes 60-375B; ❤ breakfast, lunch & dinner) Sophistication is in short supply in Nong

---

GREAT BALLS OF FIRE

Mass hysteria? Methane gas? Drunken Lao soldiers? Clever monks? Or perhaps the fiery breath of the sacred *naga*, a serpentlike being that populates folkloric waterways throughout Southeast Asia. For many Lao and Thai who live by the Mekong River, it's not a matter of whether or not to believe. Since 1983 (or for ages, depending on who you ask), the sighting of the *bâng fai pá yah nâhk* (loosely translated, 'naga fireballs') has been an annual event. Sometime in the early evening, at the end of the Buddhist Rains Retreat (October), which coincides with the 15th waxing moon of the 11th lunar month, small reddish balls of fire shoot from the Mekong River just after dusk and float a hundred or so metres into the air before vanishing without a trace. Most claim the *naga* fireballs are soundless, but others say a hissing can be heard if one is close enough to where they emerge from the surface of the river. People on both sides of the Mekong see the event as a sign that resident *naga* are celebrating the end of the holiday.

Naga fireballs have only recently come to the attention of the rest of Thailand. TV news has been reporting the annual sightings for years, but it wasn't until the 2002 release of a comedy film based on the phenomena that Thais really began to take notice. Entitled *Sìp Hâh Kâm Deuan Sìp èt* (Fifteenth Waxing Moon of the Eleventh Lunar Month; the film was released with English subtitles under the curious title *Mekhong Full Moon Party*), the debut of the film not long before the scheduled event had the expected effect. Thousands of Thais from Bangkok and the rest of the country converged on the banks of the Mekong in Nong Khai Province and waited for the show to begin. Sadly, it rained that year. But that didn't dampen enthusiasm and *naga* fireballs were witnessed right on schedule.

Khai, but it oozes out of this little restaurant. Both the menu and liquor list, the latter among the best in town, go global. Gyros, Weiner schnitzel, fish and chips, lasagne, tuna salad and smoked salmon are some of the most popular options.

Bird's Eye View Terrace (☎ 0 4242 0033; Hwy 212; dishes 70-260B; ☯ dinner) You can sample Isan food and see nearly the whole city from the Nong Khai Grand hotel's open-air rooftop restaurant.

Drinking

Gaia (☎ 0 4246 0717; below Mut Mee Garden Guesthouse; ☯ 7pm-late Wed-Mon) Much of the Mut Mee crowd and many resident *fa·ràng* fill this laid-back lounge on the Mekong. There's a great drinks list, a dreamy vibe and sometimes live music. It often hosts fundraisers for various charitable projects.

Warm Up (☎ 08 1965 7565; 476/4 Th Rimkhong; ☯ 7pm-2am) This little place rises above, both figuratively and literally, the other bars on this end of Th Rimkhong. It looks out over the river, has a free pool table and is popular with both Thais and travellers.

For something a little more Thai, follow the Mekong-hugging Th Rimkhong east past Tha Sadet Market to find a bevy of neon-lit restaurants and bars churning out dinner and drinks to an all-ages Thai crowd.

Shopping

Tha Sadet Market (Th Rimkhong) This huge market runs for most of the day and offers the usual mix of dried food, electronic items, souvenirs and assorted bric-a-brac, most of it imported from Laos and China.

Village Weaver Handicrafts (☎ 0 4242 2652; 1020 Th Prajak; ☯ 8am-6pm) This place sells high-quality, hand-woven fabrics and clothing (ready-made or made-to-order) to fund development projects around Nong Khai. The *mát·mèe* cotton is particularly good here.

Village Weaver workshop (☎ 0 4241 1236; 1151 Soi Jittapanya; ☯ 8am-5pm Mon-Sat) This workshop, where some of the nearby Village Weaver Handicrafts' products are produced, has a somewhat different inventory, with many more Lao designs.

Village Vocational Training Center (☎ 0 4299 0613; ☯ 8am-5pm Mon-Sat) Though separate from Village Weaver, this school 7km south of town (take Hwy 2 and follow the sign east) has similar goals. It's a great place to see the *mát·mèe* process from start to finish, and it also has a pottery workshop and mushroom farm.

Getting There & Away

AIR

The nearest airport is 55km south in Udon Thani, from where there are regular flights

So what, you might ask, is the real cause behind *naga* fireballs? There are many theories. One, which was aired on a Thai TV exposé-style program, claimed that Lao soldiers taking part in festivities on the other side of the Mekong were firing their rifles into the air. Interestingly, the reaction to the TV program was anger and a storm of protest from both sides of the river. Some suggest that a mixture of methane gas and phosphane, trapped below the mud on the river bottom, reaches a certain temperature at that time of year and is released. Many assume that some monks have found a way to make a 'miracle'. Whatever the real cause, few Thais will even entertain the suggestion of a hoax.

Naga fireballs have become big business in Nong Khai Province. Every year some 40,000 people invade little Phon Phisai, the locus of fireball watching, and thousands more converge on dozens of other riverside spots between Sangkhom and Khong Jiam in hopes of sightings. Special buses (28B) make the return trip at night, but don't try to leave too late or you run the risk of not getting back. Several hotels run their own buses where you'll get a guaranteed seat, plus Mut Mee Garden Guesthouse sails its boat there and back (2500B, including lunch and dinner).

If you don't come with the right mindset, you'll likely be disappointed. The fireball experience is much more than just watching a few small lights rise from the river; it's mostly about watching Thais watching a few small lights rise from the river. And even if the *naga* doesn't send his annual greeting on the day you come (it's sometimes delayed by a day due to the vagaries of calculating the arrival of the full moon), it'll be an interesting experience.

to Bangkok and a couple to Luang Prabang, Laos. See p505 for details.

Udon Kaew Tour (☎ 0 4241 1530; Th Pranang Cholpratan; ☺ 8.30am-5.30pm) travel agency runs vans (150B per person) to/from the airport. Coming into town they'll drop you at your hotel or the bridge; going back you need to get yourself to their office. It's best to buy a ticket in advance. A private driver to the airport can be hired for 700B from most travel agencies around town.

BUS

Nong Khai's **bus terminal** (☎ 0 4241 1612) is located just off Th Prajak, about 1.5km from the main pack of riverside guesthouses.

Udon Thani (ordinary/1st class 25/47B, one hour, every 45 minutes) is the most frequent destination. There are also buses for Khon Kaen (2nd/1st class 120/157B, 3½ hours, hourly) and Nakhon Phanom (ordinary/2nd class 175/220B, six hours, six daily). For Chiang Mai, you have to change at Udon's new bus terminal.

For those travelling west along the Mekong, there are usually five buses to Pak Chom, which can drop you in Sangkhom (55B, three hours, until 3pm) or anywhere else along the way. Normally only the 7.30am service travels all the way to Loei (130B, seven hours), but if there are enough passengers later departures may go too.

Bangkok (2nd/1st class 350/450B, 11 hours) buses are frequent in the late afternoon and early evening, but less so during the day. **Roongprasert Tour** (☎ 0 4241 1447; ☺ 7.45pm) and **999 VIP** (☎ 0 4241 2679; ☺ 7.30pm & 8pm), with offices on opposite sides of the bus terminal, offer daily 24-seat VIP (700B, 10 hours) services to Bangkok. There's also one bus direct to Suvarnabhumi International Airport (454B, nine hours, 8pm).

Laos

Take a túk-túk to the border crossing (50B from the bus station) where you get stamped out of Thailand. From there regular minibuses ferry passengers across the bridge (15B, or 20B from 6am to 8.30am and 4pm to 9.30pm) to the hassle-free Lao immigration checkpoint, where 30-day visas (see p754 for details) are available. From there it's 22km to Vientiane; there will be plenty of buses, túk-túk and taxis waiting for you. If you already have a visa for Laos, there are also six direct buses a day to Vientiane from Nong Khai's bus terminal (60B, one hour).

Unless you're travelling in a large group, there's no good reason to use any of the visa service agencies in town.

TRAIN

Express trains leave Bangkok daily at 6.30pm and 8pm, arriving in Nong Khai at 5.05am and 8.25am respectively. Going the other way, the express train services depart from Nong Khai at 6am (arriving at 5.10pm) and 6.20pm (arriving at 6.25am). The fares range from 1317B for a 1st-class sleeper cabin to 253/388B for a 3rd-/2nd-class seat. There's also one rapid train (213/348B 3rd /2nd class) leaving Bangkok at 6.40pm (arriving at 7.35am) and leaving for Bangkok at 7.15pm (arriving at 8am).

For information call **Nong Khai Station** (☎ 0 4241 1592), which is 2km west of town.

Getting Around

If your guesthouse doesn't hire out bikes (from 30B) or motorcycles (from 150B), someone nearby will. And it pays to shop around a bit, since brakes aren't necessarily standard equipment.

A túk-túk trip from the bus station to the Mut Mee area should be around 30B.

EAST OF NONG KHAI

Most people travelling along the Mekong rather than crossing over it into Laos head west, but there are some real rewards for bucking the trend and heading east, including one of Thailand's best homestay programs and most interesting temples.

Ban Ahong

บ้านอาฮง

Ban Ahong is a pretty riverside village at the Km115 marker on Rte 212. **Wat Ahong Silawat** (☼ daylight hr) on its west side is built amidst ruddy boulders at a river bend known as Sàdeu Námkong (the Mekong River's Navel) because of the large whirlpool that spins here from June to September. A 7m-tall copy of Phitsanulok's Chinnarat Buddha gazes over the Mekong to the simple little bòht. This is considered a highly auspicious spot to spend the evening of wan òrk pan·sǎh, the end of the Buddhist Rains Retreat (Buddhist Lent), because the bâng fai pá yah nâhk (naga fireballs) were first reported here (for more details on the fireballs see the boxed text, p514). It is also presumed to be the deepest spot along the river and there are many legends about underwater caves.

The **Ahong Mekong View Hotel** (☎ 08 6227 0465; r/f 500/800B; ☒) sits along the river on the temple grounds (all profits from the hotel go to the temple) and does most of its business with tour groups, so it's likely you'll

either find it booked out or you'll be the only guests. Prices are a bit high, but each of the 14 large rooms is well appointed and has a balcony. The monks, wanting to promote a peaceful atmosphere, requested that the rooms have no TVs.

Another overnight option is the village's **homestay** (☎ 08 7223 1544; per person incl meals 250B), though very little English is spoken. About two dozen families have guestrooms in their houses and you can partake in village life as much as you like, perhaps joining your hosts fishing on the river or out in the surrounding rubber plantations.

The buses between Nong Khai (ordinary/2nd class 80/100B, 2½ hours, hourly until 4pm) and Beung Kan pass here.

Beung Kan

บึงกาฬ

Beung Kan, a quiet, dusty town on the Mekong River 136km east of Nong Khai, is small, but it's one of the few significant centres between Nong Khai and Nakhon Phanom, so some people break the journey here. It has banks, an internet cafe and most other services you might need, plus a promenade along the river.

During the dry season the Mekong River recedes far from Beung Kan and reaches its narrowest point along the border between Thailand and Laos. People picnic on the sandbar that becomes exposed at this time. Most travellers, however, only stop long enough to catch a connecting ride to Wat Phu Tok.

There are cheaper places in town, away from the river, but the Mekong-facing **Maenam Hotel** (☎ 0 4249 1051; www.maenamhotel .com; 107/1 Th Chansin; r 350-400B; ☒), offering spotless rooms with lots of little extras, is the best located place in Beung Kan. Just about all the restaurants on Th Chansin serve inside or riverside (which can be buggy).

GETTING THERE & AWAY

Buses to Nong Khai (ordinary/2nd class 80/110B, three hours, hourly until 3.30pm) park in front of the 'Thai Beauty' shop near the old clock tower.

Although it's very rarely done, you can cross the border here to/from Pakson, Laos, but only if you already have your visa. The boat trips cost 400B.

Wat Phu Tok
วัดภูทอก

Accessed via a network of rickety staircases built in, on and around a giant sandstone outcrop, **Wat Phu Tok** (Isolated Mountain Temple; ☉ daylight hr, closed 10-16 April) is one of the region's true wonders. Six levels of steps lead past shrines and *gù·dì* that are scattered around the mountain, in caves and on cliffs. A 7th-level scramble up roots and rocks takes you to the forest at the summit, with fabulous views over the surrounding countryside and a truly soporific atmosphere. It's the cool and quiet isolation of this wát that entices monks and *mâa chee* from all over Thailand to come and meditate here; many of them do so on the summit, so be quiet and respectful up there. The route up the mountain symbolises that the path to virtue requires personal effort.

This wát used to be the domain of the famous meditation master Luang Pu Juan, a disciple of Luang Pu Man (see p533). Luang Pu Juan died in a plane crash in 1980 along with several other highly revered forest monks who were flying to Bangkok for Queen Sirikit's birthday celebration. A marble *chedi* containing Luang Pu Juan's belongings and some bone relics sits below the mountain.

Visitors who impress the monks by acting and dressing respectfully are permitted to stay the night in single-sex dorms.

GETTING THERE & AWAY

Túk-túk can be hired to go to Wat Phu Tok from Beung Kan; drivers will ask for 600B for the return journey plus a two-hour wait at the wát itself. Better still, you could take bus 225 from Beung Kan's old clock tower southward to Ban Siwilai (20B, 45 minutes) where túk-túk drivers ask for 200B to go to the wát. If you catch an early bus to Beung Kan, Wat Phu Tok can be visited as a day trip from Nong Khai. If you are driving or pedalling, a more direct route is to continue southeast along Rte 212 from Beung Kan for 27km until you reach Chaiyapon, then turn right at Rte 3024, the road signed for Chet Si, and Tham Phra waterfalls. The water-falls are in the Phu Wua Wildlife Reserve and make worthy detours, as much for the weird rock formations as the cascades. After 17.5km make a right and continue 4km more.

Ban Kham Pia
บ้านขามเปี้ย

Isan is flush with village homestay programs, and while they all let you delve deep into rural life, most are aimed at Thai tour groups. But, thanks to the help of Open Mind Projects (p49) and English-speaking Khun Bunleud, **Kham Pia** (☎ 0 4241 3578, 08 7861 0601; www.thailand wildelephanttrekking.com; per person 200B, meals 50-90B) really knows how to welcome *fa·ràng*.

The village is within walking distance of 186-sq-km **Phu Wua Wildlife Reserve**, so you can add some superb treks to the usual cultural activities in the village – another thing that helps make this one of Thailand's best homestay programs. The forest is flush with waterfalls and home to two dozen elephants, who are sometimes encountered during day walks (March and April are the best months) and often seen during overnight stays in the treehouse (not for the faint-hearted).

Kham Pia is 190km east of Nong Khai, just 3km off Hwy 212. Buses between Nong Khai (180B, 3½ hours) and Nakhon Phanom (160B, 2½ hours) will drop you at Ban Don Chik, 3km away.

WEST OF NONG KHAI

The people living west of Nong Khai are obsessed with **topiary**, and along Rte 211 you'll pass hedges and bushes sculpted by ambitious gardeners into everything from elephants to boxing matches. The river road (Th Kaew Worawut), lined with floodplain fields of tobacco, tomatoes and chillies, is another option for the first stretch of the route west, though cyclists should note that it has no shoulder.

The TAT office in Nong Khai has information about several village homestay programs (most costing about 300B with meals) along the way, and if you ask, they'll probably call to arrange your visit.

Wat Phra That Bang Phuan
วัดพระธาตุบังเผือน

Boasting a beautiful and ancient Indian-style stupa, **Wat Phra That Bang Phuan** (Map p507; ☉ daylight hr) is one of the region's most sacred sites. It's similar to the original *chedi* beneath the Phra Pathom Chedi in Nakhon Pathom, but while it's presumed that this stupa dates back to the early centuries AD, no one really knows when either was built.

In 1559 King Jayachettha of Chanthaburi (not the present Chanthaburi in Thailand, but Wiang Chan, now known as Vientiane, in Laos) extended his capital across the Mekong and built a newer, taller Lao-style *chedi* over the original as a demonstration of faith (just as King Mongkut did in Nakhon Pathom). Rain caused the *chedi* to lean precariously and in 1970 it finally fell over. The Fine Arts Department restored it in 1976 and 1977. The current *chedi* stands 34.25m high on a 17.2-sq-metre base and has several unsurfaced *chedi* around it, giving the temple an ancient atmosphere.

GETTING THERE & AWAY
The temple is 11km from Nong Khai on Hwy 211. Catch a Sangkhom-bound bus and ask for Ban Bang Phuan (20B, 40 minutes).

Tha Bo
ท่าบ่อ
pop 16,000
Prosperous Tha Bo (Map p507) is the most important market centre between Nong Khai and Loei, and the covered market, which spills out to the surrounding streets, is full of locally grown products. A large Vietnamese population lives here, and they've cornered the market on noodle production. You'll see masses of *sên lék* (flat rice noodles) drying in the sun on the west side of town near the hospital. From about 5am to 10am you can watch people at the factories making the noodles, and then around 2pm they start the cutting – all by hand.

It used to be mostly spring-roll wrappers laid out on the bamboo racks, but noodles are a better export product and most people have made the switch. Ban Hua Sai, upriver just before Si Chiangmai and directly across the Mekong from Vientiane, has picked up the slack and is now the area's spring roll–wrapper capital.

Tha Bo is mostly a day-trip destination, but there are some cheap guesthouses if you want to spend the night.

GETTING THERE & AWAY
The 'yellow bus' runs regularly between Nong Khai and Tha Bo (25B, one hour, every half-hour), taking the scenic riverside route. Pick it up in Nong Khai at the bus station or near the Hospital Food Court on Th Meechai. Alternatively, take a Sangkhom-bound bus (25B, 40 minutes).

Wat Hin Mak Peng
วัดหินหมากเป้ง
Set in a cool forest with lots of bamboo groves overlooking the Mekong, this vast forest **temple** (Map p507; ☺ daylight hr) is very quiet and peaceful. And, since the riverside mountains begin to rise right around here, it's very beautiful too. It was built above three giant boulders that form a cliff rising out of the river. From this point, a Lao forest temple can be seen directly across the river and fisherfolk occasionally drift by on house rafts.

Its *tú·dong* monks have taken ascetic vows in addition to the standard 227 precepts, eating only once a day and wearing robes sewn by hand from torn pieces of cloth. Several monuments honour Luang Pu Thet, the wát's deeply revered founding abbot, including a glistening *chedi* housing his few earthly possessions.

The current abbot requests that visitors dress politely: no shorts or sleeveless tops. Those who don't observe the code may be turned away.

GETTING THERE & AWAY
The temple is midway between Si Chiangmai and Sangkhom. Sangkhom-bound buses from Nong Khai (50B, 2¼ hours) pass the wát, and then it's a longish walk.

Sangkhom
สังคม
Seductively sleepy, the little town of Sangkhom (Map p507), facing the Lao island of Don Klang Khong, is a convenient staging post for those taking the river road (Rte 211) between Nong Khai and Loei. The Mekong dominates life here, but there are also some lovely waterfalls in the area. The largest is three-tiered **Nam Tok Than Thip** (admission free; ☺ daylight hr), 13km west of Sangkhom (2km off Rte 211). The lower level drops 30m and the second, easily reached via stairs, falls 100m. The 70m-top drop is only barely visible through the lush forest. **Nam Tok Than Thong** (admission free; ☺ daylight hr), 11km east of Sangkhom, is a wider but shorter drop with a swimmable pool at the bottom, although it dries up around April. The short nature trail takes you down by the Mekong. Than Thong is more accessible than Than Thip, but can be rather crowded on weekends and holidays.

The forest wát peering down on the town from the eastern hills, **Wat Pa Tak Sua** (☼ daylight hr), lies about 3km away as the crow flies (ask someone to point you to the footpath used by the monks every morning), but it's 19km to drive; the last 3km are on a dirt road. Take the turn-off across from Nam Tok Than Thong. It has the most amazing Mekong views we know of, and the sunset scene is wonderful in the summer months.

As the ever-smiling Buoy will tell you, Sangkhom's veteran lodge, **Bouy Guesthouse** (☎ 0 4244 1065; Rte 211; r 190-200B; 🖳), has just a few 'simple huts' (the cheaper ones sharing bathrooms), but they're popular for good reason. They come with hammocks and wooden decks and the riverside location just west of town is wonderfully relaxing. Motorbike hire is 200B.

Poopae Ruenmaithai (☎ 0 4244 1088; Rte 211; r 500-1500B; 🗙 🖳) offers some swankier digs 1.5km east of town. This gorgeous set-up, featuring wooden walkways and decorative stonework, should have made better use of the river views, though it will definitely satisfy those who demand a certain level of comfort. The cheapest rooms have a little *Being John Malkovich* about them, but most people will be able to stand up straight. The restaurant is good and there's a four-person Jacuzzi for rent (200B per hour).

GETTING THERE & AWAY
There are usually five buses a day from Nong Khai (60B, three hours) and the earliest of those continues to Loei (70B, 3½ hours).

LOEI PROVINCE

Stretching south from the sleepy arc of the Mekong River near Chiang Khan to the vast mountain plateau of Phu Kradung National Park, Loei (which means 'to the extreme') is a diverse, beautiful province untouched by mass tourism, despite all it has to offer. This isn't the wildest place in Thailand, but potholes definitely pepper the trail that will lead you from the hush of the region's tranquil national parks (there are far more good ones than we can feature here) to the hubbub of Dan Sai's annual Phi Ta Khon Festival. If Chiang Khan weren't tucked away in such a remote corner of the country, it would probably be a bustling backpacker magnet.

The terrain here is mountainous and temperatures fluctuate from one extreme to the other – hotter than elsewhere in Thailand during the hot season and chillier during the cold season. This is the only province in Thailand where temperatures drop below 0°C, a fact the tourist brochures love to trumpet. In December and January the crisp air paints leaves red and yellow at high elevations, such as around Phu Kradung and Phu Reua.

LOEI
เลย
pop 33,000
Arrive here after a sojourn in the region's dreamy countryside and Loei, the capital city, is little more than a reminder that concrete and congestion still exist. Efforts to upgrade the town, including a large city-centre lake, have helped haul Loei out of the doldrums; but, as the TAT itself says: 'the city of Loei has little to hold the traveller's interest.'

Information
A few internet cafes are spread around the city centre, while most of the banks are on or near Th Charoenrat, including **Krung Thai Bank** (Th Ua Ari; ☼ 8.30am-4.30pm), which offers exchange services and weekend hours.

The **Tourism Authority of Thailand** (TAT; ☎ 0 4281 2812; Th Charoenrat; ☼ 8.30am-4.30pm) provides a good map of the province and has helpful staff.

Sights
The little **Loei Cultural Centre** (☎ 0 4283 5224; Rte 201; admission free; ☼ 8.30am-4pm), found 5km north of town at Rajabhat University, is hardly worth the trip; but if you won't be stopping in Dan Sai, there are Phi Ta Khon festival masks and photos to see. Ask in the office down below and someone will open the door for you.

Festivals
Though Loei's farmers are fast switching to other crops, Loei Province is still Thailand's second biggest producer of cotton, so it's fitting that the city kicks off its **Blooming Cotton Flower and Sweet Tamarind Festival** (1–9 February) with cotton-decorated floats.

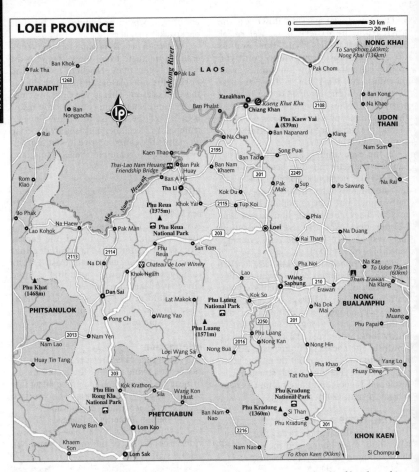

LOEI PROVINCE

Sleeping

Sugar Guesthouse (☎ 0 4281 2982; www.sugarguest house.blog.com; 4/1 Th Wisut Titep/Soi 2; r 180-380B; ✴) The cheapest place in town (the fan rooms share a hot-water bathroom) is also the friendliest. The English-speaking owner arranges trips around the province at reasonable prices, or, if you'd rather get there yourself, hires bikes (50B) and motorcycles (250B). A túk-túk from the bus station will probably cost 60B.

Thuang Sap Guesthouse (☎ 0 4281 5576; 22 Th Sathon Chiang Khan; r 350B; ✴) Hidden away in the centre of the block, rooms at this quiet, good-value place feature a fridge and quality mattresses. They also have little balconies, but there's nothing to see from them. Shining surfaces

bear testament to a clutch of hard-working, behind-the-scenes cleaners.

King Hotel (☎ 0 4281 1701; 11/8-12 Th Chumsai; r 500-1000B; ✴ 💻) Fit for a king? No, though a major overhaul has given the rooms a simple but attractive style, making it a pleasant place to stay for those who don't need the leisure activities available at the big hotels. They tell us an upgrade of the courtyard is coming next.

Loei Palace Hotel (☎ 0 4281 5668; 167/4 Th Charoenrat; r 1000-3000B; ste 5000B; ✴ 💻 ✴) Loei's flagship hotel sports some wedding-cake architecture, helpful staff, plenty of mod cons and usually a high vacancy rate, which is why you can get such big rooms for such small prices. Wi-fi covers the first two floors only. Check out the flood marker and photos next to the reception desk to see what the city suffered in September 2002.

Eating

Loei's main **night market** (🕐 4-10pm) is small, but pretty good.

Gwan Yin Jai (☎ 0 4281 4863; 34/25-26 Soi PR House; dishes 30-35B; 🕐 breakfast & lunch Sun-Fri) This friendly vegetarian restaurant serves mock-meat versions of Thai fast-food standards, like *kôw man gài* (rice with steamed chicken). They have an English menu, but can't always find it because it gets used so rarely.

Krua Nid (no roman-script sign; ☎ 0 4281 3013; 58 Th Charoenrat; dishes 20-45B; 🕐 breakfast, lunch & dinner) Fronted by a big glass buffet case, this no-frills eatery serves *hòr mòk* (soufflé-like curry steamed in banana leaves) and other central-Thai dishes. Look for the red-and-white awning.

Baan Yai (no roman-script sign; ☎ 0 4283 3361; Th Sert-Si; dishes 20-150B; 🕐 lunch & dinner) This big, leafy place with a funky variety of wooden tables and chairs is a genuine Isan restaurant where the menu (no English) has entire sections for

insects, ant eggs and frogs. They also serve *dtòhng mŏo* (pork in a sour and spicy sauce), a Loei speciality you'll probably never find anywhere else in Thailand. At night there's live music or movies and football to watch, so many people just come here to drink.

Ban Thai (☎ 0 4283 3472; 22/58-60 Th Chumsai; dishes 50-350B; 🕐 lunch & dinner) The first choice for a fix of *fa-ràng* food is a fairly attractive spot with German and Italian dishes dominating the mixed menu, but the Thai food is pretty good too.

Getting There & Away

There are no longer flights to Loei, but they may resume.

BUS

The most frequent service from Loei's **bus terminal** (☎ 0 4283 3586) is to Udon Thani (ordinary/1st class 70/113B, three hours, every half-hour). There are also buses to Khon Kaen (2nd/1st class 141/160B, 2½ hours, every half-hour), Khorat (2nd/1st class 260/321B, six hours, hourly), Phitsanulok (2nd/1st class 139/178B, four hours, hourly) and Chiang

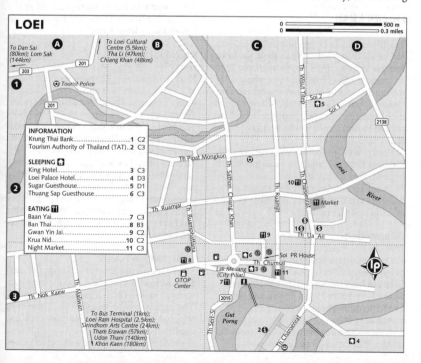

LOEI

0	500 m
0	0.3 miles

To Dan Sai (80km); Lom Sak (144km)
To Loei Cultural Centre (5.5km); Tha Li (47km); Chiang Khan (48km)

203
201
201

2138

⊙ Tourist Police

Th Wisut Thep
Soi 2
5
Soi 1

Th Pipat Mongkon

Th Sathon Chiang Khan

Th Ruamjai
Th Ruampattana

10
Th Charoenrat

Loei River

Market

Th Ruamjai

Th Ruamjai

9
Th Ua Ari

8
Soi PR House
6
Th Chumsai
11
Soi Chumsai

Lak Meuang (City Pillar)
7
3

OTOP Center

Th Nok Kaew

Th Maliwan

2015

Gut Porng

Th Sert-Si

Th Charoenrat

2
4

INFORMATION
Krung Thai Bank.................................1 C2
Tourism Authority of Thailand (TAT)..2 C3

SLEEPING 🛏
King Hotel...3 C3
Loei Palace Hotel...............................4 D3
Sugar Guesthouse...............................5 D1
Thuang Sap Guesthouse.....................6 C3

EATING 🍴
Baan Yai..7 C3
Ban Thai..8 B3
Gwan Yin Jai.....................................9 C2
Krua Nid..10 C2
Night Market....................................11 C3

To Bus Terminal (1km); Loei Ram Hospital (2.5km); Sirindhorn Arts Centre (2km); Tham Erawan (57km); Udon Thani (140km); Khon Kaen (180km)

Mai (2nd class/32-seat VIP 410/613B, 10 hours, six daily). Usually there's only one bus to Nong Khai (130B, seven hours), which leaves at 6am, and it's worth catching because it follows the scenic Mekong River route. It's faster, however, to go via Udon Thani.

Buses to Bangkok (2nd class/32-seat VIP 321/481B, 11 hours) leave frequently in the early evening, and less so in the early morning; there are 24-seat VIP buses (640B) with **Air Muang Loei** (☎ 0 4283 2042; ☼ 8.30pm) and **999 VIP** (☎ 0 4281 1706; ☼ 8.40pm).

LAOS

Foreigners can now arrange all immigration formalities at the seldom-used Thai-Lao Nam Heuang Friendship Bridge in Amphoe Tha Li, but there's no public transport and the road running north through Laos to Luang Prabang is not very good. The border is open 8am to 6pm daily.

Getting Around

Sŏrng·tăa·ou (10B) run from the bus station into town every five minutes, or you can take a túk-túk for about 30B.

CHIANG KHAN

เชียงคาน

Traditional timber houses line the streets, with old ladies sitting nattering in their shadows, and the Mekong drifts slowly by. If you have an image of a quiet riverside town where nothing much happens and no one seems to care, Chiang Khan may just be it; 7-Eleven hasn't even made it here yet, and you'll be hard pressed to find someone who isn't very happy about that.

Pretty and peaceful, with photogenic views of the river and the Laos mountains beyond, this little town has a good spread of cheap accommodation and makes a restful stopover if you fancy a couple of days of doing…well…nothing.

Information

BAAC (Rte 201; ☼ 8.30am-3.30pm Mon-Fri) Has an ATM and is an agent for Western Union, but there are no foreign-exchange facilities in town.

Baan Dok Faii Guesthouse (333/11 Soi 11; internet per hr 15B; ☼ 9.30am-9.30pm) The first choice of most travellers for checking email.

Immigration Office (☎ 0 4282 1911; Soi 26 ☼ 8.30am-4.30pm Mon-Fri) Foreigners can't cross to Laos at Chiang Khan, but you can get a visa extension.

Tourist Information Center (Kaeng Khut Khu; ☼ 8am-4.30pm) Your guesthouse will be a better source of information.

Sights & Activities
TEMPLES

Chiang Khan's wáts are modest, but have a particularly idiosyncratic style of architecture featuring colonnaded fronts. Many have sweeping Lao-style roofs and there's often a touch of French influence. A good example is **Wat Si Khun Meuang** (Th Chai Khong; ☼ daylight hr), which contains a Lao-style *chedi* and *bòht*, fronted by interesting murals, plus plenty of topiary. Similar structures, minus the bush art, are found at **Wat Thakhok** (Th Chai Khong; ☼ daylight hr) and **Wat Pa Klang** (Th Chiang Khan; ☼ daylight hr).

Wat Mahathat (Th Chiang Khan; ☼ daylight hr), in the centre of town, is Chiang Khan's oldest temple. The *bòht*, constructed in 1654, has a new roof over old walls with faded original murals on the front.

Wat Tha Khaek (☼ daylight hr) is a ramshackle, 700-year-old forest temple housing three 300-year-old stone Buddha images. They sit on a ledge over a larger, modern Buddha in the wát's still unfinished *bòht*. The temple is 2km before Kaeng Khut Khu.

KAENG KHUT KHU

แก่งคุดคู้

Next to nobody in Bangkok has ever heard of Chiang Khan, but most know the gorgeous rapids at **Kaeng Khut Khu** (admission free; ☼ 24hr), about 5km downstream. It's most beautiful in the dry, hot season, but worth the trip anytime. The surrounding park has a bevy of vendors selling Isan food into the early evening. The local speciality is coconut candy *(má·prów gàaw)*, and you will also find *gûng đen* (dancing shrimp), little bowls of live shrimp meant for slurping down just as they come, on the menu. *Sŏrng·tăa·ou* rarely come out here, so take a túk-túk (50B), or better yet, hire a bike.

BOAT TRIPS & TOURS

Most guesthouses arrange boat trips to Kaeng Khut Khu or further afield, and the mountain scenery makes these highly recommended. The rapids can be reached on a one-hour trip, but since you'll have to turn back immediately after arriving, two-hour trips are a wiser choice. Prices swing with petrol prices,

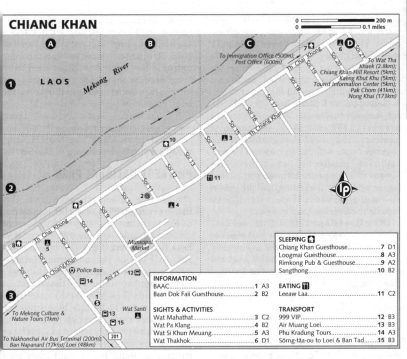

CHIANG KHAN

SLEEPING	
Chiang Khan Guesthouse	**7** D1
Loogmai Guesthouse	**8** A3
Rimkong Pub & Guesthouse	**9** A2
Sangthong	**10** B2

EATING	
Leeaw Laa	**11** C2

INFORMATION	
BAAC	**1** A3
Baan Dok Faii Guesthouse	**2** B2

SIGHTS & ACTIVITIES	
Wat Mahathat	**3** C2
Wat Pa Klang	**4** B2
Wat Si Khun Meuang	**5** A3
Wat Thakhok	**6** D1

TRANSPORT	
999 VIP	**12** B3
Air Muang Loei	**13** B3
Phu Kradung Tours	**14** A3
Sŏrng-tăa-ou to Loei & Ban Tad	**15** B3

but expect a two-hour trip in a boat that can hold three or four people to cost about 1000B. If you arrange your trip down at the rapids you're looking at 700B per hour for a boat that can hold 15 people.

Another option is to kayak the river (1500B per person, minimum four) with Mekong Culture & Nature Tours (see p524).

Most guesthouses also hire bikes (50B to 70B) and motorcycles (200B to 250B), and Huub at Chiang Khan Guesthouse and Pascal at Rimkong Guesthouse can also set you up with maps if you're a do-it-yourselfer.

Sleeping & Eating

Chiang Khan doesn't quite have a backpacker scene, but there are many traveller-focused guesthouses, so you may want to stroll Th Chai Khong before deciding on your digs for the night.

Sangthong (☎ 0 4282 1305; thepbluesthai@hotmail .com; 162/1 Th Chai Khong; s/d 200/300B; 🖳) Not the cheapest rooms on the river, but pretty close; and though simple, with shared bathrooms, they're much cheerier than anything cheaper. The whole chaotic place is stuffed with the

owner's art, and the terrace restaurant is one of the town's most attractive.

Rimkong Pub & Guesthouse (☎ 08 7951 3172; http://rimkhong.free.fr; 294 Th Chai Khong; r 200–500B) This heartily polished teak house has good rooms (with shared bathrooms) that, unlike most of the wooden oldies in town, still radiate some historic charm on the inside. French expat Pascal will tell you all you want to know about the area over breakfast or beer.

our pick Chiang Khan Guesthouse (☎ 0 4282 1691; www.thailandunplugged.com; 282 Th Chai Khong; r 300–400B; 🖳) Run by a Dutch tour guide (you'll never be short of local info) and his affable Thai wife (you'll never stop laughing), this traditional-style place with shared bathrooms is all creaking timber and tin roofing. Scores of pot plants and bucolic views from the terrace round out the scene. Meals with the family are available, as are *bohng-lahng* shows (3000B) performed by local students, who keep all the cash to put towards their studies.

our pick Loogmai Guesthouse (☎ 0 4282 2334; 112/1 Th Chai Khong; r 300–450B) Combining some minimalist modern artistic styling with oodles of French colonial class, this old-school villa offers a handful of sparse but atmospheric rooms, an airy terrace with river views and a real sense of history. The owner leaves the villa at 5.30pm (you get the key) and chances are you'll have the place to yourself. Bathrooms are shared in all but one of the rooms.

Mekong Culture & Nature Tours (☎ 0 4282 1457; mcn_thailand@hotmail.com; 407 Th Chiang Khan; campsites per person 150B, r 800-2500B; ☐) If you want some Siamese serenity, head 1km upstream to this riverside home with bungalows and shared-bathroom guestrooms out in the forest. Rooms are quite pricey for what you get, but you're paying for the setting, and off-season discounts are available. If you're travelling by bus, staff will pick you up in town.

Chiang Khan Hill Resort (☎ 0 4282 1285; www.chiang khanhill.com; r 800-3000; ☒ ☒) The best views of Kaeng Khut Khu are from the town's only swanky resort. Skip past the 800B level and the rooms are nice for the price. The Thai and Isan restaurant (dishes 25B to 250B) specialises in mushrooms, since they grow their own, and Mekong River fish.

Guesthouse restaurants serve a mix of Western and Thai food, but generally speaking if you want the latter you can eat more authentically along Th Chiang Khan at a place like **Leeaw Laa** (no roman-script sign; ☎ 08 6240 2350; 127/5 Th Chiang Khan; dishes 30-200B; ☽ lunch & dinner), a simple food-to-order shop with a few favourites on an English menu.

Getting There & Away

Sŏrng·tăa·ou to Loei (35B, 1¼ hours) depart about every 20 minutes from a stop on Rte 201, while eight buses (45B, 45 minutes) leave from Nakhonchai Air's bus terminal 250m further south. The buses continue to Khorat (2nd/1st class 231/297B, seven hours) via Chaiyaphum (2nd/1st class 165/212B, five hours).

Three companies, departing from their own offices, make the run direct to Bangkok (10 hours). **Air Muang Loei** (☎ 0 4282 1317; Rte 211), with an office at the Shell station, has 1st-class (479B) departures at 8am and 6.30pm. The other choices are **999 VIP** (☎ 0 4281 1706; Soi 9), with 24-seat VIP (694B) buses at 6.30pm and 2nd-class buses (347B) at 6.30pm; and **Phu Kradung Tours** (☎ 08 7856 5149; Rte 201), with a same-priced 2nd-class bus at 6.40pm.

No transport runs direct to Nong Khai. The quickest way there is via Loei and Udon Thani, but the river route is preferable for the scenery. To do the latter, take a Loei-bound *sŏrng·tăa·ou* south to Ban Tad (20B, 30 minutes) where you can catch the morning bus headed to Nong Khai from Loei. Because things are always changing on this trip, ask at your guesthouse for the latest news.

If you're heading west and you've got your own wheels, consider following the seldom-seen back roads along Mae Nam Heuang; they'll eventually deposit you in Dan Sai.

PHU REUA NATIONAL PARK
อุทยานแห่งชาติภูเรือ

Phu Reua means 'boat mountain', a moniker that owes its origins to a cliff jutting out of the peak that's sort of in the shape of a Chinese junk. At only 121 sq km, **Phu Reua National Park** (☎ 0 4280 1716; admission 200B) isn't one of Thailand's most impressive reserves, but it does offer some dreamy views from the summit of the mountain it surrounds. Few visitors do more than make the easy 30-minute hike from the upper visitor centre through pine forest to the summit (1365m), where in December and January temperatures can drop below freezing at night. If you want more solitude, strike out from the lower visitor centre instead. Arguably the park's most scenic waterfall, 30m-tall **Nam Tok Huai Phai**, is an easy 2.5km hike from here, or you can take a roundabout route to the summit.

As well as a **campsite** (per person with own tent 30B, 3-/4-person tent hire 405/540B), there are also some comfortable **bungalows** (☎ 0 2562 0760; www.dnp .go.th/parkreserve; 4-/6-people 2000/3000B). Many resorts around the park offer less scenery, but better value.

There are restaurants at both visitor centres.

The park is about 50km west of Loei on Rte 203. Although buses heading west from the city can drop you in the town of Phu Reua (2nd/1st class 45/60B, 1½ hours), you'll have to charter a truck for around 500B (including a few hours wait) to the park itself.

DAN SAI
ด่านซ้าย

For 362 days a year, Dan Sai is an innocuous little town, a borderline backwater community where life revolves around a small market and a dusty main street. For the remaining three days, however, it's the site of one of the country's liveliest and loudest festivals.

Falling during the fourth lunar month (usually June), Dan Sai's **Phi Ta Khon Festival** (also called Bun Phra Wet) combines the Phra Wet Festival, during which recitations of the *Mahavessantara Jataka* (past-life stories of the Buddha) are supposed to enhance the listener's chance of being reborn in the lifetime of the next Buddha, with Bun Bang Fai (Rocket Festival). For those wishing to plunge headlong into Isan life, this curious cross between the drunken revelry of Carnivale and the spooky imagery of Halloween is a must see.

The origins of the Phi Ta Khon Festival are shrouded in ambiguity, but some aspects of the festival appear to be related to tribal Thai (possibly Tai Dam) spirit cults. In fact, the dates for the festival are divined by Jao Phaw Kuan, a local spirit medium who channels the information from the town's guardian deity. On the first day Jao Phaw Kuan performs a sacrifice to invite Phra Upakud (an enlightened monk with supernatural powers who chose to transform himself into a block of white marble to live eternally on the bottom of the Man River) to come to town. Locals then don wild costumes and masks for two days of *lôw kŏw* (white whisky)–fuelled dancing that's full of sexual innuendo, before launching the rockets and heading to the temple to listen to sermons through the night and into the third day.

Information

The main road through town is Th Kaew Asa. At its north end, inside the *têt·sà·bahn* (city hall), there's an **information centre** (☎ 0 4289 1231; www.tessabandansai.com; Th Kaew Asa; ☑ 8.30am-4.30pm) with English-speaking staff and free internet. The post office, library (also with free internet plus festival photos) and municipal market are all nearby. To the south, at the junction with Rte 2013, is **Krung Thai Bank** (Rte 2013; ☑ 8.30am-4.30pm Mon-Fri), which always changes euros and usually changes dollars.

Sights & Activities

Behind the big white gate, **Wat Phon Chai** (Th Kaew Asa; ☑ daylight hr) plays a major role in the Phi Ta Khon festivities. The **Dan Sai Folk Museum** (admission free; ☑ 8.30am-4.30pm) is

also on the grounds, and has a collection of costumes worn during the celebrations, a demonstration of how the masks are made and a 20-minute video from the festival.

Phra That Si Songrak (Rte 2113; ☑ 7am-5pm) is the most highly revered stupa in Loei Province. The whitewashed Lao-style *chedi* stands 30m high and was built in 1560–63 as a gesture of unity between the Lao kingdom of Wiang Chan (Vientiane) and the Thai kingdom of Ayuthaya in their resistance against the Burmese. A pavilion in front of it contains a very old chest that supposedly contains an even older carved stone Buddha about 76cm long. You can't wear shoes, hats or the colour red, or carry food or open umbrellas if you climb up to the *chedi*. Down below is a modest **museum** (admission free; ☑ 8.30am-4pm) showing random artefacts donated by locals.

On a wooded hill overlooking Phra That Si Songrak, **Wat Neramit Wiphatsana** (☑ daylight hr) is a gorgeous (it almost looks like a Buddhist-themed resort) meditation *wát* where most of the buildings are made of unplastered laterite blocks. Famous Thai temple muralist Pramote Sriphrom spent years painting images of *jataka* tales on the interior walls of the massive *bòht,* which also hosts a copy of Phitsanulok's Chinnarat Buddha (p390). The *wát* is dedicated to the memory of the late Luang Pu Mahaphan (aka Khruba Phawana), a much-revered local monk.

Kawinthip Hattakham (☎ 0 4289 2339; 70/1 Th Kaew Asa; ☑ 6.30am-8pm) sells authentic Phi Ta Khon masks, plus a bevy of other festival-related souvenirs. It makes for a fun browse. It also has bike hire (100B per day).

Chateau de Loei (☎ 0 4280 9521; www.chateaudeloei .com; ☑ 8am-5pm), one of Thailand's most respected vineyards, is 23km out of town on Rte 203 (at Km60). The winery released the first commercially produced Thai wine in 1995 and scooped a silver medal for its Chenin Blanc dessert wine in the 2004 International Wine & Spirits Competition. Visitors are welcome and you can taste its wines, grape juices and brandies back in the main building. There's a restaurant and gift-gourmet shop on the main road.

Sleeping & Eating

As few people stay in Dan Sai outside the festival season, accommodation is limited.

Homestay (☎ 08 9077 2080; phitakhon@yahoo.com; per person 150-200B, per meal 50B) A couple of villages just outside town have been running a successful homestay program for many years, and the families dote on *fa·ràng* guests. When not at work (most of the English-speaking hosts are teachers) they'll take you out to share typical daily activities. Everything can be arranged at Kawinthip Hattakham craft shop.

Dansai Resort Hotel (☎ 0 4289 2281; Rte 2013; r 300-450B; ✗ ▯) Dan Sai's original hotel has ordinary but adequate rooms (those at the back are better), though the 300B versions don't have hot water.

SB Resort Hotel (☎ 0 4289 1918; www.sbresort.net; Rte 2013; r 450-600B; ✗ ▯) Despite the fancy name, like the Dansai it's just an ordinary hotel, though a newer and nicer one.

Phunacome (☎ 0 4289 2005; www.phunacomeresort .com; Rte 2013; r 3800-5500B; ✗ ▯ ▨) This new luxury resort makes the most of its country location, and the kitchen makes use of the organic rice and veggies grown on the grounds. Two styles of room line a row of ponds: standard hotel rooms and some cool wood-and-thatch Isan-inspired cottages. Both are plush and lovely, with nice views. The lobby has a library, massage service and restaurant with Thai and Western food. Their mascot is the buffalo, and two real ones roam grounds that also host several artistic renditions.

Im Un (no roman-script sign; ☎ 0 4289 1586; Rte 2013; dishes 30-150B; ✕ breakfast, lunch & dinner) Sizzling Thai and Isan favourites, like *gaang 'bàh* (jungle curry) and *gaang aòrm*, are served under a thatched roof in a garden setting. It's on the edge of town, 900m east of the main junction.

A mini **night market** (Th Kaew Asa; ✕ 4.30-9.30pm) sets up across from the municipal market.

Getting There & Away
Buses between Loei (2nd class 60B, 1½ hours) and Phitsanulok (ordinary/2nd class 67/94B, three hours) stop in Dan Sai about hourly and there are a few other buses that begin their journeys to these towns in Dan Sai. All stop near the junction of Th Kaew Asa and Rte 2013.

SIRINDHORN ART CENTRE
ศูนย์ศิลป์สิรินทร

Wang Saphung, 23km south of Loei, is the unlikely location of the **Sirindhorn Art Centre** (☎ 0 4284 1410; Rte 210; admission free; ✕ 8am-6pm). It was built to honour Sangkom Thongmee,

a famous local teacher (since retired) at the adjoining school whose students, mostly farmers' children, have won thousands of awards for their work. Student works (and sometimes professional pieces) are always on display and sometimes for sale in the glassy gallery. There's also a nice sculpture garden in front.

PHU KRADUNG NATIONAL PARK
อุทยานแห่งชาติภูกระดึง

Capped off by its eponymous peak, **Phu Kradung National Park** (☎ 0 4287 1333; admission 400B; ✕ trail to summit 7am-2pm Oct-May) covers a high-altitude plateau, cut through with trails and peppered with cliffs and waterfalls. Rising to 1316m, Thailand's second national park is always cool at its highest reaches (average year-round temperature 20°C), where its flora is more typical of a temperate zone. There are mixed deciduous and evergreen monsoon forests as well as patches of cloud forest.

A small visitor centre at the base of the mountain distributes detailed maps and collects your admission fee, but almost everything else is up top. The **main trail** scaling Phu Kradung is 5.5km long and takes about three to four hours to climb. It's strenuous, but not all that challenging since the most difficult parts have steps. The hike is quite scenic and there are rest stops with food vendors about every kilometre along the way. Once on top, it's another 3km to the main park **visitor centre** (✕ 24hr). You can hire porters to carry your gear balanced on bamboo poles for 15B per kilogram.

The 348-sq-km park is a habitat for various forest animals, including elephants, Asian jackals, Asiatic black bears, sambar deer, serows, white-handed gibbons and the occasional tiger. The best place to see wildlife is the **wilderness area**, which can only be entered during January to March. Many waterfalls (including **Tham Yai**, which has a cave behind it) and scenic viewpoints (some ideal for sunrises and sunsets) are scattered around the mountain.

Spending the night atop Phu Kradung is a rite of passage for many local students, so the park gets unbelievably crowded during school holidays (especially March to May). The park is closed to visitors during the rainy season (June to September) because the path to the top is considered too hazardous to climb.

SLEEPING & EATING

Atop the mountain there's **camping** (per person with own tent 30B, 3-/6-person tent hire 225-450B) space for 5000 people plus lots of **bungalows** (☎ 0 2562 0760; www.dnp.go.th/parkreserve; 6-12-person bungalow 900-3600B). There are also several small open-air eateries serving the usual stir-fry dishes. If you're arriving late in the afternoon, there's camping and one bungalow at the bottom and some resorts outside the entrance.

GETTING THERE & AWAY

Buses from Loei go to the district town of Phu Kradung (50B, 1½ hours, every half-hour). From Phu Kradung, hop on a *sŏrng·tăa·ou* (20B) to the park visitor centre at the base of the mountain, 10km away. The last *sŏrng·tăa·ou* leaves the mountain around 8pm.

THAM ERAWAN
ถ้ำเอราวัณ

High up the side of a beautiful limestone mountain, **Tham Erawan** (⏰ 6am-7pm) is a large cave shrine, featuring a vast seated Buddha. Gazing out over the mountain-studded plains below, the Buddha is visible from several kilometres away and can be reached by a winding staircase of 600 steps. The views are superb, especially at sunset. More stairs and a line of lights lead you through the massive chamber and out the other side of the mountain. Take a torch, because if the lights go out, you're screwed – we speak from experience.

The temple is along Rte 210, just across the Nong Bualamphu Province line. Buses from Loei (ordinary/2nd class 25/40B, 11/four hours, every 20 minutes) to Nong Bualamphu will drop you 2.5km away, where, if you're lucky enough to find one, a túk-túk or motorcycle taxi will shuttle you to the temple for about 25B.

NAKHON PHANOM PROVINCE

Lao and Vietnamese influences are strong in Nakhon Phanom, a province bordered by the Mekong and dotted with beautiful and revered temples. Though just about every person you see marching buffalo or tending their rice fields is ethnically Thai, many wear conical Vietnamese-style straw hats. It's not a region bristling with can't-miss attractions, but there are plenty of fine river views and some interesting diversions available; and the colossal Wat Phra That Phanom is an enchanting talisman of Isan culture.

Construction of the third Thai-Lao Friendship Bridge is under way 15km north of the capital, and it could open by 2011, but it's unlikely to alter the city's sleepy character much.

NAKHON PHANOM
นครพนม

pop 31,700

Nakhon Phanom means 'City of Mountains', but the undulating sugarloaf peaks all lie across the river in Laos, so you'll be admiring rather than climbing them. But the views are beautiful, especially during a hazy sunrise. Nothing else is quite as appealing as the distant row of hills, though there's plenty more to see and do for those who've come all the way out here. Most Thai visitors make some time to shop for silver at the places near the pier.

Information

Bangkok Bank (Tesco-Lotus, Th Nittayo; ⏰ 10am-8pm) Banks are clustered around the junction of Th Nittayo and Th Aphiban Bancha, but this one can do foreign exchange (cash only) after hours.

Crab Technology (Th Si Thep; internet per hr 15B; ⏰ 8am-10pm)

Immigration office (☎ 0 4251 1235; Th Sunthon Wijit; ⏰ 8.30am-noon & 1-4.30pm Mon-Fri) For visa extensions.

North By North-East Tours (☎ 0 4251 3572; www.north-by-northeast.com; 746/1 Th Sunthon Wijit; ⏰ 9am-5pm Mon-Sat) Leads cultural and eco tours in Isan and across the river in Laos. It can also help arrange volunteer placements in the area.

Tourism Authority of Thailand (TAT; ☎ 0 4251 3490; Th Sunthon Wijit; ⏰ 8.30am-4.30pm) Covers Nakhon Phanom, Sakon Nakhon and Mukdahan Provinces.

Sights & Activities
TEMPLES

Nakhon Phanom's temples have a distinctive style. This was once an important town in the Lan Xang Empire, and after that Thai kings sent their best artisans to create new buildings. Later, a vivid Vietnamese and French influence crossed the Mekong and jumped into the mix.

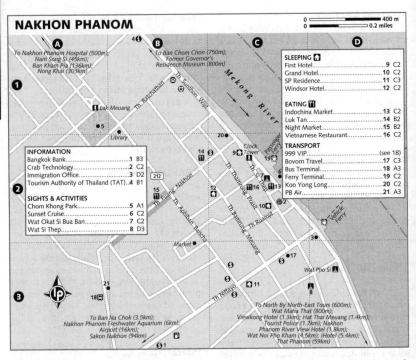

NAKHON PHANOM

One good example is **Wat Maha That** (Th Sunthon Wijit; ☼ daylight hr). Its 24m-tall, gold-and-white Phra That Nakhon *chedi* resembles the second *chedi* built at That Phanom.

Wat Okat Si Bua Ban (Th Sunthon Wijit; ☼ daylight hr) pre-dates the town and also has a touch of Chinese influence. The *wí·hǎhn* houses Phra Taew and Phra Tiam, two sacred wooden Buddha images. The amazing mural, one of our favourites in Thailand (it's like a Thai Where's Waldo; try to find the backpackers) shows the story of Phra Taew and Phra Tiam floating across the Mekong from Laos.

The interior murals of the *bòht* at **Wat Si Thep** (Th Si Thep; ☼ daylight hr) show the *jataka* along the upper portion, and kings of the Chakri dynasty along the lower part. On the back of the *bòht* is a colourful triptych done in modern style. The abbot's residence, built in 1921, won a preservation award.

BAN NA CHOK
บ้านนาจอก

The Vietnamese community in Ban Na Chok, about 3km west of town, has restored **Uncle Ho's House** (admission free; ☼ daylight hr), the simple wooden house where Ho Chi Minh lived (1928–9) while planning his resistance movement. There are a few more Ho Chi Minh displays, some labelled in English, a bit to the northwest at the **Friendship Village** (☎ 08 0315 4630; admission free; ☼ 8am-4pm) community centre. There's a celebration of his birthday every 19 May.

OTHER SIGHTS & ACTIVITIES

Nakhon Phanom's newest attraction is the **Former Governor's Residence Museum** (☎ 08 5853 8503; Th Sunthon Wijit; admission free; ☼ 10am-7.30pm Wed-Sun), a recently restored c 1925 mansion that holds photos of Nakhon Phanom past and present and, out the back, displays about the Illuminated Boat Procession (see opposite).

The city's old prison has been converted into **Chom Khong Park** (Th Ratchathan; admission free; ☼ 5am-8pm). Models of prisoners sit in some of the old cells and you can climb the guard towers.

If you like fish you'll like **Nakhon Phanom Freshwater Aquarium** (☎ 0 4251 5312; Hwy 2033; admission 30B; ☼ 9am-4pm), which houses Mekong River species, including giant Mekong catfish (*blah bèuk*). It's 5km west of town and 1km south of Hwy 22. *Sŏrng·tăa·ou* to Nakae (20B, 15 minutes) pass by.

The city runs an hour-long **sunset cruise** (☎ 08 6230 5560; per person 50B) along the Mekong on *Thesaban 1*, which docks across from the Indochina Market. Thai and Western snacks are served and, of course, there's karaoke. It sails nightly around 5pm. You can charter the boat for 1000B.

From February to April **Hat Thai Meuang** (tourism boosters call it Hat Sai Thong: 'Golden Sand Beach') rises just south of the Viewkong Hotel.

Festivals

Nakhon Phanom is famous for its **Illuminated Boat Procession** (*Lái Reua Fai*), a modern twist on the ancient tradition of sending rafts loaded with food, flowers, and candles down the Mekong as offerings for the *naga*. Today's giant bamboo rafts hold as many as 16,000 handmade lanterns, and recently some designers have added a touch of animation to the scenes. Boat races, music competitions and other festivities run for a week at the end of Ork Phansaa (the end of Buddhist Lent), but the boats are launched only on the night of the full moon. That morning, Phu Thai perform their 'peacock dance' in front of That Phanom (p531).

Sleeping

First Hotel (☎ 0 4251 1253; 16 Th Si Thep; r 160-300B; ❄) Has the cheapest beds in town, for good reason.

Grand Hotel (☎ 0 4251 1281; 210 Th Si Thep; r 190-320B; ❄) 'Grand' is a popular euphemism for 'modest' among Thailand's budget hotels. This is no duff option though. While the interior is rather spartan, potted plants and animal sculptures bring a lick of colour, and the rooms are perfectly comfortable. A few of the cheapest even have hot water.

Windsor Hotel (☎ 0 4251 1946; 272 Th Bamrung Meuang; r 250-400B; ❄ 🖥) Housed in a rather intimidating concrete block, this is never-theless one of the friendlier options in town. The fan rooms are a bit noisy, but remain fair value, and even have a minifridge.

SP Residence (☎ 0 4251 3505; 193/1 Th Nittayo; r 450-800B; ❄ 🖥) This well-run place has plain, but modern, comfortable rooms in a good location.

iHotel (☎ 0 4254 3355; Th Chayanghoon; r 450-800B; ❄ 🖥) One of Isan's most stylish ho-tels, the 'i' mixes good mattresses, 'power showers' (ground floor only), free wi-fi, a backyard garden and some artistic touches. If it wasn't 5km out of town and right along the highway it would be Nakhon Phanom's best choice.

Viewkong Hotel (☎ 0 4251 3564; www.viewkonghotel .com; 527 Th Sunthon Wijit; r 700-900B, ste 2600B; ❄ 🖥) The town's former chart-topping hotel has less pizzazz and more wear than the current champ (the Nakhon Phanom River View, 500m further downstream), but it's priced much better and feels less cold. There's a pleasant terrace overlooking the river and it has the expected business-class ameni-ties, plus karaoke, massage and all the other things Thai travellers can't live without. Riverview rooms cost no extra, so be sure to request one.

Eating

Downtown has a few fun restaurants and bars, most on or near Th Fuang Nakhon, including a couple of dinner-only joints with terraces along the Mekong. The bal-cony at the 1st-floor food court in the

---

THE BI-COLOURED RIVER

If you're coming from or heading to the north along Hwy 212, take a short break at **Nam Song Si**, 45km from Nakhon Phanom, where the greenish water of Huay Songkhram meets the muddy brown Mekong. The line between the two is very clear, especially when it's windy or rainy. And don't be swayed by any locals you meet along the way who tell you there's no such place in Nakhon Phanom, that you must be thinking of Mae Nam Song Si in Ubon Ratchathani. Just turn at the sign for 'the Bi-Coloured River.' This northern merger may be much less famous, but it's still pretty cool.

our pick **Pak Nam Chaiburi** (no roman-script sign; ☎ 0 4257 3037; dishes 30-230B; ☺ lunch & dinner) serves fish on a shaky wooden deck right at the confluence. The best way to enjoy the bucolic setting is by stopping here for lunch. The food and the scenery are superb.

Indochina Market (Th Sunthon Wijit; ☺ breakfast, lunch & dinner) has choice seats that frame the mountain views. The city's excellent **night market** (Th Fuang Nakhon; ☺ 4-9pm) rocks out a great variety of food, though there are few places to sit so consider snacking your way through dinner.

Vietnamese Restaurant (no roman-script sign; ☎ 0 4251 2087; 165 Th Thamrong Prasit; dishes 30-120B; ☺ breakfast, lunch & dinner) With coloured lights and Ronaldinho posters, this little corner shop makes a half-hearted attempt at being fashionable, but the food stays classic. It has served the same family recipes, including *năam neu·ang* (assemble-it-yourself pork spring rolls) and spicy Thai salads, for over 50 years now.

Luk Tan (☎ 0 4251 1456; 83 Th Bamrung Meuang; buffet 89B; ☺ dinner) This friendly little spot oozes quirky charm, with tables made from old sewing machines, and a carefully constructed model train built into the wall. Quirkiest of all is the food: an American home-style buffet featuring mashed potatoes and a salad bar. They also serve steak and pizza.

Ban Chom Chon (no roman-script sign; ☎ 0 4252 0399; 124 Th Sunthon Wijit; dishes 59-249B; ☺ dinner) This upscale but low-priced place next to the museum and across from the river is famous for Mekong River fish cooked in a dizzying choice of styles including *blah chôrn lui sŏo·an* (deep-fried striped snake-head 'run through the garden'; served with lots of vegetables in a lemon and chilli sauce). Both the food and service are top-notch and the wooden deck invites you to stay late into the night.

Getting There & Away

AIR

PB Air (☎ in Bangkok 0 4251 6300, 0 2261 0222; www.pbair .com; 327/12 Th Fuang Nakhon; ☺ 8.30am-5.30pm Mon, Wed & Sat, 8.30am-2pm Tue, Thu, Fri & Sun) flies at least once daily to/from Bangkok (one way 3180B, 1¼ hour). You can also buy tickets at **Bovorn Travel** (☎ 0 4251 2494; Th Nittayo; ☺ 8am-5pm Mon-Fri, to 1pm Sat & Sun), which is more conveniently located. An **airport shuttle** (☎ 08 1872 1215) costs 500B per carload.

BOAT

Between 8.30am and 6pm you can catch a boat (one way 60B, every half-hour) from the **ferry terminal** (Th Sunthon Wijit) across the Mekong to Tha Khaek in Laos. Thirty-day Lao visas (see p754 for details) are now available at the border.

BUS

Nakhon Phanom's **bus terminal** (☎ 0 4251 3444; Th Fuang Nakhon) is east of the town centre. From here buses head to Nong Khai (ordinary/2nd class 175/220B, six hours, hourly from 6am to 11am); Udon Thani (2nd/1st class 165/211B, five hours, every 45 minutes until 3pm) via Sakon Nakhon (2nd/1st class 65/85B, 1½ hours); and Mukdahan (ordinary/1st class 52/92B, two hours, hourly) via That Phanom (ordinary/1st-class 27/49B, one hour, five daily). Most Bangkok (2nd /1st class 442/569B, 12 hours) buses depart from 7am to 8am and 4.30pm to 6.30pm. **999 VIP** (☎ 0 4251 1403) sends a 24-seat VIP bus (885B) at 6pm.

Getting Around

Túk-túk drivers quote 30B per person from the bus station to most places in town and 200B per hour, which is about how long it takes to visit Ban Na Chok.

Nakhon Phanom's sparse traffic makes it a good place for biking. **Koo Yong Long** (☎ 0 4251 1118; 363 Th Sunthon Wijit; bikes per hr 10B; ☺ 8am-6pm) has bike hire.

RENU NAKHON

เรณูนคร

Renu Nakhon is known for cotton weaving, though few people in the town proper work their looms anymore. You'll need to visit a nearby village if you want to see the process. The Phu Thai, who compose the majority of the town's residents, make and market their designs here. The finished products are sold in the big **handicrafts market** on the grounds of **Wat Phra That Renu Nakhon** (☺ daylight hr), as well as at a string of nearby shops. The temple's 35m-tall *tâht* is a replica of the previous *chedi* built in That Phanom and is considered very holy.

Tour groups sometimes arrange Phu Thai folk dances on the stage across from the market. If you'd like to hire the troupe, or just have questions about Phu Thai culture, ask for **Khun Gobgab** (☎ 08 6339 1600; gobgab1234@yahoo .co.th), who lives right behind the market and speaks English.

GETTING THERE & AWAY

The turn-off to Renu Nakhon is only 8km north of That Phanom, and then it's a further 7km west on Rte 2031. There's no public transport. Túk-túk drivers in That Phanom ask 200B round trip per person with a little waiting time for you to look at the *tâht* and do some shopping, but the final price depends on your bargaining skills. You won't save much money if you travel up to the junction and bargain with a túk-túk driver there.

THAT PHANOM
ธาตุพนม

Towering over the small town, the spire of the colossal Lao-style *chedi* of Wat Phra That Phanom is one of the region's most emblematic symbols and one of the great flagpoles of Isan identity. In comparison, the little town of That Phanom itself is rather forgettable. Divided neatly in two, with the older half next to the river, it does, however, make a relatively peaceful base for a night as you explore the region.

Sights
WAT PHRA THAT PHANOM
วัดพระธาตุพนม

Wat Phra That Phanom (Th Chayangkun; ☽ 4am-8pm) is a potent and beautiful place; and even if you're feeling templed-out, this is an impressive and inspiring place. At its hub is a *tâht*, more impressive than any in present-day Laos and highly revered by Buddhists from both countries. The temple is busiest around full moons because people believe that a visit on these days bestows bountiful happiness in their life.

The *tâht* is 53m high and a five-tiered, 16kg gold umbrella laden with precious gems adds 4m more to the top. Many Thais believe that the Lord Buddha travelled to Thailand and directed that one of his breastbone relics be enshrined in a *chedi* to be built on this very site: and so it was, eight years after his death in 535 BC. Historians date the first construction, a short **satoop** (there's a replica of it in a pond in front of the temple), to the Dvaravati period (6th to 11th centuries). Modifications have been routine since then, but there have been four major constructions. The first *tâht* was 24m tall and went up in the 1st century BC; it was raised to 47m in 1690 and you'll find copies of this design all over Isan. The current design was built in 1941, but it toppled during heavy rains in 1975 and was rebuilt in 1978.

Behind the surrounding cloister is a shady little park with a giant drum and to the north sits a 30m, century-old longboat carved from a single tree. The nearby **museum** (admission free; ☽ 8.30am-4pm) tells the history of the *tâht* and also displays a hodgepodge collection of pottery, gongs, US presidential commemorative coins and more.

OTHER SIGHTS
The short road between Wat Phra That Phanom and the old town on the Mekong River passes a large **Lao arch of victory**, which is a crude miniature version of the arch in Vientiane. The short stretch of Th Kuson Ratchadamnoen between the arch and the river is interesting, with a smattering of French-Chinese architecture that's reminiscent of old Vientiane or Saigon and some shops selling Vietnamese foodstuffs. A couple of the interiors are nearly museum-quality timeless.

Hundreds of Lao merchants cross the river for a **market** (☽ 8.30am-noon Mon & Thu) north of the pier. Exotic offerings include Lao herbal medicines, forest roots and crabs. The maddest haggling occurs just before the market closes, when Thai buyers try to take advantage of the Lao's reluctance to carry unsold merchandise back home.

Festivals
During the **That Phanom Festival** in late January or early February visitors descend from all over Thailand and Laos to pay respect to the *tâht*. The streets fill with market stalls, many top *mŏr lam* (an Isan musical tradition akin to *lôok tûng*) troupes perform and the town hardly sleeps for 10 days.

Sleeping
Few tourists stick around town very long, so there are only a handful of sleeping options, and most are extremely old. During the That Phanom Festival in January/February rates soar and rooms are booked out well in advance.

Niyana Guesthouse (☎ 0 4254 0880; 65 Soi 33; r 120-160B) The town's backpacker original was temporarily closed when we last stopped by as Niyana was occupying the airport with PAD demonstrators (see p44), but it's running again. It's little more than someone's house with an English school on the ground floor, with all the good and bad that goes with that. Rooms are spartan and bathrooms are shared,

NORTHEASTERN THAILAND

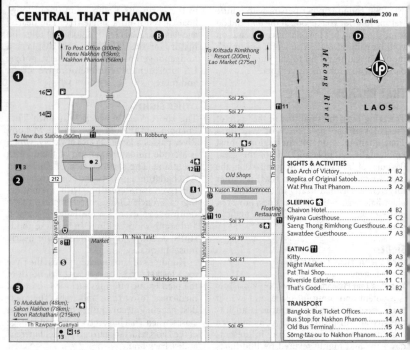

CENTRAL THAT PHANOM

To Post Office (300m);
Renu Nakhon (15km);
Nakhon Phanom (56km)

To Kritsada Rimkhong
Resort (200m);
Lao Market (275m)

Mekong River

LAOS

16
14

Soi 25
Soi 27
Soi 29

To New Bus Station (500m) Th Robbung   Soi 31

Soi 33

2

212

Old Shops

4
12

Th Kuson Ratchadamnoen

1

Floating
Restaurant

10   Soi 37

6

Th Chaiyangkun

Market

Th Naa Talat

Soi 39

Soi 41

Th Ratchadorn Utit

Soi 43

To Mukdahan (48km);
Sakon Nakhon (78km);
Ubon Ratchathani (215km)

Th Rawpaw-Guanyai   Soi 45

13   15

SIGHTS & ACTIVITIES
Lao Arch of Victory.........................1 B2
Replica of Original Satoob...............2 A2
Wat Phra That Phanom....................3 A2

SLEEPING
Chaivon Hotel.................................4 B2
Niyana Guesthouse.........................5 C2
Saeng Thong Rimkhong Guesthouse.6 C2
Sawatdee Guesthouse......................7 A3

EATING
Kitty...8 A3
Night Market.................................9 A2
Pat Thai Shop...............................10 C2
Riverside Eateries.........................11 C1
That's Good..................................12 B2

TRANSPORT
Bangkok Bus Ticket Offices............13 A3
Bus Stop for Nakhon Phanom.........14 A1
Old Bus Terminal..........................15 A3
Sörng-tåa-ou to Nakhon Phanom...16 A1

but the owner is a good source of local information. Bike hire costs 40B per day.

Chaivon Hotel (☎ 0 4254 1391; 38 Th Phanom Phanarak; r 200-300B; 🔀) This green wooden hotel is almost the definition of shabby. It's definitely not for everyone, but some people may enjoy a night here as it's a genuine historic relic.

Saeng Thong Rimkhong Guesthouse (no roman-script sign; ☎ 0 4254 1397; 507 Th Rimkhong; r 250-400B; 🔀) This so-so place just off the river steals the centre ground, with less sparkle than Kritsada and Sawatdee and less atmosphere than Niyana and Chaivon. Not all rooms are created equal, so you may want to have a look at a few before deciding. Newer rooms are planned.

Sawatdee Guesthouse (no roman-script sign; ☎ 08 1671 9717; r 400-500B; 🔀) This new place, off Th Ratchadorn Utit in the modern part of town, has a motel-style strip of somewhat sterile but well-appointed rooms. The two 400B rooms are across the street.

Kritsada Rimkhong Resort (☎ 0 4254 0088; 90-93 Th Rimkhong; r 400-600B; 🔀 🖳) More an eclectic hotel than a resort. Some of the rooms are plain while others are very attractive, but all

are comfy and have lots of little extras including free wi-fi. If the English-speaking owner is around when you call, someone will pick you up at the bus station for free, otherwise a túk-túk should cost 30B.

Eating

Pat Thai Shop (☎ 0 4254 0366; 39 Th Phanom Phanarak; dishes 30B; ⏱ breakfast, lunch & dinner) This hole-in-the-wall spins out just a few simple stir-fries like *râht nâh* (noodles in gravy) or *pàt prík bai gà prow* (spicy stir-fry with basil leaves), and frankly they're nothing special, but unlike the many similar places, the menu is in English. And the cooks are used to vegetarians.

That's Good (☎ 08 6230 6068; 37 Th Phanom Phanarak; dishes 25-80B; ⏱ dinner) We're not sure how long a place this hip (relatively speaking) can survive in little That Phanom, but as long as it does, it's a good spot for a coffee or beer after your meal.

Kitty (☎ 0 4254 0148; 419 Th Naa Talat; dishes 35-420B; ⏱ lunch & dinner) For something almost fancy, try this open-fronted place popular with local big-wigs. There are classic album covers on the wall and a long list of Thai food (a few dishes are labelled in English) on the menu. Fish is the most popular pick, and Kitty's the only place for steak.

Every evening a **night market** (4-10pm) takes over Th Robbung. It has a good variety of food, but few places to sit. Also, come nightfall, lots of small **riverside eateries** (Th Rimkhong), perched on stilts and ablaze in fairy lights, open their doors north of the promenade. For the most part, the biggest difference between them is the volume of the karaoke machine, so have a wander and pick your place.

Getting There & Away

From That Phanom's new bus station, inconveniently located west of town, there are services to Ubon Ratchathani (ordinary/1st class 102/184B, 4½ hours, hourly) via Mukdahan (ordinary/1st class 28/50B, one hour), Udon Thani (ordinary/1st class 109/196B, four hours, five daily) via Sakon Nakhon (ordinary/1st class 38/68B, 1¼ hours, hourly) and Nakhon Phanom (ordinary/1st class 27/49B, one hour, five daily). You can also catch the Nakhon Phanom buses in front of the school on Hwy 212; or take one of the frequent *sŏrng·tǎa·ou* (35B, 90 minutes, every 10 minutes) that park a bit further north and depart up to 3pm.

Bangkok buses (2nd/1st class/24-seat VIP 430/515/855B, 10 hours) also use the bus station, but currently (this may change) you should buy tickets at the old bus station (or the shops just west of it) on the south side of the city. Some of the buses start their journey here before heading to the new bus station to get more passengers. There are a few morning buses, but most depart between 5pm and 7pm.

There's an immigration office in town, but it's only for the Lao traders on market day: nobody else is allowed to cross the river here.

SAKON NAKHON PROVINCE

Many famous forest temples sit deep in the Phu Pan mountain range that runs across Sakon Nakhon Province, and among Sakon Nakhon's famous sons are several of the most highly revered monks in Thai history,

including Luang Pu (Ajahn) Man Bhuridatto (although born in Ubon Ratchathani he spent his most influential years here) and his student, Luang Pu (Ajahn) Fan Ajaro. Both were ascetic *tú-dong* monks who attained high levels of proficiency in *vipassana* meditation and are widely recognised among Thais as having been *arahants* (fully enlightened beings).

SAKON NAKHON
สกลนคร
pop 68,000
Workaday Sakon Nakhon is primarily an agricultural market and Th Ratpattana is chock-a-block with shops selling farm equipment. Although the city centre is the usual concrete mess, quiet neighbourhoods on the fringes are full of old wooden houses, and this is where you'll find the two historic temples of Wat Phra That Choeng Chum and Wat Pa Sutthawat, the town's main attractions.

Information

Most banks are found along Sukkasem and Ratpattana Sts. Branches of Bangkok Bank at **Big C** (Th Jai Phasuk) and **Tesco-Lotus** (Th Makkhalai) shopping centres open 10am to 8pm daily, though they exchange cash only. Internet cafes are spread liberally around town.

Sights
WAT PA SUTTHAWAT
วัดป่าสุทธาวาส
The grounds of **Wat Pa Sutthawat** (daylight hr), on the southwestern outskirts of town, are essentially a shrine to two of Thailand's best-known monks. Most famous of all is Luang Pu (Ajahn) Man Bhuridatto, who helped found the temple but didn't live here until just before his death in 1949. The final resting place of Ajahn Man's personal effects, the **Ajahn Man Museum**, bizarrely looks a bit like a modern Christian church, with arches and etched-glass windows. A bronze image of Ajahn Man sits on a pedestal at the back and relics that remained after his cremation are in a glass box in front.

Luang Pu (Ajahn) Lui Chanthasaro, who died in 1989, was one of Ajahn Man's most famous students and King Rama IX designed the *chedi* that holds the **Ajahn Lui Museum**. Ajahn Lui is represented in lifelike wax.

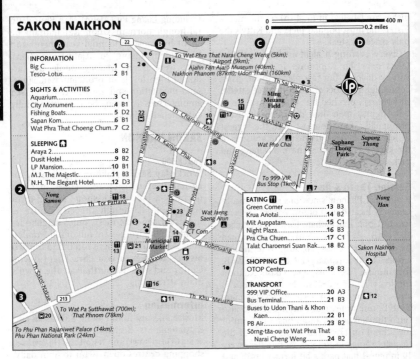

SAKON NAKHON

Both museums showcase all the monks' worldly possessions, as well as photographs and descriptions of their lives; Ajahn Man's displays, signed in English, provide a good sense of a typical monk's life.

WAT PHRA THAT CHOENG CHUM
วัดพระธาตุเชิงชุม

The most visible highlight at **Wat Phra That Choeng Chum** (Stupa of the Gathering of the Footprints; Th Reuang Sawat; daylight hr) is the 24m-high Lao-style *chedi*, which was erected during the Ayuthaya period over a smaller 11th-century Khmer *prang*. It was built above four Buddha footprints, which Thais believe were each left by different incarnations of the Lord Buddha. To view the *prang* you must enter through the adjacent *wí·hăhn*. If the door to the *chedi* is locked, ask one of the monks to open it; they're used to having visitors. *Lôok ní·mít* (spherical ordination-precinct markers that look like cannonballs and are buried under the regular boundary markers that surround most *bòht*) are lined up in the back.

Also on the grounds are a Lan Xang–era *bòht* and an octagonal *hŏr drai* that now

houses an interesting little museum. Again, the monks will be happy to get the key and let you have a look around inside. The top of the western gate resembles the wax castles carved for the Buddhist Rains Retreat (opposite), and you can usually see the temple's actual parade float parked way back in the northeast corner of the grounds behind a green screen.

WAT PHRA THAT NARAI CHENG WENG
วัดพระธาตุนารายณ์แจงแวง

About 5km west of town at Ban That, this *wát* (known as Phra That Nawaeng, a contraction of the words Narai Cheng Weng) has a 10th- to 11th-century Khmer *prang* in the early Bapuan style. Originally part of a Khmer-Hindu complex, the five-level sandstone *prang* is missing most of its top, but still features several lintels including a reclining Vishnu over its northern portico and a dancing Shiva over its eastern one. This is not a very impressive or evocative temple, but it's the most complete Khmer ruin in the province.

To get here by public transport take *sŏrng·tăa·ou* 3 (10B) from near the market or catch it heading north on Th Ratpattana. Get off at Ban That Nawaeng market and walk 500m south.

OTHER SIGHTS

The **city monument** (Th Ratpattana) at the northwestern corner of town loosely resembles Vientiane's Patuxai. The archlike structure consists of four thick cement pillars standing over a bowl filled with *naga*.

Across the park from the monument, the replica **Sapan Kom** (Khmer Bridge; Th Sai Sawang) lies along part of a Khmer road leading to Wat Phra That Narai Cheng Weng.

Along the eastern and northern edges of town is 123-sq-km **Nong Han**, Thailand's largest natural lake, which is well known among Thais due to the legend (see boxed text, p536) surrounding it. Fishermen, who tie up their boats behind Saphang Thong Park, will take you out sightseeing, including a stop to visit the monks on **Ko Don Sawan** (Paradise Island), the lake's largest island. The going rate is around 500B; the Dusit Hotel can make arrangements (see right). Don't copy the fishermen and swim in the lake: it's infested with liver flukes, which can cause a nasty infection known as opisthorchiasis.

The freshwater **aquarium** (☎ 0 4271 1447; Th Sai Sawang; admission free; 8.30am-4.30pm) at the Sakon Nakhon Fishery Station displays fish from Nong Han, as well as the Mekong and Songkhram rivers.

Festivals

Ork Phansaa (the end of Buddhist Lent – also called the Buddhist Rains Retreat) in October or November is fervently celebrated in Sakon, with the carving and display of wax castles in Ming Meuang Field the highlight. The festival also features demonstrations of *moo·ay boh·rahn*, the old and more dangerous style of Thai boxing.

Sleeping

Araya 2 (☎ 0 4271 1054; 354 Th Prem Prida; r 150-250B) This basic concrete bolt-hole is creeping towards decrepit, but it won't break your budget.

LP Mansion (no roman-script sign; ☎ 0 04271 5356; Th Charoen Meuang; r 230-320B;) LP is no beauty queen, but for just a few baht more it takes the tiara from Araya. Rooms are simple but big and bright and even have minifridges.

Dusit Hotel (☎ 0 4271 1198; www.dusitsakhon.com; 1784 Th Yuwaphattana; r 350-900B, ste 3500B;) This reborn old-timer has the loveliest lobby and cheeriest staff in town. The more you pay the more atmosphere you get, but each price category offers good value and all rooms have free wi-fi. The restaurant is good and the owner, Fiat, is a great source of local info.

NH The Elegant Hotel (☎ 0 4271 3338; www.nhonghanhotel.com; 163/32 Th Robmuang; s/d 600/650B;) Smart sums it up better than elegant, but that's really beside the point. What matters is that these newly built, well-appointed rooms are rock solid for the price, which includes breakfast *and* dinner. Its biggest drawback is the noncentral location, but there's a great coffee shop across the street.

MJ The Majestic (☎ 0 4273 3771; 399/2 Th Khu Meuang; r 440-1440B, ste 2400-3440B;) This business-class property is the reigning champ as most expensive hotel in town. The cheapest rooms are bigger than Dusit and Elegant, but not better. It's worth considering, however, if you want the full gamut of night-time entertainment (cocktail lounge, massage, snooker, karaoke) that those quieter choices can't provide.

Eating

Sakon Nakhon's biggest night market, the **Night Plaza** (Th Khu Meuang), has an excellent selection of food, but it's mostly bagged up for takeaway and the action starts to fade around 8pm. If you want to sit down and stay out late, hit **Talat Charoensri Suan Rak** (Charoensri Love Park Market; Th Tor Pattana; 5pm-2am) in the thick of the city's nightlife district.

Krua Anotai (no roman-script sign; ☎ 0 4271 1542; 1709/16-17 Th Prem Prida; dishes 25-60B; lunch & dinner) This formerly formal place serves classic Thai and Chinese fast food like stir-fries and dim sum.

Green Corner (☎ 0 4271 1073; 1773 Th Ratpattana; dishes 35-325B; breakfast, lunch & dinner) The top spot for *fa·ràng* food really distinguishes itself with its Thai and Isan choices (maoberry juice, fish *lâhp*, and ants' egg omelettes) that rarely appear on English-language menus.

Mit Auppatam (no roman-script sign; ☎ 0 4271 1633; 37 Th Sukkasem; dishes 40-160B; breakfast, lunch & dinner) This traditional place is a popular breakfast stop (with great omelettes) and later in the day it switches to curries, steaks and other dishes you wouldn't expect to find in such simple surrounds. The food is so good

---

THE LEGEND OF THE LAKE *Amaralak (Pim) Khamhong*

Phya Khom was the ruler of Ekthita city. He had a beautiful daughter named Nang Ai whose beauty was known by everyone in every land. Prince Phadaeng of Phaphong city came to visit Nang Ai secretly, and they fell in love immediately. They spent a night together and promised that they would be rightfully married soon.

In the sixth lunar month, Phya Khom arranged a rocket-shooting contest and invited people from the surrounding lands to participate. Whoever's rocket went the highest would be rewarded with treasure and his daughter's hand in marriage. Prince Phadaeng was not invited; however, he came with a great rocket anyway knowing that he must win in order to marry Nang Ai. At the contest, Phya Khom's rocket failed to fire, as did Phadaeng's. In anger Phya Khom broke his promise and gave nothing to the winner. Phadaeng then went back to his own city with great disappointment.

While the contest was taking place, the *naga* Phangkhi, son of Suttho Naga, ruler of the underground land called Muang Badan, came in disguise to witness the beauty of Nang Ai and fell deeply in love with her.

After he returned home, he was unable to eat and sleep; so, despite his father's objection, he went back again. This time he disguised himself as a white squirrel and hid in a tree near Nang Ai's window. Once Nang Ai saw the white squirrel she wanted to have it, so she ordered a soldier to catch it for her. Unable to do so, the soldier eventually killed the squirrel with a poisoned arrow. As Phangkhi was dying he made a wish: 'May my meat be very delicious and enough to feed everyone in the city'. His wish came true and all the townspeople, except the widows who had no official duties, got a share of his meat.

---

that word reached Princess Sirindhorn, who dropped in unexpectedly to dine in 2008. Unfortunately, nobody here speaks English.

our pick **Pra Cha Chuen** (no roman-script sign; ☎ 0 4271 1818; 382 Th Makkhalai; dishes 69-229B; ☽ dinner) This lovely, youthful place in an old wooden house is Sakon's most publike restaurant, but they don't slack on the food. Whether it's the fried rice or *'blah chôrn sá·mŭn·prai* (snake-head fish with herbs in chilli sauce with mango) it will be divine.

Shopping

Sakon's **OTOP Center** (☎ 0 4271 1533; Th Sukkasem; ☽ 8.30am-5pm) sells interesting hand-woven silk and cotton fabrics and clothes dyed with indigo and other natural colorants. You can also pick up maoberry and black-ginger wines.

Getting There & Away

PB Air (☎ 0 4271 5179; ☎ in Bangkok 0 2261 0222; www .pbair.com; 1438 Th Yuwaphattana; ☽ 8.30am-5.30pm Sun-Fri, 8.30am-3pm Sat) flies once or twice daily to/from Bangkok (one way 3015B, 70 minutes).

Sakon's centrally located **bus terminal** (Th Ratpattana) serves Ubon Ratchathani (ordinary/ 1st class 125/225B, five hours, nine daily), That Phanom (ordinary/air-con 38/68B, 1¼ hours, hourly), Nakhon Phanom (2nd/1st class

65/85B, 1½ hours, every 45 minutes), Udon Thani (ordinary/1st class 73/148B, 3½ hours, every half-hour), Khon Kaen (ordinary/1st class 129/188B, four hours, five daily) and Bangkok (2nd/1st class 386/497B, 11 hours, morning and late afternoon departures only).

There are also 2nd-class buses to Udon Thani (109B, every half-hour) and Khon Kaen (155B, five daily) from the Esso petrol station north of the bus terminal. **999 VIP** (☎ 0 4271 2860) sends 24-seat buses to Bangkok (773B, 8.30am, 7.30pm and 7.45pm) from a roadside stop on Th Reuang Sawat (across from Sakon Nakhon Pattana Supsa School) south of town, but if you want to reserve a seat you need to buy tickets from its office on Th Sukkasem.

AROUND SAKON NAKHON
Ajahn Fan Ajaro Museum

พิพิธภัณฑ์พระอาจารย์ฝั้นอาจาโร

Luang Pu (Ajahn) Fan Ajaro, a famous student of Ajahn Man, lived at Wat Pa Udom Somphon in his home district of Phanna Nikhom from 1964 until his death in 1977. His **museum** (admission free; ☽ 8am-5pm), inside a *chedi* with a triple-layer lotus design, commemorates his life with the usual display of relics, photos and worldly possessions. Unlike Wat Pa Sutthawat (p533), which has become a

When Phangkhi's followers, who witnessed his death, returned to Muang Badan and reported the news, Suttho Naga was so angry that he called in tens of thousands of soldiers to destroy Phya Khom's city. They headed off instantly to Ekthita.

Meanwhile, Phadaeng was so lovesick that he couldn't stay in his own city any longer and rode his horse back to see Nang Ai. When the two met again, she gave him a very warm welcome and offered him food cooked with squirrel meat. Phadaeng refused to eat and told Nang Ai that the squirrel was Phangkhi in disguise and that whoever ate his meat would die and their city would be destroyed.

Suttho Naga's army arrived at Ekthita by nightfall. The destruction they inflicted was so severe that the foundation of the city started to collapse. Phadaeng told Nang Ai to take the kingdom's rings, gong and drum and they fled on his horse. When Suttho Naga learned Nang Ai had run away, he began to follow her. The earth sank wherever he passed. Thinking that Suttho Naga was following the rings, gong and drum, Nang Ai threw them away but the Naga still followed. When the horse grew tired, Suttho Naga caught up with them and grabbed Nang Ai with his tail and carried her down to Muang Badan.

The battle had caused the whole area to sink and it became a huge lake, called Nong Han. The widows who did not eat the squirrel meat were safe and their houses were left undamaged on a small island that has been called Don Hang Mai (Widow's Island) ever since.

Phadaeng returned to Phaphong, but could not bear the sadness from the loss of Nang Ai. He chose to die in order to continue to fight for her. After his death, he became a ghost leader and his army fought the *naga* in Muang Badan. The fight lasted so long that the god Indra had to come down to stop it. Ever since, Nang Ai has been waiting for Indra to decide who should be her husband.

wát têe·o (tourist *wát*), this is still a strict forest meditation monastery. The temple is 40km from Sakon Nakhon towards Udon Thani on Hwy 22, then 2km north of Ban Phanna Nikhom on Th Srisawadwilai.

Phu Phan Rajaniwet Palace
พระตำหนักภูพานราชนิเวศน์

The grounds of the **royal family's Isan home** (☎ 0 4271 1550; admission free; ⏰ 8am-4pm) are open to the public when not in use. It's quite a modest residence compared to some of their other palaces, but the gardens are beautiful and peaceful. You can't drive around the grounds, but you can down drive to the elephant corral. Visitors are not permitted to wear shorts, short dresses or revealing tops.

The palace is 14km south of Sakon Nakhon, just off Rte 213. Take a Kalasin-bound bus (18B to 20B, 20 minutes, hourly).

Phu Phan National Park
อุทยานแห่งชาติภูพาน

Swathed in forest and tumbling over the pretty Phu Phan mountains, **Phu Phan National Park** (☎ 08 1263 5029; admission free) remains relatively undeveloped and isolated. It's no surprise that the area once provided cover for the renowned Seri Thai resistance

fighters in WWII and People's Liberation Army of Thailand (PLAT) guerrillas in the 1970s. The former used **Tham Seri Thai** as an arsenal and mess hall during WWII. As well as being a stomping ground for barking deer, monitor lizards, slow loris and monkeys, the 664-sq-km park also hosts a few elephants.

There are two main areas to visit. **Pha Nang Moen** is a vista 700m from the visitor centre and you can climb down to **Lan Sao-E** plateau, another 1.5km further on, which is great for sunsets. **Nam Tok Kam Hom**, one of four petite falls along a 600m stretch of stream (the water only runs from August to October), is 8.5km north (near Thailand's largest kilometre pillar). Seldom-visited **Tang Pee Parn** natural rock-bridge can be reached by 4WD. A park guide is recommended for trekking deep into the gorgeous mountains in the south end of the park.

Accommodation options include a **camp-site** (per person with own tent 30B, 3-6–person tent hire 150-225B) and five four-person **bungalows** (☎ 0 2562 0760; www.dnp.go.th/parkreserve; 500-600B).

Both of the principal attractions sit right off Rte 213 and any Kalasin-bound bus (18B to 20B, 45 minutes, hourly) from Sakon Nakhon will drop you off.

Talat Klang Dong Sang Kaw
ตลาดกลางดงสร้างข้อ

Twenty-five kilometres past Phu Phan National Park on Rte 213, **Talat Klang Dong Sang Kaw** (Sang Kaw Jungle Market) stocks custard apples and other foods grown on small village farms, but it's best known for the products gathered sustainably in the surrounding forest, like fruits, roots, honey, insects, bird nests (for good luck; well, not for the birds) and mushrooms. There are also locally produced whiskies and maoberry wines.

MUKDAHAN PROVINCE

MUKDAHAN
มุกดาหาร
pop 34,300

On the banks of the Mekong, directly opposite the Lao city of Savannakhet, Mukdahan is one of the region's more humdrum towns. The December 2006 opening of the Thai-Lao Friendship Bridge 2 formalised Mukdahan's status as a regional trade hub by connecting Thailand to Vietnam by road, but the city hasn't gone bridge crazy like Nong Khai did when that Mekong span was planned, and Savannakhet has reaped most of the economic reward.

Other than the bridge, Mukdahan is best known for its riverfront **Talat Indojin** (Indochina Market), which stretches under as well as along the riverfront, and most Thai tour groups on their way to Laos and Vietnam make a shopping stop at this market for cheap food, clothing and assorted trinkets.

Information
Bangkok Bank (Hwy 212, Tesco-Lotus; 10am-8pm) Changes cash only, but many banks in the centre of town are open regular banking hours and exchange travellers cheques.
Huanam Hotel (0 4261 1137; 36 Th Samut Sakdarak; internet per hr 20B; 6am-midnight) Has speedy internet connections, plus bike hire (100B/day).
Immigration office (0 4261 1074; 2 Th Song Nang Sathit; 8.30am-4.30pm Mon-Fri) Visa extensions are available here.
Tourism Information Center (0 4263 2700; Th Phitak Phanomkhet; 8.30am-4.30pm Mon-Fri) The city tourism office is in a complex with internet access, traditional Thai massage and a crafts shop.

Sights
One of the most oddly out-of-place landmarks in all of Thailand, **Ho Kaeo Mukdahan** (0 4263 3211; Th Samut Sakdarak; admission 20B; 8am-6pm) is a 65m-tall tower built for the 50th anniversary of King Rama IX's ascension to the throne. The nine-sided base has a good museum with displays (labelled in English) on typical Isan village life and the eight ethnic groups of the province. There are great views and a few more historical displays in 'The 360° of Pleasure in Mukdahan by the Mekong' room up at the 50m level. The ball on the top holds a locally revered Buddha image supposedly made of solid silver.

You can get a more organic view of Laos and the Mekong from atop **Phu Manorom** (6am-7pm) further south. There's a nice little garden and a small temple. Tourism officials try to promote sunrise-watching here, but odds are it'll be just you and the monks.

According to one of the many legends associated with it, the 2m-tall Phra Chao Ong Luang Buddha image at **Wat Si Mongkhon Tai** (Th Samron Chaikhongthi; daylight hr) is older than the city itself and was unearthed during Mukdahan's construction. The temple's ceramic-encrusted northern gate was built as a gesture of friendship by the city's large Vietnamese community in 1954. **Wat Yod Kaeo Sivichai** (Th Samron Chaikhongthi; daylight hr) just down the street stands out for having its enormous Buddha inside a glass-walled *wí·hǎhn*, and not one, but two small-sized copies of Phra That Phanom.

Festivals
The **Mukdahan Festival**, held either in December or January in the field fronting the *sǎh·lah glahng*, is a chance to see the dances and clothing of Mukdahan's eight ethnic groups.

Sleeping
Bantomkasen Hotel (no roman-script sign; 0 4261 1235; 25/2 Th Samut Sakdarak; r 150-300B;) From the outside this place looks just like your usual concrete block, but louvered doors and wooden floors give it some back-in-the-day charm. Best of all, hot water and sit-down toilets start at just 170B and air-con at 250B.

Kimjeckin 2 Hotel (0 4263 1310; 95/1 Th Phitak Phanomkhet; r 280-380B;) This travelling-salesperson's favourite is completely ordinary, except for the low prices, which is why it's

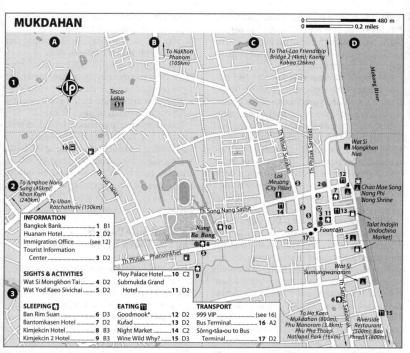

MUKDAHAN

often full. Rooms at Kimjekcin 1 across the street are 30B cheaper, and about that much scruffier, though the air-con rooms at the back do look out over a little lake.

Ban Rim Suan (☎ 0 4263 2980; Th Samut Sakdarak; r 330B; ❷ 🖳) This is the best budget deal in the city. Rooms certainly aren't stylish, but the owners have made some effort to liven things up. It's a tad south of the centre, but that makes it more convenient for dinner and drinks along the river. It offers free wi-fi.

Submukda Grand Hotel (☎ 0 4263 3444; 72 Th Samut Sakdarak; r 400-500B; ❷ 🖳) This shiny new tower was erected in 2006 to cash in on the expected rise in tour-bus business that the bridge might bring. Rooms and services are similar to Ban Rim Suan, but you can squeeze out a river view from upper-floor balconies.

Ploy Palace Hotel (☎ 0 4263 1111; www.ploypalace .com; 40 Th Phitak Phanomkhet; r 1050-1800B; ste 5500B; ❷ 🖳 🛄) Rooms at this executive sleepeasy are dated, but good value. There's plenty of marble and wood for that 'swanky' feel, a decent spread of creature comforts (including in-room wi-fi, a sauna, swimming pool and rooftop restaurant) and some friendly staff.

For something out of the ordinary, ask for the 8th- and 9th-floor rooms with beehives outside the windows.

Eating
Dining downtown is pretty pedestrian, but head out along the river and you'll find many good choices: most specialising in fish, of course.

Night market (Th Song Nang Sathit; ⏰ 4pm-10pm) Mukdahan's good night market has all the Isan classics, like *gài yâhng*, *sôm·đam* and deep-fried insects, but you'll also find lots of Vietnamese choices including *ฬòr ฬéea* (spring rolls), either *sòht* (fresh) or *tôrt* (fried).

Kufad (no roman-script sign; ☎ 0 4261 2252; 36-37 Th Samut Sakdarak; dishes 25-100B; ⏰ breakfast, lunch & dinner) This simple Vietnamese cafe is rightly quite popular and a good choice for breakfast. The picture menu takes the guesswork out of ordering, but leaves you clueless on the prices.

our pick Wine Wild Why? (☎ 0 4263 3122; 11 Th Samron Chaikhongthi; dishes 40-150B; ⏰ lunch & dinner) Housed in an atmospheric wooden building next to the river, this relaxing little spot serves delicious Thai and Isan food and has bags of character, though the wine list is history. The sociable owners, transplants from Bangkok, just add to the charm.

Bao Phradit (no roman-script sign; ☎ 0 4263 2335; 123/4 Th Samron Chaikhongthi; dishes 40-200B; ☻ lunch & dinner) It's a bit of a yomp south of the centre, but this is a real Isan restaurant where many ingredients are gathered from the forest and *hŭa ↋ĕt yâhng* (duck-head BBQ) and *gaang aòrm wǎi* (curry made with young rattan) are as common as steamed fish or pork fried rice. It's all served on a peaceful riverside deck. This is an English-free zone, so try to bring a Thai friend out here so you can enjoy the full culinary experience.

Riverside Restaurant (☎ 0 4261 1705; 103/4 Th Samron Chaikhongthi; dishes 45-150B; ☻ lunch & dinner) About 200m before Bao Phradit, this popular spot offers great views from a garden terrace and has tanks filled with examples of the kinds of Mekong River fish it has in the kitchen: if you don't want to eat the fish, it's almost worth just coming here for a biology lesson. The menu lists the many styles in which the chefs can cook it up for you, plus some nonfish dishes including wild boar. Free wi-fi, too.

Goodmook* (☎ 0 4261 2091; 414/1 Th Song Nang Sathit; dishes 70-380B; ☻ breakfast, lunch & dinner) This fun place has all the ingredients of a travellers' cafe – a mix of Thai and Western food (*dôm yam* to T-bone), free wi-fi, art on the walls – except a room full of travellers. Though many of those who do stop in Mukdahan longer than needed to change buses do cosy up here at some point. Bike hire is 100B per day and the management intends to lead tours.

Getting There & Away

Mukdahan's **bus terminal** (☎ 0 4263 0486), which has a good coffee shop to tide you over during your wait, is on Rte 212, west of town. To get there from the centre, take a yellow *sŏrng·tăa·ou* (10B, 6am to 6pm) from Th Phitak Phanomkhet near the fountain. There are buses to Nakhon Phanom (ordinary/1st class 52/92B, two hours, hourly) going via That Phanom (ordinary/air-con 28/50B, one hour), and also to Khon Kaen (2nd class 155B, 4½ hours, every half-hour), Ubon Ratchathani (ordinary/1st class 80/144B, 3½ hours, hourly) and Yasothon (2nd/1st class 81/104B, two hours, 10 daily). There are three Bangkok (2nd/1st class 390/502B, 10 hours)

departures between 8am and 9am and many more from 4.30pm until 8.45pm including a 24-seat VIP service (818B, 8.30am, 8pm and 8.15pm) with **999 VIP** (☎ 0 4261 1478).

If you're driving to Ubon Ratchathani, Hwy 212 will zip you there in about three hours, but if you can spare a whole day, take the Mekong-hugging backroads through a gorgeous and rarely visited stretch of rural Thailand.

Boats continue to connect Mukdahan with Savannakhet, Laos, though these days they're for Thai and Lao only. When taking the buses to Savannakhet (weekday/weekend 45/50B, 45 minutes, hourly 7.30am to 7pm) all border formalities for foreigners are handled during the crossing: the border-pass office at the bus station is for Thais only.

AROUND MUKDAHAN
Phu Pha Thoep National Park
อุทยานแห่งชาติภูผาเทิบ

Although little more than a speck of a reserve at just 48 sq km, hilly **Phu Pha Thoep National Park** (☎ 0 4260 1753; admission 100B), also known as Mukdahan National Park, has some beautiful landscapes and is scattered with unusual mushroom-shaped rock formations. The main rock group sits immediately behind the visitor centre, and wildflowers bloom here in October and November.

Besides the weird rocks there are several clifftop views, where pretty much only forest is visible around you. Also popular is **Nam Tok Phu Tham Phra**, a scenic waterfall (May to August only) with a grotto atop it holding hundreds of small Buddha images. It only takes a couple of hours on the well-marked trails to see all of these, though you'll need to scale some ladders to reach them. **Tham Fa Mue Daeng**, a cave with 5000-year-old hand paintings, is an 8km drive from the main park area. If you'd rather walk through the forest, you'll need a park guide.

For accommodation, you have a choice of **camping** (per person with own tent 30B, 3-/5-person tent hire 300/600B) or the three-bedroom **bungalow** (☎ 0 2562 0760; www.dnp.go.th/parkreserve; 1800B) that can sleep six.

The park is 15km south of Mukdahan off Rte 2034. *Sŏrng·tăa·ou* (20B, 30 minutes) to Amphoe Don Tan (which leave from the bus terminal in Mukdahan every half-hour) pass the turn-off to the park entrance. Hitching the last 1.3km to the visitor centre isn't tough, or you can try to bargain with the *sŏrng·tăa·ou* drivers (try for 30B) to have them detour off their route and take you. Less-frequent Kham Marat buses also pass the turn-off, and the 5pm service is your last guaranteed ride back to town.

Old Highway 212

Travelling north of town along the old route of Hwy 12, which never strays far from the Mekong, offers a lovely look at traditional Thai life and makes a fantastic bike trip: Goodmook* (opposite) and Huanam Hotel, (p538) in Mukdahan Province's oldest temples hire out bikes. There's no single road to follow, just stay as close to the river as you can. Leaving the city on the Non Ak-Na Po Yai road you'll follow a long line of fish farms before ducking under the 1.6km **Thai-Lao Friendship Bridge 2**. This is the widest reach of the Mekong along the Thai border, so this bridge stretches 400m more than the Friendship Bridge 1 in Nong Khai.

After another 10km (turn at the big orange arrow), where the greenish Chanot River meets the muddy Mekong (if you're lucky, you'll see men unloading their fish traps here), is **Wat Manophirom** (daylight hr), one of Mukdahan Province's oldest temples. The original *bòht*, now a *wí·hăhn*, was built in 1756 in Lan Xang style with an elaborately carved wooden facade and large painted eave brackets. It holds many ancient Buddha images, including eight carved into an elephant tusk.

Wat Srimahapo (daylight hr), sometimes called Wat Pho Si, is another 4.5km north in Ban Wan Yai. You'd never expect its tiny *bòht*, built in 1916, to be worth a look, but inside, elaborately carved beams hold up the tin roof and interesting naive murals cover the walls. The Buddhas that greet you once had holes cut over their hearts to receive blessings, but they have since been filled. The monks' residence is classical French style and a couple of longboats are stored here between races.

After a further 7km you'll pass the modern, glass-walled **Our Lady of the Martyrs of Thailand Shrine** (8.30am-4.30pm, 7am Mass on Sun), locally called Wat Song Khan and often incorrectly described as the largest church in Southeast Asia. It was built in 1995 to commemorate seven Thai Catholics killed by the police in 1940 for refusing to renounce their faith. Wax sculptures of the martyrs and their ashes lie under glass at the back.

Just beyond the church is **Kaeng Kabao**, a stretch of rocky shore and islets, turning to rapids when submerged during the rainy season. A variety of restaurants have set up on and along the river here, making this a good place to refuel before heading back to Mukdahan, or continuing on for another 20km to That Phanom. At the end of the dry season, from March to May, beaches emerge and people come to swim and ride inner-tubes.

Amphoe Nong Sung
อำเภอหนองสูง

Whether you want to learn about a different culture or just want to delve into rural Thailand, Nong Sung District in Mukdahan's far west is a great place to do it.

Mukdahan Province has a large Phu Thai population. Of all Isan's minority groups, the Phu Thai (who trace their heritage to southern China, near the Laos and Vietnam border) are known for having clung closest to their culture. Most villagers here still don traditional duds for festivals and funerals and their children do the same at school on Thursdays. The Phu Thai dialect dominates, so no matter how well you speak Thai or Isan, expect some verbal trip-ups here.

There are many silk- and cotton-weaving villages out here. Most women make the usual *mát·mèe* designs, which is what the market demands, but genuine Phu Thai clothes and fabrics are always available if you ask.

THAI HOUSE-ISAAN
เรือนไทยอีสาน

This friendly Australian-owned our pick **guesthouse** (08 7065 4635; www.thaihouse-isaan.com; r 700-1500B;) is a great place to dip your toes into village life without having to rough it. The nightly price includes a visit to the family farm, a foraging excursion in the forest and (for a donation direct to the local school) a children's dance performance. Day tours around the region cost 800B to 900B per person (minimum two) or you can hire a bicycle (120B per day) or motorcycle (500B per day) and see things for yourself. The rooms are comfortable and well appointed, especially the 1500B Thai-style 'chalet', and the mostly organic menu (70B to 295B) covers Thai tastes and your favourites from home. If you want, you can join Noi in the kitchen for a cooking lesson. Day guests are welcome.

Thai House Isaan is 60km out of Mukdahan on Hwy 2042. Buses between Mukdahan and Khon Kaen will drop you in Ban Kham Pok (from Mukdahan 50B, 70 minutes, every half-hour until 4.30pm).

BAN PHU
บ้านภู

Ban Phu, 6km south of Nong Sung town via Rte 2370, is a quaint village in the shadow of Phu Jaw Kor Puttakiri, and you can dig deep into village life here with its well-run **homestay** (☎ 08 9276 8961; per person incl meals 500B) program, which lets you join in daily life: cooking, weaving and farming, for example. If you want some nature with your culture, someone can take you up the mountain and into a cave. English is quite limited in the village, but Khun Puyai Pairit speaks some and will organise visits for *fa·ràng*.

You'll find a loom under most of the 300 houses, and the little shop at the temple stocks some traditional Phu Thai designs.

Sŏrng·tăa·ou head to Nong Sung (40B, 1¼ hours) every 10 minutes throughout the day from lane 16 of Mukdahan's bus terminal. Six or so of these will continue to Ban Phu (50B), but it's at the discretion of the driver. Khon Kaen-bound buses also stop in Nong Sung (2nd class 43B, one hour, every half-hour until 4.30pm). At Nong Sung you can hire a motorcycle taxi (50B to 60B) or a *sŏrng·tăa·ou* (about 100B) for the final leg.

YASOTHON & ROI ET PROVINCES

Yasothon and Roi Et, two of Thailand's most rural provinces, have little of interest to fast-track travellers, but they do show a side of Thailand that few people (including other Thais) ever see.

People looking to nose deeper into Isan culture will want to take a peek at Phra That Kong Khao Noi and purchase some pillows in Ban Si Than in Yasothon Province. Yasothon city saves all of its fireworks for the annual Rocket Festival, which completes a trifecta of Isan icons. Roi Et Province has a few enormous off-beat attractions, including a 68m standing Buddha statue, and its capital city is the far more pleasant of the two.

YASOTHON
ยโสธร
pop 23,000

Yasothon has little to offer outside the official whizz-bang period of mid-May and neither looks nor acts like a capital city. In fact, it barely feels like a city at all.

Sights

The centrepiece of **Wat Mahathat** (Th Wariratchadet; ☼ daylight hr) is Phra That Anon (aka Phra That Yasothon), a highly venerated Lao-style *chedi*. It's said to date from AD 695 and to enshrine holy relics of Phra Anan (Ananda), the Buddha's personal attendant monk. Much more interesting, however, is the gorgeous little *hŏr đrai*, dating to the 1830s and restored in 2008, which sits on stilts in a pond. If you ask a monk, he'll let you look inside.

Wat Singh Ta (Th Uthai-Rammarith; ☼ daylight hr) is rather ordinary, but the block fronting its southeast corner is a treasure trove of classic Chinese shophouses. It's 300m off the main road, west of Kasikornbank.

Festivals

The **Rocket Festival** (Bun Bâng Fai) is celebrated on the second weekend of May. Rocket Festivals are held to herald the rainy season across Isan, but nowhere as fervently as in Yasothon where it involves local dances, parades and rocket-launching contests. The largest rockets, called *bâng fai săan*, are packed with 120kg of nitrate. Those whose homemade rockets fail to launch get tossed in the mud.

Sleeping & Eating

In Town Hotel (no roman-script sign; ☎ 0 4571 3007; 614 Th Jangsanit; r 220-380B; ☼) This place, on the main road, is far enough south that it almost loses the rights to its name, but for Yasothon it's far better than the budget average. The Warotohn Hotel next door is even cheaper, though not quite as good.

Yasothon Orchid Garden (no roman-script sign; ☎ 0 4572 1000; 219 Th Prachasamphan; r 400-450B; ☼ ▣) Conveniently near the bus terminal, this is a plain but reasonable midranger with big rooms. Wi-fi is available in ground-floor rooms and the restaurant stays open until midnight.

Green Park (☎ 0 4571 4700; Th Wariratchadet; r 500-800B; ☼ ▣) Similar standards to the Orchid, but with a modern flair. It has wi-fi in all rooms and for 60B per day you can use the adjacent health club. On the downside, there are no restaurants nearby. It's 1km east of the night market on the way to Mukdahan.

JP Emerald Hotel (☎ 0 4572 4848; 36 Th Prapa; r 800-1000B, ste 1600B; 🅿 🄿 🖵) The lobby is lovely and the rooms comfy, though they've fallen behind on the upkeep of everything in between. Still, it's the best in town, and the disco will keep you busy. It's at the Roi Et end of town.

Rim Chi (no roman-script sign; ☎ 0 4571 4597; dishes 50-270B; 🕙 breakfast, lunch & dinner) Enjoy superb Isan and Thai food and bucolic Chi River views from either the tree-filled terrace or your own thatched-roof raft. The picture menu will get you through your order. It's 900m west of Krung Thai Bank.

For some more colourful eats, head to the dually misnamed **Night Barza** (Th Jangsanit; 🕙 breakfast, lunch & dinner) at the north end of downtown, which is only busy during lunch, or the proper **night market** (Th Wariratchadet; 🕙 4pm-midnight), one block northeast.

Getting There & Away

Yasothon has a **bus terminal** (☎ 0 4571 2965) on Th Rattanakhet in the heart of town, but only Khorat (2nd class 170B, 4½ hours, every half-hour until 1.30pm) buses and **999 VIP** (☎ 0 4571 2965) to Bangkok (32-/24-seat 483/644B, 8pm/8.30pm) use it. Most regular rides to Bangkok (2nd/1st class 322/425B, nine hours) leave from various spots along Hwy 23 in the northern half of town. The most frequent Ubon Ratchathani (2nd/1st class 70/90B, 1½ hours, hourly) and Khon Kaen (2nd/1st class 122/157B, 3½ hours, hourly) via Roi Et (2nd/1st class 50/65B, one hour) buses stop 100m south of the terminal next to TT&T, while some 2nd-class Ubon buses also depart in the morning from nearby, in front of Mitsubishi on Hwy 23.

AROUND YASOTHON
Phra That Kong Khao Noi
พระธาตุก่องข้าวน้อย

A rather sinister myth surrounds **Phra That Kong Khao Noi** (Small Rice Basket Stupa; 🕙 daylight hr), a brick-and-stucco *chedi* dating from the late Ayuthaya period found along Hwy 23, 5km out of town towards Ubon. According to one legend (which is taught to school children around the country as an example of why it's important to keep your emotions in check)

a young, and no doubt ravenously hungry, farmer who had toiled all morning in the hot sun murdered his mother here when she brought his lunch to the fields late, and in the smallest of sticky-rice baskets. The farmer, eating his lunch over his mother's dead body, realised that the small basket actually contained more sticky rice than he could manage to eat. To atone for his misdeed, he built this *chedi*.

Or perhaps not. Others say it was built by people who were travelling to Phra That Phanom to enshrine gold and gems, but got to Ban Tat Thong and learned they were too late; so they built this *chedi* instead. Some locals combine the myths and say that the repentant son was unable to build a *chedi* of his own and so joined forces with the pilgrims and they built it together.

Further complicating matters, most Yasothonians claim the real Small Rice Basket Stupa is a little further north in the back of **Wat Ban Sadoa**, 7km east of Yasothon on Rte 202. All that remains is the base; when the original tumbled over shortly after the redeemed son's death, locals built another petite *chedi* next to it. When we asked a monk here why Thai tourists visit the other *chedi*, he simply answered, 'Gahn meuang' (It's politics).

Ban Si Than
บ้านศรีฐาน

Residents of **Ban Si Than** can't leave their work behind when they go to sleep; this is a pillow-making village. Almost everywhere you look in the village (and most of those surrounding it) you'll see people sewing, stuffing or selling *mŏrn kít* (pillows decorated with diamond-grid *kít* patterns), most famously the triangular *mŏrn kwăhn* ('axe pillow'). They couldn't possible meet demand without using machine-made fabric, but the stuffing and some of the sewing is still done by hand. Prices here are far lower than you'll pay elsewhere in Thailand, and this is also one of the few places you can buy them unstuffed (*yang mâi sài nûn;* literally 'no kapok inserted'), which makes the big ones viable as souvenirs.

If you want to see monkeys, have someone point you to **Don Ling**, 4km out of town at Ban Tao Hi.

If you want to stay here, Ban Si Than has a **homestay** (☎ 08 7258 1991; per person incl 2 meals 300B)

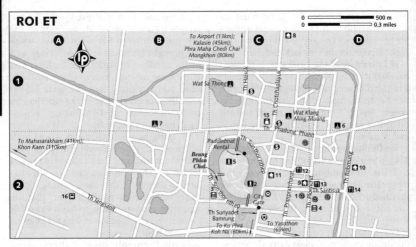

INFORMATION		SLEEPING		White	
Plaza Department Store	1 C2	Phetcharat		Elephant	14 D2
		Garden Hotel	8 C1		
SIGHTS & ACTIVITIES		Phrae Thong Hotel	9 C2	SHOPPING	
Lak Meuang	2 C2	Poon Petch Sportclub	10 D2	Craft Shops	15 C1
Roi Et Aquarium	3 C2	Saithip Hotel	11 C2		
Roi Et National Museum	4 D2			TRANSPORT	
Walking Buddha Statue	5 C2	EATING		999 VIP	(see 16)
Wat Burapha	6 D1	Night Market	12 C2	Bus	
Wat Neua	7 B1	Richi India Food	13 D2	Terminal	16 A2

program. The village is 20km from Yasothon on Rte 202, then 2.5km south of Ban Nikom. Any Amnat Charoen-bound bus can drop you at the junction (25B, 45 minutes) where a motorcycle taxi will zip you in for 20B.

ROI ET

ร้อยเอ็ด

pop 36,000

There has been a settlement at this spot for at least 2800 years, making this one of Isan's oldest cities. At one point, legend says, it had 11 city gates, and in ancient writing '11' was expressed as '10-plus-1'. Somehow this morphed into the city's name, which means 'one hundred one'.

Except for extensive stretches of the old city moat, Roi Et's long history hasn't followed it into the 21st century. Still, the city retains a charm and sense of identity all its own. You can't call Roi Et sleepy, but, perhaps taking its cue from the walking Buddha on the island in the city-centre lake, it does seem to move to its own urban beat.

Roi Et Province is known for the crafting of the quintessential Isan musical instrument, the *kaan*, a kind of Pan pipe. Many say the best *kaan* are made in the village of Si Kaew (15km northwest of Roi Et), though you can buy them (and other traditional musical instruments) at several shops in the city on Th Phadung Phanit.

Information

Banks are scattered around the centre, with several at the north end of Th Suriyadet Bamrung, which also holds the main post office and police station. Internet cafes aren't too common, but there are a few near the Plaza Department Store.

Sights

The enormous standing Buddha towering above Roi Et's squat skyline is **Phra Phuttha Ratana Mongkon Mahamuni** (Luang Po Yai for short) at **Wat Burapha** (Th Phadung Phanit; daylight hr). Despite being of little artistic significance, it's hard to ignore. Head to toe he stands 59.2m, and from the ground to the tip of the ùt·sà·nít it's 67.8m.

Wat Neua (Th Phadung Phanit; ☉ daylight hr), in the northern quarter of town, has an ancient ambience. It's known for its 1200-year-old *chedi* (Phra Satup Jedi) from the Dvaravati period, which has an unusual four-cornered bell-shaped form that's rare in Thailand. Around the *bòht* are a few old Dvaravati *sǎir·mah* and outside the main compound is an inscribed pillar, erected by the Khmers when they controlled this area during the 11th and 12th centuries.

Walking paths criss-cross the attractive, shady island in **Beung Phlan Chai** and attract the usual crowd of doting couples, joggers and picnickers. The well-known **walking Buddha statue** is on the north side and the **lak meuang** (city pillar) is to the south; many more monuments and interesting statuary stand between.

The interesting **Roi Et National Museum** (☎ 0 4351 4456; Th Ploenchit; admission 100B; ☉ 9am-4pm Wed-Sun) gives equal billing to ancient artefacts unearthed in the district and Isan cultural displays. The 3rd floor shows materials used to produce a rainbow of colours in natural-dyed fabrics.

There are a few odd-looking fish in the little **Roi Et Aquarium** (☎ 0 4351 1286; Th Sunthornthep; admission free; ☉ 8.30am-4.30pm Wed-Sun), and the walk-through tunnel is a nice touch.

Sleeping & Eating

Phrae Thong Hotel (☎ 0 4351 1127; 45-47 Th Ploenchit; r 180-350B) Insomniacs will bemoan the noise drifting up from the road (and perhaps the adjoining quarters since it offers a three-hour rate), but this no-frills spot has tidy little rooms with plenty of natural light.

Saithip Hotel (☎ 0 4351 1742; 133 Th Suriyadet Bamrung; r 240-320B; ☒) The architect tried, and failed, to splash a smidgen of glamour onto this simple place, but take a room here and your baht will be well spent; and you'll even get a real sit-down toilet.

Poon Petch Sportclub (☎ 0 4351 6391; 52 Th Robmung; r 370-438B; ☒) This newly built place is rather institutional, but the sparkling-clean rooms come with refrigerator and balconies.

Phetcharat Garden Hotel (☎ 0 4351 9000; www .petcharatgardenhotel.com; Th Chotchaplayuk; r 540-700B; ste 1740B; ☒ ▢ ▣) Some genuinely chic styling earns this attractive place several gold stars. The open-air lobby showcases serene East-meets-West decor, with wooden shutters and tall ceilings, and the immaculate staff (the men sport cool trousers) are tirelessly attentive. The rooms don't really capture the atmosphere and are starting to show their age, but are still good value. The swimming pool is huge and wi-fi is free.

White Elephant (☎ 0 4351 4778; Th Robmung; dishes 40-240B; ☉ dinner) This stylish place, just across the old moat, has a massive Thai menu, but the specialities are German, as is the owner. The outdoor terrace is surrounded by greenery.

Richi India Food (☎ 0 4352 0413; 37/1 Th Santisuk; dishes 50-250B; ☉ lunch & dinner) This colourful place looks more like a hair salon than a restaurant, and the food won't wow you, but with Indian cuisine being so rare in Isan, you take what you can get. Wi-fi is free for customers.

The main **night market** (☉ 5pm-midnight) is a covered affair with at least one cart stir-frying at all hours of the day.

Drinking

Roi Et's nightlife district, which features live music, large beer gardens and the obligatory coyote dancers, runs along Th Chotchaplayuk between the canal and Phetcharat Garden Hotel. Some more low-key tables for a tipple sit on the west side of the lake.

Getting There & Away

PB Air (☎ 0 4351 8572, in Bangkok 0 2261 0222; www.pbair .com) flies to/from Bangkok (one way 2740B, one hour) four days a week. There's a ticket office at the airport, which is 13km north of town.

From Roi Et's **bus terminal** (☎ 0 4351 1466; Th Jangsanit), buses head at least hourly to Yasothon (2nd/1st class 50/65B, one hour, hourly), Khon Kaen (2nd/1st class 80/99B, two hours, every 20 minutes), Surin (2nd class 98B, three hours, hourly) and Ubon Ratchathani (ordinary/1st class 82/148B, three hours). Many buses link Roi Et with Bangkok (2nd/1st class 314/403B, eight hours) including **999 VIP** (☎ 0 4351 1466) with 24-seat VIP buses (627B, 7½ hours, 10.45am and 9.30pm).

The bus terminal is 1km from the city centre. Túk-túk will charge 45B to Phetcharat Garden.

AROUND ROI ET

Ku Phra Koh Na

กู่พระโกนา

Sixty kilometres southeast of Roi Et town are the minor ruins of **Ku Phra Koh Na** (admission free; ☉ daylight hr), an 11th-century Khmer shrine. The monument comprises three brick *prang* facing east from a sandstone pediment surrounded by a sandstone-slab wall that once had four gates. The middle *prang* was replastered in 1928 and Buddha niches were added. A Buddha footprint shrine, added to the front of this *prang*, is adorned with the Khmer monument's original Baphuon-style *naga* sculptures. The two other *prang* have been restored (though they still look like they might tumble over any time) but retain their original forms. The northern *prang* has a reclining Narai (Vishnu) lintel over one door and a *Ramayana* relief on the inside gable.

The ruins themselves are neither impressive nor well restored, but it's interesting to see how they've been incorporated into the modern temple. And if that doesn't thrill you, spend your time watching the hundreds of monkeys that live here.

GETTING THERE & AWAY

Any Surin-bound bus from Roi Et can drop you off at Wat Ku (45B, 1½ hours), as the compound is known locally, which is 6km south of Suwannaphum on Rte 214.

Phra Maha Chedi Chai Mongkhon

พระมหาเจดีย์ชัยมงคล

This monument in the making, sometimes called **Isan Buddhist Park** (admission free; ☉ 7am-6pm), is far from finished, but it's already a sight to behold. At its heart is a gleaming white *chedi* rising a symbolic 101m. It's encircled by a 101m-wide building and sits on 101 *râi* (16 hectares) of land. Inside is a riot of gold paint and mirrored tiles, and, depending on your tastes, it's either beautiful or gaudy, but either way you're sure to love it. The *chedi* sits atop Khao Keeo (White Mountain) and the surrounding Pha Nam Yoi Forest Park reportedly still harbours a few tigers.

The *chedi* is 80km northwest of Roi Et city near Nong Phok. It's a pain to get there without your own wheels. From Roi Et take a *sŏrng·tăa·ou* to Phon Thong (40B, one hour, every 45 minutes) and then catch one of the Khon Kaen–Amnat Charoen buses to *brà·doo* Kong (Kong Gate) in Ban Tha Saat (20B, 20 minutes, 10 daily). Then it's 5km uphill.

Hitching isn't usually tough, or ask in one of the shops to arrange a ride: expect to pay 300B round trip.

Upper Southern Gulf

Most travellers slide through the upper southern gulf region, often in the middle of the night, en route to beaches and islands further south. The area's attractions may not be as dazzling or obvious as more popular destinations, but with mellow seaside towns, flashier resort destinations, the country's biggest national park and plenty of historical intrigue, this thin slice of Thailand holds its own.

Local tourists have long flocked to the region, and you can get your merrymaking on with Thai revellers on weekend sojourns in decidedly un-*fa·ràng* Cha-am. For the comforts of hotel high-rises, world-class golf courses and a buffet of international food choices, hit the brakes at modern Hua Hin, which, though firmly cosmopolitan, has been attracting Thai tourists since Rama VII built a palace retreat there in 1922.

For those more into history than holidaying, the region is pocked with cave temples seemingly lit from within by sun-dappled Buddhas, and Phetchaburi's provocative skyline of wáts and palaces is perfect to take in on a city stroll.

Wilderness and wildlife fans can challenge their quads on steep hikes that climb past waterfalls, through thick forests to savannahs and panoramic sea views.

Exercise your traveller's ingenuity and make some new Thai friends by catching local transport between the smaller towns. Sure, it's not as simple as an overnight train-ride, but it'll be worth it.

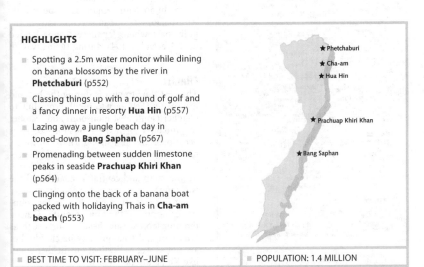

HIGHLIGHTS

- Spotting a 2.5m water monitor while dining on banana blossoms by the river in **Phetchaburi** (p552)

- Classing things up with a round of golf and a fancy dinner in resorty **Hua Hin** (p557)

- Lazing away a jungle beach day in toned-down **Bang Saphan** (p567)

- Promenading between sudden limestone peaks in seaside **Prachuap Khiri Khan** (p564)

- Clinging onto the back of a banana boat packed with holidaying Thais in **Cha-am beach** (p553)

★ Phetchaburi
★ Cha-am
★ Hua Hin

★ Prachuap Khiri Khan

★ Bang Saphan

- BEST TIME TO VISIT: FEBRUARY–JUNE
- POPULATION: 1.4 MILLION

UPPER SOUTHERN GULF

0 — 40 km
0 — 20 miles

To Ratchaburi (30km)

To Bangkok (50km)

RATCHABURI

Phetchaburi

PHETCHABURI

Hat Chao Samran

Kaeng Krachan National Park

Kheuan Karng Krachan

Hat Peuktian

Cha-am

GULF OF THAILAND

Hua Hin

Ko Singtoh

Khao Takiap

Khao Yai (1204m)

Khao Tao

Pranburi

Kheuan Pran Buri

Khao Sam Roi Yot National Park

Bang Pu

Kuiburi

Hat Laem Sala

PRACHUAP KHIRI KHAN

Ao Khan Kradai

Prachuap Khiri Khan

Ao Noi
Ao Prachuap
Ao Manao

Dan Singkhon

Ko Raet

Huay Yang Falls

Ko Phing

MYANMAR (BURMA)

Hat Wanakon

Ko Phang

Thap Sakae

Hat Laem Kum

Hat Sai Kaew

Hat Ban Krut

Hat Baw Thawng Lang

Khao Thwe (891m)

Bang Saphan Yai

Hat Sombun

Ao Bang Saphan

Bang Saphan Noi

Ko Thalu

Khao Daen Noi (582m)

Ko Sing

Ko Sang

See Prachuap Khiri Khan Province Map (p556)

Ko Wiang

GULF OF THAILAND

Pathiu

Ao Baw Mao
Ao Thung Wua Laen

Tha Sae

Ko Jarakhe

CHUMPHON

Ao Phanang Tak

Ko Ngam Yai & Ko Ngam Noi

Chumphon

Hat Pharadon Phap

Ko Samet

Kraburi

Pak Nam

Ko Maphrao

Ko Mattara

Ka Poh National Park

Hat Sairi

Ao Sawi

Ko Rang Kachiu

Sawi

To Ko Tao (75km)

Tako Estuary

Hat Arunothai

RANONG

Lang Suan

Isthmus of Kra

Ranong

Hat Tawan Chai

Lamae

Hat Suan Son

To Phuket (850km)

To Surat Thani (105km)

History

Though the region owes much of its current status as a popular Thai holiday spot to its endorsement by a long line of relatively recent kings, archaeological evidence suggests that the upper southern gulf has attracted visitors since the Dvaravati period. In particular, Phetchaburi acts as a visible timeline of historical periods, displaying evidence of the different influences enacted upon the area.

During the 11th century, the Khmer empire settled in, though their control was relatively short-lived. As Khmer power diminished, Phetchaburi became a strategic royal fort during the Sukhothai and Ayuthaya kingdoms; in fact, the Sukhothai reign marks the first true kingdom of Thais along the peninsula.

As the Ayuthaya kingdom absorbed the Sukhothai reign in the 13th and 14th centuries, the upper peninsula flourished. It saw the gradual growth of what today is called Prachuap Khiri Khan, and Phetchaburi thrived as a 17th-century trading post between Burma and Ayuthaya. The town is often referred to as a 'Living Ayuthaya', since many relics that were destroyed in the former kingdom's capital are still intact here.

When the city of Ayuthaya was taken in 1767, Prachuap Khiri Khan was abandoned. It wasn't to be reconstructed until 1845, when King Rama IV re-established the town and gave it its current name.

Prachuap Khiri Khan, and specifically Ao Manao, was one of seven points on the gulf coast where Japanese troops landed on 8 December 1941 during their invasion of Thailand.

Climate

The best time to visit is during the hot and dry season (February to June). From July to October (southwest monsoon) and October to January (northeast monsoon) there is occasional rain and strong winds. However, because this region lies between the three-monsoon season that rules northern, northeastern and central Thailand, and the two-monsoon season in the country's south, it remains drier than elsewhere in the country, even during the rainy months. During the monsoon season, beach resorts such as Hua Hin and Cha-am may be cloudy, but are not as wet as destinations further south like Ko Samui or Phuket.

National Parks

Kaeng Krachan (p552), the largest national park in Thailand, covers nearly half of Phetchaburi Province and is known for its waterfalls and birdwatching. From the tall peaks of Khao Sam Roi Yot (p562) there are views of the gulf, the coast and limestone cliffs.

Getting There & Away

Frequent air-con buses from Bangkok's southern bus station travel to all major cities in the region, including Phetchaburi, Hua Hin and Chumphon. Air-con services also connect to smaller destinations such as Prachuap Khiri Khan, Hat Ban Krut and Bang Saphan Yai on at least a daily basis. Thai Railways' southern line from Bangkok conveniently stops at most points of interest for the independent traveller. Chumphon is the major departure point for boats to Ko Tao, and there are three flights per day to/from Bangkok's Suvarnabhumi International Airport and Hua Hin.

Getting Around

Public transport is not as prolific or well organised as further south, but it's still relatively easy to get to most places. Buses and trains connect the region's major cities, and motorcycle taxis and *sŏrng·tăa·ou* (also spelt *săwngthăew*; pick-up trucks) cater for shorter trips. The exception is reaching the two national parks, where you'll either need to have your own wheels, charter a taxi or *sŏrng·tăa·ou*, or join a tour.

PHETCHABURI PROVINCE

PHETCHABURI (PHETBURI)

เพชรบุรี

pop 40,259

Most travellers see Phetchaburi (commonly known as Phetburi) as a rushed day trip from Bangkok or from the window of a southbound bus or train, but a more leisurely approach allows you to peel back the intriguing layers of Thai history. Traditional Siam can still be glimpsed in century-old teak houses, and by sampling Phetchaburi's culinary heritage. When you've had your fill of the town's tasty desserts, climb to hilltop royal palaces in what is called the 'Living Ayuthaya' or contemplate the Buddhist shrine in the cave sanctuary of Khao Luang.

Orientation

Arriving by train, follow the road southeast of the tracks until you come to Th Ratchadamnoen, then turn right. Follow Th Ratchadamnoen south to the second major intersection and turn left towards central Phetchaburi. A *săhm·lór* (also spelt *săamláw*; three-wheeled pedicab) from the train station to Saphan Chomrut (Chomrut Bridge) is 20B. If you've come by air-con bus, you'll stop near the night market on the northern edge of the centre.

Information

There's no formal information source in town, but the Rabieng Rim Nam Guest House (p551) is a great resource for both Phetchaburi and Kaeng Krachan National Park (p552). The Sun Hotel (p551) has wireless internet and one terminal (per hr 100B).

Main post office (cnr Th Ratwithi & Th Damnoen Kasem)

Police station (☎ 0 3242 5500; Th Ratwithi) Near the intersection of Th Ratchadamnoen.

Siam Commercial Bank (2 Th Damnoen Kasem) Other nearby banks also offer foreign exchange and ATMs.

Telephone office (cnr Th Ratwithi & Th Damnoen Kasem; ☉ 7am-10pm) Upstairs at the post office.

Sights & Activities

There are scores of wát in town, and a few different ways to see them. Take a walk around town – most hotels offer free basic maps, while the *Phetchaburi Attractions and Travelling Guide* (70B), published by Phetchaburi Rajabhat University, has more detailed maps and descriptions. Alternatively, you can hire a *săhm·lór* or motorbike taxi starting at around 300B. Motorbikes are for hire at the Rabieng Rim Guest House (p551). It also offers a one-day tour visiting Phetchaburi's wát and palaces (400B to 600B per person).

KHAO LUANG & KHAO BANDAI-IT CAVES

ถ้ำเขาหลวง

The main cavern in the cave sanctuary of **Khao Luang** (donation appreciated; ☉ 8am-6pm) is lined with impressive stalactites and crammed with old Buddha statues, many of which were put in place by Rama IV. Sunlight from a hole in the chamber ceiling illuminates the images

PHETCHABURI (PHETBURI)

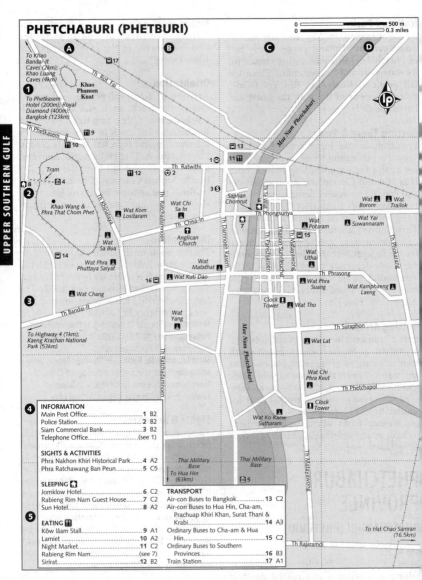

and makes for great photos. To the rear of the main cavern is an entrance to a third, smaller chamber. On the right of the entrance is Wat Bunthawi, with a *săh·lah* (often spelt *sala*; meeting hall) designed by the abbot of the *wát* himself and a *bòht* (central sanctuary) with impressively carved wooden door panels. Around the cave you'll meet brazen monkeys looking for handouts. The cave is 4km north of town.

An even more magical cave sanctuary is **Khao Bandai-It** (donation appreciated; ☉ 9am-4pm) 2km west of town. A monastery sits regally on the hill, while several large caverns pock the hillside. English-speaking guides lead tours through the caves.

From Phetchaburi catch a săhm·lór (60B to 70B) or motorcycle taxi (40B to 50B) to the sanctuaries.

KHAO WANG & PHRA NAKHON KHIRI HISTORICAL PARK
เขาวัง/อุทยานประวัติศาสตร์พระนครคีรี

You can't miss Khao Wang (Palace Hill) – it rises importantly on the northwest side of Phetchaburi, studded with wát and crowned with King Mongkut's palace, while the white point of **Phra That Chom Phet** skewers the sky. Cobblestone paths wind up and around it, leading to panoramic views of Phetchaburi's wát-smattered skyline.

Phra Nakhon Khiri (Holy City Hill; ☎ 0 3240 1006; admission 150B; ☼ 9am-4pm), the palace area on the top, is a national historical park and a good spot to take in views of the town while curious monkeys look at you (and make plays for your beverage or purse). The walk up is fairly strenuous, especially in the heat. A **tram** (one way adult/child 70/30B; ☼ 8.30am-5.30pm) is the easier way.

On Mondays a **night market** lines the street in front of Khao Wang, and besides being filled with the usual food stalls it's also a flea market. It's a fun place to peruse if you happen to be in town on a Monday.

PHRA RATCHAWANG BAN PEUN
พระราชวังบ้านปืน

Just over 1km south of the city centre, and inside a Thai military base, is the European-influenced **Phra Ratchawang Ban Peun** (Ban Peun Palace; ☎ 0 3242 8083; admission 50B; ☼ 8am-4pm Mon-Fri). Construction began in 1910 at the behest of Rama V (who died just after the project was started) and was completed in 1916. It was designed by German architects, who used the opportunity to showcase contemporary German innovations in construction and interior design. The structure is typical of the early 20th century, a period that saw a Thai passion for erecting European-style buildings in an effort to keep up with the 'modern' architecture of its colonised neighbours. The outside of the two-storey palace is not too exciting, but it's worth visiting to see the exquisite glazed tiles in the interior.

Festivals & Events

The **Phra Nakhon Khiri Fair** takes place in early February and lasts nine days. Centred on Khao Wang and Phetchaburi's historic temples, the festivities include a sound-and-light show at the Phra Nakhon Khiri Palace, temples festooned with lights, and performances of lá·kon chah·đree (Thai classical dance-drama), lí·gair (Thai folk dance-drama) and modern-style historical dramas. A twist on the usual beauty contest showcases Phetchaburi widows.

Sleeping

Jomklow Hotel (☎ 0 3242 5398; 1 Th Te Wiat; r 130-170B) A welcoming Chinese hotel on the river. The rooms are very, very basic – think super-sized jail cell – but experienced budget travellers should be OK.

Rabieng Rim Nam Guest House (☎ 08 9919 7446; fax 0 3240 1983; 1 Th Chisa-In; s/d 120/240B) Bare-bones rooms are made up for by an excellent location in a riverside teak house with a yummy restaurant. Laundry service, bicycle and motorcycle hire, and tours to Kaeng Krachan National Park are also on offer. It's a backpacker favourite.

Phetkasem Hotel (☎ 0 3242 5581; 86/1 Th Phetkasem; r 250-400B; ✷) Middle-aged dogs loll in reception at this slightly industrial place hunched under an overpass. Cheaper rooms don't have air-con and the furniture is decidedly aged.

Sun Hotel (☎ 0 3240 0100; www.sunhotelthailand.com; 43/33 Soi Phetkasem; r 800-1500B; ✷ ▢) Opposite the entrance to Phra Nakhon Khiri, this hotel has large rooms with good bathrooms, and is your best midrange bet in town. Rooms come with cable and refrigerators, and the ones facing the hill are much more pleasant than those facing a wall. There's a pleasant cafe downstairs with wireless access.

Royal Diamond (☎ 0 3241 1061; www.royaldiamondhotel.com; Mu 1, Th Phetkasem; r 1200-1800B; ✷) The carpeted rooms are a bit dingy, despite the swank lobby. Still, it's perfectly adequate, with TVs and refrigerators in the rooms.

Eating

Local dishes include kà·nŏm jeen tôrt man (thin noodles with fried spicy fishcake), the hot-season specialty kôw châa pét·bù·ree (moist chilled rice served with sweetmeats) and kà·nŏm môr gaang (egg custard). You'll find these, along with a range of standard Thai and Chinese dishes, at several good restaurants in the Khao Wang area. Lots of cheap eats are available at the night market, near the northern end of the centre of town.

Other good eating spots are along the main street, Th Panichjaroen, leading to the clock tower. North of Khao Wang, Lamiet (no roman-script sign) sells good kà·nŏm môr gaang and fŏy torng (sweet shredded egg yolk). Across the street from Khao Wang, an unnamed food stall serves delicious kôw lăam (sticky rice and coconut steamed in a length of bamboo).

Sirirat (☎ 0 3242 6305; 85 Ratwithi; breakfast, lunch & dinner; dishes 10-50B) Dishes up big, piping-hot bowls of noodles at the right price. Look for the black-and-white chequered tablecloths.

our pick **Rabieng Rim Nam** (☎ 0 3242 5707; 1 Th Chisa-In; dishes 40-180B; ☺ breakfast, lunch & dinner) This teak riverside restaurant serves up terrific food with a surprising degree of sophistication, and if you're lucky you'll spot a water monitor cruising through the river below you. The menu is enticingly long, so take your time and discover our favourite – the delicate banana-blossom salad.

Getting There & Away

There are hourly services to/from Bangkok's southern bus station (1st/2nd class 133/119B, two hours); the bus terminal for air-con buses to/from Bangkok is near the night market. Other bus destinations to/from Phetchaburi include: Cha-am (35B to 100B, 40 minutes), Hua Hin (50B to 120B, 1½ hours), Prachuap Khiri Khan (80B to 115B, three hours) and Surat Thani (300B, eight hours). These destinations are served from the bus station just east of Khao Wang. If you're coming from the south, you may be dropped off on the highway. Motorcycle taxis await and can take you into town for around 40B.

Ordinary buses to the southern provinces leave from the corner of Th Bandai-It and Th Ratchadamnoen. Local buses to Hua Hin and Cha-am depart in the town centre, on Th Matayawong.

Frequent rail services run to/from Bangkok's Hualamphong station. Fares vary depending on the train and class (3rd class 74B to 115B, 2nd class 143B to 358B, three hours).

Getting Around

Sǎhm·lór and motorcycle taxis go anywhere in the town centre for 30B to 40B, or charter them for the whole day from 300B. Sŏrng·tǎa·ou cost 10B around town. It's a 20-minute walk (1km) from the train station to the town centre.

Rabieng Rim Nam Guest House (p551) hires out bicycles (120B per day) and motorbikes (250B per day).

KAENG KRACHAN NATIONAL PARK

อุทยานแห่งชาติแก่งกระจาน

At 3000 sq km, Thailand's largest **national park** (☎ 0 3245 9293; www.dnp.go.th; admission 200B; ☺ visitors centre 8.30am-4.30pm) is home to the stunning Pa La-U waterfalls, and includes long-distance hiking trails that snake through forests and savannah-like grasslands, past cliffs, caves and mountains. Two rivers, Mae Nam Phetchaburi and Mae Nam Pranburi, a large lake and abundant rainfall keep the place green year-round. Animal life includes wild elephants, deer, tigers, bears, gibbons, boars, hornbills, dusky langurs, gaurs, wild cattle and 400 species of birds.

To explore Kaeng Krachan you really need your own transport, but it's worth the effort as this majestic place sees few tourists. The best months to visit are between November and April.

Sights

Hiking is the best way to explore the park. Try the 4km (three hours) walk from the Km36 marker on the park road to the 18-tiered **Nam Tok Tho Thip** waterfall. A longer 6km hike summits **Phanoen Thung**, the park's highest point. From the top there are lush forest views in all directions. It can be particularly spectacular in late autumn, when surrounding valleys are shrouded in early-morning mist. The hiking trail starts at the Km27 marker on the park road. Note that some trails, including the one to Phanoen Thung, are closed during the rainy season (August to October).

To the south, near La-U Reservoir, are the spectacular twin waterfalls of **Pa La-U Yai** and **Pa La-U Noi**. Water flows over their 15 tiers year-round. The waterfalls can be reached by 4WD from the south (closer to Hua Hin) along Hwy 3219.

Near the visitors centre is a reservoir where boats can be hired for 400B per hour.

Sleeping & Eating

There are various **bungalows** (☎ 0 2562 0760; reserve@dnp.go.th; bungalows from 1200B) within the park, mainly near the reservoir. These sleep from four to six people and are simple affairs with fans and fridges. There are also **camp sites** (per person 60-90B), including a pleasant grassy one near the reservoir at the visitors centre (where there's also a modest restaurant). Tents (225B to 300B) can be rented at the visitors centre.

On the road leading to the park entrance are several simple resorts and bungalows. About 3.5km before reaching the visitors centre, **A&B Bungalows** (☎ 08 9891 2328; r/bungalows 650/1500B) is scenic and popular with birdwatching groups. There is a good restaurant here that can provide you with a packed lunch.

Getting There & Away
Kaeng Krachan is around 52km southwest of Phetchaburi, with the southern edge of the park 35km from Hua Hin. From Phetchaburi, drive 20km south on Hwy 4 to the town of Tha Yang. Turn right (west) and after 38km you'll reach the visitors centre.

There is no direct public transport all the way to the park, but you can get a *sŏrng·tăa·ou* (75B, 1½ hours) from Phetchaburi (near the clock tower) to the village of Ban Kaeng Krachan, 4km before the park. Go early as the last *sŏrng·tăa·ou* leaves at 2pm. You can also charter your own *sŏrng·tăa·ou* for around 600B one way, a decent alternative if you have a group. Motorcycle taxis (40B) run from Ban Kaeng Krachan to the visitors centre. An alternative is to join a trip from Phetchaburi, Hua Hin or Cha-am. In Phetchaburi, the **Rabieng Rim Nam Guest House** (☎ 08 9919 7446; fax 0 3240 1983; 1 Th Chisa-In) runs one- and two-day trips (2600B to 4000B) that include bird- and animal-watching and trekking. Most travel agencies in Hua Hin and Cha-am offer day trips (1200B to 2200B).

CHA-AM
อำเภอชะอำ
pop 46,000
At weekends and on public holidays, Cha-am is a getaway spot for provincial families and Bangkok students. Neon-painted buses deliver holidaymakers firmly in party mode, fuelled by cheesy pop music and ready to kick back for a couple of days. Mix in beach parties under shady casuarina trees, fresh seafood and cold beers delivered to your deckchair, and rip-snorting banana boats bobbing up and down the beach and you begin to see the attraction. Subtle it's not, but hey, there's nothing wrong with a bit of raucous Thai fun.

If you're looking for something quieter, then come during the week when Cha-am returns to being a relaxed resort town and

you'll get an even better deal at the good-value guesthouses and midrange hotels. Chances are it will be just you and the ladies selling deep fried shrimps and grilled squid. Bliss…

Orientation
Phetkasem Hwy runs through Cha-am's busy centre, which includes the main bus stop, banks, the main post office, an outdoor market and the train station. About 1km east, via the main connecting road, Th Narathip, is the long beach strip where you'll be headed. The road along the beach (and where beach accommodation and services are located) is Th Ruamjit. Air-con buses from Bangkok stop one block from the beach on Th Chao Lai.

Information
You'll find plenty of banks along Th Ruamjit with ATMs and exchange services.
Communications Authority of Thailand (CAT; Th Narathip) For international phone calls.
CV Net (Th Ruamjit; per hr 40B; ☼ 9am-11pm) Internet access; on the beach road just before Soi North 7.
Post office (Th Ruamjit) On the main beach strip.
Tourism Authority of Thailand (TAT; ☎ 0 3247 1005; tatphet@tat.or.th; 500/51 Th Phetkasem; ☼ 8.30am-4.30pm) On Phetkasem Hwy, 500m south of town. The staff speak good English.

Festivals & Events
The **Cha-am Feast-Fish-Flock Seafood Festival** is a riot of Thai food stalls and kitschy pop music. It's all set in a beachfront beer garden at the eastern end of Th Narathip and not to be missed if you're around in late September/early October.

Sleeping
Cha-am has two basic types of accommodation: low-grade apartment-style hotels along the beach road (Th Ruamjit) and more expensive 'condotel' developments (condominiums with a kitchen and operating under a rental program). True bungalow operations are quite rare. Expect a 20% to 40% discount on posted rates for weekday stays. Compared to flashier Hua Hin, your money will go further in Cha-am.

BUDGET
Cha-am Villa Beach (☎ 0 3247 1241; www.chaamvilla hotel.com; 241/2 Th Ruamjit; r from 500B; 🅿 🕭 🖵) Its charm is fading a bit, but with a swimming

pool, wi-fi and air-con, this is a good deal. The 500B fan rooms are bargains.

Nirundorn 3 (☎ 0 3247 0300; 26/171 Th Ruamjit; r/bungalows 600/1000B; 🖳) One of several 'Nirundorn' cousins, this place wins with pillow-top mattresses and lounge chairs on verandahs that have peekaboo sea views. Bungalows are big, but face each other – you may as well go for the cheaper hotel-type room with a view.

our pick Charlie House (☎ 0 3243 3799; Soi 1 North, 241/60-61 Th Ruamjit; r 650-800B; 🖳) With pastel leather stools and accent lighting (even in the superbly designed bathrooms), this friendly place gets points for colour and flare. Don't confuse it with Charlie Place or Charlie TV, both on the same soi (lane).

MIDRANGE

Nana Guesthouse (☎ 0 3243 3632; www.nanahouse.net; 208/3-4 Th Ruamjit; r from 900B; 🖳 🖳) Rooms are clean and cheerful, if rather plain, and the price includes breakfast. Look for the purple and peach exterior at the north end of the beach.

Cha_Inn@Cha-am (☎ 0 3247 1879; www.cha-inn.com; 274/3 Th Ruamjit; r 900-1500B, bungalows 900-1200B; 🖳) Modern and minimalist, this is Cha-am's newest and sleekest digs. Rooms have bamboo mats over polished cement floors, honest-to-goodness art on the walls, and either a window seat or a verandah.

Dee Lek (☎ 0 3247 0145; www.deelek.com; 225/30-33 Th Ruamjit; r 1200-1500B; 🖳) Bright rooms with crisp bed linen, spacious bathrooms and upholstered furniture that brings to mind Europe. There are two Dee Leks: Dee Lek 1 (on Soi Long Beach, on the north side of town) is better than Dee Lek 2 (on Th Ruamjit).

Sweet Home (☎ 0 3241 1039; 279/1 Ruamjit; bungalows 1500B; 🖳) Sweet Home's traditional wooden bungalows sit in a tropical garden. Inside things are a little cramped, but there is no denying their rustic charm at the right price.

Kaenchan Beach Hotel (☎ 0 3247 0777; 241/4 Th Ruamjit; r 2150-3300B; bungalows 1550-3260B; 🖳 🖳) Cherry-coloured wooden buildings are ageing, but the somewhat worn pool area is splashy with kids enjoying their holiday and has good views.

TOP END

Baan Pantai Resort (☎ 0 3243 3111; www.baanpantai.com; 247/58 Th Ruamjit; r from 2200B; 🖳 🖳 🖳) This family-friendly place has a huge pool and small fitness centre. It's in the centre

of all the action – you can hear the banana boats roar by the beach across the street. The staff don't speak a lot of English, but they're very friendly.

Casa Papaya (☎ 0 3247 0678; www.casapapayathai.com; 810/4 Th Phetkasem; r 3000-5000B; 🖳 🖳) Designer Mexican chic runs riot at this terrific spot right on the beach 6km towards Hua Hin. The beachfront and sea-view bungalows have rooftop decks to enjoy the sunlight (or the moonlight), and inside there are king-size beds and bathrooms in wonderfully brave colours.

Eating

Beach vendors sell barbecued and fried seafood, and at the far northern end of the beach reasonably priced seafood restaurants can be found at the fishing pier. Along the beach road are simple Thai restaurants, all similar in ambience and price. The following are a bit different.

Rang Yen Garden (☎ 0 3247 1267; 259/40 Th Ruamjit; dishes 50-180B; 🕑 lunch & dinner Nov-Apr) This lovely patio-style restaurant is tucked away in a lush garden like a juicy secret. It serves up Thai favourites next to a burbling fish pond and is only open in the high season.

Sea_Rocco (☎ 0 3247 1879; 274/34 Th Ruamjit; dishes 80-190B; 🕑 breakfast, lunch & dinner) At the Cha_Inn@Cha-am hotel (left), Sea_Rocco maintains Cha-am's most fashionable hotel's vibe but the curry is reassuringly spicy and the prices are reasonable.

German Food House (☎ 08 7082 6252; 234/28-30 Soi Bus Station; mains 90-375B; 🕑 breakfast, lunch & dinner) Run by a butcher and baker (no candlestick maker, though), this joint is deservedly popular with expats. A carnivore's delight, this butcher shop's menu includes house-made sausages and artisan breads.

Poom Restaurant (☎ 0 3247 1036; 274/1 Th Ruamjit; dishes 120-250B; 🕑 lunch & dinner) Slightly more expensive than other nearby beach restaurants, but worth it for the fresh seafood served under tall sugar palms. It appears to be the restaurant of choice for weekending Thais – always a good sign.

Getting There & Away

Most hotels have shuttles to Hua Hin for 150/300B one way/return, and a private taxi will cost you 2500B.

Ordinary and air-con buses stop in the town centre, on Phetkasem Hwy

Some air-con buses to/from Bangkok go to the beach, stopping on Th Chao Lai a few hundred metres south of the Th Narathip intersection.

Frequent bus services operating to/from Cha-am include Bangkok (air-con/ordinary 150/130B, three hours), Phetchaburi (100B, 40 minutes) and Hua Hin (30B, 30 minutes).

The train station is inland on Th Narathip, west of Phetkasem Hwy, and a 30B motorcycle ride to/from the beach. From Bangkok two train stations have daily services to Cha-am: Hualamphong (9.20am and 3.35pm) and Thonburi (7.25am, 1.05pm and 7.15pm). Tickets cost from 60B to 150B and the journey is around four hours. Cha-am isn't listed on the English-language train schedule.

Getting Around

From the city centre to the beach it's a quick motorcycle (30B) or *sŏrng·tăa·ou* (20B) ride. Motorcycle taxis around town cost 30B. Some drivers will try to take you to another hotel that offers them a commission. Be firm.

You can hire motorcycles for 300B per day all along Th Ruamjit. Cruisy bicycles are available everywhere for 20B per hour, or 100B per day, and are a good way to get around. Travel agencies hire cars or jeeps for 1500B to 2000B per day.

AROUND CHA-AM

Midway between Cha-am and Hua Hin is **Phra Ratchaniwet Marukhathayawan** (☎ 0 3247 2482; admission by donation; ☼ 9am-4.30pm), a summer palace built during the reign of Rama VI. The one- and two-storey buildings are constructed of teak and interlinked by covered boardwalks, all high above the ground on stilts. Incorporating high tiled roofs and tall shuttered windows, the design maximises air circulation.

Unlike the current summer palace situated further south at Hua Hin, this palace is open to the public. Camp Rama VI, a military post, surrounds the palace grounds, and you need to check in at the gate. If you catch a Cha-am–Hua Hin bus to get here, ask to be dropped at the road to the palace. There are often motorcycle taxis waiting, or you can walk 2km the rest of the way.

PRACHUAP KHIRI KHAN PROVINCE

HUA HIN

อำเภอหัวหิน

pop 42,000

Once a humble fishing village, Hua Hin owes its roots as Thailand's first glamorous getaway to King Rama VII. In 1922 the king instructed his Italian architect to construct Phra Ratchawang Klai Kangwon ('Far from Worries' Palace). Today's royal family still commutes regularly to the palace to unwind from the pressures of keeping the army and politicians in line in Bangkok. Rama VII's endorsement made the town *the* place to be for Thai society, and Hua Hin (like Cha-am), settled into a low-key role as a favourite spot for holidaying Thais.

In the 1980s the renovation of the Hua Hin Railway Hotel by the luxury hotel group Sofitel sparked overseas interest and ignited development geared towards foreigners. Today all the big hotel chains have properties in Hua Hin, and in recent years a growing number of expats have chosen to live in the seaside town that's fast becoming one of Thailand's most cosmopolitan cities. High-rise condominiums and planned housing subdivisions are creeping across the surrounding hinterland, and French, Italian, German and Scandinavian restaurants create a little slice of home for sun-kissed escapees from the European winter.

With rapid development comes challenges. Hua Hin has witnessed the growth of a small sex industry, and the fishing-village ambience of the old piers has largely been swallowed by hotels, restaurants and tailor shops. Development has encroached onto government land, and trying to spot the sea is a frustrating exercise along many parts of the beach road.

Despite the development Hua Hin is bravely clinging to the beachside atmosphere that kicked things off back in 1922. Compared to Pattaya, the other main beach destination near Bangkok, Hua Hin is (relatively) serene, and is a favourite with families and older travellers. Don't come looking for a party-at-all-costs backpacker scene. Instead you can fill your time with a game of golf or go horseback riding on the beach. After dark there's a cosmopolitan restaurant scene to explore, rustic seafood restaurants on the pier to visit, or the

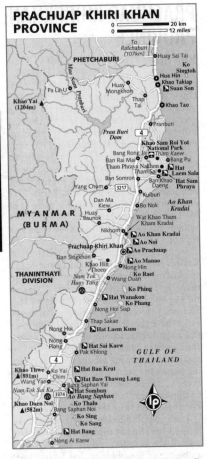

PRACHUAP KHIRI KHAN PROVINCE

0 ————— 20 km
0 ————— 12 miles

UPPER SOUTHERN GULF

To Ratchaburi (107km)

PHETCHABURI

Huay Sai Tai
Ko Singtoh
Hua Hin
Khao Takiap
Suan Son

Pa La-u
Huay Mongkhon
Thap Tai
Khao Tao

Khao Yai (1204m)

Pranburi

Mae Nam Pranburi

Pran Buri Dam

Khao Sam Roi Yot National Park
Bang Rong Jai — Tham Kaew
Ban Rai Mai — Bang Pu
Tham Phraya Nakhon — Hat Laem Sala
Ban Somron — Tham Sai
Ban Khao Daeng — Hat Sam Phraya

Yang Chum

Kuiburi

Dan Ma Kiew

Ao Khan Kradai

MYANMAR (BURMA)

Huay Baunok

Wat Khao Tham Kham Kradai

Nikhom

Ao Khan Kradai
Ao Noi
Ao Prachuap

Prachuap Khiri Khan

Dan Singkhon

Ao Manao

Khao Hin
Thoen
Nam Tok Huay Yang
Nong Hin
Wang Duan
Ko Raet

THANINTHAYI DIVISION

Ko Phing

Hat Wanakon
Ko Phang

Nong Hoi Siap

Thap Sakae

Nong Hoi

Hat Laem Kum

Nong Plong

Hat Sai Kaew

Pak Khlong

GULF OF THAILAND

Khao Thwe (891m)
Ko Yai
Wang Yao — Chim
Bang Saphan Yai

Hat Ban Krut
Hat Baw Thawng Lang
Hat Sombun

Nam Tok Sai Ku
Ao Bang Saphan

Khao Daen Noi (582m)
Bang Saphan Noi
Ko Sing
Ko Thalu
Ko Sang
Hat Bang

Nong Ai Kaew

simple culinary charms of one of Thailand's best night markets to sample. The city's 5km of beaches are the cleanest they've been for many years, swimming is safe, and Hua Hin continues to enjoy some of the peninsula's driest weather.

Orientation

From afar, Hua Hin's towering hotels make this resort town look like nothing but row upon row of high-rises. But smaller guesthouses and outdoor restaurants line the waterfront area, and little soi veer off concealing more guesthouses, lively bars and travel agencies. The backbone of the tourist centre is Th Naresdamri, which is crammed with souvenir stalls, persistent tailors and classy restaurants. If you lose your way, look for the Hilton Hotel – it makes a good landmark as it usually peeps above the smaller buildings in the centre. Th Naresdamri is a lively place and if you want some quiet time it may be best to stay elsewhere.

The best beach is in front and south of the Sofitel resort. This pleasant stretch of sand is broken up by round, smooth boulders (Hua Hin means 'stone head') and is ideal for year-round swimming. The train station lies at the western end of town and features a beautifully restored royal waiting room. The **airport** (www .huahinairport.com) is 6km north of town.

Information

BOOKSHOPS

Bookazine (☎ 0 3251 3060; 122 Th Naresdamri; 🕑 9am-10pm) Attached to a Kodak store, this has a few magazines and books in English.

Megabooks (☎ 0 3253 2071; 166 Th Naresdamri; 🕑 9am-10pm) Crammed full of new titles in English, including Lonely Planet guides.

EMERGENCY

Tourist police (☎ 0 3251 5995, emergency 1155; Th Damnoen Kasem) At the eastern end of the street.

INTERNET ACCESS

Internet access is available all over Hua Hin, in guesthouses and cafes.

Cups & Comp (☎ 0 3253 1119; 144/2 Th Chomsin; per hr 40B; 🕑 9am-midnight) Has internet, printing, faxing and overseas calls.

Sidewalk Café (☎ 0 8438 5518-7; Soi Selakam; 🕑 8.30am-1am) Has a free wi-fi network.

World News Coffee (☎ 0 3253 2475; Th Naresdamri; per hr 40B; 🕑 8am-11pm) Has fast internet connection in air-con comfort.

INTERNET RESOURCES

www.huahinafterdark.com A good resource for night-time shenanigans.

MEDIA

Free maps, pamphlets and brochures can be found in restaurants and hotels.

Hua Hin Observer (www.observergroup.net) A free, home-grown, expat-published magazine with features in English and German. Available at most hotels around town, it contains info on dining, culture and entertainment.

MEDICAL SERVICES

Hospital San Paolo (☎ 0 3253 2576; 222 Th Phetkasem) Just south of town with emergency facilities.

UPPER SOUTHERN GULF

MONEY

There are exchange booths and ATMs up and down Th Naresdamri. Near the bus stations, there are banks on Th Phetkasem.

Bank of Ayudhya (Th Naresdamri) Most convenient to the beach; near the corner of Th Damnoen Kasem.

POST & TELEPHONE

Main post office (Th Damnoen Kasem) Includes the CAT for international phone calls.

TOURIST INFORMATION

TAT office (☎ 0 3251 3885; 39/4 Th Phetkasem; ⏰ 8.30am-4.30pm) North of the tourist centre, this government office speaks English and is quite helpful.

Tourist Information Office (☎ 0 3251 1047; cnr Th Phetkasem & Th Damnoen Kasem; ⏰ 8.30am-4.30pm) Provides advice about Hua Hin and its surrounding area, and sells bus tickets. There's another branch (☎ 0 3252 2797) under the clock tower on the corner of Th Phetkasem and Th Naep Khehat.

TRAVEL AGENCIES

There are many travel agencies, most offering day trips to nearby places such as Khao Sam Roi Yot (p562) and Kaeng Krachan (p552) National Parks. Unless you're in a group, you may have to wait a day or two until enough people sign up for the trip of your choice, so keep that in mind when you make a booking. Alternatively, try forming a group with fellow tourists to ensure a prompt trip.

Hua Hin Adventure Tour (☎ 0 3253 0314; www.hua hinadventuretour.com; Th Naep Khehat; ⏰ 9am-6pm Mon-Sat) Offers more active excursions than other travel agencies. Runs kayaking trips in the Khao Sam Roi Yot National Park (2100B) as well as tours into Kaeng Krachan National Park.

Ken Diamond (☎ 0 3253 2271; www.travel-huahin .com; 162/6 Th Naresdamri; ⏰ 8.30am-7pm) Offers dozens of trips to nearby destinations, including waterfalls and national parks, and organises diving and snorkelling packages. Can arrange for German-speaking guides. Also has car hire.

Tuk Tours (☎ 0 3251 4281; www.tuktours.com; 33/5 Th Phunsuk; ⏰ 10am-7pm) Can book activities and transport all around Thailand.

Activities

A long-time favourite golf-holiday destination for Thais, Hua Hin has recently begun receiving attention from international golfers.

Hua Hin Golf Centre (☎ 0 3253 0476; www.huahingolf .com; 2/136 Nabkahards; ⏰ noon-10pm) rents golfing equipment and organises golfing tours. You'll also find loads of info at **Bernie's** (☎ 0 3253 2601; Hua Hin Bazaar, Th Damnoen Kasem).

The **Royal Hua Hin Golf Course** (☎ 0 3251 2475; green fee 2000B) is only one of several golf courses but it's definitely the best. Near the train station, it offers ocean and temple views on an elegant course.

Horseback riding (per 40min 600B) is on offer on the beach at the end of Th Damnoen Kasem; the lessons are conducted in a safe fashion.

Moo·ay tai (also spelt *muay thai*; Thai boxing) matches take place every Tuesday and Saturday at 9pm at the **Thai Boxing Garden** (☎ 0 3251 5269; 20/23 Th Phunsuk; admission 350B). On Wednesday and Friday at 9pm the action moves to the **Grand Plaza** (☎ 08 9754 7801; Th Phetkasem; admission 500B). The Grand Plaza's **gym** (www.huahingrandsport.com; admission 180B, moo·ay tai lessons 300B; ⏰ 9am-9pm) has a sauna, yoga instruction and coffee/protein-shake bar, and is a good place to burn off last night's Singha beers in authentic Thai style. See the website for information on other sporting activities offered.

Aspiring chefs should visit **Buchabun Art & Crafts Collection** (☎ 08 1572 3805; www.thai-cooking course.com; 22 Th Dechanuchit), where you can sign up for a half-day Thai cooking class. Classes cost 1500B and include a market visit and recipe book. They only run if several people are interested.

Volunteering

If you love animals and aren't afraid of a bit of hard work, then a stint at the **Wildlife Friends of Thailand Rescue Centre** (☎ 0 3245 8135; rescue centre www.wfft.org, volunteering www.wildlife volunteer.org) could be a good, fun and unique way to break up your travels. Based 35km northwest of Cha-am, the centre cares for an entire menagerie of animals that have been rescued from animal shows and exploitative owners. An average day could involve feeding sun bears, building enclosures for macaques and establishing island refuges for gibbons. Volunteers are required to stay a minimum of three weeks. Travel agencies in Cha-am and Hua Hin can organise day trips (1200B) to the centre or you can phone the centre directly, and staff can arrange return transport from Hua Hin (650B) or Cha-am (950B). From Cha-am, a taxi to the centre will cost about 400B.

The organisation also runs an elephant refuge – at €325 per week, it's a bit expensive, but you'll be trained how to work hands-on with rescued elephants.

Sleeping

All budgets are catered for in Hua Hin. Expect discounts of 20% to 40% off these rates in the low season. Prices may be hiked up on weekends and at holidays.

BUDGET

All Nations Guest House (☎ 0 3251 2747; www.geocities.com/allnationsguesthouse; 10-10/1 Th Dechanuchit; r 200-550B; ✷) Feed the backpacker within at this friendly spot with cheap beers and homemade pies. The less-expensive rooms have shared bathrooms, and there is a bar with televisions tuned to an all-day diet of sport.

Euro-Hua Hin City Hotel YHA (☎ 0 3251 3130; www.tyha.org; 15/15 Th Sasong; r incl breakfast 250-1000B; ✷) Just like any large hostel from back home, this place feels both comfortable and institutional. All rooms have air-con, even the somewhat cramped six-person dormitories (250B). If you snore we recommend a single room (1000B). Add 50B to these prices if you don't belong to HI.

ourpick Pattana Guest House (☎ 0 3251 3393; 52 Th Naresdamri; r 350-550B) This restored fisherman's house has small rooms, but a lusciously verdant bar and courtyard area. Note the whimsically carved teak sinks in the bathroom. Book ahead as it's very popular.

Tong-Mee House (☎ 0 3253 0725; tongmeehuahin@hotmail.com; 1 Soi Raumpown; r 450-550B; ✷ ▣) Hidden away in a quiet residential soi, this boutique-ish hotel is the best value in town. The rooms are small but well kept and have balconies, and the giggly owner is ever-friendly.

Cha-ba Chalet (☎ 0 3252 1181-3; www.chabachalet.com; 1/18 Th Sasong; r 600-700B; ✷) The rooms here are relatively roomy though a bit musty-smelling. Still, at a decent price and very close to the bustling night market, it's a good choice.

Supasuda Guest House (☎ 0 3251 3618; 1/8 Th Chomsin; r 800-1000B; ✷) Large rooms come with sleek black furniture and hot showers. The more expensive ones have verandahs – and a bit of road noise.

Ban Somboon (☎ 0 3251 1538; 13/4 Soi Damnoen Kasem; r 950-1200B; ✷) With family photos, a compact garden and a tiny Buddhist shrine, this place is like staying at your favourite Thai auntie's house. Prices include breakfast, which, based on the smells coming from the small bakery, seems like a sweet deal. In the same soi there are a couple of other good-value guesthouses.

Pier Guesthouses

There are several pier guesthouses lining Th Naresdamri with simple rooms overlooking the sea. You're paying for the location and the shared areas can be noisy, but hearing the tide rush in under your floorboards is an oddly soothing experience. When the tide is out you can often hear your shower water draining onto the beach – consider biodegradable soap.

Mod (☎ 0 3251 2296; Th Naresdamri; r 200-450B; ✷) Thankfully, the interior of this two-storey place is better than the shabby exterior. The upstairs rooms cost more, but are airy and have better views. The cheapest rooms just have fans.

Sirima (☎ 0 3251 1060; Th Naresdamri; r 250-650B; ✷) Sirima has an excellent exterior, with stained glass and polished wood. A long hallway leads to a common deck overlooking the water. The blue-carpeted rooms are small with basic bathrooms; hang out on the deck instead.

Bird Guest House (☎ 0 3251 1630; 31/2 Th Naresdamri; r 400-600B; ✷) Bird is smaller and quieter than the other pier guesthouses, though fairly ramshackle. The family that runs it is friendly, however, and there's a secluded pier-end deck.

MIDRANGE

Hua Hin's midrange places are small, sedate, modern hotels with air-con, fridges and cable TV. A handful of new openings are making everyone lift their game. Th Chomsin has several boutique guesthouses, just a short stroll from some of Hua Hin's best restaurants.

Rajana Garden House (☎ 0 3251 1729; www.rajana-house.com; 3/9 Th Sasong; r 1000B; ✷) The rooms may lack the designer touches of other midrangers in town, but it's a little cheaper and the air-con bus from Bangkok stops nearby. Ask for a room at the back to counter road noise from busy Th Sasong or rent the bungalow in the verdant garden for 1500B.

Sand Inn (☎ 0 3253 2060; www.sandinn-huahin.com; 38/1-4 Th Phunsuk; r 1000-1600B; ✷ ▣) The generic exterior belies the artsy interior, with the funkiest hallway lighting we've seen in a midrange joint. Some rooms come with huge balconies. The new pool looked promising but seemed rarely used when we visited.

Baan Oum-or Hotel (☎ 0 3251 5151; 77/18-19 Th Phetkasem, Soi 63; r from 1200B; ✷) The rooms are big and bright and there are only seven of them so book ahead.

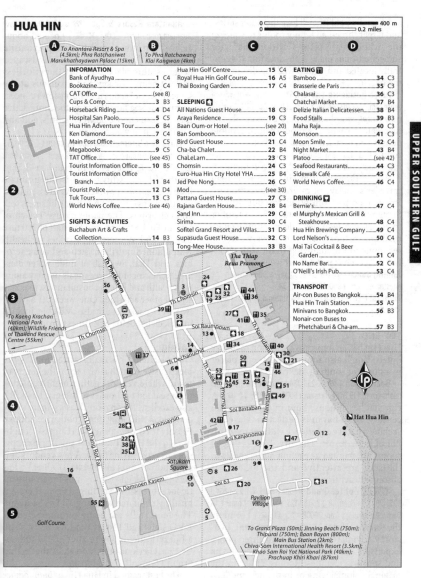

HUA HIN

0 / 400 m
0 / 0.2 miles

INFORMATION
Bank of Ayudhya	**1** C4
Bookazine	**2** C4
CAT Office	(see 8)
Cups & Comp	**3** B3
Horseback Riding	**4** D4
Hospital San Paolo	**5** C5
Hua Hin Adventure Tour	**6** B4
Ken Diamond	**7** C5
Main Post Office	**8** C5
Megabooks	**9** C5
TAT Office	(see 45)
Tourist Information Office	**10** B5
Tourist Information Office Branch	**11** B4
Tourist Police	**12** D4
Tuk Tours	**13** C3
World News Coffee	(see 46)

SIGHTS & ACTIVITIES
Buchabun Art & Crafts Collection	**14** B3
Hua Hin Golf Centre	**15** C4
Royal Hua Hin Golf Course	**16** A5
Thai Boxing Garden	**17** C4

SLEEPING
All Nations Guest House	**18** C3
Araya Residence	**19** C3
Baan Oum-or Hotel	(see 20)
Ban Somboon	**20** C5
Bird Guest House	**21** C4
Cha-ba Chalet	**22** B4
ChaLeLarn	**23** C3
Chomsin	**24** C3
Euro-Hua Hin City Hotel YHA	**25** B4
Jed Pee Nong	**26** C5
Mod	(see 30)
Pattana Guest House	**27** C4
Rajana Garden House	**28** B4
Sand Inn	**29** C4
Sirima	**30** C3
Sofitel Grand Resort and Villas	**31** D5
Supasuda Guest House	**32** C3
Tong-Mee House	**33** B3

EATING
Bamboo	**34** C3
Brasserie de Paris	**35** C3
Chalasai	**36** C3
Chatchai Market	**37** B4
Delizie Italian Delicatessen	**38** B4
Food Stalls	**39** B3
Maha Raja	**40** C3
Monsoon	**41** C3
Moon Smile	**42** C4
Night Market	**43** B4
Platoo	(see 42)
Seafood Restaurants	**44** C3
Sidewalk Café	**45** C4
World News Coffee	**46** C3

DRINKING
Bernie's	**47** C4
el Murphy's Mexican Grill & Steakhouse	**48** C4
Hua Hin Brewing Company	**49** C4
Lord Nelson's	**50** C4
Mai Tai Cocktail & Beer Garden	**51** C4
No Name Bar	**52** C4
O'Neill's Irish Pub	**53** C4

TRANSPORT
Air-con Buses to Bangkok	**54** B4
Hua Hin Train Station	**55** A5
Minivans to Bangkok	**56** B3
Nonair-con Buses to Phetchaburi & Cha-am	**57** B3

To Anantara Resort & Spa (4.5km); Phra Ratchaniwet Marukhathayawan Palace (15km)

To Phra Ratchawang Klai Kangwon (4km)

To Kaeng Krachan National Park (40km); Wildlife Friends of Thailand Rescue Centre (55km)

Tha Thiap Reua Pramong

Th Phetkasem
Th Chomsin
Th Chomsin
Th Dechanuchit
Th Sasong
Th Naebkehardt
Th Selakam
Th Naresdamri
Th Amnuaysin
Th Liap Thang Rot Fai
Soi Raumporn
Soi Bintaban
Soi Kanjanomai
Soi 63
Satukarn Square
Th Damnoen Kasem

Hat Hua Hin

Golf Course

Pavilion Village

To Grand Plaza (50m); Jinning Beach (750m); Thipurai (750m); Baan Bayan (800m); Main Bus Station (2km); Chiva-Som International Health Resort (3.5km); Khao Sam Roi Yot National Park (40km); Prachuap Khiri Khari (87km)

ChaLeLarn (☎ 0 3253 1288; www.chalelarn.com; 11 Th Chomsin; r 1200-1300B; ✷ ▭) ChaLeLarn has a beautiful lobby with wooden floors, while big rooms are equipped with king-sized beds. Verandahs, breakfast and free wi-fi are all part of the perks.

Chomsin (☎ 0 3251 5348; www.chomsinhuahin .com; 130/4 Th Chomsin; r 1300B; ✷ ▭) Close to

the beach and night market, the Chomsin has super comfortable, if somewhat bland, rooms with wood floors, clean bathrooms and cable TV. Some of the lower rooms face the neighbour's wall.

Jed Pee Nong (☎ 0 3251 2381; www.jedpeenong hotel-huahin.com; 17 Th Damnoen Kasem; r 1500-1800B; ✷ ▨) Family-oriented, this place has a small kid-friendly pool (they'll love the water slides) and larger three-bed family rooms to squeeze the whole clan into. Cartoon-character shower curtains make bath-time fun. It's centrally located and within walking distance of the beach.

Araya Residence (☎ 0 3253 1130; www.araya-residence.com; 15/1 Th Chomsin; r 1500-2000B; ✂ ☐) At this new hotel, wood and concrete are combined to create a rustic yet modern feel. Double doors open to spacious and tiled bathrooms in rooms that have special touches such as writing desks and settees. Highly recommended.

About 1km south of Hua Hin is a small traveller's enclave of midrange guesthouses. Prices (rooms from 600B to 900B July to September, from 1000B to 1350B October to June) and facilities (clean, comfortable, modern) are the same at almost every one. We recommend the following (both with pools, but the beach is just a short walk away).

Jinning Beach (☎ 0 3251 3950; www.jinningbeachguesthouse.com; r 800-1700B; ✂ ☒)

Thipurai (☎ 0 3251 2210; www.thirupai.com; r 1350B; ✂ ☒)

TOP END

Hua Hin has an impressive selection of luxury hotels. You'll also find other top-end places just north or south of the town centre.

Baan Bayan (☎ 0 3253 3544; www.beachfronthotelhuahin.com; 119 Th Phetkasem; r 6000-11,000B; ✂ ☒) A colonial beach house built in the early 20th century, Baan Bayan is perfect for travellers seeking a luxury experience without the overkill of a big resort. The airy, high-ceilinged rooms are painted a relaxing buttery yellow, the staff are attentive and the location is absolute beachfront.

our pick Sofitel Grand Resort and Villas (☎ 0 3251 2021, in Bangkok 0 2541 1125; www.sofitel.com; 1 Th Damnoen Kasem; r from 7000B; ✂ ☐ ☒) Formerly the Railway Hotel, this is a magnificent, two-storey colonial-style place with three pools, expansive grounds along the beach, a spa and sporting facilities. Rooms, either in the original colonial wing or in the new modern wing, are luxurious with old-world touches. Discounts of up to 40% may be possible during the week and in the low season, or if you book through the office in Bangkok. Also worth visiting is the lobby cafe, which doubles as a museum of the hotel's fascinating history and was part of the set in the 1984 movie *The Killing Fields*.

Anantara Resort & Spa (☎ 0 3252 0205; www.anantara.com; r from 7500B; ✂ ☒) Located about 4.5km from town, and featuring exquisite Thai-style villas and suites on 5.5 landscaped hectares, this place pulls off the effortless trick of being low key and luxurious at the same time. Gorgeous teak bungalows conceal pampering spa facilities, and the more active traveller can choose between tennis, golf and a whole raft of water sports.

Chiva-Som International Health Resort (☎ 0 3253 6536; www.chivasom.com; 74/4 Th Phetkasem; 3 nights from US$2070; ✂ ☒) Set on a private lake 3.5km south of town, Chiva-Som is the ultimate hideaway for overworked, overstressed (and just maybe overpaid) high-flying business folk and celebrities. The name means 'Haven of Life' in Thai-Sanskrit, and the staff of 200 fuse Eastern and Western approaches to health with planned nutrition, step and aqua aerobics, and Thai, Swedish or underwater massage. Rates include three meals per day along with health and fitness consultations, massage and all other activities. One-week, 10-day and two-week packages are also available, including specialist detox and fitness programs.

Eating

One of Hua Hin's major attractions is the inexpensive Chatchai Market in the centre of town, where vendors gather nightly to cook fresh seafood for hordes of hungry Thais. It's also excellent for Thai breakfasts – there's very good *jóhk* and *kôw đôm* (both rice soups). Freshly fried *bah·tôrng·gôh* (Chinese doughnuts in the Hua Hin style – small and crispy, not oily) cost 3B for three. A few vendors also serve hot soy milk in bowls (5B) – break a few *bah·tôrng·gôh* into the soy milk for an authentic local breakfast. Starting at 5pm, there is a bustling night market along Th Dechanuchit. The food stalls are being outnumbered by DVD stalls and T-shirt vendors, but it's still a buzzy scene. If you're after 100% authentic eats, check out the food stalls that set up around 5pm off Th Chomsin.

The best seafood in Hua Hin is *blah săm·lee* (cotton fish or kingfish), *blah grà·pong* (perch), *blah mèuk* (squid), *hŏy má·laang pôo* (mussels) and *boo* (crab). Fresh seafood is all over town, but the concentration of wharfside outdoor seafood restaurants is on Th Naresdamri. On the beach you can order a cold Singha and cracked crab without leaving your deckchair.

Chalasai (7 Th Naletmanley; mains 50-120B; 9am-9pm) With a small patio and a seaside location, Chalasai (no roman-script sign – it's across from Monsoon) doesn't need to put any energy into ambience. Instead, it puts it all into the delicious, cheap Thai seafood.

Sidewalk Café (0 8438 5518-7; Soi Selakam; coffee 50B, breakfast 70-130B; 8.30am-1am) Welcoming owner Tim advertises 'probably the best coffee in town', and we have to concede that he's probably right. Also excellent are the rich scrambled eggs and fresh-squeezed juice. When we visited, he was busy readying the cafe for an evening bar – we expect that when it opens you'll find excellent company in a mellow setting.

World News Coffee (0 3253 2475; 130/2 Th Naresdamri; dishes 70-130B; breakfast, lunch & dinner) This Starbucks-esque cafe serves Western breakfasts, including bagels, croissants and lots of different coffees. You can surf the web for 40B per hour and there are magazines and newspapers to complement your first cup of the day.

Moon Smile (Th Phunsuk; dishes 80-200B; lunch & dinner) The best in an enclave of well-priced Thai restaurants on Th Phunsuk that will respect your request for 'Thai spicy, please'. Try the grilled beef and eggplant salad. A few doors up, Platoo is another good choice.

Bamboo (08 9164 3526; 27/1 Th Dechanuchit; dishes 80-210B; 9am-1am) Though the name has changed from the beloved Elmar's (the old sign still hung outside when we visited), Bamboo strives to carry on the 15-year tradition of Elmar's excellent European dishes and comfort food. Sample some goulash (125B) or Wiener schnitzel (210B).

Maha Raja (0 3253 0347; 25 Th Naresdamri; dishes 90-200B; lunch & dinner) Indian cuisine usually travels well and this reasonably priced shrine to Bollywood bling is no exception.

Monsoon (0 3253 1062; 62 Th Naresdamri; dishes 120-300B, afternoon tea 120B; 2pm-midnight) An excellent wine list and mood lighting make this Vietnamese restaurant, located in a lovingly restored two-storey teak house, Hua Hin's most romantic (and expensive) spot. There's also Thai and European food, and you can treat yourself to afternoon tea from 3pm.

Delizie Italian Delicatessen (0 3253 0192; 1/13 Th Sasong; dishes 160-380B; 9am-9pm) Pick out your olives and salami, grab some pesto and baguettes, and you're all set for an Italian picnic. You can also enjoy the ambience and authentic Italian at small bistro tables inside.

Brasserie de Paris (08 1826 6814; 3 Th Naresdamri; dishes 350-500B) France comes to town with a real French chef cooking up authentic French flavours in a light and airy space with good views of *la mer* from bistro tables upstairs. Local crab is the standout dish. Reassuringly expensive.

Drinking

There are several *fa·ràng* bars under European management in the Hua Hin Bazaar. Some offer the familiar Thai-hostess atmosphere, but a few bill themselves as 'sports bars' and have wide-screen TVs. Soi Bintaban is lined with girlie bars doing their best to attract clientele. It's not a dangerous place per se, just a glimpse into the seedier side of tourism. Nearby Th Naresdamri is a bit more salubrious with a couple of classier drinking holes.

O'Neill's Irish Pub (0 3251 1517; 5 Th Phunsuk; 8.30am-midnight) Pretty authentic for so far from the Blarney Stone, O'Neill's (formerly Crawford's) offers excellent *craic* amid two levels of moody wood, with lots of hideaway nooks and crannies. Live sport is on offer on several tellies, and there's a robust menu including fish and chips. Draught beers are cheaper Monday to Thursday. *Slainte!*

Mai Tai Cocktail & Beer Garden (0 3253 3344; 33/12 Th Naresdamri; noon-1am) Attracts a casual crowd on a deck made for people-watching and chairs made for chilling. Draft Chang is only 45B.

Bernie's (0 3253 2601; Hua Hin Bazaar, Th Damnoen Kasem) The owner is a big golf nut with loads of info on swinging a club in the area. Wall-to-wall TVs show wall-to-wall sport – especially golf.

Hua Hin Brewing Company (0 3251 2888; 33 Th Naresdamri; open 5pm) Though there's no longer any beer brewed here, most nights there's a live band followed by a relatively clued-up DJ. Inside is as dark as the belly of Jonah's whale, so park yourself outside on the spacious decks and watch the passing parade on Th Naresdamri.

el Murphy's Mexican Grill & Steakhouse (0 3251 1525; 25 Soi Selakam) Serves an unlikely combo of pints and Mexican food. Come in to enjoy a tall one while you watch the game, but maybe skip dinner – it's rather what you'd expect from Thai cooks in an Irish bar trying to cook Mexican food.

Along soi Selakam between Sidewalk Café and el Murphy's there are several hostess bars, but a few don't have girls. No Name and Lord Nelson's are two of them.

Getting There & Away

SGA (☎ 0 3252 2300, in Bangkok 0 2134 3233; www.sga .co.th) flies a 12-seat shuttle at 12.30pm and 5.30pm from Bangkok's Suvarnabhumi International Airport to Hua Hin (one way 3700B, 40 minutes).

Air-con buses to/from Bangkok's southern bus station (140B to 165B, three hours) leave 70m north of Rajana Garden House on Th Sasong (outside the Siripetchkasem Hotel), every hour from 4am to 10pm.

The new main bus station is south of town, on Th Phetkasem, and has air-con buses to many destinations throughout the country. There is at least one bus per day to each destination: Phetchaburi (85B, 1½ hours), Cha-am (45B, 30 minutes), Prachuap Khiri Khan (60B to 80B, 1½ hours), Chumphon (160B, four hours) and Surat Thani (270B, seven hours). This bus station has plans to add a direct service to Chiang Mai.

Frequent nonair-con buses to Phetchaburi (50B, 1½ hours) and Cha-am (25B, 30 minutes) leave from near the intersection of Th Chomsin and Th Phetkasem.

Minivans run regularly from Bangkok's Victory Monument to Th Phetkasem (200B).

There are frequent trains running to/from Bangkok's Hualamphong train station (2nd class 292B to 382B, 3rd class 100B to 234B, four hours) and other stations on the southern railway line.

Getting Around

Even though sǎhm·lór fares in Hua Hin have been set by the municipal authorities, haggling is usually required. Sample fares include: from the train station to the beach 50B; from the air-con bus terminal to Th Naresdamri 40B to 50B (depending on size of your bags). Most drivers will push for at least twice this much.

Motorcycles (250B to 500B per day) and bicycles (100B per day) can be hired from a couple of places on Th Damnoen Kasem near the Jed Pee Nong hotel. Car and 4WD hire can be arranged at most travel agencies, including Ken Diamond (p557). Expect to pay around 1500B per day for a Suzuki 4WD and around 2000B per day for a small sedan.

KHAO SAM ROI YOT NATIONAL PARK

อุทยานแห่งชาติเขาสามร้อยยอด

Towering limestone cliffs, caves and beaches produce a dramatic landscape at this 98-sq-km **park** (☎ 0 3282 1568; adult/child 200/100B), which means Three Hundred Mountain Peaks in English. The park's lagoons and coastal marshlands are excellent for birdwatching, and with a little exercise you'll be rewarded with magnificent views of the gulf coastline.

Bring your mosquito repellent, especially during the rainy season (June to November). Rama IV and a large entourage of Thai and European guests came here on 18 August 1868 to see a total solar eclipse (apparently predicted by the monarch himself) and to enjoy a feast prepared by a French chef. Two months later the king died from malaria, contracted from mosquito bites inflicted here. Today the risk of malaria in the park is low, but the mosquitoes can be pesky.

Orientation & Information

There are three park headquarter locations: Hat Laem Sala, Ban Rong Jai and Ban Khao Daeng. There are also visitors centres at Hat Laem Sala, Hat Sam Phraya and Ban Khao Daeng. A nature-studies centre lies at the end of a 1km road leading north from Ban Rong Jai. There are a couple of checkpoints – on the road south from Pranburi and on the road east of Hwy 4. You'll need to pay admission or show proof that you already have.

Sights & Activities

BEACHES

Both of the park's beaches have plenty of facilities – from food stalls to picnic areas and toilets.

Hat Laem Sala is a sandy beach flanked on three sides by dry limestone hills and casuarinas. It has a small visitors centre, restaurant, bungalows and camp sites. Boats, taking up to 10 people, can be hired from Bang Pu to the beach (250B return, 15 minutes). The beach is about a 20-minute hike from Bang Pu, via a steep trail.

Hat Sam Phraya, 5km south of Hat Laem Sala, is a 1km-long beach with a restaurant and toilets.

CAVES

Khao Sam Roi Yot has three caves, all worth visiting. **Tham Phraya Nakhon** is the most popular and for good reason; here, a royal *săh·lah* built for Rama V in 1890 sits bathing in streams of light. The 430m trail, which starts from Hat Laem Sala, is steep, rocky and at times slick – don't wear your ballet flats. Once there you'll find two large caverns with sinkholes – the meeting hall is the second of the two.

Tham Kaew, 2km from the Bang Pu turn-off, features a series of chambers connected by narrow passageways; you enter the first cavern by means of a ladder. Stalactites and limestone formations glittering with calcite crystals (hence the cave's name, 'Jewel Cave') are plentiful. You can hire lamps, but it's better if you let a park ranger guide you as the footing is dangerous.

Tham Sai is in a hill near Ban Khung Tanot, 2.5km from the main road between Laem Sala and Sam Phraya beaches. Villagers rent out lamps (40B) at a shelter near the cave mouth. A 280m trail leads up the hillside to the cave, which features a large single cavern filled with stalactites and stalagmites. Be careful of steep drop-offs inside.

HIKING

For spectacular views of limestone cliffs against a jagged coastline, take the 30-minute step trail near the park headquarters at Ban Khao Daeng to the top of **Khao Daeng**. At sunset you might see a serow (Asian mountain goat). If you have more time and energy, climb the 605m to the top of **Khao Krachom** for even better views.

KAYAKING

In the fishing village of Ban Khao Daeng, **Horizon Adventure** (☎ 08 1820 9091) rents out kayaks for 400B per day, allowing you to explore the wildlife-filled mangroves of the area at your leisure.

WILDLIFE-WATCHING

Wildlife includes barking deer, crab-eating macaques, slow lorises, Malayan pangolins, fishing cats, palm civets, otters, serows, Javan mongooses, monitor lizards and dusky langurs. Possibly due to the rise in tourism, it can be difficult to actually spot any wild animals.

Because the park is at the intersection of the East Asian and Australian flyways, as many as 300 migratory and resident bird species have been recorded here, including yellow bitterns, cinnamon bitterns, purple swamphens, water

rails, ruddy-breasted crakes, bronze-winged jacanas, grey herons, painted storks, whistling ducks, spotted eagles and black-headed ibises. The park contains Thailand's largest freshwater marsh (along with mangroves and mudflats), and is one of only three places in the country where the purple heron breeds.

Waterfowl are most commonly seen in the cool season. Encroachment by shrimp farmers in the vicinity has sadly destroyed substantial portions of mangroves and other wetlands, thus depriving the birds of an important habitat. November to March are the best waterfowl-watching months. The birds come from as far as Siberia, China and northern Europe to winter here. You can hire a boat in the village of Khao Daeng for a cruise (400B, 45 minutes) along the canal in the morning or afternoon to spot them. Before heading out, chat with your prospective guide to see how well they speak English. Better guides will know the English names of common waterfowl and point them out to you.

Sleeping & Eating

Along with camping and bungalows, there are also a few private resort-style accommodation options.

Royal Forestry Department (☎ 0 2562 0760; www.dnp.go.th; campsite per person 30B, bungalows 5-6 people 1200-1400B, 6-9 people 1600-2200B) The forestry department hires out bungalows at Hat Laem Sala and at the visitors centre near the Khao Daeng viewpoint. You can pitch a tent at campsites near the Khao Daeng viewpoint, Hat Laem Sala or Hat Sam Phraya. There are basic restaurants at all these locations.

Dolphin Bay Resort (☎ 0 3255 9333; www.dolphinbayresort.com; 227 Mu 4, Phu Noi; r & bungalows from 1490B; ✷ ▣ ⚊) Choose between hotel-style rooms or well-appointed bungalows at this family-friendly place with two large pools and an excellent restaurant. A wide range of trips is on offer to nearby islands and the national park. From February to May pink dolphins are sometimes seen off the beach.

Long Beach Inn (☎ 0 3255 9068; www.longbeach-thailand.com; 223/4 Mu 4, Phu Noi; r 1950B; ✷ ▣ ⚊) A short walk from the eponymous Long Beach, but comfortable with air-con rooms in new villas around a pretty pool.

our pick Brassiere Beach (☎ 08 1734 4343; www.brassierebeach.com; 210 Mu 5, Cosy Beach; villas 4200-9425B; ✷) Nine stunning Mexican-style villas have (white)washed ashore at a private cove, and the funky owners have equipped them with retro furniture, CD players and playful names like La Perla and Wacoal. Brassiere Beach's uniqueness deserves your support.

Getting There & Away

The park is about 40km south of Hua Hin, and best visited by car. From Hua Hin, take Hwy 4 (Th Phetkasem) to Pranburi. In Pranburi, turn left at the main intersection, drive 2km, stay right at the fork in the road, and go another 2km. At the police substation, turn right. From there, it's 19km to the park's entrance and then another 14km to the headquarters at Hat Laem Sala. If you're trying to reach the park from the south, there's an entrance off Hwy 4 – turn right at highway marker 286.5, where there's a sign for the park, then drive another 13km to the headquarters at Ban Khao Daeng.

If you don't have your own wheels, catch a bus or train to Pranburi and then a *sŏrng·tăa·ou* (50B, every half-hour between 8am and 4pm) to Bang Pu, the small village inside the park. From Bang Pu you can walk to Hat Laem Sala or charter a boat (250B return, 15 minutes).

You can also hire a *sŏrng·tăa·ou* (350B to 500B) or a motorcycle taxi (250B) from Pranburi all the way to the park. Be sure to mention you want to go to the *ù·tá·yahn hàang châht* (national park) rather than Ban Khao Sam Roi Yot. Transport can also be arranged at travel agencies in Hua Hin (p557), most of which also run tours. **Hua Hin Adventure Tour** (☎ 0 3253 0314; www.huahinadventuretour.com) has the best selection of more intrepid activities.

PRACHUAP KHIRI KHAN

ประจวบคีรีขันธ์
pop 27,700
Prachuap Khiri Khan is a melange of pastel colours – a soft yellow corniche (beachfront walkway) that follows a deep swoop of mellow sand, silky blue water that gently bobs vibrant fishing boats – saddled between steep limestone cliffs and islands. Blur your eyes just a bit (well, maybe a bit more), and you could almost be in the south of France. This sleepy seaside town is actually the provincial capital, but the ambience is nicely small-town relaxed. Attractions, with a small 'a', include climbing to a hill-top *wát* while being shadowed by a troop of curious monkeys, taking a leisurely motorbike ride to the excellent beaches north

and south of town, or just enjoying some of Thailand's freshest (and cheapest) seafood.

Several street names around town commemorate the skirmish that ensued after Japanese troops landed on 8 December 1941: Phithak Chat (Defend Country), Salachip (Sacrifice Life) and Suseuk (Fight Battle).

Information

Bangkok Bank (cnr Th Maitri Ngam & Th Sarachip)
Police station (Th Kong Kiat) Just west of Th Sarachip.
Post office (cnr Th Maitri Ngam & Th Suseuk) By the telephone office.
Prachuap Video (Th Sarachip; per hr 30B; 🕙 9am-9pm) For internet access; near Th Maitri Ngam.
Thai Farmers Bank (Th Phitak Chat) Just north of Th Maitri Ngam.
Tourist office (☎ 0 3261 1491; Th Chai Thaleh; 🕙 8.30am-4.30pm) At the northern end of town. The staff speak English.

Sights & Activities

Visible from almost anywhere in Prachuap Khiri Khan is **Khao Chong Krajok** (Mirror Tunnel Mountain – named after the hole in the mountain that appears to reflect the sky). At the top of a long flight of stairs up the small mountain is **Wat Thammikaram**, established by Rama VI. From here there are perfect views of the town and the bay – even the border with Myanmar, just 11km away. Along the way you'll be entertained by hordes of monkeys. At the base of the mountain, the more fastidious monkeys bathe in a small pool.

Continue 4km north along the beach road and you'll come to the small village of **Ao Bang Nang Lom**, where wooden fishing vessels are still made using traditional Thai methods. The industrious folk here also catch a fish called *blah ching chang*, which they dry and store for Sri Lankan traders. A couple of kilometres north of Ao Bang Nang Lom is another bay, **Ao Noi**, with a small fishing village and the comfortable Aow Noi Sea View hotel (p566).

Six kilometres south of the city is island-dotted **Ao Manao**, a scenic bay ringed by a clean white-sand beach. A Thai air-force base guards access to the bay and every week the beach is given a military-grade clean up. There are several *săh·lah* here, along with a hotel and restaurant. You can rent chairs, umbrellas and inner tubes, and buy food and drink, while Thailand's Top Guns relax on a golf course and driving range. The beach itself is around 3km past the base entrance, where you may need to show your passport. The beach closes at 8pm.

Around 9km south of Ao Manao, **Hat Wa Kaw** is a pleasant casuarina-lined beach that's even quieter and cleaner than Ao Manao. Here you'll find the **King Mongkut Memorial Park of Science & Technology** (☎ 0 3266 1098; admission free; ⏰ 8.30am-4.30pm), which commemorates the 1868 solar eclipse that the king and his 15-year-old son Prince Chulalongkorn came south to witness. Unfortunately, not much is translated into English, but there is a good aquarium.

Sleeping

Development is coming slowly to Prachuap, and a few recent guesthouse openings have improved the level of accommodation. Bump up from budget to midrange and you should score yourself sea views and bright rooms. Head north and south for a few interesting places to stay on quieter beaches.

Yuttichai Hotel (☎ 0 3261 1055; 115 Th Kong Kiat; r 150-200B) A simple budget option, with cold-water showers, close to the train station. The cheapest rooms share baths, and there's one air-con room for 400B. The cafe downstairs has decent coffee and smells like incense.

Hadthong Hotel (☎ 0 3260 1050; www.hadthong.com; 21 Th Suseuk; r 700-1100B; ❄ ⌨ 🖥) Some rooms at this multistorey hotel have been updated with new flooring, though others still have tired carpeting. The staff are friendly and knowledgeable, and can help you plan your day in town. Budget rooms in the dungeon, er, basement go for 500B.

Sun Beach Guesthouse (☎ 0 3260 4770; www.sunbeach-guesthouse.com; 160 Th Chai Thaleh; r 800-1000B; ❄ 🖥) Neoclassical styling and bright yellow paint liven things up, while the rooms are super-clean and come with large verandahs. Frolic in the pool or Jacuzzi while gazing out to sea.

Prachuap Beach Hotel (☎ 0 3260 1288; 123 Th Suseuk; r 900-1000B; ❄ ⌨) PKK's newest hotel has crisp white linens and splashy accent walls for a bit of flair. One side has fabulous sea views, while the other has decent, though not exciting, mountain views.

NORTH OF TOWN

One kilometre north of town (just across the bridge) is a quiet beach which gets lots of Thai visitors at the weekend.

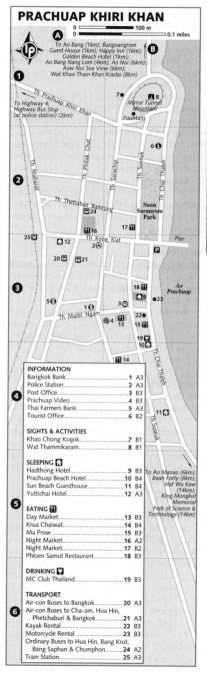

PRACHUAP KHIRI KHAN

UPPER SOUTHERN GULF

Happy Inn (☎ 0 3260 2082; 149-151 Th Suanson; bungalows 500B) Simple bungalows (no hot showers) face each other along a brick drive, and the two at the end have wooden charm and hang over the canal. The highlight here – besides the shy, friendly staff – is a sitting area over the mangrove-lined water.

Golden Beach Hotel (☎ 0 3260 1626; 113-115 Th Suanson; r 500-1200B; ☒) There's a range of rooms here; for 750B you can have picture windows as well as views of both the sea *and* the canal. For 500B you're looking at the parking garage. However, all rooms come with tiled showers and cane furniture.

Bangnangrom Guest House (☎ 0 3260 4841; 137 Th Suanson; r 700-1000B; ☒) Seven rooms are furnished in light wood, while painted brick decorates the roomy showers. All have air-con and tellies.

AO NOI BEACH
Heading 5km north from town, you reach Ao Noi Beach, where there's a small market and blue fishing boats cluttered at the southern end.

Aow Noi Sea View (☎ 0 3260 4440; www.aownoiseaview.com; 202/3 Mu 2; r 800B; ☒) A three-storey beachfront hotel that has sea breezes, large bathrooms and linen drying on the line outside.

AO KHLONG WAN
To the south of town is Ao Khlong Wan.

Baan Forty (☎ 0 3266 1437; www.baanfortyresort.com; 555 Th Prachuap-Khlong Wan; bungalows 800-1200B; ☒) Spend your nights in concrete bungalows on a private beach, and spend your days relaxing on the sand or in the shady garden waiting for another huge meal. The friendly owner arranges tours and will hire you bicycles or motorbikes.

Eating & Drinking
Because of its reputation for fine seafood, Prachuap Khiri Khan has many restaurants. A local specialty is *bˈlah săm·lee dàat dee·o* – whole cotton fish that's sliced lengthways and left to dry in the sun for half a day. It's then fried quickly and served with mango salad. It may sound awful, but the taste is sublime. An all-day market lines the street on Th Maitri Ngam, starting early in the morning. There are two excellent night markets; the more atmospheric is opposite the pier, but both are good with lots of different stalls.

Phloen Samut Restaurant (☎ 0 3261 1115; 44 Th Chai Thaleh; dishes 50-120B; ☽ breakfast, lunch & dinner) One of a few seafood restaurants along the promenade, with sea views and loads of seafood, this is a good option. The service would be better if the staff stopped watching Thai soap operas on the telly.

Ma Prow (☎ 08 5293 7278; 48 Th Chai Thaleh; dishes 80-160B; ☽ lunch & dinner) An airy wooden pavilion across from the beach that cooks up excellent *bˈlah săm·lee dàat dee·o*. The music is an intriguing mix of Western and Thai – kind of like the clientele you'll see here on a busy weekend.

Krua Chaiwat (☎ 0 3260 4534; 143/1 Th Sarachip; dishes 80-220B; ☽ breakfast, lunch & dinner) High ceilings and tiered floors appeal to those looking for a little ambience with their Thai food. The coffee isn't bad, either.

MC Club Thailand (Th Chai Thaleh; ☽ noon-late) Half-heartedly decorated with motorcycle memorabilia (look for the single tyre), this bar is a good place to kick-start a big night in PKK. During the high season, the club sets up on the promenade beside the beach.

Getting There & Away
There are frequent air-con buses to/from Bangkok (190B to 256B, five hours), Hua Hin (80B, 1½ hours), Cha-am (90B, 2½ hours) and Phetchaburi (95B to 105B, three hours) leaving from Th Phitak Chat near the centre. For southern destinations such as Phuket or Krabi, hike 2km northwest out to the police station on the highway to catch passing buses (motorcycle taxis will take you for 40B to 50B). Ordinary (slow) buses to Hua Hin (60B), Bang Krut (50B), Bang Saphan Yai (60B) and Chumphon (155B, 3½ hours) leave from the southeast corner of Ths Thetsaban Bamrung and Phitak Chat.

There are frequent train services to/from Bangkok (2nd class 210B to 357B, 3rd class 168B, six hours). A 1st-class express departs Hualamphong at 7.30pm (1100B, 5¼ hours). Trains also run to Ban Krut (one hour), Bang Saphan Yai (1½ hours) and Chumphon (two hours).

Getting Around
Prachuap is small enough to get around on foot, but you can hop on a motorcycle taxi around town for 20B to 30B. Other destinations include Ao Noi and Ao Manao (50B). At Ao Manao motorcycles aren't permitted past

---

DETOUR: DAN SINGKHON BORDER MARKET

Southwest of Prachuap Khiri Khan, near the narrowest slice of Thailand's trim waist (12km from the coast to the border), is the Burmese border town of Dan Singkhon. Once a strategic military point, Dan Singkhon is now home to a more peaceful trade: the selling of orchids.

Beginning at dawn on Saturday mornings, Burmese appear, almost mysteriously, from a bend in the road just beyond the checkpoint, pushing handcarts piled high with the usual market fare, with the exception, of course, of orchids. Hanging from wooden frames, dripping from pots and spread across fabric on the ground, orchids in various stages of bloom fill the tiny valley on the Thai side of the border.

There's not much here for tourists to buy and the plants generally don't travel well in suitcases, so you'll probably only be window shopping. However, the market has a festive vibe, with music blaring, colourful umbrellas lining the road and thatch 'sales booths' hidden under palms. You'll need to arrive before noon to enjoy it, as the market closes at midday.

To get to Dan Singkhon from Prachuap Khiri Khan, head south on Hwy 4. After several kilometres you'll see a sign for Dan Singkhon; from here you'll head west about 15km before reaching the border.

---

the gate unless both driver and passenger are wearing helmets.

You can hire motorbikes in front of the Hadthong Hotel for 250B per day. The roads in the area are very good and it's a great way to see the surrounding beaches.

Kayaks are available for hire at a pet supplies store near the Hadthong Hotel. A two-person kayak is 100B per hour, and a trip to the nearby islands should take around three hours.

AROUND PRACHUAP KHIRI KHAN
Wat Khao Tham Khan Kradai
วัดเขาถ้ำคานกระได

About 8km north of town, following the road beyond Ao Noi, is this small cave wát at one end of **Ao Khan Kradai** (also known as Ao Khan Bandai) – a long, beautiful bay. A trail at the base of the limestone hill leads up and around the side to a small cavern and then to a larger one that contains a reclining Buddha. If you have a torch you can proceed to a larger second chamber also containing Buddha images. From this trail you get a good view of Ao Khan Kradai. The beach here is suitable for swimming and is usually deserted. A motorcycle ride here costs 50B.

HAT BAN KRUT & BANG SAPHAN YAI
หาดบ้านกรูด/บางสะพานใหญ่

These two low-key destinations lie about 80km and 100km south of Prachuap Khiri Khan, respectively, and are a popular weekend and holiday destination for Thai tourists. During the week you'll have the beaches largely to yourself and a few long-tail boats.

The main beach of **Hat Ban Krut** is along a road, making the 10km beach handy to cars and services, but detracting from a 100% peaceful beach experience. North of the headland topped by the Disneyland-like spires of **Wat Tan Sai**, you'll find **Hat Sai Kaew**, which is quieter but slightly out of the way, making it a better beach experience.

Bo Thong Lang is a little cove where the still water stays clear year-round – it's good for swimming. There's a small wát and a couple of food stalls, though it's difficult to ignore the smell from the fishery nearby.

Bang Saphan Yai, 20km south of Ban Krut, is now experiencing development and there is good budget accommodation here. Islands off the coast to the south, including **Ko Thalu** and **Ko Sing**, offer good snorkelling and diving from the end of January to mid-May. Coral Hotel and Suan Luang Resort (p568) in Bang Saphan Yai can arrange half-day diving excursions to these islands.

A couple of waterfalls decorate the area; **Nam Tok Sai Ku** tumbles into a valley spotted with pineapple farms.

When booking transport, don't confuse Bang Saphan Yai with Bang Saphan Noi, which is a fisherman's village 15km further south.

Sleeping
HAT BAN KRUT

You'll struggle to find true budget options here, but if you visit on a weekday you should secure a discount of 20% to 30%. Bicycles

(100B per day) and motorcycles (300B per day) can be hired to see the surrounding area, and most accommodation places arrange snorkelling trips (350B to 450B) to nearby islands.

On the beach road south of the wát-topped headland, **Ban Klang Aow Beach Resort** (☎ 0 3269 5086; www.baanklangaowresort.com; bungalows incl breakfast 2300-3800B; ❄ ⬜ ⬚) has 79 one- and two-bedroom bungalows with large verandahs, hidden in leafy glades. Bicycles, kayaks and two swimming pools will get you hungry for your next meal at the resort's restaurant.

The following places are on Hat Sai Kaew, north of the headland. Count on running up a substantial tab on motorcycle taxis if you want to frequent the wider range of restaurants on the main beach. An alternative is to hire your own two wheels.

Ban Kruit Youth Hostel (☎ 0 3261 9103; www.thailandbeach.com; dm 350-400B, bungalows 600-2600B; ❄ ⬚) More like a resort than a hostel, this place has bungalows in a wide range of sizes. The cheapest are wooden huts with shared bathroom, and the ritzy beachfront ones have TV, air-con and hot water. Cheaper dorm rooms are available in the main building. There's lots of greenery beside the long empty beach, a postage stamp–sized pool, and plenty of activities on offer. Breakfast is included and YHA cardholders get a discount.

Bayview Beach Resort (☎ 0 3269 5566; www.bayviewbeachresort.com; bungalows 1700-4800B; ❄ ⬚) Sharing the same beach as the youth hostel, Bayview has fine bungalows amid shady grounds with a beachside pool. The spick-and-span bungalows range from small wooden numbers to large concrete ones with huge bay windows.

BANG SAPHAN YAI
There is accommodation on the beaches north and south of town. To the north are mainly midrange places, while to the south there is one flash resort and a few budget-priced bungalows. A good source of local information is www.bangsaphanguide.com; it's worth checking out before your trip.

North of Town
Van Veena Hotel (☎ 0 3269 1251; www.vanveena.com; r 400-800B; ❄) The rooms are unexciting but undeniably spacious, though the carpeted ones have a bit of a funky smell. Downstairs

there is a well-stocked minimart and across the road is a beachfront restaurant.

Sailom Resort (☎ 0 3269 1003; www.sailombangspahan.com; r 1900B; ❄ ⬚) Soft lighting, house plants, and large verandahs – add these to a curved swimming pool, sleek decor, and grounds that look like a mini-golf course, and you've got one of the sweetest spots on the beach.

South of Town
The following are about 5km south of town. There is more budget accommodation here than on the northern beach or at Hat Ban Krut.

Patty Hut (☎ 08 6171 1907; bungalows 300-700B; ❄) This funky spot is right behind the Coral Hotel. The more-expensive rooms are a bargain, while the cheaper ones have mattresses on the floor. This is one place where you can both eat dinner with the family and get a tattoo. Bus stop pick-ups and drop-offs available.

Suan Luang Resort (☎ 0 3281 7031; www.suanluang.com; bungalows 480-680B; ❄) Run by a young, hip family, Suan Luang has simple wooden bungalows with fans or air-con concrete ones with TV and hot water. You're 700m from the beach, but it's a pleasant jungle walk down a quiet road. The excellent restaurant serves Thai and French food, and there are day trips to waterfalls and parks on offer.

Coral Hotel (☎ 0 3281 7121; www.coral-hotel.com; 171 Mu 9; r 1525B, bungalows 2700-5400B; ❄ ⬜ ⬚) Set amid a coconut grove, this upmarket French-managed hotel is right on the beach. There's a huge pool, three restaurants and all rooms have TV, fridge and hot water. Fill your days with water-sports or exploring the area on an organised tour. Four-person bungalows are also available for families.

Along the beach north of Coral Hotel are several simple bungalow operations, where you can get a simple hut with a corrugated roof for around 300B.

Getting There & Around
Buses depart at least once daily from Bangkok's southern bus terminal to Ban Krut (315B, five hours) and Bang Saphan Yai (315B, six hours). Get a direct bus, otherwise you may be left on Hwy 4 (Th Phetkasem) and will need to get a motorbike taxi to the beaches (70B). Frequent buses run from Prachuap Khiri Khan to Ban Krut (50B) and Bang Saphan Yai (60B), and

a local bus (20B) trundles from Ban Krut to Bang Saphan Yai.

Ban Krut and Bang Saphan Yai are both on Thailand's southern railway line and there are at least daily departures to/from Chumphon, Prachuap Khiri Khan, Hua Hin and Bangkok. Ban Krut's train station is 4km from the beach and in Bang Saphan Yai you'll be dropped off in town. In both places you'll need to hire a motorcycle taxi (around 70B) to get to the beach.

Getting around can be a problem, as there's not much public transport between the beaches. Once you get to them, most resorts hire out motorcycles for around 300B per day, and the roads are decent for driving.

CHUMPHON PROVINCE

CHUMPHON

ชุมพร

pop 48,571

Chumphon features as a blip on many travellers' itinerary as they flit in and out of the busy transport hub en route to Ko Tao, or head west for Ranong and Phuket. Around 500km south of Bangkok, Chumphon is where southern Thailand begins and you'll begin to see mosques and start to hear different dialects.

While there's not a lot in town to keep you amused, the surrounding beaches are good places to step off the backpacker bandwagon for a few days. **Hat Tha Wua Laen** (12km

north of town) is renowned for windsurfing and kiteboarding, and has a developing travellers' scene with some good bungalows and beachside bars. Pretty **Hat Sairi** (21km east of town) is a more traditional Thai beach resort, and the best spot to arrange day trips to offshore islands.

When you're ready to move on again, Chumphon's array of enterprising travel agencies (below) can help you book transport to Ko Tao, as well as bus and train connections further south to Krabi and Surat Thani.

Information

There are banks along Th Sala Daeng with exchange facilities and ATMs.

Bangkok Bank (Th Sala Daeng) Has an ATM.

CAT office (Th Poramin Mankha) About 1km east of the post office; sells good international phone cards.

CS Leisure Travel (☎ 0 7750 3001; www.cslchumphon .com; 68/10 Th Tha Taphao; ☿ 8am-10pm) Food and drink, travel information and internet. Its website is an excellent resource for information on Chumphon and the surrounding area.

DK Book Store (☎ 0 7750 3876; Soi Sala Daeng; ☿ 8am-9pm) Carries a few titles in English, including Lonely Planet books.

Main post office (Th Poramin Mankha) In the southeastern part of town.

New Infinity Travel (☎ 0 7750 1937; new_infinity@ hotmail.com; 68/2 Th Tha Taphao; ☿ 8am-10pm) Folks here are knowledgeable and friendly, and they'll sell you paperbacks, book your travel and rent you one of four rooms. Also has wi-fi and terminal internet access.

Songserm (☎ 0 7750 6205; off Th Tha Taphao) Book your Songserm Express tickets directly here.

THE THAI CANAL

Egypt has the Suez Canal, the Panama Canal joins the Atlantic and Pacific oceans, and a waterway linking the Gulf of Thailand with the Andaman Sea has been discussed for more than 350 years.

At its narrowest point just south of Chumphon, the Isthmus of Kra (the land bridge joining mainland Asia and the Malay Peninsula) is only 44km wide. In 1677 and 1793 Thai kings championed the idea, but the technology of the times was not up to scratch. When Burma (now Myanmar) became a British colony in 1863 the idea was floated again and Ferdinand de Lesseps, the successful engineer behind the Suez Canal, visited the area in 1882. By 1897 Singapore was an important regional trading hub, and Thailand and Britain agreed to shelve any canal plans.

During the 20th century the idea surfaced again, but the preferred site was moved south to join Nakhon Si Thammarat and Trang. In 1985 a Japanese design planned to use more than 20 nuclear devices to complete the excavation work, and most recently China has planned a US$25 billion Thai canal to secure a regional strategic and commercial advantage. The US is apparently watching very closely.

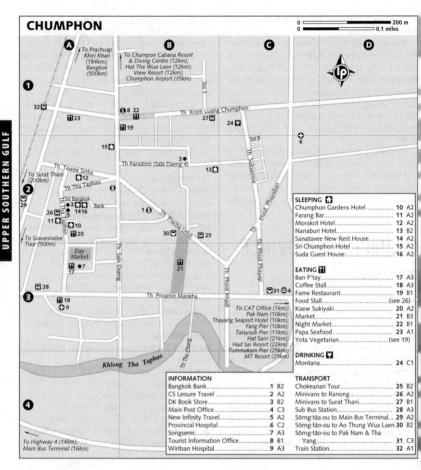

CHUMPHON

SLEEPING
Chumphon Gardens Hotel	**10** A2
Farang Bar	**11** A2
Morakot Hotel	**12** A2
Nanaburi Hotel	**13** B2
Sanatavee New Rest House	**14** A2
Sri Chumphon Hotel	**15** A2
Suda Guest House	**16** A2

EATING
Ban P'tay	**17** A3
Coffee Stall	**18** A3
Fame Restaurant	**19** B1
Food Stall	(see 26)
Kaew Sukiyaki	**20** A2
Market	**21** B3
Night Market	**22** A1
Papa Seafood	**23** A1
Yota Vegetarian	(see 19)

DRINKING
Montana	**24** C1

INFORMATION
Bangkok Bank	**1** B2
CS Leisure Travel	**2** A2
DK Book Store	**3** B2
Main Post Office	**4** C3
New Infinity Travel	**5** A2
Provincial Hospital	**6** C2
Songserm	**7** A3
Tourist Information Office	**8** B1
Wiritsan Hospital	**9** A3

TRANSPORT
Chokeanan Tour	**25** B2
Minivans to Ranong	**26** A2
Minivans to Surat Thani	**27** B1
Sub Bus Station	**28** A3
Sŏrng·tăa·ou to Main Bus Terminal	**29** A2
Sŏrng·tăo·ou to Ao Thung Wua Laen	**30** B2
Sŏrng·tăo·ou to Pak Nam & Tha Yang	**31** C3
Train Station	**32** A1

Tourist Information Office (☎ 0 7750 4833;
cnr Th Sala Daeng & Th Krom Luang Chumphon;
⊙ 8.30am-4.30pm) Speaks OK English but supplies good
information, especially about transport to/from Chumphon.
Wiratsin Hospital (☎ 0 7750 3238; Th Poramin
Mankha) Privately owned; handles emergencies.

Festivals & Events

From mid-March to the end of April the
Chumphon Marine Festival features folk-art exhibits, free shrimp, a windsurfing competition
at Hat Thung Wua Laen and a marathon. In
October, the five-day **Lang Suan Buddha Image
Parade & Boat Race Festival** includes a procession
of temple boats and a boat race on Mae Nam
Lang Suan (Lang Suan River), about 60km
south of Chumphon.

Sleeping

Instead of jumping on the next boat to Ko Tao
or the overnight train back to Bangkok, consider breaking your journey on the beaches
at Hat Thung Wua Laen or Hat Sairi. Since
most people overnighting in Chumphon are
backpackers on the way to Ko Tao, accommodation is budget priced and usually a good
deal. Most guesthouses (and restaurants) book
tickets to Ko Tao – the reason behind the common greeting, 'Hello, where you go?'

BUDGET

Sanatavee New Rest House (☎ 0 7750 2147; 4 Soi
Bangkok Bank; r 150-250B) If Suda's two doors down
is full, check the four rooms here. They're
small but clean, and have fans and shared

bath. The owners occasionally roast coffee in the back yard and the smell can be pungent.

Farang Bar (☎ 0 7750 1003; farngbar@yahoo.com; 69/36 Th Tha Taphao; r 150-300B; 🖳) A basic backpacker dive. Many travellers will find themselves deposited here for an hour or two after an all-night bus from Khao San Rd en route to Ko Tao. Rooms are ramshackle but the stone showers (for nonguests 20B) give an unexpected (and unintentional, we're sure) spa-like feel. The restaurant isn't worth bothering about.

ourpick Suda Guest House (☎ 0 7750 4366; 8 Soi Bangkok Bank; r 200-500B; 🕄) Suda, the friendly English-speaking owner, proudly advertises 'Probably the best guesthouse in town' from an earlier edition of this guidebook. She's maintaining her impeccable standards in six rooms with wooden floors and a few nice touches, such as soap in the showers, that you wouldn't expect for the price. It's very popular so phone ahead.

Sri Chumphon Hotel (☎ 0 7751 1280; Th Sala Daeng; r 280-600B; 🕄) The dark hallways feel like lights out at Alcatraz, and the rooms are a bit scruffy. Some are more cheerful than others, with wood floors and furniture, so look at a couple before deciding.

Morakot Hotel (☎ 0 7750 3629; fax 0 7757 0196; 102-112 Th Tawee Sinka; r 420-540B; 🕄) Despite a strange location behind a motorcycle dealership, the young, friendly staff make this a welcoming place. The rooms are a bit worn but bright, and the upper floors have lovely views of Chumphon and the hills around it.

Chumphon Gardens Hotel (☎ 0 7750 6888; 66/1 Th Tha Taphao; r 490B; 🕄) This recently refurbished place with spacious rooms including cable TV is excellent value – as is the 80B breakfast.

View Resort (Hat Thung Wua Laen, r 500-700B; 🕄) The nicest of a few simple bungalow operations on Hat Thung Wua Laen, the View has a good selection of fan and air-con rooms and a good restaurant.

MIDRANGE
Nanaburi Hotel (☎ 0 7750 3888; 355/9 Th Paradorn; r/ste 700/1500B; 🕄) Chumphon's newest hotel is an excellent deal, and the sleek, polished rooms come with breakfast. Though the decor is grey, black and white, rooms higher up look out to green-clad hills.

Had Sai Resort (☎ 0 7755 8028; www.hadsairesort.com; Hat Sairi; bungalows 800-2000B; 🕄) The concrete rooms are small, but the couple of bungalows on a hillside feel like tree houses. It's at the

quieter end of Hat Sairi and is a good jumping-off point for day trips to nearby islands.

MT Resort (☎ 0 7755 8153; www.mtresort-chumphon.com; Hat Tummakam Noi; bungalows incl breakfast 950-1250B; 🕄) This friendly spot on a quiet beach beside the Lomprayah ferry pier is a good place to break your journey before or after Ko Tao. Free kayaks are provided to explore offshore islands and the mangroves of the nearby Mu Ko Chumphon National Park. There's no public transport and a taxi from Chumphon will cost around 350B. Call to organise transport.

Chumphon Cabana Resort & Diving Centre (☎ 0 7756 0245; www.cabana.co.th; Hat Thung Wua Laen; r & bungalows 1500-2300B; 🕄 🖳) This place tumbles across haphazardly gardened grounds. The tangle of greenery and somewhat institutional buildings belie snazzy and immaculate rooms. There's a giant swimming pool (and PADI courses on offer) and a little one for the kiddos. Of the 20 bungalows, two are wheelchair-accessible. A private shuttle bus (150B) runs to/from Chumphon.

Eating & Drinking
Chumphon's **night market** (Th Krom Luang Chumphon) is excellent, with a huge variety and good street lighting. Come for the delicious food and linger for good photographs. Two other markets run during the day.

Beside Farang Bar on Th Tha Taphao, there is an unnamed food stall that sets up nightly at 4pm. Look for the white plastic furniture. A couple of curries with rice costs 30B. Near the corner of Th Tha Taphao and Th Poramin Mankha, a coffee stall selling Chinese doughnuts (10B) opens at dawn.

Yota Vegetarian (Th Sala Daeng; dishes 20-90B; 🍽 7am-5pm) Located beside Fame Restaurant, this hole-in-the-wall eatery has delicious self-serve vegetarian dishes. Add your own touch with overflowing plates of Vietnamese mint, holy basil and sliced cucumber.

Ban P'Tay (☎ 0 7757 0580; 45/9 Th Tha Taphao; coffee 40B; 🍽 breakfast & lunch; 🖳) An air-conditioned little cafe and bakery with sweet treats, iced coffees and giggly teenage employees. There are internet terminals and you can log on to the wi-fi network.

Kaew Sukiyaki (☎ 0 7750 6366; Th Tha Taphao; dishes 40-240B; 🍽 breakfast, lunch & dinner) Sukiyaki noodles of all kinds (cooked at your table) are the specialty here, and you can eat inside a cool room or in the large outdoor pavilion. The bar is popular with both locals and travellers.

UPPER SOUTHERN GULF

Papa Seafood (☎ 0 7750 4504; 2-2/1 Th Krom Luang Chumphon; dishes 70-150B; ☺ lunch & dinner) The food (mainly seafood, obviously) is good, without being exceptional, but it's a popular local hang-out. Next door is Papa 2000; after you've downed a few beers with your meal, you can head over to the sparkly discotheque and dance off your dinner.

Fame Restaurant (☎ 0 7757 1077; 188/20 Th Sala Daeng; dishes 80-220B; ☺ breakfast, lunch & dinner) Despite also being called Khao San Restaurant, (gee, I wonder who they're targeting), Fame has excellent Western breakfasts, tasty sandwiches using freshly baked bread, and real-deal cheeses like mozzarella and gorgonzola. Mmmm. A travel agency is attached, so you might get the hard sell mid-sandwich.

Montana (☎ 0 7750 2864; 116 Th Suksamoe; ☺ 6pm-1am) This bar has relatively authentic Western decor including stuffed animal heads (don't worry, they're fake), Budweiser neon and nightly gigs with the Big Boss Blues Band from 9.30pm. In the kitchen there are no concessions to the West with a zingy Thai menu.

Getting There & Away
BOAT
You have many options for getting to the small island of Ko Tao (p610), as several piers service different types of boats. Most travel agencies provide free transfers for all but the slowest, cheapest ferries. Following is a summary of your numerous options.

Tha Yang pier is 10km from Chumphon, while Talaysub is 1km past that; Talaysub is often lumped with Tha Yang. From Tha Yang a slow night boat (200B, six hours) departs at midnight. If you fancy sleeping on the deck of a slow boat and a lovely moon is out, this could be a memorable trip. However, if it's raining or the seas are rough, it could be a long and uncomfortable night. It's a gamble.

A car ferry leaves Tha Yang at 11pm (with cabin 300B, six hours). It's possible to get a bunk or mattress on this boat, making it a more comfortable (and fun) option than the other night ferry.

From Talaysub, the Songsrem Express (450B, 2½ hours) departs at 7am.

The **Lomprayah express catamaran** (www.lomprayah.com) leaves Tummakam pier (25km from town) at 7am and 1pm (550B, 1½ hours).

Seatran Discovery runs a catamaran out of Pak Nam pier (or Seatran Jetty), 10km from Chumphon, at 7am (550B, two hours).

A shared taxi to Tha Yang pier costs 50B. *Sŏrng·tǎa·ou* to Tha Yang and Pak Nam piers are 30B.

If you get stuck at Tha Yang pier and don't want to return to Chumphon, try the **Thayang Seaport Hotel** (☎ 0 7755 3052; r 200-450B; ☒).

BUS
The main bus terminal is on the highway, 16km from Chumphon. To get there you can catch a local bus or *sŏrng·tǎa·ou* (30B) from Th Nawaminruamjai. There's a small 'sub bus station' on Th Poramin Mankha, though there are plans to move it next to the train station. These also stop at the main bus terminal.

Much more convenient is **Chokeanan Tour** (☎ 0 7751 1757; Th Pracha Uthit), in the centre of town, with six buses a day to Bangkok (air-con 375B, VIP 419B to 550B) or **Suwannatee Tour** (☎ 0 7750 4901), 700m southeast of the train station, with 12 departures per day (2nd class/air-con/VIP 310/398/464B). Most Bangkok buses stop in town so get off there and save yourself the *sŏrng·tǎa·ou* fare from the bus station. Ask the driver or local passengers to tell you where to disembark.

Other destinations from Chumphon include Hua Hin (165B to 230B, five hours), Bang Saphan Yai (100B, two hours), Prachuap Khiri Khan (120B to 160B, 3½ hours), Ranong (100B to 110B, three hours), Surat Thani (170B, 3½ hours), Krabi (270B, eight hours), Phuket (320B, seven hours) and Hat Yai (310B to 350B, seven hours). Tickets can be bought at travel agencies.

TRAIN
There are frequent services to/from Bangkok (2nd class 292B to 382B, 3rd class 235B, 7½ hours). Overnight sleepers range from 440B to 770B.

Southbound rapid and express trains – the only trains with 1st and 2nd class – are less frequent and can be difficult to book out of Chumphon from November to February.

Getting Around
Sŏrng·tǎa·ou and motorcycle taxis around town cost 30B and 20B respectively per trip. *Sŏrng·tǎa·ou* to Hat Sairi and Hat Thung Wua Laen cost 30B.

Motorcycles can be hired at travel agencies and guesthouses for 200B to 250B per day. Car hire costs around 1500B per day from travel agencies or from Suda Guest House (p571).

Lower Southern Gulf

It really isn't fair – there are over 200 countries around the globe and Thailand has managed to snag a disproportionate amount of the world's top beaches. These creamy stretches of sand undulate along the paper-thin coast, and scallop tonnes of jungly bumps out at sea. They're everywhere. So how are we ever supposed to choose from these honey-tinged paradises when every acre boasts enough beach options to give Goldilocks a complex?

It's simple. If you're plagued by indecision, head here – to Thailand's lower southern gulf, and follow three simple steps to reach your ultimate beach-holiday nirvana.

Step 1. Before hitting the waves, start below the surface. Ko Tao is the ultimate playground for scuba neophytes, sporting shallow reefs teeming with slippery reef sharks, skulking stingrays and radiant blooms of waving coral.

Step 2. Now that you've swum with the fishes, it's time to drink like one. Ko Pha-Ngan has long been synonymous with white nights, and on the eve of every full moon, pilgrims pray to party gods with trance-like dancing, glittery body paint and bucket-sized beverages.

Step 3. An intensive detox session is a must after your lunar romp. Ko Samui is the ultimate place to pamper yourself silly, and five-star luxury is the name of the game.

If the triple threat of gulf island paradises didn't quite do the trick, then add on one of Ang Thong Marine National Park's 40-odd islets. Each craggy fleck peppering the azure ocean boasts sandy bays that gingerly await your footprint. This ethereal realm, forever immortalised in backpacker lore, is the last frontier for unbridled castaway fantasies.

LOWER SOUTHERN GULF

HIGHLIGHTS

- Finding Nemo in the technicolour kingdom off the coast of **Ko Tao** (p610)

- Dimpling the virgin sands on the hidden bleach-blonde beaches of **Ang Thong Marine National Park** (p623)

- Joining the masses of party pilgrims and trancing the night away at the Full Moon party on **Ko Pha-Ngan** (p595)

- Purring like a kitten during a five-star massage session on **Ko Samui** (p575)

- Smiling while spotting an elusive pink dolphin gliding along the shores of **Ao Khanom** (p627)

★ Ko Tao

Ang Thong Marine ★ Ko Pha-Ngan
National Park ★   ★ Ko Samui

★ Ao Khanom

| ■ BEST TIME TO VISIT: DECEMBER–APRIL | ■ POPULATION: 2.46 MILLION |

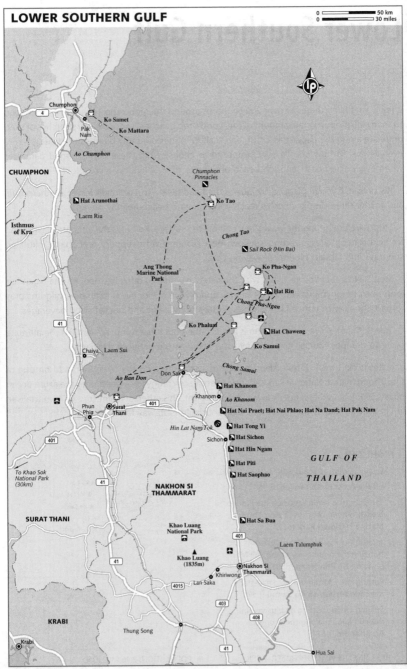

LOWER SOUTHERN GULF

0 ——— 50 km
0 ——— 30 miles

Chumphon

Ko Samet

Pak Nam

Ko Mattara

Ao Chumphon

CHUMPHON

Chumphon Pinnacles

Hat Arunothai

Ko Tao

Laem Riu

Isthmus of Kra

Chong Tao

Sail Rock (Hin Bai)

Ang Thong Marine National Park

Ko Pha-Ngan

Hat Rin

Chong Pha-Ngan

Ko Phalui

Hat Chaweng

Ko Samui

Chaiya

Laem Sui

Chong Samui

Ao Ban Don

Don Sak

Hat Khanom

Khanom

Ao Khanom

Phun Phin

Surat Thani

Hat Nai Praet; Hat Nai Phlao; Hat Na Dand; Hat Pak Nam

Hin Lat Nam Tok

Hat Tong Yi

Sichon

Hat Sichon

Hat Hin Ngam

GULF OF

Hat Piti

Hat Saophao

THAILAND

NAKHON SI THAMMARAT

SURAT THANI

Hat Sa Bua

Khao Luang National Park

Laem Talumphuk

To Khao Sok National Park (30km)

Khao Luang (1835m)

Khiriwong

Nakhon Si Thammarat

Lan Saka

KRABI

Thung Song

Krabi

Hua Sai

LOWER SOUTHERN GULF

Climate

The best time to visit the Samui islands is during the hot, dry season from February to April. From May to October, during the southwest monsoon, it can rain intermittently, and from October to January, during the northeast monsoon, there can be strong winds. However, many travellers have reported sunny weather (and fewer crowds) in September and October. November tends to get some of the rain that affects the east coast of Malaysia at this time.

The overall lack of tourism south of the Samui archipelago can be explained by the fact that the southwestern Gulf's best season (climatically) runs from April to October – the exact opposite of Thailand's typical tourist season (which coincides with the European and North American winter).

National Parks

There are a couple of notable parks in this region.

Ang Thong Marine National Park (p623), the setting for the perfect beach in the movie *The Beach* (although much of the movie was actually filmed on Ko Phi-Phi Leh; see p697), is a stunning archipelago of 40 small jagged limestone islands.

Khao Luang National Park (p631) is known for its beautiful mountain and forest walks, waterfalls and fruit orchards. It is also home to a variety of elusive animals, from clouded leopards to tigers.

Getting There & Away

Travelling to the lower southern Gulf is fairly straightforward. It's extremely easy to hop on a bus or a train in Bangkok and then catch a ferry to the Gulf islands. Several daily flights connect Bangkok, Phuket and Pattaya to Ko Samui. Bus and train travel from Bangkok is generally cheap, relatively efficient and mostly takes place overnight.

Getting Around

Numerous boats shuttle back and forth between Ko Samui, Ko Pha-Ngan, Ko Tao and Surat Thani, while buses and trains link Surat Thani with destinations further south. Consider using the port in Chumphon (p569) to access the Gulf islands from the mainland.

SURAT THANI PROVINCE

Surat Thani Province features southern Thailand's ultimate holiday trifecta, Ko Samui, Ko Pha-Ngan and Ko Tao – three idyllic island paradises hidden behind dozens of jagged islets peppered throughout the stunning Ang Thong Marine National Park.

KO SAMUI

เกาะสมุย

pop 45,800

At first glance, Ko Samui could be mistaken for a giant golf course floating in the Gulf of Thailand. The greens are perfectly manicured, sand traps are plentiful, and there's a water hazard or two thrown in for good measure. Middle-aged men strut about donning white polo shirts that contrast with their cherry-red faces, while hired help carry around their stuff. But Samui is far from being an adults-only country club – a closer look reveals steaming street-side food stalls, 2am jet-setter parties, secreted Buddhist temples, and backpacker shanties plunked down on a quiet stretch of sand.

Ko Samui is a choose-your-own-adventure kinda place that strives, like a genie, to grant every tourist their ultimate holiday wish. You want ocean views, daily massages and personal butlers? Poof – here are the keys to your private poolside villa. It's a holistic aura-cleansing vacation you're after? Shazam – take a seat on your yoga mat before your afternoon colonic. Wanna party like a rock star? Pow – trance your way down the beach with the throngs of whisky bucket–toting tourists.

Beyond the merry-making machine, the island will also offer interested visitors a glimpse into local life. Chinese merchants from Hainan Island initially settled Samui and today these unique roots have blossomed into a small community that remains hidden beneath the glossy holiday veneer.

Orientation

Ko Samui is quite large – the ring road around the island is almost 100km long. The island has been blessed with picturesque beaches on all four sides. The most crowded are Hat Chaweng (Map p582) and Hat Lamai (Map p584), both on the eastern side of the island.

The beaches on the island's north coast including Choeng Mon, Mae Nam, Bo Phut (Map p587), Bang Po and Big Buddha Beach (Bang

Rak) are starting to become busy as well, but the prices are still decent, and secluded nooks can still be found. For a quieter experience, try the secluded beaches along the southern coast, and western shore south of Na Thon.

Information
BOOKSHOPS
There are several places around the island where you can snag a paperback to read in your hammock. Many hotels also have libraries or book trades.

Bookazine (Map p582; ☎ 0 7741 3616; Hat Chaweng; ⏰ 10am-11pm) Chain outlet selling new books, magazines and loads of Lonely Planet guides.

EMERGENCY
Tourist police (Map p577; ☎ 0 7742 1281, emergency 1155) Based at the south of Na Thon.

IMMIGRATION OFFICES
During high season, the Bangkok Samui Hospital also has an immigration booth and can offer small extensions on tourist visas.
Immigration Office (Map p577; ☎ 0 7742 1069; ⏰ 8.30am-noon & 1-4.30pm Mon-Fri) Offers seven-day tourist visa extensions. Located about 2km south of Na Thon.

INTERNET ACCESS
There are countless places all over the island for internet access, even at the less popular beaches. Prices range from 1B to 2B per minute. Keep an eye out for restaurants that offer complementary wi-fi service.

INTERNET RESOURCES
The following websites cover dive centres, accommodation and tours. They also have transport timetables.
Sawadee.com (www.samui.sawadee.com)
Tourism Association of Koh Samui (www.samui tourism.com)

MEDIA & MAPS
The Siam Map Company puts out quarterly booklets including *Spa Guide*, *Dining Guide* and an annual directory that lists thousands of companies and hotels on the island. Its *Siam Map Company Samui Guide Map* is fantastic, free and easily found throughout the island. *Essential* (www.essential-samui .com) is a pocket-size pamphlet focused on promoting Samui's diverse activities. *Samui Guide* looks more like a magazine and features mostly restaurants and attractions.

MEDICAL SERVICES
Ko Samui has four private hospitals, all near the Tesco-Lotus supermarket on the east coast, where most of the tourists tend to gather. The government hospital in Na Thon has seen significant improvements in the last couple of years but the service is still a bit grim since funding is based on the number of Samui's legal residents (which doesn't take into account the heap of illegal Burmese workers).

Bangkok Samui Hospital (Map p582; ☎ 0 7742 9500, emergency 0 7742 9555) Your best bet for just about any medical problem.

Hyperbaric Chamber (Map p577; ☎ 0 7742 7427; Big Buddha Beach) The island's dive medicine specialists.

Samui International Hospital (Map p582; ☎ 0 7742 2272; www.sih.co.th; Hat Chaweng) Emergency ambulance service is available 24 hours and credit cards are accepted. Near the Amari Resort in Chaweng.

MONEY
Changing money isn't a problem on the east and north coasts, and in Na Thon. Multiple banks and foreign-exchange booths offer daily exchange services and there's an ATM every couple of hundred metres.

POST
In several parts of the island there are privately run post office branches charging a small commission. You can almost always leave your stamped mail with your accommodation.
Main post office (Na Thon) Near the TAT office; not always reliable.

TOURIST INFORMATION
Tourist Authority of Thailand office (TAT; ☎ 0 7742 0504; Na Thon) At the northern end of Na Thon; is friendly, helpful and has handy brochures and maps.

TRAVEL AGENCIES
Basically every resort and bungalow operation has travel services that can book you on tours and transport. Booking directly with a tour operator will usually save you a few baht.

Dangers & Annoyances
As on Phuket, the rate of road accident fatalities on Samui is quite high. This is mainly due to the large number of tourists who rent motorcycles only to find out that the winding roads, sudden tropical rains and frenzied traffic can be lethal. If you decide to rent a motorcycle, protect yourself by wearing a

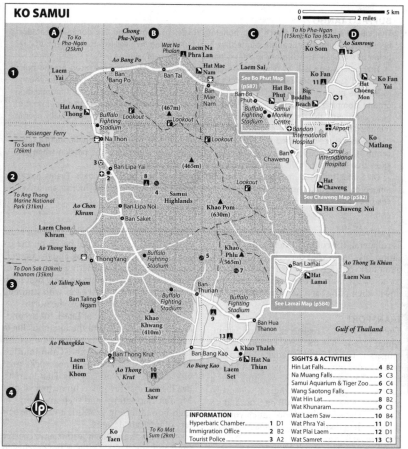

KO SAMUI

SIGHTS & ACTIVITIES		
Hin Lat Falls	4	B2
Na Muang Falls	5	C3
Samui Aquarium & Tiger Zoo	6	C4
Wang Saotong Falls	7	C3
Wat Hin Lat	8	B2
Wat Khunaram	9	C3
Wat Laem Saw	10	B4
Wat Phra Yai	11	D1
Wat Plai Laem	12	D1
Wat Samret	13	C3

INFORMATION		
Hyperbaric Chamber	1	D1
Immigration Office	2	B2
Tourist Police	3	A2

LOWER SOUTHERN GULF

helmet, and ask for one that has a plastic visor. Shoes and appropriate clothing are also a must when driving – jeans will save you from skinning your knees if you wipe out. Even if you escape unscathed from a riding experience, we've heard reports that some shops will claim that you damaged your rental and will try to extort some serious cash from you. Car rental is another option on the island – we suggest leasing a vehicle from a reputable and internationally recognised name brand.

Lately, jet-ski rentals are the newest avatar of the motorbike scam. Incidents of injury on these water scooters are high, and leasers will claim that you damaged their goods in order to collect some extra money.

Another scam that's rapidly gaining popularity involves time-shares. It's best to avoid anyone who approaches you offering a vacation deal that seems too good to be true.

Beach vendors are registered with the government and should all be wearing a numbered jacket. No peddler should cause an incessant disturbance – seek assistance if this occurs.

Theft is a continuing problem, particularly around the more populated parts of the island like Chaweng and Lamai. If you're staying in a beach bungalow, consider depositing your valuables with the management while on excursions around the island or while you're swimming at the beach. Consider asking for a receipt listing the items stored with the staff.

BUFFALO TANGO

Thai villagers just love to watch their buffaloes tussle. You won't find any pompous matadors here though – unlike its Spanish counterpart, Thai bullfighting involves two male water buffaloes being pitted against each other in a fairly harmless contest of wills.

Thai bullfighting is known to take on circus proportions. Flowers are placed on the bull's horns and sacred ropes are hung around their necks. The animals are then released to engage in a battle of wits, attempting to establish territory with shows of bravado and intimidating ground-stomping. Eventually the two contestants will lock horns and connect in a brief bout of head-wrestling – the first animal to turn and run is declared the loser. Fights are usually over in minutes and the animals are rarely injured.

Crowds get seriously riled up and wild hollering is the norm when a popular animal takes centre stage. Gambling is a big sideline activity – you can understand the passion when you know that millions of baht might be hanging on the outcome.

On Samui, bullfights mostly take place during festivals and public holidays. Events are arranged on a rotating basis at several rustic fighting rings around the island. Tourists are usually charged about 200B to 500B.

Lastly, never give your passport to anyone as collateral. If a company demands identification, give them your driver's license or any other form of ID. A fraudulent operation can try to extort money from you, or track you down when filing for a new passport.

TRANSPORT

There are over 400 registered taxis on Samui, which means that the competition for passengers is fierce. Unlike Bangkok, cabs will refuse to use their meters so you must *always* negotiate your price before stepping into a cab. A 35B taxi ride in Bangkok will probably set you back about 350B on Samui. It's a flagrant crime, but there's not much you can do other than taking a *sŏrng·tăa·ou* (also spelt *săwngthăew*) instead.

Take care when making train and bus reservations: bookings are sometimes not made at all, or the bus turns out to be far inferior to the one expected. In another scam involving air tickets, agents claim that the economy class seating is fully booked and force tourists to book in business class. When the customer boards the plane, they find out that they've been allotted an economy seat but paid for a first-class ticket.

Sights

Even though the island has over 500 resorts, there are still some interesting things hidden amongst the island's three million coconut palms.

Ko Samui is one of Thailand's premiere beach destinations and there's a reason why

Chaweng is the most popular spot – it's the longest and most beautiful beach on the island. The sand is powder soft and the water is surprisingly clear, considering the number of boats and bathers. Picture opps are best from the southern part of the beach, with stunning views of the hilly headland to the north.

At the southern end of **Lamai**, the second-largest beach, you'll find the infamous **Hin Ta** and **Hin Yai** (Map p584) stone formations (also known as Grandfather and Grandmother Rocks). These genitalia-shaped rocks provide endless mirth to giggling Thai tourists. **Hua Thanon**, just beyond, is home to a vibrant Muslim community, and their anchorage of high-bowed fishing vessels is a veritable gallery of intricate designs.

Although the **northern beaches** have coarser sand and aren't as striking as the beaches in the east, they have a laid-back vibe and stellar views of Ko Pha-Ngan. **Bo Phut** stands out with its charming Fisherman's Village: a collection of narrow Chinese shophouses that have been transformed into trendy resorts and boutique hotels.

Many visitors spend the day on the wild, rugged beaches of **Ang Thong Marine Park** (p623). This stunning archipelago might just have the most beautiful islands in all of Thailand.

WATERFALLS

At 30m, **Nam Tok Na Muang** (Map p577) is the tallest waterfall on Samui and lies in the centre of the island about 12km from Na Thon. The water cascades over ethereal purple rocks, and there's a great pool for swimming at the base. This is the most scenic, and somewhat less frequented, of Samui's falls. There are two other waterfalls in the vicinity; a smaller waterfall called Na Muang 2, and recently improved road conditions have also made it possible to visit the high drop at **Nam Tok Wang Saotong**. These chutes are situated just north of the ring road near Hua Thanon.

Nam Tok Hin Lat (Map p577), near Na Thon, is worth visiting if you have an afternoon to kill before taking a boat back to the mainland. After a mildly strenuous hike over streams and boulders, reward yourself with a dip in the pool at the bottom of the falls. Keep an eye out for the Buddhist temple that posts signs with spiritual words of moral guidance and enlightenment. Sturdy shoes are recommended.

WÁT

For temple enthusiasts, **Wat Laem Sor** (Map p577), at the southern end of Samui near Ban Phang Ka, has an interesting, highly venerated old Srivijaya-style stupa. At Samui's northern end, on a small rocky island linked by a causeway, is **Wat Phra Yai** (Temple of the Big Buddha; Map p577). Erected in 1972, the modern Buddha (sitting in the Mara posture) is 15m high and makes an alluring silhouette against the tropical sky and sea. Nearby, a new temple, **Wat Plai Laem** (Map p577), features an enormous 18-armed Buddha.

On the eastern part of Samui, near the waterfalls of the same name, **Wat Hin Lat** (Map p577; ☎ 0 7742 3146) is a meditation temple that teaches daily *vipassana* (Buddhist meditation) courses. Several temples have the mummified remains of pious monks including **Wat Khunaram** (Map p577), which is south of Rte 4169 between Th Ban Thurian and Th Ban Hua. The monk, Luang Phaw Daeng, has been dead for over two decades but his corpse is preserved sitting in a meditative pose and sporting a pair of sunglasses.

At **Wat Samret** (Map p577), near Th Ban Hua, you can see a typical Mandalay sitting Buddha carved from solid marble – a common sight in India and northern Thailand, but not so common in the south.

Activities
DIVING

If you're serious about diving, head to Ko Tao and base yourself over there for the duration of your diving adventure. If you're short on time and don't want to leave Samui, there are plenty of operators who will take you to the same dive sites (at a greater fee, of course). Try to book with a company that has its own boat (or leases a boat) – it might be slightly more expensive, but you'll be glad you did it. Companies without boats often shuttle divers on the passenger catamaran to Ko Tao, where you board a second boat to reach your dive site. These types of trips are arduous, mealless and rather impersonal.

Certification courses tend to be twice as expensive on Ko Samui as they are on Ko Tao, this is largely due to use of extra petrol, since tiny Tao is significantly closer to the preferred diving locations. You'll drop between 16,000B and 22,000B on an Open Water certification, and figure between 3200B and 6200B for a diving day trip depending on the location of the site.

The island's hyperbaric chamber is at Big Buddha Beach (Hat Bang Rak). The following dive operators are recommended:

100 Degrees East (☎ 0 7742 5936; www.100degrees east.com; Hat Bang Rak) Highly recommended.

Calypso Diving (Map p582; ☎ 0 7742 2437; www .calypso-diving.com; Chaweng)

Discovery Dive Centre (Map p582; ☎ 0 7741 3196; www.discoverydivers.com; Hat Chaweng) Based at the Amari Resort.

Samui Planet Scuba (SIDS; Map p582; ☎ 0 7723 1606; samuiplanetscuba@planetscuba.net; Chaweng)

OTHER WATER ACTIVITIES

For those interested in snorkelling and kayaking, book a day trip to the stunning **Ang Thong Marine National Park** (p623). **Blue Stars Kayaking** (Map p582; ☎ 0 7741 3231; www.bluestars.info), based in Chaweng on Ko Samui, offers guided sea-kayak trips (2000B) in the park.

For some instant gratification, head to Chaweng, from where you can hire sailboats, catamarans, snorkelling gear, boats for waterskiing and so forth. Be wary of scams involving jet-ski rentals, see p577 for details.

SPA & YOGA

Competition for Samui's five-star accommodation is fierce, which means that their spas are of the highest calibre. Pick up the Siam Map Company's free booklet, *Spa Guide* (www.siamspaguide.com), for a detailed catalogue of the top centres on the island. The following list of resort-affiliated retreats includes some of the finest places to be pampered on Samui (if not the world).

TOP FIVE TOP-END SLEEPS

Samui is the place to splurge, and there is no shortage of five-star accommodation that will make you feel like royalty. These are our faves:

- **Sila Evason Hideaway** (p585)
- **Library** (p583)
- **Anantara** (p586)
- **Baan Taling Ngam** (p588)
- **Zazen** (p586)

For top-notch pampering, try the spa at Anantara (p586), the Hideaway Spa at the Sila Evason Hideaway (p585), or the wellness centre at Tamarind Springs (p584).

The newly opened **Absolute Sanctuary** (☎ 0 7760 1190; www.absoluteyogasamui.com) is a wellness resort near the airport offering detox programs and every type of yoga under the sun.

The Spa Resort (p583), in Lamai, is the island's original health destination, and is still known for its effective 'clean me out' fasting regime.

Courses

The **Samui Institute of Thai Culinary Arts** (SITCA; Map p582; ☎ 0 7741 3434; www.sitca.net; Hat Chaweng) has daily Thai-cooking classes, and courses in the aristocratic Thai art of carving fruits and vegetables into intricate floral designs. Lunchtime classes begin at 11am, while dinner starts at 4pm (both cost 1850B for a three-hour course with three or more dishes). Of course you get to eat your projects, and even invite a friend along for the meal. DVDs with Thai cooking instruction are also available so you can practise at home.

The Health Oasis Resort (p588) offers one-to eight-day courses and certification in Thai and Swedish massage, aromatherapy, reiki, meditation and yoga for between 5500B and 9000B. The length and tuition of all courses can be adjusted to suit the individual.

Volunteering

Donations of time and/or money are hugely appreciated at the aptly named **Dog Rescue Centre Samui** (☎ 0 7741 3490; www.samuidog.org). The organisation has played an integral role in keeping the island's dog population under control through an active spaying and neutering program. The centre also vaccinates dogs against rabies. Volunteers are always needed to take care of the pooches at either of the kennel/clinics (located in Chaweng and Taling Ngam). Call the centre for volunteering details or swing by the Wave Samui (opposite) for additional info.

See p48 and p52 for more information about volunteering in Thailand.

Sleeping

'Superior', 'standard', 'deluxe', 'standard deluxe', 'deluxe superior', 'superior standard' – what does it all mean? Trying to decode Samui's obnoxious hotel lingo is like trying to decipher the ancient Mayan language (it can't be done). The island's array of sleeping options is overwhelming – we've compiled a list of our favourites, but the following inventory is by no means exhaustive.

If you're looking to splurge, there is definitely no shortage of top-end resorts sporting extravagant bungalows, charming spas, private infinity pools and first-class dining. Bo Phut, on the island's northern coast, has a charming collection of boutique lodging – the perfect choice for midrange travellers. Backpack-toting tourists will have to look a little harder, but budget digs do pop up once in a while along all of the island's beaches.

Private villa services have become quite popular in recent years. Rental companies often advertise in the various tourist booklets that circulate on the island.

This large section is organised as follows: we start on the popular east coast with Chaweng and Lamai, then move anticlockwise around the island covering the smaller beaches. These tinier areas are grouped according to location – Bo Phut and Choeng Mon, for example, are subcategories under 'Northern Beaches', and so forth.

CHAWENG

Packed end-to-end with hotels and bungalows, this beach is the eye of the tourist storm. The main street in central Chaweng feels like a nondescript soi (lane) in the heart of Bangkok. Despite the chaos, there's a striking stretch of beach, and most resorts are well protected from street noise. In the last couple of years, the beach has experienced a bit of a renaissance – new budget spots are opening their doors (although prices are still a bit high relative to the rest of the island), and previously derelict areas are getting facelifts. At the south end of the beach, a small headland separates a sliver of sand (called Chaweng Noi) from the rest of the hustle.

Budget

Green Guest House (Map p582; ☎ 0 7742 2611; www .greenguestsamui.com; r 400-1000B; ✷ ▣) If penny-pinching is your game, you won't find anything cheaper than Green, although there isn't much in the way of atmosphere…

Wave Samui (Map p582; ☎ 0 7723 0803; www .thewavesamui.com; r from 400B; ✷) The only place in Chaweng with a true backpacker vibe, the Wave is a friendly spot with a bright blue library-cum-restaurant and stack of well-maintained bedrooms upstairs. Book ahead – this place is popular!

Lucky Mother (Map p582; ☎ 0 7723 0931; r & bungalows 500-1500B; ✷) First, let's take a moment to giggle at the resort's name. OK, now we can appreciate the old utilitarian huts, a dying breed in Chaweng. For those wanting hot showers and air-con, modern hotel rooms are also available, but most of them look out onto a parking lot.

P Chaweng (Map p582; ☎ 0 7723 0684; r 700B; ✷) This cheapie doesn't even pretend to be close to the beach, but the pink-tiled rooms are spacious and squeaky clean (minus a couple of bumps and bruises on the wooden furniture). Pick a room facing away from the street – it seems a tad too easy for someone to slip through an open window and pilfer your stuff.

Queen Boutique Resort (Map p582; ☎ 0 7741 3148; queensamui@yahoo.com; Soi Colibri; s/d from 600/800B; ✷ ▣) Yes, these rooms really are less than 1000B (although probably not for long)! Queen is a brand new place to hang your hat and is luring travellers by the boatload with boutique digs at backpacker prices.

Jungle Club (off Map p582; ☎ 0 1894 2327; bungalows 600-2900B; villas 3500B; ✷ ▣ ♨) The perilous drive up the slithering dirt road is totally worthwhile once you get a load of the awesome views from the top. This isolated mountain getaway is a huge hit amongst locals and tourists alike. There's a relaxed back-to-nature vibe – guests chill around the stunning horizon pool or tuck themselves away for a catnap under the canopied roofs of an open-air *săh·lah* (often spelt *sala*). Call ahead for a pick-up; you don't want to spend your precious jungle vacation in a body cast.

Midrange

Chaweng Center Hotel (Map p582; ☎ 0 7741 3747; chawengcenter@hotmail.com; r 1200B; ✷ ▣) Although the views of McDonald's across the street are far from charming, this central cheapie has freshly refurbished rooms that are well-priced and pull off 'minimal-chic' instead of feeling spartan.

Akwa (Map p582; ☎ 08 4660 0551; www.akwaguest house.com; r 999-2599B; ✷ ▣) A charming B&B-style sleeping spot, Akwa has a few funky rooms decorated with bright colours.

our pick **Ark Bar** (Map p582; ☎ 0 7742 2047; www .ark-bar.com; bungalows 1600-2500B; ✷ ♨) You'll find two of every creature at Ark Bar – hardcore partiers, chilled-out hippies, teenagers, 40-somethings, even Canadians. Sky-blue motel units run along the thin verdant strip connecting the Bangkokian streets of Chaweng to the wildly popular restaurant-bar on the beach.

Chaweng Garden Beach (Map p582; ☎ 0 7796 0394; www.chawenggardnessamui.com; r from 1600B; ✷ ▣ ♨) A popular 'flashpacker' choice, this campus of accommodation has a large variety of room types serviced by an extra-smiley staff.

Nora Chaweng (Map p582; ☎ 0 7791 3666; www .norachawenghotel.com; r from 2500B; ✷ ▣ ♨) It's not on the beach, but this new addition to the Chaweng bustle has a great price-to-comfort ratio.

Corto Maltese (Map p582; ☎ 0 7723 0041; www.corto -samui.com; r 2000-4000B; tr 3000B; ✷ ♨) Owned by a Frenchman, this place looks like it just fell out of a comic book – maybe *Tintin and the Mystery of Surprisingly Cheap Accommodation in Chaweng?* Rooms are outfitted with cheerful pastels, wooden moulding and the occasional stone feature. It's not the best place on Chaweng, but it's definitely a spot you'll remember.

Tango Beach Resort (Map p582; ☎ 0 7742 2470; www.tangobeachsamui.com; r incl breakfast 2650-6250B; ✷ ▣ ♨) A midrange all-star, the newly completed Tango features a string of bungalows arranged along a teak boardwalk that meanders away from the beach.

Top End

Baan Chaweng Beach Resort (Map p582; ☎ 0 7742 2403; www.baanchawengbeachresort.com; bungalows 4000-7000B; ✷ ▣ ♨) A pleasant option for those who want top-end luxury without the hefty bill, Baan Chaweng is one of the new kids on the block and is keeping the prices relatively low. The immaculate rooms are painted in various

LOWER SOUTHERN GULF

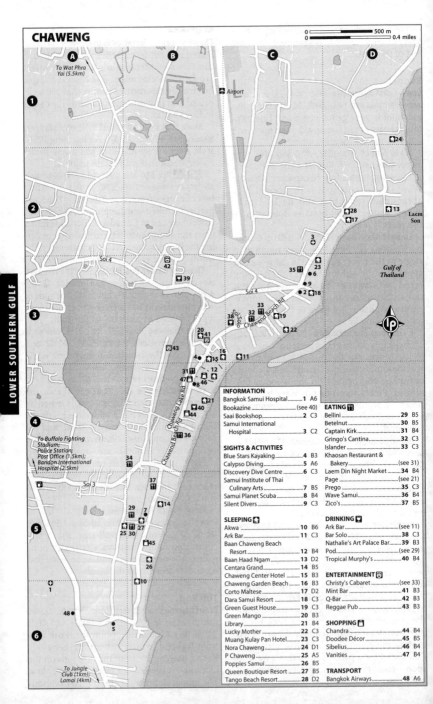

CHAWENG

0   500 m
0   0.4 miles

To Wat Phra
Yai (5.5km)

Airport

Laem
Son

Gulf of
Thailand

Soi 4

Soi 4

Chaweng Beach Rd

Chaweng Beach Rd

Chaweng Lake Rd

To Buffalo Fighting
Stadium;
Police Station;
Post Office (1.5km);
Bandon International
Hospital (2.5km)

Soi 3

To Jungle
Club (1km);
Lamai (4km)

INFORMATION
Bangkok Samui Hospital...........**1** A6
Bookazine.............................(see **40**)
Saai Bookshop...........................**2** C3
Samui International
　Hospital.................................**3** C2

SIGHTS & ACTIVITIES
Blue Stars Kayaking..................**4** B3
Calypso Diving..........................**5** A6
Discovery Dive Centre..............**6** C3
Samui Institute of Thai
　Culinary Arts.........................**7** B5
Samui Planet Scuba...................**8** B4
Silent Divers.............................**9** C3

SLEEPING
Akwa......................................**10** B6
Ark Bar...................................**11** C3
Baan Chaweng Beach
　Resort..................................**12** B4
Baan Haad Ngam.....................**13** D2
Centara Grand.........................**14** B5
Chaweng Center Hotel.............**15** B3
Chaweng Garden Beach............**16** B3
Corto Maltese..........................**17** D2
Dara Samui Resort...................**18** C3
Green Guest House..................**19** C3
Green Mango...........................**20** B3
Library....................................**21** B4
Lucky Mother..........................**22** C3
Muang Kulay Pan Hotel............**23** C3
Nora Chaweng.........................**24** D1
P Chaweng..............................**25** A5
Poppies Samui.........................**26** B5
Queen Boutique Resort............**27** B5
Tango Beach Resort.................**28** D2

EATING
Bellini.....................................**29** B5
Betelnut..................................**30** B5
Captain Kirk............................**31** B4
Gringo's Cantina......................**32** C3
Islander...................................**33** C3
Khaosan Restaurant &
　Bakery.............................(see **31**)
Laem Din Night Market............**34** B4
Page.................................(see **21**)
Prego......................................**35** C3
Wave Samui.............................**36** B4
Zico's......................................**37** B5

DRINKING
Ark Bar..............................(see **11**)
Bar Solo..................................**38** C3
Nathalie's Art Palace Bar.........**39** B3
Pod....................................(see **29**)
Tropical Murphy's....................**40** B4

ENTERTAINMENT
Christy's Cabaret.................(see **33**)
Mint Bar..................................**41** B3
Q-Bar......................................**42** B3
Reggae Pub.............................**43** B3

SHOPPING
Chandra..................................**44** B4
Doodee Décor.........................**45** B5
Sibelius...................................**46** B4
Vanities...................................**47** B4

TRANSPORT
Bangkok Airways......................**48** A6

shades of peach and pear, with teak furnishings that feel both modern and traditional.

Muang Kulay Pan Hotel (Map p582; ☎ 0 7723 0849-51; www.kulaypan.com; r incl breakfast 4725-13540B; ❄ 💻 🏊) No, that's not a rip in the wallpaper – it's all part of the design concept. The architect cites a fusion between Zen and Thai concepts, but we think the decor is completely random. The seaside grounds have been purposefully neglected to lend an additional sense of chaos to this unique resort.

Baan Haad Ngam (Map p582; ☎ 0 7723 1500, 0 7723 1520; www.baanhaadngam.com; bungalows 6400-14000B; ❄ 💻 🏊) Vibrant Baan Haad Ngam shuns the usual teak and tan – every exterior is painted in an interesting shade of green, like radioactive celery. It's sassy, classy and a great choice if you've got the dime.

Poppies Samui (Map p582; ☎ 0 7742 2419; www.poppies samui.com; r 7000-11000B; ❄ 💻 🏊) After passing through the marble lobby, a small staircase suddenly opens onto a tropical paradise that feels miles away from busy Chaweng. The charming bungalows lie hidden in the brush – only the opulent arched roofs poke through from the patchwork of climbing ferns. Small presents, such as designer soaps, are placed on the beds during the nightly turn-down service.

Dara Samui (Map p582; ☎ 0 7723 1323; www.darasamui.com; r & bungalows from 8160B; ❄ 💻 🏊) Inserted in the middle of Chaweng's seamless chain of accommodation, Dara can feel a tad cramped but the rooms are elegant and the pool area looks like a scene from a Rudyard Kipling novel.

Centara Grand (Map p582; ☎ 0 7723 0500; www.centralhotelsresorts.com; r 8900-19,500B; ❄ 💻 🏊) Centara is a massive, manicured compound in the heart of Chaweng, but the palm-filled property is so large that you can safely escape the streetside bustle. Rooms are found in a hotel-like building that is conspicuously Western in theme and decor. Grown-ups can escape to the spa, or one of the four restaurants, and leave the children at the labyrinth of swimming pools under the watchful eye of an in-house babysitter.

our pick **Library** (Map p582; ☎ 0 7742 2407; www.thelibrary.name; bungalows 9000-12,000B; ❄ 💻 🏊) This place is too cool for school, which is ironic since it's called 'The Library'. The entire resort is a sparkling white mirage accented with black trimming and slatted curtains. Besides the futuristic iMac computer in each

page (rooms are called 'pages' here), our favourite feature is the large monochromatic wall art – it glows brightly in the evening and you can adjust the colour depending on your mood. Life-size statues are engaged in the act of reading, and if you too feel inclined to pick up a book, the on-site library houses an impressive assortment of colourful art and design books. The large rectangular pool is not to be missed – it's tiled in piercing shades of red, making the term 'bloodbath' suddenly seem appealing.

LAMAI

Ten years ago, people in the know used to say 'skip Chaweng and head to Lamai', but these days Lamai has become the island's has-been and the unofficial HQ of Samui's girly bar scene. South of Lamai, Hua Thanon is a small, quieter beach with a couple of standout resorts.

Budget & Midrange

New Hut (Map p584; ☎ 0 7723 0437; newhut@hotmail.com; Lamai North; huts 200-500B) New Hut is a rare beachfront cheapie with tiny-but-charming A-frame huts. The wooden structures, including the welcoming restaurant, are covered with layers of thick black paint.

Beer's House (Map p584; ☎ 0 7723 0467; Lamai North; bungalows 200-550B) These tiny shade-covered bungalows are lined up right along the sand. Some huts have a communal toilet, but all have plenty of room to sling a hammock and laze the day away. Those with their own bathroom have freshly retiled surfaces.

Sunrise Bungalow (Map p584; ☎ 0 7742 4433; www.sunrisebungalow.com; Lamai South; bungalows 400-1300B; ❄) Steps away from the awkward giggles at Hin Ta and Hin Yai (the island's infamous genital-shaped rocks), Sunrise offers budget travellers a relaxing place to hang their backpack. The owner is a sixth-generation Samui native.

Amity (Map p584; ☎ 0 7742 4084; bungalows 350-1500B; ❄) Amity offers alluring modern bungalows and a few ramshackle cheapies with shared bathroom – there's no theme, just a mishmash of accommodation that changes style depending on the price range (we liked the 700B huts). The air-con cottages are a welcome addition to the repertoire.

Spa Resort (Map p584; ☎ 0 7723 0855; www.spasamui.com; Lamai North; bungalows 900-3500B; ❄) This health spa has a bevy of therapeutic programs on

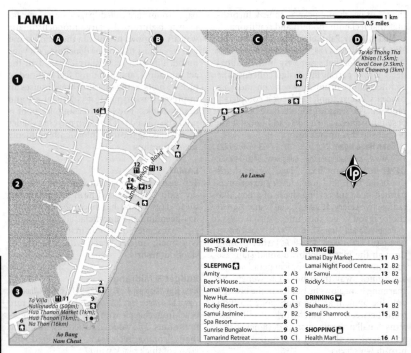

LAMAI

SIGHTS & ACTIVITIES	
Hin-Ta & Hin-Yai **1** A3	

SLEEPING	
Amity **2** A3
Beer's House **3** C1
Lamai Wanta **4** B2
New Hut **5** C1
Rocky Resort **6** A3
Samui Jasmine **7** B2
Spa Resort **8** C1
Sunrise Bungalow **9** A3
Tamarind Retreat **10** C1

EATING	
Lamai Day Market **11** A3
Lamai Night Food Centre **12** B2
Mr Samui **13** B2
Rocky's .... (see 6)

DRINKING	
Bauhaus **14** B2
Samui Shamrock **15** B2

SHOPPING	
Health Mart **16** A1

offer, and no one seems to mind that the lodging is cheap by Lamai's standards. Programs include colonics, massage, aqua detox, hypnotherapy and yoga, just to name a few. The bathrooms leave a bit to be desired, but who needs a toilet when you're doing a week-long fast? Accommodation tends to book up quickly, so it's best to reserve in advance (via email). Nonguests are welcome to partake in the programs.

Lamai Wanta (Map p584; ☎ 0 7742 4550, 0 7742 4218; www.lamaiwanta.com; r & bungalows 1600-3400B;) The pool area feels a bit retro, with its swatch book of beige- and blue-toned tiles, but in the back there are modern motel rooms and bungalows with fresh coats of white paint. On the inside, rooms tread a fine line between being minimal and sparse.

Top End
Samui Jasmine Resort (Map p584; ☎ 0 7723 2446; www.samuijasmineresort.com; r & bungalows 3800-5000B;) Pleasant Samui Jasmine is a great deal along Lamai's sun-bleached sands. Go for the lower-priced rooms – most have excellent views of the ocean and the crystal-coloured

lap pool. The design scheme features plenty of varnished teak and frilly accessories such as lavender pillows.

Tamarind Retreat (Map p584; ☎ 0 7723 0571; www.tamarindretreat.com; villas 3500-11,600B;) Tucked far away from the beach within a silent coconut palm plantation, Tamarind's small collection of villas are each elaborated with a different design schema. Some have granite boulders built into walls and floors; others offer private ponds or creative outdoor baths. There's a seven-night minimum stay (three nights in low season) and free pick-up at the airport is included. Advance reservations are a must.

our pick Rocky Resort (Map p584; ☎ 0 7741 8367; www.rockyresort.com; Hua Thanon; r 4200-14000B;) Our favourite spot in Lamai (well, actually just south of Lamai), Rocky finds the right balance between an upmarket ambience and an unpretentious, sociable atmosphere. During the quieter months the prices are a steal, since ocean views abound, and each room has been furnished with beautiful Thai-inspired furniture that seamlessly incorporates a modern twist. The pool has been carved in between a collection of boulders mimicking the rocky beach nearby (hence the name).

Villa Nalinnadda (off Map p584; ☎ 0 7723 3131; www.nalinnadda.com; Hua Thanon; bungalows 6000-6500B; 🅿 🄼) Villa Nalinnadda's exterior walls are swathed in undulating waves of white adobe that mimic the bubbling water in the rectangular plunge pool. Seven suites of various shapes and sizes face out towards the swaying ocean offering a blend of romantic solitude while also fostering a convivial atmosphere amongst guests.

NORTHERN BEACHES

Ko Samui's northern beaches have the largest range of accommodation. Choeng Mon has some of the most opulent resorts in the world, while Mae Nam and Bang Po cling to their backpacker roots. Bo Phut, in the middle, is the shining star in Samui's constellation of beaches.

Choeng Mon

While technically known as Plai Lam, this rugged outcropping is often called Choeng Mon after the largest beach in the area. If you happen to be the CEO of a Fortune 500 company, Choeng Mon is where you'll stay. These resorts are locked in an unwavering battle to out-posh one another.

Imperial Boat House Hotel (☎ 0 7742 5041-52; www .imperialhotels.com; Hat Choeng Mon; r 4000-5500B, boat ste 6000-6700B; 🅿 🄼) This sophisticated retreat has a three-storey hotel and several free-standing bungalows made from imported-teak rice barges whose bows have been transformed into stunning patios. Oxidised copper cannons blast streams of water into the boat-shaped swimming pool.

White House (☎ 0 7724 7921, 0 7724 5318; www .hotelthewhitehouse.com; r 5000-6600B; 🅿 🄼) You can check Angkor Wat off your 'to do' list – The White House feels like the seat of an ancient empire hidden deep within the thickest jungle. Sandstone temples bleed luscious tropical ferns from every crevice, and praying deity statues hide amongst the twisting jungle foliage.

Sala Samui (☎ 0 7724 5888; www.salasamui.com; bungalows US$360-1100; 🅿 🄼 🄼) Look out folks, these guys quote their room rates in US dollars instead of baht. Is the hefty price tag worth it? Probably. The design scheme is undeniably exquisite – regal whites and lacquered teaks are generously lavished throughout, while

subtle turquoise accents draw on the colour of each villa's private plunge pool.

Tongsai Bay (☎ 0 7724 5480-5500; www.tongsaibay .co.th; Hat Choeng Mon; ste 11,000-30,000B; 🅿 🄼) Expansive and impeccably maintained, the hilly grounds make the cluster of bungalows look more like a small village. Golf carts whiz around the vast landscape transporting guests to various activities like massages or dinner. All the split-level suites have day-bed rest areas, gorgeous romantic decor, stunning views, large terraces and creatively placed bathtubs (you'll see). Facilities include salt- and freshwater pools, a tennis court, the requisite spa, a dessert shop and several restaurants.

our pick **Sila Evason Hideaway** (☎ 0 7724 5678; www.sixsenses.com/hideaway-samui/index.php; bungalows from 17,000B; 🅿 🄼 🄼) Set along a rugged promontory, Sila Evason strikes the perfect balance between opulence and rustic charm, and defines the term 'barefoot elegance'. Most of the villas have stunning concrete plunge pools and offer magnificent views of the silent bay below. The regal, semi-outdoor bathrooms give the term 'royal flush' a whole new meaning. Beige golf buggies move guests between their hidden cottages and the stunning amenities strewn throughout the property – including a world-class spa and two excellent restaurants.

Big Buddha Beach (Bang Rak)

This area gets its moniker from the huge golden Buddha that acts as overlord from the small nearby quasi-island of Ko Fan. Its proximity to the airport means lower prices at the resorts.

Shambala (☎ 0 7742 5330; www.samui-shambala .com; bungalows 600-1000B; 🄼) While surrounding establishments answer the call of upmarket travellers, this laid-back, English-run place is a backpacking stalwart with a subtle hippy feel. There's plenty of communal cushion seating, a great wooden sun-deck, and the bungalows are bright and roomy. Staff doles out travel tips and smiles in equal measure.

Samui Mermaid (☎ 0 7742 7547; www.samui-mer maid.info; r 400-2500B; 🅿 🄼 🄼) Samui Mermaid is a great choice in the budget category because it feels like a full-fledged resort. There are two large swimming pools, copious beach chairs, two lively restaurants and every room has cable TV. The landing strip at Samui's airport is only a couple of kilometres away, so sometimes there's noise, but free airport transfers sweeten the deal.

Maya Buri (☎ 0 7748 4656, 08 1539 4194; www.maya buri.com; r incl breakfast 1200-1600B; ✖ 🖳 ☲) Maya Buri's inland location near the airport means that these boutique bungalows would be four times more expensive if they were situated along Chaweng. The modern resort has been designed with finesse – airy rooms, stocked with teak furniture, are focused around a cooling infinity pool.

Ocean 11 (☎ 0 7741 7118; www.o11s.com; bungalows 1900-3200B; ✖) A little slice of luxury at a very reasonable price, Ocean 11's 'residences' are a steal (get it?!). Silly film references aside, this mellow spot with modern designer details is a great midrange getaway along a relatively quiet patch of sand. Free wi-fi available.

Prana (☎ 0 7724 6362; www.pranaresorts.com; r 5600-8000B; ✖ 🖳 ☲) Vegetarians unite! This trendy crash-pad is the ultimate retreat for those who shun the carnivorous lifestyle. Beautiful oceanfront bedrooms extend along the beach beyond the infinity-edge lap pool.

Bo Phut

The beach isn't breathtaking, but Bo Phut has the most dynamic lodging in all of Samui. A string of vibrant boutique cottages starts deep within the clutter of Fisherman's Village and radiates outward along the sand.

Khuntai (Map p587; ☎ 0 7724 5118, 08 6686 2960; r 600-850B; ✖) This clunky orange guesthouse is as cheap as decent rooms get on Samui. A block away from the beach, on the outskirts of Fisherman's Village, Khuntai's 2nd-floor rooms are drenched in afternoon sunshine and feature outdoor lounging spots.

Cactus (Map p587; ☎ 0 7724 5565; cactusbung@hotmail .com; bungalows 700-1590B; ✖) Cactus does a good job of keeping up with Bo Phut's boutique crowd by offering cave-like concoctions that sizzle with burnt reds and oranges. The palpable backpacker buzz means that rooms err on the basic side, but they're still clean, comfy and sport loads of charm (the fan bathrooms could benefit from an air freshener though). Fan huts are half price in low season.

Lodge (Map p587; ☎ 0 7742 5337; www.apartmentsamui .com; r 1350-1900B; ✖ ☲) Another great choice in Bo Phut, the Lodge feels like a colonial hunting chalet with pale walls and dark wooden beams jutting across the ceiling. Every room has scores of wall hangings and a private balcony overlooking the beach. The 'pent-huts' on the top floor are very spacious. Reservations are a must – this place always seems to be full.

our pick L'Hacienda (Map p587; ☎ 0 7724 5943; www .samui-hacienda.com; r 1400-3000B; ✖ ☲) Polished terracotta and rounded archways give the entrance a Spanish mission motif. Similar decor permeates the eight adorable rooms, which sport loads of personal touches like pebbled bathroom walls and translucent bamboo lamps. There's a charming surprise waiting for you on the roof, and we're pretty sure you'll love it as much as we did.

Red House (Map p587; ☎ 0 7742 5686; www.design -visio.com; r 2000B; ✖) To reach the small reception area at the back, guests must pass through a shoe shop that looks like a sleek Chinese bordello. The four rooms are decorated with a similar spiciness. Intricate oriental patterns liven the walls and canopied beds are swathed in streamers of ruby and chartreuse. A cache of reclining beach chairs and potted plants is the perfect rooftop escape.

B1 Villa Spa (Map p587; ☎ 0 7742 7268; www.b1villa .com; ste 3500-5000B; ✖ ☲) There's a refreshing burst of character at this inn-style option along the beach in Fisherman's Village. Each room displays a unique collection of wall art, and has been given a special moniker – the 2nd-storey spaces are named after the stars in Orion's belt. Oh, and it's B1 as in 'B1 with yourself', get it?

our pick Zazen (Map p587; ☎ 0 7742 5085; www .samuizazen.com; r 5300-12,800B; ✖ 🖳 ☲) Zazen is the boutique-iest boutique resort on Samui – every inch of this charming getaway has been thoughtfully and creatively designed. It's 'Asian minimalism meets modern rococo' with a scarlet accent wall, terracotta goddesses, a dash of feng shui and a generous smattering of good taste. Guests relax poolside on comfy beach chairs gently shaded by canvas parasols. The walk-in prices are scary, so it's best to book in advance.

our pick Anantara (Map p587; ☎ 0 7742 8300; www .anantara.com; r 7000-15,000B; ✖ 🖳 ☲) Anantara's stunning palanquin entrance satisfies every fantasy of a far-flung oriental kingdom. Lowslung torches spurt plumes of unwavering fire, and the residual smoke creates a light fog around the soaring palm fronds. Clay and copper statues of grimacing jungle creatures abound on the property's wild acreage, while guests savour wild teas in an open-air pagoda, swim in the lagoon-like infinity-edged swimming pool, or indulge in a relaxing spa treatment.

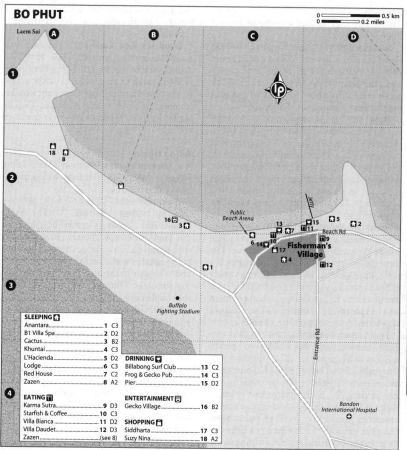

LOWER SOUTHERN GULF

Mae Nam

Mae Nam doesn't have the most beautiful tract of sand, but it offers cheap accommodation relative to the other beaches.

Shangrilah (☎ 0 7742 5189; bungalows 300-2000B;) A backpacker's Shangri-La indeed – these are some of the cheapest huts around and they're in decent condition!

Coco Palm Resort (☎ 0 7742 5095; bungalows 1200B;) The bungalows at Coco Palm have been crafted with tonnes of rattan. A rectangular pool is the centrepiece along the beach – and the price is right for a resort-like atmosphere.

Maenam Resort (☎ 0 7742 5116; www.maenamresort .com; bungalows 1200-2700B;) Palm-bark cottages are set in several rows amid a private, jungle-like garden. They're decked out in a mix of wicker and wooden furnishings, and vary in price according to their distance from the beach. Suites are a steal for families.

Harry's (☎ 0 7742 5447; www.harrys-samui.com; bungalows 1200-3000B;) Arriving here is like entering sacred temple grounds. Polished teak wood abounds in the lobby and the classic pitched roofing reaches skyward. The concrete bungalows, stashed in a verdant garden, don't retain the flamboyant architectural theme out front, but they're cute and comfortable nonetheless.

Sea Fan (☎ 0 7742 5204; www.seafanresort.com; r 2200-2700B;) Offering huge thatch and wood bungalows connected by wooden walkways, with colourful flora abounding, this is a fine place to stay. The beautiful beachside pool has a small kids' area.

Bang Po

This small enclave has a cache of budget bungalows.

Sunbeam (☎ 0 7742 0600; bungalows 500-1000B) Quiet Sunbeam has just over a dozen rustic cottages by the sea. They're spacious, comfy and offer beach views from the porch. Brick paths wind through a lush garden, and cool breezes pass through the shanty-like bar.

Moon (☎ 0 7724 7740; bungalows 600-1800B) Moon is a throwback to an earlier time when Samui was rife with seaside shacks. Several modern concrete cottages have recently sprung up on the property – they're comfortable and clean, and they don't detract from the general laid-back jungle-on-the-beach atmosphere. The large wood-beamed restaurant is the heart of the action.

Health Oasis Resort (☎ 0 7742 0124; www.healthoasis resort.com; bungalows 800-4500B; 🔀) If you're lookin' to get 'cleansed' – whether it's your aura or your colon – then you've happened upon the right place. Guests can choose from a variety of healing packages involving everything from meditation to fasting. Bungalows are modern and receive plenty of sunshine. There's also a vegetarian restaurant on site, of course.

Four Seasons Koh Samui (☎ 0 7724 3000; www .fourseasons.com/kohsamui; villas 30,000B) Four Seasons feels more like a private village than a resort. The international luxury brand has purchased an entire peninsula at the far western corner of Bang Po, and transformed it into a hilly enclave. A ridiculous amount of on-site amenities means that you'll probably never leave the grounds. Each villa has a large private plunge-pool and spacious sitting areas. Should you decide to be more social, there's a beautiful stretch of flaxen sand offering beach chairs and water sports.

WEST COAST

Largely the domain of Thai tourists, Samui's west coast doesn't have the most picturesque beaches, but it's a welcome escape from the east-side bustle.

Na Thon

The island's main settlement is dominated by the ferry pier and is not much to look at. There's really no reason to stay here, but if for some reason you feel compelled, try the following.

Jinta Hotel (☎ 0 7742 0630, 0 7723 6369; www.jinta samui.com; r 500-650B; 🔀 🖳) Jinta's white walls and linoleum floors feel a bit institutional, but they get the job done. All rooms have satellite TV.

Grand Sea View Hotel (☎ 0 7742 0441; www .grandseaviewbeachhotel.com; r 1000-2000B; 🔀 🖳) Na Thon's pick of the litter, this five-floor hotel is popular with visiting businessmen. Spacious rooms have sparkling tile floors, light wooden framing, air-conditioning and cable TV. The higher levels have great views over the town and sea.

Taling Ngam

A quiet stop south of Nathon Thon, Taling Ngam is a charming hideaway with a quaint local village nearby.

Wiesenthal (☎ 0 7723 5165; fax 0 7741 5480; bungalows incl breakfast 1500-2500B; 🔀) The name sounds like a smoky German beer hall but this Thai-owned operation is a breezy beach-side paradise. Cast modesty aside, spread your curtains wide, and welcome sunshine and sea views in through your floor-to-ceiling windows. Lounge-worthy porch furniture further contributes to the comfy, casual vibe established at the open-air restaurant and pool.

Ban Sabai (☎ 0 7742 8200; www.bansabaisunset.com; bungalows 6800-25,000B; 🔀) Beautiful Baan Sabai has 20 rooms on a secluded stretch of sand and palms. Villas along the beach have multi-room lavatories under a charming patchwork of thatching and starlight. Rooms have a private waterfall – the bathtubs receive water from a charming cascade-like faucet. The intimate common spaces and semi-detached cottages make this resort a great place to relax with friends.

our pick Baan Taling Ngam Resort (☎ 0 7742 9100; www.baan-taling-ngam.com; bungalows 8500-16,000B; 🔀) Unlike most of Samui's five-star digs, Baan Taling Ngam has been designed in a 'classic Thai' theme. Luxuriously appointed guest accommodation contains custom-made Thai-style furnishings and the service here is impeccable. As it's not right on the beach, a shuttle service transports guests back and forth; airport and ferry transfers are also provided.

SOUTH COAST

The southern end of Ko Samui is spotted with rocky headlands and smaller sandy coves. Accommodation is mostly midrange and top end.

Laem Set Inn (☎ 0 7723 3299; www.laemset.com; bungalows 1200-20,000B; ❂ 🖳 🖳) This secluded paradise offers accommodation to suit every budget. Cheaper huts have woven bamboo siding, and the midrange choices are gathered in blocks of units that have a homey vibe. The priciest options sport snazzy lacquered upholstery and are authentic southern-Thai homes that were dismantled and reconstructed at the resort.

Centara Villas Samui (Central Samui Village; ☎ 0 7742 4020; www.centralhotelsresorts.com; bungalows 4500-5500B; ❂ 🖳 🖳) Centara Villas are set right where the wild thicket meets a deserted patch of boulder-strewn sand. Pavilions and terraced boardwalks, which climb over the rocky landscape, link the chic, wooden cottages.

Eating

If you thought it was hard to pick a place to sleep, the island has even more options when it comes to dining. From roasted crickets to beluga caviar – Samui's got it and is not afraid to flaunt it.

Influenced by the mainland, Samui is peppered with *kôw gaang* (rice and curry) shops, usually just a wooden shack displaying large metal pots of southern Thai–style curries. Folks pull up on their motorcycles, lift up the lids to survey the vibrantly coloured contents, and pick one for lunch. *Kôw gaang* shops are easily found along the Ring Rd (Rte 4169) and sell out of the good stuff by 1pm. Any build-up of local motorcycles is usually a sign of a good meal in progress.

The upmarket choices are even more numerous and although Samui's swank dining scene is laden with Italian options, visitors will have no problem finding flavours from around the globe. Lured by high salaries and spectacular weather, world-class chefs regularly make an appearance on the island.

CHAWENG

Dozens of the restaurants on the 'strip' serve a mixed bag of local bites, international cuisine, and greasy fast food. For the best ambience, get off the road and head to the beach, where many bungalow operators set up tables on the sand and have glittery fairy lights at night.

Laem Din Market & Night Market (Map p582; dishes from 30B; ❧ 4am-6pm, night market 6pm-2am) A busy day market, Laem Din is packed with stalls selling fresh fruits, vegetables and meats that stock local Thai kitchens. Pick up a kilo of sweet green oranges or wander the stalls trying to spot the ingredients in last night's curry. For dinner, come to the adjacent night market and sample the tasty southern-style fried chicken and curries.

Khaosan Restaurant & Bakery (Map p582; dishes from 60B; ❧ breakfast, lunch & dinner) From *filet mignon* to flapjacks and everything in between, this chow house is popular with those looking for a cheap nosh. Hang around after your meal and catch a newly released movie on the big TV. It's everything you'd expect from a place called 'Khaosan'.

Wave Samui (Map p582; ☎ 0 7723 0803; dishes from 60B; ❧ breakfast, lunch & dinner) Everyone says that Samui is going upmarket, but the most crowded restaurants at dinnertime are still the old-fashioned budget spots, like this one. This jack-of-all trades (guesthouse-bar-restaurant) serves honest food at honest prices and fosters a travellers ambience with an in-house library and a popular happy hour (3pm to 7pm).

Islander (Map p582; ☎ 08 1788 6239; dishes 100-250B; ❧ 8am-2am) A popular, pub-style shanty with Western and Thai food, a kids' menu, outdoor tables, billiards and sports on TV – something for everyone. Breakfast is a sausage fest (literally) – the stacks of greasy meat are perfect cure-all remedy for your Singha-induced hangover.

Gringo's Cantina (Map p582; ☎ 0 7741 3267; dishes 140-280B; ❧ 2pm-midnight) Wash down a Tex-Mex classic with a jug of sangria or a frozen margarita. We liked the chimichangas (mostly because we like saying 'chimichanga'). There are burgers, pizza and veggie options too, for those who don't want to go 'south of the border'.

Captain Kirk (Map p582; ☎ 08 1270 5376; dishes 140-480B; ❧ dinner) Beam yourself up to this beautiful rooftop garden for a vast selection of international eats. Patrons often lounge on the cushioned bamboo furniture and indulge in post-repast cocktails.

Sibelius (Map p582; ☎ 08 7466 6967; dishes from 180B; ❧ dinner Mon-Sat) Named for a Finnish composer, Sibelius strives for simplicity in a sea of overreaching complexity. True to the Scandinavian reputation, the menu is spare but direct in communicating the kitchen's strengths, mainly in fresh fish dishes gently enhanced with herbal sauces.

Prego (Map p582; ☎ 0 7742 2015; www.prego-samui .com; mains 200-700B; ❧ dinner) This swankified ministry of culinary style serves up fine Italian cuisine in a barely-there dining room of cool marble and modern geometry. Reservations are accepted for seatings at 7pm and 9pm.

Bellini (Map p582; ☎ 0 7741 3831; www.bellini-samui .com; dishes from 200B; ◷ dinner) A staple on Soi Colibri, Bellini sizzles under designer mood lighting. There's Italian on the menu, but not in a pizza-pasta kind of way – think veal, rock lobster and a dainty assortment of tapas.

our pick Page (Map p582; ☎ 0 7742 2767; dishes 180-850B; ◷ breakfast, lunch & dinner) If you can't afford to stay at the ultra-swank Library (p583), have a meal at its beachside restaurant. The food is overpriced (of course) but you'll receive glances from the beach bums on the beach as they try to figure out if you're a jet-setter or movie star. Lunch is a bit more casual and affordable, but you'll miss the designer lighting effects in the evening.

Zico's (Map p582; ☎ 0 7723 1560; menu 750B; ◷ dinner) This palatial *churrascaria* puts the *'carne'* in Carnival. Vegetarians beware – Zico's is an all-you-can-eat Brazilian meat-fest complete with saucy dancers sporting peacock-like outfits.

Betelnut (Map p582; ☎ 0 7741 3370; mains 600-800B; ◷ dinner) Fusion can be confusing, and often disappointing, but Betelnut will set you straight. Chef Jeffrey Lords claims an American upbringing and European culinary training, but most importantly he spent time in San Francisco, where all good fusion food is born. The menu is a pan-Pacific mix of curries and chowder, papaya and pancetta.

LAMAI

As Samui's second-most populated beach, Lamai has a surprisingly limited assortment of decent eateries when compared to Chaweng next door. Most visitors dine wherever they're staying.

Lamai Day Market (Map p584; dishes from 30B; ◷ 6am-8pm) The Thai equivalent of a grocery store, Lamai's market is a hive of activity, selling food necessities and takeaway food. Visit the covered area to pick up fresh fruit or to see vendors shredding coconuts to make coconut milk. Or hunt down the ice-cream seller for homemade coconut ice cream. It's next door to a petrol station.

Hua Thanon Market (Map p584; ☎ 0 7742 4630; dishes from 30B; ◷ 6am-6pm) Slip into the rhythm of this village market slightly south of Lamai; it's a window into the food ways of southern Thailand. Vendors shoo away the flies from the freshly butchered meat and housewives

load bundles of vegetables into their baby-filled motorcycle baskets. Follow the market road to the row of food shops delivering edible southern culture: chicken biryani, fiery curries, or toasted rice with coconut, bean sprouts, lemongrass and dried shrimp.

Lamai Night Food Centre (Map p584; ☎ 0 7742 4630; dishes from 30B; ◷ dinner) Eating becomes a circus sideshow at Lamai's outdoor food centre, next door to a 7-Eleven. The vendor stalls whip up all the Thai standards – a spectacle in itself. And then the hostesses at the nearby girly bars crank up the music for pole dancing or a few rounds of *moo·ay tai* (Thai boxing; also spelt *muay thai*).

Mr Samui (Map p584; ☎ 0 7742 4630; dishes 100-180B; ◷ lunch & dinner) Enter Baan Soi Gemstones (look for the 'illy' sign out front) and pass the veritable garage sale of oriental knick-knacks to find a tiny cluster of tables and cushions. Savour your nutty massaman curry amid flamboyant Chinese wall art, dripping chandeliers and gaudy geometric pillows (everything's for sale).

Rocky's (Map p584; ☎ 0 7741 8367; dishes 300-800B; ◷ lunch & dinner) Easily the top dining spot on Lamai, Rocky's gourmet dishes are actually a bargain when you convert the baht into your native currency. Try the signature beef tenderloin with *bleu* cheese – it's like sending your tastebuds on a Parisian vacation. On Tuesday evenings diners enjoy a special Thai-themed evening with a prepared menu of local delicacies.

NORTHERN BEACHES

Some of Samui's finest establishments are located on the northern coast. Boho Bo Phut has several trendy eateries to match the string of yuppie boutique hotels.

Choeng Mon & Big Buddha Beach (Bang Rak)

BBC (☎ 0 7742 5264; dishes 60-200B; ◷ breakfast, lunch & dinner) No, this place has nothing to do with the BBC or *Dr Who* – BBC stands for Big Buddha Café. It's popular with expats, and there's a large international menu and exquisite ocean views from the patio.

Elephant & Castle (☎ 0 7743 0394; dishes 80-250B; ◷ lunch & dinner) The ultimate hang-out for homesick Brits, Elephant & Castle is the perfect replica of a London pub. There's beer by the pint and the steak-and-kidney pies will give you meat sweats for days.

OUR PICK **Dining on the Rocks** (☎ 0 7724 5678; reservations-samui@sixsenses.com; menus from 1500B; ⏲ dinner) The Sila Evason's (p585) ultimate dining experience takes place on nine cantilevered verandahs of weathered teak and bamboo that yawn over the gulf. After sunset (and a glass of wine), guests feel like they're dining on a wooden barge set adrift on a starlit sea. Each dish is the brainchild of the experimental cooks who regularly dabble with taste, texture and temperature. If you're celebrating a special occasion, you'll have to book well in advance to sit at 'table 99', the honeymooners' table, positioned on a private terrace.

Bo Phut

Starfish & Coffee (Map p587; ☎ 0 7742 7201; dishes 130-180B; ⏲ breakfast, lunch & dinner) This streamer-clad eatery was probably named after the Prince song, since we couldn't find any starfish on the menu (there's loads of coffee though). Evenings feature standard Thai fare and sunset views of rugged Ko Pha-Ngan.

Karma Sutra (Map p587; dishes 130-260B; ⏲ breakfast, lunch & dinner) A haze of purples and pillows, this charming chow spot in the heart of Bo Phut's Fisherman Village serves up international and Thai eats listed on colourful chalkboards. Karma Sutra doubles as a clothing boutique.

Villa Bianca (Map p587; ☎ 0 7724 5041, 08 9873 5867; dishes from 200B; ⏲ lunch & dinner) Another fantastic Italian spot on Samui, Villa Bianca is a sea of crisp white tablecloths and woven lounge chairs. Who knew wicker could be so sexy?

Villa Daudet (Map p587; dishes from 130-380B; ⏲ lunch & dinner Mon-Sat) Villa Daudet is French-owned (so you know the food's gonna be good) and sits in a quaint garden decorated with a flower trellis and elephant-themed paintings.

Zazen (Map p587; ☎ 0 7742 5085; dishes 550-850B, set menus from 1300B; ⏲ lunch & dinner) The chef describes the food as 'organic and orgasmic', and the ambient 'yums' from elated diners definitely confirm the latter. This romantic dining experience comes complete with ocean views, dim candle lighting and soft music. Reservations recommended.

Mae Nam & Bang Po

Angela's Bakery (☎ 0 7742 7396; dishes 80-200B; ⏲ breakfast & lunch) Duck through the screen of hanging plants into this beloved bakery, smelling of fresh bread and hospitality. Her sandwiches and cakes have kept many Western expats from wasting away in the land of rice.

OUR PICK **Ko-Seng** (☎ 0 7742 5365; dishes 100-300B; ⏲ dinner) Hidden down a narrow side street near Mae Nam's Chinese temple, Ko Samui's best-kept secret is a welcome escape from the island's restaurants that fuss over the decor instead of their food. It's a local haunt that dishes out top-notch soft-shell crab and plump, flash-fried prawns in a peppery sauce.

Bang Po Seafood (☎ 0 7742 0010; dishes from 100B; ⏲ dinner) A meal at Bang Po Seafood is a test for the tastebuds. It's one of the only restaurants that serves traditional Ko Samui fare (think of it as island road-kill, well, actually it's more like local sea-kill): recipes call for ingredients such as raw sea urchin roe, baby octopus, sea water, coconut and local turmeric.

WEST COAST

The quiet west coast features some of the best seafood on Samui. Nathon has a giant day market on Th Thawi Ratchaphakdi – it's worth stopping by to grab some snacks before your ferry ride.

About Art & Craft Café (☎ 08 9724 9673; Na Thon; dishes 80-180B; ⏲ breakfast & lunch) An artistic oasis in the midst of hurried Na Thon, this cafe serves an eclectic assortment of healthy and wholesome food, gourmet coffee and, as the name states, art and craft, made by the owner and her friends. Relaxed and friendly, this is also a gathering place for Samui's dwindling population of bohemians and artists.

Wiesenthal (☎ 0 7723 5165; Taling Ngam; dishes 90-250B; ⏲ breakfast, lunch & dinner) Wiesenthal is a casual open-air restaurant overlooking a quiet beach. Devour a scrumptious assortment of international cuisine in the shade of a bamboo umbrella.

Big John Seafood (☎ 0 7742 3025; www.bigjohn samui.com; Thong Yang; dishes 60-300B; ⏲ breakfast, lunch & dinner) Big John's menu looks like an encyclopaedia of marine life. The seafood is freshly caught everyday from various fishing hot spots off the coast of Samui. Dinnertime is particularly special – live entertainment kicks in around 6pm just as the sun plunges below the watery horizon.

Five Islands (☎ 0 7741 5359, 08 1447 5371; www.thefiveislands.com; Taling Ngam; dishes 150-500B, tours 5000-6500B; ⏲ lunch & dinner) Five Islands defines the term 'destination dining' and offers the most unique eating experience on the island. Before your meal, a traditional long-tail boat will take you out into the turquoise sea to visit the haunting Five Sister Islands, where you'll learn about the ancient and little-known art of harvesting bird nests to make bird's-nest soup, a Chinese delicacy. This perilous task is rewarded with large sums of cash – a kilo of bird's nests is usually sold for 100,000B to restaurants in Hong Kong (yup, that's five zeros). The lunch tour departs at 10am, and the dinner program leaves at 3pm. Customers are also welcome to dine without going on the tour.

Drinking & Entertainment

Samui's biggest party spot is, without a doubt, noisy Chaweng. Lamai and Bo Phut come in second and third respectively, while the rest of the island is generally quiet, as the drinking is usually focused around self-contained resort bars.

CHAWENG

Making merry in Chaweng is a piece of cake. Most places are open until 2am and there are a few places that go strong all night long. Soi Green Mango has loads of girly bars. Soi Colibri and Soi Reggae Pub are raucous as well.

Ark Bar (Map p582; ☎ 0 7742 2047; www.ark-bar.com) The 'it' destination for a Wednesday-night romp on Samui. Drinks are dispensed from the multicoloured bar draped in paper lanterns, and guests lounge on pyramidal pillows strewn down the beach. The party usually starts around 4pm.

Pod (Map p582; ☎ 08 3692 7911, 08 4744 9207) This hole-in-the-wall hot spot feels like a hidden metropolitan lounge whose address is known only by the poshest of jet-setters.

Bar Solo (Map p582; ☎ 0 7741 4012) A sign of things to come, Bar Solo has future-fitted Chaweng's outdoor beer halls into an urban setting with sleek cubist decor and a cocktail list that doesn't scream holiday hayseed. The evening drink specials lure in the front-loaders preparing for a late, late night at the dance clubs on Soi Solo and Soi Green Mango.

Tropical Murphy's (Map p582; ☎ 0 7741 3614; dishes 50-300B) A popular *fa·ràng* joint, Tropical Murphy's dishes out steak-and-kidney pie, fish and chips, lamb chops and Irish stew. Come night-time, the live music kicks on and this place turns into the most popular Irish bar on Samui (yes, there are a few).

Nathalie's Art Palace Bar (Map p582; ☎ 0 7723 1485) You've got to hand it to German TV personality Nathalie Gutermann for her unabashed self-promotion. She's turned a hillside apartment into a boutique hotel and bar, which primarily promote the cult of Nathalie and her 'fabulous' lifestyle. Curious about the life of an expatriate claiming aristocratic origins? Stop by for a sunset cocktail, Friday night barbecue or some of the special party events.

Green Mango (Map p582; ☎ 0 7742 2661) This place is so popular it has an entire soi named after it. Samui's favourite power-drinking house is very big, very loud and very *fa·ràng*. Green Mango has blazing lights, expensive drinks and masses of sweaty bodies swaying to dance music.

Q-Bar (Map p582; ☎ 08 1956 2742; www.qbarsamui .com) Overlooking Chaweng Lake, Q Bar is a little piece of Bangkok nightlife planted among the coconut trees. The upstairs lounge opens just before sunset treating cocktail connoisseurs to various highbrow tipples and a drinkable view of southern Chaweng – mountains, sea and sky. After 10pm, the night-crawlers descend upon the downstairs club where DJs spin the crowd into a techno amoeba. A taxi there will cost between 200B and 300B.

Reggae Pub (Map p582; ☎ 0 7742 2331) This fortress of fun sports an open-air dance floor with music spun by foreign DJs. It's a towering two-storey affair with long bars, pool tables and a live-music stage. The whole place doubles as a shrine to Bob Marley.

Mint Bar (Map p582; ☎ 08 7089 8726) The scene outside on the street is too entertaining to keep crowds corralled in this stylish club on ordinary nights. But the Mint is able to lure a few DJ heavyweights for a Samui spin on extraordinary nights. Watch the entertainment listings for special events.

Christy's Cabaret (Map p582; ☎ 0 1894 0356) This flashy joint offers free *gà·teu·i* (transgender males; also spelt *kàthoey*) cabaret every night at 11pm and attracts a mixed clientele of both sexes. Other ladyboys loiter out front and try to drag customers in, so to speak.

LAMAI

Although smaller than Chaweng, Lamai has way more girly bars than its big bro…

Bauhaus (Map p584; ☎ 0 7741 8387/8) Lamai's long-running dance club, Bauhaus' DJed beats are interspersed with short drag shows, Thai boxing demos and the occasional foam party.

Samui Shamrock (Map p584; ☎ 08 1597 8572) More classic than chic, Samui Shamrock is a good-times pub where house bands belt out dated cover tunes that inspire the tipsy crowd to sing along. At some point in the night you'll hear 'Hotel California', the ultimate foreigner tribute song.

NORTHERN BEACHES

The following joints are in Bo Phut.

Billabong Surf Club (Map p587; ☎ 0 7743 0144) Billabong's all about Aussie Rules – it's playing on the TV and the walls are smothered with memorabilia from Down Undah. There are great views of Ko Pha-Ngan and hearty portions of ribs and chops to go with your draught beer.

Frog & Gecko Pub (Map p587; ☎ 0 7742 5248) This tropical British watering hole and food stop is famous for its noodle-bending 'Wednesday Night Pub Quiz' competitions and its wide selection of music. Live sporting events are shown on the big screen.

Pier (Map p587; ☎ 0 7743 0681; dishes 200-390B; 🕑 lunch & dinner) This sleek black box sticks out amongst Bo Phut's narrow Chinese tenements. It's the hippest address in Fisherman's Village, sporting multilevel terraces, a lively bar and plenty of wide furniture to lounge around on and watch the rickety fishing vessels pull into the harbour.

Gecko Village (Map p587; ☎ 0 7724 5554) For electronica fans, Gecko Village is the original maven of beats. It's a beachfront bar and resort that has used its London connections to lure international DJs to Samui paradise. The New Year's Eve parties and Sunday sessions are now legendary thanks to the big names that grace the turntables.

Shopping

Chandra (Map p582; ☎ 08 6606 3639; Chaweng; 🕑 noon-midnight) Ethno-chic has come a long way since those embroidered hem sacks of yore. Chandra scours Asia, but mainly Bali, for wispy dresses that show off newly acquired suntans.

Doodee Décor (Map p582; ☎ 08 1633 9160; Chaweng; 🕑 11am-11pm) Ignore the name, this shop sells so much more than bathroom decor. Peruse the quality Thai-made gifts and decorations, like *dhana* vases, hand-hammered cutlery from Ayuthaya and funky embroidered handbags.

Vanities (Map p582; Chaweng; 🕑 11am-10pm) Two Bangkokian fashionistas have opened this dress boutique for the vacationing urbanite. Selections hail from Bangkok, Hong Kong and India, and are a welcome relief from the faux-hippie dress peddlers elsewhere on the beach.

Health Mart (Map p584; ☎ 0 7741 9157; Lamai; 🕑 8am-5pm) Considering the number of people wandering around the island on fasts, there are very few wellness stores. Affiliated with Spa Samui, Health Mart, only 100m from Wat Lamai, carries several natural body and beauty lines produced by royally sponsored economic-development projects. Look for the herbal shower gels and shampoos made by Khao Kho Talay Pu, Supaporn facial scrubs, Tropicana coconut shampoos and Power of Brown tea.

Siddharta (Map p587; ☎ 0 7724 5014; Bo Phut; 🕑 10am-9pm) A French import company brings its globetrotting treasures from Bali and Nepal to the shores of Samui. The racks are filled with cool geometric beach cover-ups and flower appliqué skirts – fashionable replacements, if you grow tired of the contents of your suitcase.

Suzy Nina (Map p587; ☎ 0 7724 5221; Bo Phut; 🕑 11am-9pm) Samui's version of Pier One is an interior-design shop selling silk and natural cotton bed-linens and custom-made drapes. Finger through the fabric room loaded with elegant Thai and Burmese silks.

Getting There & Away

AIR

Samui's airport (Map p582) is located in the northeast of the island near Big Buddha Beach. The monopoly that Bangkok Airways had on flights into and out of Samui ended in early 2008, and Thai Airways International has begun a Samui–Bangkok service. Other airlines are expected to follow.

Bangkok Airways (www.bangkokair.com) operates flights roughly every 30 minutes between Samui and Bangkok (2000B to 4000B, one to 1½ hours). **Thai Airways** (in Bangkok ☎ 0 2134 5403; www.thaiair.com) operates between Samui and Bangkok (5600B, twice a day). Both airlines land at Bangkok's Suvarnabhumi Airport.

There is a **Bangkok Airways office** (Map p582; ☎ 0 7742 0512-9) in Chaweng and another at the **airport** (☎ 0 7742 5011). The first (at 6am) and last (9pm) flights of the day are always the cheapest.

Bangkok Air also flies from Samui to Phuket (2000B to 3000B, one hour, three daily), Pattaya (3000B, one hour, three daily), Krabi (1600B, one hour, three times a week) and Chiang Mai (4500B to 6500B, 2½ hours, twice a week). International flights go directly from Samui to Singapore (4200B to 5400B, three hours, daily) and Hong Kong (12,000B to 6000B, four hours, five days a week).

During the high season, make your flight reservations far in advance as seats do sell out. If Samui flights are full, try flying into Surat Thani from Bangkok and taking a short ferry ride to Samui. Flights to Surat Thani are generally cheaper than a direct flight to the island.

BOAT

The ferry situation is rather convoluted: schedules and prices are always in flux, and there are tons of entry and exit points on Samui and the mainland. Your exit and entry point will probably depend on what's available when you arrive in Surat Thani (after all, you probably don't want to hang around town). The four main piers on the mainland are Ao Ban Don, Tha Thong, Don Sak and Khanom. On Samui, the three oft-used ports are Na Thon, Mae Nam and Big Buddha. Service quality can also vary greatly within the same ferry company – some boats are rusty and rundown, others are much more modern and are even outfitted with TVs.

There are frequent daily boat departures between Samui and Surat Thani. The hourly Seatran ferry is a common option. Ferries cost between 110B and 190B, and take one to three hours, depending on the boat. A couple of these departures can connect with the train station in Phun Phin (for an extra 100B to 140B). The slow night boat to Samui (150B) leaves from central Surat Thani each night at 11pm, reaching Na Thon around 5am. It returns from Na Thon at 9pm, arriving at around 3am. Watch your bags on this boat.

There are almost a dozen daily departures between Samui and Ko Pha-Ngan. These leave either from the Na Thon, Mae Nam or Big Buddha piers and take from 20 minutes to one hour (130B to 250B). On Ko Pha-Ngan there are two piers (Hat Rin and Thong Sala). The boats departing from Big Buddha service Hat Rin, and the other boats land at Thong Sala. Ferries from Mae Nam slide up Ko Pha-Ngan's remote eastern coast. From the same piers, there are also around six daily departures between Samui and Ko Tao. These take 1¼ to 2½ hours and cost from 350B to 600B.

Car ferries from Don Sak and Khanom land at Thong Yang, about 10km south of Na Thon. There are no car ferries from Samui to Ko Pha-Ngan or Ko Tao.

BUS & TRAIN

A bus-ferry combo is more convenient than a train-ferry package because you don't have to switch transport in Phun Phin (a tiny town near Surat Thani). However, the trains are much more comfortable and spacious – especially at night. If you prefer the train, you can get off at Chumphon and catch the Lomprayah catamaran service the rest of the way.

The government-bus fares from Bangkok's Southern bus terminal include the cost of the ferry. These are 500B for 2nd-class passengers. Most private buses from Bangkok charge around 450B for the same journey and include the ferry fare. From Th Khao San in Bangkok it's possible to get bus-ferry combination tickets for as little as 350B, but service is substandard and theft is very common. If an agency on Th Khao San claims to be able to get you to Samui for less, it is almost certainly a scam as no profit can be made at such low prices.

Getting Around

See p578 for information about possible transport scams when getting around the island. You can rent motorcycles (and bicycles) from almost every resort on the island. The going rate is 200B to 300B per day, but for longer periods try to negotiate a better rate.

Sŏrng·tăa·ou drivers love to try to overcharge you, so it's always best to ask a third party for current rates, as they can change with the season. These vehicles run regularly during daylight hours only. It costs about 30B to travel along one coast, and no more that 75B to travel halfway across the island. Figure about 20B for a five-minute ride on a motorcycle taxi.

TO/FROM THE AIRPORT

Taxi service on Samui is quite chaotic and prices can vary greatly depending on your driver's mood. Ask your resort about complimentary airport transfers or try the **Samui Shuttle** (www.samuishuttle.com). Taxis typically charge 300B to 500B for airport transfer. Some Chaweng travel agencies arrange minibus taxis for less.

KO PHA-NGAN
เกาะพะงัน
pop 12,100

In the family of southern Gulf islands, Ko Pha-Ngan sits in the crystal sea between Ko Samui, its business-savvy older brother, and little Ko Tao, the spunky younger brother full of dive-centric energy. Ko Pha-Ngan is the slacker middle child: a chilled out beach bum with tattered dreadlocks, a tattoo of a Chinese serenity symbol, and a penchant for white nights and bikini-clad pool parties.

The scenic cape of Hat Rin has long been the darling destination of this laid-back paradise. Sunrise Beach started hosting the world-famous Full Moon parties long before Alex Garland's *The Beach* inspired many of us to strap on a rucksack. Today, thousands still flock to the kerosene-soaked sands for an epic trance-a-thon fuelled by adrenaline and a couple of other substances…

But like any textbook teenager, this angst-ridden island can't decide what it wants to be when it grows up. Should the party personality persist or will the stunning and secluded northern beaches finally come out from under Hat Rin's shadow?

While Pha-Ngan's slacker vibe and reputation will no doubt dominate for years to come, the island is secretly starting to creep upmarket. Every year, tired old shacks are being replaced by crisp modern abodes. In Hat Rin, you will be hard-pressed to find a room on Sunrise Beach for less than 1000B. Soon, the phrase 'private infinity pool' and 'personal butler' will find a permanent place in the island's lexicon, replacing 'pass the dutch' and 'another whiskey bucket please'. But don't fret just yet – the vast inland jungle continues to feel undiscovered, and there are still plenty of secluded bays in which you can string up a hammock and watch the tide roll in.

Orientation

Ko Pha-Ngan, Thailand's fifth-largest island, is approximately 20km from Ko Samui and 100km from Surat Thai.

Most of the island's visitors stay on the thin peninsula known as Hat Rin. This mountainous cape is flanked with beautiful beaches on either side, and is home to the infamous Full Moon parties held every month (see boxed text, p598). For a detailed layout of the area, see p600. The rest of the island is noticeably quieter, although gradual development has meant an increase in population on the west and south coasts. The northern coast has a few good beaches that feature modern amenities but feel relaxed and remote. The quiet eastern shore is virtually deserted.

About half of Ko Pha-Ngan's population live in and around the small port of Thong Sala, where the ferries to and from Ko Tao, Surat Thani and Ko Samui dock.

Information

BOOKSHOPS

D's Books & Café (Map p601; ☎ 08 4667 7730) A carbon-copy of the successful bookshop-cum-cafe on Ko Phi-Phi, it's a chill spot to grab an iced coffee while catching up on your holiday reading.

EMERGENCY

Police station (Map p596; ☎ 0 7737 7114) About 2km north of Thong Sala. The police station in Hat Rin (near Hat Rin School) will not let you file a report; you must go to Thong Sala.

INTERNET ACCESS

Hat Rin and Thong Sala are centres of internet activity, but every beach with development now offers access. Rates are generally 2B per minute (3B in Hat Rin), with a 20B minimum (30B in Hat Rin) and discounts if you stay on for one hour. Places offering a rate of 1B per minute usually have turtle-speed connections.

INTERNET RESOURCES

Backpackers Thailand (www.backpackersthailand .com) A handy site managed by the island's Backpackers Information Centre. Offers info on local news, transport and Full-Moon fun.

Phangan Info (www.phangan.info) An online version of the helpful island pamphlet available at most bungalows and the Thong Sala pier.

LAUNDRY

If you got neon body paint on your clothes during your Full-Moon romp, don't bother sending them to the cleaners – the paint will never come out. Trust us, we tried. For your other washing needs, there are heaps of places that will gladly wash your clothes. Prices hover around 40B per kilo, and express cleanings shouldn't be more than 60B per kilo.

LOWER SOUTHERN GULF

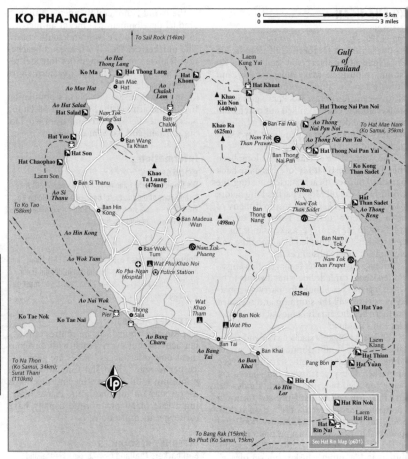

MEDICAL SERVICES

Medical services can be a little crooked in Ko Pha-Ngan – expect unstable prices and under-qualified doctors. Many clinics charge a 3000B entrance fee before treatment. Serious medical issues should be dealt with on nearby Ko Samui. All dental problems should be treated on Ko Samui as well.

Ko Pha-Ngan Hospital (Map p596; ☎ 0 7737 7034; Thong Sala; ⏰ 24hr) About 2.5km north of Thong Sala; offers 24-hour emergency services.

MONEY

Thong Sala, Ko Pha-Ngan's financial 'capital', has plenty of banks, currency converters and several Western Union offices. Hat Rin has numerous ATMs and a couple of banks at the pier. There are also ATMs in Hat Yao, Chaloklum and Thong Nai Pan.

POST

Main post office (Map p601; ⏰ 8.30am-4.30pm Mon-Fri, 9am-noon Sat) In Thong Sala; there's a smaller office right near the pier in Hat Rin.

TOURIST INFORMATION & TRAVEL AGENCIES

There are no government-run TAT offices on Ko Pha-Ngan, instead most tourists get their information from local travel agencies and pamphlets. Hat Rin has an ungodly amount of travel agencies, and there's also a cluster within eyeshot of the Thong Sala pier terminus. Price competition keeps prices relatively stable (tickets in Thong Sala tend to be slightly cheaper), although scams and faulty bookings are common throughout.

Several minimagazines also offer comprehensive information about the island's accommodation, restaurants, activities and Full Moon parties. Our favourite option is *Phangan Info* (www.phangan.info).

Backpackers Information Centre (Map p601; ☎ 0 7737 5535; www.backpackersthailand.com; Hat Rin) A must for travellers looking to book high-quality tours (diving, live-aboards, jungle safaris etc) and transport, the Backpackers Information Centre isn't just for backpackers. It's a travel agency that offers peace of mind with every purchase. The friendly owners, a husband-and-wife team, have travelled all over Thailand and dedicate their time to helping others discover the island and the rest of the country. They also run the Crystal Dive shop next door (see p612) and offer a cosy internet lounge.

Dangers & Annoyances

Some of your fondest vacation memories may be forged on Ko Pha-Ngan; just be mindful of the following situations that can seriously tarnish your experience on this hot-blooded jungle island.

DRUGS

You're relaxing on the beach when suddenly a local walks up and offers you some local herb at a ridiculously low price. 'No thanks,' you say, knowing that the penalties for drug-use in Thailand are fierce. But the vender drops his price even more and practically offers you the weed for free. Too good to be true? Obviously. As soon as you take a toke, the seller rats you out to the cops and you're whisked away to the local prison where you must pay a wallet-busting fine. This type of scenario happens all the time on Ko Pha-Ngan so it's best to avoid the call of the ganja.

Here's another important thing to remember: your travel insurance does not cover any drug-related injury or treatment. Drug-related freak-outs *do* happen – we've heard first'hand accounts of partiers slipping into extended periods of delirium. Suan Saranrom (Garden of Joys) Psychiatric Hospital in Surat Thani has to take on extra staff during full-moon periods to handle the number of *fa·ràng* who freak out on magic mushrooms, acid or other abundantly available hallucinogens.

WOMEN TRAVELLERS

Female travellers should be extra careful when partying on the island. We've received many reports about drug- and alcohol-related rape (and these situations are not limited to Full Moon parties). Another disturbing problem is the unscrupulous behaviour of some of the local motorcycle taxi drivers. Several complaints have been filed about drivers groping female passengers; there are even reports of severe sexual assaults.

MOTORCYCLES

Ko Pha-Ngan has more motorcycle accidents than injuries incurred from Full-Moon tomfoolery. Nowadays there's a system of paved roads, but much of it is a labyrinth of rutty dirt-and-mud paths. The island is also very hilly, and even if the road is paved, it can be too difficult for most to take on. The *very* steep road to Hat Rin is a perfect case in point. The island now has a special ambulance that trolls the island helping injured bikers.

SCAMS

There are no tourist police on Ko Pha-Ngan, which means that a greater percentage of tourists fall victim to various gimmicks. A common scam involves booking 'first class' bus or boat tickets only to find out that the transport is rickety at best, and the other passengers paid significantly less. Sometimes travellers fall victim to phantom bookings, in which the ticket agent made no reservations whatsoever. Many tourists have reported problems with transport between Bangkok and Ko Pha-Ngan – operators often rifle through bags placed in the luggage compartment of the bus.

Sights

For those who have grown weary of beach-bumming, this large jungle island has many natural features to explore, including mountains, waterfalls and spectacular beaches.

BEACHES & WATERFALLS

There are many **waterfalls** (Map p596) throughout the island's interior, four of which gush throughout the year. **Nam Tok Than Sadet** features boulders carved with the royal insignia of Rama V, Rama VII and Rama IX. King Rama V enjoyed this hidden spot so much that he returned over a dozen times between 1888 and 1909. The river waters of Khlong Than

THE TEN COMMANDMENTS OF FULL MOON FUN

No one knows exactly when and how these crazy parties got started – many believe it began in 1987 or 1988 as someone's 'going away party', but none of that is relevant now. Today, thousands of bodies converge monthly on the powdery sand of Hat Rin Nok to bump, grind, sweat and drink their way through a lunar-lit night filled with thumping DJed beats. Crowds can reach an outrageous 30,000 partiers in high season, while low season still sees a respectable 5000 pilgrims.

If you can't make your trip coincide with a full moon but still want to cover yourself in fluorescent paint, fear not – enterprising locals organise Black Moon parties (at Ban Khai), Half Moon parties (at Ban Tai), Moon Set parties (at Hat Chaophao) and pool parties (at Coral Bungalows; p601), which have nothing to do with the moon's position.

Critics claim that the party is starting to lose its carefree flavour, especially since the island's government is trying to charge a 100B entrance fee to partygoers. Despite the disheartening schemes hatched by money-hungry locals, the night of the Full Moon is still the ultimate partying experience, so long as one follows the unofficial Ten Commandments of Full Moon fun:

- Thou shalt arrive in Hat Rin at least three days early to nail down accommodation during the pre–Full Moon rush of backpackers (see p600 for information about sleeping in Hat Rin).
- Thou shalt double-check the party dates as sometimes they coincide with Buddhist holidays and are rescheduled.
- Thou shalt secure all valuables, especially when staying in budget bungalows.
- Thou shalt savour some delicious fried fare in Chicken Corner (p607) before the revelry begins.
- Thou shalt wear protective shoes during the sandy celebration, unless ye want a tetanus shot.
- Thou shalt cover thyself with swirling patterns of neon body paint.
- Thou shalt visit Magic Mountain or The Rock for killer views of the heathens below.
- Thou shalt not sample the drug buffet, nor shalt thou swim in the ocean under the influence of alcohol.
- Thou shalt stay in a group of two or more people, especially women, and especially when returning home at the end of the evening.
- Thou shalt party until the sun comes up and have a great time.

Sadet are now considered sacred and used in royal ceremonies. Also near the eastern coast, **Nam Tok Than Prawet** is a series of chutes that snake inland for approximately 2km.

In the centre of the island, **Nam Tok Phaeng** is protected by a national park and is a pleasant reward after a short-but-rough hike. Continue the adventure and head up to **Khao Ra**, the highest **mountain** on the island at 625m. Those with eagle-eyes will spot wild crocodiles, monkeys, snakes, deer and boar along the way, and the **viewpoint** from the top is spectacular – on a clear day you can see Ko Tao. Although the trek isn't arduous, it is very easy to lose one's way, and we *highly* recommend hiring an escort in Ban Madeua Wan (near the falls). The local guides have crude signs posted in front of their homes, and, if they're around, they'll take you up to the top for 500B. Most of them only speak Thai.

Pha-Ngan's stunning **beaches** are definitely worth visiting, however caution should also be exercised for those travelling on foot. The 'Green Dot' trail from Hat Rin to Hat Yuan is completely overgrown, as is most of the route between Chalok Lam and Hat Khuat (Bottle Beach). Save yourself the strife and charter a water taxi.

Hat Khuat, also called Bottle Beach, is a classic fave. Visitors flock to this shore for a relaxing day of swimming and snorkelling – some opt to stay the night at one of the several bungalow operations along the beach. For additional seclusion, try the isolated beaches on the east coast, which include: **Than Sadet**, **Hat Yuan**, **Hat Thian** and the teeny **Ao Thong Reng**. For more enchanting beaches, consider doing a day trip to the stunning **Ang Thong Marine National Park** (p623).

WÁT

Remember to change out of your beach clothes before visiting one of the 20 **wát** on Ko Pha-Ngan. Most temples are open during daylight hours.

The oldest temple on the island is **Wat Phu Khao Noi**, near the hospital in Thong Sala. While the site is open to visitors throughout the day, the monks are only around in the morning. **Wat Pho**, near Ban Tai, has a **herbal sauna** (admission 50B) accented with natural lemongrass. The steam bath is open from 3pm to 6pm. The **Chinese Temple** is known to give visitors good luck. It was constructed about 20 years ago after a visiting woman had a vision of the Chinese Buddha who instructed her to build a fire-light for the island. **Wat Khao Tham**, also near Ban Tai, sits high on a hill and has resident female monks. At the temple there is a bulletin board detailing a meditation retreat taught by an American-Australian couple. For additional information, write in advance to Wat Khao Tham, PO Box 8, Ko Pha-Ngan, Surat Thani 84280.

Activities

DIVING & SNORKELLING

With Ko Tao, the high-energy diving behemoth, just a few kilometres away, Ko Pha-Ngan enjoys a much quieter, more laid-back diving scene focused on fun diving rather than certifications. Prices are about 2000B to 2500B cheaper on Ko Tao for an Open Water certificate, but group sizes can be smaller on Ko Pha-Ngan since there are less divers in general. Like the other islands in the Samui Archipelago, Pha-Ngan has several small reefs dispersed around the island. The clear favourite snorkelling spot is **Ko Ma**, a small island in the northwest connected to Ko Pha-Ngan by a charming sand bar. There are also some rock reefs of interest on the eastern side of the island.

A major perk of diving from Ko Pha-Ngan is the proximity to **Sail Rock** (Hin Bai), perhaps the best dive site in the Gulf of Thailand. This large pinnacle lies about 14km north of the island. An abundance of corals and large tropical fish can be seen at depths of 10m to 30m, and there's a rocky vertical swim-through called 'The Chimney'.

Dive shops on Ko Tao sometimes visit Sail Rock, however the focus tends to swing more towards swallow reefs (for newbie divers) and the shark-infested waters at Chumphon Pinnacle. The most popular trips departing

from Ko Pha-Ngan are three-site day trips, which stop at Chumphon Pinnacle, Sail Rock and one of the other premiere sites in the area (see boxed text, p614). These three-stop trips cost around 3800B and include a full lunch. Two-dive trips to Sail Rock will set you back around 2500B.

The following local dive operators are recommended:

Haad Yao Divers (☎ 08 6279 3085; www.haadyao divers.com) Established in 1997, this dive operator has garnered a strong reputation by maintaining high standards of safety and customer service.

Lotus Diving (☎ 0 7737 4142; www.lotusdiving.net) This well-reputed dive centre has top-notch instructors, and owns not one, but two beautiful boats (that's two more vessels than most of the other operations on Ko Pha-Ngan). Trips can be booked at their office in Chalok Lam, or at the Backpackers Information Centre (p597).

Sail Rock Divers (☎ 0 7737 4321; www.sailrock diversresort.com) The responsible and friendly staff at Sail Rock satisfies customers at their purpose-facility, featuring air-con classrooms and a small wading pool. They are technically the closest dive school to Sail Rock, the Gulf's best dive site.

OTHER WATER SPORTS

Jamie passes along his infinite wakeboarding wisdom to eager wannabes at **Wake Up** (☎ 08 7283 6755; www.wakeupwakeboarding.com; ☺ Jan–Oct), his small water sports school in Chalok Lam. Fifteen minutes of 'air time' will set you back 1500B (2500B for 30 minutes), which is excellent value considering you get one-on-one instruction. Kite-boarding, wake-skating and waterskiing sessions are also available, as are round-the-island day trips (2000B per person; a six-person quorum needed).

Coral Bungalows (p601) rents out a variety of aquatic equipment such as jet skis and kayaks. The friendly staff at the Backpackers Information Centre (p597) can attend to any of your other water-sports needs.

YOGA & MASSAGE

If you're dropping the big bucks for lodging, then you probably have access to an on-site spa. Inexpensive massage parlours are aplenty in Hat Rin and Thong Sala. Others can be scouted along the main road connecting the two towns (although be wary of the shadier joints offering 'happy endings').

The Ananda Yoga Resort on Hat Chaophao, run by **Agama Yoga** (☎ 08 1397 6280, 08 9233 0217; www.agamayoga.com; Hin Kong, r 500B, bungalows 1200B,

LOWER SOUTHERN GULF

four night minimum), gets rave reviews from our readers for its holistic approach to the study of tantric yoga. The centre is often closed from September to December while its instructors travel to other locations around the world spreading the cosmic *ohm*. On the east coast, the Sanctuary (p606) is another popular retreat for yoga enthusiasts.

OTHER ACTIVITIES

The exceedingly popular **Eco Nature Tour** (☎ 08 4850 6273) offers a 'best of' island trip, which includes elephant trekking, snorkelling and a visit to the Chinese temple, a stunning viewpoint and Phang waterfall. The day trip, which costs 1500B, departs at 9am and returns around 3pm. Bookings can be made at its office in Thong Sala or at the Backpackers Information Centre (p597). **Pha-Ngan Safari** (☎ 0 7737 4159, 08 1895 3783) offers a similar trip for 1900B.

Hiking and snorkelling day trips to **Ang Thong Marine National Park** (p623) generally depart from Ko Samui, but recently tour operators are starting to shuttle tourists from Ko Pha-Ngan as well. Ask at your accommodation for details about boat trips as companies often come and go due to unstable petrol prices.

Sleeping

Ko Pha-Ngan's legendary history of laid-back revelry has solidified its reputation as *the* stomping ground for the gritty backpacker lifestyle. Recently, however, the island is starting to see a shift towards a more upmarket clientele. Many local mainstays have collapsed their bamboo huts and constructed newer, sleeker accommodation aimed at the ever-growing legion of 'flashpackers'.

On other parts of the island, new tracts of land are being cleared for Samui-esque five-star resorts. But backpackers fear not; it'll still be many years before the castaway lifestyle goes the way of the dodo. For now, Ko Pha-Ngan can revel in its three distinct classes of lodging: pinch-a-penny shacks, trendy mid-range hang-outs and blow-the-bank luxury.

Hat Rin sees an exorbitant amount of visitors relative to the rest of the island. Party pilgrims flock to this picturesque peninsula for the legendary festivities, and although most of them sleep through the daylight hours, the setting remains quite picturesque despite the errant beer bottle in the sand.

The southern part of Sunrise Beach is starting to reek of kerosene due to the nightly fire-related shenanigans at Drop-In Bar – needless to say it's best to sunbathe at the quieter northern part of the sand.

Pha-Ngan also caters to a subculture of seclusion-seekers who crave a deserted slice of sand. The northern and eastern coasts offer just that – a place to escape.

The following sleeping options are organised into five sections: we start in Hat Rin, move along the southern coast, head up the west side, across the northern beaches and down the quiet eastern shore.

HAT RIN

The thin peninsula of Hat Rin features three separate beaches. Hat Rin Nok (Sunrise Beach) is the epicentre of Full Moon tomfoolery, Hat Rin Nai (Sunset Beach) is the less impressive stretch of sand on the far side of the tiny promontory, and Hat Seekantang (also known as Hat Leela), just south of Hat Rin Nai, is a smaller, more private beach. The three beaches are linked by Ban Hat Rin (Hat Rin Town), a small inland collection of restaurants and bars.

Needless to say, the prices listed here are meaningless during periods of maximum lunar orbicularity. Also, during Full Moon events, bungalow operations expect you to stay for a minimum number of days. If you plan to arrive the day of the party (or even the day before), we strongly suggest booking a room in advance, or else you'll probably have to sleep on the beach (which you might end up doing anyway).

Budget

Sea Garden (Map p601; ☎ 0 7737 5281; www.seagarden _resort.com; Ban Hat Rin; r 200-1500B; 🌐) A campus of bungalows and motel-style accommodation, Sea Garden has a variety of rooms for every budget (although have a look at a few different room types before hanging your hat). Go for the cheap, closet-sized digs if you're just looking for a place to drop your bags during the Full Moon fun.

Seaside Bungalow (Map p601; ☎ 08 6940 3410, 0 87 266 7567; Hat Rin Nai; bungalows 300-600B; 🌐) Seaside sees loads of loyal customers who return for the mellow atmosphere, cheap drinks, free pool table and comfy wooden bungalows staggered along Sunset Beach. At 500B, we're pretty sure that these huts are the cheapest air-con rooms on the island.

Paradise Bungalows (Map p601; ☎ 0 7737 5244; Hat Rin Nok; bungalows 250-1200B; ✷) The world-famous Full Moon party was hatched at this scruffy batch of bungalows, and the place has been living on its name fame ever since. The backpackers keep on coming to wax nostalgic, although the grounds are starting to look more like a junkyard than a resort. Paradise lost.

Lighthouse Bungalow (Map p601; ☎ 0 7737 5075; Hat Seekantang; bungalows 350-800B) Hidden at the far end of Hat Rin, this low-key collection of humble huts gathers along a sloping terrain punctuated by towering palms. To access this secluded resort, walk through Leela Beach Bungalows (don't bother stopping) and follow the wooden boardwalk as it curves to the left (southeast) around the sea-swept boulders.

Coral Bungalows (Map p601; ☎ 0 7737 5023; www .coralhaadrin.com; Hat Rin Nai; bungalows 500-800B; ✷ 🖥 🖳) This party-centric paradise has firmly planted its flag in Backpackerland as the go-to resort for a holiday on a shoestring. By day, sun-worshippers straddle beachside chaises or jet skis. Then, by night, like a superhero, Coral transforms into its alter ego: a pool-party machine fuelled by gregarious employees and a couple of vodka–Red Bull buckets (see boxed text, p609).

Same Same (Map p601; ☎ 0 7737 5200; www.same -same.com; Ban Hat Rin; r 500-800B; ✷) This backpacker hang-out is targeted at Scandinavian travellers. In the party-prone restaurant, the

LOWER SOUTHERN GULF

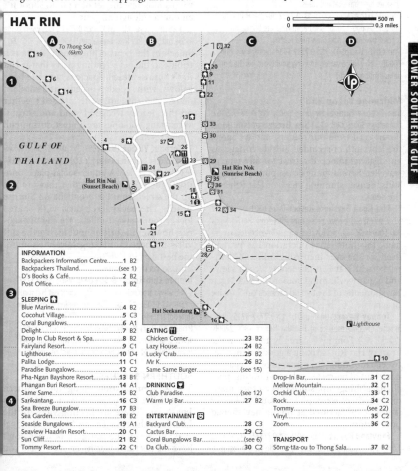

HAT RIN

0 — 500 m
0 — 0.3 miles

To Thong Sok (6km)

GULF OF THAILAND

Hat Rin Nai (Sunset Beach)

Hat Rin Nok (Sunrise Beach)

Hat Seekantang

Lighthouse

INFORMATION
Backpackers Information Centre.........**1** B2
Backpackers Thailand.....................(see 1)
D's Books & Café..............................**2** B2
Post Office.......................................**3** B2

SLEEPING 🏠
Blue Marine......................................**4** B2
Cocohut Village................................**5** C3
Coral Bungalows..............................**6** A1
Delight...**7** B2
Drop In Club Resort & Spa...............**8** B2
Fairyland Resort................................**9** C1
Lighthouse......................................**10** D4
Palita Lodge....................................**11** C1
Paradise Bungalows.........................**12** C2
Pha-Ngan Bayshore Resort..............**13** B1
Phangan Buri Resort........................**14** A1
Same Same.....................................**15** B2
Sarikantang.....................................**16** C3
Sea Breeze Bungalow......................**17** B3
Sea Garden.....................................**18** B2
Seaside Bungalows..........................**19** A1
Seaview Haadrin Resort...................**20** C1
Sun Cliff...**21** B2
Tommy Resort.................................**22** C1

EATING 🍴
Chicken Corner...............................**23** B2
Lazy House......................................**24** B2
Lucky Crab......................................**25** B2
Mr K...**26** B2
Same Same Burger........................(see 15)

DRINKING 🍷
Club Paradise................................(see 12)
Warm Up Bar..................................**27** B2

ENTERTAINMENT 🎭
Backyard Club.................................**28** C3
Cactus Bar......................................**29** C2
Coral Bungalows Bar.......................(see 6)
Da Club...**30** C2

Drop-In Bar.....................................**31** C2
Mellow Mountain............................**32** C1
Orchid Club.....................................**33** C1
Rock...**34** C2
Tommy..(see 22)
Vinyl...**35** C2
Zoom..**36** C2

TRANSPORT
Sŏrng·tǎa·ou to Thong Sala............**37** B2

affable staff work around the clock making sure that smiles (and drinks) abound. Upstairs, the no-frills motel rooms get plenty of sunlight, but they need to be renovated.

Delight (Map p601; ☎ 0 7737 5527; www.delightresort .com; Ban Hat Rin; r 700-2000B; ☒) Tucked behind the bright yellow Kodak sign in the centre of Hat Rin, Delight offers some of the best lodging around. Spic-and-span hotel rooms come with subtle designer details (like peacock murals) and are sandwiched between an inviting swimming pool and a lazy lagoon peppered with lily pads.

Also recommended:

Seaview Haadrin Resort (Map p601; ☎ 0 7737 5160; Hat Rin Nok; bungalows from 500B; ☒) Bungalows are scattered along the north end of Sunrise Beach; the cheaper huts have tatami walls.

Blue Marine (Map p601; ☎ 0 7737 5079; Hat Rin Nai; bungalows 600-1200B; ☒) Prim concrete bungalows topped by shimmering blue-tiled roofs.

Sun Cliff (Map p601; ☎ 0 7737 5134; bungalows 250-2000B; ☒) Huge variety of bungalow types perched on a palm-studded knoll.

Midrange & Top End

Sea Breeze Bungalow (Map p601; ☎ 0 7737 5162; bungalows 500-8000B; ☒) Sea Breeze gets a good report card from our readers, and we agree; the labyrinth of secluded hillside cottages is an ideal hammocked retreat for any type of traveller. Several bungalows, poised high on stilts, deliver stunning views of Hat Rin and the sea.

Pha-Ngan Bayshore Resort (Map p601; ☎ 0 7737 5227, 0 7737 5224; www.phanganbayshore.com; Hat Rin Nok; r 800-5000B; ☒ 🖳 🖵) After a much-needed overhaul, this hotel-style operation has primed itself for the ever-increasing influx of flash-packers in Hat Rin. Sweeping beach views and a giant swimming pool make Pha-Ngan Bayshore one of the top addresses on Sunrise Beach.

Tommy Resort (Map p601; ☎ 0 7737 5215; www .phangantommyresort.com; Hat Rin Nok; r 1800-2200B; ☒ 🖳 🖵) Tommy is a trendy address in the heart of Hat Rin, striking a good balance between chic boutique and carefree backpacker hang-out. The rectangular swimming pool changes things up, since every other man-made body of water on the island looks like it was manufactured at the kidney-shaped pool factory.

Fairyland Resort (Map p601; ☎ 0 7737 5076, 08 5057 1709; www.haadrinfairyland.com; Hat Rin Nok; bungalows from 1400B; ☒) Although the name sounds like a board game for six-year-old girls, these prim bungalows are serious competition for the older resorts on Sunrise Beach. Walk-ins might be lucky enough to score a 60% discount depending on the time of the month and year – be sure to ask the other vacationers how much they're paying before you decide to check in.

our pick Sarikantang (Map p601; ☎ 0 7737 5055, 0 81 444 1322; www.sarikantang.com; Hat Seekantang; bungalows 500-3500B; ☒ 🖵) Don't get too strung out over trying to pronounce the resort's name – you can simply call this place heaven. Cream-coloured cabins, framed with teak posts and lintels, are sprinkled amongst swaying palms and crumbling winged statuettes. Inside, the rooms look like the set of a photo shoot for an interior-design magazine.

Palita Lodge (Map p601; ☎ 0 7737 5172; www.palita lodge.com; Hat Rin Nok; bungalows 1500-4500B; ☒ 🖵) Smack in the heart of the action, Palita is a tribute to the never-ending party that is Hat Rin's Sunrise Beach. Spacious concrete bungalows, with wooden accents and modern design elements, are neatly pressed together on this beachy wedge of sand and shrubs. Week-long bookings are a must during Full Moon revelry.

Cocohut Village (Map p601; ☎ 0 7737 5368; www .cocohut.com; Hat Seekantang; r 600B, bungalows 1900-10,000B; ☒ 🖳 🖵) A super-social place unto itself, guests might forget that they are just up the street from the brouhaha on Sunrise Beach. The backpacker digs, with shared locker room–styled toilets, are slightly subpar, however the pricier options, like the cliff villas and beachfront bungalows, are some of the best bets in Hat Rin.

Also recommended:

Drop In Club Resort & Spa (Map p601; ☎ 0 7737 5444; www.dropinclubresortandspa.com; Bat Hat Rin; r 1500-12,000B; ☒ 🖵) Ever-expanding resort in the heart of Hat Rin.

Phangan Buri Resort (Map p601; ☎ 0 7737 5481; www.phanganburiresort.com; Hat Rin Nai; bungalows from 2700B; ☒ 🖵) Upmarket but slightly uptight.

SOUTHERN BEACHES

The accommodation along the southern coast is the best bang for your baht on Ko Pha-Ngan. There are fleeting views of the islands in the Ang Thong Marine National Park; however, the southern beaches don't have the postcard-worthy crystal waters you might be longing for. This section starts at the port in Thong Sala and follows the coast east towards Hat Rin.

Thong Sala

There's really no reason to stay in Thong Sala, unless you're paranoid about missing a morning ferry, or feeling ill and seeking medical attention nearby.

Bua Kao Inn (☎ 0 7723 7226; buakao@samart.co.th; s & d from 450-850B; ☒) If you're looking for a town vibe rather than a strip of sand, Bua Kao is your best bet. The beds are comfy and the rooms are well kempt (although some have the faint smell of cigarette smoke) and the restaurant downstairs teems with chatty ex-pats.

Pha-Ngan Chai Hotel (☎ 0 7737 7068, 0 7737 7286; r 700-1200B; ☒ ▯) Think 'Soviet tenement meets tropical holiday' and you'll immediately spot this dowdy behemoth while landing at the Thong Sala pier. The convenient location is the hotel's best feature, although you'll need some cab fare to find a swimmable beach.

Ban Tai

The waters at Ban Tai tend to be shallow and opaque, especially during low season, but lodging options are well-priced compared to other parts of the island, and you're not too far from Hat Rin.

Lifestyle Bungalows (☎ 08 5916 3852; bungalows 250-600B; ☒) A skin artist by trade, the owner has tattooed each fan bungalow with an eye-catching assortment of designs and colours. The cluster of sandy huts embodies the true essence of Ko Pha-Ngan; no capitalist nonsense here, just a sign saying 'eat, drink and chill'.

Chokana (☎ 0 7723 8085; bungalows 400-1200B; ☒) Chokana is the Jabba the Hutt of huts; these wooden beachside bungalows are enormous. The bubbly owner genuinely cares about her clientele – the cabins have loads of personal touches such as wooden carvings and mosaics, and it feels as though all of the guests are repeat customers.

Coco Garden (☎ 0 7737 7721, 08 6073 1147; www.cocogardens.com; bungalows 500-1000B; ☒) The best budget spot along the southern coast, Coco Garden one-ups the nearby resorts with well-manicured grounds and sparkling bungalows that are almost pathologically clean. Free wi-fi available.

Phangan Great Bay Resort (☎ 0 7723 8659; fax 0 7723 8697; bungalows 1250-2000B; ☒ ▯ ☒) Take

your pick from motel rooms housed in a mauve structure, or comfy bungalows further afield that also make use of ostentatious colours like radioactive carrot and lime. Idle away the day trying to anthropomorphise the curious shape of the pool, or catch a movie on the TV in the restaurant.

Milky Bay Resort (☎ 0 7723 8566; www.milkybay.com; bungalows 1400-5000B; ☒ ▯ ☒) Milky white walls, which permeate the grounds, are peppered with large black stones resembling the spots on a cow. These bovine bulwarks snake through the resort linking the airy thatched bungalows to the sea. A family favourite with an exceptionally professional staff, Milky Bay would earn a '10 out of 10' if it weren't for the restaurant's excessively expensive menu, although the food is quite tasty…

Ban Khai

Like Ban Tai, the beaches aren't the most stunning, but the accommodation is cheap and there are beautiful views of Ang Thong Marine National Park in the distance.

Lee's Garden (☎ 08 5916 3852; bungalows 250-600B) If Lee's Garden had a soundtrack, it would probably be Bob Marley's greatest hits. The clump of comfy wooden huts is a wonderful throwback to a time when Pha-Ngan attracted a grittier backpacker who wasn't fussed about hot showers or air-con.

Boom's Cafe Bungalows (☎ 0 7723 8318; www.boomscafe.com; bungalows 300-1000B; ☒) Staying at Boom's is like visiting the Thai family you never knew you had. The friendly owners lovingly tend their sandy acreage and dote on the contented clientele. No one seems to mind that there's no swimming pool, since the curling tide rolls right up to your doorstep. Boom's is located at the far eastern corner of Ban Kai, near Hat Rin.

Mac Bay (☎ 0 7723 8443; bungalows 500-1500B; ☒ ☒) Home to the Black Moon Party (another lunar excuse for Ko Pha-Ngan to go wild), Mac Bay is a sandy slice of Ban Khai where even the cheaper bungalows are spic and span. At beer o'clock, grab a shaded spot on the sand and watch the sun dance amorphous shadows over the distant islands of Ang Thong Marine National Park.

Morning Star (☎ 0 7737 7756; morningstarkpn@yahoo.com; bungalows 1190-2490B; ☒ ☒) This collection of wooden and concrete jungle cottages has spotless interiors; some rooms are furnished with noticeably ornate dressers and vanities, others

LOWER SOUTHERN GULF

have subtle dark-wood trimming. A dozen white wooden beach chairs orbit the adorable kidney bean–shaped swimming pool.

WEST COAST BEACHES

Now that there are two smooth roads between Thong Sala and Chalok Lam, the west coast has seen a lot of development. The atmosphere is a pleasant mix between the east coast's quiet seclusion and Hat Rin sociable vibe, although the beaches along the western shores aren't as picturesque as the other parts of the island.

Nai Wok to Srithanu

Close to Thong Sala, the resorts peppered along this breezy strip mingle with patches of gnarled mangroves. Despite the lack of appealing beaches, the prices are cheap and the sunsets are memorable.

Cookies Bungalows (☎ 0 7737 7499; cookies _bungalow@hotmail.com; bungalows 300-1000B; ✶) Cookie's friendly service sets this bundle of bungalows apart, although the accommodation is a standard-issue assemblage of bamboo, thatch and wooden slats.

Sea Scene (☎ 0 7737 7516; www.seascene.com; bungalows 500-1700B; ✶) Sea Scene's family-sized bungalows are sprawled along a tangle of old mangroves and offer front-row seats to the blazing sunsets over Ang Thong Marine National Park in the distance.

Grand Sea Resort (☎ 0 7737 7777; www.grand searesort.com; bungalows 1200-3000B; ✶ ✿) A good choice for those wanting a bit of sand close to Thong Sala, Grand Sea feels like a collection of wooden Thai spirit houses.

Hat Chaophao

Like Hat Yao up the coast, this rounded beach is lined with a variety of bungalow operations. There's an inland lake further south, and a 7-Eleven to cure your midnight munchies.

Sunset Cove (☎ 0 7734 9211; www.thaisunsetcove.com; bungalows 1500-3350B; ✶ ⌨ ✿) There's a feeling of Zen symmetry amongst the forested assortment of boutique bungalows; the towering bamboo shoots are evenly spaced along the cobbled paths weaving through brush and boulders. The beachside abodes are particularly elegant, sporting slatted rectangular windows and barrel-basined bathtubs.

Pha-Ngan Paragon (☎ 08 4728 6064; www.phangan paragon.com; bungalows 2500-13,000B; ✶ ⌨ ✿) A tiny hideaway with seven rooms, Paragon has decor that incorporates stylistic elements from the ancient Khmer, India and Thailand, without forfeiting any modern amenities. The 'royal bedroom' deserves a special mention – apparently the canopied bed has been imported from Kashmir.

Hat Yao & Hat Son

One of the busier beaches along the west coast, Hat Yao sports a swimmable beach, numerous resorts and a few extra conveniences like ATMs and convenience stores.

Ibiza (☎ 0 7734 9121; www.ibizabungalows.com; bungalows 150-1300B; ✶) Ibiza brings Hat Rin's youthful backpacker vibe up the west coast to Hat Yao. The no-frills bungalows are run of the mill, but the friendly staff members, appealing central garden, and cheap rates keep budget travellers coming back for more.

Tantawan Bungalow (☎ 0 7734 9108; www.tan tawanbungalow.com; bungalows 450-550B; ✿) Little Tantawan sits high up in the jungle like a tree house, boasting soaring sea views from the sprinkle of rugged bungalows. Guests can take a dip in the trapezoidal swimming pool or enjoy the sunrise on their small bamboo porch. Don't forget to try the tasty French and Thai dishes at the on-site restaurant.

High Life (☎ 0 7734 9114; www.highlifebungalow .com; bungalows 500-2000B; ✶ ✿) We can't decide what's more conspicuous: the dramatic ocean views from the infinity-edged swimming pool, or the blatant double entendre in the resort's name. True to its moniker, the 25 bungalows, of various shapes and sizes, sit on a palmed outcropping of granite soaring high above the cerulean sea. Advance bookings will set you back an extra 200B.

Haad Son Resort (☎ 0 7734 9104; www.haadson .info; bungalows 1000-8000B; ✶ ⌨ ✿) The word 'complex' has a double meaning at this vast resort; we suggest leaving a trail of breadcrumbs along the serpentine paths if you ever want to find the way back to your room. The poshest rooms aren't worth the baht, so go for the budget digs; they're simple, but you'll have access to all of the on-site amenities.

Haad Yao Bay View (☎ 0 7734 9193; www.haadyao -bayviewresort.com; r & bungalows 2000-5000B; ✶ ⌨ ✿) Sparkling after a recent facelift, this conglomeration of bungalows and hotel-style accommodation looks like a tropical mirage on Hat Yao's northern headland. Vacationers, in various states of undress, linger around the large turquoise swimming pool catching rays and Zs. Others nest in their private suites amid polished hardwood floors and wicker day-beds.

Hat Salad

One of the best beaches on the island, Hat Salad has a string of quality accommodation along the sand.

Cookies Salad (☎ 0 7734 9125, 08 3181 7125; www .cookies-phangan.com; bungalows 1500-3000B) The resort with a tasty name has delicious Balinese-style bungalows orbiting a two-tiered lap pool tiled in various shades of blue. Shaggy thatching and dense tropical foliage gives the realm a certain rustic quality, although you won't want for creature comforts.

Green Papaya (☎ 0 7737 4182; www.greenpapaya resort.com; bungalows 4000-7500B; ✂ ▢ ☎) The polished wooden bungalows at Green Papaya are a clear standout along the lovely beach at Hat Salad, however they come at quite a hefty price.

Ao Mae Hat

The northwest tip of the island has excellent ocean vistas, and little Ko Ma is connected to Pha-Ngan by a stunning sand bar.

Royal Orchid (☎ 0 7737 4182; royal_orchid_maehaad@ hotmail.com; bungalows 300-800B; ✂ ▢) Handsome backpacker bungalows are arranged like a zipper along a slender garden bath – most have fleeting views of the serene beach and idyllic sand bar that extends to scenic Ko Ma offshore.

Pha-Ngan Utopia Resort (☎ 0 7737 4093; www .phanganutopia.com; bungalows 1500-3000B; ✂ ▢ ☎) It's pretty audacious to name one's resort 'Utopia', but the owners have done an excellent job of creating an idyllic jungle retreat perched high above the sea. Our favourite rooms – the two-storey villas – slope down the mountainside and have an entire level dedicated to an extra-large Jacuzzi.

NORTHERN BEACHES

Stretching from Chalok Lam to Thong Nai Pan, the dramatic northern coast is a wild jungle with several stunning and secluded beaches – it's the most scenic coast on the island.

Chalok Lam (Chaloklum) & Hat Khom

The cramped fishermen's village at Chalok Lam is like no other place on Ko Pha-Ngan. The conglomeration of teak shanties and huts is a palpable reminder that the wide-reaching hand of globalisation has yet to touch some parts of the world. *Sŏrng·tǎa·ou* ply the route

from here to Thong Sala for around 100B per person. There's a dirt road leading from Chalok Lam to Hat Khom, and water taxis are available as well (50B to 100B).

Sarisa Place (bungalows from 250B) Trippy seashells dangle on the porches at Sarisa, which offers cheap (but lacklustre) semi-detached bungalows. Guests get a free motorbike rental to tool around the island (petrol not included).

Fanta (☎ 0 7737 4132; fantaphangan@yahoo.com; bungalows 300-700B) Not to be confused with Fantasea next-door, Fanta sits at the far eastern side of Chaloklum and boasts rows of old-school Pha-Ngan bungalows (think lots of worn wood and thatch) on a sizeable chunk of sand.

Coral Bay (☎ 0 7737 4245; bungalows 150-600B) Perched on a small promontory separating Chaloklum from Hat Khom, Coral Bay's seemingly secluded selection of classic backpacker digs can be easily accessed by road or water taxi from the heart of Chaloklum.

Mandalai (☎ 0 7737 4316; www.mymandalai.com; r 2750-5600B; ✂ ▢ ☎) Like an ash-white Riyadh from a distant Arabian land, this small boutique hotel quietly towers over the surrounding shantytown of fishermen's huts. Floor-to-ceiling windows command views of tangerine-coloured fishing boats in the bay, and there's an intimate wading pool hidden in the inner cloister.

Bottle Beach (Hat Khuat)

This isolated dune has garnered a reputation as a low-key getaway, and has thus become quite popular. During high season, places can fill up fast so it's best to try and arrive early. Grab a long-tail taxi boat from Chalok Lam for 50B to 120B (depending on the boat's occupancy).

Bottle Beach II (☎ 0 7744 5156; bungalows 350-400B) At the far eastern corner of the beach, this is the spot where penny pinchers can live out their castaway fantasies.

Smile (☎ 08 1956 3133; smilebeach@hotmail.com; bungalows 400-700B) At the far west corner of the beach, Smile features an assortment of wooden huts that climb up a forested hill. The two-storey bungalows (700B) are our favourite.

Haad Khuad Resort (☎ 0 7744 5153; www.geocities .com/haadkhuad_resort; r 1800-2200B; ✂) Although significantly more expensive than the other sleeping spots on Bottle Beach, this small hotel is worth the splurge. The rooms are fastidiously clean and they all feature floor-to-ceiling windows that face the cerulean bay.

Thong Nai Pan

The pair of rounded bays at Thong Nai Pan looks a bit like buttocks; Ao Thong Nai Pan Yai (*yai* means 'big') is the northern half, and Ao Thong Nai Pan Noi (*noi* means 'little') curves just below. These beaches have been increasing in popularity over the last few years as a pleasant alternative to the raucous in Hat Rin. See p609 for information about transport to Thong Nai Pan.

Dolphin (bungalows 500-1300B; ☒) Sorry Dolphin, we have to let the cat out of the bag…you're the best sleeping spot on the island. This hidden retreat gives yuppie travellers a chance to rough it in style, while granola types will soak up every inch of the laid-back charm. Quiet afternoons are spent lounging on the comfy cushions in one of the small pagodas hidden throughout the jungle. Lodging is only available on a first-come basis.

Havana (☎ 0 7744 5162; www.phanganhavana.com; r 3000-4500B, ste 7000-8000B; ☒ ☐) The newest spot in Thong Nai Pan features psychedelic ocean-inspired murals in the rooms, which are arranged in apartment-style complexes around an inviting swimming pool.

Santhiya (☎ 0 7723 8333; www.santhiya.com; bungalows from 10,000B; ☒ ☐ ☒) Beautiful Santhiya feels a bit out of place on Ko Samui's shabby younger brother. Ko Pha-Ngan is accustomed to bamboo huts, not maid service and flamboyant gestures of Siamese design.

EAST COAST BEACHES

Robinson Crusoe, eat your heart out. The east coast is the ultimate hermit hang-out. For the most part, you'll have to hire a boat to get to these beaches, but water taxis are available in Thong Sala and Hat Rin. Some of these secluded beaches can even be reached by taking the ferry connecting Thong Nai Pan and Mae Nam on Ko Samui (see p609).

Than Sadet & Thong Reng

Accessible by 4WD vehicles and colourful taxi boats, quiet Than Sadet and Thong Reng are the island's best-kept secrets for seclusion seekers.

Treehouse (treehouse.kp@googlemail.com; bungalows from 200B) Ko Chang (the big Ko Chang)'s legendary backpacker hang-out has recently set up shop along the secluded waters of Thong Reng. Follow the cheery plastic flowers over the hill from Than Sadet to find uberbasic digs drenched in bright shades of paint.

Plaa's (☎ 0 7744 5191; bungalows 600B; ☐) Plaa's colourful village of bungalows sits on the northern headland of Than Sadet overlooking the bay below. Grab a Corona, 'cause this is the perfect place to shoot one of those idyllic-beach beer commercials.

Mai Pen Rai (☎ 0 7744 5090; www.thansadet.com; bungalows 600B; ☐) 'Mai pen rai' is the Thai equivalent of 'don't worry, be happy', which isn't too surprising since this bay elicits nothing but sedate smiles. Bungalows mingle with Plaa's on the hilly headland, and sport panels of straw weaving with gabled roofs.

Hat Thian

Geographically, Hat Thian is quite close to Hat Rin; however, there are no roads and the crude hiking trail is lengthy and confusing. Ferry taxis are available from Hat Rin for around 150B.

Beam Bungalows (☎ 0 7927 2854, 08 6947 3205; bungalows 300-500B) Beam is set back from the beach and tucked behind a coconut palm grove. Charming wooden huts have dangling hammocks out front, and big bay windows face the ocean through the swaying palms.

Sanctuary (☎ 08 1271 3614; www.thesanctuarythailand.com; dm 120B, bungalows 400-3800B) A friendly enclave promoting relaxation, this inviting haven offers luxury lodging and also functions as a holistic retreat offering everything from yoga classes to detox sessions. Accommodation, in various manifestations of twigs, is scattered around the resort, married to the natural surroundings. You'll want to Nama-stay forever.

Hat Yuan

Hat Yuan has a few bungalow operations, and is quite secluded as there are no roads connecting this little beach to Hat Rin down the coast.

Barcelona (☎ 0 7737 5113; bungalows 200-600B) Solid wood huts come in two shades: natural wood or creamy white. They climb up the hill on stilts behind a palm garden and have good vistas and jovial staff.

Eating

Ko Pha-Ngan is no culinary capital, especially since most visitors quickly absorb the lazy lifestyle and wind up eating at their accommodation. Those with an adventurous appetite should check out Thong Sala and the island's southern coast.

HAT RIN

This bustling 'burb has the largest conglomeration of restaurants and bars on the island, yet most of them are pretty lousy. The infamous Chicken Corner (Map p601) is a popular intersection stocked with several poultry peddlers promising to cure the munchies, be it noon or midnight.

Mr K (Map p601; ☎ 0 7737 5470; dishes 50-80B; ☺ 24hr) Our favourite joint at 'Chicken Corner', Mr K offers local eats all night long. Cheesy Thai soap-operas blare on the TV, and there's dirt-cheap beer to wash down your meal.

Same Same Burger (Map p601; ☎ 0 7737 5200; www.same-same.com; burgers 180-230B; ☺ lunch & dinner) Owned by the folks who run the backpacker digs with the *same same* name, this bright-red burger joint is the *same same* as McDonald's.

Lazy House (Map p601; ☎ 0 7737 5432; dishes 90-270B; ☺ lunch & dinner) Back in the day, this joint was the owner's apartment – everyone liked his cooking so much that he decided to turn the place into a restaurant and hang-out spot. Today, Lazy House is easily one of Hat Rin's best places to veg in front of a movie with a scrumptious shepherd's pie.

Lucky Crab (Map p601; dishes 100-400B; ☺ lunch & dinner) Lucky Crab is your best bet for seafood in Hat Rin. Rows of freshly caught creatures are presented nightly atop miniature long-tail boats loaded with ice. Once you've picked your prey, grab a table inside amid dangling plants and charming stone furnishings.

SOUTHERN BEACHES

Thong Sala

our pick **Night Market** (dishes 25-180B; ☺ 6.30-10.30pm) A heady mix of steam and snacking locals, Thong Sala's night market is a must for those looking for a dose of culture while nibbling on a low-priced snack. The best place to grab some cheap grub is the stall in the far right corner with a large white banner. Hit up the vender next door for tasty seafood platters, like red snapper served over a bed of thick noodles. Banana pancakes and fruit smoothies abound for dessert (of course).

Vantana Restaurant (☎ 0 7723 8813; dishes 80-150B; ☺ breakfast, lunch & dinner) Spilling out onto Soi Krung Thai Bank, Vantana offers a hearty selection of English eats. The gut-busting Sunday Brunch (260B) is the perfect cure for homesick Brits.

Kaito (☎ 0 7737 7738; dishes from 130B; ☺ 3-9pm Thu-Mon) Authentic Japanese imports (sorry, no sushi) are the speciality here – slurp an Asahi while savouring your tangy seaweed salad and *tonkatsu* (pork cutlet). The upstairs level offers cosy cushioned seating while the main sitting area is flanked with *manga* and pocket-sized Japanese novels.

A's Coffee Shop & Restaurant (☎ 0 7737 7226; dishes 80-260B; ☺ breakfast, lunch & dinner Mon-Sat) Located on Soi Krung Thai Bank, A's is the perfect place to nab some heart-clogging British pub grub, if you're stuck in town waiting for the ferry.

Pizza Chiara (☎ 0 7737 7626; pizzas 180-320B; ☺ lunch & dinner) The quintessential chequered tables confirm it (in case you didn't guess from the name): Pizza Chiara is all about tasty Italian fare. Go for the Pizza Cecco smothered with prosciutto, salami, mushrooms and *cotto* cheese.

John's Bar & Bistro (☎ 08 7345 5417; dishes from 195B ☺ lunch & dinner) John, a professional chef and English expat, serves scrumptious roast dinners and refined European fare. Tuesday is quiz night.

Ban Tai & Ban Khai

Like in Thong Sala nearby, the small villages of Ban Tai and Ban Khai have some solid dining options as well.

Ando Loco (☎ 08 6780 7200; meals from 59B ☺ dinner) This outdoor Mexican hang-out looks like an animation cell from a vintage Hanna Barbera cartoon, with assorted kitschy accoutrements like papier-mâché cacti. Down a super-sized margarita and show your skills on the beach volleyball court.

Somtum Inter (☎ 0 7737 7334; dishes 40-80B ☺ breakfast, lunch & dinner) Housed in a breezy open-air pavilion next door to Boat Ahoy (owned by the same family; see p608), Somtum announces its speciality in the restaurant's name: spicy papaya salad (*sôm·đam*). Other Isan favourites, such as crispy fried beef, are also a big hit.

Maew Hot Pan BBQ (☎ 08 1970 4077; buffet 110B; ☺ dinner) The island's best do-it-yourself dinner joint, Maew is an all-you-can-eat affair where diners cook their meats, veggies and quail eggs (a local fave) over a gurgling hot pot. Maew can be easy to miss; it is located on the ocean side of Ban Tai's main road near the 7-Eleven.

Boat Ahoy (☎ 0 7723 8759, 0 7737 7334; dishes 100-180B ❤ breakfast, lunch & dinner) A compound of open-air pavilions encased in slats of mahogany wood, Boat Ahoy offers a night's worth of fun. After feasting on a variety of sensational Asian victuals (the beef salad and cashew chicken are especially delish), grab a drink at the boat-shaped bar, or re-enact the Spice Girls' reunion tour in your own private karaoke suite.

WEST COAST BEACHES

Tantawan (☎ 0 7734 9108; Hat Son; dishes 60-200B; ❤ lunch & dinner) This charming teak hut, nestled amongst jungle fronds, drips with clinking chandeliers made from peach coral and khaki-coloured seashells. Diners sit in a sea of geometric cushions while gobbling up some of the tastiest Thai- and French-inspired dishes on the island.

Absolute Island (☎ 0 7734 9109; Hat Yao; dishes 60-250B; ❤ breakfast, lunch & dinner) The name sounds like a Swedish vodka ad, but it's only by coincidence that the menu has some Scandinavian classics. Actually, every traveller will find a dish from his or her native country – Absolute's menu is so vast, it really needs an index.

Drinking

Every month, on the night of the full moon, pilgrims pay tribute to the party gods with trance-like dancing, wild screaming and glow-in-the-dark body paint. The throngs of bucket-sippers and fire twirlers gather on the infamous Sunrise Beach (Hat Rin Nok) and party til the sun replaces the moon in the sky.

A few other noteworthy spots can be found around the island for those seeking something a bit mellower.

HAT RIN

Hat Rin is the beating heart of the legendary Full Moon fun, and the area can get pretty wound up even without the influence of lunar phases. The following party venues flank Hat Rin's infamous Sunrise Beach from south to north:

Rock (Map p601; ☎ 0 7737 5244) Great views of the party.

Club Paradise (Map p601; ☎ 0 7737 5244) Paradise basks in its celebrity status as the genesis of the lunar *loco*-motion.

Drop-In Bar (Map p601; ☎ 0 7737 5374) This dance shack blasts the chart toppers that we all secretly love. The other nights of the year are equally as boisterous.

Zoom (Map p601) An ear-popping trance venue.

Vinyl (Map p601) Bigger than Zoom, Vinyl cranks up the beat on its epic sound system.

Cactus Bar (Map p601; ☎ 0 7737 5308) Smack in the centre of Hat Rin Nok, Cactus pumps out a healthy mix of old-school tunes, hip hop and R&B.

Da Club (Map p601) A newer spot on the sand where trance beats shake the graffitied walls.

Orchid Club (Map p601) Features drum & bass sounds rather than the usual trance.

Tommy (Map p601; ☎ 0 7737 5215) One of Hat Rin's largest venues lures the masses with black lights and trance music blaring on the sound system. Drinks are dispensed from a large ark-like bar.

Mellow Mountain (Map p601; ☎ 0 7737 5347) Also called 'Mushy Mountain' (you'll know why when you get there), this trippy hang-out sits at the northern edge of Hat Rin Nok delivering stellar views of the shenanigans below.

These haunts are located elsewhere in Hat Rin:

Coral Bungalows Bar (Map p601; ☎ 0 7737 5023) Back on Hat Rin Nai (Sunset Beach), Coral's pool-centric powwows are so raucous, they might just eclipse the Full Moon parties.

Backyard Club (Map p601) The Backyard Club separates the strong from the weak – only the most hardcore make it to their Full Moon after-parties. When Hat Rin Nok shuts down mid-morning, surviving 'Mooners' stumble over for a second round of slippery beats. And we all know there's nothing better than a beer to cure a hangover.

Warm Up Bar (Map p601; ☎ 08 9652 1778) Groove to DJed beats or shoot some pool – this sit-down joint, in the heart of Hat Rin town, is the perfect place to (yup, you guessed it) warm up for wild night out.

OTHER BEACHES

Eagle Pub (☎ 08 4839 7143; Hat Yao) At the southern end of Hat Yao, this drink-dealing shack, built right into the rock face, is tattooed with the neon graffiti of virtually every person that's passed out on the lime-green patio furniture after too many *caiparinhas*.

Amsterdam (☎ 0 7723 8447; Ao Plaay Laem) Near Hat Chaophao on the west coast, Amsterdam attracts tourists and locals from all over the island who are looking for a chill spot to watch the sunset.

Pirates Bar (☎ 08 4728 6064; Hat Chaophao) This popular and wacky drinkery is a replica of a pirate ship built into the cliffs. When you're sitting on the deck and the tide is high (and you've had a couple of drinks), you can almost believe you're out at sea. These guys host the well-attended Moon Set parties, three

---

BUCKIN' FUCKETS

Like getting drunk but hate wasting time drinking? Ko Pha-Ngan has invented the mother-of-all booze bombs: the Red Bull bucket, which contains Coke, Red Bull (a product of Thailand), and a pint of vodka or Saeng Som (local whisky). The concoction is mixed unceremoniously in a plastic pale, and festooned with straws so that your mooching buddies can share in the attack. The mixture goes down easy, real easy, and catapults drinkers from slightly tipsy to…well…put it this way: after a night of bucket bingeing, you'll be slurring words and mixing up your syllables…

---

days before Hat Rin gets pumpin' for the Full Moon fun.

Sheesha Bar (☎ 0 7737 4161; Chalok Lam) The antithesis of grungy Hat Rin, Sheesha Bar swaps buckets of Samsung for designer drinks. The enticing patchwork of beige sandstone and horizontal slats of mahogany wood fit right in with the arabesque Mandalai Hotel across the street (and owned by the same family).

Mason's Arms (☎ 08 5884 7271; Thong Sala; ☻ 10.30am-11.30pm) Suddenly, a clunky structure emerges from the swaying palms; it's a Tudor-style cottage, plucked directly from Stratford-upon-Avon and plunked down in the steamy jungle. This lodge-like lair is one blood pudding away from being an official British colony.

Getting There & Away

As always, the cost and departure times are in flux. Rough waves are known to cancel ferries between the months of October and December. Beware of travel agencies in Bangkok and Surat Thani selling fake boat-train combinations.

BANGKOK, HUA HIN & CHUMPHON

Lomprayah (www.lomprayah.com) and **Seatran Discovery** (www.seatrandiscovery.com) have bus-boat combination packages departing from Bangkok and passing through Chumphon. It is also quite hassle-free to take the train from Bangkok to Chumphon and switch to a ferry service (it works out to be about the same price). For detailed information about travelling through Chumphon see p572 or p622. Bangkok-bound passengers can choose to disembark in Hua Hin.

KO SAMUI

There are almost 10 daily departures between Ko Pha-Ngan and Ko Samui (200B to 350B). These boats leave throughout the day from 7am to 4pm and take from 30 minutes to an hour. All leave from either Thong Sala or Hat Rin on Ko Pha-Ngan and arrive either in Na Thon, Mae Nam or the Bang Rak pier on Ko Samui. If the final location matters, state your preferences while buying your ticket.

The *Haad Rin Queen* (200B) goes back and forth between Hat Rin and Big Buddha Beach. Ferry service from Samui's Mae Nam pier leaves at noon and wanders up the eastern coast of Ko Pha-Ngan, stopping in Hat Thian, Than Sadet and Thong Nai Pan. Boats running in the other direction leave Thong Nai Pan at 9am.

There are no car ferries between Ko Pha-Ngan and Ko Samui, you must return to the mainland and take a separate boat.

KO TAO

Ko Tao–bound Lomprayah and Seatran Discovery ferries depart Ko Pha-Ngan at 8.30am and 1pm and arrive at 9.45am and 2.15pm. Songserm leaves Ko Pha-Ngan at noon and arrives at 1.45pm. Note the catamaran ferry times are always in flux and it is best to check the timetable with a travel agent.

SURAT THANI & THE ANDAMAN COAST

Combination boat-bus tickets are available at any travel agency; simply tell them your desired destination and they will sell you the necessary links in the transport chain. Most travellers will pass through Surat Thani as they swap coasts. There are approximately six daily departures between Ko Pha-Ngan and Surat Thani (220B to 350B, 2½ hours) on the Raja Car Ferry, Songserm or Seatran. These boats leave from Thong Sala throughout the day from 7am to 8pm. Every night, depending on the weather, a night boat runs from Surat, departing at 11pm. Boats in the opposite direction leave Ko Pha-Ngan at 10pm. See the Backpackers Information Centre website (p597) for detailed departure times to most Andaman destinations.

Getting Around

See p597 for important information about the dangers of riding motorbikes around the island. You can rent motorcycles all over the island for 150B to 250B per day. Always wear

LOWER SOUTHERN GULF

a helmet – it's the law on Ko Pha-Ngan, and local policemen are starting to enforce it. Bicycle rentals are discouraged unless you're fit enough to take on Lance Armstrong. Car rentals are around 1000B a day.

Some places, such as Bottle Beach and some sections of the eastern coast, can only be reached by boat. If you do find trails, keep in mind that they are often overgrown and not suitable for solo navigation.

Sŏrng·tăa·ou chug along the island's major roads and the riding rates double after sunset. Ask your accommodation about free or discount transfers when you leave the island. The trip from Thong Sala to Hat Rin is 50B; further beaches will set you back around 100B.

Long-tail boats depart from Thong Sala, Chalok Lam and Hat Rin, heading to a variety of far-flung destinations like Hat Khuat (Bottle Beach) and Ao Thong Nai Pan. Expect to pay anywhere from 50B, for a short trip, to 300B for a lengthier journey. You can charter a private boat ride from beach to beach for about 150B per 15 minutes of travel.

KO TAO
เกาะเต่า
pop 5000

First there was Ko Samui, then Ko Pha-Ngan; now, the cult of Ko Tao ('Ko Taoism' perhaps?) has emerged along Thailand's crystalline Gulf Coast. Today, thousands of visitors come to worship the turquoise waters offshore, and quite often many of them stay. The secret to Ko Tao's undeniable appeal? Simple: although the island is only 21 sq km, tiny Tao sure knows how to pack it in – there's something for everyone, and nothing is in moderation. Diving enthusiasts cavort with sharks and rays in a playground of tangled neon coral. Hikers and hermits can re-enact an episode from 'Lost' in the dripping coastal jungles. And when you're Robinson Crusoe-ed out, hit the bumpin' bar scene that rages on until dawn.

Many years have already passed since the first backpacker came to the scrubby island and planted a flag in the name of self-respecting shoestring travellers everywhere, but fret not, there's still plenty of time to join the tribe. Ko Tao has many years to go before corporate resort owners bulldoze rustic cottages, and visitors start discussing stockholdings rather than sea creatures spotted on their latest dive.

Orientation

Ferries pull into Mae Hat, on the western side of the island. This seaside town has all the tourist amenities one would need: travel agencies, hotels, dive shops, restaurants, internet cafes and motorcycle rentals. The biggest village on the island is Sairee Beach (also called Hat Sai Ri), about 2km up the coast. Here, travellers will find similar amenities but in greater quantity. Chalok Ban Kao, on the muddy southern coast, is the island's third settlement.

The island's eastern and northern coasts are fairly undeveloped compared to the bustling west coast, with only a few bungalow enterprises on each little bay. A paved road connects the west coast to Tanote Bay; a four-wheel vehicle should be used when navigating any of the other rugged roads in the area.

About the only thing of historic interest on the island is a large boulder, which has the initials of King Rama V, commemorating his royal visit in 1899.

Information
EMERGENCY
Police station (☎ 0 7745 6631) At the northern end of Mae Hat near the beach.

INTERNET ACCESS
Rates are generally 2B per minute, with a 20B minimum, and discounts if you log on for one hour or longer. You may find that certain useful tourism websites have been firewalled at internet cafes affiliated with travel agencies.

INTERNET RESOURCES
Koh Tao Community (www.kohtao-community.com) A forum offering general info about the various goings-on around the island.
Koh Tao Online (www.kohtaoonline.com) An online version of the handy *Koh Tao Info* booklet.
Just Koh Tao (www.justkohtao.com) A blog focused on local diving and conservation information.

LAUNDRY
After a few dives, you'll probably want to wash your swim trunks (especially if you saw a shark and 'accidentally' peed your wetsuit). Almost every bungalow operation (and even some restaurants) offers laundry service. One kilo of laundry should be 30B, although operations closer to the beach tend to charge 40B. You may want to ask your diving instructor where he or she gets their washing

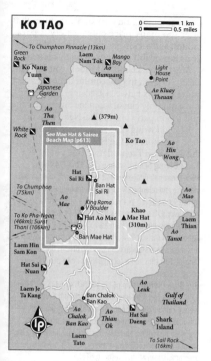

KO TAO

0 ___ 1 km
0 ___ 0.5 miles

To Chumphon Pinnacle (13km)
Green Rock
Ko Nang Yuan
Laem Nam Tok
Mango Bay
Ao Muruang
Light House Point
Japanese Garden
Ao Kluay Theuan
Ao Tha Then
▲ (379m)
White Rock
See Mae Hat & Sairee Beach Map (p613)
Ko Tao
Ao Hin Wong
Hat Sai Ri
Ban Hat Sai Ri
Ao Mao
To Chumphon (75km)
Ao Mae
King Rama V Boulder
Khao Mae Hat (310m)
Hat Ao Mae
Laem Thian
To Ko Pha-Ngan (46km); Surat Thani (106km)
Ban Mae Hat
Ao Tanot
Laem Hin Sam Kon
Hat Sai Nuan
▲
Laem Je Ta Kang
Ao Leuk
Gulf of Thailand
Ban Chalok Ban Kao
Ao Chalok Ban Kao
Ao Thian Ok
Hat Sai Daeng
Shark Island
Laem Tato
To Sail Rock (16km)

Diver Safety Support (SSS Recompression Chamber Network; Map p613; ☎ 0 7745 6572, 08 1083 0533; kohtao@sssnetwork.com; Mae Hat; ☺ on call 24hr) Has a temporary hyperbaric chamber and offers emergency evacuation services.

MONEY
As a general rule, there are 24-hour ATMs at every 7-Eleven on the island. We also found five ATMs orbiting the ferry docks at Mae Hat. There is a money-exchange window at Mae Hat's pier and a second location near Choppers in Sairee. There are several banks near the post office in Mae Hat, at the far end of town along the island's main inland road.

POST
Post Office (☎ 0 7745 6170; ☺ 9am-5pm Mon-Fri, 9am-noon Sat) A 10- to 15-minute walk from the pier; at the corner of Ko Tao's main inner-island road and Mae Hat Boulevard.

TOURIST INFORMATION & TRAVEL AGENCIES
There's no government-run TAT office on Ko Tao. Transport and accommodation bookings can be made at any of the numerous travel agencies, all of which take a commission on services rendered.

Dangers & Annoyances
There's nothing more annoying than enrolling in a diving course with your friends and then having to drop out because you scraped your knee in a motorcycle accident. The roads on Ko Tao are horrendous, save the main drag connecting Sairee Beach to Chalok Ban Kao. While hiring a moped is extremely convenient, this is not the place to learn how to drive. The island is rife with abrupt hills and sudden sand pits along gravel trails. Even if you escape unscathed from a riding experience, scamming bike shops may claim that you damaged your rental and will try to extort you for some serious bling.

Activities
DIVING
Never been diving before? Ko Tao is *the* place to lose your scuba virginity. The island issues more scuba certifications than in any other place around the world, which means that prices are low and quality is high as dozens of dive shops vie for your baht. The shallow bays that scallop the island are the perfect

done, as sometimes items get conveniently lost. Express service is usually available for 60B per kilogram.

MEDIA
The ubiquitous *Koh Tao Info* booklet lists loads of businesses on the island and goes into some detail about the island's history, culture and social issues. The pocket-sized *Sabai Jai* is a new publication on the island dedicated to ecotravel.

MEDICAL SERVICES
All divers must sign a medical waiver before exploring the sea. If you have any medical condition that might hinder your ability to dive (including mild asthma), you will be asked to get medical clearance from a doctor on Ko Tao. Consider seeing a doctor before your trip as there are no official hospitals on the island, and the number of qualified medical professionals is limited. Also, make sure your travel insurance covers scuba diving.
Bangkok Samui Hospital (Map p613; ☎ 0 7742 9500; Hat Sai Ri; ☺ on call 24hr) Offers competent medical service in a large glassy storefront.

spot for newbie divers to take their first stab at scuba. On shore, over 40 dive centres are ready to saddle you up with some gear and teach you the ropes in a three-and-a-half-day Open Water course. We know, we know, homework on a holiday sucks, but the intense competition among scuba schools means that certification prices are unbeatably low, and the standards of service are top notch.

It's no surprise that this underwater playground has become exceptionally popular with beginners; the waters are crystal clear, there are loads of neon reefs and temperatures feel like bathwater. The best dive sites are found at offshore pinnacles within a 20km radius of the island (see boxed text, p614), but seasoned scubaholics will probably prefer the top-notch sites along the Andaman Coast. The local marine wildlife includes grouper, moray eels, batfish, bannerfish, barracuda, titan triggerfish, angelfish, clownfish (Nemos), stingrays, reef sharks and frequent visits by the almighty whale sharks.

When you alight at the pier in Mae Hat, swarms of touts will try to coax you into staying at their dive resort with promises of a 'special price for you'. There are dozens of dive centres on the island, so it's best to arrive armed with the names of a few reputable dive schools. If you aren't rushed for time, consider relaxing on the island for a couple of days before making any diving decisions – you will undoubtedly bump into swarms of divers and instructors who will gladly offer their advice and opinions. Remember: the success of your diving experience (especially if you are learning how to dive) will largely depend on how much you like your instructor. There are other factors to consider as well, like the size of your diving group, the condition of your equipment and the condition of the dive sites, to name a few.

For the most part, diving prices are standardised across the island, so there's no need to spend your time hunting around for the best deal. A **PADI** (www.padi.com) Open Water course costs 9800B; an **SSI** (www.ssithailand.com) Open Water course is slightly less at 9000B, because you do not have to pay for instructional materials. An Advanced certificate will set you back 8500B, a rescue course is 9500B and the Divemaster program costs a cool 25,000B. Fun divers should expect to pay 1000B per dive, or 7000B for a 10-dive package. These rates include gear, boat, instructor and snacks. Discounts are usually given if you bring your own equipment. Be wary of dive centres that offer too many price cuts – safety is paramount, and a shop giving out unusually good deals is probably cutting too many corners.

Most dive schools can hook you up with cheap (or even free) accommodation. Expect larger crowds between December and April, and a monthly glut of wannabe divers after the Full Moon party on Ko Pha-Ngan next door.

The following dive schools are among the best operators on the island, and all support the Save Koh Tao initiative (see p615).

Ban's Diving School (Map p613; ☎ 0 7745 6466; www.amazingkohtao.com; Hat Sai Ri) A well-oiled diving machine and relentlessly expanding conglomerate, Ban's certifies more divers per year than any other scuba school in the world. Classroom sessions tend to be conducted in large groups, but there's a reasonable amount of individual attention in the water. A breadth of international instructors means that students can learn to dive in their native tongue. The affiliated resort (p616) is quite popular with party-seekers.

Big Blue Diving (Map p613; ☎ 0 7745 6415; 0 7745 6772; www.bigbluediving.com; Hat Sai Ri) If Goldilocks were picking a dive school, she'd probably pick Big Blue – this midsize operation (not too big, not too small) gets props for fostering a sociable vibe while maintaining a high standard of service. Divers of every ilk can score dirt-cheap accommodation at their resort (p616).

Buddha View (☎ 0 7745 6074; www.buddhaview -diving.com; Chalok Ban Kao) Another big dive operation on Ko Tao, Buddha View offers the standard fare of certification and special programs for technical diving (venturing beyond the usual parameters of recreational underwater exploration). Discounted accommodation is available at their friendly resort (p618).

Crystal Dive (☎ 0 7745 6107; www.crystaldive.com; Mae Hat) Crystal is the Meryl Streep of diving operators, winning all the awards for best performance. It's one of the largest schools on the island (and around the world), although high-quality instructors and intimate classes keep the school feeling quite personal. Multilingual staff members, air-conditioned classes and an on-site swimming pool sweeten the deal. Crystal offers accommodation in both Mae Hat and Sairee (see p617).

New Heaven (☎ 0 7745 6587; www.newheavendive school.com; Chalok Ban Kao) The owners of this small diving operation dedicate a lot of their time to preserving the natural beauty of Ko Tao's underwater sites by conducting regular reef checks and contributing to reef restoration efforts. They are currently spearheading the Save Koh Tao Group environmental efforts. A special Coastal Preservation & Development Foundation (CPAD) research diver–certification program is available in addition to the regular order of programs and fun dives.

LOWER SOUTHERN GULF

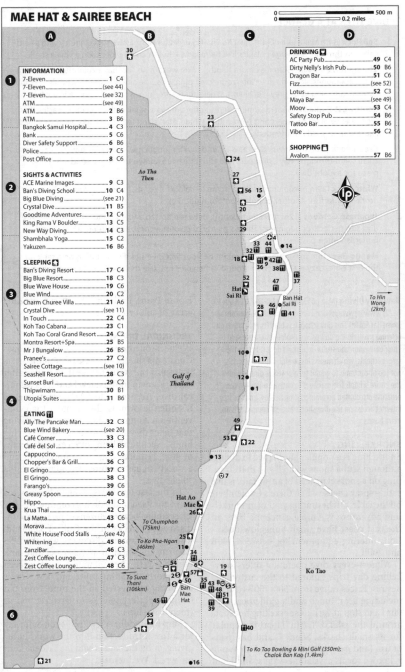

MAE HAT & SAIREE BEACH

INFORMATION	
7-Eleven................................**1** C4	
7-Eleven............................(see 44)	
7-Eleven............................(see 32)	
ATM.................................(see 49)	
ATM....................................**2** B6	
ATM....................................**3** B6	
Bangkok Samui Hospital......**4** C3	
Bank...................................**5** C6	
Diver Safety Support............**6** C5	
Police.................................**7** C5	
Post Office..........................**8** C6	

SIGHTS & ACTIVITIES
ACE Marine Images..............**9** C3
Ban's Diving School............**10** C4
Big Blue Diving.................(see 21)
Crystal Dive.....................**11** B5
Goodtime Adventures.........**12** C4
King Rama V Boulder..........**13** C5
New Way Diving.................**14** C3
Shambhala Yoga................**15** C2
Yakuzen............................**16** B6

SLEEPING
Ban's Diving Resort............**17** C4
Big Blue Resort..................**18** C3
Blue Wave House................**19** C6
Blue Wind.........................**20** C2
Charm Churee Villa..............**21** A6
Crystal Dive.....................(see 11)
In Touch............................**22** C4
Koh Tao Cabana.................**23** C1
Koh Tao Coral Grand Resort..**24** C2
Montra Resort+Spa.............**25** B5
Mr J Bungalow...................**26** B5
Pranee's............................**27** C2
Sairee Cottage..................(see 10)
Seashell Resort.................**28** C3
Sunset Buri.......................**29** C2
Thipwimarn.......................**30** B1
Utopia Suites.....................**31** B6

EATING
Ally The Pancake Man..........**32** C3
Blue Wind Bakery..............(see 20)
Café Corner.......................**33** C3
Café del Sol......................**34** B5
Cappuccino.......................**35** C6
Chopper's Bar & Grill...........**36** C3
El Gringo...........................**37** C3
El Gringo...........................**38** C3
Farango's..........................**39** C6
Greasy Spoon.....................**40** C6
Hippo...............................**41** C3
Krua Thai...........................**42** C3
La Matta............................**43** C6
Morava..............................**44** C3
'White House'Food Stalls......(see 42)
Whitening..........................**45** B6
ZanziBar............................**46** C3
Zest Coffee Lounge.............**47** C3
Zest Coffee Lounge.............**48** C6

DRINKING
AC Party Pub.....................**49** C4
Dirty Nelly's Irish Pub.........**50** B6
Dragon Bar........................**51** C6
Fizz...............................(see 52)
Lotus................................**52** C3
Maya Bar.........................(see 49)
Moov................................**53** C4
Safety Stop Pub.................**54** B6
Tattoo Bar.........................**55** B6
Vibe.................................**56** C2

SHOPPING
Avalon..............................**57** B6

LOWER SOUTHERN GULF

DIVE SITES AT A GLANCE

- **Sail Rock** (34m maximum depth), near Ko Pha-Ngan, features a massive rock chimney with a vertical swim-through, and large pelagics like barracuda, kingfish and the occasional whale shark.

- **Chumphon Pinnacle** (36m maximum depth), 13km west of Ko Tao, has a colourful assortment of sea anemones along the four interconnected pinnacles. The site is home to schools of giant trevally, tuna and large grey reef sharks. Whale sharks are known to pop up once in a while.

- **Southwest Pinnacle** (33m maximum depth) offers divers a small collection of pinnacles that are home to giant groupers and barracudas. Whale sharks and leopard sharks are sometimes spotted (pun partially intended).

- **Green Rock** (25m maximum depth) is an underwater jungle gym featuring caverns, caves and small swim-throughs. Rays, groupers and triggerfish are known to hang around. It's a great place for a night dive.

- **White Rock** (29m maximum depth) is home to colourful corals, angelfish, clown fish and territorial triggerfish. Another popular spot for night divers.

- **Japanese Gardens** (12m maximum depth), between Ko Tao and Ko Nang Yuan, is a low-stress dive site perfect for beginners. There's plenty of colourful coral, and turtles, stingray and pufferfish often pass by.

- **Mango Bay** (16m maximum depth) might be your first dive site if you putting on a tank for the first time. Lazy reef fish swim around as newbies practise their skills on the sandy bottom.

New Way Diving (Map p613; ☎ 0 7745 6527, 08 60440 0822; www.newwaydiving.com, www.scubadivingkohtao .com; Hat Sai Ri) This tiny school has built its reputation on offering small diving groups in a professional atmosphere. Their early-morning scuba excursions depart before the larger schools, which means less traffic in the water. It's not too uncommon to go out for a postdive dinner with the entire school. The manager (a native Ko Tao-ist) can organise discounted accommodation nearby, and the free internet access on the dive shop's ancient computer is an extra bonus.

SNORKELLING

Snorkelling is a popular alternative to diving, although scuba snobs will tell you that strapping on a snorkel instead of an air tank is like eating spray cheese when there's Camembert on the table. Orchestrating your own snorkelling adventure is simple, since the bays on the east coast have small bungalow operations offering equipment for between 100B and 200B.

Almost every dive operation offers snorkelling day trips tailored to the customers' desires. Prices range from 500-700B (usually including gear, lunch and a guide/boat captain) and stop at various snorkelling hot spots around the island. Laem Thian is popular for its small sharks, Shark Island has loads of fish (and ironically no sharks); Hin Wong is known for its crystalline waters; and Light House Point, in the north, offers a dazzling array of colourful sea anemones.

TECHNICAL DIVING

Well-seasoned divers and hardcore Jacques Cousteaus should contact **Trident** (www.techthai land.com), if they want to take their underwater exploration to the next level and try a technical dive. According to PADI, tec diving, as it's often known, is 'diving other than conventional commercial or recreational diving that takes divers beyond recreational diving limits'. Technical diving often exceeds depths of 40m, requires stage decompressions and a variety of gas mixtures are often used in a single dive.

In the last few years, Trident has made a name for itself in the diving community after successfully locating dozens of previously undiscovered wrecks in the Gulf of Thailand. Their most famous discovery was the USS *Lagarto*, an American naval vessel that sunk during WWII. The Gulf waters have long been an important trading route and new wrecks are being discovered all the time, from old Chinese pottery wrecks to Japanese *marus* (merchant ships).

Stop by Buddha View (p612) on Saturday for a free introduction into the world of tec diving, or hit the waters with the Trident team on 'wreck Wednesdays'.

UNDERWATER PHOTOGRAPHY & VIDEOGRAPHY

If your wallet is already full of PADI certification cards, make a stop at **ACE Marine Images** (Map p613; ☎ 0 7745 7054; www.acemarineimages.com; Sairee Beach), one of Thailand's leading underwater videography studios. Many scuba schools hire professional videographers to film Open Water certifications, and if this piques your interest, consider enrolling in their underwater video or photo course. The interactive eight-dive course (30,000B) includes an independent diver certification and one-on-one instruction in the editing room. Internships are also available for those who are truly serious about gaining field experience. The staff at ACE are starting a variety of other projects, such as whale shark tracking and tagging, and a unique photography-oriented gap-year program. Visit the website for more information or join their group on Facebook.

SPA

All of that shark ogling might leave you with a serious backache, so why not indulge in a post-scuba session? (Though be warned that a massage treatment directly after diving can be dangerous as it pushes residual nitrogen throughout your body.) If you are paying more than 2500B for your bungalow, then you probably have access to on-site spa services. Budget travellers looking to be pampered will find several good places to blow their baht.

Jamahkiri Resort & Spa (☎ 0 7745 6400/1; www.jamahkiri.com) Offers aloe-vera wraps (great for sunburn), massages, and facials atop a huge island peak. Call for free transport, or swing by their wooden storefront near the Mae Hat pier.

Charm Churee Villa (Map p613; ☎ 0 7745 6393; www.charmchureevilla.com; Mae Hat) Rejuvenation suites drip with Balinese decoration and sit close to the water's edge along a rugged escarpment of boulders.

Yakuzen (☎ 0 7745 6229, 08 4837 3385; Mae Hat; ☼ 5pm-10pm, closed Wed) Japanese-style bathhouse in Mae Hat changes things up by offering this unique form of relaxation. A 60-minute soaks cost 700B.

YOGA

Ko Tao's only fulltime yoga centre is **Shambhala** (Map p613; ☎ 08 4440 6755), housed in beautiful wooden *sāh·lah* located on the forested grounds of Blue Wind (see p616) in Sairee Beach. The two-hour classes, led by Kester, the energetic yogi, cost 300B.

OTHER ACTIVITIES

Although most activities on Ko Tao revolve around the sea, the friendly crew at **Goodtime Adventures** (Map p613; ☎ 08 7275 3604; www.gtadventures.com; Sairee Beach; ☼ noon-midnight) offers a wide variety of land-based activities to get the blood pumping. Hike through the island's jungly interior, swing from rock to rock during a climbing and abseiling session, or unleash your inner daredevil during an afternoon of cliff jumping.

Ko Tao Bowling & Mini Golf (off Map p613; ☎ 0 7745 6316; ☼ noon-midnight), on the main road between Mae Hat and Chalok Ban Kao, has several homemade bowling lanes where the employees reset the pins after every frame (300B per hour). The 18-hole minigolf course has a landmark theme – putt your ball through Stonehenge or across the Golden Gate Bridge.

Volunteering

The **Save Koh Tao Group** (☎ 0 7745 7045; www.marineconservationkohtao.com), spearheaded by New Heaven diving school (p612), is an initiative focused on keeping the island as pristine as possible by promoting sustainable tourism. They don't have a structured volunteer program, although there are always projects that need a helping hand, both on land and in the sea. Save Koh Tao's biggest endeavour is the Biorock, an artificial reef built beyond the headland at the northern end of Sairee Beach. See boxed text, p616, for more information.

The **Secret Garden** (www.secretgarden-kohtao.com) offers work opportunities for travellers who are interested in conservation and educational programs. Conservation projects include beach clean-ups, erosion-prevention initiatives and marine protection. Native English-speakers can help out in the classroom by offering English lessons to the local Thai children, or lending a hand during the yearly summer camp. Contact the Secret Garden directly via their website to learn more about volunteering.

Regular beach clean-ups attract a large number of volunteers as well. Contact Crystal Dive (p612) in Mae Hat, Big Blue (p612) in Sairee Beach, New Heaven (p612) in Chalok Ban Kao and Black Tip (p619) in Tanote Bay.

See p48 and p52 for more information about volunteering in Thailand.

LOWER SOUTHERN GULF

LOWER SOUTHERN GULF

Sleeping

If you are planning to dive while visiting Ko Tao, your scuba operator will probably offer you discounted accommodation to sweeten the deal. Some schools have on-site lodging, while others have deals with nearby bungalows. It's important to note that you only receive your scuba-related discount on the days you dive. So, for example, if you buy a 10-dive package, and decide to take a day off in the middle, your room rate will not be discounted on that evening. Also, a restful sleep is important before diving, so scope out these 'great room deals' before saying yes – some of them are one roach away from being condemned.

There are also many sleeping options that have absolutely nothing to do with the island's diving culture. Ko Tao's secluded eastern coves are dotted with stunning retreats that still offer a true getaway experience, but these can be difficult to reach due to the island's dismal network of roads. You can often call ahead of time and arrange to be picked up from the pier.

SAIREE BEACH (HAT SAI RI)

Giant Sairee Beach is the longest and most developed strip on the island, with a string of dive operations, bungalows, travel agencies, superettes and internet cafes. The narrow 'yellow brick road' stretches the entire length of beach (watch out for motorcycles).

Budget

Blue Wind (Map p613; ☎ 0 7745 6116, 0 7745 6015; bluewind_wa@yahoo.com; bungalows 300-900B; 🔀) Hidden within a clump of bodacious lodging options, Blue Wind offers a breath of fresh air from the high-intensity dive resorts strung along Sairee Beach. Sturdy bamboo huts are

---

BIOROCK

After the success of a small pilot project off the island's eastern coast, the Save Koh Tao Group (p615), implanted the Gulf of Thailand's largest Biorock (artificial reef) in the waterway between Ko Tao and the small offshore island of Ko Nangyuan. The massive lattice of steel domes, which hums with a low electrical current to attract fish and coral, measures almost 1 sq km in size and largely functions as a diver training site for scuba neophytes.

---

peppered along a dirt trail behind the beachside bakery. Large, tiled air-conditioned cabins are also available, boasting hot showers and TVs.

Big Blue Resort (Map p613; ☎ 0 7745 6050; www .bigbluediving.com; r 200-1000B; 🔀 🖳) This scuba-centric resort has a summer-camp vibe – diving classes dominate the daytime, while evenings are spent en masse, grabbing dinner or watching fire-twirling. Both the basic fan bungalows and motel-style air-con rooms offer little when it comes to views, but who has the time to relax when there's an ocean out there to explore?

In Touch (Map p613; ☎ 0 7745 6514; bungalows 500-1200B) Older bungalows are a mishmash of bamboo and dark wood, while several rounded air-con rooms have a cave theme – it's all very Flintstones, except the shower nozzle hasn't been replaced with the trunk of an elephant.

Sairee Cottage (Map p613; ☎ 0 7745 6126, 0 7745 6374; saireecottage@hotmail.com; bungalows 400-1500B; 🔀) The air-con bungalows are hard to miss since they've been painted in various hues of fuchsia. Low prices means low vacancy – so arrive early to score one of the brick huts facing out onto a grassy knoll.

Midrange

Pranee's (Map p613; ☎ 0 7745 6080; bungalows 500-2000B) Tidy budget bungalows, made of wood and rattan-woven walls, are shaded by coconut-wielding palms. A new fleet of air-con options are an uninspiring mix of white and blue, but some still have that new car smell.

Ban's Diving Resort (Map p613; ☎ 0 7745 6466, 0 7745 6061; www.amazingkohtao.com; r 400-3000; 🔀 🖳 🖳) This dive-centric party palace offers a wide range of quality accommodation, from basic backpacker digs to sleek hillside villas. Post-scuba chill sessions happen on Ban's prime slice of beach, or at one of the two swimming pools tucked within the strip of jungle between the two motel-like structures. Evenings are spent at the bar downing international cuisine and 'buckets' in equal measure.

Seashell Resort (Map p613; ☎ 0 7745 6299; www .seashell-resort.com; bungalows 450-3800B; 🔀) Several bungalows have ocean views from their porches (a rarity in Sairee), while others sit in a well-maintained garden of colourful vegetation and thin palm trunks. Seashell welcomes divers and non-divers alike.

Sunset Buri Resort (Map p613; ☎ 0 7745 6266; bungalows 700-2500B; 🔀 🖳 🖳) A long beach-bound path is studded with beautiful white bungalows featuring enormous windows and flamboyant temple-like roofing. The kidney-shaped pool is a big hit, as are the large beach recliners sprinkled around the resort.

Top End

Ko Tao Cabana (Map p613; ☎ 0 7745 6250; www.kohtao cabana.com; bungalows 3000-6300B; ✱) This prime piece of beachside property offers timber-framed villas and crinkled white adobe huts dotted along the boulder-strewn. Bric-a-brac cheers the colourful bungalows – stone gnomes greet you with a naughty smirk as you shower in the roofless bathrooms.

Koh Tao Coral Grand Resort (Map p613; ☎ 0 7745 6431; www.kohtaocoral.com; bungalows 3200-4500B; ✱ ✱) The plethora of pink facades at this family-friendly option feels a bit like Barbie's dream Thai beach-house. Cottage interiors are coated in cheery primary colours framed by white truncated beams while pricier digs have a more distinctive Thai flavour, boasting dark lacquered mouldings and gold-foiled art. Guests can participate in an array of organised off-site activities, like fishing, hiking, kayaking and boating, although it might be hard to tear yourself away from the relaxing resort and large beachside pool.

Thipwimarn (Map p613; ☎ 0 7745 6409; www.thip wimarnresort.com; bungalows 3100-4900B; ✱ ✱) North of the Sairee action, Thipwimarn occupies a secluded strip of land overlooking the quiet crystal sea. A circular restaurant with an outstanding view offers intimate, floor-level tables. Attractive bungalows spill down the hillside among boulders and greenery, with a myriad of stairs to keep you fit!

MAE HAT (HAT AO MAE)

All ferry arrivals pull into the pier at the busy village of Mae Hat. Busy village accommodation is spread throughout, but the more charming options extend in both directions along the sandy beach.

North of the Pier

Mr J Bungalow (☎ 0 7745 6066, 0 7745 6349; bungalows 250-1000B) Even though Mr J tried to charge us 50B for his business card, we still think he's well worth the visit. The eccentric owner entangles guests in a philosophical web while tending to his flock of decent bungalows. Ask him about reincarnation if you want to hear some particularly twisted conjectures.

Crystal Dive (☎ 0 7745 6107; www.crystaldive.com; bungalows 800-1500B; ✱ ✱) The bungalows and motel-style accommodation at Crystal are reserved for its divers, and prices drop significantly for those taking courses. Guests can take a dip in the refreshing pool when it isn't overflowing with bubble-blowing newbie divers. At the time of research, the construction of a newer, shmancier digs was underway.

Blue Wave House (☎ 0 7745 6287; nightly/monthly r 1000/10,000B; ✱) Hooked on Ko Tao's addictive diving vibe and planning on staying forever? These prim rooms in the heart of Mae Hat village are a good choice, if you're looking for a monthly rental.

Montra Resort & Spa (☎ 0 7745 7057; www.koh taomontra.com; r from 3500B; ✱ 🖥 ✱) Mae Hat's newest address is an upmarket affair with all the modern bells and whistles. The hotel structure is rather imposing when compared to the scatter of humble bungalows at the neighbouring resorts.

South of the Pier

Utopia Suites (☎ 0 7745 6729, 0 7745 6672; r/ste from 600/200B, monthly from 20,000B) Utopia's apartment-style accommodation is located in the charming fishing village, just a stone's throw from the pier. The beachside apartment-style accommodation is perfect for families and small groups. Ask about discounts for extended stays.

our pick Charm Churee Villa (☎ 0 7745 6393; www .charmchureevilla.com; bungalows 3200-12,200B; ✱ 🖥 ✱) Tucked gently under sky-scraping palms, the luxuriant villas of Charm Churee are dedicated to the flamboyant spoils of the Far East. Gold-foiled oriental demigods pose in arabesque positions, with bejewelled eyes frozen in a Zen-like trance. Staircases, chiselled into the rock face, dribble down a palmed slope revealing teak huts strewn across smoky boulders. The villas' unobstructed views of the swishing indigo waters are nothing short of charming.

The following sleeping spots are located further south and can be accessed by a quick ride in a boat taxi.

Sai Thong Resort (☎ 0 7745 6868; www.saithong -resort.com; bungalows 300-2500B; ✱ 🖥 ✱) As the rush of Mae Hat dwindles away along the island's southwest shore, Sai Thong emerges along sandy Hat Sai Nuan. Bungalows, in various incarnations of weaving and wood, have colourful porch hammocks and palm-filled vistas. Guests frequent the restaurant's relaxing sun deck, a favourite spot for locals too.

Tao Thong Villa (☎ 0 7745 6078; bungalows from 500B) Very popular with long-termers seeking peace and quiet, these funky, no-frills bungalows have killer views. Tao Thong actually straddles two tiny beaches on a craggy cape about halfway between Mae Hat and Chalok Ban Kao. The pair of neighbouring swim spots are the perfect place for a hermitic afternoon.

CHALOK BAN KAO
Ao Chalok Ban Kao, about 1.7km south of Mae Hat by road, is the third largest concentration of accommodation on Ko Tao, but can feel a lot more crowded because the beach is significantly smaller than Sairee and Mae Hat. The beach itself isn't tops as low tides are often muddy.

Budget
Buddha View Dive Resort (☎ 0 7745 6074; www.buddhaview-diving.com; r 300-1500B; ❄) Like the other large diving operations on the island, Buddha View offers its divers discounted on-site digs in a super-social atmosphere. If you plan on staying awhile, ask about the 'Divers Village' across the street, which offers basic accommodation from around 4000B per month.

Tropicana (☎ 0 7745 6167; www.koh-tao-tropicana-resort.com; r from 400B) Tropicana ups the ante when it comes to quality budget digs. Low-rise hotel units are peppered across a garden campus providing fleeting glimpses of the ocean between fanned fronds and spiky palms.

JP Resort (☎ 0 7745 6099; bungalows 400-700B) This little cheapie promises a colourful menagerie of prim motel-style rooms stacked on a small scrap of jungle across the street from the sea. The sun-soaked rooms have polished pastel-coloured linoleum floor, and many of the tiled bathrooms have been recently refurbished.

Freedom Beach (☎ 0 7745 6596; bungalows 400-1500B) On its own secluded beach at the eastern end of Ao Chalok Ban Kao, Freedom feels like a classic backpacker haunt, although there's a variety of accommodation to suit various humble budgets. The string of bungalows (from wooden shacks to sturdier huts with air-con) links the breezy seaside bar to the resort's restaurant high on the cliff.

Midrange & Top End
New Heaven Resort (☎ 0 7745 6422; newheavenresort@yahoo.co.th; r & bungalows 1200-3900B) Just beyond the clutter of Ao Chalok Ban Kao, New Heaven delivers colourful huts perched over impossibly clear waters. A steep path of chiselled stone tumbles down the shrubby rock face revealing views ripped straight from the pages of *National Geographic*.

Ko Tao Resort (☎ 0 7745 6133; www.kotaoresort.com; r & bungalows 1600-3000B; ❄ 🖳 🗩) The entrance is a throwback to the days when taste and architecture weren't particularly synonymous (the '70s perhaps?), but the facilities themselves fit the true definition of a resort. The rooms are well stocked, water-sports equipment is on offer, and there are several bars primed to serve an assortment of fruity cocktails.

Chintakiri Resort (☎ 0 7745 6133; www.chintakiri.com; r & bungalows 2900-4000B; ❄ 🖳 🗩) Perched high over the gulf waters overlooking Chalok Ban Kao, Chintakiri (which sounds a bit too much like the top-end fave Jamahkiri) is Ko Tao's newest luxury addition as the island furtively creeps upmarket. Rooms are spread around the inland jungle, and sport crisp white walls with lacquered finishing.

EAST COAST BEACHES
The serene eastern coast is, without a doubt, one of the best places in the region to live out your island-paradise fantasies. The views are stunning, beaches are silent, yet all of your creature comforts are 10-minutes away. Accommodation along this coast is organised from north to south.

Hin Wong
A sandy beach has been swapped for a boulder-strewn coast, but the water is crystal clear. The road to Hin Wong is paved in parts, but sudden sand pits and steep hills can toss you off your motorbike.

Hin Wong Bungalows (☎ 0 7745 6006, 08 1229 4810; bungalows from 300B) Pleasant wooden huts are scattered across vast expanses of untamed tropical terrain – it all feels a bit like *Gilligan's Island* (minus the millionaire castaways). A rickety dock, jutting out just beyond the breezy restaurant, is the perfect place to dangle your legs and watch schools of black sardines slide through the cerulean water.

View Rock (☎ 0 7745 6548/9; viewrock@hotmail.com; bungalows 300-400B) When coming down the dirt road into Hin Wong, follow the signs as they lead you north (left) of Hin Wong Bungalows. View Rock is precisely that: views and rocks. The hodgepodge of wooden huts, which looks like a secluded fishing village, is built into the steep crags, offering stunning views of the bay.

Laem Thian

Laem Thian is a scenic cape with a small patch of sand.

Laem Thian (☎ 0 7745 6477; r & bungalows 400-1500B; ✕) Nestled far from civilisation on a lush stretch of jungle, this small boulder-filled resort is the only operation on Laem Thian. The modern rooms tend to be better than the bungalows, so long as you don't mind the ugly facades. The road here is very rough; call for a pick-up.

Tanote Bay (Ao Tanot)

Tanote Bay is slightly more populated than some of the other eastern coves, but it's still quiet and picturesque. It is the only bay on the east coast that is accessible by paved road. Discounted taxis (80B to 100B) bounce back and forth between Tanote Bay and Mae Hat; ask at your resort for a timetable and price details.

Poseidon (☎ 0 7745 6735; poseidonkohtao@hotmail.com; bungalows from 300B) Poseidon keeps the tradition of the budget bamboo bungalow alive with a dozen basic-but-sleepable huts scattered near the sand.

Bamboo Huts (☎ 0 7745 6531; bungalows 300-500B) Sitting on scraggly boulders in the centre of Tanote Bay, Bamboo Huts caters to penny-pinchers with the usual crew of cheap bungalows. The sociable restaurant, serving Thai and Western fare, is an added bonus.

Diamond Beach (☎ 0 7745 6591; bungalows 300-1100B; ✕) Diamond's beachy batch of huts sits directly on Tanote's sand. There's a mix of bungalow types, including A-frames for tinier wallets.

Black Tip Dive Resort (☎ 0 7745 6488; www.blacktip-kohtao.com; bungalows 600-2800B; ✕ ☐) Part dive shop and water-sports centre, Black Tip also has a handful of lovely wooden bungalows with thatched roofing. The scuba centre is housed in a wacky structure made of rippling white adobe and strange geometric protrusions. Guests get a 50% discount when enrolled in a diving course and 'fun divers' get 25% off room rates.

Ao Leuk & Ao Thian Ok

The dirt roads to Ao Leuk and Ao Thian Ok are steep, rough and rutty, especially towards the end; don't attempt it on a motorcycle unless you're an expert. Both bays are stunning and serene.

Ao Leuk Bungalows (☎ 0 7745 6692; bungalows 400-1500B) Lodging at Ao Leuk comes in several shapes and sizes ranging from backpacker shacks to modern family-friendly options. Flickering torches and ambient cackles of curious cicadas accent the jet-black evenings.

Jamahkiri Resort & Spa (☎ 0 7745 6400; www.jamahkiri.com; bungalows 6900-13,900B) The flamboyant decor at this whitewashed estate is decidedly focused around tribal imagery. Wooden gargoyle masks and stone fertility goddesses abound amid swirling mosaics and multi-armed statues. Feral hoots of distant monkeys confirm the overarching jungle theme, as do the thatched roofs and tiki-torched soirees. The resort's seemingly infinite number of stone stairways can be a pain, so it's a good thing Ko Tao's most luxurious spa is located on the premises (p615).

NORTH COAST

This isolated rocky bay has one sleeping option in a dramatic setting of tangled jungle vines and rocky hills.

Mango Bay Grand Resort (☎ 0 7745 6097; www.mangobaygrandresortkohtaothailand.com; bungalows 1400-3000B; ✕) Spacious mahogany bungalows are perched high on stilts above the ashen boulders lining the bay. A thin necklace of mosaic-lined paths winds through the tropical shrubbery, connecting the secluded villas.

KO NANG YUAN

Photogenic Ko Nang Yuan, just off the coast of Ko Tao, is easily accessible by the Lomprayah catamaran, and by water taxis that depart from Mae Hat and Sairee.

Ko Nangyuan Dive Resort (☎ 0 7745 6088, 0 7745 6093; www.nangyuan.com; bungalows 1500-7000B; ✕) Although the obligatory 100B tax to access the island is a bit off-putting (as is the 100B water-taxi ride each way), Nangyuan Dive Resort is nonetheless a charming place to stay. The rugged collection of wood and aluminium bungalows winds its way across three coolie hat–like conical islands connected by an idyllic beige sandbar. The resort also boasts the best restaurant on the island, but then again, it's the only place to eat…

Eating

With super-sized Samui lurking on the horizon, it's hard to believe that quaint little Ko Tao is a worthy opponent in the gastronomy category. Most resorts offer on-site dining, and stand-alone establishments are multiplying at lightning speed at Sairee Beach and Mae Hat. The diverse population of divers has spawned a broad range of international cuisine, including Mexican, French, Italian, Indian and Japanese. On our quest to find the tastiest Thai fare on the island, we discovered, not surprisingly, that our favourite local meals were being dished out at small, unnamed restaurants on the side of the road.

SAIREE BEACH (HAT SAI RI)

Sairee Beach is tiny Tao's unofficial capital of cuisine, offering an impressive assortment of international flavours. Keep an eye out for rickety food carts scattered around the village serving tasty tea and treats. Stop by the 7-Eleven beside Big Blue Resort to check out Ally the Pancake Man (Map p613) as he dances around, like an Italian chef making pizza, while cooking your tasty dessert. He's become quite the local legend and has even appeared on YouTube.

White House Food Stalls (Map p613; dishes 30-70B; lunch & dinner) Plunked in front of a humble white house amid the bustling action in Sairee, these clinking metallic food stalls sling awesome *sôm·dam* and barbecue treats to crowds of hungry locals.

Café Corner (Map p613; mains 30-100B; breakfast & lunch) The flaky *pain au chocolat* can easily be mistaken for a Parisian patisserie. Customers enjoy their desserts at swirling stainless steel countertops while watching movies on a swank plasma TV. Swing by at 5pm to stock up for tomorrow morning's breakfast; the scrumptious baked breads are buy-one-get-one-free before being tossed at sunset.

Blue Wind Bakery (Map p613; ☎ 0 7745 6116; mains 50-120B; breakfast, lunch & dinner) This beachside shanty dishes out Thai favourites, Western confections and freshly blended fruit juices. Enjoy your thick fruit smoothie and flaky pastry while reclining on tattered triangular pillows.

Krua Thai (Map p613; ☎ 08 7892 9970; dishes 50-120B; lunch & dinner) Popular with the tourists who want their food '*fa·ràng* spicy' rather than 'Thai spicy', Krua Thai offers a large assortment of classic faves served in a well-maintained storefront.

El Gringo (Map p613; ☎ 0 7745 6323; dishes 80-150B; breakfast, lunch & dinner) As if there weren't already enough nicknames for Caucasians in Thailand…this self-proclaimed 'funky' Mexican joint slings burritos of questionable authenticity at two locations in Sairee Beach and a third in Mae Hat.

Chopper's Bar & Grill (Map p613; ☎ 0 7745 6641; dishes 60-200B; breakfast, lunch & dinner) A great place to widen that beer belly, Chopper's offers live music, sports on big-screen TVs, billiards, and a classier screening room upstairs. Friday night is particularly popular; the drinks are 'two for one' and dishes are half-priced. Cheers for scored goals are interspersed with the exaggerated chatter about creatures seen on the day's dive.

ourpick ZanziBar (Map p613; ☎ 0 7745 6452; sandwiches 90-140B; breakfast, lunch & dinner) The island's outpost of sandwich yuppie-dom slathers a mix of unpronounceable condiments betwixt two slices of whole-grain bread.

Hippo (Map p613; ☎ 0 7745 6021; dishes 80-300B; breakfast, lunch & dinner) A new favourite, Hippo offers tasty reminders of home: grilled steaks, fish and chips (the island's best!), burgers and omelettes.

Morava (Map p613; ☎ 0 7745 6270; dishes 200-350B; breakfast, lunch & dinner) This Sairee splurge has out-swanked the competition with smooth decor and equally stylish dishes. The recently refined menu features delicious options like tender lamb steaks and fresh-from-the-sea sashimi.

MAE HAT (HAT AO MAE)

Cappuccino (Map p613; ☎ 08 7896 8838; dishes 30-90B; breakfast & lunch) Cappuccino's decor is somewhere between the New York deli on Seinfeld and a French brasserie – it's a great place to grab a coffee and croissant while waiting for the ferry.

Zest Coffee Lounge (Map p613; ☎ 0 7745 6178; dishes 70-190B; breakfast & lunch) Indulge in the street-cafe lifestyle at Zest; idlers can nibble confections or nurse their cup of joe all the way till sunset. There's a second location in Sairee.

ourpick Whitening (Map p613; ☎ 0 7745 6199; dishes 90-160B; dinner) This sandy spot falls somewhere between being a restaurant and bar – foodies will appreciate the modern twists on indigenous dishes while beer-toters will love the beachy, bleached-white atmosphere which hums with gentle lounge music. Although menu is multicultural, diners should stick to the phenomenal assortment of Thai dishes like the garlic prawns or the slow-stewed red curry with duck.

Greasy Spoon (Map p613; ☎ 08 6272 1499; English breakfast 120B; ⏰ 7am-6pm) Although completely devoid of character, breakfast lovers will be sated by Greasy Spoon's hearty morning repast – eggs, sausage, chips and cooked veggies that'll bring a tear to any Brit's eye.

La Matta (Map p613; ☎ 0 7745 6517; dishes 80-230B; ⏰ lunch & dinner) There's an age-old rivalry between La Matta and Farango's (see below). Both serve 'authentic' (note the quotation marks) Italian cuisine and are located virtually right on top of one another. We're staunch Farango's fans, although secretly it's pretty hard to tell the difference between the two.

Farango's (☎ 0 7745 6205; dishes 80-230B; ⏰ lunch & dinner) Ko Tao's first *fa·ràng* restaurant spins tasty steaks Italian dishes much to La Matta's chagrin (see above). The cheery atmosphere drips with burnt yellows and Spanish-themed posters of flamboyant matadors.

Café del Sol (☎ 0 7745 6578; dishes 70-250B; ⏰ breakfast, lunch & dinner) Even the pickiest eater will be satisfied with the menu's expansive selection of 'world cuisine'. The focus is namely European (French and Italian) with specialties like homemade pâté, bruschetta and tender steaks imported from New Zealand. Free wi-fi available.

CHALOK BAN KAO

Tukta Thai Food (☎ 0 7745 6109; dishes 40-180B; ⏰ breakfast, lunch & dinner) On the main road coming into Chalok Ban Kao, Tukta is a solid option for Thai staples.

New Heaven Restaurant (☎ 0 7745 6462; dishes 60-350B; ⏰ lunch & dinner) The best part about New Heaven Restaurant is the awe-inducing view of Shark Bay (Ao Thian Ok) under the lazy afternoon moon. The turquoise waters below are so translucent that the curving reef is easily visible from your seat. The menu is largely international, and there are nap-worthy cushions tucked under each low-rise table.

Drinking

After diving, Ko Tao's favourite pastime is drinking, and there's definitely no shortage of places to get tanked. Fliers detailing upcoming parties are posted on various trees and walls along the west coast (check the two 7-Elevens in Sairee). Also keep an eye out for posters touting 'jungle parties' held on nondescript patches of scrubby jungle in the centre of the island. The tides also play an integral part

of the island's night scene. When the tides are high, evenings tend to be less raucous along Sairee Beach since there's not a lot of room to get wild. If you're looking for something a bit more structured, try joining up with Goodtime Adventures (p615) for a pub crawl or booze cruise

Just remember: don't drink and dive.

SAIREE BEACH (HAT SAI RI)

Fizz (Dry Bar; Map p613; ☎ 08 7887 9495) Recline in an expanse of white-and-green pillows and enjoy designer cocktails while listening to Moby, or Enya, mixed with hypnotic gushes of the rolling tide. Stick around for dinner – the tuna steaks (200B) earn top marks.

Lotus (Map p613; ☎ 0 7745 6358) This bar, next door to Fizz, is the de facto late-night hangout spot along the northern end of Sairee. Muscular fire-twirlers toss around flaming batons, and the drinks are so large there should be a lifeguard on duty.

Vibe (Map p613) Sairee's top spot for a sundowner drinks, Vibe has the largest (and best) playlist out of any drinking spot on the island.

Clumped at the southern end of Sairee Beach, these nightspots take turns reeling in the partiers throughout the week:

Moov (Map p613; ☎ 08 4849 6648; www.moov-kohtao .com) The newest of the pack, and currently the most popular. Check the website for party details.

AC Party Pub (Map p613; ☎ 0 7745 6197) Things get wild on Tuesday and Thursday.

Maya Bar (Map p613; ☎ 0 7745 6195) Bounces on Monday and Friday.

MAE HAT (AO HAT MAE)

Dirty Nelly's Irish Pub (Map p613; ☎ 0 7745 6569) True to its name, Dirty Nelly's is unapologetically Irish; the draught beers, the managers – everything's been imported straight from the motherland (except the weather).

Tattoo Bar (Map p613; ☎ 08 9291 9416) A casual affair in the heart of Mae Hat's rickety fishing village, Tattoo is a chill place to grab a beer and burger (150B).

Dragon Bar (Map p613; ☎ 0 7745 6423) This bar caters to those seeking snazzy, cutting-edge surroundings. There's happening 'Communist-chic' retro styling throughout, and everything's dimly lit, moody and relaxing. Dragon Bar is rumoured to have the best cocktails on the island – try the espresso martini for a real buzz.

LOWER SOUTHERN GULF

LEARNING THE LOCAL LINGO

Due to the steady influx of international visitors, English is spoken just about everywhere; however, the locals on this scuba-savvy island regularly incorporate diving sign language symbols into common parlance – especially at the bars.

Here are a few gestures to get you started:

- **I'm OK** – Make a fist and tap the top of your head twice.
- **Cool** – Bring together the tips of your index finger and thumb forming an 'O'.
- **I'm finished/I'm ready to go** – Hold your hand tight like a karate chop and quickly swing it back and forth perpendicular to your neck.

Safety Stop Pub (☎ 0 7745 6209) A haven for homesick Brits, this pier-side pub feels like a tropical beer garden. Stop by on Sunday to stuff your face with an endless supply of barbecued goodness. Wi-fi is available.

Shopping
If you're having trouble scrubbing the sea salt out of your hair, then stop by **Avalon** (Mae Hat; ☽ 10am-7pm Mon-Sat) for some locally made (and ecofriendly) body and hair-care products.

Getting There & Away
As always, the cost and departure times are in flux. Rough waves are known to cancel ferries between the months of October and December. Beware of travel agencies in Bangkok and Surat Thani selling fake boat/train combinations.

BANGKOK, HUA HIN & CHUMPHON
Bus-boat package tickets from Bangkok cost 900B to 1000B and are available from travel agencies on Th Khao San. Promotional bus-boat combination tickets in the opposite direction are sometimes offered for as little as 700B (watch out for scams!). Buses switch to boats in Chumphon and Bangkok-bound passengers can choose to disembark in Hua Hin.

The train is a more comfortable option than the bus, and tourists can plan their own journey by taking a boat to Chumphon and the train up to Bangkok (or any town along

the upper southern gulf); likewise in the opposite direction.

From Ko Tao, the high-speed catamaran departs for Chumphon at 10.15am and 2.45pm (550B, 1½ hours), the Seatran leaves the island at 4pm (550B, two hours), and a Songserm fast boat makes the same journey at 2.30pm (450B, three hours). There may be fewer departures if the swells are high.

There's also a midnight boat from Chumphon (600B) arriving early in the morning. It returns from Ko Tao at 11pm. Don't take this boat if there's a good chance of rain; some boats leak and you'll be wet, cold and miserable. See p572 for more information.

KO PHA-NGAN
The Lomprayah catamaran offers twice daily service, leaving Ko Tao at 9.30am and 3pm and arriving on Ko Pha-Ngan around 10.50am and 4.10pm. The Seatran Discovery ferry offers an identical service. The Songserm Express Boat departs daily at 10am and arrives on Samui at 11.30am. Hotel pick-ups are included in the price.

Ko Tao–bound Lomprayah and Seatran ferries depart Ko Pha-Ngan at 8.30am and 1pm and arrive at 9.45am and 2.15pm. Songserm leaves Ko Pha-Ngan at noon and arrives at 1.45pm.

KO SAMUI
The Lomprayah catamaran offers twice daily service, leaving Ko Tao at 9.30am and 3pm, and arriving on Samui around 11.30am and 4.40pm. The Seatran Discovery ferry offers an identical service. The **Songserm Express Boat** (www.songserm-expressboat.com) departs daily at 10am and arrives on Samui at 12.45pm. Hotel pick-ups are included in the price.

Ko Tao–bound Lomprayah and Seatran ferries depart Samui at 8am and 12.30pm and arrive at 9.45am and 2.15pm. Songserm leaves Samui at 11am and arrives at 1.45pm.

SURAT THANI & ANDAMAN COAST
Combination boat-bus tickets are available at any travel agency; simply tell them your desired destination and they will sell you the necessary links in the transport chain. Most travellers will pass through Surat Thani as they swap coasts. Daily buses to the Songserm Express Boat depart from Surat Thani (6½ hours) at 8am and arrive at 2.30pm. Return passengers leave Ko Tao at 10am and arrive

in Surat Thani at 4.30pm. Every night, depending on the weather, a boat runs between Surat Thani (Tha Thong) and Ko Tao (nine hours). From Surat, these night boats depart at 11pm. From Ko Tao the departure time is 8.30pm.

Getting Around

Sŏrng·tăa·ou crowd around the pier in Mae Hat as passengers alight. If you're a solo traveller, you will pay 100B to get to Sai Ri and Chalok Ban Kao. Groups of two or more will pay 50B each. Rides from Sai Ri to Chalok Ban Kao cost 80B per person, or 150B for solo tourists. These are non-negotiable prices, and passengers must wait until each taxi is full before it departs. If taxis are empty, you will be asked to pay for the entire cab (300B to 500B). Prices double for trips to the east coast, and drivers will raise the prices when rain makes the roads harder to negotiate. If you know where you intend to stay, call ahead for a pick-up.

If you're one to throw caution to the wind, then consider renting a motorbike to explore the island's rugged jungle. There are loads of places to lease a vehicle, but be warned that scams are common (see p611). Go with **Lederhosenbikes** (☎ 08 1752 8994; www.lederhosen bikes.com; Mae Hat; ⏰ 8.30am-6pm Mon-Sat), an expat operation that has a great selection of quality equipment, and promises honest service. Daily rental rates begin with 150B scooters; it's 200B for an automatic, larger bikes start at 350B, four-wheelers are 500B, and four-seater ATVs will set you back 1800B. It costs around 45B to fill the petrol tank on a moped.

Boat taxis depart from Mae Hat, Chalok Ban Kao and the northern part of Hat Sai Ri (near Pranee's bungalows, p616). Boat rides to Ko Nang Yuan will set you back at least 100B. Long-tail boats can be chartered for around 1500B per day, depending on the number of passengers carried.

ANG THONG MARINE NATIONAL PARK

อุทยานแห่งชาติหมู่เกาะอ่างทอง

The 40-some jagged jungle islands of Ang Thong Marine National Park stretch across the cerulean sea like a shattered emerald necklace – each piece a virgin realm featuring sheer limestone cliffs, hidden lagoons and perfect peach-coloured sands. These dream-inducing islets inspired Alex Garland's cult classic *The Beach* about dope-dabbling backpackers.

February, March and April are the best months to visit this ethereal preserve of greens and blues; crashing monsoon waves means that the park is almost always closed during November and December.

Sights

Every tour stops at the park's head office on **Ko Wua Talap**, the largest island in the archipelago. The island's **viewpoint** might just be the most stunning vista in all of Thailand. From the top, visitors will have sweeping views of the jagged islands nearby as they burst through the placid turquoise water in easily anthropomorphised formations. The trek to the lookout is an arduous 450m trail that takes roughly an hour to complete. Hikers should wear sturdy shoes and walk slowly on the sharp outcrops of limestone. A second trail leads to **Tham Bua Bok**, a cavern with lotus-shaped stalagmites and stalactites.

The **Emerald Sea** (also called the Inner Sea) on **Ko Mae Ko** is another popular destination. This large lake in the middle of the island spans an impressive 250m by 350m and has an ethereal minty tint. You can look but you can't touch; the lagoon is strictly off-limits to the unclean human body. A second dramatic **viewpoint** can be found at the top of a series of staircases nearby.

The naturally occurring stone arches on **Ko Samsao** and **Ko Tai Plao** are visible during seasonal tides and weather conditions. Because the sea is quite shallow around the island chain, reaching a maximum depth of 10m, extensive coral reefs have not developed, except in a few protected pockets on the southwest and northeast sides. There's a shallow coral reef near Ko Tai Plao and Ko Samsao that has decent but not excellent snorkelling. There are also several novice dives for exploring shallow caves and colourful coral gardens and spotting banded sea snakes and turtles. Soft powder beaches line **Ko Tai Plao**, **Ko Wuakantang** and **Ko Hintap**.

Tours

The best way to experience Ang Thong is through one of many guided tours departing from Ko Samui and Ko Pha-Ngan. The tours usually include lunch, snorkelling equipment, hotel transfers and (with fingers crossed) a knowledgeable guide. If you're staying in luxury accommodation, there's a good chance that your resort has a private boat for group

LOWER SOUTHERN GULF

tours. Some midrange and budget also have their own boats, and if not, they can easily set you up with a general tour operator. Dive centres on Ko Samui and Ko Pha-Ngan offer scuba trips to the park, although Ang Thong doesn't offer the world-class diving that can be found around Ko Tao.

Due to the tumultuous petrol prices, tour companies tend to come and go like the wind. Ask at your accommodation for a list of current operators; see also p579.

Sleeping

Ang Thong does not have any resorts; however, on Ko Wua Talap the national park has set up five bungalows, each housing between two and eight guests. The marine national park also allows campers to pitch a tent in certain designated zones. Advance reservations can be made with the **National Parks Services** (☎ 0 7728 6025, 0 7728 0222; www.dnp.go.th; bungalows 500-1400B). Online bookings are possible, although customers must forward a bank deposit within two days of making the reservation. Check out the website for detailed information.

Getting There & Around

The best way to reach the park is to catch a private day-tour from Ko Samui or Ko Pha-Ngan (located 28km and 32km away, respectively). The islands sit between Samui and the main pier at Don Sak; however, there are no ferries that stop off along the way. The park officially has an admission fee (adult/child 400/200B), although it should be included in the price of every tour. Private boat charters are also another possibility, although high gas prices will make the trip quite expensive.

SURAT THANI

อ.เมืองสุราษฎร์ธานี

pop 111,900

This busy junction has become a transport hub that indiscriminately moves cargo and people around the country. Travellers rarely linger here as they make their way to the deservedly popular islands of Ko Samui, Ko Pha-Ngan and Ko Tao. Those who are looking for an off-the-beaten-path Thai cultural experience should pick a different city.

Information

Scores of tourists pass through town every day sparking many unscrupulous travel agencies to develop innovative scams involving

substandard buses, phantom bookings and surprise 'extra' fees. Not everyone's a crook, of course, just make sure to ask a lot of questions and trust your instincts. Traffic in Surat Thani flows both ways, so when you happen upon tourists travelling in the opposite direction, ask them about the details of their trek.

Th Na Meuang has a bank on virtually every corner in the heart of downtown. If you're staying near the 'suburbs', the Tesco-Lotus has ATMs as well.

Post office (☎ 0 7727 2013, 0 7728 1966; Th Talat Mai) Across from Wat Thammabucha.

Siam City Bank (Th Chonkasem) Has a Western Union office.

Taksin Hospital (☎ 0 7727 3239; Th Talat Mai) The most professional of Surat's three hospitals. Just beyond the Talat Mai Market in the northeast part of downtown.

Tourist Authority of Thailand office (TAT; ☎ 0 7728 8817-9; tatsurat@samart.co.th; 5 Th Talat Mai; ☺ Sun-Fri) Friendly office southwest of town. Distributes useful brochures and maps, and staff speak English very well.

Sleeping

For a comfy night in Surat, escape the grimy city centre and hop on a sŏrng·tăa·ou heading towards the Phang-Nga district. When you climb aboard, tell the driver 'Tesco-Lotus', and you'll be taken about 2km to 3km out of town to a large, box-like shopping centre. At least four hotel options orbit the mall and have reasonable prices and refreshingly modern amenities.

Options in the downtown area are cheaper, but they tend to offer 'by the hour' service, so things can get a bit noisy as clients come and go. If you're on a very tight budget, consider zipping straight through town and taking the night ferry (see p626). When the weather is nice, you may even sleep better on the boat than in a noisy hotel. But if there's a chance of rain, beware – you're likely to be wet and weary in the morning.

If you are stuck in the cruddy transport junction of Phun Phin, or want to catch a very early train before the bus service begins in Surat, don't despair; there are a few tolerable options.

Queen Hotel (☎ 0 7731 1003; 916/10-13 Th Sri Sawat, Phun Phin; r 200-400B; ❄) The Queen Hotel is just a block away from Phun Phin's rail station. It's no luxury vacation, but at least you won't have to sleep on the streets. Have a look at a couple of rooms before putting down your bags – some choices are larger and less dingy than others.

100 Islands Resort & Spa (☎ 0 7720 1150; www
.roikoh.com; 19/6 Moo 3, Bypass Rd; r 590-1200B; ❄ ▢ ▣)
Across the street from the suburban Tesco-
Lotus, 100 Islands is as good as it gets in
Thailand for under 600B. This teak palace
looks out of place along the suburban highway, but inside, the immaculate rooms surround an overgrown garden and lagoon-like
swimming pool.

Wangtai Hotel (☎ 0 7728 3020; www.wangtaisurat
.com; 1 Th Talad Mai; r 790-2000B; ❄ ▢ ▣) Across the
river from the TAT office, Wangtai tries its best
to provide a corporate hotel atmosphere. Polite
receptionists and tux-clad bellboys bounce
around the vast lobby, and upstairs, rooms
have unmemorable furnishings, but there are
good views of the city from the upper floors.

Eating & Drinking

Surat Thani isn't exactly bursting with dining options. Head to the night market on
Th Ton Pho for fried, steamed, grilled or
sautéed delicacies. Don't forget to try the
crunchy insects, we hear they're a great
source of protein. During the day many food
stalls near the bus terminal sell *kŏw gài òp*
(marinated baked chicken on rice), which
is very tasty.

Crossroads Restaurant (☎ 0 7722 1525; Bypass Rd;
dishes 50-200B; ☾ 11am-1am) Located southwest
of Surat across from the Tesco-Lotus mall,
Crossroads has a quaint bluesy vibe enhanced
by dim lighting and live music. Try the oysters –
Surat Thani is famous for its giant molluscs,
and the prices are unbeatable.

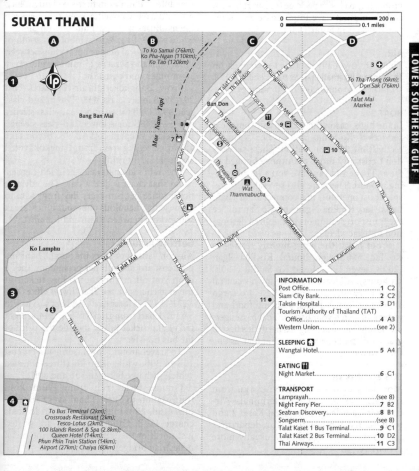

SURAT THANI

GM Pub (30/16 Th Karunrach; dishes 40-140B; ⏲ lunch & dinner) GM has a good mix of locals and *fa·ràng* English teachers who return time and time again for the mellow atmosphere, tasty international menu, and wide selection of beer and cocktails.

Getting There & Away

In general, if you are departing Bangkok or Hua Hin for Ko Samui, Ko Pha-Ngan or Ko Tao, consider taking a boat-bus package that goes through Chumphon rather than Surat. You'll save time, and the journey will be more comfortable. Travellers can also take a train south to Chumphon and then connect to a catamaran service. Those who are moving between the Andaman and Gulf Coasts will probably travel with package transport tickets, and should not have to purchase any additional tickets in Surat Thani.

AIR

There are two daily shuttles to Bangkok on **Thai Airways International** (☎ 0 7727 2610; 3/27-28 Th Karunarat) for around 3000B (70 minutes).

BOAT

In the high season there are usually bus-boat services to Ko Samui and Ko Pha-Ngan directly from the train station. These services don't cost any more than those booked in Surat Thani and can save you a lot of waiting around. There are also several ferry and speedboat operators that connect Surat Thani to Ko Tao, Ko Pha-Ngan and Ko Samui. See the transport section of your desired destination for exact details.

From Surat there are nightly ferries to Ko Tao (500B, eight hours), Ko Pha-Ngan (200B, seven hours) and Ko Samui (150B, six hours). All leave from the town's central night ferry pier at 11pm. These are cargo ships, not luxury boats, so bring food and water and watch your bags. If Thai passengers are occupying your assigned berth, it's best to grab a different one nearby rather than asking them to move.

BUS & MINIVAN

Most long-distance public buses run from the Talat Kaset 1 and 2 bus terminals. Air-con minivans leave from Talat Kaset 2 and tend to have more frequent departures than buses, although they're usually more expensive.

Air-con buses and minibuses to Khao Sok (two hours) can be booked through travel agencies and should cost no more than 100B. You can also catch certain Phuket-bound buses from the two bus terminals in town and ask to be let off at Khao Sok – a better option since some pushy minivan drivers double as touts for Khao Sok hotels.

TRAIN

When arriving by train you'll actually pull into Phun Phin, a cruddy town approximately 14km west of Surat. From Phun Phin, there are buses to Phuket, Phang-Nga and Krabi – some via Takua Pa, a junction city further west. Transport from Surat moves with greater frequency, but it's worth checking the schedule in Phun Phin first – you might luck out and save yourself a slow ride between towns. Buses in Phun Phin line up along a white wall with a Pepsi symbol just south of the station. Local orange buses chug between Phun Phin and Surat (a 25-minute ride) every 10 minutes, and cost 15B.

From Bangkok, fan/air-con fares cost 297/397B in 3rd class, 438/578B in 2nd-class seat, 498/758B for an upper 2nd-class sleeper and 548/848B for a lower 2nd-class sleeper. First-class sleepers cost 1279B. If you take an early evening train from Bangkok, you'll arrive in the morning.

The train station has a 24-hour left-luggage room that charges 20B a day. The advance ticket office is open every day from 6am to 6pm (with a nebulous one-hour lunch break somewhere between 11am and 1.30pm).

Getting Around

Air-con vans to or from the Surat Thani airport cost around 70B per person and they'll drop you off at your hotel. Buy tickets at travel agencies or the **Thai Airways office** (☎ 0 7727 2610; 3/27-28 Th Karunarat). All boat services to Samui depart from Don Sak (except the night ferry) and ticket prices include the price of the bus transfer.

To travel around town, *sŏrng·tăa·ou* cost 10B to 30B, while *săhm·lór* (three-wheeled vehicles) charge between 30B and 40B.

Orange buses run from Phun Phin train station to Surat Thani every 10 minutes (15B, 25 minutes). For this ride, taxis charge 150B. Other taxi rates are posted just north of the train station (at the metal pedestrian bridge).

AROUND SURAT THANI

Chaiya

ไชยา

pop 12,500

It's hard to believe that Chaiya, a sleepy town 60km north of Surat Thani, was once an important seat of the Srivijaya Empire. These days, most foreigners who visit are on their way to the outstanding meditation retreats held at the progressive Suan Mokkhaphalaram monastery.

Surrounded by lush forest, **Wat Suan Mokkhaphalaram** (Wat Suanmokkh; www.suanmokkh.org), whose name means 'the Garden of Liberation', charges 1500B for a 10-day program that includes food, lodging and instruction (although technically the 'teaching' is free). English retreats begin on the first day of every month and registration takes place the night before. Founded by Ajan Buddhadasa Bhikkhu, arguably Thailand's most famous monk, the temple's philosophical teachings are ecumenical in nature, comprising Zen, Taoist and Christian elements, as well as the traditional Theravada schemata.

To reach the temple, located 7km outside of Chaiya, you can catch a 3rd-class local train from Phun Phin (10B to 20B, one hour), or catch a *sŏrng·tǎa·ou* (40B to 50B, 45 minutes) from Surat's Talat Kaset 2 bus terminal. If you're heading to Surat Thani by train from Bangkok, you can get off before Surat Thani at the small Chaiya train station. Take a motorcycle taxi from the station for an additional 40B.

NAKHON SI THAMMARAT PROVINCE

While Surat Thani steals the show offering tourists the ultimate vacation paradises, Nakhon Si Thammarat tends to be a bigger hit for Thai travellers who relax along the *fa·ràng*-free shores and visit important wát in the provincial capital. The province also boasts Khao Luang National Park, a silence preserve known for its beautiful mountain and forest trails.

AO KHANOM

อ่าวขนอม

Little Khanom, halfway between Surat Thani and Nakhon Si Thammarat, quietly sits along the blue Gulf waters. Overlooked by tourists who flock to the jungle-islands nearby, this pristine region, simply called Khanom, is a worthy choice for those seeking a serene beach setting unmarred by enterprising corporations.

Information

The police station and hospital are located just south of Ban Khanom at the junction leading to Kho Khao Beach. There's a 7-Eleven (with an ATM) in the heart of Ban Khanom.

Sights

A unique feature of Khanom is the **pink dolphins**, a rare breed of albino dolphins that have a stunning pink hue. They are regularly seen from the old ferry pier and the electricity plant pier around dawn and dust.

The area is also home to a variety of pristine geological features including **waterfalls** and **caves**. The largest falls, known as **Samet Chun**, has tepid pools for cooling off, and great views of coast. To reach the falls, head south from Ban Khanom and turn left at the blue Samet Chun sign. Follow the road for about 2km and after crossing a small stream, take the next right and hike up into the mountain following the dirt road. After a 15-minute walk, listen for the waterfall and look for a small trail on the right. The scenic **Nam Tok Hin Lat** is the smallest cascade, but it's also the easiest to reach. There are pools for swimming and several huts providing shape. It's located south of Nai Phlao.

There are also two beautiful **caves** along the main road (Hwy 4014) between Khanom and Don Sak. **Khao Wang Thong** has a string of lights guiding visitors through the network of caverns and narrow passages. A metal gate covers the entrance; stop at the house at the base of the hill to retrieve the key (and leave a small donation). Turn right off the main highway at Rd 4142 to find **Khao Krot Cave**, which has two large caverns; you'll have to bring a flashlight.

For a postcard-worthy vista of the undulating coastline, head to **Dat Fa Mountain**, located about 5km west of the coast along Hwy 4014. The hillside is usually deserted, making it easy to spot along the way, and snap some photos.

Sleeping & Eating

In the last few years, construction in the area has started to take off. The area is far from booming, but large-scale development is definitely on the cards. A recent surge in Gulf oil-rigging has meant that developers are eyeing Khanom as a potential holiday destination for nearby workers.

For some cheap eats, head to Kho Khao Beach at the end of Rd 4232. You'll find a steamy jumble of barbecue stands offering some tasty favourites like *mŏo nám dòk* (spicy pork salad) and *sôm·đam*. On Wednesday and Sunday, there are markets further inland near the police station.

Talkoo Beach Resort (☎ 0 7552 8397, 08 3692 2711; bungalows 800-1500B; 🅿 🔁) This charming operation has dozens of snazzy white cottages featuring quirky fixtures such as sinks made from hollowed-out tree trunks.

Khanom Hill Resort (☎ 0 7552 9403; bungalows 800-1800B; 🅿 🔁) The seven small, red-roofed bungalows overlook the sea from various angles along this hilly property. Adorable wicker furnishings abound, and when we visited, the construction of a swimming pool was underway.

Racha Kiri (☎ 0 7552 7847; www.rachakiri.com; bungalows 3500-12,500B; 🅿 🔁) Khanom's upmarket retreat is a beautiful campus of rambling villas. The big price-tag means no crowds, which can be nice, although the resort feels like a white elephant in low season.

ourpick **One More Beer** (☎ 08 1396 4447; www.1morebeer.net; bungalows 800-1000B; 🅿 🖳) One More Beer is a chill spot to grab some delicious international cuisine. The tidy bungalows and friendly *fa·ràng* staff make One More Beer a worthy option even though it's not directly on the beach.

Getting There & Away

From Surat Thani, you can catch any Nakhon-bound bus and ask to be let off at the junction for Khanom. Catch a motorcycle taxi (70B) the rest of the way. You can get a share taxi from Nakhon Si Thammarat's share-taxi terminal to Khanom town for 85B. From Khanom town you can hire motorcycle taxis out to the beaches for about 60B. There are three separate bus stops in the vicinity. Ask your driver to stop near the fruit market or the hospital, as these are closer to the beach. Motorbikes can be rented at One More Beer for 300B per day.

NAKHON SI THAMMARAT

อ.เมือ งนครศรีธรรมราช
pop 118,100

The bustling city of Nakhon Si Thammarat (usually shortened to 'Nakhon') won't win any beauty pageants. However, travellers who stop in this historic town will enjoy a decidedly cultural experience amid some of the most important *wát* in the kingdom. Hundreds of years ago, an overland route between the western port of Trang and eastern port of Nakhon Si Thammarat functioned as a major trade link between Thailand and the rest of the world. This ancient influx of cosmopolitan

---

JATUKHAM RAMMATHEP

If you've spent more than 24 hours in Thailand, then you've probably seen a Jatukham Rammathep dangling around someone's neck – these round amulets are everywhere.

The bearers of the Jatukham Rammathep are supposed to have good fortune and protection from any harm. The origin of the amulet's name remains a mystery, although a popular theory suggests that Jatukham and Rammathep were the aliases of two Srivajaya princes who buried relics under Nakhon's Wat Phra Mahathat Woramahawihaan (opposite) some 1000 years ago.

A notorious Thai police detective first wore the precious icon, and firmly believed that the guardian spirits helped him solve a particularly difficult murder case. He tried to popularise the amulet, but it wasn't a market success until his death in 2006. Thousands of people attended his funeral including the crown prince, and the Jatukham Rammathep took off.

The talismans are commissioned at the Mahathat temple, and in the last several years, southern Thailand has seen an incredible economic boom. The first amulet was sold in 1987 for 39B, and today, over 100 million baht are spent on the town's amulets every *week*. The desire for these round icons has become so frenzied that a woman was crushed to death on the temple grounds during a widely publicised discount sale (she was not wearing her talisman).

Everyday, trucks drive along Nakhon's main roads blaring loud music to promote new shipments. These thumping beats have started to shake the ground beneath the temple, and the repeated hammering has, in an ironic metaphor, bent the main spire of Mahathat.

conceits is still palpable today, and can be found in the recipes of local cuisine, or housed in the city's temples and museums.

Orientation

Most of Nakhon's commercial activity (hotels, banks and restaurants) takes place in the northern part of the downtown. South of the clock tower, visitors will find the city's historic quarter with the oft-visited Wat Mahatat. Th Ratchadamnoen is the main thoroughfare and is loaded with cheap *sŏrng·tăa·ou* heading in both directions.

Information

Several banks and ATMs hug Th Ratchadamnoen in the northern end of the downtown. There is an English-language bookstore on the third floor of Robinson Ocean shopping mall.

Bovorn Bazaar (Th Ratchadamnoen) A mall housing a few internet cafes.

Police station (☎ 1155; Th Ratchadamnoen) Opposite the post office.

Post office (Th Ratchadamnoen; ☯ 8.30am-4.30pm)

TAT office (☎ 0 7534 6515) Housed in a 1926-vintage building in the northern end of the Sanam Na Meuang (City Park). Has some useful brochures in English. The local One Tambon One Product (OTOP) is just a block away on the west side of Sanam Na Meuang Park.

Sights

The most important *wát* in southern Thailand, **Wat Phra Mahathat Woramahawihaan** (simply known as Mahatat) is a stunning campus boasting 77 *chedi* (stupa) and an imposing 77m *chedi* crowned by a gold spire. According to legend, Queen Hem Chala and Prince Thanakuman brought relics to Nakhon over 1000 years ago, and built a small pagoda to house the precious icons. The temple has since grown into a rambling site, and today, crowds gather daily to purchase the popular Jatukham amulets (see boxed text, opposite). Mahathat's resident monks live across the street at **Wat Na Phra Boromathat**.

When the Tampaling (also known as Tambralinga) kingdom traded with merchants from Indian, Arabic, Dvaravati and Champa states, the region around Nakhon became a melting pot of crafts and art. Today, many of these relics are on display behind the run-down facade of the **national museum** (Th Ratchadamnoen; admission 30B; ☯ 9am-4pm Wed-Sun).

Nakhon's noteworthy **shadow puppets** are also worthy of exploration. Traditionally, there are two styles of puppet: *năng đà·lung* and *năng yài*. At just under 1m tall, the former are similar in size to Malay-Indonesian puppets and feature movable appendages and parts (including genitalia); the latter are unique to Thailand, nearly life-sized, and lack moving parts. Both are intricately carved from buffalo-hide. Nowadays performances are rare and usually limited to festivals.

Festivals & Events

Every year during mid-October there is a southern-Thai festival called **Chak Phra Pak Tai**, held in Nakhon Si Thammarat (as well as Songkhla and Surat Thani). In Nakhon Si the festival is focused around Wat Phra Mahathat and includes performances of *năng đà·lung* and *lá·kon lék*, as well as the parading of Buddha images around the city to collect donations for local temples.

In the third lunar month (February to March) the city holds the colourful **Hae Phaa Khun That**, in which a lengthy cloth *jataka* painting is wrapped around the main *chedi* at Wat Phra Mahathat.

Sleeping

Lodging options are limited to a few respectable options.

Thai Hotel (☎ 0 7534 1509; fax 0 7534 4858; 1375 Th Ratchadamnoen; fan r 220-270B, air-con r 340-450B, ste 750B; ✷) Thai Hotel is the most central sleeping spot in town – look for a small sign (which actually says 'Thai Hotet' in Thai) pointing down a busy side street. The walls are thin, but the air-con options are a good deal for the price. Each room has a TV and the higher floors have good views of the urban bustle.

Nakorn Garden Inn (☎ 0 7532 3777; 1/4 Th Pak Nakhon; r 445B; ✷) The motel-style Nakorn Garden Inn offers a pleasant alternative to the usual cement cube. Rooms are encased in exposed crimson brick and set around a sandy garden. Each unit is identical, sporting a TV and fridge; try to score a room that gets plenty of sunlight.

Grand Park Hotel (☎ 0 7531 7666-73; fax 0 7531 7674; 1204/79 Th Pak Nakhon; r 700-1700B; ✷) Grand Park offers fine, modern rooms with TV and fridge – nothing too fancy or luxurious. The rooms are on seven floors, some with sweeping vistas of the city. Guests can loiter in the spacious lobby and restaurant.

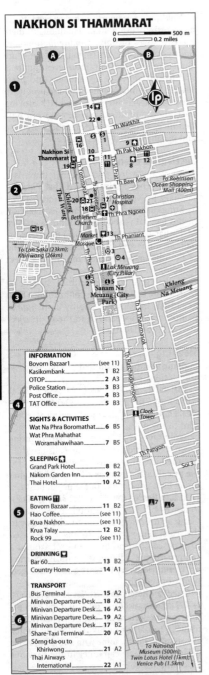

NAKHON SI THAMMARAT

Twin Lotus Hotel (☎ 0 7532 3777; www.twin lotushotel.net; 97/8 Th Phattanakan Khukhwang; r 1100-3000B; ☒ ☒ ☒) Its age is starting to show, but Twin Lotus is still a nice spot for a little pampering while visiting Nakhon. The well-equipped hotel gym is very popular with the local English teachers. This 16-storey behemoth sits several kilometres southeast of the city centre.

Eating & Drinking

Nakhon is a great place to sample cuisine with a distinctive southern twist. In the evening, Muslim food stands sell delicious *kôw mòk gài* (chicken biryani), *má·dà·bà* (*murdabag*; Indian pancake stuffed with chicken or vegetables) and roti. Several tasty options cluster around Bovorn Bazaar on Th Ratchadamnoen.

For an all-night dance fest, head south towards the Twin Lotus Hotel and you'll find the popular Venice Pub. For a tamer evening of beers and pub grub, check out Bar 60 (known as Bar Hok Sip), near the corner of Th Ratchadamnoen and Th Phra Ngoen.

Hao Coffee (☎ 0 7534 6563; Bovorn Bazaar; dishes 30-60B; ☺ breakfast & lunch) Dishes out quick and convenient breakfasts, and the coffee is pretty darn good.

Rock 99 (☎ 0 7531 7999; 1180/807, Bavorn Bazaar; dishes 40-100B; ☺ dinner) The choice *fa·ràng* out (*fa·ràng* hang-out) in Nakhon, Rock 99 has a good selection of international fare – from taco salads and steak sandwiches, to pizzas and fried potatoes. There's live music on Wednesday, Friday and Saturday nights, but expect to bump into friendly expats almost all the time.

Khrua Nakhon (☎ 0 7531 7197; Bovorn Bazaar; dishes 60-200B ☺ breakfast & lunch) This joint, next to Hao Coffee, has a great selection of traditional Nakhon cuisine. Order one of the sharing platters, which comes with five types of curry (including an unpalatable spicy fish sauce), or try the *kôw yam* (southern-style rice salad). There's one at a second location in Robinson Ocean Mall.

Krua Talay (Th Pak Nakhon; dishes 40-300B; ☺ lunch & dinner) Located near the Kukwang Market, Krua Talay is the top spot in town for succulent seafood. It can be a little pricey compared to the other nontouristy chow spots around town, but the locals agree that it's definitely worth it.

Country Home (☎ 08 1968 0762; 119/7 Th Ratchadamnoen) This large, open-air bar invokes the Wild West with saloon-style seating and an odd smattering of straw hats. There's live music every night and the joint gets packed with beer-toting locals.

Getting There & Away

Due to the burgeoning popularity of the Jatukham amulet (see boxed text, p628), transport to Nakhon is booming.

Several small carriers (plus Thai Airways) fly from Bangkok to Nakhon everyday. There are about six daily one-hour flights priced around 3500B.

There are two daily train departures from Bangkok to Nakhon (stopping through Hua Hin, Chumphon and Surat Thani along the way). They are both 12-hour night trains leaving at 5.35pm and 7.15pm. Second-class fares cost between 590B and 890B. These trains continue on to Hat Yai and Sungai Kolok.

Buses from Bangkok depart either between 6am and 8am, or between 5.30pm and 10pm. There are about seven daily departures (1st/2nd class around 700/600B, 12 to 13 hours). Ordinary buses to Bangkok leave from the bus terminal, but a couple of private buses leave from booking offices on Th Jamroenwithi, where you can also buy tickets.

When looking for minivan stops to leave Nakhon, keep an eye out for small desks along the side of the downtown roads (minivans and waiting passengers may or may not be present nearby). It's best to ask around as each destination has a different departure point. Krabi and Don Sak minivans are grouped together – just make sure you don't get on the wrong one. Stops are scattered around Th Jamroenwithi, Th Wakhit and Th Yommarat. There are frequent minivans (that leave when they're full) to Krabi (180B

to 240B, 2½ hours) and Phuket (175B to 275B, five hours), Surat Thani (100B, one hour), Khanom (85B, one hour) and Hat Yai (around 120B, three hours).

Getting Around

Sŏrng·tăa·ou run north–south along Th Ratchadamnoen and Th Si Thammasok for 10B (a bit more at night). Motorcycle-taxi rides start at 20B and cost up to 50B for longer distances.

AROUND NAKHON SI THAMMARAT
Khao Luang National Park

อุทยานแห่งชาติเขาหลวง

Known for its beautiful mountain and forest walks, cool streams, waterfalls and orchards, **Khao Luang National Park** (☎ 0 7530 9644-7; adult/child 400/200B) surrounds the 1835m peak of Khao Luang. This soaring mountain range reaches up to 1800m, and is covered in virgin forest. An ideal source for streams and rivers, the mountains show off impressive waterfalls and provide a habitat for a plethora of bird species – this place is a good spot for any budding ornithologist. Fans of flora will also get their kicks here; there are over 300 species of orchid in the park, some of which are found nowhere else on earth.

Park bungalows can be rented for between 600B and 1000B per night, and sleep six to 12 people. Camping is permitted along the trail to the summit. To reach the park, take a *sŏrng·tăa·ou* (25B) from Nakhon Si Thammarat to the village of Khiriwong, at the base of Khao Luang. The entrance to the park and the offices of the Royal Forest Department are 33km from the centre of Nakhon on Rte 4015, an asphalt road that climbs almost 400m in 2.5km to the office and a further 450m to the car park.

Andaman Coast

As airfares soar and vacation time dwindles, we tighten the grip on our 'travel bibles' in hopes of planning the best trip ever. This is a daunting task, especially for those of us on the relentless quest for '-est'. Fortunately, the Andaman Coast is the ultimate land of superlatives: the tall*est* karst formations, the long*est* beaches, the soft*est* sands, the blu*est* water – the list goes on.

Along the coast, boats from Khao Lak idle between the Similan and Surin islands, dropping scuba buffs deep down into the great*est* dive sights around. Further south, Phuket, the bigg*est* island, is the region's hedonistic launching pad, offering a glimmer of what's to come next.

The Andaman's signature pinnacles of jagged jungle-clad slate come to a stunning climax in Krabi. The region's earthen fortresses lie frozen in the sea – each one protected by a halo of neon reefs. Ko Phi-Phi Don's unimaginable beauty exceeds even the high*est* expectations. Scurry up to viewpoints for change-your-life vistas of the island's idyllic hourglass-shaped sandbar. At Railay, climbers take in the scenery as they dangle like ornaments on a giant Christmas tree.

Down in Trang, the skyscraping swell of iconic limestone starts to sink back into the deep, but not before punctuating the coastline with a handful of anthropomorphic islets. This quiet getaway, the Andaman's b*est*-kept secret (until now), is the mystical stomping ground of the local sea gypsies, who cast their lines amongst the fin*est* blooms of snorkel-worthy coral. Save these islands for the end of your journey – we guarantee you'll be impr*est*.

HIGHLIGHTS

- Cavorting with curious pufferfish in the necklaces of fiery coral draped around each of the **Trang Islands** (p709)
- Tooling around on your motorbike uncovering local markets and desolate beaches on **Ko Lanta** (p698)
- Tempting your tastebuds with a heady mix of gourmet treats and street-side eats on **Phuket** (p672)
- Slinking into the sea for a sunrise dive while cruising through Thailand's top scuba sites on a live-aboard from **Khao Lak** (p641)
- Spotting colourful hornbills and prancing monkeys from your wooden canoe while paddling between the peaks of **Khao Sok National Park** (p639)
- Floating in a sea of lapis lazuli while staring up at the astounding limestone crags on **Ko Phi-Phi** (p692)

★Khao Sok National Park
★Khao Lak
Phuket ★
★Ko Phi-Phi
★ Ko Lanta
★Trang Islands

■ BEST TIME TO VISIT: DECEMBER–APRIL	■ POPULATION: 1.13 MILLION

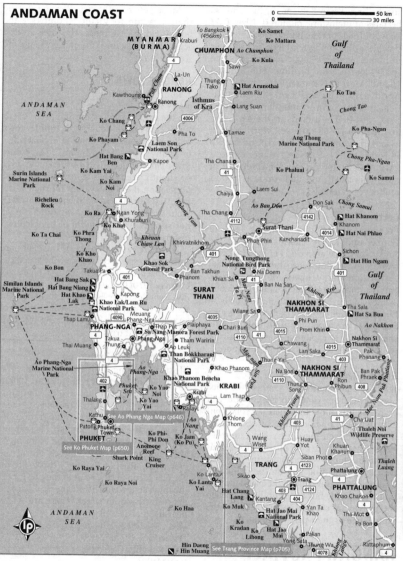

Climate

A main concern when visiting Thailand's southern provinces is the weather. The Andaman Coast receives more rain than the southern gulf provinces – with May to October being the months of heaviest downpours. During this time, passenger boat frequency to the islands slows, and in many instances ferries suspend their service (most in the far south).

National Parks

This region has more than its share of national parks. Ao Phang-Nga (p647) offers limestone cliffs, islands and caves to explore by sea kayaking, scuba diving or snorkelling. Khao Sok (p639) has endless hectares of prehistoric rainforest. Khao Lak/Lam Ru (p641) offers hiking past cliffs and beaches, while multiple islands and throngs of mangroves and jungle make Laem Son (p638) perfect for birding. The Similan Islands Marine National Park (p645) is a world-class diving and snorkelling destination, as is the Surin Islands Marine National Park (p644). The islands in the Ko Lanta archipelago (p698) are well worth a visit, as are the jungly islets surrounding Ko Phi-Phi (p697). Sa Nang Manora Forest Park (p648) has a fairyland setting of moss-encrusted roots and rocks, as well as multilevel waterfalls.

Getting There & Away

Frequent flights from Bangkok land in Phuket and Krabi, making travel to the Andaman Coast a breeze. Phuket also services a slew of domestic and international destinations like Chiang Mai, Ko Samui, Pattaya, Singapore, Kuala Lumpur, Seoul, Sydney and several destinations in northern Europe. A well-trodden network of trains and buses are a popular (and only slightly cheaper) way to explore the rest of Thailand or head down to Malaysia and Singapore.

Getting Around

If you're planning to play 'connect the dots' and travel from island to island, you will be pleased to know that there's a solid (but expensive) transportation infrastructure in place. In fact, these ferry links improve every season – it's now possible to island-hop from Phuket to Langkawi (in Malaysia) without ever setting foot on the mainland. Those who do travel along the mainland will find manageable bus and train links through the provincial capitals (which all have the same name as their parent province).

RANONG PROVINCE

The first piece in the Andaman's puzzle of curvy coastal provinces is Thailand's least populated region and also its most rainy, logging in with up to eight months of showers per year. As a result, Ranong's forests are lush and green (although it's swampy near the coastline and mainland beaches are almost nonexistent).

Most people only visit Ranong during their visa run to Victoria Point (see the boxed text, p636); those who stick around seek out the relaxing vibe on Ko Chang and Ko Phayam.

RANONG TOWN

ระนอง
pop 24,500

On the eastern bank of the Sompaen River's turbid, tea-brown estuary, the frontier town of Ranong is no more than a short boat ride – or a filthy swim – from Myanmar. This border town *par excellence* (shabby, frenetic, ever so slightly seedy) has a thriving Burmese population (keep an eye out for men wearing traditional *longyi*; Burmese sarong), a clutch of mildly interesting (and stinky) hot springs, and a handful of tumbledown historic buildings.

An increasing number of travellers are showing up specifically to dive the spectacular Burma Banks (in the Mergui Archipelago), 60km north of the Surin Islands. A number of dive operators have established themselves in Ranong (which does lend the city a pinch of an expat feel), using it as a jumping-off point for live-aboard trips.

Orientation & Information

Most of Ranong lies just west of Hwy 4, about 600km south of Bangkok and 300km north of Phuket. For information about immigration and visa runs, see the boxed text on p636. The main Thai immigration office is on the road to Saphan Plaa, about halfway between town and the main piers, although you can get stamped out at the pier itself. Most of Ranong's banks are on Th Tha Meuang (the road to the pier), near the intersection with Th Ruangrat, Ranong's main north–south street. There are ATMs near the pier as well.

J Net (☎ 0 7882 2877; Th Ruangrat; per hr 40B;
🕑 9am-9pm)

Main post office (Th Chonrau; 🕑 9am-4pm Mon-Fri, to noon Sat)

Sights & Activities

HOT SPRINGS

Ranong is rural Thailand's version of a spa town – stinky and charmless. You can sample the waters at Wat Tapotaram, where **Ranong Mineral Hot Springs** (Th Kamlangsap; admission 10B; 🕑 8am-5pm) offers pools hot enough to boil an

ANDAMAN COAST

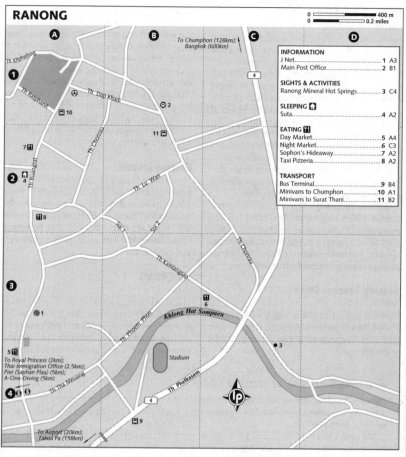

RANONG

To Chumphon (128km);
Bangkok (600km)

INFORMATION	
J Net	1 A3
Main Post Office	2 B1

SIGHTS & ACTIVITIES	
Ranong Mineral Hot Springs	3 C4

SLEEPING	
Suta	4 A2

EATING	
Day Market	5 A4
Night Market	6 C3
Sophon's Hideaway	7 A2
Taxi Pizzeria	8 A2

TRANSPORT	
Bus Terminal	9 B4
Minivans to Chumphon	10 A1
Minivans to Surat Thani	11 B2

Th Kitphadung
Th Ratphanit
Th Dap Khadi
Th Chonrau
Th Ruangrat
Th Lu Wan
Th Kamlangsap
Th Chonrau
Soi 1
Soi 2
Th Phoem Phon
Khlong Hat Sompaen
Stadium
Th Tha Meuang
Th Phetkasem

To Royal Princess (2km);
Thai Immigration Office (2.5km);
Pier (Saphan Plaa) (5km);
A-One-Diving (5km)

To Airport (20km);
Takua Pa (158km)

ANDAMAN COAST

egg (65°C). Like the three bears of Goldilocks fame, the names of the three springs translate as Father Spring, Mother Spring and Baby Spring, and each has its own distinct smell (all horrid). The spring water is thought to be sacred, as well as having miraculous healing powers.

DIVING

Live-aboard diving trips run from Ranong to world-class bubble-blowing destinations including the Burma Banks (Mergui Archipelago) and the Surin and Similan islands. Prices start at around 16,000B for a four-day package. Try **A-One-Diving** (☎ 0 7783 2984; www.a-one-diving.com; 77 Saphan Plaa). Several operators in Khao Lak (p641) are starting up live-aboard services to the stunning Burma Banks.

Sleeping

If you are doing your visa run through an agency, they'll ship you in and out of town without having to spend the night.

Suta (☎ 0 7783 2707; Th Ruangrat; r 350B; ⁕) One of the comfier choices in Ranong (and popular with repeat visa-running expats), this off-the-road place has a clump of simple bungalows overlooking a small garden/car park.

Royal Princess (☎ 0 7783 5240; www.royalprincess .com; r 990-2900B; ⁕ ⁑) As good as it gets in the hotel category, Royal Princess has a gym, pool and mineral water bathroom, but the trimmings are starting to look a bit tatty.

Eating & Drinking

On Th Kamlangsap, not far from Hwy 4, is a night market with several food stalls selling great Thai dishes at low prices; across the street is a modest noodle stand. The day market, on Th Ruangrat towards the southern end of town, offers inexpensive Thai and Burmese meals, as well as fresh produce, fish and meats. A cluster of decent eateries can also be found at the northern end of Th Ruangrat.

Taxi Pizzeria (☎ 0 7782 5730; Th Ruangrat; dishes 60-180B; ✆ lunch & dinner) Completed framed jigsaws provide the decoration at this spartan pizzeria. The food won't have Mum amending her recipe book, but the chef does make an attempt at rustling up a reasonable margarita.

Sophon's Hideaway (☎ 0 7783 2730; Th Ruangrat; dishes 60-200B; ✆ lunch & dinner) This expat fave has everything, including internet access, a free pool table, a pizza oven and rattan furnishings aplenty. The menu spans the East–West divide and cocktails are served come sundown.

Getting There & Away

AIR

Ranong airport is 20km south of town, off Hwy 4. **Air Asia** (www.airasia.com) has three or four flights to Bangkok (one way around 1900B) per week.

BUS

The bus terminal is on Th Phetkasem towards the southern end of town, though some buses stop in town before proceeding to the terminal. *Sŏrng·tăa·ou* (also spelt *săwngthăew*; pick-up truck) 2 (blue) passes the terminal. Bus services include Bangkok (220B to 700B, 10 hours), Chumphon (120B to 150B, three hours), Hat Yai (410B to 430B, five hours), Krabi (190B to 220B, six hours), Phuket (180B to 250B, 5½ hours) and Surat Thani (100B to 200B, 4½ hours).

Getting Around

Motorcycle taxis will take you almost anywhere in town for 20B, to the hotels along Th Phetkasem for 25B and to the pier for boats to Ko Chang, Ko Phayam and Myanmar for 50B. **Pon's Place** (☎ 0 7782 3344; Th Ruangrat; ✆ 7.30am-midnight) can assist with motorcycle and car rentals.

KO CHANG

เกาะช้าง

If you're looking for the big Ko Chang, you've come to the wrong place. But if your suitcase is overflowing with novels and you're seeking a silent stretch of sand on which to read them, then welcome! Unlike most of the Andaman's

---

RENEWING YOUR VISA AT VICTORIA POINT

The name Victoria Point sounds so regal, but in reality the southernmost tip of mainland Myanmar is a dusty, tumbledown hellhole. The Burmese call it Kawthoung, a corruption of the Thai name, Ko Song (Second Island).

The easiest way to renew your visa is to opt for one of the 'visa trips' offered by travel agencies in Ranong. You probably aren't vacationing in Ranong, so ask about special visa runs where you are – be it Phuket, Khao Lak, Ko Phi-Phi, Ko Samui or Ko Pha-Ngan – before boarding a bus to Ranong Town. If you're already in town you can also renew your visa on your own steam. This can be slightly cheaper and faster, although prepare to be hassled and harangued during the entire process. If you do go on your own, tobacco-smacking Burmese boatswains will try to sell you cases of Viagra (to 'bring you up') or Valium (to 'bring you down') – the trip itself will be enough of a rollercoaster ride.

All travellers need to have their passport, a photocopy of their passport and US$10. Organised visa trips will take care of the last two items for you. Boats leave from the pier (signs throughout Ranong mark it well), where there is a small Thai **immigration booth** (✆ 8.30am-6pm) that will stamp you out (and back in when you return). The one-hour long-tail boat ride to the Burmese checkpoint costs 200B each way. Those travelling with a visa run company will be herded onto a wooden ferry. Solo travellers are allowed to board these ferries as well for around 70B each way. Before arriving at Victoria Point, your boat will pass two checkpoints where the boat driver will flash your passport to authorities.

If you're just coming to renew your Thai visa, the whole process will take between 1½ and 4½ hours, depending on how you are travelling. Bear in mind that Myanmar's clocks are 30 minutes behind Thailand time. Oh, and bring an umbrella and some bottled water – there's very little shade on the trip.

islands, Ko Chang enjoys its back-to-basics kinda lifestyle – there are no ATMs, no internet and no rush to acquire them.

When you're done with your book, spend your time exploring the island's tiny village 'capital' (and we use that word lightly), or wind your way around on one of the dirt trails. Sea eagles, Andaman kites and hornbills all nest here, and, if you're lucky, you'll catch sight of them floating above the mangroves.

Bungalow operators can arrange boat trips to Ko Phayam and other nearby islands for around 200B per person (including lunch) in a group of six or more. Dive trips are also possible. **Aladdin Dive Cruise** (☎ 0 7782 0472; www .aladdindivecruise.de), on Ko Chang, runs PADI courses and offers a range of live-aboard dive safaris.

SLEEPING & EATING

Bamboo and thatch are the norm on rustic Ko Chang and, for the most part, they're only open from November to April. Electricity is limited although a few spots use solar power.

Ko Chang Resort (☎ 0 7782 8177; Ao Yai; bungalows 200-300B) Bright colours and bamboo slats perch on the rocks above a patch of peach sand. The pricier bungalows have split-level decks, and the bathrooms are some of the best around.

Cashew Resort (☎ 0 7782 4741; Ao Yai; bungalows 200-600B) Cashew is Ko Chang's most venerable resort. Choose from cheap A-frame huts or larger, more robust bungalows.

Sawadee (☎ 0 7782 0177; Ao Yai; bungalows 300-400B) This is about as upmarket as things get on the little Chang. Dark-wood interiors contrast with attached bathrooms, which are set ablaze with a palette of bright colours. The restaurant serves Thai standards under the stars.

GETTING THERE & AWAY

From central Ranong Town, take a *sŏrng·tǎa·ou* (15B) or taxi (50B) to Saphan Plaa. Two boats (150B) leave every morning from mid-October to May; turn up around 9am to see when they're going, as they don't usually leave before this hour. During the high season (November to April) there's a daily noon departure. Boats return to Ranong at 8am the next day. Long-tails can be chartered from Ko Phayam for around 1000B to 1200B.

KO PHAYAM
เกาะพยาม

While technically part of Laem Son National Park (p638), little Ko Phayam swims in the sea amid other verdant flecks of sand and limestone. It's a welcoming place, whose small population is a friendly mix of Thais and Burmese, expats and a few dozen ethnic *chow lair* (also spelt *chao leh*; sea gypsies) who earn a living baiting prawns or plucking savoury cashew nuts. Everyone gathers along the two main bays, flanked by strands of flaxen sand, where the soundtrack is a delightful blend of lapping waves and hooting hornbills.

The island has one 'village', where you will find the main pier, a couple of simple eateries, small grocery stalls and a bar. From the pier area, motorcycle taxis scoot you to your basic bungalow along the motorcycle 'highway', running down the middle of the island.

Sleeping & Eating

Fan-cooled, rustic bungalows are the staple on Ko Phayam; electricity is usually only available from sunset to 10pm or 11pm. Most of the bungalow operations stay open throughout the year – although the shutters will come down if business becomes too slow. Most spots have attached eateries serving standard backpacker fare.

Vijit (☎ 0 7783 4082; www.kohpayam-vijit.com; Ao Khao Fai; bungalows 200-500B; 🖳) Towards the southern end of the bay, Vijit has a dozen basic bungalows around a sandy lot peppered with young trees. Each bungalow has been built in a slightly different style, but all have schmancy indoor/outdoor bathrooms. At high tide, the beach here thins out. Contact the staff for free transport from Ranong.

Bamboo Bungalows (☎ 0 7782 0012; Ao Yai; bungalows 300-500B) Opt for the more expensive, but sturdier (read: monsoon-proof) concrete-and-tile bungalows. It is run by an Israeli-Thai couple, offers oodles of atmosphere and attracts plenty of backpackers – when they are in town. There's a solid eatery, a pleasant, leafy garden and you can hire bodyboards if you fancy a boogie in the surf.

Mountain Resort (☎ 0 7782 0098; Ao Khao Fai; bungalows 350B) Located in a shady palm grove, this has some of the glossiest bungalows on the island – they are also some of the most pleasant. With only a handful of bungalows on offer, you can count on plenty of privacy

ANDAMAN COAST

and lashings of peace and quiet. Mountain Resort is at the northern end of the bay.

Also try:

Mr Gao (☎ 0 7787 0222; www.mr-gao-phayam.com; Ao Khao Kwai; bungalows from 350B) Classic bamboo crash pad for couples. Smiles are at a minimum though.

Coconuts (☎ 0 7782 0011; Ao Yai; bungalows 350-500B) No-fuss, no-muss housing when Bamboo is full.

Drinking

Beach-bars line both of the island's strips of sand; most of them look like piles of ocean debris.

Oscar's (☎ 0 7782 4236; Ao Khao Fai; ⏰ 10am-11pm) Located in the main village, this modern bar looks a little incongruous in its backwater setting. If you're after late-night (for a remote island) shenanigans, however, it is *the* place to go – the beer might even be cold.

Getting There & Around

There are daily boats from Saphan Plaa to Ko Phayam's pier at around 9am and 2pm (150B, 1½ to two hours). From Ko Phayam back to Ranong the boats run at 8am and 1pm. During the high season there may be three runs daily. Long-tail boat charters to the island cost 1500B to 2000B. A charter to Ko Chang is around 1250B.

Motorcycle taxis provide the transport around Ko Phayam; there are no cars or trucks (yet), and roads are pleasantly motorcycle-sized. A ride to your bungalow will cost 50B to 100B. Walking is possible but distances are long – it's about 45 minutes from the pier to Ao Khao Fai, the nearest bay.

Motorcycle rentals are available at **Oscar's** (☎ 0 7782 4236; per day approx 250B), the only bar in Ko Phayam's village – you can't miss it. Some of the bigger guesthouses might be able to arrange rentals, too.

LAEM SON NATIONAL PARK

อุทยานแห่งชาติแหลมสน

Covering 315 sq km of land shared by Ranong and Phang-Nga Provinces, the **park** (☎ 0 7782 4224; www.dnp.go.th; adult/child 400/200B) also includes around 100km of Andaman Sea coastline – the longest protected shore in the country – as well as over 20 idyllic islets. Much of the coast here is covered with mangrove swamps, home to various species of birds, fish, deer and monkeys (including crab-eating macaques), often seen while you're driving along the road to the park headquarters.

The most accessible beach is **Hat Bang Ben**, just down the street from the park's rusty gates. (Note that you only have to pay the national park fee if you enter the park here.) This long, sandy beach, backed by shady casuarinas, is a great place to get wet. From Hat Bang Ben you can see several of the park's protected islands, including the nearby Ko Kam Yai, Ko Kam Noi, Mu Ko Yipun, Ko Khang Khao and, to the north, Ko Phayam. The park staff can arrange boat trips out to any of these islands for 1500B per boat per day, although private tours can be scouted for a much cheaper rate (see the Wasana Resort, below).

Ko Khang Khao is known for the beach on its northern end that is covered with colourful pebbles. Although underwater visibility isn't great here, it's a little better than on Ko Chang as it's further from the mouth of the Sompaen River. The beach on **Ko Kam Noi** has relatively clear water for swimming and snorkelling (April is the best month), plus the added bonus of fresh water year-round and plenty of grassy areas for camping. One island on the other side of Ko Kam Yai, which can't be seen from the beach, is **Ko Kam Tok** (also called Ko Ao Khao Khwai). It's only about 200m from Ko Kam Yai, and, like Ko Kam Noi, has a good beach, coral, fresh water and a camping ground. **Ko Kam Yai** is 14km southwest of Hat Bang Ben. It's a large island with some accommodation (camping and bungalows), a pretty beach and great snorkelling.

About 3km north of Hat Bang Ben, across the canal, is another beach, **Hat Laem Son**, which is almost always deserted since the only way to get here is to hike over from Hat Bang Ben. In the opposite direction, about 60km south of Hat Bang Ben, is **Hat Praphat**, very similar to Bang Ben, with casuarinas backing the long beach. Sea turtles lay eggs on Hat Praphat. There is a second park office here, which can be reached by road via Hwy 4 (Phetkasem Hwy).

Sleeping & Eating

ourpick Wasana Resort (☎ 0 7786 1434; bungalows 450-600B; ✷) Rather than staying at the cruddy (and overpriced) national park bungalows, try the Wasana Resort, near the park's front ticketing gate off Hwy 4. A perennial favourite amongst the more intrepid do-it-yourself backpacker crowd, this family-run resort features a small ring of cosy bungalows wrapping around the colourful on-site restaurant. The owners, a Dutch-Thai couple, have plenty of great ideas for exploring Laem Son (ask about the stunning 10km trek around the headland) and can take you out on a day trip to the islands for 550B per person (excellent lunch included; four person minimum).

Getting There & Away

The turn-off for Laem Son National Park is about 58km from Ranong down Hwy 4 (Phetkasem Hwy), between the 657km and 658km markers. Buses heading south from Ranong can drop you off here (ask for Hat Bang Ben). Once you're off the highway, however, you'll have to flag down a pick-up truck going towards the park. If you can't get a ride all the way, it's a 10km walk from Hwy 4 to the park entrance. At the police box at the junction you may be able to hire a motorcycle taxi for 50B; the road is paved, so if you're driving it's a breeze. Private car is undoubtedly the best way to get around these parts – local renters charge 1000B.

For detailed information about getting around the mainland portion of the park, check out the www.vwvagabonds.com/Bike/CycleTouringRouteBangkokPhuket.html website. Boats out to the various islands can be chartered from the park's visitor centre; the general cost is 1500B per day.

PHANG-NGA PROVINCE

Wounds take a long time to heal, but Phang-Nga is finally on the mend. It's been five years since the tsunami and, although the tales are still being told here, there's a palpable sense of progress as hot spots like Khao Lak return to the well-trodden backpacker route.

From November to April the water is very clear, the sun shines and soda-white beaches beckon. In the rainy season, however, many places shut down and the area can feel a bit haunted. Offshore, the Surin and Similan island marine national parks harbour some of the world's top diving destinations.

KHAO SOK NATIONAL PARK

อุทยานแห่งชาติเขาสก

Welcome to Jurassic Park – you can almost hear the theme song playing in surround sound while you pass between the soaring karst formations. Add a prancing T Rex and Thailand's first protected preserve would

be a dead ringer for Crichton's prehistoric Disneyland. This dripping juicy jungle is part of the oldest rainforest in the world, where snakes, monkeys and tigers mingle within the tangle of lazy vines.

Although technically part of Surat Thani Province, **Khao Sok National Park** (☎ 0 7739 5025; www.khaosok.com; admission 400B) is much closer to the Andaman Sea, and possesses the classic Andaman topography: signature ferny cliffs that shoot straight up into the air like crocodile teeth.

Orientation & Information

The **park headquarters** (☎ 0 7739 5025) and visitor centre are 1.8km off Rte 401, close to the Km109 marker. Myriad tour operators from Phuket and Khao Lak offer day trips into the wilds of the park, but you can make the trek under your own steam as the highway has decent signage.

The best time of year to visit is between December and May – the dry season. During the June to November wet season, trails can be extremely slippery and waterlogged, and flash flooding is a common and sometimes fatal occurrence. On the other hand, animals leave their hidden reservoirs throughout the wet months, so you're more likely to stumble across some big fauna.

Sights & Activities

Khao Sok's vast terrain makes it one of the last viable habitats for **large mammals** requiring large areas in order to subsist. During the wetter months you may happen upon bears, boars, gaurs, tapirs, gibbons, deer, wild elephants and perhaps even a tiger. There are also over 180 species of bird, as well as the world's largest flower, the rare *Rafflesia kerrii*. Found only in Khao Sok, these **giant flowers** can reach 80cm in diameter. It has no roots or leaves of its own; instead it lives parasitically inside the roots of the liana, a jungle vine.

The stunning **Chiaw Lan Lake** sits about an hour's drive east of the visitor centre. The lake was created in 1982 by an enormous shale-clay dam called Ratchaprapha (Kheuan Ratchaprapha or Kheuan Chiaw Lan). The limestone outcrops protruding from the lake reach a height of 960m, over three times higher than the formations in the Phang-Nga area.

A cave known as **Tham Nam Thalu** contains striking limestone formations and subterranean streams, while **Tham Si Ru** features four converging passageways used as a hideout by communist insurgents between 1975 and 1982. The caves can be reached on foot from the southwestern shore of the lake. You can rent boats from local fishermen to explore the coves, canals, caves and cul-de-sacs along the lakeshore.

Elephant trekking, kayaking and rafting are popular park activities. The hiking is also excellent, and you can arrange park tours from any guesthouse – just be sure you get a certified guide (they wear an official badge). Various hiking trails from the visitors centre lead to the waterfalls of **Sip-Et Chan** (4km), **Than Sawan** (9km) and **Than Kloy** (9km), among other destinations.

Sleeping & Eating

The road leading into the park is lined with charming fan bungalows offering comfortable digs in natural surroundings. Try to arrive in the daytime, so you can walk along the short road leading up to the park and pick where you want to stay.

Art's Riverview Jungle Lodge (☎ 0 7739 5009; bungalows 350-550B) Art's has a pleasant range of simple, solid and airy rooms with mosquito nets. The more expensive ones have verandahs and hammocks, and all are in a beautiful, tranquil and lush setting. You can watch wild macaques from the riverside restaurant.

Khao Sok Rainforest Resort (☎ 0 7739 5006; www .krabidir.com/khaosokrainforest; bungalows 400-600B) Huts perched high on stilts along the snaking river. In-house conservation programs target low-impact hiking and forest restoration.

Morning Mist Resort (☎ 0 7885 6185; bungalows 600B) Plenty of twigs and thatch with views of the jagged rock formations. Bookings should be made through the National Park Services.

Cliff & River Jungle Resort (☎ 08 7271 8787; www.thecliffandriver.com; bungalows 1800B) A beautiful property set just below the jagged silver cliffs. The plunge pool and steam spa are extra perks.

Getting There & Around

Khao Sok is about 100km from Surat Thani. Transport to the park by minivan from Surat Thani (80B, one hour, at least twice daily) can be arranged through most travel agents in Surat, but be aware that some minivan companies work with specific bungalow outfitters and will try to convince you to stay at that place. Otherwise, from the Surat Thani area you can catch a bus going towards Takua Pa – you'll be getting off well before hitting this destination (tell the bus driver 'Khao Sok'). You can also come from the west coast by bus, but you'll have to go to Takua Pa first. Buses from Takua Pa to the park (25B, one hour, nine daily) drop you off on the highway, 1.8km from the visitor centre. If guesthouse touts don't meet you, you'll have to walk to your chosen guesthouse (from 50m to 2km). The roads within the main parts of the park are well paved, so personal vehicles will have no problems getting around.

To arrive at Chiaw Lan Lake, go east on Rte 401 from the visitor centre and take the turn-off between the Km52 and Km53 markers, at Ban Takum. It's another 14km to the lake. If you don't have your own wheels, you'll have to bus it to Ban Takum, then hope to hitch a ride to the lake. The best option without private transport would be to join a tour, which any guesthouse can arrange for 1000B (2000B to 2500B with an overnight stay).

KHAO LAK & AROUND
เขาหลัก/บางเนียง/นางทอง

Khao Lak is a one-horse town. And that lone horse is a one-trick pony. Diving drives the economy here, and beyond that, there isn't a whole lot to do – sure, the beach is nice, but the reefs are nicer. These days, the big draw is live-aboard diving trips, which explore the stunning Similan and Surin Archipelagos. The air in Khao Lak is thick with anticipation as visitors gear up to swim with the fishes.

Orientation & Information

Khao Lak sits on a long stretch of coastline scalloped by long, attractive beaches. Hwy 4 runs parallel to the beach about 1.5km inland, connecting several little clumps of businesses and accommodation. This section encompasses four beaches (from south to north): Khao Lak, Nang Thong, Bang Niang and Bang Sak. Most of the action takes place around Nang Thong. Khao Lak/Lam Ru National Park is just south of Khao Lak Beach.

For diving-related emergencies, call the **SSS Ambulance** (☎ 08 1081 9444) emergency, which rushes injured persons down to Phuket for treatment. The ambulance can also be used for car or motorcycle accidents. There is also one nurse in Bang Niang who caters to diving related injuries.

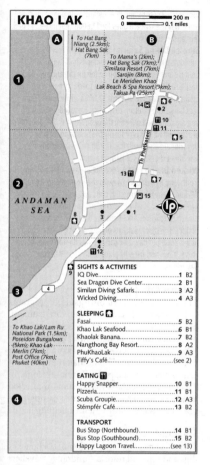

KHAO LAK

SIGHTS & ACTIVITIES	
IQ Dive.....................................1 B2	
Sea Dragon Dive Center...............2 B1	
Similan Diving Safaris.....................3 A2	
Wicked Diving................................4 A3	
SLEEPING	
Fasai...5 B2	
Khao Lak Seafood.........................6 B1	
Khaolak Banana............................7 B2	
Nangthong Bay Resort....................8 A3	
PhuKhaoLak..................................9 A3	
Tiffy's Café..............................(see 2)	
EATING	
Happy Snapper...........................10 B1	
Pizzeria......................................11 B1	
Scuba Groupie............................12 A3	
Stémpfér Café.............................13 B2	
TRANSPORT	
Bus Stop (Northbound)................14 B1	
Bus Stop (Southbound)................15 B2	
Happy Lagoon Travel...............(see 13)	

There are numerous travel agencies scattered about – many just a desk on the side of the road – and most of these do laundry and rent motorbikes for around 250B per day. The post office is in Tabla Mu near the Khao Lak Merlin resort.

Sights

While travelling along the Andaman Coast, you will undoubtedly still hear whispers of the 2004 Boxing Day Tsunami. Of Thailand's beach destinations damaged by the wave, the area around Khao Lak suffered the most. A **police boat**, slightly north of central Khao Lak, was brought by the tide to its present location (about 2km inland) when the giant wave ploughed through the harbour. The boat remains on the hill – a monument to those lost and a reminder of nature's raw power.

The area immediately south of Hat Khao Lak has been incorporated into the 125-sq-km **Khao Lak/Lam Ru National Park** (☎ 0 7642 0243; www.dnp.go.th; adult/child 200/100B; ⏰ 8am-4.30pm), a beautiful collection of sea cliffs, 1000m hills, beaches, estuaries, forested valleys and mangroves. Wildlife seen in the park includes hornbills, drongos, tapirs, gibbons, monkeys and Asiatic black bears. The visitor centre, just off Hwy 4 between the 56km and 57km markers, has little in the way of maps or printed information, but there's a very nice open-air restaurant perched on a shady slope overlooking the sea.

Guided treks along the coast or inland can be arranged through Poseidon Bungalows (p642), as can long-tail boat trips up the scenic **Khlong Thap Liang** estuary. The latter afford opportunities to view mangrove communities of crab-eating macaques. Between Khao Lak and Bang Sak is a network of sandy beach trails – some of which lead to deserted beaches – which are fun to explore on foot or by rented motorcycle. Most of the hotels in town rent out motorbikes for 250B per day.

Activities
DIVING

Khao Lak is the official gateway to the underwater paradise in the Similan and Surin islands. Diving and snorkelling day trips are quite popular, but the live-aboard excursions are out of this world. On these two-, three-, four- or five-day trips, you'll wake up with the dawn and slink below the ocean's surface up to four times per day to cavort with slippery reef sharks, sly rays and surly barracuda in what's commonly considered to be one of the top 10 diving realms in the world. Longer live-aboard trips visit **Richelieu Rock** – the *crème de la crème* of the region's sites. Discovered by Jacques Cousteau (he was led there by local fishermen), the horseshoe-shaped pinnacle rises dramatically from the ocean floor. Only a finger of stone manages to poke through the sea's churning surface so you really feel like you're diving in the middle of nowhere. **Ko Bon** and **Ko Ta Chai** are two other popular spots due to the traffic of giant manta rays that gracefully swoop through and use the sites as cleaning stations. Divers aren't guaranteed to see one (we didn't) but in the height of high season it's a safe bet that you'll see one soar

ANDAMAN COAST

by like a possessed pancake. Day trippers can usually get out to Ko Bon, but most trips make a beeline for the Similan Islands (p645).

Choosing a live-aboard may seem tricky at first, especially since there are so many options. There are two important things to consider: your price range and the desired length of your trip. Live-aboards range from backpacker-friendly three-day trips priced at 12,000B, to lavish luxury yachts that charge upwards of 25,000B for three days at sea. Part of the live-aboard magic involves bonding with the other divers on the boat, so beware of schools that regularly return to shore to swap passengers before your expedition is over. Before signing your cheque, ask your dive operator of choice if there are any additional fees (national park permits, equipment rental etc); some schools have lots of fine print to make their prices seem competitive. Check out www.backpackersthailand.com for information about several live-aboard options. If your schedule is flexible, try to book a trip in the later part of the season – your dive tour guide/divemaster will have a better knowledge of the reefs if this is their first season in the Similans. The turnover rate is quite high since the area's diving is seasonal (starting in late October and ending in May; dates vary depending on the year and the ever-changing park restrictions).

Newbie divers can tackle a smattering of PADI courses as well, although Ko Tao (p610), on the gulf coast, is cheaper and the dive sites are closer to shore. A PADI Open Water course here will set you back around 16,000B – Khao Lak is better suited for 'fun dives' or divemaster training programs.

Snorkellers can hop on selected dive excursions or live-aboards for a discount of around 40%; otherwise, tour agencies all around town offer even cheaper snorkelling trips starting at around 2500B, but these are generally over-crowded and of poor quality.

Khao Lak has two dozen diving operations vying for your baht. The following dive schools are highly recommended:

IQ Dive (☎ 0 7648 5614; www.iq-dive.com; Th Phetkasem) A quality operation that focuses on diving and snorkelling day trips. Diving day trips start at 5100B (all-inclusive). The website has good information about the gamut of live-aboards operating in the region.

Sea Dragon Diver Center (☎ 0 7648 5420; www.seadragondivecenter.com; Th Phetkasem) One of the older operations in Khao Lak, Sea Dragon has maintained high standards throughout the years and continues to offer top-notch day trips and live-aboards. The penny-pincher three-day live-aboard goes for 11,800B (not including park fees and equipment).

Similan Diving Safaris (☎ 0 7648 5470; www.similan-diving-safaris.com) Joe, the owner, is half-Jamaican, half-Chinese and half-British (you do the math), and approaches life like a Rastafarian Lao Tzu. The speciality here is the high-quality four-day live-aboard (17,800B all-inclusive) that regularly attracts return customers. Knowledgeable staff and amazing food sweeten the deal. As far as live-aboards are concerned, this is probably the best bang for your baht. Day trips are also available. The office is located down the side street that leads to Happy Lagoon.

Wicked Diving (☎ 0 7648 5868; www.wickeddiving.com; Hwy 4) Relatively new to the Khao diving scene, Wicked is already garnering oohs and aahs for its seriously awesome staff, well-run excursions and eco-friendly approach to tourism. Ask about the whale shark exploration project. The three-day live-aboard (15,900B; plus equipment, 300B per day, and park fees) is the top seller here. This is a fun and friendly place to do your PADI coursework. Day trips are also available.

Volunteering

There are a couple of disorganised programs in the area that toss around the word tsunami, but if you're interested in some make-a-difference volunteering, contact **Grassroots HRED** (☎ 0 7642 0351; www.ghre.org) in Takua Pa, 25km north of Khao Lak. This human rights organisation strives to help the Burmese people in Thailand, particularly in the tsunami-affected areas. Their successful summer camps programs are a great way to lend a helping hand.

Sleeping

Khao Lak has a great selection of backpacker digs and top-end resorts – midrange travellers will be forced to choose sides.

BUDGET

For the cheapest sleeps in town, head to Sea Dragon Diver Center (left) and ask about the dorm beds at Tiffy's Café, which go for 180B per night.

Fasai (☎ 0 7648 5867; r 500-700B; 🕹) The best budget choice in Khao Lak, Fasai has immaculate motel-style rooms and smiling staff members who coyly giggle like geishas.

Khaolak Banana (☎ 0 7648 5889; www.khaolakbanana.com; r 500-1200B) These adorable little bungalows have swirls painted on the cement floors and sun-filled indoor-outdoor bathrooms. A cute pool with deckchairs sweetens the deal. Ask the other guests how much they are paying before you check in – prices fluctuations are a tad dubious.

Khao Lak Seafood (☎ 0 7642 0318; r 600B) Affiliated with the restaurant of the same name, these fresh-faced bungalows are a solid choice for small wallets.

Poseidon Bungalows (☎ 0 7644 3258; www.similantour.com; bungalows from 900B) On the other side of the headland near Khao Lak/Lam Ru National Park, about 5km south of Hat Khao Lak, this quiet spot features a gaggle of huts scattered throughout coastal forest.

Also recommended:

PhuKhaoLak (☎ 0 7648 5141; bungalows 600-1800B; ❑ ▣ ▨) Service oriented operation with comfy huts and great food. A five-minute walk south of central Khao Lak.

MIDRANGE & TOP END

[our pick] **Nangthong Bay Resort** (☎ 0 7648 5088; bungalows 2000-3000B; ❑ ▣ ▨) Nangthong is an excellent place to stay and it's no secret – this place fills up fast. Rooms are designed with a sparse black-and-white decor that feel chic rather than spartan. Terracotta sculptures shoot water into the cerulean swimming pool while contented vacationers watch the tide roll in. All room types are excellent value.

Similana Resort (☎ 0 7648 7166; www.similanaresort.com; r from 3000B; ❑ ▣ ▨) Each bungalow is a small work of art, with handcrafted furnishings, dark-wood floors, quilted bedcovers, bay windows and private decks with panoramic views. Try the traveller-recommended tree houses nestled in the beach-facing forest.

Khao Lak Merlin (☎ 0 7642 8300; www.merlinphuket.com; Hwy 4; r from 6800B; ❑ ▣ ▨) This giant resort, 7km south of town, features a maze of swimming pools and colonial-style rooms stretched along six hectares of lush tropical gardens.

[our pick] **Le Meridien Khao Lak Beach & Spa Resort** (☎ 0 7642 7500; www.khaolak.lemeridien.com; Hwy 4; r/bungalows from 7000B; ❑ ▣ ▨) Located along the secluded sands of Bang Sak, Khao Lak's proliferation of the Le Meridien chain was completely demolished during the tsunami, but today it's back and better than ever. Epic in size, this rambling resort has hundreds of rooms orbiting several different swimming pools (including a family-friendly pool), and an endless beachfront flanked by tropical gardens and private villas.

[our pick] **Sarojin** (☎ 0 7642 7900; www.sarojin.com; r from 12,500B; ▨) The style of this serene retreat mixes Japanese austerity with sumptuous Thai decor, creating a resort that is both elegant and intimate. We especially love the pool, with

its stylish lounging huts that hover like islands above the crystal blue water. The Sarojin is located in Bang Sak.

Eating & Drinking

This is no culinary capital, but there are a few local haunts where tourists congregate to rehash the day's diving yarns. Early-morning divers will be hard-pressed to find a place to grab a bite before 8.30am.

Takua Pa market (5am-6pm) This colourful market 25km north of town is a great place for snacking. A lot of rainforest tours departing from Khao Lak make a stop here before delving into the jungle.

Stémpfer Café (Th Phetkasem; dishes 90-150B; ☼ 9am-10pm) Great coffee, tasty sandwiches, and a speedy wireless internet connection – what more could an email junky as for?

Happy Snapper (☎ 0 7642 3540; Th Phetkasem; dishes 90-290B; ☼ breakfast, lunch & dinner) Wooden statues lie frozen as patrons bop their heads to the nightly live-music acts. There's a small Thai canteen attached to the bar that serves up tasty usuals.

Pizzeria (☎ 0 7648 5271; dishes 200-300B; ☼ lunch & dinner) By Giorgio, these Italian dishes are phenomenal! Stuff your face with authentic eats like homemade gnocchi or thin-crust pizzas, and we guarantee you'll be back for seconds.

Also recommended:

Mama's (mains 40-120B; breakfast, lunch & dinner) Mama whips up honest-to-goodness home-cooked meals. Located next to the 7-Eleven in Bang Niang.

Scuba Groupie (☼ 4.30pm-1am) Friendly bartender dispenses post-dive drinks. Located on the ground floor of the 'big yellow building' (you can't miss it).

Getting There & Away

Any bus running along Hwy 4 between Takua Pa (50B, 45 minutes) and Phuket (80B, two hours) will stop at Hat Khao Lak if you ask the driver. Make sure not to get off at Kokloi (about 40km south of Khao Lak); travellers have been known to disembark here by accident. VIP Buses in either direction breeze through town in the early morning (6am to 8am), while regular buses pass by every hour. VIP sleeper buses direct to Bangkok leave at 5pm, 7pm, 8pm and 9pm everyday and cost 750B to 1100B. Buses will also stop near the Merlin Resort and the Khao Lak/Lam Ru National Park headquarters. All transportation queries can be answered with a smile at Happy Lagoon Travel on Hwy 4 in the centre of town (two doors down from Stémpfer Café).

SURIN ISLANDS MARINE NATIONAL PARK

อุทยานแห่งชาติหมู่เกาะสุรินทร์

The five gorgeous islands that make up this **national park** (www.dnp.go.th; admission 400B; ☉ mid-Nov–mid-May) sit about 60km offshore, a measly 5km from the Thai–Burma marine border. Healthy rainforest, pockets of white-sand beach in sheltered bays and rocky headlands that jut into the ocean characterise these granite-outcrop islands. The clearest of water makes for great marine life, with underwater visibility often up to 35m. The islands' sheltered waters also attract *chow lair* – sea gypsies – who live in a village onshore during the monsoon season from May to November. Around here they are known as Moken, from the local word *oken* meaning 'salt water'.

Ko Surin Nuea (north) and Ko Surin Tai (south) are the two largest islands. Park headquarters and all visitor facilities are at Ao Chong Khad on Ko Surin Nuea, near the jetty. Khuraburi is the jumping-off point for the park. The pier is about 9km north of town, as is the mainland **national park office** (☎ 0 7649 1378; ☉ 8am-5pm) with good information, maps and helpful staff.

Sights & Activities

MOKEN VILLAGE

On Ko Surin Tai, the Moken village at **Ao Bon** welcomes visitors; take a long-tail boat from headquarters (100B). Post-tsunami, Moken have settled in this one sheltered bay where a major ancestral worship ceremony (Loi Reua) takes place in April. Painted *law bong* – protective totem poles – stand at the park entrance.

DIVING & SNORKELLING

Dive sites in the park include **Ko Surin Tai** and **HQ Channel** between the two main islands. In the vicinity is **Richelieu Rock** (a seamount 14km southeast), where whale sharks are often spotted during March and April. Sixty kilometres northwest of the Surins are the famed **Burma Banks**, a system of submerged seamounts in the Mergui Archipelago. Separately run diving live-aboard trips visit these pristine waters. The three major banks, **Silvertip**, **Roe** and **Rainbow**, provide five-star diving experiences, with coral gardens laid over flat plateaus and large oceanic and smaller reef marine species.

The best way to explore these all-star dive sites is by joining a multiday live-aboard departing from Khao Lak (p641).

Snorkelling is excellent due to relatively shallow reef depths of 5m to 6m, and most coral survived the tsunami intact. Two-hour snorkelling trips by boat (per person 80B; gear per day 150B) leave the island headquarters daily at 9am and 2pm.

WILDLIFE & HIKING

Around the park headquarters you can explore the forest fringes, looking out for crab-eating macaques (cheeky monkeys!) and some of the 57 resident bird species, which include the fabulous Nicobar pigeon, endemic to the islands of the Andaman Sea. Along the coast you're likely to see the chestnut Brahminy kite soaring, and reef herons on the rocks. Twelve species of bat live here, most noticeably the tree-dwelling fruit bats, also known as flying foxes.

A rough-and-ready **walking trail** – not for the unsteady – winds 2km along the coast and through forest to the beach at **Ao Mai Ngam**, where there's good snorkelling. At low tide it's easy to walk between the bays near headquarters.

Sleeping & Eating

Sleeping on the Surins is significantly more comfortable than shacking up on the Similans. Park accommodation is simple and fine, but because of the island's short, narrow beaches it's *very* close together and can feel seriously crowded when full (around 300 people).

For park accommodation, book online at www.dnp.go.th or with the mainland **national park office** (☎ 0 7649 1378) in Khuraburi. **Bungalows** (with fan, bathroom & balcony 2000B) and **tents** (1-/2-person 300/450B) are available at Ao Chong Khad, and tents are also available at Ao Mai Ngam. You can pitch your own **tent** (80B). There's generator power until about 10pm. A park **restaurant** (dishes from 60B) serves authentic Thai food.

If you need to stay overnight in Khuraburi, there's basic accommodation at **Tararin Resort** (☎ 0 7649 1789; r from 300-500B; ⊠) or try **Boon Piya Resort** (☎ 08 1752 5457; bungalows 600B; ⊠), beside Tom & Am Tour. A more luxurious option, **Kuraburi Greenview Resort** (☎ 0 7640 1400; www.kuraburigreenview.co.th; d from 1900B; ⊠ 💻 🏊), 15km south of town, is set among forest and river, with comfortable slate-and-cobblestone bungalows.

Getting There & Away

A 'big boat' (return 1200B, 2½ hours one way) leaves the Khuraburi pier at 9am daily, returning at 1pm (though it didn't go when we passed through). Tour operators use speedboats (return 1700B, one hour one way) and will transfer independent travellers on their daily runs.

Several tour operators, all located near the pier, run day/overnight tours (around 2800/3800B) to the park; agencies in Khao Lak (p642) and Phuket (p659) can make bookings for these and other trips. Popular live-aboard diving trips departing from Khao Lak stop around several different islands in the archipelago. In Khuraburi town, try the affable **Tom & Am Tour** (☎ 08 6272 0588; www.surinislandtour.com) for on-spec bookings. Tour operators include transfers from Khao Lak in their prices.

Three to six daily buses run between Phuket and Khuraburi (160B, 3½ hours) and between Khuraburi and Ranong (60B, 1½ hours).

SIMILAN ISLANDS MARINE NATIONAL PARK

อุทยานแห่งชาติหมู่เกาะสิมิลัน

The fluorescent playground of Khao Lak's booming live-aboard industry, beautiful **Similan Islands Marine National Park** (www.dnp.go.th; admission 400B; ☺ Nov-May) lies 70km offshore, offering some of the finest diving in Thailand, if not the world. Its smooth granite islands are as impressive above water as below, topped with rainforest, edged with white-sand beaches and fringed with coral reef.

Two of the nine islands, Ko Miang (Island 4) and Ko Similan (Island 8), have ranger stations and accommodation; park headquarters and most visitor activity centres on Ko Miang. 'Similan' comes from the Malay word *sembilan*, meaning nine, and while each island has a proper name; they are usually referred to by their number.

The jumping-off point for the park is the pier at Thap Lamu (or Tabla Mu), about 10km south of Khao Lak. The mainland **national park office** (☎ 0 7659 5045; ☺ 8am-4pm) is about 500m before the pier, but there's no information in English available – it's best to head to Khao Lak (p642) to get all the info you need about exploring these nine magical islets and the reefs that surround them.

Sights & Activities

DIVING & SNORKELLING

The Similans offer exceptional diving for all levels of experience, at depths from 2m to 30m. There are seamounts (at **Fantasy Rocks**), rock reefs (at **Ko Payu**) and dive-throughs (at **Hin Pousar**, known as 'Elephant Head'), with marine life ranging from tiny plume worms and soft corals to schooling fish and whale sharks. Popular sites on live-aboard trips also include East of Eden, West of Eden, Hide Away and Breakfast Bend. The uber-popular **Ko Bon** and **Ko Ta Chai**, north of the nine Similans, are cleaning stations for large mantas. There are dive sites at each of the six islands north of Ko Miang; the southern part of the park is off limits to divers. No facilities for divers exist in the national park itself, so you'll need to take a dive tour. Agencies in Khao Lak (p642) and Phuket (p659) book dive trips (three-day live-aboards from around 15,000B).

Snorkelling is good at several points around **Ko Miang**, especially in the main channel; you can hire snorkel gear from the park (per day 100B). Day-tour operators usually visit three or four different snorkelling sites. Loads of diving operators and travel agencies in Khao Lak can hook up with snorkelling-only trips (day trips around 2500B to 3000B).

WILDLIFE & WALKS

The forest around the park headquarters on Ko Miang has a couple of walking trails and some great wildlife. The fabulous Nicobar pigeon, with its wild mane of grey-green feathers, is common here. Endemic to the islands of the Andaman Sea, it's one of some 39 bird species in the park. Hairy-legged land crabs and fruit bats are relatively easily seen in the forest, as are flying squirrels.

Small Beach Track, with information panels, leads 400m to a tiny, pretty snorkelling bay. Detouring from it, the **Viewpoint Trail** – 500m or so of steep scrambling – has panoramic vistas from the top. A 500m walk to **Sunset Point** takes you through forest to a smooth granite platform facing – obviously – west.

On Ko Similan there's a 2.5km forest hike to a **viewpoint**, and a shorter, steep scramble off the main beach to the top of **Sail Rock**.

Sleeping & Eating

Accommodation in the park is available for all budgets, although none of it is spectacular. Book online at www.dnp.go.th or with

ANDAMAN COAST

the mainland **national park office** (☎ 0 7659 5045) south of Khao Lak.

On Ko Miang there are sea-view **bungalows** (r 2000B; ❄) with balconies, two dark five-room wood-and-bamboo **longhouses** (r 1000B) with fans, and crowded on-site **tents** (2-person 570B). There's electricity from 6pm to 6am.

On-site tents are also available on Ko Similan.

A **restaurant** (dishes 100B) near park headquarters serves simple Thai food.

Getting There & Away

There's no public transport to the park, and if you book accommodation through the national park you'll have to find your own way there. Agencies in Khao Lak (p642) and Phuket (p659) book day/overnight tours (from around 2500/3500B) and dive trips (three-day live-aboards from around 15,000B) – this is about how much you would pay if you tried to get to the islands on your own steam. You can try to link up with a dive trip and pay for the excursion sans diving equipment, but operators will only cooperate if their boats are relatively empty.

PHANG-NGA TOWN & AO PHANG-NGA

พังงา/อ่าวพังงา

pop 9700

In Phang-Nga, it's extremely easy to tell the difference between a tourist and a local – tourists are looking up. Jaw-dropping limestone rock towers stretch towards the afternoon clouds, leaving visitors almost as awestruck as when they see a local going about their business completely unfazed by the region's ethereal gifts. It's hard not to stop dead in one's tracks and gaze at these crags for hours – the blend of soda-white sand and jagged stone is intoxicating.

A cameo in *The Man with the Golden Gun* has lured loads of James Bond fanatics and spy wannabes out to this serene realm, which has prompted the government to step in and protect the land under a national park mandate. The area is lacking in quality accommodation, so it may be best to visit on a day trip – there are heaps of tours out of Phuket (p660) and Khao Lak; ask at any of the local travel agencies. Most trips are advertised on chalkboards and posters as 'trips to James Bond Island'. Tours start at around 550B depending on season and demand.

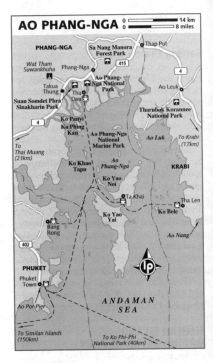

Information

Phang-Nga town doesn't have a tourist office, but the **Tourism Authority of Thailand** (TAT; ☎ 0 7621 2213; www.tat.or.th; 73-65 Th Phuket; ☺ 8.30am-4.30pm) office in Phuket Town provides maps and good information on the region. The post office is about 2km south of the centre. There are numerous places around town to log on to update your blog.

Immigration office (☎ 0 7641 2011; ☺ 8.30am-4.30pm Mon-Fri) A few kilometres south of town; you'll probably never find it on your own, so take a motorcycle taxi.

Siam Commercial Bank (Hwy 4; ☺ 9am-4pm Mon-Fri) On the main road through town; has an ATM and change facilities.

Sights & Activities

The old 'city of contrasts' cliché really does apply to the town of Phang-Nga: it is a scruffy, luckless town in a sublime location. The main street is a downtrodden, rather sad-looking strip, but it backs up against breathtaking limestone cliffs.

About 8.5km south of the town centre is **Tha Dan**. From here, you can charter boats to see half-submerged caves, oddly shaped islands and Ko Panyi, a Muslim village on stilts. There are tours to **Ko Phing Kan** ('James Bond Island'; the island rock depicted in Roger Moore's Bond escapade, *The Man with the Golden Gun*). These tours also visit Ao Phang-Nga National Park (per person for a two- to three-hour tour 500B to 600B). **Takua Thung**, another pier area about 10km further west of Tha Dan, also has private boats for hire, for similar prices; ask at the restaurants. The park office inside Ao Phang-Nga Marine National Park offers boat tours as well.

Unless you enjoy haggling with boatmen, it's much easier (and not too expensive) to go with an organised tour through an agency in town. **Sayan Tours** (☎ 0 7643 0348) has been doing tours of Ao Phang-Nga for many years now, and continues to receive good reviews from travellers. Half-day/day tours cost from 500/800B per person and include Tham Lawt (a large water cave), Ko Phing Kan and Ko Panyi, among other destinations. Meals and very rustic accommodation on Ko Panyi are part of the longer packages. The overnight trip (2500B) is recommended as tourists will see a great deal more, although tourists have given us negative feedback about their homestay experience in the Muslim village. Sayan Tours also offers canoe trips and tours to other nearby destinations, including Sa Nang Manora Forest Park and the various caves near town.

Sleeping

Phang-Nga doesn't have much in the way of quality sleeping – most folks choose to swing by on a day trip.

Phang-Nga Inn (☎ 0 7641 1963; 2/2 Soi Lohakit; r 400-1600B; ☒) This converted residential villa comes up trumps in the town's hotel stakes. Expect pleasant surrounds, comfy beds and homey welcomes. It's well furnished and there's a little eatery out front. Rooms range from basic fan options to swish air-con suites.

Old Lukmuang Hotel (☎ 0 7641 2125; fax 0 7641 1512; 1/2 Moo 1, Th Phetkasem; r 450B) This choice is rather dingy, but Bond fanatics will be interested to know that it housed some of the crew from *The Man with the Golden Gun* when they based themselves here during filming.

Eating

Several food stalls on the main street of Phang-Nga sell delicious *kà nŏm jeen* (thin wheat noodles) with chicken curry, *nám yah* (spicy ground-fish curry) or *nám prík* (spicy sauce). There's also a small night market on Tuesday, Wednesday and Thursday evenings just south of Soi Lohakit.

Cha-Leang (☎ 0 7641 3831; Th Phetkasem; dishes 40-90B; ☒ lunch & dinner) The best – and often busiest – eatery in town cooks up a smorgasbord of well-priced seafood dishes – try the clams with basil leaf and chilli or 'edible inflorescence of banana plant salad'. There's a pleasant verandah out back.

Bismilla (☎ 08 1125 6440; Th Phetkasem; dishes 60-120B; ☒ lunch & dinner) With dishes like 'yum fish's spawn' on the menu, how can you resist a night at this basic, Thai-Muslim outfit? The food is good, the prices are excellent and the crowds are boisterous.

Getting There & Around

If you're arriving in the Ao Phang-Nga area from Krabi on Hwy 4, you can go two ways. At 2km before Thap Put, you can either continue straight on Hwy 4 (also known as Old Road) or go left onto Hwy 415. Turning onto Hwy 415 (New Road) will keep you on the shorter, straighter path, while staying on Hwy 4 will take you onto a narrow, very curvy and pretty stretch of highway that is 5km longer than the direct route. It's a choice between boring but straight or pretty but longer.

Phang-Nga's bus terminal is located just off the main street on Soi Bamrung Rat. There are usually seven daily buses between Bangkok and Phang-Nga (380B to 740B, 12 hours).

AROUND PHANG-NGA
Ao Phang-Nga Marine National Park

อุทยานแห่งชาติอ่าวพังงา

Established in 1981 and covering an area of 400 sq km, **Ao Phang-Nga Marine National Park** (☎ 0 7641 2188; 80 Moo 1, Ban Tha Dan; admission 200B) is noted for its classic karst scenery, created by mainland fault movements that pushed massive limestone blocks into geometric patterns. As these blocks extended southward into Ao Phang-Nga, they formed more than 40 islands with huge vertical cliffs. The bay itself is composed of large and small tidal channels that originally connected with the mainland fluvial system. The main tidal channels – Khlong Ko Phanyi, Khlong Phang-Nga, Khlong Bang Toi and Khlong Bo Saen – run through vast mangroves in a north–south direction and today are used by fisherfolk and island inhabitants as aquatic highways. These mangroves are the largest remaining primary mangrove forest in Thailand. The Andaman Sea covers more than 80% of the area within the park boundaries.

The biggest tourist spot in the park is so-called James Bond Island, known to Thais as **Ko Phing Kan** (Leaning on Itself Island). Once used as a location setting for *The Man with the Golden Gun*, the island is now full of vendors hawking coral and shells, along with butterflies, scorpions and spiders encased in plastic.

The Thai name for the island refers to a flat limestone cliff that appears to have tumbled sideways to lean on a similar rock face, which is in the centre of the island. Off one side of the island, in a shallow bay, stands a tall, slender limestone formation that looks like a big rock spike that has fallen from the sky. There are a couple of caves you can walk through and some small sand beaches, often littered with rubbish from the tourist boats. Improve your trash karma and pick up some junk while passing through.

About the only positive development in recent years has been the addition of a concrete pier so that tourist boats don't have to moor directly on the island's beaches, but this still happens when the water level is high and the pier is crowded with other boats.

Two types of forest predominate in the park: limestone scrub forest and true evergreen forest. The marine limestone environment favours a long list of reptiles, including the Bengal monitor, flying lizard, banded sea snake, dogface water snake, shore pit viper and Malayan pit viper. Keep an eye out for the two-banded (or water) monitor (*Varanus salvator*), which looks like a crocodile when seen swimming in the mangrove swamp and can measure up to 2.2m in length (only slightly smaller than the komodo dragon, the largest lizard in the Varanidae family). Like its komodo cousin, the water monitor (called *hêea* by the Thais, who generally fear or hate the lizard) is a carnivore that prefers to feed on carrion but occasionally preys on live animals.

Amphibians in the Ao Phang-Nga area include the marsh frog, common bush frog and crab-eating frog. Avian residents of note are the helmeted hornbill (the largest of Thailand's 12 hornbill species, with a body length of up to 127cm), the edible-nest swiftlet (*Aerodramus fuciphagus*), osprey, white-bellied sea eagle and Pacific reef egret.

Over 200 species of mammal reside in the mangrove forests and on some of the larger islands, including the white-handed gibbon, serow, dusky langur and crab-eating macaque.

For information on Ko Yao, which is part of Ao Phang-Nga Marine National Park, see p680.

SLEEPING & EATING

National Park Bungalows (☎ 0 2562 0760; reserve@dnp .go.th; bungalows 700–900B; 🖫) The cheaper bungalows sleep four and are fan-cooled; the pricier air-con bungalows sleep two. At the time of research camping was permitted in certain areas within park boundaries but you should ask permission at the bungalow office first as several other parks in the area have recently put a ban on camping.

There's a small, clean restaurant in front of the bungalow office with views over the mangroves.

GETTING THERE & AROUND

From the centre of Phang-Nga, drive south on Hwy 4 about 6km, then turn left onto Rte 4144 and go 2.6km to the park headquarters; the visitors centre sits 400m beyond the 'gate'. See p660 for tour operators on Phuket that run day trips to the park.

Sa Nang Manora Forest Park

สวนป่าสระนางมโนราห์

The fairyland setting at this beautiful and little-visited **park** (admission free) is nothing short of fantastic. Moss-encrusted roots and rocks, dense rainforest and rattan vines provide a delicious backdrop for swimming in pools beneath multilevel waterfalls. The park's name comes from a local folk belief that the mythical Princess Manora bathes in the pools when no one else is around.

Primitive trails meander along (and at times through) the falls, climbing level after level, and seem to go on forever – you could easily get a full day's hiking in without walking along the same path twice. Bring plenty of drinking water – although the shade and the falls moderate the temperature, the humidity in the park is quite high. Facilities include some picnic tables, plus a small restaurant.

To get here, catch a motorcycle taxi from Phang-Nga (50B). If you have your own wheels, head north out of town on Hwy 4, go 3.2km past the Shell petrol station, then turn left and go down a curvy road another 4km.

PHUKET PROVINCE

The reigning granddaddy of Thailand beach vacations, Phuket Province features one giant island – the Andaman's drop zone of quintessential tropical fun.

PHUKET

ภูเก็ต

pop 83,800

The island of Phuket has long been misunderstood. First of all, the 'h' is silent. Ahem. And second, Phuket doesn't feel like an island at all. It's so huge (it's the biggest in the country) that you never really get the sense that you're surrounded by water, which is probably the reason why the 'Ko' (meaning 'island') was dropped from its name. Dubbed the 'pearl of the Andaman' by savvy marketing execs, this is Thailand's original flavour of tailor-made fun in the sun.

Phuket's beating heart can be found in Patong. Located halfway down the western coast, Thailand's 'sin city' is the ultimate gong show where podgy beach-aholics sizzle like rotisserie chickens and gogo girls play ping-pong…without paddles…

These days, however, Phuket's affinity to luxury far outshines any of the island's other stereotypes; jet-setters come through in droves, getting pummelled during swanky spa sessions and swigging sundowners at one of the many fashion-forward nightspots. But you don't have to be an heiress or an Oscar-winner to tap into Phuket's trendy to-do list. There's deep-sea diving, high-end dining, soda-white beaches that beckon your book and blanket – whatever your heart desires. Visitors never say *ph*uket to Phuket.

History

Phuket has always had a reputation for welcoming foreigners. After all, Indian merchants founded Phuket Town in the 1st century BC. Ptolemy, a Greek geographer who visited in the 3rd century AD, tabbed it 'Jang Si Lang', which later became 'Jung Ceylon', the name you'll find on ancient maps of Thailand (it's also the name of the unavoidably massive shopping complex in Patong, p674).

Among Phuket's original locals were now-extinct primitive tribes similar to Malaysia's surviving Semang pygmies. They lived in triple-canopy virgin rainforest and survived by hunting and eating jungle fruits and roots.

Meanwhile, the nomadic *chow lair* populated the coastal areas of Phuket, living off the sea's spoils.

In the 16th century, copious lodes of tin inspired Portuguese, French and British traders to set up makeshift colonies. A century later the British contemplated using Phuket as a base in order to control the vital Strait of Malacca. They sent Captain Francis Light to scout it out, where he was swept up in Phuket's most important historical event.

The year was 1785, and Burma and Thailand were locked in a series of wars for regional supremacy. Thai soldiers had repelled Burmese forces from Phuket a year earlier, but now the Burmese were returning in an enormous fleet. Captain Light spotted them and alerted the governor's office. But the governor had recently passed away, so his wife, Kunying Jan, took charge. She and her sister, Mook, assembled the forces, and, according to legend, disguised the local women as male soldiers, which made Phuket's military manpower seem invincible to the Burmese scouts. They attacked anyway, but quickly lost heart and left after a short siege. King Rama I awarded Kunying Jan with the royal title of 'Thao Thep Kasattri', and she and her sister are honoured with the **Heroines Monument** at the Thalang roundabout.

In the early 19th century the tin-mining boom took Phuket by storm and attracted thousands of Chinese labourers. The Chinese brought their culinary and spiritual traditions with them, and when they intermarried among the Thai, a new culture was born. The first and future generations of the ethnic Thai-Chinese are also known as the Baba people. Although their roots were in the mines, many Baba descendents became merchants. They built up Phuket Town (p652), erecting enormous homes with Portuguese and Chinese accents. Tin, along with rubber, remained the dominant industry in Phuket until the 1970s, when the beachcombers began arriving en masse after Club Med invested in Hat Kata and Thai Airways began offering daily flights from Bangkok.

Tourism remained strong until the tsunami hit on 26 December 2004. On Phuket, 250 people died as Patong, Kamala, Kata, Karon, Nai Thon and Nai Yang all suffered major damage. As a result, Phuket's economy briefly suffered, but in 2006 resort development skyrocketed once more.

ANDAMAN COAST

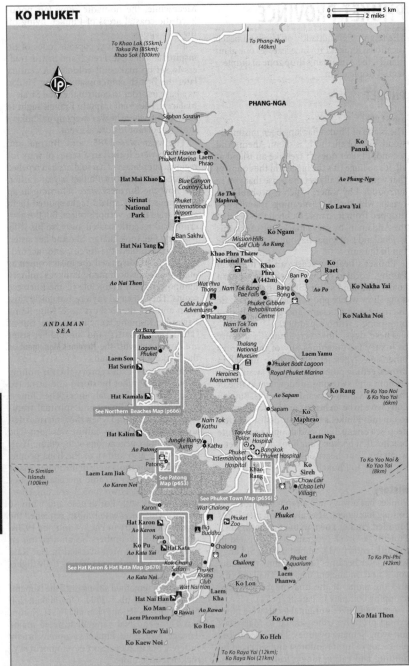

KO PHUKET

ANDAMAN COAST

0 — 5 km
0 — 2 miles

To Khao Lak (55km);
Takua Pa (85km);
Khao Sok (100km)

To Phang-Nga
(40km)

Saphan Sarasin

PHANG-NGA

Ko Panuk

Yacht Haven
Phuket Marina
Laem
Phrao

Ao Phang-Nga

Hat Mai Khao

Blue Canyon
Country Club

**Sirinat
National
Park**

*Ao Tha
Maphran*

Phuket
International
Airport

Ko Lawa Yai

Ban Sakhu

Ao Nai Thon

Hat Nai Yang

Mission Hills
Golf Club

Ko Ngam

Ao Kung

**Khao Phra Thaew
National Park**

**Khao
Phra**
▲(442m)

Ban Po

*Ko
Raet*

Ko Nakha Yai

Wat Phra
Thong

Nam Tok Bang
Pae Falls

Bang
Bong

Ao Po

Cable Jungle
Adventures

Phuket Gibbon
Rehabilitation
Centre

Ko Nakha Noi

Thalang

**ANDAMAN
SEA**

*Ao Bang
Thao*

Nam Tok Ton
Sai Falls

Thalang
National
Museum

Laguna
Phuket

Laem Son
Hat Surin

Heroines
Monument

Laem Yamu

Phuket Boat Lagoon
Royal Phuket Marina

Hat Kamala

See Northern Beaches Map (p666)

Ao Sapam

Ko Rang

To Ko Yao Noi
& Ko Yao Yai
(6km)

Sapam

*Ko
Maphrao*

Hat Kalim

Nam Tok
Kathu

Laem Nga

To Similan
Islands
(100km)

Jungle Bungy
Jump

Kathu

Tourist
Police

Wachira
Hospital

To Ko Yao Noi &
Ko Yao Yai
(8km)

Ao Patong

Phuket
International
Hospital

Bangkok
Phuket Hospital

Patong

Laem Lam Jiak

**See Patong
Map (p653)**

Khao
Rang

*Ko
Sireh*

Ao Karon Noi

Chow Lair
(Chao Leh)
Village

Karon

See Phuket Town Map (p656)

Wat Chalong

*Ao
Phuket*

Hat Karon

Ao Karon

Phuket
Zoo

Kata

Big
Buddha

Ko Pu

Hat Kata

Ao Kata Yai

Chalong

*Ao
Chalong*

Phuket
Aquarium

To Ko Phi-Phi
(42km)

See Hat Karon & Hat Kata Map (p670)

Ao Kata Noi

Kok Chang
Safari

Phuket
Riding
Club

Phuket
Aquarium

Laem
Phanwa

Wat Nai Han

Laem
Kha

Hat Nai Han

Ko Man

Ko Lon

Ao Rawai

Laem Phromthep

Rawai

Ko Aew

Ko Mai Thon

Ko Kaew Yai

Ko Bon

Ko Heh

Ko Kaew Noi

To Ko Raya Yai (12km);
Ko Raya Noi (21km)

Orientation

Phuket's stunning west coast, scalloped by its trademark sandy bays, faces the crystal Andaman Sea. The island's quieter east coast features gnarled mangroves rather than silky sand.

Patong, about halfway down the west coast, is the eye of the tourist storm, while Phuket Town, in the southeast part of the Phuket, is the provincial capital.

Phuket International Airport is in the northern part of the island, while most long-distance buses arrive and depart in Phuket Town. For information on getting around the island, see p678.

We have organised Phuket's sleeping section to follow the island's natural geography. Listings start with the northern beaches (from south of Hat Nai Thon down to Hat Kamala), moving south to Patong, then the southern beaches (Karon, Kata, Nai Han and Rawai), and finally the inland Phuket Town. The island's eating section is organised in a similar manner.

Information

BOOKSHOPS

Bookazine Karon (Map p670; ☎ 0 7633 3273; 23/7 Th Karon, Karon; ⏲ 10am-11pm) The Bookazine chain's Karon location where you can to buy English-language maps, guidebooks, magazines and newspapers.

Bookazine Patong (Map p653; ☎ 0 7634 5833; 18 Th Bangla, Patong; ⏲ 9.30am-11.30pm) If you need more beach reading, you'll find a wealth of English-language titles – from bestsellers to regional fiction and nonfiction – at this local chain.

Books (Map p656; ☎ 0 7621 1115; www.thebooks phuket.com; 53-55 Th Phuket, Phuket Town; ⏲ 8.30am-9.30pm) Offers English-language magazines, guidebooks and novels.

Kata Bookshop (Map p670; ☎ 0 7633 0109; 82 Th Kata, Kata; ⏲ 10am-9pm) Great selection of new and used books, and helpful service.

EMERGENCY

Police (Map p656; ☎ 191, 0 7622 3555; cnr Th Phang-Nga & Th Phuket, Phuket Town)

Tourist police (Map p653; ☎ 0 7634 0244; Th Thawi-wong, Patong)

INTERNET ACCESS

Wi-fi access is widely available on Phuket. Most hotels and guesthouses offer free wi-fi connection for their guests, and several cafes (including the zillion Starbucks) and bars do the same. If you're travelling without a computer, it won't be hard to locate an internet cafe. They can be found everywhere and net access costs anywhere from 40B to 150B an hour.

Phuket CAT office (Map p656; Th Phang-Nga, Phuket Town; ⏲ 8am-midnight)

TA Internet (Map p653; ☎ 0 7634 9014; Th Bangla, Patong; per min 2B; ⏲ 9am-3pm)

INTERNET RESOURCES

Check out the following useful websites:

1 Stop Phuket (www.1stopphuket.com) A mini travel guide to Phuket on the web.

Jamie's Phuket (www.jamie-monk.blogspot.com) A great blog featuring loads of info about hotels and activities around the island.

Phuket.com (www.phuket.com) Offers a sophisticated compendium of many kinds of information, including accommodation on the island.

Phuket-Info.com (www.phuket-info.com) You'll find more info on Phuket Province here.

Phuket.Net (www.phuket.net) An internet service that provides forums for tourism and business-oriented exchange, and has limited listings.

Phuket Gazette (www.phuketgazette.net) The local newspaper offering news online.

Saltwater Dreaming (www.saltwater-dreaming.com) The go-to website for surfing info on Phuket.

MEDICAL SERVICES

Both hospitals listed are equipped with modern facilities, emergency rooms and outpatient-care clinics. For dive-related medicine, see p659.

Bangkok Phuket Hospital (off Map p656; ☎ 0 7625 4425; Th Yongyok Uthit, Phuket Town) Reputedly the favourite with locals.

Phuket International Hospital (Map p650; ☎ 0 7624 9400, emergency 7621 0935; Airport Bypass Rd, Phuket Town) International doctors rate this hospital as the best on the island.

MONEY

Phuket has banks and ATMs littered across the entire island, with heavy concentrations in Patong and Phuket Town – you won't be hard-pressed to find one. As a general rule, all 7-Elevens have a money machine.

POST

DHL World Wide Express (Map p656; ☎ 0 7625 8500; 61/4 Th Thepkasatri, Phuket Town) Swift and reliable courier service (everything goes by two-day delivery), but rates are about 25% higher than at the post office.

ANDAMAN COAST

Main post office (Map p656; Th Montri, Phuket Town; ☿ 8.30am-4pm Mon-Fri, 9am-noon Sat)
Post office (Map p670; Rte 4028, Kata; ☿ 9am-4.30pm Mon-Fri, to noon Sat)

TOURIST INFORMATION

The weekly English-language *Phuket Gazette* (20B) publishes lots of information on activities, events, dining and entertainment around the island.
Immigration office (Map p653; ☎ 0 7634 0477; Th Hat Kalim, Patong; ☿ 10am-noon & 1-3pm Mon-Fri) Does visa extensions.
TAT office (Map p656; ☎ 0 7621 2213; www.tat.or.th; 73-65 Th Phuket, Phuket Town; ☿ 8.30am-4.30pm) Has maps, information brochures, a list of standard shared-taxi fares out to the various beaches and also the recommended charter costs for a vehicle.

Dangers & Annoyances

Drownings are common on Phuket's beaches, especially on the west coast (Karon, Surin, Laem Singh and Kamala). Red flags are posted on beaches to warn bathers of rip tides and other dangerous conditions. If a red flag is flying at a beach, don't go into the water (even if anyone says or does otherwise). Especially during the May to October monsoon, the waves on the west coast of Phuket sometimes make it too dangerous to swim. Hat Rawai, on the southern edge of the island, is usually a safe bet any time of the year.

Keep an eye out for jet skis when you're in the water. Although the Phuket governor declared jet skis illegal in 1997, enforcement of the ban is cyclic.

Renting a motorcycle can be a high-risk proposition – rental cars are a relatively safer option. Thousands of people are injured or killed every year on Phuket highways, and some have been travellers who weren't familiar with riding motorcycles and navigating the island's roads, highways and traffic patterns. If you must rent a motorcycle, make sure you at least know the basics and wear a helmet. Late-night motorcycle muggings are also on the rise, so keep an eye out in the evenings.

Sights

When your legs start to itch after one too many days of baking on the beach, why not inject a bit of culture (or nature) into your holiday itinerary with a visit to a Thai temple or one of the island's national parks.

PATONG
ป่าตอง

Some call Patong (Map p653) a city, we call it a sight. You say you love Patong's frenzy of neon lights? Great! See p667 for an assortment of lodging options. You hate it? We're not surprised – Phuket's capital of hedonism isn't everyone's cup of tea. You see, we measure globalisation in Patong by Starbucks rather than 7-Elevens, so that perfect slice of sandy paradise you saw on a poster on your travel agent's wall is somewhere else on the island. But don't get us wrong, even though this beachside wonderland is a testament to unchecked tourism instead of paradise with a capital 'P', it is definitely a must see. Besides the much-talked-about unsavoury tourism, Patong promises smiles with colourful cabarets (p677), endless shopping, boisterous boxing rings, watersports, see-and-be-seen resorts and amazing dining options from hot tin shacks to schmancy high-end eats (p674).

PHUKET TOWN

Long before boardshorts or flip-flops, Phuket was an island of rubber trees, tin mines and cash-hungry merchants. Attracting entrepreneurs from as far away as the Arabian Peninsula, China, India and Portugal, Phuket Town (Map p656) was a colourful blend of cultural influences, cobbled together by tentative compromise and cooperation. After a visit to Phuket Town you can put a tick in the culture category of your Phuket checklist. If you're interested in staying longer, there are plenty of quality places to spend the night (see p671), not to mention a heap of great eating options (p676) if you're spending the day.

Phuket's historic **Sino-Portuguese architecture** is the town's most evocative sight: stroll along Ths Thalang, Dibuk, Yaowarat, Ranong, Phang-Nga, Rasada and Krabi for a glimpse of some of the best buildings on offer. The most magnificent examples in town are the **Standard Chartered Bank** (Map p656; Th Phang-Nga), Thailand's oldest foreign bank; the **THAI office** (Map p656; Th Ranong); and the **old post office building**, which now houses the **Phuket Philatelic Museum** (Map p656; Th Montri; admission free; ☿ 9.30am-5.30pm), a first stop for stamp boffins. The best-restored residential properties are found along Th Dibuk and Th Thalang.

ANDAMAN COAST

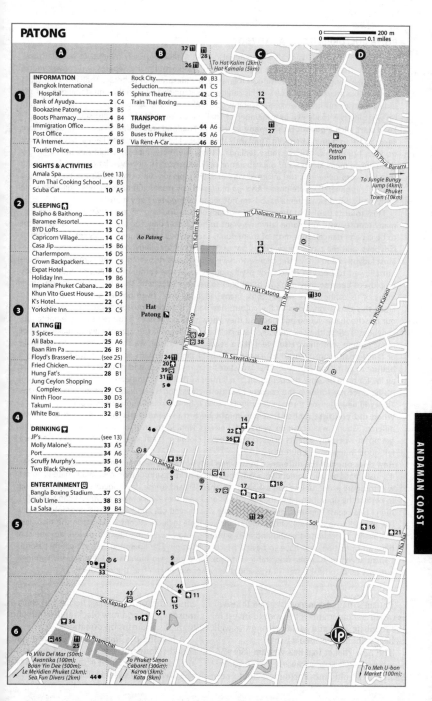

PATONG

0 — 200 m
0 — 0.1 miles

INFORMATION
Bangkok International
  Hospital...................................**1** B6
Bank of Ayudya.........................**2** C4
Bookazine Patong......................**3** B5
Boots Pharmacy.........................**4** B4
Immigration Office....................**5** B4
Post Office.................................**6** B5
TA Internet................................**7** B5
Tourist Police............................**8** B4

SIGHTS & ACTIVITIES
Amala Spa...........................(see 13)
Pum Thai Cooking School......**9** B5
Scuba Cat................................**10** A5

SLEEPING
Baipho & Baithong..................**11** B6
Baramee Resortel.....................**12** C1
BYD Lofts................................**13** C2
Capricorn Village.....................**14** C4
Casa Jip...................................**15** B6
Charlermporn...........................**16** D5
Crown Backpackers...................**17** C5
Expat Hotel..............................**18** C5
Holiday Inn.............................**19** B6
Impiana Phuket Cabana...........**20** B4
Khun Vito Guest House............**21** D5
K's Hotel..................................**22** C4
Yorkshire Inn...........................**23** C5

EATING
3 Spices...................................**24** B3
Ali Baba..................................**25** A6
Baan Rim Pa............................**26** B1
Floyd's Brasserie.................(see 25)
Fried Chicken...........................**27** C1
Hung Fat's...............................**28** B1
Jung Ceylon Shopping
  Complex................................**29** C5
Ninth Floor..............................**30** D3
Takumi.....................................**31** B4
White Box................................**32** B1

DRINKING
JP's....................................(see 13)
Molly Malone's........................**33** A5
Port...**34** A6
Scruffy Murphy's......................**35** B4
Two Black Sheep.....................**36** C4

ENTERTAINMENT
Bangla Boxing Stadium............**37** C5
Club Lime................................**38** B3
La Salsa...................................**39** B4

Rock City..................................**40** B3
Seduction.................................**41** C5
Sphinx Theatre.........................**42** C3
Train Thai Boxing.....................**43** B6

TRANSPORT
Budget.....................................**44** A6
Buses to Phuket........................**45** A6
Via Rent-A-Car.........................**46** B6

ANDAMAN COAST

POP'S CULTURE: LIFE AS A LADYBOY

Pop, age 45, is what Thais call a *gà·teu·i* (also spelt *kàthoey*), usually referred to as a 'ladyboy' in English. Thailand's transgender population is the subject of many debates and conversations, especially amongst tourists. Although tolerance is widespread in Buddhist Thailand, concealed homophobia prevails – for *gà·teu·i*, this can be a challenging life, with the entertainment and sex industries the only lucrative career avenues open. We spent the day with Pop and got the skinny on what life was really like as a member of Thailand's oft-talked-about 'third sex'.

Let's start with a question that many tourists in Thailand would like to ask: why does there seem to be so many *gà·teu·i* in Thailand? Well, that's like asking me why I am a ladyboy! I have no idea. I didn't ask to have these feelings. I think the more important thing to notice is why there are so many ladyboys in the cabaret or sex industry. First, however, let me start by staying that the word *gà·teu·i* is the informal way of saying 'person with two sexes'; the term *phuying kham pet* is generally more polite. Also, *gà·teu·i* is strictly reserved for people who still have male body parts but dress as female, so I am not technically *gà·teu·i* any more.

Most tourists think that there are tons of ladyboys in Thailand because they are in places that many tourists visit. Yes, some ladyboys want to be cabaret dancers, just like some women want to be cabaret dancers, but most of them don't. These types of jobs are the only ones available to ladyboys, and the pay is lousy. Life is not as 'Hollywood' for a ladyboy as it may seem on stage. Most ladyboys don't have the chance to have a job that is respected by the community. We are not allowed to become doctors or psychologists and most corporations do not allow ladyboy employees because they don't want *gà·teu·i* to be associated with their company's image. Since many of us cannot have proper jobs, many ladyboys don't even bother going to school, and lately this educational gap in the culture has become huge. You see many *gà·teu·i* dropping out of school at a young age because they know they don't have a future in a respectable job. Ladyboys work in the sex industry because they aren't given the opportunity to make a lot of money doing something else. I feel like a second-class citizen; we are not allowed to use male *or* female bathrooms! I used to have to climb 14 flights of stairs to use the special ladyboy's bathroom at my old job! Also, Thai law states that my ID cards and passport must always have an 'M' for male because the definition of a female in Thailand is someone who can bear children. It's hard for me to leave the country because my passport says 'male' but I look like a female. They will never let me through security because it looks like a fraudulent passport.

When did you first realise that you might be a transgender person? I realised that I was different when I was about six years old. I always wanted to dress up like my sister and would get upset when my parents dressed me in boys' clothing. It felt wrong being in boys' clothes. I felt good in my sister's outfits.

How does one tell the difference between a ladyboy and a woman on the street? Sometimes it's really hard to tell…sometimes a ladyboy can be more beautiful than a woman! There is no set way to figure it out, unless you ask them for their ID card. These days, doctors are really starting to perfect the operations, and the operations are expensive – mine was 150,000B! I had the 'snip', then I had breast implants, my Adam's apple was shaved off, and I also had a nose job (I didn't like my old nose anyway). Other operations available include silicone implants in the hips, jaw narrowing, cheekbone shaving and chin sculpting – to make it rounder. But before anyone can have an operation, you have to have a psych evaluation. The operation was extremely painful. I spent seven days in the hospital and it took me about two months to fully recover. Younger patients tend to heal faster – I was about 40 years old when I had the operation.

Phuket's main **day market** (Map p656; Th Ranong) is worth a wander and is the spot to invest in the requisite Thai and Malay sarongs, as well as baggy Shan fishermen's pants.

The new **Phuket Thai Hua Museum** (Map p656; www.thaihua.net; Th Krabi; admission free; ﹀ 1-8pm Tue-Sun), set in an old Sino-Portuguese home, cel-

ebrates the town's Chinese heritage. It consists mostly of old and new black-and-white photographs and runs on donations.

A handful of Chinese temples inject some added colour into the area. Most are standard issue, but the **Shrine of the Serene Light** (Map p656; Saan Jao Sang Tham; ﹀ 8.30am-noon & 1.30-5.30pm),

Why didn't you have the operation earlier? I didn't 'change' earlier because I didn't want to give up my job, and I knew that after the operation I would be forced to quit. I was working as a software instructor at a university, and university teachers are not allowed to be transgender. I also waited until my father passed away so that it would be easier on my family when I made the transition.

How has your family handled the transition? Well, contrary to what some tourists believe, no family particularly *wants* a transgender child, even a family with only boys. Some of my close friends no longer speak to their families. My mother was always very comforting. A month before my operation she told me, 'You will always be my child, but never lie to anyone about who you are – accept who you are.' I have two adopted sons who are now quite grown up, and after I made the change, they bought me presents on Mother's Day instead of Father's Day – I thought that was very sweet. My father, on the other hand, was never very supportive. When he found out I was sleeping with men, he…well…let's put it this way, he practised his *moo·ay tai* boxing on me.

What was the first thing that passed through your mind when you woke up after the operation? How has life been since the operation? I woke up with a big smile. Life is great. I am happy that I can be on the outside what I am on the inside – I can stop feeling sad every time I look down! Finding a job after my surgery was hard. I wrote on my CV 'transgender post-op' so that there would be no surprises in the interview, but I never heard back from any companies. Oh, actually one company asked me to come in for an interview, but they spent the meeting asking me inappropriate questions about my personal life. It was very disheartening. I finally found a queer-friendly company, where I am employed as a hospitality software implementer, meaning that I go around to hotels around Thailand and teach front-desk staff how to use the hotel's computer system. I adore my job.

Now that my surgery is far behind me, I have to take female hormones regularly until I die. I take a pill twice per week, but some male-to-females take one injection per month (I hate needles). Some people have bad reaction to the medication at first. I have had friends who got a lot of pimples and got really fat. Sometimes it takes a while before you find the right amount of hormones. Besides the hormones, there is a certain amount of…maintenance…that needs to take place in order to keep my new parts working. Put it this way, when you get your ears pierced, if you don't regularly wear earrings…well… Anyway, my aunt, who moved to the United States, asked me if I wanted to move too, but I am happy in Thailand. Even though transgender individuals don't have a lot of rights, I'm not convinced that it is that much better anywhere else.

And finally, what do you feel is the biggest misconception about *gà·teu·i* in Thailand? This is an easy question. The biggest misconception is that we are all promiscuous whores and liars. Like any human being, we are just looking for love. It is true that many ladyboys do try to trick the people around them, but this is because they are afraid of being rejected for who they really are. Also, many of them lie because they desperately want to be real women, but they will never be real women. I know that – that's why I always show the real me – I am comfortable with who I am. I wish everyone else would be too.

For more information about ladyboys in Thailand, visit www.thailadyboyz.net (although the site is currently in Thai only).

tucked away at the end of a 50m alley near the Bangkok Bank of Commerce on Th Phang-Nga, is a cut above the rest. You'll see Taoist etchings on the walls, the vaulted ceiling stained from incense plumes, and the altar is always alive with fresh flowers and burning candles. The shrine, which has been restored, is said to have been built by a local family in the mid-1880s, and the sense of history is tangible.

The namesake of the **Phra Phitak Chyn Pracha Mansion** (Map p656; 9 Th Krabi) used to own a number of tin mines in the early 20th century. Today the ochre-tinged house sits forlorn, in

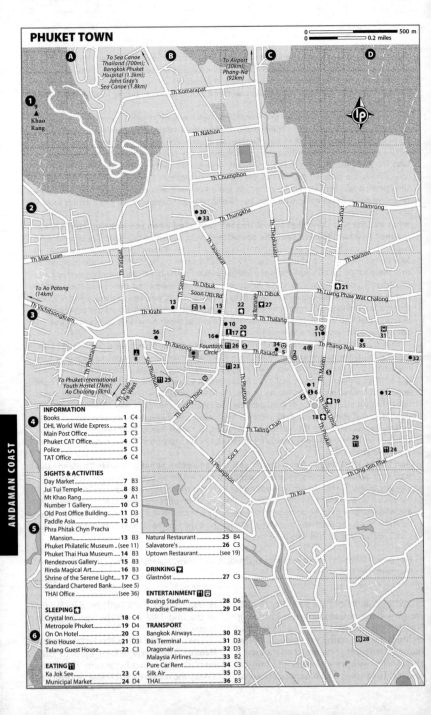

PHUKET TOWN

ANDAMAN COAST

need of a Thai Scarlett O'Hara (it certainly has the grounds for it). The iron gates are open, so proceed at your own risk. If you do breach the threshold, and dogs bark, don't worry as they're probably just growling at the ghosts.

Phuket Town is also known for its whimsical galleries tucked behind charming Chinese shopfronts. At **Rinda Magical Art** (Map p656; ☎ 08 9289 8852; www.rindamagicalart.com; 27 Th Yaowarat; admission free; 10am-7pm) you step inside a surrealistic realm run by a chatty artist. Distinctly modern interpretations of traditional themes can be found at **Number 1 Gallery** (Map p656; ☎ 08 7281 5279; www.number1gallery.com; 32 Th Yaowarat; admission free; 10.30am-7.30pm), a branch of one of Bangkok's best-loved fine-art galleries. Gold leaf and acrylic formed evocative images of blooming lotuses and Asian elephants when we visited. The **Rendezvous Gallery** (Map p656; ☎ 0 7621 9095; 69 Th Yaowarat; 10am-7pm) features fantastic psychedelic Buddhist art on canvas, batik, paper and wood.

For a bird's-eye view of the city, climb up pretty **Khao Rang** (Phuket Hill; Map p656), northwest of the town centre. It's at its best during the week, when the summit is relatively peaceful, but keep an eye out for the mobs of snarling dogs. If, as many people say, Phuket is a corruption of the Malay word *bukit* (hill), then this is probably its namesake.

BIG BUDDHA

Set on a hilltop just northwest of Chalong circle and visible from almost half of the island, the Big Buddha (Map p650) sits at the best viewpoint on Phuket. To get here you'll follow the red signs from the main highway (Hwy 402) and wind up a country road, passing terraced banana groves and tangles of jungle. Once you're on top, pay your respects at the tented golden shrine, then step up to Big Buddha's glorious plateau where you can peer into Kata's perfect bay, glimpse the shimmering Karon strand and, on the other side, survey the serene Chalong harbour where the channel islands look like pebbles.

Of course, you'll be forgiven if you disregard the view for a few minutes to watch local craftsmen put the finishing touches on their 60 million baht Buddha, dressed in Burmese alabaster. Over the last 20 years construction on Phuket hasn't stopped, so it means something when locals refer to the Big Buddha project as Phuket's most important development in the last 100 years.

Visitors can help complete the Big Buddha by purchasing small tablets of white stone for 200B each. You can sign the stone, which will eventually be cemented into the facade.

WÄT

Phuket has many centres for Buddhist worship; just remember to ditch your beach clothes before stepping on temple grounds. Donations are warmly accepted at all wát.

One of our favourite wát on Phuket, **Wat Chalong** (Map p650; Hwy 4021, Chalong; 6am-6pm) is a bustling, tiered temple with 36 Buddhas that are seated, reclining or meditating on the first two floors. Concrete serpents line the banisters and the lotus pond outside. It's not an antique, but it does have a heady spiritual vibe, especially when worshippers come to pay their respects.

Located near Thalang Town, **Wat Phra Thong** (Map p650; 6am-6pm) is known as the 'Temple of the Gold Buddha'. The image is half-buried so that only the head and shoulders are visible above ground. According to local legend, those who have tried to excavate the image have become gravely ill soon after. The temple is particularly revered by Thai Chinese, many of whom believe the image hails from China. During Chinese New Year the temple is an important focus for Phang-Nga and Krabi provinces. In addition to Phra Thong, there are several other Buddhas, including seven representing the different days of the week, plus a Phra Praket (an unusual pose in which the Buddha is touching his own head).

Although the architecture is rather uninspiring, **Wat Nai Han** (Map p650; Hat Nai Han; 6am-6pm) is a working monastery, so if you show up at dawn you can watch, or even join in, as the monks chant scripture. Just make sure to ask permission from a monk the day before.

Set back from the road, **Wat Karon** (Map p670; Th Patak East, Karon; 6am-6pm) is a relatively new temple complex with a small shine occupied by a seated, black-stone Buddha. Behind it is the striking crematorium with its tiered roof – which only opens on ceremonial days. The grounds are lush with banana, palm and mango trees.

LAEM PROMTHEP
แหลมพรหมเทพ

You won't be alone, but that won't matter once you scan the 270 degrees of Andaman Sea, noticing how elegantly it arcs around the

ANDAMAN COAST

cape below, where local fishermen cast into the waves from the jutting rocks. With the possible exception of the Big Buddha, **Laem Phromthep** (Map p650; Hwy 4233) is the best place to watch the sunset. Take it from the crowds, most of whom are Thai tourists. They spill onto the concrete platform, make offerings to the fantastic elephant shrine and climb to the top deck of the modern lighthouse shaped like a crab.

If you really crave privacy, follow the handful of locals down the fishermen's trail that hugs the ridge and ends on the rocks just a few metres above the sea. Although it looks like a thin strand from above, the peninsula – the island's true southernmost point – spreads out quite nicely, and you will easily find a nook of your own.

THALANG DISTRICT

อำเภอถลาง

Those interested in the island's colonial history can visit the **Thalang National Museum** (Map p650; ☎ 0 7631 1426; admission 40B; 🕑 8.30am-4pm). The museum contains five exhibition halls chronicling southern themes such as the history of Thalang-Phuket and the colonisation of the Andaman Coast. The museum's biggest draw is the 2.3m-tall Vishnu, which dates to the 9th century and was found near Takua Pa in the early 1900s.

When travelling to the museum, you will most likely pass the **Heroines Monument** (Map p650); see p649 for the story behind the statues. Also in Thalang District is Wat Phra Thong (p657).

KHAO PHRA THAEW ROYAL WILDLIFE & FOREST RESERVE

อุทยานสัตว์ป่าเขาพระแทว

Phuket isn't just sand and sea. Khao Phra Thaew (Map p650), in the northern part of the island, is a preserve protecting 23 sq km of virgin rainforest. There are several pleasant jungle hikes leading to a couple of photogenic waterfalls, **Ton Sai** and **Bang Pae** in particular. The falls are best seen in the rainy season between June and November; in the dry months they slow to a trickle. The highest point in the preserve is **Khao Phra**, rising to 442m. The park has royal status, so it is better protected than the average national park in the kingdom.

A German botanist discovered a rare and unique species of palm in Khao Phra Thaew about 50 years ago. Called the white-backed palm or *langkow* palm, the fan-shaped plant stands 3m to 5m tall and is found only here and in Khao Sok National Park (p639).

Tigers, Malayan sun bears, rhinos and elephants once roamed the forest here, but nowadays resident mammals are limited to humans, gibbons, monkeys, slow loris, langurs, civets, fruit bats, squirrels, mouse-deer and other smaller animals. Watch out for cobras and wild pigs.

The **Phuket Gibbon Rehabilitation Centre** (Map p650; ☎ 0 7626 0492; www.gibbonproject.org; admission by donation; 🕑 9am-4pm), near Bang Pae, is a must-see for park visitors. Funded by donations (1500B will care for a gibbon for one year), the volunteer-run centre adopts gibbons that have been kept in captivity and reintroduces them into the wild after they find a mate. When the gibbons are ready to forage and live in holy matrimony, they're released into the forest nearby. Once free, they swing from branch to branch at 25km/h, eating fruit, nuts, insects and lizards.

SIRINAT NATIONAL PARK

อุทยานแห่งชาติสิรินาถ

Comprising the beaches of Nai Thon, Nai Yang and Mai Khao, as well as the former Nai Yang National Park and Mai Khao wildlife reserve, **Sirinat National Park** (Map p650; ☎ 0 7632 8226; www.dnp.go.th; admission 200-400B; 🕑 8am-5pm) encompasses 22 sq km of coastal land, plus 68 sq km of sea. It runs from the western Phang-Nga provincial border south to the headland that separates Nai Yang from Nai Thon.

A visitor centre with toilets, showers and picnic tables is located at Hat Mai Khao, Phuket's longest beach. Short trails lead from the centre into the mangroves and down to a steep beach. Between November and February sea turtles lay their eggs along the beach.

The area between Nai Yang and Mai Khao is largely given over to **shrimp farming**, which can be an interesting practice to watch. Fortunately, shrimp farmers here don't dig artificial lagoons into the beach or mangroves (like they do on Ko Chang or at Khao Sam Roi Yot), but rather they raise the spawn in self-contained concrete tanks, a method significantly less harmful to the environment.

The park is easily accessible from Phuket International Airport.

PHUKET AQUARIUM

At the tip of Laem Phanwa, **Phuket Aquarium** (Map p650; ☎ 0 7639 1126; adult/child 100/50B; 🕑 8.30am-4pm) displays a varied collection of tropical fish and other sea creatures. There are 32 tanks and you can experience underwater life with a stroll along the walk-through tunnel. Follow Rte 4021 south and turn on Rte 4023 outside of Phuket Town.

Activities
DIVING

Phuket enjoys an enviable central location relative to the Andaman's top diving destinations. The much-talked-about Similans sit to the north, while dozens of dive sites orbit Ko Phi-Phi (p693) and Ko Lanta (p700) to the south. Of course, this means that trips from Phuket to these awesome destinations cost slightly more since you'll be forking over some extra dough for your boat's petrol. Most operators on Phuket take divers to the nine decent sites orbiting the island, like Ko Raya Noi and Ko Raya Yai (also called Ko Racha Noi and Ko Racha Yai); however, these spots rank lower on the wow-o-meter. The reef off the southern tip of Raya Noi is particularly good for experienced divers. It's a deep site where soft corals cling to boulders, around which pelagic fish species, like barracuda, rainbow runners and trevally, roam. Manta and marble rays are also frequently glimpsed here, and if you're lucky, you may even see a whale shark.

A typical two-dive day trip (including equipment) to nearby sites costs around 3000B to 4000B. Nondivers (and snorkellers) are permitted to join such dive trips for a significant discount. A four-day PADI Open Water certification course costs around 12,500B to 15,000B. The best diving months are December to May, when the weather is good and the sea is at its clearest (and boat trips are less rocky).

At first glance, it seems like are hundreds of dive shops on the island, when in fact the number is much, much smaller. Most of these 'operators' are merely booking agencies that charge a hefty fee and find you a spot on a random boat with some random school. Customers tend to be dissatisfied as these companies are usually involved in un-savoury money-making schemes. On Phuket it is always best to book directly with a dive school that has its own boat and accreditation. Like in any diving destination, picking a diving school can be tricky and will greatly affect your experience underwater. Read the Ko Tao diving section (p611) for pointers about choosing a diving operation.

The Phuket dive operations listed below are recommended, and specialise in a variety of day trips to nearby sites. For information about quality live-aboards to the Similan and Surin islands see p642. If you are interested in diving Hin Daeng/Hin Muang (and have time to swing down to Ko Lanta) see p700.

Dive Asia (Map p670; ☎ 0 7633 0598; www.diveasia .com; 24 Th Karon, Kata) There is a second location at 623 Th Karon near Karon Beach.

Scuba Cat (Map p653; ☎ 0 7629 3120; www.scubacat .com; 94 Th Thawiwong, Patong)

Sea Bees (☎ 0 7638 1765; www.sea-bees.com; 69 1/3 Moo 9 Viset, Ao Chalong) Also operates out of Khao Lak.

Sea Fun Divers (off Map p653; ☎ 0 7634 0480; www.seafundivers.com; 29 Soi Karon Nui, Patong) An outstanding and very professional diving operation. Standards are extremely high and service is impeccable. There's an office at the Le Meridien resort in Patong, and a second location at the Katathani Resort (p669) in Kata Noi.

There are three hyperbaric chambers on Phuket.

Bangkok International Hospital (Map p653; ☎ 0 7634 2518; 231-233 Th Rat Uthit, Patong)

Phuket International Hospital (Map p650; ☎ 0 7624 9400, emergency 0 7621 0935) Just outside Phuket Town.

Wachira Hospital (Map p650; ☎ 0 7621 1114) Outside Phuket Town.

SNORKELLING

Snorkelling is best along Phuket's west coast, particularly at the rocky headlands between beaches. Mask, snorkel and fins can be rented for around 250B a day. As with scuba diving, you'll find better snorkelling, with greater visibility and variety of marine life, along the shores of small outlying islands such as Ko Raya Yai and Ko Raya Noi.

Recommended snorkel tour operators:

Offspray Leisure (☎ 08 1894 1274; www.offspray leisure.com; 43/87 Chalong Plaza; trips from 2950B) This dive and snorkelling excursion company specialises in trips to the reefs around Ko Phi-Phi. Its high-speed boat will get you there in 45 minutes, compared to the usual 1½ hours (minimum), which leaves you more time to enjoy the water. It also keeps its client loads small, which lends an intimate feel – something missing among most other dive operators on Phuket.

Oi's Longtail (☎ 08 1978 5728; 66 Moo 3, Hat Nai Yang; tours 1600B) Oi specialises in two-hour snorkelling tours of the reefs around Ko Waeo. Cost includes snorkelling gear. Located at Bank restaurant, opposite the long-tail boat harbour.

SURFING

Phuket is a secret surfing paradise. Once the monsoons bring their midyear swell, glassy seas fold into barrels. The best waves arrive between June and September, when Hat Kata becomes the island's unofficial surf capital. An annual competition is held here in late August (sometimes early September). The best waves on Kata are found at the south end, and they typically top out at 2m. Nai Han is known to get huge waves too (up to 3m), mostly near the beach's yacht club. Be warned: both Kata and Nai Han have vicious undertows that can claim lives.

Hat Kalim, just north of Patong, is sheltered and has a consistent break that also gets up to 3m. The **Phuket Boardriders Club** (www.phuket-boardriders.com) sponsors an August contest here. Hat Kamala's northernmost beach has a nice 3m break, and Laem Singh, just up the coast in front of the Amanpuri Resort, gets very big and fast, plus it's sheltered from wind by the massive headland.

Hat Nai Yang may have the best waves in all of Phuket. They are more than 200m offshore, so you'll have to paddle a bit, but the reef provides a consistent break, swells get up to 3m high and there is no undertow.

Surfing isn't a major draw on Phuket, so the island isn't exactly brimming with surf schools or board shops. But if you bring your own stick and skills, and arrive with the wind, you'll find some nice waves all the way up the west coast.

Recommended operators:

Blujelly (Map p666; ☎ 08 5880 7954; www.blujelly .com; Bang Thao) Offers kids' lessons and is a good source of info about surfing around Bang Thao.

Phuket Surf (Map p670; ☎ 08 1002 2496; www .phuketsurf.com; Kata) Offers surf lessons starting at 1500B, as well as board rentals; on Kata Yai's southern cove.

Saltwater Dreaming (Map p666; ☎ 0 7627 1050; www.saltwater-dreaming.com; Surin) Undoubtedly the island's best surf shop. Ask about surfing classes and check out the website to answer any of your surfing questions.

KITEBOARDING

If you've never tried this up-and-coming sport, now's your chance. Lessons with **Kiteboarding Asia** (off Map p666; ☎ 08 1591 4593; www.kiteboardingasia.com; 74/10 Moo 3, Th Hat Nai Yang; lessons from 4000B) take place in the sheltered bay and prices include all equipment hire. For a bit more time and money you can become certified by the International Kiteboarding Organisation – a necessary step to be able to hire equipment from most outfitters around the world. Bob, the owner/instructor, also gives traditional surfing lessons (and hires boards) when the swell arrives (best between June to September). The waves here are just as good as in Kata and Nai Han, without the lethal undertow.

KAYAKING & CANOEING

Several companies based on Phuket offer canoe tours of scenic Ao Phang-Nga (p646). The kayaks are able to enter semisubmerged caverns (known in Thai as 'rooms'), which are inaccessible to the trademark long-tail boats. A day paddle will set you back around 3000B per person, which includes meals, equipment and hotel transfers. Many outfitters also run three-day all-inclusive trips (from 13,000B).

Operators based in or around Phuket Town:

John Gray's Sea Canoe (off Map p656; ☎ 0 7625 4505; www.johngray-seacanoe.com; 124 Soi 1, Th Yaowarat, Phuket Town; trips 3950-57,800B) Phuket's original kayak outfitter, John Gray and his team of local guides lead ecotours to Ao Phang-Nga's hidden islands, lagoons and *hongs* (caves semisubmerged in the sea), where guests learn about this fragile ecosystem. The Hong By Starlight tour, a guided, evening paddle through bat caves into bioluminescent lagoons, is unforgettable. Overnight camping trips are also available. Trips leave from Ao Por.

Paddle Asia (Map p656; ☎ 0 7624 0952; www.paddle asia.com; 19/3 Th Rasdanusorn, Phuket Town) Caters to beginners and those who don't enjoy being surrounded by noisy tour groups. Groups are small (two to six people) and multiday tours are offered.

Sea Canoe Thailand (off Map p656; ☎ 0 7621 2172; www.seacanoe.net; 367/4 Th Yaowarat, Phuket Town) Has a great reputation despite the unoriginal name.

YACHTING

Phuket is one of Southeast Asia's main yachting destinations, and you'll find all manner of craft anchored along its shores – from 80-year-old wooden sloops that look like they can barely stay afloat to the latest in hi-tech motor cruisers. Marina-style facilities with year-round anchorage are available at a few locations. Port clearance is rather complicated; the marinas will take care of the paperwork (for a fee of course) if notified of your arrival in advance.

Phuket Boat Lagoon (Map p650; ☎ 0 7623 9055; fax 0 7623 9056) Located at Ao Sapam, about 10km north of

Phuket Town on the east coast. It has an enclosed marina with tidal channel access, serviced pontoon berths, 60- and 120-tonne travel lifts, hard stand area, plus a resort hotel, laundry, coffee shop, fuel, water, repairs and maintenance services.

Rolly Tasker Sailmakers (☎ 0 7628 0347; www .rollytasker.com; 26/2 Th Chaofa, Ao Chalong) If you need sails, Rolly Tasker can outfit you. Riggings, spars and hardware are also available.

Royal Phuket Marina (Map p650; ☎ 0 7623 9762; www.royalphuketmarina.com) This US$25 million marina is located just south of Phuket Boat Lagoon. Luxury villas, town houses and a hotel join 190 berths and a spa here.

Yacht Haven Phuket Marina (Map p650; ☎ 0 7620 6705; www.yacht-haven-phuket.com) At Laem Phrao on the northeastern tip of the island. The Yacht Haven boasts 130 berths and a scenic restaurant, and also does yacht maintenance.

The **TAT office** (Map p656; ☎ 0 7621 2213; www.tat .or.th; 73-65 Th Phuket, Phuket Town; ◷ 8.30am-4.30pm) in Phuket Town has an extensive list of yacht charters and brokers. For insurance purposes, it's a good idea to see if the boat you want to charter is registered in Thailand. Expect to pay from 20,000B per day for a high-season, bareboat charter. The following companies can help with information on yacht charters (both bareboat and crewed), yacht sales and yacht deliveries:

Dream Yacht Charter (☎ 0 7620 6492; www .dreamyachtcharter.com; Yacht Haven Phuket Marina) This French-run company charters large bare-boat catamarans with and without crews. They aren't cheap, but sailing between limestone karsts in Ao Phang-Nga is the type of moment worth paying for.

Faraway Sail & Dive Expeditions (☎ 0 7628 0701; www.far-away.net; 112/8 Moo 4, Th Taina, Hat Karon)

Sunsail Yacht Charters (☎ 0 7623 9057; www .sunsailthailand.com; Phuket Boat Lagoon)

Thai Marine Leisure (☎ 0 7623 9111; www.thai marine.com; Phuket Boat Lagoon)

Yachtpro International (☎ 0 7623 2960; www.sailing -thailand.com; Yacht Haven Phuket Marina)

GOLF

Blue Canyon Country Club (Map p650; ☎ 0 7632 8088; www.bluecanyonclub.com; 165 Moo 1, Th Thep-kasatri; 18 holes 5300B) A luxury country club with two championship golf courses that have hosted two dramatic (and one record setting) Tiger Woods tournament wins. There is also a full-service spa, two restaurants and luxury apartments on the property. The facilities are showing their age, but you'll come for the golf course. It's a good one. Club hire and lessons are available.

Dino Park (Map p670; ☎ 0 7633 0625; www.dino park.com; Th Patak West, Karon; adult/child 240/180B; ◷ 10am-midnight) Jurassic Park meets minigolf at this bizarre park on the southern edge of Hat Karon. It's a maze of caves, lagoons, leafy gardens, dinosaur statues and, of course, putting greens. Kids will dig it the most.

Mission Hills Golf Club (Map p650; ☎ 0 7631 0888; www.missionhillsphuket.com; 195 Moo 4, Pla Khlok; 18 holes 3800B) Twenty-seven more holes of tournament-calibre golf can be found at this Jack Nicklaus–designed course near the east coast. It, too, has a spa and hotel rooms and two swimming pools.

Thailand Tours & Paradise Golf (☎ 084 8433677; www.golfinphuket.com; Centara Mall, Th Patak East) Swed-ish owned and operated, it arranges custom-golf trips (and deep-sea fishing trips) for independent travellers. If you are into golf, these guys are the island's authority.

HORSE RIDING

Bangthao Beach Riding Club (Map p666; ☎ 0 7632 4199; 394 Moo 1, Th Hat Bang Thao; horseback rides from 1000B, elephant rides from 350B) Aptly named, this club offers everything from half-day horseback rides through forest, marsh and along virgin beach to serious riding lessons, and 10-minute elephant rides. It's located near the Laguna Phuket entrance.

Phuket Riding Club (Map p650; ☎ 0 7628 8213; www.phuketridingclub.com; 95 Th Vises; rides from 650B; ◷ 7am-6.30pm) Ride the jungle trails and white sands of the south coast atop Australian horses. The stables, gear and horses are all top quality. Lessons are also available.

ELEPHANT RIDES

Arawan Bukit Elephant Trekking (☎ 08 6809 4780; Th Patong-Karon; tours 400-1200B; ◷ 9am-6pm) Gulong, Peter and their mates are logging-industry refugees. They sleep five hours a day, eat six hours a day and will carry you to commanding views of Ao Patong.

Kok Chang Safari (Map p650; ☎ 08 4841 9794; www. kokchangsafari.com; 287 Moo 2, Th Kata Sai Yuan Hwy 4233; tours from 600B; ◷ 8.30am-5.30pm) This well-run, attrac-tive elephant camp is easily one of the best on Phuket, if not the best. The animals are healthy. Tours last 20 minutes to an hour. If you do the full hour (1000B), you'll have a magical view from the top of the mountain. Or you could always ditch the elephants and have a drink with Charlie, a friendly and damn handsome monkey. He'll be at the bar.

Phuket Elephant Ride (☎ 08 4058 3276; 25/19 Moo 1, Hwy 4233; elephant tours from 800B, snake show 400B, monkey show 400B; ◷ 9am-7pm) If you can't be both-ered to drive the extra few kilometres to the superior Kok Chang Safari (see above), you can book a similar trip here. Tours last 20, 30 or 60 minutes. The camp also features a snake show starring a king cobra and another somewhat depressing show with a trained monkey.

ANDAMAN COAST

Phuket Zoo (Map p650; ☎ 0 7638 1227; www
.phuketzoo.com; 23/2 Moo 3 Soi, Th Phalai Chaofa, near
Chalong; admission 200B; ☼ 8.30am-6pm) Young animal
enthusiasts will enjoy the elephant shows.

MOO·AY TAI (THAI BOXING)

Rawai has several well-known *moo·ay tai*
(also spelt *muay thai*) schools. There is one
popular (but fairly touristy) training centre
in Patong (p677).

Rawai Muay Thai (☎ 08 1078 8067; www
.rawaimuaythai.com; 43/42 Moo 7, Th Sai Yuan, Rawai;
☼ 7.30-9.30am & 4-6pm; group class/private session
500/800B) A former *moo·ay tai* champion opened this gym,
and tourists from around the world come here to learn
how to fight alongside professional Thai fighters. Most are
college kids who live in on-site dorms, but you're welcome
to drop in for lessons. Be warned: it's immediately addictive.

Sinbi Muay Thai (☎ 08 3391 5535; www.sinbi
-muaythai.com; 100/15 Moo 7, Th Sai Yuan, Rawai;
☼ 7.30-9.30am & 4-6pm; per day/week/month
500/3000/10,000B) Another well-respected boxing training
camp in Rawai. Open to both sexes.

ADRENALIN SPORTS

Cable Jungle Adventures (☎ 08 1977 4904; 232/17
Moo 8, Th Bansuanneramit; per person 1600B; ☼ 9am-
6pm) Tucked into the hills behind a quilt of pineapple
fields, rubber plantations and mango groves is this maze of
eight zip lines linking cliffs to ancient ficus trees. The zips
range from 6m to 23m above the ground and the longest
run is 100m long. Closed-toe shoes are a must.

Jungle Bungy Jump (Map p650; ☎ 0 7632 1351;
www.phuketbungy.com; 61/3 Moo 6, Kathu; jump 1600B)
In operation since 1992, this 20-storey bungy jump inland
from Patong is built and operated to Kiwi standards. Jump-
ers have the option to dunk in the water, leap in pairs or
experience the Rocket Man, where you'll be shot 50m into
the air, then do the bungy thing on the way down.

SPAS

For the skinny on spas check out the boxed
text, below.

Amala Spa (Map p653; ☎ 0 7634 3024; www.bydlofts
.com; 5/28 Th Rat Uthit, Patong; treatments from 600B;
☼ 9am-8pm) Like the rest of the BYD property (p668),
this spa offers luxurious urban design, as well as Thai, oil

THE LOW-DOWN ON THE BEST RUB-DOWN

There seems to be a massage parlour on every *soi* on Phuket, with an eager employee in the
doorway yelling, 'Massaaaaaaaaaage!' with a Fran Drescher–esque nasal squeak. Most of these
shops are low-key family affairs where rub-downs go for 250B and a quick mani-pedi will set
you back a measly 100B. The quality of service at these joints varies, and changes rapidly as staff
turnover is high. Go with your gut and ask your fellow travellers – at these bargain prices it's
hard to go wrong, but don't expect fireworks.

If you're looking for a more Westernised spa experience, head to one of Phuket's plentiful spa
resorts. These places are often affiliated with a ritzy hotel (but nearly all are open to nonguests).
They are snazzy affairs with gorgeous Zen designs and huge treatment menus. Prices vary depending on location, but treatments generally start at around 1000B and go up and up from there.
Our three favourite spas:

- The **Banyan Tree Spa** (Map p666; www.banyantree.com) at the Banyan Tree Phuket (p665) is the
  clear winner. The spa runs a world-renowned massage school and all specialists at the centre
  have completed the lengthy training. Special Indian energy treatments have been recently
  added to the laundry list of therapies. Try the signature three-hour Royal Banyan treatment
  (US$195). It includes a mint footbath, a cucumber and lemongrass rub, Thai herbal massage
  and a soak in a petal-filled tub.

- The **Six Senses Spa** (www.sixsenses.com) at the Evason Phuket Resort (p671) is sublimely back-
  to-nature in setting, yet cutting edge as far as treatments are concerned. Try the 'Sensory Spa
  Journey' (90 minutes, 8000B), which includes a four-hand massage (two therapists), luxurious
  footbaths and a goody bag of product samples used in your treatment.

- One of Phuket's first spas, **Hideaway Day Spa** (☎ 0 7627 1549; ☼ 11am-9pm) still enjoys an
  excellent reputation. More reasonably priced than many hotel counterparts, the Hideaway
  offers traditional Thai massage, sauna and mud body wraps in a tranquil wooded setting at
  the edge of a lagoon. Treatments start at 1500B.

For a list of additional spas, see above.

and reflexology massage, a white-clay body wrap or a detoxifying green tea body polish.

Amanpuri Spa (Map p666; ☎ 0 7632 4333; www .amanresorts.com; 118/1 Moo 3, Th Srisoonthorn, Surin; treatments from 3500B; ☺ 9am-9pm) Therapy mingles with luxury at this cliff-side spa, set in a secluded coconut grove. Treatment rooms are all wood and glass with private steam chambers and meditation gardens. The spa uses its own brand of all-natural organic products and resort guests can wake up with an early-morning yoga class.

Aspasia (Map p670; ☎ 0 7633 3033; www.aspasia phuket.com; 1/3 Th Laem Sai; treatments from 1000B; ☺ 9am-9pm) A brilliant day spa option is hidden away at this unique condo resort on the headland between Kata and Karon. The interior is cosy and very Zen with sliding rice-paper doors dividing the treatment rooms. Try the red sweet body scrub, a mixture of sesame, honey and fresh orange juice. Or maybe you'd rather the coconut and pas-sionfruit exfoliation? It also has a full-service beauty salon and offers a variety of massage styles.

Atsumi Healing (☎ 08 1272 0571; www.atsumihealing .com; 34/18 Soi Pattana, Rawai; spa treatments from 1000B) Atsumi isn't just a spa, it's an earthy fasting and detox retreat centre. Most guests come to fast on water, juice and/or herbs for days at a time. Massages are also part of the program, and the regularly eating public is welcome to book massages here. In addition to traditional Thai, oil and deep-tissue treatments, you can have the signature ThaiAtsu massage (think Thai meets shiatsu) or meditative and gentle yoga classes with a touch of t'ai chi. Staff call it their Morning Ritual.

Indigo Spa (☎ 0 7632 7006; www.indigo-pearl.com; Hat Nai Yang; treatments from 1500B; ☺ 9am-9pm) Set in the mega Indigo Pearl resort (p665) that doubles as an avant-garde monument to Phuket's tin-mining past, treatments at this fantastic spa include a moist chocolate-pudding scrub (don't eat it!) and a pearl wrap featuring the vegetal extracts of local cultured pearls.

Spa Royale (Map p670; ☎ 0 7633 3568; www.villa royalephuket.com; 12 Th Kata Noi; treatments from 1200B; ☺ 9am-8pm) With organic spa products, seaside treat-ment rooms and highly skilled therapists, this is one of the top spas in southern Phuket. Its 90-minute aromatherapy massage is an all-timer.

Courses

Beach House Cooking School (Map p666; ☎ 089 6511064; Hat Surin; class per person 1900B; ☺ 9am-10pm) Peruse the menu, circle the intriguing dishes at this chic beach cafe and you'll learn to make them during your three-hour class run by the owner/chef. The dining room has live trees rising through the roof, and the student kitchen has ocean views.

Mom Tri's Cooking Class (Map p670; ☎ 0 7633 0015; www.boathousephuket.com; Th Patak West, Kata; 2 classes incl lunch 3200B; ☺ 10am-1pm Sat & Sun) The Boathouse's award-winning executive chef, Tummanoon Punchun, carves a bit of time out of his schedule to teach the basics of Thai cooking. Classes take place just off the Boathouse dining room, so you will cook with a view.

Pum Thai Cooking School (Map p653; ☎ 0 7634 6269; www.pumthaifoodchain.com; 204/32 Tha Rat Uthit, Patong) Runs excellent Thai restaurants in Phuket, Ko Phi-Phi and France. At the Phuket branch you can learn easy haute cuisine the Thai way for 450B for a one-dish class, 900B for a two-dish class and up to 4650B for an over-six-hour, five-dish class.

Tours

The following tours are geared towards 4WD enthusiasts:

Bang Pae Safari (☎ 0 7631 1163; 12/3 Moo 5, Th Srisoonthorn; tours from 800B; ☺ 7.30am-5pm) Based on the outskirts of the Khao Phra Thaew Royal Wildlife & Forest Reserve, this elephant trek, 4WD and canoe outfitter takes guests through the nearby rubber plantations and canals. The tour is fairly soft as far as adventure goes, and is best done in the wet season.

Phuket Paradise 4WD Tour (☎ 0 7628 8501; 24/1 Moo 1, Hwy 4233; tours from 1500B; ☺ 8.30am-6pm) Here's your chance to 4WD on dirt roads through the jungles of Phuket. You can be a passenger or driver, and tours last either one or two hours.

Volunteering

Soi Dog Foundation (☎ 08 7050 8688; www.soidog.org) is a well-organised unit aimed at sterilising and caring for stray dogs. Volunteers are needed for feeding the dogs but it's just as helpful to donate funds towards the projects. Check the website for updates and details.

Starfish Volunteers (☎ 08 1723 1403; www.starfish volunteers.com) runs three volunteer projects in Phuket: child care, dog rescue and gibbon reha-bilitation. Those working with children spend their time at a daycare for kids under the age of five whose parents are below the poverty line. The dog centre has now neutered over 14,000 dogs but there is still much work to be done to safely control the pet population. At the gibbon centre, volunteers work with animals that have been rescued from the tourism industry before they are released into the wild.

Festivals & Events

The **Vegetarian Festival** (www.phuketvegetarian.com) is Phuket's most important event and usually takes place during late September or October. The TAT office (p652) in Phuket Town prints a helpful schedule of Vegetarian Festival events; check out the festival website and see the boxed text on p664 for more info.

UM...DO THOSE WOUNDS HEAL?

Ever seen a picture of Phuket's yearly Vegetarian Festival? If you have, you would definitely remember – daggers piercing cheeks, razorblades cutting tongues – the makings of a child's nightmare. Basically, the festival celebrates the beginning of the month of 'Taoist Lent', when devout Chinese abstain from eating all meat and meat products. In Phuket Town, the festival activities are centred on five Chinese temples, with the Jui Tui temple on Th Ranong the most important.

After the abstention from meat eating, the Vegetarian Festival involves various processions culminating in incredible acts of self-mortification – walking on hot coals, piercing the skin with sharp objects and so on. Shop owners along Phuket Town's central streets set up altars in front of their shopfronts offering nine tiny cups of tea, incense, fruit, candles and flowers to the nine emperor gods invoked by the festival. Those participating as mediums bring the nine deities to earth for the festival by entering into a trance state and piercing their cheeks with a variety of objects – tree branches, spears, slide trombones and so forth. Some even hack their tongues with saw or axe blades...

During the street processions, these mediums stop at the shopfront altars, where they pick up the offered fruit and either add it to the objects piercing their cheeks or pass it on to bystanders as a blessing. They also drink one of the nine cups of tea and grab some flowers to stuff in their waist belts.

The entire atmosphere is one of religious frenzy, with deafening firecrackers, ritual dancing and bloody T-shirts. Oddly enough, there is no record of this kind of activity associated with Taoist Lent in China...

Sleeping

When it comes to sleeping on Phuket, the options are endless and there's something for every wallet size, from swish five-star resorts to orphanage-like dormitories. With over a thousand places to crash, picking your ultimate Phuket crash pad may seem like a tricky process, but it can actually be pretty straightforward.

When choosing your all-important accommodation, you have to start by selecting the location that suits you best. Hat Patong (p667) is the most densely populated resort area. It's got the hottest nightlife, some terrific dining and the beaches are packed all day (300B for a beach chair and umbrella!). Hat Rawai and Hat Nai Han (p671) in the far south are rather quiet and sport loads of local food stalls offering street-side cookin'. Hat Kata (p669) and Hat Karon (p669) tend to cater to Scandinavian package tourists, but it's generally a fun, young crowd. Kata's beaches are particularly gorgeous and there are some terrific boutique hotels in the area.

Reasonably priced Hat Kamala (p666), just north of Patong, is perfect for long-term and self-catering guests. Hat Surin (p666) is undeniably chic. Sprinkled with five-star properties and great beachfront dining, you'd do well to base yourself here if you have the cash. The beach at Ao Bang Thao (opposite) is stunning and the area strikes a funny balance between being an exclusive vacationing paradise and a rural fishing village – it's not uncommon to spot cows grazing on the greens of a golf course.

Further up the coast, the beaches get even better and more secluded. If you're looking for a quiet, shoes-optional retreat, try Hat Nai Thon (opposite), Hat Nai Yang or Hat Mai Khao (opposite). Or you can do as the native Phuketians do and call inland Phuket Town (p671) home.

Once you've decided on a location (and a sense of your budget constraints), you can then start sorting through the myriad lodging options available in the area. Scores of websites and booking pages provide a glut of information on sleeping on Phuket.

While it's always best to book in advance during high season, the island is starting to experience a bit of overdevelopment, which means that last-minute bookings are still often possible. This surplus of hotel rooms has meant a slight drop in prices, but the island is still one of the most expensive vacation destinations in Thailand.

During the slightly quieter low season, haggling over walk-in prices is quite common. Politely push for a discount and if the price is still too high, ask for the room without breakfast; they might knock off an extra 200B.

NORTHERN BEACHES

Lately, Phuket's gorgeous northern beaches are a veritable who's who of world-class resorts. Penny-pinchers fret not, there are still a couple cheapies tucked into the mix.

Hat Nai Yang & Hat Mai Khao

Both Hat Nai Yang and Hat Mai Khao belong to the supremely serene Sirinat National Park (p658). Camping is allowed on both beaches without a permit. See p672 for eating options nearby.

Nai Yang Beach Resort (☎ 0 7632 8300; www.naiyangbeachresort.com; bungalows 1000-7000B; ❄) This resort is clean, quiet and near the beach, and has swimming pools and wi-fi. Cheaper digs are fan-cooled, while higher-priced pads have chic Thai-style decor.

Golddigger's Resort (☎ 08 1892 1178; www.airport-phuket.com; r 1200-1500B; ❄ 🖳 🖳) Despite its unsavoury name, Golddigger's is one of the best midrange options on this beach. The Swiss-run hotel has just 16 rooms, and their decor, spaciousness and choice furniture take them a step above most beachside sleeping spots in this price bracket.

our pick **Indigo Pearl** (☎ 0 7632 7006; www.indigo-pearl.com; r/bungalows 5600-26,000B; ❄ 🖳 🖳) The most unique and hip of Phuket's high-end resorts takes its design cues from the island's tin-mining history – although it sounds weird, this industrial theme fused with tropical luxe creates a spectacularly beautiful and soothing place to stay. Hardware, such as vices, scales and other mining equipment, is used in the decor to the tiniest detail – even the toilet paper rolls are fashioned out of oversized bolts. The Sunday brunch (p672) here is epic.

JW Marriott Phuket Resort & Spa (☎ 0 7633 8000; www.marriott.com; r from 8100B; ❄ 🖳 🖳) Don't let the name discourage you: this Marriott once held the honour of being one of the best hotels in the world, according to *Condé Nast Traveler*. Among the most appreciated assets are mammoth rooms boasting superior sea views, raised open-air pavilions, triangular back cushions, massage mats and polished wood floors. A cooking school and pub with live music round out the deal. A rub-down at the spa is a must.

Hat Nai Thon

Improved roads to Hat Nai Thon have brought only a small amount of development to this broad expanse of pristine sand backed by casuarinas and pandanus trees. Down on the beach, umbrellas and sling chairs are available from vendors. Swimming is quite good here except at the height of the monsoon, and there is some coral near the headlands at either end of the bay. See p672 for eating options in Nai Thon.

Naithon Beach Resort (☎ 0 7620 5379; cottages 1000-1500B; ☯ Nov-May; ❄) This resort has large, tastefully designed wooden cottages. The resort closes in the rainy season. It is on the opposite side of the access road from the beach.

Trisara (☎ 0 7361 0100; www.trisara.com; villas from US$700; ❄ 🖳 🖳) If you can afford to stay here, do so. A tranquil oasis far removed from Patong's chaos, uber-exclusive Trisara's villas take in some of Phuket's most stunning views and are nestled in an idyllic location between the jungle and the cerulean sea. Honeymoon anyone?

Bang Thao

If we were forced to pick our favourite beach, it would probably be Bang Thao – an 8km stunner with flaxen dunes that glisten under the tropical sun. Most of Bang Thao's luxury superstars unite under the corporate Laguna Phuket, which looks exactly like a glitzy California gated community. If you have the bucks, and aren't too fussed about experiencing the local culture, then Laguna is the place for you. See p672 for eating options around Bang Thao.

Sheraton Grande Laguna Phuket (Map p666; ☎ 0 7632 4101; www.starwoodhotels.com; r from 4000B; ❄ 🖳 🖳) A city within a city, the 400-room Sheraton will appeal to families and energetic vacationers. The hotel features loads of watersports, a huge beachfront and a gigantic pool (more like lagoon) – the biggest swimming pool in Asia.

Andaman Bangtao Bay Resort (Map p666; ☎ 0 7627 0246; www.andamanbangtaobayresort.com; bungalows incl breakfast 5000-7000B; ❄ 🖳 🖳) Every bungalow has a sea view and there's a summer-camp vibe at this pleasant little resort. The design is very Thai, with woodcarvings on the walls and coconuts hanging from the eaves of the roofs, but for this price we expected a little more luxury.

our pick **Banyan Tree Phuket** (Map p666; ☎ 0 7632 4374; www.banyantree.com; villas US$550-2500; ❄ 🖳 🖳) One of Asia's finest hotels, and the first on Phuket to introduce bungalows with their

ANDAMAN COAST

own private pool, the Banyan Tree Phuket (in Laguna Phuket) is an oasis of sedate, understated luxury. Accommodation is in rambling villas, the most indulgent being the 'double-pool villas' (aka the ultimate shag pad). A trip to the spa is a must – it's one of the continent's best (see p662). If you have the bling to drop on a place like this, do it now – Banyan Tree books up fast.

Surin

Surin is upmarket but completely unpretentious. A distinctly Thai spirit lingers here along with the lazy, pampered vacationers – which is probably why expats love this area so much. Trees line the pretty shore and dozens of cheap food shacks shelter beneath them. (See p673 for details about eating in and around Surin.) If you're looking for five-star luxury, you've come to the right place.

Capri Beach Resort (Map p666; ☎ 0 7627 0597; r 1500-2900B; ☒) A little temple to Italian kitsch, this welcoming spot offers great home cooking, snug rooms and more Italiana than you can likely stomach. Expect opera, giant pepper grinders and high standards. It's a short hop from the beach.

Surin Bay Inn (Map p666; ☎ 0 7627 1601; www.surin bayinn.com; r 2000B; ☒ ▣) Right next to Capri Beach, this is another welcoming midranger. There's an eatery serving fabulous breakfasts below; clean, spacious rooms above (although a sea view costs a bit extra); and a useful book exchange.

Benyada Lodge (Map p666; ☎ 0 7627 1261; www.benyadalodge-phuket.com; r 2500-5000B; ☒ ▣ ▣) Chic, modern rooms have black louvred closets, terracotta tiles and silk, pastel-coloured throw pillows scattered in the lounging corner. Service is stellar and we loved the high-end details, like ice water service every time you sit anywhere in the lobby.

Twin Palms (Map p666; ☎ 0 7631 6500; www.twin palms-phuket.com; r from 6800B; ☒ ▣ ▣) Twin Palms is the Audrey Hepburn of Phuket's hotels – it's classic yet contemporary, and oozes oodles of class. There's a pervasive feeling of space with minimalist, artsy swimming pools fringed by delicate white frangipani. Even the simplest rooms are extra spacious and have oversized bathrooms, sublimely comfortable beds and a supreme sense of calm.

Chedi (M Map p666; ☎ 0 7632 4017; www.ghmhotels.com; r/bungalows from 17,000B; ☒ ▣) Any hotel located on a private beach this stunning would

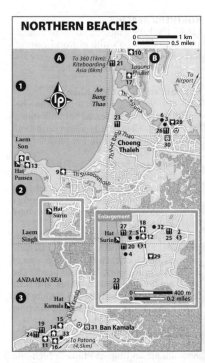

NORTHERN BEACHES

make our top picks list, but Chedi's bungalows, with their naturalistic wooden exteriors that hide within a jungly hillside, further enhance the property's Garden of Eden vibe. You'll have to be in decent shape for walking around the resort, since it can be quite a hoof up hills and over wooden walkways to get to your bungalow.

Amanpuri Resort (Map p666; ☎ 0 7632 4333; www.amanresorts.com; villas US$750-10,000; ☒ ▣ ▣) Phuket's number one celebrity magnet, the Amanpuri offers lashings of glamour and palatial luxury (what else would you expect from the former Shah of Iran's winter palace architect?). With a staggering 3½ staff members assigned to every guest, this is as close most of us will get to royalty. Accommodation is in private villas and you can even book your own private cook.

Kamala

Location, location, location. Sandwiched in between Patong and the tranquil north bays, Hat Kamala is a good spot to call home if you're looking to make naughty and nice. See p673 for eating options in Kamala.

Benjamin Resort (Map p666; ☎ 0 7638 5145; www .phuketdir.com; r incl breakfast 1000-1500B; 😵) With c 1970 construction, but right on the beach, friendly Benjamin is showing its age despite the fresh layers of paint. Rooms all come with TVs and minifridges, and you'll fork over an extra few hundred baht for a view.

Orchid House (Map p666; ☎ 0 7638 5445; treepoppa nat_kwan@yahoo.com; r 1000-1500B; 😵) Orchid House is clean and cutesy with patterned tiles and gussied curtains. Blooming potted plants abound and there's a sweet downstairs bar-cafe. It one-ups Benjamin and is only about 20m further away from the sand.

Kamala Dreams (Map p666; ☎ 0 7629 1131; www .kamala-beach.net; r 2500-3000B; 😵) One giant stride from the sea, Kamala Dreams has sparkling surfaces and spotless (though slightly dowdy) rooms with tiled floors and bleached-white walls. The grounds are small but well kept, and are sprinkled with flowers and statues of praying Buddhas.

Layalina Hotel (Map p666; ☎ 0 7638 5942; www.layalina hotel.com; r incl breakfast 5500-7700B; 😵 💻 🔊) This tiny beachfront boutique hotel earns top marks, especially for the split-level suites with very private rooftop terraces, perfect for romantic sunset gazing. The decor is decisively Thai, with honey-toned wooden furnishings. The only downside is the pool is hilariously small – but that turquoise ocean *is* only steps away.

PATONG

Phuket's Costa del Soul-less is a seething beachside city that crams thousands of hotel rooms between its craggy headlands. Check out p674 for a selection of excellent eats. When sizzling neon lights the sky after the sun has set, the beach's heady party scene fires up; see p677 for entertainment details.

Budget

Budget rooms have pretty much gone the way of the dodo, although if you wander around the soi behind the Jung Ceylon shopping complex, you're bound to find something for less than 1000B.

Crown Backpackers (Map p653; ☎ 0 7634 2297; crown_hostel@yahoo.com; 169/3 Soi Sansabai; female-only dm 250B, r from 500B; 😵) Expect bare-bones basics and late-night rumblings in this hostel in the heart of the Patong war zone…er…we mean bar zone.

Capricorn Village (Map p653; ☎ 0 7634 0390; 2/29 Th Rat Uthit; bungalows from 700B; 😵 🔊) Capricorn is a rare cheapie in Patong's inflated sleeping scene. Bright little bungalows with terraces wind back into a quiet garden. Guests can take a dip in the pool at K's Hotel next door.

Casa Jip (Map p653; ☎ 0 7634 3019; www.casajip.com; 207/10 Th Rat Uthit; r 1000B; 😵) Italian-run and great value, this place has very big, luxurious rooms (for the price bracket) with comfy beds and a taste of Thai style. You get cable TV and there's even a special breakfast room service.

Swarms of low-priced accommodation hovers around Th Nanai. The following are recommended:

Khun Vito Guest House (Map p653; ☎ 0 7629 7061; www.khunvito.com; 74/7 Soi Nanai; s/d from 600/1000B; 😵) Friendly Vito offers a dozen spic-and-span rooms.

Chalermporn (Map p653; ☎ 0 7629 6994; chalerm porn9@hotmail.com; 74/32 Soi Nanai; r 1000B; 😵) Standard-issue rooms are spotless.

ANDAMAN COAST

Midrange

Expat Hotel (Map p653; ☎ 0 7634 0300; expat@loxinfo .co.th; r 890-3000B; ✕) At the end of a bar-packed alley, this popular spot is a hit with unfussy foreigners – there's a communal, buddy-buddy feeling between staff and guests. Monthly rates are available, too.

K's Hotel (Map p653; ☎ 0 7634 0832; www.k-hotel.com; 180 Th Rat Uthit; r from 1500B; ✕ 🖵) Although K's caters mainly to Germans, everyone is made to feel plenty *willkommen*. Beer aficionados will adore the on-site *biergarten*. Upstairs, standard rooms have been gussied up with plasma TVs and stone-tile bathrooms. It's a popular spot for families.

Villa Del Mar (off Map p653; ☎ 0 7634 5698; www .villa-delmar.com; r 1600-2800B, ste 3600-6300B; ✕) Like a weathered Mediterranean ship, Villa Del Mar has a lot of shabby-chic charm but can sometimes feel a bit mildewy.

Yorkshire Inn (Map p653; ☎ 0 7634 0904; www .yorkshireinn.com; 169/16 Soi Saen Sabai; r from 1800B; ✕ 🖵) About as Thai as the Queen Mother, this is one of a string of unabashedly British outfits courting homesick visitors. The Yorkshire offers a flicker of homey B&B charm, and can put together a mean fry-up – the Yorkshire pudding is a little less successful. The rooms are spotless and come with cable TV.

Baipho & Baithong (Map p653; ☎ 0 7629 2074; www .baipho.com; 205/12 & 205/14 Th Rat Uthit; r incl breakfast 1800-3300B; ✕ 🖵) This much style isn't usually found in this price range – particularly since 'chic' isn't really in Patong's vocabulary. Zen trimmings mingle with modern urban touches in the dimly lit, nest-like rooms of these twin hotels. Guests can use the pool at the unsightly Montana Grand Phuket next door.

Baramee Resortel (Map p653; ☎ 0 7634 0010; info@ barameeresortel.com; 266 Th Phra Barami; r 2700-3300B, ste 5700B; ✕) Brand-new Baramee is one of the best midrange deals in Patong. Spacious rooms have crisp white furnishings befitting a chic, top-end resort. Although not located directly on the beach, the hotel has many rooms with ocean views (the others look out onto a parking lot).

Top End

Holiday Inn (Map p653; ☎ 0 7634 0608; www.phuket .holiday-inn.com; Th Rat Uthit; r from 4500B; ✕ 🖵 🎤) What? A Holiday Inn in a Lonely Planet guide? Don't worry – this hotel is way glitzier than those Holiday Inns near your hometown's airport. Beach-resort amenities come standard here, plus there's an upmarket spa to repair your post-Patong battle wounds.

BYD Lofts (Map p653; ☎ 0 7634 3024; www.bydlofts .com; 5/28 Th Hat Patong; apt from 5000B; ✕ 🖵 🎤) Style and comfort reign supreme at BYD, whose urban-chic apartments feature loads of white (floors, walls, curtains), which feels angelic when compared to Patong's seedy street scene.

Baan Yin Dee (off Map p653; ☎ 0 7629 4104; www.baanyindee.com; 7/5 Th Muean Ngen; r from 6000B; ✕ 🖵 🎤) On a hill overlooking town, this is Patong's premier boutique getaway. It's small but perfectly put together: spacious rooms with balconies, magazine-worthy styling and bikini-clad model-wannabes lazing out around the pool. If you're partying all night, come here to repair your soul (plus there's a fabulous restaurant that provides hangover-curing culinary delights).

Le Meridien Phuket (off Map p653; ☎ 0 7634 0480; www.lemeridien.com; r from 8000B; ✕ 🖵 🎤) Close to the Patong chaos, yet secluded on its own private (and spectacular) beach, Le Meridien offers everything that the international globetrotter could ask for, housed in a bright green compound that reeks of the '70s (in the most charming way possible). Tennis courts and swimming pools abound – a great hotel for families. It remains one of Phuket's most popular great escapes.

Avantika (off Map p653; ☎ 0 7629 2802; www .avantika-phuket.com; 4/1 Th Thawiwong; r 8900B; ✕) Down on the quieter south side of Patong, this beach-facing resort is a new player on pricey Phuket, sporting standard-issue high-end hotel accommodation. You'll be satisfied with your stay but you won't be blown away. Prices drop to 3800B in low season – that's when Avantika really shines.

Impiana Phuket Cabana (Map p653; ☎ 0 7634 0138; www.impiana.com; Th Thawiwong; r from 8900B; ✕ 🖵 🎤) …And winner of the 'best beachfront location' award goes to Impiana. This campus of comfy rooms is practically in the heart of the action.

SOUTHERN BEACHES

The beaches south of Patong are not as stunning as their northern counterparts, but there are some good deals to be had along these flaxen strips of sand.

Karon

Stuck between Patong and Kata, Karon draws a bit of its personality from both, and that chilled-out-yet-slightly-sleazy vibe can make the beach feel wonderfully peaceful or depressingly backwater, depending on your attitude. Sleeping cheapies tend to be a bit of a trek from the beach. See p675 for eating options in Karon.

Karon Café (Map p670; ☎ 0 7639 6217; www.karon
-phuket-hotels.com; 526/17 Soi Islandia Park Resort; r 800-1000B; ❄) Way less sexy than its neighbours, Karon Café has clean, no-fuss rooms above a friendly eatery.

Karon Living Room (Map p670; ☎ 0 7628 6618; www.karonlivingroom.com; 481 Th Patak; r incl breakfast 900-2000B; ❄ 💻) Karon Living Room provides sparkling clean rooms with air-con set to cryogenic levels. The rooms don't have oodles of personalised pizazz, but it's a solid pick at the low end of the midrange category. Pricing is sometimes all over the board so contact it ahead of time and ask about discounts.

Casa Brazil (Map p670; ☎ 0 7639 6317; www
.phukethomestay.com; 9 Th Luang Pho Chuan; r 1100-1600B; ❄ 💻) Simple rooms have *Carnivale* styling, which makes this friendly spot a standout operation. There's a whimsically styled and very social cafe on the ground level, and the 20-odd rooms are spacious and tastefully decorated. It's a short walk to both Kata and Karon beaches.

Baan Suay (Map p670; ☎ 08 9594 4633; www
.baansuayphuket.com; 381 Th Patak; r 1300-1900B, ste 3200-4300B; ❄ 💻 🏊) A popular spot with divers, Baan Suay offers comfortable, modern surroundings with a tinge of Thai decor thrown in for good measure. It's not the cheapest place on the block, but the service is excellent and the wading pool is perfect for when the beach gets too crowded. Free wi-fi abounds.

Mövenpick (Map p670; ☎ 0 7639 6139; www.moevenpick-hotels.com; 509 Th Patak West; r from 8000B; ❄ 🏊) Grab a secluded villa and choose from a private plunge pool or outdoor rainforest shower; alternatively, chill in the ultramod rooms with huge floor-to-ceiling windows (in some cases covering two entire walls). Besides a prime location across the street from a pretty stretch of beach, the Mövenpick offers artistic decor, top-end linens, a big pool with swim-up bar and a top-notch spa.

Kata

Kata attracts travellers of all ages with its shopping, surfing and lively beach, and without the seedy hustle endemic to Patong up the coast. While you might not find a secluded strip of sand, you will find plenty to do and plenty of easy-going folks to clink beers with. The area has a large number of Scandinavian expats – you can't go 50m without seeing a cartoon logo of a horned helmet.

The beach is actually split into two distinct sections, separated by a rocky headland: Hat Kata Yai to the north and Hat Kata Noi to the south. Both offer loads of bleach-blond sand and attract chilled-out beach-goers. Like Patong, these beaches are losing their under-1000B accommodation as the entire area gently creeps upmarket.

See p675 for eating options in Kata.

Lucky Guesthouse (Map p670; ☎ 0 7633 0572; lucky
guesthousekata@hotmail.com; 110/44 Moo 4 Th Taina; r 450B) Phuket penny-pinchers usually wind up at Lucky, which offers the basic necessities for beach holidays on a shoestring: a bed and a bathroom. The extra-friendly staff strive to help you to the best of their ability and can offer insider tips about the island.

Kata On Sea (Map p670; ☎ 0 7633 0594; bungalows 450-1000B; ❄) 'On Sea'? Hardly. It's a steep 100m climb to this clutch of modest bungalows dotting a quiet green hilltop, but for the price, it's well worth the effort. Spacious bungalows have massive picture windows that maximise views. Air-con rooms start at 800B.

Sugar Palm Resort (Map p670; ☎ 0 7628 4404; www.sugarpalmphuket.com; 20/10 Th Kata; r 1800-6000B; ❄ 💻 🏊) It's a 'chic, chill-out world' as this Miami-meets-Thailand-style resort claims. Sleek rooms mix beachy whisps of colour with the whites and blacks of an old-school photo. Outside you'll find a U-shaped black-bottomed pool – the perfect spot to shoot an MTV music video.

CC Bloom's (Map p670; ☎ 0 7633 3322; www.ccblooms
hotel.com; 84/21 Th Patak; r 3500-3900B; ❄ 💻 🏊) This American-run gay-friendly boutique hotel (strangely named after Bette Midler's character in the movie *Beaches*) has a fab location overlooking Kata. Stylish rooms are done up in creamy Indochine yellows. If you have a hankerin' for waves (it is a bit of a hike from the beach), a free shuttle makes multiple runs to the beach.

Katathani Resort (Map p670; ☎ 0 7633 0124; www
.katathani.com; 14 Th Kata Noi; r from 7000B; ❄ 🏊)

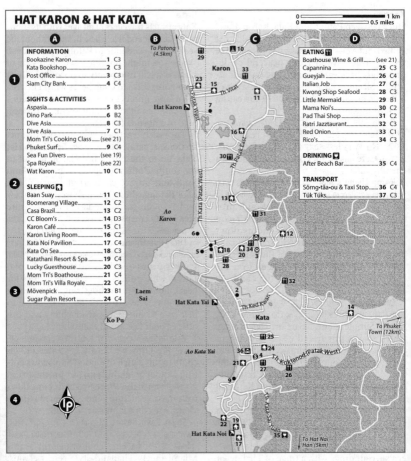

HAT KARON & HAT KATA

INFORMATION		
Bookazine Karon	1	C3
Kata Bookshop	2	C3
Post Office	3	C3
Siam City Bank	4	C4
SIGHTS & ACTIVITIES		
Aspasia	5	B3
Dino Park	6	B2
Dive Asia	8	C3
Dive Asia	7	C1
Mom Tri's Cooking Class	(see 21)	
Phuket Surf	9	C4
Sea Fun Divers	(see 19)	
Spa Royale	(see 22)	
Wat Karon	10	C1
SLEEPING		
Baan Suay	11	C1
Boomerang Village	12	C2
Casa Brazil	13	C2
CC Bloom's	14	D3
Karon Café	15	C1
Karon Living Room	16	C2
Kata Noi Pavilion	17	C4
Kata On Sea	18	C3
Katathani Resort & Spa	19	C4
Lucky Guesthouse	20	C3
Mom Tri's Boathouse	21	C4
Mom Tri's Villa Royale	22	C4
Mövenpick	23	B1
Sugar Palm Resort	24	C4

EATING		
Boathouse Wine & Grill	(see 21)	
Capannina	25	C3
Gueyjah	26	C4
Italian Job	27	C4
Kwong Shop Seafood	28	C3
Little Mermaid	29	B1
Mama Noi's	30	C2
Pad Thai Shop	31	C2
Ratri Jazztaurant	32	C3
Red Onion	33	C1
Rico's	34	C3
DRINKING		
After Beach Bar	35	C4
TRANSPORT		
Sörng•tăa•ou & Taxi Stop	36	C4
Túk Túks	37	C3

Down on quieter Hat Kata Noi, this glitzy spa resort offers all the usual trimmings in stylish surrounds. It features a spa, a handful of pools, a beauty salon and heaps of space. Excellent low-season deals are on offer to top hagglers.

Mom Tri's Boathouse (Map p670; ☎ 0 7633 0015; www.theboathousephuket.com; 2/2 Th Patak West; r 8000-20,000B; ✖ ▢ ☎) For Thai politicos, pop stars, artists and celebrity authors, the intimate boutique Boathouse is still the only place to stay on Phuket. Rooms were remodelled after the tsunami and are spacious affairs sporting large breezy verandahs. Critics complain the Boathouse is a bit stiff-lipped old-fashioned for this century, but no one can deny that the main reason to sleep at the Boathouse is for

the food. The three on-site restaurants are the best on the island.

Mom Tri's Villa Royale (Map p670; ☎ 0 7633 3568; www.villaroyalephuket.com; ste incl breakfast from 10,000B; ✖ ▢ ☎) Tucked away in a secluded Kata Noi location with the grandest of views, Villa Royale opened in 2006 to nearly instant acclaim. The romantic place with fabulous food offers beautiful rooms straight out of the pages of *Architectural Digest*. Guiltless pleasures include an attached spa and a saltwater pool – a tamer version of the real thing, which is just a few steps away.

Also recommended:

Kata Noi Pavilion (Map p670; ☎ 0 7628 4346; www .katanoi-pavilion.com; bungalows 1150-1500B; ✖) Slightly generic, but the rooms are spic and span.

Boomerang Village (Map p670; ☎ 0 7628 4480; www
.phuket-boomerang.com; 9/11 Soi 10 Th Patak; r from
2000B; 🅿 🖳 🏊) An immensely popular spot strung up
the side of a hill overlooking Kata (750m from the beach).

Nai Han & Rawai

Rawai was one of Phuket's first tourist developments, but this was mostly due to the
fact that it was close to Phuket Town. As
better beaches were discovered, tourist traffic in Rawai dwindled, and today it's a quiet
spot. Tourists often chat about visiting the
chow lair village here – it's worth giving it
a miss, unless you're a fan of barking dogs
and old car parts (most of the sea gypsies
have moved).

Nai Han, on the other hand, is cloistered
from the tourist frenzy, and hosts a beach
full of local snack shacks. Except for the
yacht club, there's not much accommodation
with views of the beach. For eating options
around Nai Han and Rawai, see p676.

For something a bit quieter, grab a long-
tail boat to nearby Ko Heh and stay at the
secluded **Coral Island** (☎ 0 7628 1060; www.coralis
landresort.com; bungalows from 2000B; 🅿 🏊). A lot of
snorkelling day trippers visit the island, but
after sunset it's absolutely serene.

Nai Harn Garden Resort (☎ 0 7628 8319; www
.naiharngardenresort.com; 15/12 Moo 1, Th Viset; r 2000-
8000B; 🅿 🖳 🏊) Back from the beach, on
the far side of the reservoir, this resort offers
a range of bungalows and villas in a spacious garden setting. The atmosphere is a
little suburban cul-de-sac, but standards are
high, there are plenty of masseuses at hand –
massage is something of a hotel speciality –
and prices are fairly reasonable.

Sabana (☎ 0 7628 9327; www.sabana-resort.com; 14/53
Moo 1, Th Viset; r 3500-8000B; 🅿 🖳 🏊) Right on
the yacht club's doorstep, Sabana is a less-
expensive stunt double. The decor is all primary colours and Thai motifs, and while the
cheaper rooms are a little ordinary, the pricier
'Thai Sala' options are beautifully designed.
There's also an on-site spa.

Royal Phuket Yacht Club (☎ 0 7638 0200; www
.phuket.com/yacht-club; 23/3 Moo 1, Th Viset; r from 7500B;
🅿 🖳 🏊) When the Le Meridien brand
decided to let this property go, the owners
changed the 'le' to a 'the' and kept on goin'.
There's not a yacht in sight, but the resort does
feel grand in a country club kinda way. If you
can cadge one of the low-season discounts, it
really is excellent value.

Evason Phuket Resort (☎ 0 7638 1010; www.sixsenses
.com; 100 Th Viset; r 7500-38,000B; 🅿 🖳 🏊) This spa
hotel extraordinaire offers copious amounts of
luxury. Hip and heavily designed, it is the type
of place that appeals to rock stars and moneyed
media types. Expect beautiful people tapping
away at their wireless gadgetry beside the infinity pool, and immaculately turned-out staff.
Room prices – opulent villas top the billing –
stretch from pricey to impossibly expensive.

PHUKET TOWN

Phuket Town has a healthy assortment of
budget-friendly lodging options. Although
you're nowhere near the beach, foodies will
adore the small bundle of kick-ass restaurants
(p676) tucked between the town's vibrant architectural remains of its multicultural past.
Get the low-down on Phuket Town's attractions on p652.

On On Hotel (Map p656; ☎ 0 7621 1154; 19 Th Phang-
Nga; r from 200B; 🅿) This bare-bones classic
snapped up a cameo in *The Beach* (2000),
playing a shitty backpacker dive. It's been a full
decade since Leo's sandy foray, and the travellers are still comin' to experience the droopy
beds, creaking fans and hole-for-a-toilet bathrooms. Smell that? Yup, that's the gritty stink
of Thailand's original shoestringer spirit.

Phuket International Youth Hostel (off Map p656;
☎ 0 7628 1325; www.phukethostel.com; 73/11 Th Chao Fa,
Ao Chalong; dm 250B, r from 600B; 🅿) As a bona fide
Hostelling International outfit, this contemporary spot offers comfy sleeps in typically
sterile surrounds. 'Reliable' is the buzzword
here, and while you won't be dazzled by
charming decor, you will sleep safe knowing
that you're not being stalked by bed bugs. It
is 7km south of Phuket Town.

Talang Guest House (Map p656; ☎ 0 7621 4225; ta-
langgh@phuket.ksc.co.th; 37 Th Thalang; r 250-420B; 🅿)
This decrepit shophouse is something of an
architectural classic. Creature comforts are
at a premium, but it bags extra points for
character and charm. If you really want to
soak up the atmosphere, check in to the 3rd-
floor room overlooking the street. It's a fan
room with a large verandah and is ideal for
nostalgia junkies.

Crystal Inn (Map p656; ☎ 0 7625 6789; www.phuket
crystalinn.com; 2/1-10 Soi Surin, Th Phuket; r from 1000B;
🅿 🖳) It may not age well, but for now this
is a slick midrange option. With its attractive
Rothko-esque murals, it's a stylish alternative
to the midrange dreck nearby.

Sino House (Map p656; ☎ 0 7622 1398; www.sino housephuket.com; 1 Th Montri; r 2000-2500B; 🔀 🖵) Like a swank Shanghai bordello (in a good way…), Sino House's rooms are massive and dimly lit, and the attached bathrooms feature handmade ceramic basins and quarter-moon-shaped tubs. Staff members are friendly and speak excellent English.

Metropole Phuket (Map p656; ☎ 0 7621 5050; www .metropolephuket.com; 1 Soi Surin, Th Montri; r from 3000B; 🔀 🖵) The Metropole fancies itself as the big cheese; however, it feels a bit more like the big cheesy. The seahorse fountain is a little kitsch and the rooms are a tad frumpy (think matching drapes and duvets – all floral prints). It's a decent choice if you need to be in central Phuket Town, and the top-floor views are pretty darn cool.

Eating & Drinking

Choosing a restaurant on Phuket can be a mind-numbing task. At the top of the totem pole is the island's much-lauded haute cuisine – designer eats created by a legion of world-class chefs. Patong (p674) has a slew of dining all-stars, as do the high-end resorts in Bang Thao (right) and Surin (opposite) to the north.

The swarms of Thai seafood restaurants are a must. You'll find at least one on every beach (although avoid the overpriced schlock in Patong and Karon) serving fresh crab, fish and prawns plucked directly from the sea. You can often choose your platter as it swims around a tank.

And then there's the street food. You can find it in night markets, in dark sweaty soi and in steamy sand-covered shacks along the beach. Turn off that inner monologue and go for the gusto without fearing the gastro. Muslim fried chicken and Isan's *sôm dam* (spicy papaya salad) are usually safe and delicious bets, although why not go for the eyeball soup that you've been staring at (and that's been looking back at you).

Many of Phuket's sit-down restaurants tread a fine line between restaurant and bar. It's not uncommon to find a gang of tourists grabbing beers beside a family gorging on wholesome platters of *pàt tai* noodles. If you're looking to crank things up a notch and get down with your dirt-ay self, check out p677 for the island's top nightclubs and dance-oriented bars.

TOP FIVE SPOTS FOR A SUNDOWNER COCKTAIL

Ask any local expat: sipping sundowner cocktails is an official sport on Phuket. Any west-facing joint will do the trick, but after some serious field research, we've found five seriously special spots to enjoy that 6pm snifter:

- **Rockfish** (opposite)
- **White Box** (p674)
- **After Beach Bar** (p676)
- **Watermark** (p677)
- **360** (opposite)

NORTHERN BEACHES

If you're staying along Phuket's northern beaches, there are dozens of excellent eating options within arm's reach.

Hat Nai Yang, Hat Mai Khao & Hat Nai Thon

Chao Lay Bistro (☎ 0 7620 5500; 9 Moo 4, Tambon Sakhu; dishes from 100B; ☺ noon-10.30pm) Tasty Thai food in a hip, open-air dining room. Try the *pá·nang tá·lair*, prawns or squid in red curry with lime leaves and coconut milk.

our pick Indigo Pearl (☎ 0 7632 7006; brunch 1300-1600B; ☺ breakfast, lunch & dinner) On Sunday, do not pass Go, do not collect $200 (you won't need to – the bill will be way less); head directly to Indigo Pearl for the ultimate in weekend brunching. Every delicious dish imaginable – sushi, foie gras, roast lamb, green curry, crab legs, fried chicken, pasta, fondue, chocolate cake, ice cream – is at your disposal in the culinary labyrinth that leads to your martini-covered table. This will be a meal you won't soon forget.

Bang Thao

Despite what some local hoteliers would have you believe, there is good food to be had outside the confines of Bang Thao's luxury hotels.

Lotus Restaurant (Map p666; dishes 50-120B; ☺ lunch & dinner) An open-walled eatery 500m west of the entrance to Banyan Tree Phuket, this is the first in a row of beachside Thai and seafood restaurants that stretches to the south. It's clean, breezy and friendly, and has an amazing assortment of live crab, lobster, shrimp, fish and other visual and culinary delights in well-tended tanks.

Tawai (Map p666; ☎ 0 7632 5381; Moo 1, Laguna Phuket entrance; dishes from 150B; ☽ dinner) Set in a lovely old house decorated with traditional art is this gem of a Thai kitchen serving classics like roast duck curry and pork *larb* (minced pork salad mixed with chilli, mint and coriander), and steamed, grilled and fried seafood.

Rain-Hail (Map p666; ☎ 08 1979 1967; 21 Moo 2, Choeng Thaleh; dishes from 180B; ☽ 11.30am-2am) Modernists will appreciate the black-bottom fountain in the entry, which juxtaposes a white marble and limestone dining room on one side and a classic mod lounge on the other. The cuisine is all Pacific Rim, with a *tamago* roll of miso, mango and crab, and a lovely bluefin tuna tartare.

Tatonka (Map p666; ☎ 0 7632 4349; Th Srisoonthorn; dishes 250-350B; ☽ dinner Thu-Tue) This is the home of 'globetrotter cuisine', which owner-chef Harold Schwarz developed by taking fresh local products and combining them with techniques learned in Europe, Colorado and Hawaii. The eclectic, tapas-style selection includes creative vegetarian and seafood dishes like Peking duck pizza (230B). There's also a tasting menu (per person 750B, minimum two people) which lets you nibble a little of everything. Call ahead in the high season. Tatonka arranges free transportation for guests of the resort complex.

our pick Tre (Map p666; ☎ 0 7632 4374; dishes 550-3000B; ☽ dinner) This French–Vietnamese fusion masterpiece is located on a silent lagoon in the heart of Laguna's Banyan Tree Resort (p665). Savour perfected recipes for succulent steaks and lobster while the strum of a lyre idles nearby. You'll need a torch (provided, of course) to read your menu after the sun has set, and as the scenery fades to black, Thai canvas hot-air balloons and glittery stars accent the sky. If you're feting any special occasion while visiting Phuket, have your celebratory dinner here.

360 (off Map p666; ☎ 0 7631 7600; Phuket Pavilions Resort) This open-air patio, covered with giant rattan lounge chairs, sits high above the gnarled jungle trees. The lychee Bellini goes down real easy while admiring the 360-degree views as the sun sets over the manicured Laguna grounds.

English Pub (Map p666; ☎ 0 8987 21398; Th Srisoonthorn) Aka 'The Whispering Cock', this timber-and-thatch watering hole is the most authentic English pub on the island – even

the toilets smell. It has a sunny beer garden, a snug interior, a good range of beers and some decent pub grub.

Surin

Patacharin (Map p666; ☎ 08 1892 8587; dishes from 60B; ☽ lunch & dinner) This local fish grill is built into the headland at the southernmost end of Hat Surin. Other fish grills and cafes unfurl north of here like a strand of delicious pearls.

La Plage (Map p666; ☎ 08 1184 7719; dishes from 150B; ☽ 11am-10pm) When two Paris-raised Laotian polyglots (what?) open a fusion restaurant on the sand, you have to swing by to see what it's all about. It serves a fine nicoise salad and a savoury green curry with a kick.

Silk (Map p666; ☎ 0 7627 1705; Hwy 4025; dishes from 200B; ☽ 11am-11pm) This expansive, stylish place is one of several upmarket restaurants in Surin Plaza, and an expat magnet. The decor is a hip cocktail of burgundy paint, wood and exotic flowers, while the menu focuses on beautifully executed Thai specialities.

Catch (Map p666; ☎ 0 7631 6500; dishes from 250B; ☽ 11am-11pm) Slip on your spaghetti-strapped dress or a linen suit to blend in at this cabana-style eatery right on the beach. It's part of Twin Palms (p666), and has the same classy attributes as the hotel both in ambience and cuisine. The attached lounge-bar attracts an excellent assortment of live acts.

Liquid Lounge (Map p666; ☎ 08 1537 2018; ☽ 4pm-1am) A stylish, loft-style martini lounge with premium liquor, occasional live jazz and wi-fi.

Kamala

Basilico (Map p666; ☎ 0 7638 5856; 125 Moo 3, Th Hat Kamala; dishes from 180B; ☽ dinner) Another member of Phuket's ever-growing legion of tasty Italian restaurants. Basilico has good wood-fired pizza, but try the grilled tiger prawns in a parsley and garlic marinade, served on a chickpea and rosemary mash.

our pick Rockfish (Map p666; ☎ 0 7627 9732; 33/6 Th Hat Kamala; dishes from 240B; ☽ dinner) Kamala's best dining room, a rumoured favourite of pop diva Mariah Carey, is perched above bobbing long-tails offering diners excellent beach, bay and mountain views. Its eclectic brand of fusion won it Phuket's Restaurant of the Year in 2005, and it's still rolling out gems like fried red crab or seafood wontons wrapped in a rice crêpe with apple, guava and cinnamon compote.

PATONG

Patong comes up trumps in the gastronomy category, offering the island's widest selection of memorable feasts. We've separated the following listings into two separate categories: restaurants and bars, although many of Patong's establishment exist somewhere in between. See p677 for a list of dance-prone joints and nightclubs.

Restaurants

From street shacks to seven-course dinners, Patong's colourful gamut of eats features all-star options for every taste and wallet. For delicious seafood, try the local market on Th Nanai called Meh U-Bon.

our pick Fried Chicken (Map p653; 63/5 Th Phra Barami; dishes from 45B; 10am-7pm) The name on the sign, though it is written in Thai script, doesn't lie. Three huge fryers are bubbling and splattering with juicy, crispy 'yard bird'. It's Muslim owned, so Halal doctrine dictates that this joint is clean. The chicken is served with a tangy hot sauce and sticky rice. It's impossible to overstate this. If you like fried chicken (all non-veggies raise your hand), this place is a must.

Jung Ceylon Shopping Complex (Map p653; Th Rat Uthit; dishes 60-160B; lunch & dinner) When the sweltering beach heat becomes too much to handle, head to air-conditioned paradise in Jung Ceylon for tasty standards.

Ali Baba (Map p653; 0 7634 5024; 38 Th Ruamchai; dishes from 70B; lunch & dinner) A favourite with Patong's resident Indians, Ali Baba serves up delicious subcontinental specialities (the island's best) to diners swathed in hookah smoke.

Takumi (Map p653; 0 7634 1654; Th Thawiwong; dishes from 160B; lunch & dinner) This fantastic find, with a blubbery Sumo mascot, specialises in *yakiniku* (Japanese barbecue). You'll sit around granite tables embedded with hibachi broilers and self-cook crab, prawns, eel, squid and tenderloin sliced paper-thin. Wash it down with one of the many varieties of cold sake. It has a sushi menu, but broiling is its thing, so stick to what it does best.

3 Spices (Map p653; 0 7634 2100; Impiana Phuket Cabana; dishes 175-600B; lunch & dinner) Welcome to well-dressed Asian fusion on the Patong strip. Enjoy miso and crab-meat soup and wok-fried snapper with coconut curry among other stellar dishes.

Hung Fat's (Map p653; 0 7629 0313; 314 Th Phra Barami; dishes 200-380B; 6.30pm-midnight Tue-Sun) The newest offering from those behind the adjacent Baan Rim Pa restaurant group serves dim sum and southern Szechuan Chinese cuisine garnished with live jazz. Brand new at the time of research, this spot was generating a ton of buzz.

Baan Rim Pa (Map p653; 0 7634 4079; dishes 215-475B; lunch & dinner) Soft piano music sets the mood for a romantic evening at this restaurant built high above a thicket of mangrove trees. It offers stunning ocean-view tables and specialises in Thai cuisine that's only slightly toned down for foreign palates. Book ahead, and consider ironing your shirt.

Floyd's Brasserie (Map p653; 0 7637 0000; 18/110 Th Ruamchai; dishes 220-410B; dinner) Keith Floyd, one of England's favourite celebrity chefs, is the man behind the Burasari resort's popular restaurant. If duck breast braised in champagne, eggs poached in red wine and Phuket lobster thermidor gets you salivating, then this is your place.

our pick White Box (Map p653; 0 7634 6271; 247/5 Th Phra Barami; dishes 280-480B; lunch & dinner) Who cares if the food at White Box is good or not (although if you are wondering, it is delish); dining at this high-energy supper club is like spending an evening on the starship *Enterprise*. This chic realm is housed in, quite literally, a white box, which teeters on the rocky shoreline.

Ninth Floor (Map p653; 0 7634 4311;; 47 Th Rat Uthit; dishes from 300B; dinner) To get some perspective on just how massive Patong has become, come on up to the 9th floor of the Sky Inn Condotel building, where you can watch the sea of lights through sliding-floor-to-ceiling glass doors. This rising star of Phuket's dining scene is the highest open-air restaurant on the island, but its perfectly prepared steaks and chops are what make it a Patong institution.

Bars

Despite Patong's reputation, not all of the area's bars are of the gogo-girl variety.

Port (Map p653; Th Thawiwong, Baan Thai Resort) An outdoor bar smack in the heart of the action, the Port features glowing blue-and-green lounge chairs that match the designer cocktails and pulsates all evening long. Complimentary bar snacks are served throughout the night.

Two Black Sheep (Map p653; 08 9872 2645; 172 Th Rat Uthit) Owned by a fun Aussie couple, this old-school pub is a great find. It has good grub and live music nightly. From 8pm to 10pm there's an acoustic set, then Chilli Jam, the house band, gets up and rocks till last call. Towards the wee hours local musicians, fresh off their gigs, filter in and spontaneous jams ensue. And bar girls are banned, which keeps everything rated PG.

Molly Malone's (Map p653; ☎ 0 7629 2771; Th Thawiwong) Wildly popular with tourists, this pub rocks with Irish gigs every night at 9.45pm. There's a good atmosphere, great pub food and some excellent outdoor tables perfect for people-watching. Guinness is available for a mere 349B per pint.

Scruffy Murphy's (Map p653; ☎ 0 7629 2590; 5 Th Bangla) A Molly Malone's facsimile, Scruffy's offers live acts and sports on the big screen. If you're keen to escape the girly-bar scene, this is one of the better bets.

JP's (Map p653; ☎ 0 7634 3024; 5/28 Th Rat Uthit) This hipster indoor-outdoor lounge at BYD Lofts (p668) definitely brings a touch of style and panache to Patong. There's a low-slung bar, outdoor sofa booths, happy hours (with free tapas) from 10pm and weekly DJ parties.

SOUTHERN BEACHES

From Karon to Rawai, each beach caters to all budget types with heaps of hidden Thai gems and tons of expat-owned joints.

Karon

When compared to Patong or Kata next door, Karon loses the culinary contest. As usual, almost every place to stay has a restaurant but you'll have to look hard to find memorable eats.

Pad Thai Shop (Map p670; Th Patak East; noodles from 40B; lunch) On the busy main road behind Karon, just north of the tacky Ping Pong Bar, is this glorified food stand that spills from the owners' home onto a dirt lot. It's only open for lunch, when you can find chicken-feet stew, beef-bone soup and the best *pàt tai* on earth. Spicy and sweet, packed with prawns, tofu, egg and peanuts, and wrapped in a fresh banana leaf – you'll be back for seconds, we promise.

Mama Noi's (Map p670; ☎ 0 7628 6272; Karon Plaza, 291/1-2 Moo 3, Th Patak East; dishes 50-190B; breakfast, lunch & dinner) Repeat visitors adore this place, which churns out fantastic Thai and Italian pasta dishes. It does a superb *gaeng som* (southern Thai curry with fish and prawns),

bakes its own baguettes every morning and has the best banana shake on the island.

Red Onion (Map p670; ☎ 0 7639 6827; dishes 80-160B; 4-11pm) High on tasty food, low on atmosphere, this slap-shut eatery, housed in a garage, is a bona fide expat magnet. Cocktail selections complement the international meals – or an extra one to blur the bad music humming in the background. It's about 300m east of the roundabout – look for the coloured lights.

Little Mermaid (Map p670; ☎ 0 7639 6580; 643 Th Patak East; dishes 80-300B; breakfast, lunch & dinner) The UN of speedy grub, Little Mermaid features menus in six languages, free wi-fi, hearty Western breakfasts and evening barbecues – you're likely to have at least one meal here if you're sleeping in Karon. There are lamb chops on Monday, ribs on Wednesday and Phuket lobster on Saturday night.

Kata

Although nearby Karon is a culinary snooze-fest, Kata cooks up several decent places to tempt the taste buds. All of the following options are a safe bet for satisfaction.

Kwong Shop Seafood (Map p670; ☎ 08 1273 3707; Th Thai Na; dishes 40-130B; lunch & dinner) Kwong, the friendly owner, utters a big 'OK!' when you order (we're pretty sure it's the only English word he knows), and minutes later out comes tasty Thai treats. Although small on atmosphere, this humble joint is big on smiles.

Gueyjah (Map p670; dishes from 40B; lunch & dinner) Tucked away on a side road off Rte 4028, Gueyjah is tops for quick and cheap Thai eats, and it's known only to locals.

Italian Job (Map p670; 179/1 Th Koktanod; dishes from 75B; 7am-9pm) Though Charlize Theron is nowhere to be found, this hip coffee lounge has wi-fi, decent pastries, delicious Italian espresso and a loyal morning following.

Rico's (Map p670; Th Thai Na; dishes 120-350B; lunch & dinner) The smartest kid on this block features fine New Zealand steaks, pizzas and a huge collection of black-and-white film star snaps (very 1980s).

Ratri Jazztaurant (Map p670; ☎ 0 7633 3538; Th Chalong-Karon; dishes from 140B; lunch & dinner) If you like jazz, you should wind your way up to this hillside terrace to listen to local and international acts blow like they mean it. It's especially sweet at sunset, and the food comes highly recommended as well.

Capannina (Map p670; dishes 150-350B; ☽ lunch & dinner) The chefs at this hip, open-air bistro with moulded concrete booths and imported olive oil on the tables start prepping early in the day. Everything here – from the pasta dishes to the sauces – is made fresh. It gets crowded during the high season, so you may want to book ahead.

our pick **Boathouse Wine & Grill** (Map p670; ☎ 0 7633 0015; Th Patak West; dishes 450-850B; ☽ lunch & dinner) The perfect place to wow a fussy date, the Boathouse has been the critic's champion for some time. The Mediterranean fusion food is fabulous (think vodka-marinated lobster and foie gras with black-truffle oil), the wine list is endless and the sea views are sublime. It's a fancy place – this is the closest Phuket gets to old-school dining – so put away that Hawaiian-print shirt!

our pick **After Beach Bar** (Map p670; ☎ 08 1894 3750; Hwy 4233; ☽ 11am-midnight) It's difficult – make that impossible – to overstate how glorious the view is from this stilted, thatched patio bar hanging off a cliff above Kata. Now turn on the Bob Marley and you've got the best reggae bar on Phuket. The menu is packed with Thai faves, and at sunset the sky performs a light show – when the fireball finally drops, lights from the distant fishing boats blanket the horizon.

Nai Han & Rawai

Besides the restaurants attached to the resorts in Rawai, there are oodles of seafood and noodle vendors along the roadside near Hat Rawai. The following listings are sit-down restaurants.

Rawai Seafood (Hat Rawai; dishes 60-340B) Located next to the local municipal building at the west end of the beach, this haphazard assortment of benches and tables is the top spot for fresh seafood in Rawai. Try the local Phuketian dishes, like bean-curd soup and steamed kale.

Freedom Pub (☎ 0 7628 7402; Hat Rawai; dishes 80-200B; ☽ lunch & dinner) More watering hole than eatery, this Rawai boozer features outdoor seating, a pool table, live music on the weekends, a free barbecue on Friday night and – strangely – an on-site tattoo parlour.

Don's Mall & Cafe (☎ 0 7638 3100; 48-5 Soi Sai Yuan; dishes 100-650B) This Texan-run food-and-entertainment complex showcases hearty American meat feast barbecued over a mesquite-wood fire. It also has an extensive wine list and freshly baked goods. It's about 3km from the beach in Rawai.

Los Amigos (☎ 08 9472 9128; Nai Han; dishes 130-230B) This is as close to real Tex-Mex as you're going to get in Thailand. Orders available for takeaway as well.

Rum Jungle (☎ 0 7638 8153; 69/8 Th Sai Yuan; dishes from 180B; ☽ 5-11pm Mon-Sat) The thatched dining room is patrolled by a fun Thai crew who effortlessly make you feel at home. Oh, and the food is dynamite too. Who knew penne and meatballs or fish and chips could be this fine? The Argentinean tenderloin is also divine, and so is the world-beat soundtrack.

PHUKET TOWN

Meals in Phuket Town cost a lot less than those at the beach – as much as 50% less. Southeast of the centre, on Th Ong Sim Phai, is the town's municipal market where you can buy fresh fruit and vegetables.

our pick **Uptown Restaurant** (Map p656; ☎ 0 7621 5359; Th Tilok Uthit; dishes 30-60B; ☽ 10am-9pm) It may not look fancy, but this breezy joint is a favourite spot for the 'hi-so' (high society) folk. If you look closely you'll notice that the waitresses jot down your order on a slick PalmPilot, and the walls have mounted photos of Thai celebrities who have stopped by Uptown to slurp the spectacular noodles.

Natural Restaurant (Map p656; ☎ 0 7622 4287; 62/5 Soi Phuthon; dishes 80-200B; ☽ lunch & dinner) Travel round the world in 80 plates at this dazzlingly green Phuket Town eatery. If you're a fan of the Swiss Family Robinson, this treehouse-cum-restaurant will become your new favourite joint.

Salavatore's (Map p656; ☎ 08 9871 1184; 15 Th Rasada; dishes 140-620B; ☽ lunch & dinner Tue-Sun) This authentic Italian restaurant (chequered tablecloths, giant pepper grinders, opera and a portly owner) cooks up all of Mama's favourites, from a mean pizza to a sizzling steak fillet.

our pick **Ka Jok See** (Map p656; ☎ 0 7621 7903; kajoksee@hotmail.com; 26 Th Takua Pa; dishes 180-480B; ☽ dinner Tue-Sun) Dripping old Phuket charm and creaking under the weight of the owner's fabulous trinket collection, this atmospheric little eatery offers great food, top-notch music and – if you're lucky – some sensationally camp cabaret. Enjoy your dinner, sip down some wine and then dance the night away. Book ahead.

Glastnöst (Map p656; ☎ 08 4058 0288; 14 Soi Rommani) With the unusual moniker 'Law & Notary Public Bar', this place doubles as an attorney's office, but don't let that dissuade you from stopping by. It's about as laid-back and intimate a setting as you could find, and spontaneous jazz jam sessions are the norm.

EAST COAST

Often overlooked by tourists, Phuket's east coast has a few must-eat gems.

Kachang Floating Restaurant (dishes 90-320B; ☒ lunch & dinner) Set adrift in Ao Phuket, rickety Kachang is only a few minutes east of Phuket Town, but it's far off the beaten tourist trail. Free long-tail boats shuttle grumbling bellies to the floating restaurant surrounded by schools of corralled fish. Enjoy soft-shell crab in the waning light as the sun dips behind the hills.

Chalong Night Market (Hwy 402 near Chalong Circle; dishes from 35B; ☒ 6-11pm Wed) One of the most popular night markets on the island, where vendors, farmers and local chefs converge under the gas lamps. Bring an appetite – that pumpkin curry looks good – and a shopping bag, as it's always nice to have a mango in the morning.

Kan Eang (☎ 0 7638 1212; Chalong Pier; dishes 100-300B; ☒ lunch & dinner) This Thai favourite, steps away from Chalong's soaring pier, has been satisfying customers for over 30 years. The atmosphere is modern and elegant, but the food is still very authentic.

Watermark (☎ 0 7623 9730; 22/1 Th Thepkrassartri, Phuket Boat Lagoon) Although it's located at the Phuket Boat Lagoon marina on the east coast, Watermark is one of the best spots on the island for a sundowner cocktail (see the boxed text on p672 for other suggestions). The espresso martini and passionfruit margarita are the house specials, although the tome-sized wine list is also very tempting. This chic venue is the island's preferred address for jet-setters and, for the last six years it has been featured in the *Thailand Tatler* as one of the country's best restaurants.

Entertainment

This is no sleepy jungle island lost at sea; Phuket keeps the party going long after the sun has set.

NORTHERN BEACHES

Phuket Fantasea (Map p666; ☎ 0 7638 5000; www .phuket-fantasea.com; admission with/without dinner 1900/1500B; ☒ 5.30-11.30pm Wed-Mon) The island's biggest entertainment attraction is a US$60 million 'cultural theme park' just north of Hat Kamala. Despite the billing, there aren't any rides, but there is a truly magical show that manages to capture the colour and pageantry of traditional Thai dance and costumes, and combine them with state-of-the-art light-and-sound techniques rivalling anything found in Las Vegas (think 30 elephants). All of this takes place on a stage dominated by a full-scale replica of a Khmer temple reminiscent of Angkor Wat. Kids especially will be captivated by the spectacle; adults may find it a tad cheesy. There is a good collection of souvenir shops in the park offering Thai handicrafts. The Thai buffet dinner has a bad reputation amongst tourists, so consider taking in the show sans meals. Tickets can be booked through most hotels and tour agencies.

If you're looking to mix things up a bit (and are too lazy to head down to Patong), try **Jackie O** (Map p666; ☎ 08 9474 0431; ☒ 6pm-1am) at the entrance of Laguna Phuket, which serves up live rock acts three nights a week, or swig a martini at **Liquid Lounge** (Map p666; ☎ 08 1537 2018; ☒ 4pm-1am), Surin's resident jazz lounge.

PATONG

A walk around Patong at night is an entertaining experience in itself. Th Bangla is the centre of the action, with loud techno music blaring out of exhausted sound systems while go-go girls shake it till they make it (and ladyboys fake it till they make it) on beer-slicked tabletops. Thai boxing matches and ladyboy cabarets draw in a lot of tourists. To learn more about ladyboys, see the boxed text on p654.

Club Lime (Map p653; ☎ 08 5798 1850; www.clublime .info; ☒ 10pm-2am) A new hot spot gaining steam, this place attracts the beautiful people and a rotating roster of Thai and international DJs.

La Salsa (Map p653; ☎ 0 7634 0138; admission 500B; ☒ 10pm-4am) Located beside the Impiana Resort, this is another of Patong's hot spots. Take a break from the dance floor and try the designer cocktails and tapas treats.

Seduction (Map p653; 39/1 Th Bangla; admission 500B; ☒ 10pm-4am) Patong's newest and most popular dance hall comes courtesy of a Finnish club impresario. Known for buying up the best clubs in Helsinki, he opened this one in 2006 and has since attracted international party people dancing to well-known global DJs.

Rock City (Map p653; Th Kalim Beach Rd) The giant guitar out front makes it look like a Hard Rock wannabe; the inside is far less wholesome. This dark den keeps the faded glory of old rock groups alive.

Phuket Simon Cabaret (off Map p653; ☎ 0 7634 2011; www.phuket-simoncabaret.com; admission 550B) About 300m south of town on Th Sirirach, this cabaret offers entertaining transvestite shows. The 600-seat theatre is grand, the costumes are gorgeous and the ladyboys are convincing. It's often a full house. Performances are at 7.30pm and 9.30pm nightly – book ahead.

Sphinx Theatre (Map p653; ☎ 0 7634 1500; 120 Th Rat Uthit; admission 350B) There's more cabaret on offer at the Sphinx, where shows kick off at 9pm and 10.30pm nightly.

Bangla Boxing Stadium (Map p653; ☎ 0 7275 6364; Th Bangla; admission 1000B) Boxing bouts are held nightly at 8pm.

Train Thai Boxing (Map p653; ☎ 0 7629 2890; Soi Kepsap; ☽ 8am-9pm) Watch a riveting round of boxing battling or learn a few moves of your own at Train Thai Boxing, where a 90-minute lesson costs 300B and a blow to your ego (and ribcage).

PHUKET TOWN
Head to skinny soi Rommani for a good mix of the town's top chill-out spots.

Paradise Cinemas (Map p656; ☎ 0 7622 0174; Th Tilok Uthit; tickets 80B) For those addicted to celluloid, Paradise plays English-language blockbusters.

Boxing Stadium (Map p656; tickets 500-1000B) Thai boxing can be seen Tuesday and Friday nights at 8pm. Ticket prices vary depending on where you sit and include one-way transport. The stadium is at the southern edge of town near the pier; a túk-túk (pronounced đúk đúk; motorised transport) costs 70B. Get your tickets at the On On Hotel (p671).

Getting There & Away
AIR
Phuket International Airport is situated at the northwest end of the island, 30km from Phuket Town. It takes around 45 minutes to an hour to reach the southern beaches from here, and you could wait over an hour for the mythic metered taxis, which supposedly exist but are quite rare. The best bet is to hire a private car; alternatively, pay 120B and hop

in a minivan destined for Phuket's Old Town, or 180B if you're headed to Patong, Karon or Kata. The minivans only leave when they have 10 passengers, so you may have to wait.

Thai Airways International (THAI; Map p656; ☎ 0 7621 1195; www.thaiairways.com; 78/1 Th Ranong, Phuket Town) operates about a dozen daily flights to Bangkok (one way from 2800B); it also has regular flights to/from 11 other cities in Thailand and international destinations including Penang, Langkawi, Kuala Lumpur, Singapore, Hong Kong, Taipei and Tokyo.

Bangkok Airways (Map p656; ☎ 0 7622 5033; www .bangkokair.com; 58/2-3 Th Yaowarat, Phuket Town) has daily flights to Ko Samui (one way 2600B), Bangkok (one way 2800B) and Utapau for Pattaya (one way 3100B).

Nok Air (☎ 1318; www.nokair.co.th; Phuket International Airport) links Phuket with Bangkok, as do **One-Two-Go** (☎ 1141, ext 1126; www.fly12go.com; Phuket International Airport) and web-based **Air Asia** (www .airasia.com), from 2000B one way. Air Asia also flies to Kuala Lumpur (one way from 25,000B) and Singapore (one way 2500B).

Other international airlines with offices in Phuket's Old Town:

Dragonair (Map p656; ☎ 0 7621 5734; Th Phang-Nga)

Malaysia Airlines (Map p656; ☎ 0 7621 6675; 1/8-9 Th Thungkha)

Silk Air (Map p656; ☎ 0 7621 3891; www.silkair.com; 183/103 Th Phang-Nga)

BOAT
Ferries link Phuket Town to Ko Phi-Phi three times per day at 8.30am, 1.30pm and 2.30pm (400B). Boats depart in the opposite direction at 9am, 2.30pm and 3pm. Ask at the airport about cheap buses linking Phuket International Airport to the ferry pier.

MINIVAN
Minivan services (plus a ferry connection) link Phuket to Ko Samui, Ko Pha-Ngan and Ko Tao on the gulf coast. Air-con minivans to Krabi, Ranong and Trang are also available. Departure locations vary – see the TAT office (p652) in Phuket Town for more info. Prices are slightly higher than the buses (see below).

Getting Around
Phuket is quite large and public transport leaves a lot to be desired, so most tourists opt to hire cars (per day 1200B to 1500B) or motorbikes (per day 250B to 500B). Both are rea-

BUSES FROM PHUKET TOWN			
Destination	**Bus type**	**Fare (B)**	**Duration (hr)**
Bangkok	air-con	630	13-14
	VIP	970	13
Chumphon	air-con	320	6½
Hat Yai	ordinary	250	8
	air-con	370	6-7
Ko Samui	air-con	500	8 (bus & boat)
Krabi	air-con	150	3½
Nakhon Si Thammarat	air-con	300	7
Phang-Nga	air-con	100	2½
Ranong	air-con	240	5
Surat Thani	air-con	200	5
Takua Pa	air-con	120	3
Trang	air-con	240	5

sonably priced and easy to find. All you need is a current driving license from your home country. Remember to keep it with you at all times, because checkpoints pop up – especially in Patong. Helmets are also required, and if you don't wear one (which is monumentally stupid considering the prevalence of motorbike accidents on Phuket), you'll pay a fine.

There are regular *sŏrng·tăa·ou* (also spelt *săwngthăew*), the Thai version of local buses, which run between resort areas and Phuket Town. They're cheap, but can be packed and are very slow. A trip from Kata to Phuket's Old Town takes nearly two hours. With private transport you can get there in 20 minutes.

Taxis and túk-túks are good alternatives, but they are surprisingly expensive. They don't have meters, so you should negotiate a fare before you leave. Most rides between resort areas cost at least 300B, and sometimes up to 500B one way. There's virtually no price break for choosing a túk-túk over a much faster and safer automobile, so unless you crave the novelty ride (and you will…once), get in a car.

BOAT

Long-tail boats are easily hired on the sand for remote beach locations. There are also daily public boats to Ko Yao from Bang Rong and Phuket Town harbours.

CAR

Driving around Phuket looks complicated when you're bleary-eyed from a long flight,

but it's a snap. The main roads are wide, the roundabouts are easy to manoeuvre and traffic snarls only occasionally. There are cheap car-hire agencies on Th Rasada in Phuket's Old Town near Pure Car Rent. Suzuki jeeps and Toyota sedans go for anywhere from 1000B to 1500B per day (including insurance), though in the low season the rates can come down to 750B. If you hire for a week or more, you'll pay near the low end of the range.

Some car-hire agencies sport international names like Budget, but if you book through an agent (rather than directly through the company) you must pay cash up front to receive the car, and it will usually bring the car to you. No matter which you choose, it's always a good idea to reserve in advance.

Andaman Car Rent (☎ 0 7632 4422; www.andamancarrent.com; Moo 2, Cheangtalay, Thalang)

Budget (☎ 0 7620 5396; www.budget.co.th; Phuket International Airport) Also a branch in Patong (Map p653).

Phuket New Car Rent (☎ 0 7637 9571; www.phuketnewcarrent.com; 111/85 Moo 8, Th Tharua-Muang mai, Thalang)

Pure Car Rent (Map p656; ☎ 0 7621 1002; www.purecarrent.com; 75 Th Rasada, Phuket Town)

Via Rent-A-Car (Map p653; ☎ 0 7638 5718; www.via-phuket.com; 189/6 Th Rat Uthit, Patong) Also a branch in Kamala (Map p666).

There are many petrol stations around the island, but only one in Patong (and it's always very busy).

SŎRNG·TĂA·OU & TÚK-TÚK

In Phuket Town, large *sŏrng·tăa·ou* run regularly from Th Ranong near the day market to the various Phuket beaches for 40B to 70B per person. They operate from 7am to 5pm; outside these times you have to charter a túk-túk to the beaches, which will set you back 250B to Patong, 280B to Karon and Kata, and 340B for Nai Han and Kamala. For a ride around Phuket's Old Town, túk-túk drivers should charge 30B for an hour. In Patong, a quick ride shouldn't set you back more than 25B. You can also charter túk-túk between beach resorts. Rides cost 300B to 500B.

TAXI

If only Phuket had a fleet of metered taxis with published fares. Instead they have private cars, whose drivers can charge more for a 10-minute ride to Rawai from Kata than a 20-minute ride from Rawai to Phuket Town.

Don't try to make sense of it, just negotiate the fare before you leave. Rides generally cost 300B to 500B one way. Motorcycle taxis are much cheaper, and can cost as little as 30B per ride, but most work exclusively in Phuket's Old Town.

KO YAO
เกาะยาว

Ko Yao Yai (Big Long Island) and Ko Yao Noi (Little Long Island) are actually part of the Ao Phang-Nga Marine National Park (p647), but are more easily accessible from Phuket. Together they encompass 137 sq km of forest, beach and rocky headland, with views of the surrounding karst formations characteristic of Ao Phang-Nga.

Ko Yao Noi is more populated than its sister. **Hat Pa Sai** and **Hat Tha Khao**, both on Yao Noi, are the best beaches. **Ta Khai**, the largest settlement on the island, is a subdistrict seat and a source of minimal supplies.

Ko Yao Yai is more isolated and rustic than its smaller neighbour. Please remember to respect the Muslim culture on both islands by wearing modest clothing outside beach areas.

Boat trips to neighbouring islands, bird-nest caves and *chow nám* funeral caves are possible. **Ko Bele**, a small island east of the twin Ko Yao, features a large tidal lagoon, three white-sand beaches, and easily accessible caves and coral reefs. Make sure to bring enough cash when visiting Ko Yao, as there is only one ATM and it's often out of cash.

Sleeping
KO YAO NOI
Koh Yao Noi Eco-Tourism Club (☎ 0 7659 7409, 0 1089 5413; www.koh-yao-noi-eco-tourism-club.com) This model ecotourism project has been developed in partnership with Responsible Ecological Social Tours Project (REST), a Bangkok-based NGO. Participants stay with a host family and learn about small-scale fishing methods and local ecology. With postcard views of Ao Phang-Nga's limestone mountains, the island is poised between a traditional way of life and a mushrooming tourist industry. Through the homestay program, visitors can contribute to the island's economic development without undermining the village atmosphere. A night of accommodation costs 400B per person and includes meals.

Sabai Corner Bungalow (☎ 08 1892 7827; www.sabaicornerbungalows.com; bungalows 500-2000B) Sturdy thatch-and-wood bungalows with small verandahs are managed by a long-time British expat. The restaurant is pretty good and comes with the usual fabulous views.

Tha Khao Bungalow (☎ 08 1676 7726; www.kohyaobungalow.com; bungalows 550-1200B) On Hat Tha Khao, this small place features five solid thatch-and-wood bungalows, including two family-size ones (with three bedrooms). The small restaurant does tasty food and also rents out bicycles and kayaks – a recommended way to explore the area.

Lom Lea (☎ 08 9868 8642; www.lomlae.com; bungalows 2100-5000B) Lom Lea's bungalows jive perfectly with the natural surroundings. The resort edges a secluded stretch of beach offering unobstructed views of Ao Phang-Nga's idyllic limestone karst formations.

Koyao Island Resort (☎ 0 1606 1517; www.koyao.com; villas from 8000B; ▓ 🖳 🐭) With some of the most glamorous beds on the island, this outfit features slick service, luxurious villas and a fine line of sundowners at the bar. If you're fed up with the stunning views (unlikely), you can always go and watch satellite TV and crank up the air-con.

KO YAO YAI
Halavee Bungalows (☎ 08 7881 1238; bungalows 500-1000B) Perched on an inland hill with panoramic vistas, this run-of-the-mill sleeping spot is well run and well priced.

Yao Yai Island Resort (☎ 08 9471 9110; www.yaoyairesort.com; bungalows from 1200B) Located on the western side of the island, Yao Yai offers spectacular sunset views from its beachfront bungalows.

Getting There & Around
Although both islands fall within the Phang-Nga Province boundaries, the easiest places to find boat transport are in Phuket and Krabi provinces. In Phuket Town, catch a *sŏrng·tăa·ou* from in front of the day market to Bang Rong (on Ao Po) for 50B. From the public pier there are up to six daily boats (50B, one hour) between 8am and 5pm. Between departures or after hours you can charter a long-tail boat for about 1500B one way. Once you arrive on Ko Yao Noi, it costs an additional 70B to 100B to get to your resort.

To go from Ko Yao Noi to Ko Yao Yai, catch a shuttle boat from Tha Manaw (20B, 15 minutes). On the islands, túk-túk provide transport for about 80B.

KRABI PROVINCE

When travellers talk about the amazing Andaman, they are probably talking about Krabi, with its trademark karst formations curving along the coast like a giant limestone fortress. Rock climbers will find their nirvana in Railay, while castaway wannabes should head to Ko Lanta, Ko Phi-Phi or any of the other 150 islands swimming off the bleach-blonde shores.

KRABI TOWN

กระบี่

pop 27,500

Most travellers just breeze through Krabi's grid-iron of travel agencies, optical shops and knick-knack shacks, using the provincial capital as a jumping-off point for wonderful surrounding destinations – Ko Lanta to the south, Ko Phi-Phi to the southwest and Railay to the west.

The town sits on the western bank of Mae Nam Krabi, about 1000km from Bangkok and 180km from Phuket. The eastern bank of the river is covered in dense mangroves and north of town are the twin limestone massifs of Khao Khanap Nam, which emerge from the water like breaching whales. The population is mainly Taoist-Confucian and Muslim, and Krabi is an important transport hub for ferries to the islands along the coast.

Orientation & Information

Th Utarakit is the main road into and out of Krabi and most places of interest are on the soi that branch off it. Ferries to Ko Phi-Phi and Ko Lanta leave from a passenger jetty at Khlong Chilat, about 5km north of town. Krabi's bus terminal is north of the centre at Talat Kao, near the junction of Th Utarakit. The airport is 17km south. Many of Krabi's guesthouses and restaurants offer internet access for 40B to 60B per hour. There are numerous banks and ATMs.

Immigration office (☎ 0 7561 1350; Th Chamai Anuson; ☘ 8.30am-4pm Mon-Fri) Handles visa extensions.

Krabi Hospital (☎ 0 7561 1210; Th Utarakit) 1km north of town.

Pakaran (☎ 0 7561 1164; 151 Th Utarakit; ☘ 9am-8pm) Good place to stock up on second-hand books before you head for the islands.

Sights & Activities

Thailand has a lot of wát, but **Wat Tham Seua** (Tiger Cave Temple), in the forest 8km northeast of Krabi, is unique. The main hall is built into a long, shallow limestone cave. On either side of the cave, dozens of *gùdì* (monks' cells) are built into various cliffs and caves. The large cave features portraits of Ajahn Jamnien Silasettho (the wát's abbot, who had quite a cult following) and close-up pictures of human entrails and internal organs, which are meant to remind guests of the impermanence of the body. Skulls and skeletons scattered around the grounds are meant to serve the same educational purpose. Troops of hungry monkeys liven the awkward silences. Private taxis to the wát from Krabi cost 250B each way; túk-túks charge about 200B.

Sea Kayak Krabi (☎ 0 7563 0270; www.seakayak-krabi.com; 40 Th Ruen Rudee) offers a wide variety of sea-kayaking tours, including to Ao Thalane (half/full day 800/1400B), which has looming sea cliffs; Ko Hong (full day 1500B), famed for its emerald lagoon; and Ban Bho Tho (full day 1500B), which has sea caves with 2000- to 3000-year-old cave paintings. All rates include guides, lunch, fruit and drinking water.

Tours

Chen Phen Tour (☎ 0 7561 2004; Th Utarakit) and others offer birdwatching tours in the mangroves around Krabi for about 600B per boat per hour (early morning is best); alternatively, you can hire a boat at the main pier for around 350B per hour. Keep an eye out for fiddler crabs and mudskippers on the exposed mud.

Various companies offer day trips to Khlong Thom, about 45km southeast of Krabi on Hwy 4, taking in some nearby hot springs and freshwater pools. Expect to pay around 950B to 1100B, including transport, lunch and beverages; bring a swimsuit and good walking shoes. Various other 'jungle tour' itineraries are available.

Sleeping

New guesthouses are appearing all over Krabi and most offer large, clean, tiled rooms with windows and shared bathrooms.

KR Mansion (☎ 0 7561 2761; krmansion@yahoo.com; 52/1 Th Chao Fah; r 300-600B; ☒ ☐) There's a great funky rooftop beer garden with panoramic views over Krabi, just perfect for a sundowner. The rooms in this bright-pink building are quite comfortable.

Chan Cha Lay (☎ 0 7562 0952; www.geocities.com/chan_cha_lay; 55 Th Utarakit; r 300-650B; ☒ ☐) This place has very helpful staff, and its relaxing

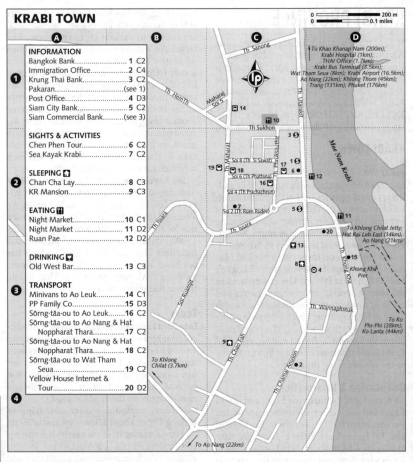

KRABI TOWN

white and baby-blue decor has an appealing Mediterranean feel. The tiled rooms are immaculate and the cafe has dainty trimmings, artistic photos and other bits of art on the walls. It's a great place to stay.

Eating & Drinking

Some might say the town's less than appetising, but they don't say the same about the food. Krabi offers a number of quality venues.

Night Market (Th Khong Kha; meals 20-50B; ☼ dinner) Found near the Khong Kha pier, this is one of the best places to eat. The menus are in English but the food is authentic and excellent. Stalls here sell papaya salad, fried noodles, *dôm yam gûng* (prawn and lemon-grass soup with mushrooms), fresh seafood and all

manner of things on satay sticks, plus sweet milky Thai desserts. There's a similar night market just north on Th Sukhon, near the intersection with Th Phruksauthit.

Ruan Pae (☎ 0 7561 1956; Th Utarakit; dishes 60-150B; ☼ lunch & dinner) This old-fashioned floating restaurant is a fine place to watch the evening mist gather around the mangroves, though the atmosphere is sometimes better than the food. Mosquitoes can be a problem in the evening.

Old West Bar (Th Chao Fah; ☼ 1pm-2am) Bamboo and wood inside and out, this Wild West-themed bar booms music nightly and is one popular place for a tipple. There's a lively scene most nights and the cocktail list is long enough to keep you sampling for a while.

Getting There & Away

AIR

Most domestic carriers offer service between Bangkok and Krabi International Airport (one way around 2400B to 3100B, 1¼ hours). **Bangkok Air** (www.bangkokair.com) has daily service to Ko Samui for around the same price. Discounts can be hunted down at local travel agencies and online. See www.domesticflights thailand.com for more information.

BOAT

Boats to Ko Lanta and Ko Phi-Phi leave from the passenger pier at Khlong Chilat, about 5km north of Krabi. Travel agencies will arrange free transfers when you buy a boat ticket with them.

The largest boat operator is **PP Family Co** (☎ 0 7561 2463; Th Khong Kha), which has a ticket office right beside the pier in town. In the high season there are boats to Ko Phi-Phi (450B to 490B, 1½ hours) at 9am, 10.30am and 2.30pm. In the low season, boats run at 9am and 2.30pm only.

From September to May, there are boats to Ko Lanta (450B, 1½ hours) leaving Krabi at 10.30am and 1.30pm. These can also stop at Ko Jam (one hour), where long-tails will shuttle you to shore (though you'll pay the full 450B fare). During the off season, boats to Ko Lanta are replaced by air-con vans (250B, 2½ hours), which leave at 9am, 11am, 1pm and 4pm.

If you want to get to Railay, head to Ao Nang by taxi (100B) or catch a long-tail boat from Krabi's Khong Kha pier to Hat Rai Leh East from 7.45am to 6pm (200B, 45 minutes); from here it is only a five-minute walk along a paved path to the more appealing Hat Rai Leh West. The boatmen will wait until they can fill a boat with 10 people before they leave; if you want to go before then you can charter the whole boat for 2000B.

BUS

With fewer eager touts and guaranteed departure times, taking a government bus from the **Krabi bus terminal** (☎ 0 7561 1804; cnr Th Utarakit & Hwy 4) in nearby Talat Kao, about 4km from Krabi, is an altogether more relaxing option than taking a private bus. Air-con government buses leave for Bangkok (700B, 12 hours) at 7am, 4pm and 5.30pm. There's a very plush 24-seat VIP bus to Bangkok (1100B) departing at 5.30pm daily. From Bangkok's southern bus terminal, buses leave at 7.30am and between 7pm and 8pm. Regular, air-con government buses also service Hat Yai (170B to 210B, three hours), Phang-Nga (70B to 80B, two hours), Phuket (120B to 140B, 3½ hours), Surat Thani (130B to 150B, 2½ hours) and Trang (100B, two hours).

Dozens of travel agencies in Krabi run air-con minivans and VIP buses to popular tourist centres throughout southern Thailand, but staff can be very pushy and you may end up crammed cheek to jowl with other backpackers.

MINIVAN

Minivans are booked through travel agencies in town. Prices can vary widely; shop around to get an idea. Some sample fares are Ao Leuk (50B, one hour), Hat Yai (280B, three hours), Ko Lanta (250B, 1½ hours), Trang (280B, two hours) and Satun (400B, five hours). Minivans leave when full.

SŎRNG·TĂA·OU

Useful *sŏrng·tăa·ou* run from the bus station to central Krabi and on to Hat Noppharat Thara (40B), Ao Nang (40B) and the Shell Cemetery at Ao Nam Mao (50B). There are services from 6am to 6.30pm. In the high season there are less frequent services until 10pm for 70B. For Ao Leuk (50B, one hour) there are frequent *sŏrng·tăa·ou* from the corner of Th Phattana and Th Phruksauthit; the last service leaves at around 3pm. Occasional *sŏrng·tăa·ou* to Wat Tham Seua leave from opposite the 7-Eleven on Th Maharat and cost 20B.

Getting Around

Krabi Town is easy to explore on foot, but the bus terminal and airport are both a long way from the centre. A taxi from the airport to town will cost 350B to 500B. In the reverse direction, taxis or túk-túk cost 400B. Agencies in town can also arrange minivans to the airport for 150B. *Sŏrng·tăa·ou* between the bus terminal and downtown Krabi cost 20B.

CAR & MOTORCYCLE

Most of the travel agencies and guesthouses in town can rent you a Honda Dream motorcycle for around 150B per day. **Yellow House Internet & Tour** (☎ 0 7562 2809; 5 Th Chao Fa) hires out reliable bikes and provides helmets. A few of the travel agencies along Th Utarakit rent out small 4WDs for 1200B to 2000B per day.

KHAO PHANOM BENCHA NATIONAL PARK

อุทยานแห่งชาติเขาพนมเบญจา

This 50-sq-km **national park** (admission 400B) protects a dramatic area of virgin rainforest along the spine of 1350m-high Khao Phanom Bencha, just 20km north of Krabi. The name means 'Five-Point Prostration Mountain', a reference to the mountain's profile, which resembles a person prostrate in prayer, with hands, knees and head touching the ground.

The park is full of scenic waterfalls, including the 11-tiered **Nam Tok Huay To**, just 500m from the park headquarters. Close by and almost as dramatic are **Nam Tok Huay Sadeh** and **Nam Tok Khlong Haeng**. On the way into the park you can visit **Tham Khao Pheung**, a fantastic cave with shimmering mineral stalactites and stalagmites. Numerous trails snake through the park providing excellent opportunities for hiking. You can discover lesser-known streams and waterfalls, too.

Clouded leopards, black panthers, tigers, Asiatic black bears, barking deer, serow, Malayan tapirs, leaf monkeys, gibbons and various tropical birds – including the helmeted hornbill, argus pheasant and extremely rare Gurney's pitta – make their home here.

There is no public transport to the park, and it doesn't offer any lodging or eating options. But the park is an easy day trip from Krabi by hired motorcycle; just follow the signposted turn-off from Hwy 4. Alternatively, you can hire a túk-túk for around 400B return.

AO NANG

อ่าวนาง

pop 12,400

Don't let the resorts and package holiday deals fool you. Ao Nang isn't a destination, it's an uninspired link in the transport chain (as the zillions of travel agencies in town will attest). The town's main street, which makes an 'L' as it hits the sand, feels like one giant mall that hawks cheesy souvenirs and tailored suits. Every evening, the blur of neon lights competes with the setting sun (the spectacular sunset usually wins) as cocktails are blended street-side and locals wave *moo·ay tai* tickets to hungry passers-through.

Ao Nang serves as the main jumping-off point for Railay, only a 20-minute long-tail ride away. For your money, Railay is a heaps nicer place to stay. Ao Nang is appealing, however, if you want to partake in popular island-hopping tours or sea-kayaking adventures, as most companies are based here. Plus, if having booze with meals is paramount, Ao Nang will do a better job quenching your thirst: many of Railay's resorts are Muslim-owned and don't serve alcohol in their restaurants (although you can buy beer at the local store and take it into restaurants that don't serve alcohol).

Orientation & Information

Locals give directions using the McDonald's and Burger King as landmarks, so it's safe to say that tourists will find all of life's creatures comforts in Ao Nang – internet aplenty, ATMs, foreign-exchange windows etc. For police and medical attention, it is best to head to Krabi Town. Due to the high influx of travel agencies, finding friendly and polite service is easier here as the competition is fierce amongst businesses. Feel free to shop around and bargain – although you'll rarely find discounts on boat services.

Hwy 4203 heads west into town, runs north along the beach for about 500m and then heads back inland for a bit before curving towards the coast again at Hat Nopphnarat Thara.

Sights

About 9km east of Ao Nang at the western end of Ao Nam Mao is the **Shell Cemetery** (admission 50B; ☼ 8.30am-4.30pm), also known as Gastropod Fossil or Su-San Hoi. Here you can see giant slabs formed from millions of tiny 75-million-year-old fossil shells. There's a small visitor centre with geological displays and various stalls selling snacks. Public transport from Ao Nang costs around 30B.

Activities

Loads of activities are possible at Ao Nang, and children under 12 typically get a 50% discount. **Elephant trekking** is a popular activity, and most tour operators arrange jungle excursions. Before you participate, however, make sure the elephants don't look abused.

KAYAKING

At least seven companies offer sea-kayaking tours to mangroves and islands around Ao Nang. Popular destinations include the lofty sea cliffs and wildlife-filled mangroves at Ao Thalane (half/full day 1000/1500B), and to the sea caves and 2000- to 3000-year-old paintings at Ban Bho Tho (1500B) – the caves are also filled with layers of archaeological shell forma-

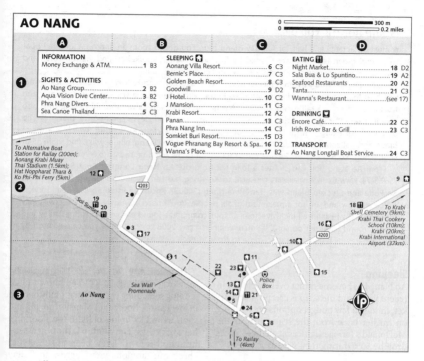

AO NANG

INFORMATION	
Money Exchange & ATM	1 B3

SIGHTS & ACTIVITIES

Ao Nang Group	2 B2
Aqua Vision Dive Center	3 B2
Phra Nang Divers	4 C3
Sea Canoe Thailand	5 C3

SLEEPING

Aonang Villa Resort	6 C3
Bernie's Place	7 C3
Golden Beach Resort	8 C3
Goodwill	9 D2
J Hotel	10 C2
J Mansion	11 C3
Krabi Resort	12 A2
Panan	13 C3
Phra Nang Inn	14 C3
Somkiet Buri Resort	15 D3
Vogue Phranang Bay Resort & Spa	16 C3
Wanna's Place	17 B2

EATING

Night Market	18 D2
Sala Bua & Lo Spuntino	19 A2
Seafood Restaurants	20 A2
Tanta	21 C3
Wanna's Restaurant	(see 17)

DRINKING

Encore Café	22 C3
Irish Rover Bar & Grill	23 C3

TRANSPORT

Ao Nang Longtail Boat Service	24 C3

tions. All rates include lunch, fruit, drinking water, sea kayaks and guides. **Sea Canoe Thailand** (☎ 0 7569 5387) and **Ao Nang Group** (☎ 0 7563 7660/1) are two recommended companies.

DIVING & SNORKELLING

Ao Nang has numerous dive schools offering trips to dive sites at nearby Railay's Laem Phra Nang. It costs about 2200B for two dives. Ko Mae Urai is one of the more unique local dives, with two submarine tunnels lined with soft and hard corals. Other trips run further afield to sites around Ko Phi-Phi or Hin Daeng and Hin Muang, southwest of Ko Lanta (around 4000B for two dives). A PADI Open Water course will set you back 15,000B to 18,000B. Reliable dive schools include **Phra Nang Divers** (☎ 0 7563 7064; www.pndivers.com) and **Aqua Vision Dive Center** (☎ 0 7563 7415; www.aqua -vision.net). Dive companies can also arrange snorkelling trips in the area.

Courses

About 10km from Ao Nang between Wat Sai Thai and Ao Nam Mao, **Krabi Thai Cookery School** (☎ 0 7569 5133; www.thaicookeryschool.net; 269 Moo 2, Ao Nang, Rte 4204) offers one-day Thai-cooking courses for 1000B; transfers are included in the price.

Tours

Any agency worth its salt can book you on one of the popular four- or five-island tours (see the boxed text, p686), which cost between 400B and 500B for a day trip. Several tour agencies offer tours to **Khlong Thom**, including visits to freshwater pools, hot springs and the **Wat Khlong Thom Museum**; the price per adult/child is 750/400B. So-called 'mystery tours' visit local snake farms, rural villages, crystal pools and rubber, pineapple, banana and papaya plantations, and cost around 900/450B per adult/ child. Tour agencies also offer trips to attractions around Ao Phang-Nga and to a number of dubious animal shows around Ao Nang.

You can also arrange day tours to Ko Phi-Phi on the **Ao Nang Princess** (per adult/child 1100/850B). The boat leaves from the Hat Noppharat Thara National Park headquarters at 9am and visits Bamboo Island, Phi-Phi Don and Phi-Phi Leh. Free transfers from Ao Nang to Hat Noppharat Thara are included in the price.

ANDAMAN COAST

ISLAND HOP 'TIL YOU DROP

A must-do activity is a half- or full-day island tour. You get to zoom around on a long-tail boat to several green isles that are fringed by luscious beaches, snorkel around vibrant coral, and explore impressive caves and cliffs – it's a perfect day out.

Tours visit **Ko Hua Khwan** (Chicken Island), with excellent snorkelling reefs and a rock formation that looks surprisingly like poultry; **Ko Poda**, with a handsome stretch of white beach; and **Ko Taloo**, which is a tall rock formation that has an underwater swim-through. These trips also take in **Tham Phra Nang** (Princess Cave), the location of a 'princess's spirit house' that's revered by locals; **Ko Hong**, with a hidden lagoon surrounded by cliffs; **Ko Lading**, which is a major bird's-nest collection point and has sublime beaches; and **Ko Daeng**, where you'll find more great snorkelling. **Ko Rai** and **Ko Pakiba** are other island gems often tacked onto a tour.

From Ao Nang you can charter a long-tail from the **Ao Nang Longtail Boat Service** (☎ 0 7569 5474; www.aonanglongtailboatservice.com) to Ko Hong, Ko Lading and Ko Daeng (2500B) or to Ko Poda and Chicken Island with Tam Phra Nang (2000B). Prices are listed on the 'Boat Service' office window and are for a maximum of six people. You'll need your own gear. Otherwise pay more for a five-island all-inclusive tour at tour companies found all over Ao Nang, Railay and Krabi (around 850B per person). If you're willing to pay 200B to 400B extra you can even go by speedboat, which gives you more time to frolic at each destination.

Sleeping

Ao Nang has become rather overdeveloped in recent years and the strip is creeping upmarket, though a few budget options are hanging on further back from the seafront near the McDonald's (cringe!). Prices at all these places drop by 50% during the low season.

BUDGET

There are loads of under-1000B spots lining the main road into town; as you venture away from the beach the price goes down and the quality goes up.

Bernie's Place (☎ 0 7563 7093; r 200-600B) Bernie's will excite the penniless in high season – rooms max out at just 600B. You'll have to share a bathroom, and the mattresses are droopy, but the rooms themselves are actually quite decent considering the price. The big bar and backpacker-priced buffets (all you can eat for 250B) foster a burgeoning travellers' vibe.

J Hotel (☎ 0 7563 7878; j_hotelo@hotmail.com; r 350-1800B; ❄️ 🖵) J Mansion's sister property (owned by the same friendly family) is nearly as good as the original, and it's just up the street. Rooms in an old shophouse are huge, atmospheric and endearingly shabby chic. The staff isn't as friendly here, which is probably why there are rooms available.

Panan (☎ 0 7563 8105; r 400-500B; ❄️) Crisp white rooms are small but cooled by generous amounts of air-con. Watch satellite TV or glimpse at fleeting views of the sea. Overall it's a great pick for the price.

J Mansion (☎ 0 7563 7876, 7569 5128; j_mansion10@hotmail.com; r 800-1000B; ❄️ 🖵) You know a place is doing something right when it's fully booked in low season. Rooms at J Mansion are big and spotless and let in lots of light; top-floor digs have sea views. The rooftop is the best asset – head up here with a few beers at sunset and check out fabulous views across to Railay (constant breezes make it almost as cool as swimming in a pool). Advance bookings are an absolute must, as frequent tour groups gobble up most of the hotel space. J Mansion also runs an honest, fairly priced travel agency and does day trips to Ko Phi-Phi.

MIDRANGE & TOP END

North of the McDonald's (away from the beach), travellers will find several brand-new buildings that house various high-quality hotel rooms. They're all pretty much the same – spotless rooms, TV, air-con and wi-fi – though **Goodwill** (www.aonanggoodwill; r 1550B) is a safe bet if you're feeling indecisive. Lately, the midrange and top-end resorts outside of Ao Nang's core (1km to 4km away) are earning higher marks than the spots in the town. See p688 for a couple of options; construction is booming though, so a quick web search is bound to reveal more.

Somkiet Buri Resort (☎ 0 7563 7320; www .somkietburi.com; r 2000-3000B; ❄️ 🏊) This place just might inspire you to slip into a yoga pose. The lush jungle grounds are filled with ferns and orchids, while lagoons, streams and meandering wooden walkways guide you to the 26 large and creatively designed rooms. A great swimming pool is set amid it all – balconies either face this pool or a peaceful pond. The service everywhere is first rate.

Vogue Phranang Bay Resort & Spa (☎ 0 7563 7635; www.vogueresort.com; r 2100-6800B; 🔀 🖭) Rooms have big windows – ask for one facing the sea – and mix tiles and wooden floors in a Zen architectural collage. Baths have separate showers (complete with doors – rare here). The only fault was the softness of the mattress. We really liked the grounds, however; they were peaceful with lots of jungle foliage. There is a big round swimming pool, with sea and sunset views.

Phra Nang Inn (☎ 0 7563 7130; phranang@sun.phuket .ksc.co.th; r incl breakfast 2300-5500B; 🔀 🖭) The beautiful interior decor – a unique bamboo theme with eclectic designs in shell and tilework – is Phra Nang's forte. There are two pools, and a second, similarly designed branch is across the road from the original.

Krabi Resort (☎ 0 7563 7030, in Bangkok 0 2208 9165; www.krabiresort.com; r/bungalows 4200-8900B; 🔀 🖭) The original Ao Nang luxury resort is ageing gracefully, maintaining quality rooms and luxury bungalows on peaceful, landscaped grounds, some right near the beach. There is an on-site dive school, a restaurant and a bar.

Golden Beach Resort (☎ 0 7563 7870-4; www.krabi goldenbeach.com; r 4500-6000B, bungalows 6000-10,000B; 🔀 🖭) This swanky modern resort is made up of large hotel blocks and stylish bungalows arranged in a tidy garden around a big pool. The outdoor restaurant is lit up like a Christmas tree at night and hosts slightly cheesy live music (think electric keyboards and '80s covers).

Also recommended:

Wanna's Place (☎ 0 7563 7322; www.wannasplace .com; r 1875-1975B, bungalows 2290-2390B; 🔀) Popular but not the pick of the litter.

Aonang Villa Resort (☎ 0 7563 7270; www.aonang villaresort.com; r 3400-7500B; 🔀 🖭) A swank seaside affair.

Eating

At the western end of the beach is Soi Sunset, a narrow alley housing a number of identical seafood restaurants. They all have bamboo seating abutting the ocean, and model boats at the entrance showing off the day's catch.

Wanna's Restaurant (dishes 60-190B; 🕑 breakfast, lunch & dinner) Casual and inexpensive, it's worth stopping by for the variety of food on offer – everything from burgers to cheese selections to Swiss specialities, along with Thai cuisine and breakfast.

our pick Sala Bua & Lo Spuntino (☎ 0 7563 7110; dishes 80-520B; 🕑 10am-11pm) Located deep within the bustle of 'Seafood Street', this excellent ocean-facing restaurant serves the best of both worlds – East and West – accompanied by a long list of wines. A resident Italian chef and a Thai chef whip up traditional masterpieces in the steamy kitchen while diners coddle their chardonnay and watch the sunset. Simple pleasures, like vegetable rice, are cooked to perfection, as are the big ticket items: seafood 'baskets' (for two) and Florentine sirloins.

Tanta (☎ 0 7563 7118; dishes 180-350B; 🕑 lunch & dinner) The thin-crust pizza is divine and not too doughy, and the service is discreet (you get your meal but aren't pushed to order every 10 minutes). Tanta offers a great selection of Thai and international dishes. It's a popular modern place with a raised covered terrace and wood accents.

Drinking & Entertainment

Have a drink – there's no shortage of bars in Ao Nang.

Irish Rover Bar & Grill (☎ 0 7563 7607) Readers like this typical Irish pub specialising in draught Guinness and Kilkenny, along with brews like Singapore's Tiger and Thailand's high alcohol–content (but headache-inducing) Chang. Sports fans will appreciate the telly broadcasting English footy matches and South African cricket. The place also features live music, tropical cocktails and pool tables.

Encore Café (🕑 4pm-2am in high season) Very popular with holidaying Thais, this live-music club is a fun and modern spot. It has pool tables and special themed evenings – from ladies' night to speed pool. Readers like the Tex-Mex pub food.

Aonang Krabi Muay Thai Stadium (☎ 0 7562 1042; admission 500B, ringside incl 1 beer 1200B) If you get tired of the beach-bars and pirated movies playing on the strip, this place has boisterous *moo·ay tai* bouts on multiple nights each week from around 8.45pm. A free (and hard-to-miss) *sŏrng·tǎa·ou* runs along the strip at Ao Nang, collecting punters before the bouts.

Getting There & Around

A ferry service to Ko Phi-Phi runs year-round (450B to 490B, two hours) at 9am and includes a ride to/from the pier in nearby Hat Noppharat Thara.

Long-tail boats to the Hat Rai Leh area run daily in good weather and cost 80B (120B after 6pm). In bad weather head to Ao Nam Mao and then catch a long-tail boat (90B), which runs even in choppy weather.

A good way to get around is by *sŏrng·tăa·ou*. Destinations include Krabi (40B), Hat Noppharat Thara (10B) and Ao Nam Mao (20B). Look for them on the main road. Taxis from Ao Nang *to* Krabi airport cost 600B (though you can bargain down), but *from* the airport can cost up to 900B.

AROUND AO NANG
Hat Noppharat Thara
หาดนพรัตน์ธารา
About 4km from Ao Nang, at the end of Rte 4203, Hat Noppharat Thara used to feel like a completely separate destination; a quieter alternative to the touristy hub nearby. These days the casuarina-lined beach is a little suburb getting pulled in by Ao Nang's magnet tourism energy. If you're island-bound from Ao Nang, chances are high that you'll pass through this little beach, as the headquarters for Ko Phi-Phi Marine National Park are located here. Several resorts falsely advertise a 'central Ao Nang' location – so if you don't like reading fine print, you might end up sleeping out here (though most will argue that it's better out in Noppharat Thara than sleeping next door to a McDonald's in town).

SLEEPING
Laughing Gecko (☎ 0 7569 5115; bungalows 100–500B) One of several basic bungalow operators down a lane just before the national park office. It features beachy bungalows and an artistically decorated restaurant filled with chattering backpackers (the all-you-can-eat buffets for under 200B are a big hit with small wallets).

Government Bungalows (☎ 0 7563 7200; 2-6-person tents 300B, 2-person bungalows 600B, 6-8-person bungalows 1200B or per person 200B) Well-maintained bungalows come with fans, bathrooms and mosquito nets on the windows. Tents are also available if you want the full primitive experience. A small canteen serves meals in the evenings.

At the other end of the scale, **Red Ginger** (☎ 0 7563 7999; www.redgingerkrabi.com; r 5450–9450B; ❄ 🖥 🏊) and **Pakasai Resort** (☎ 0 7563 7777; www.pakasai.com; r 6700–8000B; ❄ 🖥 🏊) are excellent upmarket choices sporting all the amenities of a luxury resort.

Around the national park headquarters there are several restaurants serving snacks such as fried chicken and papaya salad.

GETTING THERE & AWAY
Sŏrng·tăa·ou between Krabi and Ao Nang stop in Hat Noppharat Thara; the fare is 40B from Krabi or 10B from Ao Nang. From October to May the *Ao Nang Princess* runs between Ko Phi-Phi Marine National Park headquarters and Ko Phi-Phi (450B to 490B, two hours). The boat leaves from the national park jetty at 9am, returning from Ko Phi-Phi at 3.30pm. It also stops at Railay's Hat Rai Leh West. This boat can also be used for day trips to Ko Phi-Phi. During the high season there's also a direct boat to Phuket, leaving from the same pier at 3.30pm (450B), and to Ko Lanta at 10.30am (450B).

RAILAY
ไร่เล
Krabi's fairytale limestone crags come to a dramatic climax at Railay (also spelled Rai Leh), the ultimate jungle gym for rock-climbing fanatics. This quiet slice of paradise fills in the sandy gaps between each craggy flourish, and although it's just around the bend from chaotic tourist hustle in Ao Nang, the atmosphere here is nothing short of laid-back, Rasta-Thai haven. Recent construction has added a slew of five-star digs, but there's still plenty of time to quietly soak up the sun under dangling daredevils before Railay goes corporate.

Information
There are now a couple of ATMs in Railay – an easy one is on the path between Hat Rai Leh West and Hat Rai Leh East. Several of the bigger resorts can also change cash and travellers cheques. A few shops have internet for a whopping 3B per minute; connections are usually unreliable, so you may be better off checking your email in Ao Nang or Krabi Town. For minor climbing injuries there's a small clinic at Railay Bay Resort on Hat Rai Leh West. Check out www.railay.com for more info about the area.

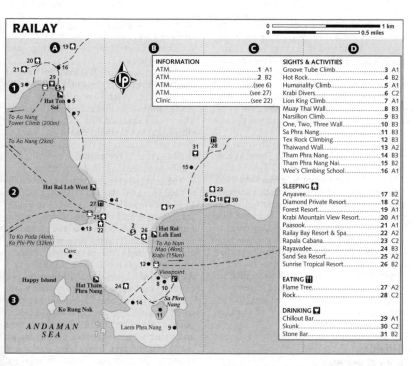

RAILAY

INFORMATION	
ATM	1 A1
ATM	2 B2
ATM	(see 6)
ATM	(see 27)
Clinic	(see 22)

SIGHTS & ACTIVITIES	
Groove Tube Climb	3 A1
Hot Rock	4 B2
Humanality Climb	5 A1
Krabi Divers	6 C2
Lion King Climb	7 A1
Muay Thai Wall	8 B3
Narsillion Climb	9 B3
One, Two, Three Wall	10 B3
Sa Phra Nang	11 B3
Tex Rock Climbing	12 B3
Thaiwand Wall	13 A2
Tham Phra Nang	14 B3
Tham Phra Nang Nai	15 B2
Wee's Climbing School	16 A1

SLEEPING	
Anyavee	17 B2
Diamond Private Resort	18 C2
Forest Resort	19 A1
Krabi Mountain View Resort	20 A1
Paasook	21 A1
Railay Bay Resort & Spa	22 A2
Rapala Cabana	23 C2
Rayavadee	24 B3
Sand Sea Resort	25 A2
Sunrise Tropical Resort	26 B2

EATING	
Flame Tree	27 A2
Rock	28 C2

DRINKING	
Chillout Bar	29 A1
Skunk	30 C2
Stone Bar	31 B2

Sights

Railay's most alluring beach is **Hat Rai Leh West**. It's also the best place to watch the sun go down (bring a camera – the sunsets are ethereal). Tastefully designed midrange resorts line a long stretch of golden sand beach and dozens of long-tail boats make pick-ups and drop-offs from here to nearby Ao Nang. The water is perfect for swimming (even at low tide it's deep enough), and we'd suggest floating on your back, staring up at the cliffs and contemplating life for a while – it's very Zen.

At the southern end of the beach is the mighty Thaiwand Wall, a sheer limestone cliff offering some of Railay's most challenging climbing routes (see p690).

Boats from Krabi arrive at **Hat Rai Leh East**. The shallow, muddy beach is lined with mangroves and is not really suitable for swimming, but there are plenty of bungalows, bars and facilities onshore. It's only a short walk (less than five minutes) across the deer neck of Laem Phra Nang to Hat Rai Leh West, so don't feel you're trapped on this beach if you're arriving from Krabi.

Hat Ton Sai is the backpacker retreat and is reached by long-tail (either directly from Ao Nang or from Hat Rai Leh West) or by a sweaty 20-minute scramble over limestone rocks. While the beach here is mediocre, the dozens of cheap bungalow outfits and excellent access to some of the best climbs around keeps it lively with climbers and backpackers. There are occasional Full Moon parties here during the high season.

Near the tip of the peninsula is **Hat Tham Phra Nang**, a splendid strip of whispering white sand, framed by looming cliffs. If you just want to sunbathe, this is the spot to go – it's the most beautiful beach around and just a few minutes' walk from Hat Rai Leh East. The plush Rayavadee resort dominates the eastern end of the beach but the rest of Hat Tham Phra Nang is untouched. A huge cavern punches straight through the cliffs at the western end of the beach, emerging halfway up Thaiwand Wall. Immediately offshore are Happy Island and Ko Rung Nok (Bird Nest Island), which offer some good snorkelling.

At the eastern end of Hat Tham Phra Nang is **Tham Phra Nang** (Princess Cave), an

ANDAMAN COAST

important shrine for local fishermen. Legend has it that a royal barge carrying an Indian princess foundered in a storm here during the 3rd century BC. The spirit of the drowned princess came to inhabit the cave, granting favours to all who came to pay respect. Local fishermen – Muslim and Buddhist – place carved wooden phalluses in the cave as offerings in the hope that the spirit will provide plenty of fish.

About halfway along the path from Hat Rai Leh East to Hat Tham Phra Nang, a crude path leads up the jungle-cloaked cliff wall to a hidden lagoon known as **Sa Phra Nang** (Holy Princess Pool). There's a dramatic viewpoint over the peninsula from the nearby cliff top, but be warned that this is a strenuous hike with some serious vertigo-inducing parts.

Above Hat Rai Leh East is another large cave called **Tham Phra Nang Nai** (Inner Princess Cave; adult/child 20/10B; ☺ 5am-8pm), also known as Diamond Cave. A wooden boardwalk leads through a series of illuminated caverns full of beautiful limestone formations, including a splendid 'stone waterfall' of sparkling gold-coloured quartz.

Activities
ROCK CLIMBING

With nearly 700 bolted routes and unparalleled cliff-top vistas, it's no surprise these dramatic rock faces are among the top climbing spots in the world. There are routes here ascending to the roofs of massive caverns and following cascades of stalactites up 300m-high cliffs. Climbing options are so plentiful (and new routes are being 'discovered' all

the time!), ranging from beginner routes to challenging advanced climbs, that you could spend months climbing and exploring – and many people do.

Most climbers start off at **Muay Thai Wall** and **One, Two, Three Wall**, at the southern end of Hat Rai Leh East, which have at least 40 routes graded from 4b to 8b on the French system. The mighty **Thaiwand Wall**, a sheer limestone cliff, sits at the southern end of Hat Rai Leh West and has some of the most challenging climbing routes. For a list of some of the best climbs here, see the boxed text, below.

The going rate for climbing courses is 800B to 1200B for a half day and 1500B to 2200B for a full day. Three-day courses (5000B to 6000B) involve some lead-climbing (where you clip into bolts on the rock face as you ascend) as well as multipitch routes. Experienced climbers can hire lead kits from any of the climbing schools for 600/1000B for a half/full day – the standard kit consists of a 60m rope, two climbing harnesses, two pairs of rock boots, a belaying device and 12 quickdraws. You could consider bringing your own climbing boots and a collection of loose slings, nuts and cams to provide extra protection on thinly bolted routes. If you leave anything at home, all the climbing schools sell imported climbing gear.

Several locally published books detail climbs in the area, but *Rock Climbing in Thailand* (1000B) is one of the more popular guides.

Recommended climbing schools:

Hot Rock (☎ 0 7562 1771; www.railayadventure.com; Hat Rai Leh West) Unabashedly the most expensive climb-

TOP FIVE CLIMBS

With nearly 700 climbs to choose from, picking a few of the best ones is no easy task, but here's a list we've whittled down. Grades are based on the French grading system.

Climb	Grade	Height	Description
Groove Tube	6a	25m	A great climb for beginner to intermediate levels; lots of big gaps and pockets to grab.
Humanality	6a-6b	120m	This multipitch scramble is one of the most popular here; you may have to queue to climb it.
Lion King	6b+	18m	A good, challenging climb, with a slight overhang and zigzags up a crack; requires lots of strength and agility.
Narsillion	6c+	30m	Accessible only at low tide, this climb has a steep wall with small pockets. The beach below this rock is lovely.
Ao Nang Tower	6b-6c	68m	You have to start this climb from a long-tail boat! The last 6c stretch here is a long one so save your strength.

ing school in Railay, but the longstanding reputation keeps the operation busy. The owner, Luang, is a bit of a Railay climbing legend.

Tex Rock Climbing (☎ 0 7563 1509; Rai Leh East) A tiny, venerable school where the owner still climbs and runs the school directly from the shop.

Wee's Climbing School (Hat Ton Sai) A friendly and professional outfit.

WATER SPORTS

Several dive operations in Railay run trips to Ko Poda and other neighbouring sites. **Krabi Divers** (☎ 0 7562 1686/7; www.viewpointresort66.com; Hat Rai Leh East), at Railay Viewpoint Resort, charges 6000B for dives at outlying islands.

Snorkelling trips to Ko Poda and Ko Hua Khwan (Chicken Island) can be arranged through any of the resorts for about 900B by long-tail or 1200B by speedboat. Longer multi-island trips cost 1000/1900B per half-/full day. If you just want to snorkel off Railay, most resorts can rent you a mask set and fins for 150B each.

The Flame Tree (right) at Hat Rai Leh West rents out **sea kayaks** for 200B per hour, as do many midrange and top-end resorts around Railay. Overnight trips to deserted islands can be arranged with local boat owners but you'll need to bring your own camping gear and food.

Sleeping & Eating
HAT RAI LEH WEST

Rai Leh West is beautiful and developers know it – you'll only find midrange and top-end resorts around here. Rates drop by 30% in the low season. You can't go wrong with any of the resorts' restaurants.

Sand Sea Resort (☎ 0 7562 2170; www.krabisandsea .com; bungalows 1800-6000B; 🞩 🖳 🖭) Solid, well-appointed concrete bungalows with veran-dahs line a snaking, foliage-laced pathway. A full buffet breakfast at the hotel restaurant is included; nonguests should stop by at lunch or dinner, as the food is quite good. These are cheapest digs around. Sand Sea is alcohol free.

Railay Bay Resort & Spa (☎ 0 7581 9401; www .krabi-railaybay.com; bungalows 3500-19,000B; 🞩 🖭) It's worth staying here for the pool alone. The amoeba-shaped, sparkling blue creation faces onto the best bit of the beach so you can easily switch between salt and fresh water. The cam-pus of charming timber-framed bungalows stretches all the way to Rai Leh East along well

manicured grounds. Trips to both the on-site restaurant and spa will not disappoint.

Flame Tree (dishes 150B) Flame Tree has a bit of a monopoly on nightlife in Rai Leh West, so the prices are inflated and the food is medio-cre at best, but it's still a chilled place to relax with your climbing buddies at beer o'clock.

HAT RAI LEH EAST

Often referred to as Sunrise Beach, the 'beach' here is riddled with gnarled man-groves and tends to be quite muddy. It's not the end of the world, as Hat Rai Leh West is just a 10-minute walk away. The resorts on the hillside above the beach get sea breezes, but down by the water it can feel like a sauna.

Rapala Cabana (☎ 08 6957 8096; bungalows 200B) Superbly located deep in the jungle and high in the hills in a bowl of karst cliff, this uber-rustic, Rasta-run place is the cheapest place to crash in Railay.

Anyavee (☎ 08 1537 5517; www.anyavee.com; r/bun-galows 1500-3000B) Anyavee doesn't know what it wants to be – some parts of the resort feel backpackery, other parts feel decidedly high-end. The rooms fall somewhere in the mid-dle, sporting modern, comfortable amenities on tiled surfaces.

Diamond Private Resort (☎ 0 7562 1729; www .diamondprivate-railay.com; r 1800-3500B; 🞩 🖭) Although the name sounds a bit like a strip joint, Diamond Private is a family-friendly resort with a swimming pool high on the hilltop with a deck that sports great views of the bay below. The rooms and bungalows come with TVs, hot showers and minibars, and are set in well-landscaped gardens.

Sunrise Tropical Resort (☎ 0 7562 2599; www.sunrise tropical.com; bungalows 3500-5500B; 🞩 🖭) Likely the first place you'll come across after dis-embarking from the Krabi boat (look for it just beyond the mooring area). Sunrise has stylish Thai villas with neat decor and very swanky bathrooms. Breakfast is included. The restaurant does not serve alcohol.

Rock (dishes 120B; 🕑 breakfast, lunch & dinner) Our favourite lunchtime spot in all of Railay sits up on a small clearing in the karst formaton-filled jungle. The sea views are divine and the large selection of Thai food never gets complaints. Try the refreshing basil smooth-ies on especially hot days. The 99B do-it-yourself barbecues are quite popular – stop by for more information.

HAT THAM PHRA NANG

Rayavadee (☎ 0 7562 0740; www.rayavadee.com; r 30,000-55,000B; ✲ ◨ ▣ ✿) Yes, you read those prices correctly. But if you have serious baht to burn, we can't think of a better place. This exclusive colonial-style five-star resort monopolises 10 hectares of stunning beachfront property clad with seven types of luxury bungalows; all are two-storey and fabulously decked out in traditional Thai style. Champagne breakfasts, afternoon tea amid wafting classical music, and romantic sunset dinners are the norm.

HAT TON SAI

Covered from rock to rock in dangling climbers, Ton Sai is a fun place to hang your hat. The beach isn't spectacular, but there's a welcoming backpacker vibe that'll keep a smile on your face. In the low season, rates for bungalows plummet as low as 150B.

Forest Resort (☎ 08 9290 0262; bungalows 300-500B) Tucked up in the woods away from the fray and dangling climbers, this friendly resort has a cluster of basic bungalows scattered on a small hill. The on-site Indian restaurant is an added bonus.

Paasook (☎ 08 9645 3013; bungalows 500B) At the far western end of the beach, Paasook has basic bungalows with large picture windows.

Krabi Mountain View Resort (☎ 0 7562 2610; bungalows 1100-1900B; ✲) Cheery and immaculate with mint-green walls, tiled floors and crisp linen – these are Ton Sai's best-value air-con digs.

Drinking

Although many of the resorts don't serve alcohol, there are a few places on the beaches where you can celebrate the day's climb with a frosty one…or seven…

Skunk (Hat Rai Leh East) Scratchy roots reggae is the name of the game as chilled-out locals twirl their dreads with their fingers.

Chillout Bar (Hat Ton Sai) Climbers like to chill here after a long day on the rocks. The place flies Rasta colours and serves cold beers as fast as you can drink them.

Stone Bar (Rai Leh East) Swig your Tiger beer in the rounded gazebo sitting under a massive climbing wall. The parties go late and buzz with ambient electronica beats.

Getting There & Around

If you're not aboard the ferry connecting Ao Nang and Ko Phi-Phi Don, then the only way to get to Railay is by long-tail boat, either from the seafront at Ao Nang or at Khong Ka (Chao Fa) in Krabi. Boats between Krabi and Hat Rai Leh East leave every 1½ hours (or when they have 10 passengers) from 7.45am to 6pm (200B, 45 minutes).

Boats to Hat Rai Leh West or Ton Sai (80B, 15 minutes) leave from the eastern end of the promenade at Ao Nang during daylight hours. After dark you'll pay 120B. If seas are very rough, boats leave from a sheltered cove just west of Krabi Resort in Ao Nang. You can be dropped at Hat Tham Phra Nang or Hat Ton Sai for the same fare.

During exceptionally high seas, the boats from both Ao Nang and Krabi stop running, but you may still be able to get from Hat Rai Leh East to Ao Nam Mao (90B, 15 minutes), where you can catch a ride to Krabi or Ao Nang.

KO PHI-PHI DON

เกาะพีพีดอน

Ko Phi-Phi is uncanny. One glimpse of the island's otherworldly crests and cliffs will turn brutes into poets, and sceptics into believers.

A beacon for backpackers from all over the planet, this menagerie of towering crags sits frozen in a shimmering tapestry of emerald and jade, inviting daydreamers to idle in the shallow bays and climb the soaring cliffs. Viewpoints reveal soul-altering vistas of the sandy hourglass isthmus that plays host to these legions of visitors and their hedonistic pursuits.

Even though Ko Phi-Phi may seem a bit expensive compared to the rest of Thailand, if you compare it to other gorgeous islands around the planet, we think you'll discover this paradise actually comes pretty damn cheap.

Orientation & Information

Ko Phi-Phi Don (usually just referred to as Ko Phi-Phi) is part of the Ko Phi-Phi Marine National Park, which also includes uninhabited Ko Phi-Phi Leh next door (p697).

Ko Phi-Phi Don is actually two islands joined together by a narrow isthmus flanked by the stunning **Ao Ton Sai** and **Ao Lo Dalam** on either side. Boats dock at the large concrete pier at Ao Ton Sai and a narrow path, crammed full of tour operators, bungalows, restaurants, bars and souvenir shops, stretches along the beach towards **Hat Hin Khom**. The maze of small streets in the middle of this sand bar is equally packed and is known as **Tonsai**

Village (or the Tourist Village). The swimmer-friendly **Hat Yao** (Long Beach) faces south and has some of Phi-Phi Don's best coral. The beautifully languid and long eastern bays of **Hat Laem Thong** and **Ao Lo Bakao** are reserved for several top-end resorts, while the smaller bays of **Hat Phak Nam** and **Hat Rantee** play host to a few simple, low-key bungalow affairs.

Tonsai Village is a patchwork of travel agencies, superettes, restaurants, internet cafes and guesthouses. There's a Western Union bank and a 24-hour ATM at the southern tip of Ao Ton Sai.

Sights & Activities

The strenuous and sweaty climb to Phi-Phi's **viewpoint** is a rewarding short hike. The path up the mountain begins near Phi Phi Casita (p695) and wends its way up a steep crag – most people will need to stop for a short break (don't forget to bring some water), but once you reach the top you'll be treated to postcard-worthy views of the twin bays, soaring karst formations and quiet Phi-Phi Leh off in the distance. Pinned to a sturdy tree is a small photograph taken from the viewpoint only hours after the tsunami – a graphic reminder of the tragedy that haunts the island's consciousness.

DIVING

Crystal Andaman water and abundant marine life make the perfect recipe for top-notch scuba. Popular sights include the **King Cruiser Wreck**, sitting a mere 12m below the surface; **Anemone Reef**, teeming with hard corals and clownfish; **Hin Bida**, a submerged pinnacle attracting turtles and large pelagic fish; and **Ko Bida Nok**, with its signature karst massif luring leopard sharks. Hin Daeng and Hin Muang (p700), to the south, are expensive ventures from Ko Phi-Phi – it's cheaper to link up with a dive crew in Ko Lanta.

All dive shops in Tonsai Village have standardised their pricing – an Open Water

certification course costs 12,400B, while the standard two-dive trips cost 2200B. Trips out to Hin Daeng/Hin Muang will set you back 5500B.

Recommended dive operators:

Adventure Club (☎ 08 1970 0314, 08 1895 1334; www.divingphi.com) Our favourite diving operation on the island runs an excellent assortment of educational, eco-focused diving, hiking and snorkelling tours. You won't mind getting up at 6am for the much-loved shark-watching snorkel trips on which you are guaranteed to cavort with at least one curious reef shark. Ask about the top-secret 007 tours – we could tell you, but then we'd have to kill you...

Phi Phi Scuba (☎ 0 7561 2665; www.ppscuba.com) One of the largest operators on the island, churning out dive certifications by the boatload. There's a sociable and professional atmosphere, although nervous newbies might feel as though they aren't getting enough hand-holding.

SNORKELLING

Snorkelling around Ko Phi-Phi is equally amazing, especially around Ko Phi-Phi Leh. It is worth shelling out the 800B to 2000B (depending on boat type and trip length) to join a day trip and explore the reefs. Most trips include lunch and take you to a number of spots around the marine park. Any travel agency on the island can arrange snorkelling day trips.

If you're going at it on your own, most bungalows and resorts rent out a snorkel, mask and fins for 150B to 200B per day. There is good snorkelling along the eastern coast of **Ko Nok**, near Ao Ton Sai and along the eastern coast of **Ko Nai**.

ROCK CLIMBING

Yes, there are good limestone cliffs to climb on Ko Phi-Phi, and the view from the top is spectacular. The main climbing areas are **Ton Sai Tower**, at the western edge of Ao Ton Sai, and **Hin Taak**, a short long-tail boat ride around the bay. There is a handful of good climbing shops on the island and most places charge around 900B for a half day of climbing or 1600B for a full day, including instruction and gear. **Cat's Climbing Shop** (☎ 08 1787 5101; www.catsclimbingshop.com), in Tonsai Village, is a French-run operation that gets a thumbs up from tourists. **Spider Monkey** (☎ 08 9728 1608) in Tonsai Village also gets a good report card. Hardcore climbing buffs should head to Railay (p690).

SHE SELLS SEASHELLS

Numerous souvenir shops on Ko Phi-Phi Don sell seashells, which are poached from the surrounding marine national parks. These local shell species are quickly becoming extinct, so please don't buy shell-related souvenirs.

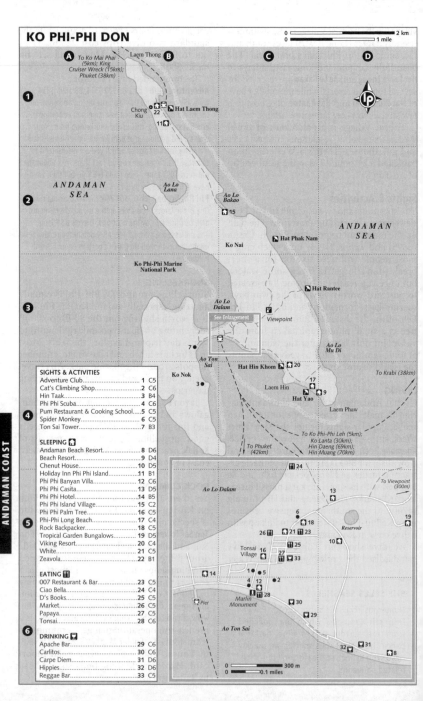

KO PHI-PHI DON

To Ko Mai Phai (5km); King Cruiser Wreck (15km); Phuket (38km)

Laem Thong

Chong Kiu

22

Hat Laem Thong

11

ANDAMAN SEA

Ao Lo Lana

Ao Lo Bakao

15

ANDAMAN SEA

Ko Nai

Hat Phak Nam

Ko Phi-Phi Marine National Park

Hat Rantee

Ao Lo Dalam

See Enlargement

Viewpoint

Ao Lo Mu Di

7

Ao Ton Sai

Ko Nok

Hat Hin Khom

20

To Krabi (38km)

3

17

Laem Hin

9

Hat Yao

Laem Phaw

To Ko Phi-Phi Leh (5km); Ko Lanta (30km); Hin Daeng (69km); Hin Muang (70km)

To Phuket (42km)

SIGHTS & ACTIVITIES
Adventure Club	1 C5
Cat's Climbing Shop	2 C6
Hin Taak	3 B4
Phi Phi Scuba	4 C6
Pum Restaurant & Cooking School	5 C5
Spider Monkey	6 C5
Ton Sai Tower	7 B3

SLEEPING
Andaman Beach Resort	8 D6
Beach Resort	9 D4
Chenut House	10 D5
Holiday Inn Phi Phi Island	11 B1
Phi Phi Banyan Villa	12 C6
Phi Phi Casita	13 D5
Phi Phi Hotel	14 B5
Phi Phi Island Village	15 C2
Phi Phi Palm Tree	16 C5
Phi-Phi Long Beach	17 C4
Rock Backpacker	18 C5
Tropical Garden Bungalows	19 D5
Viking Resort	20 C4
White	21 C5
Zeavola	22 B1

EATING
007 Restaurant & Bar	23 C5
Ciao Bella	24 C4
D's Books	25 C5
Market	26 C5
Papaya	27 C5
Tonsai	28 C6

DRINKING
Apache Bar	29 C6
Carlitos	30 C6
Carpe Diem	31 D6
Hippies	32 D6
Reggae Bar	33 C5

Ao Lo Dalam

24

To Viewpoint (300m)

13

6

18

19

Reservoir

26

21 23

25

10

Tonsai Village

16

27

33

14

1 5

2

12

28

30

Pier

Marlin Monument

29

Ao Ton Sai

32 31

8

0 ——— 300 m
0 ——— 0.1 miles

Courses

Thai-food fans can take cooking courses at the newly renovated **Pum Restaurant & Cooking School** (☎ 0 1521 8904; www.pumthaifoodchain.com; full day 2500B) in Tonsai Village. Students learn to make some of the excellent dishes that are served in its restaurant, and the take-home recipe book is a nice keepsake.

Tours

Ever since Leo smoked a spliff in Alex Garland's *The Beach,* Phi-Phi Leh (p697) has become a pilgrimage site for backpackers around the world. Any travel agency on Phi-Phi Don can arrange your half-day, full-day or sunset trip. Tours to Ko Mai Phi (Bamboo Island), Monkey Bay and the beach at Wang Long are also popular choices. Figure between 500B to 800B.

We highly recommend the unique tours offered by Adventure Club (p693).

Sleeping

If you are coming to Phi-Phi in peak season, you *must* book a room in advance. You'll often see travellers arrive on the morning boat and leave on the afternoon boat when they fail to find a place to crash (sleeping on the beach is strictly prohibited). Swarms of touts flock to the docking ferries – if you're going to follow them to a resort, make sure you arm yourself with a couple of hotel names so you don't end up in a dive. Posters at the pier list the island's accommodation with prices attached – a handy tool if you want to make a go of it on your own.

TONSAI VILLAGE

The flat, hourglass-shaped land between Ao Ton Sai and Ao Lo Dalam is crowded with loads of lodging options.

Rock Backpacker (☎ 0 7561 2402; therockbackpacker@ hotmail.com; dm/r 350/800B) Solo penny-pinchers will like it here. The funky restaurant, on a boat dry-docked on the hillside, is conducive to mingling. The 16-bed dorm room is a real rarity on Ko Phi-Phi, and digs are clean, if rather cramped. Rock Backpacker is inland, but close to Ao Lo Dalam.

Tropical Garden Bungalows (☎ 08 9729 1436; r from 800B; 🖾) If you don't mind walking 10 minutes to eat, drink or sunbathe, then you'll love Tropical Garden. At the far end of the main path from Ao Ton Sai, it feels pretty isolated in its fragment of flourishing hillside jungle.

The great cabins are frontier-style log affairs and there's even a lofty pool, surrounded by flora, halfway up the hill.

White (☎ 0 7560 1300; www.whitephiphi.com; r 1600-1900B; 🖾 🖳) Geared towards the 'flashpacker' crowd, the White has two locations in Tonsai Village with squeaky clean rooms – everything's white (duh).

Phi Phi Casita (☎ 0 7560 1214; www.phiphi-hotel.com; bungalows 2000-3000B; 🖾 🖳) A step back from Ao Lo Dalam beach, this place looks like a classy fishermen's village, with tiny wooden bungalows hovering over weathered planks and flower-planted mud flats. There's not much privacy but the stylish infinity pool and proximity to the beach are major draws.

Phi Phi Banyan Villa (☎ 0 7561 1233; www.phiphi -hotel.com; r 2500-2800B; 🖾 🖳) These comfy quarters have all the mod cons and some have a balcony overlooking a garden-lined path. There's a seaside restaurant and the hotel's namesake, a large gnarled banyan tree, sits out front.

Phi Phi Palm Tree (☎ 0 7561 1233; www.phiphi -hotel.com; r 3100-5400B; 🖾 🖳 🖳) In Tonsai Village, Palm Tree uses the inland location well by organising its accommodation around a tranquil interior courtyard and inviting swimming pool. The rooms are lavish and mix mod cons with one-of-a-kind paintings by one of Thailand's best-known classical painters.

Also recommended:

Chenut (☎ 08 1894 1026; bungalows from 1000B) Friendly, family-run spot with woodsy timber-framed bungalows.

Phi Phi Hotel (☎ 0 7561 1233; www.phiphi-hotel .com; r from 1700B; 🖾 🖳) Guests love this hotel, which has amazing views and all the amenities of a posh resort.

HAT HIN KHOM

Between Hat Yao and Tonsai Village, this quieter patch of sand is a great choice if you want to be near the action but also value a quiet night's sleep.

Viking Resort (☎ 0 7581 9399; tak_blobk@hotmail .com; bungalows 800-2000B; 🖳) Viking Resort has oodles of tiki-chic charm on a great beach for swimming and tanning.

Andaman Beach Resort (☎ 0 7562 1427; www .andamanbeachresort.com; bungalows 1650-4350B; 🖾 🖳) A U-shape of pistachio-toned huts sits around a large spartan lawn. The best asset is the small amoeba-shaped pool with great views of Phi-Phi Leh.

HAT YAO

Hat Yao (Long Beach) is a short boat ride (80B) or long sweaty hike (45 minutes) from Ao Ton Sai. The beach here is fantastic and not as crowded as the double bays around Tonsai Village.

Phi-Phi Long Beach (☎ 08 6281 4349; bungalows 500-1000B) Standard-issue bungalows are nothing to write home about, but the price is right (cheap!) and there's a chill backpacker vibe along the sand.

Beach Resort (☎ 0 7561 8267; bungalows 3950-5900B; ✂ ▯ ▣) An ever-expanding class act with a good pool and chic bar, this resort swarms with package tourists looking for (and finding) comfort. It's relatively new, so good service can be off and on, but management seems eager to iron out the kinks.

AO LO BAKAO

Ao Lo Bakao has a beautiful and secluded beach on Phi-Phi's remote northeastern shore. The resort here arranges boat transfers for guests (there's a thin dirt trail for hikers). Long-tails from Ao Ton Sai cost 500B (one way).

Phi Phi Island Village (☎ in Phuket 0 7621 5014, in Bangkok 0 2276 6056; www.ppisland.com; bungalows from 6500B; ✂ ▯ ▣) This place really is a village unto itself: its whopping 104 bungalows take up much of the beachfront with only a few lonely palms swaying between them. This is the full-service deal with all the trimmings – it's particularly popular with the Japanese jet set.

HAT LAEM THONG

At the northern end of Ko Nai, Hat Laem Thong features Phi-Phi's who's who of glitzy five-star resorts. There's also a small *chow lair* settlement of corrugated-metal shacks at the end of the beach. A long-tail charter from Ao Ton Sai costs 600B. The following resorts can also arrange transfers.

Holiday Inn Phi Phi Island (☎ 0 7521 1334; www.phiphi-palmbeach.com; bungalows 7500-9000B; ✂ ▣) Amid coconut palm at the southernmost point of the beach, this tastefully decorated resort has large Thai-Malay–style bungalows sitting on 2m-high stilts. On the grounds are tennis courts, a spa, dive centre, restaurant and hilltop bar.

Zeavola (☎ 0 7562 7024; www.zeavola.com; bungalows 15,000-37,000B; ✂ ▯ ▣) If you have money to burn, let this be your pyre. Gorgeous teak bungalow mansions incorporate traditional Thai style with simple, sleek modern design. Each comes with glass walls on three sides (with remote-controlled bamboo shutters for privacy), beautiful 1940s fixtures, antique furniture, a patio and impeccable service. Some villas have a private pool.

Eating

We hope you're in the mood for Thai or Italian food, 'cause there's plenty of it on Ko Phi-Phi. If a shopfront isn't a travel agency then it's probably selling food. The local fresh-food market, tucked into the fray of Tonsai Village, is great spot to scout out takeaway meals for pennies.

D's Books (☎ 08 4667 7730; coffee 50-110B; ☼ breakfast, lunch & dinner) In the beating heart of Tonsai Village, this classy cafe has amazing coffee drinks and stacks of cheap reading. Good luck finding a seat – the free wi-fi attracts email-aholics from all over the island.

Papaya (dishes 80-180B; ☼ lunch & dinner) Near Reggae Bar, Papaya is where to go for perfectly cooked Thai standards.

Tonsai (☎ 0 7561 1233; dishes 80-300B; ☼ lunch & dinner) The best seafood restaurant on Ao Ton Sai serves a mouth-watering assortment of the day's catch.

007 Restaurant & Bar (dishes 120-200B; ☼ breakfast, lunch & dinner) Owned by a talkative Scot named James, 007 features ultramodern chrome tables, red cushion booths and, of course, all the Bond paraphernalia you could want. There's a big selection of beer (including British favourites) on tap, and food from the motherland is cooked in a sparkling kitchen.

Ciao Bella (☎ 08 1894 1246; dishes 150-300B; ☼ breakfast, lunch & dinner) Italian-run Ciao Bella is a long-time expat and traveller fave serving excellent pizzas and seafood in a romantic location by the sea. Try the chef's mystery pastas if you're looking for a little adventure. At night, twinkling candles and stars provide the atmosphere for alfresco dining, while lapping waves provide the soundtrack. Ciao Bella is on the sand in Ao Lo Dalam and has a couple of charming bungalows in the back if you're looking for accommodation.

Drinking & Entertainment

Phi-Phi gives Ko Pha-Ngan some serious competition in the party department.

Reggae Bar (Tonsai Village) The most popular nightspot waves its Rasta flags high. Drinking competitions, *moo·ay tai* boxing and the occasional *gà·teu·i* (ladyboy) cabaret get patrons out of their chairs.

Carpe Diem (☎ 08 4840 1219; Hat Hin Khom) Sit on pillows in the upstairs lounge and watch the sun go down (locals say this is the best spot for sundowners). Carpe Diem rocks well into the night with fire shows, dance parties and live music on the beach. It's very popular, and an easy spot for mingling if you're travelling alone.

Hippies (☎ 08 1970 5483; Hat Hin Khom) Hippies is a good place to end the evening. There are candlelit tables on the beach and chill-out tunes on the sound system. Moon parties are thrown throughout the month.

Apache Bar (Ao Ton Sai) With a strange Native American theme (think the Village People) lit by fluorescent lights, this long-time favourite is definitely campy. It fills up early and blasts loud music to all hours (to the annoyance of people sleeping nearby). Look for a new instalment of Apache in Tonsai Village.

Carlitos (☎ 08 9927 3772; Ao Ton Sai) This fairy-light-lit beachside bar, which puts on impressive fire shows, attracts *fa·ràng* seeking beers and a chair in the sand. It gets rowdy and packs in major crowds on dance-party nights. We like how Carlitos does its bit for the environment by recycling.

Getting There & Away

Boats link Ko Phi-Phi to Krabi, Phuket, Ao Nang, Ko Lanta, the Trang Islands and Ko Lipe. Most boats moor at Ao Ton Sai, though a few from Phuket use the isolated northern pier at Laem Thong. The Phuket and Krabi boats operate year-round while boats to Ao Nang, Ko Lanta, the Trang Islands and Ko Lipe only run in the November-to-May high season.

Boats depart from Krabi for Ko Phi-Phi at 9am, 10.30am and 2.30pm (450B to 490B, 1½ hours). From Phuket, boats leave at 8.30am, 1.30pm and 2.30pm, and return from Ko Phi-Phi at 9am, 2.30pm and 3pm (400B, 1¾ to two hours). Speedy bus links on Phuket have made it possible to make a beeline to/from Phuket International Airport. A boat departs from the Ko Phi-Phi Marine National Park headquarters jetty (near Ao Nang) at 9am, returning from Ko Phi-Phi (via Railay) at 3.30pm (450B to 490B, two hours). Prices often drop by 50B in the low season. To Ko Lanta (with continuing service to Ko Lipe and the Trang Islands), boats leave Phi-Phi at 11.30am and 2pm, and return from Ko Lanta at 8am and 1pm (450B, 1½ hours). Rumour has it that a Phi-Phi–Ko Yao ferry will start running soon – ask around for details.

Getting Around

There are no roads on Phi-Phi Don so transport is mostly by foot. If you want to visit a remote beach, long-tails can be chartered at Ao Ton Sai for 100B to 500B depending on how far you go. Chartering a long-tail boat costs 1200B for three hours or 3000B for the whole day.

KO PHI-PHI LEH
เกาะพีพีเล

Like a giant earthen crown rising up from the ocean floor, Ko Phi-Phi Leh is truly a sight for sore eyes. The smaller and scruffier of the Phi-Phi sisters, the island features rounded soaring cliffs that cut through crystalline waters and gorgeous blooms of coral. Two lovely lagoons hide in the island's interior – **Pilah** on the east coast and the legendary **Ao Maya** on the west. Ao Maya hit the jackpot in 1999 when it starred as 'the perfect beach' in the movie version of Alex Garland's cult classic *The Beach*. Visitor numbers continue to soar.

At the northeastern tip of the island, **Viking Cave** (Tham Phaya Naak; admission 20B) is a major collection point for swiftlet nests. Bamboo scaffolding reaches its way to the roof of the cave as nimble collectors scamper up to gather the nests built high up the cliffs. Before ascending the scaffolds, the collectors pray and make offerings of tobacco, incense and liquor to the cavern spirits. This cave gets its misleading moniker from the 400-year-old graffiti made by crews of passing Chinese fishing junks.

There are no places to stay at on Phi-Phi Leh and most people come here on one of the ludicrously popular day trips out of Phi-Phi Don (p695). Tours last between three and eight hours, and include snorkelling stops at various points around the island, with detours to Viking Cave and Ao Maya. Long-tail trips cost around 800B; by motorboat you'll pay around 2000B to 2500B.

KO JAM & KO SI BOYA
เกาะจำ(ปู)/เกาะศรีบอยา

Like Lanta's two baby brothers, Ko Jam (also called Ko Pu) and Ko Si Boya eagerly wait for tourists to come play on their streamers of white sand. The islands share a relaxed ambience where travellers can wander around friendly Muslim fishing villages or fill up their vacation days with afternoons of blissful nothingness.

ANDAMAN COAST

Sleeping & Eating

Limited transportation forces most resorts to close between June and October. Most accommodation has an on-site restaurant.

Siboya Bungalows (☎ 0 7561 8026; www.siboya bungalows.com; bungalows 200-1200B) The well-designed huts sit on a lush lawn and are shaded by expansive palm and rubber trees. Verandahs and hammocks come as standard, and there are also a couple of self-contained houses that are ideal for long-term rentals.

Oon Lee Lodge (☎ 08 7200 8053; www.koh-jum-resort .com; bungalows 700-3800B) The timber bungalows at this Swiss Family Robinson-esque resort (well, actually the owners are a French-Thai family) sit along quiet dunes of the Ko Pu part of Ko Jam. You'll love the restaurant's excellent fusion food.

Koh Jum Lodge (☎ 0 7561 8275; www.kohjumlodge .com; bungalows 4000-5000B) An ecolodge with style: imagine lots of hard woods and bamboo, gauzy mosquito netting, manicured grounds and a hammock-strewn curve of white sand out front. Bliss.

Getting There & Away

From December to April, boats between Krabi and Ko Lanta can drop you at Ko Jam, but you'll pay full fare (450B, one hour). In November and May, only the early-morning boat will make the stop. The islands can also be accessed by boat from Ban Laem Kruat, a village about 30km from Krabi, at the end of Rte 4036, off Hwy 4. The cost is 80B to Ko Si Boya and 100B to Ko Jam.

KO LANTA

เกาะลันตา

pop 20,000

Long and thin, and covered in bleach-blond tresses, Ko Lanta is Krabi's sexy beach babe. The largest of the 50-plus islands in the local archipelago, this relaxing paradise effortlessly caters to all budget types with its west-coast parade of peach sand – each beach better than the next.

Ko Lanta is relatively flat compared to the karst formations of its neighbours, so the island can be easily explored by motorbike. A quick drive around reveals a colourful crucible of cultures – fried-chicken stalls sit below slender minarets, creaking *chow lair* villages dangle off the island's side, and small Thai *wát* hide within green-brown tangles of curling mangroves.

Orientation & Information

Ko Lanta is technically called Ko Lanta Yai, the largest of 52 islands in an archipelago protected by the Ko Lanta Marine National Park (below). Almost all boats pull into Ban Sala Dan, a dusty two-street town at the northern tip of the island.

The village has plenty of restaurants, mini-marts, internet cafes, travel agencies, dive shops and motorcycle rentals. There are five 7-Elevens spread along the island's west coast – each one has an ATM. The *Lanta Biker Map* (below) is a must for anyone who wants to get off the beach and explore the island.

Ko Lanta Hospital (☎ 0 7569 7085) The hospital is 1km south of Ban Lanta (Old Town).

Police station (☎ 0 7569 7017)

Sights
BAN LANTA (OLD TOWN)

Halfway down the eastern coast, **Ban Lanta** (Old Town) was the island's original port and commercial centre, and provided a safe harbour for Arabic and Chinese trading vessels sailing between the larger ports of Phuket, Penang and Singapore. Some of the gracious and well-kept wooden stilt houses and shopfronts here are over 100 years old, and are a pleasure to stroll through. A few pier restaurants offer up fresh catches of the day and have prime views over the sea. A stop at the **Hammock House** (☎ 0 4847 2012; www.jumbohammock.com; ☉ 10am-5pm) is a must. The friendly owners have amassed the largest selection of quality hammocks in Thailand. They are stunning and unique creations woven by indigenous hill tribes. Don't forget to pick up a copy of their awesome (and free) *Lanta Biker Map*, a free leaflet detailing some of the coolest spots to stop if you're tooling around on a motorbike.

Old Town can be a charming place to spend the night if you're looking for a calm retreat from the frenetic package-holiday vibe on some of Ko Lanta's west-facing beaches. Check out www.lantaoldtown.com, a site developed by the local expat community, for more information about things to do and see in Old Town.

KO LANTA MARINE NATIONAL PARK

อุทยานแห่งชาติเกาะลันตา

Established in 1990, this **marine national park** (adult/child 400/200B) protects 15 islands in the Ko Lanta group, including the southern tip of Ko Lanta Yai. The park is

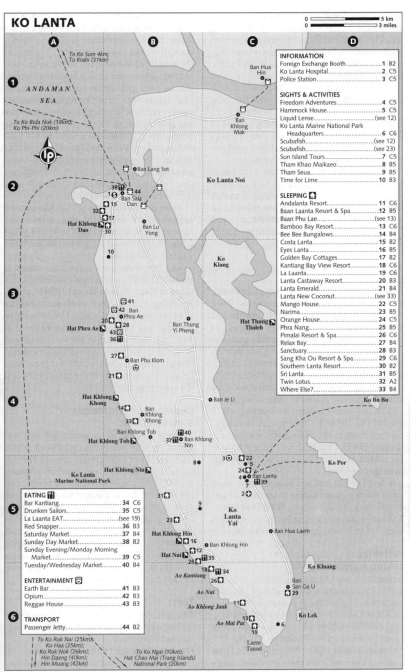

KO LANTA

ANDAMAN COAST

increasingly threatened by the runaway development on the western coast of Ko Lanta Yai. The other islands in the group have fared slightly better – **Ko Rok Nai** is still very beautiful, with a crescent-shaped bay backed by cliffs, fine coral reefs and a sparkling white-sand beach. Camping is permitted on Ko Rok Nok and nearby **Ko Haa**, with permission from the national park headquarters. On the eastern side of Ko Lanta Yai, **Ko Talabeng** has some dramatic limestone caves that you can visit on sea-kayaking tours. The national-park fee applies if you visit any of these islands.

The **national park headquarters** is at Laem Tanod, on the southern tip of Ko Lanta Yai, reached by a steep and corrugated 7km dirt track from Hat Nui. There are some basic hiking trails and a **scenic lighthouse**, and you can hire long-tails here for island tours during the low season.

THAM KHAO MAIKAEO
ถ้ำเขาไม้แก้ว

Monsoon rains – pounding away at limestone cracks and crevices for millions of years – have created this complex of forest caverns and tunnels. There are chambers as large as cathedrals, dripping with stalactites and stalagmites, and tiny passages that you have to squeeze through on hands and knees. There's even a subterranean pool you can take a chilly swim in. Sensible shoes are essential and total coverage in mud is almost guaranteed.

Tham Khao Maikaeo is reached via a guided trek through the jungle. A local family runs treks to the caves (with torches) for around 200B. The best way to get here is by rented motorcycle, or most resorts can arrange transport.

Close by, but reached by a separate track from the dirt road leading to the marine national park headquarters, **Tham Seua** (Tiger Cave) also has interesting tunnels to explore; elephant treks run up here from Hat Nui.

Activities
DIVING & SNORKELLING
Sometimes Ko Lanta can feel like the dark horse in Thailand's diving scene. Newbies flock to Ko Tao off the gulf coast, others head to Khao Lak (the gateway to the Similans), and holidaymakers who want a side order of scuba wind up on Phuket or Ko Phi-Phi. Vacationers here will be delighted to find that some of Thailand's top spots are within arm's reach. The best diving can be found at the undersea pinnacles called **Hin Muang** and **Hin Daeng**, about 45 minutes away. These world-class dive sites have lone coral outcrops in the middle of the sea, and act as important feeding stations for large pelagic fish such as sharks, tuna and occasionally whale sharks and manta rays. Hin Daeng is commonly considered to be Thailand's second-best dive site after Richelieu Rock, near the Burmese border (p641). The sites around **Ko Haa** have consistently good visibility, with depths of 18m to 34m, plenty of marine life and a cave known as 'the Cathedral'. Lanta dive outfitters also run trips up to the King Cruiser Wreck, Anemone Reef and Ko Phi-Phi (p693).

Trips out to Hin Daeng/Hin Muang cost around 5000B to 6000B, while trips to Ko Haa tend to be around 3500B to 4500B. PADI Open Water courses will set you back around 14,000B to 17,000B.

The best dive operation on the island is **Scubafish** (☎ 0 7566 5095; www.scuba-fish.com), located at Baan Laanta Resort (p702) on Ao Kantiang; there's also a small second office at the Narima resort (p702). Unlike some of the large and impersonal operators based in Ban Sala Dan, Scubafish runs personal and personable programs tailored to one's needs, including the Liquid Lense program (see below). The three-day dive packages (9975B) are quite popular.

UNDERWATER PHOTOGRAPHY & VIDEOGRAPHY
If you're looking to try something new underwater, why not enrol in an underwater photography or videography course? The colourful reefs at Hin Daeng and Hin Muang are the perfect spots to click a camera, and the friendly staff at **Liquid Lense** (www.liquidlense.co.uk) can show you how. This digital-imaging academy runs a slew of hands-on courses from one-day, two-dive seminars (7100B) to six-day, nine-dive videography tutorials (32,900B). The Tips & Tricks course (2700B) is a popular option for those who already have a bit of photo experience.

Tours
Boat tours are a popular way to discover the quieter islands orbiting Ko Lanta. Highly recommended operators:

Freedom Adventures (☎ 08 4910 9132; www.freedom-adventures.net; Hat Khlong Nin) This family-run company focuses on day trips to the Trang Islands (p709). Day trips cost 1400B to 1700B. Overnight camping trips to Ko Ngai, Ko Kradan and Ko Rok cost 2300B to 2800B.

Scubafish (☎ 0 7566 5095; www.scuba-fish.com; Baan Lanta Resort, Ao Kantiang) This professional and friendly dive operator offers an interesting array of marine-life classes and site visits through its Aqualogy program.

Sun Island Tours (☎ 08 7891 6619; www.lantalong tail.com; Ban Lanta) Run by a husband-and-wife team, these high-quality tours meander around the Trang Islands or the eastern islands in the Ko Lanta archipelago. A full-day trip costs 1500B per person and includes a traditional Thai meal. Overnight camping trips to Ko Nui are also available upon request.

Courses

Time for Lime (☎ 0 7568 4590; www.timeforlime.net), on Hat Khlong Dao, has a huge, professional kitchen with plenty of room to run amok. It offers cooking courses with a slightly more exciting selection of dishes than most cookery schools in Thailand; half-day courses cost from 1400B to 1800B.

Sleeping

Ko Lanta has some of the best accommodation in southern Thailand. The prices are reasonable, the quality is high and there's an excellent range of lodging to suit any wallet size. Expect 50% discounts in low season

HAT KHLONG DAO

With perfect white sand stretching for over 2km, it's no wonder this was one of the first beaches to attract tourists and developers.

Golden Bay Cottages (☎ 0 7568 4161; www .goldenbaylanta.com; bungalows 1200-2800B; ✷ ☲) Bungalows surrounding a leafy courtyard. The air-con rooms offer the best bang for your baht.

Southern Lanta Resort (☎ 0 7568 4174-7; www .southernlanta.com; bungalows incl breakfast 1800-5000B; ✷ ☲) Loads of shade in the tropical garden and a good-sized beachfront. The pool has a water slide and the bungalows come with TVs, hot showers and minibars. The resort is family friendly and you can organise horse riding from here for 600B per hour.

Twin Lotus (☎ 0 7560 7000; www.twinlotusresort .com; bungalows 5100-21,300B; ✷ ☲ ☲) Although not as avant-garde as Costa Lanta next door, Twin Lotus is a stunning resort that features Balinese-style architecture with a modern twist. Interiors are lavished with lacquered dark-wood panels and roofs have towering,

canvas-coloured thatch that looks a bit like Marge Simpson's hair. The angular infinity-edge pool features panels of concrete and marble – a perfect centrepiece to this intriguing retreat.

Costa Lanta (☎ 0 2662 3550; www.costalanta.com; r 6050-9460B; ✷ ☲ ☲) You'll either adore or abhor this attempt at cutting-edge design. The spartan grounds and near-militant security further add to the austerity of these minimalist concrete bungalows plunked in the middle of the beach-facing forest. The cabin walls can unhinge, offering unobstructed views of the sea (and other cabins).

HAT PHRA AE

The beach at Hat Phra Ae (Long Beach) is only mediocre, but the ambience is lively. A large travellers' village has set up camp and there are loads of *fa-ràng*-oriented restaurants, beach bars, internet cafes and tour offices.

Sanctuary (☎ 0 1891 3055; bungalows 400-800B) A delightful place to stay. There are artistically designed wood-and-thatch bungalows with lots of grass and a hippyish atmosphere that's low key and friendly. The restaurant offers Indian and vegetarian eats among the Thai usuals. The resort holds yoga classes and has a small art gallery displaying local talent.

Lanta Castaway Resort (☎ 0 7568 4851; www.lanta castaway.com; bungalows 750-4000B) A good mid-range find, Castaway has a cottage-clad garden that winds inland away from the beach. Bungalows are spotless and sport lots of Thai paintings and murals. We liked the 2000B rooms the most.

Relax Bay (☎ 0 7568 4194; www.relaxbay.com; bungalows 900-1600B; ✷ ☲) A friendly French-run spot. Could use a little freshening up.

HAT KHLONG KHONG

Stick to the northern end of the rather rocky beach. There are a few good spots for backpackers.

ourpick **Bee Bee Bungalows** (☎ 08 1537 9932; www.diigii.de; bungalows 300-700B; ✷ ☲ ☲) Easily the best budget pick on the island, Bee Bee's super-friendly staff care for a dozen Bali-inspired cabins perched high in the trees. The on-site restaurant has a library of tattered paperbacks to keep you busy while you wait for your delicious Thai staples.

Lanta New Coconut (☎ 08 1537 7590; bungalows 500B) Simple huts surrounded by swaying palms. It's not much, but it's darn cheap.

Lanta Emerald (☎ 7566 7037; www.lantaemerald resort.com; bungalows from 500B; ⛶ 🖳 🍴) Lanta Emerald has all the trappings of a resort, but it's tailored to smaller budgets. Concrete air-con bungalows mix with a handful of comfy bamboo huts on the well-manicured grounds. It's 1km south of the 7-Eleven in Khlong Khong.

Where Else? (☎ 0 1536 4870; www.whereelse-lanta .com; bungalows 500-1500B) Make your way here for Ko Lanta's little slice of bohemia. The bungalows may be a bit shaky but there is great mojo here and the place buzzes with backpackers. The restaurant is a growing piece of art in itself, but the bamboo and coconut knick-knacks are threatening to take over. The pricier bungalows are all unique multilevel abodes sleeping up to four people.

HAT KHLONG NIN

Halfway down the island, the tarmac road forks – head inland towards Ban Khlong Nin or continue south along the coast to the marine national park headquarters at Laem Tanod. The first beach here is lovely Hat Khlong Nin, which gets progressively nicer the further south you travel.

Sri Lanta (☎ 0 7569 7288; www.srilanta.com; villas from 4000B; ⛶ 🖳 🍴) On the southern (and best) bit of the beach, this sophisticated (but slightly overpriced) resort consists of roomy wooden villas in a hillside garden, set back from the shore. There's a very stylish beachside area with a restaurant and pool.

HAT NUI

There are several small beaches around here with upmarket places to stay.

Narima (☎ 0 7566 2668; www.narima-lanta.com; bungalows 1800-2900B; ⛶ 🖳 🍴) Five years ago Narima was Ko Lanta's best resort – every guest would say, 'Don't change a thing!' and, well, the lovely owners have taken those words a bit too literally. The atmosphere is eco-chic, but the bungalows are starting to fade into the brush. The wooden restaurant is lit by lanterns and has some massive gnarled wood furniture.

Eyes Lanta (☎ 0 7566 5119; www.eyeslanta.com; bungalows 3800-5000B; ⛶ 🖳 🍴) Brand spankin' new, Eyes Lanta still has that new-car smell. This self-proclaimed 'lifestyle resort' mixes traditional Asian decoration (think tin gongs, and Chinese paper lanterns dangling from gabled Balinese roofs) for a truly unique ambience.

AO KANTIANG

This bay's tip-top beach has a good sprinkling of sand, and a couple of excellent sleeping options.

Kantiang Bay View Resort (☎ 0 1787 5192; bungalows 400-1500B; ⛶) The staff can be dreadfully rude, the food is mediocre at best, but Kantiang Bay View remains a popular spot for backpackers, probably because the bungalows are decent and they sit right in the centre of the stunning beach.

Baan Laanta Resort & Spa (☎ 0 7566 5091; www .baanlaanta.com; bungalows 3500-4500B; ⛶ 🖳 🍴) Fragrant, green landscaped grounds wind around stylish wooden bungalows and an inviting central pool. The gorgeous bungalows are distinctly Thai in style and feature enormous beds covered in white linen. The attached bathrooms are exceptionally modern with polished fixtures and charming bamboo towel racks. The evening seafood barbecues get rave reviews.

Phra Nang (☎ 0 7566 5025; www.vacationvillage.co.th; r 8000B; ⛶ 🖳 🍴) Charming Mallorca-style digs – they're a bit pricey though.

Pimalai Resort & Spa (☎ 0 7560 7999; www.pimalai .com; r/bungalows 11,500-31,000B; ⛶ 🍴) The sprawling, manicured gardens are interspersed with splendid water features and fountains. The Thai villas all have slick, modern Thai furnishings and excellent views of the beautiful bay below. There are several pools and restaurants on the grounds, a spa and small library.

AO KHLONG JAAK

The splendid beach here is named after the inland waterfall.

Andalanta Resort (☎ 0 7566 5018; www.andalanta .com; bungalows 2500-6500B; ⛶ 🖳 🍴) You'll find a large campus of comfortable and modern air-con bungalows (some with a loft), which all face out onto the sea. The garden is a delight, there's an alluring restaurant, and the waterfall is a 30- to 40-minute walk away. Overall, Andalanta is one of the top spots for families. Call ahead and the staff will pick you up at Ban Sala Dan.

AO MAI PAI

There are only three resorts on this lovely isolated beach.

Bamboo Bay Resort (☎ 0 7561 8240; www.bamboo bay.net; bungalows 700-1700B) Clinging to the hillside above Ao Mai Pai beach, this place has a variety of brick and concrete bungalows on stilts and a fine restaurant down on the sand. The best bungalows come with balconies and grand sea views – it's worth paying the extra baht to stay in one.

Baan Phu Lae (☎ 08 1201 1704; www.baanphulae .com; bungalows 900-1200B; 🐾) The restaurant and many of the bungalows sit right on the semi-private beach and have perfect sunset views. The thatch bungalows come with bamboo-framed beds and rustic porches made for slinging up a hammock.

ourpick La Laanta (☎ 0 7566 5066; www.lalaanta .com; bungalows 2900-6300B; 🐾 🖳 🛋) The southernmost resort on the island, La Laanta is perhaps the friendliest spot in the Land of Smiles, and it isn't saccharine sweet – the owners are genuine folks who make sure all of their guests are enjoying their stay. The bungalows aren't the island's best, but they're very reasonably priced for what you get: creamy walls decorated with swirling floral murals, comfy beds covered in overstuffed pillows, and modern bathrooms with stylish bucket sinks. The resort is a popular spot for families and honeymooners.

EAST COAST

Often snubbed for the strips of Andaman-facing beach on the island's other coast, Ko Lanta's east side has a couple of gems if honey-toned dunes aren't your first priority.

Ban Lanta (Old Town)

These options inhabit old Chinese shophouses near the pier.

Orange House (☎ 08 3104 3109; bungalows 800-1200B; 🐾) If you want to stay in Old Town, but can't afford to stay at Mango House, this friendly spot offers a couple of quaint rooms that look out over the lazy long-tail boats tied to the wooden pier.

ourpick Mango House (☎ 08 1968 6477; r 2000B) Mango House puts the 'teak' in boutique with several well-appointed rooms that feel decidedly old-school. It's like sleeping in an old fisherman's home, except the beds feel like clouds, and the bathrooms have been modernised with the savvy use of sleek concrete and stainless-steel fixtures. Enjoy breakfast on the beautiful terrace that yawns over the ocean.

Ban Sang Ga U

ourpick Sang Kha Ou Resort & Spa (☎ 08 1443 3232; bungalows 500-3500B; 🐾 🛋) It's like you stumbled into Alice in Jungleland – the rooms

DETOUR: KO POR

If Ko Lanta's western coastline is a bit too touristy for your taste, inject a dose of culture into your beach vacation with a home-stay on **Ko Por** (☎ 08 7474 3247; sanae.yamae@ yahoo.com). The small islet, within eyeshot of Ko Lanta, is home to a tiny Muslim fishing village. Guests on the island will stay with one of the local families and participate in the daily chores – cutting rubber and fishing for crab. The homestays cost 350B per day and visitors are politely asked not to bring booze or bikinis to the island. A long-tail picks up (and drops off) homestayers at the pier in Old Town.

are in the trees, the trees are in the rooms – it's all so deliciously nonsensical. The smiley owner (a dead ringer for the Buddha statue at the front desk) knows that his resort is a little quirky, and chortles as wide-eyed backpackers stumble through the twilight zone of classical statues, terracotta warriors and indiscernible papier-mâché projects. Lodging gets a bit lacklustre as the prices go up, so it's best to stick with one of the treehouses, or try one of the beached boats transformed into two-storey suites.

Eating

Ko Lanta's many markets are a great choice for cheap eats. The island's Sunday day market is held in Ban Sala Dan, the Sunday evening/Monday morning market can be found in Old Town, the Tuesday/Wednesday market is in Jae Lee, and you'll find the Saturday market near Khlong Nin. Every resort in Ko Lanta has an on-site restaurant – many of them are excellent. If you can muster up the energy to leave the beach, the following options are worth the trip.

Bar Kantiang (dishes 50-150B; 🕑 dinner) Excellent Thai food comes out of this ramshackle kitchen near Ao Kantiang. It's exceptionally popular with the local expat crowd, who secretly come for the karaoke.

Red Snapper (☎ 0 7885 6965; dishes 90-240B; 🕑 dinner) Excellent fusion tapas fare is served in open-air pavilions dipped in red paint.

Drunken Sailors (☎ 0 7566 5076; dishes 100-200B; 🕑 breakfast, lunch & dinner) This hip, ultra-relaxed, octagonal pad is smothered with beanbags. The coffee drinks are top-notch and go well

ANDAMAN COAST

with interesting bites like the chicken green curry sandwich.

our pick La Laanta (☎ 0 7566 5066; dishes 100–290B; ☙ breakfast, lunch & dinner) The owners of La Laanta, located at the like-named resort, are from all over Southeast Asia, and their fusion cuisine is a blend of secret family recipes. The wonton soup is out of this world, as are the spring rolls and smoothies. If you call ahead, they'll pick you up at your hotel free of charge.

Drinking & Entertainment

If you're looking for roaring discotheques, pick another island. If you want a more low-key bar scene with music wafting well into the night, then head to Ao Phra Ae, where you'll find a cluster of fun spots like Opium, Earth Bar and Reggae House.

Getting There & Away

Most people come to Ko Lanta by boat or air-con minivan. If you're coming under your own steam, you'll need to use the vehicle ferries between Ban Hua Hin and Ban Khlong Mak (Ko Lanta Noi) and on to Ko Lanta Yai. These run frequently between 7am and 8pm daily (motorcycle/car 20/70B).

BOAT

There are two piers at Ban Sala Dan. The passenger jetty is about 300m from the main strip of shops; vehicle ferries leave from a second jetty that's several kilometres further east.

Passenger boats between Krabi's Khlong Chilat passenger pier and Ko Lanta run when there are enough passengers and supplies to go through, and take 1½ hours. Boats depart from Ko Lanta at 8am and 1pm (450B). In the reverse direction boats leave at 10.30am and 1.30pm.

Boats between Ko Lanta and Ko Phi-Phi run as long as there are enough passengers, which means that services peter out in the low season. Boats usually leave Ko Lanta at 8am and 1pm (450B, 1½ hours); in the opposite direction boats leave Ko Phi-Phi at 11.30am and 2pm.

Two high-speed ferries connect Ko Lanta and Ko Lipe (p725; 1800B). One service stops at Ko Ngai (600B), Ko Muk (1200B) and Ko Bulon Leh (1600B); the other stops at Hat Yao in Trang Province. Daily boats run during high season and leave at 1pm. If business is slow, the boats will run every other day.

MINIVAN

This is the main way of getting to/from Ko Lanta, and vans run year-round. Daily minivans to Krabi operate between 7am and 8am (350B, 1½ hours). Check for afternoon services at 1pm and 3.30pm. From Krabi, vans depart at 9am, 11am, 1pm and 4pm. There are also daily air-con vans to Trang (250B, two hours).

Getting Around

Most resorts send vehicles to meet the ferries and you'll get a free ride *to* your resort. In the opposite direction, expect to pay 80B to 180B. Motorcycles can be rented almost anywhere on the island. Always ask for a helmet. The going rate is 250B per day – you might have to bargain. The roads along the western coast are in pretty good shape, making Ko Lanta one of the better islands for tooling around.

TRANG PROVINCE

With its own set of jagged jungly karst formations and lonely islets in the crystalline sea, Trang feels like 'Krabi Lite'. Lately, travellers are getting wise to the province's hidden charms, so it won't be long before the region experiences a tourist boom like neighbouring Krabi did several years back. Trang's shining stars are the constellation of fabled offshore isles known simply as the Trang Islands.

TRANG TOWN

ตรัง

pop 64,700

A glorified launch pad for the Trang Islands of Hat Chao Mai National Park nearby, humble Trang is short on attractions. Foodies will find a gaggle of excellent local markets and Hokkien coffeehouses dotting the town's mishmash of imported architectural styles. Travellers with the Trang Islands in mind should swing through – local travel agencies are dedicated to helping you hop to your island of choice as fast as possible. Many of the Trang Island resorts maintain satellite offices here that can assist with bookings and transfers to islands.

Information

There are several banks on Th Praram VI between the train station and the clock tower.

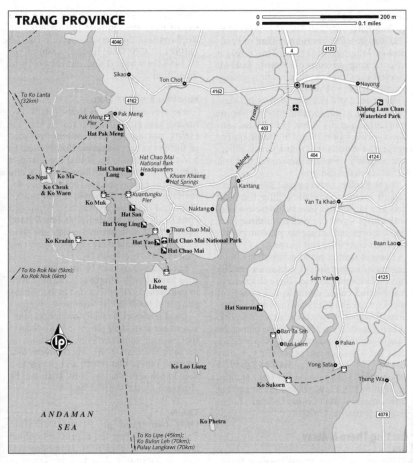

TRANG PROVINCE

0   200 m
0   0.1 miles

To Ko Lanta (32km)

Sikao

Ton Chot

Trang

Nayong

Khlong Lam Chan Waterbird Park

Pak Meng Pier

Pak Meng

Hat Pak Meng

Hat Chao Mai National Park Headquarters

Khuen Khaeng Hot Springs

Kantang

Hat Chang Lang

Ko Ngai

Ko Ma

Ko Cheuk & Ko Waen

Ko Muk

Kuantungku Pier

Naktang

Yan Ta Khao

Baan Lao

Hat San

Hat Yong Ling

Tham Chao Mai

Ko Kradan

Hat Yao

Hat Chao Mai National Park

Hat Chao Mai

To Ko Rok Nai (5km); Ko Rok Nok (6km)

Ko Libong

Sam Yaen

Hat Samran

Ban Ta Seh

Ban Laem

Palian

A N D A M A N   S E A

Ko Lao Liang

Yong Sata

Thung Wa

Ko Sukorn

Ko Phetra

To Ko Lipe (45km); Ko Bulon Leh (70km); Pulau Langkawi (70km)

ANDAMAN COAST

Ani's (☎ 08 1397 4574; 285 Th Ratchadamnoen; ⏰ 9am-10pm) Stock up on English- and European-language titles here.

Post office (cnr Th Praram VI & Th Kantang) Also sells CAT cards for international phone calls.

TAT office (☎ 0 7521 5867; tattrang@tat.or.th; Th Ruenrom) New tourist office located near the night market.

Tosit (285 Th Visetkul; per hr 20B) Fast computers, knowledgeable staff and a cafe serving real coffee.

Sights

Trang is more of a business centre than a tourist town. **Wat Tantayaphirom** (Th Tha Klang) has a huge white *chedi* (stupa) enshrining a footprint of the Buddha that's mildly interesting. The Chinese **Meunram Temple**, between Soi 1 and Soi 3, sometimes sponsors performances

of southern Thai shadow theatre. It's also worth strolling around the large **wet & dry markets** on Th Ratchadamnoen and Th Sathani.

Activities

Boat trips to the mythical Trang Islands in Hat Chao Mai National Park start at 800B per person and take in Ko Muk, Ko Cheuk and Ko Kradan, with lunch and drinks. National-park fees are extra. There are also **sea-kayaking** tours to Tham Chao Mai (850B), where you can explore mangrove forests and canoe under commanding stalactites. **Snorkelling** trips to Ko Rok (1300B to 1500B) can also be arranged by most agencies. For a cultural fix you can spend a day **trekking** in the Khao Banthat Mountains to visit villages of the Sa Kai mountain people (1400B).

Sleeping & Eating

Ko Teng Hotel (☎ 0 7521 8148; 77-79 Th Praram VI; r 180-300B; 🕸) The undisputed king of backpacker lodgings in Trang. Don't forget to pack your adventurous spirit, 'cause if you left it on the bus, these slightly grungy rooms will get you down.

My Friend (☎ 0 7522 5447; 25/17-20 Th Sathani; r 430B; 🕸 🖳) Comfortable modern rooms sport air-con and TV, but not all have windows – check first. There are some quirky decorative flourishes (weird Greek pillars and an oddly mounted aquarium) that will definitely make you grin.

Night Market (noodles per bowl 20B) This excellent market has stalls selling the local delicacy of *kà·nǒm jeen* (Chinese noodles with curry) – you can pick from three spicy curry sauces and spruce up your soup with chopped vegetables and leaves.

Trang is famous for its coffee shops *(ráhn gah·faa or ráhn goh-pée)*, which are usually run by Hokkien Chinese. These shops serve real filtered coffee along with a variety of snacks, typically Chinese buns and dumplings, Trang-style sweets or barbecued pork. When you order coffee in these places, be sure to use the Hokkien word *goh-pée* rather than the Thai *gah·faa,* otherwise you may end up with Nescafé. Try **Sin Ocha Bakery** (Th Sathani; dishes 25-50B) next to the train station, or head to 183 Th Wisek-kul for something truly unique at Mae Chuan Leekpai's house (see the boxed text, p708).

Getting There & Away

AIR

THAI and Air Asia operate regular flights from Bangkok to Trang (around 3000B), but there have been some problems with landing at this airport in rain. The **THAI office** (☎ 0 7521 9923; 199/2 Th Visetkul) is open weekdays only. The airport is 4km south of Trang; air-con minivans meet flights and charge 80B to town. In the reverse direction a taxi or túk-túk will cost 100B to 150B.

BUS

Public buses leave from the well-organised **bus terminal** (Th Huay Yot). Air-con buses from Trang to Bangkok cost 600B to 700B (12 hours, morning and afternoon). More comfortable are the VIP 24-seater buses at 5pm and 5.30pm (1050B). From Bangkok, VIP/air-con buses leave between 6.30pm and 7pm. Buses to Satun (130B) and La-Ngu depart from the southern bus terminal on Th Ratsada. Other services include Hat Yai (110B to 135B, three hours), Krabi (130B to 145B, two hours) and Phuket (240B to 265B, four hours).

MINIVAN & SHARE TAXI

There are share taxis to Krabi (180B, two hours) and air-con minivans to Hat Yai (160B, two hours) from offices just west of the Trang bus terminal. Hourly vans to Surat Thani (200B, 2½ hours) leave from a **depot** (Th Tha Klang), just before Th Tha Klang crosses the railway tracks. There are also departures directly to Ko Samui (220B) and Ko Pha-Ngan (320B) every day at 12.30pm and 3pm from the same depot. **KK Tour & Travel** (☎ 0 7521 1198; 40 Th Sathani), opposite the train station, has several daily air-con vans to Ko Lanta (220B, two hours).

Local share taxis can be hired for custom trips from depots; sample fares include 500B to Pak Meng, 700B to Hat Yao or Hat Chang Lang, and 800B to Hat Samran.

Local transport is mainly by air-con minivan rather than *sŏrng·tǎa·ou.* For Ko Sukorn there are air-con vans from Th Ratsada to the jetty at Palian (60B). Alternatively, take a van to Yan Ta Khao (30B) and change to a Ban Ta Seh *sŏrng·tǎa·ou* (50B); boats can be chartered on the shore at Ta Seh.

TRAIN

Only two trains go all the way from Bangkok to Trang: the express 83, which leaves from Bangkok's Hualamphong station at 5.05pm and arrives in Trang at 7.35am the next day; and the rapid 167, which leaves from Hualamphong station at 6.20pm, arriving in Trang at 10.11am. From Trang, trains leave at 1.45pm and 5.30pm. Fares are 1280/731B for a 1st-/2nd-class air-con sleeper and 521B for a 2nd-class (fan) sleeper.

Getting Around

Túk-túks can be found near the intersection of Th Praram VI and Th Kantang, and charge 30B for local trips. Motorcycles can be rented at travel agencies or at **Ani's** (☎ 08 1397 4574; 285 Th Ratchadamnoen; 🕙 9am-10pm) for about 200B per day. Most agencies can also help you arrange car rental for around 1100B to 1500B per day.

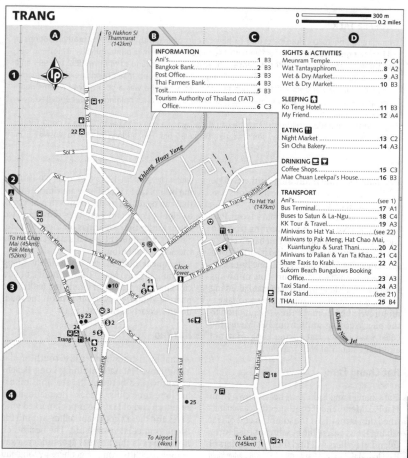

TRANG

0	300 m
0	0.2 miles

INFORMATION
Ani's..1 B3
Bangkok Bank..............................2 B3
Post Office..................................3 B3
Thai Farmers Bank.........................4 B3
Tosit..5 B3
Tourism Authority of Thailand (TAT)
Office....................................6 C3

SIGHTS & ACTIVITIES
Meunram Temple...........................7 C4
Wat Tantayaphirom.......................8 A2
Wet & Dry Market..........................9 A3
Wet & Dry Market........................10 B3

SLEEPING
Ko Teng Hotel............................11 B3
My Friend.................................12 A4

EATING
Night Market.............................13 C2
Sin Ocha Bakery..........................14 A3

DRINKING
Coffee Shops.............................15 C3
Mae Chuan Leekpai's House............16 B3

TRANSPORT
Ani's.................................(see 1)
Bus Terminal.............................17 A1
Buses to Satun & La-Ngu.................18 C4
KK Tour & Travel.........................19 A3
Minivans to Hat Yai..................(see 22)
Minivans to Pak Meng, Hat Chao Mai,
    Kuantungku & Surat Thani...........20 A2
Minivans to Palian & Yan Ta Khao......21 C4
Share Taxis to Krabi....................22 A2
Sukorn Beach Bungalows Booking
    Office................................23 A3
Taxi Stand...............................24 A3
Taxi Stand...........................(see 21)
THAI.....................................25 B4

ANDAMAN COAST

TRANG BEACHES

Trang Province's string of quiet beaches are the jumping-off points for the Trang Islands floating in the turquoise waters of the Andaman Sea.

Hat Pak Meng
หาดปากเม็ง

Thirty-nine kilometres from Trang in Sikao District, Hat Pak Meng serves as the main jumping-off point for several of the Trang Islands. There's a wild-looking stretch of coastline here, with a couple of so-so pockets of sand, but much of the seashore is rather marred by a big concrete sea wall. The main pier is at the northern end of the beach, where Rte 4162 meets the coast.

There are good fresh seafood restaurants in the vicinity.

Tour agencies at the jetty and the Lay Trang Resort organise one-day boat tours to Ko Muk, Tham Morakot (Emerald Cave, on Ko Muk), Ko Cheuk, Ko Ma and Ko Kradan for 750B per person (minimum three people), including lunch and beverages. There are also snorkelling day tours to Ko Ngai (650B) and Ko Rok (1000B to 1200B, plus national-park fees).

Run by a staunch supporter of the Thai royal family, **Lay Trang Resort** (☎ 0 7527 4027/8; www.laytrang.com; bungalows 1000-1500B; ❀) boasts smart bungalows in a tidy garden and a very good patio restaurant. The hard-to-miss **Yok Ya Restaurant** (dishes 40-300B), near the pier, is a

---

COFFEE TALK

Imagine going to London expecting to have a cup of tea with Tony Blair's mother. Sounds a li'l crazy right? Well in Trang, coffee with the mother of a former prime minister is nothing out of the ordinary. After serving two terms, Chuan Leekpai, Thailand's PM from 1992 to 1995 and 1997 to 2001, returned home to humble Trang, where he found Mae Chuan Leekpai (or 'Mama Chuan') sipping her coffee with friends like she did when he was a young boy. When Chuan Leekpai was little, he'd often invite friends over for a drink; after holding office, he invited over the entire country.

And the invitation still holds. Anyone can drop by for a cup of joe with Mama – don't forget to wish her a happy birthday, she's nearly 100 years old. Her address is 183 Th Wisek-kul in Trang Town.

---

local haunt serving traditional southern-style cuisine. It might just be the most famous restaurant in all of Trang.

There are several daily boats from Pak Meng to Ko Ngai at 10am, returning from Ko Ngai between 8am and 9am. You have a choice of a 30-minute ride by speedboat (400B) or a slower ride by 'big boat' (150B, one hour).

There are very regular air-con minivans from Th Kha Klang in Trang to Hat Pak Meng (100B, 45 minutes). You may have to take a motorcycle taxi from the Rte 4162 junction to the pier. Heading south from Pak Meng, the coast road passes Hat Chang Lang, Hat Yao and Hat Chao Mai National Park.

Hat Chang Lang
เกาะช้างหลัง

Hat Chang Lang is the next beach down from Hat Pak Meng, and it continues the casuarina-lined dunes motif. At the southern end of Hat Chang Lang, where the beachfront road turns inland, travellers will find the headquarters of **Hat Chao Mai National Park** (☎ 0 7521 3260; adult/child 400/200B; ☟ 6am-6pm).

The 231-sq-km park covers the shoreline from Hat Pak Meng to Laem Chao Mai, and encompasses the islands of Ku Muk, Ko Kadran and Ko Cheuk (plus a host of small islets). In various parts of the park you may see endangered dugong and rare black-necked storks, as well as more common species such as sea otters, macaques, langurs, wild pigs, pangolins, little herons, Pacific reef egrets, white-bellied sea eagles and monitor lizards.

You usually only need to pay the national-park fees if you visit the park headquarters, Ko Kadran, Hat San or Hat Yong Ling (the next two beaches south of Hat Chang Lang).

The **national park headquarters** (☎ 0 7521 3260, in Bangkok 0 2562 0760; www.dnp.go.th/index_eng.asp;

camping free, tent hire 150B, r 800B, cabins 800-1500B) is the best place to stay. There are simple cabins that can be rented by the room – they sleep six to eight people and have fans. You can also camp under the casuarinas on the foreshore. There's a restaurant and a small shop near the accommodation.

Frequent minivans run from Th Kha Klang in Trang to Chao Mai (60B, one hour), or you can charter a taxi from Trang for 650B. The park headquarters is about 1km off the road, down a clearly signposted track.

Hat Yao
หาดยาว

A shabby fishing hamlet just south of Hat Yong Ling, Hat Yao (meaning Long Beach) is sandwiched between the sea and imposing limestone cliffs. A rocky headland at the southern end of Hat Yao is pockmarked with caves and there's good snorkelling around the island immediately offshore. The best beach in the area is the tiny **Hat Apo**, hidden away among the cliffs; you can get here by long-tail or wade around from the sandy spit in front of Sinchai's Chaomai Resort.

Apparently, pirates used to hoard their treasure south of Hat Yao at **Tham Chao Mai**, a vast cave full of crystal cascades and impressive stalactites and stalagmites, which can be explored by boat. To visit Tham Chao Mai, you can charter a long-tail for 400B per hour from Yao pier. Haad Yao Nature Resort offers sea-kayaking trips to the cave, including lunch, for around 700B to 1100B per person, including guide. You can also rent a kayak and self-explore the cave for 550B (map included).

Haad Yao Nature Resort (☎ 0 1894 6936; www .trangsea.com; r 400-600B, bungalows 800B; 🖳) is run by enthusiastic naturalists and offers a variety of environmental tours in the region. Very orderly and homey bungalows come with shared baths, while the better self-contained bungalows have verandahs and frilly extras. There's also a great pier restaurant here where you can watch the fishermen ply their trade over tasty Thai victuals.

Sinchai's Chaomai Resort (☎ 0 7520 3034; bungalows 300-1500B; 🛁) offers a handful of bungalows nestled under the rocky cliffs at the northern end of Hat Yao. The family that owns it arranges kayaking tours (600B), rents mountain bikes (per day 100B) and runs multiday-tour packages around Trang and the Andaman Coast (prices vary).

From Hat Yao you can charter a long-tail to Ko Kradan (1000B, 1¼ hours) or catch one of the regular long-tail boats to Ko Libong (50B to 100B, 20 minutes). A charter to Ko Libong is 300B. The long-tail jetty is just before the new Yao pier.

Motorcycles (200B) can be rented at Sinchai's Chaomai Resort.

TRANG ISLANDS

The mythical Trang Islands are the last iteration of the Andaman's iconic limestone peaks before they tumble into the sea like sleeping giants. Shrouded in mystery and steeped in local legend (see the boxed text, p710), these stunning island Edens are home to roving sea gypsies and technicolour reefs.

Ko Ngai
เกาะไหง(ไห)

Locals can't seem to decide whether to call the island Ko Ngai or Ko Hai, so we came up with a suggestion – how about 'Perfection'? It's a dishy destination, with a dramatic interior jungle and squeaky-clean beaches that drape around the eastern coast. There is no indigenous population on the island, but there are a few spiffy resorts. A ring of bright coral, excellent for snorkelling, circles Ko Ngai and the visibility in the turquoise water is excellent. Masks, snorkels and fins can be rented from resorts for 50B each, or you can take half-day snorkelling tours to nearby islands (per person 850B). Trips to Ko Rok Nok, 29km southwest of Ko Ngai, cost 1500B by speedboat (plus the marine national park fee).

SLEEPING
There's little here for budgetarians; most places are decidedly midrange and come

with restaurants and 24-hour electricity. The boat pier is at Koh Ngai Resort, but if you book ahead resorts on the other beaches will arrange transfers.

Koh Ngai Resort (☎ 0 7520 6924; bungalows 1500-15,000B; 🛁 🖥 🛏) In a separate cove at the southern end of the island, this resort has its own private jetty and elegant wooden bungalows with huge verandahs. The garden is immense and the resort has a small beach all to itself.

Coco Cottages (☎ 0 7521 2375; www.coco-cottage .com; bungalows 1600-4500B; 🛁) The beach here is a tad thin, but the rest is exquisite: stylish coconut-and-bamboo bungalows, artistically designed grounds and smiley service. There are no manmade materials in sight, massage huts dot the beach and a groovy restaurant/ bar saddles a stream.

GETTING THERE & AWAY
Even though Ko Ngai is technically a part of Krabi Province, the island is most easily accessible from Pak Meng. The resorts provide daily boats from Hat Pak Meng to Ko Ngai at 10am, returning from Ko Ngai between 8am and 9am. Speedboat transfers cost 350B (30 minutes), while the slower 'big boats' cost 150B (one hour). Unless you're staying at Koh Ngai Resort you'll have to take a long-tail for the ship-to-shore ride (40B) or arrange for one of the other resorts to provide transfers. You can also privately charter a long-tail from Pak Meng for 900B.

In the high season, Koh Ngai is a stop on the Ko Lanta–Ko Lipe route (600B). The southbound boats also stop intermittently at Ko Muk, Hat Yao and Ko Bulon Leh (but never all three on one journey) – have your resort call ahead to the ferry service if you are planning to alight before arriving in Ko Lipe. See p725 for more info.

Ko Muk
เกาะมุก

The pearl of Trang (*muk* means 'pearl') is a golden paradise with soaring trees that shelter the local settlement of *chow-lair*. While Charlie Beach Resort has thus far achieved near total domination of wide and white **Hat Farang** (Hat Sai Yao) on the west coast, a Bangkok company has recently bought up the other handful of resorts on this beach with plans to go even bigger. A few lower-end accommodation places remain back in the

---

LEGEND OF THE TRANG ISLANDS

Long ago a young fisherman fell in love with a beautiful girl from a wealthy Chinese merchant family. Her parents lived on the shores of Trang, and when the fisherman and the beautiful girl married, he moved in with her family. The fisherman never talked about his own family because they were poor fisherfolk and he was afraid that his wife would be embarrassed. After his wife pleaded to meet her in-laws, the fisherman finally agreed, and they packed their essential belongings into a small boat for the journey up the coast – a rope, a plank, a liquor bottle, her pearl and his ring. As they paddled up to the fisherman's village, he became fearful once more and turned the boat around. The fisherman's parents were waiting for their son on the beach, and when they saw him turn his boat around his mother cursed them out of sadness and anger. Hours later an epic storm tore through Trang, ravaging the fisherman's boat and killing the two young lovers. In the morning, all that was left were their humble belongings floating on the calm sea: the rope (cheu), the plank (kradan), the liquor bottle (ngai), the pearl (muk) and the ring (wan).

---

bush. The interior of the island is filled with soaring rubber plantations and you are likely to see rubber collection going on throughout the island. The east coast is home to the main village, a handful of quiet midrange options and the island's newest and most swanky resort. Note that much of Ko Muk shuts down in the low season.

Good snorkelling opportunities lie offshore and the archipelago's star attraction, **Tham Morakot** (Emerald Cave), hides at the northern end of the island. This cave is a beautiful limestone tunnel that leads 80m to a mint-green sea lagoon. You have to swim through here at high tide, part of the way in pitch blackness, to a small concealed white-sand beach surrounded by lofty limestone, with a chimney that lets in a piercing shaft of light around midday. Boats can enter at low tide and the cave features on most tour itineraries; it can get pretty crowded in high season, and during the busiest month can reek of urine.

Between Ko Muk and Ko Ngai are the small karst islets of **Ko Cheuk** and **Ko Waen**, which have good snorkelling and small sandy beaches.

SLEEPING

The following places are a short walk north from the pier on a shallow beach.

Mookies (tents 200B) These aren't bungalows, they're 'tent-alows'! The Australian owner Brian claims to sell the coldest beer in Thailand and checks his stock regularly to ensure that he stays true to his claim. It's open year-round and is always a fun place to grab a meal or a drink.

Ko Mook Resort (☎ in Trang 0 7520 3303; 45 Th Praram VI; bungalows 500-1000B) These comfortable huts are excellent value and lie concealed in a thick

garden covered with wild-looking ferns. The design here is unadorned and the tropical isolation is perfect for those searching for a romantic getaway. There's a free daily boat to Hat Farang and snorkelling can be arranged for 350B.

Charlie Beach Resort (☎ 0 7520 3281-3; www.koh mook.com; bungalows 1000-4000B; 🍴 🖵) This place has a bit of an ego – it tried to change the name of the beach from Hat Farang to Hat Charlie. There's a bunch of different bungalow options, ranging from basic shacks to swish air-con deals with little decorations and big porches. It's starting to get a little crowded, but the beach here is lovely. Staff can organise snorkelling tours to Tham Morakot and other islands for around 1000B. It's open year-round.

Sivalai (☎ 08 9723 3355; www.komooksivalai.com; bungalows 5500-9000B) If you're coming from the mainland, you'll spot Sivalai long before you dock on Ko Muk – it guards an enviable position on a spear-shaped peninsula lavished with white sand. Like many of the resorts in the Trang Islands, it seems a bit overpriced for what you get (gardens need to be tended to), but it still ranks high on our list.

GETTING THERE & AWAY

Boats to Ko Muk now leave from the pier at Kuantungku, a few kilometres south of the national park headquarters. There are several ferries to Ko Muk leaving around noon and returning at 8am (55B, 30 minutes). A chartered long-tail from Kuantungku to Ko Muk costs from 700B (800B to Hat Farang). Chartered long-tails from Pak Meng cost around 1000B. Air-con vans run frequently from Trang to Kuantungku for 100B (one hour). Contact your resort ahead of time and ask about transport updates and any possible discounts or deals (perhaps other people are looking to charter a long-tail as well).

From November to May, Ko Muk is one of the stops on the speedboats connecting Ko Lanta and Ko Lipe; see p725 for details.

Ko Kradan
เกาะกระดาน

With a juicy inner jungle and the best house reef in the region (if not all of Thailand), sand-strewn Ko Kradan takes home the sash and crown. This beauty queen is protected under the Hat Chao Mai National Park mandate, so development has been limited to a couple resorts. While day tripping is popular, you can really only appreciate the island's natural splendour as the sun rises and sets over the easily anthropomorphised karst formations along the horizon.

SLEEPING

Paradise Lost Resort (☎ 08 9587 2409/1391; www .kokradan.com; bungalows 600-1200B; ❄) Wally, a friendly American, has built a veritable summer camp of rustic bungalows deep within the island's interior jungle. Locals say the woods are haunted, but all we heard in the evenings was friendly laughter and delicious Thai platters sizzling in the crock-pot. Wally's been around these parts for ages and has great tips on uncovering the islands' secrets.

our pick **Seven Seas** (☎ in Bangkok 0 2250 4526; www.sevenseasresorts.com; r/bungalows 5000-10,000B;

❄ 🖵 ❄) A stunning new addition to the island, this small luxury resort has ultra-slick rooms with enormous beds that could sleep four (if you're into that). Long-tail outings to Ko Kra Rok and the Emerald Cave on Ko Muk (around 2000B) are popular ways to pass the day. Beach bums will adore the local stretch of sand out front, where cotton hammocks link the curling mangroves that lightly pepper the shore. The breezy on-site restaurant, hugging the jet-black infinity-edge pool, serves a mix of gourmet Western dishes (Caesar salads are a big hit) and excellent southern-style curries (spicy!). Overall, it's a tad pricey, but the amazing staff more than make up for it.

GETTING THERE & AWAY

The best way to reach Ko Kradan is to contact your desired accommodation in advance and ask if they can lend a helping hand – sometimes you can hitch a ride with a supply vessel, or if other guests are arriving you can split a long-tail. Solo long-tail charters cost 1000B from Pak Meng and it's about the same price from Kuantungku. If you're short on cash you can take a ferry from Kuantungku to Ko Muk (or from Hat Yao to Ko Libong) and then finish the journey in a long-tail. The 'public' boats that shuttle fishermen to Ko Muk and Ko Libong usually don't go as far as Ko Kradan – the island does not have a local community.

Ko Libong
เกาะลิบง

Thais believe that if you wear the tears of the dugong as perfume, you'll attract your soul mate. Perhaps this is why Trang's largest island, while less-visited than its neighbours, receives a subset of offbeat tourists, as Ko Libong is known for its fertile beds of sea grass (the rare dugong's habitat) more than its beaches, which aren't the most stunning in the region. The island is home to a small Muslim fishing community and has a few resorts on the isolated western coast. The sensitive development here is a real breath of fresh air compared with other islands in the bay.

On the eastern coast of Ko Libong at **Laem Ju Hoi** is a large area of mangroves protected by the Botanical Department as the **Libong Archipelago Wildlife Reserve** (☎ 0 7525 1932). The grass-filled sea channels here are one of the dugong's last habitats, and around 40 of them graze on the sea grass that flourishes in the bay. The nature resorts in Hat Yao (p708)

ANDAMAN COAST

and here on Ko Libong offer dugong-spotting tours by sea kayak, led by trained naturalists, for around 1000B. Sea kayaks can also be rented at most resorts for 200B per hour.

If you want to spend the night, **Le Dugong Libong Resort** (☎ 0 7972 7228; www.libongresort.com; bungalows 350-800B) is a neat little budget affair dripping with thatch from its many charming, beachfront bamboo huts – each partly concealed by luxuriant greenery and palms. Indoor-outdoor bathrooms enhance the naturalistic flair. Motorbikes can be rented for 300B per day.

Owned by the same friendly and environmentally conscious people running the nature resort in Hat Yao (p708), **Libong Nature Beach Bungalow** (☎ 0 1894 6936; www.trangsea.com; bungalows 600-1000B; 🔀) is set on a lovely grassy garden and surrounded by rubber plantations. There's a simple restaurant with tasty food and the owners run excellent sea-kayaking tours of the mangroves. The resort is closed in the low season.

GETTING THERE & AWAY

Long-tail boats to Ban Ma Phrao on the eastern coast of Ko Libong leave regularly from Hat Yao (per person 70B to 100B) during daylight hours. On Ko Libong, motorcycle taxis run across to the resorts on the western coast for 70B. A chartered long-tail directly to either resort will cost around 1000B each way.

Ko Lao Liang
เกาะเหลาเหลียง

Two little limestone karst outcroppings – Nong and Pi – make up gorgeous Ko Lao Liang, which technically sits in the Ko Phetra Marine National Park (p719). The only place to stay is **Laoliang Island** (☎ 08 4304 4077; www.laoliangisland.com; 3-day/2-night package per person 5500B) and, so far, this place is more popular with Thais than Westerners. Lodging is in luxury beachside tents equipped with mattresses, fans and electricity. There are plenty of activities on offer, including snorkelling through some amazing house reefs, shimmying up the islands' karst cliffs and sea kayaking across crystal horizons. At night there's a small bar and the restaurant sometimes puts together seafood barbecues. Package rates include all meals, gear and a few activities are available. Transport to/from Hat Yao is included in the price. A 200-person ferry leaves Hat Yao at 1pm, and departs from the island at noon.

Ko Sukorn
เกาะสุกร

Sukorn means 'pig', which is a tad ironic since the island is home to a small Muslim community. Keeping these fisherfolk company are four cars, three dogs (locals don't like 'em) and hundreds of water buffalo. Ko Sukorn is a place to take in the local culture as well as a few rays. The beaches here are a deep golden colour and, although less flashy than those more popular islands, are more intimate and good for swimming. Clean and friendly little villages are strewn between rubber plantations and rice paddies in the interior, and watermelon fields and coconut palms near the coast.

The best way to see the island is by renting a mountain bike for the day (about 50B) – with few hills, stunning panoramas, lots of shade and plenty of opportunities to meet locals, this will get you right into the slower pace of life here. Covering up is an absolute must when you go off the beach because this is a strongly Muslim island.

SLEEPING

There's limited electricity on Sukorn so expect power only in the evenings. For serious backpackers, ask around at the Sukorn boat pier for homestay opportunities. **Pawadee Guesthouse** (☎ 0 8988 74756; r 100B) is recommended.

Sukorn Beach Bungalows (☎ 07520 7707; www.sukorn-island-trang.com; bungalows 850-1950B) This is easily the most professionally run place on the island, sporting comfy concrete and wooden bungalows perfectly positioned for memorable sunsets. The friendly Dutch owner is chock-full of information and can arrange excellent tailor-made island-hopping tours throughout the region. The resort is open year-round (rates drop by 60% in low season), and the booking office near the train station in Trang can arrange transfers to Sukorn as well as other islands.

GETTING THERE & AWAY

The easiest way to get to Sukorn is by private transfers available with the resort of your choice for around 1800B per person. Adventurous types can head to Palian (a 60B ride on public transportation from Trang) and catch a cheaper long-tail here for around 300B.

From Ko Sukorn you can also charter long-tail boats to get to Ko Bulon Leh or Ko Libong (2500B), as well as to Ko Kradan, Ko Ngai or Ko Muk (3000B).

ANDAMAN COAST

Deep South

Where is Mr DeMille? – the Deep South is ready for its close-up. After years of waiting in the wings while diva destinations shone under the sun's tropical spotlight, Thailand's southern frontier is taking the stage, hungry for attention.

The kingdom's Deep South darling is Ko Tarutao Marine Park, whose sand-fringed isles swirl in a tapestry of infinite aqua and jade. Head straight to tiny Ko Lipe, then discover the wilds of the neighbouring islands with a troop of local *chow lair* (sea gypsies).

Exploring the mainland is like opening a clock – a trip to Hat Yai reveals what makes the region tick under the ambient holiday veneer. This trade and transport hub is a rowdy and raucous burg that clangs to the sound of incoming traffic, outgoing produce and haggling in the crowded local markets. The pace is slower in nearby Songkhla, whose urban soundtrack mixes the rhythmic lapping of the tides with the muezzin's call to prayer.

For the past few years, the political situation in the southernmost provinces (Yala, Pattani and Narathiwat) has been unstable, and travelling here can be a risky venture. Sect violence and bouts of terror-inducing attacks are the norm, and although tourists aren't the targets of these aggressive outbursts, it's better not to risk it. It's a shame though – these sleepy towns silently simmer in 2000 years' worth of mystical kingdoms, aromatic spice markets and imperialist mercantilism. If, by the time you read this, the heated situation has cooled, consider editing your itinerary to include a little look-see. If not, thumb through the end of this chapter – you might learn a bit more about the many faces in the 'land of smiles'.

HIGHLIGHTS

- Clicking your camera at a colourful long-tail boat bobbing in the perfect cerulean waters around **Ko Lipe** (p722)

- Rummaging through endless market merchandise of questionable authenticity in **Hat Yai** (p726)

- Letting the local *chow lair* guide you to hidden beaches on **Ko Adang** and **Ko Rawi** (p726)

- Enjoying your steaming street-stall noodles on the sands of **Songkhla** (p731)

- Swinging in a cotton hammock while swishing your fingers in the warm sand of one of the many islands in **Ko Phetra Marine National Park** (p719)

★ Songkhla
★ Hat Yai
Ko Phetra Marine ★
National Park
Ko Rawi ★ ★Ko Adang
★ Ko Lipe

DEEP SOUTH

| ▦ BEST TIME TO VISIT: DECEMBER–APRIL | ▦ POPULATION: 3.91 MILLION |

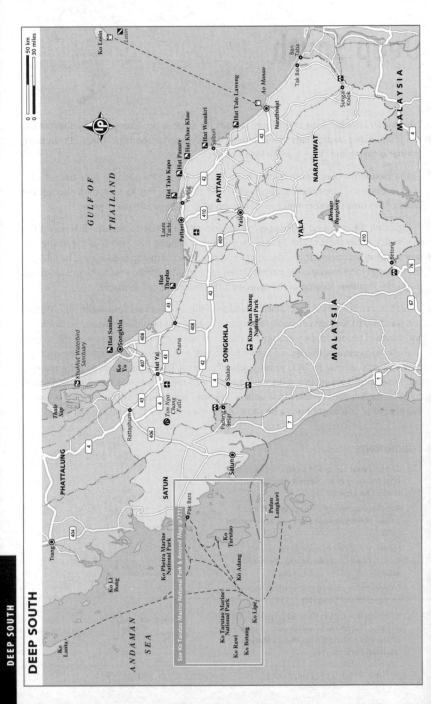

DEEP SOUTH

History

Indian traders first visited the region around 600 BC and introduced Hinduism, which rapidly became the principal faith in the area. By 230 BC, when Chinese traders showed up on the southern shores, large parts of Thailand had been incorporated into the kingdom of Funan, the first state in Southeast Asia. At its peak, the state included large parts of Thailand, Laos, Cambodia and Vietnam. However, most of Thailand's Deep South belonged to a kingdom known as Langka Suka, which neighboured Kedah (in modern-day Malaysia). The area would forever remain linked to the Malay kingdoms rather than the proto-Thai kingdoms.

Sumatra's Srivijaya kingdom, a confederation of maritime states, annexed southern Thailand and Malaysia in the 7th century and held the land until the 13th century. The kingdom became hugely wealthy from tolls extracted from traffic through the Strait of Malacca. As the Islamic sultanate of Kedah rose and assumed power near the present Thai-Malay border, the majority of Thailand (including Tambralinga and nearby states) adopted Buddhism. Islam was well woven into the region's fabric of society by the 14th century, spreading as far north as present-day Songkhla. The Malay dialect of Yawi became the main language of the Deep South and Islam replaced Buddhism throughout the region. This religious and linguistic boundary further cemented the great rift between these future provinces and the rest of Thailand further north.

During the 18th and 19th centuries, after the fall of Ayuthaya, the Malay sultanate of Pattani acted as a fully independent entity until 1909 when the Anglo-Siamese Treaty divvied up the blurred borders of Pattani and Kedah. Pattani went to the King of Siam, as did Narathiwat, Yala, Satun and Songkhla. The rest of the region went to the British and would later become part of Malaysia.

Culturally quite different from the rest of the country, these provinces were comprehensively neglected by the central government over the next 50 years. Islamic traditions and the Yawi language were discouraged by the region's non-Malay administrators, and systematic abuses of power contributed to growing separatist sentiments.

In 1957 Muslim resentment against the ruling Buddhist government reached boiling point and separatists initiated a guerrilla war with the aim of creating a separate Muslim state in southern Thailand. The main armed faction was the Pattani United Liberation Organisation (PULO), which launched a campaign of bombings and armed attacks throughout the 1970s and '80s. The movement began to decline in the 1990s, when Bangkok presented a peace deal consisting of greater cultural freedom and autonomy for the south.

Current Events

After many years of relative peace, the Thai government reduced the strength of their grip in Pattani by annulling their police state–like control. In 2004 tensions quickly heightened as separatist sentiments flourished anew. These antigovernment feelings came at a time when job numbers were dwindling as corporate fisheries ploughed through, wrecking family-run operations. Terrorist attacks had a distinctive communist slant reminiscent of demonstrations many decades ago.

The first major incident that signified a notable rise in antigovernment sentiments occurred in late April 2004, when a string of organised attacks blasted through 11 government buildings across the region at dawn. Insurgents gathered in the Krua Se mosque and held off military forces for nine long hours until the army wore them down and killed everyone inside. Critics argued that such severe force was completely unnecessary and that negotiations should have taken place before the mass killing. Only six months later, at the end of 2004, the Tak Bai incident further created a worrisome rift between the government and its Muslim citizens. Upon the arrest of six southern men, crowds of young locals gathered to demand their release. The demonstrators were met with brute military force and were promptly rounded up and taken to nearby Pattani. Over 80 locals died during the ordeal from severe beatings and mistreatment.

By 2006, when a political coup ejected prime minister Thaksin Shinawatra from office, the death toll in the border provinces had reached over 1400 victims. Unfortunately, the sudden shift in government did not put an end to the violence in the south. By mid-2007 the body count had virtually doubled to roughly 2600, despite the resurrection of the Southern Border Provinces' Administrative

DEEP SOUTH

THAILAND'S DEEP SOUTH: SHOULD I GO?

You're probably thinking, 'Why should I risk my life to find a *fa·ràng*-less beach when there are so many other amazing beach destinations in Thailand?' Well…you have a really good point. The last thing we want is for you to return from your tropical adventure in a cedar box. But don't dismiss Thailand's Deep South so quickly, intrepid traveller; there are many places in the region that have never experienced the 'terrorism' detailed in the global newspapers.

One quick thing before we give you the low-down: we (of course) cannot promise that any destination is *always* safe (you'll find lengthy 'Dangers & Annoyances' sections in our coverage of Thailand's most popular vacation spots), so when we refer to a place as being tourist-friendly, we mean that they are just as safe as, say, Phuket or Chiang Mai.

Satun Province has never been consumed in the political turmoil endemic to its next-door neighbours. The province's *pièce de résistance* is the must-see Ko Tarutao Marine National Park (p720), a collection of 50-some scruffy jungle islands. Songkhla Province is also safe, save for the province's four southernmost 'counties', which have had blips on the police radar. The bustling business town of Hat Yai (p726) is a great spot for market oglers, while Songkhla Town (p729) is a haven for laid-back types who are looking to step off the tourist trail.

As far as the other provinces go? They are untouched hinterlands swathed in thousands of years of religious history. But, like you mentioned before, there are plenty of other beaches and temple towns awaiting the flash of your camera, so it's probably best to start elsewhere. See p715 for more information. Those who are contemplating a visa run across the Malaysian border should consider traversing on the Ko Lipe–Langkawi circuit; however, if you're on a Butterworth-bound train it's not the end of the world to hop the border elsewhere.

Centre (dismantled by Thaksin in 2002) and a public apology to the local Muslim population by Surayud Chulanont, the new prime minister, for the mistakes of the Thaksin government. The intensification of the violence in the Deep South was targeted towards places of learning – palpable reminders of the Thai Buddhist government's unwavering grip on the region. By 2008 angry rebels had incinerated over 200 schools and murdered almost 80 teachers, bringing the five-year death toll up to 3500.

Today the terror-inducing demonstrations continue. Most of the attacks today are firecracker bombs or other small exploding devices that harm few but ignite fear. The number of attacks always increases in the month of November – right after the prime minister passes through for his yearly survey and visit. Victims are chosen at random – men playing cards in a coffee shop are dragged out onto the street and shot, a farmer working in a rubber field gets his head cut off, or passengers in a van are stopped, searched and beaten beyond recognition. It's the pure randomness of these acts that causes the high amount of local anguish. Thai authorities keep a watchful eye on the main perpetrators – Yawi-speaking young males fuelled by severe drug addiction and a lack of formal education. However, until authorities are more proactive in reducing these random acts of violence, the media will continue to blame these traumatic blips of terror on the parliament's lack of control rather than erratic behaviour of muddled separatists. While motives remain unclear, most people believe that violence will only end when all Buddhists have been driven away, and the provinces of Yala, Pattani and Narathiwat can re-establish the sultanate they had over a century ago.

Climate

If you are planning to visit the islands in Satun Province, it is best to plan your trip between early November and mid-May – the seas tend to be quite choppy during the low season and ferry services drastically dwindle. Monsoon rains between June and October make travel along the Andaman Coast rather unappealing. On the other hand, the region's gulf-facing provinces experience the most rain between October and December.

National Parks

Wild islands, pristine beaches and azure seas provide plenty of opportunities for snorkelling and diving in remote Ko Tarutao (p720) and Ko Phetra (p719) Marine National Parks.

Language
Roughly three million citizens in Thailand's Deep South speak Yawi. Also called Pattani Malay, the dialect is commonly spoken in the Muslim community, who make up approximately 80% of the local population.

Dangers & Annoyances
For the last few years, a continuous string of violent incidents have made travel in Pattani, Yala and Narathiwat provinces a potentially risky enterprise. For more information, see the boxed text, opposite, and consult your home country's consular website.

Tourists have not been the targets of the insurgency; however, the oft-unfocused nature of the political unrest has made it difficult to predict where and when the next incident will occur.

Getting There & Away
Regular air, bus and train services connect Bangkok and Hat Yai (p728). Boats connect Ko Lipe and Ko Bulon Leh to popular Andaman destinations like Phuket, Ko Phi-Phi and Ko Lanta. Due to the tense security issues in several regional provinces, most travellers making a 'visa run' across the border to extend their Thai visas pass through Satun Province – the Ko Lipe–Langkawi (p725) route has become particularly popular.

Getting Around
Getting around Thailand's Deep South has become quite straightforward in recent years. Land transport gets funnelled through Hat Yai (p728), while maritime transport along the Andaman Coast passes through the port town of Pak Bara (p719). The gulf waters are rather quiet, other than foreign oil-drilling prospects. Transport to the Ko Tarutao Marine National Park generally shuts down during wet season.

SATUN PROVINCE

If you only have time to visit one province in Thailand's Deep South, make it Satun (often pronounced stoon). The Andaman Coast's southernmost region is rather quiet compared to the tourist rush further north, and the local highlight is the dozens of deserted islands swimming in the turquoise sea. Although they lack the Andaman's trademark limestone karsts, these jungle-clad islets have those perfect peach-coloured beaches you've seen in all the postcards.

Satun has experienced almost none of the political turmoil that plagues the neighbouring regions of Yala, Pattani and Narathiwat.

SATUN
สตูล
pop 33,400
If you're island-hopping your way up or down the coast you probably won't stop in Satun, a town that embodies both meanings of the phrase 'provincial capital'. Tears won't be shed if you have to give this place a miss – Satun only has one real attraction, the **Ku Den Museum** (Satun National Museum; Soi 5, Th Satun Thanee; admission by donation; ⏰ 8.30am-4.30pm Wed-Sun). Housed in a lovely old Sino-Portuguese mansion, this excellent museum was constructed to house King Rama V during a royal visit but the governor snagged the roost when the king failed to show up. The building has been lovingly restored and the exhibits feature dioramas with soundtracks covering every aspect of southern Muslim life.

Sleeping & Eating
Sinkiat Thani Hotel (☎ 0 7473 0255; 50 Th Burivanich; r 663B; ❄) Satun's most comfortable choice is right in the centre of town. It's housed in a tall building and big rooms have plenty of mod cons – the best have fantastic views over the town and jungle.

On's (48 Th Burivanich; dishes from 40B; ⏰ breakfast, lunch & dinner) Popular with visiting yachties, On's is a Western-oriented joint serving up plenty of international eats. There's beer on tap and plenty of local insight from the friendly staff.

Chinese and Muslim bites can be scouted on Th Burivanich and Th Samanta Prasit. Try the 'red pork' with rice at the Chinese food stalls or the southern-style roti offered at most Muslim restaurants (around 50B each). Satun's popular **night market** (off Th Satun Thanee) comes to life around 5pm and serves great Thai curries.

Getting There & Away
BOAT
Boats to Malaysia and Tarutao leave from Tammalang pier, about 7km south of Satun along Th Sulakanukoon. Ferry services are

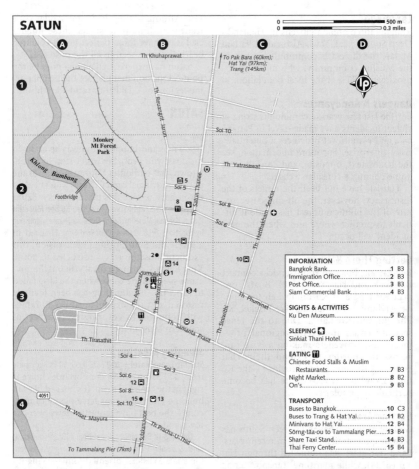

SATUN

INFORMATION
Bangkok Bank..............................**1** B3
Immigration Office.......................**2** B3
Post Office..................................**3** B3
Siam Commercial Bank................**4** B3

SIGHTS & ACTIVITIES
Ku Den Museum..........................**5** B2

SLEEPING 🏠
Sinkiat Thani Hotel......................**6** B3

EATING 🍴
Chinese Food Stalls & Muslim
  Restaurants.............................**7** B3
Night Market..............................**8** B2
On's..**9** B3

TRANSPORT
Buses to Bangkok.......................**10** C3
Buses to Trang & Hat Yai............**11** B2
Minivans to Hat Yai....................**12** B4
Sŏrng·tăa·ou to Tammalang Pier..**13** B4
Share Taxi Stand........................**14** B3
Thai Ferry Center........................**15** B4

dwindling in Satun as Pak Bara (opposite), further up the coast, is priming itself to become the region's major port town. Large long-tail boats run regularly to Kuala Perlis in Malaysia (200B, one hour) between 8am and 2pm. From Malaysia the fare is RM$20.

For Pulau Langkawi in Malaysia, boats leave from Tammalang pier daily at 9.30am, 1.30pm and 4pm (250B, 1½ hours). In the reverse direction, boats leave Pulau Langkawi at 8.30am, 12.30pm and 4pm, and cost RM$27. Remember that there is a one-hour time difference between Thailand and Malaysia.

BUS

Buses to Bangkok leave from a small depot on Th Hatthakham Seuksa, just east of the centre. Air-con services (820B, 14 hours) leave at 7am and 2.30pm. A single VIP bus leaves at 4.30pm (1030B). Ordinary and air-con buses to Hat Yai (80B, two hours) and Trang (100B, 1½ hours) leave regularly from in front of the 7-Eleven on Th Satun Thanee.

MINIVAN & SHARE TAXI

There are regular vans to the train station in Hat Yai (150B, one hour) from a depot on Th Sulakanukoon. Occasional minivans run to Trang, but buses are much more frequent. If you're arriving by boat at Tammalang pier, there are direct air-con vans to Hat Yai (180B), Hat Yai airport (220B) and Trang (220B).

Share taxis can be hired to Pak Bara (400B, 45 minutes) or Hat Yai (400B, one hour).

DEEP SOUTH

Getting Around

Small orange *sŏrng·tăa·ou* (also spelt *săwngthăew*; pick-up trucks) to Tammalang pier (for boats to Malaysia) cost 50B and leave every 20 minutes or so between 8am and 5pm from a depot opposite the Thai Ferry Centre. A motorcycle taxi from the same area costs 60B.

PAK BARA
ปากบารา

Satun's quiet coastline has a few small towns that serve as jumping-off points for the islands in the Ko Phetra and Ko Tarutao Marine National Parks, but the fishing community of Pak Bara is the main point of transit. There is a sense of anticipation in the air here as new businesses open their doors and transport links continue to expand. Plans are in the works to cut a deep-water channel across the peninsula from Pak Bara to Songkhla that would eliminate the need for vessels to travel down to Singapore when passing from Thailand's gulf to the Andaman Sea. If these plans are realised, Pak Bara and its new deep-water seaport will become an important point on the map. Currently, there are no ATMs in Pak Bara (the closest one is in La-Ngu).

Travellers planning to visit the quieter islands of the Ko Tarutao National Park should stop by the **park headquarters** (☎ 0 7478 3485) just behind the pier, where you can book accommodation and obtain permission for camping. Travel agencies at the pier will gladly sell you a ticket to wherever you want to go, and many of these businesses also offer kayaking and snorkelling day trips (from 1500B).

We wouldn't recommend putting Pak Bara on your trip's itinerary, but if you get stuck in town, there are a couple of places to stay, including **Best House Resort** (☎ 0 7578 3058; bungalows 590B; 🅿), which is the closest to the pier. The friendly owner manages a cluster of bungalows surrounding a pond. If you're waiting for a speedboat to one of the islands, there are a few Muslim restaurants huddling around the pier – the best one is next to Andrew Tour.

Getting There & Away

There are hourly minibuses from Hat Yai (southern Thailand's main transport hub) to the pier at Pak Bara (150B, two hours) between 7am and 4pm. They also operate a reverse service. A private taxi from Hat Yai will cost roughly 1500B. A taxi from Trang costs 600B,

and a taxi from Satun will set you back around 400B. There are also vans to Trang (250B, 1½ hours) and Krabi (400B, four hours).

The following ferry information is relevant in high season only (1 November to 15 May); a skeleton crew of slow ferries operates during low season. If you are on the mainland and want to get to Ko Lipe, Ko Bulon Leh or one of the other islands nearby, you must pass through Pak Bara. If you are already on an island (like Ko Lanta, Ko Phi-Phi or Ko Ngai) and want to travel to these southern islands, there are speedboats that will take you there directly. A coterie of ferries and speedboats leave Pak Bara between 11.30am and 3.30pm for the islands in the Ko Tarutao and Ko Phetra Marine National Parks. Ferries to Ko Bulon Leh cost around 350B and speedboats to Ko Lipe cost 650B (or 1200B return), stopping at Ko Tarutao along the way.

KO PHETRA MARINE NATIONAL PARK
อุทยานแห่งชาติหมู่เกาะเภตรา

Often outshone by the Ko Tarutao Marine National Park next door, **Ko Phetra Marine National Park** (☎ 0 7478 1582; adult/child 400/200B) is a stunning archipelago that includes Ko Khao Yai, Ko Lao Liang (p712), Ko Bulon Leh (the park's only island with privately run accommodation; see p720) and 19 other furry green isles.

The park headquarters is located 3km southeast of Pak Bara at Ao Nun. Make sure to stop by if you plan on pitching a tent on one of the park's deserted islands.

Ko Bulon Leh
เกาะบุโหลนเล

Floating in the sea between the Trang Islands and Ko Tarutao Marine Park, Ko Bulon Leh (also called Bulon) is surrounded by crystal-clear waters that mingle with its powder-soft beaches. The island is in that perfect state of limbo where it's developed enough to offer comfortable facilities, yet not so popular that you have to fight for your own patch of sand.

The southern part of the island is where you'll find scenic **Mango Bay**, while in the north there is a rocky bay that's home to small settlements of *chow lair* (also spelt *chao leh*). The island is perfect for hiking – the interior is interlaced with tracks and trails lined with rubber plantations that are thick with birds, and you can reach most places on the island within half an hour. There are also some bizarre rock

DEEP SOUTH

formations along the coastline reminiscent of a Salvador Dalí dream. A fine golden-sand beach runs along the eastern coast, with good coral reefs immediately offshore.

Resorts can arrange snorkelling trips to other islands in the Ko Bulon group for around 900B, and fishing trips for 300B per hour. You can also hire masks and snorkels (100B), fins (70B) and sea kayaks (150B per hour).

SLEEPING & EATING

Most places here shut down in the rainy season. There are a few local restaurants and a small shop in the Muslim village next to Bulon Viewpoint.

Bulone Resort (☎ 08 1897 9084; www.bulone-resort .com; bungalows 600-1200B) My Bulone has a first name, it's b-e-a-c-h...(sorry, we couldn't resist). The pick of the bunch when it comes to budget options, this simple affair has airy cottages in various sizes, all with plenty of shade under the tall casuarinas that line the northern part of the beach.

Pansand Resort (☎ 0 7521 8035; www.pansand-resort .com; 82-84 Th Visetkul; cottages incl breakfast 1000-1700B) Pansand sits on the island's prime bit of beach. There are amiable colonial-style bungalows, and prim cottages lined up along green grounds. The restaurant here is great and staff can arrange snorkelling trips to White Rock Island (1500B for up to eight people). It's popular – call ahead.

GETTING THERE & AWAY

As the number of ferries continues to expand during high season, it is best to contact your resort on the island for the most up-to-date transport information. A speedboat departs Pak Bara every day at 1.30pm (400B) and arrives on the island at around 3pm. Boats in the reverse direction leave at 9am. Ferries to Ko Bulon Leh from Ko Lipe depart at 2.30pm (550B); ferries to Ko Lipe from Ko Bulon Leh depart at 10am. Additional speedboat services between Ko Lipe and Ko Bulon Leh are available when there is enough demand.

KO TARUTAO MARINE NATIONAL PARK

อุทยานแห่งชาติหมู่เกาะตะรุเตา

Like with any good secret, it's only a matter of time before someone lets the cat out of the bag. In this case, that someone was a producer from *Survivor*, America's eminent reality show, who chose this stunning ma-

rine park for the fifth instalment of the hit series. Fortunately, stringent Thai law has protected **Ko Tarutao Marine National Park** (☎ 0 7478 1285; adult/child 400/200B; ☺ Nov–mid-May) from preying developers – the national park is still one of the most exquisite and unspoiled regions in Thailand. The massive archipelago features myriad coral reefs, and 51 islands covered with well-preserved virgin rainforest teeming with dusky langurs, crab-eating macaques, mouse deer, wild pigs, sea otters, fishing cats, water monitors, tree pythons, hornbills and kingfishers.

The park officially closes in the low season (May through October), when virtually all boats stop running.

Ko Tarutao

เกาะตะรุเตา

Most of Ko Tarutao's whopping 152 sq km is covered in dense, old-growth jungle that rises sharply up to the park's 713m peak. Mangrove swamps and impressive limestone cliffs circle much of the island, and the western coast is lined with quiet white-sand beaches.

Tarutao has a sordid history that partly explains its great state of preservation today. Between 1938 and 1948, more than 3000 Thai criminals and political prisoners were incarcerated here, including interesting inmates like So Setabutra, who compiled the first Thai-English dictionary while imprisoned on the island. During WWII food and medical supplies from the mainland were severely depleted and hundreds of prisoners died from malaria. The prisoners and guards mutinied, taking to piracy in the nearby Strait of Malacca until they were suppressed by British troops in 1944.

SIGHTS & ACTIVITIES

The overgrown ruins of the camp for political prisoners can be seen at **Ao Taloh Udang**, in the southeast of the island, reached via a long overgrown track. The prison camp for civilian prisoners was over on the eastern coast at **Ao Taloh Waw**, where the big boats from Satun's Tammalang pier now dock. A concrete road runs across the island from Ao Taloh Waw to **Ao Pante Malacca** on the western coast, where you'll find the park headquarters, bungalows and the main camping site. Boats travel between Ao Pante Malacca and Pak Bara on the mainland.

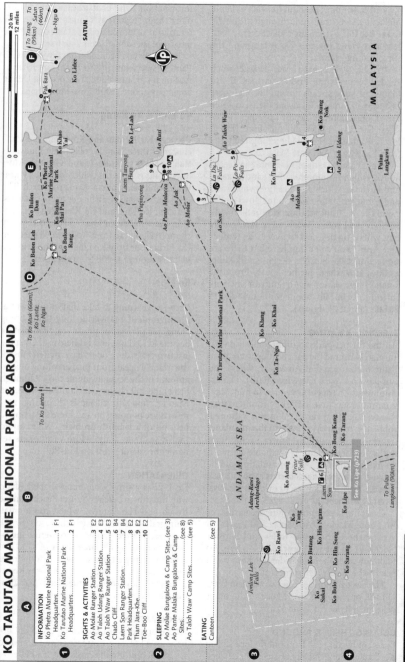

KO TARUTAO MARINE NATIONAL PARK & AROUND

INFORMATION

Ko Phetra Marine National Park
Headquarters..................................1 F1
Ko Tarutao Marine National Park
Headquarters..................................2 F1

SIGHTS & ACTIVITIES

Ao Molae Ranger Station......................3 E2
Ao Taloh Udang Ranger Station............4 E3
Ao Taloh Waw Ranger Station..............5 E3
Chado Cliff...6 B4
Laem Son Ranger Station......................7 B4
Park Headquarters................................8 E2
Tham Jara-khe.....................................9 E2
Toe-Boo Cliff......................................10 E2

SLEEPING

Ao Molae Bungalows & Camp Sites....(see 3)
Ao Pante Malaka Bungalows & Camp
Sites...(see 8)
Ao Taloh Waw Camp Sites..................(see 5)

EATING

Canteen..(see 5)

Next to the park headquarters at Ao Pante Malacca, a steep trail leads through the jungle to **Toe-Boo Cliff**, a dramatic rocky outcrop with fabulous views towards Ko Adang and the surrounding islands.

Ao Pante Malacca has a lovely alabaster beach shaded by pandanus and casuarinas. If you follow the large stream flowing through here inland, you'll reach **Tham Jara-Khe** (Crocodile Cave), once home to deadly saltwater crocodiles. The cave is navigable for about 1km at low tide and can be visited on long-tail tours from the jetty at Ao Pante Malacca.

Immediately south of Ao Pante Malacca is **Ao Jak**, which has another fine sandy beach; and **Ao Molae**, which also has fine white sand and a ranger station with bungalows and a camp site. A 30-minute boat ride or 8km walk south of Ao Pante is **Ao Son**, an isolated sandy bay where turtles nest between September and April. You can camp here but there are no facilities. Ao Son has decent snorkelling, as does **Ao Makham**, further south. From the small ranger station at Ao Son you can walk inland to **Lu Du Falls** (about 1½ hours) and **Lo Po Falls** (about 2½ hours).

SLEEPING & EATING

All the formal park accommodation on Ko Tarutao is around the park headquarters at Ao Pante Malacca and at Ao Molae, where you can pay your park entry fee (400B). The accommodation (open November to mid-May) is far more sensitive to the environment than the average Thai resort. Water is rationed, rubbish is transported back to the mainland, lighting is provided by power-saving light bulbs, and electricity is available between 6pm and 7am only. Accommodation can be booked at the **park headquarters** (☎ 0 7478 3485; cabins 600–1200B) in Pak Bara, or through the **Royal Forest Department** (☎ 0 2561 4292/3) in Bangkok.

Camping is permitted under casuarinas at Ao Pante Malacca, Ao Molae and Ao Taloh Waw, where there are toilet and shower blocks, or on the wild beaches at Ao Son, Ao Makham and Ao Taloh Udang, where you'll need to be totally self-sufficient.

The park authorities run two **canteens** (dishes 40–120B), one at Ao Pante Malacca, the other near the jetty at Ao Taloh Waw.

GETTING THERE & AROUND

Boats connecting Pak Bara and Ko Lipe stop at Ko Tarutao along the way; see p725 for detailed information. One boat from Satun departs daily (high season) at 11am and makes the return trip at 3pm, at a comparable price to the ferry (not speedboat) from Pak Bara.

Long-tails can be hired from the jetty at Ao Pante Malacca for trips to Tham Jara Khae or Ao Son for around 600B. To Ao Taloh Udang you'll pay about 1500B for a round trip.

Ko Khai & Ko Klang
เกาะไข่/เกาะกลาง

Between Ko Tarutao and Ko Adang is a small cluster of three islands collectively known as **Muu Ko Klang** (Middle Island Group). Most interesting is Ko Khai, which has a very neat white-sand beach and a scenic rock arch. The coral here has suffered a bit due to boat anchors, but both Ko Khai and Ko Klang have crystal-clear water for swimming. You can get here by chartered long-tail from Ao Pante Malacca on Ko Tarutao, or from Ko Lipe; a round-trip fare will cost around 1500B from either end.

Ko Lipe
เกาะหลีเป๊ะ

If you're yearning to take that quintessential photograph of a tangerine long-tail bobbing along in a perfect turquoise sea, then make a beeline to Ko Lipe, and get here fast! Over the last two years, developers have snared most of the island's oceanfront property (and a good amount of the scraggly jungle too). Although little Lipe still clings to its laid-back vibe, the island's *chow lair* village is shrinking, new resorts are popping up and there's starting to be a bit of a rubbish problem. We're afraid that it won't be long before vacationers rename the island 'mini Ko Phi-Phi'…

ORIENTATION

Ko Lipe is a tiny boomerang-shaped island with three main beaches: Sunset Beach, Sunrise Beach and Hat Pattaya, which has a small immigration office during high season (p725). A series of paved pathways criss-cross the island, connecting all three strips of sand – it is best to bring a torch at night as sometimes these roads can be confusing. Castaway Resort (p725) has the best map of the island – a charming faux treasure map.

INFORMATION

At the time of research, Ko Lipe still did not have an ATM. Some midrange and high-end resorts accept credits cards but it's better to

KO LIPE

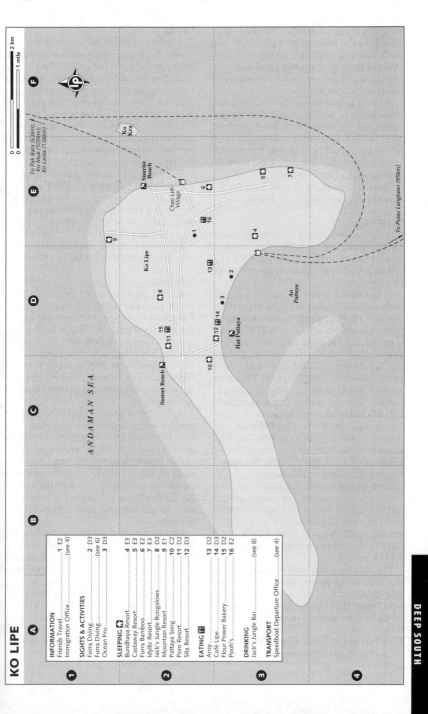

INFORMATION
Friends Travel...........................1 E2
Immigration Office.............(see 4)

SIGHTS & ACTIVITIES
Forra Diving.............................2 D3
Forra Diving.........................(see 6)
Ocean Pro..............................3 D3

SLEEPING 🛏
Bundhaya Resort......................4 E3
Castaway Resort......................5 E3
Forra Bamboo..........................6 E2
Idyllic Resort...........................7 E3
Jack's Jungle Bungalows..........8 D2
Mountain Resort......................9 E1
Pattaya Song.........................10 C2
Porn Resort...........................11 D2
Sita Resort............................12 D3

EATING 🍴
Aroy......................................13 D2
Café Lipe...............................14 D3
Flour Power Bakery.................15 D2
Pooh's...................................16 E2

DRINKING
Jack's Jungle Bar................(see 8)

TRANSPORT
Speedboat Departure Office...(see 4)

ANDAMAN SEA

To Pak Bara (63km);
Ko Muk (105km);
Ko Lanta (136km)

Ko
Kra

Sunrise
Beach

Chao Leh
Village

Ko Lipe

Sunset Beach

Ao
Pattaya

Hat Pattaya

To Pulau Langkawi (95km)

DEEP SOUTH

bring lots of baht, just to be on the safe side. The island also does not have a 7-Eleven (see the boxed text, opposite), so the local convenience shops tend to gouge customers with highly inflated prices – buy your sunscreen before arriving on Ko Lipe.

When it comes to getting transportation information or booking tours, find the girl named Boi. She owns **Friends Travel** (Boi's Travel; ☎ 08 9464 5854; www.kohlipethailand.com), located on the paved road between Hat Pattaya and Sunrise Beach. She also sells some fantastic homemade Ko Lipe souvenirs.

There is a threat of dengue fever on Ko Lipe; see p774 for more information.

ACTIVITIES

If you have your sights set on exploring nearby Ko Adang or Ko Rawi (p726), you can do it under your own steam (long-tail rides cost 50B each way) or you can join up with a tour (see right).

Divers with a Lipe bias will tell you that there are dozens of sites in the area. What they won't tell you is that the visibility can be pretty hit-and-miss – sometimes the water is crystal-clear, at other times hard currents drag in clouds of sand. Nevertheless, Ko Lipe is a chilled-out place to do some scuba – there aren't zillions of divers (like on Phuket or Ko Tao) and the reefs are comparatively unharmed. The region's top dive spots include **Eight Mile Rock**, a submerged pinnacle that lures large pelagic fish; the **Yong Hua Shipwreck**, now covered in marine growth; and **Ko Bu Tang**, with its aptly named Stingray City site. There are also pleasant diving spots dotting the channel between Ko Adang and Ko Rawi.

Most diving schools run trips from early November to mid-May and charge around 2200B to 2500B for a two-dive excursion. A PADI Open Water course will set you back around 12,000B to 13,500B (that's about 2500B more expensive than the schools on Ko Tao; p611)

The following dive operators are recommended, using proper boats rather than long-tails:

Forra Diving (☎ 08 4407 5691; www.forradiving.com) Friendly French-run school with an office on Sunrise and Pattaya Beaches.

Ocean Pro (☎ 08 9733 8068; www.oceanprodivers .net) Professional and knowledgeable staff run a seamless operation.

TOURS

Day trips and overnight camping trips on nearby Ko Adang and Ko Rawi have been quite popular in the last couple of years. The local *chow lair* offer excellent trips on which tourists can snorkel through virgin reefs, sunbathe on lonely beaches and learn about the unique lifestyle of the sea gypsies through their stories and cuisine. Most day trips involve an authentically cooked meal of smoked fish steamed in bamboo over an open fire. If this type of adventure sounds like your cup of tea, you can often find a *chow lair* guide who will lead you on a multiday camping adventure. It is important to ask around before joining a tour as the quality of the guides varies and there are no tour offices. Day trips start at around 400B.

Boi (see p722) also runs quality snorkel trips (550B to 650B) from her travel shop.

SLEEPING

Space and electricity on Ko Lipe are at a premium, so accommodation is way overpriced. Bungalows that go for 300B on other islands are double the price on Ko Lipe during high season. Most resorts close between May and October, when the seas become rather choppy and the speedboats stop running. Virtually every resort has an on-site eatery, and several of our eating options (opposite) also rent out bungalows.

At the time of research, the construction of two five-star resorts was well under way, so if your wallet runneth over, consider checking to see if the Sita or Idyllic resorts are complete.

Porn Resort (☎ 08 9464 5765; Sunset Beach; bungalows 700-800B) This collection of weathered bungalows is the only resort on the comely Sunset Beach. Its bungalow verandahs are ideal for admiring the sun's nightly dip into the ocean.

Forra Bamboo (☎ 08 4407 5691; www.forradiving.com; Sunrise Beach; bungalows 700-1200B) Giant bamboo bungalows sit in a thicketed patch of land facing Sunrise Beach, providing the quintessential Ko Lipe views of languid long-tails and jungle islets further in the distance. Discounts are offered when diving with Forra (left).

Jack's Jungle Bungalows (www.jacksjjunglebar .com; bungalows 950B) Located 150m inland from Sunset Beach, these brand-new bungalows sit in the heart of a vine-tangled rainforest. If you're looking for ocean views, this is not the place for you; however, Jack's Jungle offers a pretty good bang for your baht.

Pattaya Song (☎ 0 7472 8034; www.pattayasongresort.com; bungalows 1200-1800B) Above the rocks at the western end of the beach, this Italian-run pad has decent wood and concrete huts strung out either along the ocean or a little way up the hill. The Pattaya Seafood restaurant here serves excellent food and the resort can organise fishing and island-hopping trips around the area.

Mountain Resort (☎ 0 7472 8131; Sunrise Beach; bungalows 1600B; ✂) This big resort has outstanding views of Ko Adang from its hillside location. Winding wooden walkways lead up from the beach, where you'll find a terraced restaurant with equally spectacular vistas. Recent sewage problems (or rather the lack of a sewerage system) have left a section of the resort smelling a tad funny, so poke your nose around before dropping your bags. Beach massages (300B) and snorkel gear (50B) are always on offer.

Bundhaya Resort (☎ 0 7475 0248; www.bundhayaresort.com; Hat Pattaya; bungalows incl breakfast 1600-4000B; ✂ 🖳) Corporate Bundhaya is a necessary evil on a laid-back island like Ko Lipe. The uber-organised resort doubles as a speedboat ticket and immigration office. Soulless wooden bungalows are comfortable but overpriced, although the complimentary buffet breakfast will keep you full until dinner.

Castaway Resort (☎ 08 3138 7472; www.castaway-resorts.com; Sunrise Beach; bungalows 3000-6250B; 🖳) You're probably wondering why the heck there's no air-con for a room that costs 3000B. Well, it's all part of the bamboo-chic charm. Everything at Castaway feels decidedly upmarket, from the candlelit restaurant to the breezy, teak-adorned bedrooms stocked with myriad pillows.

EATING & DRINKING

Flour Power Bakery (☎ 08 9464 5884; baked goods from 40B; 🕑 breakfast & lunch) Located behind Sabye Sport on Sunset Beach, Flour Power uses imported ingredients to craft delicious homemade cakes and brownies – just like Mum's recipe back home.

Café Lipe (☎ 0 7472 8036; www.cafe-lipe.com; dishes from 90B; 🕑 breakfast & lunch) A local breakfast legend, the Swiss-run Café Lipe whips up stellar morning repasts – the unfinishable muesli topples over with fresh fruit and colourful grains. A group of brand-new bamboo bungalows (500B; no running water) squats in the backyard.

THE 7-ELEVEN GAME

In Bangkok 7-Eleven stores are thick on the ground, but as you venture further afield these palpable markers of globalisation start to disappear – it's like an off-the-beaten-path-o-meter.

If you're stuck on a long bus ride with nothing to do, play the 7-Eleven Game: try to recall the number of superettes seen in each place you visited. We counted one on Ko Phi-Phi (the busiest 7-Eleven in Thailand), four on Ko Tao and five on Ko Lanta. You'll be happy to know that there are none on Ko Lipe (for now)…

Aroy (☎ 08 7621 9488; dishes 80-180B) True to its name (*aroy* means 'delicious'), this popular Thai restaurant sits along the inland road connecting Sunrise and Pattaya Beaches. The sign is small so you might have to ask around, but you'll be happy you made the effort once you sample the dishes.

Pooh's (☎ 0 7472 8019; www.poohlipe.com; dishes from 120B) Pooh's is a one-stop shop for all of your island needs: a lively restaurant, a bar, internet, a travel agency and a few so-so rooms in the back.

For a round of beers, try **Jack's Jungle Bar** (www.jacksjunglebar.com), a friendly spot in the heart of the jungle that also serves a few killer curries.

GETTING THERE & AWAY

There is no pier on Ko Lipe. Ferries park near the beach (either at Hat Pattaya or Sunrise Beach) and you hop to shore (or on a day with rough seas, a long-tail will pick you up from the ferry). During high season (1 November to 15 May) there are daily boat services departing from Pak Bara (11.30am and 1.30pm, 2½ hours, 600B) and Pulau Langkawi (8am and 9am, 1½ hours, 600B). Boats from Ko Lipe head to Pak Bara at 9.30am, 10am and 1pm, and to Pulau Langkawi at 3.30pm, 4pm and 4.30pm. It is extremely important to note that if you are doing your visa run from Ko Lipe to Langkawi you must stay overnight in Langkawi before returning to Ko Lipe. The boats running between Pak Bara and Ko Lipe almost always stop at Ko Tarutao and Ko Bolun Leh.

DEEP SOUTH

A speedboat from Ko Phi-Phi departs at 8am, stopping in Ko Lanta (at 9.30am) and Hat Yao (12.30pm) before arriving at Ko Lipe at around 3.30pm. Boats going in the opposite direction leave Ko Lipe at 10am, arriving on Ko Phi-Phi at around 5.30pm. A second speedboat service operates between Ko Lanta and Ko Lipe, stopping at Ko Bulon Leh, Koh Muk and Koh Ngai along the way. Ko Lipe–bound boats leave Ko Lanta at 1pm; Ko Lanta–bound boats leave Ko Lipe at 9am. The interisland speedboats cost around 2000B. See www.kohlipethailand.com for more information.

GETTING AROUND

Motorbike taxis whiz around the island offering rides for 50B per person (there are no cars on Ko Lipe); however, it's so small that taxi hire is only necessary if you're hauling some serious luggage. Long-tail taxis whoosh around the island for the same price.

Ko Adang & Ko Rawi
เกาะอาดัง/เกาะราวี

Like Rabelais' Gargantua and Pantagruel, giant Ko Adang and Ko Rawi could clobber little Lipe next door. The best way to explore these islands is on a boat tour guided by a local *chow lair*; see p724 for details.

Ko Adang has brooding, densely forested hills and white-sand beaches, and is said to be haunted by the spirits of dead elephants. When the wind is blowing, the trees shake in a manner that eerily resembles the sound of a pachyderm's cry.

Five stellar beaches, each one more beautiful than the next, flank the island's western coast. Inland, visitors will find a network of rutty trails that lead to highlights like **Pirate's Falls**, a freshwater source for marauders long ago, and **Chado Cliff**, which offers excellent views of the sandy dunes below. There is a ranger station at **Laem Son**, although it's not always occupied. Accommodation can be sorted out at the **park headquarters** (☎ 0 7478 3485; www .dnp.go.th) in Pak Bara (see the website for more details). When the park-affiliated restaurant is open, don't miss out on the spicy *sôm·dam* (spicy green papaya salad).

Ko Rawi is 11km west of Ko Adang and has similar limestone hills and dense jungle, with first-rate beaches and large coral reefs offshore. There is a ranger station on Ko Rawi, and Crusoe wannabes must pay 400B to explore the interior of the island. Wild camping is allowed…much to the park ranger's chagrin.

Other excellent snorkelling spots include the northern side of **Ko Yang** and tiny **Ko Hin Ngam**, which is known for its unique stripy pebbles. Legend has it that the stones are cursed and anyone who takes one away will experience bad luck until the stones are returned to their source.

Long-tails from Ko Lipe will take you to Ko Adang and Ko Rawi for 50B per person, although you might have to do a little bargaining.

SONGKHLA PROVINCE

Songkhla's postal code is 90210, but this ain't no Beverly Hills! The province's two main commercial centres, Hat Yai and Songkhla, are not usually affected by the political turmoil plaguing the cities further south. Intrepid travellers will be able to count the number of other tourists on one hand as they wander through local markets, savour Muslim-Thai fusion cuisine and relax on breezy beaches.

HAT YAI
หาดใหญ่
pop 193,732

Welcome to backcountry Thailand's version of big city livin'. Songkhla Province's liveliest town has long been a favourite stop for Malaysian men on their weekend hooker tours. These days Hat Yai gladly shakes hands with globalisation – Western-style shopping malls stretch across the city, providing local teenagers with a spot to loiter and middle-aged ladies with a place to do their cardio. Tourists usually only get a glimpse of the city's winking commercial lights from the window of their train carriage as they connect the dots along the peninsula, but those who decide to explore will be rewarded with excellent local cuisine (the city has hundreds of restaurants), shopping (DVDs anyone?) and an evening bar scene that brilliantly mixes cosy pubs and bouncing discotheques.

Information

Bangkok Hatyai Hospital (☎ 0 7436 5780-9; bhhimc@bgh.co.th; 75 Soi, 15 Th Phetkasem) One of the best health-care providers in southern Thailand, it offers full medical care and has English-speaking staff.

DEEP SOUTH

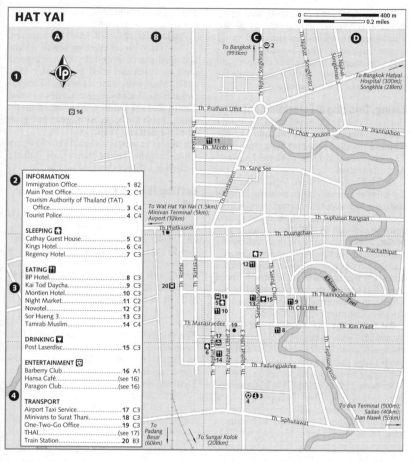

HAT YAI

0 — 400 m
0 — 0.2 miles

To Bangkok (993km)

To Bangkok Hatyai Hospital (300m); Songkhla (28km)

Th Pratham Uthit

Th Jirannakhon

Th Chuti Anuson

Th Montri 1

Th Sang See

Th Suphasan Rangsan

To Wat Hat Yai Nai (1.5km); Minivan Terminal (5km); Airport (12km)

Th Phetkasem

Th Duangchan

Th Prachathipat

Th Thamnoonvithi

Th Chi Uthit

Th Kim Pradit

Th Manasruedee

Th Padungpakdee

To Bus Terminal (500m); Sadao (40km); Dan Nawk (53km)

Th Siphunawat

To Padang Besar (60km)

To Sungai Kolok (208km)

Immigration office (☎ 0 7425 7079; Th Phetkasem) Near the railway bridge; handles visa extensions.

Tourism Authority of Thailand (TAT; ☎ 0 7424 3747; tatsgkhla@tat.or.th; 1/1 Soi 2, Th Niphat Uthit 3) Very helpful staff here speak excellent English and have loads of info on the area.

Tourist police (☎ 0 7424 6733; Th Niphat Uthit 3; ⏰ 24hr) Near the TAT office.

Sights

If you aren't into shopping malls and cabarets, then Hat Yai falls short in the attraction department. **Wat Hat Yai Nai**, 1.5km out of town, features a 35m reclining Buddha (Phra Phut Mahatamongkon). Inside the image's gigantic base is a curious little museum and mausoleum with a souvenir shop. To get here, catch a

motorcycle taxi (40B) near the intersection of Th Niphat Uthit l and Th Phetkasem, and get off after crossing the river; it costs about 15B.

Sleeping

Hat Yai has dozens of hotels within walking distance of the train station.

Cathay Guest House (☎ 0 7424 3815; 93/1 Th Niphat Uthit 2; r 160-250B) Ludicrously helpful staff and plentiful information about onward travel make up for the slightly scary rooms at this popular cheapie.

Kings Hotel (☎ 0 7422 0966; 126-134 Th Niphat Uthit; s/d 450/50B; ❄) It's no royal palace, but Kings offers prim rooms stocked with TVs, minifridges and dated decorations (c 1983). It's two blocks from the train station.

Regency Hotel (☎ 0 7435 3333-47; www.regency-hatyai.com; 23 Th Prachathipat; r 800-1400B; ❄ ⬛ ⬛) This beautiful hotel has that grand old-world charm that's so very rare nowadays. Rooms in the old wing are smaller (and cheaper) and feature attractive wood furnishings, while the new wing boasts amazing views.

Eating, Drinking & Entertainment

Hat Yai is the capital of southern Thailand's cuisine, offering Muslim roti and curries, Chinese noodles and dim sum, and fresh Thai-style seafood from both the Gulf and Andaman coasts.

On Th Niyomrat, between Niphat Uthit 1 and 2, starting at Tamrab Muslim, is a string of casual and inexpensive Muslim restaurants open from about 7am to 9pm daily. Meals at these places cost between 20B to 60B. The extensive **night market** (Th Montri 1) specialises in fresh seafood and Hat Yai–style chicken. After gorging on street-stall food, try hitting one of Hat Yai's upmarket hotels. Great meals can be found at the Montien Hotel, BP Hotel and the splurge-worthy Novotel, which features an amazing all-you-can-eat sushi dinner on Saturday evenings (450B).

Kai Tod Daycha (☎ 08 1098 3751; Th Chi Uthit; dishes 30-50B; ☾ lunch & dinner) Hat Yai–style fried chicken is a dish known across Thailand, and locals claim that Daycha does it best. Enjoy your spicy bird over fragrant yellow rice.

Sor Hueng 3 (☎ 08 1896 3455; 79/16 Th Thamnoonvithi; dishes 30-120B; ☾ 4pm-3am) This popular local legend with branches all over town prepares heaps of delicious Thai-Chinese and southern Thai faves. Simply point to whatever looks good or order something freshly wok-fried from the extensive menu.

Post Laserdisc (☎ 0 7423 2027; 82/83 Th Thamnoonvithi; ☾ 9am-1am) With an excellent sound system and well-placed monitors, this is a great joint to watch the latest blockbuster after dark; music videos are shown as fillers between films. Rockers replace movies on some nights, and the bands tend to be relatively good. Quash the booze with cheap pub grub from the East and West.

Cabaret enthusiasts should visit Barberry Club, Paragon Club or Hansa Café – all are located in a cluster downtown.

Getting There & Away

AIR

There are 12 daily flights connecting Hat Yai to Bangkok (2800B to 3000B). Operators include **THAI** (☎ 0 7423 3433; 182 Th Niphat Uthit 1), **One-Two-Go** (☎ in Bangkok 0 2229 4260 ext 1126, elsewhere 1141; www.fly12go.com; New World Hotel, 152-156 Th Niphat Uthit 2), with one daily flight (1850B), **Nok Air** (☎ 0 2900 9955; www.nokair.com) and **Air Asia** (☎ 0 2515 9999; www.airasia.com).

BUS

The minibus station is 2km southeast of the town centre, though many buses make stops in town. It costs around 50B to take a túk-túk (pronounced dúk dúk) to the bus junction. Destinations from Hat Yai include Bangkok (740B to 1075B, 14 hours), Krabi (235B, five hours), Ko Samui (combined bus/boat 380B, eight hours), Kuala Lumpur (350B to 450B, nine hours) and Phuket (370B, eight hours).

MAKING A (VISA) RUN FOR THE BORDER FROM HAT YAI

The Malaysian border is about 60km south of Hat Yai, and many travellers come through town just to extend their Thai visas. To get an in-and-out stamp, head to Padang Besar, the nearest Malaysian border town (you do not need to head to Sungai Kolok). Buses are the most efficient option, costing 39B (two hours, every 25 minutes from 6am to 6pm); minivans are 50B (1½ hours, hourly from 6am to 6pm).

On the Thai side, the **immigration office** (☎ 0 7452 1020) is open daily from 5am to 9pm. There's another border at Dan Nawk, south of Sadao (open 6am to 6pm), which can be reached by minivan (50B, 1½ hours), but this route sees more through traffic than day trippers. On the Thai side, the **immigration office** (☎ 0 7430 1107) is open daily from 5am to 11pm. If you need a longer Thai visa, you'll have to see the Thai consulate in Georgetown, on Penang Island (accessible through the mainland town of Butterworth). Buses from Hat Yai to Butterworth are run by private tour companies and start from 250B (four hours). Trains from Hat Yai to Butterworth are slower and less frequent.

If you're not in a rush to stamp your passport, try doing your visa run in style by taking the ferry that runs between Ko Lipe and the Malaysian island of Langkawi; see p725 for details.

DEEP SOUTH

TRAIN

There are four daily overnight trains to/from Bangkok, and the journey takes roughly 16 hours. Prices range from 399B for a 3rd-class seat to 1594B for a 1st-class sleeper. There are also daily trains to Sungai Kolok (43B to 284B), Butterworth (180B to 322B) and Padang Besar (57B to 272B).

There is an advance-booking office and left-luggage office at the train station; both are open 6am to 6pm daily.

Getting Around

An **Airport Taxi Service** (☎ 0 7423 8452) makes the run to/from the airport (80B, four daily, during daylight hours). A private taxi for this run costs about 300B.

Sŏrng·tăa·ou run along Th Phetkasem and charge 5B per person. A túk-túk around town should cost you 10B per person, though drivers do like to try to charge foreigners 20B instead.

SONGKHLA & AROUND

สงขลา

pop 87,822

'The great city on two seas' lends itself perfectly to the click of a visitor's camera; however, slow-paced Songkhla doesn't see much in the way of tourist traffic. Although the town hasn't experienced any of the Muslim separatist violence plaguing the provinces further south, it's still catching the same bad press. This is a darn shame, since it's the last safe city where travellers can experience the unique flavour of Thailand's predominately Muslim Deep South. The population is a mix of Thais, Chinese and Malays, and the local architecture and cuisine reflect this fusion at every turn.

Big-name international petroleum companies and their exploration interests offshore bring an influx of multinational (particularly British and Canadian) oil-company employees to the region. The result is a strong Western presence in Songkhla that has helped create a relatively open-minded and prosperous town.

Orientation

The city has a split personality, with the charming older section west of Th Ramwithi towards the waterfront, and a modern mix of business and suburbia to the east. If you enter town from the north, or leave town heading north, you'll pass through Ko Yo and cross the Tinsulanonda Bridges – the longest concrete bridges in Thailand.

Information

Banks can be found all over town.

Immigration office (☎ 0 7431 3480; Th Laeng Phra Ram; ☻ 8.30am-4.30pm Mon-Fri) Visa extensions can be filed here.

Malaysian consulate (☎ 0 7431 1062; 4 Th Sukhum)

Police station (☎ 0 7431 2133)

Post office (Th Wichianchom) Opposite the market; international calls can be made upstairs.

Sights

CITY CENTRE

Songkhla's top site is the excellent **national museum** (☎ 0 7431 1728; Th Wichianchom; admission 150B; ☻ 9am-4pm Wed-Sun, closed public holidays), which was constructed in 1878 in a Thai-Chinese architectural style that's as delightful as the art inside. Design highlights include curved rooflines and thick walls. The grounds are quiet and shady with a tranquil garden at the front – the perfect place to sit under a tree and write in your journal. Inside there are exhibits from all national art-style periods. The most intriguing is on Srivijaya, a 7th- to 9th-century Shivalingam found in Pattani.

If museums aren't your style, head to the beach. The residents have begun taking better care of the strip of white sand along **Hat Samila**, and it is now quite pleasant for strolling or flying a kite (a local obsession). A bronze **Mermaid sculpture**, depicted squeezing water from her long hair in tribute to Mae Thorani (the Hindu-Buddhist earth goddess), sits atop some rocks at the northern end of the beach. Locals treat the figure like a shrine, tying the waist with coloured cloth and rubbing the breasts for good luck. Next to that are the **Cat and Rat sculptures**, named for the Cat and Rat Islands (Ko Yo and Ko Losin). Fragments of a dragon statue are sliced up and placed around the city. The **Nag Head** (dragon head), which shoots water into the ocean, is said to bring prosperity and fresh water – it's a popular meeting spot for locals.

Kids will enjoy cuddling with baby tigers at the **zoo** (Khao Rup Chang; adult/child 30/5B; ☻ 9am-6pm), feeding monkeys on Monkey Mountain (at the north end of town), and pointing at clown fish in Songkhla's brand-new **aquarium** (www.songkhlaaquarium.com; admission 200B).

DEEP SOUTH

SONGKHLA

0 ————— 500 m
0 ————— 0.3 miles

INFORMATION
Immigration Office.................... 1 B3
Malaysian Consulate.................. 2 C3
Police Station............................ 3 A3
Police Station............................ 4 B5
Post Office............................... 5 B5

SIGHTS & ACTIVITIES
Aquarium................................. 6 A1
Cat and Rat Sculptures.............. 7 C3
Khao Noi.................................. 8 C3
Khao Tang Kuan (Monkey Mountain).9 C3
Mermaid Sculpture.................... 10 A1
Nag Head................................. 11 A1
National Museum...................... 12 B4

SLEEPING
BP Samila Beach Hotel.............. 13 C3
Romantic Guest House............... 14 B5
Yoma Guest House.................... 15 B4

EATING
Crown Bakery........................... 16 C4
J Glass..................................... 17 B5
Jetty Restaurant Departure Point....18 A1
Khao Nawy............................... 19 B4
Naa Suan Night Market.............. 20 C6
Parlang.................................... 21 C4
Pavilion Hotel Market................ 22 C4
Roti Stand................................ 23 C4
Seafood Restaurants................. 24 C3
Wachira Night Market............... 25 D6

DRINKING
Baan Kafae.............................. 26 C4
Corner Bier.............................. 27 C4

TRANSPORT
Buses and Minivans to Hat Yai......28 C5
Buses to Nakhon Si Thammarat......29 C6
Minivans to Pattani & Yala.........30 C5
Sŏrng·tăa·ou to Ko Yo................(see 28)
Taxi Stand...............................(see 27)

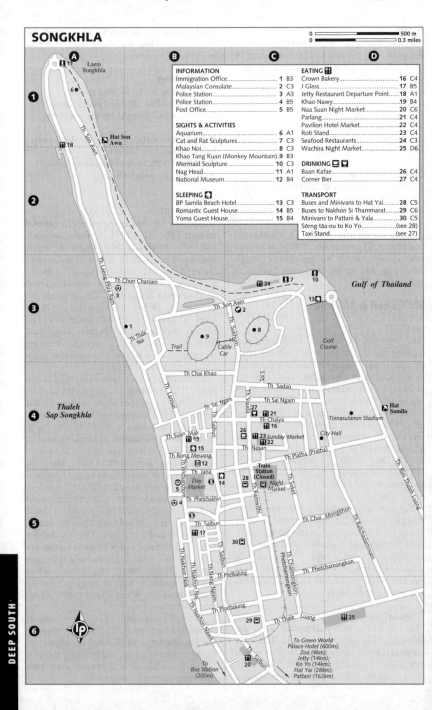

Gulf of Thailand

Thaleh Sap Songkhla

KO YO
เกาะยอ

A popular day trip from Songkhla, this island in the middle of Thale Sap is actually connected to the mainland by bridges and is famous for its cotton-weaving industry. There's a roadside market selling cloth and ready-made clothes at excellent prices. The must-see **Thaksin Folklore Museum** (☎ 0 7459 1618; admission 60B; ⊙ 8.30am-4.30pm) – no relation to the former prime minister – actively aims to promote and preserve the culture of the region. The pavilions here are reproductions of southern Thai–style houses and contain folk art, handicrafts and traditional household implements.

Sleeping
Songkhla's hotels tend to be lower priced than other areas in the gulf, which makes going up a budget level a relatively cheap splurge.

Yoma Guest House (☎ 0 7432 6433; Th Rong Meuang; r 250-350B; 🍴) Like staying in the home of the Thai grandmother you never knew you had, this homey option offers a batch of cutesy, brightly coloured rooms.

Romantic Guest House (☎ 0 7430 7170; 10/1-3 Th Platha; r 250-380B; 🍴) Substantial, airy abodes smell fresh and all come with TVs. The bamboo beds are a charming extra touch. The cheapest rooms have shared toilets.

Green World Palace Hotel (☎ 0 7443 7900-8; 99 Th Samakisukson; r 750-900B; 🍴 🖥 🛒) When expats say that sleeping in Songkhla is a steal, they're not lying – Green World is the proof. This classy affair boasts chandeliers, a spiralling staircase in the lobby and a 5th-floor swimming pool with views. Rooms are immaculate and filled with all the mod cons of a hotel twice the price. Look for it a few hundred metres south of town.

our pick **BP Samila Beach Hotel** (☎ 0 7444 0222; www.bphotelsgroup.com; 8 Th Ratchadamnoen; r 1500B; 🍴 🖥 🛒) A landmark in quaint Songkhla, the city's poshest address is actually a really good deal – you'd pay nearly double for the same amenities on the islands. The beachfront establishment offers large rooms with fridges, satellite TVs and a choice of sea or mountain views (both are pretty darn good). BP can arrange a caddie for the neighbouring golf course.

Eating & Drinking
For quality seafood, head to the street in front of the BP Samila Beach Hotel – the best spot is the restaurant directly in the roundabout.

If market munching is your game, you'll find a place to sample street food every day of the week. On Sundays try the bustling market that encircles the Pavilion Hotel. Monday, Tuesday and Wednesday feature a night market (which closes around 9pm) near the local fish plant and bus station, and the Friday-morning market sits diagonally opposite the City Hall.

Khao Nawy (☎ 0 7431 1805; 14/22 Th Wichianchom; dishes 30-50B; ⊙ breakfast & lunch) Songkhla's most lauded curry shop serves up an amazing variety of authentic southern-style curries, soups, stir-fries and salads. Look for the glass case holding several stainless-steel trays of food just south of the sky-blue Chokdee Inn.

J Glass (☎ 0 7444 0888; Th Nakhon Nai; dishes 50-420B; ⊙ lunch & dinner) J Glass is one of the top fa·ràng hang-outs in town. Only the 1st floor is open for lunch, while the welcoming upstairs patio is reserved for dinner. Enjoy Thai faves (that have admittedly been slightly westernised) while watching the quirky artificial waterfalls gush over the windows.

Jetty Restaurant (dishes 150-250B; ⊙ breakfast, lunch & dinner) Jetty offers a special dining experience on Saturday evenings. At 6pm diners are invited to board a boat that wends its way up the river from the Nag Head to Ko Yo and back. The menu features tasty Thai and international standards and waiters speak excellent English as most of them are students at the local university.

If you're looking for some friendly expats, head to Th Sisuda (north of Th Palatha), where you will find a cluster of tasty spots frequented by the local fa·ràng gang. Corner Bier is a local fave, as is Parlang next door; Parlang is Isan-run, so go for the strips of dried meat or the spicy sôm·đam. The Crown Bakery, across the street from Parlang, is Songkhla's Starbucks-iest spot, featuring free wi-fi, and modern furnishings that orbit a mesmerising fish tank. Go round the corner to find Baan Kafae, where you can sip tea by candlelight, and the best roti stand in town sitting directly across the street.

Getting There & Around
From Songkhla you'll have to go to Hat Yai to reach most long-distance destinations in the south (trains no longer pass through town).

The government bus station is located a few hundred metres south of the Viva Hotel. Three 2nd-class buses go daily to Bangkok (593B), stopping in Chumphon (312B), Nakhon Si

Thammarat (136B) and Surat Thani (207B), among other places. One VIP bus to Bangkok leaves at 5pm (1125B).

To Hat Yai, buses (19B) and minivans (25B) take around 40 minutes and leave from Th Ramwithi. *Sǒrng·tǎa·ou* also leave from here for Ko Yo. Minivans to Pattani (90B) and Yala (100B) leave from the southern part of Th Ramwithi from 6am to 5pm.

Motorcycle taxis around town cost around 20B during the day; rates double at night. There's a taxi and motorcycle taxi stand beside Corner Bier.

YALA PROVINCE

YALA
ยะลา
pop 99,954

Landlocked Yala feels quite different from the neighbouring towns. The city's gaping boulevards and well-organised street grid feels distinctly Western, especially since Yala is predominantly a university town. Thailand's 'cleanest city', as it's known, attracts bright minds from all over the kingdom.

Yala's biggest attraction is **Wat Kuha Pi Muk** (also called Wat Na Tham or Cave-Front Temple), 8km west of town on the road connecting Yala to Hat Yai (Hwy 409). This Srivijaya-period cave temple features a reclining Buddha that dates back to AD 757. A statue of a giant guards the temple's entrance, and inside small natural openings in the cave's roof let in the sun's rays to illuminate a variety of ancient Buddhist cave drawings. Kuha Pi Muk is one of the most important pilgrimage points in southern Thailand.

Take a breather from wát ogling and check out what is known as the largest mail box in Thailand, built in the township of Betong in 1924.

Sleeping & Eating
The lack of tourism means great bargains for a comfy bed.

Chang Lee Hotel (☎ 0 7324 4600; 318 Th Sirirot; r 300B; 🌐 🍴) A 15-minute walk from the train station, the Chang Lee has plush rooms that cater to business travellers. Facilities include a karaoke nightclub and coffee shop.

Although inland, Yala has several excellent seafood restaurants – there's a cluster around Th Pitipakdee and Th Sribumrung. Rice and noodle stalls abound near the train station.

Getting There & Around
Buses to Hat Yai (150B, 2½ hours) stop several time a day on Th Sirirot, outside the Prudential TS Life office. Across the street is the stop for other short- to medium-distance buses north. Daily train destinations from Yala include Bangkok (600B to 1700B) and Sungai Kolok (3rd class 65B).

PATTANI PROVINCE

PATTANI
ปัตตานี
pop 44,800

Like a rebellious child that can never get along with his stepmother, Pattani has never quite adjusted to Thai rule. It was once the heart and soul of a large Muslim principality that included the nearby provinces of Yala and Narathiwat. Although today's political situation has stunted the area's development, Pattani has a 500-year history of trading with world's most notorious imperial powerhouses. The Portuguese established a trading post here in 1516, the Japanese passed through in 1605, the Dutch in 1609, and the British flexed their colonial muscle in 1612.

Orientation & Information
Mae Nam Pattani (Pattani River) acts as a divider between the older town to the east and the newer town to the west. Along Th Ruedi you can see what is left of old Pattani architecture – the Sino-Portuguese style that was once so prevalent in this part of southern Thailand. On Th Arnoaru there are several very old, but still quite intact, Chinese-style homes. There are several banks along the southeastern end of Th Pipit, near the Th Naklua Yarang intersection.

Internet cafe (cnr Th Pipit Talattewiwat 2 & Th Pipit; per hr 20B)
Le Rich Travel (☎ 0 7331 3699; fax 0 7331 3911; 78/13 Th Makrut) Friendly agency that can help arrange everything from safe beach destinations to good local eats.
Pattani Hospital (☎ 0 7332 3411-14; Th Nong Jik)
Police station (☎ 0 7334 9018; Th Pattani Phirom)

Sights
If it weren't for the political unrest in the region, Pattani could be one of the better beach destinations in southern Thailand. Unfortunately, exploring much of the area independently is not a safe option at this time,

---

DEEP SOUTH UNCOVERED

While riding in a taxi through Thailand's Deep South, we got the inside scoop from our taxi driver, Yeats Chaiyarat, on what really goes on when the bombs aren't going off.

In your opinion, what would a traveller enjoy the most during a trip to Thailand's Deep South? I think the best thing for a tourist to see here is the local culture and way of life – how people live and work. The region is 90% Muslim, and Muslim families from all over Thailand send their children to study at the universities in Yala, Pattani and Songkhla. A lot of the places in the Deep South are university towns. The area's history is really fascinating too. You see, before the area was split up between Thailand and Malaysia, it was known as Pattani Darusalam – a completely separate kingdom. And before Pattani, over 600 years ago, the area was called Langka Suka, and included Penang and Langkawi. These days we don't hear a lot about the area's history, but long ago these ancient kingdoms used to trade with the main imperialists from around the world!

Besides the local culture and history, are there any sights that you would recommend? The region's centres of worship are definitely the most interesting things to see on a trip in this area. Outside of Pattani (about 5km) there is a Chinese temple called San Jao Meh Lim and a mosque called Mas Jud Kreu-seh, which have been crumbling beside one another for the last 450 years or so. The Chinese temple was built on the site where a young Chinese girl hanged herself when her brother converted to Islam. There is a wooden statue of the young woman, carved from the same tree which she used to hang herself. The most famous temple in the region is 30km outside of Yala, and is called Wat Chang Hai. It's famous because a monk named Luang Po Tuad used to live here and many people carry around an amulet with his image on it for good luck and protection from harm. It is sort of like the Jatukham Rumanthep amulet from Nakhon Si Thammarat (see the boxed text, p628). I also like Wat Kuha Pi Muk (8km from Yala; opposite), an old temple which the locals call Wat Tham – 'tham' means cave. I don't really like beaches, but I know that a lot of locals go to Hat Narathat (p734), Narathiwat's most popular beach. It's honestly not that nice, but there are no *fa·ràng* tourists. Hat Samila (p729) in Songkhla is probably the best beach for travellers.

What is the biggest misconception about the Thai-Malaysian border? Most tourists probably think that the border is empty and that no one is crossing, but the border at Sungai Kolok is always really crowded. Malaysian men are always lining up to cross the border into Thailand to look for women and karaoke bars. Malaysia has cheaper petrol prices, so you will find tons of people going in the opposite direction too.

Yeats Chaiyarat, originally from Phang-Nga Province, moved to Yala to study at the local university. Today he is a private taxi driver.

---

and there are plenty of pretty beaches further north that are perfectly safe.

Locals frequent **Laem Tachi**, a sandy cape that juts out over the northern end of Ao Pattani. It can be reached by boat taxi from Pattani pier. **Hat Talo Kapo**, 14km east of Pattani near Yaring Amphoe, is another hot spot. And although it's technically in Songkhla Province, **Thepha district**, 35km northwest of Pattani, is the most developed beach destination in the area. There you'll find a few slightly aged resorts that cater mostly to middle-class Thais. At **Hat Soi Sawan**, near the Songkhla-Pattani border, several families have set up informal beachfront restaurants that are popular with weekend visitors. To reach Thepha, hop on any Songkhla-bound bus from Pattani (or vice

versa); mention the name of your resort and you'll be deposited at the side of the road for the brief walk to the beach.

When you're finishing toeing the crystal gulf waters, see the boxed text, above, for a couple of cultural suggestions in the area.

Sleeping & Eating

PATTANI TOWN

CS Pattani Hotel (☎ 0 7333 5093/4; cspatani@cscoms .com; 299 Moo 4, Th Nong Jik; r from 1500B; ❄ ▢ ▣) If you are spending the night in Pattani, you might as well enjoy it. The CS Pattani features a gorgeous colonial lobby, two pools, an excellent restaurant, a sauna and steam room…the list goes on. Breakfast is included. Ask about discounts.

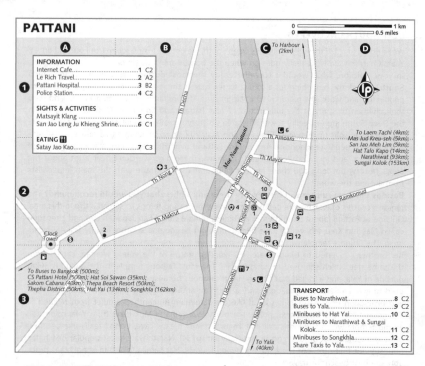

PATTANI

INFORMATION
Internet Cafe..........................1 C2
Le Rich Travel........................2 A2
Pattani Hospital......................3 B2
Police Station.........................4 C2

SIGHTS & ACTIVITIES
Matsayit Klang 5 C3
San Jao Leng Ju Khieng Shrine...........6 C1

EATING
Satay Jao Kao........................7 C3

TRANSPORT
Buses to Narathiwat....................8 C2
Buses to Yala..........................9 C2
Minibuses to Hat Yai...................10 C2
Minibuses to Narathiwat & Sungai
  Kolok...............................11 C2
Minibuses to Songkhla..................12 C2
Share Taxis to Yala....................13 C2

Satay Jao Kao (☎ 08 9737 5417; 37/20 Th Udomwithi; dishes 20-30B; ⏰ 10am-6pm) This well-respected open-air restaurant serves beef satay local style with cubes of rice and a sweet dipping sauce.

Several other restaurants along Th Udomwithi come highly recommended by Pattani's Muslim foodies.

THEPHA DISTRICT

Sakom Cabana (☎ 0 7431 8065; 136 Moo 4, Tambon Sakom; r 600-1000B; 🍴) Located 40km from Pattani town, this basic resort features a clean compound with several attractive wooden duplex bungalows a short walk from the beach.

Thepa Beach Resort (☎ 0 7432 5551; 255 Moo 4, Tambon Thepha; bungalows 1140B; 🍴 🏊) Located near the Pattani-Songkhla border, this resort features attractive bungalows (get one by the lotus pond), not to mention a pool and calm stretch of ocean.

Getting There & Around

Minivans are the region's most popular mode of transport and there are several terminals around Pattani town. As they regularly change location, you will have to ask around for the latest arrival and departure points. Minivans run during daylight hours. Buses to Bangkok depart from the small lot beside a petrol station near the CS Pattani Hotel; call ☎ 0 7334 8816 for ticket purchase and reservations. The trip takes 15 to 16 hours and costs between 650B and 1200B depending on the quality of the bus. Local taxis can take you anywhere in town for 10B per person.

NARATHIWAT PROVINCE

NARATHIWAT
นราธิวาส
pop 44,200
Originally known as Ban Bang Nara, this small provincial capital was renamed after a visit from King Rama VI. He found the locals to be so welcoming and friendly that he gave the town its present moniker, meaning 'home of good people'.

Just north of town is **Hat Narathat**, a 5km-long sandy beach fronted by towering pines, which serves as a veritable public park for locals. Annual long-tail races are held here. The beach is only 3km from of the town centre; you can easily walk there or take a taxi. Five kilometres south of town, **Ao Manao** used to be a popular sun and sand destination, but today it's the stomping ground of local fishermen.

The tallest seated-Buddha image in southern Thailand is at **Wat Khao Kong**, 6km southwest on the way to the train station in Tanyongmat. The image is 17m long and 24m high, and made of reinforced concrete covered with tiny gold-coloured mosaic tiles that glint magically in the sun.

The **TAT office** (☎ 0 7352 2411) is inconveniently located a few kilometres south of town, just across the bridge on the road to Tak Bai.

Sleeping & Eating
Most of the town's accommodation is located on and around Th Phupha Phakdi (signposted as 'Puphapugdee') along the Bang Nara River.

Ocean Blue Mansion (☎ 0 7351 1109; 297 Th Phupha Phakdi; r 350-450B; ❄) Comparatively new, and the only spot in town to really take advantage of the riverfront view. Rooms include a huge fridge and cable TV.

Jay Sani (☎ 08 9657 1546; 50/1 Th Sophaphisai; dishes 30-60B; ☯ breakfast, lunch & dinner) This is where locals go for excellent Thai-Muslim food. Point to whatever curry or stir-fry looks good, but be sure not to miss the sublime beef soup.

Every evening a ragtag **night market** (Th Pichitbamrung) forms north of the clock tower.

Getting There & Around
Air Asia (☎ 0 2515 9999; www.airasia.com) operates one daily flight to and from Bangkok (3800B, 11.10am or 11.35am).

Air-con buses to Bangkok and Phuket and most minivans now leave from the bus terminal 2km south of town on Th Rangae Munka. The buses to Phuket (530B, 12 hours) originate in Sungai Kolok, pass Narathiwat three times daily (7am, 9am and 6.30pm) and continue via Pattani, Hat Yai, Songkhla, Trang, Krabi and Pha-Ngan. Buses to Bangkok (VIP/1st/2nd class 1295/833/669B) take at least 15 hours and depart several times during the day.

Minivans heading to Hat Yai (150B, three hours), Pattani (100B, 1½ hours), Songkhla (150B, two hours), Sungai Kolok (70B, one hour) and Yala (100B, 1½ hours) generally leave on an hourly basis from 5am to 5pm.

Narathiwat is small enough to navigate by foot, although motorcycle taxis only charge 20B to get around. Keep an eye out for the new buses (9B) that circle around town and stop near Hat Narathat. Look for the light-blue bus-stop signs along Th Phupha Phakdi and Th Pichitbamrung.

SUNGAI KOLOK
สุไหงโก-ลก
pop 40,500
This soulless border town isn't a destination unto itself so there's really no reason to spend any time here. Also, the only train that stops in town gets in around 10am, so you'll have the greater part of a day to find a way out (can you tell how much we love this li'l town?). Sungai Kolok has become quite the mini Pattaya – the border, which opens at 5am and closes at 9pm (6am to 10pm Malaysian time) is clogged during the daylight hours with Malaysian men who snip across country lines for some afternoon delight. In the opposite direction you'll find savvy Thais who step over to Malaysia for the discounted petrol.

Information
There are two immigration offices in Sungai Kolok: one at the **border** (☎ 0 7336 1414; ☯ 5am-9pm) and a larger **office** (☎ 0 7361 1231; Th Charoenkhet; ☯ 8.30am-4.30pm Mon-Fri) across from the Merlin Hotel. A tourist police office sits at the border. There are plenty of banks with ATMs in town as well as foreign-exchange booths, which are open during border-crossing hours.

CS Internet (Th Asia 18; internet per hr 20B; ☯ 10am-9pm) Across from the Genting Hotel.

Sleeping
If you must stay the night in Sungai Kolok, there's a large assortment of hotels to choose from – most cater to the 'by-the-hour' clientele.

Genting Hotel (☎ 0 7361 3231; 250 Th Asia 18; r 550-1520B; ❄ ❒) Geared towards the conference trade, the Genting comes equipped with a pub and a karaoke lounge. There are some good, only slightly scuffed, midrange rooms, and it's away from the seedier areas.

Getting There & Away
BUS & MINIVAN
The long-distance **bus station** (☎ 0 7361 2045) is located east of downtown, from where there are three daily air-con buses for the 18-hour trip to Bangkok (720B to 1400B). From

ISLAM IN THAILAND

At approximately 4% of the population, Muslims make up Thailand's largest religious minority, living side by side with the majority Theravadin Buddhists. There are some 3000 mosques in Thailand – over 200 in Bangkok alone. Of these mosques, 99% are associated with the Sunni branch of Islam (in which Islamic leadership is vested in the consensus of the Ummah, or Muslim community), and 1% with the Shi'ite branch (in which religious and political authority is given to certain descendants of the Prophet Mohammed).

Islam was introduced to Thailand's southern region between AD 1200 and AD 1500 through the influence of Indian and Arab traders and scholars. To this day, most of Thailand's Muslims reside in the south, concentrated in the regions of Pattani, Narathiwat, Satun and Yala. These southerners trace their heritage to the former Kingdom of Pattani, an Islamic kingdom whose territory straddled the present-day border between Thailand and Malaysia. Accordingly, the south shares both a border and a cultural heritage with its predominantly Muslim neighbour. Indeed, most of Thailand's southern Muslims are ethnically Malay and speak Malay or Yawi (a dialect of Malay written in the Arabic script) in addition to Thai. These cultural differences, inflamed by a history of perceived religious and linguistic discrimination, have led to a feeling of disconnection from the Buddhist mainland among a radical few of the southern Muslims. Some have called for secession, and fewer still have, in the past, taken up armed insurgency.

Proper etiquette in Thai Muslim communities is simple and predictable. Islam forbids the consumption of pork and alcohol. In very conservative communities, multigender groups will be split off into separate rooms upon arrival. Men and women will be reunited as they depart. Just as is the case when visiting wát, mosques will not permit entry to those in shorts or shoes. Women should not wear short skirts, sleeveless tops or any particularly revealing clothing; simply think conservative. Unless invited to do so, avoid entering the mosque's main prayer hall, as this is a sacred space intended for Muslims. Do not bring cameras, and remember to turn off mobile phones.

Friday is the day of the Sabbath, with religious activities culminating between 11am and 2pm. Locals may be too busy on Friday for visitors and most restaurants close during this time.

Bangkok, the VIP bus leaves at 5.15pm, three 1st-class buses leave between 9pm and 10pm, and the 2nd-class leaves at 9pm. There are two early-morning buses that head to Phuket (580B), stopping in Krabi (460B) along the way. Minivans to Narathiwat (80B) depart on the half-hour from across from the train station. Minivans heading to Pattani (120B), Yala (90B) and Hat Yai (180B) depart hourly during daylight hours, and leave from the Genting Hotel.

TRAIN
Trains from Bangkok to Sungai Kolok leave in the early afternoon and take 20 hours (180B to 1000B) – you'll arrive at around 10am, which will give you plenty of time to get the heck out of town. If you are on a train

passing between Thailand and Malaysia (in either direction) there is really no reason to disembark here. Daily departures connect Sungai Kolok to Surat Thani, Nakhon Si Thammarat and Hat Yai – all of them continue on to Bangkok.

From Rantau Panjang (Malaysian side), a share taxi to Kota Bharu will cost about RM$8 per person (about 80B) or about RM$30 to charter the whole car yourself. The ride takes around an hour.

Getting Around
The border is about 1km from the centre of Sungai Kolok or the train station. Motorcycle taxis zoom around town – it'll cost you around 30B to make the ride between the city centre and the border.

Directory

CONTENTS

ACCOMMODATION

Thailand offers a wide variety of accommodation from cheap and basic to pricey and luxurious. Accommodation rates listed in this book are high-season prices for either single or double rooms. Icons are included to indicate where internet access, swimming pools or air-con are available; otherwise, assume that there's a fan.

A two-tiered pricing system has been used in this book to determine budget category (budget, midrange, top end). In big cities and beach resorts, rates under 1000B are budget, under 3000B are midrange, with top end over 3000B. For small towns, rates under 600B are budget, under 1500B are midrange and top end over 1500B.

In places where spoken English might be limited, it is handy to have the following:

hôrng pát lom (room with fan) and *hôrng aa* (room with air-con).

The following are descriptions of the types of lodging you'll find in Thailand.

Guesthouses

Guesthouses are generally the cheapest accommodation in Thailand and can be found all along the backpacker trail. In areas like the northeast and parts of the southeast, guesthouses (as well as tourists) are not as widespread.

Rates vary according to facilities, from a rock-bottom 150B for a room with shared bathroom and a rickety fan to over 600B for a room with private facilities, air-con and a TV. Many guesthouses make their bread and butter from their onsite restaurants that serve the classic backpacker fare (banana pancakes and fruit shakes). Although these restaurants are convenient and a good way to meet other travellers, don't measure Thai food based on dishes you've eaten in famously mediocre guesthouses.

Most guesthouses cultivate a travellers' ambience with friendly knowledgeable staff and minor amenities like tourist information and book exchanges. But there are also plenty of guesthouses with grumpy, often disgruntled, clerks who let customers know that they dislike their jobs.

Increasingly guesthouses can handle advance reservations, but due to inconsistent cleanliness and quality it is advisable to always look at a room in person before committing. In tourist centres, if your preferred place is full, there are usually a dozen alternatives nearby. Guesthouses typically only accept cash payments.

A subset of the traditional guesthouse is the beach bungalow, which occupies the backpacker destinations along the Thai coastline.

BOOK ACCOMMODATION ONLINE

For more accommodation reviews and recommendations by Lonely Planet authors, check out the online booking service at www.lonelyplanet.com. You'll find the true, insider lowdown on the best places to stay. Reviews are thorough and independent. Best of all, you can book online.

Increasingly rare are the simple palm thatch and bamboo huts, which have been replaced by sturdier wooden or concrete bungalows. Regardless of quality, many bungalows are usually smack dab on the beach or built on a hillside overlooking the ocean.

Hotels & Resorts

In provincial capitals and small towns, the only options are often older Thai-Chinese hotels, once the standard in all of Thailand. Most cater to Thai guests and English is usually limited.

These hotels are multistorey buildings and might offer a range of rooms from midrange options like private bathrooms, air-con and TV to cheaper ones with shared bath facilities and a fan. In some of the older hotels, the toilets are squats and the 'shower' is a *klong* jar (a large terracotta basin from which you scoop out water for bathing). Although the Thai-Chinese hotels have got tons of accidental retro charm, unless the establishment has been recently refurbished, we've found that they are too old and worn to represent good value compared to the guesthouses.

In recent years, there has been a push to fill the budget gap for ageing backpackers or young affluent travellers who want the ambience of a guesthouse with the comforts of a hotel. Now in major tourist towns, new 'flashpacker' hotels have dressed up the utilitarian options of the past with stylish decor and creature comforts.

International chain hotels can be found in Bangkok, Chiang Mai, Phuket and other high-end beach resorts. Many of these upscale resorts incorporate traditional Thai architecture with modern minimalism.

Most top-end hotels and some midrange hotels add a 7% government tax (VAT) and an additional 10% service charge. The additional charges are often referred to as 'plus plus'. A buffet breakfast will often be included in the room rate. If the hotel offers Western breakfast, it is usually referred to as 'ABF', a strange shorthand meaning American breakfast.

Midrange and chain hotels, especially in major tourist destinations, can be booked in advance and some offer internet discounts through their websites or online agents. They also accept most credit cards, but only a few deluxe places accept American Express.

In most countries, 'resort' refers to hotels that offer substantial recreational facilities (eg tennis, golf, swimming and sailing) in addition to accommodation and dining. In Thai hotel lingo, however, the term simply refers to any hotel that isn't in an urban area. Hence a few thatched beach huts or a cluster of bungalows in a forest may be called a 'resort'. Several places in Thailand fully deserve the resort title under any definition – but it will pay for you to look into the facilities before making a reservation.

National Parks Accommodation

Most national parks have bungalows or campsites available for overnight stays. Bungalows typically sleep as many as 10 people and rates range from 800B to 2000B, depending on the park and the size of the bungalow. These are popular with extended Thai families who bring enough provisions to survive the Apocalypse. A few parks also have *reu·an tăa·ou* (longhouses).

Camping is available at many parks for 60B per night. Some parks rent tents (300B a night) and other sleeping gear, but the condition of the equipment can be poor.

The **National Parks' department** (www.dnp.go.th/parkreserve) now has a comprehensive, if slightly clunky online booking system for all parks. Do note that reservations for camp sites and bungalows are handled on different pages within the website. Advance bookings can be made a month ahead and are recommended for popular parks, especially on holidays and weekends.

ACTIVITIES

Thailand has developed a thriving soft-adventure scene that matches a low-impact activity with sightseeing. Most tours are glorified highlight trips in a minivan but a few allow people to sweat and strain in the jungle.

Cycling & Mountain Biking

Long-distance cycling is becoming a popular touring option. **Biking Southeast Asia with Mr Pumpy** (www.mrpumpy.net) contains route suggestions, tips and other details from 'spoke folks'. There are also countrywide cycling and mountain biking tour programs available through **SpiceRoads** (spiceroads.com) as well as tours operators out of Bangkok and Chiang Mai. Cycling around certain cities in Thailand is a great alternative to public transport; for details on bicycle hire see p762.

Diving & Snorkelling

Thailand's two coastlines and countless islands are popular among divers for their warm and calm waters and colourful marine life. Lonely Planet's richly illustrated *Diving & Snorkelling Thailand* is full of vital information for serious divers.

Reef dives along the Andaman Coast are particularly rewarding – with hundreds of hard corals and reef fish catalogued in this fertile marine zone. The most spectacular diving is in the marine parks of the Similan Islands (p645) and Surin Islands (p644). Most dive operators run live-aboard trips out of Phuket (p649) and Khao Lak (p640).

Diving on the Gulf Coast is available just about anywhere foreigners rest their luggage. Ko Tao (p610) has the reputation of providing the cheapest dive training but most courses feel like factories instead of classrooms. Although the water conditions are not the best, Pattaya (p234) is the closest dive spot to Bangkok, with several wreck dives.

Most islands have easily accessible snorkelling amid offshore reefs that are covered by water no deeper than 2m. Local fisherman will also take out groups for day-long snorkelling tours to various sites around the islands. Masks, fins and snorkels are readily available for rent at dive centres and guesthouses in beach areas. If you're particular about the quality and condition of the equipment you use, however, you might be better off bringing your own mask and snorkel – some of the stuff for rent is second rate.

Other Watersports

The most dramatic scenery for kayaking is along the Andaman Coast. It's littered with bearded limestone mountains and semi-submerged caves. Many sea-kayaking tours take visitors to scenic Ao Phang-Nga (p647). Krabi (p681) is the one-stop beach destination for sporty types, and sea-kayaking tours explore emerald lagoons and sea caves. Kayaking trips through the Ang Thong Marine Park (p623), off the coast of Ko Samui, is the Gulf's premier paddling spot.

Most tour operators use open-deck kayaks since water and air temperatures in Thailand

---

SAFETY GUIDELINES FOR DIVING

Before embarking on a scuba diving, skin diving or snorkelling trip, carefully consider the following points to ensure a safe and enjoyable experience:

- Possess a current diving-certification card from a recognised scuba diving instructional agency.

- Obtain reliable information about physical and environmental conditions at the dive site (eg from a reputable local dive operation).

- Be aware of local laws, regulations and etiquette about marine life and the environment.

- Dive only at sites within your realm of experience; if available, engage the services of a competent, professionally trained dive instructor or dive master.

- Be aware that underwater conditions vary significantly from one region, or even site, to another. Seasonal changes can significantly alter any site and dive conditions. These differences influence the way divers dress for a dive and what diving techniques they use.

- Ask about the environmental characteristics that can affect your diving and how trained local divers deal with these considerations.

DIRECTORY

are warm. When signing up for a tour, find out if you or a guide is the primary paddler; some are more sightseeing than exercise.

The rivers of northern Thailand offer white-knuckle white-water trips during and after the monsoon season. Trips are organised out of Pai (p441), Chiang Mai (p299) and to a lesser extent in Nan province.

Windsurfing enjoys a modest following in Pattaya (p237) and Phuket (p649). In general the windy months on the Gulf of Thailand are from mid-February to April. On the Andaman Sea side of the peninsula the winds are strongest from September to December. At certain times of year on Phuket, the normally subdued Andaman roars into shore with enough energy to steer a surfboard.

Rock Climbing

Way back before the Stone Age, Thailand sat at the bottom of a vast ocean that lapped against the Tibetan Plateau. When the ocean eventually receded and mainland Southeast Asia popped up, the skeletons of deceased marine life left behind a swath of chalk-white caves and cliffs the whole length of Thailand. While the Tibetans lost backyard surfing rights, the Thais got the milky-white, pock-marked, medium-hard limestone perfect for chalky fingers and Scarpa-clad toes. *Fa·ràng* backpackers were the first to slam bolt to stone in the mid-1980s, but the Thais have quickly followed suit. Rock climbing has become so popular that the Thais have begun sending climbers to amateur contests in the USA and Australia.

Krabi's Hat Railay (p688) is Thailand's climbing mecca. The huge headland and tiny islands nearby offer high-quality limestone with steep pocketed walls, overhangs and the occasional hanging stalactite. But what makes climbing here so popular are the views. Your reward for a vertical assault on a cliff isn't just the challenge to gravity but also a bird's eye perspective of a sparkling blue bay and humpbacked mountains.

If the crowds in Krabi are too much, check out Ko Phi-Phi or head north to Chiang Mai (p299).

Trekking

Wilderness walking or trekking is one of northern Thailand's biggest draws. Many routes feature daily walks through forested mountain areas coupled with overnight stays in hill-tribe villages and elephant rides to satisfy both ethno-

and ecotourism urges. Chiang Mai and Chiang Rai are the primary base points for these tours. Other trekking areas in the north include Mae Hong Son, Pai, Chiang Dao, Tha Ton, Nan and Um Phang. In southwestern Thailand, Kanchanaburi has become an outdoor trekking destination with easier access to Bangkok.

These adventures rank high on most travellers' to-do lists, but the final verdict is often mixed. Hill-tribe trekking has many detractors because of concerns over exploitation and tourism overload. Some companies and guesthouses in less-touristed areas are actually able to live up to travellers' expectations of providing an authentic cultural exchange with hill-tribe villagers and intense jungle experiences but we're not big fans of running off to the most far-flung place to find 'same same but different'.

It is difficult to recommend a particular trekking company as guides often float between companies and the participants will vary each trip. Officially all guides should be licensed by the Tourism Authority of Thailand (TAT). This means they have received at least regional and survival training, and they are registered, which is useful if there are problems later. The guide should be able to show you their licence and certificate. Green licences are for trekking only, pink are for sightseeing only and silver ones are for guides licensed to do both. In general tour companies are safer and better regulated now than years past but you should still talk to fellow travellers for recommendations.

If an organised trek doesn't appeal to you, consider travelling to Mae Salong (p358), an interesting highland town where you can arrange independent trekking trips.

The best time to trek is during the cool season (roughly November to February) when the weather is refreshing, the landscape is still green, the waterfalls are full from the monsoon rains and the wildflowers are in bloom. Between March and May the hills are dry and the weather is quite hot. The second-best time is early in the rainy season, between June and July, before the dirt roads become too saturated.

For a discussion about the responsibility issues of entering hill-tribe villages see p47.

BUSINESS HOURS

Most government offices are open from 8.30am to 4.30pm weekdays. Some government offices close from noon to 1pm for lunch, while others have Saturday hours (9am-3pm). Banking hours are typically 9.30am to 3.30pm Monday to Friday. ATMs are usually accessible 24 hours a day and bank branches with extended hours can be found at the big department stores such as Tesco Lotus and Big C.

Privately owned stores usually operate between 10am and 5pm daily. Most local restaurants are open 10am until 10pm, with an hour's variation on either side. Some restaurants, specialising in morning meals close by 3pm.

Please note that all government offices and banks are closed on public holidays (see p748).

CHILDREN

Thais love children and will shower attention and sweets on them as if they were celebrities. Children can easily find ready playmates among their Thai counterparts and a 'temporary' nanny service at practically every stop. Thais are so family focused that you'll find otherwise disinterested parties wanting to pinch at your children's cheeks and play a game of peekaboo (called '*já ăir*') with amusable babies.

To smooth out the usual road bumps of dragging children from place to place, check out Lonely Planet's *Travel with Children,* which contains useful advice on how to cope with kids on the road, with a focus on travel in developing countries.

Health & Safety

For the most part parents needn't worry too much about health concerns, although it pays to lay down a few ground rules (such as regular hand washing) to head off potential medical problems. Children should be warned not to play with animals as rabies is relatively common in Thailand and many dogs are better at being barkers and garbage eaters than pets. All the usual health precautions apply (see p771).

Practicalities

Amenities specially geared towards young children – such as child-safety seats for cars, high chairs in restaurants or nappy-changing facilities in public restrooms – are virtually nonexistent in Thailand. Therefore parents will have to be extra resourceful in seeking out substitutes or just follow the example of Thai families (which means holding smaller children on their laps much of the time).

TYPICAL OPENING HOURS

- Bars – 6pm-midnight or 1am (times vary depending on local enforcement of national curfew laws)
- Department stores – 10am-8pm or 9pm Monday to Sunday
- Discos – 8pm-2am
- Live-music venues – 6pm-1am
- Restaurants – 10am-10pm
- Local shops – 10am-6pm Monday to Saturday, some open Sunday

---

Baby formula and nappies (diapers) are available at minimarkets and 7-Elevens in the larger towns and cities, but the sizes are usually small, smaller and smallish. If your kid wears size 3 or larger, head to Tesco Lotus, Big C or Tops Market stores. Nappy rash cream is sold at the pharmacies.

Hauling around little ones can be a challenge. Thailand's footpaths are oftentimes too crowded to push a pram, especially today's full-sized SUV versions. Instead opt for a compact umbrella stroller that can squeeze past the fire hydrant and the mango cart and that can be folded up and thrown in a *túk-túk*. A baby pack is also useful but make sure that the child's head doesn't sit higher than yours: there are lots of hanging obstacles poised at forehead level.

Although you might be in food heaven, kids can be a little resistant to culinary adventures. In general Thai children don't start to eat spicy food until elementary school, before then they seemingly survive on *kôw nĕe·o* and jelly snacks. Other kid-friendly meals include chicken in all of its non-spicy permutations – *gài yâhng* (grilled chicken), *gài tôrt* (fried chicken) and *gài pàt mét má·môo·ang* (chicken stir-fried with cashew nuts) – as well as *kôw pàt* (fried rice), *kài jee·o* (Thai-style omelette) and *gŏo·ay dĕe·o* (noodle soups). See also p90.

Sights & Activities

Of the many destinations in Thailand, children will especially enjoy the beaches, as most are in gentle bays good for beginner swimmers. Animal amusements abound in Thailand, but animal conditions and treatment are often below par compared with standards in the West. Elephant rides, bamboo rafting and other outdoor activities around Chiang Mai and Kanchanaburi are more animal- and kid-friendly. Older children might enjoy the northeastern town of Khon Kaen (p493), which is decorated with dinosaur statues and boasts a nearby national park and museum with dinosaur bones *in situ*. Bangkok is great fun for those in awe of construction sites: the city is filled with cranes, jackhammers and concrete-pouring trucks. Kids on a train kick might like an overnight journey. On the train they can walk around and they're assigned the lower sleeping berths with views of the stations. For other itinerary ideas, see p28.

CLIMATE CHARTS

See p18 for further information on choosing the best time of year for your visit to Thailand.

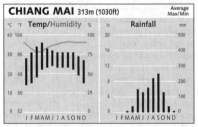

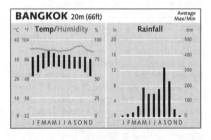

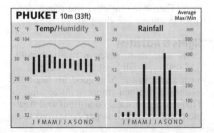

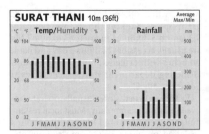

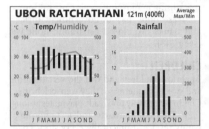

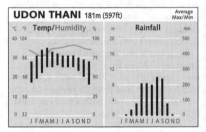

COURSES
Cooking

Cooking courses pop up wherever there are tourists willing to dice some shallots. Bangkok's courses (p144) tend to be more formal, with dedicated kitchen facilities and individual work stations; but Chiang Mai is the undisputed cooking-course capital (see p300). Elsewhere, a resourceful entrepreneur might hang a sign on the front door and students join the rhythm of a typical Thai kitchen. See the individual destination chapters for recommended schools.

Language

Formal, university-affiliated language programs are available in Bangkok (p145) and Chiang Mai (p301). Both cities also offer an array of short-term coursework tailored to suit different communication needs from business Thai to reading and writing.

Moo·ay Tai (Thai Boxing)

One of the fastest growing sectors of Thailand's educational tourism, *moo·ay tai* (Thai boxing; also spelt *muay thai*) training takes place at dozens of camps around the country. Traditional *moo·ay tai* camps, especially in the rural areas, are in the business of training winning fighters, who elevate the prestige and earnings of the teacher and the school. The training sessions are gruelling, the diet is rudimentary and the facilities are little more than a dusty ring for sparring and a few shared cabins. Some foreign fighters with the potential for competitive success have trained in these schools but they did so through personal introductions and a dedication to the sport.

Better suited for the athlete interested in the sport rather than becoming a potential prize fighter are the camps that specialise in training Westerners. Many of these facilities have English-speaking trainers and better equipment, and subsidise the training through increased tuition fees. Training periods can range from a one-day course to multi-week sessions. Do be aware that the potential for some camps to be interested only in tuition fees is a concern and it pays to do a lot of advance research. Bangkok and Chiang Mai have long-established foreigner-friendly training camps. Phuket and other resort towns have less serious schools intended for less serious students.

Meditation

Thailand has long been a popular place for Buddhist meditation study. Unique to Buddhism, particularly Theravada and to a lesser extent Tibetan Buddhism, is a system of meditation known as *vipassana* (*wí·bàt·sà·nah* in Thai), a Pali word that roughly translates as 'insight'. Foreigners who come to Thailand to study *vipassana* can choose from dozens of temples and meditation centres specialising in these teachings. Teaching methods vary but the general emphasis is on observing mind-body processes from moment to moment. Thai language is usually the medium of instruction but several places also provide instruction in English.

Contact details for some of the more popular meditation-oriented temples and centres are given in the destination chapters of this guide. Instruction and accommodation are free of charge at temples, although donations are expected.

Some places require that you wear white clothes when staying overnight. For even a brief visit, wear clean and neat clothing (ie long trousers or skirt and sleeves that cover the shoulders).

Thai Massage

Thai massage is more like a yoga workout than a deep-tissue massage. The theory behind the tradition is to promote health by manipulating certain *sên* (pressure points) along the body meridians so that energy is distributed evenly throughout the nervous system. The dynamic aspects of Thai massage also address the muscular-skeletal system in a way that is often compared to modern physiotherapy and chiropractic. Training in Thai massage is available in Bangkok and Chiang Mai. The centre of Thai massage pedagogy is at Wat Pho (p146) in Bangkok.

CUSTOMS REGULATIONS

Thailand prohibits the import of firearms and ammunition (unless registered in advance with the police department), illegal drugs and pornographic media. A reasonable amount of clothing, toiletries and professional instruments are allowed in duty free. Up to 200 cigarettes and 1L of wine or spirits can be brought into the country duty free. The **customs department** (www.customs.go.th) maintains a helpful website with more specific information.

When leaving Thailand, you must obtain an export licence for any antiques or objects of art, including newly cast Buddha images. Export licence applications can be made by submitting two front-view photos of the object(s), a photocopy of your passport, along with the purchase receipt and the object(s) in question, to the **Department of Fine Arts** (DFA; ☎ 0 2628 5032). Allow three to five days for the application and inspection process to be completed.

DANGERS & ANNOYANCES

Although Thailand is in not a dangerous country to visit, it is smart to exercise caution, especially when it comes to dealing with strangers (both Thai and foreigners) and travelling alone. In reality, you are more likely to be ripped off or have a personal possession surreptitiously stolen than you are to be physically harmed.

Assault

Assault of travellers is rare in Thailand, but it does happen. We've received letters detailing fights between travellers and Thai guesthouse workers or other Thai youths. While both parties are probably to blame (and alcohol is often a factor), do be aware that causing a Thai to 'lose face' (feel public embarrassment or humiliation) might elicit an inexplicably strong and violent reaction. While a good cuss-out might be an acceptable way to vent anger in the West, it is an invitation for fisticuffs, a sneak attack or worse by a Thai. While gun violence is almost unheard of in Thailand, there have been a few instances of foreigners getting into fights with off-duty police officers who have used their weapons in retaliation.

There is a surprising amount of assaults in Ko Samui and Ko Pha-Ngan considering their idyllic settings. Oftentimes alcohol is the number one contributor to bad choices and worse outcomes. Ko Pha-Ngan's Full Moon party is becoming increasingly violent and dangerous. There are often reports of fights, rapes and robbings.

Women, especially solo travellers in Samui or Pha-Ngan, need to be smart and somewhat sober when interacting with the opposite sex, be they Thai or *fa·ràng*. Opportunists pounce when too many whisky buckets are involved. Also be aware that an innocent flirtation might convey firmer intentions to a recipient who does not share your culture's sexual norms.

Border Issues

Thailand enjoys much better relations with its neighbours than it did a decade ago and many land borders are now functional and safe passages for goods and people. The ongoing violence in the Deep South (see right) has made the once popular crossing at Sungai Kolok a potentially dangerous proposition.

Cross-border relations with Thailand and Myanmar during the Thaksin era have resulted in increased cooperation between the two governments and the discontinuation of the Thai army providing assistance to minority resistance groups in Myanmar. Many of the border crossings between Thailand and Myanmar are day-use only and attract people renewing their visas or poking around the border markets. On rare occasions the Myanmar government has impetuously closed these points without notice, leaving day-pass visitors stranded. More likely closures are due to news-making events like Thailand's 2006 coup. Keeping abreast of current events prior to arriving at the border will prevent potential problems.

The long-contested border temple of Khao Phra Wihan (known as 'Preah Vihear' in Cambodia), in the far northeast of the country, resulted in a military build-up and violent clashes between Thai and Cambodian forces in 2007. Although tensions have relaxed since, the temple is still closed to visitors.

Deep South Violence

Currently Thailand's southernmost Muslim-majority provinces (Yala, Pattani and Narathiwat) experience frequent occurrences of violence believed to be connected to an amorphous but ongoing ethno-nationalist struggle. Since 2002, violence has escalated from attacks on perceived symbols of the government (provincial officials, soldiers, teachers and monks) to seemingly random (though possibly vendetta-motivated) killings on average citizens, and increasingly sophisticated, coordinated bombings of market-places, banks and train stations. From 2004 to 2007 there was an average of 160 violent occurrences per month. Attacks varied from insurgent-style activity to gang-like shootings, further complicating attempts to clearly define the groups and their intentions. Most violence is confined to the three provinces known collectively as the Deep South and primarily to more rural districts within these provinces, though bombings have occurred in downtown sections of the provincial capitals of Yala and Pattani provinces.

Periodic bombings have also occurred in the southern commercial and transport hub of Hat Yai and in border districts of Songkhla Province. Although the Thai government has political motivations to connect the violence in the Deep South to global terror networks such as Al Qaeda and regional militant groups such as Jemaah Islamiyah, most observers do not believe that the region's insurgents are closely linked to these groups.

At the time of writing, no foreign tourists had been directly targeted, but civilian attacks have increased and it is a distinct possibility that an unsuspecting traveller might get caught in the wrong place. We would discourage taking the train through the Thai–Malaysian border at Sungai Kolok – a popular crossing for tourists heading to the Perhentian Islands in Malaysia. It would be safer to cross the border on the western side of the peninsula, either by bus or train from Hat Yai or by boat from Satun.

Although Hat Yai is considered a target for bombings, it is still a functioning city and for now is safe enough to travel in and out of, though this situation should be monitored. The provincial capital of Songkhla should also be fairly safe for visitors, although caution should be exercised. It is not advisable to travel between Hat Yai and Songkhla after dark.

Druggings & Drug Possession

More common amongst sex tourists than backpackers, male travellers have reported accepting cigarettes, drinks or food from flirtatious Thai women only to wake up sometime later with a headache and without their valuables. Inviting a prostitute to your hotel room can have the same results.

It is illegal to buy, sell or possess opium, heroin, amphetamines, hallucinogenic mushrooms and marijuana in Thailand. A new era of vigilance against drug use and possession was ushered in by former Prime Minister Thaksin's 2003 war on drugs; during the height of the campaign police searched partygoers in Bangkok nightclubs and effectively scared many of the recreational drug users into abstinence for a time. Things have relaxed somewhat since the 2006 coup but the country is no longer a chemical free-for-all.

Belying Thailand's anything-goes atmosphere are severely strict punishments for possession and trafficking that are not relaxed for foreigners. Possession of drugs can result in at least one year or more of prison time. Drug smuggling – defined as attempting to cross a border with drugs in your possession – carries considerably higher penalties, including execution.

During citywide festivals, such as Bangkok's New Year's Eve and Ko Pha-Ngan's Full Moon parties, police set up road blocks and inspection stations in an attempt to apprehend drug suppliers and their contraband. In some cases, enforcement of the drug laws is merely leverage for exacting massive bribes. Ko Pha-Ngan's police are notorious for bribable 'sting' operations in which a drug dealer makes an exchange with a customer, followed shortly by a police bust and an on-site demand of 70,000B to avoid arrest.

Another party town, Pai has seen a recent revival of the Thaksin-era urine drug tests on bar patrons by police. As of writing, the strong-arm gift of freedom in such cases is 10,000B. The Pai police have been following a policy of intimidation towards foreign revellers, often fining bars for creative applications of the entertainment prohibitions and entering establishments visibly carrying weapons.

Scams

Thais can be so friendly and laid-back that some visitors are lulled into a false sense of security making them vulnerable to scams of all kinds. Bangkok is especially good at long-involved frauds that dupe travellers into thinking that they've made a friend and are getting a bargain.

Most scams begin in the same way: a friendly and well-dressed Thai, or sometimes even a foreigner, approaches you and strikes up a conversation. Invariably your destination is closed or being cleaned, but your new friend offers several alternative activities, such as sightseeing at smaller temples or shopping at authentic markets. After you've come to trust the person, you are next invited to a gem and jewellery shop because your new-found friend is picking up some merchandise for himself. Somewhere along the way he usually claims to have a connection, often a relative, in your home country (what a coincidence!) with whom he has a regular gem export-import business. One way or another, you are convinced that you can turn a profit by arranging a gem purchase and reselling the merchandise at home. After all, the jewellery shop just happens to be offering a generous discount today – it's a government or religious holiday, or perhaps it's the shop's 10th anniversary, or maybe they've just taken a liking to you!

There are seemingly infinite numbers of variations on the scam described above, almost all of which end up with you making a purchase of small low-quality gems and posting them to your home country. Once you return home, of course, the cheap jewels turn out to be worth much less than you paid for them (perhaps one-tenth to one-half).

The Thai police are usually no help whatsoever, believing that merchants are entitled to whatever price they can get.

Card games are another way to separate travellers from their money. A friendly stranger approaches the lone traveller on the street, strikes up a conversation and then invites them to their house or apartment for a drink or meal. After a bit of socialising a friend or relative of the con arrives on the scene; it just so happens a little high-stakes card game is planned for later that day. Like the gem scam, the card game has many variations, but eventually the victim is shown some cheating tactics to use with help from the 'dealer', some practise sessions take place and finally the game gets under way with several high rollers at the table. And if you don't know how this ends, we suggest you watch the movie *The Hustler*. Again, the police won't take any action because gambling is illegal in Thailand and you've actually broken the law.

Other minor scams involve túk-túk drivers, hotel employees and bar girls who take new arrivals on city tours; these almost always end up in high-pressure sales situations at silk, jewellery or handicraft shops. In this case the victim's greed isn't the ruling motivation – it's simply a matter of weak sales resistance.

Follow TAT's number-one suggestion to tourists: *Disregard all offers of free shopping or sightseeing help from strangers*. These invariably take a commission from your purchases.

Contact the **tourist police** (☎ 1155) if you have any problems with consumer fraud.

Theft & Fraud

Exercise diligence when it comes to your personal belongings. Ensure that your room is securely locked and carry your most important effects (passport, money, credit cards) on your person. Take care when leaving valuables in hotel safes.

Follow the same practise when you're travelling. A locked bag will not prevent theft on a long-haul bus when you're snoozing and the practised thief has hours alone with your luggage. This is a common occurrence on the tourist buses from Khao San Rd to the southern beaches or north to Chiang Mai.

When using a credit card, don't let vendors take your credit card out of your sight to run it through the machine. Unscrupulous merchants have been known to rub off three or four or more receipts with one purchase. Sometimes they wait several weeks – even months – between submitting each charge receipt to the bank, so that you can't remember whether you'd been billed by the same vendor more than once.

To avoid losing all of your travel money in an instant, always use a credit card that is not directly linked to your bank account back home so that the operator doesn't have access to immediate funds.

Touts

Touting is a long-time tradition in Asia, and while Thailand doesn't have as many touts as, say, India, it has its share.

In the popular tourist spots you'll be approached, sometimes surrounded, by guesthouse touts who get a commission for bringing in potential guests. While it is annoying for the traveller, it is an acceptable form of advertising among small-scale businesses. Take anything a tout says with scepticism. Since touts get paid for delivering you to a guesthouse or hotel (whether you check in or not), they'll say anything to get you in the door. Some places refuse to pay commissions so in return the touts will steer customers to places that do pay. This type of commission work is not limited to low-budget guesthouses. Travel agencies are notorious for talking newly arrived tourists into staying at badly located, overpriced hotels.

Travel agencies often masquerade as TAT, the government-funded tourist information office. They might put up agents wearing fake TAT badges or have signs that read TAT in big letters to entice travellers into their offices where they can sell them overpriced bus and train tickets. Be aware that the official TAT offices do not make hotel or transport bookings. If such a place offers to do this for you then they are a travel agent not a tourist information office.

When making transport arrangements, talk to several travel agencies to look for the best price, as the commission percentage varies greatly between agents. Also resist any highsales tactics from an agent trying to sign you up for everything: plane tickets, hotel, tours etc. The most honest Thais are typically very low-key and often sub-par salespeople.

EMBASSIES & CONSULATES

Foreign embassies are located in Bangkok; some nations also have consulates in Chiang Mai.

Australia (Map p124; ☎ 0 2344 6300; www.aust embassy.or.th; 37 Th Sathon Tai, Bangkok)

Cambodia (Map pp110-11; ☎ 02957 5851-2; 518/4 Pracha Uthit/Soi Ramkamhaeng 39, Bangkok)

Canada Bangkok (Map p124; ☎ 0 2636 0540; www .dfait-maeci.gc.ca/bangkok; 15th fl, Abdulrahim Bldg, 990 Th Phra Ram IV); Chiang Mai (Map pp276-7; ☎ 0 5385-0147; 151 Superhighway, Tambon Tahsala) Consulate only at Chiang Mai.

China Bangkok (Map pp110-11; ☎ 0 2245 7044; www .chinaembassy.or.th; 57 Th Ratchadaphisek); Chiang Mai (Map pp284-5; ☎ 0 5327 6125; 111 Th Chang Lor) Consulate only at Chiang Mai.

Denmark (Map p124; ☎ 0 2343 1100; www.amb bangkok.um.dk; 10 Soi 1, Th Sathon Tai; Bangkok) Consulates in Pattaya and Phuket.

France Bangkok (Embassy Map pp118-19; ☎ 0 2657 5100; www.ambafrance-th.org; 35 Soi 36, Th Charoen Krung; Consular Section Map p124; ☎ 0 2627 2150; 29 Th Sathon Tai); Chiang Mai (Map pp284-5; ☎ 0 5328 1466; 138 Th Charoen Prathet) Consulates only in Chiang Mai, Phuket and Surat Thani.

Germany (Map p124; ☎ 0 2287 9000; www.german -embassy.or.th; 9 Th Sathon Tai, Bangkok)

India Bangkok (Map pp122-3; ☎ 0 2258 0300-6; 46 Soi Prasanmit/Soi 23, Th Sukhumvit); Chiang Mai (Map pp276-7; ☎ 0 5324 3066; 344 Th Charoenrat) Consulate only in Chiang Mai.

Indonesia (Map pp120-1; ☎ 0 2252 3135; www.kbri -bangkok.com; 600-602 Th Phetchaburi, Bangkok)

Ireland (Map p124; ☎ 0 2677 7500; www.irelandinthai land.com; 28th fl, Q House, Th Sathon Tai, Bangkok) This is a consulate only; the nearest Irish embassy is in Kuala Lumpur.

Israel (Map pp122-3; ☎ 0 2204 9200; Ocean Tower 2, 25th fl, 25 Soi 19, Th Sukhumvit, Bangkok)

Japan Bangkok (Map p124; ☎ 0 2207 8500; www .th.emb-japan.go.jp; 177 Th Withayu); Chiang Mai (Map pp276-7; ☎ 0 5320 3367; 104-107 Airport Business Park, Th Mahidon) Consulate only in Chiang Mai.

Laos (Map pp110-11; ☎ 0 2539 6678; www.bkklao embassy.com; 502/1-3 Soi Sahakarnpramoon, Pracha Uthit/Soi 39, Th Ramakamhaeng, Bangkok)

Malaysia (Map p124; ☎ 0 2679 2190-9; 35 Th Sathon Tai, Bangkok) There's also a consulate in Songkhla.

Myanmar (Burma; Map pp118-19; ☎ 0 2233 2237, 0 2234 4698; www.mofa.gov.mm; 132 Th Sathon Neua, Bangkok)

Nepal (Map pp110-11; ☎ 0 2391 7240; www.immi.gov .np; 189 Soi 71, Th Sukhumvit, Bangkok)

Netherlands (Map pp120-1; ☎ 0 2309 5200; www.nether landsembassy.in.th; 15 Soi Tonson, Th Ploenchit, Bangkok)

New Zealand (Map pp120-1; ☎ 0 2254 2530; www .nzembassy.com; 14th fl, M Thai Tower, All Seasons Pl, 87 Th Withayu, Bangkok)

Philippines (Map pp122-3; ☎ 0 2259 0139; www.phil embassy-bangkok.net; 760 Th Sukhumvit, Bangkok)

Singapore (Map pp118-19; ☎ 0 2286 2111; www.mfa .gov.sg/bangkok; 129 Th Sathon Tai, Bangkok)

South Africa (Map p124; ☎ 0 2253 8473; www.saemb bangkok.com; 12A fl, M Thai Tower, All Seasons Place, 87 Th Withayu, Bangkok)

Spain (Map pp122-3; ☎ 0 2661 8284; 23 fl, Lake Ratch-ada Office Complex, 193 Th Ratchadaphisek, Bangkok)

Switzerland (Map pp120-1; ☎ 0 2253 0156; 35 Th Withayu, Bangkok)

UK Bangkok (Map pp120-1; ☎ 0 2305 8333; www.british embassy.gov.uk; 14 Th Withayu); Chiang Mai (Map pp284-5; ☎ 0 5326 2015; British Council, 198 Th Bamrungrat) Consulate only in Chiang Mai.

USA Bangkok (Map pp120-1; ☎ 0 2205 4000; http://bang kok.usembassy.gov; 95 Th Withayu); Chiang Mai (Map pp284-5; ☎ 0 5310 7700; 387 Th Wichayanon) Consulate only in Chiang Mai.

Vietnam (Map pp120-1; ☎ 0 2251 5836-8; www.vietnam embassy-thailand.org; 83/1 Th Withayu, Bangkok)

FESTIVALS & EVENTS

Thai festivals tend to be linked to the agricultural seasons or to Buddhist holidays. The general word for festival in Thai is *ngahn têt·sà·gahn*. See the Events Calendar (p21) for more information.

FOOD

Most restaurants in Thailand are inexpensive by international standards and food prices tend to hold steady throughout the year. The 2007 global spike in oil prices resulted in one of the first nationwide increases of food in almost a decade: a bowl of *gŏo·ay đĕe·o* in Bangkok jumped from 30B to 35B.

A typical meal at a street stall should cost 25B to 40B; a meal at a typical mum-and-dad Thai restaurant for one should be about 80B to 150B. Guesthouses and restaurants catering to foreigners tend to charge more than local restaurants. See p83 for thorough descriptions of the cuisine and the kinds of restaurants you'll find in Thailand.

GAY & LESBIAN TRAVELLERS

Thai culture is relatively tolerant of both male and female homosexuality. There is a fairly prominent gay and lesbian scene in Bangkok, Pattaya and Phuket. With regard to dress or mannerism, lesbians and gays are generally accepted without comment. However, public displays of affection – whether heterosexual or homosexual – are frowned upon. **Utopia** (www.utopia-asia.com) posts lots of Thailand information for gay and lesbian visitors and publishes a guidebook to the kingdom for homosexuals.

HOLIDAYS

Government offices and banks close on the following days.

January 1 New Year's Day

April 6 Chakri Day, commemorating the founder of the Chakri dynasty, Rama I

May 5 Coronation Day, commemorating the 1946 coronation of HM the King and HM the Queen

July (date varies) Khao Phansaa, the beginning of Buddhist 'lent'

August 12 Queen's Birthday

October 23 Chulalongkorn Day

October/November (date varies) Ork Phansaa, the end of Buddhist 'lent'

December 5 King's Birthday

December 10 Constitution Day

INSURANCE

A travel-insurance policy to cover theft, loss and medical problems is a good idea. Policies offer differing medical-expense options. There is a wide variety of policies available, so check the small print. Be sure that the policy covers ambulances or an emergency flight home.

Some policies specifically exclude 'dangerous activities', which can include scuba diving, motorcycling or even trekking. A locally acquired motorcycle licence is not valid under some policies.

You may prefer a policy that pays doctors or hospitals directly rather than you having to pay on the spot and claim later. If you have to claim later make sure you keep all documentation.

See p771 for recommendations on health insurance and p766 for details on vehicle insurance. Worldwide travel insurance is available at www.lonelyplanet.com/travel_services. You can buy, extend and claim online anytime – even if you're already on the road.

INTERNET ACCESS

You'll find plenty of internet cafes in most towns and cities, and in many guesthouses and hotels as well. The going rate is anywhere from 40B to 120B an hour, depending on how much competition there is. Connections tend to be pretty fast and have been sped up with the proliferation of wireless access, which is fairly widespread throughout the country including the rural northeast. Only Bangkok has been slow to make wi-fi affordably accessible. Most guesthouses will offer wi-fi for free while high-end hotels offer it only in lobbies for a usage fee.

LEGAL MATTERS

In general Thai police don't hassle foreigners, especially tourists. If anything they generally go out of their way not to arrest a foreigner breaking minor traffic laws, instead taking the approach that a warning will suffice.

One major exception is drugs, which most Thai police view as either a social scourge against which it's their duty to enforce the letter of the law, or an opportunity to make untaxed income via bribes.

If you are arrested for any offence, the police will allow you the opportunity to make a phone call to your embassy or consulate in Thailand, if you have one, or to a friend or relative if not. There's a whole set of legal codes governing the length of time and manner in which you can be detained before being charged or put on trial, but a lot of discretion is left to the police. In the case of foreigners the police are more likely to bend these codes in your favour. However, as with police worldwide, if you don't show respect you will make matters worse.

Thai law does not presume an indicted detainee to be either 'guilty' or 'innocent' but rather a 'suspect', whose guilt or innocence will be decided in court. Trials are usually speedy.

The **tourist police** (☎ 1155) can be very helpful in cases of arrest. Although they typically have no jurisdiction over the kinds of cases handled by regular cops, they may be able to help with translations or with contacting your embassy. You can call the hotline number 24 hours a day to lodge complaints or to request assistance with regards to personal safety.

MAPS

ThinkNet (www.thinknet.co.th) produces a high-quality city and country maps series, including interactive-map CDs to Bangkok. For GPS users in Thailand, most prefer the Garmin units and the associated map products that are accurate and fully routed. An online world map showing adequate street detail for Thailand can be found at **Multimap** (www.multimap.com).

Do-it-yourself trekkers or anyone with a keen interest in geography may find sheet maps issued by the Thai military to be helpful. These maps are available at a number of scales, complete with elevations, contour lines, place names (in both Thai and roman script) and roads. These maps can be purchased at the

Royal Thai Survey Department (Krom Phaen Thi Thahan; Map pp114–15; ☎ 0 2222 8844; www.rtsd.mi.th/service; Th Kanlayana Maitri, Bangkok), opposite the Interior Ministry on the western side of Th Ratchini in Ko Ratanakosin. You can survey the survey's maps at the website.

MONEY

The basic unit of Thai currency is the *baht*. There are 100 *satang* in one baht; coins include 25-satang and 50-satang pieces and baht in 1B, 2B, 5B and 10B coins. Older coins have Thai numerals only, while newer coins have Thai and Arabic numerals. The 2B coin was introduced in 2007 and is confusingly similar in size and design to the 1B coin. The two satang coins are typically only issued at supermarkets where prices aren't rounded up to the nearest baht, which is the convention elsewhere.

Paper currency is issued in the following denominations: 20B (green), 50B (blue), 100B (red), 500B (purple) and 1000B (beige). In the 1990s, the 10B bills were phased out in favour of the 10B coin but occasionally you might encounter a paper survivor.

ATMs & Credit/Debit Cards

Debit and ATM cards issued by a bank in your own country can be used at ATM machines around Thailand to withdraw cash (in Thai baht only) directly from your account back home. ATMs are widespread throughout the country and can be relied on for the bulk of your spending cash. You can also use ATMs to buy baht at foreign-exchange booths at some banks.

Credit cards as well as debit cards can be used for purchases at many shops, hotels and restaurants. The most commonly accepted cards are Visa and MasterCard. American Express is typically only accepted at high-end hotels and restaurants.

To report a lost or stolen credit/debit card, call the following hotlines in Bangkok.

American Express (☎ 0 2273 5544)
Diners Club (☎ 0 2238 3660)
MasterCard (☎ 001 800 11887 0663)
Visa (☎ 001 800 441 3485)

Changing Money

Banks or the rarer private moneychangers offer the best foreign-exchange rates. When buying baht, US dollars are the most accepted currency, followed by British pounds and euros. Most banks charge a commission and duty for each travellers cheque cashed.

Current exchange rates are printed in the *Bangkok Post* and the *Nation* every day, or you can walk into any Thai bank to see a daily rate chart.

See p18 for information on the cost of travel in Thailand.

Foreign Exchange

There is no limit to the amount of Thai or foreign currency you may bring into the country.

There are certain monetary requirements for foreigners entering Thailand; demonstrations of adequate funds varies per visa type but typically does not exceed a traveller's estimated trip budget. Rarely will you be asked to produce such financial evidence, but be aware that such laws do exist. For specific amounts for each visa type, visit the website of the **Ministry of Foreign Affairs** (www.mfa .go.th).

Upon leaving Thailand, you're permitted to take out a maximum of 50,000B per person without special authorisation; export of foreign currencies is unrestricted. An exception is made if you're going to Cambodia, Laos, Malaysia, Myanmar or Vietnam, where the limit is 500,000B.

It's legal to open a foreign-currency account at any commercial bank in Thailand. As long as the funds originate from out of the country, there aren't any restrictions on maintenance or withdrawal.

Tipping

Tipping is not generally expected in Thailand. The exception is loose change from a large restaurant bill; if a meal costs 488B and you pay with a 500B note, some Thais will leave the 12B change. It's not so much a tip as a way of saying 'I'm not so money grubbing as to grab every last baht'. Apart from this, it is not customary to leave behind the change if it is less than 10B.

At many hotel restaurants or other upmarket eateries, a 10% service charge will be added to your bill. When this is the case, tipping is not expected. Bangkok has adopted some standards of tipping, especially in restaurants frequented by foreigners.

PHOTOGRAPHY & VIDEO

Thais are gadget fans and most have made the transition to digital. Memory cards for digital cameras are generally widely available in the more popular formats and available in the

---

BARGAINING

If there isn't a sign stating the price for an item then the price is negotiable. Bargaining for non-food items is common in street markets and some mum-and-dad shops. Prices in department stores, minimarts, 7-Elevens and so forth are fixed.

Thais respect a good haggler. Always let the vendor make the first offer then ask 'Can you lower the price?'. This usually results is an immediate discount from the first price. Now it's your turn to make a counteroffer; always start low but don't bargain at all unless you're serious about buying.

It helps immeasurably to keep the negotiations relaxed and friendly, and always remember to smile. Don't loose your temper or raise your voice as drama is not a good leverage tool.

---

electronic sections of most shopping malls. In the tourist areas, many internet shops have CD-burning software if you want to offload your pictures. Alternatively, most places have sophisticated enough connections that you can quickly upload digital photos to a remote storage site.

Print film is still available but not as ubiquitous as it once was. Slide film can be hard to find outside Bangkok and Chiang Mai. Dependable E6 processing is available at several labs in Bangkok but is untrustworthy elsewhere. **Image Quality Lab** (IQ Lab; Map pp118-19; ☎ 0 2266 4080; www.iqlab.co.th; 160/5 ITF Bldg, Th Silom, Bangkok) offers the widest range of professional services, with all types of processing for print and digital printing.

Be considerate when taking photographs of the locals. Learn how to ask politely in Thai and wait for an embarrassed nod. In some of the regularly visited hill-tribe areas be prepared for the photographed subject to ask for money in exchange for a picture. Other hill tribes will not allow you to point a camera at them.

POST

Thailand has a very efficient postal service and local postage is inexpensive. Typical provincial post offices keep the following hours: 8.30am to 4.30pm weekdays and 9am to noon on Saturdays. Larger main post offices in provincial capitals may also be open for a half-day on Sundays.

Most provincial post offices will sell do-it-yourself packing boxes, and some will pack your parcels for you for a small fee. Don't send cash or other valuables through the mail.

Thailand's poste restante service is generally very reliable, though these days few tourists use it. When you receive mail, you must show your passport and fill out some paperwork.

SHOPPING

Many bargains await you in Thailand but don't go shopping in the company of touts, tour guides or friendly strangers as they will inevitably take a commission on anything you buy, thus driving prices up beyond an acceptable value and creating a nuisance for future visitors.

Antiques

Real antiques cannot be taken out of Thailand without a permit. No Buddha image, new or old, may be exported without the permission of the Department of Fine Arts. See p743 for information.

Real Thai antiques are increasingly rare. Today most dealers sell antique reproductions or items from Myanmar. Bangkok and Chiang Mai are the two centres for the antique and reproduction trade.

Ceramics

Many kinds of hand-thrown pottery, old and new, are available throughout the kingdom. The best-known ceramics are the greenish celadon products, red-earth clay of Dan Kwian, and central Thailand's ben·jà·rong or 'five-colour' style. Ben·jà·rong is based on Chinese patterns while celadon is a Thai original that has been imitated throughout China and Southeast Asia. Rough unglazed pottery from the north and northeast can also be very appealing. Bangkok is full of modern ceramic designs while Chiang Mai sticks to traditional styles.

Clothing

Clothes tend to be inexpensive in Thailand but ready-made items are not usually cut to fit Westerners' body types. Increasingly larger-sized clothes are available in metropolitan malls, like Bangkok's MBK and

Central Department Store as well tourist-oriented shops throughout the country. Markets sell cheap everyday items and are handy for picking up something when everything else is dirty. For chic clothes, Bangkok and Ko Samui lead the country with design-minded fashions. Finding shoes that fit larger feet is also a problem. The custom of returns is not widely accepted in Thailand, so be sure everything fits before you leave the store.

Thailand has a long sartorial tradition, practised mainly by Thai-Indian Sikh families. You're more likely to get a good fit from a custom-made piece by a tailor. But this industry is filled with cut-rate operators and commission-paying scams. Be wary of the quickie 24-hour tailor shops; they often use inferior fabric and have poor workmanship. It's best to ask Thai or long-time foreign residents for a recommendation and then go for two or three fittings.

Fakes

In Bangkok, Chiang Mai and other tourist centres there's a thriving black-market street trade in fake designer goods. No-one pretends they're the real thing, at least not the vendors. Technically it is illegal for these items to be produced and sold and Thailand has often been pressured by intellectual-property enforcement agencies to close down the trade. Rarely does a crackdown by the police last and often the vendors develop more surreptitious means of distribution, further highlighting the contraband character of the goods. In the Patpong market, for example, a vendor might show you a picture of a knock-off watch, you pay for it and they go around the corner to fetch it. They usually come back but you'll wait long enough to wonder.

Furniture

Rattan and hardwood furniture items are often good purchases and can be made to order. Chiang Mai is the country's primary furniture producer with many retail outlets in Bangkok. Due to the ban on teak harvesting and the subsequent exhaustion of recycled teak, 70% of export furniture produced in Thailand is made from parawood, a processed wood from rubber trees that can no longer be used for latex production.

Gems & Jewellery

Thailand is the world's largest exporter of gems and ornaments, rivalled only by India and Sri Lanka. Although rough-stone sources in Thailand have decreased dramatically, stones are now imported from Myanmar, Sri Lanka and other countries to be cut, polished and traded.

Although there are a lot of gem and jewellery stores in Thailand, it has become so difficult to dodge the scammers that the country no longer represents a safe and enjoyable place to buy these goods. See p745 for a detailed warning on gem fraud.

Lacquerware

Northern Thailand has long produced regionally distinctive lacquerware thanks to the influence of ancient artisans originally from Burma. Chiang Mai is known for gold-on-black lacquerware. Lacquerware furniture and decorative items were traditionally made from bamboo and teak but these days mango wood might be used as the base. Resin from the *Melanorrhea usitata* (Burmese lacquer) tree is mixed with paddy-husk ash to form a light, flexible, waterproof coating. If the item is top quality, only the frame is bamboo and horse or donkey hairs will be wound round it. With lower-quality lacquerware, the whole object is made from bamboo. The lacquer is then coated over the framework and allowed to dry. After several days it is sanded down with ash from rice husks, and another coating of lacquer is applied. A high-quality item may have seven layers of lacquer. The piece is then engraved and painted and polished to remove the paint from everywhere except in the engravings. Multicoloured lacquerware is produced by repeated applications.

From start to finish it can take five or six months to produce a high-quality piece of lacquerware, which may have as many as five colours. Flexibility is one characteristic of good lacquerware: a well-made bowl can have its rim squeezed together until the sides meet without suffering damage. The quality and precision of the engraving is another thing to look for.

Textiles

Each region in Thailand has its own distinctive silk-weaving tradition and colour palette that can often be divided even further into village characteristics. In ancient times woven textiles might have functioned much like business cards do today – demarcating tribal identity and sometimes even married status. Today village weaving traditions continue but have become less geographically specific. Silk shops throughout the country sell a variety of styles, from the iridescent, single-colour smooth silk to the naturally dyed raw silk with its knubby texture. Woven silk pieces still retain their regional characteristics.

The northeast is famous for *mát·mèe* cloth – a thick cotton or silk fabric woven from tie-dyed threads, similar to Indonesia's *ikat* fabrics. Surin Province is renowned for its *mát·mèe* silk often showcasing colours and geometric patterns inherited from Khmer traditions.

In the north, silks reflect the influence of the Lanna weaving traditions, brought to Chiang Mai and the surrounding mountains by the various Tai tribes.

Fairly nice *ʻbah ʻdé* (batik) is available in the south in patterns that are more similar to the batik found in Malaysia than in Indonesia.

Each hill tribe has a tradition of embroidery that has been translated into the modern marketplace as bags and jewellery. Much of what you'll find in the marketplaces have been machine made but there are many NGO cooperatives that help villagers get their handmade goods to the consumers. Chiang Mai and Chiang Rai are filled with handicraft outlets.

TELEPHONE

The telephone system in Thailand has been deregulated and the once state-owned entities have been privatised. The telecommunications sector is dominated by the now private TOT Public Company Limited (formerly Telephone Organisation of Thailand or TOT) and CAT Telecom Public Company Limited (formerly Communications Authority of Thailand or CAT). For domestic service, TOT and its subsidiary TT&T are the primary service providers, while CAT and TOT compete for international service.

The telephone country code for Thailand is ☎ 66 and is used when calling the country from abroad. You must also dial an international exchange prefix (for Australia it is ☎ 0011, for the UK ☎ 00 and for the US ☎ 001) before the country code.

Thailand no longer uses separate area codes for the provinces, so all phone numbers in the country use eight digits (preceded by a '0' if you're dialling domestically). To accommodate the growth in mobile (cell) phone usage, Thailand has introduced an '8' prefix to all mobile numbers; ie ☎ 01 234 5678 is now ☎ 081 234 5678. If you're calling a mobile phone from overseas you would omit the initial '0' for both mobile and landline numbers.

International Calls

If you want to call an international number from a telephone in Thailand, you must first dial an international access code before dialling the country code followed by the subscriber number.

In Thailand, there are varying international access codes charging different rates per minute. The standard direct-dial prefix is ☎ 001; it is operated by CAT and is considered to have the best sound quality; it connects to the largest number of countries but is the most expensive. The next best is ☎ 007, a prefix operated by TOT with reliable quality and slightly cheaper rates. Economy rates are available with ☎ 008 and ☎ 009; both of which use Voice over Internet Protocol (VoIP), with varying but adequate sound quality.

Many expats are now using **DeeDial** (www .deedial.com), a direct-dial service that requires a prepaid account managed through the internet. The cheapest service they offer is the 'ring-back' feature, which circumvents local charges on your phone.

There are also a variety of international phonecards available through **CAT** (www.cthai .com) offering promotional rates as low as 1B per minute.

Dial ☎ 100 for operator-assisted international calls. To make a reverse-charges (or collect) call, use this prefix. Alternatively contact your long-distance carrier for their overseas operator number, a toll-free call, or try ☎ 001 9991 2001 from a CAT phone and ☎ 1 800 000 120 from a TOT phone.

Phones

If you don't have access to a private landline you can use a somewhat old-fashioned way to call overseas through a service called Home Country Direct, available at some post offices and CAT centres throughout the country. This service offers an easy one-button connection to international operators in countries around the world.

Calling overseas through phones in most hotel rooms usually incurs additional surcharges (sometimes as much as 50% over and above the CAT rate); however sometimes local calls are free or at standard rates. Some guesthouses will have a mobile phone or landline that customers can use for a per-minute fee for overseas calls.

There are also a variety of public payphones that use prepaid phonecards for calls (both international and domestic) and coin-operated pay phones for local calls. Using the public phones can be a bit of a pain: they are typically placed beside a main thoroughfare where you're cooked by the sun and the conversation is drowned out by traffic noise.

The red and blue public phones are for local calls and are coin-operated; it typically costs 5B to initiate a call. Then there are the phonecard phone booths that accept only certain kinds of cards. The green phones take domestic TOT phonecards. The yellow phones (labelled either domestic or international) take the respective Lenso phonecards. These phonecards can be bought from 7-Elevens in 300B and 500B denominations and rates vary between 7B and 10B per call.

Mobile Phones

Thailand is on a GSM network. Mobile (cellular) phone operators in Thailand include AIS, DTAC and True Move (formerly Orange). You have two hand-phone options: you can either buy a mobile phone in Thailand at one of the shopping malls, like Bangkok's MBK, or you can use an imported phone that isn't SIM-locked. Most mobile users in Thailand use the prepaid services of a particular carrier (AIS and DTAC are the most popular). To get started buy a SIM card, which includes an assigned telephone number. Once your phone is SIM-enabled you can buy minutes with prepaid phonecards. SIM cards and refill cards can be bought from 7-Elevens throughout the country. There are various promotions but rates typically hover around 2B to 3B per minute anywhere in Thailand and between 5B and 7B for international calls. SMS is usually 5B per message, making it the cheapest 'talk' option for baht-strapped mobile users.

TIME

Thailand's time zone is seven hours ahead of GMT/UTC (London). At government offices and local cinemas, times are often expressed according to the 24-hour clock, eg 11pm is written '2300'. See also the World Time Zone map at the end of this book.

The official year in Thailand is reckoned from 543 BC, the beginning of the Buddhist Era, so that AD 2009 is BE 2552, AD 2010 is BE 2553 etc.

TOILETS

As in many other Asian countries, the 'squat toilet' is the norm except in hotels and guesthouses geared towards tourists and international business travellers. These sit more-or-less flush with the surface of the floor, with two footpads on either side. For travellers who have never used a squat toilet, it takes a bit of getting used to.

Toilet users scoop water from an adjacent bucket or tank with a plastic bowl and use it to clean their nether regions while still squatting over the toilet. A few extra scoops of water must be poured into the toilet basin to flush waste into the septic system.

Even in places where sit-down toilets are installed, the septic system may not be designed to take toilet paper. In such cases the usual washing bucket will be standing nearby or there will be a waste basket where you're supposed to place used toilet paper.

TOURIST INFORMATION

The government-operated tourist information and promotion service, **Tourism Authority of Thailand** (TAT; www.tourismthailand.org), was founded in 1960 and produces excellent pamphlets on sightseeing, accommodation and transport. TAT's head office is in Bangkok and there are 22 regional offices spread throughout the country. Check the destination chapters for the TAT office in the towns you're planning to visit.

The following are a few of TAT's overseas information offices; check TAT's website for contact information in Hong Kong, Taipei, Seoul, Tokyo, Osaka, Fukuoka, Stockholm and Rome.

Australia (☎ 02 9247 7549; www.thailand.net.au; Level 20, 75 Pitt St, Sydney, NSW 2000)

France (☎ 01 53 53 47 00; tatpar@wanadoo.fr; 90 Ave des Champs Elysées, 75008 Paris)

Germany (☎ 069 138 1390; www.thailandtourismus.de; Bethmannstrasse 58, D-60311 Frankfurt/Main)

Malaysia (☎ 603 216 23480; www.thaitourism.com.my; Ste 22.01, Level 22, Menara Citibank, 165 Jalan Ampang, 50450 Kuala Lumpur)

Singapore (☎ 65 6235 7901; tatsin@signnet.com.sg; c/o Royal Thai Embassy, 370 Orchard Rd, 238870)

UK (☎ 020 7925 2511; www.tourismthailand.co.uk; 3rd fl, Brook House, 98-99 Jermyn St, London SW1Y 6EE) USA New York (☎ 212 432 0433; tatny@tat.or.th; 61 Broadway, Ste 2810, New York, NY 10006); Los Angeles (☎ 323 461 9814; tatla@ix.netcom.com; 1st fl, 611 North Larchmont Blvd, Los Angeles, CA 90004)

TRAVELLERS WITH DISABILITIES

Thailand presents one large, ongoing obstacle course for the mobility impaired. With its high curbs, uneven footpaths and nonstop traffic, Bangkok can be particularly difficult. Many streets must be crossed via pedestrian bridges flanked with steep stairways, while buses and boats don't stop long enough even for the fully abled. Rarely are there any ramps or other access points for wheelchairs.

A number of more expensive top-end hotels make consistent design efforts to provide disabled access to their properties. Other deluxe hotels with high employee-to-guest ratios are usually good about accommodating the mobility impaired by providing staff help where building design fails. For the rest, you're pretty much left to your own resources.

Counter to the prevailing trends, **Worldwide Dive & Sail** (www.worldwidediveandsail.com) offers liveaboard diving programs for the deaf and hard of hearing.

Some organisations and publications that offer tips on international travel include the following.

Accessible Journeys (☎ 610 521 0339; www.disability travel.com; 35 West Sellers Ave, Ridley Park, PA 19078, USA)
Mobility International USA (☎ 541 343 1284; www .miusa.org; 132 E Broadway, Suite 343, Eugene, OR 97401, USA)
Society for Accessible Travel & Hospitality (☎ 212 447 7284; www.sath.org; 347 Fifth Ave, Suite 605, New York, NY 10016, USA)

VISAS

The **Ministry of Foreign Affairs** (www.mfa.go.th) oversees immigration and visas issues. Check the website or the nearest Thai embassy or consulate for application procedures and costs. In the past five years there have been some shifting rules on visas and visa extensions; **Thaivisa** (www.thaivisa.com) stays abreast of any changes and developments.

Tourist Visas & Exemptions

The Thai government allows tourist-visa exemptions for 41 different nationalities, including those from Australia, New Zealand, the USA and most of Europe, to enter the country without a prearranged visa. Do note that in 2008, the length of stay for citizens from exempted countries was slightly altered from years past. For those arriving in the kingdom by air, a 30-day visa is issued without a fee. For those arriving via a land border, the arrival visa has been shortened to 15 days (no fee is charged). The exception to this rule is for Malaysian nationals who will still receive a 30-day visa if arriving via a land border.

Without proof of an onward ticket and sufficient funds for one's projected stay any visitor can be denied entry, but in practise your ticket and funds are rarely checked if you're dressed neatly for the immigration check.

If you plan to stay in Thailand longer than 30 days (or 15 days for land arrivals), you should apply for the 60-day tourist visa from a Thai consulate or embassy before your trip. Obtaining a tourist visa is a good idea for overland travellers who need more time in Thailand than the land-arrival visa allows. Alternatively you can extend your visa in Thailand (see Visa Extensions & Renewals below), but it will be cheaper and you'll get more time if you arrange for a tourist visa before your arrival. Contact the nearest Thai embassy or consulate to obtain application procedures and fees for tourist visas.

Non-Immigrant Visas

The Non-Immigrant Visa is good for 90 days and is intended for foreigners entering the country for business, study, retirement and extended family visits. There are multiple-entry visas available in this visa class; you're more likely to be granted multiple entries if you apply at a Thai consulate in Europe, the US or Australia than elsewhere. If you plan to apply for a Thai work permit, you'll need to possess a Non-Immigrant Visa first.

Visa Extensions & Renewals

You can apply at any immigration office in Thailand for visa extensions. Most foreigners use the **Bangkok immigration office** (Map p124; ☎ 0 2287 3101; Soi Suan Phlu, Th Sathon Tai; ☼ 9am-noon & 1-4.30pm Mon-Fri, 9am-noon Sat) or the **Chiang Mai immigration office** (Map pp276-7; ☎ 0 5320 1755-6; Th Mahidon; ☼ 8.30am-4.30pm Mon-Fri) for extensions of most types of visa. The usual fee for a visa extension is 1900B.

Those issued with a standard stay of 15 or 30 days can extend their stay for seven to 10 days (depending on the immigration office) if the extension is handled before the visa expires. The 60-day tourist visa can be extended by up to 30 days at the discretion of Thai immigration authorities.

Another visa renewal option is to cross a land border. Since 2006, Thailand has been tweaking the border visa rules in an attempt to crackdown on foreigners who work or live in the country illegally (ie without the proper documentation). As of 2008, passport holders from visa-exempt countries could only obtain a 15-day visa upon arrival at a land border. The 30-day visa is still available if you arrive by air and many expats have been booking flights to nearby Kuala Lumpur for their 'visa runs'. There was a short-lived limit placed on the number of times immigration would grant a stay to visitors crossing the land borders, but this seems to have been lifted with the new 15-day land visas. If you're arriving in Thailand via a land border and would like to stay longer than 15 days, you should consider securing a tourist visa from a Thai embassy or consulate in whichever country you'll be visiting prior to your arrival in the kingdom.

For all types of visa extensions, bring along two passport-sized photos and one copy each of the photo and visa pages of your passport. Remember to dress neatly and do all visa extensions yourself, rather than hiring a third party.

If you overstay your visa, the usual penalty is a fine of 500B per day, with a 20,000B limit. Fines can be paid at the airport or in advance at an immigration office. If you've overstayed only one day, you don't have to pay. Children under 14 travelling with a parent do not have to pay the penalty.

Foreign residents in Thailand should arrange visa extensions at the immigration office closest to their in-country address; this is a recent procedural change so check with the Ministry of Foreign Affairs for more details.

WOMEN TRAVELLERS

Women make up nearly half of all foreign visitors to Thailand, a much higher ratio than the worldwide average, and female travellers generally face few problems. With the great amount of respect afforded to women, an equal measure should be returned.

In the provincial towns, it is advisable to dress conservatively, covering shoulders, belly buttons and thighs. Outside of Bangkok, most Thai women cover up in the sun to avoid unnecessary exposure since lighter skin is considered more beautiful. That Westerners believe the opposite is an endless source of amusement and confusion.

Attacks and rapes are not common in Thailand, but incidents do occur, especially when an attacker observes a vulnerable target: a drunk or solo woman. If you return home from a bar alone, be sure to have your wits about you. The regular Full Moon party at Ko Pha-Ngan is a common trouble spot. Avoid accepting rides from strangers late at night or travelling around in isolated areas by yourself – common sense stuff that might escape your notice in a new environment filled with hospitable people.

While Bangkok might be a men's paradise to some, foreign women are finding their own Romeos on the Thai beaches. As more couples emerge, more Thai men will make themselves available. Women who aren't interested in such romantic encounters should not presume that Thai men have merely platonic motives. Women should not encourage frivolous flirting as some Thai men might feel a loss of face if attention is then diverted to another person and, in some cases where alcohol is involved, violence can ensue.

Transport

GETTING THERE & AWAY

ENTERING THE COUNTRY

Entry procedures for Thailand, by air or by land, are straightforward: you'll have to show your passport (see p754 for information about visa requirements); and you'll need to present completed arrival and departure cards. Blank arrival and departure cards are usually distributed on the incoming flight or, if arriving by land, can be picked up at the immigration counter.

You do not have to fill in a customs form on arrival unless you have imported goods to declare. In that case, you can get the proper form from Thai customs officials at your point of entry. See p749 for Thai customs information about minimum funds requirements.

Flights, tours and rail tickets can be booked online at www.lonelyplanet.com/travel _services.

AIR
Airports

The Suvarnabhumi Airport (p181; sù·wan·ná·poom) opened in September 2006 and has replaced the airport at Don Muang for all international flights and some domestic flights. It is located in the Nong Ngu Hao area of Samut Prakan – 30km east of Bangkok and 60km from Pattaya. The airport code for Suvarnabhumi is BKK.

The old international airport, Don Muang Airport (p181) in Bangkok, is now used for some domestic flights by Thailand's national carrier, Thai Airways International (THAI), as well as by Nok Air and One-Two-Go. The airport code is DMK. When booking connecting flights, always check which Bangkok airport you will be using.

While most international flights arrive at and depart out of Bangkok, there are a few routes using Thailand's other 'international' airports. Moderately up-to-date information about these airports is available online at www.airportthai.co.th. The country's second-busiest airport for passenger service is Phuket International Airport (p678). Flights to certain Asian destinations operate from here without a layover in Bangkok.

Other airports with limited connections to Asian capitals can be found in Chiang Mai (with services to Taipei, Singapore, Kuala Lumpur, Luang Prabang and Vientiane), Udon Thani (with services to Luang Prabang), Ko Samui (with services to Singapore and Hong Kong) and Hat Yai (with services to Kuala Lumpur).

Airlines Travelling to/from Thailand

Bangkok is one of the cheapest cities in the world to fly into and out of, because of the Thai government's loose restrictions on airfares, and close competition between airlines and travel agencies. The following airlines fly to and from Thailand.

Air Asia (☎ 0 2515 9999; www.airasia.com; Suvarnabhumi International Airport)

DEPARTURE TAX

For international departures from Bangkok's Suvarnabhumi Airport, there is no longer a separate departure tax. Do note however, that international flights out of Ko Samui do still incur a departure tax (300B).

CLIMATE CHANGE & TRAVEL

Climate change is a serious threat to the ecosystems that humans rely upon, and air travel is the fastest-growing contributor to the problem. Lonely Planet regards travel, overall, as a global benefit, but believes we all have a responsibility to limit our personal impact on global warming.

Flying & Climate Change

Pretty much every form of motor travel generates CO_2 (the main cause of human-induced climate change) but planes are far and away the worst offenders, not just because of the sheer distances they allow us to travel, but because they release greenhouse gases high into the atmosphere. The statistics are frightening: two people taking a return flight between Europe and the US will contribute as much to climate change as an average household's gas and electricity consumption over a whole year.

Carbon Offset Schemes

Climatecare.org and other websites use 'carbon calculators' that allow jetsetters to offset the greenhouse gases they are responsible for with contributions to energy-saving projects and other climate-friendly initiatives in the developing world – including projects in India, Honduras, Kazakhstan and Uganda.

Lonely Planet, together with Rough Guides and other concerned partners in the travel industry, supports the carbon offset scheme run by climatecare.org. Lonely Planet offsets all of its staff and author travel.

For more information check out our website: lonelyplanet.com.

TRANSPORT

Air Canada (Map pp118-19; ☎ 0 2670 0400; www .aircanada.com; Ste 1708, River Wing West, Empire Tower, 195 Th Sathon Tai)

Air China (Map pp118-19; ☎ 0 2634 8991; www .fly-airchina.com; Bangkok Union Insurance Bldg, 175-177 Th Surawong)

Air France (Map pp118-19; ☎ 0 2635 1191; www .airfrance.fr; 20th fl, Vorawat Bldg, 849 Th Silom)

Air New Zealand (Map pp118-19; ☎ 0 2235 8280; www .airnewzealand.com; 11th fl, 140/17 ITF Tower, Th Silom)

American Airlines (Map pp120-1; ☎ 0 2263 0225; www.aa.com; 11th fl Ploenchit Tower, 898 Th Ploenchit)

Bangkok Airways (☎ 1771; www.bangkokair.com; Suvarnabhumi International Airport)

British Airways (Map pp118-19; ☎ 0 2627 1701; www.britishairways.com; 21st fl, Charn Issara Tower, 942/160-163 Th Phra Ram IV)

Cathay Pacific Airways (Map pp120-1; ☎ 0 2263 0606; www.cathaypacific.com; 11th fl, Ploenchit Tower, 898 Th Ploenchit)

China Airlines (Map pp120-1; ☎ 0 2250 9898; www.china-airlines.com; 4th fl, Peninsula Plaza, 153 Th Ratchadamri)

Emirates (Map pp122-3; ☎ 0 2664 1040; www.emirates .com; 2nd fl, BB Bldg, 54 Soi 21/Asoke, Th Sukhumvit)

Eva Air (Map pp110-11; ☎ 0 2269 6288; www.evaair .com; 2nd fl, Green Tower, 3656/4-5 Th Phra Ram IV)

Garuda Indonesia (Map p124; ☎ 0 2679 7371; www .garuda-indonesia.com; 27th fl, Lumphini Tower, 1168/77 Th Phra Ram IV)

Gulf Air (Map pp120-1; ☎ 0 2254 7931-4; www.gulf airco.com; 10th fl, Maneeya Center, 518/5 Th Ploenchit)

Japan Airlines (Map pp120-1; ☎ 0 2649 9520; www .jal.co.jp; 1st fl, Nantawan Bldg, 161 Th Ratchadamri)

Jetstar Airways (Map p189; ☎ 0 2267 5125; www .jetstar.com; Suvarnabhumi International Airport)

KLM-Royal Dutch Airlines (Map pp118-19; ☎ 0 2635 2300; www.klm.com; 20th fl, Vorawat Bldg, 849 Th Silom)

Korean Air (Map pp118-19; ☎ 0 2635 0465; www .koreanair.com; 1st fl, Kongboonma Bldg, 699 Th Silom)

Lao Airlines (Map pp118-19; ☎ 0 2236 9822; www .laoairlines.com; 1st fl, Silom Plaza, 491/17 Th Silom)

Lufthansa Airlines (Map pp122-3; ☎ 0 2264 2484, reservations 0 2264 2400; www.lufthansa.com; 18th fl, Q House, Soi 21/Asoke, Th Sukhumvit)

Malaysia Airlines (Map pp120-1; ☎ 0 2263 0565; www.mas.com.my; 20th fl, Ploenchit Tower, 898 Th Ploenchit)

Myanmar Airways International (Map pp122-3; ☎ 0 2261 5060; www.maiair.com; 8th fl, BB Bldg, 54 Soi 21/Asoke, Th Sukhumvit)

Northwest Airlines (Map pp120-1; ☎ 0 2660 6999; www.nwa.com; 4th fl, Peninsula Plaza, 153 Th Ratchadamri)

Orient Thai (Map pp118-19; ☎ 0 2229 4260; www .orient-thai.com; 17th fl, Jewellery Centre Bldg, 138/70 Th Naret)

Philippine Airlines (Map pp110-11; ☎ 0 2633 5713; Manorom Bldg, 3354/47 Th Phra Ram IV)

Qantas Airways (Map pp118-19; ☎ 0 2236 2800; www.qantas.com.au; Tour East, 21st fl, Charn Issara Tower, 942/160-163 Th Phra Ram IV)

Royal Brunei Airlines (Map p124; ☎ 0 2637 5151; www.bruneiair.com; 17th fl, U Chu Liang Bldg, 968 Th Phra Ram IV)

Royal Nepal Airlines (Map pp112-13; ☎ 0 2216 5691-5; www.royalnepal-airlines.com; 9th fl Phayathai Plaza Bldg, 128 Th Phayathai)

Scandinavian Airlines (Map pp122-3; ☎ 0 2645 8200; www.scandinavian.net; 8th fl, Glas Haus Bldg, Th Sukhumvit)

Singapore Airlines (Map pp118-19; ☎ 0 2353 6000; www.singaporeair.com; 12th fl, Silom Center Bldg, 2 Th Silom)

South African Airways (Map pp118-19; ☎ 0 2635 1410; www.flysaa.com; 20th fl, Vorawat Bldg, 849 Th Silom)

Thai Airways International (www.thaiair.com) Banglamphu (Map pp114-15; ☎ 0 2356 1111; 6 Th Lan Luang); Silom (Map pp118-19; ☎ 0 2232 8000; 1st fl, Bangkok Union Insurance Bldg, 175-177 Soi Anuman Rajchathon, Th Surawong)

United Airlines (Map pp118-19; ☎ 0 2353 3900; www.ual.com; 6th fl, TMB Bank Silom Bldg, 393 Th Silom)

Vietnam Airlines (Map pp120-1; ☎ 0 2655 4137-40; www.vietnamair.com.vn; 10th fl, Wave Place Bldg, 55 Th Withayu)

Tickets

Tickets can be purchased cheaply on the internet through booking and airline websites, which often list fare sales or special internet prices. In Thailand, most travel arrangements are made through an agent. Most firms are honest and solvent, but there are some rogue fly-by-night outfits around. What varies most is the amount of commission an agent will charge; shop around to gauge the discrepancy in prices. Paying by credit card generally offers protection, because most card issuers provide refunds if you can prove you didn't get what you paid for. Agents who accept only cash should hand over the tickets straight away and not tell you to 'come back tomorrow'. After you've made a booking or paid your deposit, call the airline and confirm that the booking was made.

Booking flights in and out of Bangkok during the high season (from December to March) can be difficult and expensive. For air travel during these months you should make your bookings as far in advance as you possibly can.

Also, be sure to reconfirm return or on-going tickets when you arrive in Thailand. Failure to reconfirm can mean losing your reservation.

ROUND-THE-WORLD (RTW) TICKETS

A round-the-world (RTW) ticket – where you pay a single discounted price for several connections – may be the most economical way to go.

Here are a few online companies that can arrange RTW tickets.

Airtreks (www.airtreks.com)

Air Brokers International (www.airbrokers.com)

Around the Worlds (www.aroundtheworlds.com)

Avia Travel (www.aviatravel.com)

Asia

There are regular flights to Suvarnabhumi International Airport from almost every major city in Asia. With the emergence of budget airlines, quick hops from, say, Bangkok to Kuala Lumpur, Singapore or Hong Kong are now commonly used in Asia for a weekend getaway. Air Asia and Dragon are two discount carriers that run frequent promotions.

Recommended booking agencies for reserving flights from Asia include **STA Travel** (www.statravel.com), which has offices in Bangkok, Hong Kong, Japan and Singapore. Another resource in Japan is **No1 Travel** (www.no1-travel.com); in Hong Kong try **Four Seas Tours** (www.fourseastravel.com). In India, try **STIC Travels** (www.stictravel.com), which has offices in dozens of Indian cities.

Australia

THAI and Qantas both have direct flights to Bangkok. Qantas' low-budget subsidiary, Jetstar, travels to Thailand from Sydney and Melbourne. Garuda Indonesia, Singapore Airlines, Philippine Airlines, Malaysia Airlines, China Airlines, Cathay Pacific Airways and Emirates Airlines also have frequent flights to Bangkok from Australia.

Online ticket sites include the following.

Expedia (☎ 1 300 397 3342; www.expedia.com.au)

Flight Centre (☎ 133 133; www.flightcentre.com.au)

STA Travel (☎ 134 782; www.statravel.com.au)

Canada

Air Canada, THAI, Cathay Pacific, Japan Airlines, Singapore Airlines and several US-based airlines fly from various Canadian cities to Bangkok. **Travel Cuts** (☎ 866 246 9762; www.travelcuts.com) is Canada's national student travel agency. **North South Travel** (www.northsouthtravel.com) is an independent travel agency located in Vancouver.

Continental Europe

Following are some recommended agencies across Europe.

France

Anyway (☎ 0 892 302 301; www.anyway.fr)
Lastminute (☎ 0 466 923 029; www.lastminute.fr)
Nouvelles Frontières (☎ 0 149 206 587; www.nouvelles-frontieres.fr)
Voyageurs du Monde (www.vdm.com)

Germany

Just Travel (☎ 089 747 3330; www.justtravel.de)
Lastminute (☎ 0 1805 284 366; www.lastminute.de)
STA Travel (☎ 0 6974 303 292; www.statravel.de)

Italy

CTS Viaggi (☎ 06 462 0431; www.cts.it) Specialises in student and youth travel.

Netherlands

Airfair (☎ 0 900 7717 717; www.airfair.nl)

Spain

Barcelo Viajes (☎ 902 116 226; www.barceloviajes.com)

Middle East

Egypt Panorama Tours (☎ 2359 0200; www.eptours.com) is a long-running agency located in Cairo.

New Zealand

Air New Zealand, British Airways, THAI and Australian-based airlines have direct flights to Bangkok. Malaysia Airlines, Qantas and Garuda Indonesia also have flights to Bangkok, with stopovers.

Both **Flight Centre** (☎ 0800 243 544; www.flightcentre.co.nz) and **STA Travel** (☎ 0800 474 400; www.statravel.co.nz) have branches throughout the country. **Go Holidays** (www.goholidays.co.nz) is recommended for online bookings.

South America

Some recommended agencies include the following.
ASATEJ (www.asatej.com) In Argentina.
Student Travel Bureau (☎ 3038 1555; www.stb.com.br) In Brazil.

UK

At least two dozen airlines fly between London and Bangkok, although only three of them – British Airways, EVA Airways and THAI – fly nonstop. Discount air-travel ads

---

appear in *Time Out*, the *Evening Standard* and in the free magazine *TNT*. **Low Cost Lux** (www.lowcostlux.com) discusses stopover ideas and nonstop travel between London and Bangkok.

Recommended travel agencies include the following.
Ebookers (☎ 0871 223 5000; www.ebookers.com)
Expedia (www.expedia.co.uk)
Flight Centre (☎ 0870 499 0040; flightcentre.co.uk)
STA Travel (☎ 0871 230 0040; www.statravel.co.uk)
Trailfinders (☎ 0845 058 5858; www.trailfinders.co.uk)
Travel Bag (☎ 0800 804 8911; www.travelbag.co.uk)
Quest Travel (☎ 0845 263 6963; www.questtravel.com)

US

It's cheaper to fly to Bangkok from West Coast cities than from the East Coast. The airlines that generally offer the lowest fares from the US include China Airlines, EVA Airways, Korean Air and Northwest. EVA Airways (Taiwan) offers the 'Evergreen Deluxe' class between the US and Bangkok, via Taipei, which has business class–sized seats and personal movie screens for about the same cost as regular economy fares on most other airlines.

Reliable discounters include the following.
Cheap Tickets (☎ 888 922 8849; www.cheaptickets.com)
Expedia (☎ 800 397 3342; www.expedia.com)
Lowest Fare (☎ 800 678 0998; www.lowestfare.com)
Orbitz (☎ 888 656 4546; www.orbitz.com)
Smarter Living (☎ 617 886 5555; www.smarterliving.com)
STA Travel (☎ 800 781 4040; www.sta.com)
Travelocity (☎ 888 872 8336; www.travelocity.com)

BOAT

You can cross into and out of Thailand via public boat from the west coast of Malaysia. For visa-run purposes you can do a one-day crossing from the Andaman coast town of Ranong to Myanmar's Victoria Point (also known as Kawthoung).

All foreign-registered private vessels, skippers and crew must check in with the relevant Thai authorities as soon as possible after entering Thai waters. Although major ports throughout Thailand offer port check-ins, most leisure-boating visitors check in at Phuket, Krabi, Ko Samui, Pranburi or Pattaya. Before departing from Thailand by boat, you must also check out with immigration, customs and the harbourmaster.

LAND

Thailand shares land borders with Laos, Malaysia, Cambodia and Myanmar. Travel between all of these countries can be done by land via sanctioned border crossings. With improved highways, it is also becoming easier to travel from Thailand to China. See right for specific border crossing immigration points and transport summaries.

Bicycle

Many visitors bring their own touring bicycles to Thailand. No special permits are needed for bringing a bicycle into the country, although it may be registered by customs – which means if you don't leave the country with your bicycle, you'll have to pay a customs duty. See p762 for more information about travelling by bike. It's advisable to bring a well-stocked repair kit.

Bus, Car & Motorcycle

Road connections exist between all of Thailand's neighbours, and these routes can be travelled by bus, shared taxi and private car. In some cases, you'll take a bus to the border point, pass through immigration and then pick up another bus or shared taxi on the other side. In other cases, especially when crossing the Malaysian border, the bus will stop for immigration formalities and then continue to its destination across the border.

Private passenger vehicles (eg cars, vans, trucks or motorcycles) can be brought into Thailand for tourist purposes for up to six months, provided that you have a valid International Driving Permit, a passport, vehicle registration papers (or in the case of a borrowed or hired vehicle, authorisation from the owner) and a cash or bank guarantee equal to the value of the vehicle plus 20%. For entry through Khlong Toey Port or Suvarnabhumi International Airport, this means a letter of bank credit; for overland crossings via Malaysia, Cambodia or Laos a 'self-guarantee' filled in at the border is sufficient.

Train

If everything goes according to plan, Thailand will soon have a new international rail link with Laos. Slated for completion in April 2009, the extended 3.5km rail line will go from the Nong Khai station in Thailand across the Thai-Lao Friendship bridge to Ban Tanalaeng, which is just north of Vientiane. The rail line offers very little advantage for passenger service as surface roads are faster and easier ways to cross the border, but it may help expedite cargo transport.

Other rail services that travel across international borders can be found on the western part of the Malay peninsula between Thailand and Malaysia. The two countries' state railways meet at Butterworth (93km south of the Thai-Malaysian border), which is a transfer point to Penang (by boat) or to Kuala Lumpur and Singapore (by Malaysian train).

There are several border crossings for which you can take a train to the border and then switch to automobile transport on the other side. The Thai-Cambodian border is accessible by train from Bangkok to the border town of Aranya Prathet. There is talk of restoring the train line on the Cambodian side all the way to Sisophon, though little has materialised.

Another rail line travels to the Malaysian east coast border town of Sungai Kolok, but because of ongoing violence in Thailand's deep south we don't recommend this route for travellers.

BORDER CROSSINGS
Cambodia

Between Cambodia and Thailand, most visitors cross from Poipet (Cambodia) to Aranya Prathet (Thailand; p272). This is the most direct land route between Bangkok and Angkor Wat. Cambodian visas can be arranged upon arrival at the Cambodian immigration office. Do note however, that there are many transport and visa scams on the Poipet side of the border; read up on some of the common problems online before setting off. **Tales of Asia** (www.talesofasia.com) monitors this Cambodian border crossing.

If you're travelling along the southeastern coast of Thailand, you can cross into Cambodia from Hat Lek to Koh Kong, which has boat access to Sihanoukville. Cambodian visas are available upon arrival. For more information, see p257.

Several more remote crossings exist between southeastern Thailand and southwestern Cambodia, including O Smach–Chong Chom, Chong Sa Ngam–Anlong Veng, Ban Laem–Daun Lem, Ban Phakkat–Pailin and Ban Laem–Deun Lem. Private or hired transport is required to access most of these crossings; Ban Phakkat is an exception because minibuses connect this border crossing to Chanthaburi, making it an underutilised crossing point to Battambang.

China

Land and rail links between China and member countries of the Association of Southeast Asian Nations (ASEAN), including Thailand, Laos, Myanmar and Vietnam, have been increasing since the turn of the millennium, making overland travel between Southeast Asia and the interior of southern China an easier proposition than in years past.

The China–Thailand highway (also called Rte 3) officially opened in mid-2008. Following a former opium smuggling trail, it comprises 1800km of paved road intended to link Kunming, in China's Yunnan Province, to Bangkok. The once rough tracks, mainly in Laos and southern China, are now modern enough to handle passenger and freight shipping, with only a slight interruption by the Mekong River at the Thai–Lao border (at Chiang Khong–Huay Xai). The river crossing is now done by boat, but a planned Mekong River bridge is due to be completed in 2011. For more information about this crossing, see p374.

The ambitious China–Myanmar highway plans to reopen stretches of the old Stillwell Rd (an invasion route built during WWII by Allied forces), which would eventually link China's Yunnan province to India's Assam state through the Pangsaw Pass. Although portions of road are now functional, the project has stalled because of the diverging political and economic interests of the three countries. It was once also possible to travel overland from the Thai town of Mae Sai through Myanmar and across the border near Mong La to the Chinese town of Daluo, but this border has been closed since 2005.

You can also take a slow boat along the Mekong River from the northern Thai town of Chian Saen to Jinghong in China's Yunnan Province. See p369 for more information.

Laos

The Thai-Lao Friendship Bridge (1174m) spans a section of the Mekong River between Nong Khai, Thailand, and Tha Na Leng (near Vientiane), Laos, and is the main transport gateway between the two countries. The border crossing is currently undertaken by hired or public transport across the bridge. A planned rail link along this route is expected to open in mid-2009, but it will offer little advantage to travellers heading to Vientiane and would require a Lao visa in advance; while for the bridge crossing, Lao visas can be obtained on arrival. For more information, see p515.

A second Mekong bridge, between Mukdahan and Savannakhet, opened in 2006 and provides a fundamental trilateral link between Thailand, Laos and Vietnam. This crossing is done by bus. A Lao visa is available on arrival, and many Bangkok-based expats use this route for visa runs. See p540 for more information.

It's legal for non-Thais to cross the Mekong River by ferry between Thailand and Laos at the following points: Chiang Khong (opposite Huay Xai), Nakhon Phanom (opposite Tha Khaek) and Beung Kan (opposite Pakson), although this route is used less frequently. Lao visas are available upon arrival at Huay Xai and Tha Khaek, but not at Pakson.

The only land crossing open to foreigners is from Chong Mek into the Laos town of Vangtao. On the Thai side, the border is best accessed via bus from Ubon Ratchathani; Lao visas are available upon arrival. See p489 for more information.

Another crossing is via little-visited Loei Province; a bridge links the Thai town of Thai Li to the Lao town of Nam Hoeng. We've heard conflicting reports about issuances of Lao visas on arrival here, and only private or chartered transport is available. Expats who live in the area have used this as a hassle-free visa run.

Malaysia

The train line heading into Malaysia from Bangkok splits at Hat Yai. One spur heads west through Padang Besar to Butterworth,

TRANSPORT

which is the transfer point to Penang or other destinations along the west coast of Malaysia. Another spur heads east to the border town of Sungai Kolok, which was once a popular traveller migration point through Malaysia's Kota Bahru and on to the Perhentian Islands. Due to unrest in the far southern provinces of Thailand, it is not advisable to take the train east; stick to the western side of the peninsula.

Buses and minibuses also cross the border into the Malaysian towns of Padang Besar and Dan Nawk (south of Thailand's Sadao). By boat you can cross to several points along the Malaysian west coast, including Pulau Langkawi, from the mainland town of Satun or from Ko Lipe. See p728 for more details. There are also a few lesser-used land crossings, but those mentioned here are the easiest to reach with public transport.

Myanmar

Most of the land crossings into Myanmar have restrictions that don't allow full access to the country. These border points are also subject to unannounced closures, which can last anywhere from a day to years.

The crossing at Mae Sai–Tachileik is the only land point through which foreigners can travel into portions of Myanmar. From the border you can continue to Kengtung, as far as Mong La on the Thai–China border (see p365). Prior to 2005, foreigners could continue on to China as long as they had the appropriate visas beforehand, but this is no longer an option. Interestingly, the bridge that spans the two border towns is Lo Hsing-han's former 'Golden Triangle' passageway for the opium and heroin trade. Many travellers use this border as a way to renew their Thai visas, especially if they are based in or have just visited Chiang Mai and Chiang Rai.

The Mae Sot–Myawadi border crossing is open to foreigners only as a day trip into a Burmese border market, even though the road continues to Mawlamyaing (Moulmein) via Kawkareik. This border is also a busy crossing for renewing Thai visas. For more information, see p411.

Once a gateway for various invading armies and an important smuggling route, Three Pagodas Pass (p226) has been closed to foreigners since 2006. Prior to its closure, the border was open for day-pass trips to the

Burmese border market only and no visa extensions/renewals were issued.

In the southern part of Thailand, you can legally enter Myanmar by boat from Ranong to the island of Kawthoung, but you can't travel onward from here into mainland Myanmar. Many people use this crossing only as a day trip in order to renew their Thai visas; see the boxed text, p636, for more information.

GETTING AROUND

AIR

Hopping around the country by air is becoming more and more affordable thanks to airline deregulation. Most routes originate from Bangkok, but Chiang Mai, Ko Samui and Phuket all have routes to other Thai towns. See the Thai Airfares and Rail Lines map (p763) for routes and estimated costs; for airline contact information, see the respective city sections.

THAI operates many domestic air routes from Bangkok to provincial capitals. Bangkok Air is another established domestic carrier. One-Two-Go, Nok Air and Air Asia all tend to be cheaper than the older carriers.

BICYCLE

For travelling just about anywhere outside Bangkok, bicycles are an ideal form of local transport – cheap, nonpolluting and slow moving enough to allow travellers to see everything.

Bicycle touring is also a popular way to see the country, and most roads are sealed and have roomy shoulders. Grades in most parts of the country are moderate; exceptions include the far north, especially Mae Hong Son and Nan Provinces.

You can take bicycles on the train for a little less than the equivalent of one 3rd-class fare. On ordinary buses they'll place your bike on the roof, and on air-con buses it will be put in the cargo hold. **Biking Southeast Asia with Mr Pumpy** (www.mrpumpy.net) contains route suggestions, tips and other details from 'spoke folks'. The **Thailand Cycling Club** (☎ 08 1555 2901; www.thaicycling.com), established in 1959, serves as an information clearing house on biking tours and cycle clubs.

See p760 for more information on bringing a bike into Thailand.

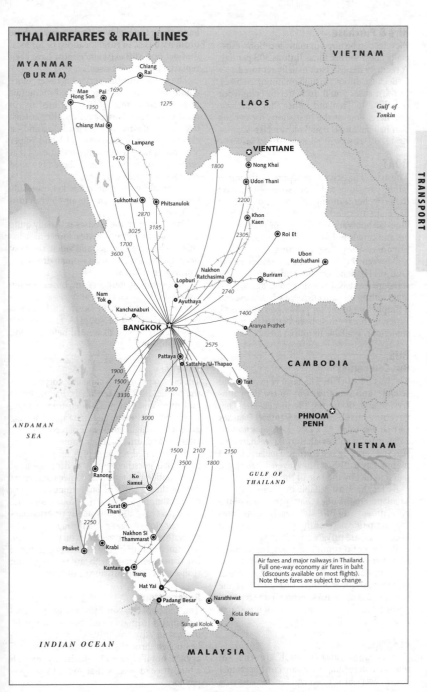

THAI AIRFARES & RAIL LINES

MYANMAR (BURMA)

VIETNAM

LAOS

Gulf of Tonkin

Chiang Rai

Mae Hong Son

Pai   1690

1350

1275

Chiang Mai

Lampang

1470

VIENTIANE

Nong Khai

Udon Thani

1800

2200

Sukhothai

Phitsanulok

2870

3025

3185

Khon Kaen

2305

Roi Et

Ubon Ratchathani

1700

3600

Nam Tok

Kanchanaburi

Lopburi

Ayuthaya

Nakhon Ratchasima

2740

Buriram

BANGKOK

1400

Aranya Prathet

2575

Pattaya

Sattahip/U-Thapao

CAMBODIA

1900

1500

3330

3550

Trat

3000

PHNOM PENH

VIETNAM

ANDAMAN SEA

1500   2107   2150

3500   1800

GULF OF THAILAND

Ranong

Ko Samui

Surat Thani

2250

Nakhon Si Thammarat

Phuket

Krabi

Kantang   Trang

Hat Yai

Padang Besar   Narathiwat

Kota Bharu

Sungai Kolok

INDIAN OCEAN

MALAYSIA

Air fares and major railways in Thailand.
Full one-way economy air fares in baht
(discounts available on most flights).
Note these fares are subject to change.

TRANSPORT

Hire & Purchase

Bicycles can be hired in many locations, especially guesthouses, for as little as 50B per day. A security deposit isn't usually required.

Because duties are high on imported bikes, in most cases you'll do better to bring your own bike to Thailand rather than purchase one here. One of the best shops for cycling gear in Thailand is Bangkok's **Probike** (Map p124; ☎ 0 2253 3384; www.probike.co.th; 237/1 Soi Sarasin).

BOAT

The true Thai river transport is the *reu·a hǎhng yow* (long-tail boat), so-called because the propeller is mounted at the end of a long drive shaft extending from the engine. The long-tail boats are a staple of transport on rivers and canals in Bangkok and neighbouring provinces. See p185 for details.

Between the mainland and islands in the Gulf of Thailand or the Andaman Sea, the standard craft is a wooden boat, 8m to 10m long, with an inboard engine, a wheelhouse and a simple roof to shelter passengers and cargo. Faster, more expensive hovercraft or jetfoils are sometimes available in tourist areas.

BUS
Bus Companies

The bus network in Thailand is prolific and reliable, and is a great way to see the countryside and sit among the locals. The Thai government subsidises the **Transport Company** (bò·rí·sàt kǒn sòng; ☎ 0 2936 2841; www.transport .co.th), usually abbreviated to Baw Khaw Saw (BKS). Every city and town in Thailand linked by bus has a BKS station, even if it's just a patch of dirt by the side of the road.

By far the most reliable bus companies in Thailand are the ones that operate out of the government-run BKS stations. In some cases the companies are entirely state owned, in others they are private concessions.

We do not recommend using bus companies that operate directly out of tourist centres, like Bangkok's Th Khao San, because of repeated instances of theft. Be sure to read the Dangers & Annoyances section in the relevant destination chapter to be aware of bus scams and problems.

CLASSES

The cheapest and slowest are the *rót tam·má·dah* (ordinary non air-con buses) that stop in every little town and for every waving hand along the highway. Only a few of these ordinary buses, in rural locations or for local destinations, still exist since most have been replaced by air-con buses.

The bulk of the bus service is faster, more comfortable air-con buses, called *rót aa* (air bus), *rót ฿ràp ah·gàht* (air-con bus) or *rót too·a* (tour bus). Longer routes offer at least two classes of air-con buses: 2nd class and 1st class; the latter have toilets. 'VIP' and 'Super VIP' buses have fewer seats so that each seat reclines further. Sometimes these are called *rót norn* (sleeper bus).

It is handy to bring along a jacket, especially for long-distance trips, as the air-con can turn the cabin into a deep freeze.

The service on these buses is usually quite good and on certain routes sometimes includes a beverage service and video, courtesy of an 'air hostess', a young woman dressed in a polyester uniform.

On overnight journeys the buses usually stop somewhere en route and passengers are awakened to get off the bus for a free meal of fried rice or rice soup. A few companies even treat you to a meal before a long overnight trip.

SAFETY

The most reputable bus companies depart from the public, BKS bus terminals. Private buses and minivans that pick up customers from tourist centres such as Th Khao San in Bangkok experience a higher incidence of reported theft, lateness and unreliability. Sometimes these tourist-oriented services pick up passengers from their guesthouse only to drop them off at the public bus terminal. Other complaints include the alleged 'VIP' bus turning out to be a cramped minibus that arrives four hours late.

Readers have also consistently reported having their stowed bags rifled through and valuables stolen. Keep all valuables on your person, not stored in your luggage because even locked bags can be tampered with and you might not realise anything is missing until days later.

Reservations

You can book air-con BKS buses at any BKS terminal. Ordinary (fan) buses cannot be booked in advance. Privately run buses can be booked through most hotels or any travel agency, but it's best to book directly through a bus office to be sure that you get what you pay for.

ROAD DISTANCES (KM)

	Aranya Prathet	Ayuthaya	Bangkok	Chiang Mai	Chiang Rai	Chumphon	Hat Yai	Hua Hin	Khon Kaen	Mae Hong Son	Mae Sai	Mukdahan	Nakhon Ratchasima	Nakhon Sawan	Nong Khai	Phitsanulok	Phuket	Sungai Kolok	Surat Thani	Tak	Trat
Aranya Prathet	⋮																				
Ayuthaya	246	⋮																			
Bangkok	275	79	⋮																		
Chiang Mai	844	607	685	⋮																	
Chiang Rai	1014	777	775	191	⋮																
Chumphon	727	531	452	1138	1308	⋮															
Hat Yai	1268	1072	993	1679	1849	555	⋮														
Hua Hin	458	262	183	869	1039	269	810	⋮													
Khon Kaen	432	397	440	604	774	902	1443	633	⋮												
Mae Hong Son	1013	767	800	225	406	1298	1839	1029	829	⋮											
Mae Sai	1082	845	746	259	68	1376	1917	1107	842	474	⋮										
Mukdahan	601	524	680	917	1087	1029	1570	760	313	1142	1155	⋮									
Nakhon Ratchasima	239	204	257	744	914	709	1250	440	193	969	982	320	⋮								
Nakhon Sawan	409	163	242	444	614	694	1235	425	408	604	682	692	372	⋮							
Nong Khai	598	563	516	720	890	799	1609	799	166	945	958	347	359	546	⋮						
Phitsanulok	535	298	420	309	479	829	1370	560	295	578	547	608	435	135	411	⋮					
Phuket	1125	929	862	1536	1706	412	474	667	1300	1696	1774	1427	1107	1092	1466	1227	⋮				
Sungai Kolok	1555	1359	1210	1966	2136	842	287	1097	1730	2126	2204	1857	1357	1522	1896	1657	761	⋮			
Surat Thani	927	731	635	1338	1508	214	401	469	1102	1498	1576	1229	909	894	1268	1029	286	791	⋮		
Tak	581	335	435	280	460	866	1407	597	441	432	528	754	544	172	557	146	1264	1694	557	⋮	
Trat	285	392	313	999	1169	765	1306	496	717	1397	1237	886	524	555	883	690	1163	1593	965	727	⋮
Ubon Ratchathani	444	367	620	881	1051	872	1413	603	277	1106	1119	157	163	535	443	572	1270	1700	1072	707	729

SAMPLE BUS FARES TO BANGKOK

Destination	Distance from Bangkok	VIP (B)	1st class (B)	2nd class (B)
Chiang Mai	685km	695	596	(n/a)
Kanchanaburi	130km	(n/a)	139	112
Krabi	817km	1100	700	(n/a)
Hat Yai	993km	1075	740	(n/a)
Trat	313km	(n/a)	260	223

CAR & MOTORCYCLE
Bring Your Own Vehicle
See p760 for information on how to bring a private vehicle into Thailand for tourist purposes.

Driving Licence
Short-term visitors who wish to drive vehicles (including motorcycles) in Thailand need an International Driving Permit. Long-term visitors can apply for a Thai driver's licence through the provincial office of the **Department of Land Transport** (☎ 0 2272 3814). Contact the main office to determine the location of your assigned office (based on residence).

Fuel & Spare Parts
Modern petrol (gasoline) stations are in plentiful supply all over Thailand wherever there are paved roads. In more-remote, off-road areas *ben·sin*/*nám·man rót yon* (petrol containing benzene) is usually available at small roadside or village stands. All fuel in Thailand is unleaded, and diesel is used by trucks and some passenger cars. Because of the global increase in petrol prices, Thailand has introduced several alternative fuels, including gasohol (a blend of petrol and ethanol that comes in different ratios, either 91% or 95%) and compressed natural gas, used by taxis with bifuel capabilities. For news and updates about fuel options, and other car talk, see the website of **BKK Auto** (www.bkkautos.com).

If you're driving a motorcycle for distances of more than 100km, take an extra supply of motor oil; if riding a two-stroke machine, carry two-stroke engine oil.

If you're bringing your own vehicle, you'd be wise to bring a box of crucial spare parts that might not be available in Thailand. The same goes for motorcycles – especially so for bikes larger than 125cc.

Hire & Purchase
Cars, jeeps and vans can be rented in most major cities and airports from local companies as well as international chains. Local companies tend to have cheaper rates than the international chains, but their fleets of cars tend to be older and not as well maintained. Check the tyre treads and general upkeep of the vehicle before committing.

Motorcycles can be rented in major towns and many smaller tourist centres from guesthouses and small mum-and-dad businesses. Renting a motorcycle in Thailand is relatively easy and a great way to independently tour the countryside, especially in northern Thailand and on the southern beaches. For daily rentals, most businesses will ask that you leave your passport as a deposit. Before renting a motorcycle, check the vehicle's condition and ask for a helmet (which is required by law).

Many tourists are injured riding motorcycles in Thailand because they don't know how to handle the vehicle and are unfamiliar with road rules and conditions. Drive sensibly to avoid damage to yourself and to the vehicle, and be sure to have adequate health insurance. If you've never driven a motorcycle before, stick to the smaller 100cc step-through bikes with automatic clutches. Remember to distribute weight as evenly as possible across the frame of the bike to improve handling.

It is also possible to buy a new or used motorcycle and sell it before you leave the country.

Insurance
Thailand requires a minimum of liability insurance for all registered vehicles on the road. The better hire companies include comprehensive coverage for their vehicles. Always verify that a vehicle is insured for liability before signing a rental contract; you should also ask to see the dated insurance documents. If you have an accident while

driving an uninsured vehicle, you're in for some major hassles.

If you need auto insurance, a policy can be purchased inexpensively through local companies. Two of the more reliable ones are **Bangkok Insurance** (☎ 0 2285 8888; www.bki .co.th) and **AIA Thailand** (www.aiathailand.com).

Road Rules & Hazards

Thais drive on the left-hand side of the road (most of the time!). Other than that, just about anything goes, in spite of road signs and speed limits.

The main rule to be aware of is that right of way goes to the bigger vehicle; this is not what it says in the Thai traffic law, but it's the reality. Maximum speed limits are 50km/h on urban roads and 80km/h to 100km/h on most highways – but on any given stretch of highway you'll see various vehicles travelling as slowly as 30km/h and as fast as 150km/h. Speed traps are common along Hwy 4 in the south and Hwy 2 in the northeast.

Indicators are often used to warn passing drivers about oncoming traffic. A flashing left indicator means it's OK to pass, while a right indicator means that someone's approaching from the other direction. Horns are used to tell other vehicles that the driver plans to pass. When drivers flash their lights, they're telling you not to pass.

In Bangkok traffic is chaotic, roads are poorly signposted and motorcycles and random contra flows mean you can suddenly find yourself facing a wall of cars coming the other way.

Outside of the capital, the principal hazard when driving in Thailand, besides the general disregard for traffic laws, is having to contend with so many different types of vehicles on the same road – 18-wheelers, bicycles, túk-túk (motorised pedicabs) and motorcycles. This danger is often compounded by the lack of working lights. In village areas the vehicular traffic is lighter but you have to contend with stray chickens, dogs and water buffaloes.

HITCHING

Hitching is never entirely safe in any country and we don't recommend it. Travellers who decide to hitch should understand that they are taking a small but potentially serious risk. Hitching is rarely seen these days in Thailand, so most passing motorists might not realise the intentions of the for-eigner standing on the side of the road with a thumb out. Firstly, Thais don't 'thumb it', instead when they want a ride they wave their hand with the palm facing the ground and the arm slightly outstretched. This is the same gesture used to flag a taxi or bus, which is why some drivers might stop and point to a bus stop if one is nearby.

In general, hitching isn't worth the hassle as buses are frequent and cheap. In some of the national parks where there isn't public transport Thais are often willing to pick up a passenger standing by the side of the road.

LOCAL TRANSPORT

City Bus & Sŏrng·tăa·ou

Bangkok has the largest city-bus system in the country. Elsewhere, public transport is typically supplied by *sŏrng·tăa·ou* that run established routes, although Udon Thani and a few other provincial capitals have city buses.

The etiquette for riding public transport is to hail the vehicle by waving your hand palm-side downward, You typically pay the fare once you've taken a seat or when you disembark.

A *sŏrng·tăa·ou* (literally, 'two rows') is a small pick-up truck with two rows of bench seats down both sides of the truck bed. They sometimes operate on fixed routes, just like buses, but they may also run a share-taxi service where they pick-up passengers going in the same general direction. In tourist centres, *sŏrng·tăa·ou* can be chartered individually just like a regular taxi, but you'll need to negotiate the fare beforehand. Occasionally in tourist centres, drivers operating a *sŏrng·tăa·ou* intended for shared use will try to convince foreigners to 'charter' the vehicle by quoting a large fare before boarding.

Depending on the region, *sŏrng·tăa·ou* might also run a fixed route from the centre of town to outlying areas or even points within the provinces. Sometimes these vehicles are converted pick-up trucks, while in other cases they are larger six-wheeled vehicles (sometimes called '*rót hòk lór*').

Mass Transit

Bangkok is the only city in Thailand to have either an above-ground or underground light-rail public transport system. Known as the Skytrain and the Metro, respectively, both systems have helped to alleviate the capital city's notorious traffic jams.

TRANSPORT

Motorcycle Taxi

Many cities in Thailand also have *mor·đeu·sai ráp jâhng* (100cc to 125cc motorcycles) that can be hired, with a driver, for short distances. They're not very suitable if you're carrying more than a backpack or small suitcase, but if you're empty-handed they can't be beaten for quick transport over short distances. In addition to the lack of space for luggage, motorcycle taxis also suffer from lack of shelter from rain and sun. Although most drivers around the country operate at safe, sane speeds, the kamikaze drivers of Bangkok are a major exception.

In most cities, you'll find motorcycle taxis clustered near street intersections, rather than cruising the streets looking for fares. Usually they wear numbered jerseys. Fares tend to run from 10B to 50B, depending on distance.

Săhm·lór & Túk·túk

Săhm·lór means 'three wheels' and that's just what they are – three-wheeled vehicles. There are two types of săhm·lór – motorised and nonmotorised.

You'll find motorised săhm·lór (better known as túk-túk) throughout the country. They're small utility vehicles, powered by horrendously noisy engines (usually LPG-powered); if the noise and vibration don't get you, the fumes will.

The nonmotorised săhm·lór, ie the bicycle rickshaw or pedicab, is similar to what you may see in other parts of Asia. There are no bicycle săhm·lór in Bangkok, but you will find them elsewhere in the country. With either form of săhm·lór the fare must be established by bargaining before departure.

Readers interested in pedicab lore and design may want to have a look at Lonely Planet's hardcover pictorial book, *Chasing Rickshaws*, by Lonely Planet founder Tony Wheeler.

Taxi

Bangkok has the most formal system of metered taxis. In other cities, a taxi can be a private vehicle with negotiable rates. You can also travel between cities by taxi but you'll need to negotiate a price as few taxi drivers will run a meter for intercity travel.

TOURS

Many operators around the world can arrange guided tours of Thailand. Most of them simply serve as brokers for tour companies based in Thailand; they buy their trips from a wholesaler and resell them under various names in travel markets overseas. Long-running, reliable tour wholesalers in Thailand include the following.

Asian Trails (Map pp120-1; ☎ 0 2626 2000; www .asiantrails.net; 9th fl, SG Tower, 161/1 Soi Mahatlek Leung 3, Th Ratchadamri, Bangkok)

Diethelm Travel (Map p124; ☎ 0 2660 7000; www .diethelmtravel.com; 12th fl, Kian Gwan Bldg II, 140/1 Th Withayu, Bangkok)

World Travel Service (Map pp118-19; ☎ 0 2233 5900; www.wts-thailand.com; 1053 Th Charoen Krung, Bangkok)

Overseas Companies

The better overseas tour companies build their own Thailand itineraries from scratch and choose their local suppliers based on which best serve these itineraries. Of these, several specialise in adventure and/or ecological tours.

Asia Transpacific Journeys (☎ 800 642 2742; www .southeastasia.com; 2995 Center Green Dr, Boulder, CO 80301, USA) Small group highlight tours and speciality trips.

Club Adventure (☎ 514 527 0999; www.clubaventure .com; 757 ave du Mont-Royal Est, Montreal, QUE H2J 1W8, Canada) French-language tour operators.

Exodus (☎ 800 843 4272; www.exodustravels.co.uk; 1311 63rd St, Ste 200, Emeryville, CA 94608, USA) Award-winning agency for its environmentally responsible tours.

Hands Up Holidays (☎ 0 800 783 3554; www.hands upholidays.com; 5 Kendal Pl, London SW15 2QZ, UK) Volunteer and sightseeing programmes for comfort travellers.

Intrepid Travel (www.intrepidtravel.com) Specialises in small-group travel geared toward young people; visit the website for country-specific contact details.

I-to-I (☎ 800 985 4852; www.i-to-i.com) Volunteer and sightseeing tours.

Starfish Ventures (☎ 44 800 1974817; www .starfishvolunteers.com) Organises a gap year volunteer and sightseeing package.

Tours with Kasma Loha-Unchit (☎ 510 655 8900; www.thaifoodandtravel.com; PO Box 21165, Oakland, CA 94620, USA) This Thai cookbook author offers personalised 'cultural immersion' tours of Thailand.

TRAIN

The government rail network, operated by the **State Railway of Thailand** (SRT; ☎ 1690; www.railway.co.th), covers four main lines: the northern, southern, northeastern and eastern lines (see Map p763 for major routes). The train is most convenient as an alternative to buses for the long journey north to Chiang

Mai or south to Surat Thani. The train is also ideal for trips to Ayuthaya and Lopburi from Bangkok.

Although they can take longer (trains generally don't run on time), the trains offer many advantages over buses. To start with, there is more room to move and stretch out and the scenery rolling by the windows is grander from the vantage point of rail than highway. On the 3rd-class trains there's also more local commotion: hawkers selling food and drinks, babies staring wide-eyed at foreigners, sarong-clad villagers – to name just a few.

Main Terminals & Routes

Almost all the long-distance trains originate from Bangkok's Hualamphong station. Bangkok Noi station in Thonburi serves the commuter and the short-line trains running to Kanchanaburi/Nam Tok and Nakhon Pathom. You can also get to Nakhon Pathom by train from Hualamphong. Thonburi's Wong Wian Yai station runs a short commuter line to Samut Songkhram.

Four main rail lines cover 4500km along northern, southern, northeastern and eastern routes. There are several side routes, notably from the Bangkok Noi station in Thonburi (p183) to Nam Tok (stopping in Kanchanaburi and Nakhon Pathom), and between Thung Song and Kantang (stopping in Trang) in the south. The southern line splits at Hat Yai: one route goes to Sungai Kolok on the Malaysian east coast border, via Yala; the other goes to Padang Besar in the west, also on the Malaysian border. A Bangkok–Pattaya spur exists but is slower and less convenient than a bus.

Classes

The SRT operates passenger trains in three classes – 1st, 2nd and 3rd – but each class varies considerably depending on whether you're on an ordinary, rapid or express train.

THIRD CLASS

A typical 3rd-class carriage consists of two rows of bench seats divided into facing pairs. Each bench seat is designed to seat two or three passengers, but on a crowded rural line nobody seems to care about design considerations. On some ordinary 3rd-class-only trains, seats are sometimes made of hard wooden slats, although these cars are being phased out.

Express trains do not carry 3rd-class carriages at all. Commuter trains in the Bangkok area are all 3rd class.

SECOND CLASS

The seating arrangements in a 2nd-class, nonsleeper carriage are similar to those on a bus, with pairs of padded seats, usually recliners, all facing toward the front of the train.

On 2nd-class sleeper cars, pairs of seats face one another and convert into two fold-down berths, one over the other. Curtains provide a modicum of privacy and the berths are fairly comfortable, with fresh linen for every trip. The lower berth has more headroom than the upper berth and this is reflected in a higher fare. Children are always assigned a lower berth.

Second-class carriages are found only on rapid and express trains. Air-con 2nd class is more common nowadays than ordinary (fan) 2nd class (with the latter available only on rapid lines).

FIRST CLASS

Each private cabin in a 1st-class carriage has individually controlled air-con (older trains also have an electric fan), a washbasin and mirror, a small table and long bench seats that convert into beds. Soap is provided free of charge. First-class carriages are available only on rapid, express and special-express trains.

Costs

Fares are determined on a base price with surcharges added for distance, class and train type (special express, express, rapid, ordinary). There is a 150B surcharge above the basic fare for rót dòo·an (express trains) and 110B for rót re·ou (rapid trains). These trains are somewhat faster than the ordinary trains, as they make fewer stops. Note that there are no 3rd-class carriages on either rapid or express trains. For the rót dòo·an pí·sèht (special-express trains) that run between Bangkok and Padang Besar, and between Bangkok and Chiang Mai, there is a 170B to 180B surcharge.

For distances under 300km, the base price is 50B to 80B; over 301km, 110B.

Some 2nd- and 3rd-class cars have aircon, in which case there is a 60B to 110B surcharge. Sleeping berths in 2nd class accrue another 120B to 240B surcharge.

TRANSPORT

For a 1st-class cabin the surcharge is 300/500B for upper/lower berth. Single 1st-class cabins are not available, so if you're travelling alone you may be paired with another passenger, although the SRT takes great care not to mix genders.

TRAIN PASSES

The SRT issues a Thailand Rail Pass that may save on fares if you plan to use the trains extensively over a relatively short interval. This pass is only available in Thailand and may be purchased at Bangkok's Hualamphong station.

The cost for 20 days of unlimited 2nd- or 3rd-class train travel is 3000/1500B per adult/child including all supplementary charges (ie type of train, air-con, etc). Passes must be validated at a local station before boarding the first train. The price of the pass includes seat reservations that, if required, can be made at any SRT ticket office.

TRAIN DINING

Meal service is available in *rót sà·beeang* (dining carriages) and at your seat in 2nd- and 1st-class carriages. Menus change as frequently as the SRT changes catering services. All the meals seem a bit overpriced (80B to 200B on average) by Thai standards. Many Thai passengers bring along their own meals and snacks to avoid the relatively high cost of SRT-catered meals.

Reservations

Advance bookings can be made from one to 60 days before your intended date of departure. It is advisable to make advanced bookings for long-distance sleeper trains between Bangkok and Chiang Mai or from Bangkok to Surat Thani during holidays – especially around Songkran in April, Chinese New Year and during the peak tourist-season months of December and January.

You can make bookings from any train station. Throughout Thailand SRT ticket offices are generally open 8.30am to 6pm on weekdays, and 8.30am to noon on weekends and public holidays. Train tickets can also be purchased at travel agencies, which usually add a service charge to the ticket price.

All advance bookings need to be made in person. If you are planning long-distance train travel from outside the country, you should email the **State Railway of Thailand** (passenger-ser@railway.co.th) at least two weeks before your journey. You will receive an email confirming the booking. Pick up and pay for tickets an hour before leaving at the scheduled departure train station.

For short-distance trips you should purchase your ticket at least a day in advance for seats (rather than sleepers).

Partial refunds on tickets are available depending on the number of days prior to your departure you arrange for a cancellation. These arrangements can be handled at the train station booking office.

Station Services

You'll find that all train stations in Thailand have baggage-storage services (or 'cloak rooms'). The rates and hours of operation vary from station to station – rates being anywhere from 20B to 70B. Most stations have a ticket window that will open between 15 and 30 minutes before train arrivals. There are also newsagents and small snack vendors, but no full-service restaurants.

Most train stations have printed timetables in English; although this isn't always the case for smaller stations. Bangkok's Hualamphong station is a good spot to load up on timetables. There are two types of timetable available: four condensed English timetables with fares, schedules and routes for rapid, express and special express trains on the four trunk lines; and four Thai timetables for each trunk line, and side lines. These latter timetables give fares and schedules for all trains – ordinary, rapid and express. The English timetables only display a couple of the ordinary routes; eg they don't show all the ordinary trains that go to Ayuthaya and as far north as Phitsanulok.

Health Dr Trish Batchelor

Health risks and the quality of medical facilities vary enormously depending on where and how you travel in Thailand.

The majority of major cities and popular tourist areas are well developed, however, travel to more remote rural areas can expose you to health risks and less adequate medical care.

Travellers tend to worry most about contracting exotic infectious diseases when visiting the tropics, but such infections are a far less common cause of serious illness or death in travellers than pre-existing medical conditions such as heart disease, and accidental injury (especially as a result of traffic accidents).

Becoming ill in some way is common, however. Respiratory infections, diarrhoea and dengue fever are particular hazards in Thailand.

Fortunately most common illnesses can either be prevented with some commonsense behaviour or are easily treated with a well-stocked traveller's medical kit.

The following advice should be read as a general guide only and does not replace the advice of a doctor trained in travel medicine.

BEFORE YOU GO

Pack medications in clearly labelled original containers. A signed and dated letter from your physician describing your medical conditions and medications, including generic names, is a good idea. If carrying syringes or needles be sure to have a physician's letter documenting their medical necessity. If you have a heart condition, bring a copy of your ECG taken just prior to travelling.

If you take any regular medication bring double your needs in case of loss or theft. In Thailand you can buy many medications over the counter without a doctor's prescription, but it can be difficult to find the exact medication you are taking. It is safer to bring adequate supplies from home.

INSURANCE

Even if you're fit and healthy, don't travel without health insurance – accidents *do* happen. Declare any existing medical conditions you have – insurance companies *will* check if your problem is pre-existing and won't cover you if it is undeclared. You may require extra cover for adventure activities such as rock climbing or diving, as well as scooter/motorcycle riding. If your health insurance doesn't cover you for medical expenses abroad, ensure you get specific travel insurance. If you're uninsured, emergency evacuation is expensive; bills of over US$100,000 aren't uncommon. Most hospitals require an upfront guarantee of payment (from yourself or your insurer) prior to admission.

In many countries doctors expect payment in cash. Keep all documentation (medical reports, invoices etc) for claim purposes. Some policies ask you to call back (reverse charges) to a centre in your home country where an immediate assessment of your problem is made. It is always wise to inform your insurance company if you seek medical advice whilst abroad.

VACCINATIONS

Specialised travel-medicine clinics are your best source of information; they stock all available vaccines and will usually have

HEALTH

medical kits and other products such as impregnated mosquito nets available. The doctors will take into account factors such as your past vaccination history, the length of your trip, activities you may be undertaking and underlying medical conditions, such as pregnancy, before making their individualised recommendations.

Most vaccines don't produce immunity until around two weeks after they're given. Ideally you should visit a doctor six to eight weeks before departure, but it is never too late. Ask your doctor for an International Certificate of Vaccination (otherwise known as the yellow booklet), which will list all the vaccinations you've received.

Recommended Vaccinations

The following vaccinations are those recommended by the World Health Organization (WHO) for travellers to Thailand:

Adult Diphtheria, Tetanus & Pertussis Single booster recommended if none in the previous 10 years. Side effects include sore arm and fever.

Hepatitis A Provides almost 100% protection for up to a year, a booster after six to 12 months likely provides lifetime protection. Mild side effects such as headache and sore arm occur in 5% to 10% of people.

Hepatitis B Now considered routine for most travellers. Given as three shots over six months. A rapid schedule is available, as is a combined vaccination with Hepatitis A. Side effects are mild and uncommon, usually headache and sore arm. Lifetime protection occurs in 95% of people.

Measles, Mumps & Rubella Two doses of MMR required unless you have had the diseases. Occasionally a rash and flu-like illness can develop a week after receiving the vaccine. Many young adults require a booster.

Polio There have been no cases for many years in Thailand so no booster required. Note that only one booster is required as an adult for lifetime protection.

Typhoid Recommended unless your trip is less than a week and only to the major cities. The vaccine offers around 70% protection, lasts for two to three years and comes as a single shot. Tablets are also available, however the injection is usually recommended as it has fewer side effects. Sore arm and fever may occur.

Varicella If you haven't had chickenpox, discuss this vaccination with your doctor.

The following immunisations are recommended for long-term travellers (more than one month) or those at special risk:

Influenza Particularly recommended for travellers over 55 years of age or with underlying medical conditions such as diabetes or heart disease. Influenza is however common in all ages and the vaccine should be considered by all travellers.

Japanese B Encephalitis Three injections in all. Booster recommended after three years. Sore arm and headache are the most common side effects. Rarely, an allergic reaction comprising hives and swelling can occur up to 10 days after any of the three doses.

Rabies Three injections in all. No booster required for travellers. Those at continued risk (animal workers etc) should discuss booster recommendations with their doctor. Side effects are rare – occasionally headache and sore arm.

Tuberculosis A complex issue. Adult long-term travellers or expats are usually recommended to have a TB skin test or Quantiferon blood test before and after travel, rather than vaccination. For expatriate children under five, BCG vaccination is highly recommended. Only one vaccine given in a lifetime.

Required Vaccinations

The only vaccine required by international regulations is yellow fever. Proof of vaccination will only be required if you have visited a country in the yellow-fever zone within the six days prior to entering Thailand. If you are travelling to Thailand *from* Africa or South America you should check to see if you require proof of vaccination.

MEDICAL CHECKLIST

Recommended items for a personal medical kit include:

- antifungal cream, eg Clotrimazole
- antibacterial cream, eg Muciprocin
- antibiotic for skin infections, eg Amoxicillin/Clavulanate or Cephalexin
- antibiotics for diarrhoea include Norfloxacin, Ciprofloxacin or Azithromycin for bacterial diarrhoea; for giardiasis or amoebic dysentery Tinidazole
- antihistamine – there are many options, eg Cetrizine for daytime and Promethazine for night
- antiseptic, eg Betadine
- antispasmodic for stomach cramps, eg Buscopan
- contraceptives
- decongestant
- DEET-based insect repellent
- oral rehydration solution for diarrhoea (eg Gastrolyte), diarrhoea 'stopper' (eg Loperamide) and antinausea medication (eg Prochlorperazine)

- first-aid items such as scissors, Elasto-plasts, bandages, gauze, thermometer (but not mercury), sterile needles and syringes, safety pins and tweezers
- hand gel (alcohol based) or alcohol-based hand wipes
- ibuprofen or another anti-inflammatory
- indigestion medication, eg Quick Eze or Mylanta
- laxative, eg Coloxyl
- migraine sufferer – take along your personal medicine
- paracetamol
- Permethrin to impregnate clothing and mosquito nets if at high risk
- steroid cream for allergic/itchy rashes, eg 1% to 2% hydrocortisone
- sunscreen, hat and sunglasses
- throat lozenges
- thrush (vaginal yeast infection) treatment, eg Clotrimazole pessaries or Diflucan tablet
- Ural or equivalent if you are prone to urine infections

INTERNET RESOURCES

There is a wealth of travel-health advice on the internet. For further information, **Lonely Planet** (www.lonelyplanet.com) is a good place to start. *International Travel & Health* is a superb book published by the WHO (www.who.int/ith), which is revised annually and is available online at no cost. The **Centers for Disease Control & Prevention** (CDC; www.cdc.gov) website has good general information and country-specific advice.

Check your own country's Department of Foreign Affairs page for any current travel warnings, and register your trip if this facility is available. Registering greatly helps if there is an event such as a tsunami that requires the tracing of missing people.

FURTHER READING

Lonely Planet's *Healthy Travel – Asia & India* is a handy pocket-size book that is packed with useful information including pretrip planning, emergency first aid, immunisation and disease information and what to do if you get sick on the road. Other recommended references include *Traveller's Health* by Dr Richard Dawood and *Travelling Well* by Dr Deborah Mills – check out the website www.travellingwell.com.au.

The Thai Red Cross produces an excellent book *Healthy Living in Thailand* which is strongly recommended, particularly for those staying long term.

IN TRANSIT

DEEP VEIN THROMBOSIS

Deep vein thrombosis (DVT) occurs when blood clots form in the legs during long trips such as flights, chiefly because of prolonged immobility. The longer the journey, the greater the risk. Though most blood clots are reabsorbed uneventfully, some may break off and travel through the blood vessels to the lungs, where they can cause life-threatening complications.

The chief symptom of DVT is swelling or pain of the foot, ankle or calf, usually but not always on one side. When a blood clot travels to the lungs, it may cause chest pain and difficulty in breathing. Travellers with any of these symptoms should immediately seek medical attention.

To prevent the development of DVT on long flights you should walk about the cabin, perform isometric compressions of the leg muscles (ie contract the leg muscles while sitting) and drink plenty of fluids (nonalcoholic). Those at higher risk should speak with a doctor about extra preventive measures such as compression socks or medication.

JET LAG & MOTION SICKNESS

Jet lag is common when crossing more than five time zones; it results in insomnia, fatigue, malaise or nausea. To avoid jet lag try drinking plenty of fluids (nonalcoholic) and eating light meals. Upon arrival, seek exposure to natural sunlight and readjust your schedule (for meals, sleep etc) as soon as possible. Some people find melatonin helpful but it is not available in all countries.

Sedating antihistamines such as dimenhydrinate (Dramamine), Prochlorperazine (Phenergan) and others depending on your country of residence are usually the first choice for treating motion sickness. Their main side effect is drowsiness. A herbal alternative is ginger, which works like a charm for some people. Scopolamine patches are considered the most effective prevention but again are unavailable in many countries.

HEALTH

IN THAILAND

AVAILABILITY & COST OF HEALTH CARE

Bangkok is considered the nearest centre of medical excellence for many countries in Southeast Asia (such as Cambodia, Laos and Vietnam) and there are a number of excellent hospitals in the city. Some of them have specific staff available for liaising with foreign patients. They are usually more expensive than other medical facilities but are worth using as they will offer a superior standard of care. They can also liaise with insurance companies more easily. Such facilities are listed under Information in the city sections of this book. The cost of health care is relatively cheap in Thailand compared to most Western countries, which makes it even more sensible to ensure you utilise one of the better hospitals if you do require medical care.

In rural areas, however, it remains difficult to find reliable medical care. Your embassy and insurance company can be good contacts.

Self-treatment may be appropriate if your problem is minor (eg traveller's diarrhoea), you are carrying the appropriate medication and you cannot attend a recommended clinic or hospital. If you think you may have a serious disease, especially malaria, do not waste time – travel to the nearest quality facility to receive attention. It is always better to be assessed by a doctor than to rely on self-treatment.

Buying medication over the counter is not recommended, because fake medications and poorly stored or out-of-date drugs are common.

INFECTIOUS DISEASES

Avian Influenza

Thailand has recorded a total of 25 cases of 'bird flu' since 2004 – the majority of which occurred in 2004. At the time of writing there have been no cases reported since January 2007.

The risk of travellers catching bird flu is minimal – it remains that most of those infected have had close contact with sick or dead birds.

To avoid bird flu the following recommendations come from the CDC and WHO:

- avoid direct contact with poultry and wild birds
- avoid bird markets and poultry farms
- only eat thoroughly cooked bird meat or products (chicken, duck, eggs)
- wash hands frequently with alcohol-based hand gel
- seek medical care quickly if you have a fever, sore throat and cough – especially if you may have been exposed

Cutaneous Larva Migrans

This disease, caused by dog or cat hookworm, is particularly common on the beaches of Thailand. The rash starts as a small lump, and then slowly spreads like a winding line. It is intensely itchy, especially at night. It is easily treated with medications and should not be cut out or frozen.

Dengue Fever

This mosquito-borne disease is becoming increasingly problematic throughout Southeast Asia, especially in the cities. As there is no vaccine available it can only be prevented by avoiding mosquito bites. The mosquito that carries dengue is a daytime biter, so use insect-avoidance measures at all times. Symptoms include high fever, severe headache (especially behind the eyes), nausea and body aches (dengue was previously known as 'breakbone fever'). Some people develop a rash (which can be very itchy) and experience diarrhoea. The southern islands of Thailand are particularly high risk. There is no specific treatment, just rest and paracetamol – do not take aspirin or ibuprofen as they increase the risk of haemorrhaging. See a doctor to be diagnosed and monitored. Dengue can progress to the more severe and life threatening dengue haemorrhagic fever, however this is very uncommon in tourists. The risk of this increases substantially if you have previously been infected with dengue and are then infected with a different serotype.

Filariasis

A mosquito-borne disease that is common in the local population, yet very rare in travellers. Mosquito-avoidance measures are the best way to prevent this disease.

Hepatitis A

The risk in Bangkok is decreasing but there is still significant risk in most of the country. This food- and water-borne virus infects the liver, causing jaundice (yellow skin and eyes), nausea and lethargy. There is no specific treatment for hepatitis A, you just need to allow time for the liver to heal. Rarely, it can be fatal in those over the age of 40. All travellers to Thailand should be vaccinated against hepatitis A.

Hepatitis B

The only sexually transmitted disease (STD) that can be prevented by vaccination, hepatitis B is spread by body fluids, including sexual contact. In some parts of Thailand up to 20% of the population are carriers of hepatitis B, and usually are unaware of this. The long-term consequences can include liver cancer, cirrhosis and death.

Hepatitis E

Hepatitis E is transmitted through contaminated food and water and has similar symptoms to hepatitis A, but is rare in travellers. It is a severe problem in pregnant women and can result in the death of both mother and baby. There is currently no vaccine, and prevention is by following safe eating and drinking guidelines.

HIV

HIV is now one of the most common causes of death in people under the age of 50 in Thailand. Heterosexual sex is the main method of transmission. Always practice safe sex, avoid getting tattoos or using unclean needles.

Influenza

Present year-round in the tropics, influenza (flu) symptoms include high fever, muscle aches, runny nose, cough and sore throat. Flu is the most common vaccine-preventable disease contracted by travellers and everyone should consider vaccination. There is no specific treatment, just rest and paracetamol. Complications such as bronchitis or middle ear infection may require antibiotic treatment.

Japanese B Encephalitis

While a rare disease in travellers, at least 50,000 locals are infected each year in Southeast Asia. This viral disease is transmitted by mosquitoes. Most cases occur in rural areas and vaccination is recommended for travellers spending more than one month outside of cities, or long-term expats. There is no treatment, and a third of people infected will die, while another third will suffer permanent brain damage. Thailand is a high-risk area.

Leptospirosis

Leptospirosis is contracted from exposure to infected fresh water – most commonly after river rafting or canyoning. Early symptoms are very similar to the flu and include headache and fever. It can vary from a very mild ailment to a fatal disease. Diagnosis is made through blood tests and it is easily treated with Doxycycline.

Malaria

For such a serious and potentially deadly disease, there is an enormous amount of misinformation concerning malaria. Ensure you get expert advice as to whether your trip actually puts you at risk. Most parts of Thailand visited by tourists, particularly city and resort areas, have minimal to no risk of malaria, and the risk of side effects from taking anti-malarial tablets is likely to outweigh the risk of getting the disease itself. For some rural areas, however, the risk of contracting the disease outweighs the risk of any tablet side effects. Remember that malaria can be fatal. Before you travel, seek proper medical advice on the right medication and dosage for you.

Malaria is caused by a parasite transmitted by the bite of an infected mosquito. The most important symptom of malaria is fever, but general symptoms such as headache, diarrhoea, cough or chills may also occur – the same symptoms as many other infections. A diagnosis can only be made by taking a blood sample.

Two strategies should be combined to prevent malaria – mosquito avoidance and antimalarial medications. Most people who catch malaria are taking inadequate or no antimalarial medication.

Travellers are advised to prevent mosquito bites by taking these steps:

- use a DEET-containing insect repellent on exposed skin (20% to 30% is ideal), washing it off at night (as long as you are sleeping under a mosquito net); natural repellents such as citronella can be effective, but must be applied more frequently than products containing DEET

HEALTH

- sleep under a mosquito net, ideally impregnated with Permethrin
- choose accommodation with screens and fans (if not air-conditioned)
- impregnate clothing with Permethrin in high-risk areas
- wear long sleeves and trousers in light colours
- use mosquito coils
- spray your room with insect repellent before going out for your evening meal

There are a variety of medications available:

Artesunate Derivatives of Artesunate are not suitable as a preventive medication. They are useful treatments under medical supervision.

Chloroquine & Paludrine The effectiveness of this combination is now limited in Thailand. It is not recommended.

Doxycycline This daily tablet is a broad-spectrum antibiotic that has the added benefit of helping to prevent a variety of tropical diseases, including leptospirosis, tick-borne disease, typhus and meliodosis. The potential side effects include photosensitivity (a tendency to sunburn), thrush in women, indigestion, heartburn, nausea and interference with the contraceptive pill. More serious side effects include ulceration of the oesophagus – you can help prevent this by taking your tablet with a meal and a large glass of water, and never lying down within half an hour of taking it. Must be taken for four weeks after leaving the risk area.

Lariam (Mefloquine) Lariam has received much bad press; some of it justified, some not. This weekly tablet suits many people. Serious side effects are rare but include depression, anxiety, psychosis and having fits. Anyone with a history of depression, anxiety, other psychological disorders or epilepsy should not take Lariam. It is considered safe in the second and third trimesters of pregnancy. There is however significant resistance in parts of northern Thailand. Tablets must be taken for four weeks after leaving the risk area.

Malarone This drug is a combination of Atovaquone and Proguanil. Side effects are uncommon and mild, most commonly nausea and headache. It is an excellent tablet, however it is expensive, which can limit its use long term. It must be taken for one week after leaving the risk area.

A final option is to take no preventive medication but to have a supply of emergency medication should you develop the symptoms of malaria. This is less than ideal, and you'll need to get to a good medical facility within 24 hours of developing a fever. If you choose this option the most effective and safest treatment is Malarone (four tablets once daily for three days). Riamet is another good option

but is not available in some countries. Other options such as Mefloquine and Quinine are less desirable due to side effects. Fansidar is no longer recommended.

Measles

This highly contagious viral infection is spread through coughing and sneezing. Most people born before 1966 are immune as they had the disease in childhood. Measles starts with a high fever and rash and can be complicated by pneumonia and brain disease. There is no specific treatment. Ensure you are fully vaccinated.

Meliodosis

This infection is contracted by skin contact with soil. It is rare in travellers, but in some parts of northeast Thailand up to 30% of the local population are infected. The symptoms are very similar to those experienced by tuberculosis (TB) sufferers. There is no vaccine but it can be treated with medications.

Rabies

This uniformly fatal disease is spread by the bite or lick of an infected animal – most commonly a dog or monkey. You should seek medical advice immediately after any animal bite and commence post-exposure treatment. Having a pre-travel vaccination means the post-bite treatment is greatly simplified. If an animal bites you, gently wash the wound with soap and water, and apply iodine-based antiseptic. If you are not pre-vaccinated you will need to receive rabies immunoglobulin as soon as possible, followed by five shots of vaccine over 28 days. If pre-vaccinated you need just two shots of vaccine given three days apart. Immunoglobulin is in short supply and you may well have to travel to Bangkok to get it.

STDs

Sexually transmitted diseases most common in Thailand include herpes, warts, syphilis, gonorrhoea and chlamydia. People carrying these diseases often have no signs of infection. Condoms will prevent gonorrhoea and chlamydia but not warts or herpes. If after a sexual encounter you develop any rash, lumps, discharge or pain when passing urine seek immediate medical attention. If you have been sexually active during your travels have an STD check on your return home.

Strongyloides

This parasite, also transmitted by skin contact with soil, is common in Thailand but rarely affects travellers. It is characterised by an unusual skin rash called *larva currens* – a linear rash on the trunk which comes and goes. Most people don't have other symptoms until their immune system becomes severely suppressed, when the parasite can cause an overwhelming infection. It can be treated with medications.

Tuberculosis

While rare in travellers, medical and aid workers and long-term travellers who have significant contact with the local population should take precautions. Vaccination is usually only given to children under the age of five, and is highly recommended for children spending more than three months in Thailand. Adults at risk are recommended pre- and post-travel TB testing – either with the Mantoux test or Quantiferon blood test, depending on your country's guidelines. The main symptoms are fever, cough, weight loss, night sweats and tiredness. Treatment is available with long-term multi-drug regimens.

Typhoid

This serious bacterial infection is spread via food and water. It gives a high and slowly progressive fever, severe headache, and may be accompanied by a dry cough and stomach pain. It is diagnosed by blood tests and treated with antibiotics. Vaccination is recommended for all travellers spending more than a week in Thailand, or travelling outside of the major cities. Be aware that vaccination is not 100% effective so you must still be careful with what you eat and drink.

Typhus

Murine typhus is spread by the bite of a flea whereas scrub typhus is spread via a mite. These diseases are rare in travellers. Symptoms include fever, muscle pains and a rash. You can avoid these diseases by following general insect-avoidance measures. Doxycycline will also prevent them.

TRAVELLER'S DIARRHOEA

Traveller's diarrhoea is by far the most common problem affecting travellers – between 30% and 50% of people will suffer from it within two weeks of starting their trip. In over 80% of cases, traveller's diarrhoea is caused by a bacteria (there are numerous potential culprits), and therefore responds promptly to treatment with antibiotics. Treatment with antibiotics will depend on your situation – how sick you are, how quickly you need to get better, where you are etc.

Traveller's diarrhoea is defined as the passage of more than three watery bowel movements within 24 hours, plus at least one other symptom such as vomiting, fever, cramps, nausea or feeling generally unwell.

Treatment consists of staying well hydrated; rehydration solutions like Gastrolyte are the best for this. Antibiotics such as Norfloxacin, Ciprofloxacin or Azithromycin will kill the bacteria quickly.

Loperamide is just a 'stopper' and doesn't get to the cause of the problem. It can be helpful, for example if you have to go on a long bus ride. Don't take Loperamide if you have a fever, or blood in your stools. Seek medical attention quickly if you do not respond to an appropriate antibiotic.

Amoebic Dysentery

Amoebic dysentery is very rare in travellers but may be misdiagnosed by poor-quality labs. Symptoms are similar to bacterial diarrhoea, ie fever, bloody diarrhoea and generally feeling unwell. You should always seek reliable medical care if you have blood in your diarrhoea. Treatment involves two drugs; Tinidazole or Metronidazole to kill the parasite in your gut and then a second drug to kill the cysts. If left untreated complications such as liver abscesses can occur.

Giardiasis

Giardia lamblia is a parasite that is relatively common in travellers. Symptoms include nausea, bloating, excess gas, fatigue and intermittent diarrhoea. 'Eggy' burps are often attributed solely to giardiasis, but work in Nepal has shown that they are not specific to this infection. The parasite will eventually go away if left untreated but this can take months. The treatment of choice is Tinidazole, with Metronidazole being a second-line option.

ENVIRONMENTAL HAZARDS
Air Pollution

Whilst Bangkok has terrible traffic the good news is the petrol is generally lead free. Air pollution can still be a problem however and

HEALTH

if you have severe respiratory problems speak with your doctor before travelling. This pollution can also cause minor respiratory problems such as sinusitis, dry throat and irritated eyes. If you are troubled by the pollution leave the city for a few days and get some fresh air.

Diving

Divers and surfers should seek specialised advice before they travel to ensure their medical kit contains treatment for coral cuts and tropical ear infections as well as the standard problems. Divers should ensure their insurance covers them for decompression illness; get specialised dive insurance through an organisation such as **Divers Alert Network** (DAN; www.danseap.org). Have a dive medical before you leave your home country – there are certain medical conditions that are incompatible with diving and economic considerations may override health considerations for some dive operators in Thailand.

Food

Eating in restaurants is the biggest risk factor for contracting traveller's diarrhoea. Ways to avoid it include eating only freshly cooked food, and avoiding shellfish and food that has been sitting around in buffets. Peel all fruit, cook vegetables, and soak salads in iodine water for at least 20 minutes. Eat in busy restaurants with a high turnover of customers.

Heat

Many parts of Thailand are hot and humid throughout the year. For most people it takes at least two weeks to adapt to the hot climate. Swelling of the feet and ankles is common, as are muscle cramps caused by excessive sweating. Prevent these by avoiding dehydration and excessive activity in the heat. Take it easy when you first arrive. Don't eat salt tablets (they aggravate the gut) but drinking rehydration solution or eating salty food helps. These measures will help prevent heat exhaustion. Treat cramps by stopping activity, resting, rehydrating with rehydration solution and gently stretching.

Heat stroke is a serious medical emergency and requires immediate medical treatment. Symptoms come on suddenly and include weakness, nausea, a hot dry body with a body temperature of over 41°C, dizziness, confusion, loss of coordination, fits and eventually collapse and loss of consciousness.

Prickly heat is a common skin rash in the tropics, caused by sweat being trapped under the skin. The result is an itchy rash of tiny lumps. Treat by moving out of the heat and into an air-conditioned area for a few hours and by having cool showers. Creams and ointments clog the skin so they should be avoided. Locally bought prickly-heat powder can be helpful.

Tropical fatigue is common in long-term expats based in the tropics. It's rarely due to disease and is caused by the climate, inadequate mental rest, excessive alcohol intake and the demands of daily work in a different culture.

Insect Bites & Stings

Bedbugs don't carry disease but their bites are very itchy. They live in the cracks of furniture and walls and then migrate to the bed at night to feed on you. You can treat the itch with an antihistamine. Lice inhabit various parts of your body but most commonly your head and pubic area. Transmission is via close contact with an infected person. They can be difficult to treat and you may need numerous applications of an anti-lice shampoo such as Permethrin. Pubic lice are usually contracted from sexual contact.

Ticks are contracted when walking in rural areas. Ticks are commonly found behind the ears, on the belly and in armpits. If you have had a tick bite and experience symptoms such as a rash at the site of the bite or elsewhere, fever or muscle aches you should see a doctor. Doxycycline prevents tick-borne diseases.

Leeches are found in humid rainforest areas. They do not transmit any disease but their bites are often intensely itchy for weeks afterwards and can easily become infected. Apply an iodine-based antiseptic to any leech bite to help prevent infection.

Bee and wasp stings mainly cause problems for people who are allergic to them. Anyone with a serious bee or wasp allergy should carry an injection of adrenaline (eg an Epipen) for emergency treatment. For others, pain is the main problem – apply ice to the sting and take painkillers.

Parasites

Numerous parasites are common in local populations in Thailand; but most of these are rare in travellers. The two rules to follow if you wish to avoid parasitic infections are

JELLYFISH STINGS

It is difficult to get accurate statistics on the incidence of serious or fatal jellyfish stings in Thailand, however there have been at least 10 tourist deaths in the past 20 years. Of note, between December 2007 and May 2008 there were nine serious envenomations in four separate incidents reported from popular tourist beaches (on Ko Tao, Ko Samet, Ko Lanta and Pattaya). One of these victims died.

Not all box jellyfish are dangerous, and stings range from minor to deadly. A good rule of thumb, however, is to presume a box jelly is dangerous until proven otherwise. There are two main types of box jellyfish – multi-tentacled and single-tentacled.

Multi-tentacled box jellyfish are present in Thai waters – these are potentially the most dangerous of jellyfish and a severe envenomation can kill an adult within two minutes. They are generally found on sandy beaches near river mouths and mangroves during the warmer months but can be found at any time of the year.

There are many types of single-tentacled box jellyfish, some of which can cause severe symptoms known as the Irukandji syndrome. The initial sting can seem minor; however severe symptoms such as back pain, nausea, vomiting, sweating, difficulty breathing and a feeling of impending doom can develop between five and 40 minutes later. There has been the occasional death reported from this syndrome as a result of high blood pressure causing strokes or heart attacks.

There are many other jellyfish in Thailand that cause irritating stings but no serious effects. The only effective way to prevent these stings is to provide a barrier between human skin and the jellyfish. This can be achieved most effectively with protective clothing. For example in the tropical waters of Australia it is recommended to wear a 'stinger suit' – a full length lycra suit. Multi tentacled jellyfish stinger nets at beaches are also effective, however, these are not yet found on Thai beaches.

First Aid for Severe Stings

For severe life-threatening envenomations the first priority is keeping the person alive. Stay with the person, send someone to call for medical help, and start immediate CPR if they are unconscious. If the victim is conscious douse the stung area liberally with vinegar – simple household vinegar is fine – for 30 seconds. Keep a close eye on their conscious state and get them immediately to medical care. For single-tentacled jellyfish stings pour vinegar onto the stung area as above; early application can make a huge difference. It is best to seek medical care quickly in case any other symptoms develop over the next 40 minutes.

Australia and Thailand are now working in close collaboration to identify the species of jellyfish in Thai waters, as well as their ecology – hopefully enabling better prediction and detection of the jellyfish.

Thanks to Dr Peter Fenner for the information in this boxed text.

HEALTH

to wear shoes and to avoid eating raw food, especially fish, pork and vegetables. A number of parasites are transmitted via the skin by walking barefoot, including strongyloides, hookworm and cutaneous *larva migrans*.

Skin Problems

Fungal rashes are common in humid climates. Two fungal rashes commonly affect travellers. The first occurs in moist areas that get less air such as the groin, armpits and between the toes. It starts as a red patch that slowly spreads and is usually itchy. Treatment involves keeping the skin dry, avoiding chafing and using an antifungal cream such as Clotrimazole or Lamisil. *Tinea versicolor* is also common – this fungus causes small and light-coloured patches, most commonly on the back, chest and shoulders. Consult a doctor.

Cuts and scratches become easily infected in humid climates. Take meticulous care of any cuts and scratches to prevent complications such as abscesses. Immediately wash all wounds in clean water and apply antiseptic. If you develop signs of infection (increasing pain and redness) see a doctor. Divers and surfers should be particularly careful with coral cuts as they can easily become infected.

HEALTH

Snakes

Over 175 species of snake have been identified in Thailand, of which 85 are at least mildly venomous. Various snakes in the viper, krait and cobra families are responsible for the majority of serious envenomations. It is best to assume any snake is poisonous and never try to catch one. Always wear boots and long pants if walking in an area that may have snakes. First aid in the event of a snake bite involves 'pressure immobilisation' using an elastic bandage firmly wrapped around the affected limb, starting at the hand or foot (depending on the limb bitten) and working up towards the chest. The bandage should not be so tight that the circulation is cut off, and the fingers or toes should be kept free so the circulation can be checked. Immobilise the limb with a splint and carry the victim to medical attention. It is very important that the victim stays immobile. Do not use tourniquets or try to suck the venom out. Leave the bandage in place and go to the nearest hospital for evaluation. The Thai Red Cross produces antivenom for many of the poisonous snakes in Thailand. Antivenom is not given automatically and the hospital will assess the severity of the envenomation. Snake bites are rare in travellers.

Sunburn

Even on a cloudy day sunburn can occur rapidly. Use a strong sunscreen (at least factor 30), making sure to reapply after a swim, and always wear a wide-brimmed hat and sunglasses outdoors. Avoid lying in the sun during the hottest part of the day (10am to 2pm). If you become sunburnt stay out of the sun until you have recovered, apply cool compresses and take painkillers for the discomfort. One per cent hydrocortisone cream applied twice daily is also helpful.

TRAVELLING WITH CHILDREN

Thailand is a great place to travel with children; it is relatively safe from a health point of view if you don't venture too far off the beaten track. It is wise to consult a doctor who specialises in travel medicine prior to travel to ensure your child is appropriately prepared. Children are not mini adults and it is important that you carry a medical kit designed specifically for them. In particular have adequate paracetamol or Tylenol syrup for fevers, an antihistamine, itch cream, first-aid supplies, nappy-rash treatment and plenty of age-appropriate sunscreen and insect repellent. It is a good idea to carry

a general antibiotic (best used under medical supervision) – Azithromycin is ideal as it comes in a paediatric formula and can be used to treat bacterial diarrhoea, ear, chest and throat infections. Some medications that are avoided in countries such as Australia and the US are used frequently in Asia (for example anti-nausea medications). By carrying your own medical kit you can avoid using useless or even potentially dangerous medication. Good resources are the Lonely Planet publication *Travel with Children*, and for those spending longer away Jane Wilson-Howarth's book *Your Child's Health Abroad* is excellent.

WOMEN'S HEALTH

Pregnant women should receive specialised advice before travelling. The ideal time to travel is in the second trimester (16 and 28 weeks), when the risk of pregnancy-related problems are at their lowest and pregnant women generally feel at their best. During the first trimester there is a risk of miscarriage and in the third trimester complications such as premature labour and high blood pressure are possible. It's wise to travel with a companion. Always carry a list of quality medical facilities available at your destination and ensure you continue your standard antenatal care at these facilities. Avoid rural travel in areas with poor transportation and medical facilities. Most of all, ensure travel insurance covers all pregnancy-related possibilities, including premature labour.

Malaria is a high-risk disease in pregnancy. Advice from the WHO recommends that pregnant women do *not* travel to those areas with Chloroquine-resistant malaria. None of the more effective antimalarial drugs is completely safe in pregnancy.

Traveller's diarrhoea can quickly lead to dehydration and result in inadequate blood flow to the placenta. Many of the drugs used to treat various diarrhoea bugs are not recommended in pregnancy. Azithromycin is considered safe.

In Thailand's urban areas, supplies of sanitary products are readily available. Your personal birth-control option may not be available so bring adequate supplies of your own. Heat, humidity and antibiotics can all contribute to thrush. Treatment of thrush is with antifungal creams and pessaries such as Clotrimazole. A practical alternative is one tablet of fluconazole (Diflucan). Urinary-tract infections can be precipitated by dehydration or long bus journeys without toilet stops; bring suitable antibiotics.

Language

CONTENTS

Learning some Thai is indispensable for travel in the kingdom; naturally, the more you pick up, the closer you get to Thailand's culture and people. Your first attempts to speak Thai will probably meet with mixed success, but keep trying. Listen closely to the way the Thais themselves use the various tones – you'll catch on quickly. Don't let laughter at your linguistic forays discourage you; this apparent amusement is really an expression of appreciation. Travellers are particularly urged to make the effort to meet Thai college and university students. Thai students are, by and large, eager to meet visitors from other countries. They will often know some English, so communication isn't as difficult as it may be with shop owners, civil servants etc, and they're generally willing to teach you useful Thai words and phrases.

DIALECTS

Thailand's official language is effectively the dialect spoken and written in central Thailand, which has successfully become the lingua franca of all Thai and non-Thai ethnic groups in the kingdom.

All Thai dialects are members of the Thai half of the Thai-Kadai family of languages. As such, they're closely related to languages spoken in Laos (Lao, Northern Thai, Thai Lü), northern Myanmar (Shan, Northern Thai), northwestern Vietnam (Nung, Tho), Assam (Ahom) and pockets of south China (Zhuang, Thai Lü).

Modern Thai linguists recognise four basic dialects within Thailand: Central Thai (spoken as a first dialect through central Thailand and throughout the country as a second dialect); Northern Thai (spoken from Tak Province north to the Myanmar border); Northeastern Thai (northeastern provinces towards the Lao and Cambodian borders); and Southern Thai (from Chumphon Province south to the Malaysian border). There are also a number of Thai minority dialects such as those spoken by the Phu Thai, Thai Dam, Thai Daeng, Phu Noi, Phuan and other tribal Thai groups, most of whom reside in the north and northeast.

VOCABULARY DIFFERENCES

Like most languages, Thai distinguishes between 'polite' and 'informal' vocabulary, so that *tahn*, for example, is a more polite everyday word for 'eat' than *gin*, and *sĕe-sà* for 'head' is more polite than *hŏo·a*. When given a choice, it's better to use the polite terms, since these are less likely to lead to unintentional offence.

SCRIPT

The Thai script, a fairly recent development in comparison with the spoken language, consists of 44 consonants (but only 21 separate sounds) and 48 vowel and diphthong possibilities (32 separate signs). Though learning the alphabet is not difficult, the writing system itself is fairly complex, so unless you're planning a lengthy stay in Thailand it should perhaps be foregone in favour of actually learning to speak the language. The names of major places and food items included in this book are given in both Thai and roman script, so that you can at least 'read' the names of destinations or dishes, or point to them if necessary.

LANGUAGE

TONES

In Thai the meaning of a single syllable may be altered by means of different tones – in standard Central Thai there are five: low tone, mid tone, falling tone, high tone and rising tone. For example, depending on the tone, the syllable *mai* can mean 'new', 'burn', 'wood', 'not?' or 'not'; ponder the phrase *mái mài mâi mâi măi* (New wood doesn't burn, does it?) and you begin to appreciate the importance of tones in spoken Thai. This makes it a rather tricky language to learn at first, especially for those of us unaccustomed to the concept of tones.

Even when we 'know' what the correct tone in Thai should be, our tendency to denote emotion, verbal stress, the interrogative etc through tone modulation often interferes with producing the correct tone. Therefore the first rule in learning to speak Thai is to divorce emotions from your speech, at least until you've learned the Thai way to express them without changing essential tone value.

The following is visual representation in chart form to show relative tone values:

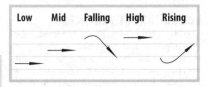

Low	Mid	Falling	High	Rising

The list below is a brief attempt to explain the tones. The only way to really understand the differences is by listening to a native or fluent non-native speaker. The range of all five tones is relative to each speaker's vocal range so there is no fixed 'pitch' intrinsic to the language.

low tone – 'Flat' like the mid tone, but pronounced at the relative bottom of one's vocal range. It is low, level and has no inflection, eg *bàht* (baht – the Thai currency).

mid tone – Pronounced 'flat', at the relative middle of the speaker's vocal range, eg *dee* (good); no tone mark is used.

falling tone – Starting high and falling sharply, this tone is similar to the change in pitch in English when you are emphasising a word, or calling someone's name from afar, eg *mâi* (no/not).

high tone – Usually the most difficult for Westerners. It's pronounced near the relative top of the vocal range, as level as possible, eg *máh* (horse).

rising tone – starting low and gradually rising, sounds like the inflection used by English speakers to imply a question – 'Yes?', eg *săhm* (three).

PRONUNCIATION

The following is a guide to the phonetic system that's been used for the words and phrases in this chapter (and throughout the rest of the book when transcribing directly from Thai). The dots indicate syllable breaks within words, including compound vowels.

Consonants

The majority of consonants correspond closely to their English counterparts. Here are a few exceptions:

g	similar to the 'g' in 'good'
b̶	a hard 'p' sound, almost like a 'b'; sounds something like the sound made when you say 'hi**p-b**ag'
đ	a hard 't' sound, like a sharp 'd'; sounds something like the sound made when you say 'mi**d-t**one'
k	as the 'k' in 'kite'
p	as the 'p' in 'pie'
t	as the 't' in 'tip'
ng	as the 'nging' in 'singing'; can occur as an initial consonant (practise by saying 'singing' without the 'si')
r	similar to the 'r' in 'run' but flapped (ie the tongue touches palate); in everyday speech it's often pronounced like 'l'

Vowels

i	as in 'bit'
ee	as the 'ee' in 'feet'
ai	as in 'aisle'
ah	as the 'a' in 'father'
a	as in 'about'; half as long as '**ah**'
aa	as the 'a' in 'bat' or 'tab'
e	as in 'hen'
air	as in English but with no final 'r' sound (for American speakers)
eu	as the 'er' in 'fern' (without the 'r' sound)
u	as the 'u' in 'put'
oo	as the 'oo' in 'food'
ow	as the 'ow' in 'now'
or	as the 'or' in 'torn' (without the 'r' sound)
o	as the 'o' in 'hot'
oh	as the 'o' in 'toe'
eu·a	a combination of 'eu' and 'a'

ee·a	as 'ee-ya'
oo·a	as the 'our' in 'tour'
oo·ay	sounds like 'oo-way'
ew	as the 'ew' in 'new'
ee·o	as the 'io' in 'Rio'
aa·ou	like the 'a' in 'cat' followed by a short 'u' as in 'put'
eh·ou	like the 'e' in bed, followed by a short 'u' as in 'put'
oy	as the 'oi' in 'coin'

TRANSLITERATION

Writing Thai in roman script is a perennial problem – no wholly satisfactory system has yet been devised to assure both consistency and readability. The Thai government uses the Royal Thai General System of transcription for official government documents in English and for most highway signs. However, local variations crop up on hotel signs, city street signs, menus and so on in such a way that visitors often become confused. Added to this is the fact that even the government system has its flaws.

Generally, names in this book follow the most common practice or simply copy their roman script name, no matter what devious process was used in its transliteration! When this transliteration is markedly different from actual pronunciation, the pronunciation is included (according to the system outlined in this chapter) in parentheses after the transliteration. Where no roman model was available, names have been transliterated phonetically, directly from Thai.

ACCOMMODATION

I'm looking for a ...	ผม/ดิฉัน กำลังหา...	pŏm/dì·chăn gam·lang hăh ...
guesthouse	บ้านพัก/ เกสต์เฮาส์	bâhn pák/ gèt hów
hotel	โรงแรม	rohng raam
youth hostel	บ้าน เยาวชน	bâhn yow·wá·chon

Where is a cheap hotel?
โรงแรมที่ราคาถูกอยู่ที่ไหน
rohng raam têe rah·kah tòok yòo têe năi

What is the address?
ที่อยู่คืออะไร
têe yòo keu à·rai

Could you write the address, please?
เขียนที่อยู่ให้ได้ไหม
kĕe·an têe yòo hâi dâi măi

Do you have any rooms available?
มีห้องว่างไหม
mee hôrng wâhng măi

I'd like (a) ...
อยากได้...
yàhk dâi ...

bed	เตียงนอน	đee·ang norn
single room	ห้องเดี่ยว	hôrng dèe·o
double room	ห้องคู่	hôrng kôo
room with two beds	ห้องที่มีเตียง สองตัว	hôrng têe mee đee·ang sŏrng đoo·a
room with a bathroom	ห้องที่มีห้องน้ำ	hôrng têe mee hôrng nám
ordinary room (with fan)	ห้องธรรมดา (มีพัดลม)	hôrng tam·má· dah (mee pát lom)
to share a dorm	พักในหอพัก	pák nai hŏr pák

How much is it ...? ...เท่าไร? ... tôw rai

| per night | คืนละ | keun lá |
| per person | คนละ | kon lá |

May I see the room?
ดูห้องได้ไหม
doo hôrng dâi măi

Where is the bathroom?
ห้องน้ำอยู่ที่ไหน
hôrng nám yòo têe năi

I'm/We're leaving today.
ฉัน/พวกเราจะออกวันนี้
chăn/pôo·ak row jà òrk wan née

toilet	ห้องส้วม/ ห้องน้ำ	hôrng sôo·am/ hôrng nám
room	ห้อง	hôrng
hot	ร้อน	rórn
cold	เย็น	yen
bath/shower	อาบน้ำ	àhp nám
towel	ผ้าเช็ดตัว	pâh chét đoo·a

CONVERSATION & ESSENTIALS

When being polite, the speaker ends his or her sentence with *kráp* (for men) or *kâ* (for women). It is the gender of the speaker that is being expressed here; it is also the common way to answer 'yes' to a question or show agreement.

Hello.	สวัสดี (ครับ/ค่ะ)	sà·wàt·dee (kráp/kâ)
Goodbye.	ลาก่อน	lah gòrn
Yes.	ใช่	châi
No.	ไม่ใช่	mâi châi
Please.	ขอ	kŏr
Thank you.	ขอบคุณ	kòrp kun
That's fine.	ไม่เป็นไร/	mâi ben rai/
(You're welcome)	ยินดี	yin·dee
Excuse me.	ขออภัย	kŏr à·pai
Sorry. (Forgive me)	ขอโทษ	kŏr tôht
I'm from ...	มาจาก...	mah jàhk ...
I like ...	ชอบ...	chôrp ...
I don't like ...	ไม่ชอบ...	mâi chôrp ...
Just a minute.	รอเดี๋ยว	ror dĕe·o
I/me (for men)	ผม	pŏm
I/me (for women)	ดิฉัน	dì·chăn
I/me (informal, men and women)	ฉัน	chăn
You (for peers)	คุณ	kun

How are you?
สบายดีหรือ? — sà·bai dee rĕu
I'm fine, thanks.
สบายดี — sà·bai dee
What's your name?
คุณชื่ออะไร? — kun chêu à·rai
My name is ...
ผมชื่อ... — pŏm chêu ... (men)
ดิฉันชื่อ... — dì·chăn chêu ... (women)
Where are you from?
มาจากที่ไหน — mah jàhk têe năi
See you soon.
เดี๋ยวเจอกันนะ — dĕe·o jeu gan ná
Do you have ...?
มี...ไหม/...มีไหม? — mee ... măi/... mee măi

SIGNS	
ทางเข้า	Entrance
ทางออก	Exit
ที่ติดต่อสอบถาม	Information
เปิด	Open
ปิด	Closed
ห้าม	Prohibited
สถานีตำรวจ	Police Station
ห้องน้ำ	Toilets
ชาย	Men
หญิง	Women

(I) would like ... (+ verb)
อยากจะ... — yàhk jà ...
(I) would like ... (+ noun)
อยากได้... — yàhk dâi ...

DIRECTIONS

Where is (the) ...?
...อยู่ที่ไหน? — ... yòo têe năi
(Go) Straight ahead.
ตรงไป — đrong bai
Turn left.
เลี้ยวซ้าย — lée·o sái
Turn right.
เลี้ยวขวา — lée·o kwăh
at the corner
ตรงมุม — đrong mum
at the traffic lights
ตรงไฟแดง — đrong fai daang

behind	ข้างหลัง	kâhng lăng
in front of	ตรงหน้า	đrong nâh
far	ไกล	glai
near	ใกล้	glâi
not far	ไม่ไกล	mâi glai
opposite	ตรงข้าม	đrong kâhm
left	ซ้าย	sái
right	ขวา	kwăh
beach	ชายหาด	chai hàht
bridge	สะพาน	sà·pahn
canal	คลอง	klorng
countryside	ชนบท	chon·ná·bòt

hill	เขา	kŏw
island	เกาะ	gò
lake	ทะเลสาบ	tá·leh sàhp
mountain	ภูเขา	poo kŏw
paddy (field)	(ทุ่ง) นา	(tûng) nah
palace	วัง	wang
pond	หนอง/บึง	nŏrng/beung
river	แม่น้ำ	mâe nám
sea	ทะเล	tá·lair
temple	วัด	wát
town	เมือง	meu·ang
track	ทาง	tahng
village	(หมู่) บ้าน	(mòo) bâhn
waterfall	น้ำตก	nám đòk

HEALTH

I need a (doctor).

ต้องการ(หมอ) *đôrng gahn (mŏr)*

dentist

หมอฟัน *mŏr fan*

hospital

โรงพยาบาล *rohng pá·yah·bahn*

chemist/pharmacy

ร้านขายยา *ráhn kăi yah*

I'm ill.

ฉันป่วย *chăn bòo·ay*

It hurts here.

เจ็บตรงนี้ *jèp đrong née*

I'm pregnant.

ตั้งครรภ์แล้ว *đâng kan láe·ou*

I feel nauseous.

รู้สึกคลื่นไส้ *róo·sèuk klêun sâi*

I have a fever.

เป็นไข้ *ben kâi*

I have diarrhoea.

ท้องเสีย *tórng sĕe·a*

I'm ...

ผม/ดิฉัน... *pŏm/dì·chăn ...*

asthmatic

เป็นโรคหืด *ben rôhk hèut*

diabetic

เป็นโรคเบาหวาน *ben rôhk bow wăhn*

epileptic

เป็นโรคลมบ้าหมู *ben rôhk lom bâh mŏo*

EMERGENCIES

There's been an accident.

มีอุบัติเหตุ *mee ù·bàt·đi·hèt*

I'm lost.

ฉันหลงทาง *chăn lŏng tahng*

Help!

ช่วยด้วย *chôo·ay dôo·ay*

Go away!	ไปซิ	bai sí
Stop!	หยุด	yùt!
Call ...!	เรียก...	rêe·ak ...
	หน่อย	nòy
a doctor	หมอ	mŏr
the police	ตำรวจ	đam·ròo·at

I'm allergic to ...

ผม/ดิฉันแพ้... *pŏm/dì·chăn páa ...*

antibiotics

ยาปฏิชีวนะ *yah bà·đi·chee·wá·ná*

aspirin

ยาแอสไพริน *yah àat·sà·pai·rin*

bees

ตัวผึ้ง *đoo·a pêung*

peanuts

ถั่วลิสง *tòo·a lí·sŏng*

penicillin

ยาเพนิซิลลิน *yah pair·ní·sin·lin*

antiseptic

ยาฆ่าเชื้อ *yah kâh chéu·a*

aspirin

ยาแอสไพริน *yah àat·sà·pai·rin*

condoms

ถุงยางอนามัย *tŭng yahng a·nah·mai*

contraceptive

การคุมกำเนิด *gahn kum gam·nèut*

medicine

ยา *yah*

mosquito coil

ยากันยุงแบบจุด *yah gan yung bàap jùt*

mosquito repellent

ยากันยุง *yah gan yung*

painkiller

ยาแก้ปวด *yah gâe bòo·at*

sunblock cream
ครีมกันแดด *kreem gan dàat*
tampons
แทมพอน *taam·porn*

LANGUAGE DIFFICULTIES

Do you speak English?
คุณพูดภาษาอังกฤษได้ไหม
kun pôot pah·săh ang·grit dâi măi
Does anyone here speak English?
ที่นี่มีใครพูดภาษาอังกฤษได้ไหม
têe née mee krai pôot pah·săh ang·grit dâi măi
How do you say ... in Thai?
...ว่าอย่างไรภาษาไทย
... wâh yàhng rai pah·săh tai
What do you call this in Thai?
นี่ภาษาไทยเรียกว่าอะไร
née pah·săh tai rêe·ak wâh à·rai
What does ... mean?
...แปลว่าอะไร
... plaa wâh à·rai
Do you understand?
เข้าใจไหม
kôw jai măi
A little.
นิดหน่อย
nít nòy
I understand.
เข้าใจ
kôw jai
I don't understand.
ไม่เข้าใจ
mâi kôw jai
Please write it down.
ขอเขียนให้หน่อย
kŏr kĕe·an hâi nòy
Can you show me (on the map)?
ให้ดู(ในแผนที่) ได้ไหม
hâi doo (nai păan têe) dâi măi

NUMBERS

0	ศูนย์	*sŏon*
1	หนึ่ง	*nèung*
2	สอง	*sŏrng*
3	สาม	*săhm*
4	สี่	*sèe*
5	ห้า	*hâh*
6	หก	*hòk*
7	เจ็ด	*jèt*
8	แปด	*bàat*
9	เก้า	*gôw*
10	สิบ	*sìp*
11	สิบเอ็ด	*sìp·èt*
12	สิบสอง	*sìp·sŏrng*
13	สิบสาม	*sìp·săhm*
14	สิบสี่	*sìp·sèe*
15	สิบห้า	*sìp·hâh*
16	สิบหก	*sìp·hòk*
17	สิบเจ็ด	*sìp·jèt*
18	สิบแปด	*sìp·bàat*
19	สิบเก้า	*sìp·gôw*
20	ยี่สิบ	*yêe·sìp*
21	ยี่สิบเอ็ด	*yêe·sìp·èt*
22	ยี่สิบสอง	*yêe·sìp·sŏrng*
30	สามสิบ	*săhm·sìp*
40	สี่สิบ	*sèe·sìp*
50	ห้าสิบ	*hâh·sìp*
60	หกสิบ	*hòk·sìp*
70	เจ็ดสิบ	*jèt·sìp*
80	แปดสิบ	*bàat·sìp*
90	เก้าสิบ	*gôw·sìp*
100	หนึ่งร้อย	*nèung róy*
200	สองร้อย	*sŏrng róy*
300	สามร้อย	*săhm róy*
1000	หนึ่งพัน	*nèung pan*
2000	สองพัน	*sŏrng pan*
10,000	หนึ่งหมื่น	*nèung mèun*
100,000	หนึ่งแสน	*nèung săan*
one million	หนึ่งล้าน	*nèung láhn*
one billion	พันล้าน	*pan láhn*

PAPERWORK

name	ชื่อ	*chêu*
nationality	สัญชาติ	*săn·châht*
date of birth	เกิดวันที่	*gèut wan têe*
place of birth	เกิดที่	*gèut têe*
sex (gender)	เพศ	*pêt*
passport	หนังสือเดิน	*năng·sĕu deun*
	ทาง	*tahng*
visa	วีซ่า	*wee·sâh*

SHOPPING & SERVICES

I'd like to buy ...
อยากจะซื้อ...   *yàhk jà séu ...*
How much?
เท่าไร   *tôw raí*
How much is this?
นี่เท่าไร/กี่บาท   *nêe tôw rai/gèe bàht*
I don't like it.
ไม่ชอบ   *mâi chôrp*
May I look at it?
ดูได้ไหม   *doo dâi mǎi*
I'm just looking.
ดูเฉยๆ   *doo chěr·i chěr·i*
It's cheap.
ราคาถูก   *rah·kah tòok*
It's too expensive.
แพงเกินไป   *paang geun bai*
I'll take it.
เอา   *ow*

Can you reduce the price a little?
ลดราคาหน่อยได้ไหม
lót rah·kah nòy dâi mǎi
Can you come down just a little more?
ลดราคาอีกนิดหนึ่งได้ไหม
lót rah·kah èek nít·nèung dâi mǎi
Do you have something cheaper?
มีถูกกว่านี้ไหม
mee tòok gwàh née mǎi
Can you lower it more?
ลดอีกได้ไหม
lót èek dâi mǎi
How about ... baht?
...บาทได้ไหม
... bàht dâi mǎi
I won't give more than ... baht.
จะให้ไม่เกิน...บาท
jà hâi mâi geun ... bàht

Do you accept ...?
รับ...ไหม   *ráp ... mǎi*
  credit cards
  บัตรเครดิต   *bàt krair·dìt*
  travellers cheques
  เช็คเดินทาง   *chék deun tahng*

more   อีก   *èek*
less   น้อยลง   *nóy long*
smaller   เล็กกว่า   *lék gwàh*

bigger   ใหญ่กว่า   *yài gwàh*
too expensive   แพงไป   *paang bai*
inexpensive   ราคา   *rah·kah*
  ประหยัด   *brà·yàt*

I'm looking for ...
ผม/ดิฉันกำลังหา...   *pǒm/dì·chǎn gam·lang hǎh ...*
  a bank
  ธนาคาร   *tá·nah·kahn*
  the city centre
  ใจกลางเมือง   *jai glahng meu·ang*
  the ... embassy
  สถานทูต...   *sà·tǎhn tôot ...*
  the market
  ตลาด   *đà·làht*
  the museum
  พิพิธภัณฑ์   *pí·pít·tá·pan*
  the post office
  ไปรษณีย์   *brai·sà·nee*
  a public toilet
  ห้องน้ำสาธารณะ   *hôrng nám sǎh·tah·rá·ná*
  a restaurant
  ร้านอาหาร   *ráhn ah·hǎhn*
  a temple
  วัด   *wát*
  the telephone centre
  ศูนย์โทรศัพท์   *sǒon toh·rá·sàp*
  the tourist office
  สำนักงานท่อง   *sǎm·nák ngahn tôrng*
   เที่ยว   *têe·o*

I want to change ...
ต้องการแลก...   *đôrng gahn lâak ...*
  money
  เงิน   *ngeun*
  travellers cheques
  เช็คเดินทาง   *chék deun tahng*

Can I/we change money here?
แลกเงินที่นี่ได้ไหม
lâak ngeun têe née dâi mǎi
What time does it open?
เปิดกี่โมง
bèut gèe mohng
What time does it close?
ปิดกี่โมง
bìt gèe mohng

LANGUAGE

TIME & DATES

Telling the time in Thai can be very challenging for an outsider to master. While the Western 12-hour clock divides the day between two time periods, am and pm, the Thai system has four periods. The 24-hour clock is also commonly used by government and media. The list below shows hours of the 12-hour clock translated into the Thai system.

What time is it?

กี่โมงแล้ว   *gèe mohng láa·ou*

12 midnight	หกทุ่ม/	*hòk tûm/*
	เที่ยงคืน	*têe·ang keun*
1am	ตีหนึ่ง	*đee nèung*
2am	ตีสอง	*đee sŏrng*
3am	ตีสาม	*đee sǎhm*
4am	ตีสี่	*đee sèe*
5am	ตีห้า	*đee hâh*
6am	หกโมงเช้า	*hòk mohng chów*
7am	หนึ่งโมงเช้า	*nèung mohng chów*
11am	ห้าโมงเช้า	*hâh mohng chów*
12 noon	เที่ยง	*têe·ang*
1pm	บ่ายโมง	*bài mohng*
2pm	บ่ายสองโมง	*bài sŏrng mohng*
3pm	บ่ายสามโมง	*bài sǎhm mohng*
4pm	บ่ายสี่โมง/	*bài sèe mohng*
	(lit: afternoon four hours)	
	สี่โมงเย็น	*sèe mohng yen*
	(lit: four hours evening)	
5pm	ห้าโมงเย็น	*hâh mohng yen*
6pm	หกโมงเย็น	*hòk mohng yen*
7pm	หนึ่งทุ่ม	*nèung tûm*
8pm	สองทุ่ม	*sŏrng tûm*
9pm	สามทุ่ม	*sǎhm tûm*
10pm	สี่ทุ่ม	*sèe tûm*
11pm	ห้าทุ่ม	*hâh tûm*

For times after the hour, just add the number of minutes following the hour.

4.30pm

บ่ายสี่โมงครึ่ง

bài sèe mohng krêung (lit: four afternoon hours half)

4.15pm

บ่ายสี่โมงสิบห้านาที

bài sèe mohng sìp·hâh nah·tee (lit: four afternoon hours 15)

To give times before the hour, add the number of minutes beforehand.

3.45pm

อีกสิบห้านาทีบ่ายสี่โมง

èek sìp·hâh nah·tee bài sèe mohng (lit: another 15 minutes four afternoon hours)

When?	เมื่อไร	*mêu·a·rai*
today	วันนี้	*wan née*
tomorrow	พรุ่งนี้	*prûng née*
yesterday	เมื่อวาน	*mêu·a wahn*
Monday	วันจันทร์	*wan jan*
Tuesday	วันอังคาร	*wan ang·kahn*
Wednesday	วันพุธ	*wan pút*
Thursday	วันพฤหัสฯ	*wan pá·réu·hàt*
Friday	วันศุกร์	*wan sùk*
Saturday	วันเสาร์	*wan sŏw*
Sunday	วันอาทิตย์	*wan ah·tít*
January	มกราคม	*má·ga·rah·kom*
February	กุมภาพันธ์	*gum·pah·pan*
March	มีนาคม	*mee·naa·kom*
April	เมษายน	*mair·sǎh·yon*
May	พฤษภาคม	*préut·sà·pah·kom*
June	มิถุนายน	*mí·tù·nah·yon*
July	กรกฎาคม	*ga·rák·gà·đah·kom*
August	สิงหาคม	*sǐng·hǎh·kom*
September	กันยายน	*gan·yah·yon*
October	ตุลาคม	*đù·lah·kom*
November	พฤศจิกายน	*préut·sà·jì·gah·yon*
December	ธันวาคม	*tan·wah·kom*

TRANSPORT
Public Transport

What time does the ... leave?

...จะออกกี่โมง

... jà òrk gèe mohng

What time does the ... arrive?

...จะถึงกี่โมง

... jà tĕung gèe mohng

boat	เรือ	reu·a
bus (city)	รถเมล์/	rót mair/
	รถบัส	rót bát
bus (intercity)	รถทัวร์	rót too·a
plane	เครื่องบิน	krêu·ang bin
train	รถไฟ	rót fai

I'd like ...

ผม/ดิฉันอยากได้...

pŏm/dì·chăn yàhk dâi ...

a one-way ticket

ตั๋วเที่ยวเดียว đŏo·a têe·o dee·o

a return ticket

ตั๋วไปกลับ đŏo·a bai glàp

two tickets

ตั๋วสองใบ đŏo·a sŏrng bai

1st class

ชั้นหนึ่ง chán nèung

2nd class

ชั้นสอง chán sŏrng

I'd like a ticket.

อยากได้ตั๋ว yàhk dâi đŏo·a

I want to go to ...

อยากจะไป... yàhk jà bai ...

The train has been cancelled.

รถไฟถูกยกเลิกแล้ว rót fai tùk yók lêuk láa·ou

The train has been delayed.

รถไฟช้าเวลา rót fai cháh wair·lah

airport

สนามบิน sa·năhm bin

bus station

สถานีขนส่ง sa·tăh·nee kŏn sòng

bus stop

ป้ายรถเมล์ bâi rót mair

taxi stand

ที่จอดรถแท็กซี่ têe jòrt rót táak·sêe

train station

สถานีรถไฟ sa·tăh·nee rót fai

platform number ...

ชานชาลาที่... chahn·chah·lah têe ...

ticket office

ตู้ขายตั๋ว đôo kăi đŏo·a

timetable

ตารางเวลา đah·rahng wair·lah

the first

ที่แรก têe râak

the last

สุดท้าย sùt tái

Private Transport

I'd like to hire a/an ...

ผม/ดิฉันอยากเช่า...

pŏm/dì·chăn yàhk chôw ...

car

รถยนต์ rót yon

4WD

รถโฟร์วีล rót foh ween

motorbike

รถมอเตอร์ไซค์ rót mor·đeu·sai

bicycle

รถจักรยาน rót jàk·gà·yahn

Is this the road to ...?

ทางนี้ไป...ไหม tahng née bai ... măi

Where's a service station?

ปั๊มน้ำมันอยู่ที่ไหน bám nám man yòo têe nài

Please fill it up.

ขอเติมให้เต็ม kŏr đeum hâi đem

I'd like (30) litres.

เอา(สามสิบ)ลิตร ow (săhm sìp) lít

diesel

น้ำมันโซล่า nám man soh·lâh

unleaded petrol

น้ำมันไร้สารตะกั่ว nám man rái săan đà·gòo·a

Can I park here?

จอดที่นี่ได้ไหม jòrt têe née dâi măi

How long can I park here?

จอดที่นี่ได้นานเท่าไร jòrt têe née dâi nahn tôw·rai

Where do I pay?

จ่ายเงินที่ไหน jài ngeun têe nài

I need a mechanic.

ต้องการช่าง đôrng gahn châhng

I have a flat tyre.

ยางแบน yahng baan

I've run out of petrol.

หมดน้ำมัน mòt nám man

I've had an accident.

มีอุบัติเหตุ

mee ù·bàt·đì·hèt

The car/motorbike has broken down (at ...)

รถ/มอเตอร์ไซค์เสียที่...

rót/mor·đeu·sai sĕe·a têe ...

The car/motorbike won't start.

รถ/มอเตอร์ไซค์สตาร์ทไม่ติด

rót/mor·đeu·sai sa·đáht mâi đìt

TRAVEL WITH CHILDREN

Is there (a/an) ...

มี...ไหม

mee ... măi

baby change room

ห้องเปลี่ยนผ้าเด็ก

hôrng blèe·an pâh dèk

car baby seat

เบาะนั่งในรถสำหรับเด็ก

bò nâng nai rót săm·ràp dèk

child-minding service

บริการเลี้ยงเด็ก

bor·rí·gahn lée·ang dèk

children's menu

รายการอาหารสำหรับเด็ก

rai gahn ah·hăhn săm·ràp dèk

(disposable) nappies/diapers

ผ้าอ้อม(แบบใช้แล้วทิ้ง)

pâh ôrm (bàap chái láa·ou tíng)

formula (milk)

นมผงสำหรับเด็ก

nom pŏng săm·ràp dèk

(English-speaking) babysitter

พี่เลี้ยงเด็ก(ที่พูดภาษาอังกฤษได้)

pêe lée·ang dèk (têe pôot pah·săh ang·grìt dâi)

highchair

เก้าอี้สูง

gôw·êe sŏong

potty

กระโถน

grà·tŏhn

stroller

รถเข็นเด็ก

rót kĕn dèk

Are children allowed?

เด็กอนุญาตให้เข้าไหม

dèk à·nú·yâht hâi kôw măi

Also available from Lonely Planet:
Thai phrasebook

Glossary

This glossary includes Thai, Pali (P) and Sanskrit (S) words and terms frequently used in this guidebook. For definitions of food and drink terms, see p92.

ah·hǎhn – food

ah·hǎhn bàh – 'jungle food', usually referring to dishes made with wild game

ajahn – *(aajaan)* respectful title for 'teacher'; from the Sanskrit term *acarya*

amphoe – *(amphur)* district, the next subdivision down from province

amphoe meu·ang – provincial capital

AUA – American University Alumni

bâhn – *(ban)* house or village

baht – *(bàat)* the Thai unit of currency

bàht – a unit of weight equal to 15g; rounded bowl used by monks for receiving alms food

bai sěe – sacred thread used by monks or shamans in certain religious ceremonies

ben·jà·rong – traditional five-coloured Thai ceramics

BKS – Baw Khaw Saw (Thai acronym for the Transport Company)

BMA – Bangkok Metropolitan Authority; Bangkok's municipal government

bodhisattva (S) – in Theravada Buddhism, the term used to refer to the previous lives of the Buddha prior to his enlightenment

bòht – central sanctuary in a Thai temple used for the monastic order's official business, such as ordinations; from the Pali term *uposatha (ubohsòt);* see also *wí·hǎhn*

bòr nám rórn – hot springs

Brahman – pertaining to Brahmanism, an ancient religious tradition in India and the predecessor of Hinduism; not to be confused with 'Brahmin', the priestly class in India's caste system

BTS – Bangkok Transit System (Skytrain); Thai: *rót fai fáh*

bah·dé – batik

bàk đâi – southern Thailand

bèe·pâht – classical Thai orchestra

bohng·lahng – northeastern Thai marimba (percussion instrument) made of short logs

CAT – CAT Telecom Public Company Limited (formerly Communications Authority of Thailand)

chedi – see *stupa*

chow – folk; people

chow lair – *(chow nám)* sea gypsies

chow nah – farmer

CPT – Communist Party of Thailand

doy – mountain in the Northern Thai dialect; spelt 'Doi' in proper names

đà·làht – market

đà·làht nám – water market

đam·bon – *(tambol)* precinct, next governmental subdivision under *amphoe*

đròrk – *(trok)* alley, smaller than a soi

fa·ràng –a Westerner (person of European origin); also guava

gà·teu·i – *(kàthoey)* Thailand's 'third gender', usually cross-dressing or transsexual males; also called ladyboys

gopura (S) – entrance pavilion in traditional Hindu temple architecture, often seen in Angkor-period temple complexes

góo·ay hâang – Chinese-style work shirt

grà·bèe grà·borng – a traditional Thai martial art employing short swords and staves

gù·đì – monk's dwelling

hàht – beach; spelt 'Hat' in proper names

hǐn – stone

hǒr đrai – a Tripitaka (Buddhist scripture) hall

hǒr glorng – drum tower

hǒr rá·kang – bell tower

hôrng – *(hong)* room; in southern Thailand this refers to semi-submerged island caves

hôrng tǎa·ou – rowhouse or shophouses

Isan – *(ee·sǎhn)* general term used for northeastern Thailand

jataka (P) – *(chah·đòk)* stories of the Buddha's previous lives

jeen – Chinese

jeen hor – literally 'galloping Chinese', referring to horse-riding Yunnanese traders

jôw meu·ang – principality chief; *jôw* means lord, prince or holy being

kaan – reed instrument common in northeastern Thailand

kàthoey – see *gà·teu·i*

klorng – canal; spelt 'Khlong' in proper nouns

kǒhn – masked dance-drama based on stories from the Ramakian

kon ee·săhn – the people of northeastern Thailand; *kon* means person

kŏw – hill or mountain; spelt 'Khao' in proper names

kôw – rice

KMT – Kuomintang

KNU – Karen National Union

kràbìi-kràbawng – see *grà·bèe grà·borng*

ku – small *chedi* that is partially hollow and open

kúay hâeng – see *góo·ay hâang*

kùtì – see *gù·đî*

lăam – cape; spelt 'Laem' in proper names

làk meu·ang – city pillar

lá·kon – classical Thai dance-drama

lék – little, small (in size); see also *noi*

lí·gair – Thai folk dance-drama

longyi – Burmese sarong

lôok tûng – Thai country music

lôw kŏw – white whisky, often homemade rice brew

lôw tèu·an – illegal (homemade) whisky

mâa chee – Thai Buddhist nun

mâa nám – river

Mahanikai – the larger of the two sects of Theravada Buddhism in Thailand

mahathat – *(má·hăh tâht)* common name for temples containing Buddha relics; from the Sanskrit-Pali term *mahadhatu*

má·noh·rah – Southern Thailand's most popular traditional dance-drama

masjid – *(mát·sà·yít)* mosque

mát·mèe – technique of tie-dyeing silk or cotton threads and then weaving them into complex patterns, similar to Indonesian *ikat*; the term also refers to the patterns themselves

metta (P) – *(mêt·đah)* Buddhist practice of loving-kindness

meu·ang – city or principality

mon·dòp – small square, spired building in a wát; from Sanskrit *mandapa*

moo·ay tai – *(muay thai)* Thai boxing

mŏr lam – an Isan musical tradition akin to *lôok tûng*

mŏrn kwăhn – wedge-shaped pillow popular in northern and northeastern Thailand

MRTA – Metropolitan Rapid Transit Authority, Bangkok's subway system; Thai: *rót fai fáh đâi din*

naga (P/S) – *(nâhk)* a mythical serpent-like being with magical powers

ná·kon – city; from the Sanskrit-Pali *nagara;* spelt 'Nakhon' in proper nouns

nám – water

nám đòk – waterfall; spelt 'Nam Tok' in proper nouns

năng đà·lung – Thai shadow play

neun – hill; spelt 'Noen' in proper names

ngahn têt·sà·gahn – festival

nibbana (P/S) – nirvana; in Buddhist teachings, the state of enlightenment; escape from the realm of rebirth; Thai: *níp·pahn*

noi – *(nóy)* little, small (amount); see also *lék*

nôrk – outside, outer; spelt 'Nok' in proper names

ow – bay or gulf; spelt 'Ao' in proper nouns

pâh ka·máh – cotton sarong worn by men

pâh mát·mèe – *mát·mèe* fabric

pâh sîn – cotton sarong worn by women

pâhk glahng – central Thailand

pâhk něua – northern Thailand

pâhk tâi – see *bàk đâi*

pěe – ghost, spirit

pin – small, three-stringed lute played with a large plectrum

pìi-phâat – see *bèe·pâht*

pík·sù – a Buddhist monk; from the Sanskrit *bhikshu,* Pali *bhikkhu*

PLAT – People's Liberation Army of Thailand

pleng koh·râht – Khorat folk song

pleng pêu·a chee·wít – 'songs for life', Thai folk-rock music

ponglang – see *bohng·lahng*

poo kŏw – mountain

pôo yài bâhn – village chief

prá – an honorific term used for monks, nobility and Buddha images; spelt 'Phra' in proper names

prá krêu·ang – amulets of monks, Buddhas or deities worn around the neck for spiritual protection; also called *prá pim*

prá poom – earth spirits or guardians

prang – *(brahng)* Khmer-style tower on temples

prasada – blessed food offered to Hindu or Sikh temple attendees

prasat – *(brah·sàht)* small ornate building, used for religious purposes, with a cruciform ground plan and needle-like spire, located on temple grounds; any of a number of different kinds of halls or residences with religious or royal significance

PULO – Pattani United Liberation Organization

râi – an area of land measurement equal to 1600 sq metres

reu·a hăhng yow – long-tail boat

reu·an tăa·ou – longhouse

reu·sĕe – an ascetic, hermit or sage (Hindi: *rishi*)

rót aa – blue-and-white air-con bus

rót bràp ah·gàht – air-con bus

rót fai fáh – Bangkok's Skytrain system

rót fai tâi din – Bangkok's subway system

rót norn – sleeper bus

rót tam·má·dah – ordinary (non air-con) bus or train

rót too·a – tour or air-con bus

săh·lah – open-sided, covered meeting hall or resting place; from Portuguese term *sala*, literally 'room'
săhm·lór – three-wheeled pedicab
săhn prá poom – spirit shrine
săm·nák sŏng – monastic centre
săm·nák wí·ʼbàt·sà·nah – meditation centre
samsara (P) – in Buddhist teachings, the realm of rebirth and delusion
sangha – (P) the Buddhist community
satang – (sà·ʼdahng) a Thai unit of currency; 100 *satang* equals 1 *baht*
sèe yâak – intersection, often used to give driving directions
sĕmaa – boundary stones used to consecrate ground used for monastic ordinations
serow – Asian mountain goat
sêua môr hôrm – blue cotton farmer's shirt
soi – lane or small street
Songkran – Thai New Year, held in mid-April
sŏo·an ah·hăhn – outdoor restaurant with any bit of foliage nearby; literally 'food garden'
sŏrng·tăa·ou – (literally 'two rows') common name for small pick-up trucks with two benches in the back, used as buses/taxis; also spelt 'săwngthăew'
SRT – State Railway of Thailand
stupa – conical-shaped Buddhist monument used to inter sacred Buddhist objects
sù·săhn – cemetery

tâh – pier, boat landing; spelt 'Tha' in proper nouns
tâht – four-sided, curvilinear Buddha reliquary, common in Northeastern Thailand; spelt 'That' in proper nouns
tâht grà·dòok – bone reliquary, a small *stupa* containing remains of a Buddhist devotee
tàlàat náam – see *đà·làht nám*
tâm – cave; spelt 'Tham' in proper nouns
tam bun – to make merit
tambon – see *đam·bon*
TAT – Tourism Authority of Thailand
têt·sà·bahn – a governmental division in towns or cities much like municipality
THAI – Thai Airways International; Thailand's national air carrier

thammájàk – Buddhist wheel of law; from the Pali *dhammacakka*
Thammayut – one of the two sects of Theravada Buddhism in Thailand; founded by King Rama IV while he was still a monk
thanŏn – (tà·nŏn) street; spelt 'Thanon' in proper noun and shortened to 'Th'
T-pop – popular teen-music
tràwk – see *đròrk*
trimurti (S) – collocation of the three principal Hindu deities, Brahma, Shiva and Vishnu
Tripitaka (S) – Theravada Buddhist scriptures; (Pali: *Tipitaka*)
tú·dong – a series of 13 ascetic practices (for example eating one meal a day, living at the foot of a tree) undertaken by Buddhist monks; a monk who undertakes such practices; a period of wandering on foot from place to place undertaken by monks
túk-túk – (đúk-đúk) motorised săhm·lór

ùt·sà·nít – flame-shaped head ornament on a Buddha

vipassana (P) – (wí·ʼbàt·sà·nah) Buddhist insight meditation

wâi – palms-together Thai greeting
wan prá – Buddhist holy days, falling on the days of the main phases of the moon (full, new and half) each month
wang – palace
wát – temple-monastery; from the Pali term *avasa* meaning 'monk's dwelling'; spelt 'Wat' in proper nouns
wá·tá·ná·tam – culture
wát ʼbàh – forest monastery
wí·hăhn – (wihan, viharn) any large hall in a Thai temple, usually open to laity; from Sanskrit term *vihara*, meaning 'dwelling'

Yawi – traditional language of Malay parts of Java, Sumatra and the Malay Peninsula, widely spoken in the most southern provinces of Thailand; the written form uses the classic Arabic script plus five additional letters
yài – big
yâhm – shoulder bag

The Authors

CHINA WILLIAMS

Coordinating Author
Getting Started, Events Calendar, Itineraries,
Thailand & You, The Culture, Arts, Chiang Mai Province,
Northern Thailand (Lamphun Province), Directory, Transport, Glossary

For many years China hopped across the Pacific Ocean to work on Lonely Planet's guidebooks to Bangkok. But a baby in 2007 segued her career from dusty backpack to dirty nappies. After a year's 'retirement', China has resumed the twice annual pilgrimage with her son in tow. With each visit she falls in love with a different region of Thailand and for now her heart is pledged to Chiang Mai, a city that suits her post–flower child temperament. She first came to Thailand to teach English in Surin more than a decade ago. In between trips, China lives in Baltimore, Maryland, with her husband, Matt, and son, Felix.

MARK BEALES

Central Thailand

Mark moved to Thailand in 2004, leaving behind life as a journalist in England. Various jobs, including English teacher, TV presenter and freelance writer, have given him a chance to explore almost every part of the country. During his trips, Mark has swum with whale sharks, been bitten by leeches and watched gibbons threaten to invade his log cabin. When Mark isn't on the road he teaches English near Bangkok and attempts to improve his Thai with help from his ever-patient wife, Bui.

TIM BEWER

Northeastern Thailand

While growing up, Tim didn't travel much except for the obligatory pilgrimage to Disney World and an annual summer week at the lake. He's spent most of his adult life making up for this, and has since visited over 50 countries, including most in Southeast Asia. After university he worked briefly as a legislative assistant before quitting Capitol life in 1994 to backpack around West Africa. It was during this trip that the idea of becoming a freelance travel writer and photographer was hatched, and he's been at it ever since. This is his 11th book for Lonely Planet. During the half of the year that he isn't shouldering a backpack somewhere for work or pleasure, he lives in Khon Kaen.

LONELY PLANET AUTHORS

Why is our travel information the best in the world? It's simple: our authors are passionate, dedicated travellers. They don't take freebies in exchange for positive coverage so you can be sure the advice you're given is impartial. They travel widely to all the popular spots, and off the beaten track. They don't research using just the internet or phone. They discover new places not included in any other guidebook. They personally visit thousands of hotels, restaurants, palaces, trails, galleries, temples and more. They speak with dozens of locals every day to make sure you get the kind of insider knowledge only a local could tell you. They take pride in getting all the details right, and in telling it how it is. Think you can do it? Find out how at **lonelyplanet.com**.

CATHERINE BODRY
Southeastern Thailand, Upper Southern Gulf

Catherine grew up in the Pacific Northwest and moved to Alaska in her early 20s, so it's no surprise that frequent, extended tropical vacations were often in order. She first visited Thailand in 2004 as part of a round-the-world trip (which included only countries where the temperature stayed firmly above 30°C) and returned a year later to perfect her bargaining skills and eat as much curry as possible. This research trip marked Catherine's third visit to the country, and she's probably still sweating curry from it. When Catherine isn't flagging down 2nd-class buses and learning local slang on Lonely Planet research trips, she's usually tromping around the mountains near her home in Seward, Alaska.

AUSTIN BUSH
Food & Drink, Bangkok, Northern Thailand

After graduating from the University of Oregon in 1999 with a degree in linguistics, Austin received a scholarship to study Thai at Chiang Mai University and has remained in Thailand ever since. After working several years at a stable job, he made the questionable decision to pursue a career as a freelance writer and photographer, endeavours that have taken him as far as Pakistan's Karakoram Highway and as near as Bangkok's Or Tor Kor Market. Austin enjoys writing about and taking photos of food most of all because it's a great way to connect with people. Samples of his work can be seen at www.austinbushphotography.com.

BRANDON PRESSER
Lower Southern Gulf, Andaman Coast, Deep South

Growing up in a land where bear hugs are taken literally, this wanderlusty Canadian always craved swaying palms and golden sand. A trek across Southeast Asia as a teenager was the clincher – he was hooked, returning year after year to scuba dive, suntan and savour spoonfuls of spicy *sôm-đam* (papaya salad). Brandon was primed to research Thailand's top holiday destinations, but it wasn't all fun and games – there were beaches to be judged, curries to be sampled and kiteboards to be test-ridden. Brandon spends most of the year writing his way around the world and has co-authored several other Lonely Planet guides to Southeast Asia, including *Thailand's Islands & Beaches* and *Malaysia, Singapore & Brunei*.

CONTRIBUTING AUTHORS

Dr Trish Batchelor is a general practitioner and travel medicine specialist who currently works in Canberra and is Medical Advisor to the Travel Doctor New Zealand clinics. She has just returned from working in Vietnam and has previously worked in Nepal and India. Trish teaches travel medicine through the University of Otago, and is interested in underwater and high-altitude medicine, and the impact of tourism on host countries. She has travelled extensively through Southeast and East Asia.

David Lukas is a naturalist who lives on the edge of Yosemite National Park. He has contributed chapters on the environment and wildlife for nearly 30 Lonely Planet guides, including for *Vietnam, Cambodia, Laos & the Greater Mekong, Thailand's Islands & Beaches, Bangkok* and the Environment chapter for this edition of *Thailand*.

Bhawan Ruangsilp wrote the History chapter. She is a native of Bangkok and a published historian of the Ayuthaya period at Chulalongkorn University. She finds 17th-century Western travel literature on Siam fascinating and leapt at the chance to lend her expertise to this edition of Lonely Planet's *Thailand* guide.

Behind the Scenes

THIS BOOK

This 13th edition of Thailand was researched and written by China Williams (coordinating author), Mark Beales, Tim Bewer, Catherine Bodry, Austin Bush, Brandon Presser, Bhawan Ruangsilp, David Lukas and Trish Batchelor. This guidebook was commissioned in Lonely Planet's Melbourne office, and produced by the following:

Commissioning Editors Carolyn Boicos, Tashi Wheeler
Coordinating Editor Nigel Chin
Coordinating Cartographer Peter Shields
Coordinating Layout Designer Aomi Hongo
Managing Editor Geoff Howard
Managing Cartographer David Connolly
Managing Layout Designer Sally Darmody
Assisting Editors Janet Austin, Janice Bird, Monique Choy, Victoria Harrison, Rowan McKinnon, Anne Mulvaney, Diana Saad, Angela Tinson, Saralinda Turner
Assisting Cartographers Enes Bašić, Valeska Cañas, Corey Hutchison, David Kemp, Joanne Luke
Assisting Layout Designers Paul Iacono
Cover Designer Rebecca Dandens
Project Manager Chris Love

Thanks to Lucy Birchley, Nicholas Colicchia, Jessica Crouch, Bruce Evans, Chris Girdler, Nicole Hansen, Carol Jackson, Laura Jane, Indra Kilfoyle, Robyn Loughnane, Kirsten Rawlings, Erin Richards, Alison Ridgway, Kate Whitfield

THANKS
CHINA WILLIAMS

Thanks immeasurably to Nong, so glad to have met you. Gratitude to Pong, Pim, Andrew, Alex, Panupan, Pichai, Duen, Sara, Aidan, Olly, Tom and Ken. Also to Joon, Jane and the staff at Buri Gallery for being so sweet to Felix. Thanks in Bangkok to Kaneungnit, Tom, Anne, Ruengsang, Mason, Jane and the staff at Seven. More thanks to my husband, Matt, who drove the little car that could and to Felix, my trustworthy if temperamental sidekick. And to Tashi Wheeler, the LP production team and lucky 13's dedicated co-authors.

MARK BEALES

Many thanks go to the Lonely Planet team, especially Tashi, China and Brandon, for their fantastic support and guidance. In Ayuthaya, I'm grateful to Ajarn Monthorn of Classic Tours for his expert knowledge and for Duncan Stearn's help with history. In Kanchanaburi my appreciation goes to Khun Chalee, Mickey, Airin and Noi of Good Times. And in Lopburi, I'd be very thankful if the monkey

---

THE LONELY PLANET STORY

Fresh from an epic journey across Europe, Asia and Australia in 1972, Tony and Maureen Wheeler sat at their kitchen table stapling together notes. The first Lonely Planet guidebook, *Across Asia on the Cheap*, was born.

Travellers snapped up the guides. Inspired by their success, the Wheelers began publishing books to Southeast Asia, India and beyond. Demand was prodigious, and the Wheelers expanded the business rapidly to keep up. Over the years, Lonely Planet extended its coverage to every country and into the virtual world via lonelyplanet.com and the Thorn Tree message board.

As Lonely Planet became a globally loved brand, Tony and Maureen received several offers for the company. But it wasn't until 2007 that they found a partner whom they trusted to remain true to the company's principles of travelling widely, treading lightly and giving sustainably. In October of that year, BBC Worldwide acquired a 75% share in the company, pledging to uphold Lonely Planet's commitment to independent travel, trustworthy advice and editorial independence.

Today, Lonely Planet has offices in Melbourne, London and Oakland, with over 500 staff members and 300 authors. Tony and Maureen are still actively involved with Lonely Planet. They're travelling more often than ever, and they're devoting their spare time to charitable projects. And the company is still driven by the philosophy of *Across Asia on the Cheap*: 'All you've got to do is decide to go and the hardest part is over. So go!'

who stole my car's wing mirror would return it at some point. Most of all, thanks to my amazing wife, Bui, for her fact-checking and constant support.

TIM BEWER

A hearty kòrp jai lăi lăi dĕu to the people of Isan who rarely failed to live up to their reputation for friendliness and hospitality when faced with my incessant questions. In particular, Kritsada Kaewkhiew, Amaralak (Pim) Khamhong, Tommy Manophaiboon, June Niampan, Veena Puntace, Suphanuch Rathising, Nuan Sarnsorn, Supawadee Srifa, Naiyarat Techasetthawit, Julian Wright and Jinda Yatan all provided good help and good company. And a special thanks to Worapanyaporn Taranop for all the little things.

CATHERINE BODRY

First, huge thanks to Carolyn Boicos for commissioning me for this project, and to Tashi Wheeler for competently taking the reigns midstream. A big thanks to China Williams for always promptly responding with level-headed advice, and for teaching me some very helpful Thai phrases. Thanks to all my co-authors for insight and information, particularly Brandon Presser and Mark Beales. Brett Atkinson left me with great text to work with. In Thailand, I received help from more people than I could ever thank, but I have to give a special shout-out to Tim and Pat in Hua Hin, Are and Suda in Chumphon, Morn in Trat, Kor and her fam in Bang Saphan and the TAT staff in Nakhon Nayak. The travellers I met were invaluable with their info (and their company): Alex and Jasmine, Stephanie and Sonia. Thanks to Leif for after-work, on-the-road entertainment. Finally, thanks to Lael for Buddha-like patience and unconditional support.

AUSTIN BUSH

Thanks muchly to commissioning editors Carolyn Boicos and Tashi Wheeler, coordinating author China Williams, map expert David Connolly and language guru Bruce Evans, not to mention people on the ground here in Thailand, including but not limited to Andrew Burke, Yuthika Charoenrungruang, Joe Cummings, Nick Grossman, Richard Hermes, Wes and Ann Hsu, Paul Hutt, Sivaporn Ngarmsittichoke, John Spies, Chenchira Suntharwirat and Maylee Thavat.

BRANDON PRESSER

Thanks to Neal & Rashi for a (beach) home away from home (congrats on little Jorge!), to Tash for adding a few too many martinis to my Phuket research, to Songkran for showing me Trang and its spicy cuisine, and to Golf for your generosity. Additional thanks to Wayne Lunt, Hans Ulrich, Robyn Hasson, Rene Balot, Joe Hue, Rick Gamble, Matt Bolton, Palm on PP, Amar Mungcal, Paul Clammer, JYSK, TAT, and a special shout out to Celeste Brash – my phone buddy in absentia. Lastly, to my co-authors, it was a pleasure working with all of you, and China – huge thanks for your support and suggestions. Big 'thank you's to Tashi Wheeler, Dave Connolly, Carolyn Boicos and the rest of the savvy crew at Lonely Planet HQ.

OUR READERS

Many thanks to the travellers who used the last edition and wrote to us with helpful hints, useful advice and interesting anecdotes:

A Daan Albers, Sara Alereza, Jeff Allen, Nic Allen, Myriam Altmeyer, Malin Andersson, Rockin' Angels, Jessica Arial, Shelley Arnoldi, Rahul Asave, Luc Assame, Jenny Austin **B** John Bailey, David Bailward, Cindy Bakker , Makarand Bakshi, Julien Balmer, Kristina Barker, Antony Barton, Andrew Bates, Mary Beaumier, Ronald Beck, Manfred Becker, Peter Bennetton, Angelique Berhault, Maurizio Bettini, Burjis Bhathena, Rudi Blacker, Andrew Bodman, Charlotte Boegh, Boudewijn Boers, Stacy Bold, Achim Boltz, Julie Booth, Stanley Bootsaraporn, David Boulding, Josephine Bradley, M Bradshaw, Barry Bravenboer, Anna Brechbuehl-Belart, Charlotte Breinersdorf, Anne Brock, David Brock, Matthew Brock, Jade Brockley, Adrian Brophy, Lena Brühne, Tobias Brühne, Joanne Burrell **C** Sandra Caillet, Duncan Cameron, Lara Cameron, Alison Campbell, Gianni Caramma, William Chambers, Christopher Chaw, Mason Cheyne, Stephen Chittum, Amelia Cleary, Jon Clements, Edward Cook, Catherine Cornish, Ursula Cornu, Jasmin Croome, Jennifer Cudnik, Sophie Curtis, Corey Cusson **D** Eric Danell, Nik Daum, Stuart Davie, Vaughan Davies, Ingrid De Vries, Petr Dedek, Brooke Dekker, Catherine Delahunty, Rj Demers, Brigette Dempsey, Sofie Depraeter, Jeroen Diederen, Anja Dijkema, John Dillard, James Dimond, Colette Dixon, Kate Dixon, Willem Dohmen, Chris Donnelly, Ben Dopkins, Ellen Douglas, Arne-Joost Douma, Roberto Jung Drebes, Fred Duprat **E** Marente En Tolik Smirnoff, Andreana Engler, Krister Errikson, Rachel Esse, Lucy Evans **F** Michael Falvella, Sebastien Ferenczi, Kristen Fitzgerald, Dianne Fleischer, Paul Foulkes, David Fowler, Lib Fox, Adrienne Frazer, Claudia Freeman **G** Gintare G, Dee Gadaria, Lubbe Garell, John Garretson, Ben Garrison, Ted Gault, Joaquin Gausachs, Michelle Gee, Lia Genovese, Helen Gerald, James Gibbs, Mary-Margaret Gibson, Tanja Gilb, David Gohla, Abigail Gonzalez, Sarah Jane Goodall, Hans Goudriaan, Mary Grimson, Alain Grootaers, Mario Guajardo, Nadia Gunardisurya, Krishnan Guruswamy **H** Jano Ha, Friedemann Hagen, Glen Hall, Ari Halpern, Monica Hampton, Becky Hanke, Miriam Hanley, David Hanna, Nicole Hansen, William Hanson, Paul & Jo Harris, Jonathan Harth, Remo Hartmann, Fred Harvey, Richard Harvey, Tom Healy, Francois Hebrard De Veyrinas, Still Heel, Peter Heron, Martin Hine, Nina Holst, Sompong Hongbin, Erik Hoogcarspel, Anneloes Hoorneman, Johnny Hopper, Pien Huang, Raymond Hudson, Esmaralda Huijbregts, Jakobien Huisman,

Zara Hulscher, Andrew Hunt **I** Amy Iacopi, Nabeel Ibrahim, Claire Ingram, Kate Introna, Dan Isander-Wahlberg **J** Sven Jacobs, J A Jarzabek, Cara Jedell, Gudrun Jehle, Rich Jenkins, Frank & Daan Jochems Verleg, Amanda Johnsen, Judith Johnson, Marissa Johnson, Marla Johst, Andrew Jones, Jeff Jones, Popelka Herzfeld Juan Carlos **K** Jamie Kadamani, Eva Kamenz, John Kennedy, Rob Kent, Philip Keulemans, Majid Khan, Kritsana Khumwong, Joyce Kim, Sirinud Kitikan, Jesper Nicolaj Birger Kjolseth, Darl Kleinbach, Merel & Ian Kneepkens, Gösta Knochenhauer, Kendra Kreider, Ivar Sonbo Kristiansen, Mireille Kruse, Andrew Kukowski **L** Philippe Labonte, David Laine, Richard Lam, Claus Lang, Alexandre Langlois, Silke Lassen, Julie Lawson, James Lee, Patricia Lichtenberg, Chengxuan Liu, Silvia Lopes, Suzanne Lowrie, B Ludwig **M** Suzanne MacRae, Daniel Magliola, Gilles Maguin, Florent Mahieu, Karen Malaca, Farida Man-Nga, Lauren Marlow, Antonio Marreiros, Patsy Martin, Mr Mashore, Mrs Mashore, Steven Mathers, Sebastien Maury, Jo McArthur, John McAully, Rosemary McAully, Lianne McElhone, David McGee, Peter McIntosh, Patrick Meijer, Kathryn Merry, Ronald Meyerq, Andrea Mikleova, Jaime Milgram, Wouter Moerman, Dennis Mogerman, Marina Mogli, Nakaret Montienmanee, Mark Moore, Ivor Morgan, Jeffrey Morrisey, Debbie Morton, Melanie Mosa, Robbert Most, Susan Mulholland, Aoife Murtagh, Terry Murtha **N** Johannes Nagelhout, Naoko Nakagawa, Saowalax Nakagawa, Surajit Narang, Kim Nash, Ema Nate, Colette Nevin, Karola Noebel, Joachim Norum **O** Simon O'Brien, Richard O'Bryen, Susan O'Connor, Petra O'Neill, Sarah O'Sullivan, Lisa Oglesby, Ted Olander, Yvonne Oostrijk **P** Kate Palmer, Sarah Palmer, Romano Paparazzo, Sridhar Pappu, Tim Parkin, Martina Pasic, Trent Paton, Barry Peacock, Victoria Pearson, Terry Penney, Matthew Pepe, Dieter Petermichl, Vivian Peters, Dave Peterson, Gabriel Pilotto, John Piper, Marieke Pol, Patrakamon Pongsiriwan, Chanel Pranic, Isabelle Prentice, Jean Pugh **Q** Moin Qazi **R** Pascal Raats, Alexis Raimbault, Nickolay Rashev, Michael Raue, Leni Reeves, Stephanie Reid, Linda Renland, Natasha Reus, Allan Rickmann, Margaret Rickmann, Sarah Riordan, Renee Rivest, Eric Rochard, Nick Rogers, Vena Rosa, Mandelberg Roslyn, Nick Rowlands, Stacey Rudd, Barry Russell **S** Allon Sacks, Jintana Sakran, Gunilla Samuelsson, Matilda Sandén, Carrie Sauer, Simon Scheurer, Rose Marie Schillings-Hagen, Andreas Schmidt, Scholten family, Anne Schoone, John Schulpen, Rainer Schulze, Anna Schweizer, Irmi Seidl, Tim Severino, Jim Seymour, Bill Shaw, Wannee Shaw, Eddie Shroff, Aruna Singh, Jan Sisperda, Gemma State, Judith Slot, Gijsbert Smit, Sandy Smith, Doris Spiers, Sonya Spry, Lydia Stables, Anna Stenek, Peter Stripp, Anna Sumik, Lisa Sutcliffe, Du-Fung Suwa, Mark Swider, Lange Sylvie, Istvan Szucs **T** Dan Taylor, Ken Taylor, Geiser Thomas, Robin Thomsen, Alex Tidd, Katri Toivonen, Cristina Topham, Christina Tunnah , Ed Turner, Jason Turner, Lee Tyson, Waltraud Tzschoeckel **U** Antoni P Uni **V** Andrej Valena, Cor Valk, Maike Van De Weijer, Marc Van Der Heijde, Bas Van Der Slikke, Monique Van Druten, Marte Van Haperen, Peggy Van Huis-Versteeg, Walter Van Paassen, Marja Van Weeren, Jazz Vanderbilt, Bruce Vanderkooi, Francine Vandersteen, Emma Varney, Roy Verbrugge, Dirk Verbruggen, Dirk Verlinde, Ubonpon Vibunsalanee, Adriano Vincenzi, Thomas Vogel, John Voight **W** Jay Wachrasetkul, Aine Wade, Linus Waerner, Melissa Wagstaff, Pitak Waiyasilpa, Vanessa Walker, Erlend Walseth, Jamie Waterhouse, Stephanie Weinzierl, Michael Weitzman, Kim Wejendorp, Dan Welch, Nicolas Welzl, Ben Wilks, Al Williams, Jabbar Williams, Wee Win, Moritz Winnen, Wai San Wong **Y** Nihat Yasartuerk, Aycan Yeniley, Deborah Young **Z** Karyn Zlatkovic, Marc Zonruiter, Anthony Zuza, Jord Zwaal.

SEND US YOUR FEEDBACK

We love to hear from travellers – your comments keep us on our toes and help make our books better. Our well-travelled team reads every word on what you loved or loathed about this book. Although we cannot reply individually to postal submissions, we always guarantee that your feedback goes straight to the appropriate authors, in time for the next edition. Each person who sends us information is thanked in the next edition – and the most useful submissions are rewarded with a free book.

To send us your updates – and find out about Lonely Planet events, newsletters and travel news – visit our award-winning website: **lonelyplanet.com/contact**.

Note: we may edit, reproduce and incorporate your comments in Lonely Planet products such as guidebooks, websites and digital products, so let us know if you don't want your comments reproduced or your name acknowledged. For a copy of our privacy policy visit lonelyplanet.com/privacy.

BEHIND THE SCENES

ACKNOWLEDGMENTS
Many thanks to the following for the use of their content:

Globe on title page ©Mountain High Maps 1993 Digital Wisdom, Inc.

All other photographs by Lonely Planet Images, or as credited, and by Austin Bush; p430 (#3), p436 (#1); Michael Aw p431 (#2); Sean Caffrey p430 (#1); Tom Cockrem p429, p432 (#3); Paul Dymond p433 (#6); John Elk III p435 (#5); Mick Elmore p434 (#1), (#3); Felix Hug p432 (#2).

Index

INDEX

000 Map pages
000 Photograph pages

INDEX

000 Map pages
000 Photograph pages

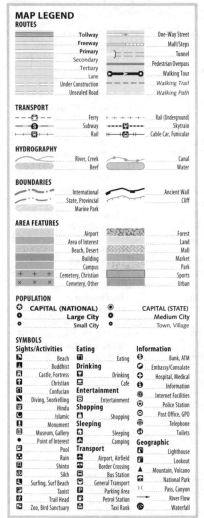

MAP LEGEND
ROUTES

Tollway	One-Way Street
Freeway	Mall/Steps
Primary	Tunnel
Secondary	Pedestrian Overpass
Tertiary	Walking Tour
Lane	Walking Trail
Under Construction	Walking Path
Unsealed Road	

TRANSPORT

Ferry	Rail (Underground)
Subway	Skytrain
Rail	Cable Car, Funicular

HYDROGRAPHY

River, Creek	Canal
Reef	Water

BOUNDARIES

International	Ancient Wall
State, Provincial	Cliff
Marine Park	

AREA FEATURES

Airport	Forest
Area of Interest	Land
Beach, Desert	Mall
Building	Market
Campus	Park
Cemetery, Christian	Sports
Cemetery, Other	Urban

POPULATION

CAPITAL (NATIONAL)	CAPITAL (STATE)
Large City	Medium City
Small City	Town, Village

SYMBOLS

Sights/Activities
Beach
Buddhist
Castle, Fortress
Christian
Confucian
Diving, Snorkelling
Hindu
Islamic
Monument
Museum, Gallery
Point of Interest
Pool
Ruin
Shinto
Sikh
Surfing, Surf Beach
Taoist
Trail Head
Zoo, Bird Sanctuary

Eating
Eating
Drinking
Drinking
Cafe
Entertainment
Entertainment
Shopping
Shopping
Sleeping
Sleeping
Camping
Transport
Airport, Airfield
Border Crossing
Bus Station
General Transport
Parking Area
Petrol Station
Taxi Rank

Information
Bank, ATM
Embassy/Consulate
Hospital, Medical
Information
Internet Facilities
Police Station
Post Office, GPO
Telephone
Toilets
Geographic
Lighthouse
Lookout
Mountain, Volcano
National Park
Pass, Canyon
River Flow
Waterfall

LONELY PLANET OFFICES
Australia
Head Office
Locked Bag 1, Footscray, Victoria 3011
☎ 03 8379 8000, fax 03 8379 8111
talk2us@lonelyplanet.com.au

USA
150 Linden St, Oakland, CA 94607
☎ 510 250 6400, toll free 800 275 8555,
fax 510 893 8572
info@lonelyplanet.com

UK
2nd fl, 186 City Rd,
London EC1V 2NT
☎ 020 7106 2100, fax 020 7106 2101
go@lonelyplanet.co.uk

Published by Lonely Planet Publications Pty Ltd
ABN 36 005 607 983

© Lonely Planet Publications Pty Ltd 2009

© photographers as indicated 2009

Cover photograph: Festival participants holding large paper lanterns at Loi Krathong festival, Felix Hug/Lonely Planet Images. Many of the images in this guide are available for licensing from Lonely Planet Images: www.lonelyplanetimages.com.

Printed through Colorcraft Ltd, Hong Kong.
Printed in China.

Mixed Sources
Product group from well-managed forests and other controlled sources
www.fsc.org   Cert no. SGS-COC-005002
© 1996 Forest Stewardship Council